MANAGEMENT 15E

Stephen P. Robbins
San Diego State University

Mary Coulter
Missouri State University

With contributions by

Amy Randel
San Diego State University

 Pearson

Please contact https://support.pearson.com/getsupport/s/contactsupport with any queries on this content.

Library of Congress Cataloging-in-Publication Data

Names: Robbins, Stephen P., author. | Coulter, Mary K., author.
Title: Management / Stephen P. Robbins, Mary Coulter.
Description: 15 Edition. | Hoboken, NJ : Pearson, [2020] | Revised edition
    of the authors' Management, [2018]
Identifiers: LCCN 2019020717 (print) | LCCN 2019980991 (ebook) |
    ISBN 9780135581858 | ISBN 9780135581872 (ebook other)
Subjects: LCSH: Management.
Classification: LCC HD31 .R5647 2020 (print) | LCC HD31 (ebook) |
    DDC 658—dc23
LC record available at https://lccn.loc.gov/2019020717
LC ebook record available at https://lccn.loc.gov/2019980991

1 2019

ISBN 10:   0-13-558185-0
ISBN 13: 978-0-13-558185-8

To my wife, Laura
Steve

To my husband, Ron
Mary

Brief Contents

Contents

Chapter 9: Managing Strategy 220

Part 4 Organizing 274

Welcome to the 15th edition of *Management*. First published in 1984, this book has become one of the world's most popular introductory management textbooks. It's used by hundreds of US colleges and universities; it's translated into Spanish, French, Russian, Dutch, Bahasa, Korean, and Chinese; and there are adapted editions for Australia, Canada, India, and the Arab World.

New to This Edition

We've added a number of new topics to this 15th edition of *Management*. The following overview highlights some of those topics.

Rethinking Globalization

Globalization has long been promoted by economists and the media as a win-win proposition for all countries. However, recent developments have challenged this belief and indicate signs of growing anti-globalization attitudes. Chapter 4 provides a history of globalization and the growth of a nationalism movement.

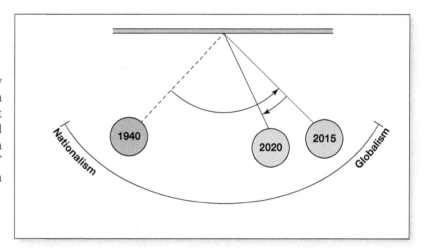

The "Me-Too" Movement

The recent "me-too" movement has drawn global attention to gender inequities in the workplace.[40] It essentially began in 2017, when more than a dozen women accused film producer Harvey Weinstein of sexual harassment, assault, or rape. What began as a trickle, soon became a flood of accusations. The movement ended Weinstein's reign at his film studio, but also brought to light abuses of power by dozens of prominent men, including *Today* co-host Matt Lauer, TV journalists Bill O'Reilly and Charlie Rose, Pixar head John Lasseter, and casino magnate Stephen Wynn.

The recent "me-too" movement has drawn global attention to gender inequities in the workplace and revealed organizational cultures that are hostile to women. In Chapter 5, gender inequities in the workplace are reviewed.

The Widespread Impact of Social Media

This edition provides insights into how social media is reshaping management practices—including ethical behavior, communication, motivation, and control.

Focus on Social Media

You probably can't imagine a time when employees did their work without smart devices, email, apps, or internet access. Yet, some twenty-five years ago, as these tools were becoming more common in workplaces, managers struggled with the challenges of providing guidelines for using the internet and email in their organizations. Today, a tool that nearly all organizations use is **social media**, forms of electronic communication through which users create online communities to share ideas, information, personal messages, and other content. And employees don't just use these on their personal time, but also for work purposes. That's why managers need to understand and manage the power and peril of social media.

There is also a downside to social media. As noted by Berkshire Hathaway CEO Warren Buffet, "It takes twenty years to build a reputation and five minutes to ruin it."[23] Internally, social media also becomes problematic when it becomes a way for boastful employees to brag about their accomplishments, for managers to publish one-way messages to employees, or for employees to argue or gripe about something or someone.

In the remainder of the book, we'll look at how social media is impacting how managers manage, especially in the areas of ethics, communication, motivation, and strategy.

Big Data and Artificial Intelligence

As the Cleveland Clinic found, IBM's supercomputer, Watson, can do things faster and more accurately than many professionals. For instance, it can diagnose cancers four times more accurately than doctors and can provide legal advice in seconds with 90 percent accuracy, compared to 70 percent accuracy by lawyers.[32] The secret to Watson's talents? Big data and artificial intelligence.

Big data is a term that refers to huge and complex sets of data.[33] These data sets are composed of so much information that traditional data-processing application software is unable to deal with them. For instance, cloud-computing capacity now can allow a room full of legal opinions to be put online. What used to take a lawyer several days or even weeks to find relevant cases to support a client's case can now be done in seconds. Similarly, even football and basketball coaches and managers are using big data to guide drafting decisions and even play calling.

Big data has opened the door to widespread use of **artificial intelligence (AI)**. As noted in Chapter 1, AI is using the power of computers to replicate the reasoning functions of humans.[34] It goes well beyond the simple "if-then" processing of computer software. AI has the ability to learn and solve complex problems.

You already know how big data and AI are changing the lives of consumers with products like Siri, Google Maps, Uber, and the rapid advancements being made toward self-driving cars. But big data and AI, along with machine learning, deep learning, and analytics are rapidly changing how managers make decisions.

How Big Data, Analytics, and AI Are Changing the Manager's Job

Big data, analytics, and artificial intelligence are changing how managers make decisions and design their organizations. The topic is addressed in several chapters of this edition.

Additional Chapter-by-Chapter Changes in This Edition

Chapter 1

- Rewrote Why Are Managers Important?
- New Managerial Challenge: Focus on Disruptive Innovation
- New Managerial Challenge: Focus on Ethics
- New Managerial Challenge: Focus on Political Uncertainty
- New: Employability Skills
- Added Learning from Failure box: Successful Managers Learn from Their Failures

History Module

- Updated to Include Technology/Computerization Era

Chapter 2

- New: Decision Styles
- New: Big Data, AI, Analytics
- New: Machine Learning, Deep Learning
- Added Learning from Failure box: James Dyson: A Man of a Thousand Failures

Chapter 3

- Expanded Discussion of Environmental Uncertainty
- Expanded Discussion of Elements in the Specific Environment
- Added Learning from Failure box: A Corrupt Culture at Wells Fargo

Chapter 4

- Total Rewrite to Reflect Growing Anti-Globalization Movement
- Added Learning from Failure box: Disney Learns That France Isn't Florida

Chapter 5

- New: "Me-Too" Movement and Gender Diversity
- New: Critical Questions About Diversity
- Added Learning from Failure box: Denny's Answer to Its Diversity Problem

Chapter 6

- New: Social Responsibility and Economic Performance
- New Current Issues: Protecting Whistle-Blowers
- New Current Issues: Social Media and Social Responsibility

Chapter 8

- New: Virtual Reality as a Planning Tool
- Added Contingency Factors in Planning
- Added Learning from Failure box: US Army Corps of Engineers and Hurricane Katrina

Chapter 9

- New Competitive Advantage: Mass Customization
- New Competitive Advantage: Social Media
- Added Learning from Failure box: Coke Panics After the Pepsi Challenge

Chapter 10

- New: A Hybrid Path to Entrepreneurship
- Added Learning from Failure box: The Third Time Is a Charm for Vera Wang

Chapter 11
- Added Learning from Failure box: Working at Home Doesn't Work at IBM

Chapter 12

- New: Bullying in the Workplace
- New: Material on Socialization
- New: Career Development
- Rewrote Compensation and Benefits section
- Added Learning from Failure box: Forced Rankings Bomb at Microsoft

Chapter 14

- New: Cybersecurity
- Added Learning from Failure box: GM's Catastrophic Communication Breakdown

Chapter 15
- New: Dark Triad Personality

Chapter 16
- Added Learning from Failure box: NSPS: Pay-for-Performance Gone Bad

Chapter 17

- New: Servant Leadership
- New: Followership
- New: Comparing Leadership Theories for Their Validity
- Added Learning from Failure box: The Firing of Steve Jobs at Apple

Chapter 18
- New: Social Media as a Control Tool
- New: Compliance Offices and Positions

POM Module
- New: Robotics

Our Three Guiding Principles

What has allowed this book to flourish for thirty-five years? We think the answer is in our three guiding principles: (1) offer cutting-edge topic coverage, (2) ensure that the writing is readable and conversational, and (3) make certain the presentation is relevant to students.

Cutting-Edge Topic Coverage

This book has always sought to provide the *latest topic coverage*. It was, for instance, the first introductory management book to discuss organizational culture, the symbolic view of management, behavioral decision making, sustainability, and value-chain management. This edition continues in that tradition, with cutting-edge topics like the changing attitudes toward globalization, the "me-too" movement, disruptive innovation, decision analytics, and the effects of social media. And, of course, the entire research base for this edition has been fully updated.

High Readability

Every textbook author claims his or her books are *highly readable*. The reality is that few actually are. Most appear to be written more for professors than for students. From the first edition of this book, we were determined to make the field of management interesting and engaging for students. How did we do this? First, we committed to a conversational writing style. We wanted the book to read like normal people talk. And second, we relied on an extensive use of examples. As your senior author learned early in his teaching career, students often forget theories but they remember stories. So you'll find a wealth of current examples in this book.

Relevance

Since this book's inception, we have subjected every theory and concept to our "So What?" test. We ask ourselves: Why is a specific concept relevant? Why should a student need to know this? This test has guided us in deciding what to include and exclude over these many editions, as well as reminding us to explain the importance and relevance of concepts when it might not be obvious.

Solving Learning and Teaching Challenges

Speaking of relevance, if there is one component of this book that instructors will find important, it's our focus on providing job-relevant skills for students.

In the typical introductory management class, only about 20 percent of students are management majors. The rest are majoring in accounting, finance, marketing, information systems, or some other business discipline. As a result, instructors tell us that one of their most challenging obstacles in teaching the introductory management class is convincing these non-management majors of the course's importance. These non-management majors often question the course's relevance to their career goals. As one accounting student put it, "Why do I have to take this class? I have no interest in being a manager. My time would be better spent taking another course in tax or auditing."

We have an answer for those students: This book and your management class are relevant to anyone who plans to work in an organization. How? In addition to describing what effective managers do and offering insights into how organizations work, we include features that will help students develop the specific skills employers are looking for in job candidates and provide guidance to help students survive and thrive in the workplace. Let's highlight what those features are.

Specific Employability Skills

Research studies have identified five specific skills that employers are looking for in job candidates. These are critical thinking, communication, collaboration, knowledge application, and ethics/social responsibility. So in this edition, chapters 2 through 18 each begin with an Employability Skills Matrix. The matrix identifies how components in the chapter build on one or more of the five employability skills.

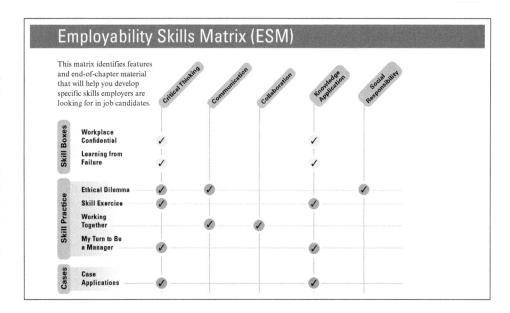

WORKPLACE CONFIDENTIAL   Adjusting to a New Job or Work Team

Almost all of us have made transitions in our lives. Maybe your parents moved and you had to make new friends and adjust to a new school. Or you joined a new church, social club, or sports team. As a result, you'd think that most of us would be pretty confident and successful in making the transition into a new job. This is often not the case, especially for younger employees.

For our discussion, we'll focus on the outsider-to-insider transition and both external (between organizations) and internal (between horizontal departments or vertical promotions) adjustments.

The importance of this issue is underlined by research that tells us that the typical individual changes jobs 10.2 times over 20 years—so you need to be prepared to do a lot of adjusting to new work situations.

One of your goals in any new job situation should be to make the adjustment successful. What does that entail? You've made a successful transition if, after six months in your new position, you can say that you feel comfortable, confident, and accepted by your peers. And the evidence tells us that this is most likely to occur where you know what is required to function in your job, you have confidence that you have the knowledge and skills to perform it, and you know what the job demands are in terms of relationships with others. Moreover, successful adjustment should result in satisfaction with your job and a minimal degree of anxiety and stress.

Successful adjustment should begin by assessing the new situation. Assuming you have concluded that the job is a good fit for you, you need to determine the following: What's the history of the organization or work unit? Which individuals are held in high esteem, and what factors have led to their influence? And what does the culture value? Learning to read the organization's culture (see the earlier "It's Your Career" box) can provide you with answers to many of these questions.

Organizations have a variety of socialization options that they use to shape employees and help them adjust to the organization. Let's briefly review some options and consider their impact on you:

Formal vs. Informal. Specific orientation and training programs are examples of formal socialization. The informal variety puts new employees directly into the job.

Individual vs. Collective. When you're grouped with others and processed through an identical set of experiences, it's collective. Most small organizations socialize new members individually.

Fixed vs. Variable. A fixed schedule establishes standardized time targets for transition, such as a six-month probationary period or a rotational training program. Variable schedules have no advance notice of transitions; for instance, you'll be promoted when you're "ready."

Serial vs. Random. In serial socialization, you'll have a role model who will train and encourage you.

Apprenticeship and mentoring programs are examples. In random socialization, you're left on your own to figure things out.

Investiture vs. Divestiture. When the organization wants to affirm and support your qualities and qualifications, they basically leave you alone. But in divestiture, the organization will attempt to strip away certain characteristics. For instance, fraternities and sororities use divestiture rites when they put "pledges" through rituals to shape new members into the proper role.

As you move into your new job, be aware that the socialization programs, or lack of such programs, you'll be exposed to will have a significant influence on your adjustment. For instance, if you see yourself as a conformist and want a job that fits you, choose a job that relies on institutional socialization—one that is formal, collective, fixed, serial, and shapes you through divestiture rites. In contrast, if you see yourself as a "wave-maker" who likes to develop your own approaches to problems, choose a job that focuses on individualized socialization—one that is informal, individual, variable, and random and affirms your uniqueness through investiture.

The evidence indicates most people end up more satisfied with, and committed to, their job when they go through institutional socialization. This is largely because its structured learning helps reduce the uncertainty inherent in a new situation and smooths the transition into the new job.

An additional insight on new-job adjustment is the value of organizational insiders as a valuable resource for information. Colleagues, supervisors, and mentors are more useful as sources for accurate information about your job and the organization than formal orientation programs or organizational literature. People give you a better and more accurate reading of "the ropes to skip and the ropes to know."

Finally, don't forget the power of first impressions. A positive first impression on your transition. Think about can both speed up and smooth your transition. Think about the image you want to convey and make sure your clothes, posture, attitude, and speech fit that image.

So what are the specific implications of all this? How can you use this information to increase the probability that you'll have a successful adjustment in a new job? The answer is to focus on those things you can control. First, to summarize, choose a job where the socialization process matches up well with your personality. And, based on the evidence, choosing a job with institutionalized socialization will reduce uncertainty, lessen stress, and facilitate adjustment. Second, use insiders to provide background information and to reduce surprises. Lastly, start off on the right foot by making a good first impression. If colleagues like and respect you, they are more likely to share with you key insights into the organization's values and culture.[22]

Advice for Surviving and Thriving in the Workplace

Regardless of whether one is working in an organization employing three people or 300,000, there are common challenges that employees will encounter. We provide students with guidance for dealing with these challenges in our "Workplace Confidential" features.

IT'S YOUR CAREER

Learning Your Strengths and Weaknesses

Do you know your personal strengths and weaknesses? You need to for at least two reasons. The first is that job interviewers commonly ask what you consider your strengths and weaknesses, and you want to be prepared to answer those questions. Second, by knowing your strengths and weaknesses you can size up where you stand in your career and make good decisions about what you need to do to keep advancing.

Here are some suggestions to help you learn your strengths and weaknesses:

1. *Identify your strengths.* Your strengths are your individual personal positive attributes and characteristics. As you look at your strengths, assess the following: skills (what you are good at), interests (what you enjoy doing), educational background (what qualifications you have), your values (what things are important to you), and your personality (what characteristics you have). As you evaluate these, think in terms of what sets you apart. What things do you like to do? What things do you do well? What things do you do better than others? It's also helpful to ask others you trust what they see as your strengths.

2. *Take a look at your weaknesses.* It's sometimes hard to admit, but we all have weaknesses. What things could you improve about yourself? What are your negative personal/work habits? What things do you not like to do? What skills, training, or qualifications are you lacking, the possession of which would make you a more valuable employee? Are you lacking career direction or focus? What things do others do better than you do? Again, it's helpful to ask others you trust what they see as your weaknesses.

3. *As discussed later in this chapter's "Workplace Confidential," develop a strategy to do something about your strengths and weaknesses.* What actions can you take to get the job you want or to best meet the requirements of your current job or a promotion you're seeking? Accentuate your positives! You want to leverage, emphasize, and capitalize on your strengths.

Here's an insight that many young people don't realize: You can go a long way on just a few strengths. In school, to be an outstanding student, you have to be a generalist. You have to be good at everything: math, science, history, geography, languages, the arts, and so forth. But "the real world" pays off for specialization. You only have to excel in one or two areas to have an amazing career. So find your niche and exploit that strength.

4. *Update your list of strengths and weaknesses periodically.* As you gain new experiences and as your life circumstances change, you'll want to revise your list of strengths and weaknesses. Sharpen your self-awareness so you can craft the kind of life—professionally and personally—you want to live.

Career Guidance

We've found that students appreciate career guidance. Toward that end, we included "It's Your Career" boxes that address skills that will enhance career progress. These include identifying your strengths and weaknesses, managing your time, developing your negotiation skills, and learning to read an organization's culture.

Developing Resilience

In this edition of *Management*, we added "Learning From Failure" boxes to illustrate how people like Steven Spielberg, J. K. Rowling, and Vera Wang, as well as companies like Apple, Disney, and GM, have encountered setbacks, assessed what went wrong, gained new insights from their experience, and bounced back.

Resilience is a valuable quality for students and employees. These boxes can help students see the positive side of failures and how individuals and organizations have learned from their mistakes.

Learning from
FAILURE   Disney Learns That France Isn't Florida

The Walt Disney Company had a proven record of creating and operating highly successful theme parks in southern California and Orlando, Florida. So how difficult would it be to transfer that success to Paris? What worked in Florida should work in France, right? Unfortunately, Disney found out that success doesn't necessarily transfer when they opened Euro Disney Resort (now called Disneyland Paris) in 1992.

The French aren't like Americans in a number of ways. For instance, Americans typically travel to theme parks in their cars. The French tend to use buses. The result was large, empty parking lots while facilities for bus drivers to park their buses and rest were inadequate.

Disney parks in the US don't serve alcohol. But the French consider wine a part of their daily life and a glass of wine for lunch a necessity. Visitors were astonished that no wine was available at the park and complained en masse.

Not only was the lack of wine a problem at lunch, so was the time when the French want their midday meal. There is no fixed time for Americans to each lunch. And Americans are comfortable grabbing something on the go and eating while they wander around the park. In contrast, the majority of European visitors would converge on restaurants at 12:30 p.m., expect to be seated, and treat the meal as a leisurely event. Disneyland Paris's managers failed to properly staff their restaurants for the one- or two-hour "rush hours."

Disney executives also failed to understand that, while American park visitors' average stay was four days, the French typically arrived early in the morning, spent the day at the park, checked into their hotel late at night, then checked out early the next morning. The difference was largely due to the multiple theme parks—SeaWorld, Knott's Berry Farm, Universal Studios—near the Florida and California parks. There were no such options in Paris. The result was long lines in the hotel lobbies with people all checking-in and checking-out at the same time.

In response to these mistakes, Disney executives initiated a number of changes in Paris. Bus areas were expanded, corporate policy was modified to make wine and beer available, restaurant staffing was adjusted, and additional computer stations were installed at park hotels to reduce waiting lines.

What did Disney learn from their failures at Euro Disneyland? Culture matters![24]

Continued Focus on Practical Applications

This edition of *Management* continues our commitment to provide instructors with a comprehensive set of in-text exercises that allow students to translate what they've learned into practical applications. These include, for example, end-of-chapter cases, ethical dilemmas, and team-building exercises, plus a part-ending integrative case. Here's a brief summary of these applications.

CASE APPLICATION 1 — Environmental Uncertainty at HBO

HBO is one of those company names everyone knows. It's the oldest and second-largest pay TV station in the US. Since the early 1990s, it has been developing original programming. That's much longer than Netflix and Amazon. HBO shows like *Game of Thrones*, *The Sopranos*, and *Westworld* have won Emmy and Golden Globe awards. HBO includes seven 24-hour channels as well as the streaming service HBO Now. It has about 130 million subscribers worldwide.[25]

That all sounds like HBO is doing well, right? Looking more deeply, though, there is a lot happening in HBO's environment.

Over a million households got rid of their cable TV subscriptions during a three-month period in 2017. That's much faster change than experts expected. By 2030, the cable and satellite TV market is estimated to shrink by 26 percent. That would leave only 60 percent of American households as subscribers to pay TV.[26]

Meanwhile, smart phone usage keeps climbing worldwide each year. The number of smart phone users in 2018 was estimated at 2.53 billion. By 2020, that number is expected to climb to 2.87 billion.[27]

Case Applications

There are two new case applications at the end of each chapter.

Starbucks Integrative Case

Each of the six parts of this book concludes with the Starbucks integrative case. This case helps students see how concepts can be applied in an organization with which most are familiar as well as see the integrative nature of management. The case has been totally updated from the previous edition.

Continuing Case

Starbucks—Introduction

Community. Connection. Caring. Committed. Coffee. Five Cs that describe the essence of Starbucks Corporation—what it stands for and what it wants to be as a business. With nearly 30,000 stores in 77 countries, Starbucks is the world's number one specialty coffee retailer. The company also owns Seattle's Best Coffee, Teavana, Starbucks VIA, Starbucks Refreshers, Evolution Fresh, La Boulange, Verismo, and Torrefazione Italia brands. It's a company that truly epitomizes the challenges facing managers in today's globally competitive environment. To help you better understand these challenges, we're going to take an in-depth look at Starbucks through these continuing cases, which you'll find at the end of every part in the textbook. Each of these six part-ending continuing cases will look at Starbucks from the perspective of the material presented in that part. Although each case "stands alone," you'll be able to see the progression of the management process as you work through each one.

Skill Exercises

It's not enough to "know" something. Students need to be able to apply that knowledge. Skill Exercises at the end of each chapter are designed to help achieve that goal. Some of these exercises include developing your skills at politicking, creativity, collaboration, building trust, interviewing, motivating others, and acquiring power.

SKILLS EXERCISE   Developing Your Collaboration Skill

About the Skill

Collaboration is the teamwork, synergy, and cooperation used by individuals when they seek a common goal. In many cross-cultural settings, the ability to collaborate is crucial. When all partners must work together to achieve goals, collaboration is critically important to the process. However, cultural differences can often make collaboration a challenge.

Steps in Practicing the Skill

- *Look for common points of interest.* The best way to start working together in a collaborative fashion is to seek commonalities that exist among the parties. Common points of interest enable communications to be more effective.

- *Listen to others.* Collaboration is a team effort. Everyone has valid points to offer, and each individual should have an opportunity to express his or her ideas.

- *Check for understanding.* Make sure you understand what the other person is saying. Use feedback when necessary.

- *Accept diversity.* Not everything in a collaborative effort will "go your way." Be willing to accept different ideas and different ways of doing things. Be open to these ideas and the creativity that surrounds them.

- *Seek additional information.* Ask individuals to provide additional information. Encourage others to talk and more fully explain suggestions. This brainstorming opportunity can assist in finding creative solutions.

- *Don't become defensive.* Collaboration requires open communications. Discussions may focus on things you and others may not be doing or need to do better. Don't take the constructive feedback as personal criticism. Focus on the topic being discussed, not on the person delivering the message. Recognize that you cannot always be right!

Practicing the Skill

Interview individuals from three different nationalities about the challenges of collaborating with individuals from different cultures. What challenges do different cultures create? How have they dealt with these challenges? What advice do they have for improving collaboration across cultural differences? Based on your interviews, what are some general ideas you learned to improve your ability to collaborate?

ETHICS DILEMMA

In many ways, technology has made all of us more productive. However, ethical issues do arise in how and when technology is used. Take the sports arena. All kinds of technologically advanced sports equipment (swimsuits, golf clubs, ski suits, etc.) have been developed that can sometimes give competitors/players an edge over their opponents. We saw it in swim meets at the Summer Olympics and on the ski slopes and ice rinks at the Winter Olympics.

3-8. What do you think? Is this an ethical use of technology?

3-9. What if your school (or country) were competing for a championship and couldn't afford to outfit athletes in such equipment and it affected your ability to compete? Would that make a difference?

3-10. What ethical guidelines might you suggest for such situations?

Ethics Dilemmas

Each chapter presents students with an ethical dilemma and encourages them to practice their skills in ethical decision making and critical decision making.

Team Exercises

Work in today's organizations is increasingly being done in groups and teams. And being a "team player" has become an important quality in the hiring process. To help students build their collaboration skills, we have included team exercises at the end of each chapter.

WORKING TOGETHER   Team Exercise

Almost a third of employees who leave their companies within the first ninety days say they left because they didn't fit into the company's culture.[24] This suggests that learning about a company's culture before you accept a job could save you a considerable amount of grief. To increase the chances that you'll fit with the culture of the company you next work for, form groups of three or four and share the characteristics of an organizational culture each wants

(and don't want) in an employer. Compare your lists for common factors. Now choose one of the group member's lists and discuss: What could you do when visiting a company for an interview to find out whether it has the characteristics on the list? What questions could be asked during the interview? What clues could be looked for when walking around the company to understand what the culture is like? Be ready to share your analysis with the class.

"My Turn to Be a Manager" Exercises

Additional opportunities for students to apply management concepts introduced in each chapter are the "My Turn to Be a Manager" exercises.

MY TURN TO BE A MANAGER

- Find current examples in any popular business periodical of both the omnipotent and symbolic views of management. Write a paper describing what you found and how the examples you found represent these views of management.
- Consider a business that you frequent (for example, a restaurant or coffee shop) and review the six aspects of the external environment discussed in the text. Create a list of factors in the external environment that could affect the management of the business you selected.

- Choose an organization with which you're familiar or one you would like to know more about. Create a table identifying potential stakeholders of this organization. Then indicate what particular interests or concerns these stakeholders might have.
- If you belong to a student organization, evaluate its culture by answering the following: How would you describe the culture? How do new members learn the culture? How is the culture maintained? If you don't belong to a student organization, talk to another student who does and evaluate it using the same questions.

For more information and resources, visit www.pearson.com.

Acknowledgments

Writing and publishing a textbook is a team effort. While there are only two names on the cover, there are dozens of people who helped to create the book you have before you.

In addition to your two authors, this edition was greatly aided by Prof. Amy Randel at San Diego State University. She was instrumental in providing research suggestions, examples, and developing the end-of-chapter materials.

Our team at Pearson continues to provide your authors with amazing support and help in turning our files into a finished textbook. We want to specifically thank Stephanie Wall, Kris Ellis-Levy, Yasmita Hota, Lynn Huddon, Beth Kaufman, Lacey Vitteta, Adrienne D'Ambrosio, Erin Kelly, and Nayke Heine. We also want to thank our project manager, Denise Forlow at Integra-Chicago, and photo editor, Melissa Pellerano. We would be remiss not to also acknowledge and thank the phenomenal sales and marketing people at Pearson who have been supporting the Robbins brand around the globe for more than forty-five years.

Finally, we want to thank our reviewers—past and present—for the insights they have provided us:

Reviewers of 15th Edition

Kennedy Amofa, *Columbia College, MO*

Jessie Bellflowers, *Fayetteville Technical Community College, NC*

Margaret Deck, *Virginia Polytechnic Institute, VA*

Tom Deckelman, *Owens Community College, OH*

Steve Diasio, *University of South Florida, FL*

Lauren M. Donovan, *Delaware County Community College, DE*

Barbara Garrell, *Delaware County Community College, DE*

Scott Geiger, *University of South Florida St. Petersburg, FL*

Lacey Gonzalez, *Lehigh Carbon Community College, PA*

Anne Hoel, *University of Wisconsin–Stout, WI*

Edward Hoeppner, *University of South Florida St. Petersburg, FL*

Greg Hoffeditz, *Southern Illinois University Carbondale, IL*

Stephen P. Robbins
Mary Coulter

About the Authors

STEPHEN P. ROBBINS received his Ph.D. from the University of Arizona. He previously worked for the Shell Oil Company and Reynolds Metals Company and has taught at the University of Nebraska at Omaha, Concordia University in Montreal, the University of Baltimore, Southern Illinois University at Edwardsville, and San Diego State University. He is currently professor emeritus in management at San Diego State. A full bio is available at stephenprobbins.com.

Dr. Robbins's research interests have focused on conflict, power, and politics in organizations, behavioral decision making, and the development of effective interpersonal skills. His articles on these and other topics have appeared in such journals as *Business Horizons*, the *California Management Review, Business and Economic Perspectives, International Management, Management Review, Canadian Personnel and Industrial Relations*, and *The Journal of Management Education.*

Dr. Robbins is the world's best-selling textbook author in the areas of management and organizational behavior. His books have sold more than 12 million copies and have been translated into 20 languages. His books are currently used at more than 1,500 U.S. colleges and universities, as well as hundreds of schools throughout Canada, Latin America, Australia, New Zealand, Asia, Europe, and the Arab World.

Dr. Robbins also participates in masters' track competition. Since turning 50 in 1993, he's won 23 national sprint championships and 14 world sprint titles. He was inducted into the U.S. Masters Track & Field Hall of Fame in 2005.

MARY COULTER received her Ph.D. from the University of Arkansas. She held different jobs including high school teacher, legal assistant, and city government program planner before completing her graduate work. She has taught at Drury University, the University of Arkansas, Trinity University, and Missouri State University. She is currently professor emeritus of management at Missouri State University. In addition to *Management*, Dr. Coulter has published other books with Pearson including *Fundamentals of Management* (with Stephen P. Robbins), *Strategic Management in Action*, and *Entrepreneurship in Action.*

When she's not busy writing, Dr. Coulter enjoys puttering around in her flower gardens, trying new recipes, reading all different types of books, and enjoying many different activities with husband Ron, daughter Sarah and her husband, James, and son-in-law Matt, and most especially with her two grandkids, Brooklynn and Blake, who are the delights of her life!

Chapter 1

Managers and You in the Workplace

Learning Objectives

1.1 **Tell** who managers are and where they work.
1.2 **Explain** why managers are important to organizations.
1.3 **Describe** the functions, roles, and skills of managers.

1.4 **Describe** the factors that are reshaping and redefining the manager's job.
1.5 **Explain** the value of studying management.
1.6 **Describe** the benefits of the Employability Skills Matrix (ESM).

Like many students, you've probably had a job (or two) while working on your degree. And your work experiences are likely to have been significantly influenced by the skills and abilities of your managers. What makes successful managers and what skills do they possess? A good manager can make your job at worst tolerable and, at best, a joy. A poor manager can make your life miserable. In this chapter, we introduce you to managers and management by looking at (1) who managers are, (2) where they work, (3) why they're important, and (4) what tasks they perform. We wrap up the chapter by looking at the factors reshaping and redefining the manager's job and discussing why the field of management is important to you.

TELL who managers are and where they work

LO1.1 You'll find managers in a variety of settings. They run large corporations, medium-sized businesses, and entrepreneurial start-ups. They're found in government departments, hospitals, not-for-profit agencies, museums, schools, and even nontraditional organizations such as political campaigns and music tours. Managers can also be found doing managerial work in every country on the globe. And managers today are just as likely to be women as they are men.

Who Is a Manager?

It used to be fairly simple to define who managers were: They were the organizational members who told others what to do and how to do it. It was easy to differentiate *managers* from *nonmanagerial employees*. Now, it isn't quite that simple. In many organizations, the changing nature of work has blurred the distinction between managers and nonmanagerial employees. Many traditional nonmanagerial jobs now include managerial activities and many organizations have done away with having formal managers. For example, the gaming company Valve Corporation doesn't have job titles, and there is little formal supervision. All projects are started by an individual employee or a group pitching an idea, then they put together a team. If projects have a "leader," he or she just keeps track of information and organizes tasks—but doesn't give orders.

So, how *do* we define who managers are? A **manager** is someone who coordinates and oversees the work of other people so organizational goals can be accomplished. A manager's job is not about *personal* achievement—it's about helping *others* do their work. That may mean coordinating the work of a departmental group, or it might mean supervising a single person. It could involve coordinating the work activities of a team with people from different departments or even people outside the organization such as temporary employees or individuals who work for the organization's suppliers. Keep in mind that managers may also have work duties not related to coordinating and overseeing others' work. For example, an insurance claims supervisor might process claims in addition to coordinating the work activities of other claims clerks.

How can managers be classified in organizations? In traditionally structured organizations (often pictured as a pyramid because more employees are at lower organizational levels than at upper organizational levels), managers can be classified as first-line, middle, or top. (See Exhibit 1-1.) At the lowest level of management, **first-line (or frontline) managers** manage the work of nonmanagerial employees who typically are involved with producing the organization's products or servicing the organization's customers. These managers typically have titles such as *supervisor, shift manager, district manager, department head*, or *office administrator*. **Middle managers** are those between first-line managers and the top level of the organization. They may have titles such as *regional manager, store manager*, or *division manager*. Middle managers are mainly responsible for turning the organization's strategy into action. At the upper levels of the organization are the **top managers**, who are responsible for making organization-wide decisions and establishing the strategy and goals that affect the entire organization. These individuals typically have titles such as *executive vice president, president, managing director, chief operating officer*, or *chief executive officer*.

Not all organizations are structured to get work done using a traditional pyramidal form. Some organizations—for example, W. L. Gore, Zappos, and GitHub—are more loosely configured, with work done by ever-changing teams of employees who move from one project to another as work demands arise. Although it's not as easy to tell who the managers are in these organizations, we do know that someone must fulfill that role—that is, someone must coordinate and oversee the work of others, even if that "someone" changes as work tasks or projects change or that "someone" doesn't necessarily have the title of manager.

Where Do Managers Work?

Managers work in organizations, but what *is* an **organization**? It's a deliberate arrangement of people to accomplish some specific purpose. Your college or university is an organization; so are fraternities and sororities, government departments, churches, Amazon.com, your neighborhood grocery store, the United Way, the St. Louis Cardinals baseball team, and the Mayo Clinic. All these entities have three common characteristics. (See Exhibit 1-2.)

Carnival Corporation CEO Arnold Donald is the top manager of the world's largest cruise line, with over 100,000 employees from different cultures and countries, 10 cruise line brands, and 100 ships. His challenging job involves making decisions and developing plans that help Carnival achieve its goal: "To show our guests the kind of fun that memories are made of."
Source: Rick Wilking/Reuters/Newscom

manager
Someone who coordinates and oversees the work of other people so organizational goals can be accomplished

first-line (frontline) managers
Managers at the lowest level of management who manage the work of nonmanagerial employees

middle managers
Managers between first-line managers and the top level of the organization

top managers
Managers at or near the upper levels of the organization structure who are responsible for making organization-wide decisions and establishing the strategy and goals that affect the entire organization

organization
A deliberate arrangement of people to accomplish some specific purpose

Exhibit 1-1
Levels of Management

Top Managers

Middle Managers

First-Line Managers

Nonmanagerial Employees

Exhibit 1-2
Characteristics of Organizations

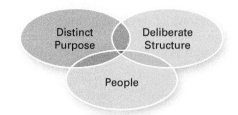

First, an organization has a distinct purpose that is typically expressed through goals the organization seeks to accomplish. Second, each organization is composed of people. It takes people to perform the work that's necessary for the organization to achieve its goals. Third, all organizations develop a deliberate structure within which members do their work. That structure may be open and flexible, with no specific job duties or strict adherence to explicit job arrangements. For instance, most big projects at Alphabet (the parent of Google) are tackled by small, focused employee teams that set up in an instant and complete work just as quickly. Or the structure may be more traditional—like that of Procter & Gamble—with clearly defined rules, regulations, job descriptions, and some members identified as "bosses" who have authority over other members. In the military, there is a well-defined hierarchy. In the US Air Force, the General of the Air Force is the highest ranking officer and Second Lieutenant is the lowest ranking officer. Between the two are nine officer ranks.

Many of today's organizations are structured more like Alphabet, with flexible work arrangements, employee work teams, open communication systems, and supplier alliances. In these organizations, work is defined in terms of tasks to be done. And workdays have no time boundaries since work can be—and is—done anywhere, anytime. However, no matter what type of approach an organization uses, some deliberate structure is needed so work can get done, with managers overseeing and coordinating that work.

WHY are managers important?

LO1.2 Managers are important to organizations. Why? Let's look at three reasons.

The first is that *organizations need their managerial skills and abilities* more than ever in uncertain, complex, and chaotic times. As organizations deal with today's challenges—changing workforce dynamics, the worldwide economic uncertainty, changing technology—managers play an important role in identifying critical issues and crafting responses.

A second is that *they're critical to getting things done.* They create and coordinate the workplace environment and work systems so that others can perform their tasks. Or, if work isn't getting done or isn't getting done as it should be, managers are the ones who find out why and get things back on track.

Third, *managers make a difference in an organization's performance.* How do we know that? The Gallup Organization, which has polled millions of employees and tens of thousands of managers, has found that the single most important variable in employee productivity and loyalty isn't pay or benefits or workplace environment—it's the quality of the relationship between employees and their direct supervisors.[2] (See Exhibit 1-3.) In addition, global consulting firm Towers Watson found that the way a company manages and engages its people can significantly affect its financial performance.[3] Companies that hire managers based on talent realize a 48 percent increase in profitability, a 22 percent increase in productivity, a 30 percent increase in employee engagement scores, a 17 percent increase in customer engagement scores, and a 19 percent decrease in turnover.[4] And another study by the Gallup Organization found leadership to be the single largest influence on employee engagement.[5]

Exhibit 1-3
Managers Make a Difference

MANAGEMENT vs. managers

What Is Management?

LO1.3 **Management** involves coordinating and overseeing the work activities of others so their activities are completed efficiently and effectively. We already know that coordinating and overseeing the work of others is what distinguishes a managerial position from a nonmanagerial one. However, this doesn't mean that managers or their employees can do what they want anytime, anywhere, or in any way. Instead, management involves ensuring that work activities are completed efficiently and effectively by the people responsible for doing them, or at least that's what managers should be doing.

Efficiency refers to getting the most output from the least amount of inputs or resources. Managers deal with scarce resources—including people, money, and equipment—and want to use those resources efficiently. Efficiency is often referred to as "doing things right," that is, not wasting resources. For instance, Southwest Airlines has achieved operating efficiency through a variety of practices, which include using one aircraft model (Boeing 737) throughout its fleet. Using one model simplifies scheduling, operations, and flight maintenance, and the training costs for pilots, ground crew, and mechanics are lower because there's only a single aircraft to learn.[6] These efficient work practices have paid off, as Southwest has made a profit for forty-two consecutive years![7]

It's not enough, however, just to be efficient. Management is also concerned with employee effectiveness. **Effectiveness** is often described as "doing the right things," that is, doing those work activities that will result in achieving goals. Besides being efficient, Southwest Airlines' mission is "dedication to the highest quality of Customer Service delivered with a sense of warmth, friendliness, individual pride, and Company Spirit."[8] Two of the many reasons cited for the airlines' effectiveness are permitting two checked bags for free and permitting a change in itinerary without incurring a penalty.[9]

Whereas efficiency is concerned with the *means* of getting things done, effectiveness is concerned with the *ends*, or attainment of organizational goals (see Exhibit 1-4). In successful organizations, high efficiency and high effectiveness typically go hand in hand.

management
Coordinating and overseeing the work activities of others so their activities are completed efficiently and effectively

efficiency
Getting the most output from the least amount of inputs or resources

effectiveness
Doing those work activities that will result in achieving goals

Exhibit 1-4
Efficiency and Effectiveness in Management

Exhibit 1-5
Four Functions of Management

Planning	Organizing	Leading	Controlling	Lead to
Setting goals, establishing strategies, and developing plans to coordinate activities	Determining what needs to be done, how it will be done, and who is to do it	Motivating, leading, and any other actions involved in dealing with people	Monitoring activities to ensure that they are accomplished as planned	Achieving the organization's stated purposes

Leading is an important function of The Container Store manager Jaimie Moeller (left). She influences the behavior of employees by leading them in a team huddle before they begin their work day. Coaching employees to succeed in the store's team-selling environment helps Moeller achieve the store's sales performance and customer service goals.
Source: James Borchuck/Tampa Bay Times/ Zumapress.com/Alamy Stock Photo

planning
Management function that involves setting goals, establishing strategies for achieving those goals, and developing plans to integrate and coordinate activities

organizing
Management function that involves arranging and structuring work to accomplish the organization's goals

leading
Management function that involves working with and through people to accomplish organizational goals

controlling
Management function that involves monitoring, comparing, and correcting work performance

What Do Managers Do?

Now let's take a more detailed look at what managers do. Describing what managers do isn't easy. Just as no two organizations are alike, no two managers' jobs are alike. In spite of this, management researchers have developed three approaches to describe what managers do: functions, roles, and skills.

MANAGEMENT FUNCTIONS According to the functions approach, managers perform certain activities or functions as they efficiently and effectively coordinate the work of others. What are these functions? Henri Fayol, a French businessman in the early part of the twentieth century, suggested that all managers perform five functions: planning, organizing, commanding, coordinating, and controlling.[10] (See Management History Module for more information.) Today, we use four functions to describe a manager's work: planning, organizing, leading, and controlling (see Exhibit 1-5). Let's briefly look at each.

If you have no particular destination in mind, then any road will do. However, if you have someplace in particular you want to go, you've got to plan the best way to get there. Because organizations exist to achieve some particular purpose, someone must define that purpose and the means for its achievement. Managers are that someone. As managers engage in **planning**, they set goals, establish strategies for achieving those goals, and develop plans to integrate and coordinate activities.

Managers are also responsible for arranging and structuring the work that employees do to accomplish the organization's goals. We call this function **organizing**. When managers organize, they determine what tasks are to be done, who is to do them, how the tasks are to be grouped, who reports to whom, and where decisions are to be made.

Every organization has people, and a manager's job is to work with and through people to accomplish goals. This is the **leading** function. When managers motivate subordinates, help resolve work group conflicts, influence individuals or teams as they work, select the most effective communication channel, or deal in any way with employee behavior issues, they're leading.

The final management function is **controlling**. After goals and plans are set (planning), tasks and structural arrangements are put in place (organizing), and people are hired, trained, and motivated (leading), there has to be an evaluation of whether things are going as planned. To ensure goals are met and work is done as it should be, managers monitor and evaluate performance. Actual performance is compared with the set goals. If those goals aren't achieved, it's the manager's job to get work back on track. This process of monitoring, comparing, and correcting is the controlling function.

Just how well does the functions approach describe what managers do? Do managers always plan, organize, lead, and then control? Not necessarily. What a manager does may not always happen in this sequence. However, regardless of the order in which these functions are performed, managers do plan, organize, lead, and control as they manage.

Exhibit 1-6
Mintzberg's Managerial Roles
Source: Based on H. Mintzberg, *The Nature of Managerial Work* (New York: Prentice Hall, 1983).

MANAGEMENT ROLES Another perspective has been offered by Henry Mintzberg, a well-known management researcher who studied actual managers at work. In his first comprehensive study, Mintzberg concluded that what managers do can best be described by looking at the managerial roles they engage in at work.[11] The term **managerial roles** refers to specific actions or behaviors expected of and exhibited by a manager. As shown in Exhibit 1-6, Mintzberg found ten roles, grouped around interpersonal relationships, the transfer of information, and decision making.

The **interpersonal roles** involve people (subordinates and persons outside the organization) and other ceremonial and symbolic duties. The three interpersonal roles include figurehead, leader, and liaison. The **informational roles** involve collecting, receiving, and disseminating information. The three informational roles include monitor, disseminator, and spokesperson. Finally, the **decisional roles** entail making decisions or choices and include entrepreneur, disturbance handler, resource allocator, and negotiator. As managers perform these roles, Mintzberg proposed that their activities included both reflection (thinking) and action (doing).[12]

A number of follow-up studies have tested the validity of Mintzberg's role categories, and the evidence generally supports the idea that managers—regardless of the type of organization or level in the organization—perform similar roles.[13] However, the emphasis that managers give to the various roles seems to change with organizational level.[14] At higher levels of the organization, the roles of disseminator, figurehead, negotiator, liaison, and spokesperson are more important, while the leader role (as Mintzberg defined it) is more important for lower-level managers than it is for either middle or top-level managers.

So which approach is better, managerial functions or Mintzberg's propositions? Although each does a good job of depicting what managers do, the functions approach still seems to be the generally accepted way of describing the manager's job. "The classical functions provide clear and discrete methods of classifying the thousands of activities managers carry out and the techniques they use in terms of the functions they perform for the achievement of goals."[15] Still, managerial roles provide insights into what managers do while planning, leading, organizing, and controlling.

MANAGEMENT SKILLS UPS is a company that understands the importance of management skills.[16] The company's new on-road supervisors are immersed in a new manager orientation where they learn people and time management skills. The company started an intensive eight-day offsite skills training program for first-line managers as a way to improve its operations. What have supervisors learned from the skills training?

managerial roles
Specific actions or behaviors expected of and exhibited by a manager

interpersonal roles
Managerial roles that involve people and other duties that are ceremonial and symbolic in nature

informational roles
Managerial roles that involve collecting, receiving, and disseminating information

decisional roles
Managerial roles that revolve around making choices

Exhibit 1-7
Skills Needed at Different
Managerial Levels

Top Managers	Conceptual		Interpersonal	Technical

Middle Managers	Conceptual		Interpersonal		Technical

Lower-Level Managers	Conceptual	Interpersonal		Technical

technical skills
Job-specific knowledge and techniques
needed to proficiently perform work
tasks

interpersonal skills
The ability to work well with other people
individually and in a group

conceptual skills
The ability to think and to conceptualize
about abstract and complex situations

Some things they mentioned learning were how to communicate more effectively and how to comply with safety laws and labor practices.

What types of skills do managers need? Robert L. Katz proposed that managers need three critical skills in managing: technical, human, and conceptual.[17] (Exhibit 1-7 shows the relationships of these skills to managerial levels.) **Technical skills** are the job-specific knowledge and techniques needed to proficiently perform work tasks. These skills tend to be more important for first-line managers because they typically manage employees who use tools and techniques to produce the organization's products or service the organization's customers. Often, employees with excellent technical skills get promoted to first-line manager. For example, Dean White, a production supervisor at Springfield ReManufacturing, started as a parts cleaner. Now, Dean manages twenty-five people in six departments. He noted that at first it was difficult to get people to listen, especially his former peers. "I learned I had to gain respect before I could lead," White said. He credits mentors—other supervisors whose examples he followed—with helping him become the type of manager he is today.[18] Dean is a manager who has technical skills, but also recognizes the importance of **interpersonal skills**, which involve the ability to work well with other people both individually and in a group. Because all managers deal with people, these skills are equally important to all levels of management. Managers with good human skills get the best out of their people. They know how to communicate, motivate, lead, and inspire enthusiasm and trust. Finally, **conceptual skills** are the skills managers use to think and to conceptualize about abstract and complex situations. Using these skills, managers see the organization as a whole, understand the relationships among various subunits, and visualize how the organization fits into its broader environment. Managers then can effectively direct employees' work. For example, Ian McAllister, general manager at Amazon, indicates that a successful general manager understands the whole business. With this understanding, managers can get everyone on the same page. In turn, employees will make a substantial number of decisions in support of the company's vision.[19] These skills are most important to top managers.

MANAGERIAL challenges today and into the future

LO1.4 In today's world, managers are dealing with a host of challenges. We want to briefly focus on six of these: technology, disruptive innovation, social media, ethics, political uncertainty, and the customer.

Focus on Technology

Managers increasingly face challenges in their work because technology has been changing how things get done.[20] Cloud computing, artificial intelligence, and robotics are examples of technology. Keeping employees updated on new technologies presents a challenge to many managers. Managers need to work with employees to help them understand why new technology is an improvement over present ways of conducting business. According to Didier Bonnet, coauthor of *Leading Digital*, "The job

IT'S YOUR CAREER

The ABC's of Managing Your Time

Do you feel constantly busy? Do you always seem to have a lot to do and never enough time to do it? If you're like most people, the answer to these questions is YES! Well, maybe in a management textbook we need to do something about that by focusing on one aspect of management that can be tremendously useful to you ... TIME MANAGEMENT!

Time is a unique resource. If it's wasted, it can never be replaced. People talk about saving time, but time can never actually be saved. And unlike resources such as money or talent, which are distributed unequally in this world, time is an equal-opportunity resource. Each one of us gets exactly the same amount: twenty-four hours per day and 168 hours each week. Some people are just a lot more efficient in using their allotment. Here are some suggestions to help you better use your time:

1. *List your current and upcoming goals.* Know what needs to be done daily, weekly, and monthly.

2. *Rank your goals according to importance.* Not all goals are of equal importance. Make sure you give highest priority to the most important goals.

3. *List the activities/tasks necessary to achieve your goals.* What specific actions do you need to take to achieve your goals?

4. *Divide these activities/tasks into categories using an A, B, and C classification.* The As are important and urgent. Bs are either important or urgent, but not both. Cs are routine—not important nor urgent, but still need to be done.

5. *Schedule your activities/tasks according to the priorities you've set.* Prepare a daily plan. Every morning, or at the end of the previous workday, make a list of the five or so most important things you want to accomplish for the day. Then set priorities for the activities listed on the basis of importance and urgency.

6. *Recognize that technology can be a time waster.* Think for a moment how many phone calls, e-mails, texts, and postings on social media you receive on a typical day. Some are essential, while others are distractions that don't require immediate attention. Prioritize the importance of this information.

7. *Realize that priorities may change as your day or week proceeds.* New information may change a task's importance or urgency. As you get new information, reassess your list of priorities.

of a manager is to help people cross the bridge—to get them comfortable with the technology, to get them using it, and to help them understand how it makes their lives better."[21]

Focus on Disruptive Innovation

There are few managerial challenges today more critical than coping with disruptive innovations. Regardless of what business an organization is in, there's a very good chance that they're either a disruptive innovator or competing against a disruptive innovator.

Technology has provided opportunities for small, upstart companies to take on long-standing and well-established businesses. For instance, Uber and Lyft have made it difficult for taxi companies to compete. Expedia, TripAdvisor and the like have basically eliminated storefront travel agents. Hulu and Sling have stolen a good portion of the network and cable TV audience. And LegalZoom has become a major competitor to law firms.

In Chapter 7, we more fully explore disruptive innovation, the opportunities it creates, and what the management of established businesses can do in response.

Focus on Social Media

You probably can't imagine a time when employees did their work without smart devices, email, apps, or internet access. Yet, some twenty-five years ago, as these tools

Learning from
F A I L U R E   Successful Managers Learn from Their Failures

Microsoft cofounder Bill Gates says, "It's fine to celebrate success, but it is more important to heed the lessons of failure." And Jeff Bezos, founder and CEO of Amazon, actually prides himself on his failures. He says, "I've made billions of dollars of failures." Bezos embraces risk, and Amazon has created a culture that has an extreme tolerance for failure. For instance, Amazon Destinations tried to sell hotel rooms and bombed. So did Amazon's effort to create a mobile wallet, offer songs, and allowing customers to test out apps before buying. One of its biggest failures was Fire Phone, which lost $170 million, but led to Echo—its popular voice-activated speaker.

Behind thousands of success stories are paths strewn with setbacks and often failures. Remember: No one goes undefeated all the time. But out of those setbacks, for those individuals and organizations with persistence and the willingness to evaluate, change, and adapt—success frequently prevails. And what applies to managers and companies also applies to you. You're going to make mistakes, have setbacks, and sometimes fail in your endeavors. You need to learn from these and move on. For instance:

J. K. Rowling was a single mother, living on welfare, who had her manuscripts rejected by more than a dozen publishers before she found one to publish *Harry Potter*. Ms. Rowling, now a billionaire, is one of the richest women in Britain.

After being fired early in her TV career, Oprah went on to find great success in her field, where she is now known by her first name.

Source: JStone/Shutterstock

Early in her career, Oprah Winfrey was fired from her Baltimore TV news reporter job and told by her producer that she was "unfit for television news." But that reporter job and television experience prepared her for her incredibly successful TV talk show.

While classmates in high school, Bill Gates and Paul Allen started Traf-O-Data. They designed a computerized microprocessor that would analyze traffic data and create reports for Washington state highway department's traffic engineers. The goal was to optimize traffic and end road congestion. Unfortunately, their first demo didn't work and the idea later became obsolete when the state of Washington offered to tabulate the tapes for cities for free. While the concept failed, it provided Gates and Allen with the software skills that would lead to their creating a new start-up called "Micro-Soft."

Heart surgeon Toby Cosgrove, the former president and CEO of the Cleveland Clinic, made an excellent case for the value of failure in his graduation address to Case Western University's Class of 2018: "Failure is a great teacher ... In my more than 20,000 heart operations, it is difficult to remember the successful outcomes. It is the one percent of patients who do not survive that are remembered ... From this one percent, most of my lessons were learned. You learn vastly more from your mistakes ... Failure is an opportunity to learn. We may learn that our present strategy won't work; we may learn that our goal was not worthy; we may learn that we quit too soon ... Our instinct is to hide our failures [but] failure is temporary. It is a source of experience and most importantly, failure is an event in each person's life, but it is not the person."

We think there's a lot for you to learn through reading about others' failures. So throughout this book we include examples that illustrates major failures, what individuals and organizations learned, and the changes they made in response.[22]

social media

Forms of electronic communication through which users create online communities to share ideas, information, personal messages, and other content

were becoming more common in workplaces, managers struggled with the challenges of providing guidelines for using the internet and email in their organizations. Today, a tool that nearly all organizations use is **social media**, forms of electronic communication through which users create online communities to share ideas, information, personal messages, and other content. And employees don't just use these on their personal time, but also for work purposes. That's why managers need to understand and manage the power and peril of social media.

There is also a downside to social media. As noted by Berkshire Hathaway CEO Warren Buffet, "It takes twenty years to build a reputation and five minutes to ruin it."[23] Internally, social media also becomes problematic when it becomes a way for boastful employees to brag about their accomplishments, for managers to publish one-way messages to employees, or for employees to argue or gripe about something or someone.

In the remainder of the book, we'll look at how social media is impacting how managers manage, especially in the areas of ethics, communication, motivation, and strategy.

Focus on Ethics

It's the unusual week that the business press doesn't report a story about unethical practices by a firm, an executive, or a group of employees. A major bank is found to be creating fake accounts in the name of real customers. A car dealer is caught rolling back the odometers on used vehicles. A pharmaceutical company raises the price 500 percent on a drug that has been around for twenty years. An employee is found to have turned in fake receipts on his expense account.

The long-term success of an organization depends on building trust with customers, clients, suppliers, and employees. Leaders need to take responsibility for setting high ethical standards and creating ethical workplaces. In Chapter 6, we address the ethical challenge. And the end of each chapter includes an ethical dilemma to help you focus on the importance of ethical behavior and for coping with ethical challenges.

Focus on Political Uncertainty

Democratic societies like the US, Canada, Australia, and the UK historically faced stable and relatively predictable political environments. The last decade has seen a significant shift toward uncertainty. With this arise new challenges for management. A few examples of changes in the US include major business tax reform that significantly cut corporate tax rates but also limited the deduction for interest expense; renegotiation of the US, Canada, and Mexico trade agreement (NAFTA); imposition of trade tariffs on certain industrial products that resulted in retaliatory tariffs from foreign countries on US products; continual reinterpretations of immigration policies; and changes in federal laws affecting corporate healthcare plans.

In Europe, UK voters surprisingly chose in 2016 to exit the European Union. Among other things, for many European firms that had head offices in London, this meant reorganizing so as to better serve European customers.

And political uncertainty hasn't been limited to the federal level. States have been imposing new laws and regulations that affect business. California, for instance, has continually imposed new regulations on business in the areas of the environment, labor laws, minimum wage, land use, and consumer protection. Cities, too, have added to political uncertainty. As an example, in 2018, the city of Seattle imposed an annual tax of $275 for every Seattle employee of businesses with $20 million or more in yearly revenue. Under pressure from business firms, a month later, the city repealed the tax. For a company like Amazon, that has 45,000 employees in Seattle, the tax would have added more than $12 million to its cost of doing business.

> ## fyi
>
> - 18 percent of top executives identify global political uncertainty as one of the top 10 challenges they face.
> - The challenge mentioned by the most executives (64 percent) is developing leaders in their organizations.[24]

Focus on the Customer

John Legere, CEO of T-Mobile, likes to listen to customers. "My business philosophy is listen to your employees, listen to your customers. Shut up and do what they tell you. And each of our Un-carrier moves and the way I run my company is completely aligned with that."[25] This manager understands the importance of customers and clearly believes that focusing on customers is essential to success. Without them, most organizations would cease to exist. Yet, focusing on the customer has long been thought to be the responsibility of marketing types. "Let the marketers worry about the customers" is how many managers felt. That sentiment is out of date. Companies like Costco, Nordstrom, Dunkin' Donuts, Tesla, and Zappos stand out for their outstanding customer service and loyal customers.

Today, the majority of employees in developed countries work in service jobs as teachers, nurses, technical support reps, food servers, housekeepers, consultants, financial planners, and the like. For instance, 77.2 percent of the US labor force is employed in service industries.[26] In Australia and Canada, similarly, 78 percent work in service industries.[27] And as service economies have become dominant, managers realize that delivering consistent, high-quality customer service is essential for their organization's survival and success.

With the growing popularity of tourism in the Dominican Republic, a large percentage of the labor force works in service jobs for resorts, attractions, and tourist-related activities such as the food service workers shown here presenting fruit in an artistic fashion for tourists. To succeed in the service industry, managers must create a customer-responsive organization.
Source: Lucas Vallecillos/Alamy Stock Photo

universality of management
The reality that management is needed in all types and sizes of organizations, at all organizational levels, in all organizational areas, and in organizations, no matter where located

Importantly, the evidence indicates that good customer care pays off. A recent study found that nearly all customers (92 percent) whose issue was resolved during first contact with customer service would likely continue using the company.[28] That number drops to about half (51 percent) for customers whose issue was not resolved during first contact. Employees are an important part of that equation.[29] The implication is clear: managers must create a customer-responsive organization where employees are friendly and courteous, accessible, knowledgeable, prompt in responding to customer needs, and willing to do what's necessary to please the customer.[30] We'll look at customer service management in other chapters.

WHY study management?

LO1.5 If you're not a management major nor planning on a career in management, you might rightly ask: Why should I study management? We can give you four reasons: the universality of management, the reality of work, the rewards from being a manager, and the insights it can provide you into life at work.

The Universality of Management

We can say with absolute certainty that management is needed in all types and sizes of organizations, at all organizational levels, in all organizational work areas, and in all organizations, regardless of where they're located. This is known as the **universality of management**. (See Exhibit 1-8.) In all these organizations, managers must plan, organize, lead, and control. However, that's not to say that management is done the same way. What a supervisor in an applications testing group at Twitter does versus what the CEO of Twitter does is a matter of degree and emphasis, not function. Because both are managers, both will plan, organize, lead, and control. How much and how they do so will differ.

Management is universally needed in all organizations. And organizations that are well managed—and we'll share many examples of these throughout the text—develop a loyal customer base, grow, and prosper, even during challenging times. Those that are poorly managed find themselves losing customers and revenues. By studying management, you'll be able to recognize poor management and work to get it corrected.

The Reality of Work

Another reason for studying management is the reality that for most of you, once you graduate from college and begin your career, you will either manage or be managed. For those who plan to be managers, an understanding of management forms the foundation

Exhibit 1-8
Universal Need for Management

- Create a work environment in which organizational members can work to the best of their ability
- Have opportunities to think creatively and use imagination
- Help others find meaning and fulfillment in work
- Support, coach, and nurture others
- Work with a variety of people
- Receive recognition and status in organization and community
- Play a role in influencing organizational outcomes
- Receive appropriate compensation in the form of salaries, bonuses, and stock options

Exhibit 1-9
Rewards from Being a Manager

upon which to build your management knowledge and skills. For those of you who don't see yourself managing, you're still likely to have to work with managers. Our experience tells us that you can gain a great deal of insight into the way your boss (and fellow employees) behave and how organizations function by studying management.

Rewards from Being a Manager

There are real rewards from holding a managerial position. (See Exhibit 1-9.) There's the satisfaction of creating a work environment in which organizational members can do their work to the best of their ability and thus help the organization achieve its goals. You help others find meaning and fulfillment in their work. You get to support, coach, and nurture others and help them make good decisions. In addition, as a manager, you often have the opportunity to think creatively and use your imagination. You'll get to meet and work with a variety of people—both inside and outside the organization. Other rewards may include receiving recognition and status in your organization and in the community, playing a significant role in influencing organizational outcomes, and receiving attractive compensation in the form of salaries, bonuses, and stock options.

Gaining Insights into Life at Work

A good number of students regularly remind your authors that they're not planning a career in management. These students' career goals are to be accountants or financial analysts or marketing researchers or computer programmers. They ask us: Why do I need to take a management course? Our answer is: Because understanding management concepts and how managers think will help you get better results at work and enhance your career. And who knows, you may become a manager someday. Oftentimes, successful employees are promoted to managerial roles. For example, you may begin your career as an auditor with a major accounting firm and find, a few years later, you're overseeing an audit team or you're a partner thrust into managing a regional office.

Throughout this book you'll encounter pages that we call "Workplace Confidential." This feature will introduce you to challenges you're likely to face at work—like organizational politics, an uncommunicative boss, or an unfair performance review—and offer you specific suggestions on how to deal with these challenges.

If you expect to work with others—whether it's in a Fortune 100 corporation or in a three-person start-up—studying management can pay demonstrable dividends.

EMPLOYABILITY SKILLS

LO1.6 It's one thing to *know* something and another to be able to *apply* that knowledge. We want to prepare you for your career in the working world by helping you learn and practice key skills that hiring managers identify as important to success in a variety of organizational settings—small and large businesses, profit and nonprofit organizations, and entrepreneurial endeavors. Here are the skills we'll be focusing on and a brief definition:

WORKPLACE CONFIDENTIAL Dealing with Organizational Politics

In an ideal world, the good guys always win, everyone tells the truth, and job promotions and generous pay raises go to the most deserving candidate. Unfortunately, we don't live in such an ideal world. The world we live in is a political one.

Politics is a fact of life in organizations. People who ignore this fact do so at their own peril. But why, you may wonder, must politics exist? Isn't it possible for an organization to be politics free? It's possible, but most unlikely.

Organizations are made up of individuals and groups with different values, goals, and interests. This sets up the potential for conflict over resources. Departmental budgets, office allocations, project responsibilities, promotion choices, and salary adjustments are just a few examples of the resources about whose allocation organizational members will disagree.

Resources in organizations are also limited, which turns potential conflict into real conflict. If resources were abundant, then all the various constituencies within the organization could satisfy their goals. But because they're limited, not everyone's interests can be provided for. Furthermore, whether true or not, gains by one individual or group are often perceived as being at the expense of others within the organization. These forces create a competition among members for the organization's limited resources.

Maybe the most important factor leading to politics within organizations is the realization that most of the facts that are used to allocate the limited resources are open to interpretation. What, for instance, is good performance? What's an adequate improvement? What constitutes an unsatisfactory job? One person's team player is another's "yes man." So it is in the large and ambiguous middle ground of organizational life—where the facts don't speak for themselves—that politics flourish.

The above explains why some people in the workplace lie, misrepresent, conceal, backstab, play favorites, scheme, pass the buck, deny responsibility, form alliances, or engage in similar political actions.

If you want to improve your political skills at work, we offer the following suggestions:

- *Frame arguments in terms of organizational goals.* People whose actions appear to blatantly further their own interests at the expense of the organization are almost universally denounced, are likely to lose influence, and often suffer the ultimate penalty of being expelled from the organization. Make sure your actions appear to be in the best interests of the organization.

- *Develop the right image.* Make sure you understand what your organization wants and values from its employees—in terms of dress, associates to cultivate and those to avoid, whether to appear to be a risk-taker or risk averse, the importance of getting along with others, and

so forth. Because the assessment of your performance is rarely a fully objective process, you need to pay attention to style as well as substance.

- *Gain control of organizational resources.* The control of organizational resources that are scarce and important is a source of influence. Knowledge and expertise are particularly effective resources to control. These resources make you more valuable to the organization and, therefore, more likely to gain security, advancement, and a receptive audience for your ideas.

- *Make yourself appear indispensable.* You don't have to be indispensable as long as key people in your organization think that you are. If the organization's prime decision makers believe there is no ready substitute for what you bring to the organization, your job is likely safe and you're likely to be treated well.

- *Be visible.* If you have a job that brings your accomplishments to the attention of others, that's great. However, if not—without creating the image of a braggart—you'll want to let others know what you're doing by giving progress reports to your boss and others, having satisfied customers relay their appreciation to higher-ups, being seen at social functions, and being active in your professional associations.

- *Develop powerful allies.* It is often beneficial to have friends in high places. Network by cultivating contacts with potentially influential people above you, at your own level, and in the lower ranks. These allies often can provide you with information that's otherwise not readily available and provide you with support if and when you need it. Having a mentor in the organization who is well respected is often a valuable asset.

- *Avoid "tainted" members.* In almost every organization, there are fringe members whose status is questionable. Their performance and/or loyalty are suspect. Or they have strange personalities. Keep your distance from such individuals. Given the reality that effectiveness has a large subjective component, your own effectiveness might be called into question if you're perceived as being too closely associated with tainted members.

- *Support your boss.* Your immediate future is in the hands of your current boss. Because that person evaluates your performance, you'll typically want to have your boss on your side. You should make every effort to help your boss succeed, make her look good, support her if she is under siege, and spend the time to find out the criteria she will use to assess your effectiveness. Don't undermine your boss. And don't speak negatively of her to others.[31]

Critical thinking involves purposeful and goal-directed thinking used to define and solve problems, make decisions, or form judgments across a variety of situations.

Communication is defined as effective use of oral, written, and nonverbal skills; effective listening; and use of technology to convey both information and understanding.

Collaboration is a skill in which individuals can actively work together on a task, negotiate differences, and produce final outcomes reflective of their joint and interdependent actions.

Knowledge application and analysis is defined as the ability to learn a concept and then apply that knowledge in another setting to achieve a higher level of understanding.

Social responsibility includes skills related to both ethical behavior and corporate obligations. Ethics includes sets of guiding principles that influence the way individuals and organizations behave. Corporate obligations is a form of ethical behavior that requires organizations understand, identify, and eliminate unethical economic, social, and environmental behaviors.

Each of the following chapters will start with what we are calling the Employability Skills Matrix (ESM). As you can see in Exhibit 1-10, this matrix links the five employability skills to specific features in each chapter—including It's Your Career, Workplace Confidential, Ethical Dilemma, Working Together, My Turn to Be a Manager, and the Case Applications. Within these sections, you will practice thinking critically and applying your knowledge of concepts. You will also learn how to improve your collaboration and communication skills by learning what you might do or say in these given situations to navigate the work world positively and effectively. You'll be confronted with dilemmas in which you will consider the ethics of particular issues in the workplace. We recommend that you review and consider the ESM in advance of reading the chapter so that you'll have a better idea of the skills you'll be developing from each chapter.

Exhibit 1-10
Employability Skills Matrix (ESM)

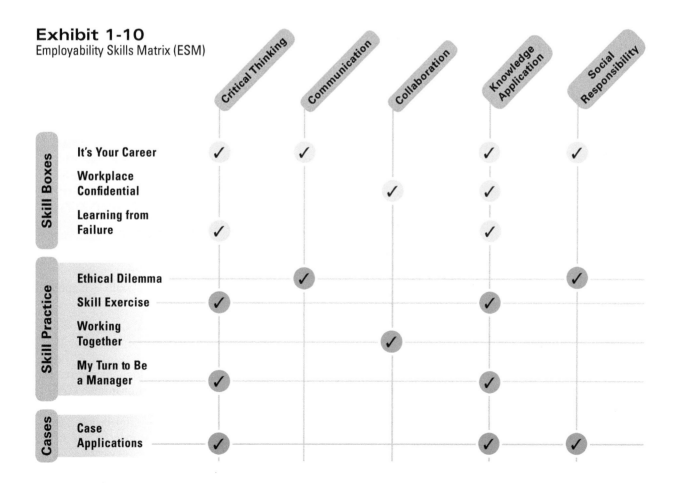

		Critical Thinking	Communication	Collaboration	Knowledge Application	Social Responsibility
Skill Boxes	It's Your Career	✓	✓		✓	✓
	Workplace Confidential			✓	✓	
	Learning from Failure	✓			✓	
Skill Practice	Ethical Dilemma		✓			✓
	Skill Exercise	✓			✓	
	Working Together			✓		
	My Turn to Be a Manager	✓			✓	
Cases	Case Applications	✓			✓	✓

Chapter 1 PREPARING FOR: Exams/Quizzes

CHAPTER SUMMARY by Learning Objectives

LO1.1 **TELL** who managers are and where they work.

Managers coordinate and oversee the work of other people so that organizational goals can be accomplished. Nonmanagerial employees work directly on a job or task and have no one reporting to them. In traditionally structured organizations, managers can be first-line, middle, or top. In more loosely structured organizations, managers may be less easy to identify, but managers still are needed to coordinate the work.

Managers work in an organization, which is a deliberate arrangement of people to accomplish some specific purpose. Organizations have three characteristics: they have a distinctive purpose, they are composed of people, and they have a deliberate structure. Organizations range from sororities and online companies like Amazon.com to nonprofits and local retail stores.

LO1.2 **EXPLAIN** why managers are important to organizations.

Managers are important to organizations for three reasons. First, organizations need their managerial skills and abilities in uncertain, complex, and chaotic times. Second, managers are critical to getting things done in organizations. Finally, managers make a difference in an organization's performance. The way employees are managed can affect the organization's financial performance by affecting employee productivity, loyalty, and engagement, and managerial ability has been shown to be important in creating organizational value.

LO1.3 **DESCRIBE** the functions, roles, and skills of managers.

Broadly speaking, management is what managers do and involves coordinating and overseeing the efficient and effective completion of others' work activities. Efficiency means doing things right; effectiveness means doing the right things.

The four functions of management include planning (setting goals, establishing strategies, and developing plans), organizing (arranging and structuring work), leading (working with and through people), and controlling (monitoring, comparing, and correcting work performance).

Mintzberg's managerial roles include interpersonal, which involves people and other ceremonial/symbolic duties (figurehead, leader, and liaison); informational, which involves collecting, receiving, and disseminating information (monitor, disseminator, and spokesperson); and decisional, which involves making choices (entrepreneur, disturbance handler, resource allocator, and negotiator).

Katz's managerial skills include technical (job-specific knowledge and techniques), interpersonal (ability to work well with people), and conceptual (ability to think and express ideas). Technical skills are most important for lower-level managers, while conceptual skills are most important for top managers. Interpersonal skills are equally important for all managers.

LO1.4 **DESCRIBE** the factors that are reshaping and redefining the manager's job.

The changes impacting managers' jobs include changing technology, disruptive innovation, social media, ethical issues, political uncertainties, and customer service. Managers must focus on technology in order to keep up to date on how things get done in organizations. Managers must focus on disruptive innovation because their organization may be competing against a disruptive innovator or may be one itself.

Managers must focus on social media because both organizations and employees use this form of communication to share information and create connections with others. Managers must focus on ethics to establish an ethical culture and ensure laws and regulations are followed. And finally, managers must focus on customer service because employee attitudes and behaviors play a big role in customer satisfaction.

LO1.5 **EXPLAIN** the value of studying management.

It's important to study management for four reasons: (1) the universality of management, which refers to the fact that managers are needed in all types and sizes of organizations, at all organizational levels and work areas, and in all global locations; (2) the reality of work—that is, you will either manage or be managed; (3) the significant rewards (such as creating work environments to help people work to the best of their ability, supporting and encouraging others, helping others find meaning and fulfillment in work, helping the organization achieve its goals, etc.) in being a manager; and (4) gaining an understanding of how managers think and how organizations operate.

LO1.6 **DESCRIBE** the benefits of the Employability Skills Matrix (ESM).

The ESM identifies chapter content relating to five crucial employment skills—critical thinking, communication, collaboration, knowledge application, and social responsibility.

REVIEW AND DISCUSSION QUESTIONS

1-1. What is a manager? How do managers differ from nonmanagerial employees?

1-2. Why are managers important to organizations?

1-3. What is the difference between efficiency and effectiveness?

1-4. Is your course instructor a manager? Discuss in terms of managerial functions, managerial roles, and skills.

1-5. What is an example of a disruptive innovation that managers might have to cope with in the future?

1-6. Why is it important for managers to focus on the customer?

1-7. Explain why the universality of management concept still holds true or doesn't hold true today.

1-8. Which of the reasons for studying management is most important to you and why?

Writing Assignments

1-9. Is there one best "style" of management? Why or why not?

1-10. Researchers at Harvard Business School found that the most important managerial behaviors involve two fundamental things: enabling people to move forward in their work and treating them decently as human beings. What do you think of these two managerial behaviors? What are the implications for someone, like yourself, who is studying management?

PREPARING FOR: My Career

ETHICS DILEMMA

• The gap between career development opportunities managers intend to provide and what they actually deliver to employees has grown to 12 percent • Millennials place more importance on career development opportunities and job training than older generations • Forty percent of managers never talk with employees about career goals and how to meet them • Thirty-seven percent of employees would like to have career-related discussions with their managers more frequently.[32] Moving to a management position isn't easy.

1-11. Does an organization have an ethical responsibility to provide career development advice to employees? Explain your position.

1-12. If career opportunities in an organization are limited, do managers have a responsibility to convey this information to employees? Explain your position.

SKILL EXERCISE Developing Your Skills as a Manager

About The Skill

Research has shown that there are skills that most managers should have. Unfortunately, as many as 90 percent of managers don't have these skills.[33] Managers who have these skills can set themselves apart from those without them. If you aren't yet a manager, developing these skills can be just what you need to get higher-level jobs and show others that you have management potential.

Steps in Practicing the Skill

- *Ask for feedback.* Managers often think they need to be in complete control without asking for feedback. Make it a habit to ask how you could do a better job or how you could be a more effective teammate. Get used to doing this now and then continue this skill once you are a manager.

- *View matters from employees' point of view.* Practice asking yourself what others at work might think of situations that arise. Ask people in different jobs or departments outside of your friendship group. Having these different perspectives will help you to make better decisions. You also score points by asking people for their input.

- *Understand the big picture.* Managers should think about not just their department, but also the company as a whole. Increase your understanding of how your job fits into what your company does. Then, go even bigger by researching trends in your company's industry.

- *Manage your own emotions.* When you are a manager, frustration and anger affect your employees. If you feel like you need to vent, do so outside of work. Practice treating everyone at work as if they are customers and work on stress management techniques so you don't take your emotions out on others.

- *Acknowledge employees for good work.* Appreciation goes a long way toward improving morale. Let people at work know when they have done a good job or have made your work easier in some way.

- *Support employees in front of others.* Managers sometimes feel pressure to go along with their bosses rather than support their employees. Look for opportunities to stand up for people you work with when others aren't giving them the credit they deserve.

- *Manage your own career.* Develop a long-term career plan that you revisit regularly. Write in your calendar every three months that it is time to check your career plan and make any needed adjustments.

- *Recognize possible biases you may have and communicate with people different than yourself.* Most people have biases that they don't realize they have. When you are about to make a decision, ask yourself if there are any possible biases that might be relevant and ask someone with a different personality type, age, race, or background what they think.

- *Build trust and communication at work.* Get to know people at work beyond what must be said or done as a part of the job. Establish relationships with them and show that you care about them as people. Working with them will be much easier as a result.

Practicing the Skill

Select two of the skills that managers don't often have and spend one week working on them. Write notes describing your experiences—good and bad. What did you notice that was different after practicing these skills? What could you have done to practice these skills even more effectively? What steps could you take to improve these skills in the future?

WORKING TOGETHER Team Exercise

If you've worked for a manager, played for a coach, or been part of a group that had a leader, you've probably noticed management skills that those individuals could have improved. In groups of three or four, each student should describe a specific situation where the management skills they observed could have been improved. As a group, decide what commonalities, if any, exist in the various situations. Using Mintzberg's roles, where were these individuals deficient? Now, brainstorm ways that these individuals might improve their skills. Be prepared to share what you learned with the class.

MY TURN TO BE A MANAGER

- Use the most current *Occupational Outlook Handbook* (US Department of Labor, Bureau of Labor Statistics) to research three different categories of managers. For each, prepare a bulleted list that describes the following:

the nature of the work, training and other qualifications needed, earnings, and job outlook and projections data.

- Get in the habit of reading at least one current business periodical (*Wall Street Journal, Bloomberg Businessweek, Fortune, Fast Company, Forbes,* etc.). Sign up to follow a few of these publications on Twitter.

- Explore the social media presence of your favorite company. Like them on Facebook and follow them on Twitter, Instagram, and/or any other social media outlet the company uses.

- Interview two different managers and ask them the following questions: What are the best and worst parts about being a manager? What's the best management advice you ever received? Type up the questions and their answers to turn in to your professor.

- Accountants and other professionals have certification programs to verify their skills, knowledge, and professionalism. What about managers? Two certification programs for managers include the Certified Manager (Institute of Certified Professional Managers) and the Certified Business Manager (Association of Professionals in Business Management). Research each of these programs. Prepare a bulleted list of what each involves.

- If you have work experience, consider managers who you have encountered. Did you work with any good managers? Did you work with any bad managers? Based on your experience, create a list of traits or skills that good managers possess.

CASE APPLICATION 1 — Working with Artificial Intelligence

For most people, artificial intelligence brings to mind *replacing* jobs with robots. However, 1,500 companies studied by the management consulting firm Accenture found that the largest performance gains were when humans and machines *worked together*.[34]

What does humans and machines working together look like? At clothing retailer H&M, human buyers and planners use artificial intelligence (AI) to guide their work. They rely on data to figure out what styles will be purchased, by which types of customers, and what their customers might need in future seasons. Buyers and planners then build on that data to make final decisions.

A similar process is used by Nathan Cates, a buyer at Bombfell, an online styling service for men that sends customers boxes of clothing that they can keep or return. Before buying an item, Cates insists on touching the fabric and testing it for features such as fabric sheerness and fit.[35] But, in contrast to H&M, these tasks are not currently accomplished well by machines.

If you call your pharmacy to refill a prescription and don't talk to a human, pharmacy employees are freed up to spend their time on customer questions that are more complex. Some companies, like the Swedish bank SEB, use AI to monitor customer calls handled by humans to see how similar problems might be resolved or even prevented in the future.

It's also possible to see humans and computers working together to increase employees' physical capabilities. At Hyundai, robotic devices are worn by some manufacturing employees that give them more strength and endurance than any normal human.

While it's difficult to predict exactly how artificial intelligence will affect jobs in the future, there are some aspects of jobs that may be impossible to automate effectively. As CEO Chida Khatua of the asset-management firm EquBot put it, "If I'm the customer explaining what I want, humans need to be involved. Sometimes I don't know what I really want."

DISCUSSION QUESTIONS

1-13. In what ways do machines add to the work of managers and other employees (instead of replacing them)?

1-14. How might AI change a manager's job in 2030?

1-15. What kind of skills or tasks do you think are least likely to be done by machines or computers in the future?

1-16. What can you do to make yourself more valuable to companies so that they need you (and not a machine) to get work done?

CASE APPLICATION 2

Nike: Taking a Customer Focus to a New Level

It's one thing to ensure that customers feel that their concerns are resolved quickly. It's something else to *revamp* how a company reaches customers. That's what Nike has been up to lately. This approach seems to be paying off with sales growth as well as record-high stock prices.[36]

Nike CEO Mark Parker calls their Nike Direct effort a "massive transformation" of the company.[37] Selling to customers directly has changed processes throughout the company—including design, manufacturing, sales and more.

They rolled out the Nike SNKRS app to alert superfans about limited-edition releases. Nike cultivated closer relationships with superfans with a suite of new experiences. They also used SNKRS as a lab for how to better connect with customers digitally.

As Nike learns what their customers want, they are injecting that information into the first step of their process: creating new shoes. In the summer of 2018, they opened their first Nike Live store in Los Angeles.[38] Sneakers and apparel made just for this neighborhood are being sold there. Nike figured out what residents in this area like based on data from their six apps.

Nike Live stores are all about a new kind of focus on the customer. A pair of shoes are waiting for you in a locker that pops open upon your arrival in the store. Then, you can take the shoes for a run on an in-store treadmill. Have questions? No problem! Feel free to ask Nike athletes who are ready to answer those questions. If you know what you want, you can schedule curbside pick-up from the store via the app.

Special offers also await customers visiting Nike Live stores. Scan your profile bar code in a store at a special vending machine and gifts like Dri-Fit socks are yours for free. Nike wants these stores to make shoppers feel special. And they offer what online shopping can't: trying on items and getting in-person service.

Building a one-on-one relationship with consumers comes with perks. Nike doesn't have to spend months working with retailers on how to target customers. And, based on data from their apps, they can keep a step ahead figuring out what customers want.

DISCUSSION QUESTIONS

1-17. What makes Nike's focus on the customer different from most companies?

1-18. If you were in charge of taking Nike's focus on the customer to the next level, what you would you do?

1-19. What advantages of online shopping and in-person shopping do Nike Live stores try to combine? Why (or why not) do you think they will be successful?

1-20. What do you think a focus on the customer will look like for companies in 2025?

ENDNOTES

1. US Bureau of Labor Statistics, *Occupational Outlook Handbook*, April 13, 2018.
2. R. Beck and J. Harter, "Why Great Managers Are So Rare," March 25, 2014, businessjournal.gallup.com.
3. "Work USA 2008/2009 Report: Driving Business Results through Continuous Engagement," Watson Wyatt Worldwide, Washington, DC.
4. A. Adkins, "Report: What Separates Great Managers from the Rest," Gallup Organization, May 12, 2015.
5. "The New Employment Deal: How Far, How Fast and How Enduring? Insights from the 2010 Global Workforce Study," Towers Watson, Washington, DC.
6. M. Srinivasan, "Southwest Airlines Operations—A Strategic Perspective," Airline Industry Articles, September 11, 2014, http://airline-industry.malq.net/.
7. Southwest, "Southwest Corporate Fact Sheet," January 10, 2016, http://www.swamedia.com/channels/Corporate-Fact-Sheet/pages/corporate-fact-sheet.
8. From "The Mission of Southwest Airlines." Copyright (c) 2016 Southwest Airlines. January 5, 2016. https://www.southwest.com/html/about-southwest/index.html?clk=GFOOTER-ABOUT-ABOUT.
9. D. Landsel, "11 Reasons Why Southwest Is the Best Airline You're Probably Not Flying," *Airfarewatchdog* (website), April 20, 2015, https://www.airfarewatchdog.com/blog/22975194/11-reasons-why-southwest-is-the-best-airline-youre-probably-not-flying/.
10. H. Fayol, *Industrial and General Administration* (Paris: Dunod, 1916).

11. J. T. Straub, "Put on Your Manager's Hat," *USA Today Online*, October 29, 2002, www.usatoday.com; and H. Mintzberg, *The Nature of Managerial Work* (New York: Harper & Row, 1973).

12. H. Mintzberg and J. Gosling, "Educating Managers Beyond Borders," *Academy of Management Learning and Education* (September 2002): pp. 64–76.

13. See, for example, M. J. Martinko and W. L. Gardner, "Structured Observation of Managerial Work: A Replication and Synthesis," *Journal of Management Studies* (May 1990):, pp. 330–357; A. I. Kraut, P. R. Pedigo, D. D. McKenna, and M. D. Dunnette, "The Role of the Manager: What's Really Important in Different Management Jobs," *Academy of Management Executive* (November 1989): pp. 286–293; and C. M. Pavett and A. W. Lau, "Managerial Work: The Influence of Hierarchical Level and Functional Specialty," *Academy of Management Journal* (March 1983): pp. 170–177.

14. Pavett and Lau, "Managerial Work."

15. S. J. Carroll and D. J. Gillen, "Are the Classical Management Functions Useful in Describing Managerial Work?" *Academy of Management Review*, January 1987, p. 48.

16. K. Tyler, "Train Your Front Line," *HR Magazine,* December 2013, pp. 43–45.

17. R. L. Katz, "Skills of an Effective Administrator," *Harvard Business Review*, September/October 1974, pp. 90–102.

18. K. Fivecoat-Campbell, "Up the Corporate Ladder," *Springfield (Missouri) Business Journal*, March 12–18, 2012, pp. 9+.

19. I. McAllister, "What Does It Take to Be a Great General Manager for a Web Company?" *Forbes*, October 22, 2013, https://www.forbes.com/sites/quora/2013/10/22/what-does-it-take-to-be-a-great-general-manager-for-a-web-company/#286ed2c1136e.

20. W. F. Cascio and R. Montealegre, "How Technology is Changing Work and Organizations," in *Annual Review of Organizational Psychology and Organizational Behavior* (Palo Alto, CA: Annual Reviews, 2016), pp. 359–75.

21. R. Knight, "Convincing Skeptical Employees to Adopt New Technology," March 19, 2015, https://hbr.org/2015/03/convincing-skeptical-employees-to-adopt-new-technology.

22. Based on B. Lenz, "Failure is Essential to Learning," *Edutopia*, April 8, 2015; D. Streitfeld, "Behind Success, Amazon Finds Room for Risk," *New York Times*, June 18, 2017, 1; J. Lee and P. Miesing, "How Entrepreneurs Can Benefit From Failure Management," *Organizational Dynamics*, July–September 2017, pp. 157–64; T. Cosgrove, "Embrace the Dreaded 'F Word.' Failure is a Wonderful Teacher," *Cleveland Plain Dealer*, May 27, 2018, p. E2; O. Babur, "Talking About Failure Is Crucial for Growth," *New York Times*, August 19, 2018, p. BU-3; and M. Korn, "Failure 101: Teaching Resilience," *Wall Street Journal*, December 19, 2018, p. A6.

23. A. Goodman, "Top 40 Buffett-isms: Inspiration to Become a Better Investor," September 25, 2013, https://www.forbes.com/sites/agoodman/2013/09/25/the-top-40-buffettisms-inspiration-to-become-a-better-investor/#fa0634b7ccb2.

24. "Global Leader Forecast 2018. 25 Research Insights to Fuel Your People Strategy." The Conference Board. www.ey.com/Publication/vwLUAssets/ey-the-global-leadership-forecast/$FILE/ey-the-global-leadership-forecast.

25. A. Stevenson, "T-Mobile CEO to Cramer: 'Shut Up and Listen'," CNBC.com, updated April 29, 2015, https://www.cnbc.com/2015/04/28/t-mobile-ceo-to-cramer-shut-up-and-listen.html.

26. US Bureau of Labor Statistics, "The Employment Situation—December 2017," (USDL-16-0001), January 8, 2018.

27. Data from *The World Factbook 2018*, https://www.cia.gov/library/publications/resources/the-world-factbook.

28. C. J. Grimm, "Good Customer Care Pays Off," *CX Act 2014 Touch Point Study,* May 19, 2015, hbr.org.

29. C. B. Blocker, D. J. Flint, M. B. Myers, and S. F. Slater, "Proactive Customer Orientation and Its Role for Creating Customer Value in Global Markets," *Journal of the Academy of Marketing Science* (April 2011): pp. 216–233; D. Dougherty and A. Murthy, "What Service Customers Really Want," *Harvard Business Review*, September 2009, p. 22; and K. A. Eddleston, D. L. Kidder, and B. E. Litzky, "Who's the Boss? Contending with Competing Expectations from Customers and Management," *Academy of Management Executive* (November 2002): pp. 85–95.

30. See, for instance, J. W. Grizzle, A. R. Zablah, T. J. Brown, J. C. Mowen, and J. M. Lee, "Employee Customer Orientation in Context: How the Environment Moderates the Influence of Customer Orientation on Performance Outcomes," *Journal of Applied Psychology* (September 2009): pp. 1227–1242; B. A. Gutek, M. Groth, and B. Cherry, "Achieving Service Success through Relationships and Enhanced Encounters," *Academy of Management Executive* (November 2002): pp. 132–144; S. D. Pugh, J. Dietz, J. W. Wiley, and S. M. Brooks, "Driving Service Effectiveness through Employee-Customer Linkages," *Academy of Management Executives* (November 2002): pp. 73–84; and T. Dalgic and T. Yeniceri, *Customer-Oriented Marketing Strategy* (New York: Business Expert Press, 2013).

31. L. Solomon, "Two-Thirds of Managers Are Uncomfortable Communicating with Employees," *Harvard Business Review*, March 9, 2016, https://hbr.org/2016/03/two-thirds-of-managers-are-uncomfortable-communicating-with-employees.

32. Based on G. R. Ferris, S. L. Davidson, and P. L. Perrewé, *Political Skill at Work: Impact on Work Effectiveness* (UK: Nicholas Brealey, 2011); M. Powers, *Politics at Work* (Cupertino, CA: Happy About, 2017); and E. Landells and S. Albrecht, "The Positives and Negatives of Organizational Politics: A Qualitative Study," *Journal of Business and Psychology* (February 2017): pp. 41–58.

33. L. Ryan, "Ten Skills Every Manager Needs—But 90% of Managers Lack," *Forbes*, February 11, 2018, https://www.forbes.com/sites/lizryan/2018/02/11/ten-skills-every-manager-needs-but-90-of-them-lack/#bcbeb6e16149.

34. H. J. Wilson and P. R. Daugherty, "Collaborative Intelligence: Humans and AI Are Joining Forces," *Harvard Business Review*, July/August 2018, pp. 114–23.

35. N. Scheiber, "A.I. Comes into Fashion," *New York Times*, July 8, 2018, New York edition.

36. A. Cheng, "5 Takeaways from Nike's Earnings as Its Shares Hit a Record," *Forbes*, June 29, 2018, https://www.forbes.com/sites/andriacheng/2018/06/29/five-things-nike-is-doing-to-stay-no-1/#3e4c88f214ea.

37. J. Ringen, "Nike Has a New Digital Playbook—And It Starts with Sneakerheads," *Fast Company,* May 2018, pp. 21–24.

38. R. Witte, "Nike Is Leveraging Data to Create Local Culture-Specific Retail Locations," *Forbes,* July 16, 2018, https://www.forbes.com/sites/raewitte/2018/07/16/nike-is-leveraging-data-to-create-local-culture-specific-retail-locations/#2ce5c94ad4f7.

Management History *Module*

The United Parcel Service relies on a management-efficiency system that was devised more than 100 years ago.[1] Early in the twentieth century, Frederick Taylor, an engineer in the steel industry, conducted extensive time and motion studies with the objective of improving worker efficiency. Today, UPS's management applies many of Taylor's findings as they train their drivers to minimize wasteful motions. UPS management, for example, carefully defines and stipulates every driver's behavior—from calculating the optimal route to take, to the best way to lock and unlock truck doors, to the speed at which drivers should walk.

In this module, we will provide a brief summary of how the field of study called management evolved. As with UPS, you're going to see that today's managers still utilize many techniques that were introduced 30, 50, or even 100 years ago. This module will help you put into historical perspective much of what you'll learn in future chapters.

Learning Objectives

MH1.1 **Describe** some early management examples.

MH1.2 **Explain** the various theories in the classical approach.

MH1.3 **Discuss** the development and uses of the behavioral approach.

MH1.4 **Describe** the quantitative approach.

MH1.5 **Explain** various theories in the contemporary approach.

3000 BC – 1776	1911 – 1947	Late 1700s – 1950s	1940s – 1950s	1960s – present
Early Management	Classical Approach	Behavioral Approach	Quantitative Approach	Contemporary Approaches

MH1.1 EARLY Management

Management has been practiced a long time. Organized endeavors directed by people responsible for planning, organizing, leading, and controlling activities have existed for thousands of years. Let's look at some of the most interesting examples.

The Egyptian pyramids and the Great Wall of China are proof that projects of tremendous scope, employing tens of thousands of people, were completed in ancient times.[2] For instance, it took more than 100,000 workers some

It took more than 100,000 workers some 20 years to construct an Egyptian pyramid.
A project like this could not have been completed without managers.
Source: Stephen Studd/The Image Bank/Getty Images

twenty years to construct a single pyramid. Who told each worker what to do? Who ensured there would be enough stones at the site to keep workers busy? The answer is *managers.* Someone had to plan what was to be done, organize people and materials to do it, make sure those workers got the work done, and impose some controls to ensure that everything was done as planned.

In 1776, Adam Smith published *The Wealth of Nations*, in which he argued the economic advantages that organizations and society would gain from the **division of labor** (or **job specialization**)—that is, breaking down jobs into narrow and repetitive tasks. Using the pin industry as an example, Smith claimed that ten individuals, each doing a specialized task, could produce a total of about 48,000 pins a day. However, if each person worked alone, performing each task separately, it would be quite an accomplishment to produce even ten pins a day! Smith concluded that division of labor increased productivity by increasing each worker's skill and dexterity, saving time lost in changing tasks, and creating labor-saving inventions and machinery. Job specialization continues to be popular. For example, think of the specialized tasks performed by members of a hospital surgical team, meal preparation tasks done by workers in restaurant kitchens, or positions played by players on a football team.

Starting in the late eighteenth century, when machine power was substituted for human power—a point in history known as the **industrial revolution**—it became more economical to manufacture goods in factories rather than at home. These large, efficient factories needed someone to forecast demand, ensure that enough material was on hand to make products, assign tasks to people, direct daily activities, and so forth. That "someone" was a manager. These managers would need formal theories to guide them in running these large organizations. In response, beginning in the early 1900s, the first steps toward developing formal management theories were taken.

In this module, we'll look at four major approaches to management theory: classical, behavioral, quantitative, and contemporary. (See Exhibit MH-1.) Keep in mind that each approach is concerned with trying to explain management from the perspective of what was important at that time in history and the backgrounds and interests of the researchers. Each of the four approaches contributes to our overall understanding of management, but each is also a limited view of what it is and how to best practice it.

division of labor (job specialization)
The breakdown of jobs into narrow and repetitive tasks

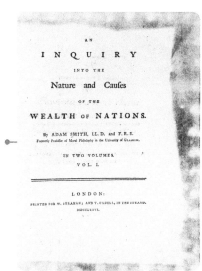

In 1776, Adam Smith published The Wealth of Nations, in which he argued the economic advantages that organizations and society would gain from the division of labor.
Source: Fotosearch/Archive Photos/Getty Images

Starting in the late eighteenth century, when machine power was substituted for human power–a point in history known as the industrial revolution–it became more economical to manufacture goods in factories rather than at home.
Source: North Wind Picture Archives/Alamy Stock Photo

3000 BC – 1776	1911 – 1947	Late 1700s – 1950s	1940s – 1950s	1960s – present
Early Management	Classical Approach	Behavioral Approach	Quantitative Approach	Contemporary Approaches

CLASSICAL Approach

Although we've seen how management has been used in organized efforts since early history, the formal study of management didn't begin until early in the twentieth century. These first studies of management, often called the **classical approach**, emphasized rationality and making organizations and workers as efficient as possible. Two major theories compose the classical approach: scientific management and general administrative theory. The two most important contributors to scientific management theory were Frederick W. Taylor and the husband-wife team of Frank and Lillian Gilbreth. The two most important contributors to general administrative theory were Henri Fayol and Max Weber. Let's take a look at each of these important figures in management history.

Scientific Management

If you had to pinpoint when modern management theory was born, 1911 might be a good choice. That was when Frederick W. Taylor's *Principles of Scientific Management*

Exhibit MH-1
Major Approaches to Management

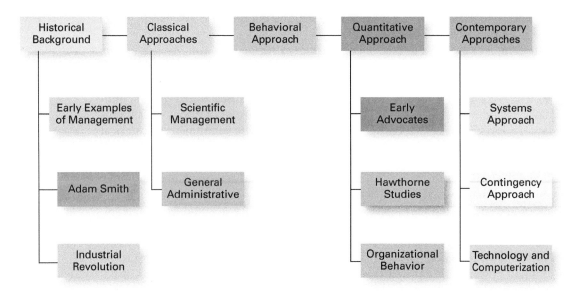

Frederick Taylor
Frederick Taylor's *Principles of Scientific Management*, published in 1911, described his theory of scientific management.
Source: Jacques Boyer/Roger-Viollet/The Image Works

industrial revolution
A period during the late eighteenth century when machine power was substituted for human power, making it more economical to manufacture goods in factories than at home

classical approach
First studies of management, which emphasized rationality and making organizations and workers as efficient as possible

scientific management
An approach that involves using the scientific method to find the "one best way" for a job to be done

was published. Its contents were widely embraced by managers around the world. Taylor's book described the theory of **scientific management**: the use of scientific methods to define the "one best way" for a job to be done.

Taylor worked at the Midvale and Bethlehem steel companies in Pennsylvania. As a mechanical engineer with a Quaker and Puritan background, he was continually appalled by workers' inefficiencies. Employees used vastly different techniques to do the same job. Virtually no work standards existed, and workers were placed in jobs with little or no concern for matching their abilities and aptitudes with the tasks they were required to do. They often "took it easy" on the job, and Taylor believed that worker output was only about one-third of what was possible. Taylor's solution was to apply the scientific method to shop-floor jobs. He spent more than two decades passionately seeking the "one best way" for each job to be done.

Taylor's experiences at Midvale led him to define clear guidelines for improving production efficiency. He argued that these four principles of management (see Exhibit MH-2) would result in prosperity for both workers and managers.[3] How did these scientific principles really work? Let's look at an example.

Probably the best-known example of Taylor's scientific management efforts was his pig iron experiment. Workers loaded "pigs" of iron (each weighing 92 pounds) onto rail cars. Their daily average output was 12.5 tons. However, Taylor believed that by scientifically analyzing the job to determine the "one best way" to load pig iron, output could be increased to 47 or 48 tons per day. After scientifically applying different combinations of procedures, techniques, and tools, Taylor succeeded in getting that level of productivity. How? By putting the right person on the job with the correct tools and equipment, having the worker follow his instructions exactly, and motivating the worker with an economic incentive of a significantly higher daily wage. Using similar approaches for other jobs, Taylor was able to define the "one best way" for doing each job. Overall, Taylor achieved consistent productivity improvements in the range of 200 percent or more. Based on his groundbreaking studies of manual work using scientific principles, Taylor became known as the "father" of scientific management. His ideas spread in the United States and to other countries and inspired others to study and develop methods of scientific management. His most prominent followers were Frank and Lillian Gilbreth.

1. Develop a science for each element of an individual's work to replace the old rule-of-thumb method.
2. Scientifically select and then train, teach, and develop the worker.
3. Heartily cooperate with the workers to ensure that all work is done in accordance with the principles of the science that has been developed.
4. Divide work and responsibility almost equally between management and workers. Management does all work for which it is better suited than the workers.

Source: F. W. Taylor, *Principles of Scientific Management* (New York: Harper, 1911).

Exhibit MH-2
Taylor's Scientific Management Principles

A construction contractor by trade, Frank Gilbreth gave up that career to study scientific management after hearing Taylor speak at a professional meeting. Frank and his wife, Lillian, a psychologist, focused their studies on eliminating inefficient hand-and-body motions. The Gilbreths also experimented with the design and use of the proper tools and equipment for optimizing work performance.[4]

Frank is probably best known for his bricklaying experiments. By carefully analyzing the bricklayer's job, he reduced the number of motions in laying exterior brick from eighteen to about five, and in laying interior brick from eighteen to two. Using Gilbreth's techniques, a bricklayer was far more productive and less fatigued at the end of the day.

The Gilbreths were among he first researchers to use motion pictures to study hand-and-body motions. They invented a device called a microchronometer that recorded a worker's hand-and-body motions and the amount of time spent doing each motion. Wasted motions missed by the naked eye could be identified and eliminated. The Gilbreths also devised a classification scheme to label seventeen basic hand motions (such as search, grasp, hold), which they called **therbligs** ("Gilbreth" spelled backward, with the *th* transposed). This scheme gave the Gilbreths a more precise way of analyzing a worker's exact hand movements.

therbligs
A classification scheme for labeling basic hand motions

General administrative theory
An approach to management that focuses on describing what managers do and what constitutes good management practice

principles of management
Fundamental rules of management that could be applied in all organizational situations and taught in schools

bureaucracy
A form of organization characterized by division of labor, a clearly defined hierarchy, detailed rules and regulations, and impersonal relationships

HOW TODAY'S MANAGERS USE SCIENTIFIC MANAGEMENT As noted earlier at UPS, many of the guidelines and techniques Taylor and the Gilbreths devised for improving production efficiency are still used in organizations today. When managers analyze the basic work tasks that must be performed, use time-and-motion study to eliminate wasted motions, hire the best-qualified workers for a job, or design incentive systems based on output, they're using the principles of scientific management.

General Administrative Theory

General administrative theory focused more on what managers do and what defined good management practice.

We introduced Henri Fayol in Chapter 1 because he first identified five functions that managers perform: planning, organizing, commanding, coordinating, and controlling.[5] Fayol wrote during the same time period as Taylor. While Taylor was concerned with first-line managers and the scientific method, Fayol's attention was directed at the activities of *all* managers. He wrote from his personal experience as the managing director of a large French coal-mining firm.

Fayol described the practice of management as something distinct from accounting, finance, production, distribution, and other typical business functions. His belief that management was an activity common to all business endeavors, government, and even the home led him to develop fourteen **principles of management**—fundamental rules of management that could be applied to all organizational situations and taught in schools. These principles are shown in Exhibit MH-3.

Max Weber (pronounced VAY-ber) was a German sociologist who studied organizations.[6] Writing in the early 1900s, he developed a theory of authority structures and relations based on an ideal type of organization he called a **bureaucracy**—a form of organization characterized by division of labor, a clearly defined hierarchy, detailed

Henry Fayol's
Henry Fayol's general administrative theory focused on what managers do and what defined good management practice.
Source: Historic Collection/Alamy Stock Photo

Exhibit MH-3
Fayol's Fourteen Principles of Management

1. **Division of work.** Specialization increases output by making employees more efficient.
2. **Authority.** Managers must be able to give orders, and authority gives them this right.
3. **Discipline.** Employees must obey and respect the rules that govern the organization.
4. **Unity of command.** Every employee should receive orders from only one superior.
5. **Unity of direction.** The organization should have a single plan of action to guide managers and workers.
6. **Subordination of individual interests to the general interest.** The interests of any one employee or group of employees should not take precedence over the interests of the organization as a whole.
7. **Remuneration.** Workers must be paid a fair wage for their services.
8. **Centralization.** This term refers to the degree to which subordinates are involved in decision-making.
9. **Scalar chain.** The line of authority from top management to the lowest ranks is the scalar chain.
10. **Order.** People and materials should be in the right place at the right time.
11. **Equity.** Managers should be kind and fair to their subordinates.
12. **Stability of tenure of personnel.** Management should provide orderly personnel planning and ensure that replacements are available to fill vacancies.
13. **Initiative.** Employees allowed to originate and carry out plans will exert high levels of effort.
14. **Esprit de corps.** Promoting team spirit will build harmony and unity within the organization.

Source: Based on Henri Fayol's 1916 "Principles of Management," in *Administration Industrielle et Générale,* translated by C. Storrs as *General and Industrial Management* (London: Sir Isaac Pitman & Sons, 1949).

Max Weber
Max Weber developed a theory of authority structures and relations based on an ideal type of organization he called a bureaucracy.
Source: Keystone Pictures USA/ ZumaPress/Alamy Stock Photo

rules and regulations, and impersonal relationships. (See Exhibit MH-4.) Weber recognized that this "ideal bureaucracy" didn't exist in reality. Instead, he intended it as a basis for theorizing about how work could be done in large groups. His theory became the structural design for many of today's large organizations.

Bureaucracy, as described by Weber, is a lot like scientific management in its ideology. Both emphasized rationality, predictability, impersonality, technical competence, and authoritarianism. Although Weber's ideas were less practical than Taylor's, the fact that his "ideal type" still describes many contemporary organizations attests to their importance.

HOW TODAY'S MANAGERS USE GENERAL ADMINISTRATIVE THEORY Several of our current management ideas and practices can be directly traced to the contributions of general administrative theory. For instance, the functional view of the manager's job can be attributed to Fayol. In addition, his fourteen principles serve as a frame of reference from which many current management concepts—such as managerial authority, centralized decision making, reporting to only one boss, and so forth—have evolved.

Weber's bureaucracy was an attempt to formulate an ideal prototype for organizations. Although many characteristics of Weber's bureaucracy are still evident in large organizations, his model isn't as popular today as it was in the twentieth century. Many managers feel that a bureaucratic structure hinders individual employees' creativity and limits an organization's ability to respond quickly to an increasingly dynamic environment. However, even in flexible organizations of creative professionals—such as Apple, Samsung, or Cisco Systems—bureaucratic mechanisms are necessary to ensure that resources are used efficiently and effectively.[7]

Exhibit MH-4
Characteristics of Weber's Bureaucracy

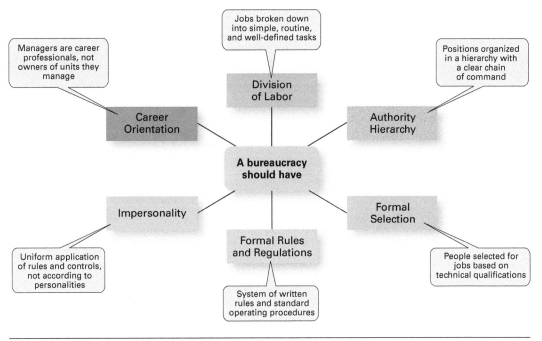

Managers are career professionals, not owners of units they manage

Jobs broken down into simple, routine, and well-defined tasks

Positions organized in a hierarchy with a clear chain of command

Division of Labor

Career Orientation

Authority Hierarchy

A bureaucracy should have

Impersonality

Formal Selection

Formal Rules and Regulations

Uniform application of rules and controls, not according to personalities

People selected for jobs based on technical qualifications

System of written rules and standard operating procedures

Source: Based on *Essays in Sociology* by Max Weber, translated, edited, and introduced by H. H. Gerth and C. Wright Mills (New York: Oxford University Press, 1946).

3000 BC – 1776	1911 – 1947	Late 1700s – 1950s	1940s – 1950s	1960s – present
Early Management	Classical Approach	Behavioral Approach	Quantitative Approach	Contemporary Approaches

BEHAVIORAL Approach

MH1.3

As we know, managers get things done by working with people. This explains why some writers have chosen to look at management by focusing on the organization's human factors. The field of study that researches the actions (behavior) of people at work is called **organizational behavior (OB)**. Much of what managers do today when managing people—motivating, leading, building trust, working with a team, managing conflict, and so forth—has come out of OB research.

Although a number of individuals in the early twentieth century recognized the importance of people to an organization's success, four stand out as early advocates of the OB approach: Robert Owen, Hugo Münsterberg, Mary Parker Follett, and Chester Barnard. Their contributions were varied and distinct, yet all believed that people were the most important asset of the organization and should be managed accordingly. Their ideas provided the foundation for such management practices as employee selection procedures, motivation programs, and work teams. Exhibit MH-5 summarizes each individual's most important ideas.

Without question, the most important historical contribution to the OB field came out of the **Hawthorne Studies**, a series of studies conducted at the Western Electric Company Hawthorne Works in Cicero, Illinois. These studies, which started in 1924, were initially designed by Western Electric industrial engineers as a scientific management experiment. They wanted to examine the effect of various lighting levels on worker productivity. Like any good scientific experiment, control and experimental groups were set up, with the experimental group exposed to various lighting intensities and the control group working under a constant intensity. If you were the industrial engineers in charge of this experiment, what would you have expected to happen? It's logical to think that individual output in the experimental group would be directly related to the intensity of the light. However, they found

organizational behavior (OB)
The study of the actions of people at work

Hawthorne Studies
A series of studies during the 1920s and 1930s that provided new insights into individual and group behavior

Western Electric Employees
Workers at the Western Electric Company were subjects of an important series of studies that initiated the behavioral approach to management.
Source: Hawthorne Works Museum of Morton College

Exhibit MH-5
Early OB Advocates

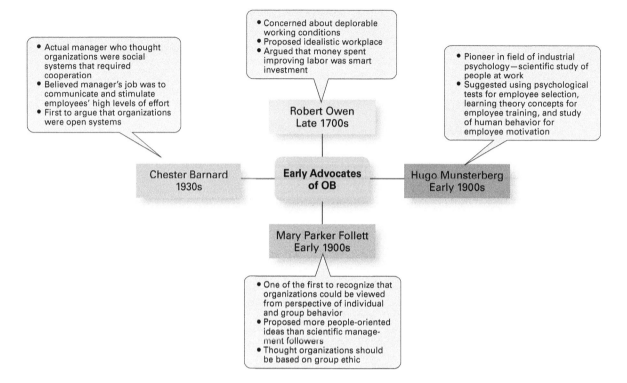

that as the level of light was increased in the experimental group, output for both groups increased. Then, much to the surprise of the engineers, as the light level was decreased in the experimental group, productivity continued to increase in both groups. In fact, a productivity decrease was observed in the experimental group *only* when the level of light was reduced to that of moonlight. What would explain these unexpected results? The engineers weren't sure, but concluded that lighting intensity was not directly related to group productivity and that something else must have contributed to the results. They weren't initially able to pinpoint what that "something else" was, though.

In 1927, the Western Electric engineers asked Harvard professor Elton Mayo and his associates to join the study as consultants. Thus began a relationship that would last through 1932 and encompass numerous experiments in the redesign of jobs, changes in workday and workweek length, introduction of rest periods, and individual versus group wage plans.[8] For example, one experiment was designed to evaluate the effect of a group piecework incentive pay system on group productivity. The results indicated that the incentive plan had less effect on a worker's output than group pressure, acceptance, and security. The researchers concluded that social norms or group standards were the key determinants of individual work behavior. In terms of the original lighting experiment, the researchers learned that just the awareness of being observed alters the behavior of people.

Scholars generally agree that the Hawthorne Studies had a game-changing impact on management beliefs about the role of people in organizations. Mayo concluded that people's behavior and attitudes are closely related, that group factors significantly affect individual behavior, that group standards establish individual worker output, and that money is less a factor in determining output than group standards, group attitudes, and security. These conclusions led to a new emphasis on the human behavior factor in the management of organizations.

HOW TODAY'S MANAGERS USE THE BEHAVIORAL APPROACH   The behavioral approach has largely shaped how today's organizations are managed. From the way managers design jobs to the way they work with employee teams to the way they communicate, we see elements of the behavioral approach. Much of what the early OB advocates proposed, and the conclusions from the Hawthorne Studies, have provided the foundation for our current theories of motivation, leadership, group behavior and development, and numerous other behavioral approaches.

3000 BC – 1776	1911 – 1947	Late 1700s – 1950s	1940s – 1950s	1960s – present
Early Management	Classical Approach	Behavioral Approach	Quantitative Approach	Contemporary Approaches

QUANTITATIVE Approach

MH1.4

Although passengers bumping into each other when trying to find their seats on an airplane can be a mild annoyance for them, it's a bigger problem for airlines because lines get backed up, slowing down how quickly the plane can get back in the air. Based on research in space-time geometry, one airline innovated a unique boarding process called "reverse pyramid" that has saved at least two minutes in boarding time.[9] This is an example of the **quantitative approach**, which is the use of quantitative techniques to improve decision making. This approach also is known as *management science.*

The quantitative approach evolved from mathematical and statistical solutions developed for military problems during World War II. After the war was over, many of these techniques used for military problems were applied to businesses. For example, one group of military officers, nicknamed the Whiz Kids, joined Ford Motor Company in the mid-1940s and immediately began using statistical methods and quantitative models to improve decision making.

What exactly does the quantitative approach do? It involves applying statistics, optimization models, information models, computer simulations, and other quantitative techniques to management activities. Linear programming, for instance, is a technique that managers use to improve resource allocation decisions; work scheduling can be more efficient as a result of critical-path scheduling analysis; and the economic order quantity model helps managers determine optimal inventory levels. Each of these is an example of quantitative techniques being applied to improve managerial decision making. Another area where quantitative techniques are used frequently is in total quality management.

A quality revolution swept through both the business and public sectors in the 1980s and 1990s.[10] It was inspired by a small group of quality experts, the most famous being W. Edwards Deming (pictured at right) and Joseph M. Juran. The ideas and techniques they advocated in the 1950s had few supporters in the United States but were enthusiastically embraced by Japanese organizations. As Japanese manufacturers began beating US competitors in quality comparisons, however, Western managers soon took a more serious look at Deming's and Juran's ideas, which became the basis for today's quality-management programs.

Total quality management, or **TQM**, is a management philosophy devoted to continual improvement and responding to customer needs and expectations. (See Exhibit MH-6.) The term *customer* includes anyone who interacts with the organization's product or services, internally or externally. It encompasses employees and suppliers, as well as the people who purchase the organization's goods or services. *Continual improvement* isn't possible without accurate measurements, which require statistical techniques that measure every critical variable in the organization's work processes. These measurements are compared against standards to identify and correct problems.

HOW TODAY'S MANAGERS USE THE QUANTITATIVE APPROACH The quantitative approach contributes directly to management decision making in the areas of planning and control. For instance, when managers make budgeting, queuing, scheduling, quality control, and similar decisions, they typically rely on quantitative techniques. Specialized software has made the use of these techniques less intimidating for managers, although many still feel anxious about using them.

This tabulating machine, used in the 1920 United States census, was a predecessor of electronic computers and worked by mechanically reading punch cards with coded information.
Source: Everett Collection Inc/ Alamy Stock Photo

W. Edwards Deming
W. Edwards Deming was one of the founders of the quality revolution.
Source: Richard Drew/AP Images

quantitative approach
The use of quantitative techniques to improve decision making

total quality management (TQM)
A philosophy of management that is driven by continuous improvement and responsiveness to customer needs and expectations

Exhibit MH-6
What Is Quality Management?

1. **Intense focus on the customer.** The customer includes outsiders who buy the organization's products or services and internal customers who interact with and serve others in the organization.
2. **Concern for continual improvement.** Quality management is a commitment to never being satisfied. "Very good" is not good enough. Quality can always be improved.
3. **Process focused.** Quality management focuses on work processes as the quality of goods and services is continually improved.
4. **Improvement in the quality of everything the organization does.** This relates to the final product, how the organization handles deliveries, how rapidly it responds to complaints, how politely the phones are answered, and the like.
5. **Accurate measurement.** Quality management uses statistical techniques to measure every critical variable in the organization's operations. These are compared against standards to identify problems, trace them to their roots, and eliminate their causes.
6. **Empowerment of employees.** Quality management involves the people on the line in the improvement process. Teams are widely used in quality management programs as empowerment vehicles for finding and solving problems.

3000 BC – 1776	1911 – 1947	Late 1700s – 1950s	1940s – 1950s	1960s – present
Early Management	**Classical Approach**	**Behavioral Approach**	**Quantitative Approach**	**Contemporary Approaches**

MH1.5 CONTEMPORARY **Approaches**

As we've seen, many elements of the earlier approaches to management theory continue to influence how managers manage. Most of these earlier approaches focused on managers' concerns *inside* the organization. Starting in the 1960s, management researchers began to look at what was happening in the external environment *outside* the boundaries of the organization. Two contemporary management perspectives—systems and contingency—are part of this approach. Systems theory is a basic theory in the physical sciences, but had never been applied to organized human efforts. In 1938, Chester Barnard, a telephone company executive, first wrote in his book, *The Functions of an Executive,* that an organization functioned as a cooperative system. However, it wasn't until the 1960s that management researchers began to look more carefully at systems theory and how it related to organizations.

A **system** is a set of interrelated and interdependent parts arranged in a manner that produces a unified whole. The two basic types of systems are closed and open. **Closed systems** are not influenced by and do not interact with their environment. In contrast, **open systems** are influenced by and do interact with their environment. Today, when we describe organizations as systems, we mean open systems. Exhibit MH-8 shows a diagram of an organization from an open systems perspective. As you can see, an organization takes in inputs (resources) from the environment and transforms or processes these resources into outputs that are distributed into the environment. The organization is "open" to and interacts with its environment.

How does the systems approach contribute to our understanding of management? Researchers imagined organizations as complex systems comprised of many components, including individuals, groups, structure, goals, status, and authority. What this means is that as managers coordinate work activities in the various parts of the organization, they ensure that all these parts are working together so the organization's goals can be achieved. For example, the systems approach recognizes that, no matter how efficient the production department, the marketing group must anticipate changes in customer tastes and work with product development in creating products customers want—or the organization's overall performance will suffer.

system
A set of interrelated and interdependent parts arranged in a manner that produces a unified whole

closed systems
Systems that are not influenced by and do not interact with their environment

open systems
Systems that interact with their environment

Exhibit MH-7
Great Moments in American Business

- **The $5 Workday (1914).** Ford doubles its employees' pay and helps create the middle class.
- **Comprehensive Employee Benefits (1928).** Kodak grants benefits that were lavish for the time—such as life insurance, tuition assistance, and a retirement annuity.
- **The Innovation Lab (1944).** 3M set up the Products Fabrication Laboratory for lab technicians to dream big without constraints.
- **ENIAC (1946).** The first digital computer begins operation.
- **The Personal Computer (1977).** The Apple II is introduced, starting the era of the personal computer.
- **Flexible Workplaces (1993).** Ad agency Chiat/Day builds new offices designed to boost creativity by eliminating assigned desks and replacing them with mobile workstations.
- **Domestic-Partner Benefits (1996).** IBM extends healthcare benefits to its employees' gay and lesbian partners.
- **Going Green (2005).** GE introduces Ecomagination, a suite of environmentally friendly products.

Based on D. Lidsky, "10 Big Bets on Optimism That Changed the Business World," *Fast Company*, February 2018, p. 96.

In addition, the systems approach implies that decisions and actions in one organizational area will affect other areas. For example, if the supply-chain group fails to acquire the right quantity and quality of inputs, the production department won't be able to do its job.

Finally, the systems approach recognizes that organizations are not self-contained. They rely on their environment for essential inputs and as outlets to absorb their outputs. No organization can survive for long if it ignores government regulations, supplier relations, or the varied external constituencies on which it depends.

The early management theorists came up with management principles they generally assumed to be universally applicable. Later research found exceptions to many of these principles. For example, division of labor is valuable and widely used, but jobs can become *too* specialized. Bureaucracy is desirable in many situations, but in some circumstances, other structural designs are *more* effective. Management is not (and cannot be) based on simplistic principles to be applied in all situations. Different and changing situations require managers to use different approaches and techniques. The **contingency approach** (sometimes called the *situational approach*) says that organizations are different, face different situations (contingencies), and require different ways of managing.

contingency approach
A management approach that recognizes organizations as different, which means they face different situations (contingencies) and require different ways of managing

Exhibit MH-8
Organization as an Open System

A good way to describe contingency is "if, then." *If* this is the way my situation is, *then* this is the best way for me to manage in this situation. It's intuitively logical because organizations and even units within the same organization differ—in size, goals, work activities, and the like. It would be surprising to find universally applicable management rules that would work in *all* situations. But, of course, it's one thing to say that the way to manage "depends on the situation" and another to say what the situation is. Management researchers continue working to identify these situational variables. Exhibit MH-9 describes four popular contingency variables. Although this list is far from comprehensive—more than 100 different variables have been identified—it represents those most widely used and gives you an idea of what we mean by the term *contingency variable.* The primary value of the contingency approach is that it stresses there are no simplistic or universal rules for managers to follow.

Finally, no contemporary history of management would be complete without recognizing the important influence that technology and computerization have played in defining current practices.[11] We'll highlight just a few.

Your grandfather could get a good job in a factory with a high school education or less. The demands of those jobs required little skill. Today's factories are highly computerized and require employees with the skills to operate complex equipment. Technology has made *computerized manufacturing* a mainstay of today's "factory." Managing today's skilled technicians is different than managing a group of unskilled, minimum-wage workers.

Technology has made it possible for organizations to create *virtual teams*—people who work together but are geographically dispersed. In response, managers have had to learn how to manage people from a distance. The internet, email, Skype, meeting software, and other technological innovations allow managers and employees to instantly communicate, meanwhile breaking down the barriers between work and nonwork hours. Today's professional, for instance, is now essentially "on call" 24/7.

An increasing number of organizations—small as well as large—are relying on Big Data to help managers make decisions. *Big Data* refers to large data sets—which are too large and complex for traditional software—that can be analyzed by computers to reveal patterns, trends, and behaviors. Contemporary managers are using Big Data, among other things, to predict what customers might want to buy, identify potential problems before they occur, and allocate scarce resources.

Maybe the most profound impact that technology has had on business firms has been its ability to make established businesses obsolete. Managers must now be constantly attuned to new competitors who are using technology to disrupt long-established products and services. *Disruptive innovation* is reshaping markets as diverse as advertising, financial services, and retail sales.

Technology has made it possible for managers and employees to instantly communicate. Here, virtual teams work together while being geographically dispersed.
Source: Rocketclips, Inc/Shutterstock

Exhibit MH-9
Popular Contingency Variables

Organization Size. As size increases, so do the problems of coordination. For instance, the type of organization structure appropriate for an organization of 50,000 employees is likely to be inefficient for an organization of 50 employees.

Routineness of Task Technology. To achieve its purpose, an organization uses technology. Routine technologies require organizational structures, leadership styles, and control systems that differ from those required by customized or nonroutine technologies.

Environmental Uncertainty. The degree of uncertainty caused by environmental changes influences the management process. What works best in a stable and predictable environment may be totally inappropriate in a rapidly changing and unpredictable environment.

Individual Differences. Individuals differ in terms of their desire for growth, autonomy, tolerance of ambiguity, and expectations. These and other individual differences are particularly important when managers select motivation techniques, leadership styles, and job designs.

PREPARING FOR: Exams/Quizzes

CHAPTER SUMMARY by Learning Objectives

MH1.1 **DESCRIBE** some early management examples.

Studying history is important because it helps us see the origins of today's management practices and recognize what has and has not worked. We can see early examples of management practice in the construction of the Egyptian pyramids and the Great Wall of China. One important historical event was the publication of Adam Smith's *The Wealth of Nations*, in which he argued the benefits of division of labor (job specialization). Another was the industrial revolution, where it became more economical to manufacture in factories than at home. Managers were needed to manage these factories, and these managers needed formal management theories to guide them.

MH1.2 **EXPLAIN** the various theories in the classical approach.

Frederick W. Taylor, known as the "father" of scientific management, studied manual work using scientific principles—that is, guidelines for improving production efficiency—to find the one best way to do those jobs. The Gilbreths' primary contribution was finding efficient hand-and-body motions and designing proper tools and equipment for optimizing work performance. Fayol believed the functions of management were common to all business endeavors but also were distinct from other business functions. He developed fourteen principles of management from which many current management concepts have evolved. Weber described an ideal type of organization he called a bureaucracy—characteristics that many of today's large organizations still have. Today's managers use the concepts of scientific management when they analyze basic work tasks to be performed, use time-and-motion study to eliminate wasted motions, hire the best qualified workers for a job, use adaptive robotics to boost worker efficiency, and design incentive systems based on output. They use general administrative theory when they perform the functions of management and structure their organizations so that resources are used efficiently and effectively.

MH1.3 **DISCUSS** the development and uses of the behavioral approach.

The early OB advocates (Robert Owen, Hugo Munsterberg, Mary Parker Follett, and Chester Barnard) contributed various ideas, but all believed that people were the most important asset of the organization and should be managed accordingly. The Hawthorne Studies dramatically affected management beliefs about the role of people in organizations, leading to a new emphasis on the human behavior factor in managing. The behavioral approach has largely shaped how today's organizations are managed. Many current theories of motivation, leadership, group behavior and development, and other behavioral issues can be traced to the early OB advocates and the conclusions from the Hawthorne Studies.

MH1.4 **DESCRIBE** the quantitative approach.

The quantitative approach involves applications of statistics, optimization models, information models, and computer simulations to management activities. Today's managers use the quantitative approach, especially when making decisions, as they plan and control work activities such as allocating resources, improving quality, scheduling work, or determining optimum inventory levels. Total quality management—a management philosophy devoted to continual improvement and responding to customer needs and expectations—also makes use of quantitative methods to meet its goals.

EXPLAIN the various theories in the contemporary approach.

The systems approach says that an organization takes in inputs (resources) from the environment and transforms or processes these resources into outputs that are distributed into the environment. This approach provides a framework to help managers understand how all the interdependent units work together to achieve the organization's goals and that decisions and actions taken in one organizational area will affect others. In this way, managers can recognize that organizations are not self-contained, but instead rely on their environment for essential inputs and as outlets to absorb their outputs.

The contingency approach says that organizations are different, face different situations, and require different ways of managing. It helps us understand management because it stresses there are no simplistic or universal rules for managers to follow. Instead, managers must look at their situation and determine that *if* this is the way my situation is, *then* this is the best way for me to manage.

Technology and computerization are dramatically changing the manager's job. Every element of management—planning, organizing, leading, and controlling—has been reshaped to some degree by technology.

REVIEW AND DISCUSSION QUESTIONS

MH-1. Explain why studying management history is important.

MH-2. What is the significance of the industrial revolution?

MH-3. What is a bureaucracy? Do bureaucracies still exist today?

MH-4. What did the early advocates of OB contribute to our understanding of management?

MH-5. Why were the Hawthorne Studies so critical to management history?

MH-6. Explain what the quantitative approach has contributed to the field of management.

MH-7. Describe total quality management.

MH-8. How has technology impacted how managers use the quantitative approach in today's workplace?

MH-9. How do systems theory and the contingency approach make managers better at what they do?

MH-10. How do societal trends influence the practice of management? What are the implications for someone studying management?

PREPARING FOR: My Career

MY TURN TO BE A MANAGER

• Conduct research and identify a new or emerging management theory. Do you think the new theory will have an impact on future management practices?

• Can scientific management principles help you be more efficient? Choose a task you do regularly (such as laundry, fixing dinner, grocery shopping, studying for exams, etc.). Analyze it by writing down the steps involved in completing that task. See if any activities could be combined or eliminated. Find the "one best way" to do this task. And the next time you have to do the task, try the scientifically managed way! See if you become more efficient (keeping in mind that changing habits isn't easy to do).

• How do business organizations survive for 100+ years? Obviously, they've seen a lot of historical events come and go. Choose one of these companies and research its history: Coca-Cola, Procter & Gamble, Avon, or General Electric. How has it changed over the years? From your research on this company, what did you learn that could help you be a better manager?

• Pick one historical event from this century and do some research on it. Write a paper describing the impact this event might be having or has had on how workplaces are managed.

• Come on, admit it: You multitask, don't you? And if not, you probably know people who do. Multitasking is also common in the workplace. But does it make employees more efficient and effective? Pretend you're the manager in charge of a loan-processing department. Describe how you would research this issue using each of the following management approaches or theories: scientific management, general administrative theory, quantitative approach, behavioral approach, systems theory, and contingency theory.

ENDNOTES

1. A. Hagan, "Frederick Taylor Has Been Reincarnated, and He Works for UPS Now," *Kienco* (blog), May 5, 2014, http://www.kienco.com.au/blog/workforce-analytics-and-neotaylorism.
2. C. S. George, Jr., *The History of Management Thought*, 2nd ed. (Upper Saddle River, NJ: Prentice Hall, 1972), p. 4.
3. F. W. Taylor, *Principles of Scientific Management* (New York: Harper, 1911).
4. See, for example, F. B. Gilbreth, *Motion Study* (New York: Van Nostrand, 1911); and F. B. Gilbreth and L. M. Gilbreth, *Fatigue Study* (New York: Sturgis and Walton, 1916).
5. H. Fayol, *Industrial and General Administration* (Paris: Dunod, 1916).
6. M. Weber, *The Theory of Social and Economic Organizations*, ed. T. Parsons, trans. A. M. Henderson and T. Parsons (New York: Free Press, 1947); and M. Lounsbury and E. J. Carberry, "From King to Court Jester? Weber's Fall from Grace in Organizational Theory," *Organization Studies* 26, no. 4 (2005): pp. 501–525.
7. B. Sanner and J. S. Bunderson, "The Truth About Hierarchy," *MIT Sloan Management Review*, Winter 2018, pp. 49–52.
8. E. Mayo, *The Human Problems of an Industrial Civilization* (New York: Macmillan, 1933); and F. J. Roethlisberger and W. J. Dickson, *Management and the Worker* (Cambridge, MA: Harvard University Press, 1939).
9. N. Zamiska, "Plane Geometry: Scientists Help Speed Boarding of Aircraft," *Wall Street Journal*, November 2, 2005, p. A1+.
10. See, for example, A. Gabor, *The Man Who Discovered Quality* (New York: Random House, 1990); J. W. Dean, Jr., and D. E. Bowen, "Management Theory and Total Quality: Improving Research and Practice through Theory Development," *Academy of Management Review* (July 1994): pp. 392–418; T. C. Powell, "Total Quality Management as Competitive Advantage: A Review and Empirical Study," *Strategic Management Journal* (January 1995): pp. 15–37; J. R. Hackman and R. Wageman, "Total Quality Management: Empirical, Conceptual, and Practical Issues," *Administrative Science Quarterly* (June 1995): pp. 309–342; and T. A. Stewart, "A Conversation with Joseph Juran," *Fortune*, January 11, 1999, pp. 168–170.
11. C. Mims, "Inside the New Industrial Revolution," *Wall Street Journal*, November 13, 2018, p. R1.

Chapter 2   Making Decisions

Learning Objectives

2.1 Describe the eight steps in the decision-making process.

2.2 Explain the five approaches managers can use when making decisions.

2.3 Classify decisions and decision-making styles.

2.4 Describe how biases affect decision making.

2.5 Identify cutting-edge approaches for improving decision making.

Employability Skills Matrix (ESM)

This matrix identifies features and end-of-chapter material that will help you develop specific skills employers are looking for in job candidates.

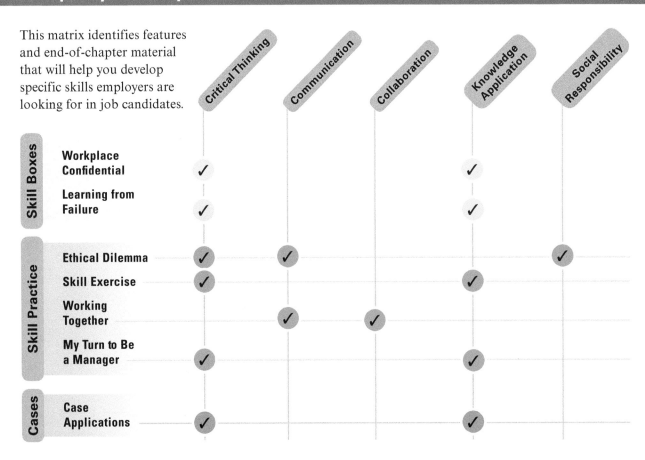

		Critical Thinking	Communication	Collaboration	Knowledge Application	Social Responsibility
Skill Boxes	Workplace Confidential	✓			✓	
	Learning from Failure	✓			✓	
Skill Practice	Ethical Dilemma	✓	✓			✓
	Skill Exercise	✓			✓	
	Working Together		✓	✓		
	My Turn to Be a Manager	✓			✓	
Cases	Case Applications	✓			✓	

If there were a decision-making Hall of Fame, Google's decision to buy YouTube in 2006 would definitely be included.[1] YouTube, at the time, was only a year and half old. Its future was uncertain. Yet Google's CEO, Eric Schmidt, thought it was worth paying $1.65 billion to buy it. Most analysts and competitors at the time thought Schmidt drastically overpaid. By conventional standards, they were probably right. But Schmidt saw the potential that others didn't. Today, YouTube earns more than $10 billion a year from selling display and video ads. And estimates place YouTube's value at more than $100 billion!

Decision making is the essence of management. And all managers would like to make good decisions because they're judged on the outcomes of those decisions. In this chapter, we examine the concept of decision making and how managers make decisions.

THE decision-making process

LO2.1 Executives make tough decisions all the time. For example,[2] ABC Entertainment President Channing Dungey cancelled the hit TV show *Roseanne* only hours after the show's star, Roseanne Barr, went on a vitriolic and racist Twitter rant. In spite of the show's ratings—it was the top-rated scripted TV series in the 2018 season—and profits of some $65 million, Dungey was not afraid to make a quick decision. As she concluded, "Roseanne's Twitter statement is abhorrent, repugnant, and inconsistent with our values, and we have decided to cancel her show."

Managers at all levels and in all areas of organizations make **decisions**. That is, they make choices among alternatives. For instance, top-level managers make decisions about their organization's goals, where to locate manufacturing facilities, what new markets to move into, or whether to cancel hit TV shows. Middle- and lower-level managers make decisions about production schedules, product quality problems, pay raises, and employee discipline. Our focus in this chapter is on how *managers* make decisions. But making decisions isn't something that just managers do. *All* organizational members make decisions that affect their jobs and the organization they work for.

Decision making is best understood as a process rather than just a choice. Even for something as straightforward as deciding where to go for lunch, you do more than just choose burgers or pizza or hot dogs. Granted, you may not spend a lot of time contemplating your lunch decision, but you still go through the process when making that decision. Exhibit 2-1 shows the eight steps in the decision-making process. This process is as relevant to personal decisions as it is to corporate decisions. We'll use an example—a manager deciding which laptop computers to purchase—to illustrate the steps in the process.

Step 1: Identify a Problem

Every decision starts with a **problem**, a discrepancy between an existing and a desired condition.[4] Let's work through an example. Amanda is a sales manager whose reps need new laptops because their old ones are outdated and inadequate for doing their job. To make it simple, assume it's not economical to add memory to the old computers and it's the company's policy to purchase, not lease. Now we have a problem—a disparity between the sales reps' current computers (existing condition) and their need to have more efficient ones (desired condition). Amanda has a decision to make.

How do managers identify problems? Unfortunately, in the real world, problems don't come with neon signs flashing "problem." When her reps started complaining about their computers, it was pretty clear to Amanda that something needed to be done, but few problems are that obvious.

Managers have to be cautious not to confuse problems with symptoms of the problem. For instance, is a 5 percent drop in sales a problem? Or are declining sales merely a symptom of the real problem, such as poor-quality products, high prices, bad advertising, or shifting consumer preferences?

Channing Dungey, ABC Entertainment president, acted quickly in her decision-making process to cancel TV show "Roseanne" after the star posted controversial comments online.
Source: FayesVision/WENN.com/Alamy Stock Photo

decision
Making choices among alternatives

- A study of 500 managers and executives found that 98 percent fail to apply best practices when making decisions.[3]

problem
A discrepancy between an existing and a desired condition

Exhibit 2-1
Decision-Making Process

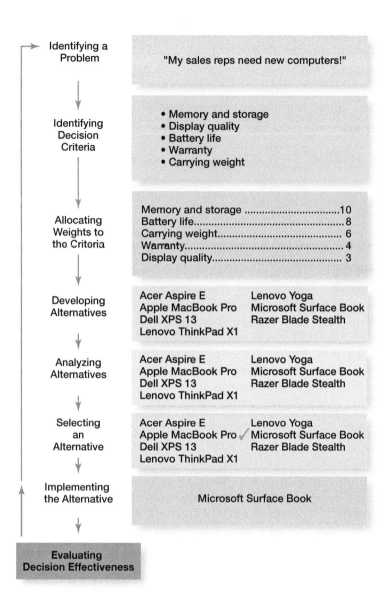

Identifying a Problem — "My sales reps need new computers!"

Identifying Decision Criteria
- Memory and storage
- Display quality
- Battery life
- Warranty
- Carrying weight

Allocating Weights to the Criteria
Memory and storage 10
Battery life...8
Carrying weight.. 6
Warranty.. 4
Display quality... 3

Developing Alternatives
Acer Aspire E	Lenovo Yoga
Apple MacBook Pro	Microsoft Surface Book
Dell XPS 13	Razer Blade Stealth
Lenovo ThinkPad X1	

Analyzing Alternatives
Acer Aspire E	Lenovo Yoga
Apple MacBook Pro	Microsoft Surface Book
Dell XPS 13	Razer Blade Stealth
Lenovo ThinkPad X1	

Selecting an Alternative
Acer Aspire E	Lenovo Yoga
Apple MacBook Pro ✓	Microsoft Surface Book
Dell XPS 13	Razer Blade Stealth
Lenovo ThinkPad X1	

Implementing the Alternative — Microsoft Surface Book

Evaluating Decision Effectiveness

Step 2: Identify Decision Criteria

decision criteria
Criteria that define what's important or relevant to resolving a problem

Once a manager has identified a problem, he or she must identify the **decision criteria** important or relevant to resolving the problem. Whether explicitly stated or not, every decision maker has criteria guiding his or her decisions. In our example, Amanda decides after careful consideration that memory and storage capabilities, display quality, battery life, warranty, and carrying weight are the relevant criteria in her decision.

Exhibit 2-2
Important Decision Criteria

Memory and storage	10
Battery life	8
Carrying weight	6
Warranty	4
Display quality	3

Step 3: Allocate Weights to the Criteria

Rarely are the relevant criteria equally important. So the decision maker needs to weight the items in order to give them the correct priority in the decision. How? A simple way is to give the most important criterion a weight of 10 and then assign weights to the rest using that standard. Of course, you could use any number as the highest weight. The key is assessing the *relative* importance of the criteria. The weighted criteria for our example are shown in Exhibit 2-2.

Step 4: Develop Alternatives

The fourth step in the decision-making process requires the decision maker to list viable alternatives that could resolve the problem. In this step, a decision maker needs to be creative, and the alternatives are only listed—not evaluated just yet. Our sales manager, Amanda, has identified seven laptops as possible choices. (See Exhibit 2-3.)

Step 5: Analyze Alternatives

Once alternatives have been identified, a decision maker must evaluate each one. How? By using the criteria established in step 2. Exhibit 2-3 shows the assessed values that Amanda gave each alternative after doing some research on them. [Reminder: This is *just* an example. Our apologies to any laptop manufacturer who might disagree with Amanda's analysis].

Keep in mind that this data represents an assessment of the seven alternatives using the decision criteria, but *not* the weighting. When you multiply each alternative by the assigned weight, you get the weighted alternatives as shown in Exhibit 2-4. The total score for each alternative, then, is the sum of its weighted criteria.

Sometimes a decision maker might be able to skip this step. If one alternative scores highest on every criterion, you wouldn't need to consider the weights because that alternative would already be the top choice. Or, if the weights were all equal, you could evaluate an alternative merely by summing up the assessed values for each one. (Look again at Exhibit 2-3.) For example, the score for the Acer Aspire E would be 36, and the score for the Apple MacBook Pro would be 40.

The eight-step decision-making process begins with identifying a problem and ends with evaluating the result of the decision. After identifying the need to buy new laptop computers for her sales reps, the manager must identify relevant criteria such as battery life, display quality, and memory that will help guide her final decision.
Source: Alex Segre/Alamy Stock Photo

	Memory and Storage	Battery Life	Carrying Weight	Warranty	Display Quality
Acer Aspire E	10	3	10	8	5
Apple MacBook Pro	8	5	7	10	10
Dell XPS 13	8	7	7	8	7
Lenovo ThinkPad	7	8	7	8	7
Lenovo Yoga	8	3	6	10	8
Microsoft Surface Book	10	7	8	6	7
Razer Blade Stealth	4	10	4	8	10

Exhibit 2-3
Possible Alternatives

	Memory and Storage	Battery Life	Carrying Weight	Warranty	Display Quality	Total
Acer Aspire E	100	24	60	32	15	231
Apple MacBook Pro	80	40	42	40	30	232
Dell XPS 13	80	56	42	32	21	231
Lenovo ThinkPad	70	64	42	32	21	229
Lenovo Yoga	80	24	36	40	24	204
Microsoft Surface Book	100	56	48	24	21	249
Razer Blade Stealth	40	80	24	32	30	206

Exhibit 2-4
Evaluation of Alternatives

Step 6: Select an Alternative

The sixth step in the decision-making process is choosing the best alternative or the one that generated the highest total in step 5. In our example (Exhibit 2-4), Amanda would choose the Microsoft Surface Book because it scored higher than all other alternatives (249 total).

Step 7: Implement the Alternative

In step 7, the decision is put into action by conveying it to those affected and getting their commitment to it. Research evidence indicates that if the people who must implement a decision participate in the process, they're more likely to support it than if you just tell them what to do.[5]

Step 8: Evaluate Decision Effectiveness

The last step in the decision-making process involves evaluating the outcome or result of the decision to see whether the problem was resolved. If the evaluation shows that the problem still exists, then the manager needs to assess what went wrong. Was the problem incorrectly defined? Were errors made when evaluating alternatives? Was the right alternative selected but poorly implemented?

APPROACHES to decision making

LO2.2 Although everyone in an organization makes decisions, decision making is particularly important to managers. As Exhibit 2-5 shows, it's part of all four managerial functions. That's why managers—when they plan, organize, lead, and control—are called *decision makers*.

The fact that almost everything a manager does involves making decisions doesn't mean that decisions are always time-consuming, complex, or evident to an outside observer. Most decisions are routine. For instance, every day of the year you make a

Exhibit 2-5
Decisions Managers May Make

Planning
- What are the organization's long-term objectives?
- What strategies will best achieve those objectives?
- What should the organization's short-term objectives be?
- How difficult should individual goals be?

Organizing
- How many employees should I have report directly to me?
- How much centralization should there be in an organization?
- How should jobs be designed?
- When should the organization implement a different structure?

Leading
- How do I handle employees who appear to be unmotivated?
- What is the most effective leadership style in a given situation?
- How will a specific change affect worker productivity?
- When is the right time to stimulate conflict?

Controlling
- What activities in the organization need to be controlled?
- How should those activities be controlled?
- When is a performance deviation significant?
- What type of management information system should the organization have?

decision about what to eat for dinner. It's no big deal. You've made the decision thousands of times before. It's a pretty simple decision and can usually be handled quickly. It's the type of decision you almost forget *is* a decision. And managers also make dozens of these routine decisions every day; for example, which employee will work what shift next week, what information should be included in a report, or how to resolve a customer's complaint. Keep in mind that even though a decision seems easy or has been faced by a manager a number of times before, it's still a decision. Let's look at five perspectives on how managers make decisions.

Rationality

We assume that managers will use **rational decision making**; that is, they'll make logical and consistent choices to maximize value.[6] After all, if managers are anything, it should be that they're rational. This, for example, should preclude allowing emotions or expediency to influence their choices.

ASSUMPTIONS OF RATIONALITY   What does it mean to be a "rational" decision maker? A rational decision maker would be fully objective and logical. The problem faced would be clear and unambiguous, and the decision maker would have a clear and specific goal and know all possible alternatives and consequences. Finally, making decisions rationally would consistently lead to selecting the alternative that maximizes the likelihood of achieving that goal. These assumptions apply to any decision—personal or managerial. However, for managerial decision making, we need to add one additional assumption—decisions are made in the best interests of the organization. These assumptions of rationality aren't very realistic. Managers don't always act rationally, but the next concept can help explain how most decisions get made in organizations.

Bounded Rationality

Despite the unrealistic assumptions, managers are *expected* to be rational when making decisions.[7] They understand that "good" decision makers are supposed to do certain things and exhibit logical decision-making behaviors as they identify problems, consider alternatives, gather information, and act decisively but prudently. When they do so, they show others that they're competent and that their decisions are the result of intelligent deliberation. However, a more realistic approach to describing how managers make decisions is the concept of **bounded rationality**, which says that managers make decisions rationally but are limited (bounded) by their ability to process information.[8] Because they can't possibly analyze all information on all alternatives, managers **satisfice** rather than maximize. That is, they accept solutions that are satisfactory and sufficient or "good enough." They're being rational within the limits (bounds) of their ability to process information. Let's look at an example.

Suppose you're a finance major and upon graduation you want a job, preferably as a personal financial planner at a major investment bank with a minimum salary of $65,000 and within 100 miles of your hometown. You accept a job offer as a business credit analyst—not exactly a personal financial planner but still in the finance field—at a regional bank fifty miles from home at a starting salary of $57,500. If you had done a more comprehensive job search, you would have discovered a job in personal financial planning at an investment bank seventy-five miles from your hometown and starting at a salary of $65,000. You weren't a perfectly rational decision maker because you didn't maximize your decision by searching all possible alternatives and then choosing the best. But because the first job offer was satisfactory (or "good enough"), you behaved in a bounded-rationality manner by accepting it.

rational decision making
Describes choices that are logical and consistent and maximize value

bounded rationality
Decision making that's rational but limited (bounded) by an individual's ability to process information

satisfice
Solutions that are satisfactory and sufficient or "good enough"

Netflix CEO Reed Hastings relies on what he calls "informed intuition" in the development of original programming, which plays a major role in the company's international growth. Although Netflix invests heavily in data analytics, Hastings says that intuition is as important as data in making final decisions.
Source: Tobias Hase/picture alliance/dpa/ Newscom

Intuition

When Travis Kalanick, former CEO of Uber, conceived of the idea of surge pricing, many of his executives and a good portion of customers thought it was a stupid idea.[9] Charging customers more for service when demand is highest or driving more difficult seemed foolish and sure to alienate customers. When all your competition has uniform pricing, modifying Uber's prices to match demand seemed irrational and certain to kill business. But Kalanick stuck to his guns, and his decision proved smart. Business boomed, and dynamic pricing is now an accepted aspect of Uber's business model. And companies like Disney are now experimenting with the concept at its theme parks.

intuitive decision making
Making decisions on the basis of experience, feelings, and accumulated judgment

Like Travis Kalanick, managers often use their intuition to help their decision making. What is **intuitive decision making**? It's making decisions on the basis of experience, feelings, and accumulated judgment. Researchers studying managers' use of intuitive decision making have identified five different aspects of intuition, which are described in Exhibit 2-6.[10] How common is intuitive decision making? One survey found that almost half of the executives surveyed "used intuition more often than formal analysis to run their companies."[11]

Intuitive decision making can complement both rational and bounded rational decision making.[12] First of all, a manager who has had experience with a similar type of problem or situation often can act quickly with what appears to be limited information because of that past experience. In addition, evidence indicates that individuals who experienced intense feelings and emotions when making decisions actually achieved higher decision-making performance, especially when they understood their feelings as they were making decisions. The old belief that managers should ignore emotions when making decisions may not be the best advice.[13]

Evidence-Based Management

Much of Amazon's success can be directly attributable to its reliance on data-driven decisions.[14] For instance, based on what customers have bought in the past, the items in their virtual shopping cart, what items a customer has ranked or reviewed after purchase, and what products a customer has viewed when visiting its site, Amazon is able to provide relevant recommendations to customers and increase sales.

The logic of data-driven management decisions owes a lot to medical research. If a patient is exhibiting unusual physical symptoms, doctors will rely on the best available evidence for proper diagnosis and treatment. The same applies to every decision maker. Any decision-making process can be enhanced through the use of relevant and

Exhibit 2-6
What Is Intuition?

Source: Based on L. A. Burke and M. K. Miller, "Taking the Mystery Out of Intuitive Decision Making," *Academy of Management Executive,* October 1999, pp. 91–99.

reliable evidence, whether it's buying a cell phone plan or deciding on a new office location. That's the reasoning behind **evidence-based management (EBMgt)**, the systematic use of the best available evidence to improve management practice.[15] And that evidence might be hard computer data, opinions of experts, or the prior experience of colleagues. In essence, EBMgt is an attempt to operationalize rationality.

evidence-based management (EBMgt)
The systematic use of the best available evidence to improve management practice

Let's Get REAL

The Scenario:

Juan Hernandez is a successful business owner. His landscaping business is growing, and a few months ago he decided to bring in somebody to manage his office operations since he had little time to keep on top of that activity. However, this individual can't seem to make a decision without agonizing about it over and over and on and on.

What could Juan do to help this person become a better decision maker?

Juan could give his office assistant a more complete picture of the tasks at hand for the day/week/month as well as timelines for each. It would force his decision to be made within a certain timeframe as well as give him a bigger-picture view of the workload. It would make him realize that there are many more tasks to accomplish.

◀ **Prudence Rufus**
Business Owner/Photographer

Source: Prudence Rufus

EBMgt is obviously relevant to managerial decision making. Its four essential elements are (1) the decision maker's expertise and judgment; (2) external evidence that's been evaluated by the decision maker; (3) opinions, preferences, and values of those who have a stake in the decision; and (4) relevant organizational (internal) factors such as context, circumstances, and organizational members. The strength or influence of each of these elements on a decision will vary with each decision. Sometimes, the decision maker's intuition (judgment) might be given greater emphasis in the decision; other times it might be the opinions of stakeholders; and at other times, it might be ethical considerations (organizational context). The key for managers is to recognize and understand the mindful, conscious choice as to which elements are most important and should be emphasized in making a decision.

- Eighty-one percent of executives believe that "data should be at the heart of all decision-making."[16]

Crowdsourcing

Our final approach to decision making is called **crowdsourcing**.[17] In a decision-making context, the term refers to relying on a network of people outside the organization's traditional set of decision makers to solicit ideas via the internet.

The Hershey Co., for instance, needed to find a way to keep their chocolates cool when shipping during the summer months or in warmer climates.[18] To meet this challenge, Hershey turned to the crowd. Instead of looking for a solution within the company, management used an innovation competition to solve this supply chain management problem. Anyone could submit an idea, and the contest winner got $25,000 in development funds and the opportunity to collaborate with Hershey to develop the proposed solution.

Finding innovative solutions to problems is one of several uses of crowdsourcing in organizations. Crowdsourcing can help managers gather insights from customers, suppliers, or other groups to help make decisions such as what products to develop, where they should invest, or even who to promote. Powered by the collective experiences and ideas of many, crowdsourcing can help managers make better-informed decisions by getting diverse input from sources outside the typical management hierarchy.

crowdsourcing
Relying on a network of people outside the organization's traditional set of decision makers to solicit ideas via the internet

TYPES **of decisions**

LO2.3 In a very simple sense, the problems managers encounter can be classified as routine and familiar or new and unusual. In response, managers will use one of two different types of decisions.

Structured Problems and Programmed Decisions

Some problems are straightforward. The decision maker's goal is clear, the problem is familiar, and information about the problem is easily defined and complete. Examples might include when a customer returns a purchase to a store, when a supplier is late with an important delivery, how a news team responds to a fast-breaking event, or how a college handles a student wanting to drop a class. Such situations are called **structured problems** because they're straightforward, familiar, and easily defined. For instance, a restaurant server spills a drink on a customer's coat. The customer is upset and the manager needs to do something. Because it's not an unusual occurrence, there's probably some standardized routine for handling it. For example, the manager offers to have the coat cleaned at the restaurant's expense. This is what we call a **programmed decision**, a repetitive decision that can be handled by a routine approach. Because the problem is structured, the manager doesn't have to go to the trouble and expense of going through an involved decision process. The "develop-the-alternatives" stage of the decision-making process either doesn't exist or is given little attention. Why? Because once the structured problem is defined, the solution is usually self-evident or at least reduced to a few alternatives that are familiar and have proved successful in the past. The spilled drink on the customer's coat doesn't require the restaurant manager to identify and weigh decision criteria or develop a long list of possible solutions. Instead, the manager relies on one of three types of programmed decisions: procedure, rule, or policy.

A **procedure** is a series of sequential steps a manager uses to respond to a structured problem. The only difficulty is identifying the problem. Once it's clear, so is the procedure. For instance, a supply-chain manager receives a request from a warehouse manager for fifteen tablets for the inventory clerks. The purchasing manager knows how to make this decision by following the established purchasing procedure.

A **rule** is an explicit statement that tells a manager what can or cannot be done. Rules are frequently used because they're simple to follow and ensure consistency. For example, rules about lateness and absenteeism permit supervisors to make disciplinary decisions rapidly and fairly.

The third type of programmed decisions is a **policy**, a guideline for making a decision. In contrast to a rule, a policy establishes general parameters for the decision maker rather than specifically stating what should or should not be done. Policies typically contain an ambiguous term that leaves interpretation up to the decision maker. Here are some sample policy statements:

- The customer always comes first and should always be *satisfied.*
- We promote from within, *whenever possible.*
- Employee wages shall be *competitive* within community standards.

Notice that the terms *satisfied, whenever possible*, and *competitive* require interpretation. For instance, the policy of paying competitive wages doesn't tell a company's human resources manager the exact amount he or she should pay for a specific job, but it does guide the manager in making the decision.

Unstructured Problems and Nonprogrammed Decisions

Not all the problems managers face can be solved using programmed decisions. Many organizational situations involve **unstructured problems**, new or unusual problems for which information is ambiguous or incomplete. The 2017 US tax reform law imposed a one-time 10 percent "repatriation" tax on offshore earnings. This compared with the standard 35 percent corporate rate. General Electric has been holding $83 billion in cash overseas. The change in the tax law now gave GE's chief financial officer an unstructured problem—what to do with all this money that could now be brought back to the US?

structured problems
Straightforward, familiar, and easily defined problems

programmed decision
A repetitive decision that can be handled by a routine approach

procedure
A series of sequential steps used to respond to a well-structured problem

rule
An explicit statement that tells managers what can or cannot be done

policy
A guideline for making decisions

unstructured problems
Problems that are new or unusual and for which information is ambiguous or incomplete

Exhibit 2-7
Programmed Versus
Nonprogrammed Decisions

Characteristic	Programmed Decisions	Nonprogrammed Decisions
Type of problem	Structured	Unstructured
Managerial level	Lower levels	Upper levels
Frequency	Repetitive, routine	New, unusual
Information	Readily available	Ambiguous or incomplete
Goals	Clear, specific	Vague
Time frame for solution	Short	Relatively long
Solution relies on. . .	Procedures, rules, policies	Judgment and creativity

When problems are unstructured, managers must rely on nonprogrammed decision making in order to develop unique solutions. **Nonprogrammed decisions** are unique and nonrecurring and involve custom-made solutions.

nonprogrammed decisions
Unique and nonrecurring decisions that require a custom-made solution

Comparing Decision Types

Exhibit 2-7 describes the differences between programmed and nonprogrammed decisions. Lower-level managers mostly rely on programmed decisions (procedures, rules, and policies) because they confront familiar and repetitive problems. As managers move up the organizational hierarchy, the problems they confront become more unstructured. Why? Because lower-level managers handle the routine decisions and let upper-level managers deal with the unusual or difficult decisions. Also, upper-level managers delegate routine decisions to their subordinates so they can deal with more difficult issues.[19]

DECISION-MAKING styles

Put Maria and Jessica into the same decision situation, and Jessica almost always seems to take longer to come to a solution. Jessica's final choices aren't necessarily always better than Maria's, she's just slower in processing information. Additionally, if there's an obvious risk dimension in the decision, Maria seems to consistently prefer a riskier option than does Jessica. What this illustrates is that all of us bring our individual style to the decisions we make.

Research on decision styles has identified four different individual approaches to making decisions.[20] The basic foundation of this model is recognition that people differ along two dimensions. One of these dimensions is an individual's way of *thinking*. This builds on our previous discussion of approaches to decision making by proposing that we have a preferred or fallback style. Some of us tend to be more rational and logical in the way we think or process information. Rational types look at information in order to make sure that it's logical and consistent before proceeding to make a decision. Others tend to be more creative and intuitive. Intuitive types don't have to process information in a certain order but are comfortable looking at it as a whole.

The other dimension describes an individual's *tolerance for ambiguity*. Again, some of us have a low tolerance for ambiguity and prefer order and certainty in the way we structure information so that ambiguity is minimized. In contrast, some of us can tolerate high levels of ambiguity and can process many thoughts at the same time. When these two dimensions are diagrammed, they form four styles of decision-making (see Exhibit 2-8). These are directive, analytic, conceptual, and behavioral.

People using the *directive* style have low tolerance for ambiguity and seek rationality. They are efficient and logical, but their efficiency concerns result in decisions being made with minimal information and with few alternatives assessed. Directive types make decisions fast and they focus on the short run.

The *analytic* type has a much greater tolerance for ambiguity than do directive decision makers. This means that analytic types are more comfortable than directives when uncertainty is involved in a decision. Analytic managers would be best characterized as careful decision makers with the ability to adapt to or cope with new situations.

Exhibit 2-8
Decision-Style Model

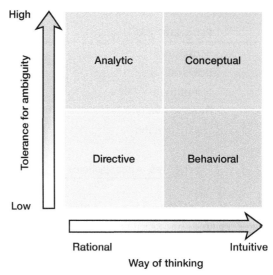

Source: A. J. Rowe and J. D. Boulgarides, *Managerial Decision Making* (Upper Saddler River, NJ: Prentice Hall, 1992), p. 29.

Individuals with a *conceptual* style tend to be very broad in their outlook and consider many alternatives. Their focus is long range and they are very good at finding creative solutions to problems.

The final category—the *behavioral* style—characterizes decision makers who work well with others. They're concerned with the achievement of peers and those working for them and are receptive to suggestions from others, relying heavily on meetings for communicating. This type of manager tries to avoid conflict and seeks acceptance by others.

Although these four categories are distinct, most managers have characteristics that fall into more than one. It's probably best to think in terms of a manager's dominant style and his or her backup styles. Some managers rely almost exclusively on their dominant style; however, more flexible managers can make shifts depending on the situation.

Business students and people in the managerial ranks tend to score highest on the analytic style. That's not surprising given the emphasis that formal education, particularly business education, gives to developing rational thinking. For instance, courses in accounting, statistics, economics, and finance all stress rational analysis.

Learning from
FAILURE James Dyson: A Man of a Thousand Failures

Sir James Dyson is a firm believer in failure. In fact, he says it's an essential part of his success. He has successfully internalized the famous quote by Thomas Edison: "I have not failed. I've just found 10,000 ways that won't work."

Dyson's revolutionary Dual Cyclone vacuum cleaner, which came out in 1993, was fifteen years in the making. He says he created 5,126 versions, which all failed, before he made one that worked.

This acceptance of failure permeates the firm he created, Dyson Ltd. His technology company now employs 5,000 people that design and manufacture vacuum cleaners, hand dryers, bladeless fans, heaters, and hair dryers.

Dyson says he hires people who "embrace the fact that failure is interesting." He views it as the essence of creativity. He argues that creativity means creating something that no one could have devised, something that hasn't existed before and solves problems that haven't been solved before. Dyson recognizes that the creative process inherently comes with setbacks and dead ends. But he accepts those setbacks and dead ends as worth the effort in order to create something revolutionary. And Dyson's approach proves that you can consistently create innovative products if you're willing to let people fail in the process.[21]

DECISION-MAKING biases and errors

LO2.4 When managers make decisions, they may use shortcuts, or **heuristics**, to simplify or speed up their decision making. Heuristics can be useful because they help make sense of complex, uncertain, and ambiguous information.[22] Even though managers may use heuristics, that doesn't mean those shortcuts are reliable. Why? Because they may lead to errors and biases in processing and evaluating information. Exhibit 2-9 identifies twelve common decision errors of managers and biases they may have. Let's look at each.[23]

heuristics
Shortcuts that managers use to simplify or speed up decision making

Exhibit 2-9
Common Decision-Making Biases

1. When decision makers think they know more than they do or hold unrealistically positive views of themselves and their performance, they're exhibiting the *overconfidence bias.*
2. The *immediate gratification bias* describes decision makers who want immediate rewards and would like to avoid immediate costs. For these individuals, decision choices that provide quick payoffs are more appealing than those with payoffs in the future.
3. The *anchoring effect* describes how decision makers fixate on initial information as a starting point and then, once set, fail to adequately adjust for subsequent information. First impressions, ideas, prices, and estimates carry unwarranted weight relative to information received later.
4. When decision makers selectively organize and interpret events based on their biased perceptions, they're using the *selective perception bias.* This influences the information they pay attention to, the problems they identify, and the alternatives they develop.
5. Decision makers who seek out information that reaffirms their past choices and discounts information that contradicts past judgments exhibit the *confirmation bias.* These people tend to accept at face value information that confirms their preconceived views and are critical and skeptical of information that challenges these views.
6. The *framing bias* occurs when decision makers select and highlight certain aspects of a situation while excluding others. By drawing attention to specific aspects of a situation and highlighting them, while at the same time downplaying or omitting other aspects, they distort what they see and create incorrect reference points.

In annual performance reviews, many managers fall victim to the availability bias when they focus on recent employee behaviors rather than behaviors over the entire year.
Source: New Africa/Shutterstock

7. The *availability bias* happens when decision makers tend to remember events that are the most recent and vivid in their memory. This distorts their ability to recall events in an objective manner and results in skewed judgments and probability estimates.

8. When decision makers assess the likelihood of an event based on how closely it resembles other events or sets of events, that's the *representation bias.* Managers exhibiting this bias draw analogies and see identical situations where they don't exist.

9. The *randomness bias* describes the actions of decision makers who try to create meaning out of random events. They do this because most decision makers have difficulty dealing with chance even though random events happen to everyone, and there's nothing that can be done to predict them.

10. The *sunk costs error* occurs when decision makers forget that current choices can't correct the past. They incorrectly fixate on past expenditures of time, money, or effort in assessing choices rather than on future consequences. Instead of ignoring sunk costs, they can't forget them.

11. Decision makers who are quick to take credit for their successes and to blame failure on outside factors are exhibiting the *self-serving bias.*

12. Finally, the *hindsight bias* is the tendency for decision makers to falsely believe that they would have accurately predicted the outcome of an event once that outcome is actually known.

Managers avoid the negative effects of these decision errors and biases by being aware of them and then not using them! Fortunately, some research shows that training can successfully help employees to recognize particular decision-making biases and reduce subsequent biased decision making over the long term.[25] Beyond that, managers also should pay attention to "how" they make decisions and try to identify the heuristics they typically use and critically evaluate the appropriateness of those heuristics. Finally, managers might want to ask trusted individuals to help them identify weaknesses in their decision-making style and try to improve on those weaknesses.

CUTTING-EDGE APPROACHES for
improving decision making

LO2.5　The last twenty years has seen a dramatic change in the ability of managers to access information. A major impetus for this change has been technology. Few organizations do a better job at providing their executives and other decision makers with quality information than the Cleveland Clinic. The Clinic is a leader at using technology to give it a competitive advantage in providing efficient, safe, and cost-effective medical services.[26] For instance, it has partnered with IBM to use Watson, IBM's artificial intelligence system that can understand spoken or written language in the course of analyzing data and making predictions. As the Clinic's CEO noted, "Digital technology will allow us to deliver smarter, more affordable and more accessible care."

In this section, we look at some of the cutting-edge approaches for improving decision making, much of which is derived from technology.

design thinking
Approaching management problems as designers approach design problems

The Cleveland Clinic is using IBM's Watson (AI system) to improve its ability to deliver better care.
Source: Drserg/Shutterstock

Design Thinking

The way managers approach decision making—using a rational and analytical mind-set in identifying problems, coming up with alternatives, evaluating alternatives, and choosing one of those alternatives—may not be the best, and is certainly not the only choice in today's environment. That's where design thinking comes in. **Design thinking** has been described as "approaching management problems as designers approach design problems."[27] To think like a designer means to consider how an object or process might

WORKPLACE CONFIDENTIAL Making Good Decisions

Life comes with tough decisions. And so do jobs. The tough decisions start with choosing whether to accept an initial job offer. They often continue with deciding who to befriend and trust at work, whether or not to join a new work team or accept a promotion to a new city, how to respond to a situation that might compromise your ethics, or how to relay bad news to your boss.

Let's begin with the basic tenet that you can't avoid tough decisions by ignoring them. The decision to do nothing *is still a decision.* It's a decision to maintain the status quo.

You can maintain the status quo by following either of two paths—one active and the other passive. You can rationally assess your current situation, identify your options, carefully review the strengths and weaknesses of these options, and conclude that no new alternative is superior to the path you're currently taking. This active approach is fully consistent with rational decision making. Our concern here, however, is with the passive approach—where the current path is followed only because you fail to consider your other options. You don't, for instance, want to find yourself regretting having spent twenty years in a go-nowhere job that you disliked because you avoided looking for other opportunities.

How do you counter the nondecision decision? The first step is awareness. You can't opt out of decisions by ignoring them. To do so is merely choosing to continue along the path you're on. That path may be the one you want, but the astute decision maker recognizes that there are costs associated with maintaining the status quo as well as with change. You also need to directly challenge the status quo. It's not merely enough to know that doing nothing is a decision. You also need to occasionally justify why you *shouldn't* pursue another path that's different from the one you're currently following. Why aren't you looking for other job opportunities? Are the stocks, bonds, and mutual funds in your retirement portfolio properly aligned to recent changes in the economy? Finally, consider the costs of inaction. Too often we focus only on the risks associated with change. You're less likely to get caught up in decision inaction if you also address the risks related to doing nothing.

We should also take a look at arguably the three most critical errors you're likely to make in your decision making: overconfidence, a short-term focus, and the confirmation bias. While each is briefly mentioned in this chapter, let's take a closer look at them.

It has been said that no problem in judgment and decision making is more prevalent and more potentially catastrophic than overconfidence. Almost all of us suffer from it. When we're given factual questions and asked to judge the probability that our answers are correct, we tend to be far too optimistic. In general, we overestimate our knowledge, undervalue risk, and overestimate our ability to control events.

Studies have found that when people say they're 65 percent to 70 percent confident that they're right, they're actually correct only about 50 percent of the time. And when they say they're 100 percent sure, they tend to be only 70 percent to 85 percent correct.

To reduce overconfidence, begin by recognizing this tendency and expect it to most likely surface when your confidence is extremely high or when accurate judgments are difficult to make. Next, adjust your confidence awareness to reflect your level of expertise on an issue. You're most likely to be overconfident when you're considering issues outside your expertise. Finally, directly address this bias by challenging yourself to look for reasons why your predictions or answers might be wrong.

A lot of us suffer from the tendency to want to grab for immediate rewards and avoid immediate costs. If it feels good, we want to do it now; if it implies pain, we want to postpone it. This immediate gratification bias explains why it's so hard to diet, quit smoking, avoid credit card debt, or save for retirement. Each comes with an immediate reward—tasty food, an enjoyable cigarette, an immediate purchase, or extra disposable money to spend. And each delays its costs to some nebulous future.

If you see yourself as vulnerable to the immediate gratification bias, what can you do? First, set long-term goals and review them regularly. This can help you focus on the longer term and help you to justify making decisions whose payoff may be far into the future. If you don't know where you want to be in ten or twenty years, it's easier to discount your future and live for the moment. Second, pay attention to both rewards *and costs.* Our natural tendency is to inflate immediate rewards and underplay future costs. For instance, think about what it would be like to be retired with no savings and trying to live on a $1,200-a-month Social Security check. Or look around for examples of people who didn't plan for their future and now are suffering the consequences.

Finally, the rational decision-making process assumes that we objectively gather information. But we don't. We *selectively* gather information so it confirms our current beliefs, and we dismiss evidence that challenges those beliefs. We also tend to accept at face value information that confirms our preconceived views, while being critical and skeptical of information that challenges these views.

Overcoming this confirmation bias begins by being honest about your motives. Are you seriously trying to get information to make an informed decision, or are you just looking for evidence to confirm what you'd like to do? If you're serious about this, then you need to purposely seek out contrary or disconfirming information. That means you have to be prepared to hear what you don't want to hear. You'll also need to practice skepticism until it becomes habitual. In the same way that a defense attorney seeks contradictory evidence to disprove a plaintiff's case, you have to think of reasons why your beliefs might be wrong and then aggressively seek out evidence that might prove them to be so.[28]

be redesigned—sometimes to the point of being completely redone. And an increasing number of organizations are beginning to recognize how design thinking can benefit them.[29] For instance, PepsiCo designers created the Pepsi Spire, which is a high-tech beverage dispensing machine with a futuristic design. Then-PepsiCo CEO Indra Nooyi, commenting on design thinking, said: "Other companies with dispensing machines have focused on adding a few more buttons and combinations of flavors. Our design guys essentially said that we're talking about a fundamentally different interaction between consumer and machine."[30]

While many managers don't deal specifically with product or process design decisions, they still make decisions about work issues; and design thinking can help them be better decision makers. What can the design thinking approach teach managers about making better decisions? It begins with the first step of identifying problems. Design thinking says that managers should look at problem identification collaboratively and integratively, with the goal of gaining a deep understanding of the situation. They should look not only at the rational aspects, but also at the emotional elements. As a by-product of this broader approach, design thinking influences how managers identify and evaluate alternatives. "A traditional manager would take the options that have been presented and analyze them based on deductive reasoning and then select the one with the highest net present value. However, using design thinking, a manager would say, 'What is something completely new that would be lovely if it existed but doesn't now?'"[31] Design thinking means opening up your perspective and gaining insights by using observation and inquiry skills and not relying simply on rational analysis.

Big Data and Artificial Intelligence

As the Cleveland Clinic found, IBM's supercomputer, Watson, can do things faster and more accurately than many professionals. For instance, it can diagnose cancers four times more accurately than doctors and can provide legal advice in seconds with 90 percent accuracy, compared to 70 percent accuracy by lawyers.[32] The secret to Watson's talents? Big data and artificial intelligence.

Big data is a term that refers to huge and complex sets of data.[33] These data sets are composed of so much information that traditional data-processing application software is unable to deal with them. For instance, cloud-computing capacity now can allow a room full of legal opinions to be put online. What used to take a lawyer several days or even weeks to find relevant cases to support a client's case can now be done in seconds. Similarly, even football and basketball coaches and managers are using big data to guide drafting decisions and even play calling.

Big data has opened the door to widespread use of **artificial intelligence (AI)**. As noted in Chapter 1, AI is using the power of computers to replicate the reasoning functions of humans.[34] It goes well beyond the simple "if-then" processing of computer software. AI has the ability to learn and solve complex problems.

You already know how big data and AI are changing the lives of consumers with products like Siri, Google Maps, Uber, and the rapid advancements being made toward self-driving cars. But big data and AI, along with machine learning, deep learning, and analytics are rapidly changing how managers make decisions.

AI increasingly facilitates **machine learning** and deep learning. The former is a method of data analysis that automates analytical model building.[35] It's a branch of AI based on the idea that systems can learn from data, identify patterns, and make decisions with little or no human assistance. Amy Hood, CFO at Microsoft, is credited with reshaping the way her company allocates spending and wins contracts by using machine learning tools.[36] For instance, she analyzed historical data from 750,000 customers to forecast sales opportunities for each product, customer, and city worldwide. Another system Hood installed predicts which customers need more attention and which are at risk of defecting.

Deep learning is a subset of machine learning.[37] It uses algorithms to create a hierarchical level of artificial neural networks that simulate functions of the human

big data
Huge and complex sets of data

artificial intelligence
Using the power of computers to replicate the reasoning functions of humans

machine learning
A method of data analysis that automates analytical model building

deep learning
Use of algorithms to create a hierarchical level of artificial neural networks that simulate functions of the human brain

Amy Hood, CFO at Microsoft, uses big data to determine how to allocate spending and forecast sales opportunities for the company.
Source: Jason Redmond/Reuters/Newscom

brain. Imitating the human brain, the nodes are connected like a web. This enables machines to process data in a nonlinear fashion. A deep-learning system, for instance, has allowed computers to identify skin cancers at a level equivalent to the best experts. A deep-learning system was fed more than 100,000 images of malignant melanomas and harmless moles. The AI program was then put up against fifty-eight highly experienced dermatologists. The AI program found 95 percent of the 300 melanomas versus 87 percent by the doctors.[38]

A final term you should know is **analytics**. This is the use of mathematics, statistics, predictive modeling, and machine learning to find meaningful patterns and knowledge in a data set.[40] The 2018 Super Bowl winner, the Philadelphia Eagles, uses analytics more than any other team in the NFL.[41] For instance, they frequently go on fourth downs rather than kick. The coaches found, using analytics, that many situations where common sense says "kick" were more likely to eventually result in team victories if the team either passed or ran the ball.

In many ways, the future is here. AI is doing functions that managers previously did. For instance, 200 Russian companies are using the AI software "Vera," which recruits and finds new employees.[42] Vera can talk to 1,500 candidates in a single day and sends customized follow-up emails. She can also call applicants and, using her conversational skills gained through machine learning, conduct an eight-minute conversation to determine a candidate's interest and job suitability. Candidates can ask her questions, and she's accurate about 82 percent of the time.

Currently, about 24 percent of businesses are implementing or plan to implement AI.[43] Among large corporations, that number is more than 97 percent![44] We can state, unequivocally, that AI usage among all businesses is sure to expand in the near future. And with this trend toward using technology to access and interpret information, managers will be less dependent on inconsistent and incomplete data. There will be less need to rely on intuition. Maybe most exciting, because AI software can learn through experience, decisions will increasingly reflect the values and goals of the manager. The result will be managerial decisions that more closely approach the assumptions of rationality.

fyi

- Machine learning and deep learning are among the top three most in-demand skills on Monster.com.[39]

analytics
Mathematics, statistics, predictive modeling, and machine learning to find meaningful patterns and knowledge in a data set

Chapter 2 | PREPARING FOR: Exams/Quizzes

CHAPTER SUMMARY by Learning Objectives

LO2.1 DESCRIBE the eight steps in the decision-making process.
A decision is a choice. The decision-making process consists of eight steps: (1) identify the problem; (2) identify decision criteria; (3) allocate weights to the criteria; (4) develop alternatives; (5) analyze alternatives; (6) select an alternative; (7) implement the alternative; and (8) evaluate decision effectiveness.

LO2.2 EXPLAIN the five approaches managers use when making decisions.
The assumptions of rationality are as follows: the problem is clear and unambiguous; a single, well-defined goal is to be achieved; all alternatives and consequences are known; and the final choice will maximize goal achievement. Bounded rationality says that managers make rational decisions but are bounded (limited) by their ability to process information. Satisficing happens when decision makers accept solutions that are good enough. Intuitive decision making means making decisions on the basis of experience, feelings, and accumulated judgment. Using evidence-based management, a manager makes decisions systematically based on

the best available evidence. A manager using crowdsourcing solicits ideas via the internet from people outside the organization.

L02.3

CLASSIFY decisions and decision-making styles.

Programmed decisions are repetitive decisions that can be handled by a routine approach and are used when the problem being resolved is straightforward, familiar, and easily defined (structured). Nonprogrammed decisions are unique decisions that require a custom-made solution and are used when the problems are new or unusual (unstructured) and for which information is ambiguous or incomplete. Individuals' decision-making styles can be classified according to two dimensions: way of thinking (rational or intuitive) and tolerance for ambiguity (low or high). These dimensions result in four styles of decision making: directive, analytic, conceptual, and behavioral.

L02.4

DESCRIBE how biases affect decision making.

The twelve common decision-making errors and biases include overconfidence, immediate gratification, anchoring, selective perception, confirmation, framing, availability, representation, randomness, sunk costs, self-serving bias, and hindsight. Ways to minimize these biases include increasing awareness of the biases, training to recognize biases, paying attention to how decisions are made, and asking others to identify weaknesses in decision making.

L02.5

IDENTIFY cutting-edge approaches for improving decision making.

Design thinking is "approaching management problems as designers approach design problems" and considering how an object or process might be redesigned. It can be useful when identifying problems and when identifying and evaluating alternatives. Using big data, decision makers have powerful tools to help them make decisions. Artificial intelligence uses the power of computers to replicate humans' reasoning functions. Machine learning and deep learning are facilitated by artificial intelligence. Analytics uses math, statistics, modeling, and machine learning to find patterns in data sets. However, no matter how comprehensive these approaches are, they need to be accompanied by good judgment.

REVIEW AND DISCUSSION QUESTIONS

2-1. Why is decision making often described as the essence of a manager's job?

2-2. Describe the eight steps in the decision-making process.

2-3. Compare and contrast the five ways managers make decisions.

2-4. Explain the two types of problems and decisions. Contrast the four decision-making styles.

2-5. How can managers blend the guidelines for making effective decisions in today's world with the rationality and bounded rationality models of decision making, or can they? Explain.

2-6. Is there a difference between wrong decisions and bad decisions? Why do good managers sometimes make wrong decisions? Bad decisions?

2-7. All of us bring biases to the decisions we make. What are the drawbacks of having biases? Could there be any advantages to having biases? Explain. What are the implications for managerial decision making?

PREPARING FOR: My Career

ETHICS DILEMMA

IKEA's sleekly designed Sladda bike was launched in 2016 to great acclaim. It was marketed as helping customers to drive less. It had a click-in system to add baskets and racks. It would require less maintenance since there wasn't any chain to oil. However, in May 2018, IKEA recalled the Sladda. The bike's belt drive—which replaced the traditional bike chain—had snapped for some consumers. Two bike riders reported minor injuries.

IKEA reported that there was no feasible way to repair the Sladda belt drives. While some bike experts think a chain could have been added to the Sladda, such a change on every bike would have been expensive. Yet some companies might have repaired the bikes. Jon Goulet, director of quality for the bike company Specialized, said in an interview that even if a problem was costly to fix, "we would probably still just choose to make it right, because it's part of our brand proposition to be rider-centric." Not fixing the bikes doesn't seem like it's part of the sustainability solution IKEA claimed at the bike's launch. Some skeptics wonder whether the Sladda's slow sales might be partly to blame for IKEA's decision to recall it and stop production.[45]

2-8. Was the decision by Ikea to recall and stop production of the Sladda appropriate? Explain both "why" and "why not."

2-9. If you were a manager, how would you use this incident to "teach" employees about ethics and decision making?

SKILLS EXERCISE **Developing Your Creativity Skill**

About the Skill

The "develop alternative" stage in the decision process can benefit from creativity. Your ability to envision a multitude of options, especially ones that are outside the mainstream, increase the probability that you will find a superior choice. Additionally, creativity can help identify problems that others can't see.

To be creative, you need to open your mind to new ideas. Each of us has the ability to be creative but, too often, we simply don't try to develop that ability. Developing your creative skills can help you become a better problem solver and contributor in the workplace.[46]

Steps in Practicing the Skill

- *Think of yourself as creative.* Although it's a simple suggestion, research shows that if you think you can't be creative, you won't be. Believing in yourself is the first step in becoming more creative.

- *Pay attention to your intuition.* Sometimes answers come to you when least expected. For example, when you are about to go to sleep, your relaxed mind sometimes whispers a solution to a problem you're facing. Listen to that voice. In fact, most creative people keep a notepad near their bed and write down ideas when they occur. That way, they don't forget them.

- *Move away from your comfort zone.* Every individual has a comfort zone in which certainty exists. But creativity and the known often don't mix. To be creative, you need to move away from the status quo and focus your mind on something new.

- *Engage in activities that put you outside your comfort zone.* You not only must think differently; you need to do things differently and thus challenge yourself. Learning to play a musical instrument or learning a foreign language, for example, opens your mind to a new challenge.

- *Find several right answers.* In the discussion of bounded rationality, we said that people seek solutions that are good enough. Being creative means continuing to look for other solutions even when you think you have solved the problem.

- *Play your own devil's advocate.* Challenging yourself to defend your solutions helps you to develop confidence in your creative efforts. Second-guessing yourself may also help you find more creative solutions.

- *Brainstorm with others.* Being creative is not a solitary activity. Divergent input from others increases the chances for a breakthrough idea.

- *Step away for a time.* A period of time away from an unresolved problem can often stimulate a solution unseen at first. This "incubation effect" often produces a sudden "a-ha" moment. So it sometimes helps, when stymied, to take a break, go for a walk, or sleep on it.

Practicing the Skill

Developing your creative skills is similar to building your muscles through exercise; it requires effort over time. Every week pick a new activity to develop your creative skills. Try something new, take an art class, practice brainstorming, or spend some time with a new group of people. Keep a journal of creative ideas or insights.

WORKING TOGETHER   Team Exercise

What are some problems on your campus? Are students tired of the food options available? Do you have trouble finding a parking space? In groups of three or four students, use the decision-making process to identify a solution to a problem on your campus. Work through the first six steps of the process: (1) identify the problem; (2) identify your decision criteria; (3) weight the criteria; (4) develop alternatives; (5) analyze alternatives; and finally (6) select an alternative. Be prepared to share your problem and the solution you decided on with the class. If you have a great idea, share it with the administration at your school!

MY TURN TO BE A MANAGER

- Consider a big decision that you have made. Write a description of the decision using the steps in the decision-making process as your guide. What could you have done differently in the process to improve your decision?

- Write a procedure, a rule, and a policy for your instructor to use in your class. Be sure that each one is clear and understandable. And be sure to explain how it fits the characteristics of a procedure, a rule, or a policy.

- Find three examples of managerial decisions described in any of the popular business periodicals (*Wall Street Journal, Bloomberg Businessweek, Fortune*, etc.). Write a paper describing each decision and any other information, such as what led to the decision, what happened as a result of the decision, etc. What did you learn about decision making from these examples?

- Interview two managers and ask them for suggestions on what it takes to be a good decision maker. Write down their suggestions and be prepared to present them in class.

- Do a web search on the phrase "8 of the biggest business mistakes in history." Pick three of the examples and describe what happened. What's your reaction to the examples? How could the managers have made better decisions?

- Visit the Mindtools website (www.mindtools.com) and find the decision-making toolkit. Explore the decision-making tools suggested and select one tool to use the next time you need to make a decision.

CASE APPLICATION 1   Making Decisions with Bad Data

Decisions should be better with *more* data, but what if *bad* data is used to make those decisions? For Amazon, the problem was fake data. Third-party sellers on Amazon were paying people to post positive reviews even when they hadn't used a product. These fake reviews raised product ratings to lure more customers. Amazon had to spend considerable time and money correcting this problem by verifying customer reviews.[47]

Outdated data is another form of "bad data." United Airlines made forecasts of seating demand based on data they collected years earlier. It turned out that the data was based on assumptions about flying habits that weren't true anymore. United figures it lost $1 billion in missed revenue from this mistake.

Other companies might transfer data from one part of the company to another with problems arising as a result. For example, prescriptions sent from one hospital's neo-natal intensive care unit to the hospital's pharmacy were not interpreted correctly. The pharmacy's data system hadn't accounted for babies so young. This resulted in too much medicine being prescribed for them.[48]

Data also might be collected in a company—about customer complaints, for instance. But if that data is not shared with people who take action on those complaints, it doesn't do much good.

A recent study found that 77 percent of the 800 bankers surveyed said that their bank is not well-prepared to deal with bad data.[49] More than half of this same survey's respondents said that their banks don't verify the data they are using to make important decisions. Results like these are sounding the alarms that data used to make decisions better be good.

DISCUSSION QUESTIONS

2-10. What should managers and companies do to minimize their use of bad data?

2-11. How might intuition, the analytical decision style, and the conceptual decision style help to work against problems arising from using bad data?

2-12. What does this case illustrate about big data and analytics?

CASE APPLICATION 2

Bringing Sports Analytics into the Thick of Things

Major league baseball has been using analytics—by hiring math whizzes—for a while now to make decisions. The math whizzes bury themselves in data. With their computers and fancy degrees, they seem a world apart from the rest of the baseball staff.

During the 2017 season, the Houston Astros tried something new to break down this "us" versus "them" dynamic between analytics and baseball staff. They hired Sig Mejdal, a big-time analytics expert, to assist Morgan Ensberg, the coach of the minor league team—the Tri-City ValleyCats.

Mejdal might not have played baseball since he was in Little League, but now he was placed as coach at first base. He travelled with the team on long bus rides, staying in cheap hotels.

What did this get the ValleyCats? Ensberg could ask Mejdal for in-the-moment game advice and get answers based on analytics. After games, Ensberg could ask "what if I did this" type questions. Mejdal then could add those scenarios into his statistical models to inform decisions for the next game.

Also, sharing long bus rides can do a lot to build trust between statistics wonks and baseball players. For instance, Mejdal showed a player how he pitched 1.5 seconds slower when men were on base, which allowed runners to steal. The pitcher was receptive to this advice coming from someone he knew.

Getting analysts in the trenches seems to be catching on. The Philadelphia Phillies and Tampa Bay Rays tried out analysts in the dugout during spring 2018 exhibition games. Ensberg predicts, "The reality is this is going to be the norm in baseball . . . If other teams really look at what the future's going to look like, it's going to be having an analyst on the bench."[50]

DISCUSSION QUESTIONS

2-13. What do you think the analyst and head coach need to do to make this approach of adding analysts to the bench as effective as possible?

2-14. How might rational and intuitive decision making both be involved when analysts join the coaching staff?

2-15. What decision-making errors might analysts help coaches minimize by being close by?

ENDNOTES

1. V. Luckerson, "A Decade Ago, Google Bought YouTube—and It Was the Best Tech Deal Ever," *The Ringer* (website), October 10, 2016, https://www. theringer.com/2016/10/10/16042354/google-youtube-acquisition-10-years-tech-deals-69fdbe1c8a06; and E. Jhonsa, "How Much Could Google's YouTube Be Worth? Try More Than $100 Billion," *The Street* (website), May 12, 2018, https://www.thestreet.com/investing/youtube-might-be-worth-over-100-billion-14586599.

2. L. Goldberg, "'Roseanne' Canceled at ABC Following Racist Tweet," *Hollywood Reporter*, May 29, 2018, https://www.hollywoodreporter.com/live-feed/roseanne-canceled-at-abc-racist-tweet-1115412.

3. E. Larson, "Don't Fail at Decision Making Like 98% of Managers Do," *Forbes*, May 18, 2017, https://www.forbes.com/sites/eriklarson/2017/05/18/research-reveals-7-steps-to-better-faster-decision-making-for-your-business-team/#361212aa40ad.

4. W. Pounds, "The Process of Problem-Finding," *Industrial Management Review* (Fall 1969): pp. 1–19.

5. S. Fuchs and R. Prouska, "Creating Positive Employee Change Evaluation: The Role of Different Levels of Organizational Support and Change Participation," *Journal of Change Management* (September 2014): pp. 361–83.

6. See H. A. Simon, "Rationality in Psychology and Economics," *Journal of Business* (October 1986): pp. 209–24; and A. Langley, "In Search of Rationality: The Purposes Behind the Use of Formal Analysis in Organizations," *Administrative Science Quarterly* (December 1989): pp. 598–631.

7. J. G. March, "Decision-Making Perspective: Decisions in Organizations and Theories of Choice," in A. H. Van de Ven and W. F. Joyce (eds.), *Perspectives on Organization Design and Behavior* (New York: Wiley-Interscience, 1981), pp. 232–33.

8. See N. M. Agnew and J. L. Brown, "Bounded Rationality: Fallible Decisions in Unbounded Decision Space," *Behavioral Science* (July 1986): pp. 148–61; D. R. A. Skidd, "Revisiting Bounded Rationality," *Journal of Management Inquiry* (December 1992): pp. 343–47; P. Hemp, "Death by Information Overload," *Harvard Business Review*, September 2009, pp. 82–89; and P. Puranam, N. Stieglitz, M. Osman, and M. M. Pillutla, "Modeling Bounded Rationality in Organizations: Progress and Prospects," *Academy of Management Annals* (January 2015): pp. 337–92.

9. S. Bonnell, "4 Leaders Who Won by Following Their Instincts (Despite Being Told They Were Crazy)," *Inc.*, January 22, 2018, https://www.inc.com/sunny-bonnell/how-to-follow-your-instincts-in-business-even-when-people-say-youre-crazy.html.

10. E. Sadler-Smith and E. Shefy, "The Intuitive Executive: Understanding and Applying 'Gut Feel' in Decision Making," *Academy of Management Executive* (November 2004): pp. 76–91; E. Dane and M. G. Pratt, "Exploring Intuition and Its Role in Managerial Decision Making," *Academy of Management Review* (January 2007): pp. 33–54; and R. M. Hogarth, "Deciding Analytically or Trusting Your Intuition? The Advantages and Disadvantages of Analytic and Intuitive Thought," in T. Betsch and S. Haberstroh (eds.), *The Routines of Decision Making* (East Sussex, UK: Psychology Press, 2014).

11. C. C. Miller and R. D. Ireland, "Intuition in Strategic Decision Making: Friend or Foe," *Academy of Management Executive* (February 1, 2005): p. 20.

12. J. L. Risen and A. D. Nussbaum, "Believing What You Don't Believe," *New York Times*, October 30, 2015, Opinion, https://www.nytimes.com/2015/11/01/opinion/believing-what-you-dont-believe.html; and G. P. Hodgkinson and E. Sadler-Smith, "The Dynamics of Intuition and Analysis in Managerial and Organizational Decision Making," *Academy of Management Perspectives* (November 2018): pp. 472–92.

13. M. G. Seo and L. Feldman Barrett, "Being Emotional During Decision Making—Good or Bad? An Empirical Investigation," *Academy of Management Journal* (August 2007): pp. 923–40; and R. L. Martin and T. Golsby-Smith, "Management Is Much More Than a Science: The Limits of Data-Driven Decision Making," *Harvard Business Review*, September-October 2017, pp. 128–35.

14. "The Evolution of Decision Making: How Leading Organizations Are Adopting a Data-Driven Culture," *Harvard Business Review*, April 20, 2016, https://hbr.org/sponsored/2016/04/the-evolution-of-decision-making-how-leading-organizations-are-developing-a-data-driven-culture.

15. T. Reay, W. Berta, and M. K. Kohn, "What's the Evidence on Evidence-Based Management?" *Academy of Management Perspectives* (November 2009): p. 5; and D. M. Rousseau, "Making Evidence-Based Organizational Decisions in an Uncertain World," *Organizational Dynamics*, July-September 2018, pp. 135–46.

16. R. L. Martin & T. Golsby-Smith. "Management Is Much More Than a Science: The Limits of Data-Driven Decision Making," *Harvard Business Review*, September-October 2017, pp. 128–135.

17. B. Power, "Improve Decision-Making with Help from the Crowd," *Harvard Business Review*, April 8, 2014, https://hbr.org/2014/04/improve-decision-making-with-help-from-the-crowd; A. Flostrand, "Finding the Future: Crowdsourcing versus the Delphi Technique," *Business Horizons* (March-April 2017): pp. 229–36; and A. Afuah, C. L. Tucci, and G. Viscusi (eds.), *Creating and Capturing Value Through Crowdsourcing* (Oxford, UK: Oxford University Press, 2018).

18. "Hershey Launches Innovative Technology Contest to Solve Summertime Shipping Dilemma," news release, January 14, 2016, https://www.businesswire.com/news/home/20160114005151/en/Hershey-Launches-Innovative-Technology-Contest-Solve-Summertime.

19. K. R. Brousseau, M. J. Driver, G. Hourihan, and R. Larsson, "The Seasoned Executive's Decision-Making Style," *Harvard Business Review*, February 2006, pp. 111–21.

20. A. J. Rowe, J. D. Boulgarides, and M. R. McGrath, *Managerial Decision Making*, Modules in Management Series (Chicago: SRA, 1984), pp. 18–22.

21. Based on N. Goodman, "James Dyson on Using Failure to Drive Success," *Entrepreneur*, November 5, 2012, https://www.entrepreneur.com/article/224855.

22. D. Kahneman and A. Tversky, "Judgment Under Uncertainty: Heuristics and Biases," *Science* 185 (1974): pp. 1124–1131; P. Johnson, "Avoiding Decision Paralysis in the Face of Uncertainty," *Harvard Business Review*, March 11, 2015, https://hbr.org/2015/03/

avoiding-decision-paralysis-in-the-face-of-uncertainty; J. Fox, "From 'Economic Man' to Behavioral Economics," *Harvard Business Review*, May 2015, pp. 78–85; and D. Kahneman, A. M. Rosenfield, L. Gandhi, and T. Blaser, "How to Overcome the High, Hidden Cost of Inconsistent Decision Making," *Harvard Business Review*, October 2016, pp. 38–46.

23. Information in this section taken from D. Kahneman, D. Lovallo, and O. Sibony, "Before You Make That Decision ...," *Harvard Business Review*, June 2011, pp. 50–60; and S. P. Robbins, *Decide & Conquer*, 2nd ed. (Upper Saddle River, NJ: Pearson Education, 2015).

24. "How Does Unconscious Bias Impact Your Decision-Making at Work?" *Great Manager* (blog), July 18, 2018, https://greatmanager.co/how-does-unconscious-bias-impact-your-decision-making-at-work-220d7efb723b.

25. C. K. Morewedge, "How a Video Game Helped People Make Better Decisions," *Harvard Business Review*, October 13, 2015, https://hbr.org/2015/10/how-a-video-game-helped-people-make-better-decisions.

26. J. Van Wagenen, "Cleveland Clinic Targets Telemedicine, Big Data and AI to Improve the Future of Care," *HealthTech*, April 18, 2018, https://healthtechmagazine.net/article/2018/04/cleveland-clinic-targets-telemedicine-big-data-and-ai-improve-future-care.

27. D. Dunne and R. Martin, "Design Thinking and How It Will Change Management Education: An Interview and Discussion," *Academy of Management Learning & Education* (December 2006): p. 512.

28. Based on S. P. Robbins, *Decide & Conquer: The Ultimate Guide for Improving Your Decision Making*, 2nd ed. (Upper Saddle River, NJ: Pearson Education, 2015).

29. R. Martin and J. Euchner, "Design Thinking," *Research Technology Management* (May-June 2012) pp. 10–14; and J. Kolko, "Design Thinking Comes of Age," *Harvard Business Review*, September 2015, https://hbr.org/2015/09/design-thinking-comes-of-age.

30. A. Ignatius, "How Indra Nooyi Turned Design Thinking into Strategy," *Harvard Business Review*, September 2015, p. 84.

31. D. Dunne and R. Martin, "Design Thinking and How It Will Change Management Education," *Academy of Management Learning and Education* 5, No. 4 (2006) p. 514.

32. I. Steadman, "IBM's Watson Is Better at Diagnosing Cancer than Human Doctors," *Wired*, February 11, 2013, https://www.wired.co.uk/article/ibm-watson-medical-doctor; and J. Sobowale, "How Artificial Intelligence Is Transforming the Legal Profession," April 2016, abajournal.com.

33. See, for instance, A. Agrawal, J. Gans, and A. Goldfarb, "How AI Will Change the Way We Make Decisions," *Harvard Business Review*, July 26, 2017, https://hbr.org/2017/07/how-ai-will-change-the-way-we-make-decisions; M. H. Jarrahi, "Artificial Intelligence and the Future of Work: Human-AI Symbiosis in Organizational Decision Making," *Business Horizons*, July-August 2018, pp. 577–86; and G. Colvin, "25 Ways A.I. Is Changing Business," *Fortune*, November 1, 2018, pp. 97–108.

34. See T. Greenwald, "How AI Is Transforming the Workplace," *Wall Street Journal*, March 13, 2017, p. R1.

35. "Machine Learning: What It Is and Why It Matters," SAS Institute, https://www.sas.com/en_us/insights/analytics/machine-learning.html.

36. "Amy Hood," *Bloomberg Businessweek*, December 10, 2018, p. 59.

37. A. Somani, "Deep Learning Can Improve Your Decision Making," *Global Real Estate Experts* (website), September 12, 2017, https://www.globalrealestateexperts.com/2017/09/deep-learning-can-improve-decision-making/.

38. "Diagnosis by Artificial Intelligence," *The Week*, June 15, 2018, p. 19.

39. K. Utermohlen, "15 Artificial Intelligence (AI) Stats You Need to Know in 2018," *Towards Data Science*, April 13, 2018, https://towardsdatascience.com/15-artificial-intelligence-ai-stats-you-need-to-know-in-2018-b6c5eac958e5.

40. "Analytics: What It Is and Why It Matters," SAS Institute, https://www.sas.com/en_sa/insights/analytics/what-is-analytics.html.

41. T. McManus, "Eagles' Secret Weapon? An Analytics-Fueled Attack," January 18, 2018, espn.com.

42. "Innovation of the Week," *The Week*, May 11, 2018, p. 18.

43. Cited in "How Artificial Intelligence Will Change Decision-Making for Business," *Becoming Human* (blog), September 1, 2017, https://becominghuman.ai/how-artificial-intelligence-will-change-decision-making-for-businesses-96d47cde98df.

44. R. Bean, "How Big Data and AI are Driving Business Innovation in 2018," *MIT Sloan Management Review*, February 5, 2018, https://sloanreview.mit.edu/article/how-big-data-and-ai-are-driving-business-innovation-in-2018/.

45. A. Peters, "IKEA's Bike Was Good—But Now They're All Been Recalled," *Fast Company*, June 5, 2018, https://www.fastcompany.com/40580222/ikeas-bike-was-good-but-now-theyre-all-being-recalled.

46. Based on T. M. Amabile, "Motivating Creativity in Organizations," *California Management Review* (Fall 1997) pp. 42–52; S. Caudron, "Creativity 101," *Workforce*, March 2002, pp. 20, 24; S. Weinschenck, "Why 'Stepping Away' Increases Your Creativity," *Psychology Today*, March 7, 2014, https://www.psychologytoday.com/us/blog/brain-wise/201403/why-stepping-away-increases-your-creativity; and S. Harvey, "Creative Synthesis: Exploring the Process of Extraordinary Group Creativity," *Academy of Management Review* (July 2014): pp. 324–43.

47. Y. Lepant, "Why Fake Data Could Be the Biggest Threat to Decision Making," *Computer Business Review Online*, July 18, 2018, https://www.cbronline.com/opinion/fake-data-decision-making.

48. C. Newcomb, "When Bad Data Happens to Good Companies," *SAS Best Practices* (2013), SAS Institute, https://www.sas.com/content/dam/SAS/en_us/doc/whitepaper1/bad-data-good-companies-106465.pdf.

49. A. McIntyre, "In Age of Big Data, Banks Face Tricky New Challenges, *Forbes*, May 16, 2018, https://www.forbes.com/sites/alanmcintyre/2018/05/16/in-age-of-big-data-banks-face-tricky-new-challenges/#177953b42b0d.

50. J. Diamond, "The Data Wonk Who Became a Coach," Sports, *Wall Street Journal*, March 29, 2018, https://www.wsj.com/articles/the-data-wonk-who-became-a-coach-1522234800.

PART 1

Management Practice

A Manager's Dilemma

Selina Lo loves her job as the manager of a toy store in San Francisco. She loves the chaos and the excitement of kids as they wander around the store searching for their favorite toys. Teddy bears pulled off the shelves and toy trucks left on the floor are part and parcel of managing a toy store. Yet her biggest challenge, which is a problem faced by many retailers, is employee turnover. Many of her employees leave after just a few months on the job because of hectic schedules and long work hours. Selina is always looking for new ways to keep her employees committed to their jobs. She also takes care of customers' requests and complaints and tries to address them satisfactorily. This is what Selina's life as a manager is like. However, retailers are finding that people with Selina's skills and enthusiasm for store management are few and far between. Managing a retail store is not the career that most college graduates aspire to. Attracting and keeping talented managers continues to be a challenge for all kinds of retailers.

> *Suppose you're a recruiter for a large retail chain and want to get college graduates to consider store management as a career option. Using what you learned in Part 1, how would you do that?*

Global Sense

Who holds more managerial positions worldwide, women or men? Statistics tell an interesting story. In the United States, women held 40 percent of all managerial positions and 21 percent held senior leadership roles, but only 4.8 percent of the Fortune 500 CEO spots. Interestingly, emerging economies have high proportions of women in top positions. In Africa, 89 percent of businesses have at least one woman in senior management, while women are in senior management positions in 87 percent of Eastern European businesses. In Western Europe, 79 percent of French businesses have at least one woman in a senior leadership role, while the United Kingdom has 75 percent. Germany fares worse, with no women CEOs leading their top 30 companies and women holding only 9 percent of positions on executive boards of top companies. Two countries in Asia with high percentages of women CEOs are Thailand (40 percent) and Vietnam (25 percent). By contrast, 10 percent of CEOs in Singapore are women. In Australia, 16.5 percent of CEOs or heads of businesses are women.

As you can see, companies across the globe continue to have a large gender gap in leadership. Men far outnumber women in senior business leadership positions. These circumstances exist despite efforts and campaigns to improve equality in the workplace. Where there has been significant progress is Europe. Many countries there require corporations to allocate a specified percentage of board seats to women. For example, since 2008 Norway has required 40 percent of board seats to be held by women. But women in Norway still only make up 7 percent of CEOs, so progress hasn't spread evenly across all kinds of leadership positions. To address leadership inequality outside the boardroom, companies like Deutsche Telekom in Germany have set recruiting goals to increase the number of women in their talent pipeline. Deutsche Telekom strives for women to comprise half of their new trainees and for women to make up at least 30 percent of those short-listed for management positions.

Some women who have been on track to CEO positions say the problem is not with the leadership pipeline. Instead, it's at least partly about biases— often *unconscious* biases—that women face. Women can be penalized for acting forcefully, looked over for challenging assignments, and not fully heard during meetings. Chevron thinks part of the answer to these problems is teaching executives about how unconscious biases may be leading women to opt out of the path to top leadership positions. Chevron invested $5 million in a "Men Advocating Real Change" training effort and has increased the percentage of women on its board to 36 percent. Chevron's CEO, Mike Wirth, says the company has seen increased innovation as a result of their diversity and inclusion efforts.[1]

> *Discuss the following questions in light of what you learned in Part 1:*
>
> - *What issues might Deutsche Telekom face in recruiting women for new trainee positions?*
> - *How could it address those issues?*
> - *What issues might Chevron face with their approach to addressing the gender gap in leadership, and how could it address those issues?*
> - *What are other possible advantages of a company's diversity and inclusion efforts besides increased innovation?*
> - *What could other organizations around the globe learn from Chevron?*

Continuing Case

Starbucks—Introduction

Community. Connection. Caring. Committed. Coffee. Five Cs that describe the essence of Starbucks Corporation— what it stands for and what it wants to be as a business. With nearly 30,000 stores in 77 countries, Starbucks is the world's number one specialty coffee retailer. The company also owns Seattle's Best Coffee, Teavana, Starbucks

VIA, Starbucks Refreshers, Evolution Fresh, La Boulange, Verismo, and Torrefazione Italia brands. It's a company that truly epitomizes the challenges facing managers in today's globally competitive environment. To help you better understand these challenges, we're going to take an in-depth look at Starbucks through these continuing cases, which you'll find at the end of every part in the textbook. Each of these six part-ending continuing cases will look at Starbucks from the perspective of the material presented in that part. Although each case "stands alone," you'll be able to see the progression of the management process as you work through each one.

The Beginning

"We aren't in the coffee business, serving people. We're in the people business, serving coffee." That was the philosophy of Howard Schultz, chief executive officer emeritus of Starbucks. It's a philosophy that has shaped—and continues to shape—the company.

The first Starbucks, which opened in Seattle's famous Pike Place Market in 1971, was founded by Gordon Bowker, Jerry Baldwin, and Zev Siegl. The company was named for the coffee-loving first mate in the book *Moby Dick,* which also influenced the design of Starbucks's distinctive two-tailed siren logo. Schultz, a successful New York City businessperson, first walked into Starbucks in 1981 as a sales representative for a Swedish kitchenware manufacturer. He was hooked immediately. He knew that he wanted to work for this company, but it took almost a year before he could persuade the owners to hire him. After all, he *was* from New York, and he hadn't grown up with the values of the company. The owners thought Schultz's style and high energy would clash with the existing culture. But Schultz was quite persuasive and was able to allay the owners' fears. They asked him to join the company as director of retail operations and marketing, which he enthusiastically did. Schultz's passion for the coffee business was obvious. Although some of the company's employees resented the fact that he was an "outsider," Schultz had found his niche and he had lots of ideas for the company. As he says, "I wanted to make a positive impact."

About a year after joining the company, while on a business trip to Milan, Schultz walked into an espresso bar and right away knew that this concept could be successful in the United States. He said, "There was nothing like this in America. It was an extension of people's front porch. It was an emotional experience. I believed intuitively we could do it. I felt it in my bones." Schultz recognized that although Starbucks treated coffee as produce, something to be bagged and sent home with the groceries, the Italian coffee bars were more like an experience—a warm, community experience. That's what Schultz wanted to recreate in the United States. However, Starbucks's owners weren't really interested in making Starbucks big and didn't really want to give the idea a try. So Schultz left the company in 1985 to start his own small chain of espresso bars in Seattle

and Vancouver called Il Giornale. Two years later, when Starbucks's owners finally wanted to sell, Schultz raised $3.8 million from local investors to buy them out. That small investment eventually made him a billionaire!

Company Facts

Starbucks's main product is coffee—more than 30 blends and single-origin coffees. In addition to fresh-brewed coffee, here's a sampling of other products the company also offers:

- **Handcrafted beverages:** Hot and iced espresso beverages, coffee and noncoffee blended beverages, and smoothies
- **Merchandise:** Home espresso machines, coffee brewers and grinders, premium chocolates, coffee mugs and coffee accessories, and other assorted items
- **Fresh food:** Baked pastries, sandwiches, salads, hot breakfast items, and yogurt parfaits
- **Global consumer products:** Starbucks Frappuccino® coffee drinks, Starbucks Iced Coffee drinks, Starbucks Liqueurs, and a line of super-premium ice creams
- **Starbucks card and My Starbucks Rewards® program:** A reloadable stored-value card and a consumer rewards program
- **Brand portfolio:** Starbucks Entertainment, Ethos™ Water, Seattle's Best Coffee, Teavana teas, and Fontana syrups

As of June 2018, the company had 277,000 full- and part-time partners (employees) around the world. Kevin Johnson is the President and CEO of Starbucks. Some of the other "interesting" executive positions include chief operating officer; global chief marketing officer; chief creative officer; executive vice president of partner resources and chief community officer; global responsibility chief, global supply chain; executive vice president, global coffee; learning business partner; and international partner resource coordinator.

Decisions, Decisions

After running the show for 15 years at Starbucks, Howard Schultz, at age 46, stepped out of the CEO job for the first time in 2000 (he remained as chairman of the company) because he was "a bit bored." By stepping down as CEO—which he had planned to do, had prepared for, and had no intention of returning to—essentially he was saying that he agreed to trust the decisions of others.

At first the company thrived, but then the perils of rapid mass-market expansion began to set in and customer traffic began to fall for the first time ever. As he watched what was happening, there were times when he felt the decisions being made were not good ones. Schultz couldn't shake his gut feeling that Starbucks had lost its way. In fact, in a memo dubbed the "espresso shot heard round the world," he wrote to his top managers explaining in detail how the company's unprecedented growth had led to many minor compromises that when added up led to a "watering down of the Starbucks experience." Among his complaints: sterile "cookie cutter" store layouts, automatic espresso machines that robbed the "barista theater" of roasting and brewing a cup of coffee, and flavor-locked packaging that didn't allow customers to inhale and savor that distinctive coffee aroma. Schulz felt Starbucks had lost its "cool" factor, and his criticism of the state of the company's stores was blunt and bold. There was no longer a focus on coffee, only on making the cash register ring. Within a year of the memo (and eight years after he left the CEO position), Schultz was back in charge and working to restore the Starbucks experience. His goals were to fix the troubled stores, to reawaken the emotional attachment with customers, and to make long-term changes like reorganizing the company and revamping the supply chain. The first thing he did, however, was to apologize to the staff for the decisions that had brought the company to this point. In fact, his intention to restore quality control led him to a decision to close all (at that time) 7,100 US stores for one evening to retrain 135,000 baristas on the coffee experience . . . what it meant, what it was. It was a bold decision, and one that many "experts" felt would be a public relations and financial disaster. But Schultz felt doing so was absolutely necessary to revive and reenergize Starbucks. Another controversial decision was to hold a leadership conference with all store managers (some 8,000 of them) and 2,000 other partners—all at one time and all in one location. Why? To energize and galvanize these employees around what Starbucks stands for and what needed to be done for the company to survive and prosper. Schultz was unsure about how Wall Street would react to the cost, which was around $30 million total (airfare, meals, hotels, etc.), but again, he didn't care because he felt doing so was absolutely necessary and critical. In the interim years, Starbucks grew and prospered. In 2017, Schultz stepped down again as CEO and completely cut his management ties to the company in June 2018, although he remains the single largest shareholder.

Schultz helped to choose the new Starbucks president and CEO, Kevin Johnson. Johnson has had to figure out how to handle the reality of stiff competition and slow same-store sales growth. One of his first actions as CEO was to close all 379 Teavana stores and sell off the Tazo tea brand. Johnson also had to determine how to respond when two African Americans were arrested at a Philadelphia Starbucks while waiting for a friend. This received a huge amount of media attention—most of it negative and suggesting the company was racist. Johnson earned praise for making a face-to-face apology to the two men and closing nearly 8,000 Starbucks stores for anti-bias training. Johnson also has overseen extending paid paternity leave and paid time off to care for sick family members for hourly employees.[2]

So we're beginning to see how Starbucks epitomizes the five Cs—community, connection, caring, committed, and coffee. In this Continuing Case in the Management

Practice section at the end of Parts 2–6, you'll discover more about Starbucks's unique and successful ways of managing. As you work on these remaining continuing cases, keep in mind that there may be information included in this introduction you might want to review.

Discussion Questions

P1-1. What management skills do you think would be most important for Kevin Johnson to have? Why? What skills do you think would be most important for a Starbucks store manager to have? Why?

P1-2. How might the following management theories/approaches be useful to Starbucks: scientific management, organizational behavior, quantitative approach, systems approach?

P1-3. Choose three of the current trends and issues facing managers and explain how Starbucks might be impacted. What might be the implications for first-line managers? Middle managers? Top managers?

P1-4. Give examples of how Kevin Johnson might perform interpersonal roles, informational roles, and decisional roles.

P1-5. Look up Kevin Johnson and notice what is mentioned about him. How might his experiences and background affect the way the company is managed?

P1-6. Go to the company's website, www.starbucks.com, and find the list of senior officers. Pick one of those positions and describe what you think that job might involve. Try to envision what types of planning, organizing, leading, and controlling this person would have to do.

P1-7. Look up the company's mission and guiding principles at the company's website. What do you think of the mission and guiding principles?

P1-8. Describe how these would influence how a barista at a local Starbucks store does his or her job. Describe how these would influence how one of the company's top executives does his or her job.

P1-9. What made Starbucks's response to the Philadelphia crisis a non-programmed decision? To ensure that store managers across the company use programmed decisions in order to respond in a consistent way to non-buying customers, what would need to be done?

P1-10. Which decision style best describes Kevin Johnson's approach to decision making? Which decision style best summarizes Howard Schultz's decision-making approach? Explain your answer.

P1-11. How might biases and errors affect the decision making done by Starbucks executives? By Starbucks store managers? By Starbucks partners?

P1-12. How might design thinking be important to a company like Starbucks? Do you see any indication that Starbucks uses design thinking? Explain.

Notes for the Part 1 Continuing Case

1. Sources: "Quick Take: Women in Management," *Catalyst*, July 30, 2018, https://www.catalyst.org/research/women-in-management/; A. Sullivan, "Report Highlights Lack of Female Leaders in German Business," *DW*, May 14, 2018, https://www.dw.com/en/report-highlights-lack-of-female-leaders-in-german-business/a-43747520; "Will We See the First Female CEO of a DAX Company in 2019?" *Handelsblatt Today*, January 10, 2019, https://www.handelsblatt.com/today/companies/gender-equality-will-we-see-the-first-female-ceo-of-a-dax-company-in-2019/23845800.html?ticket=ST-375857-U2Nt0ulWByb4oiH77fXu-ap3; Grant Thornton, "Gender Balance Remains Elusive," press release, https://www.grantthornton.global/en/press/press-releases-2018/Gender-balance-remains-elusive/; N. Ashpole, "Women in Business: New Perspectives on Risk and Reward," International Business Report, *Grant Thornton* (website), March 8, 2017, https://www.grantthornton.co.th/insights/articles/women-in-business-2017/; M. Nga, "Vietnam Leads Region for Ratio of Female Business Leaders," *VN Express*, January 2, 2018, https://e.vnexpress.net/news/business/vietnam-leads-region-for-ratio-of-female-business-leaders-3693035.html; R. Milne, "Enlightened Norway's Gender Paradox: A Decade of Mandatory 40 Per Cent Female Quotas for Boards Has Mixed Outcomes," *Financial Times*, September 20, 2018; Deutsche Telekom, https://www.telekom.com; S. Chira, "Why Women Aren't C.E.O.s, According to Women Who Almost Were," *New York Times*, July 21, 2017, https://www.nytimes.com/2017/07/21/sunday-review/women-ceos-glass-ceiling.html; "Chevron Thinks Men Can Fix the Diversity Problem," DealBook, *New York Times*, February 26, 2019, https://www.nytimes.com/2019/02/26/business/dealbook/chevron-diversity-men.html.

2. Information from Starbucks company website, https://www.starbucks.com; Wikipedia, s.v. "Starbucks," accessed March 5, 2019, https://en.wikipedia.org/wiki/Starbucks; H. Schultz (with J. Gordon), *Onward: How Starbucks Fought for Its Life Without Losing Its Soul* (New York: Rodale, 2011); R. Gulati, S. Huffman, and G. Neilson, "The Barista Principle," *Strategy and Business*, Third Quarter 2002, pp. 58–69; and H. Schultz and D. Jones Yang, *Pour Your Heart into It: How Starbucks Built a Company One Cup at a Time* (New York: Hyperion, 1997); "Number of Starbucks Stores Worldwide from 2013 to 2018," *Statista*, https://www.statista.com/statistics/266465/number-of-starbucks-stores-worldwide/; P. N. Danziger, "Starbucks Makes the Right Call, Scales Back Plans for 1,000 Upscale Reserve Stores," *Forbes*, January 8, 2019, https://www.forbes.com/sites/pamdanziger/2019/01/08/starbucks-is-scaling-back-its-plans-for-1000-upscale-reserve-stores/#61c77d672f89; C. C. Miller, "Walmart and Now Starbucks: Why More Big Companies Are Offering Paid Family Leave," *New York Times*, January 24, 2018, https://www.nytimes.com/2018/01/24/upshot/parental-leave-company-policy-salaried-hourly-gap.html; E. Sherman, "Another Starbucks Refused to Let a Black Customer Use the Bathroom," *Inc.*, February 18, 2018, https://www.inc.com/erik-sherman/another-starbucks-racism-video-training-will-be-harder-than-management-expected.html; N. Luna, "Starbucks Closing 8,000 Locations Tuesday Afternoon After Racial Profiling Incident," Nation's Restaurant News, May 30, 2018, https://www.nrn.com/quick-service/starbucks-closing-8000-locations-tuesday-afternoon-after-racial-profiling-incident; and P. Mourdoukoutas, "Starbucks' Problems at Home and Abroad," *Forbes*, June 27, 2018, https://www.forbes.com/sites/panosmourdoukoutas/2018/06/27/starbucks-problems-at-home-and-abroad/#3671cb0d64b5.

Chapter 3

Influence of the External Environment and the Organization's Culture

Learning Objectives

3.1 *Contrast* the actions of managers according to the omnipotent and symbolic views.

3.2 *Describe* the constraints and challenges facing managers in today's external environment.

3.3 *Discuss* the characteristics and importance of organizational culture.

Employability Skills Matrix

This matrix identifies features and end-of-chapter material that will help you develop specific skills employers are looking for in job candidates.

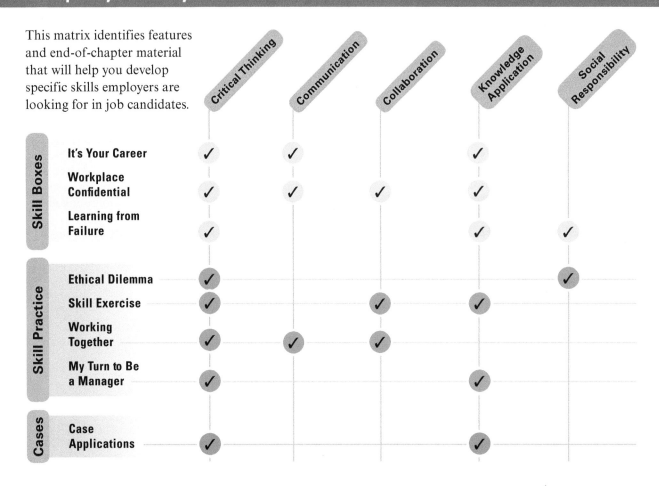

		Critical Thinking	Communication	Collaboration	Knowledge Application	Social Responsibility
Skill Boxes	It's Your Career	✓	✓		✓	
	Workplace Confidential	✓	✓	✓	✓	
	Learning from Failure	✓			✓	✓
Skill Practice	Ethical Dilemma	✓				✓
	Skill Exercise	✓		✓	✓	
	Working Together	✓	✓	✓		
	My Turn to Be a Manager	✓			✓	
Cases	Case Applications	✓			✓	

Nick Gracey owns a Shell service station in Salt Lake City. As an independent station owner, he's free to charge "whatever the market will bear" for his gas. But his options are constrained by one fact: Nick has two competitive stations at his same intersection—an Exxon and a Chevron. As Nick put it, "I'm a prisoner to what my two competitors do. If either one drops the price a nickel, I have to respond in kind." Nick is acknowledging that his options—when it comes to pricing his gas—are not just dependent on the price he has to pay his Shell distributor. They're also influenced by the actions of his competitors. As we'll show, competitors are forces in an organization's external environment.

In this chapter, we're going to look at the challenges incurred by the external environment and discuss the characteristics of organizational culture. But before we address these topics, we first need to look at two perspectives on the degree to which managers actually influence an organization's success or failure.

THE MANAGER: omnipotent or symbolic?

L03.1 How much difference does a manager really make in how an organization performs? The dominant view in management theory and society in general is that managers are directly responsible for an organization's success or failure. We call this perspective the **omnipotent view of management**. In contrast, others have argued that much of an organization's success or failure is due to external forces outside managers' control. This perspective is called the **symbolic view of management**. Let's look at each perspective to try and clarify just how much credit or blame managers should get for their organization's performance.

omnipotent view of management
The view that managers are directly responsible for an organization's success or failure

symbolic view of management
The view that much of an organization's success or failure is due to external forces outside managers' control

The Omnipotent View

In Chapter 1, we stressed how important managers were to organizations. Differences in an organization's performance are assumed to be due to the decisions and actions of its managers. Good managers anticipate change, exploit opportunities, correct poor performance, and lead their organizations. When profits are up, managers take the credit and are rewarded with bonuses, stock options, and the like. When profits are down, top managers are often fired in the belief that "new blood" will bring improved results. For instance, Twitter Chief Executive Jack Dorsey fired the head of engineering, summoning "bold rethinking" as the company's growth has slowed.[1] In the omnipotent view, someone has to be held accountable when organizations perform poorly regardless of the reasons, and that "someone" is the manager. Of course, when things go well, managers also get the credit—even if they had little to do with achieving the positive outcomes.

This view of managers as omnipotent is consistent with the stereotypical picture of the take-charge business executive who overcomes any obstacle in seeing that the organization achieves its goals. And this view isn't limited to business organizations. It also explains turnover among college and professional sports coaches, who are considered the "managers" of their teams. Coaches who lose more games than they win are usually fired and replaced by new coaches who are expected to correct the poor performance.

The Symbolic View

Levitz Furniture was founded in 1910 in Lebanon, Pennsylvania. It became widely successful selling moderately priced brand-name furniture from warehouse-style stores. But the furniture market suffered a huge and rapid downturn in late 2007 when the subprime mortgage crisis brought on the collapse of the US housing market—a collapse almost no one saw coming. New residential construction came to a halt. People didn't move because they couldn't sell their homes. Demand for furniture dried up, and Levitz sales plummeted. In October 2008, Levitz filed for bankruptcy and liquidated its business. Unfortunately, Levitz management was in the wrong place (the furniture business) at the wrong time (2007–08). Little of what Levitz management did or didn't do could affect the decline in the demand for furniture.

The symbolic view says that a manager's ability to affect performance outcomes is influenced and constrained by external factors over which it has little or no control.[2] According to this view, it's unreasonable to expect managers to significantly affect an organization's performance. Instead, performance is influenced by factors such as the economy, customers, governmental policies, competitors' actions, industry conditions, and decisions made by previous managers.

Following the symbolic view, management has, at best, only a limited effect on *substantive organizational outcomes*. What management does affect greatly are *symbolic* outcomes. Management's role is seen as creating meaning out of randomness, confusion, and ambiguity. Management creates the illusion of control for the benefit of stockholders, customers, employees, and the public. When things go right, we need someone to praise. Management plays that role. Similarly, when things go wrong, we need someone to blame. Management plays that role, too. However, according to the symbolic view, the *actual* part management plays in success or failure is minimal.

Reality Suggests a Synthesis

In reality, managers are neither helpless nor all-powerful. Internal constraints that restrict a manager's decision options exist within every organization. These internal constraints are derived from the organization's culture. In addition, external constraints impinge on the organization and restrict managerial freedom. The external constraints come from the organization's environment.

Exhibit 3-1 shows the manager as operating within constraints. The organization's culture and environment press against the manager, restricting his or her options. Yet in spite of these constraints, managers are not powerless. There still remains an area of discretion in which managers can exert a significant amount of influence on an organization's performance—an area in which good managers differentiate themselves from poor ones.

Exhibit 3-1
Constraints on Managerial Discretion

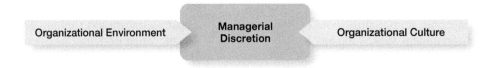

Organizational Environment → Managerial Discretion → Organizational Culture

THE EXTERNAL ENVIRONMENT:
constraints and challenges

LO3.2 The recognition that no organization operates independently was a major contribution of the systems approach to management (see History Module). In this section we want to demonstrate how forces in the environment play a major role in shaping and limiting managers' actions.

Defining the Environment and Environmental Uncertainty

environment
Institutions or forces that are outside the organization and potentially affect the organization's performance

environmental uncertainty
The degree of change and complexity in an organization's environment

The term **environment** refers to institutions or forces that are outside the organization and potentially affect the organization's performance. The reason the environment is important is because not all environments are the same. They differ by what we call their degree of **environmental uncertainty**.

		Degree of Change	
		Stable	**Dynamic**
Degree of Complexity	**Simple**	**Cell 1** Stable and predictable environment Few components in environment Components are somewhat similar and remain basically the same Minimal need for sophisticated knowledge of components	**Cell 2** Dynamic and unpredictable environment Few components in environment Components are somewhat similar but are continually changing Minimal need for sophisticated knowledge of components
	Complex	**Cell 3** Stable and predictable environment Many components in environment Components are not similar to one another and remain basically the same High need for sophisticated knowledge of components	**Cell 4** Dynamic and unpredictable environment Many components in environment Components are not similar to one another and are continually changing High need for sophisticated knowledge of components

Exhibit 3-2
Environmental Uncertainty Matrix

ENVIRONMENTAL UNCERTAINTY Environmental uncertainty refers to the degree of change and complexity in an organization's environment. The matrix in Exhibit 3-2 shows these two aspects.

The first dimension of uncertainty is the *degree of change*. If the components in an organization's environment change frequently, it's a *dynamic* environment. If change is minimal, it's a *stable* one. A stable environment might be one with no new competitors, few technological breakthroughs by current competitors, little activity by pressure groups to influence the organization, and so forth. For instance, Zippo Manufacturing, best known for its Zippo lighters, faces a relatively stable environment, with few competitors and little technological change. The main external concern for the company is probably the declining numbers of tobacco smokers and the increased popularity of e-cigarettes, which rely on lithium batteries rather than fire. In contrast, the recorded music industry faces a dynamic (highly uncertain and unpredictable) environment. Digital formats and music-downloading sites turned the industry upside down and brought high levels of uncertainty. And now, music streaming services such as Spotify and Pandora have added doubt to the equation.

If change is predictable, is that considered dynamic? No. Think of department stores that typically make one-quarter to one-third of their sales in November and December. The drop-off from December to January is significant. But because the change is predictable, the environment isn't considered dynamic. When we talk about degree of change, we mean change that's unpredictable. If change can be accurately anticipated, it's not an uncertainty for managers.

The other dimension of uncertainty describes the degree of **environmental complexity**, which looks at the number of components in an organization's environment and the extent of the knowledge that the organization has about those components. An organization with fewer competitors, customers, suppliers, government agencies, and so forth faces a less complex and uncertain environment. Organizations deal with environmental complexity in various ways. For example, the Hasbro toy company simplified its environment by acquiring many of its competitors, like Parker Brothers and Milton Bradley.

Complexity is also measured in terms of the knowledge an organization needs about its environment. For instance, managers at Pinterest must know a great deal about their internet service provider's operations if they want to ensure their website is available, reliable, and secure for their customers. On the other hand, managers of college bookstores have a minimal need for sophisticated knowledge about their suppliers.

environmental complexity
The number of components in an organization's environment and the extent of the organization's knowledge about those components

How does the concept of environmental uncertainty influence managers? Looking again at Exhibit 3-2, each of the four cells represents different combinations of degree of complexity and degree of change. Cell 1 (stable and simple environment) represents the lowest level of environmental uncertainty and Cell 4 (dynamic and complex environment), the highest. Not surprisingly, managers have the greatest influence on organizational outcomes in Cell 1 and the least in Cell 4. Because uncertainty poses a threat to an organization's effectiveness, managers try to minimize it.[3] Given a choice, managers would prefer to operate in the least uncertain environments.

The environment can also be analyzed at two levels. The next sections look at those two levels: the *general* environment and the *specific* one.

Let's Get REAL

Anooja Rangnekar ▶
Manager, Medicaid Business Development

Source: Anooja Rangnekar

The Scenario:

Leon DeNeve is a program manager at Home Box Office (HBO), which is experiencing a lot of change. Part of his job is to determine the new programs viewers will want to see, but it's difficult to make decisions when it's not clear how viewers' habits will change. More companies are getting in on producing new content to stream—like Amazon and Netflix—and there are still cable and network TV companies on the scene. How should Leon make a decision about what programs or forms of entertainment to even invest in when no one really knows how things will shake out in this industry?

How can Leon stay as informed as possible to the uncertainty and change affecting his company and industry?

As with many industries, change is inevitable, and this is especially true in the entertainment/ television industry. Part of overcoming the challenges with uncertainty is to remain nimble and allow oneself to embrace the future and new opportunities. As a manager in one of the nation's longest operating pay television services, Leon has a unique opportunity to help take the name "HBO" to the next level. One suggestion for Leon is to "learn from his viewers." Conducting viewer surveys or focus groups are great ways for Leon to connect with his customers and learn about what they might be interested in seeing from HBO in the future. Leon also could utilize data and analytics to identify trends in viewership and understand how his competitors are performing.

Monitoring the General Environment

general environment
Everything outside the organization

The **general environment** includes everything outside the organization. As shown in Exhibit 3-3, it includes a number of different components. The *economic* component encompasses factors such as interest rates, inflation, changes in disposable income, stock market fluctuations, and business cycle stages. The *demographic* component is concerned with trends in population characteristics such as age, race, gender, education level, geographic location, income, and family composition. The *political/ legal* component looks at federal, state, and local laws as well as global laws and the laws of other countries. It also includes a country's political conditions and stability. The *sociocultural* component is concerned with societal and cultural factors such as values, attitudes, trends, traditions, lifestyles, beliefs, tastes, and patterns of behavior. The *technological* component is concerned with scientific or industrial innovations. The *global* component encompasses those issues associated with globalization and a world economy.

Exhibit 3-3
Components of External
Environment

The general environment encompasses conditions that *may* affect the organization but whose relevance isn't clear. The strength of the US dollar against the pound and yen, for instance, is likely to be an environmental force for companies like Apple and Boeing, who sell in Great Britain and Japan. But the strength of the dollar isn't likely to have much impact on companies whose customers and suppliers are all within the US.

The Specific Environment

The bulk of management's attention is usually given to the organization's **specific environment**. This is the part of the environment that is directly relevant to the achievement of an organization's goals. It consists of the crucial constituencies or stakeholders that can positively or negatively influence an organization's effectiveness. The specific environment for most organizations include one or more of the following: suppliers, customers, competitors, government agencies, and special-interest groups. Let's briefly elaborate on each and why it's important.

SUPPLIERS Suppliers include any entity that provides the organization with labor, materials, and equipment. For pizza restaurants, it would include those sources that provide flour, tomatoes, meats, vegetables, and sodas. It would also probably include banks, insurers, and maybe labor unions. In contrast, for hospitals, suppliers include medical equipment distributors, drug companies, medical and nursing schools, and insurance companies.

Why are suppliers important? Management seeks to ensure a steady flow of needed inputs at the lowest price possible. Because these inputs represent uncertainties—that is, their unavailability or delay can significantly reduce the organization's effectiveness—management typically goes to great efforts to ensure a steady reliable flow.

CUSTOMERS Organizations exist to meet the needs of customers. It's the customer or client who absorbs the organization's output. This is true even for governmental organizations. They exist to provide services, and we are reminded, especially at election time, that we indicate by the way we vote how satisfied we actually are as customers.

Customers obviously represent potential uncertainty to an organization because customers can be fickle. Big-brand consumer goods companies like Campbell Soup, Kraft Heinz, PepsiCo, and Procter & Gamble, for instance, are all suffering from a change in consumer buying preferences. Private-label store-brand products at retailers like Walmart, Family Dollar, Costco, and Aldi have taken a lot of big brand-name business by offering similar products to the big brands but at significantly lower prices.

COMPETITORS All organizations, even monopolies, have one or more competitors. The US Postal Service has a monopoly on mail service, but it competes against FedEx, United Parcel Service, and other forms of communications, such as the telephone, email, and text messaging. Nike dominates the athletic shoe business

fyi

According to Ram Charan, one of the world's leading advisors to CEOs and boards of directors, the best CEOs are attuned to the external environment and detect early warning signals and opportunities.[4]

specific environment
The part of the environment consisting of crucial constituencies or stakeholders that can positively or negatively influence an organization's effectiveness

Wal-Mart's private label store brand of oatmeal has taken sales from major oatmeal brands like PepsiCo's Quaker Oats.
Source: Sheila Fitzgerald/Shutterstock

but still competes against Adidas, Puma, Asics, and Under Armour, among others. Coca-Cola competes against Pepsi and other soft drink companies as well as firms that sell bottled water and energy drinks. Not-for-profit organizations like the Charlotte Symphony Orchestra and the Girl Scouts also compete for dollars, volunteers, and customers.

Managers can ill afford to ignore the competition. When they do, they pay dearly. Up until the early 1980s, the three major TV broadcasting networks—ABC, CBS, and NBC—virtually controlled what you watched on television and essentially only had to worry about each other. Today, their market share and profits have been aggressively eaten away by Fox, cable networks, Hulu, and local stations that rely on syndicated programming. This illustrates that competitors—in terms of pricing, services offered, accessibility, new products developed, and the like—represent an important environmental force that management must monitor and to which it must be prepared to respond.

GOVERNMENT Federal, state, and local governments influence what organizations can and cannot do. Some federal legislation has had significant implications. For example, the Americans with Disabilities Act of 1990 was designed to make jobs and public facilities more accessible to people with disabilities. This, in turn, has altered hiring practices and resulted in facility-layout changes. The Lilly Ledbetter Fair Pay Act of 2009 changed the 180-day statute of limitations for filing a pay discrimination lawsuit to reset with each new paycheck. Companies responded by reassessing, and often changing, their pay practices. And the Dodd-Frank Wall Street Reform and Consumer Protection Act of 2010 placed the regulation of banks and other financial firms in the hands of the federal government and required firms to enact new transparency and accountability procedures. The federal government, of course, isn't the only source of legal regulations that govern organizations. State and local governmental regulations also extend and modify many federal standards. For instance, the city of San Francisco recently raised the minimum hourly wage to $15 an hour, considerably higher than California's minimum of $11. This significantly increased costs for many firms doing business in San Francisco.

Organizations spend a great deal of time and money to meet government regulations. But the effects of these regulations go beyond time and money. They also reduce managerial discretion. They limit the choices available to managers.

PRESSURE GROUPS Managers must recognize the special-interest groups that attempt to influence the actions of organizations. Black Lives Matter protesters attacked Starbucks and demanded changes in policies when a Philadelphia store manager called police who then arrested two black men that were sitting at a table

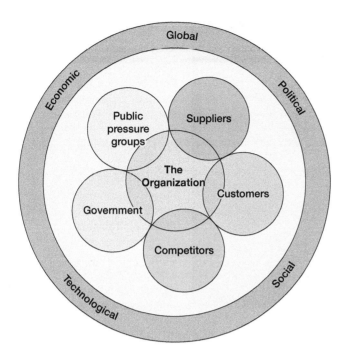

Exhibit 3-4
The Organization and Its Environment

without ordering anything. Gun manufacturers are regularly vilified by groups like the Coalition to Stop Gun Violence. Conservative citizen action groups have successfully pressured publishers of elementary and secondary-level American history textbooks to change content that their members have found offensive. And it would be an unusual week if we didn't read that pro-life or pro-choice advocates were picketing, boycotting, or just threatening some organization in order to get management to change its policies.

Managing the Environment

As we've seen, organizations are not self-contained or self-sufficient. They interact with and are influenced by their environment. (Exhibit 3-4 summarizes that environment.) Organizations depend on their environment as a source of inputs and as a recipient of its outputs. Organizations must also abide by the laws and regulations and respond to groups that challenge the organization's actions. However, while the environment constrains managers, it certainly doesn't completely tie their hands.[5]

What can management do to lessen these constraints and gain some control over their environment? They can identify key external constituencies and build a relationship with them. It makes sense, for instance, for Lockheed to hire former high-ranking military officers to lobby the Pentagon for defense contracts. The management at Kraft Heinz can respond to lower-priced store brands by engaging in advertising that builds customer loyalty for products like its ketchup and Cheez Whiz. And Apple can reduce the likelihood that the supply of memory modules for its iPhones aren't disrupted by building business relationships with multiple suppliers.

ORGANIZATIONAL CULTURE: constraints and challenges

L03.3   Each of us has a unique personality—traits and characteristics that influence the way we act and interact with others. When we describe someone as warm, open, relaxed, shy, or aggressive, we're describing personality traits. An organization, too, has a personality, which we call its *culture*. And that culture influences the way employees act and interact with others.

A Gore-Tex representative holds footwear with Gore-Tex Surround product technology at the Outdoor Retailer's summer show in Salt Lake City. Gore-Tex employees are able to thrive in the self-sufficient, people-oriented culture encouraged by its founder, Bill Gore.
Source: Rick Bowmer/AP Images

organizational culture
The shared values, principles, traditions, and ways of doing things that influence the way organizational members act and that distinguish the organization from other organizations

What Is Organizational Culture?

W. L. Gore & Associates is known for Gore-Tex and high-quality fabrics among its many products. It also is famous for its strong organizational culture.[7] Since its founding in 1958, Gore has used employee teams in a flexible, nonhierarchical organizational arrangement to develop its innovative products. Associates (employees) at Gore are committed to four basic principles articulated by company founder, Bill Gore: (1) fairness to one another and everyone you come in contact with; (2) freedom to encourage, help, and allow other associates to grow in knowledge, skill, and scope of responsibility; (3) the ability to make your own commitments and keep them; and (4) consulting other associates before taking actions that could affect the company's reputation. These principles have contributed to creating the type of independent, people-oriented culture Bill Gore wanted. And it works well for the company. It has an annual voluntary turnover rate among full-time employees of just 3 percent. It has also earned a position on *Fortune*'s annual list of "100 Best Companies to Work For" every year since the list began in 1998.

Organizational culture has been described as the shared values, principles, traditions, and ways of doing things that influence the way organizational members act and that distinguish the organization from other organizations. In most organizations, these shared values and practices have evolved over time and determine, to a large extent, how "things are done around here."[8]

Our definition of culture implies three things. First, culture is a *perception*. It's not something that can be physically touched or seen, but employees perceive it on the basis of what they experience within the organization. Second, organizational culture is *descriptive*. It's concerned with how members perceive the culture and describe it, not with whether they like it. Finally, even though individuals may have different backgrounds or work at different organizational levels, they tend to describe the organization's culture in similar terms. That's the *shared* aspect of culture.

Research indicates six dimensions that appear to capture the essence of an organization's culture:[9]

1. **Adaptability**—The degree to which employees are encouraged to be innovative and flexible and to take risks and experiment.
2. **Attention to detail**—The degree to which employees are expected to exhibit precision, analysis, and focus on details.
3. **Outcome orientation**—The degree to which management emphasizes results rather than on the techniques and processes used to achieve them.
4. **People orientation**—The degree to which management decisions consider the effect of outcomes on people within and outside the organization.
5. **Team orientation**—The degree to which collaboration is encouraged and work activities are organized around teams rather than individuals.
6. **Integrity**—The degree to which people exhibit honesty and high ethical principles in their work.

Each of the six dimensions range from low to high, meaning it's not very typical of the culture (low) or is very typical of the culture (high). Describing an organization using these six dimensions gives a composite picture of the organization's culture. Exhibit 3-5 describes how the dimensions can create significantly different cultures.

Organization A

 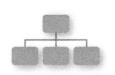

Exhibit 3-5
Contrasting Organizational Cultures

This organization is a manufacturing firm. Managers are expected to fully document all decisions, and "good managers" are those who can provide detailed data to support their recommendations. Creative decisions that incur significant change or risk are not encouraged. Because managers of failed projects are openly criticized and penalized, managers try not to implement ideas that deviate much from the status quo. One lower-level manager quoted an often-used phrase in the company: "If it ain't broke, don't fix it."

There are extensive rules and regulations in this firm that employees are required to follow. Managers supervise employees closely to ensure there are no deviations. Management is concerned with high productivity, regardless of the impact on employee morale or turnover.

Work activities are designed around individuals. There are distinct departments and lines of authority, and employees are expected to minimize formal contact with other employees outside their functional area or line of command. Performance evaluations and rewards emphasize individual effort, although seniority tends to be the primary factor in the determination of pay raises and promotions. Evaluations also focus on results, and management recognizes that ends can sometimes justify means.

Organization B

 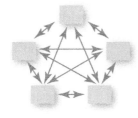 

This organization is also a manufacturing firm. Here, however, management encourages and rewards risk-taking and change. Decisions based on intuition are valued as much as those that are well rationalized. Management prides itself on its history of experimenting with new technologies and its success in regularly introducing innovative products. Managers or employees who have a good idea are encouraged to "run with it," and failures are treated as "learning experiences." The company prides itself on being market driven and rapidly responsive to the changing needs of its customers.

There are few rules and regulations for employees to follow, and supervision is loose because management believes its employees are hardworking, trustworthy, and will act with high moral standards. Management is concerned with high productivity but believes this comes through treating its people right. The company is proud of its reputation as a good place to work.

Job activities are designed around work teams, and team members are encouraged to interact with people across functions and authority levels. Employees talk positively about the competition between teams. Individuals and teams have goals, and bonuses are based on achievement of outcomes. Employees are given considerable autonomy in choosing the means by which the goals are attained.

Strong Cultures

All organizations have cultures, but not all cultures equally influence employees' behaviors and actions. **Strong cultures**—those in which the key values are intensely held and widely shared—have a greater influence on employees than weaker cultures. (Exhibit 3-6 contrasts strong and weak cultures.) The more employees accept the

strong cultures
Organizational cultures in which the key values are intensely held and widely shared

Exhibit 3-6
Strong Versus Weak Cultures

Strong Cultures	Weak Cultures
Values widely shared	Values limited to a few people—usually top management
Culture conveys consistent messages about what's important	Culture sends contradictory messages about what's important
Most employees can tell stories about company history or heroes	Employees have little knowledge of company history or heroes
Employees strongly identify with culture	Employees have little identification with culture
Strong connection between shared values and behaviors	Little connection between shared values and behaviors

Apple's strong culture of product innovation and customer-responsive service reflects the core values of its visionary cofounder, Steve Jobs. Jobs instilled these core values in all employees, from top executives to sales associates, such as the Genius Bar employee shown here training a customer at the Apple Store in Manhattan.
Source: B.O'Kane/Alamy Stock Photo

organization's key values and the greater their commitment to those values, the stronger the culture.

Most organizations have moderate to strong cultures; that is, there is relatively high agreement on what's important, what defines "good" employee behavior, what it takes to get ahead, and so forth. The stronger a culture becomes, the more it affects the way managers carry out their jobs.[10]

Research suggests that strong cultures are associated with high organizational performance.[11] When values are clear and widely accepted, employees know what they're supposed to do and what's expected of them, so they can act quickly to take care of problems. On the other hand, a strong culture can also prevent employees from trying new approaches, especially when conditions change rapidly.[12]

Where Culture Comes From and How It Continues

Exhibit 3-7 illustrates how an organization's culture is established and maintained. The original source of the culture usually reflects the vision of the founders. For instance, as we described earlier, W. L. Gore's culture reflects the values of founder Bill Gore. Company founders are not constrained by previous customs or approaches and can establish the early culture by articulating a vision of what they want the organization to be. Also, the small size of most new organizations makes it easier to instill that vision in all organizational members.

Once the culture is in place, however, certain organizational practices help maintain it. The selection process is one of these. The explicit goal of the selection process is to identify and hire individuals with the knowledge, skills, and abilities to perform successfully.

Exhibit 3-7
Establishing and Maintaining Culture

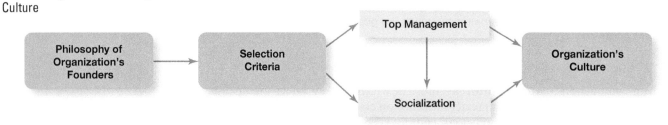

The final decision, however, includes a judgment call: How well will the individual fit into the organization? In essence, the organization seeks to identify individuals whose values are consistent with at least a good portion of the organization's.[13] The selection process also provides information to applicants. Those job candidates who perceive a conflict between their values and those of the organization can self-select themselves out of the applicant pool.[14] Selection thus becomes a two-way street, allowing both the organization and job candidates to avoid a mismatch and sustain the organization's culture by weeding out those who might undermine or attack its core values.

The actions of top managers also have a major impact on the organization's culture.[15] Through words and actions, senior executives establish norms that filter through the organization about, for instance, whether risk-taking is desirable; how much freedom managers give employees; appropriate dress; and what actions earn pay raises, promotions, and other rewards.

Finally, organizations help employees adapt to the culture through **socialization**, a process that helps new employees learn the organization's way of doing things.[16] Popular socialization processes include apprenticeships, internships, formal orientation programs, appointing mentors to guide and advise new entrants, training programs, rotating assignments, and assigning new entrants a high-performing performing employee to shadow and learn from.

socialization
a process that helps new employees learn the organization's way of doing things

Let's Get REAL

The Scenario:

Paulo, the manager of a web communications agency, is discovering that hiring employees can be frustrating. His last three hires are having trouble fitting in with the other twelve employees. For instance, one of the individuals—who's actually been there for six months now—doesn't want to jump in and help out the other team members when a deadline is fast approaching. And this same person doesn't say anything in team meetings and lets everyone else make decisions. And then there's the way they dress. "I don't expect them to 'suit up' or wear ties, but ripped cargo shorts and tattered flip-flops are a little too casual. Why don't these people 'get it'?"

◄ **Alfonso Marrese**
Retail Executive

Source: Alfonso Marrese

What advice about organizational culture would you give Paulo?

During the interview process, Human Resources needs to explain the company's brand values and how the company works as a team to meet goals. Depending on what level or position the candidate is being hired for, maybe a second interview with a senior manager would help to see if the candidate will fit in with the group. During the interview process, dress code, policies, and procedures should be explained to the candidate. During the first week or two on the job, the manager should be giving the new hire feedback on how he/she is doing. If there are any issues, they need to be addressed.

How Employees Learn Culture

Employees "learn" an organization's culture in a number of ways. The most common are stories, rituals, material artifacts and symbols, and language.

STORIES Organizational "stories" typically contain a narrative of significant events or people, including such things as the organization's founders, rule breaking, reactions to past mistakes, and so forth.[18] At 3M Company, the product innovation stories are legendary. There's the story about the 3M scientist who spilled chemicals on her tennis shoe and came up with Scotchgard. Then there's the story about Art Fry, a 3M researcher who wanted a better way to mark the pages of his church hymnal and invented the Post-It Note. At Nike, a number of senior executives spend much of their time serving as corporate storytellers. For instance, they often tell how cofounder (and Oregon track coach)

Learning from
FAILURE   A Corrupt Culture at Wells Fargo

Wells Fargo is one of the largest banks in the US. That, however, didn't stop thousands of its employees from engaging in practices that have embarrassed the company and cost it more than a billion dollars in fines. And, as you'll see, the source appears to be a sales-oriented culture that encouraged employees to mislead customers and cover up illegal behavior.

Going back to the 1990s, Wells Fargo's top management decided that the bank needed to increase profits. And the best way they thought to do this was to create a sales-oriented culture. Wells Fargo's locations were no longer branches; they were stores. Clients were now customers—who were to be squeezed as much as possible. Employees were pressured to cross-sell products—ATM cards, checking accounts, credit cards, loans. Top management set a goal to sell eight banking products per customer in an industry where the average was two or three.

This culture led to a number of illegal practices. For instance, employees opened up millions of fake accounts in customers' names. Thousands of customers who bought cars with loans from Wells Fargo were forced to buy unnecessary insurance policies from the bank with premiums that topped $1,000 a year. And customers were forced to pay for extending the length of mortgage interest rate lock-ins, even when the bank was responsible for delays in the application process.

The pressure on employees was unceasing. Branch managers were required to report sales data every hour in calls to their district managers, and individual employees were constantly ranked against each other, as were branches, districts, and regions. One branch manager described the pressure: "We were constantly told we would end up working for McDonald's if we didn't meet quotas."

When Wells Fargo's corrupt culture became exposed and huge fines were imposed, the bank's board took action. The CEO was fired, as was the head of the unit where the misconduct occurred. More importantly, Wells Fargo learned it needed to overhaul its compensation system to reward employees based on customer satisfaction and achievement of team goals rather than product sales goals. The branches aren't stores anymore; they're branches. And no one at the bank gets evaluated on products per customer.[17]

Bill Bowerman went to his workshop and poured rubber into his wife's waffle iron to create the sole of a lighter, faster running shoe. The message: Nike values innovation. To help employees learn the culture, organizational stories like these anchor the present in the past, provide explanations and legitimacy for current practices, exemplify what is important to the organization, and provide compelling pictures of an organization's goals.

RITUALS   Rituals are repetitive sequences of activities that express and reinforce the key values and goals of the organization.[19] Fraternities and sororities are famous for putting pledges through initiation rituals to develop camaraderie and discipline. Military boot camps are designed to do the same thing. In the corporate world, many firms develop rituals that are a rite of passage for new employees. For instance, Boston-based Gentle Giant Moving Company has new recruits run the steps at Harvard Stadium as a test of fitness and determination.

MATERIAL ARTIFACTS AND SYMBOLS   When you walk into different businesses, do you get a "feel" for what type of work environment it is—uptight, casual, fun, serious, and so forth? These reactions demonstrate the power of material symbols or artifacts in creating an organization's personality.[20] The layout of an organization's facilities, the size of offices, the elegance of furnishings, what pictures or personal objects are displayed on desks, how employees dress, the types of automobiles provided to top executives, the availability of corporate aircraft, and perks offered are examples of material symbols. For instance, a number of companies are known for the perks they provide employees. Google's bocce courts, FactSet's cupcake trucks, Autodesk's bring-your-dog-to-work days, and REI's free equipment rentals all say something about what it's like to work at these firms and the importance they place on employee satisfaction. These material symbols convey to employees who is important, what is important, and the kinds of behavior that are expected and appropriate.

IT'S YOUR CAREER

Reading an Organization's Culture: Find One That Is a Right Fit for You

Organizational cultures differ and so do individuals. Choosing an organization where you'll be comfortable and that values what you bring to the job is often the difference between you being a "fast tracker" and a disappointment—both to you and your employer. Being able to "read" an organization's culture should help you find one that's right for you. By matching your personal preferences to an organization's culture, you are more likely to find satisfaction in your work, are less likely to leave, and have a greater probability of receiving positive performance evaluations. Here's a list of things you can do to "read" culture:

1. *Do background work.* Check out the organization's website. What impression do you get from it? Are the organization's values listed? Mission statement? Then look for current news items, especially for evidence of high turnover or recent management shake-ups. Look for clues in stories told in annual reports and other organizational literature. Get the names of former employees if you can and talk with them. You might also talk with members of professional trade associations to which the organization's employees belong.

2. *Observe the physical surroundings and corporate symbols.* When you interview, pay attention to logos, signs, posters, pictures, photos, style of dress, length of hair, degree of openness between offices, and office furnishings and arrangements. Where do employees park? What does the physical condition of the buildings and offices look like? What does the office layout look like? What activities are encouraged or discouraged by the physical layout? What do these things say about what the organization values? Could you see yourself working there—and enjoying it?

3. *How would you characterize the people you meet?* Are they formal? Casual? Serious? Jovial? Open? Restrained in providing information? What stories are repeated? Are jokes/anecdotes used in conversation? How are employees addressed? What do job titles say about the organization? Does the organization's hierarchy appear to be strict or loose? What do these things say about what the organization values?

4. *Look at the organization's HR manual (if available).* Are there formal policies, rules, and regulations? How detailed are they? What do they cover? Could you see yourself working within these parameters?

5. *Ask questions of the people you meet.* For instance: What's the background of current senior managers? Were they promoted from within or hired from outside? What does the organization do to get new employees up and running? How is job success defined/determined? What rituals are important, and what events get commemorated? Why? Describe a decision that didn't work out well, and what the consequences were for that decision maker. Describe a crisis or critical event that occurred recently in the organization and how top management responded.

LANGUAGE Many organizations and subunits within organizations use language as a way to identify and unite members of a culture. By learning this language, members attest to their acceptance of the culture and their willingness to help preserve it.[21] Over time, organizations develop unique terms to describe equipment, locations, key personnel, suppliers, customers, processes, or products related to its business. While new employees are frequently overwhelmed with acronyms and jargon, after a short period of time these terms become a natural part of their language. And once learned, this language acts as a common denominator that bonds members. Walmart offers an example. "Action Alley" refers to the wider aisles that receive the most foot traffic. "The Cross" is the cross-section of tile and cement that separates all apparel departments. And the "Bowling Alley" is the section at the front of stores that is before the cash registers. Anyone working in a Walmart store for more than a week knows this terminology.

WORKPLACE CONFIDENTIAL Adjusting to a New Job or Work Team

Almost all of us have made transitions in our lives. Maybe your parents moved and you had to make new friends and adjust to a new school. Or you joined a new church, social club, or sports team. As a result, you'd think that most of us would be pretty confident and successful in making the transition into a new job. This is often not the case, especially for younger employees.

For our discussion, we'll focus on the outsider-to-insider transition and both external (between organizations) and internal (between horizontal departments or vertical promotions) adjustments.

The importance of this issue is underlined by research that tells us that the typical individual changes jobs 10.2 times over 20 years—so you need to be prepared to do a lot of adjusting to new work situations.

One of your goals in any new job situation should be to make the adjustment successful. What does that entail? You've made a successful transition if, after six months in your new position, you can say that you feel comfortable, confident, and accepted by your peers. And the evidence tells us that this is most likely to occur where you know what is required to function in your job, you have confidence that you have the knowledge and skills to perform it, and you know what the job demands are in terms of relationships with others. Moreover, successful adjustment should result in satisfaction with your job and a minimal degree of anxiety and stress.

Successful adjustment should begin by assessing the new situation. Assuming you have concluded that the job is a good fit for you, you need to determine the following: What's the history of the organization or work unit? Which individuals are held in high esteem, and what factors have led to their influence? And what does the culture value? Learning to read the organization's culture (see the earlier "It's Your Career" box) can provide you with answers to many of these questions.

Organizations have a variety of socialization options that they use to shape employees and help them adjust to the organization. Let's briefly review some options and consider their impact on you:

Formal vs. Informal. Specific orientation and training programs are examples of formal socialization. The informal variety puts new employees directly into the job.

Individual vs. Collective. When you're grouped with others and processed through an identical set of experiences, it's collective. Most small organizations socialize new members individually.

Fixed vs. Variable. A fixed schedule establishes standardized time targets for transition, such as a six-month probationary period or a rotational training program. Variable schedules have no advance notice of transitions; for instance, you'll be promoted when you're "ready."

Serial vs. Random. In serial socialization, you'll have a role model who will train and encourage you.

Apprenticeship and mentoring programs are examples. In random socialization, you're left on your own to figure things out.

Investiture vs. Divestiture. When the organization wants to affirm and support your qualities and qualifications, they basically leave you alone. But in divestiture, the organization will attempt to strip away certain characteristics. For instance, fraternities and sororities use divestiture rites when they put "pledges" through rituals to shape new members into the proper role.

As you move into your new job, be aware that the socialization programs, or lack of such programs, you'll be exposed to will have a significant influence on your adjustment. For instance, if you see yourself as a conformist and want a job that fits you, choose a job that relies on institutional socialization—one that is formal, collective, fixed, serial, and shapes you through divestiture rites. In contrast, if you see yourself as a "wave-maker" who likes to develop your own approaches to problems, choose a job that focuses on individualized socialization—one that is informal, individual, variable, and random and affirms your uniqueness through investiture.

The evidence indicates most people end up more satisfied with, and committed to, their job when they go through institutional socialization. This is largely because its structured learning helps reduce the uncertainty inherent in a new situation and smooths the transition into the new job.

An additional insight on new-job adjustment is the value of organizational insiders as a valuable resource for information. Colleagues, supervisors, and mentors are more useful as sources for accurate information about your job and the organization than formal orientation programs or organizational literature. People give you a better and more accurate reading of "the ropes to skip and the ropes to know."

Finally, don't forget the power of first impressions. A positive first impression on your boss and new colleagues can both speed up and smooth your transition. Think about the image you want to convey and make sure your clothes, posture, attitude, and speech fit that image.

So what are the specific implications of all this? How can you use this information to increase the probability that you'll have a successful adjustment in a new job? The answer is to focus on those things you can control. First, to summarize, choose a job where the socialization process matches up well with your personality. And, based on the evidence, choosing a job with institutionalized socialization will reduce uncertainty, lessen stress, and facilitate adjustment. Second, use insiders to provide background information and to reduce surprises. Lastly, start off on the right foot by making a good first impression. If colleagues like and respect you, they are more likely to share with you key insights into the organization's values and culture.[22]

How Culture Affects Managers

At Zappos' quarterly meetings, managers are asked, "What would you do to change the Zappos shoe box?" They are challenged to come up with ideas, with cash prizes to grease their creative juices. In contrast, for managers at many other companies, quarterly meetings mean a lot of listening to presentations. Zappos also doesn't have a dress code. Having visible tattoos or body piercings is perfectly acceptable.[23]

As we've learned, all employees of organizations—including managers—are influenced by the organization's culture. That influence—in shaping how decisions are made, what kind of behaviors to exhibit, the proper dress attire, and the like—doesn't have to be written down. In fact, it rarely is. But through their selection criteria, socialization processes, artifacts, rituals, and jargon, organizations convey to managers a number of things. One of those things is to the right way to make decisions: whether risk-taking is rewarded, whether to be an individual hero or a team player, or which choice of a preferred decision style.

Successful managers quickly learn what to do and not do in their organization. You won't, for instance, find the following values written down, but each comes from a real organization.

- Look busy, even if you're not.
- If you take risks and fail around here, you'll pay dearly for it.
- Before you make a decision, run it by your boss so that he or she is never surprised.
- We make our product only as good as the competition forces us to.
- What made us successful in the past will make us successful in the future.
- If you want to get to the top here, you have to be a team player.

The link between values such as these and managerial behavior is fairly straightforward. If an organization's culture supports the belief that profits can be increased by cost cutting and that the company's best interests are served by achieving slow but steady increases in quarterly earnings, managers are unlikely to pursue programs that are innovative, risky, long term, or expansionary. In an organization whose culture conveys a basic distrust of employees, managers are more likely to use an authoritarian leadership style than a democratic one.

As shown in Exhibit 3-8, a manager's decisions are influenced by the culture in which he or she operates. An organization's culture, especially a strong one, shapes and constrains the way managers plan, organize, lead, and control.

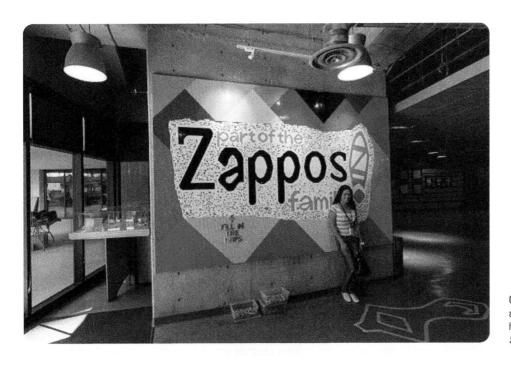

Casual dress and a relaxed atmosphere are evident at Zappos' new corporate headquarters in downtown Las Vegas.
Source: James Leynse/Corbis/Getty Images

Exhibit 3-8
Types of Managerial Decisions
Affected by Culture

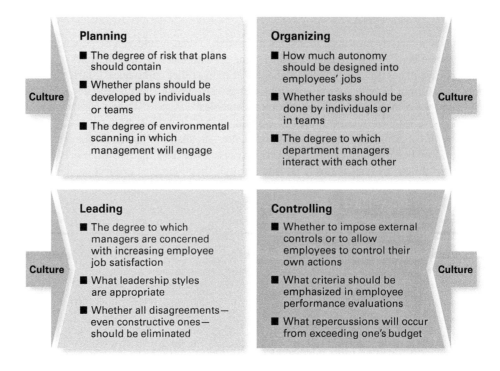

Planning
- The degree of risk that plans should contain
- Whether plans should be developed by individuals or teams
- The degree of environmental scanning in which management will engage

Culture

Organizing
- How much autonomy should be designed into employees' jobs
- Whether tasks should be done by individuals or in teams
- The degree to which department managers interact with each other

Culture

Leading
- The degree to which managers are concerned with increasing employee job satisfaction
- What leadership styles are appropriate
- Whether all disagreements— even constructive ones— should be eliminated

Culture

Controlling
- Whether to impose external controls or to allow employees to control their own actions
- What criteria should be emphasized in employee performance evaluations
- What repercussions will occur from exceeding one's budget

Culture

Chapter 3 | PREPARING FOR: Exams/Quizzes

CHAPTER SUMMARY by Learning Objectives

LO3.1 CONTRAST the actions of managers according to the omnipotent and symbolic views.

According to the omnipotent view, managers are directly responsible for an organization's success or failure. The symbolic view argues that much of an organization's success or failure is due to external forces outside managers' control. The two constraints on managers' discretion are the organization's culture (internal) and the environment (external). Managers aren't totally constrained by these two factors since they can and do influence their culture and environment.

LO3.2 DESCRIBE the constraints and challenges facing managers in today's external environment.

The external environment includes those factors and forces outside the organization that affect its performance. The main components of an organization's general environment include economic, demographic, political/legal, sociocultural, technological, and global. An organization's specific environment is directly relevant to achieving goals and can include suppliers, customers, competitors, government agencies, and special-interest groups. Managers face constraints and challenges from these components because of the impact they have on jobs and employment, environmental uncertainty, and stakeholder relationships.

LO3.3 DISCUSS the characteristics and importance of organizational culture.

The six dimensions of culture are adaptability, attention to detail, outcome orientation, people orientation, team orientation, and integrity. A culture is maintained by employee selection practices, norms created by senior executives, and socialization processes. Also, culture is transmitted to employees through stories, rituals, material symbols, and language. In organizations with strong cultures, employees are more loyal and performance tends to be higher. The stronger a culture becomes, the more it affects the way managers do their job.

REVIEW AND DISCUSSION QUESTIONS

3-1. Describe the two perspectives on how much impact managers have on an organization's success or failure.

3-2. "Businesses are built on relationships." What do you think this statement means? What are the implications for managing the external environment?

3-3. Refer to Exhibit 3-5. How would a first-line manager's job differ in these two organizations? How about a top-level manager's job?

3-4. Classrooms have cultures. Describe your classroom culture using the six dimensions of organizational

culture. Does the culture constrain your instructor? How? Does it constrain you as a student? How?

3-5. Can culture be a liability to an organization? Explain.

3-6. Discuss the impact of a strong culture on organizations and managers.

3-7. What are the four ways an organization communicates its culture to employees?

PREPARING FOR: My Career

ETHICS DILEMMA

In many ways, technology has made all of us more productive. However, ethical issues do arise in how and when technology is used. Take the sports arena. All kinds of technologically advanced sports equipment (swimsuits, golf clubs, ski suits, etc.) have been developed that can sometimes give competitors/players an edge over their opponents. We saw it in swim meets at the Summer Olympics and on the ski slopes and ice rinks at the Winter Olympics.

3-8. What do you think? Is this an ethical use of technology?

3-9. What if your school (or country) were competing for a championship and couldn't afford to outfit athletes in such equipment and it affected your ability to compete? Would that make a difference?

3-10. What ethical guidelines might you suggest for such situations?

SKILL EXERCISE Developing Your Environmental Scanning Skill

About the Skill
Anticipating and interpreting changes that take place in the environment is an important skill managers need. Information that comes from scanning the environment can be used in making decisions and taking actions. And managers at all levels of an organization need to know how to scan the environment for important information and trends.

Steps in Practicing the Skill
You can be more effective at scanning the environment if you use the following suggestions:

- *Decide which type of environmental information is important to your work.* Perhaps you need to know changes in customers' needs and desires, or perhaps you need to know what your competitors are doing. Once you

know the type of information you'd like to have, you can look at the best ways to get that information.

- *Regularly read and monitor pertinent information.* There is no scarcity of information to scan, but what you need to do is read pertinent information sources. How do you know which information sources are pertinent? They're pertinent if they provide you with the information you identified as important.

- *Incorporate the information you get from your environmental scanning into your decisions and actions.* Unless you use the information you're getting, you're wasting your time getting it. Also, the more you use information from your environmental scanning, the more likely it is that you'll want to continue to invest time and other resources into gathering it.

- *Regularly review your environmental scanning activities.* If you're spending too much time getting information you can't use, or if you're not using the pertinent information you've gathered, you need to make some adjustments.

- *Encourage your associates and colleagues to be alert to information that is important.* Your colleagues and employees can be your "eyes and ears" as well.

Emphasize to them the importance of gathering and sharing information that may affect your work unit's performance.

Practicing the Skill

Identify several different sources of business information and start practicing regularly collecting information from those sources. Subscribe to a news feed or follow a news organization on Twitter. Incorporate checking the external environment somewhere in your daily routine.

WORKING TOGETHER **Team Exercise**

Almost a third of employees who leave their companies within the first ninety days say they left because they didn't fit into the company's culture.[24] This suggests that learning about a company's culture before you accept a job could save you a considerable amount of grief. To increase the chances that you'll fit with the culture of the company you next work for, form groups of three or four and share the characteristics of an organizational culture each wants

(and don't want) in an employer. Compare your lists for common factors. Now choose one of the group member's lists and discuss: What could you do when visiting a company for an interview to find out whether it has the characteristics on the list? What questions could be asked during the interview? What clues could be looked for when walking around the company to understand what the culture is like? Be ready to share your analysis with the class.

MY TURN TO BE A MANAGER

- Find current examples in any popular business periodical of both the omnipotent and symbolic views of management. Write a paper describing what you found and how the examples you found represent these views of management.

- Consider a business that you frequent (for example, a restaurant or coffee shop) and review the six aspects of the external environment discussed in the text. Create a list of factors in the external environment that could affect the management of the business you selected.

- Choose an organization with which you're familiar or one you would like to know more about. Create a table identifying potential stakeholders of this organization. Then indicate what particular interests or concerns these stakeholders might have.

- If you belong to a student organization, evaluate its culture by answering the following: How would you describe the culture? How do new members learn the culture? How is the culture maintained? If you don't belong to a student organization, talk to another student who does and evaluate it using the same questions.

CASE APPLICATION 1   Environmental Uncertainty at HBO

HBO is one of those company names everyone knows. It's the oldest and second-largest pay TV station in the US. Since the early 1990s, it has been developing original programming. That's much longer than Netflix and Amazon. HBO shows like *Game of Thrones*, *The Sopranos*, and *Westworld* have won Emmy and Golden Globe awards. HBO includes seven 24-hour channels as well as the streaming service HBO Now. It has about 130 million subscribers worldwide.[25]

That all sounds like HBO is doing well, right? Looking more deeply, though, there is a lot happening in HBO's environment.

Over a million households got rid of their cable TV subscriptions during a three-month period in 2017. That's much faster change than experts expected. By 2030, the cable and satellite TV market is estimated to shrink by 26 percent. That would leave only 60 percent of American households as subscribers to pay TV.[26]

Meanwhile, smart phone usage keeps climbing worldwide each year. The number of smart phone users in 2018 was estimated at 2.53 billion. By 2020, that number is expected to climb to 2.87 billion.[27]

Also, HBO is now officially part of the AT&T-Time Warner family. The merger became official as of July 12, 2018.[28] Other companies in media and telecommunications industries, like Comcast and 20th Century Fox, are talking about combining forces. Meanwhile, Apple has set aside $1 billion to get in on the action of streaming original content. Competing in these industries is different than it used to be.

John Stankey, the AT&T executive in charge of HBO, has made it clear that there will be a lot of change in the company. "It's going to be a tough year. It's going to be a lot of work to alter and change direction a little bit,"[29] said Stankey. At a recent town hall meeting, Stankey talked about HBO increasing its subscriber numbers and the amount of content offered. This is a different approach from HBO's emphasis on quality over quantity.

Focusing on quality worked for almost two decades. HBO had the most Emmy nominations from 1999 to 2017. Then, in 2018, Netflix beat out HBO with a higher number of Emmy nominations. The sheer volume of Netflix's shows is credited as the reason for its launch to the top.[30] Plus, HBO only spends about one-quarter to one-third of what Netflix spends on developing new content. Some of HBO's productions in the past have taken years to develop and cost millions per episode.

Stankey wants HBO to try new approaches and add other types of content than what is currently offered on HBO Now, its streaming service. He offered these glimpses of the future saying that there would be fewer streaming companies. Figuring out how not to just survive but to thrive in this industry will be the challenge.

DISCUSSION QUESTIONS

3-11. Which of the cells in Exhibit 3-2 applies most clearly to the environmental uncertainty faced by HBO?

3-12. Using Exhibit 3-4, what components of HBO's external environment and specific environment are having an impact on the company? Why?

3-13. What, if anything, can HBO do to manage its environment and reduce it uncertainty exposure?

3-14. How might HBO's organizational culture change as a result of the changes described in this case?

CASE APPLICATION 2   Organizational Culture at Vice Media

Vice Media—a multimedia conglomerate—built its organizational culture around some features that were attractive to its young employees. It was a media company on the edge of digital content. It provided more opportunities to people in their 20s than other companies in the same industry. Vice's co-founder, Shane Smith, had the appealing pitch to employees to "come with me and change the world."[31] The company kept growing. It started as a free magazine but then became the tenth-highest-valued private company in the US. At its height, it had 3,000 employees, a cable network, many websites, two HBO shows, an ad agency, a film studio, a record label, and even a bar in London. And it was full of energetic, young employees.

There was another side to the culture at Vice. Sometimes the company was less than honest with clients as it grew. When a meeting with Intel was on the calendar, Smith convinced the architecture company next store to move out to make the office look larger. The day that Intel visited, Vice employees were asked to bring friends to work with laptops. Everyone was told to act more professional than usual. The company grew so fast that it led to a chaotic atmosphere that sometimes crossed the line. Acknowledging this at some level, they asked employees to sign a "Non-Traditional Workplace Agreement." The agreement said employees wouldn't find the workplace environment to be offensive or disturbing. Beyond allegations of harassment, there was tension from widespread consensual interoffice romances.

Departing employees have described Vice Media as a creative environment that provided professional growth, but also included low pay and overwork. A senior manager was once quoted saying that the company had a "22 Rule" hiring strategy: "Hire 22-year-olds, pay them $22,000, and work them 22 hours a day." All the while, Vice Media was valued at $2.5 billion. Smith told employees often that most of them had stock options and would be rich soon. But the stock options and high pay never seemed to pan out. When Smith bought a $23 million house in Los Angeles, employees decided to unionize.

Change in the culture at Vice Media was reportedly underway when the *New York Times* reported multiple confidential settlements with employees for gender pay inequities as well as misconduct. Company founders wrote a letter to employees apologizing for the company's culture and promising change. The company promised to pay men and women equally by the end of 2018.

Vice Media co-founder Suroosh Alvi described part of the company's problem, saying that "there was never any specific plan that took us anywhere. We have not followed any path other than growth. We didn't adhere to any business philosophy other than 'survive.'"

Nancy Dubuc, who used to be the top executive at A+E Networks, took the helm of Vice Media in April 2018. Dubuc calls being CEO at Vice Media "the opportunity of a lifetime."[32] Smith will remain at the company as executive chairman, focusing on creating content and partnerships.

DISCUSSION QUESTIONS

3-15. Which of the six organizational culture dimensions apply most clearly to Vice Media's culture?

3-16. How do you think the new Vice Media CEO needs to help employees learn about changes she decides to make in the organization's culture?

3-17. If you were the new CEO at Vice Media, what actions would you take to improve the culture?

3-18. Other high-tech firms have been accused of creating "college dorm" cultures. These type of cultures were unheard of in start-ups thirty years ago. What might have changed? How do you make cultures like this more professional?

ENDNOTES

1. Reuters, "Top Twitter Executives to Leave Company, CEO Dorsey Tweets," *New York Times* online, January 25, 2016, www.nytimes.com.

2. For insights into the symbolic view, see J. Pfeffer, "Management as Symbolic Action: The Creation and Maintenance of Organizational Paradigms," in *Research in Organizational Behavior* 3, ed. L. L. Cummings and B. M. Staw (Greenwich, CT: JAI Press, 1981), 1–52; J. R. Meindl and S. B. Ehrlich, "The Romance of Leadership and the Evaluation of Organizational Performance," *Academy of Management Journal* 30, no. 1 (March 1987): 91–109; J. A. Byrne, "The Limits of Power," *Businessweek*, October 23, 1987, 33–35; D. C. Hambrick and S. Finkelstein, "Managerial Discretion: A Bridge Between Polar Views of Organizational Outcomes," in *Research in Organizational Behavior* 9, ed. L. L. Cummings and B. M. Staw (Greenwich, CT: JAI Press, 1987), 369–406; and C. R. Schwenk, "Illusions of Management Control? Effects of Self-Serving Attributions on Resource Commitments and Confidence in Management," *Human Relations* (April 1990): 333–347.

3. W. R. Dill, "Environment as an Influence on Managerial Autonomy," *Administrative Science Quarterly* (March 1958): 409–43.

4. M. Merino, "You Can't Be a Wimp," *Harvard Business Review*, November 2013, 72–78.

5. See, for instance, A. Gafni, S. Walter, and S. Birch, "Uncertainty and the Decision Maker: Assessing and Managing the Risk of Undesirable Outcomes," *Health Economics* (November 2013): 1287–94; R. W. Spencer, "Managing Under Uncertainty," *Research-Technology Management* (September–October 2014): 53–54; and F. Samsami, S. Hosseini, A. Kordnaeji, and A. Azar, "Managing Environmental Uncertainty: From Conceptual Review to Strategic Management Point of View," *International Journal of Business and Management* 10, no. 7 (2015): 215–29.

6. "Workplace Culture Drives Company's Financial Performance," September 12, 2017, http://www.cxotoday.com/story/workplace-culture-drives-companys-financial-performance/.

7. D. Roberts, "At W. L. Gore, 57 Years of Authentic Culture," *Fortune*, posted March 5, 2015, http://fortune.com/2015/03/05/w-l-gore-culture/.

8. See, for example, B. Schneider, M. G. Ehrhart, and W. H. Macey, "Organizational Climate and Culture," *Annual Review of Psychology* 64, (2013): 361–88; and S. Giorgi, C. Lockwood, and M. A. Glynn, "The Many Faces of Culture: Making Sense of 30 Years of Research on Culture in Organization Studies," *Academy of Management Annals*, October 2017.

9. J. A. Chatman and K. A. Jehn, "Assessing the Relationship Between Industry Characteristics and Organizational Culture: How Different Can You Be?" *Academy of Management Journal* (June 1994): 522–53; and J. A. Chatman,

D. F. Caldwell, C. A. O'Reilly, and B. Doerr, "Parsing Organizational Culture: How the Norm for Adaptability Influences the Relationship Between Culture Consensus and Financial Performance in High Technology Firms," *Journal of Organizational Behavior* (August 2014): 785–808.

10. E. H. Schein, *Organizational Culture and Leadership* (San Francisco: Jossey-Bass, 1985), 314–15; and Y. Berson, S. Oreg, and T. Dvir, "CEO Values, Organizational Culture, and Firm Outcomes," *Journal of Organizational Behavior* (July 2008): 615–33.

11. See, for example, J. P. Kotter and J. L. Heskett, *Corporate Culture and Performance* (New York: Free Press, 1992), 15–27; G. G. Gordon and N. DiTomaso, "Predicting Corporate Performance from Organizational Culture," *Journal of Management Studies* (November 1992): 793–98; and J. B. Sorensen, "The Strength of Corporate Culture and the Reliability of Firm Performance," *Administrative Science Quarterly* 47, no. 1 (2002): 70–91.

12. Chatman, et al., "Parsing Organizational Culture" [see note 9]; and Sorensen, "The Strength of Corporate Culture and the Reliability of Firm Performance." [see note 11]

13. W. Arthur Jr., S. T. Bell, A. J. Villado, and D. Doverspike, "The Use of Person-Organization Fit in Employment Decision Making: An Assessment of Its Criterion-Related Validity," *Journal of Applied Psychology* (July 2006): 786–801; and W.-D. Li, Y.-L. Wang, P. Taylor, K. Shi, and D. He, "The Influence of Organizational Culture on Work-Related Personality Requirement Ratings: A Multilevel Analysis," *International Journal of Selection and Assessment* (December 2008): 366–84.

14. B. R. Dineen, S. R. Ash, and R. A. Noe, "A Web of Applicant Attraction: Person-Organization Fit in the Context of Web-Based Recruitment," *Journal of Applied Psychology* (August 2002): 723–34.

15. D. C. Hambrick, "Upper Echelons Theory: An Update," *Academy of Management Review* (July 2007): 334–43; and H. Wang, A. S. Tsui, and K. R. Xin, "CEO Leadership Behaviors, Organizational Performance, and Employees' Attitudes," *The Leadership Quarterly* (February 2011): 92–105.

16. T. N. Bauer, T. Bodner, B. Erdogan, D. M. Truxillo, and J. S. Tucker, "Newcomer Adjustment During Organizational Socialization: A Meta-Analytic Review of Antecedents, Outcomes, and Methods," *Journal of Applied Psychology* (May 2007): 707–21; and Y. Song, Y. Liu, J. Shi, and M. Wang, "Use of Proactive Socialization Tactics and Socialization Outcomes: A Latent Growth Modeling Approach to Understanding Newcomer Socialization Process," *Academy of Management Discover* (March 2017): 42–63.

17. Based on B. McLean, "How Wells Fargo's Cutthroat Corporate Culture Allegedly Drove Bankers to Fraud," *Vanity Fair*, May 31, 2017, https://www.vanityfair.com/news/2017/05/wells-fargo-corporate-culture-fraud; G. Colvin, "Inside Wells Fargo's Plan to Fix Its Culture Post-Scandal," *Fortune*, June 11, 2017, http://fortune.com/2017/06/11/wells-fargo-scandal-culture/; and M. Goldstein, "With Deal, Wells Fargo Will Pay Big Penalty," *New York Times*, April 21, 2018, B3, and "Wells Fargo Retail Bank Compensation Plan Eliminates Product Sales Goals," *New York Times*, May 6, 2018, 14.

18. S. Denning, "Telling Tales," *Harvard Business Review*, May 2004, 122–29; P. Guber, "The Four Truths of the Storyteller," *Harvard Business Review*, December 2007, 53–59; S. L. Dailey and L. Browning, "Retelling Stories in Organizations: Understanding the Functions of Narrative Repetition," *Academy of Management Review* (January 2014): 22–43; and S. R. Martin, "Stories About Values and Valuable Stories: A Field Experiment of the Power of Narratives to Shape Newcomers' Actions," *Academy of Management Journal* (October 2016): 1707–24.

19. G. Islam and M. J. Zyphur, "Rituals in Organizations: A Review and Expansion of Current Theory," *Group and Organization Management* (February 2009): 114–39; and M. J. Rossano, "The Essential Role of Ritual in the Transmission and Reinforcement of Social Norms," *Psychological Bulletin* (May 2012): 529–49.

20. M. G. Pratt and A. Rafaeli, "Artifacts and Organizations: Understanding Our 'Objective' Reality," in A. Rafaeli and M. G. Pratt (eds.), *Artifacts and Organizations: Beyond Mere Symbolism* (Mahwah, NJ: Lawrence Erlbaum, 2006), 279–88; and C. Jones, *How Matter Matters: Objects, Artifacts, and Materiality in Organization Studies* (Oxford, UK: Oxford University Press, 2013).

21. Z. Kalou and E. Sadler-Smith, "Using Ethnography of Communication in Organizational Research," *Organizational Research Methods* (October 2015): 629–55; and S. B. Srivastava and A. Goldberg, "Language as a Window Into Culture," *California Management Review* (Fall 2017): 56–69.

22. Based on B. Ashforth, "Socialization and Newcomer Adjustment: The Role of Organizational Context," *Human Relations* (July 1998): 897–926; T. N. Bauer et al., "Newcomer Adjustment During Organizational Socialization: A Meta-Analytic Review of Antecedents, Outcomes, and Methods," *Journal of Applied Psychology* (May 2007): 707–721; and S. Batistic and R. Kase, "The Organizational Socialization Field Fragmentation: A Bibliometric Review," *Scientometrics* (July 2015): 121–46.

23. H. Burns, "Zappos' Christa Foley Can Teach You a Thing or Two About How to Make a Company (Even a Really Big One) Fun," Bizwomen, updated December 26, 2014. _____ https://www.bizjournals.com/atlanta/bizwomen/news/profiles-strategies/2014/12/zappos-christa-foley-can-teach-you-a-thing-or-two.html?page=all.

24. S. Vozza, "This is Why New Hires Leave Within the First 90 Days," fastcompany.com, June 19, 2018

25. "HBO," Wikipedia entry, https://en.wikipedia.org/wiki/HBO; accessed December 2, 2018.

26. C. Mills, "Sorry, But Cable TV Won't Exist by 2030," BGR, December 4, 2017, https://bgr.com/2017/12/04/cable-tv-cord-cutting-streaming-services-omg-what/.

27. "Number of Smartphone Users Worldwide from 2014 to 2020"; Statista, https://www.statista.com/statistics/330695/number-of-smartphone-users-worldwide/.

28. C. Kang and E. Lee, "AT&T-Time Warner Deal Approval Gets Justice Department Challenge," *New York Times,* July 12, 2018, AT&T-Time Warner Deal Approval Gets Justice Department Challenge.

29. E. Lee and J. Koblin, "New Overseer of HBO Warns Growing Pains Are On the Way," *New York Times,* July 9, 2018, New York edition.

30. J. Press, "2018 Emmy Nominations: Netflix, Hulu, and Amazon Hit a TV Tipping Point," *Vanity Fair,* July 12, 2018, https://www.vanityfair.com/hollywood/2018/07/2018-emmy-nominations-netflix-nabs-most-nominations-in-tv-streaming-wars.

31. R. Wiedeman, "A Company Built on a Bluff," *New York Magazine*, June 11, 2018.

32. P. White, "Vice CEO Nancy Dubuc Calls Running Youth-Skewing Brand 'Opportunity of a Lifetime,'" *Deadline Hollywood*, June 15, 2018.

Chapter 4

Managing in a Global Environment

Learning Objectives

4.1 Define globalization, nationalism, and parochialism; and contrast ethnocentric, polycentric, and geocentric attitudes.

4.2 Describe the history of globalization.

4.3 Summarize the case for and against globalization.

4.4 Explain the different types of international organizations.

4.5 Describe the structures and techniques organizations use as they go international.

4.6 Explain the relevance of the political/legal, economic, and cultural environments to global business.

Employability Skills Matrix

This matrix identifies which features and end-of-chapter material will help you develop specific skills employers are looking for in job candidates.

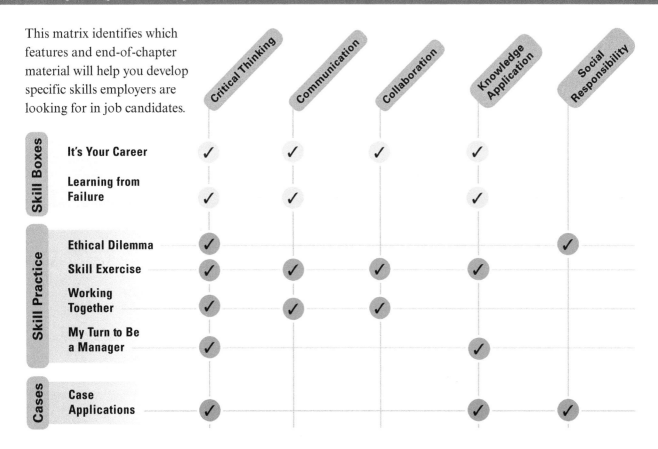

	Critical Thinking	Communication	Collaboration	Knowledge Application	Social Responsibility
Skill Boxes					
It's Your Career	✓	✓	✓	✓	
Learning from Failure	✓	✓		✓	
Skill Practice					
Ethical Dilemma	✓				✓
Skill Exercise	✓	✓	✓	✓	
Working Together	✓	✓	✓		
My Turn to Be a Manager	✓			✓	
Cases					
Case Applications	✓			✓	✓

None of us are free from the global marketplace. Look around. Millions of Americans are driving a "Japanese" car—although it was probably built in Ohio, Kentucky, or Texas. Chinese construction firms build hotels and apartments in Dubai. The movie you recently saw was filmed in New Zealand. Your smartphone was probably assembled in China and your shoes made in Italy. And the lettuce you bought at your supermarket was likely grown in Mexico. In spite of an increasing focus on the downside of globalization—and we'll discuss this at length in this chapter—business firms, universities, charities, and most not-for-profit organizations are increasingly operating across national boundaries.

One way to see how global the marketplace has become is to consider the country of origin for some familiar products. You might be surprised to find that many products you thought were made by US companies aren't! Take the following quiz and then check your answers at the end of the chapter on page 106.

1. Volvo Cars is owned by a company based in:

   a. Norway **b.** Sweden **c.** China **d.** Germany

2. Burger King restaurants are part of a company based in:

   a. Canada **b.** United Kingdom **c.** United States **d.** Germany

3. Trader Joe's is part of a company based in:

   a. United States **b.** Brazil **c.** Germany **d.** Switzerland

4. Dos Equis, Tecate, and Sol beer products are owned by a company based in:

   a. The Netherlands **b.** Mexico **c.** United States **d.** Colombia

5. The America's Got Talent show is a part of a franchise based in:

   a. United States **b.** United Kingdom **c.** Italy **d.** Spain

6. Chobani Greek yogurt is owned by a company based in:

   a. Japan **b.** France **c.** United States **d.** India

7. The manufacturer of the Swatch watch is based in:

   a. Germany **b.** United States **c.** Switzerland **d.** Brazil

8. 7-Eleven stores are part of a company based in:

   a. United States **b.** United Kingdom **c.** South Africa **d.** Japan

9. Spotify is owned by a company located in:

   a. Sweden **b.** United Kingdom **c.** United States **d.** Canada

10. Budweiser beer is owned by a company based in:

   a. United States **b.** Belgium **c.** Germany **d.** Sweden

How well did you do on the quiz? Were you aware of how many products or services we use every day that are made by companies not based in the United States? Probably not! Most of us don't fully appreciate the truly global nature of today's marketplace and how global companies operate throughout the world.

CLARIFYING TERMINOLOGY

LO4.1 To fully understand the history of globalization and where we are today, we need to agree on a common vocabulary. Let's look at some key terms related to the globalization movement.

There's no better place to start than the term **globalization** itself. What does it actually mean? Globalization refers to a process by which organizations develop influence or operations across international borders. Its distinct features are that it assumes open borders between countries and free trade. That means, for instance, that

globalization
Refers to a process by which organizations develop influence or operations across international borders

nationalism
Refers to patriotic ideals and policies that glorify a country's values

parochialism
Viewing the world solely through your own perspectives, leading to an inability to recognize differences between people

ethnocentric attitude
The parochial belief that the best work approaches and practices are those of the home country

polycentric attitude
The view that the managers in the host country know the best work approaches and practices for running their business

geocentric attitude
A world-oriented view that focuses on using the best approaches and people from around the globe

governments implement minimal trade tariffs on goods entering one country from another. When fully operating, globalization would allow for the free movement of people, goods, investments, and information technology to flow across borders.

A counterpoint to globalization is **nationalism**. It refers to patriotic ideals and policies that glorify a country's values. It advocates for independence from other countries and places a country's people and businesses first and primary. Globalization and nationalism represent two distinct and contrary views toward relationships with other countries. Extreme nationalism rejects dependence of one country on another. While globalization requires governments to work together in an interdependent network of relationships, nationalism builds walls. Nationalistic policies typically include a broad range of tariffs to protect a country's businesses and workers from foreign competition.

Countries pursuing nationalistic policies often have a population that suffers from **parochialism**—viewing the world solely through one's own eyes and perspectives. People with a parochial attitude do not recognize that others have different ways of living and working. They ignore others' values and customs and rigidly apply an attitude of "ours is better than theirs" to foreign cultures. Parochial views act as a severe restriction on implementing globalization.

Managers have been found to basically have one of three attitudes that shape their acceptance or resistance to globalization and their style of management. These are ethnocentric, polycentric and geocentric.

An **ethnocentric attitude** is the parochial belief that the best work approaches and practices are those of the *home* country (the country in which a company's headquarters are located). Managers with an ethnocentric attitude believe that people in foreign countries don't have the needed skills, expertise, knowledge, or experience to make business decisions as well as people in the home country do. They don't trust foreign employees with key decisions or technology.

A **polycentric attitude** is the view that employees in the *host* country (the foreign country in which the organization is doing business) know the best work approaches and practices for running their business. Managers with this attitude view every foreign operation as different and hard to understand. Thus, they're likely to let employees in those locations figure out how best to do things.

The final type of global attitude managers might have is a **geocentric attitude**, a *world-oriented* view that focuses on using the best approaches and people from around the globe. Managers with this type of attitude have a global view and look for the best approaches and people regardless of origin. A geocentric attitude requires eliminating parochial attitudes and developing an understanding of cross-cultural differences. This is the type of attitude typically sought out by international companies in their selection of global managers.

A BRIEF HISTORY OF GLOBALIZATION

L04.2   Globalization has gone in and out of favor for centuries. For instance, globalization was much in fashion during the nineteenth century. Industrialization fostered low-cost manufacturing, and economies of scale encouraged reaching out to global markets. Great Britain was a global economic superpower with colonies throughout the world. France, meanwhile, was imposing colonial rule over most of Africa. After World War I, however, there was a return to protectionist policies. And those held until the mid-1940s and the end of World War II.

So began a long period of growing globalization. The Bretton Woods conference in 1944 produced an agreement that established a set of rules for commercial and financial relations among the US, Canada, Western Europe, Australia, and Japan. It was the first example of a negotiated monetary order that would govern financial relations between independent countries. It opened the door to an ongoing set of agreements, institutions, and events that shaped global trade. Here are some highlights:

THE INTERNATIONAL MONETARY FUND (IMF) (ESTABLISHED IN 1945) The **IMF** is an organization made up of 189 countries. It provides temporary loans to its members, facilitates international trade, and seeks to promote economic growth and reduce poverty around the world. Member countries contribute funds to a pool from which countries experiencing balance of payment problems can borrow. It has been a recent source of stability when countries like Greece, Portugal, and Cyprus faced financial crises.

THE WORLD BANK (1945) The **World Bank** is an international financial institution that provides assistance to developing countries. It seeks to promote long-term economic development and poverty reduction by offering members technical and financial support.

GENERAL AGREEMENTS ON TARIFFS AND TRADE (GATT) (1948) **GATT** is an agreement between countries that seeks to substantially reduce or eliminate tariffs and other trade barriers. It was superseded in 1995 by the World Trade Organization.

ORGANISATION FOR ECONOMIC CO-OPERATION AND DEVELOPMENT (OECD) (1961) Composed of thirty-seven developed countries, the **OECD** was created to stimulate economic growth and world trade. Its main functions include seeking answers to common problems, identifying good practices, and coordinating domestic and international economic policies.

ASSOCIATION OF SOUTHEAST ASIAN NATIONS (ASEAN) (1967) **ASEAN** is composed of 10 Southeast Asian countries: Indonesia, Malaysia, the Philippines, Singapore, Thailand, Brunei, Cambodia, Laos, Myanmar, and Vietnam. Its principal goals include accelerating economic growth, regional stability, and providing a mechanism for member countries to resolve differences.

WORLD ECONOMIC FORUM (1974) The **World Economic Forum** is a Swiss non-profit foundation, best known for its annual meeting in Devos, Switzerland. Sometimes seen as arrogant and elitist, this meeting brings together several thousand of the world's leaders in business, government, economics, and journalism to find solutions to the economic, social, and political factors that shape and disrupt the world.

MARGARET THATCHER ELECTED PM IN GREAT BRITAIN (1979) Prime minister of the UK from 1979 to 1990, Thatcher was a major voice in promoting free trade. She introduced a series of economic policies to foster deregulation, flexible labor markets, privatization of state-owned companies, and reducing the power of trade unions.

RONALD REAGAN ELECTED US PRESIDENT (1980) What Thatcher sought to do in the UK, Reagan sought in the US. He introduced policies to reduce government regulations and stimulate the economy. He cut taxes and promoted global trade. He is widely credited with setting the foundation for the reunification of Germany and the collapse of the Soviet Union.

THE FALL OF THE SOVIET UNION (1991) In December 1991, the Soviet Union was officially dissolved. Self-governing independence was granted to former Soviet republics, and the Commonwealth of Independent States was created. This commonwealth is now composed of nine member states: Armenia, Azerbaijan, Belarus, Kazakhstan, Kyrgyzstan, Moldova, Russia, Tajikistan, and Uzbekistan. Members of the commonwealth coordinate trade, finance, lawmaking, and security.

International Monetary Fund (IMF)
An organization of 189 countries that provides temporary loans to its members, facilitates international trade, and seeks to promote economic growth and reduce poverty

World Bank (1945)
A financial institution that provides assistance to developing countries

General Agreements on Tariffs and Trade (GATT)
An agreement between countries that seeks to reduce or eliminate tariffs and other trade barriers

Organisation for Economic Co-operation and Development (OECD)
An international economic organization that helps its 37 member countries achieve sustainable economic growth and employment

Association of Southeast Asian Nations (ASEAN)
A trading alliance of 10 Southeast Asian nations

World Economic Forum
Annual meeting that brings together several thousand of the world's leaders to find solutions to economic, social, and political problems

British Prime Minister Margaret Thatcher after meeting with President Ronald Reagan at the White House in 1983, discussing economic matters, as well as relations with the Soviet Union and the Middle East.
Source: Mark Reinstein/Shutterstock

Exhibit 4-1
European Union Map

Source: Data based on: "EU Member Countries on the Road to EU Membership,"
www.europa.eu

European Union (EU)
A union of 28 European nations created as a unified economic and trade entity

The European Union has been involved in one-third of world exports, making it the largest regional trade agreement in the world.[1]

North American Free Trade Agreement (NAFTA)
An agreement among the Mexican, Canadian, and US governments in which barriers to trade have been eliminated

World Trade Organization (WTO)
A global organization of 164 countries that deals with the rules of trade among nations

Shanghai Cooperation Organization
An eight-nation cooperative made up of China, India, Pakistan, Kazakhstan, Kyrgyzstan, Russia, Tajikistan, and Uzbekistan

THE EUROPEAN UNION (EU) (1992)   The **EU** is an economic and political partnership of 28 democratic European countries (see Exhibit 4-1). By combining forces, these countries sought to better compete against the US and Japan. Before the EU, each country had border controls, taxes, and subsidies; nationalistic policies; and protected industries. These barriers to travel, employment, investment, and trade had prevented European companies from developing economic efficiencies.

NORTH AMERICAN FREE TRADE AGREEMENT (NAFTA) (1994)   **NAFTA** sought to eliminate barriers to free trade among the US, Canada, and Mexico, plus strengthen the economic power of the three countries.

WORLD TRADE ORGANIZATION (WTO) (1995)   The **WTO** is the only *global* organization that deals with trade rules among nations. It replaced the GATT. The WTO regulates trade in goods, services, and intellectual property for 164 member countries. It provides a framework of rules for negotiating trade agreements and for resolving trade disputes.

SHANGHAI COOPERATION ORGANIZATION (2003)   The **Shanghai Cooperation Organization** is an eight-nation cooperative made up of China, India, Pakistan, Kazakhstan, Kyrgyzstan, Russia, Tajikistan, and Uzbekistan. It was primarily created to provide security in the region by safeguarding the members' independence, sovereignty, territorial integrity, and social stability. Representing nearly half the world's population, its members have also pledged to cooperate on free trade.

"WE ARE THE 99%" PROTEST MOVEMENT (2011)   This movement attacked income and wealth inequality in the United States. Protesters claimed that the top 1 percent of wealthiest people in society controlled a disproportionate share of capital, political influence, and the means of production.

MADE IN CHINA 2025 (2015) The Chinese government launched a state-led industrial policy, called "Made in China 2025," in 2015 to make China dominant in global high-tech manufacturing. It was designed to use government subsidies, state-owned enterprises, and the acquisition of intellectual properties to catch up with, and then surpass, Western technological prowess in advanced industries. Among those industries targeted were electric cars, next-generation IT and telecommunications, and advanced robotics and AI. Additionally, the policy had the goal of increasing Chinese-domestic content of core materials to 70 percent by 2025.

BRITISH VOTE TO EXIT THE EU (2016) Citizens of the UK voted in June 2016 to remove themselves from the European Union. Referred to as "Brexit," it was a response to a feeling that the UK's needs and interests had been shifted to the greater EU. UK voters appeared to be particularly disenchanted with the EU's immigration, legal, and economic policies, as well as domination by Germany.

DONALD TRUMP ELECTED US PRESIDENT (2016) The surprise victory by Donald Trump in November 2016 has been attributed to distrust in established politicians, frustration with middle-class wage stagnation, and liberal US immigration policies. He has sought to reduce government regulation of business, cut taxes, renegotiate previous trade agreements, limit immigration, and foster "America First" policies.

Brexit was sparked by the discontent felt by citizens of the UK regarding the practices of the European Union.
Source: Alterov/Shutterstock

TRANS-PACIFIC PARTNERSHIP (2016) The **TPP** was a trade agreement between Australia, Brunei, Canada, Chile, Japan, Malaysia, Mexico, New Zealand, Peru, Singapore, Vietnam, and the US. It was designed to lower trade barriers and reduce the member countries' dependence on Chinese trade. It was never fully implemented after the US withdrew its support.

TPP
A trade agreement among 12 nations, including the US, Canada, Mexico, and Japan

NAFTA 2.0 OR USMCA (2018) This agreement modified the original NAFTA agreement. Called the United States-Mexico-Canada Agreement **(USMCA)**, among its provisions: it gives the US increased access to Canada's dairy markets, establishes new labor requirements for Mexico, increases environmental regulations, and updates intellectual property and data trade protections. Negotiating this agreement was part of the Trump administration's goal to enhance and protect US jobs.

USMCA
An update on the original NAFTA agreement between the US, Mexico, and Canada

As the above indicates, recent developments—Brexit, the election of Trump, the failure of the TPP—are signs of growing anti-globalization attitudes. Add in recent efforts to renegotiate NAFTA and a potential trade war between the US and China, and it appears that the pendulum has begun swinging away from unfettered belief in the value of globalization (see Exhibit 4-2).[2]

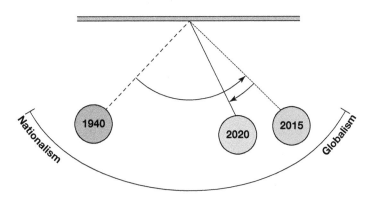

Exhibit 4-2
Nationalism vs. Globalism Pendulum

THE CASE FOR AND AGAINST GLOBALIZATION

LO4.3 As you've seen, the period from the mid-1940s to the early 2000s was generally one of pro-globalization. There was general consensus among economists that open borders and free trade would benefit all countries—the rich, the poor, the developed, and the developing.

The Win-Win Argument

law of comparative advantage
The economic proposition that a country should produce goods or service for which it has the lowest opportunity costs

The "every country wins" argument was largely based on the **law of comparative advantage**—that a country should produce goods or services for which it has the lowest opportunity costs. By specializing in the products or services for which it has the lowest cost of production, a country is best able to compete in global markets.

Economists were in near total agreement that globalization would unleash an economic "tide" that would raise all boats.[3] It would boost every nation's economy, increase wages, and result in lower-priced goods for all consumers. Importantly, it would be a major force for reducing poverty within developing nations.

Evidence of globalization's benefits abounded in the 1990s and early 2000s. Goods and capital were moving unfettered across borders. Improvements in communications and shipping technology made global outsourcing more feasible. And as developing countries prospered and moved millions of people into the middle class, new markets opened up for rich countries. Hundreds of millions of people worldwide were enjoying a significant increase in their standards of living. Meanwhile, consumers in developing countries benefited with lower prices.

By the early 2000s, any critics of globalization had essentially been silenced. Politicians and the media had joined the economists' pro-globalization bandwagon. Except for the occasional challenge—for instance, in 1999, anti-trade unionists and environmentalists protested and succeeded in shutting down the WTO meeting in Seattle—the globalization movement seemed unstoppable. Almost no one saw the coming backlash.

> **fyi**
>
> The countries that have gained the most financially from increased globalization over the last three decades are Switzerland, Japan, and Finland.[4]

The Downside of Globalization

Things started to change around 2015.[5] Critics began arguing that globalization was the major reason that the middle class in North America and Europe was suffering from wage stagnation. They also charged that global companies were shipping production (and jobs) from countries with high labor costs to developing countries where low wages prevailed. Further, globalization's free movement of labor was keeping wages down in countries like the US and the UK by allowing an inflow of immigrants. At the extreme, these factors have been used to argue that globalization and capitalism together have worked to enhance inequality in much of the Western countries.

In 2016, voters in Great Britain chose to exit the European Union—essentially saying that it didn't work in Britain's favor. A few months later, Donald Trump won the US presidency on his "America First" platform. Around the same time, the US rejected the Trans-Pacific Partnership; Italy began turning away African immigrants; and Trump sought to renegotiate NAFTA and impose tariffs on numerous imported products. In a little over twenty-four months, globalization had lost much of its charisma. It was now being called out as the primary cause of every nation's problems; and nationalism, protectionist policies, and increased border controls were being said to be the solution. For many, protectionism is being seen as the solution to problems as varied as unemployment, terrorism, stagnant economies, and trade imbalances.

The critics of globalization have considerable evidence to support their case. Contrary to the "win-win" thesis, certain countries, communities, and job groups *are* adversely affected by free markets and open borders. Inequality in developed countries has increased. The middle class has been squeezed as the bulk of globalization's benefits have gone to large global corporations and the power elite. As many US politicians proclaimed, little of the benefit has flowed to "hard-working Americans." And it's true that average wages in the US have been flat or fallen for at least a dozen years.

Linked to the inequality argument has been the immigration issue. Anti-immigration sentiment has grown in places as varied as the US, Spain, Italy, Hungary, the Czech Republic, and Australia. Critics of open borders claim that immigrants are taking jobs, holding down wages, are a threat to security, and resist fitting in.

Voters in developed countries appear to be frustrated and are taking their frustration out at the polls. Political candidates who advocate populist agendas, including nationalistic policies, have begun winning elections. A growing portion of people in developed countries have lost faith in institutions, particularly government.[6]

Many Americans feel that they're at a disadvantage due to open border policies. They feel that they're losing jobs and are facing security threats. This has led to demonstrations against immigration.
Source: Spencer Grant /Alamy Stock Photo

Even capitalism itself has come under assault for creating winners and losers. The "Occupy Wall Street" movement attacked the elite 1 percent with the chant, "We are the 99 percent!" Bernie Sanders, in the US, proposed a populist inequality agenda in his run for the White House in 2016. And recent surveys indicate that some 44 percent of millennials in the US have a positive view of socialism.[7] Stagnant job opportunities, low wages, job insecurity, and the like have soured many young people on capitalism and the global economy. They believe alleviating inequality is more important than economic growth as a societal goal and that more government and less market forces will reduce inequality and provide improved lives for all.

Globalization Today

The voices of nationalism and protectionism are the loudest they've been in eighty years. The pendulum has swung away from unbridled belief in globalism. But globalization is far from dead.[8] Contrary to the strong backlash against free trade and open markets in recent years, globalization is here to stay. Here's why:

First, it took decades to build the infrastructure and supply chains that support today's global companies. These are not easily dismantled. Global firms like Apple, IKEA, Royal Dutch Shell, and KPMG have offices, stores, manufacturing facilities, or key suppliers in dozens of different countries. And these global companies employ tens of millions of workers worldwide. There is little political will to undo what has taken decades to build.

Second, the evidence is overwhelming that free trade is *not* the cause of unemployment. The actual culprit is technology. Research has shown, for instance, that just 13 percent of manufacturing job losses in the US from 2000 to 2010 was due to trade; the rest is enhanced productivity attributable to automation.[9]

Finally, most people still believe that the benefits of globalization exceed its costs. Consumers like the lower prices. Investors like the fatter profits. And workers in developing nations like the higher wages, as do the high-skilled workers in developed countries.

What Does This Mean for Managers?

With globalization apparently here to stay, managers and manager-wannabes need to ensure they have the attitudes and skills that global management requires.

Managers need to continue to develop a geocentric attitude and build their cross-cultural sensibilities. They have to be comfortable working with people from other cultures. And they have to be flexible—open to accepting differences in languages, personalities, motivation, work habits, and management styles.

Ambitious managers need to gain international experience by working with global firms and seeking out foreign assignments. For those who want to move up in global companies, spending time in multiple foreign locales will be a must.

While it's not uncommon for Europeans to speak three or four languages, most Americans speak only English. This puts Americans at a distinct disadvantage in global organizations. Regardless of where you're from, those who only speak a single language can increase their likelihood for success by developing a second or third language.[10] The ability to speak Russian, Mandarin, Spanish, or German, for instance, is likely to open up doors for decades to come.

Finally, for managers of small businesses and those with entrepreneurial interests, it's important to gain an understanding of global markets and learn how to take their business international. In the following sections, we discuss the different forms that global organizations take and various options for turning a national organization into an international one.

DIFFERENT TYPES OF INTERNATIONAL ORGANIZATIONS

LO4.4 Companies doing business globally aren't new. DuPont started doing business in China in 1863. H. J. Heinz Company was manufacturing food products in the United Kingdom in 1905. Ford Motor Company set up its first overseas sales branch in France in 1908. By the 1920s, other companies, including Fiat, Unilever, and Royal Dutch Shell, had gone international. But it wasn't until the mid-1960s that international companies became quite common. Today, few companies don't do business internationally. However, there's not a generally accepted approach to describe the different types of international companies; different authors call them different things. We use the terms *multinational, multidomestic, global*, and *transnational*. A **multinational corporation (MNC)** is any type of international company that maintains operations in multiple countries.

One type of MNC is a **multidomestic corporation**, which decentralizes management and other decisions to the local country. This type of globalization reflects the polycentric attitude. A multidomestic corporation doesn't attempt to replicate its domestic successes by managing foreign operations from its home country. Instead, local employees typically are hired to manage the business, and marketing strategies are tailored to that country's unique characteristics. For example, Switzerland-based Nestlé is a multidomestic corporation. With operations in almost every country on the globe, its managers match the company's products to its consumers. In parts of Europe, Nestlé sells products that are not available in the United States or Latin America. Another example is Frito-Lay, a division of PepsiCo, which markets a Dorito chip in the British market that differs in both taste and texture from the US and Canadian version.

Another type of MNC is a **global company**, which centralizes its management and other decisions in the home country. This approach to globalization reflects the ethnocentric attitude. Global companies treat the world market as an integrated whole and focus on the need for global efficiency and cost savings. Although these companies may have considerable global holdings, management decisions with company-wide implications are made from headquarters in the home country. Some examples of global companies include Sony, Deutsche Bank AG, Marriott International, and Merrill Lynch.

Other companies use an arrangement that eliminates artificial geographical barriers. This type of MNC is often called a **transnational, or borderless, organization** and reflects a geocentric attitude. For example, Ford Motor Company is pursuing the second generation of what it calls the One Ford concept as it integrates its operations around the world and has achieved efficiencies by reducing the number of vehicle platforms from 27 to 9.[11]

multinational corporation (MNC)
A broad term that refers to any and all types of international companies that maintain operations in multiple countries

multidomestic corporation
An MNC that decentralizes management and other decisions to the local country

global company
An MNC that centralizes management and other decisions in the home country

transnational or borderless organization
An MNC in which artificial geographical barriers are eliminated

Deutsche Bank is one of many global companies with offices worldwide. However, the firm maintains management decisions from its headquarters in Frankfurt, Germany.
Source: JPstock/Shutterstock

HOW ORGANIZATIONS GO INTERNATIONAL

LO4.5 When organizations do go international, they often use different approaches. (See Exhibit 4-3.) Managers who want to get into a global market with minimal investment may start with **global sourcing** (also called global outsourcing), which is purchasing materials or labor from around the world wherever it is cheapest. The goal: take advantage of lower costs in order to be more competitive. For instance, many large American and Canadian hospitals now use radiologists in India to interpret CT scans. Although global sourcing may be the first step in going international for many organizations, they often continue to use this approach because of the competitive advantages it offers. Each successive stage of going international beyond global sourcing, however, requires more investment and thus entails more risk for the organization.

The next step in going international may involve **exporting** the organization's products to other countries—that is, making products domestically and selling them abroad. In addition, an organization might do **importing**, which involves acquiring products made abroad and selling them domestically. Both usually entail minimal investment and risk, which is why many small businesses often use these approaches to doing business globally.

Managers also might use **licensing** or **franchising**, which are similar approaches involving one organization giving another organization the right to use its brand name, technology, or product specifications in return for a lump-sum payment or a fee usually based on sales. The only difference is that licensing is primarily used by manufacturing organizations that make or sell another company's products and franchising is primarily used by service organizations that want to use another company's name and operating methods. For example, Chicago consumers can enjoy Guatemalan Pollo Campero fried chicken, South Koreans can indulge in Dunkin' Donuts coffee, and Hong Kong residents can dine on Shakey's Pizza—all because of *franchises* in these countries. On the other hand, Anheuser-Busch InBev has *licensed* the right to brew and market its Budweiser beer to brewers such as Kirin in Japan and Crown Beers in India.

When an organization has been doing business internationally for a while and has gained experience in international markets, managers may decide to make more of a direct foreign investment. One way to increase investment is through a **strategic alliance**, which is a partnership between an organization and a foreign-company partner or partners in which both share resources and knowledge in developing new products or building production facilities. For example, German camera company Leica teamed up with Italian luxury fashion brand Moncler to create a limited-edition fashion camera. A specific type of strategic alliance in which the partners form a separate, independent organization for some business purpose is called a **joint venture**. For example, British automaker Jaguar Land Rover and Chinese automaker

global sourcing
Purchasing materials or labor from around the world wherever it is cheapest

exporting
Making products domestically and selling them abroad

importing
Acquiring products made abroad and selling them domestically

licensing
An organization gives another organization the right to make or sell its products using its technology or product specifications

franchising
An organization gives another organization the right to use its name and operating methods

Japanese consumers can enjoy their favorite McDonald's menu items locally, as McDonald's brand is licensed in Japan, among many US companies featured abroad.
Source: Iain Masterton /Alamy Stock Photo

Global Investment	
Significant	Foreign Subsidiary
	Strategic Alliance – Joint Venture
	Franchising
	Licensing
	Exporting and Importing
Minimal	Global Sourcing

Exhibit 4-3
How Organizations Go Global

strategic alliance
A partnership between an organization and foreign company partner(s) in which both share resources and knowledge in developing new products or building production facilities

joint venture
A specific type of strategic alliance in which the partners agree to form a separate, independent organization for some business purpose

China's Lenovo CEO Yang Yuanqing (left) and Japan's NEC President Nobuhiro Endo formed a strategic alliance to create a new joint venture called NEC Lenovo Japan Group to sell personal computers in Japan. The joint venture gives the two electronics firms the opportunity to expand their business in Japan, the third-largest PC market in the world. *Source: Newscom*

foreign subsidiary
Directly investing in a foreign country by setting up a separate and independent production facility or office

Chery created a joint venture, which aims to combine the experience of Britain's luxury vehicle manufacturer with Chery's deep understanding of the Chinese markets and customer preferences.

Finally, managers may choose to directly invest in a foreign country by setting up a **foreign subsidiary** as a separate and independent facility or office. This subsidiary can be managed as a multidomestic organization (local control) or as a global organization (centralized control). This arrangement involves the greatest commitment of resources and poses the greatest amount of risk. For instance, United Plastics Group of Houston, Texas, built two injection-molding facilities in Suzhou, China, to fulfill its mission of being a global supplier to its global accounts.

MANAGING in a global environment

LO4.6 Assume for a moment that you're a manager going to work for a branch of a global organization in a foreign country. You know that your environment will differ from the one at home, but how? What should you look for?

Any manager who finds himself or herself in a new country faces challenges. In this section, we'll look at some of these challenges. Although our discussion is presented through the eyes of a US manager, this framework could be used by any manager, regardless of national origin, who manages in a foreign environment.

The Political/Legal Environment

As implied in our discussion on the changing views of globalization, the political and legal landscapes in the international environment are key sources of uncertainty. Managers need to know the laws in the various countries in which their organization operates and stay on top of legal changes. For instance, managers working for global businesses contend with a growing and changing tide of employment legislation that cuts across national boundaries. In Vietnam and Indonesia, it's almost impossible to fire someone. And in the EU, layoffs must be negotiated with worker representatives and approved by the appropriate government authority. Meanwhile, in early 2018, French President Emmanuel Macron successfully pushed through major changes in France's rigid labor laws that gave employers *more* flexibility to hire and fire employees.

Laws in some countries can be challenging to executives from North America who seek to transfer people internationally. Saudi Arabia, for instance, won't grant a visa to single women or homosexuals. And doing business in different countries comes with different rules. In India, a foreign firm can only set up a subsidiary if one of the directors is an India resident. China provides preferential treatment to protect and promote domestic firms and state-owned companies. And while bribing government officials to get around regulations or to secure contracts is illegal in most of North America and Western Europe, it's a common practice in Cambodia, Yemen, and Ukraine.

Clearly there are political risks in doing business globally. And a recent report indicates that these political risks are on the rise.[12] Doing business in a number of Latin American and African countries, for instance, comes with increased political uncertainty. The governments in these nations are subject to coups, dictatorial rule, and corruption. And while Brexit creates issues for those global companies with European headquarters in London, global firms with major operations in places like Rome and Madrid have to monitor the increasing possibility that Italy and Spain may follow the UK out of the European Union.

The Economic Environment

A global manager must be aware of economic issues when doing business in other countries. First, it's important to understand a country's type of economic system. The two major types are a free market economy and a planned economy. A **free market economy** is one in which resources are primarily owned and controlled by the private sector. A **planned economy** is one in which economic decisions are planned by a central government. The US economy is free market, based on capitalism. This economic system relies on market forces in which supply and demand for products, services, and labor determine monetary value. In contrast, China's political and economic systems are tightly intertwined. It's essentially a socialist republic ruled by the Communist Party and draws on the principle of community ownership. That is, all property, businesses, and natural resources are community owned, but these items are controlled by the single political party (Communist Party). In China, the government provides basic necessities based on need. In recent decades, China's economy has become more diverse. While maintaining communist control, economic growth has been fueled by market forces and capitalism. As a result, a growing segment of the population has gained considerable wealth and is adopting lifestyles similar to those in the United States.

Why do global managers need to know about a country's economic system? Because it, too, has the potential to constrain decisions. Other economic issues managers need to understand include currency exchange rates, inflation rates, and tax policies.

A multinational's profits can vary dramatically, depending on the strength of its home currency and the currencies of the countries in which it operates. For instance, a rise in the value of the yen against the dollar reduces the profits of a company like KFC when it converts yen into dollars.

Inflation means that prices for products and services are increasing but it also affects interest rates, exchange rates, the cost of living, and the general confidence in a country's political and economic system. Country inflation rates can, and do, vary widely. In 2018, for instance, the inflation rate in Argentina was 23 percent, while less than 1 percent in Israel.[13] Managers need to monitor inflation trends so they can anticipate possible changes in a country's monetary policies and make good business decisions regarding purchasing and pricing.

free market economy
An economic system in which resources are primarily owned and controlled by the private sector

planned economy
An economic system in which economic decisions are planned by a central government

Let's Get REAL

The Scenario:

Renata Zorzato, head of new product development for a global recruiting company, is preparing to move from São Paulo to San Diego to head up a team of executive recruiters. Her newly formed team will include company employees from Berlin, London, Shanghai, Mexico City, Kuala Lumpur, New York, and San Diego. The team will be designing and launching an innovative new global executive recruiting tool. But first, Renata has to get the team members all working together, each bringing his or her unique strengths and perspectives to the project.

◄ **Katie Pagan**
Accounting and HR Manager

Source: Katie Pagan

What's the best way for Renata to get this culturally diverse team up and running?
I would organize an off-site luncheon; food is a universal language. While at the luncheon, I would have each team member go around the room and introduce themselves, and being that the group is from all over the world, I would have each person speak a little about where they are from. After the lunch I would have an interactive game of some sort that requires the team to slowly begin working together—the idea would be for them to have more fun as opposed to work and get to know each other.

An ability to operate in different cultural settings has been identified as one of the most important skills needed by the workforce in 2020.[15]

national culture
The values and attitudes shared by individuals from a specific country that shape their behavior and beliefs about what is important

Top executives of French car manufacturer PSA Peugeot Citroen participate in a Hindu puja ritual during a ceremony celebrating the firm's plan to re-enter the Indian market with the construction of a new plant. The spiritual ritual is an integral part of India's national culture, which research shows has a greater effect on employees than an organization's culture.
Source: Sam Panthaky/AFP/Getty Images

Finally, tax policies in countries where multinationals operate can be a major economic concern. For instance, the 2017 change in US tax law that significantly reduced the tax rate on profits held overseas by American firms encouraged many multinationals to bring back those funds to the US.

The Cultural Environment

Imagine the challenges facing a German executive with Siemens who is transferred to a company facility in Japan. She's likely to be in for a bit of a shock.[14] For instance, her communication style is probably very different from her Japanese counterparts. She's used to being direct and saying what she thinks. In contrast, the Japanese tend to be subtle. They're likely to find the German executive style as rude or abrasive. Similarly, Japanese executives are unlikely to appreciate the German executive leaving every workday at 5 p.m. But that's what she did in Germany, where everyone goes home around that time to have dinner with their families. Japanese executives typically stay until 8 or 9 p.m. and then frequently go out with coworkers afterward to socialize.

As we described in the previous chapter, *organizations* have different cultures. But so, too, do *countries*. **National culture** includes the values and attitudes shared by individuals from a specific country that shape their behavior and their beliefs about what is important.[16] National culture is steeped in a country's history, and it's based on a society's social traditions, political and economic philosophy, and legal system.

Which is more important to a manager—national culture or organizational culture? For example, is an IBM facility in Germany more likely to reflect German culture or IBM's corporate culture? Research indicates that national culture has a greater effect on employees than their organization's culture.[17] German employees at an IBM facility in Munich will be influenced more by German culture than by IBM's culture.

Legal, political, and economic differences among countries are fairly obvious. The Japanese manager who works in the United States or his or her American counterpart who works in Japan can get information about laws or tax policies without too much effort. Getting information about cultural differences isn't quite that easy! The primary reason? It's difficult for natives to explain their country's unique cultural characteristics to someone else. For instance, if you were born and raised in the United States, how would you describe US culture? In other words, what are Americans like? Think about it for a moment and see which characteristics in Exhibit 4-4 you identified.

IT'S YOUR CAREER

Developing Your Global Perspective—Working with People from Other Cultures

A key to success in management and in your career is becoming comfortable with cultural differences. Becoming culturally competent is a process. It takes time, and you'll make mistakes. But it's a skill you'll want to develop.

- Nearly 70 percent of executives and management professionals say that developing global competencies is very important or extremely important to the future success of their companies.[18]
- The five most important attitudes, knowledge, skills, and abilities for effective global leadership include:

  Multicultural sensitivity/awareness
  Communicates effectively
  Strategic thinking
  Leadership; influences others
  Respect for differences[19]

You can be certain that during your career you will work with individuals who were born in a different country than you were. Their first language is likely to be different from yours. And they will probably exhibit habits and customs that differ significantly from those familiar to you. You may find it hard to understand some of those people's behaviors, and you may find your differences make it difficult to communicate and work together. But this is today's reality. It's important for you to develop your global perspective—especially your cultural intelligence.

So what can you do to increase your ability to work with people from different cultures?[20]

1. *Become aware of your own level of openness to and confidence in cross-cultural experiences.* Some people just aren't as open to and comfortable with new and different experiences as others are. For instance, do you try new foods with unfamiliar or exotic ingredients? Are you comfortable with class project teams that have individuals from other countries? Do you dread having to communicate with individuals who don't speak your native language? If you're one of those who isn't comfortable with new and different experiences, try to overcome your fear and reluctance by starting small. Practice listening closely to those who struggle with your language. Maybe try a new and unusual menu item or get to know individuals in your classes who are from other cultures. Your goal should be expanding your comfort zone.

2. *Assume differences until similarity is proven.* Most of us have a tendency to assume people are like us until proven otherwise. Try to think the reverse. Assume that individuals from different cultures will interpret communication or behaviors differently. Carefully observe how individuals from other cultures relate to each other and how those interactions differ from how people within your culture relate.

3. *Emphasize description rather than interpretation or evaluation.* Delay making judgments until you have observed and interpreted the situation from the perspectives of all cultures involved. Description emphasizes observation and being nonjudgmental. Some customs may be different from what you're used to, but different doesn't make them wrong or inferior.

4. *Show empathy.* Try to put yourself in "others' shoes." When assessing the words, motives, and actions of a person from another culture, try to interpret them from the perspective of that culture rather than your own. If the relationship is important and potentially long-lasting, read up on the individual's culture to learn his or her customs and practices.

5. *Treat your initial interpretations as working hypotheses.* Treat your first interpretations as working hypotheses rather than facts, and pay careful attention to feedback in order to avoid serious miscommunication. If you're in doubt, don't be afraid to reach out and ask others if your evaluation of a specific behavior is accurate.

6. *Educate yourself on cross-cultural issues and approaches.* Here are three ways to improve your cultural intelligence: First, get international experience through traveling. Invest in short-term study trips abroad. Consider a semester abroad where you can immerse yourself in a different culture. Second, take the initiative to get to know international students at your school and learn about their countries. Consider attending one or more cultural or multicultural events, which are typically hosted by a single cultural or multicultural student organization. Third, take advantage of online tools to learn more about cross-cultural differences. A good place to begin is reading global news stories.

HOFSTEDE'S FRAMEWORK FOR ASSESSING CULTURES   Geert Hofstede developed one of the most widely referenced approaches to helping managers better understand differences between national cultures. His research found that countries vary on five dimensions of national culture.[21] These dimensions are described in Exhibit 4-5, which also shows some of the countries characterized by those dimensions.

Exhibit 4-4
What Are Americans Like?

- Americans are *very informal.* They tend to treat people alike even when great differences in age or social standing are evident.
- Americans are *direct.* They don't talk around things. To some foreigners, this may appear as abrupt or even rude behavior.
- Americans are *competitive.* Some foreigners may find Americans assertive or overbearing.
- Americans are *achievers.* They like to keep score, whether at work or at play. They emphasize accomplishments.
- Americans are *independent and individualistic.* They place a high value on freedom and believe that individuals can shape and control their own destiny.
- Americans like *personal space.* They keep a distance when speaking and are uncomfortable when people are too close.
- Americans *dislike silence.* They would rather talk about the weather than deal with silence in a conversation.
- Americans *value punctuality.* They keep appointment calendars and live according to schedules and clocks.
- Americans *value cleanliness.* They often seem obsessed with bathing, eliminating body odors, and wearing clean clothes.

Sources: Based on M. Ernest, ed., *Predeparture Orientation Handbook: For Foreign Students and Scholars Planning to Study in the United States* (Washington, DC: US Information Agency, Bureau of Cultural Affairs, 1984), pp. 103–105; and "Basic Characteristics of Americans and American Culture," March 20, 2014, https://www.globalimmersions.com/go-global-blog/basics-of-americans-and-american-culture.

Exhibit 4-5
Hofstede's Five Dimensions of National Culture

Source: Based on Geert Hofstede, *Culture's Consequences: International Differences in Work-Related Values,* © Geert Hofstede, 1980 (Newbury Park: SAGE Publications, Inc., 1980).

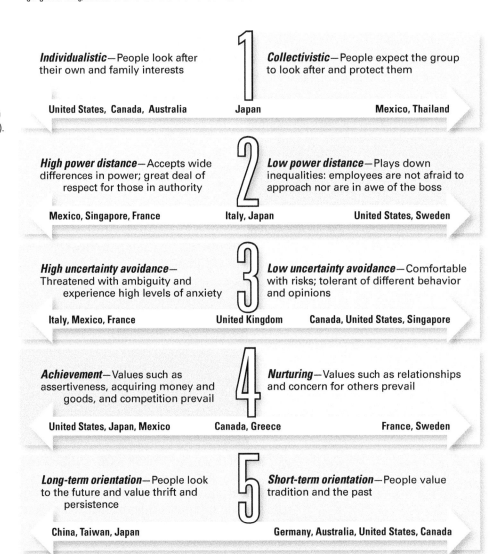

1 *Individualistic*—People look after their own and family interests

United States, Canada, Australia   Japan   Mexico, Thailand

Collectivistic—People expect the group to look after and protect them

2 *High power distance*—Accepts wide differences in power; great deal of respect for those in authority

Mexico, Singapore, France   Italy, Japan   United States, Sweden

Low power distance—Plays down inequalities: employees are not afraid to approach nor are in awe of the boss

3 *High uncertainty avoidance*—Threatened with ambiguity and experience high levels of anxiety

Italy, Mexico, France   United Kingdom   Canada, United States, Singapore

Low uncertainty avoidance—Comfortable with risks; tolerant of different behavior and opinions

4 *Achievement*—Values such as assertiveness, acquiring money and goods, and competition prevail

United States, Japan, Mexico   Canada, Greece   France, Sweden

Nurturing—Values such as relationships and concern for others prevail

5 *Long-term orientation*—People look to the future and value thrift and persistence

China, Taiwan, Japan   Germany, Australia, United States, Canada

Short-term orientation—People value tradition and the past

THE GLOBE FRAMEWORK FOR ASSESSING CULTURES The **Global Leadership and Organizational Behavior Effectiveness (GLOBE) program** is an ongoing research program that extended Hofstede's work by investigating cross-cultural leadership behaviors and giving managers additional information to help them identify and manage cultural differences. Using data from more than 18,000 managers in sixty-two countries, the GLOBE research team identified nine dimensions on which national cultures differ.[22] Two dimensions (power distance and uncertainty avoidance) fit directly with Hofstede's. Four are similar to Hofstede's (assertiveness, which is similar to achievement-nurturing; humane orientation, which is similar to the nurturing dimension; future orientation, which is similar to long-term and short-term orientation; and institutional collectivism, which is similar to individualism-collectivism). The remaining three (gender differentiation, in-group collectivism, and performance orientation) offer additional insights into a country's culture. Here are descriptions of these nine dimensions. For each of these dimensions, we have indicated which countries rated high, which rated moderate, and which rated low.

- **Power distance:** the extent to which a society accepts that power in institutions and organizations is distributed unequally. (*High:* Russia, Spain, and Thailand. *Moderate:* England, France, and Brazil. *Low:* Denmark, the Netherlands, and South Africa.)
- **Uncertainty avoidance:** a society's reliance on social norms and procedures to alleviate the unpredictability of future events. (*High:* Austria, Denmark, and Germany. *Moderate:* Israel, United States, and Mexico. *Low:* Russia, Hungary, and Bolivia.)
- **Assertiveness:** the extent to which a society encourages people to be tough, confrontational, assertive, and competitive rather than modest and tender. (*High:* Spain, United States, and Greece. *Moderate:* Egypt, Ireland, and Philippines. *Low:* Sweden, New Zealand, and Switzerland.)
- **Humane orientation:** the degree to which a society encourages and rewards individuals for being fair, altruistic, generous, caring, and kind to others. (*High:* Indonesia, Egypt, and Malaysia. *Moderate:* Hong Kong, Sweden, and Taiwan. *Low:* Germany, Spain, and France.)
- **Future orientation:** the extent to which a society encourages and rewards future-oriented behaviors such as planning, investing in the future, and delaying gratification. (*High:* Denmark, Canada, and the Netherlands. *Moderate:* Slovenia, Egypt, and Ireland. *Low:* Russia, Argentina, and Poland.)
- **Institutional collectivism:** the degree to which individuals are encouraged by societal institutions to be integrated into groups within organizations and society. (*High:* Greece, Hungary, and Germany. *Moderate:* Hong Kong, United States, and Egypt. *Low:* Denmark, Singapore, and Japan.)
- **Gender differentiation:** the extent to which a society maximizes gender role differences as measured by how much status and decision-making responsibilities women have. (*High:* South Korea, Egypt, and Morocco. *Moderate:* Italy, Brazil, and Argentina. *Low:* Sweden, Denmark, and Slovenia.)
- **In-group collectivism:** the extent to which members of a society take pride in membership in small groups, such as their family and circle of close friends, and the organizations in which they're employed. (*High:* Egypt, China, and Morocco. *Moderate:* Japan, Israel, and Qatar. *Low:* Denmark, Sweden, and New Zealand.)
- **Performance orientation:** the degree to which a society encourages and rewards group members for performance improvement and excellence. (*High:* United States, Taiwan, and New Zealand. *Moderate:* Sweden, Israel, and Spain. *Low:* Russia, Argentina, and Greece.)

The GLOBE studies confirm that Hofstede's dimensions are still valid and extend his research rather than replace it. GLOBE's added dimensions provide an expanded and updated measure of countries' cultural differences. It's likely that cross-cultural studies of human behavior and organizational practices will increasingly use the GLOBE dimensions to assess differences among countries.[23]

APPLYING CULTURAL GUIDELINES   What does all this mean for practicing managers? At a simplistic level, it says, "When in Rome, do as the Romans do." On an analytical level, Hofstede and the GLOBE studies provide managers with guidance in determining what "the Romans do." If or when managers are given a foreign assignment or merely have to work with someone from a different culture, these frameworks can alert them to areas where potential problems might surface.

Learning from
FAILURE   Disney Learns That France Isn't Florida

The Walt Disney Company had a proven record of creating and operating highly successful theme parks in southern California and Orlando, Florida. So how difficult would it be to transfer that success to Paris? What worked in Florida should work in France, right? Unfortunately, Disney found out that success doesn't necessarily transfer when they opened Euro Disney Resort (now called Disneyland Paris) in 1992.

The French aren't like Americans in a number of ways. For instance, Americans typically travel to theme parks in their cars. The French tend to use buses. The result was large, empty parking lots while facilities for bus drivers to park their buses and rest were inadequate.

Disney parks in the US don't serve alcohol. But the French consider wine a part of their daily life and a glass of wine for lunch a necessity. Visitors were astonished that no wine was available at the park and complained en masse.

Not only was the lack of wine a problem at lunch, so was the time when the French want their midday meal. There is no fixed time for Americans to each lunch. And Americans are comfortable grabbing something on the go and eating while they wander around the park. In contrast,

the majority of European visitors would converge on restaurants at 12:30 p.m., expect to be seated, and treat the meal as a leisurely event. Disneyland Paris's managers failed to properly staff their restaurants for the one- or two-hour "rush hours."

Disney executives also failed to understand that, while American park visitors' average stay was four days, the French typically arrived early in the morning, spent the day at the park, checked into their hotel late at night, then checked out early the next morning. The difference was largely due to the multiple theme parks—SeaWorld, Knott's Berry Farm, Universal Studios—near the Florida and California parks. There were no such options in Paris. The result was long lines in the hotel lobbies with people all checking-in and checking-out at the same time.

In response to these mistakes, Disney executives initiated a number of changes in Paris. Bus areas were expanded, corporate policy was modified to make wine and beer available, restaurant staffing was adjusted, and additional computer stations were installed at park hotels to reduce waiting lines.

What did Disney learn from their failures at Euro Disneyland? Culture matters![24]

Chapter 4   PREPARING FOR: Exams/Quizzes

CHAPTER SUMMARY by Learning Objectives

 DEFINE globalization, nationalism, and parochialism; and contrast ethnocentric, polycentric, and geocentric attitudes.

Globalization refers to a process by which organizations develop influence or operations across international borders. Its counterpoint has been nationalism—which refers to patriotic ideals and policies that glorify a country's values. Parochialism is viewing the world solely through your own eyes and perspectives and not recognizing that others have different ways of living and working. An ethnocentric attitude is the parochial belief that the best work approaches and practices are those of the home country. A polycentric attitude is the view that the managers in the host country know the best work approaches and practices for running their business. And a geocentric attitude is a world-oriented view that focuses on using the best approaches and people from around the globe.

LO4.2 **DESCRIBE** the history of globalization.

Beginning after World War II, and through to around 2015, globalization was the dominant political and economic perspective. It had become generally accepted that globalization provides benefits for all countries. However, in recent years, globalization has come under attack from nationalism. Nationalism's focus is on enhancing a country's specific self-interest. In contrast to globalization's emphasis on inter-country cooperation, nationalism puts its people and business first and primary. Attacks on globalization have emphasized the loss of jobs to countries with low-cost labor and the need for tariffs and trade agreements that protect domestic jobs.

LO4.3 **SUMMARIZE** the case for and against globalization.

The case *for* globalization is largely based on the law of comparative advantage. By specializing in the products or services for which it has the lowest cost of production, a country is best able to compete in global markets. Globalization benefits all countries by boosting the economy, increasing wages, and providing lower-cost goods to all consumers. It has been given credit for raising the standard of living for hundreds of millions of people worldwide. In contrast, the case *against* globalization holds it responsible for wage stagnation in North America and Europe; for shipping jobs to low labor-cost countries; for undermining the middle class in Western countries; and for increasing economic inequality. It has largely been the stimulus for the Brexit vote, the renegotiation of NAFTA, and the "We Are the 99%" protest movement.

LO4.4 **EXPLAIN** the different types of international organizations.

Multinational corporations are international companies that maintain operations in multiple countries. Multidomestic corporations decentralize management and other decisions to the local country. A global company centralizes its management and other decisions in the home country. And transnational organizations eliminate artificial geographical barriers and reflect a geocentric attitude.

LO4.5 **DESCRIBE** the structures and techniques organizations use as they go international.

A multinational corporation is an international company that maintains operations in multiple countries. A multidomestic organization is an MNC that decentralizes management and other decisions to the local country (the polycentric attitude). A global organization is an MNC that centralizes management and other decisions in the home country (the ethnocentric attitude). A transnational organization (the geocentric attitude) is an MNC that has eliminated artificial geographical barriers and uses the best work practices and approaches from wherever. Global sourcing is purchasing materials or labor from around the world wherever it is cheapest. Exporting is making products domestically and selling them abroad. Importing is acquiring products made abroad and selling them domestically. Licensing is used by manufacturing organizations that make or sell another company's products and use the company's brand name, technology, or product specifications. Franchising is similar but is usually used by service organizations that want to use another company's name and operating methods. A global strategic alliance is a partnership between an organization and foreign company partners in which they share resources and knowledge to develop new products or build facilities. A joint venture is a specific type of strategic alliance in which the partners agree to form a separate, independent organization for some business purpose. A foreign subsidiary is a direct investment in a foreign country that a company creates by establishing a separate and independent facility or office.

 EXPLAIN the relevance of the political/legal, economic, and cultural environments to global business.

The laws and political stability of a country are issues in the global political/legal environment with which managers must be familiar. Likewise, managers must be aware of a country's economic issues such as currency exchange rates, inflation rates, and tax policies. Geert Hofstede identified five dimensions for assessing a country's culture, including individualism-collectivism, power distance, uncertainty avoidance, achievement-nurturing, and long-term/short-term orientation. The GLOBE studies identified nine dimensions for assessing country cultures: power distance, uncertainty avoidance, assertiveness, humane orientation, future orientation, institutional collectivism, gender differentiation, in-group collectivism, and performance orientation. The main challenges of doing business globally in today's world include (1) the openness associated with globalization and the significant cultural differences between countries and (2) managing a global workforce, which requires cultural intelligence and a global mind-set.

REVIEW AND DISCUSSION QUESTIONS

4-1. Contrast ethnocentric, polycentric, and geocentric attitudes toward global business.

4-2. How have attitudes toward globalization changed over the last century?

4-3. Contrast multinational, multidomestic, global, and transnational organizations.

4-4. What are the managerial implications of a borderless organization?

4-5. Describe the different ways organizations can go international.

4-6. Can the GLOBE framework presented in this chapter be used to guide managers in a Russian hospital or a government agency in Egypt? Explain.

4-7. What challenges might confront a Mexican manager transferred to the United States to manage a manufacturing plant in Tucson, Arizona? Will these issues be the same for a US manager transferred to Guadalajara? Explain.

4-8. How might the cultural differences in the GLOBE dimensions affect how managers (a) use work groups, (b) develop goals/plans, (c) reward outstanding employee performance, and (d) deal with employee conflict?

Writing Assignments

4-9. Explain how the global political/legal and economic environments affect managers of global organizations.

4-10. Is globalization good for business? For consumers? Discuss.

PREPARING FOR: My Career

ETHICS DILEMMA

Face-recognition technology is on the rise. Amazon is marketing its face-recognition technology to law enforcement and private businesses.[25] Two start-up companies in China, SenseTime and Megvii, are developing face-recognition technology powered by artificial intelligence.[26] Their goal is to be able to recognize anyone in any location. They haven't accomplished that goal yet, but they have received billions of dollars in funding to try to make that a reality.

Currently, face-recognition technology needs to be linked to a database of faces and names to be useful. Driver's license photos provide just that kind of information for law enforcement to use. Some Amazon investors and the American Civil Liberties Union are trying to convince Amazon not to sell its face-recognition technology to law enforcement, although there are no state or federal laws on the books that limit law enforcement's tracking people using face recognition. Even though the Supreme Court has ruled that phone tracking without reason is unconstitutional, there are no current limits on tracking people via their faces.

Privacy concerns are not voiced in China as much as they are in the US. The Chinese government is a major investor in face recognition as a means of citizen surveillance. Industries in China where face recognition already is being used include financial services (to prevent fraud), ride sharing, and real estate.

4-11. In what industries or situations do you think using face-recognition technology is acceptable? When does it violate people's privacy?

4-12. Is it ethical to use face-recognition technology if you are doing business in a culture where privacy concerns are not raised as much (like China)? Why or why not?

SKILLS EXERCISE Developing Your Collaboration Skill

About the Skill
Collaboration is the teamwork, synergy, and cooperation used by individuals when they seek a common goal. In many cross-cultural settings, the ability to collaborate is crucial. When all partners must work together to achieve goals, collaboration is critically important to the process. However, cultural differences can often make collaboration a challenge.

Steps in Practicing the Skill
- *Look for common points of interest.* The best way to start working together in a collaborative fashion is to seek commonalities that exist among the parties. Common points of interest enable communications to be more effective.

- *Listen to others.* Collaboration is a team effort. Everyone has valid points to offer, and each individual should have an opportunity to express his or her ideas.

- *Check for understanding.* Make sure you understand what the other person is saying. Use feedback when necessary.

- *Accept diversity.* Not everything in a collaborative effort will "go your way." Be willing to accept different ideas and different ways of doing things. Be open to these ideas and the creativity that surrounds them.

- *Seek additional information.* Ask individuals to provide additional information. Encourage others to talk and more fully explain suggestions. This brainstorming opportunity can assist in finding creative solutions.

- *Don't become defensive.* Collaboration requires open communications. Discussions may focus on things you and others may not be doing or need to do better. Don't take the constructive feedback as personal criticism. Focus on the topic being discussed, not on the person delivering the message. Recognize that you cannot always be right!

Practicing the Skill
Interview individuals from three different nationalities about the challenges of collaborating with individuals from different cultures. What challenges do different cultures create? How have they dealt with these challenges? What advice do they have for improving collaboration across cultural differences? Based on your interviews, what are some general ideas you learned to improve your ability to collaborate?

WORKING TOGETHER Team Exercise

In many jobs today, you'll work with people from other countries even if your job is based in the US. To better prepare yourself for cultural differences, look at the GLOBE dimensions on pages 99–100 and find examples of your home country being different from another country that you know about. In groups of three to four students, discuss how interactions you have had (or could have) with people from other countries could be interpreted in light of differences on GLOBE cultural dimensions. List several ways that interactions with individuals from countries that differ on GLOBE dimensions could be made more comfortable for everyone involved despite cultural differences. Be prepared to share your interpretations of cultural difference interactions and ways to improve those interactions with the class.

MY TURN TO BE A MANAGER

- Find two current examples of each of the ways that organizations go international. Write a short paper describing what these companies are doing.

- The UK-based company Commisceo Global has several cultural awareness "quizzes" on its website (www.commisceo-global.com/resources/quizzes). Go to the website and try two or three of them. Were you surprised at your score? What does your score tell you about your cultural awareness?

- On another website, you'll also find Intercultural Management Guides (www.kwintessential.co.uk/resources-types/guides). Pick two countries to study (from different regions), and compare them. How are they the same? Different? How would this information help a manager?

- Interview two or three professors or students at your school who are from other countries. Ask them to describe what the business world is like in their country. Write a short paper describing what you found out.

- Take advantage of opportunities you might have to travel to other countries, either on personal trips or on school-sponsored trips.

- Sign up for a foreign language course.

- Suppose you were sent on an overseas assignment to another country (you decide which one). Research that country's economic, political/legal, and cultural environments. Write a report summarizing your findings.

- If you don't have your passport yet, go through the process to get one. (The current fee in the United States is $145.)

- It is important to understand basic etiquette when traveling internationally for business (e.g., how does one greet someone new, and is a handshake appropriate?). Identify three countries that you would like to travel to and conduct research to learn about business etiquette for those countries. Summarize your findings.

- Identify a company that operates internationally and has locations in more than two countries. Explore the "Career" page of the company's website. Write a brief report about the career opportunities available at the company and the required qualifications of applicants.

CASE APPLICATION 1

Glencore: Conducting Business in Countries Where Others Might Not

International business sounds fun. Experiencing foreign cultures, travelling, experiencing new and different ways of living and working. But what if international business brings you face-to-face with corruption? That's entirely possible, since bribes and other forms of corruption can be acceptable business practices in some countries.[27] A big red flag for Americans when conducting international business is that you can't be a part of bribes or corruption without violating the Foreign Corrupt Practices Act (FCPA). The FCPA says anyone with connections to the US can't engage in corrupt practices.[28]

Doing business in developing countries often come with the risk of corruption. Glencore, one of the most powerful commodities, mining and trading empires, found out in July 2018 that it was under investigation for money laundering in violation of FCPA.[29] Swiss-based Glencore does business in mineral-rich countries like the Democratic Republic of the Congo, Nigeria, and Venezuela—countries that some firms are unwilling to do business in. These countries provide access to minerals like cobalt, which is used in smartphones, electric vehicle batteries, and other electronic devices. The US says cobalt is essential for American national security. And Glencore is responsible for a quarter of the world's cobalt production.[30]

For Glencore, doing business in resource-rich countries means dealing with companies in international markets. In the Congo, Glencore formed ties with Israeli mining billionaire Dan Gertler in order to gain access to mines. The US Treasury Department imposed sanctions on Gertler in December 2017 for underpricing mining assets that he bought resulting in a $1.36 billion revenue loss for the Congolese government. Glencore tried paying debts to Gertler in euros in order to avoid US penalties, but this looked to others like an unethical practice to the US.[31]

DISCUSSION QUESTIONS

4-13. How can Glencore be subject to a US law when it is based in Switzerland? Is the US justified in launching this investigation?

4-14. Some people think that Glencore should change its business practices because of this corruption investigation. What if there is no other way to get access to resources without brushing up against corruption?

4-15. Can the ends (providing a much-needed mineral like cobalt) ever justify the means (corrupt practices)? If so, when?

4-16. What are other examples of international companies that have been linked to corruption? What defense did they use to justify their practices?

CASE APPLICATON 2 Tariffs: Helping or Hurting General Motors?

It sounds straightforward. Since steel and aluminum have been hurt by the low cost of imports, increase prices on imported steel and aluminum and you save US jobs. You might even call that "Tariffs 101" if there were actually a class offered on the topic. Those in favor of tariffs argue that the US imposition of 25 percent tariffs on imported steel and aluminum in 2018 should increase the competitiveness of many US industries.[32]

Managers at General Motors appreciate efforts to make their products more competitive. But being a global company makes tariffs more complicated. GM's supply chain depends on 20,000 businesses worldwide. About 30 percent of GM's cars were made outside the US in 2017.[33] GM buys imported steel and aluminum on a scale that the US might not be able to produce on its own. GM's market is global too. However, tariffs work two ways. When the US enacts tariffs, affected countries fight back with retaliatory tariffs. Because of the US steel and aluminum tariffs, China, Canada, Mexico, Turkey, and the European Union placed tariffs on $28.5 billion worth of US exports.[34]

When European or Asian countries impose tariffs on US firms, the cost of their products in these foreign markets go up and sales go down. Millions of American cars are sold each year outside the US. With tariffs, the cost of an American car sold outside the country would increase by $5,800 and annual sales across all American car companies would decrease by one to two million vehicles.[35] Without healthy foreign sales, GM would suffer.

The US appealed to the World Trade Organization, claiming that these retaliatory tariffs from other countries are illegal. The US argued that tariffs on steel and aluminum were necessary for national security reasons, as many important industries—such as autos, aerospace, and electronics—depend on these metals.

GM also is confronting uncertainty in other areas related to global trade. If the US pulls out of the North American Free Trade Agreement (NAFTA), GM's cross-country supply chain could be thrown into disarray. GM has operations that span the US, Canada, and Mexico. GM's supply chain is "like a Rubik's Cube," according to GM North American President Alan Batey.[36] Anytime a change happens in one part of the supply chain, there is a ripple effect that affects the entire process of making cars.

GM doesn't just sit back and watch what happens in the global trade arena. GM CEO Mary Barra has urged the US president not to get rid of NAFTA.[37] GM submitted some of the more than 2,500 comments to the US Commerce Department about the steel and aluminum tariffs. GM argued that the tariffs would increase car prices for cars bought by consumers who can't afford such increases. GM as a company also might become much smaller due to increased prices and lower market share.[38]

DISCUSSION QUESTIONS

4-17. What are the pros and cons of tariffs as a part of global trade?

4-18. What roles do regional trading alliances and global trade mechanisms play in the events affecting General Motors highlighted in this case?

4-19. With so many external environmental forces affecting General Motors, what could executives at General Motors do to manage this uncertainty?

4-20. What do you think General Motors might need to do better to navigate the changes happening in the global marketplace (including the pendulum swinging away from globalism toward nationalism)?

ANSWERS TO "WHO OWNS WHAT" QUIZ

1. c. **China**
   While made in Sweden, Volvo Cars is a subsidiary of Chinese auto company Geely.

2. a. **Canada**
   Burger King is part of Restaurant Brands International.

3. c. **Germany**
   Trader Joe's is owned by Aldi Nord, a German supermarket chain.

4. a. **The Netherlands**
   Mexico's second-largest beer producer was acquired by Heineken N.V. in January 2010.

5. b. **United Kingdom**
   The television show *America's Got Talent* premiered in June 2006, and it is a part of the British franchise *Got Talent*, owned by SYCOtv company.

6. c. **United States**
   Chobani LLC is a US company that manufactures and distributes Greek yogurt, and prior to 2012 it was named Agro-Farma Inc.

7. c. **Switzerland**
   The Swatch Group Ltd. was established through the merger of two Swiss watch companies— ASUAG and SSIH—in 1983.

8. d. **Japan**
   7-Eleven is part of Seven & I Holdings.

9. a. **Sweden**
   Spotify is a service of Spotify AB, which was established in 2008.

10. b. **Belgium**
    Anheuser-Busch was acquired by AB InBev in 2008.

ENDNOTES

1. "Highlights of World Trade in 2017," *World Trade Statistical Review 2018,* World Trade Organization, 2018, https://www.wto.org/english/res_e/statis_e/wts2018_e/wts2018chapter02_e.pdf.

2. See N. Saval, "Globalisation: The Rise and Fall of an Idea That Swept the World," *Guardian,* July 14, 2017, https://www.theguardian.com/world/2017/jul/14/globalisation-the-rise-and-fall-of-an-idea-that-swept-the-world; G. Ip, "A Fractured World: Nationalism Is Growing—and Changing," *Wall Street Journal,* January 23, 2018, p. R1; and I. Bremmer, "Rage at Globalism Is Just the Beginning," *Fortune,* May 1, 2018, p. 12.

3. See, for example, "The Case for Globalisation," *Economist,* September 23, 2000, p. 19.

4. T. Petersen and C. Jungbluth, "Globalization Report 2018: Who Benefits Most from Globalization?," *New Perspectives on Global Economic Dynamics,* June 8, 2018, https://ged-project.de/research/studies/globalization-report-2018-who-benefits-most-from-globalization/?cn-reloaded=1.

5. See, for instance, I. Talley and W. Mauldin, "Globalization on the Skids," *Wall Street Journal,* October 7, 2016, p. A1; P. S. Goodman and J. Kanter, "Globalization Grinds to a Halt," *New York Times,* October 22, 2016, p. B1; and B. Davis and J. Hilsenrath, "Globalization Backers Face End of an Era," *Wall Street Journal,* March 30, 2017, p. A1.

6. See L. Vavreck, "The Long Decline in Trust in Government, and Why That Can Be Patriotic," July 3, 2015, https://www.nytimes.com/2015/07/04/upshot/the-long-decline-of-trust-in-government-and-why-that-can-be-patriotic.html; and B. Bishop, "Americans Have Lost Faith in Institutions. That's Not Because of Trump or 'Fake News,'" *Washington*

Post, March 3, 2017, https://www.washingtonpost.com/posteverything/wp/2017/03/03/americans-have-lost-faith-in-institutions-thats-not-because-of-trump-or-fake-news/?utm_term=.633d54a04cfa.

7. B. Richardson, "Millennials Would Rather Live in Socialist or Communist Nation Than Under Capitalism: Poll," *Washington Times,* November 4, 2017, https://www.washingtontimes.com/news/2017/nov/4/majority-millennials-want-live-socialist-fascist-o/.

8. M. Schuman, "Globalization Isn't Going Away," *Bloomberg Businessweek*, March 19, 2018, pp. 14–16.

9. G. Griswold, "Globalization Isn't Killing Factory Jobs. Trade Is Actually Why Manufacturing Is Up 40%," *Los Angeles Times,* August 1, 2016, https://www.latimes.com/opinion/op-ed/la-oe-griswold-globalization-and-trade-help-manufacturing-20160801-snap-story.html; and C. C. Miller, "What's Really Killing Jobs? It's Automation, Not China," *New York Times,* December 22, 2016, p. A3.

10. O. Shoshan, "The 6 Top Languages Global-Minded CEOs Should Know," *Entrepreneur*, April 3, 2015, https://www.entrepreneur.com/article/244233.

11. J. Henry, "One Ford, Part Two; Tweaking the Master Plan," *Forbes,* August 30, 2015, https://www.forbes.com/sites/jimhenry/2015/08/30/one-ford-part-two-tweaking-the-master-plan/#36fc517a7361.

12. R. Smith, "Political Risk on the Rise in 2018—Marsh," *Insurance Business Magazine,* February 22, 2018, https://www.insurancebusinessmag.com/us/news/breaking-news/political-risk-on-the-rise-in-2018-marsh-92946.aspx.

13. "Inflation Rates," 2018, statista.com.

14. See P. Rudlin, "4 Differences Between Japanese and German Approaches to Work, Communication, and Customer Service," Japanese Culture Business Blog, *Japan Cultural Consulting*, October 31, 2014, https://www.japanintercultural.com/en/blogs/default.aspx?blogid=240.

15. "Future Work Skills 2020," Institute for the Future, 2011, http://www.iftf.org/futureworkskills/.

16. See G. Hofstede, *Culture's Consequences: International Differences in Work-Related Values*, 2nd ed. (Thousand Oaks, CA: Sage Publications, 2001), pp. 9–15.

17. G. Hofstede, "The Cultural Relativity of Organizational Practices and Theories," *Journal of International Business Studies* (Fall 1983): pp. 75–89; Hofstede, *Culture's Consequences* [see note 16]; and S. Bhaskaran and N. Sukumaran, "National Culture, Business Culture and Management Practices: Consequential Relationships?," *Cross Cultural Management: An International Journal* 14, no. 7 (2007): pp. 54–67.

18. B. Leonard, "Study Examines the Importance of Globally Competent Leaders," Society for Human Resource Management, May 21, 2015, https://www.shrm.org/resourcesandtools/hr-topics/behavioral-competencies/leadership-and-navigation/pages/global-leadership-study.aspx.

19. "Compete and Connect: Developing Globally Competent Leaders," *Human Capital Institute Report*, Kenan-Flagler Business School Executive Development, University of North Carolina, 2015, https://www.kenan-flagler.unc.edu/~/media/Files/documents/executive-development/unc-white-paper-developing-global-competence-final.pdf.

20. M. E. Mendenhall, A. A. Arnardottir, G. R. Oddou, and L. A. Burke-Smalley, "Developing Cross-Cultural Competencies in Management Education via Cognitive-Behavior Therapy," *Academy of Management Learning & Education* (September 2013): pp.436–451; N. Jesionka, "Why Knowing About the World Can Help Your Career," *The Muse*, June 14, 2013, https://www.themuse.com/advice/why-knowing-about-the-world-can-help-your-career; A. Solomon and R. Steyn, "Exploring Cultural Intelligences Truths: A Systematic Review," *South African Journal of Human Resource Management* (March 2017): pp. 1–11; E. Meyer, "Being the Boss in Brussels, Boston, and Beijing: If You Want to Succeed, You'll Need to Adapt," *Harvard Business Review*, July/August 2017, pp. 70–77; J. Jyoti and S. Kour, "Cultural Intelligence and Job Performance," *International Journal of Cross Cultural Management* (December 2017): pp. 305–26; and A. B. I. Bernardo and A. Presbitero, "Cognitive Flexibility and Cultural Intelligence: Exploring the Cognitive Aspects of Effective Functioning in Cultural Diverse Contexts," *International Journal of Intercultural Relations* (September 2018): pp. 12–21.

21. M. Minkov and G. Hofstede, "The Evolution of Hofstede's Doctrine," *Cross Cultural Management* (February 2011): pp. 10–20.

22. R. J. House, P. J. Hanges, M. Javidan, P. W. Dorfman, and V. Gupta, *Culture, Leadership, and Organizations: The GLOBE Study of 62 Societies* (Thousand Oaks, CA: Sage Publications, 2004); and J. S. Chhokar, F. C. Brodbeck, and R. J. House, *Culture and Leadership Across the World: The GLOBE Book of In-Depth Studies of 25 Societies* (Philadelphia: Lawrence Erlbaum Associates, 2007).

23. See, for instance, A. E. Munley, "Culture Differences in Leadership," *IUP Journal of Soft Skills* (March 2011): pp. 16–30; and D. A. Waldman, M. S. de Luque, and D. Wang, "What Can We Really Learn About Management Practices Across Firms and Countries?," *Academy of Management Perspectives* (February 2012): pp. 34–40.

24. Based on W. Yue, "The Fretful Euro Disneyland," *International Journal of Marketing Studies*, November 2009, pp. 87–91.

25. C. Mims, "Amazon and Other Companies Sell Face-Scanning Software to Anyone with a Credit Card, from Shopkeepers to Federal Agents; Very Little Is Prohibited by the User Agreement for Recognition," *Wall Street Journal*, June 23, 2018.

26. H. Jacobs and P. Ralph, "Inside the Creepy and Impressive Startup Funded by the Chinese Government That Is Developing AI That Can Recognize Anyone, Anywhere," *Business Insider*, July 8, 2018, https://www.businessinsider.com/china-facial-recognition-tech-company-megvii-faceplusplus-2018-5.

27. B. Graham and C. Stroup, "Does Anti-bribery Enforcement Deter Foreign Investment?," *Applied Economics Letters*, 2016.

28. Wikipedia, s.v. "Foreign Corrupt Practices Act," accessed August 21, 2018, https://en.wikipedia.org/wiki/Foreign_Corrupt_Practices_Act.

29. S. Reed and M. J. De la Merced, "Swiss Commodities Giant Faces U.S. Subpoena in Corruption Inquiry," *New York Times*, July 4, 2018, New York edition, p. B3.

30. J. Kollewe, "Glencore Hit with US Subpoena Over Alleged Money Laundering," *Guardian*, July 3, 2018, https://www.theguardian.com/business/2018/jul/03/glencore-subpoena-us-department-of-justice.

31. N. Hume, D. Sheppard, and H. Sanderson, "Glencore: An Audacious Business Model in the Docks," *Financial Times*, July 6, 2018, https://www.ft.com/content/c9e674b0-8105-11e8-bc55-50daf11b720d.

32. P. Nicholas, "Trump Says His Tariffs Will Rescue the U.S. Steel Industry," *Wall Street Journal*, August 15, 2018, https://www.wsj.com/articles/trump-says-his-tariffs-will-rescue-u-s-steel-industry-1534377855?mod=hp_lead_pos3.

33. D. Shepardson, "GM Says U.S. Import Tariffs Could Mean 'Smaller' Company, Fewer Jobs," Reuters Business News, June 29, 2018, https://www.reuters.com/article/us-usa-trade-autos/gm-says-u-s-import-tariffs-could-mean-smaller-company-fewer-jobs-idUSKBN1JP2PZ.

34. T. Tsu, "G.M. Tells Trump Tariff Plan Puts U.S. Jobs at Risk," *New York Times*, June 30, 2018, New York edition, p. A1.

35. Reuters, "US Launches Five WTO Challenges to Retaliatory Tariffs," CNBC, July 17, 2018, https://www.cnbc.com/2018/07/17/us-launches-five-wto-challenges-to-retaliatory-tariffs.html.

36. S. Szymkowski, "GM's Alan Batey Talks NAFTA, China Trade Tariffs," *GM Authority*, June 26, 2018, http://gmauthority.com/blog/2018/06/gms-alan-batey-talks-nafta-china-trade-tariffs/.

37. N. E. Boudette, "G.M. Chief Cautions Trump Administration on Upending NAFTA," *New York Times*, January 16, 2018, https://www.nytimes.com/2018/01/16/business/gm-nafta.html.

38. C. Isidore, "Why Steel and Aluminum Tariffs Matter to the U.S. Economy," CNNMoney, March 7, 2018, https://money.cnn.com/2018/02/19/news/economy/steel-aluminum-us-economy/index.html.

Chapter 5   Managing Diversity

Learning Objectives

5.1 *Define* workplace diversity and explain why managing it is so important.

5.2 *Describe* the changing makeup of workplaces in the United States and around the world.

5.3 *Explain* the different types of diversity found in workplaces.

5.4 *Discuss* the challenges managers face in managing diversity.

5.5 *Describe* various workplace diversity initiatives.

Employability Skills Matrix

This matrix identifies which features and end-of-chapter materials will help you develop specific skills employers are looking for in job candidates.

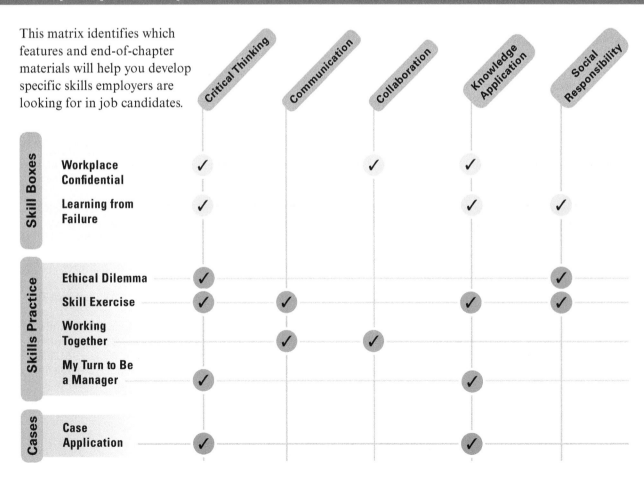

		Critical Thinking	Communication	Collaboration	Knowledge Application	Social Responsibility
Skill Boxes	Workplace Confidential	✓		✓	✓	
	Learning from Failure	✓			✓	✓
Skills Practice	Ethical Dilemma	✓				✓
	Skill Exercise	✓	✓		✓	✓
	Working Together		✓	✓		
	My Turn to Be a Manager	✓			✓	
Cases	Case Application	✓			✓	

Automobile manufacturers were long led and dominated by white males. That is certainly not true anymore at General Motors. In June 2018, the company appointed Dhivya Suryadevara as its first female chief financial officer.[1] She joined an executive team that is now widely represented by females. GM's CEO, Mary Barra, is the first woman to head a major auto company. Additionally, five of GM's directors are women, and women now also hold the positions of manufacturing chief and head of human resources.

The GM example illustrates increasing corporate diversity by expanding the number of women in key executive positions. But as we will show in this chapter, the term workforce diversity *encompasses a large number of groups beyond gender.*

GM has increased its corporate diversity by appointing women to executive-level positions, such as Dhivya Suryadevara, its recently named chief financial officer.
Source: Larry Kinsel

DIVERSITY 101

L05.1 Walk around the lobby of the MGM Mirage hotel in Las Vegas and you'll hear a variety of different languages. Because its guests come from all over the world, the Mirage is committed to reflecting that diversity in its workforce. MGM Resorts International, the hotel's parent company, has had a comprehensive diversity initiative in place for twenty years.[2] It's designed to ensure diversity at all levels—from the board and senior management to front-line personnel. Among its components, it includes workshops, networking groups, and a formal mentoring program. The initiative even includes ensuring diversity among the company's suppliers. And all of this effort isn't just public relations. There are payoffs for MGM Resorts. For instance, research shows companies in the hospitality business that boast gender-diverse workforces have a 19 percent higher average quarterly profit than hospitality businesses with less diversity.[3]

What Is Workplace Diversity?

With its basis in civil rights legislation and social justice, the word *diversity* often invokes a variety of attitudes and emotional responses in people. Diversity has traditionally been considered a term used by human resources departments, associated with fair hiring practices, discrimination, and inequality. But diversity today is considered to be so much more.[4] Exhibit 5-1 illustrates a historical overview of how the concept and meaning of workforce diversity has evolved.

We define **workforce diversity** as the ways in which people in an organization are different from and similar to one another. Notice that our definition not only focuses on the differences, but also the similarities of employees. This recognizes that managers and organizations should view employees as having qualities in common as well as differences that separate them. It doesn't mean that those differences are any less important, but that our focus is in finding ways for managers to develop strong relationships with and engage their entire workforce.

One final point: The demographic characteristics that we tend to think of when we think of diversity—age, race, gender, ethnicity, and so on—are just the tip of the iceberg. These demographic differences reflect **surface-level diversity**, which includes easily perceived differences that may trigger certain stereotypes but don't necessarily reflect the ways people think or feel. Such surface-level differences in characteristics can affect the way people perceive others, especially when it comes to assumptions or stereotyping.

workforce diversity
The ways in which people in an organization are different from and similar to one another

surface-level diversity
Easily perceived differences that may trigger certain stereotypes, but that do not necessarily reflect the ways people think or feel

Exhibit 5-1

Timeline of the Evolution of Workforce Diversity

1960s to 1970s	**Focus on complying with laws and regulations:** Title VII of Civil Rights Act; Equal Employment Opportunity Commission; affirmative-action policies and programs
Early 1980s	**Focus on assimilating minorities and women into corporate setting:** Corporate programs developed to help improve self-confidence and qualifications of diverse individuals so they can "fit in"
Late 1980s	**Concept of workforce diversity expanded from compliance to an issue of business survival:** Publication of *Workforce 2000* opened business leaders' eyes about the future composition of workforce—that is, more diverse; first use of term *workforce diversity*
Late 1980s to Late 1990s	**Focus on fostering sensitivity:** Shift from compliance and focusing only on women and minorities to include everyone; making employees more aware and sensitive to the needs and differences of others
New Millennium	**Focus on diversity and inclusion for business success:** Workforce diversity seen as core business issue; important to achieve business success, profitability, and growth

Sources: Based on "The New Global Mindset: Driving Innovation Through Diversity," by Ernst & Young, January 27, 2010.

As people get to know one another, these surface-level differences become less important and **deep-level diversity**—differences in values, personality, and work preferences—becomes more important. These deep-level differences can affect the way people view organizational work, rewards, communicate, react to leaders, negotiate, and generally behave at work. As organizations seek to improve workplace diversity, the focus is on developing appreciation and acceptance at a deep level.

deep-level diversity
Differences in values, personality, and work preferences

Benefits of Workforce Diversity

It isn't hard to build a case for organizations to develop and introduce diversity programs. The benefits fall into three main categories: people management, organizational performance, and strategic. (See Exhibit 5-2.)

Exhibit 5-2

Benefits of Workforce Diversity

People Management

- Better use of employee talent
- Increased creativity in team problem-solving
- Ability to attract and retain employees of diverse backgrounds

Organizational Performance

- Reduced costs associated with high turnover, absenteeism, and lawsuits
- Enhanced problem-solving ability
- Improved system flexibility

Strategic

- Increased understanding of the marketplace, which improves ability to better market to diverse consumers
- Potential to improve sales growth and increase market share
- Potential source of competitive advantage because of improved innovation efforts
- Viewed as moral and ethical; the "right" thing to do

Sources: Based on G. Robinson and K. Dechant, "Building a Business Case for Diversity," *Academy of Management Executive,* August 1997, pp. 21–31; O. C. Richard, "Racial Diversity, Business Strategy, and Firm Performance: A Resource-Based View," *Academy of Management Journal* (April 2000): pp. 164–177; J. A. Gonzalez and A. S. DeNisi, "Cross-Level Effects of Demography and Diversity Climate on Organizational Attachment and Firm Effectiveness," *Journal of Organizational Behavior* (January 2009): pp. 21–40; and M.-E. Roberge and R. van Dick, "Recognizing the Benefits of Diversity: When and How Does Diversity Increase Group Performance," *Human Resource Management Review* (December 2010): pp. 295–308.

PEOPLE MANAGEMENT When all is said and done, diversity *is*, after all, about people, both inside and outside the organization. The people management benefits that organizations get because of their workforce diversity efforts revolve around attracting and retaining a talented workforce. Organizations rely on capable employees with the right skills, abilities, and experiences to achieve their goals.

Positive and explicit workforce diversity efforts can help organizations draw from a larger applicant pool and utilize the best of the talents those individuals can bring to the workplace. In addition, as organizations rely more on employee teams, those work teams with diverse backgrounds often bring different and unique perspectives to discussions, which can result in more creative ideas and solutions.

ORGANIZATIONAL PERFORMANCE The performance benefits that organizations get from workforce diversity include cost savings and improvements in organizational functioning. The cost savings can be significant when organizations that cultivate a diverse workforce reduce employee turnover, absenteeism, and exposure to lawsuits. For instance, Target was fined $2.8 million for discriminating against female and racially diverse job candidates over several years.[5] Fox News similarly settled a recent racial and gender discrimination suit for $10 million.[6] UPS paid out $2 million after being sued for disability discrimination.[7] And Darden Restaurants recently paid nearly $3 million to settle a suit claiming the company hiring practices discriminated against older applicants.[8] The US Equal Employment Opportunity Commission reported that 84,254 workplace discrimination claims were filed in 2017. The monetary relief obtained for victims totaled $398 million.[9] Workforce diversity efforts can reduce the risk of such lawsuits.

In addition, a report by recruiting firm Korn Ferry International found that US companies waste $64 billion annually by losing and replacing employees who leave their jobs "solely due to failed diversity management."[11] That same report noted that 34 percent of those who left jobs because of diversity-related issues would have stayed if managers had recognized their abilities. Another study showed that when organizational biases manifest themselves in incivility toward those who are different, organizational performance is hindered.[12] However, on the positive side, organizational performance can be *enhanced* through workforce diversity because of improved problem-solving abilities and system flexibility. An organization with a diverse workforce can tap into the variety of skills and abilities represented, and just the fact that its workforce is diverse requires that processes and procedures be more accommodative and inclusive. Research confirms that diverse leadership teams make better decisions, generate higher sales, and produce better financial returns.[13]

> **fyi**
>
> - Companies with the most ethnically/culturally diverse executive teams are 33 percent more likely to outperform their peers on profitability.
> - Companies in the top quartile for gender diversity on executive teams are 21 percent more likely to outperform the national industry median.[10]

STRATEGIC Organizations also benefit strategically from a diverse workforce when they extract the best talent, performance, market share, and suppliers from a diverse country and world. A distinct strategic benefit is that with a diverse workforce, organizations can better anticipate and respond to changing consumer needs. Diverse employees bring a variety of points of view and approaches to opportunities, which can improve how the organization markets to a variety of consumers. For instance, Hispanics currently make up 18 percent of the US population and account for almost half of US population growth.[14] And as the Hispanic population has grown, so have organizational efforts to market products and services to that demographic group. Having Hispanic employees can be a fertile source of insights for reaching this market. Food service companies, retailers, financial services companies, and automobile manufacturers are just a few of the industries that have seen sales and market share increases because firms paid attention to the needs of diverse consumers using information from employees.

A diverse workforce also can be a powerful source of competitive advantage, primarily because innovation thrives in such an environment. A report by Ernst & Young stated that "cultural diversity offers the flexibility and creativity we need to re-create the global economy for the twenty-first century."[15] Tapping into differing voices and viewpoints can be powerful factors in steering innovation. Companies that seek to lead their

Let's Get REAL

Leya Ramey ▶
HR Business Partner

Source: Leya Ramey

The Scenario

As the district manager for a region of retail discount clothing stores, Henry Banks is preparing for a quarterly meeting with all of the store managers in his district. As part of a presentation about company hiring practices, he plans to stress the importance of diversity. He knows the company needs a diverse workforce to meet the needs of the company's diverse customer base; however, he is not sure how to convey this to the group of store managers.

What do you think Henry should say in his presentation?

Henry should take this opportunity to review the company's values and to consider how diversity is a critical aspect of a dynamic culture. He could provide data that indicate that diverse companies perform better than less diverse companies, overall. With a diverse customer base, Henry should provide real-life examples of situations in which diversity helped with a customer's shopping experience or increased a sale, as well as examples in which lack of diversity had a negative impact on the business. Lastly, Henry should explain how the store managers' incentives are tied to the overall performance of the store; the better the store performs, the greater incentive opportunity they have.

industries need to find ways to "stir the pot"—to generate the lively debate that can create those new ideas. And research shows that diverse viewpoints can do that. "Diversity powers innovation, helping businesses generate new products and services."[16]

Finally, from an ethical perspective, a commitment to workforce diversity can be said to be the right thing to do. Businesses have an ethical imperative to build relationships that value and enable all employees to be successful. Managers need to view workforce diversity as a way to bring different voices to the table and to build an environment based on trusting relationships.

THE CHANGING workplace

LO5.2   We opened this chapter by describing how women now hold numerous key positions at General Motors. Women also now head up companies as varied as IBM, General Dynamics, Hershey, and Occidental Petroleum. African Americans currently head up Merck, TIAA, and JCPenny; and Asian Americans now lead Microsoft, Google, and Adobe. But these examples are the exception. We see more women and minorities in organizations, but rarely at the top. Change is happening, but it has been slow. The past forty years have seen a transition from a white male managerial workforce to one that is more gender balanced and multi-ethnic. Yet we still have a ways to go—especially in the upper management ranks—for the workforce to reflect changes in the overall population. In this section, we want to look at some of these changes. Let's first look at the changing characteristics of the US population and then at global diversity trends.

Characteristics of the US Population

Since 2014, racial and ethnic minority babies have become the majority in the US. By 2044, this trend is predicted to make non-Hispanic whites the minority in the country.[17] By 2060, Hispanics alone will go from 11 percent of the population to over 28 percent.[18]

African Americans are being more represented in leadership positions at major companies, such as Ken Frazier, Chairman and CEO at Merck & Co.
Source: Brendan Mcdermid/Reuters/Newscom

WORKPLACE CONFIDENTIAL Dealing with Diversity

This chapter looks at diversity from the standpoint of management, specifically: What can *management* do to create a workplace that welcomes and appreciates differences? But this chapter doesn't offer *you* direct guidance on how to deal with coworker diversity. While management and the organization are largely responsible for fostering an inclusive culture that values diversity, you play a vital part.

Let's begin with the realization that many individuals have difficulty accepting others who are different from themselves. Human nature is such that we tend to be attracted to and feel more comfortable with people who are like us. It's not by chance, for example, that new immigrants gravitate to communities where there is a sizeable population of people from their country of origin. But "embracing differences" has become an unquestioned goal in most advanced economies and a mantra within organizations. It's increasingly difficult to survive in today's workplace if you can't accept differences and function effectively with a diverse workforce.

As described in this chapter, a strong argument can be made for a diverse workforce. From your standpoint, that argument would include being part of more effective work groups through a broader perspective in decision making; gaining a better understanding of diverse markets and customer preferences; improved ability to work comfortably with others in your workplace; and promoting fairness for individuals from underrepresented groups. Furthermore, we would be naive to ignore that supporting diversity is, for lack of a better term, "politically correct." Today's workplace is sensitive to appearances of prejudice or unfairness. If you expect to be a valued and accepted member of today's labor force, you need to recognize that supporting diversity is the ethical and morally right thing to do.

Research tells us that we all have biases. Demographics mostly reflect surface-level diversity and can lead you to perceive others through stereotypes and assumptions. In contrast, when you get to know others, you become less concerned about demographic differences if you can see yourself sharing more important, deeper-level characteristics. Let's elaborate on the difference between surface- and deep-level diversity.

Most of us typically define diversity in terms of surface-level characteristics. As noted in the chapter, surface-level diversity relates to those characteristics that are easily noticeable. So when a 20-year-old sees someone who's 70 and quickly classifies him as "old," that person is operating at a surface level. In contrast, deep-level diversity refers to characteristics that are not easily noticeable. Examples of deep-level differences would include personality, moods, attitudes, values, and beliefs. As you get to know a person, especially someone you like and bond with, you tend to forget surface differences and focus on your deeper commonalities.

An interesting illustration of the difference between these two types of diversity is the typical college campus. For more than forty years, most college admissions personnel have actively sought to expand surface diversity by considering race or ethnicity in their decision criteria. In addition, other factors such as gender, sexual orientation, socioeconomic status, or geographic background might also be applied to expand diversity. When these other factors can be visibly assessed by the way someone looks, dresses, or talks, then they are also surface-level variables. But here's the interesting observation: While college administrators try to increase diversity through admission selection, students themselves tend to undermine surface diversity by gravitating to others like themselves. Fraternities and sororities choose members who are like themselves. And friends tend to be those with similar majors, or living in the same dorm wing, or belonging to a common on-campus affinity group. So what we find is that campuses do a very good job at promoting surface-level diversity through admission decisions, but this breaks down once students are on campus. Natural student groupings tend to be defined more by deep-level characteristics.

So what can you do to more effectively deal with coworker diversity? At the surface level, start by confronting your biases and assumptions about others. You can't deal with your prejudices unless you recognize them. Then consider the positives of diversity. As we have noted in this chapter, a diverse workforce has numerous pluses. You need to recognize, accept, and value the unique contributions of those who are different from you in terms of appearance, culture, skills, experiences, and abilities.

At the deep level, the good news is that as we get to know people, most of us look beyond the surface to find common bonds. Specifically, the evidence shows that the longer individuals work together, the less the effects of surface diversity. So your first reaction might be to assume you have nothing in common with a colleague who is thirty years older, or raised in a different country, or whose first language is different from yours. But start with the basics. You're both working for the same employer. That alone suggests a common bond. Both of you saw something in your employing organization that drew you to it. Then, if you're having trouble dealing with someone's differences, look beyond the surface and try to get to know the individual's personality, interests, and beliefs. You're likely to be pleasantly surprised. You might initially think someone isn't like you or won't understand you, but as you dig deeper and spend more time with the person, you'll often find common bonds.

In addition to working one-on-one with a diverse set of coworkers, you'll likely have to deal with diversity within work teams. Occasionally, diversity within teams can create problems known as "faultlines." Faultlines are subgroups that develop naturally within teams, typically along various demographic lines. The behavior of the team leader and the way in which she structures the leadership role is essential for promoting communication and cohesiveness across the subgroups and for rallying the membership to meet a common cause.[19]

Exhibit 5-3

Changing Population Makeup of the United States

	2018	2050
Foreign-born	14%	19%
Racial/Ethnic Groups		
White*	72%	47%
Hispanic	12%	29%
Black*	12%	13%
Asian*	4%	9%

*= Non-Hispanic
American Indian/Alaska Native not included.
Source: www.census.gov

The previous statistics are just the tip of the iceberg. The US is an increasingly diverse society, and that diversity will continue to reshape the makeup of the workforce. Let's look at some of the most dramatic of these changes.

- **Total population of the United States.** The total population is projected to increase to 438 million by the year 2050, up from 327 million in 2018; 82 percent of that increase will be due to immigrants and their US-born descendants. Nearly one in five Americans will be an immigrant in 2050, compared with one in eight in 2018.
- **Racial/ethnic groups.** In addition to total population changes, the components of that population are projected to change as well. Exhibit 5-3 provides the projected population breakdown. As the projections show, the main changes will be in the percentages of the Hispanic and white population. But the data also indicate that the Asian population will more than double, primarily due to net migration.
- **An aging population.** As a nation, the US population is aging. Boomers continue to age and are slowly outnumbering children as the birth rate has declined steadily over the last decade.[20] Couples that were choosing to have three or more children in the 1950s now appear content with one or none. By 2050, one in every five persons will be age 65 or over. The "oldest" of this group—those age 80 and over—will be the most populous age group, comprising 8 percent of the entire US population. "Aging will continue to be one of the most important defining characteristics of the population."[21]

Such population trends will have a major impact on US workplaces. What workplace changes might we see?

According to the US Bureau of Labor Statistics, by the year 2024, 47 percent of the labor force will be women and 23 percent will be black, Asian/Pacific Islander, and all other racial groups.[22] Hispanics are projected to increase their numbers most rapidly among all ethnic groups—by 28 percent. In addition, between 2018 and 2024, workers age 16 to 24 will decline by 24 percent, while workers age 55 and older will increase by 19.8 percent. The immigration issue is also likely to be a factor in a changing workplace. According to an analysis released by the US Census Bureau, nearly one in seven American workers is foreign-born, the highest proportion since the 1920s. They represented 17.1 percent of the US labor force in 2018.[23]

Businesses will need to accommodate and embrace these workforce changes. Interestingly, although America historically has been known as a "melting pot," where people of different nationalities, religions, races, and ethnicities have blended together to become one, current attitudes and practices emphasize recognition and celebration of differences. Organizations need to recognize that they can't expect employees to assimilate into the organization by adopting uniform attitudes and values. Instead, there needs to be acknowledgment and appreciation for the differences that people bring to the workplace. Later in this chapter, we'll discuss initiatives that organizations can implement to foster this appreciation for differences.

What About Global Workforce Changes?

Some significant worldwide population trends also are likely to affect global workforces. According to United Nations forecasts, "The world is in the midst of an epochal demographic shift that will reshape societies, economies, and markets over the next century."[24] Let's look at two of these trends.[25]

- *Total world population.* The total world population in 2018 is estimated at over 7.6 billion individuals. However, that number is forecasted to reach 8.6 billion in 2030 and 9.8 billion by 2050, at which point the United Nations predicts the total population will either stabilize or peak after growing for centuries at an ever-accelerating rate. The main reason for this plateau is the decline in birth rates as nations advance economically. However, in developing countries in Africa, Asia, Latin America, the Caribbean, and Oceania, birth rates are likely to remain high. One of the benefits is that many of these countries are likely to experience a rising proportion of young people entering the workforce, which should drive productivity and economic growth.
- *An aging population.* The world's older population continues to grow at an unprecedented rate.[26] Today, 8.5 percent of people worldwide are aged 65 and over. This percentage is projected to jump to nearly 17 percent of the world's population by 2050.

An aging world population will bring about a lot of changes. Young workers will be in short supply and advanced nations will be reliant on immigrants from developing countries to fill job openings. And employers may be forced to hire workers in their 70s and 80s, if for no other reason than there will be lots of them: the world's population age 80 and over is projected to increase 233 percent by 2040! The implication for societies and businesses are profound—from changing family structures to shifting patterns of work and retirement to emerging economic challenges based on increasing demands on social entitlement programs, dwindling labor supply, and declining total global savings rates. Such demographic shifts will reshape the global workforce and organizational workplaces.

TYPES of workplace diversity

LO5.3   What types of dissimilarities—that is, diversity—do we find in the workplace? Exhibit 5-4 shows several types of workplace diversity. Let's work our way through the different types.

Age

The negative stereotypes of older workers—lethargic, poor mental functioning, lower job performance, resistant to change—has undoubtedly discouraged many employers from hiring and retaining people over 50. These stereotypes arguably underlie many claims of job discrimination. While both Title VII of the Civil Rights Act of 1964 and the Age Discrimination in Employment Act of 1967 prohibit age discrimination, claims of job discrimination by employers have only grown over the past fifteen years.[27]

Contrary to the stereotypes, the evidence indicates that increasing diversity by hiring and retaining older workers makes good business sense.[28] They bring experience, skills, and continuity to the workplace. Keeping older workers also provides other workers access to key institutional knowledge and history. Moreover, as implied in our previous discussion of declining birth rates and potential upcoming labor shortages, holding on to aging Baby Boomers may be critical if organizations are to keep key job positions filled.

Older employees can be valued at an organization, as demonstrated by the Fire Department Museum in Stendal, Germany. Gunter Hornke, 87 years old, is the oldest member of the team and is happy to keep active and share his experience with others.
Source: Zentralbild/dpa/Alamy Stock Photo

Exhibit 5-4
Types of Diversity Found in
Workplaces

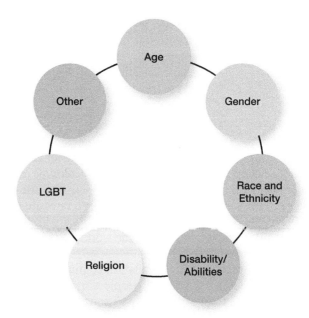

A few specifics can illuminate on the value of older workers and demonstrate many of the fallacies of age stereotypes. For instance, older workers are more stable. They stay put.[29] So management need spend less time and money on recruiting new employees. Older workers have lower rates of avoidable absences than their younger colleagues.[30] And maybe most important, studies have shown that there is virtually no relationship between age and job performance.[31] That is, there is no significant decline with age. Any drop off in physical or mental acuity appears to be more than offset by experience. These factors make a strong case for organizations to hire older workers and to implement diversity initiatives like flexible hours and skill-updating programs that will attract and keep them. As a case in point, executives at global bank Barclays believe that hiring older workers makes good business sense. To help find and select seniors, they launched an internship program for individuals age 50 or older.[32]

There is also a flip side to the older worker stereotype. That's the negative stereotype of younger workers—specifically millennials (those born between 1980 and 1996)—as being impatient, lazy, and entitled.[33] These millennials will make up about 75 percent of the global workforce by 2025.[34] And while they may have been raised in a more protective environment than their older counterparts, they bring strengths in technology know-how, communication, and curiosity, and they make great team players.[35]

Managers need to ensure that they take into account differing norms between generations. Effectively managing an organization's diverse age groups can lead to their working well with each other, learning from each other, and taking advantage of the different perspectives and experiences that each has to offer.

Gender

Look around a college campus. If it's typical, the majority of students are women.[36] And that fact has fed into the workforce. In 1950, less than 30 percent of the workforce was female. It's currently 47 percent.[37] And those statistics don't capture the nature of the jobs women now hold. In 1950, women dominated jobs like secretary, nurse, and school teacher. Few could be found in the management ranks of business firms. Today, women are an increasing proportion of professionals—as physicians, lawyers, pharmacists, college professors, and corporate executives.

In spite of the progress that has been made, the workplace is still far from being gender-neutral. For instance, one study found that men start their careers at higher levels than women. And after starting out behind, women don't ever catch up. Men move up the career ladder further and faster as well.[38] Another study, encompassing 34,000 men and women at 132 global companies, found men get more promotions, more challenging assignments, and more access to top leaders than women do.[39] And a significant share of the women in this study said that they didn't get credit for their contributions, and that their gender had been a factor in missed raises and promotions.

The recent "me-too" movement has drawn global attention to gender inequities in the workplace.[40] It essentially began in 2017, when more than a dozen women accused film producer Harvey Weinstein of sexual harassment, assault, or rape. What began as a trickle, soon became a flood of accusations. The movement ended Weinstein's reign at his film studio, but also brought to light abuses of power by dozens of prominent men, including *Today* co-host Matt Lauer, TV journalists Bill O'Reilly and Charlie Rose, Pixar head John Lasseter, and casino magnate Stephen Wynn.

The "me-too" movement, which began in 2017, has brought to light the abuses of power at many organizations. From sexual harassment to a boys' club atmosphere, women have spoken up about feeling unsafe at work, as well as the difficulties they face vying for promotions.
Source: Sundry Photography/Shutterstock

The "me-too" movement additionally revealed organizational cultures, like Fox News, that are hostile to women.[41] And investigations into Silicon Valley tech firms such as Uber, Tesla, Squarespace, and Tinder found a "boy's club" environment more suited to a fraternity house than a business organization. Women in these firms are vastly outnumbered by men and complain about being excluded from key meetings, being subject to lewd language and sexual harassment, and passed over for promotions.[42]

Clearly, there continue to be gender inequities in the workplace. But recent revelations have enacted changes. Language and behavior that was acceptable ten years ago is not acceptable today.[43] Those men or women who create a hostile environment for either sex are less likely to be tolerated. And we can expect organizational cultures that continue to be hostile, especially toward women, will attract unfavorable media attention and face serious legal consequences.

Race and Ethnicity

Race is a controversial issue in society and in organizations. We define **race** as physical characteristics, such as bone structure, skin, or eye color. **Ethnicity** is the social and culture factors—including nationality, regional culture, and ancestry—that define the groups a person belongs to. Typically, we associate race with biology and ethnicity with culture, but there is a history of self-identifying for both classifications. Laws against race and ethnic discrimination are in effect in many countries, including Australia, the UK, and the US.[44]

As we saw earlier in Exhibit 5-3, the racial and ethnic diversity of the US population is increasing at an exponential rate. We're also seeing this same effect in the composition of the workforce. Most of the research on race and ethnicity as they relate to the workplace has looked at hiring decisions, performance evaluations, pay, and workplace discrimination. However, much of that research has focused on the differences in attitudes and outcomes between whites and African Americans.

Individuals in workplaces tend to slightly favor colleagues of their own race in performance evaluations, promotion decisions, and pay raises. Although such effects are small, they are consistent.[45] Members of racial and ethnic minorities report higher levels of discrimination in the workplace.[46] African Americans generally fare worse than whites in employment decisions (a finding that may not apply outside the US). They receive lower ratings in employment interviews, lower job performance ratings, less pay, and fewer promotions.[47] While this does not necessarily prove overt racial discrimination, African Americans are often discriminated against. For instance, one study of low-wage jobs found that African American applicants with no criminal history received fewer job offers than white applicants with criminal records.[48] Not surprisingly, research shows substantial racial differences in attitudes toward affirmative action, with African Americans favoring such programs to a greater degree than whites.[49]

Race
Physical characteristics, such as bone structure, skin, or eye color, that people use to identify themselves

Ethnicity
The social and culture factors—including nationality, regional culture, and ancestry—that define the groups a person belongs to

Some industries differ significantly in terms of racial makeup. For instance, US advertising and media organizations suffer from a lack of racial diversity in their management ranks even though their client base is increasingly ethnically diverse.[50] In contrast, among technology firms in Silicon Valley, Asians are significantly over-represented relative to their percentage of the US population.[51]

Disabilities

According to the US Census Bureau, people with disabilities are the largest minority in the United States. About 12.6 percent of the US population has disabilities.[52]

The year 1990 was a watershed year for persons with disabilities. That was the year the Americans with Disabilities Act (ADA) became law. The ADA prohibits discrimination against an individual who is "regarded as" having a disability and requires employers to make reasonable accommodations so their workplaces are accessible to people with physical or mental disabilities and enable them to effectively perform their jobs. With the law's enactment, individuals with disabilities became a more representative and integral part of the US workforce.

What defines a disability? The US Equal Employment Opportunity Commission (EEOC) classifies a person as *disabled* who has any physical or mental impairment that substantially limits one or more major life activities. Examples would include missing limbs, seizure disorder, Down syndrome, autism, deafness, schizophrenia, alcoholism, diabetes, depression, and chronic back pain.

A survey by the Society for Human Resource Management found that 61 percent of the HR professionals responding said that their organizations now include disabilities in their diversity and inclusion plans. However, only 47 percent said that their organizations actively recruit individuals with disabilities. And 40 percent said that their senior managers demonstrate a strong commitment to do so.[53] Even after thirty years of the ADA, organizations and managers still have fears about employing disabled workers. A survey by the US Department of Labor looked at these unfounded fears.[54] Exhibit 5-5 describes some of those fears as well as the reality; that is, what it's really like. These fears undoubtedly lead to some employers discriminating against the disabled in the hiring process.

Overall, the disabled are highly rated by employers for traits such as dependability and conscientiousness.[55] But not to be overlooked, in some jobs people with disabilities bring talents that actually give them an edge. For instance, ambient noise can be distracting in jobs that require intense concentration. This suggests, all other things equal,

Alicia Kiser
Director of Human Resources ▶

Source: Alicia Kiser

Let's Get REAL

The Scenario:

Katelyn Morris is a manager in a branch office of a large insurance claims company. She has just hired Brian, a new employee who is on the autism spectrum, to help process insurance claims. Brian will be starting his new position at the branch office in two weeks. Katelyn's other staff members do not have prior experience working with someone with autism or with any other disability.

What should Katelyn do to ensure that Brian has a positive experience joining her branch office staff?

It's very important in this situation that Katelyn help educate her team on what to expect from Brian to set everyone up for success in working together. Katelyn should bring her team together to openly share information about Brian's strengths and areas of opportunities in addition to her expectations around how the team works together. Katelyn also should consider bringing in an expert to speak with the team and answer questions they have about how to best work with Brian.

FEAR: Hiring people with disabilities leads to higher employment costs and lower profit margins

REALITY: Absentee rates for sick time are virtually equal between employees with and without disabilities; workers' disabilities are not a factor in formulas calculating insurance costs for workers' compensation

FEAR: Workers with disabilities lack job skills and experience necessary to perform as well as their abled counterparts

REALITY: Commonplace technologies such as the Internet and voice-recognition software have eliminated many of the obstacles for workers with disabilities; many individuals with disabilities have great problem-solving skills from finding creative ways to perform tasks that others may take for granted

FEAR: Uncertainty over how to take potential disciplinary action with a worker with disabilities

REALITY: A person with a disability for whom workplace accommodations have been provided has the same obligations and rights as far as job performance

FEAR: High costs associated with accommodating disabled employees

REALITY: Most workers with disabilities require no accommodation but for those who do, more than half of the workplace modifications cost $500 or less

Exhibit 5-5
Employers' Fears About Disabled Workers
Sources: Based on R. Braum, "Disabled Workers: Employer Fears Are Groundless," Bloomberg Businessweek, *October 2, 2009; and "Survey of Employer Perspectives on the Employment of People with Disabilities," US Department of Labor/Office of Disability Employment Policy, November 2008.*

that the hearing impaired would have an advantage in doing jobs that require high concentration such as computer programmer or radiologist. Similarly, autistic workers are sought out at companies like JPMorgan Chase, Microsoft, IBM, and SAP for software testing and cybersecurity. One executive at Chase, where more than seventy autistic employees had been hired in the previous three years, commented, "Our autistic employees achieve, on average, 48 percent to 140 percent more work than their typical colleagues. . . . They are highly focused and less distracted by social interactions."[56]

Madison's Cafe employee Dan Patstone figures out change from a gift certificate with a little help from co-owner Nicole Grant McCoomb during lunch hour. Their sign reads, "Madison's Cafe, where all people matter." The eatery hires people with special needs.
Source: Deb Cram/Portsmouth Herald/AP Images

Religion

Title VII of the Civil Rights Act prohibits discrimination on the basis of religion. Today, the greatest religious diversity issue in the United States arguably revolves around Islam, especially after 9/11.[57]

Islam is one of the world's most popular religions, and it is the majority religion in many countries. In the United States, Muslims are a minority group, but growing. There are nearly 3 million Muslims in the United States, and the number is predicted to double by 2030.[58] At that point, there will be as many Muslims in the US as there are Jews and Episcopalians.[59] Despite these numbers, there is evidence that people are discriminated against for their Islamic faith in the workplace. For instance, nearly 4 in 10 US adults admit they harbor negative feelings or prejudices toward US Muslims.[60] Part of this prejudice may be explained by unique accommodations that some Muslims seek on the job. The top three are: (1) time to perform Friday prayers; (2) flexibility in dress code to cover the hair or grow a beard; and (3) time and space to perform daily prayers.[61] Since 2002, Muslims have made up a disproportionate amount of the EEOC's religious-based discrimination charges, hovering around 20 percent.[62]

Of course, there are religious challenges for employers beyond adapting to Muslim employees. Many conservative Jews, for instance, believe they should not work on Saturdays; and some Christians do not want to work on Sundays. Drug chains like CVS and Walgreens have had to deal with pharmacists who refused to give out certain kinds of contraceptives on the basis of their religious beliefs.[63]

LGBT: Sexual Orientation and Gender Identity

The acronym LGBT—for lesbian, gay, bisexual, and transgender people—relates to the diversity of sexual orientation and gender identity. Approximately 4.1 percent of American adults identify themselves as LGBT. And among Americans born between 1980 and 1998, the number is 7.3 percent.[64] It's estimated that there are 5.4 million LGBT employees in the US private sector.[65]

The status of LGBTs in the workplace has been in flux. Until 2015, US federal law did not prohibit discrimination against employees on the basis of sexual orientation, although many states and municipalities did. In two separate US Supreme Court cases, the justices held that transgendered (gender identity) and lesbian, bisexual, and gay (sexual orientation) individuals were protected under Title VII of the Civil Rights Act's prohibition against sexual discrimination.[66] In 2017, the Trump administration argued that Title VII was not intended to provide protections to gay workers. That, however, was overturned in 2018 by a US appeals court. The court said that a worker's sex is necessarily a factor in discrimination based on sexual orientation.[67] In Europe, the Employment Equality Directive requires all European Union member states to introduce legislation making it unlawful to discriminate on grounds of sexual orientation.[68]

Now let's look at the research. One study found more than 40 percent of gay and lesbian employees indicated they had been unfairly treated, denied a promotion, or pushed to quit their job because of their sexual orientation.[69] Another study found 19 percent of lesbian, gay, and bi employees had experienced verbal bullying on the job because of their sexual orientation.[70] And more than one-third of LGBT workers felt they had to lie about their personal lives while at work, while about the same percentage expressed that they felt exhaustion from spending time and energy hiding their gender identity.[71]

According to a report from the Human Rights Campaign Foundation, 91 percent of the largest corporations in the United States now prohibit employment discrimination based on sexual orientation, and 61 percent prohibit bias based on gender identity.[72] An increasing number of large companies are implementing policies and practices to protect the rights of LGBT employees in the workplace. For instance, Ernst & Young and S. C. Johnson & Sons, Inc., among others, provide training to managers on ways to prevent sexual orientation discrimination.

CHALLENGES in managing diversity

L05.4 Despite the benefits that we know workforce diversity brings to organizations, managers still face challenges in creating accommodating and safe work environments for diverse employees. In this section, we're going to look at three of those challenges: personal bias, the glass ceiling, and pay inequity.

Personal Bias

Working mothers. Professional athletes. Blondes. Conservatives. Liberals. Immigrants. What impressions come to mind when you read these words? Based on your background and experiences, you probably have pretty specific ideas and things you would say, maybe even to the point of characteristics you think that all professional athletes or all immigrants share. Each of us has biases—often hidden from others.[73] Employees can and do bring such generalizations about various groups of people with them into the workplace. These ideas can lead to prejudice, discrimination, and stereotypes. And research is pointing to a troubling fact: Eliminating bias is a lot more difficult than previously thought.[74]

bias
A tendency or preference toward a particular perspective or ideology

Bias is a tendency or preference toward a particular perspective or ideology. It's generally seen as a "one-sided" perspective. Our personal biases cause us to have preconceived opinions about people or things. Such preconceived opinions can create all kinds of inaccurate judgments and attitudes. Let's take a look at how our personal biases affect the way we view and respond to diversity.

One outcome of our personal biases can be **prejudice**, a preconceived belief, opinion, or judgment toward a person or a group of people. Our prejudice can be based on all the types of diversity we discussed: race, gender, ethnicity, age, disability, religion, sexual orientation, or even other personal characteristics.

A major factor in prejudice is **stereotyping**, which is judging a person on the basis of one's perception of a group to which he or she belongs. For instance, "married persons are more stable employees than single persons" is an example of stereotyping. While some stereotypes are accurate, they are often wrong and distort our judgment.

Both prejudice and stereotyping can lead to someone treating others who are members of a particular group unequally. That's what we call **discrimination**, which is when people act out their prejudicial attitudes toward people who are the targets of their prejudice. You'll find in Exhibit 5-6 definitions and examples of different types of discrimination. Many of these actions are prohibited by law, so you won't find them discussed in employee handbooks or organizational policy statements. However, you can still see these actions in workplaces. As discrimination has increasingly come under both legal scrutiny and social disapproval, most overt forms have faded, which may have resulted in an increase in more covert forms like incivility or exclusion.

Discrimination, whether intentional or not, can lead to serious negative consequences for employers. But it's not just the potential financial consequences

prejudice
A preconceived belief, opinion, or judgment toward a person or a group of people

stereotyping
Judging a person based on a perception of a group to which that person belongs

discrimination
When someone acts out their prejudicial attitudes toward people who are the targets of their prejudice

Type of Discrimination	Definition	Examples from Organizations
Discriminatory policies or practices	Actions taken by representatives of the organization that deny equal opportunity to perform or unequal rewards for performance	Older workers may be targeted for layoffs because they are highly paid and have lucrative benefits.
Sexual harassment	Unwanted sexual advances and other verbal or physical conduct of a sexual nature that create a hostile or offensive work environment	Salespeople at one company went on company-paid visits to strip clubs and fostered pervasive sexual rumors.
Intimidation	Overt threats or bullying directed at members of specific groups of employees	African American employees at some companies have found nooses hanging over their workstations.
Mockery and insults	Jokes or negative stereotypes; sometimes the result of jokes taken too far	Arab Americans have been asked at work whether they were members of terrorist organizations.
Exclusion	Exclusion of certain people from job opportunities, social events, discussions, or informal mentoring; can occur unintentionally	Many women in finance claim they are assigned to marginal job roles or are given light workloads that don't lead to promotion.
Incivility	Disrespectful treatment, including behaving in an aggressive manner, interrupting the person, or ignoring his or her opinions	Female team members are frequently cut off in meetings.

Exhibit 5-6
Forms of Discrimination

fyi

- Resumes with white-sounding names received 50 percent more calls for interviews than identical resumes with black-sounding names.
- Seventy-nine percent of applicants with a man's name are considered worthy of hiring compared to only 49 percent of women, even though the men and women had identical resumes.[75]

Source: S. Robbins and T. Judge, *Organizational Behavior*, 18th ed. (New York: Pearson, 2019), p. 49.

organizations face for discriminatory actions. It's the reduced employee productivity, negative and disruptive interpersonal conflicts, increased employee turnover, and overall negative climate that should be of concern to managers.

Glass Ceiling

Fact: In the US, women have gained more college degrees than men every single year for more than three decades.[76] And like their male counterparts, women have entered the business world with an eye toward moving up the corporate ladder. Yet the number of women who make it to the top levels of the companies they work for is noticeably low. For instance, in 2018, women held just 4.8 percent of Fortune 500 CEO roles.[77] Importantly, the evidence clearly indicates women's performance on the job and in managerial positions is equally as effective as men.[78] If women can handle senior management jobs as well as men, is something else going on? A strong case can be made that the something else is a glass ceiling.

A **glass ceiling** is a metaphor used to describe an invisible barrier that limits the level to which a woman or another member of a demographic minority can advance within the hierarchy of an organization. The idea of a *ceiling* means something is blocking upward movement, and the idea of *glass* is that whatever's blocking the way isn't immediately apparent. While the term is typically used to address limits that women face, gay men and African Americans also report similar barriers in their careers.[79]

Research on the glass ceiling has looked at identifying the organizational practices and interpersonal biases that have specifically blocked women's advancement. Findings from those studies have offered a number of potential factors: failure to build networks, lack of effective mentoring, sex stereotyping, associating masculine traits with leader effectiveness, and placing home life and family above career.[80]

Whatever is believed to be the reason, decision makers in organizations—particularly senior executives and boards of directors—need to shatter the glass ceiling. And their motivation shouldn't be merely because "it's the right thing to do." It makes good business sense. According to Credit Suisse Research, companies with 50 percent women in senior operating roles show a 19 percent higher return on equity on average. And a study by a major consulting firm found that companies with gender diversity on their executive teams were 21 percent more likely to have above average profitability.[82]

Pay Inequities

No contemporary discussion of diversity would be complete without addressing the issue of pay inequity between men and women. The topic gets a lot of attention.[83] Is it a fact or is it a myth? And if it's true, is it due to discrimination or something else?

First, US law explicitly makes pay inequality illegal. The Equal Pay Act of 1963 made it a legal federal requirement that pay scales for identical work be the same regardless of whether the employee doing the job is male or female. Nevertheless, almost all studies show a disparity between men and women doing the same job.

Going back to 1980, the research showed that women made only 64 percent of what men earned in comparable jobs. By 2017, that gap had closed to 82 percent.[84] For young women, the gap had narrowed even more over time. In 1980, women ages 25 to 34 earned 33 cents less than their male counterparts, compared with 11 cents in 2017.[85] Analysis as to why this gap exists has focused on the 82 percent.

There has been no shortage of analysis trying to explain this gap. Most of the attention has narrowed in on differences in educational attainment, career choices, work experience, family caregiving responsibilities, and preference for flexibility.[86] Closer examination, however, has minimized education and experience as culprits. Two factors seem to explain most of the difference: the kind of job and women's desire for flexibility.[87] One study attributed 54 percent of the gender wage gap to different jobs in different industries. Yet, still controlling for type of job, education, and experience,

glass ceiling
The invisible barrier that limits the level to which women and minorities can advance within an organization

There are fewer women among CEOs of Fortune 500 companies than there are men CEOs named James.[81]

researchers found that 33 percent of the pay gap remained "unexplained."[88] While flexibility is difficult to measure, studies show women prefer jobs that offer benefits that increase flexibility—like telecommuting, flex-hours, and sabbaticals.[89] This flexibility is likely to come with a pay penalty.

When all is said and done, even when factoring in career and industry choices and the desire for flexibility, there still remains a 3 to 5 percent gap between the pay of men and women. That can probably be attributed to discrimination.

The challenge of eliminating this gap is seen in the experience at Salesforce, a tech company with 30,000 employees.[90] The company's CEO, Marc Benioff, prides himself on the company being selected by Fortune as the number one best place to work among big companies and his firm's commitment to pay equality. He was shocked, therefore, when his head of human resources told him they had a pay-gap problem. He didn't believe it but agreed to an audit. The audit found that, largely as a result of Salesforce having bought more than a dozen companies in the previous year, inequalities had seeped in. Corrections were immediately made, and more than 10 percent of the women at the company got pay increases. The lesson Benioff learned: In spite of a strong commitment to pay equality, it's a never-ending process. Salesforce now reviews its gender pay issue on an ongoing basis.

Salesforce founder and CEO Marc Benioff is committed to pay equality. After an audit revealed a pay-gap problem at the company, 10 percent of the women at the company got pay increases, and the firm continues to review this issue.
Source: Karl Mondon/Bay Area News Group/ TNS/Newscom

The good news about the goal of gender pay equity is that it's improving. But it still has a way to go. Additionally, as seen by the Salesforce example, success requires both an organization's top management commitment and ongoing evaluations.

WORKPLACE diversity initiatives

LO5.5 Marriott International takes diversity seriously. A company spokesperson said that "we leverage our core values to embed diversity and inclusion so deeply that it is integral to how we do business globally."[91] Arne Sorenson, the company's president and CEO, is a visible force and advocate for diversity both in the company and externally. For instance, he publicly spoke against Indiana's anti-LGBT Religious Freedom Restoration Act, saying: "This is just plain wrong . . . and we will not stand for it ... the notion that you can tell businesses that somehow they are free to discriminate is not right."[92] The company also has mandatory diversity training every month and a number of employee resource groups that provide input and advice. Their diversity management efforts have earned the company the number two spot on the Top 50 Companies for Diversity list for 2018.

As the Marriott example shows, some businesses *are* effectively managing diversity. In this section, we look at various workplace diversity initiatives.

Top Management Commitment to Diversity

As noted with our previous example at Salesforce, top management commitment is an important—if not *the most* important—factor in achieving a diverse workforce. It all starts at the top. If management isn't "all in," the goal is likely to receive only lip service. But when top management makes it a priority and designs reward systems to reflect it, employees throughout the organization will take notice.

Top management needs to make sure that diversity and inclusion are part of the organization's purpose, goals, and strategies. Diversity needs to be integrated into every aspect of the business—from the workforce, customers, and suppliers to products, services, and the communities served. Policies and procedures must be in place to ensure that grievances and concerns are addressed immediately. Finally, the organizational culture needs to be one where diversity and inclusion are valued, including ensuring individual performance is measured and rewarded on diversity accomplishments.

Learning from FAILURE
Denny's Answer to Its Diversity Problem

It came to a head with a single incident. In April 1993, six black Secret Service agents assigned to Bill Clinton went into a Denny's restaurant in Annapolis, Maryland. They waited nearly an hour for breakfast. Meanwhile, as they were ignored, a group of white colleagues sitting at a nearby table were warmly received, had their orders quickly taken, and were enjoying seconds. The black agents went public with their experience in a lawsuit. The reaction was devastating for Denny's reputation. And unfortunately, it was not a unique incident. This would become the third discrimination suit against the company in a year. Clearly, Denny restaurants were hostile to minorities. However, this event in Annapolis would be the tipping point. Denny's culture had to change. And it did.

There was a major shake-up among the company's top executives. New people were brought in, and within three years the number of minorities in key management positions went from zero to 11 percent. In the same time period, the number of African American franchisees went from one to sixty-five. Additionally, numerous policies and practices changed. The company created a team to oversee its diversity programs. All employees were required to attend workshops on racial sensitivity; diversity was made a performance criterion for all restaurant and regional managers; and random checks were made at restaurants to make sure all customers and employees were being treated properly.

Denny's provides proof that organizational cultures can learn and change. Within seven years of the Annapolis episode, Denny's was ranked among the top, if not *the* top, companies in America for minorities.[93]

Mentoring

One of the consequences of having few women and minorities in top corporate leadership positions is that lower-level women and minority employees lack someone to turn to for support or advice. That's where a mentoring program can be beneficial. **Mentoring** is a process whereby an experienced (typically senior) organizational member (a mentor) provides advice and guidance to a less-experienced member (a protégé). Mentors usually provide two unique forms of mentoring functions: career development and social support.[94] (see Exhibit 5-7).

mentoring
A process whereby an experienced (typically senior) organizational member (a mentor) provides advice and guidance to a less-experienced member (a protégé)

Exhibit 5-7
Functions of a Mentor

Having a mentor makes you more likely to be promoted and increases the quality of your network.[95]

Career Development Functions
- Lobbies to get the protégé challenging and visible assignments
- Coaches the protégé to help develop his or her skills and achieve work objectives
- Provides exposure to influential individuals within the organization
- Advises the protégé on the organization's politics
- Protects the protégé from possible risks to his or her reputation
- Sponsors the protégé by nominating him or her for potential advances or promotions
- Acts as a sounding board for ideas the protégé might be hesitant to share with a direct supervisor

Social Support Functions
- Counsels the protégé to bolster his or her self-confidence
- Shares personal experiences with the protégé
- Provides friendship and acceptance
- Acts as a role model

A good mentoring program should be aimed at all employees with high potential to move up the organization's career ladder. But in terms of improving diversity, mentors who are women or minorities are often best equipped to offer advice to others like themselves. And protégés are more likely to relate to someone who they see as similar to themselves; mentors often see in their protégés the challenges they once faced earlier in their careers.

Diversity Training

It's not an exaggeration to state that American organizations spend billions of dollars a year on diversity training.[96] That's a lot of money and begs three questions: What is this training composed of? Is the training effective? And if it does work, what conditions favor this success?

Diversity training ideally should focus on knowledge, attitudes, and behavior. Programs typically include a review of diversity issues and the value of diversity, followed by exercises to help individuals become aware of their own cultural values and unconscious biases, to experience what it feels like to be discriminated against, and to practice appropriate responses in interactions with diverse groups of people. Of course, diversity programs vary widely. There is no one-size-fits-all "package" that guarantees success.

What *does* lead to success? A comprehensive integration of some 40 years of research on diversity training provides some answers.[97] Diversity training has been found to have a positive effect on knowledge, attitudes, and actions, but in different ways. After training, people remember the new knowledge; but their beliefs and behaviors tend to revert back, over time, to how they were before the training. That said, the change from training is more likely to last if it's reinforced by other diversity-related initiatives such as top-management commitment, diverse hiring goals, and a formal mentoring program. Additional research suggests that diversity training is likely to *fail* when it's mandatory rather than voluntary, when it's justified on legal grounds, and when it's provided specifically to managers as opposed to all employees.[98] Unfortunately, about 75 percent of organizations with diversity-training programs fall into at least one of these categories.[99]

Members of the Asian Pacific ERG at the US Agency for International Development competed in the DC Dragon Boat Festival in 2018 and took home gold in the 250-meter race.
Source: Barney Low/Alamy Stock Photo

Employee Resource Groups

In the 1960s, Xerox Corporation's Rochester, New York, headquarters launched a Black Caucus Group. This was an early example of an Employee Resource Group (ERG). Approximately 90 percent of Fortune 500 companies now have ERGs, and they've become an important structural device for supporting diversity.[100] For instance, the financial services and insurance giant Prudential has ERGs for military veterans, LGBT people, blacks, Hispanics, and Asian/Pacific Islanders.[101] Probably the most popular ERGs continue to be organized for women and African Americans.

An **employee resource group** (also frequently called an *affinity group*) is a voluntary, employee-led subgroup within an organization that shares distinctive qualities, interests, or goals. Although membership is totally voluntary, and initiated by employees, ERGs are typically sponsored by a senior executive who is connected to the group's issue and who ensures that the ERG's goals and concerns are heard by senior-level decision makers.

ERGs have multiple purposes. They are a sounding board for common concerns, but they also help attract and recruit diverse talent, increase employee engagement, and even run mentorship programs. The African American ERG at AT&T, as an example, has over 12,000 members and is credited with the company having an 85.6 percent black retention rate.[102]

An interesting finding about ERGs is that not all employees find the concept appealing. Interest appears to be related to age.[103] A recent study found that almost half of workers under the age of 34 were interested in ERGs. This may be due to their general strong group orientation. In contrast, less than 20 percent of workers in the 55–64 age bracket showed similar interest.

employee resource group (ERG)
A voluntary, employee-led subgroup within an organization that shares distinctive qualities, interests, or goals

Some Final Thoughts and Questions

We conclude this chapter by offering questions about workforce diversity that have no concrete answers. We propose them to reflect on the debate that continues around diversity and to challenge your critical thinking.

HAS IDENTITY POLITICS LED TO AN OBSESSION WITH CELEBRATING DIFFERENCES? Some critics have argued that we've lost the concern for unity of purpose and celebrating our common strengths. Have we become so concerned with promoting differences—race, color, gender, sexual orientation—that we have lost sight of creating and binding an organization's culture around common values? Do these subcultures emphasize placating special groups' unique needs at the expense of a unifying bond? Don't successful organizations need to unify people around common goals rather than unique differences?

DO LONG-ESTABLISHED PRACTICES UNDERMINE DIVERSITY? There are popular practices that would appear to work against diversity. Two examples would be employee referrals and corporate team-building exercises.

One of the most popular and effective recruiting sources is recommendations by current employees. Organizations have come to increasingly rely on referrals because the evidence indicates that good workers tend to know others like themselves. And employees don't tend to recommend individuals who would reflect badly on themselves. But this practice reinforces the past. If an organization is made up predominantly of white males, aren't referrals likely to be other white males?

Another practice that can undermine diversity is corporate team-building activities. These have become increasingly popular as organizations have come to rely on teams to get work done. These activities are designed to increase trust and openness among team members, improve coordination efforts, and increase team performance. However, doesn't team-building celebrate common goals and values rather than differences?

DOES SUPPORTING DIVERSITY CONFLICT WITH REWARDING MERIT? If you believe that hiring, development, and compensation decisions in organizations should be based on merit, is using diversity as a criterion in these decisions at odds with merit? We like to believe that corporate policies are fair and favor no special group. Much of the logic behind diversity is to correct a long history of decisions that led to unfair results—such as a scarcity of women and minorities in the upper echelons of organizations. But are efforts to increase diversity in organizations a threat to rewarding merit?

Chapter 5 · PREPARING FOR: Exams/Quizzes

CHAPTER SUMMARY by Learning Objectives

DEFINE workplace diversity and explain why managing it is so important.

Workplace diversity is the ways in which people in an organization are different from and similar to one another. Managing workforce diversity is important for three reasons: (1) people management benefits—better use of employee talent, increased quality of team problem-solving efforts, and ability to attract and retain diverse employees; (2) organizational performance benefits—reduced costs, enhanced problem-solving ability, and improved system flexibility; and (3) strategic benefits—increased understanding of a diverse marketplace, potential to improve sales and market share, and competitive advantage.

DESCRIBE the changing makeup of workplaces in the United States and around the world. `LO5.2`

The main changes in the workplace in the United States include the total increase in the population; the changing components of the population, especially in relation to racial/ethnic groups; and an aging population. The most important changes in the global population include the total world population and the aging of that population.

EXPLAIN the different types of diversity found in workplaces. `LO5.3`

The different types of diversity found in workplaces include age (older workers and younger workers), gender (male and female), race and ethnicity (racial and ethnic classifications), disability/abilities (people with a disability that limits major life activities), religion (religious beliefs and religious practices), sexual orientation and gender identity (gay, lesbian, bisexual, and transgender), and other (for instance, socioeconomic background, team members from different functional areas, physical attractiveness, obesity, job seniority, and so forth).

DISCUSS the challenges managers face in managing diversity. `LO5.4`

The three main challenges managers face are personal bias, the glass ceiling, and pay inequity. Bias is a tendency or preference toward a particular perspective or ideology. Our biases can lead to prejudice, which is a preconceived belief, opinion, or judgment toward a person or a group of people; stereotyping, which is judging a person on the basis of one's perception of a group to which he or she belongs; and discrimination, which is when someone acts out prejudicial attitudes toward people who are the targets of that person's prejudice. The glass ceiling refers to the invisible barrier that separates women and minorities from top management positions. Pay inequities refer to unfair pay differences based on gender or race. Gender differences in pay have been found to be based on discrimination, the kind of job, and a desire for flexibility.

DESCRIBE various workplace diversity initiatives. `LO5.5`

Workplace diversity management initiatives include top-management commitment to diversity; mentoring, which is a process whereby an experienced organizational member provides advice and guidance to a less-experienced member; diversity training; and employee resource groups, which are groups made up of employees connected by some common dimension of diversity.

REVIEW AND DISCUSSION QUESTIONS

5-1. Why is it important for an organization to have a clear definition of diversity?

5-2. Distinguish between surface-level diversity and deep-level diversity. Why is it important to understand the difference between the two?

5-3. What are the major trends in the changing populations of the United States and the world?

5-4. Distinguish between race and ethnicity.

5-5. What legal protection do employees have against discrimination based on sexual orientation?

5-6. Explain the relationship among bias, prejudice, stereotyping, and discrimination.

5-7. What other practices (besides employee referrals and corporate team building) might hurt a company's diversity efforts?

5-8. Why do you think the glass ceiling has proven to be a barrier to women and minorities?

PREPARING FOR: My Career

ETHICS DILEMMA

People with disabilities. A group about whom much has been written and discussed, especially when it comes to workplaces. The Americans with Disabilities Act prohibits employment discrimination against qualified individuals with disabilities. Yet many jobs are difficult and expensive to refit for people with disabilities. For instance, adding a lift and hand controls to a school bus so as to allow a wheelchair-bound person to be a driver can add upwards of $15,000 to the cost of a bus.

5-11. Do school districts have an ethical responsibility to refit buses for disabled applicants? Explain.

5-12. What ethical issues might arise in workplaces with disabled workers? As a manager, how might you handle such issues?

SKILLS EXERCISE Developing Your Valuing Diversity Skill

About the Skill
Understanding and managing people who are similar to us can be challenging—but understanding and managing people who are dissimilar from us and from each other can be even tougher.[104] The diversity issues a manager might face are many. They may include issues such as communicating with employees whose familiarity with the language may be limited; creating career-development programs that fit the skills, needs, and values of a particular group; helping a diverse team cope with a conflict over goals or work assignments; or learning which rewards are valued by different groups.

Steps in Practicing the Skill
- *Fully accept diversity.* Successfully valuing diversity starts with each individual accepting the principle of diversity. Accept the value of diversity for its own sake—not simply because it's the right thing to do. And it's important that you reflect your acceptance in all you say and do.

- *Recruit broadly.* When you have job openings, work to get a diverse applicant pool. Although referrals from current employees can be a good source of applicants, that source tends to produce candidates similar to the present workforce.

- *Select fairly.* Make sure the selection process doesn't discriminate. One suggestion is to use job-specific tests rather than general aptitude or knowledge tests. Such tests measure specific skills, not subjective characteristics.

- *Provide orientation and training for diverse employees.* Making the transition from outsider to insider can be particularly difficult for a diverse employee. Provide support either through a group or through a mentoring arrangement.

- *Sensitize nondiverse employees.* Not only do you personally need to accept and value diversity, as a manager you need to encourage all your employees to do so. Many organizations do this through diversity training programs. In addition, employees can also be part of ongoing discussion groups whose members meet monthly to discuss stereotypes and ways of improving diversity relationships. The most important thing a manager can do is show by his or her actions that diversity is valued.

- *Strive to be flexible.* Part of valuing diversity is recognizing that different groups have different needs and values. Be flexible in accommodating employee requests.

- *Seek to motivate individually.* Motivating employees is an important skill for any manager; motivating a diverse workforce has its own special challenges. Managers must strive to be in tune with the background, cultures, and values of employees.

- *Reinforce employee differences.* Encourage individuals to embrace and value diverse views. Create traditions and ceremonies that promote diversity. Celebrate diversity by accentuating its positive aspects. However, also be prepared to deal with the challenges of diversity such as mistrust, miscommunication, lack of cohesiveness, attitudinal differences, and stress.

Practicing the Skill
Read through the following scenario. Write down some notes about how you would handle the situation described. Be sure to refer to the eight behaviors described for valuing diversity.

Scenario
You have recently taken over the management of a team assigned to implement a new information technology system at your company. Read through the descriptions of

the following employees who are on your team. Consider the steps you can take to ensure that your team successfully works together. What types of employee issues might you face as the team's manager? How can you ensure your team works together successfully and benefits from the diversity of the team? Make some notes of your plans on how you will manage your new team.

- *Lester.* Lester is 64 years old, a college graduate, and has been with the company for more than 30 years. His two children are married, and he is a grandparent of three grandchildren. He lives in a condo with his wife, who does volunteer work and is active in their church. Lester is healthy and likes to stay active, both physically and mentally.

- *Sanjyot.* Sanjyot is a 30-year-old who joined the company after she came to the United States from Indonesia ten years ago. She completed high school after moving to the United States and has begun to attend evening classes at a local community college. Sanjyot is a single parent with two children under the age of 8. Sanjyot is hearing impaired, and one of her children suffers from a severe learning disability.

- *Yuri.* Yuri is a recent immigrant from one of the former Soviet republics and is new to the company. He is 42, and his English communication skills are quite limited. He is unmarried and has no children but feels obligated to send much of his paycheck to relatives back in his home country. As a result, he is willing to work extra hours to increase his pay.

- *Beth.* Beth joined the company two years ago when she graduated from college. She is recently married and is very involved in the local community, volunteering with several local nonprofit organizations when she is not at work. She grew up in a nearby community and also has responsibility for caring for her aging parents who have recently developed several health problems.

WORKING TOGETHER **Team Exercise**

One of the best ways to better understand and improve your interactions with people who are different from yourself is to imagine yourself in their shoes. Take a few minutes to write a few sentences that describe challenges that a racial minority or LGBT individual might face in the workplace. Then, in groups of three or four students, take turns sharing the sentences you each wrote and brainstorm what managers and coworkers could do to improve the situation involved with each challenge. If training is needed, what needs to be trained specifically? What else besides training could be done?

My Turn to Be a Manager

- Describe your experiences with people from other backgrounds. What challenges have you faced? What have you learned that will help you in understanding the unique needs and challenges of a diverse workplace?

- Go to DiversityInc.com (www.diversityinc.com) and find the latest list of Top 50 Companies for Diversity. Select three companies from this list. Describe and evaluate what they're doing as far as workplace diversity is concerned.

- Think of times when you may have been treated unfairly because of stereotypical thinking. What stereotypes were being used? How did you respond to the treatment?

- The Job Accommodation Network is a free resource for employers to identify ways to provide work accommodations to allow disabled workers to be productive and hold a wider variety of jobs. Visit www.askjan.org and search the accommodation database to find examples of accommodations for specific disabilities.

- Assume you are designing a mentoring program for an organization. Conduct some research on mentoring programs that currently exist in different organizations and identify characteristics of an effective mentoring program.

- What can you do as a manager to make it clear that there is no conflict between promoting diversity and rewarding merit?

CASE APPLICATION 1 — Gusto: Making a Difference in Gender Diversity

If you were the only female engineer at a start-up in San Francisco, you could work hard and hope more women are hired. Or you could do what Julie Lee did in the spring of 2015. She asked to meet with Edward Kim, Gusto's cofounder and chief technology officer. Kim was "extraordinarily receptive" to Lee's explanation that she loved her work, but struggled being the only woman on an 18-person engineering team.[105] Kim saw solving this problem as an opportunity ... and as a source of competitive advantage.

Gusto developed a plan to attract women engineers. The obvious ingredient of this plan was to get more women engineers to apply for job openings. But Gusto didn't just do the obvious. They changed phrases like "Ninja rock star coder" in some of their job descriptions that were unnecessarily masculine. Gusto was a step ahead of a recent study that found that masculine wording, sexist jokes, and presentation slides of only men were common in recruiting efforts in tech companies.[106]

Gusto also recruited women applicants with an email from Lee inviting them to have an initial talk with her. Lee also wrote a blog post that publicized Gusto's goal of hiring more women engineers. Since 85 percent of jobs are filled through networking and referrals, Lee's involvement was a way to signal to other women that Gusto is a place where women work as engineers.[107] Gusto also made gender diversity a priority in other parts of the company, including hiring on the executive team and beefing up their benefits for working parents.

In six months, Gusto was able to exceed their gender diversity hiring goals. Their work isn't over, however. They still have big strides to make in increasing racial diversity. They don't have Latinos or African Americans on their engineering team. As Kim put it, "The way we make progress is by focusing on one problem and then move on to the next."

DISCUSSION QUESTIONS

5-13. What were the most important steps that Gusto took to increase gender diversity?

5-14. Even though Julie Lee was so helpful to Gusto's gender diversity efforts, what demands does this case illustrate are involved in being the only woman?

5-15. Now that Gusto has hired more women engineers, what should they do to ensure that they don't leave the company?

5-16. What can Gusto do to improve its racial diversity?

CASE APPLICATION 2

Bring in Diversity ... and Then What?

Many colleges have a wide range of diversity among their students. Less advantaged students and affluent students are on the same campus. Different races, ethnicities, gender identities, political preferences, and international backgrounds are all at the same college. But, if you look around many college campuses, you see students sticking with others like themselves. There are themed dorms for certain majors, interests, and demographic backgrounds. Student organizations also tend to include students who are similar to one another.

Colleges devote a lot of effort to increasing diversity on their campuses, but then most students "spend the bulk of their time on one of many homogeneous islands."[108] The benefits of diversity don't happen automatically just because colleges bring diversity to their campuses.

It's true that companies are different from college campuses in many ways. But, just like college campuses, companies can't reap the benefits of diversity just by bringing diversity on board. There is so much that companies need to do *after* they attract diverse talent to come work for them.

Diverse employees want to feel like they belong at a company and have a future there.[109] But women and minorities often aren't well represented in top-level positions in many companies. Women hold about 26.5 percent of executive or senior-level positions in S&P 500 companies while women of color are represented in 5 percent of these top-level positions.[110]

One action companies can take is to ensure that employees can openly talk about diversity. "You can be diverse and hire a lot of people, but you are not inclusive if people don't feel like they can talk about the tough issues like race at work that affect their lives," said Julie Sweet, Accenture North America CEO. Accenture—a global management consulting firm—realized the need for open conversations about race after several police shootings of African Americans in 2016. They held meetings via webcast for all employees followed by in-person discussions in eight US cities. The conversations involved employees of all races and "surfaced far more real talk about race than the typical bias training or sensitivity program."

Many companies prioritize both diversity and inclusion. They want to make sure that everyone in the company—regardless of race, gender, personality, or any other source of difference—feel like they are included in the company. However, when companies seem to focus on certain employees, other employees can feel excluded. Research shows that the more that inclusion efforts are framed as benefiting all employees, the less resistance is found to such efforts.[111]

Accenture implemented an inclusion initiative framed for all employees in May 2017.[112] It began as an internal video entitled "Inclusion Starts with I" that was shown to its "next generation leaders" in a leadership development program. The video shows different employees holding up signs with examples of how bias—and a lack of inclusion—can occur in unexpected ways. These employees included a wide variety of employees, from childless employees, transgender individuals, African American women, disabled employees, and men with children. The video explains that it takes just one person to make a difference in creating inclusion at work. Those who watched the video tended to have an emotional response. Many discussions about inclusion ensued throughout the company as a result of the video. Ultimately, the video was shared more broadly within and outside of company walls.

DISCUSSION QUESTIONS

5-17. What can colleges do so that students spend more of their time interacting with students who are different from themselves?

5-18. What are some of the ways that companies can increase the chances that diverse employees want to keep working for them?

5-19. Companies offer "diversity and inclusion" programs and hire "chief diversity and inclusion officers." Does it make sense to include "diversity" and "inclusion" in the same phrase? Is inclusion an approach to diversity or is it something different?

5-20. Does framing inclusion efforts as "involving everyone" make a diverse workplace better? Or does including everyone dilute efforts to attract and retain diverse employees? Support your position.

ENDNOTES

1. A. Al-Muslim, "GM Names New Finance Chief," *Wall Street Journal*, June 14, 2018, p. B3.
2. B. Davis, "MGM Resorts International Pioneer of Workplace Diversity," *Las Vegas Business Press*, April 4, 2017, p. 1.
3. S. Bharadwaj Badal, "How Hiring a Gender-Diverse Workforce Can Improve a Company's Bottom Line," January 20, 2014, gallup.com/businessjournal.
4. Q. Roberson, A. M. Ryan, and B. R. Ragins, "The Evolution and Future of Diversity Work," *Journal of Applied Psychology* (March 2017): pp. 483–99.
5. C. Zillman, "Target to Pay $2.8 Million for Discriminatory Hiring Tests," *Fortune*, August 24, 2015, http://fortune.com/2015/08/24/target-discriminatory-hiring/.
6. E. Steel, "Fox Settles Discrimination Lawsuits for Roughly $10 Million," *New York Times*, May 15, 2018, https://www.nytimes.com/2018/05/15/business/media/fox-news-discrimination-lawsuits.html.
7. A. Elejalde-Ruiz, "UPS Agrees to $2 Million Settlement in Disability Discrimination Lawsuit," *Chicago Tribune*, August 8, 2017, https://www.chicagotribune.com/business/

ct-ups-eeoc-disability-discrimination-settlement-0809-biz-20170808-story.html.

8. P. Brinkmann and K. Arnold, "Darden to Pay $2.85 Million to Settle 'Old White Guys' Discrimination Suit," *Orlando Sentinel*, May 3, 2018, https://www.orlandosentinel.com/business/brinkmann-on-business/os-bz-darden-eeoc-settlement-20180503-story.html.

9. EEOC press release; January 25, 2018.

10. V. Hunt, S. Prince, S. Dixon-Fyle, and L. Yee, "Delivering Through Diversity," McKinsey & Company, January 2018, https://www.mckinsey.com/business-functions/organization/our-insights/delivering-through-diversity.

11. D. Gilgoff, "Investing in Diversity," *U.S. News & World Report*, November 2009, pp. 72–74.

12. E. B. King, J. F. Dawson, M. A. West, V. I. Gilrane, C. I. Peddie, and L. Bastin, "Why Organizational and Community Diversity Matter: Representativeness and the Emergence of Incivility and Organizational Performance," *Academy of Management Journal* (December 2011): pp. 1103–1118.

13. See, for instance, A. Joshi, H. Liao, and S. E. Jackson, "Cross-Level Effects of Workplace Diversity on Sales Performance and Pay," *Academy of Management Journal* (June 2006): pp. 459–81; and T. Kochan et al., "The Effects of Diversity on Business Performance: Report of the Diversity Research Network," *Human Resource Management* (Spring 2003): pp. 3–21.

14. P. Morse, "Six Facts About the Hispanic Market That May Surprise You," Forbes Agency Council, *Forbes*, January 9, 2018, https://www.forbes.com/sites/forbesagencycouncil/2018/01/09/six-facts-about-the-hispanic-market-that-may-surprise-you/#5d627abe5f30.

15. Ernst & Young, "The New Global Mindset: Driving Innovation Through Diversity," EYGM Limited, 2010, p. 1.

16. Ernst & Young, "New Global Mindset," p. 1.

17. "Babies Born in the US By Race," US Census Bureau, March 24, 2018, census.gov.

18. "Hispanics in the US Fast Facts," *CNN*, updated March 6, 2019, https://www.cnn.com/2013/09/20/us/hispanics-in-the-u-s-/index.html.

19. Based on D. A. Harrison, K. H. Price, and M. P. Bell, "Beyond Relational Demography: Time and the Effects of Surface- and Deep-Level Diversity on Work Group Cohesion," *Academy of Management Journal* (February 1998): pp. 96–107; D. C. Lau and J. K. Murnighan, "Demographic Diversity and Faultlines: The Compositional Dynamics of Organizational Groups," *Academy of Management Review* (April 1998): pp. 325–340; M-E. Roberge, E. Petrov, and W.-R. Huang, "Students' Perceptions of Their Attitudes and Behaviors Toward Different Cultures/Ethnicities Before and After a Diversity Training Program," *Journal of Business Diversity* (August 2014): pp. 80–90; and J. S. Lublin, "How to Cope When Undermined at Work," *Wall Street Journal*, August 23, 2018.

20. Bloomberg, "How U.S. Demographics Are Changing: America Got Less White, Older, and More Urban Last Year," *Fortune*, June 21, 2018, http://fortune.com/2018/06/21/america-older-less-white-more-diverse-census-bureau/; and C. C. Miller, "A Baby Bust, Rooted in Economic Insecurity," *New York Times*, July 6, 2018, p. B1.

21. "The Changing Demographic Profile of the United States," Congressional Research Service, March 31, 2011, p. 16.

22. US Bureau of Labor Statistics, "Labor Force Projections to 2024: The Labor Force Is Growing, But Slowly," *Monthly Labor Review* online, US Department of Labor, December 2015, https://www.bls.gov/opub/mlr/2015/article/labor-force-projections-to-2024.htm.

23. US Bureau of Labor Statistics, "Labor Characteristics of Foreign-Born Workers Summary," news release no. USDL-18-0786, US Department of Labor, May 17, 2018, https://www.bls.gov/news.release/forbrn.nr0.htm/Labor-Force-Characteristics-of-Foreign-Born-Workers-Summary.

24. Y. Hori, J. P. Lehmann, T. Ma Kam Wah, and V. Wang, "Facing Up to the Demographic Dilemma," *Strategy + Business* online, Spring 2010.

25. United Nations Department of Economic and Social Affairs, *World Population Prospects: 2017 Revision*, publication no. ESA/P/WP/248, https://esa.un.org/unpd/wpp/publications/files/wpp2017_keyfindings.pdf.

26. This section is based on National Institutes of Health, "World's Older Population Grows Dramatically," March 28, 2016, https://www.nih.gov/news-events/news-releases/worlds-older-population-grows-dramatically.

27. Equal Employment Opportunity Commission, "Charge Statistics FY 1997 Through FY 2015," accessed February 20, 2019, www.eeoc.gov.

28. R. Eisenberg, "How Age-Smart Employers See the Value of Older Workers," January 18, 2018, nextavenue.org.

29. T. W. H. Ng and D. C. Feldman, "Re-Examining the Relationship Between Age and Voluntary Turnover," *Journal of Vocational Behavior* (December 2009): pp. 283–94.

30. T. W. H. Ng and D. C. Feldman, "The Relationship of Age to Ten Dimensions of Job Performance," *Journal of Applied Psychology* (March 2008): pp. 392–423.

31. Ibid., and A. Tergesen, "Why Everything You Know About Aging Is Probably Wrong," *Wall Street Journal*, December 1, 2014, p. B1.

32. H. Ruthven, "Barclays Shifts Perception by Rolling Out Apprenticeship Scheme for Those Over 50," *Real Business*, February 9, 2015, https://realbusiness.co.uk/barclays-shifts-perception-by-rolling-out-apprenticeship-scheme-for-those-over-50/.

33. J. Stein, "The Me Me Me Generation," *Time*, May 20, 2013, pp. 46–51.

34. P. Ketter, "Value Proposition? Oh, Yes!" *T&D*, November 2011, p. 10; and "Most Common Gen Y Job Titles Today," *T&D*, April 2012, p. 23.

35. S. Patel, "The 5 Most Underappreciated Skills of Millennial Workers," November 22, 2016, inc.com; and D. Jones, "Millennial Managers: 7 Skills for the Next Generation of Leaders," July 20, 2017, business.udemy.com.

36. J. Marcus, "Why Men Are the New College Minority," *Atlantic*, August 8, 2017, https://www.theatlantic.com/education/archive/2017/08/why-men-are-the-new-college-minority/536103/.

37. U.S. Bureau of Labor Statistics, "Look at the Future of the U.S. Labor Force to 2060," January 31, 2017.

38. N.M. Carter and C. Silva, "Women in Management: Delusions of Progress," *Harvard Business Review*, March 2010, pp. 19–21.

39. Cited in N. Waller, "How Men and Women See the Workplace Differently," *Wall Street Journal*, September 27, 2016, p. R1.

40. See, for instance, *Time* magazine Person of the Year 2017: "The Silence Breakers," December 18, 2017; P. Mahdavi, "How #Me Too Became a Global Movement," *Foreign Affairs*, March 6, 2018, https://www.foreignaffairs.com/articles/2018-03-06/how-metoo-became-global-movement; and V. Fuhrmans, "What #MeToo Has to Do With the Workplace Gender Gap," *Wall Street Journal*, October 23, 2018, p. R1.

41. L. Ali, "Scandal, Sexism and the Role of Women at Fox News," *Los Angeles Times*, April 6, 2017, https://www.latimes.com/entertainment/tv/la-et-st-bill-oreilly-sexual-harrassment-fox-news-women-20170405-story.html.

42. D. Shafrir, "Tech Companies Prove the Old Boys' Club Is Alive and Well," April 29, 2017, https://nypost.com/2017/04/29/tech-companies-prove-the-old-boys-club-is-alive-and-well/; and E. Chang, *Brotopia: Breaking Up the Boys' Club of Silicon Valley* (New York: Portfolio, 2018).

43. C. Hymowitz, L. I. Alpert, and S. Vranica, "The Workplace After Harvey Weinstein: Harassment Scandals Prompt Raid Changes," *Wall Street Journal*, November 10, 2017, p. B1.

44. L. Turner and A. Suflas, "Global Diversity—One Program Won't Fit All," *HR Magazine*, May 2014, pp. 59–61.

45. G. N. Powell and D. A. Butterfield, "Exploring the Influence of Decision Makers' Race and Gender on Actual Promotions to Top Management," *Personnel Psychology* (June 2002): pp. 397–428.

46. D. R. Avery, P. F. McKay, and D. C. Wilson, "What Are the Odds? How Demographic Similarities Affects the Prevalence of Perceived Employment Discrimination," *Journal of Applied Psychology* (March 2008): pp. 235–49.

47. P. Bobko and P. L. Roth, "Reviewing, Categorizing, and Analyzing the Literature on Black-White Mean Differences for Predictors of Job Performance: Verifying Some Perceptions and Updating/Correcting Others," *Personnel Psychology* (Spring 2013): pp. 91–126.

48. S. Mullainathan, "The Measuring Sticks of Racial Bias," *New York Times*, January 4, 2015, New York edition, p. 6.

49. T. Rosentiel, "Public Backs Affirmative Action, but Not Minority Preferences," June 2, 2009, Pew Research Center, http://www.pewresearch.org/2009/06/02/public-backs-affirmative-action-but-not-minority-preferences/.

50. T. Vega, "With Diversity Still Lacking, Industry Focuses on Retention," *New York Times*, September 4, 2012, New York edition, p. B3.

51. J. Desjardins, "Silicon Valley's Diversity By the Numbers," Business Insider, August 15, 2017, https://www.businessinsider.com/infographic-tech-diversity-companies-compared-2017-8.

52. Bureau of Labor Statistics, "Persons with a Disability: Labor Force Characteristics," US Department of Labor, June 21, 2018.

53. D. Meinert, "Opening Doors," *HR Magazine*, June 2012, pp. 55–57.

54. US Department of Labor, "Survey of Employer Perspectives on the Employment of People with Disabilities," November 2008, www.dol.gov.

55. B. S. Bell and K. J. Klein, "Effects of Disability, Gender, and Job Level on Ratings of Job Applicants," *Rehabilitation Psychology* (August 2001): pp. 229–46; and E. Louvet, "Social Judgment Toward Job Applicants with Disabilities:

56. D. Eng, "Where Autistic Workers Thrive," *Fortune*, July 3, 2018, pp. 38–39.

57. S. Greenhouse, "Muslims Report Rising Discrimination at Work," *New York Times*, September 23, 2010, https://www.nytimes.com/2010/09/24/business/24muslim.html.

58. T. Audi, "A New Mosque Rises in Anchorage," *Wall Street Journal*, August 15, 2014, p. A5.

59. Audi, "A New Mosque Rises."

60. Greenhouse, "Muslims Report Rising Discrimination" [see note 57].

61. S. Khalifa, "Muslims in the Workplace," February 2018, naylornetwork.com.

62. K. Lakhani, "Workplace Discrimination Against Muslims," *On Labor* (blog), February 15, 2017, https://onlabor.org/workplace-discrimination-against-muslims/.

63. A. Barker, "Pharmacists Refusing to Fill Spark National Controversy," *Pharmacy Times*, August 11, 2015, https://www.pharmacytimes.com/contributor/alex-barker-pharmd/2015/08/pharmacists-refusing-to-fill-spark-national-controversy.

64. S. Allen, "Just How Many LGBT Americans Are There?," *Daily Beast*, January 14, 2017, https://www.thedailybeast.com/just-how-many-lgbt-americans-are-there.

65. Movement Advancement Project, Human Rights Campaign, and Center for American Progress, "A Broken Bargain," June 4, 2013, https://www.americanprogress.org/issues/lgbt/reports/2013/06/04/65133/a-broken-bargain/.

66. US Equal Employment Opportunity Commission, "EEOC and Enforcement Protections for LGBT Workers," February 21, 2016, eeoc.gov.

67. D. Wiessner, "U.S. Appeals Court Says Title VII Covers Discrimination Based on Sexual Orientation," Reuters, February 26, 2018, https://www.reuters.com/article/us-usa-lgbt/u-s-appeals-court-says-title-vii-covers-discrimination-based-on-sexual-orientation-idUSKCN1GA201.

68. F. Colgan, T. Wright, C. Creegan, and A. McKearney, "Equality and Diversity in the Public Services: Moving Forward on Lesbian, Gay, and Bisexual Equality?," *Human Resource Management Journal* (July 2009): pp. 280–301.

69. J. Hempel, "Coming Out in Corporate America," *Bloomberg Businessweek*, December 15, 2003, pp. 64–72.

70. "LGBT Facts and Figures," March 8, 2016, stonewall.org.

71. Human Rights Campaign Foundation, "The Cost of the Closet and the Rewards of Inclusion," May 2014, https://assets2.hrc.org/files/assets/resources/Cost_of_the_Closet_May2014.pdf.

72. Ibid.

73. J. S. Lubin, "Do You Know Your Hidden Work Biases?" *Wall Street Journal*, January 10, 2014, p. B1.

74. T. Henneman, "You, Biased? No. It's Your Brain," *Workforce*, February 2014, p. 28.

75. J. Dewar, "Where Unconscious Bias Creeps into the Recruitment Process," *Lever* (blog), July 26, 2018, https://www.lever.co/blog/where-unconscious-bias-creeps-into-the-recruitment-process.

76. Marcus, "New College Minority" [see note 36].

77. C. C. Miller, "The Number of Female Chief Executives Is Falling," May 23, 2018, https://www.nytimes.com/2018/05/23/upshot/why-the-number-of-female-chief-executives-is-falling.html.

78. P. L. Roth, K. L. Purvis, and P. Bobko, "A Meta-Analysis of Gender Group Differences for Measures of Job Performance in Field Studies," *Journal of Management* (March 2012): pp. 719–39; S. C. Paustian-Underdahl, L. S. Walker, and D. J. Woeher, "Gender and Perceptions of Leadership Effectiveness: A Meta-Analysis of Contextual Moderators," *Journal of Applied Psychology* (November 2014): pp. 1129–45; and E. Zell, Z. Krizan, and S. R. Teeter, "Evaluating Gender Similarities and Differences Using Metasynthesis," *American Psychologist* (January 2015): pp. 10–20.

79. R. L. Brooks, *The Racial Glass Ceiling* (New Haven: Yale University Press, 2017); and C. Glover, "Glass Ceilings Are Hindering Advancement in the Workplace for Gay Men," *NewNowNext*, June 20, 2018, http://www.newnownext. com/glass-ceilings-are-hindering-advancement-in-the-workplace-for-gay-men/06/2018/.

80. A. M. Morrison and M. A. Von Glinow, "Women and Minorities in Management," *American Psychologist* (February 2009): pp. 200–08; J. M. Hoobler, S. J. Wayne, and G. Lemmon, "Bosses' Perceptions of Family-Work Conflict and Women's Promotability: Glass Ceiling Effects," *Academy of Management Journal* (October 2009): pp. 939–57.

81. C. C. Miller, K. Quealy, and M. Sanger-Katz, "The Top Jobs Where Women Are Outnumbered by Men Named John," *New York Times*, April 24, 2018, https://www.nytimes. com/interactive/2018/04/24/upshot/women-and-men-named-john.html.

82. Cited in J. Bickford, "To Eliminate Pay Inequity, We Must Change Corporate Culture," *Medium*, April 10, 2018, https://medium.com/@p4parity/to-eliminate-pay-inequity-we-must-change-corporate-culture-cda5812e8252.

83. See, for instance, K. Dragovich, "Hired Releases Third Annual 'The State of Wage Inequality in the Workplace' Report," *Hired*, April 4, 2018, https://hired.com/blog/highlights/third-annual-wage-inequality-workplace-report/.

84. N. Graf, A. Brown, and E. Patten, "The Narrowing, But Persistent, Gender Gap in Pay," Pew Research Center, April 9, 2018, http://www.pewresearch.org/fact-tank/2018/04/09/gender-pay-gap-facts/.

85. Ibid.

86. Ibid.; and K. Bellstrom, "Don't Believe These 5 Myths About the Gender Pay Gap," *Fortune*, April 10, 2018, http://fortune.com/2018/04/10/gender-pay-gap-myths/.

87. Cited in Bellstrom, "Don't Believe These 5 Myths" [see note 86].

88. Ibid.

89. R. Greszler, "'Pay Gap' Myth Ignores Women's Intentional Job Choices," Heritage Foundation, April 9, 2018, https://www.heritage.org/jobs-and-labor/commentary/pay-gap-myth-ignores-womens-intentional-job-choices.

90. C. Zillman, "Salesforce CEO Marc Benioff: We're Erasing Our Gender Pay Gap—Again," *Fortune*, January 20, 2017, http://fortune.com/2017/01/20/salesforce-marc-benioff-gender-pay-gap-davos/; and interview on CBS "60 Minutes," April 15, 2018.

91. "Top Companies for Diversity: Marriott International," *DiversityInc.*, April 23, 2016, p. 39.

92. Ibid.

93. Based on S. Labaton, "Denny's Restaurants to Pay $54 Million Race Bias Suits," *New York Times*, May 25, 1994, https://www.nytimes.com/1994/05/25/us/denny-s-restaurants-to-pay-54-million-in-race-bias-suits.html; F. Rice, "Denny's Changes Its Spots Not So Long Ago, The Restaurant Chain Was One of America's Most Racist Companies. Today It Is a Model of Multicultural Sensitivity. Here Is the Inside Story of Denny's About-Face," *Fortune*, May 13, 1996, http://archive.fortune.com/magazines/fortune/fortune_arch ive/1996/05/13/212386/index.htm; and P. Siddhartha and I. Chakraborty, *Diversity at Denny's: The Turnaround Strategy*, IBS Research Center Case Study, 2008.

94. K. E. Kram, *Mentoring at Work: Developmental Relationships in Organizational Life* (Glenview, Il: Scott Foresman, 1985); and L. J. Zachary, *Creating a Mentoring Culture: The Organization's Guide* (San Francisco: Jossey-Bass, 2005).

95. L. Schumer, "Why Mentoring Matters, and How to Get Started," *New York Times*, September 26, 2018, https://www.nytimes.com/2018/09/26/smarter-living/why-mentoring-matters-how-to-get-started.html.

96. Cited in J. Lipman, "How Diversity Training Infuriates Men and Fails Women," *Time*, January 25, 2018, http://time.com/5118035/diversity-training-infuriates-men-fails-women/.

97. K. Bezrukova, C. S. Spell, J. L. Perry, and K. A. Jehn, "A Meta-Analytical Integration of Over 40 Years of Research on Diversity Training Evaluation," *Psychological Bulletin* (November 2016): pp. 1227–74.

98. F. Dobbin and A. Kalev, "Why Diversity Programs Fail: And What Works Better," *Harvard Business Review*, July-August 2016, pp. 52–60.

99. Ibid.

100. *Employee Resource Groups* (Bentley University, 2014).

101. https://www.prudential.com/links/about/diversity-resource-groups.

102. L. Fraser, "7 Corporations Maximizing Employee Resource Groups," November 10, 2016, blackenterprise.com.

103. *Employee Resource Groups*.

104. Based on J. Greenberg, *Managing Behavior in Organizations: Science in Service to Practice*, 2nd ed. (Upper Saddle River, NJ: Prentice Hall, 1999); C. Harvey and J. Allard, *Understanding and Managing Diversity: Readings, Cases, and Exercises*, 3rd ed. (Upper Saddle River, NJ: Prentice Hall, 2005); and P. L. Hunsaker, *Training in Management Skills* (Upper Saddle River, NJ: Prentice Hall, 2009).

105. S. Adams, "Cracking the Code," *Forbes,* February 28, 2018.

106. B. Myers, "Women and Minorities in Tech, by the Numbers," *Wired*, March 27, 2018, https://www.wired.com/story/computer-science-graduates-diversity/.

107. D. Yang and N. Maru, "We Need More Women in Tech In Order to Get More Women in Tech," *Recode*, June 21, 2018, https://www.recode.net/2018/6/21/17489450/tech-diversity-inclusion-women-leadership-engineer-culture.

108. F. Bruni, "The Lie About College Diversity," *New York Times*, December 13, 2015, https://www.nytimes.com/2015/12/13/opinion/sunday/the-lie-about-college-diversity.html.

109. J. McGregor, "How Corporate America Is Trying to Foster More Real Talk about Race," *Washington Post*, May 17, 2018, https://www.washingtonpost.com/.

110. Catalyst, "Women in S&P 500 Companies," September 2018, catalyst.org.

111. K. Smith and D. Rock, "Diversity Makes Inclusion Harder, But Here's What to Do About It," *Fast Company*, April 27, 2018, https://www.fastcompany.com/40559837/diversity-makes-inclusion-harder-but-heres-what-to-do-about-it; and L. Zou and S. Cheryan, "When Whites' Attempts to be Multicultural Backfire in Intergroup Interactions," *Social and Personality Psychology Compass*, November 2015, pp. 581–592.

112. S. Estrada, "Accenture says 'Diversity Starts with I,'" *DiversityInc*, June 26, 2017, https://www.diversityinc.com/news/accenture-says-inclusion-starts.

Chapter 6 | Managing Social Responsibility and Ethics

Learning Objectives

6.1 ***Discuss*** *what it means to be socially responsible and what factors influence that decision.*

6.2 ***Explain*** *green management and how organizations can go green.*

6.3 ***Discuss*** *the factors that lead to ethical and unethical behavior.*

6.4 ***Describe*** *management's role in encouraging ethical behavior.*

6.5 ***Discuss*** *current social responsibility and ethics issues.*

Employability Skills Matrix (ESM)

This matrix identifies which features and end-of-chapter material will help you develop specific skills employers are looking for in job candidates.

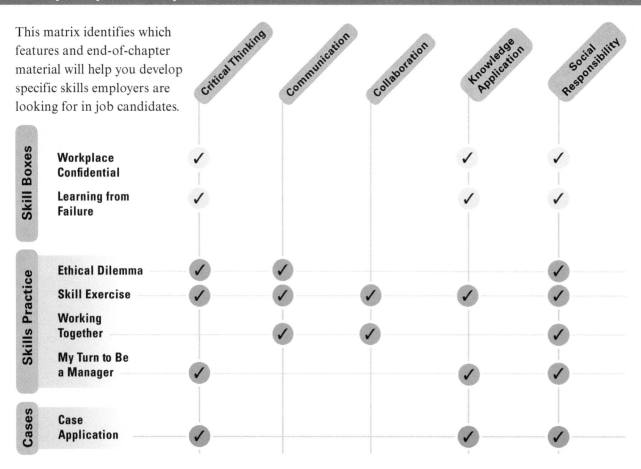

		Critical Thinking	Communication	Collaboration	Knowledge Application	Social Responsibility
Skill Boxes	Workplace Confidential	✓			✓	✓
	Learning from Failure	✓			✓	✓
Skills Practice	Ethical Dilemma	✓	✓			✓
	Skill Exercise	✓	✓	✓	✓	✓
	Working Together		✓	✓		✓
	My Turn to Be a Manager	✓			✓	✓
Cases	Case Application	✓			✓	✓

It's not hard to make the case that there is an ethics crisis in many organizations. Price gouging by major pharmaceutical companies. Engineers at Germany's largest auto company manipulating emissions tests. A top executive at South Korea's largest corporation found guilty of embezzlement and bribery. University administrators looking the other way when students reported sexual assaults by a campus employee.

In this chapter, we look at factors that determine ethical and unethical behavior and what organizations can do to create an ethical culture. First, however, we consider an organization's responsibilities to the communities in which it operates.

WHAT is social responsibility?

L06.1 How do you interpret these actions? An organization professes its commitment to sustainability yet packages its products in nonrecyclable materials. A company pays its CEO 800 times that of its average employee. A global corporation lowers its costs by outsourcing US jobs to a country with significantly lower wages. What if that country is known for abusing human rights? Are these companies being socially responsible?

Managers regularly face decisions that have a dimension of social responsibility in areas such as employee relations, philanthropy, pricing, resource conservation, product quality and safety, and doing business in countries that devalue human rights. But what does it mean to be socially responsible?

Two Opposing Views

Few terms have been defined in as many ways as *social responsibility*. Some of the more popular meanings include "going beyond profit making," "voluntary activities," "concern for the broader social system," and "social responsiveness." Most of the debate has focused at the extremes. On one side, there is the classical—or purely economic—view that management's only responsibility is to maximize profits. On the other side stands the socioeconomic position, which holds that management's responsibility goes well beyond making profits to include protecting and improving society's welfare.

THE CLASSICAL VIEW The most outspoken advocate of the **classical view** was economist and Nobel Laureate Milton Friedman.[1] He argued that most managers today are professional managers, which means that they don't own the businesses they run. They're employees, responsible to the stockholders. Their primary charge is, therefore, to conduct the business in the interests of the stockholders. And what are those interests? Friedman argued that the stockholders have a single concern: financial return.

According to Friedman, when managers take it upon themselves to spend their organization's resources for the "social good," they undermine the market mechanism. Someone has to pay for this redistribution of assets. If socially responsible actions reduce profits and dividends, stockholders are the losers. If wages and benefits have to be reduced to pay for social action, employees lose. If prices are raised to pay for social actions, consumers lose. If higher prices are rejected by the market and sales drop, the business might not survive—in which case, *all* the organization's constituencies lose. Moreover, Friedman contended that when professional managers pursue anything other than profit, they implicitly appoint themselves as nonelected policymakers. He questioned whether managers of business firms have the expertise for deciding how society *should* be. That, Friedman argued, is what we elect political representatives to decide.

THE SOCIOECONOMIC VIEW The socioeconomic position counters that society has higher expectations of business. This is inherent in the legal formation of corporations. Corporations are chartered by state governments. The same government

classical view
The view that management's only social responsibility is to maximize profits

socioeconomic view
The view that management's social responsibility goes beyond making profits to include protecting and improving society's welfare

that creates a charter can take it away. So corporations are not independent entities, responsible only to stockholders. They also have a responsibility to the larger society that creates and sustains them.

One author, in supporting the **socioeconomic view**, once noted that "maximizing profits is a company's second priority, not its first. The first is ensuring its survival."[2]

A major flaw in the classicists' view, as seen by socioeconomic proponents, is their time frame. Supporters of the socioeconomic view contend that managers should be concerned with maximizing financial return over the *long run*. To do that, they must accept some social obligations and the costs that go with them. They must protect society's welfare by *not* polluting, *not* discriminating, *not* engaging in deceptive advertising, and the like. They must also play an affirmative role in improving society by involving themselves in their communities and contributing to charitable organizations.

Exhibit 6-1 summarizes the major arguments for and against business assuming social responsibilities.

Exhibit 6-1
Arguments For and Against Social Responsibility

FOR

Public expectations
Public opinion now supports businesses pursuing economic and social goals.

Long-run profits
Socially responsible companies tend to have more secure long-run profits.

Ethical obligation
Businesses should be socially responsible because responsible actions are the right thing to do.

Public image
Businesses can create a favorable public image by pursuing social goals.

Better environment
Business involvement can help solve difficult social problems.

Discouragement of further governmental regulation
By becoming socially responsible, businesses can expect less government regulation.

Balance of responsibility and power
Businesses have a lot of power and an equally large amount of responsibility is needed to balance against that power.

Stockholder interests
Social responsibility will improve a business's stock price in the long run.

Possession of resources
Businesses have the resources to support public and charitable projects that need assistance.

Superiority of prevention over cures
Businesses should address social problems before they become serious and costly to correct.

AGAINST

Violation of profit maximization
Business is being socially responsible only when it pursues its economic interests.

Dilution of purpose
Pursuing social goals dilutes business's primary purpose—economic productivity.

Costs
Many socially responsible actions do not cover their costs and someone must pay those costs.

Too much power
Businesses have a lot of power already; if they pursue social goals, they will have even more.

Lack of skills
Business leaders lack the necessary skills to address social issues.

Lack of accountability
There are no direct lines of accountability for social actions.

From Obligations to Responsiveness to Responsibility

Now it's time to narrow in on precisely what we mean when we talk about **social responsibility**. It is a business firm's obligation, beyond that required by the law and economics, to pursue long-term goals that are good for society.[3] Note that this definition assumes that the business obeys the law and pursues economic interests. We take as a given that all business firms—those that are socially responsible and those that aren't—will obey all laws that society imposes. Also note that this definition views business as a moral agent. In its effort to do *good* for society, it must differentiate between right and wrong.

We can understand social responsibility better if we compare it with two similar concepts: social obligation and social responsiveness. A business has fulfilled its **social obligation** when it meets its economic and legal responsibilities and no more. It does the minimum that the law requires. A firm pursues social goals only to the extent that they contribute to its economic goals. In contrast to social obligation, both social responsibility and social responsiveness go beyond merely meeting basic economic and legal standards.

Social responsibility adds an ethical imperative to do those things that make society better and *not* to do those that could make it worse. **Social responsiveness** refers to the capacity of a firm to adapt to changing societal conditions.

As Exhibit 6-2 describes, social responsibility requires businesses to determine what is right or wrong and thus seek fundamental ethical truths. Social responsiveness is guided by social norms. The value of social norms is that they can provide managers with a more meaningful guide for decision making.

When a company meets pollution control standards established by the federal government or doesn't discriminate in hiring against older employees, it is meeting its social obligation and nothing more. Contrasting responsiveness with responsibility is a little less clear. But Starbucks provides an example.[4] In July 2018, Starbucks announced that it would stop using disposable plastic straws by 2020. The company was reacting to the growing public concern that plastic straws were hurting the environment. The straws were ending up in landfills and polluting the ocean. At the same time that Starbucks made their announcement, other organizations such as SeaWorld, McDonald's, and Alaska Airlines were similarly banning or limiting the use of these straws. Starbucks' action is clearly an illustration of a company being socially responsive. However, had Starbucks done this ten years earlier, it probably would have been accurately characterized as a socially responsible action.

Social Responsibility and Economic Performance

In this section, we seek to answer the question: Do socially responsible activities lower a company's economic performance?

Numerous studies have examined the relationship between social involvement and a company's economic performance.[5] Most of these studies have found a small positive relationship, although some critics have challenged the direction of causation.[6] If a study shows that social involvement and economic performance are positively related, this correlation doesn't necessarily mean that social involvement *caused* higher

social responsibility
A firm's obligation, beyond that required by the law and economics, to pursue long-term goals that are good for society

social obligation
Meeting economic and legal responsibilities and no more

social responsiveness
Adapting to changing societal conditions

Exhibit 6-2

Social Responsibility Versus Social Responsiveness

	Social **Responsibility**	Social **Responsiveness**
Major consideration	Ethical	Pragmatic
Focus	Ends	Means
Emphasis	Obligation	Responses
Decision framework	Long-term	Medium- and short-term

Source: Adapted from Steven L. Wartick and Philip L. Cochran, "The Evolution of the Corporate Social Performance Model," *Academy of Management Review* (October 1985): p. 766.

economic performance—it could simply mean that high profits afford companies the "luxury" of being socially involved.

The strongest argument in support of managers being socially responsible is a comprehensive summary of 53 studies that encompassed practices at more than 16,000 companies.[7] The results of this summary found overwhelming support for the argument that social responsibility is linked to financial performance. Of the 53 studies, 71.7 percent showed a positive result and only 3.1 percent were negative.

So what can we conclude about social involvement and economic performance? There is little evidence that social actions actually *hurt* a company's economic performance. And even if the positive effect is small, being socially responsible makes good sense. Given the current political and social pressures on business to pursue social goals, this may have the greatest significance for managerial decision making. So, to answer our opening question, do socially responsible activities lower a company's economic performance? The answer appears to be "No!"

GREEN management and sustainability

LO6.2 Nike has launched an app called Making, which allows its design engineers to see the environmental effects of their material choices on water, energy, and waste.[9] Did you know that planning a driving route with more right-hand turns than left can save fuel? UPS does. That's just one of many stats that UPS can quote about how research-based changes in its delivery route design contribute to the sustainability of the planet.[10] Being green is in!

Until the late 1960s, few people (and organizations) paid attention to the environmental consequences of their decisions and actions. Although some groups were concerned with conserving natural resources, about the only reference to saving the environment was the ubiquitous printed request "Please Don't Litter." However, a number of environmental disasters have brought a new spirit of environmentalism to society and organizations. Increasingly, managers have begun to consider the impact of their organization on the natural environment, which we call **green management**.

Today, managers are making a more substantial effort to consider the impact of their organization on the natural environment. For example, UPS considers ways to save on fuel when planning a driving route, contributing to the sustainability of the planet.
Source: Victor Maschek/Shutterstock

green management
Managers consider the impact of their organization on the natural environment

How Organizations Go Green

A number of organizations have radically changed their products and production processes as part of their efforts to protect and preserve the natural environment.[11] For instance, Fiji Water uses renewable energy sources, preserves forests, and conserves water. Carpet-maker Mohawk Industries uses recycled plastic containers to produce fiber used in its carpets. Adidas is working with social awareness-raising network Parley for the Oceans to make sportswear from recycled ocean waste. Although interesting, these examples don't tell us much about how organizations go green. We'll use the *shades of green* model to describe the different environmental approaches that organizations can take.[12] (See Exhibit 6-3.)

The first approach, the *legal (or light green) approach,* is simply doing what is required legally. In this approach, which illustrates social obligation, organizations exhibit little environmental sensitivity. They obey laws, rules, and regulations without legal challenge, and that's the extent of their being green.

As an organization becomes more sensitive to environmental issues, it may adopt the *market approach* and respond to the environmental preferences of customers. Whatever customers demand in terms of environmentally friendly products will be what the organization provides. For example, SC Johnson collaborated with a European company to develop an environmentally friendly alternative to the original

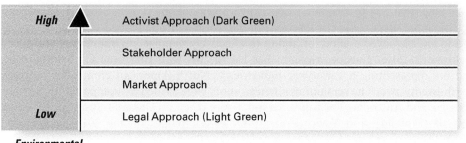

Exhibit 6-3
Green Approaches
Source: Based on R. E. Freeman, J. Pierce, and R. Dodd, *Shades of Green: Business Ethics and the Environment* (New York: Oxford University Press, 1995).

formulation of Saran Wrap, which had come under criticism for containing polyvinyl chloride (PVC). Even though the reformulated Saran Wrap product does not work as well as the original in keeping food odors within the wrapping, SC Johnson decided not to return to the original formulation.[13] This is a good example of social responsiveness, as is the next approach.

In the *stakeholder approach*, an organization works to meet the environmental demands of multiple stakeholders such as employees, suppliers, or community. For instance, L'Oreal has not only committed to sustainable practices across all aspects of its business—shortening transit routes, using biodegradable packaging, converting manufacturing facilities to run on renewable energy—the company has set stringent requirements on its thousands of worldwide suppliers. These requirements set standards for the suppliers' carbon footprint, water usage, water quality, biodiversity, acidification, resource depletion, air quality, and ozone depletion.[14]

Finally, if an organization pursues an *activist (or dark green) approach*, it looks for ways to protect the earth's natural resources. The activist approach reflects the highest degree of environmental sensitivity and illustrates social responsibility. For example, Switzerland's Climeworks has recently built a geothermal power plant in Iceland that can capture CO_2 directly from the air. This is the first system that verifiably achieves negative carbon emissions by converting the emissions into stone.[15]

Evaluating Green Management Actions

As businesses become "greener," they often release detailed reports on their environmental performance. More than 7,500 companies around the globe now voluntarily report their efforts in promoting environmental sustainability using the guidelines developed by the Global Reporting Initiative (GRI). These reports describe the numerous green actions of these organizations. A recent study revealed, for instance, that 67 percent of the world's 250 largest companies have set specific targets to cut their carbon emissions.[16] Also, 154 US companies voluntarily signed the American Business Act on Climate Pledge in 2015 to demonstrate their additional commitment to promoting environmental sustainability.[17] Among the companies signing the pledge, Alcoa has committed to reducing absolute greenhouse emissions by 50 percent by 2025 and Google has committed to tripling its purchase of renewable energy also by 2025.

Another way organizations show their commitment to being green is through pursuing standards developed by the nongovernmental International Organization for Standardization (ISO). Although ISO has developed more than 18,000 international standards, it's probably best known for its ISO 9000 (quality management) and ISO 14000 (environmental management) standards. Organizations that want to become ISO 14000 compliant must develop a total management system for meeting environmental challenges. In other words, it must minimize the effects of its activities on the environment and continually improve its environmental performance. If an organization can meet these standards, it can state that it's ISO 14000 compliant—an accomplishment achieved by organizations in over 155 countries.

fyi

Over 90 percent of the world's largest corporations report on their sustainability performance using Global Reporting Initiative standards.[18]

One final way to evaluate a company's green actions is to use the Global 100 list of the most sustainable corporations in the world.[19] To be named to this list, a company has displayed a superior ability to effectively manage environmental and social factors. In 2018, European companies led the list with fifty-nine Global 100 companies representing a variety of industries.[20] North American companies followed with twenty-two. The remaining nineteen spots were earned by companies from Asia, Africa, and Australia. The top three spots were taken by Dassault Systèmes (France), Nestlé (Finland), and Valeo (France). Other companies on the 2018 list included BMW (Germany) and Cisco Systems (USA).

Let's Get REAL

Karen Heger
Manager, Organizational
Development and Training

Source: Karen S. G. Heger

The Scenario:

Carol Borg is concerned about the waste at the coffee shop where she works as the assistant manager. She has made suggestions to the store manager on how the store could have less of a negative impact on the environment by taking steps such as encouraging customers to recycle their paper cups or by using ceramic cups for customers who aren't taking their coffee to go. However, the store manager insists that these ideas are too costly and refuses to invest in new recycling bins or ceramic cups.

What can Carol say to convince her manager that these are worthwhile investments?

Change is never easy, but a well-researched cost-benefit analysis that details the achievable cost savings and risk management strategy can change the challenge to "Go Green" into a positive opportunity. Knowing the numbers is important: provide specifics on how much money the company would save, statistics on what competitors have done (are you a leader or behind the curve?), what—if any—government benefits are available, and how the change will be positive for the company's reputation and marketing opportunities in the community. Proposing a pilot program to test the green options will also allow for a practical comparative analysis of both practices and demonstrate that there's proof in the pudding—or coffee!

MANAGERS and ethical behavior

LO6.3 We opened this chapter by suggesting that there's an ethics crisis in many organizations. Let's now turn from our discussion about social responsibility to look specifically at the issue of ethics. (See Exhibit 6-4 for some ethical guides.) Here are some ethical dilemmas. How would you handle them? Is it ethical for pharmaceutical sales representatives to provide doctors with lavish gifts as an inducement to buy? Would it make a difference if the bribe came out of the sales rep's commission? Is it ethical to use company email for personal correspondence or use the company phone to make personal phone calls? As an employee, would it be all right to award a lucrative contract to a company in which you hold a significant financial interest? Is it unethical to lie to someone in a negotiation in order to gain an advantage? Or here's a question you may have already confronted or are likely to soon: If asked during a job interview how much you made on your previous job, is it unethical to give a higher number?

What do we mean by **ethics**? We define it as the moral principles that define right and wrong conduct.[21] Many decisions that managers make require them to consider both the process of how the decision is made and who's affected by the result. To better understand the ethical issues involved in such decisions, let's look at the factors that determine whether a person acts ethically or unethically.

ethics
Moral principles that define right and wrong conduct

When faced with an ethical dilemma, consider using one or more of these tests:

- The Golden Rule Test: Would I want people to do this to me?
- The What-If-Everybody-Did-This Test: Would I want everyone to do this? Would I want to live in that kind of world?
- The Family Test: How would my parents/spouse/significant other/children feel if they found out I did this?
- The Conscience Test: Does this action go against my conscience? Will I feel guilty afterwards?
- The Front Page/Social Media Test: How would I feel if this action was reported on the front page of my hometown newspaper or splashed across social media outlets for all to see?

Source: Based on T. Lickona, *Character Matters: How to Help Our Children Develop Good Judgment Integrity, and Other Essential Virtues* (New York: Touchstone Publishing, 2004); A. Goodman, "The Dilemma: Addicted and Conflicted About Laughing at the Afflicted," Institute for Global Ethics, June 3, 2013, globalethics.org; and G. Enck, "Six-Step Framework for Ethical Decision Making," *Journal of Health Services Research and Policy* (January 2014): pp. 62–64.

Exhibit 6-4
Helping You Make Ethical Decisions

Factors That Determine Ethical and Unethical Behavior

Whether a manager acts ethically or unethically is the result of a complex interaction between the manager's stage of moral development and the moderating variables of individual characteristics, the organization's structural design, the organization's culture, and the intensity of the issue (see Exhibit 6-5). People who lack a strong moral sense are much less likely to do the wrong things if they are constrained by rules, policies, job descriptions, or strong cultural norms that frown on such behaviors. Conversely, very moral people can be corrupted by an organizational structure and culture that permit or encourage unethical practices. Moreover, managers are more likely to make ethical decisions on issues where high moral intensity is involved. Let's look at the various factors that eventually influence whether managers behave ethically or unethically.

STAGE OF MORAL DEVELOPMENT There is a substantial body of research that confirms the existence of three levels of moral development, each comprised of two stages.[22] At each successive stage, an individual's moral judgment grows less and less dependent on outside influences. The three levels and six stages are described in Exhibit 6-6.

The first level is labeled *preconventional*. At this level, individuals respond to notions of right or wrong only when there are personal consequences involved, such as physical punishment, reward, or exchange of favors. Reasoning at the *conventional* level indicates the moral value resides in maintaining the conventional order and the expectations of others. In the *principled* level, individuals make a clear effort to define moral principles apart from the authority of the groups to which they belong or society in general.

Research on these stages of moral development allows us to draw several conclusions.[23] First, people proceed through the six stages in a lockstep fashion. They gradually

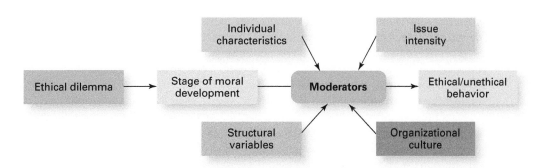

Exhibit 6-5
Factors That Determine Ethical and Unethical Behavior

Exhibit 6-6

Stages of Moral Development
Source: L. Kohlberg, "Moral Stages and Moralization: The Cognitive-Development Approach," in *Moral Development and Behavior: Theory, Research, and Social Issues,* ed. T. Lickona (New York: Holt, Rinehart & Winston, 1976), pp. 34–35.

Level		Description of Stage
	Principled	6. Following self-chosen ethical principles even if they violate the law
		5. Valuing rights of others and upholding absolute values and rights regardless of the majority's opinion
	Conventional	4. Maintaining conventional order by fulfilling obligations to which you have agreed
		3. Living up to what is expected by people close to you
	Preconventional	2. Following rules only when doing so is in your immediate interest
		1. Sticking to rules to avoid physical punishment

Nearly half of millennials believe that CEOs need to take a stance on issues important to society. In contrast, only 28 percent of Generation Xers and Baby Boomers share that belief.[24]

values
Basic convictions about what is right and wrong

ego strength
A personality measure of the strength of a person's convictions

locus of control
A personality attribute that measures the degree to which people believe they control their own fate

Nonhlanhla Joye has high ego strength. Based on her strong convictions, she developed a vegetable gardening system in a disadvantaged neighborhood of her hometown in South Africa for residents to grow their own organic vegetables. She now runs her own business, Umgibe Farming Organics and Training Institute.
Source: Bernard Menigault/Alamy Stock Photo

move up a ladder, stage by stage. They don't jump steps. Second, there is no guarantee of continued moral development. Development can terminate at any stage. Third, the majority of adults are at stage 4. They're limited to obeying the rules and laws of society. Finally, the higher the stage a manager reaches, the more he or she will be predisposed to behave ethically. For instance, a stage 3 manager is likely to make decisions based on peer approval; a stage 4 manager will try to be a "good corporate citizen" by making decisions that respect the organization's rules and procedures; and a stage 5 manager is likely to challenge organizational practices that he or she believes to be wrong.

INDIVIDUAL CHARACTERISTICS   Every person enters an organization with a relatively entrenched set of personal **values**, which represent basic convictions about what is right and wrong. Our values develop from a young age based on what we see and hear from parents, teachers, friends, and others. Thus, employees in the same organization often possess very different values.[25] Note that while *values* and *stage of moral development* may seem similar, they're not. The former are broad and cover a wide range of issues, while the latter is specifically a measure of independence from outside influences.

Two personality variables have also been found to influence an individual's actions according to his or her beliefs about what is right or wrong. They are ego strength and locus of control.

Ego strength measures the strength of a person's convictions. People with high ego strength are likely to resist impulses to act unethically and instead follow their convictions. That is, individuals high in ego strength are more likely to do what they think is right. We would expect managers with high ego strength to demonstrate more consistency between moral judgment and moral action than those with low ego strength.

Locus of control is a personality attribute that measures the degree to which people believe they control their own fate. People with an *internal* locus of control believe they control their own destinies. They're more likely to take responsibility for consequences and rely on their own internal standards of right and wrong to guide their behavior. They're also more likely to be consistent in their moral judgments and actions. People with an *external* locus of control believe what happens to them is due to luck or chance. From an ethical perspective, externals are less likely to take personal responsibility for the consequences of their behavior and more likely to rely on external forces.[26]

STRUCTURAL VARIABLES   An organization's structural design can influence whether employees behave ethically. Some structures provide strong guidance, while others only create ambiguity. Structural designs that minimize ambiguity and continuously remind employees of what is "ethical" are more likely to encourage ethical behavior.

Formal rules and regulations reduce ambiguity. Job descriptions and written codes of ethics are examples of formal guides that promote consistent behavior. Research continues to indicate, though, that the behavior of superiors is the strongest single influence on an individual's own ethical or unethical behavior.[27] People check to see what those in authority are doing and use that as a benchmark for acceptable practices and what is expected of them. Some performance appraisal systems focus exclusively on outcomes. Others evaluate means as well as ends. Where people are appraised only on outcomes, there will be increased pressures to do "whatever is necessary" to look good on the outcome variables. And closely associated with the appraisal system is the way rewards are allocated. The more rewards or punishments depend on specific goal outcomes, the more pressure there is to reach those goals and compromise ethical standards. Structures also differ in the amount of time, competition, cost, and similar pressures they place on job incumbents. The greater the pressure, the more likely it is that people will compromise their ethical standards.

ORGANIZATION'S CULTURE   The content and strength of an organization's culture also influence ethical behavior.[28]

A culture that is likely to shape high ethical standards is one that is high in adaptability, people orientation, and integrity. Employees in such a culture will be encouraged to be innovative, thoughtful of others, and free to openly challenge demands or expectations they consider to be unrealistic or personally distasteful.

A strong culture will exert more influence on people than a weak one. If the culture is strong and supports high ethical standards, it should have a very powerful and positive influence on employees' ethical behavior. In a weak culture, however, people are more likely to rely on subculture norms as a behavioral guide. Work groups and departmental standards will strongly influence ethical behavior in organizations that have weak overall cultures.

ISSUE INTENSITY   A student who would never consider breaking into an instructor's office to steal an accounting exam doesn't think twice about asking a friend who took the same course from the same instructor last semester what questions were on an exam. Similarly, a manager might think nothing about taking home a few office supplies, yet be highly concerned about the possible embezzlement of company funds. These examples illustrate the final factor that influences ethical behavior: the intensity of the ethical issue itself.[30]

As Exhibit 6-7 shows, six characteristics determine issue intensity or how important an ethical issue is to an individual:

1. How great a harm (or benefit) is done to victims (or beneficiaries) of the ethical act in question? *Example*: An act that puts a thousand people out of work is more harmful than one affecting ten people.
2. How much consensus is there that the act is evil (or good)? *Example*: More Americans agree that it is evil to bribe a customs official in Texas than agree that it is evil to bribe a customs official in Mexico.

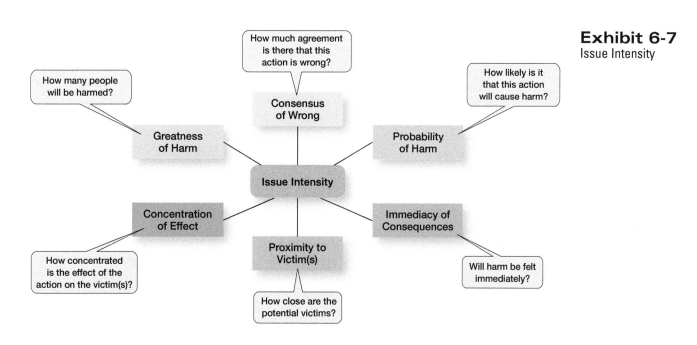

Exhibit 6-7
Issue Intensity

3. What is the probability that the act will actually take place and will actually cause the harm (or benefit) predicted? *Example*: Selling a gun to a known armed robber has greater probability of harm than selling a gun to a law-abiding citizen.

4. What is the length of time between the act in question and its expected consequences? *Example*: Reducing the retirement benefits of current retirees has greater immediate consequences than reducing retirement benefits of current employees who are under age 45.

5. How close do you feel (socially, psychologically, or physically) to the victims (or beneficiaries) of the evil (beneficial) act in question? *Example*: Layoffs in one's own work unit hit closer to home than layoffs in a remote city.

6. How large is the concentrated effect of the ethical act on the people involved? *Example*: A change in the warranty policy denying coverage to ten people with claims of $10,000 has a more concentrated effect than a change denying coverage to 10,000 people with claims of $10.

Following these guidelines, the larger the number of people harmed, the greater the consensus that an act is evil, the higher the probability that an act will take place and actually cause harm, the shorter the length of time until the consequences of the act surface, and the closer the observer feels to the victims of the act, the great the issue intensity. In aggregate, these six components determine how important an ethical issue is. And we should expect managers to behave more ethically when a moral issue is important to them than when it is not.

Ethics in an International Context

Are ethical standards universal? Although some common moral beliefs exist, social and cultural differences between countries are important factors that determine ethical and unethical behavior.[31]

Should Coca-Cola employees in Saudi Arabia adhere to US ethical standards, or should they follow local standards of acceptable behavior? If Airbus (a European company) pays a "broker's fee" to an intermediary to get a major contract with a Middle Eastern airline, should Boeing be restricted from doing the same because such practices are considered improper in the United States?

In the case of payments to influence foreign officials or politicians, US managers are guided by the Foreign Corrupt Practices Act (FCPA), which makes it illegal to make payments to foreign government officials to assist in obtaining or retaining business. However, this law doesn't always reduce ethical dilemmas to black and white. In some countries, government bureaucrat salaries are low because custom dictates that they receive small payments from those they serve. Payoffs to these bureaucrats "grease the machinery" and ensure that things get done. The FCPA does not expressly prohibit small payoffs to foreign government employees whose duties are primarily administrative or clerical *when* such payoffs are an accepted part of doing business in that country. Any action other than this is illegal. In 2017, the US Department of Justice brought 13 FCPA corporate enforcement actions, collecting $1.13 billion in fines.[32]

It's important for individual managers working in foreign cultures to recognize the social, cultural, and political-legal influences on what is appropriate and acceptable behavior.[33] And international businesses must clarify their ethical guidelines so that employees know what's expected of them while working in a foreign location.

Another ethical guide in international business is the United Nations Global Compact, which is an initiative created by the United Nations outlining principles for doing business globally in the areas of human rights, labor, the environment, and anticorruption (see Exhibit 6-8). More than 9,700 participants and stakeholders from over 160 countries have committed to the UN Global Compact, making it the world's largest voluntary corporate citizenship initiative.[34] The goal of the UN Global Compact is a more sustainable and inclusive global economy. Organizations making this commitment do so because they believe that the world business community plays a significant

Learning from
FAILURE   Siemens Atones for Its Sins

Between 2002 and 2006, a senior accountant at German engineering giant Siemens oversaw an annual bribery budget of between $40 million and $50 million. Company managers and sales staff used the slush fund to grease the palms of corrupt government officials worldwide. Hundreds of employees participated in creating phony consultants' contracts, false bills, and shell firms to win contracts.

Once discovered, the company's reputation was badly hurt. Additionally, the company paid more than $2.6 billion in fines and fees in Germany and the US.

Siemens' response to the scandal has been widely praised by many independent anti-corruption and ethics experts. The company spent upward of a billion dollars for investigations and reforms. What the investigations uncovered were several systematic elements that contributed to the scandal. Specifically, there was an aggressive growth strategy that encouraged managers to do whatever was necessary to meet tough performance targets; an organization structure that allowed divisions to essentially run themselves; poor accounting controls; and a corporate culture that not only tolerated bribes but implicitly encouraged them.

What followed first was a shake-up of the company's top management. Gone were the company's CEO and chairman. The new executive team authorized four external investigations, hired a major New York law firm to conduct a rigorous internal inquiry, and appointed a leading anti-corruption expert to serve as its adviser. Based on what was found, management made a number of changes. Strict new rules and anticorruption processes were instituted. Over 500 full-time compliance officers were hired, up from just 86 previously. Compliance hotlines were established. Training and education programs on anti-corruption practices were launched. In the first two years, more than 200,000 company employees underwent training on anti-corruption issues. Siemens withdrew from doing business in countries known for corruption or unethical practices. A new organization structure was put in place with tight controls. And finally, the company initiated over 900 internal disciplinary actions, including dismissals. The result has been a change in corporate culture at Siemens to one driven by ethical standards.[35]

The UN Global Compact asks companies to embrace, support, and enact, within their sphere of influence, a set of core values in the areas of human rights, labor standards, the environment, and anti-corruption:

Exhibit 6-8

The Ten Principles of the United Nations Global Compact

Human Rights

Principle 1:	Business should support and respect the protection of internationally proclaimed human rights within their sphere of influence; and
Principle 2:	Make sure they are not complicit in human rights abuses.

Labor Standards

Principle 3:	Business should uphold the freedom of association and the effective recognition of the right to collective bargaining;
Principle 4:	The elimination of all forms of forced and compulsory labor;
Principle 5:	The effective abolition of child labor; and
Principle 6:	The elimination of discrimination in respect to employment and occupation.

Environment

Principle 7:	Business should support a precautionary approach to environmental challenges;
Principle 8:	Undertake initiatives to promote greater environmental responsibility; and
Principle 9:	Encourage the development and diffusion of environmentally friendly technologies.

Anti-Corruption

Principle 10:	Business should work against corruption in all its forms, including extortion and bribery.

Source: United Nations Global Compact (www.unglobalcompact.org). Copyright © 2012 United Nations Global Compact.

role in improving economic and social conditions. In addition, the Organisation for Economic Co-operation and Development (OECD) has made fighting bribery and corruption in international business a high priority. The centerpiece of its efforts is the Anti-Bribery Convention (or set of rules and guidelines), which was the first global instrument to combat corruption in cross-border business deals. To date, significant gains have been made in fighting corruption in the forty-three countries that have ratified or agreed to it.[36]

ENCOURAGING ethical behavior

LO6.4 Managers can do a number of things if they're serious about encouraging ethical behaviors—for instance, hire employees with high ethical standards, establish codes of ethics, and lead by example. By themselves, such actions are not likely to have much of an impact. But if an organization has a comprehensive ethics program in place, it can potentially improve its ethical climate. The key term, however, is *potentially*. There are no guarantees that a well-designed ethics program or publicly espoused values will lead to the desired outcome. For instance, Enron, often referred to as the "poster child" of corporate wrongdoing, outlined values in its final annual report that most would consider ethical—communication, respect, integrity, and excellence. Yet the way top managers behaved didn't reflect those values at all.[37] Let's look at some specific ways that managers can encourage ethical behavior and create a comprehensive ethics program.

Let's Get REAL

Justin T Kidwell ▶
Management Consultant

Source: Justin T Kidwell

The Scenario:

All through university, Finlay Roberts wasn't sure what he really wanted to do. But now he had found what he thought was a great job, one where he could enhance his leadership skills in a competitive environment with teams of employees who sold security systems over the phone. What he soon discovered, though, was that competing to meet sales goals often led to unethical actions. After learning about ethics in pretty much every management class he took, Finlay wanted to show his employees that he was committed to an ethical workplace.

What advice would you give Finlay?
One of the cornerstones to professional success is to maintain and demonstrate strong ethics—often by exceeding the standards set by the organization. One potential path for Finlay is to remember that damaging the company's brand can risk destroying his career, but missing sales/performance targets will only impede his career. Over the long run, professionals with strong reputations will outlast those with questionable character.

Employee Selection

Wanting to reduce workers' compensation claims, Hospitality Management Corp. did pre-employment integrity testing at one hotel to see if the tests could "weed out applicants likely to be dishonest, take dangerous risks or engage in other undesirable behaviors." After six months, claims were down among new hires.[38] Integrity tests can evaluate an applicant's honesty and trustworthiness, including attitudes toward risky workplace behavior, theft, lying, misuse of company resources, email and internet abuse, use of drugs and alcohol, and trust with confidential information.[39]

In addition to integrity testing, the entire selection process should be viewed as an opportunity to learn about an individual's trustworthiness. Starting with the job announcement, management should consider conducting reference and background checks, as well as proposing ethical dilemmas to applicants as part of the employment interview.[40]

You should state in the job announcement that background and reference checks will be conducted and ethics will be part of annual performance appraisals. This is likely to discourage applicants with previous or dubious ethical issues.

The best predictor of future behavior is past behavior. This argues for following up on references and background information. Check with previous employers for information on a candidate's past attendance and discipline record as well as other pertinent data indicating work-history problems. In addition, search public criminal records databases and Google the candidate. Most job applicants today will have an internet footprint.

Use the interview to mine a candidate's experience with ethical choices. Ask, for instance, for applicants to describe how they managed an ethical dilemma at a previous job. Or offer a real-life ethical dilemma that a current employee might be facing and ask how they would respond.

French Justice Minister Francois Bayrou demonstrates the importance of a code of ethics for an organization. Becoming more popular globally, this is a formal statement of an organization's primary values and the ethical rules it expects its employees to follow.
Source: Philippe Wojazer/Reuters

Codes of Ethics

Uncertainty about what is and is not ethical can be a problem for employees. A **code of ethics** is a formal statement of an organization's values and the ethical rules it expects employees to follow. It's a popular device for providing employees with guiding principles and helping to define proper behavior in ambiguous situations. Research shows that 90 percent of US corporations have a written code of ethics.[41] And codes of ethics are becoming more popular globally. Approximately 86 percent of *Fortune* Global 200 companies have a code of ethics.[42]

code of ethics
A formal statement of an organization's primary values and the ethical rules it expects its employees to follow

What should a code of ethics look like? The *Fortune* Global 200 offer some insights.[43] The most commonly cited core values cited in the codes are integrity, teamwork, respect, innovation, and client focus. And when asked for why the company had a code, the three top answers were: to comply with legal requirements; to create a shared company culture; and to protect/improve company reputation.

Unfortunately, codes are not ethical cure-alls. A survey of employees in US businesses found that 41 percent of those surveyed had observed ethical or legal violations in the previous twelve months, including such things as conflicts of interest, abusive or intimidating behavior, and lying to employees. And 37 percent of those employees didn't report observed misconduct.[44]

Do these statistics mean that codes of ethics shouldn't be developed? No. It just tells us that, in isolation, ethical codes aren't likely to be much more than legal protections and public relations statements. Their effectiveness depends heavily on whether management supports them and how employees who break the codes are treated. When management considers them to be important, regularly reaffirms their content, and publicly reprimands rule breakers, codes can supply a strong foundation for an effective ethics program.

Leadership at the Top

Codes of ethics require a commitment from top management. Why? Because it's the top managers who set the cultural tone. They're role models in terms of both words and actions—though what they *do* is far more important than what they *say*. If top managers, for example, take company resources for their personal use, inflate their expense accounts, or give favored treatment to friends, they imply that such behavior is acceptable for all employees.

The board of directors at Texas Instruments made that perfectly clear when they forced the resignation of CEO Brian Crutcher.[45] After less than two months in the job as chief executive, Crutcher was fired for personal behavior described as inconsistent with TI's ethics and core values. The board chairman said the company has "no tolerance for violations of our code of conduct."

Top managers also set the cultural tone for their organization by their reward and punishment practices. The choices of whom and what are rewarded with pay increases and promotions send a strong signal to employees. The promotion of a manager for achieving impressive results in questionable ways indicates to everyone that those questionable ways are acceptable. When it uncovers wrongdoing, management must not only punish the wrongdoer but publicize the fact and make the outcome visible for all to see. This sends another message: "Doing wrong has a price, and it's *not* in your best interests to act unethically!"

Job Goals and Performance Appraisal

Employees should have tangible and realistic goals. Work-related goals can create ethical problems if employees see them as unrealistic. Under the stress of unrealistic goals, otherwise ethical employees may feel they have no choice but to do whatever is necessary to meet those goals. Also, goal achievement is usually a key issue in performance appraisal. If performance appraisals focus only on economic goals, ends will begin to justify means. To encourage ethical behavior, both ends *and* means should be evaluated. For example, a manager's annual review of employees might include a point-by-point evaluation of how their decisions measured up against the company's code of ethics as well as how well goals were met.

Ethics Training

Most large organizations have set up seminars, workshops, and similar ethics training programs to encourage ethical behavior. For instance, a study of 71 US-based global organizations with at least 5,000 employees found that 70 of them had employee ethics training.[46] These training programs were typically less than two hours in length and usually administered as part of new employee orientation or as an annual refresher.

Many firms offer ethics training to their employees, either as part of orientation for new hires or on an annual basis. This is one way organizations can encourage ethical behavior and emphasize the value placed on it.
Source: Fizkes/Shutterstock

But does ethics training work? The failures, unfortunately, get the most attention.[47] Arthur Andersen made millions selling ethical consulting services to its clients, before it was revealed to be helping its client, Enron, hide its losses. And Andersen was embarrassed again when it put out videos on the importance of ethics, including one featuring supermarket entrepreneur Stew Leonard speaking earnestly about integrity shortly before he was imprisoned for massive tax fraud.

In spite of some high-publicity failures, the overall evidence is generally positive when training is combined with a code of ethics, top-management role models, accountability policies, and regular ethics audits.[48] However, ethics training doesn't appear to have a significant impact on participants when it relies on abstract dilemmas and stories, which have little relevance to real situations; uses multiple-choice formats rather than requiring actual deliberation and judgment; is conducted sporadically; and conflicts with reward systems that emphasize outcomes at the expense of means.[49] When those issues are addressed, we should expect ethics training to reduce unethical behavior.

The Walt Disney Company was recently ranked number 3 among Forbes' list of the world's most reputable companies.[50] Two big reasons for this ranking are the company's ethics code and training.[51] Disney has an ethics code that covers virtually all areas and issues relating to how employees should behave and conduct themselves. It's referred to as their "Standards of Business Conduct," runs forty-three pages, and specifies expectations regarding ethics and compliance with the law. When new employees are hired, they are indoctrinated with training videos and oral explanations of the policies within the conduct code. And all employees are trained in the sections of the code that relate to the company's internal responsibility to employees, customers, the community, and other stakeholders.

Independent Social Audits

The fear of being caught can be an important deterrent to unethical behavior. Independent social audits, which evaluate decisions and management practices in terms of the organization's code of ethics, increase that likelihood.[52] Such audits can be regular evaluations, or they can occur randomly with no prior announcement. An effective ethics program probably needs both. To maintain integrity, auditors should be responsible to the company's board of directors and present their findings directly to the board. This arrangement gives the auditors clout and lessens the opportunity for retaliation from those being audited.

CURRENT issues in social responsibility and ethics

LO6.5 Today's managers continue to face challenges and opportunities in being socially responsible and ethical. Here we examine four current issues: protecting whistle-blowers, promoting social entrepreneurship, social media and social responsibility, and corporate philanthropy.

Protecting Whistle-Blowers

What would you do if you saw other employees doing something illegal, immoral, or unethical? Would you step forward? Many of us wouldn't because of the perceived risks. That's why it's important for organizations to have a comprehensive anti-retaliation program in place that allows employees to raise ethical concerns without personal or career risks. These employees, called *whistle-blowers*, require protection.

Whistle-blowing is defined as an act of an individual within an organization who discloses information in order to report and correct corruption.[54] In the US, federal legislation offers some legal protection to employees. There are 22 federal statutes that protect employees who raise or report a variety of activities—including workplace safety hazards, environmental violations, and financial manipulations.[55] The provisions of these statutes are enforced by the Occupational Safety and Health Administration (OSHA). For instance, according to the Sarbanes-Oxley Act, any manager who retaliates against an employee for reporting violations faces a stiff penalty: a ten-year jail sentence.

OSHA has proposed that employers create an anti-retaliation program, and they suggest it contain five key elements:[56]

1. *Management commitment.* Senior management needs to demonstrate that it is committed to addressing employees' concerns regarding potential violations of the law and commitment to preventing retaliation.
2. *Compliance concern response system.* Management needs to establish procedures and enable employees to confidentially report concerns, provide for fair and transparent evaluation of the concerns, offer a timely response, and ensure a fair and effective resolution.
3. *Anti-retaliation response system.* There needs to be clearly designated and independent channels for reporting the retaliation that bypass the manager who is believed to have retaliated. If unsatisfied, the reporting employee should have the ability to elevate the matter to higher levels.
4. *Anti-retaliation training.* All employees, including management, need training to ensure they know the law, their rights, and applicable organizational procedures.
5. *Program oversight.* Rigorous oversight needs to be enacted in the form of monitoring processes and independent audits to ensure that the program is working as intended.

Fifty-three percent of US employees who report wrongdoing internally face retaliation at work.[53]

whistle-blowing
An act of an individual within an organization who discloses information in order to report and correct corruption

Promoting Social Entrepreneurship

The world's social problems are many and viable solutions are few. But numerous people and organizations are trying to do something. For instance, take John Schoch, the former CEO of Profile Products, which is a profitable manufacturer and distributor of products for soil and water management. As CEO, he decided to invest some of the company's resources to help address a global crisis—a lack of clean water. He established a nonprofit subsidiary of Profile Products that put millions of dollars into research and development of a product called ProCleanse, which is a water filtration device. Schoch had chosen to pursue a purpose as well as a profit.[57] He is an example of someone pursuing **social entrepreneurship**, an entrepreneurial activity with an embedded social purpose.[58]

social entrepreneurship
An entrepreneurial activity with an embedded social purpose

Social entrepreneurship has the potential to impact economic systems as it creates solutions to social problems and leads the beneficiaries to a better standard of living. And some of the most striking examples have originated in developing countries. For instance, microfinance in Bangladesh has provided tiny loans to women so they could start small businesses. These loans have reportedly been a big factor in reducing rural poverty.[59] In the US, TOMS Shoes demonstrates social entrepreneurship with its one-for-one business model.[60] For every pair of shoes the company sells, an item is given to someone in need. Another example: Seattle-based PATH (Program for Appropriate Technology in Health) is an international nonprofit organization that uses low-cost technology to provide needed healthcare solutions for poor, developing countries. By collaborating with public groups and for-profit businesses, PATH has developed simple life-saving solutions such as clean birthing kits, credit card–sized lab test kits, and disposable vaccination syringes that can't be reused.[61]

Mrs. Kiki opened an ice cream shop in Butare to give employment opportunities to women in Rwanda.
Source: Claudia Wiens/Alamy Stock Photo

Social Media and Social Responsibility

Social media has impacted all our lives. Not surprisingly, there's increasing evidence that it can be a viable vehicle for management to communicate and promote its socially responsible actions and enhance the organization's reputation.

For instance, a study was done of twenty highly ranked global aerospace and defense companies. The researchers looked at their social media platforms for evidence of one or more social initiatives—environment, community relations, diversity, employee relations, human rights, and client comments. All twenty companies published at least four of these initiatives, leading the researchers to conclude that social media can enhance a company's reputation.[62]

As the print and broadcast media has drawn increased attention to wrongdoings in both private and public organizations, management should be looking for ways to increase transparency.[63] Transparency builds trust, and trust enhances an organization's reputation. Social media is now one of the best means for promoting transparency. It's the ideal vehicle for sharing the organization's mission statement, values, code of ethics, human resource policies, diversity initiatives, community involvement, and the like. It also offers an excellent means for customers, suppliers, employees, and potential employees to communicate with the organization and for the organization to communicate with its stakeholders.

Social media provides management the means to shape its image and reputation. As two public relations experts put it, "There is a good chance that somebody, somewhere, is using social media to talk about your organization right now."[64] Why shouldn't management, then, use social media to take the initiative and convey its story?

Corporate Philanthropy

What do Walmart, Google, and ExxonMobil have in common? In addition to being large, public organizations, they rank among the top 10 of the Fortune 500 list of the most charitable companies.[65]

Corporate philanthropy can be an effective way for companies to address societal problems.[66] For example, Google's foundation donates $100 million a

WORKPLACE CONFIDENTIAL Balancing Work and Personal Life

Several business critics have proposed that business firms have a social responsibility to help employees balance their work demands with their family and personal commitments. A number of companies, usually large ones and often in high-tech industries, have responded by making work-life balance an important corporate goal. They've introduced flexible work hours; offered paid leaves for both new dads and moms; built on-site childcare facilities, and introduced similar policies that make it easier for employees to balance their personal life and work. But such workplace benefits are probably more the exception than the rule. Unfortunately, most of us face situations more accurately described as work-life *imbalance*.

If you're going to achieve balance, responsibility is most likely to fall largely on your own shoulders. So what can you do?

In an ideal world, you would seek a progressive employer that sees the benefits of providing its employees with the flexibility to balance work and personal responsibilities. As we've noted, there are such firms. *Fortune* magazine publishes an annual list of the 100 best companies to work for. Many of these companies make the *Fortune* list in large part because of their progressive human resource policies that include options to facilitate work-life balance.

Our next suggestion asks you to assess your priorities. What trade-offs are you prepared to make between your work and personal life? Keep in mind that the answer to this question often changes over time. At age 25, your career might be your highest priority and working 70 hours a week might be a price you're willing to pay to move up the career ladder. At 35, you might not feel the same way. There is nothing wrong with going "all in" on your job. Just realize that there are trade-offs. If you have high career aspirations, recognize that you will need to make personal sacrifices. Consider where you want to be in 5, 10, 20, and even 30 years. If you decide that pursuing a rich personal life outside of work is important to you, consider this fact when seeking a job. And per Chapter 3, choose an organization whose culture is compatible with your values. If your non-work activities are your highest priority, choose an organization and a job where your preference will be honored.

Take a look back at the "It's Your Career" box in Chapter 1. It provides a brief summary of time-management techniques. To successfully manage conflicts that might arise between your work and non-work life, few activities are more valuable than effective use of your time.

As noted in Chapter 1, time is a unique resource in that, if it's wasted, it can never be replaced. Importantly, every one of us is allotted the same 24 hours a day, seven days a week. Some people just use their allotments better than others. That is, they do a better job of managing their time. For instance, you can reduce work-life conflicts by prioritizing both work and personal activities by importance and urgency.

Besides prioritizing activities, here are three additional time-management suggestions:

Follow the 80/20 principle. Most of us produce 80 percent of our results using only 20 percent of our time. It's easy to get caught in an activity trap and confuse actions with accomplishments. Those who use their time well make sure that the crucial 20 percent gets highest priority.

Know your productivity cycle. Each of us has a daily energy cycle that influences when we feel most productive or unproductive. Some of us are morning people, while others are late afternoon or evening people. Don't fight your natural cycle. Understand it and use it to your advantage. Handle your most demanding problems during the high part of your energy cycle, when you are most alert and productive. Relegate routine and undemanding tasks to your low periods.

Group less-important activities together. Set aside a regular time period each day to make phone calls, respond to emails, do follow-ups, and perform other kinds of "busy work." Ideally, this should be during your low cycle. This avoids duplication, waste, and redundancy; it also prevents trivial matters from crowding out high-priority tasks.

The following are a few additional practices that can help you balance your work-life commitments.

- ***Set specific time targets for leaving work.*** Make it a habit to leave work at a set time each day. As this pattern is established, colleagues will become increasingly aware of your schedule and learn to interact with you during your specific work hours.

- ***Separate work and personal cell phones.*** Use two separate cell phones or cell accounts. Respond to your work number during working hours and your personal number at other times. Turn off your business phone when you're outside your work hours.

  Avoid checking emails or responding to work-related texts outside work hours. Don't let your work hours become 24/7. In our digital world, it's increasingly common for people to assume we're always available. Make clear to others that you separate your personal life from your work. In reality, most "urgent" messages aren't urgent. Most replies can be delayed ten or twelve hours with minimal effects.

- ***Our final suggestion recognizes that working for others always requires giving up some degree of control.*** No matter how progressive your employer, the employment agreement implies a trade-off: You give up some of your freedom in return for compensation. You can potentially maximize control of your work-life conflicts by becoming your own boss. While this rarely lessens demands on your time, it can allow you to dictate how you will spend your time. You may end up working longer hours than you would if you worked for someone else, but that decision will be yours rather than someone else's.[70]

year in grants. It recently made grants of $2.4 million to an organization that provides direct cash to the poor; $750,000 to help a school for the blind create a navigation app; and $1 million to a group that advocates for criminal-justice reform.[67]

One could argue, following the classical view of social responsibility, that for-profit businesses should not be using stockholder's money to support corporate philanthropy. Yet charity can be consistent with the profit motive. For instance, a Nielsen study found that 55 percent of online consumers stated that they would pay more for products and services from companies that are committed to positive social and environmental impact.[68] Additionally, there is evidence that philanthropy is good for employee morale. It can be a source of pride and increase a company's ability to attract and recruit qualified staff. Thus, corporate philanthropy can be a win-win situation. Business firms "are able to meet their customers' demand while increasing long-term profits through positive public relations."[69] The fact that corporate philanthropy is now so widespread suggests that regardless of the motivation—increased sales, good marketing, concern for community and society, long-term profits, image and reputation, or employee morale—corporate executives appear committed to it.

Aside from benefiting the community, corporate philanthropy can contribute to numerous benefits for a firm, including increased sales, image and reputation, and employee morale. Here we see representatives from Ralphs, a west coast supermarket chain, at a donation event for Los Angeles families in need.
Source: Jordan Strauss/AP Images

Chapter 6   PREPARING FOR: Exams/Quizzes

CHAPTER SUMMARY by Learning Objectives

LO6.1 **DISCUSS** what it means to be socially responsible and what factors influence that decision.

Social responsibility is a business's obligation, beyond its economic and legal obligations, to pursue long-term goals that are good for society. The classical view of social responsibility is that managers' primary charge is to ensure financial returns for the company. A firm pursues social goals as they contribute to economic goals. The socioeconomic view of social responsibility involves the belief that organizations have a responsibility to society. Both views suggest that businesses have an ethical obligation to make society better and *not* to engage in activities to make it worse. A socially responsive company might decide to do something because of social norms expecting them to; a socially responsible business decision is guided by a decision about what they themselves think is right or ethical. Determining whether organizations should be socially responsible can be done by looking at arguments for and against it. We can conclude that a company's social responsibility doesn't appear to hurt its economic performance.

LO6.2 **EXPLAIN** green management and how organizations can go green.

Green management is when managers consider the impact of their organization on the natural environment. Organizations can "go green" in different ways. The light green approach is doing what is required legally, which is social obligation. Using the market approach, organizations respond to the environmental preferences of their customers. Using the stakeholder approach, organizations respond to the environmental demands of multiple stakeholders. Both the market and stakeholder approaches can be viewed as social responsiveness. With an activist or dark green approach, an organization looks for ways to respect and preserve the earth and its natural resources, which can be viewed as social responsibility.

Green actions can be evaluated by examining reports that companies compile about their environmental performance, by looking for compliance with global standards for environmental management (ISO 14000), and by using the Global 100 list of the most sustainable corporations in the world.

LO6.3 **DISCUSS** the factors that lead to ethical and unethical behavior.

Ethics refers to the principles, values, and beliefs that define right and wrong decisions and behavior. The factors that affect ethical and unethical behavior include an individual's level of moral development (preconventional, conventional, or principled), individual characteristics (values and personality variables—ego strength and locus of control), structural variables (structural design, use of goals, performance appraisal systems, and reward allocation procedures), organizational culture, and issue intensity (greatness of harm, consensus of wrong, probability of harm, immediacy of consequences, proximity to victims, and concentration of effect).

Since ethical standards aren't universal, managers should know what they can and cannot do legally as defined by the Foreign Corrupt Practices Act. It's also important to recognize any cultural differences and to clarify ethical guidelines for employees working in different global locations. Finally, managers should know about the principles of the Global Compact and the Anti-Bribery Convention.

LO6.4 **DESCRIBE** management's role in encouraging ethical behavior.

The behavior of managers is the single most important influence on an individual's decision to act ethically or unethically. Some specific ways managers can encourage ethical behavior include paying attention to employee selection, creating an organizational culture that positively influences ethical behavior, having and using a code of ethics, recognizing the important ethical leadership role they play and how what they do is far more important than what they say, making sure that goals and the performance appraisal process don't reward goal achievement without taking into account how those goals were achieved, and using ethics training and independent social audits.

LO6.5 **DISCUSS** current social responsibility and ethics issues.

Managers can protect whistle-blowers (employees who raise ethical issues or concerns) by encouraging them to come forward, by setting up toll-free ethics hotlines, and by establishing a culture in which employees can complain and be heard without fear of reprisal. Managers also can promote social entrepreneurship, which involves creating solutions to social problems through entrepreneurship activity. Social entrepreneurs want to make the world a better place and have a driving passion to make that happen. Social media is a good vehicle for management to use to communicate and promote socially responsible actions. Businesses can promote positive social change through corporate philanthropy efforts.

REVIEW AND DISCUSSION QUESTIONS

6-1. Differentiate between social responsiveness, social responsibility, and social obligation.

6-2. What does social responsibility mean to you personally? Do *you* think business organizations should be socially responsible? Explain.

6-3. Compare the stakeholder and the activist approach to green management. Why would a company choose one approach instead of the other?

6-4. What factors influence whether a person behaves ethically or unethically? Explain all relevant factors.

6-5. What is the Foreign Corrupt Practices Act?

6-6. What are some problems that could be associated with employee whistle-blowing for (a) the whistle-blower and (b) the organization?

6-7. Describe the characteristics and behaviors of someone you consider to be an ethical person. How

could the types of decisions and actions this person engages in be encouraged in a workplace?

6-8. Do you think promoting social responsibility through social media shows that a company is mostly concerned with enhancing its reputation rather than really being ethical? Why or why not?

PREPARING FOR: My Career

ETHICS DILEMMA

A coworker takes credit for the excellent job you've performed. Frustrating! It's probably happened to you or someone you know. How did it happen? Perhaps you shared an idea with a coworker and then hear her present it as her own in a meeting. Or perhaps you worked during the weekend to ensure that a project report is completed on time and your coworker takes credit for your initiative. Or maybe you resolved a conflict with a customer, but your department head reports the resolution as his own.

6-9. What are some of the possible reasons for others taking credit for your work? Are any of the reasons justifiable? Why or why not?

6-10. Do you think that those who take credit for your work know that what they're doing is wrong?

6-11. How would you respond to your coworker or boss? Explain.

SKILLS EXERCISE   Developing Your Trust Building Skill

About the Skill

Trust plays an important role in the manager's relationships with his or her employees.[71] Given the importance of trust in setting a good ethical example for employees, today's managers should actively seek to develop it within their work group.

Steps in Practicing the Skill

- *Practice openness.* Mistrust comes as much from what people don't know as from what they do. Being open with employees leads to confidence and trust. Keep people informed. Make clear the criteria you use in making decisions. Explain the rationale for your decisions. Be forthright and candid about problems. Fully disclose all relevant information.

- *Be fair.* Before making decisions or taking actions, consider how others will perceive them in terms of objectivity and fairness. Give credit where credit is due. Be objective and impartial in performance appraisals. Pay attention to equity perceptions in distributing rewards.

- *Speak your feelings.* Managers who convey only hard facts come across as cold, distant, and unfeeling. When you share your feelings, others will see that you are real and human. They will know you for who you are and their respect for you is likely to increase.

- *Tell the truth.* Being trustworthy means being credible. If honesty is critical to credibility, then you must be perceived as someone who tells the truth. Employees

are more tolerant of hearing something "they don't want to hear" than of finding out that their manager lied to them.

- *Be consistent.* People want predictability. Mistrust comes from not knowing what to expect. Take the time to think about your values and beliefs, and let those values and beliefs consistently guide your decisions. When you know what's important to you, your actions will follow, and you will project a consistency that earns trust.

- *Fulfill your promises.* Trust requires that people believe that you are dependable. You need to ensure that you keep your word. Promises made must be promises kept.

- *Maintain confidences.* You trust those whom you believe to be discreet and those on whom you can rely. If people open up to you and make themselves vulnerable by telling you something in confidence, they need to feel assured you won't discuss it with others or betray that confidence. If people perceive you as someone who leaks personal confidences or someone who can't be depended on, you've lost their trust.

- *Demonstrate competence.* Develop the admiration and respect of others by demonstrating technical and professional ability. Pay particular attention to developing and displaying your communication, negotiation, and other interpersonal skills.

Practicing the Skill

Building trust in teams you work on for class projects is a great way to practice your skills in building trust. It's important to quickly develop trust among your teammates if the project is to succeed. Using the steps above, create a plan that you can use to more quickly build and maintain trust in team projects. Make a list of steps you can take at the beginning of the project to begin building trust. Next, make a list of behaviors you are willing to commit to during the team project in order to continue to build and maintain trust. For example, you may want to commit to responding to your teammates' communications within a certain time period. Implement your plans with your next team project.

WORKING TOGETHER **Team Exercise**

Identify a company that you work at or do business with on a regular basis (for example, a restaurant or retail store). Consider the socially responsible behavior of the company you selected. Does the company provide any support to the local community, for example, donating items for fundraisers or participating in local events? Does the company engage in any green management practices, for example, recycling or using alternative energy sources?

Create a list of the company's socially responsible actions. Next, divide into groups of three to four students and share your lists. Compare and discuss the socially responsible actions of each of the companies your group considered. How do these actions benefit each company? Are there other steps that each company could take to become more socially responsible?

MY TURN TO BE A MANAGER

- Go to the Global Reporting Initiative website (www.globalreporting.org) and choose three businesses from the list that have filed reports. Look at those reports and describe/evaluate what's in them. In addition, identify the stakeholders who might be affected and how they might be affected by the company's action.

- Identify three companies that are known for being socially responsible. List and compare the types of socially responsible behavior that each company engages in.

- Research careers in sustainability. Visit the Occupational Information Network (O*Net) at www.onetcenter.org and search for careers using the terms "sustainability" or "green management." Create a list of the types of jobs or careers you can pursue. Identify the skills and abilities that are required for a career in sustainability.

- Find five different examples of organizational codes of ethics. Compare and contrast the examples.

- Using the examples of codes of ethics you found, create what you feel would be an appropriate and effective organizational code of ethics. In addition, create your own *personal code of ethics* you can use as a guide to ethical dilemmas.

- Over the course of two weeks, see what ethical "dilemmas" you observe. These could be ones you face personally, or they could be ones that others (friends, colleagues, other students talking in the hallway or before class, and so forth) face. Write these dilemmas down and think about what you might do if faced with that dilemma.

- Interview two different managers about how they encourage their employees to be ethical. Write down their comments and discuss how these ideas might help you be a better manager.

CASE APPLICATION 1 Chobani: A Different Kind of Yogurt Company

If a company you founded in a small town in the United States grew so quickly that hiring candidates from the area still left you in need of more employees, what would you do? Hamdi Ulukaya, the founder of Chobani (which sells the top-selling brand of Greek yogurt in the US), decided in 2010 to contact a refugee center that was thirty miles away from his business in upstate New York.[72] He figured he could solve his staffing shortage while also helping people in need.

It was an experiment that started out with a few temporary workers. There were challenges to resolve: cultural differences, language barriers, and transportation needs. Eight years later, 30 percent of the company's 2,000 employees are immigrants, with more than twenty languages spoken at the company's plants in New York and Idaho.[73]

Ulukaya, who is a Turkish immigrant himself, explained his hiring strategy: "This was not about politics ... this was about hiring from our community."

There have been unexpected benefits of this hiring approach. First, the motivation of the workforce at Chobani has helped the business. "These are the most hardworking, patriotic, honest people. They will give everything they have," according to Ulukaya.[74] Also, there is a sense of community and high employee morale at Chobani since the company seems to be doing more than only increasing profits.

Hiring immigrants is not Chobani's only uncommon business approach. Chobani has always given 10 percent of its post-tax profits to charitable causes.[75] The average worker's wages are double the federal minimum wage. In 2016, Chobani began giving employees shares of the company based on tenure in the company. Employees now own 10 percent of the company, which works out to an average of $150,000 per employee. "The staff was always proud, but this ownership piece was missing. This is probably one of the smartest, most tactical things you can do for a company. You're faster, you're more passionate. Your people are happier,"[76] Ulukaya says. In 2017, Chobani instituted a six-week parental leave for both mothers and fathers, including adoption and foster parents.[77] Chobani's hourly employees get the same parental leave as salaried employees. That's unlike other companies, such as Netflix, that provide shorter parental leave for hourly employees.

DISCUSSION QUESTIONS

6-12. Is Chobani a better example of social responsibility or social responsiveness? Provide reasons why.

6-13. What actions has Chobani taken that illustrate the socioeconomic view of social responsibility? What ways (if any) could Chobani be considered an example of the classical view of social responsibility?

6-14. Which of the arguments for and against social responsibility apply to Chobani (see Exhibit 6-1)?

6-15. Do you think Chobani's approaches to business would attract customers? Why or why not?

CASE APPLICATION 2

Every Kid Fed: Addressing Childhood Hunger Through Social Entrepreneurship

While in graduate school, Shanay Thompson volunteered to work with at-risk high school students. Shanay noticed that students increasingly asked her for food. Some said they were bullied at school when they ate the free lunches provided. Others said there was no food available at home. Shanay already knew that a lack of food makes it nearly impossible for kids to learn. But hearing these kids' stories in person was different ... and she found it to be too difficult to just hand them a snack and get back to her own life.

Shanay had the idea of a food pantry—a place where students (or someone else from their family) could get needed food before or after school or at lunch without feeling embarrassed. The principal of the school where Shanay was volunteering approved the idea. Before long, Shanay realized that she couldn't stop with just one school. She targeted low-income schools and started an organization called Every Kid Fed.

To get her first pantry started, Shanay chipped in her own money. She needed more food, though, so she started spending her weekends asking ten to fifteen grocery store managers for gift cards. That approach lasted for about three months. Teachers and counselors were referring students in need to the pantries, and the food was going fast.

Shanay thought her next move should be to write grant proposals. But she was concerned about the competition for grants and the slow grant approval process. As she put it, she was "competing with a ton of wonderful nonprofits for grants through this same standard process, so I said what the heck, I'm going to start emailing the CEOs of these big companies. To my surprise, it actually worked."[78] CEOs of companies, such as Amazon and Salesforce, put her in touch with their community outreach departments. And Shanay was able to quickly acquire funds.

One year into running Every Kid Fed, Shanay taught herself to code so students could access boxed meals during the summer using an app.[79] Shanay has done it all—founding and operating Every Kid Fed while simultaneously attending medical school. She recently was recognized with an award from "Black Girls Rock" for making a difference.[80]

DISCUSSION QUESTIONS

6-16. You read about TOMS Shoes as an example of social entrepreneurship. How is Every Kid Fed a different kind of example of social entrepreneurship than TOMS Shoes?

6-17. What barriers did Shanay confront in creating Every Kid Fed? How did she overcome them?

6-18. Building on the example of Shanay Thompson, what personal qualities and behaviors does it take to be a social entrepreneur?

6-19. What are other examples of social entrepreneurship? Look up some examples.

ENDNOTES

1. M. Friedman, *Capitalism and Freedom* (Chicago: University of Chicago Press, 1962); and "The Responsibility of Business Is to Increase Its Profits," *New York Times Magazine,* September 13, 1970, p. 33.

2. S. W. Gellerman, "Why 'Good' Managers Make Bad Ethical Choices," *Harvard Business Review*, July–August 1986, p. 89.

3. See, for example, R. A. Buchholz, *Essentials of Public Policy for Management*, 2nd ed. (Upper Saddle River, NJ: Prentice Hall, 1990); and V. Fuhmans and R. Feintzeig, "CEOs Risk Speaking Up—Taking a Stand on Pressing Societal Issues Can Mean Hurting Business," *Wall Street Journal*, March 2, 2018, B3.

4. C. Caron, "Starbucks to Stop Using Disposable Plastic Straws by 2020," *New York Times*, July 9, 2018, https://www.nytimes.com/2018/07/09/business/starbucks-plastic-straws.html; and A. Farley, "The Last (Plastic) Straw," *Fast Company*, September 2018, p. 24.

5. See, for instance, P. Cochran and R. A. Wood, "Corporate Social Responsibility and Financial Performance," *Academy of Management Journal* (March 1984): pp. 42–56; K. Aupperle, A. B. Carroll, and J. D. Hatfield, "An Empirical Examination of the Relationship Between Corporate Social Responsibility and Profitability," *Academy of Management Journal* (June 1985): pp. 446–463; J. B. McGuire, A. Sundgren, and T. Schneeweis, "Corporate Social Responsibility and Firm Financial Performance," *Academy of Management Journal* (December 1988): pp. 854–872; B. A. Waddock and S. B. Graves, "The Corporate Social Performance–Financial Performance Link," *Strategic Management Journal* (April 1997): pp. 303–319; and G. Balabanis, H. C. Phillips, and J. Lyall, "Corporate Social Responsibility and Economic Performance in the Top British Companies: Are They Linked?" *European Business Review* (January 1998): pp. 25–44.

6. B. Seifert, S. A. Morris, and B. R. Bartkus, "Having, Giving, and Getting: Slack Resources, Corporate Philanthropy, and Firm Financial Performance," *Business & Society* (June 2004): pp. 135–161; and McGuire, Sundgren, and Schneeweis, "Corporate Social Responsibility" [see note 5].

7. M. Mikolajek-Gocejna, "The Relationship Between Corporate Social Responsibility and Corporate Financial Performance—Evidence from Empirical Studies," *Comparative Economic Research* (December 2016): pp. 67–84.

8. R. Derousseau, "Good Behavior, Heavenly Returns," *Fortune*, September 1, 2018, p. 46.

9. G. Christ, "Sustainability: Just Do It," *Industry Week*, February 2014, pp. 22–23.

10. S. Rosenbush and L. Stevens, "At UPS, the Algorithm Is the Drive," *Wall Street Journal*, February 16, 2015, https://www.wsj.com/articles/at-ups-the-algorithm-is-the-driver-1424136536; and "The Total Package," *Bloomberg Businessweek,* March 19–March 25, 2012, p. 6.

11. C. Deutsch, "For Fiji Water, a Big List of Green Goals," *New York Times*, November 7, 2007, https://www.nytimes.com/2007/11/07/business/07fiji.html; T. Casey, "UPS Sustainability Report Proves It: Carbon Management Is Good Business," August 4, 2014, https://www.triplepundit.com/story/2014/ups-sustainability-report-proves-It-carbon-management-good-business/42016; E. Jervell, "Adidas Moves to Address Environmental Worries," *Wall Street Journal*, September 24, 2015, https://www.wsj.com/articles/adidas-moves-to-address-environmental-worries-1443075134; and J. Herlihy, "Mohawk SmartStrand Expands 'Green'

Carpet Features," *Floor Covering Weekly*, April 25, 2018, https://www.floorcoveringweekly.com/main/business-builder/mohawk-smartstrand-expands-green-carpet-features-22810.

12. The concept of shades of green can be found in R. E. Freeman, J. Pierce, and R. Dodd, *Shades of Green: Business Ethics and the Environment* (New York: Oxford University Press, 1995).

13. F. Johnson, "SC Johnson's CEO on Doing the Right Thing, Even When It Hurts Business," *Harvard Business Review*, April 2015, https://hbr.org/2015/04/sc-johnsons-ceo-on-doing-the-right-thing-even-when-it-hurts-business.

14. "Linking Products to Values," *Fast Company*, May 2018, p. 82.

15. A. Rathi, "The World's First 'Negative Emissions' Plant Has Begun Operation—Turning Carbon Dioxide into Stone," October 12, 2017, https://qz.com/1100221/the-worlds-first-negative-emissions-plant-has-opened-in-iceland-turning-carbon-dioxide-into-stone/.

16. "The Road Ahead: The KPMG Survey of Corporate Responsibility Reporting 2017," KPMG, https://home.kpmg/xx/en/home/insights/2017/10/the-kpmg-survey-of-corporate-responsibility-reporting-2017.html.

17. "White House Announces Additional Commitments to the American Business Act on Climate Package," White House, December 1, 2015, www.whitehouse.gov.

18. G. Kell, "The Future of Corporate Responsibility," *Forbes*, June 18, 2018, https://www.forbes.com/sites/georgkell/2018/06/18/the-future-of-corporate-responsibility/#230797746105.

19. The Global 100 list is a collaborative effort of Corporate Knights Inc. and Innovest Strategic Value Advisors. Information from Global 100 website, Winter 2018, www.global100.org.

20. "2018 Global 100 Issue," *Corporate Knights*, January 22, 2018, https://www.corporateknights.com/magazines/2018-global-100-issue/.

21. See, for example, J. Thiroux and K. W. Krasemann, *Ethics: Theory and Practice*, updated 11th ed. (New York: Pearson, 2015); and B. MacKinnon and A. Fiala, *Ethics: Theory and Contemporary Issues*, 9th ed. (Stamford, CT: Cengage, 2018).

22. L. Kohlberg, *Essays in Moral Development: The Philosophy of Moral Development*, vol. 1 (New York: Harper & Row, 1981); L. Kohlberg, *Essays in Moral Development: The Psychology of Moral Development*, vol. 2 (New York: Harper & Row, 1984); and D. L. Krebs and K. Denton, "Explanatory Limitations of Cognitive-Developmental Approaches to Morality," *Psychological Review* (May 2006): pp. 672-75.

23. See, for example, J. Weber, "Managers' Moral Reasoning: Assessing Their Responses to Three Moral Dilemmas," *Human Relations* (July 1990) pp. 687–702.

24. V. Fuhmans and R. Feintzeig, "CEOs Risk Speaking Up—Taking a Stand on Pressing Societal Issues Can Mean Hurting Business," *Wall Street Journal*, March 2, 2018, p. B3.

25. J. H. Barnett and M. J. Karson, "Personal Values and Business Decisions: An Exploratory Investigation," *Journal of Business Ethics* (July 1987) pp. 371–82; and W. C. Frederick and J. Weber, "The Value of Corporate Managers and Their Critics: An Empirical Description and Normative Implications," in W. C. Frederick and L. E. Preston (eds.), *Business Ethics: Research Issues and Empirical Studies* (Greenwich, CT: JAI Press, 1990), pp. 123–44.

26. L. K. Treviño and S. A. Youngblood, "Bad Apples in Bad Barrels: A Causal Analysis of Ethical Decision-Making Behavior," *Journal of Applied Psychology* (August 1990): pp. 378–385.

27. B. Z. Posner and W. H. Schmidt, "Values and the American Manager: An Update," *California Management Review* (Spring 1984): pp. 202–16; and J. Jordan, M. E. Brown, L. K. Treviño, and S. Finkelstein, "Someone to Look Up To: Executive-Follower Ethical Reasoning and Perceptions of Ethical Leadership," *Journal of Management* (March 2013): pp. 660–83.

28. B. Victor and J. B. Cullen, "The Organizational Bases of Ethical Work Climates," *Administrative Science Quarterly* (March 1988): pp. 101–25; R. R. Sims, "The Challenge of Ethical Behavior in Organizations," *Journal of Business Ethics* (July 1992): pp. 505–13; and A. Simha, "Ethical Climates and Their Effects on Organizational Outcomes Implications From the Past and Prophecies for the Future," *Academy of Management Perspectives* (November 2012): pp. 20–34.

29. C. C. Verschoor, "Survey of Workplace Ethics," *Strategic Finance*, July 2018, https://sfmagazine.com/post-entry/july-2018-survey-of-workplace-ethics/.

30. T. M. Jones, "Ethical Decision Making by Individuals in Organizations: An Issue-Contingent Model," *Academy of Management Review* (April 1991): pp. 366–395; and T. Barnett, "Dimensions of Moral Intensity and Ethical Decision Making: An Empirical Study," *Journal of Applied Social Psychology* (May 2001): pp. 1038–1057.

31. R. L. Sims, "Comparing Ethical Attitudes Across Cultures," *Cross Cultural Management: An International Journal* (March 2006): pp. 101–113; W. Bailey and A. Spicer, "When Does National Identity Matter? Convergence and Divergence in International Business Ethics," *Academy of Management Journal* (December 2007): pp. 1462–1480; and J. L. Bierstaker, "Differences in Attitudes About Fraud and Corruption Across Cultures," *Cross Cultural Management: An International Journal* (July 2009): pp. 241–50.

32. "Trends and Developments in Anti-Corruption Enforcement,", Covington, January 25, 2018, https://www.cov.com/en/news-and-insights/insights/2018/01/trends-and-developments-in-anti-corruption-enforcement.

33. L. Paine, R. Deshpande, J. D. Margolis, and K. E. Bettcher, "Up to Code: Does Your Company's Conduct Meet World-Class Standards?," *Harvard Business Review,* December 2005, pp. 122–133; A. Molinsky, "Becoming a Manager in a New Country," *Harvard Business Review*, September 14, 2015, https://hbr.org/2015/09/becoming-a-manager-in-a-new-country; and N. R. Abramson and R. T. Moran, *Managing Cultural Differences: Global Leadership for the 21st Century*, 10th ed. (New York: Routledge, 2018).

34. United Nations Global Compact 2018, https://www.unglobalcompact.org/.

35. Based on S. Schubert and T. C. Miller, "At Siemens, Bribery Was Just a Line Item," *New York Times*, December 20, 2008, https://www.nytimes.com/2008/12/21/business/worldbusiness/21siemens.html; and G. Dietz and N. Gillespie, "Rebuilding Trust: How Siemens Atoned for Its Sins," *Guardian*, March 26, 2012, https://www.theguardian.com/sustainable-business/recovering-business-trust-siemens.

36. Organisation for Economic Co-operation and Development, "OECD Convention on Combating Bribery of Foreign Public Officials in International Business Transactions," December 2018, www.oecd.org.

37. The Enron example is taken from P. M. Lencioni, "Make Your Values Mean Something," *Harvard Business Review,* July 2002, p. 113.

38. B. Roberts, "Your Cheating Heart," *HR Magazine,* June 2011, pp. 55–60.

39. "Hiring Ethical Employees," *Strategic Finance*, July 1, 2016, https://sfmagazine.com/post-entry/july-2016-hiring-ethical-employees/.

40. Here's How to Hire Ethical Employees," January 21, 2011, *Hampton Roads Business Journal*, https://pilotonline.com/inside-business/news/columns/article_3421a96e-fdda-5e90-b127-18b457c32a22.html.

41. Cited in "Code of Ethics," May 5, 2014, rampinelli.eu.

42. KPMG, "Business Codes of the Global 200," October 2014, http://www.ethicsmanagement.info/content/Business%20codes%20Fortune%20200.pdf.

43. Ibid.

44. National Business Ethics Survey of the US Workforce 2013, *Ethics Resource Center*, March 2014, ethics.org.

45. M. Armental and E. Brown, "Chips CEO Resigns Over Conduct," *Wall Street Journal*, July 18, 2018, p. B1.

46. J. Weber, "Investigating and Assessing the Quality of Employee Ethics Training Programs Among US-Based Global Organizations," *Journal of Business Ethics* (June 2015), pp. 27–42.

47. Cited in "Does Business Ethics Training Do Any Good?," August 17, 2012, http://www.philosophyforlife.org/does-ethics-training-do-any-good/.

48. M. Kaptein, "The Effectiveness of Ethics Programs: The Role of Scope, Composition, and Sequence," *Journal of Business Ethics* (October 2015): pp. 415–31.

49. A. Beerel, "Why Ethics Training Doesn't Work," January 24, 2014, nhbr.com.

50. K. Strauss, "The World's Most Reputable Companies in 2017," *Forbes*, February 28, 2017, https://www.forbes.com/sites/karstenstrauss/2017/02/28/the-worlds-most-reputable-companies-in-2017/#7b4743a62fe3.

51. UK Essays, "Walt Disney Company Ethics Audit," March 23, 2015, https://www.ukessays.com/essays/business/walt-disney-company-ethics-audit-business-essay.php.

52. S. Roy, "The Intellectual Roots of the Social Audit," *Management Accountant* (September 2012): pp. 1024–31.

53. H. Stolowy, L. Paugam, Y. Gendron, J. Moll, and D. Brown, "Whistleblowers: Endangered but Vital to the Corporate World," *Forbes*, November 20, 2018, https://www.forbes.com/sites/hecparis/2018/11/20/whistleblowers-endangered-but-vital-to-the-corporate-world/#467e7adb2e86.

54. D. Schultz and K. Harutyunyan, "Combating Corruption: The Development of Whistleblowing Laws in the United States, Europe, and Armenia," *International Comparative Jurisprudence* (December 2015): p. 89.

55. Occupational Safety & Health Administration, "Recommended Practices for Anti-Retaliation Programs," US Department of Labor, https://www.whistleblowers.gov/recommended_practices.

56. Ibid.

57. K. Flynn, "A New Pursuit for Social Entrepreneurship: Profits," *Forbes*, June 20, 2014, https://www.forbes.com/sites/kerryflynn/2014/06/20/a-new-pursuit-for-social-entrepreneurship-profits/#296837262540.

58. A. Nigam and R. K. Ghai, "Social Entrepreneurship: An Overview," *Splint International Journal of Professionals* (March 2016): pp. 107–11.

59. Ibid.

60. M. Orlic, "7 Businesses That Prove 2016 Is the Year of Social Entrepreneurship," *Search Engine Journal* (website), July 9, 2016, https://www.searchenginejournal.com/7-businesses-prove-2016-year-social-entrepreneurship/165994/.

61. Path.org.

62. D. McGunagle, D. Button, and L. Zizka, "The Impact of Corporate Social Responsibility Communication on Corporate Reputation," *Journal of Management* (March-May 2016): pp. 37–44.

63. C. Zucal, "Why Transparency Matters to Your Business," *Social Media Today* (website), March 18, 2016, https://www.socialmediatoday.com/social-business/why-transparency-matters-your-business-1.

64. G. L. Johnson and N. Larsen, "The Ever-Evolving Ethics of Social Media," *Public Relations Tactics*, September 1, 2015, http://apps.prsa.org/Intelligence/Tactics/Articles/view/11199/1115/The_Ever_Evolving_Ethics_of_Social_Media.

65. C. Preston, "The 20 Most Generous Companies of the Fortune 500," *Fortune*, June 22, 2016, http://fortune.com/2016/06/22/fortune-500-most-charitable-companies/.

66. A. Gautier and A-C. Pache, "Research on Corporate Philanthropy: A Review and Assessment," *Journal of Business Ethics* (February 2015): pp. 343–69.

67. Preston, "20 Most Generous Companies" [see note 65].

68. Cited in K. Diggs, "Why Corporate Philanthropy Is the 21st Century Standard," *Huffington Post*, April 13, 2016, https://www.huffingtonpost.com/kallen-diggs/why-corporate-social-resp_1_b_9671642.html.

69. Ibid.

70. Based on M. A. O'Connor, "Corporate Social Responsibility for Work/Family Balance," *St. John's Law Review* (Fall 2005): pp. 1193–1220; T. Kalliath and P. Brough, eds., "Achieving Work-Life Balance," special issue, *Journal of Management and Organization* (July 2008): pp. 224–327; and B. Tracy, *Time Management* (New York: AMACOM, 2014).

71. Skills Exercise based on F. Bartolome, "Nobody Trusts the Boss Completely—Now What?," *Harvard Business Review*, March–April 1989, pp. 135–42; and J. K. Butler Jr., "Toward Understanding and Measuring Conditions of Trust: Evolution of a Condition of Trust Inventory," *Journal of Management* (September 1991): pp. 643–63.

72. R. Brunner, "How Chobani's Hamdi Ulukaya Is Winning America's Culture War," *Fast Company*, March 20, 2017.

73. C. Lagorio-Chafkin, "This Billion-Dollar Founder Says Hiring Refugees Isn't a Political Act," *Inc.*, June 2018.

74. Ibid.

75. D. Callahan, "A Yogurt Tycoon Steps Up His Philanthropy, Going Where Other Funders Won't," *Inside Philanthropy*, October 10, 2014, https://www.insidephilanthropy.com/home/2014/10/10/a-yogurt-tycoon-steps-up-his-philanthropy-going-where-other.html.

76. Ibid.

77. E. Margolin, "Chobani Offers Moms, Dads 6 Weeks of Parental Leave at Full Pay," NBC News, October 6, 2016, https://www.nbcnews.com/business/business-news/chobani-offers-moms-dads-6-weeks-parental-leave-full-pay-n660701.

78. J. C. Hervey, "How One Social Entrepreneur Took Childhood Hunger into Her Own Hands," *Forbes*, February 28, 2018, https://www.forbes.com/sites/janeclairehervey/2018/02/28/how-one-social-entrepreneur-took-childhood-hunger-into-her-own-hands/#564c1853682b.

79. S. Thompson, "'Every Kid Fed' Isn't Just a Name, It's a Mission," Inspire, *Mandatory* (website), https://www.mandatory.com/inspire/1410183-former-model-fights-child-hunger.

80. "Black Girls Rock: Social Entrepreneur Shanay Thompson," September 9, 2018, bet.com.

Chapter 7

Managing Change and Disruptive Innovation

Learning Objectives

7.1 **Describe** making the case for change.
7.2 **Compare** and contrast views on the change process.
7.3 **Classify** areas of organizational change.
7.4 **Explain** how to manage change.

7.5 **Discuss** contemporary issues in managing change.
7.6 **Describe** techniques for stimulating innovation.
7.7 **Explain** why managing disruptive innovation is important.

Employability Skills Matrix (ESM)

This matrix identifies which features and end-of-chapter material will help you develop specific skills employers are looking for in job candidates.

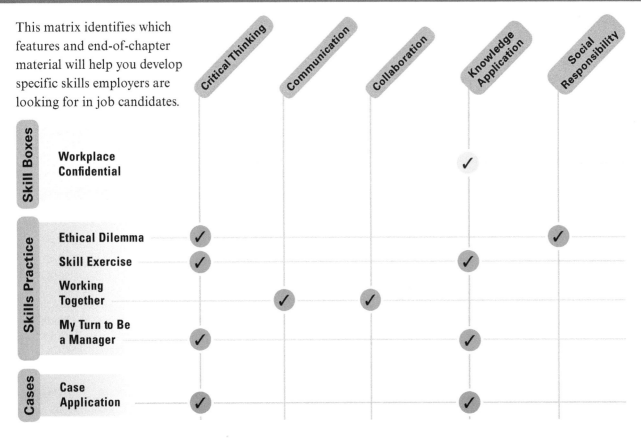

	Critical Thinking	Communication	Collaboration	Knowledge Application	Social Responsibility
Skill Boxes — Workplace Confidential				✓	
Skills Practice — Ethical Dilemma	✓				✓
Skills Practice — Skill Exercise	✓			✓	
Skills Practice — Working Together		✓	✓		
Skills Practice — My Turn to Be a Manager	✓			✓	
Cases — Case Application	✓			✓	

Someone once said, "Most people resist any change that doesn't jingle in their pockets!" There's some truth to this. Most of us are not big fans of change. We like our routine and its predictability. When it comes to organizations, managers have a challenge: Introducing change tends to face resistance among a large portion of the workforce. Yet, organizations that don't change with the times face extinction. Just ask the former executives and investors at Toys "R" Us, Blockbuster Video, or Borders Books.

This chapter looks at the change process, why people resist it, and what managers can do to overcome that resistance. Then we turn our attention to innovation; specifically, how to stimulate it in organizations. Finally, we address the subject of disruptive innovation. We'll show that disruptive innovation is arguably the greatest challenge facing today's top executives.

THE CASE for change

LO7.1 When we use the term **organizational change**, we mean any alteration of people, structure, or technology.[1] And organizational changes need someone to act as a catalyst and assume the responsibility for managing the change process—this is a **change agent**. Internally, change agents can come in many forms—top executives, middle managers, project managers, team leaders, or specialists within human resources. For major changes, organizations often hire outside consultants to provide advice and assistance. As outsiders, they can provide an objective perspective that insiders may lack. But outside consultants typically have a limited understanding of the organization's history, culture, operating procedures, and people. They're also more likely to initiate drastic changes because they don't have to deal with the repercussions after the changes are implemented. In contrast, internal change agents may be more thoughtful, but possibly overly cautious, because they have to live with the consequences of their decisions.

Senior executives at Ford Motor Company are taking on the role of change agent. Making changes has become necessary as people's needs and preferences for travel are shifting. The company recently conducted a series of experiments to better understand customers' and prospective customers' needs and preferences.[2] Ford's experiments revealed differences in how members of the younger generation prefer to get around compared to members of older generations. As a result, Ford is broadening its scope from selling cars and trucks to include car-sharing services, offering foldable electric bikes that can be charged while in the vehicle, and an app that determines the best mode of transportation to a destination (for example, driving part of the way, then riding a bike for the remainder).

Living with VUCA

Ford's executives recognize the reality of today's unpredictable and dynamic world. It's what military planners have called **VUCA**—an environment of nonstop volatility, uncertainty, complexity, and ambiguity.[3] It's a world where "change is the only constant."

If managers had their choice, they almost certainly would opt for a static and predictable world. For, if it weren't for change, a manager's job would be relatively easy. Planning would be simple because tomorrow would be no different from today. The issue of effective organizational design would also be resolved because the environment would be static and there would be no need to redesign the structure. Similarly, decision making would be dramatically streamlined because the outcome of each alternative could be predicted with almost certain accuracy. But that's not the way it is. Organizations face change because of external and internal forces (see Exhibit 7-1).

organizational change
Any alteration of people, structure, or technology in an organization

change agent
Someone who acts as a catalyst and assumes the responsibility for managing the change process

VUCA
An acronym describing an environment of nonstop volatility, uncertainty, complexity, and ambiguity

Campaigners in London call for the government to back the Agent of Change policy to prevent the closure of grassroots music venues. In organizations, managers serve as effective change agents because they have a good understanding of their organization's history, culture, procedures, employees, and customers.
Source: Mark Kerrison/Alamy Live News/Alamy Stock Photo

Exhibit 7-1

External and Internal Forces for Change

External

- Consumer needs and wants
- New governmental laws
- Technology
- The economy

Internal

- New organizational strategy
- Composition of the workforce
- New equipment
- Employee attitudes

External Forces for Change

CONSUMER NEEDS AND WANTS   Ford Motor Company understands the importance of being responsive to its customers. The company's experiments will also enable them to attract a new breed of customers, helping to secure the company's future. But sometimes a company may make changes that fail to meet customer preferences. Burger King learned that lesson by rapidly expanding its menu with items that were not popular with its customers. It had to drop its lower calorie fries, called "Satisfries," and its apple cranberry salads after one year because of poor sales. Burger King's president Jose Cil admitted, "It's not what our guests were looking for."[4]

NEW GOVERNMENTAL LAWS   Government laws require changes in how managers must conduct business. Five broad categories of governmental laws include truth in advertising, employment and labor fair practices, environmental protection, privacy, and safety and health. For example, the US Environmental Protection Agency (EPA) enforces several laws, including the Clean Air Act, which is aimed at protecting the environment and public welfare. Management must ensure that harmful emissions into the atmosphere do not exceed safe levels set forth by the EPA. Safety and health is promoted by the US Occupational Safety and Health Act, which requires that companies provide safe and healthful working conditions.

fyi

Eighty percent of CEOs think that artificial intelligence will significantly change the way their company does business by 2024.[5]

TECHNOLOGY   What do the Chevrolet Volt and the Tesla Motors Model S have in common? Both are examples of electric-powered vehicles. Compared to gas-powered vehicles, electric cars have shorter driving ranges; however, ongoing research and development into improving battery capacity to extend their range is a high priority. While most electric vehicles rely on lithium-ion batteries, Toyota and Volkswagen are considering alternatives, including solid-state batteries, in order to extend driving ranges.[6]

THE ECONOMY   Managers must respond to changes in economic forces. Consider the impact of an economic recession. According to the US Bureau of Labor Statistics, recessions are characterized by a general slowdown in economic activity, a downturn in the business cycle, and a reduction in the amount of goods and services produced and sold.[7] The Great Recession of 2007 to 2009 was considered to be one of the most severe economic downturns since the Great Depression of the 1930s. In the United States, the unemployment rate jumped from 5 percent to 10.8 percent. In response, executives in many organizations sought to protect profits by cutting costs, which often included mass employee layoffs. Ironically, ten years later, the US economy was booming and many of these same executives were offering attractive incentives to keep employees from jumping ship and aggressively searching to find candidates to fill vacant positions.

Economic changes, of course, are not limited to the US. Forecasts for slower economic growth in China have prompted China's Labor Ministry to call for "steady and cautious control" over minimum wage increases.[8] The rationale behind this practice is to help companies manage rising labor costs. With these actions come long-term risks: Chinese consumers' ability to purchase many goods and services will likely diminish, and companies will have to consider additional cost-cutting methods, such as reductions in hiring.

Internal Forces for Change

NEW ORGANIZATIONAL STRATEGY   When top management changes their organization's strategy, it can affect all segments of the business. For example, Walmart has aggressively responded to increased online competition from Amazon and Target.[9] The CEO of Walmart's e-commerce business has focused his strategy on acquisitions, reorganization, and leveraging Walmart's strengths. He has accelerated growth by buying Bonobos, Moosejaw, ShoeBuy, and ModCloth. He has elevated the importance of customer service by having executives responsible for Customer Care and Customer Experience report directly to him. And he's leveraged Walmart's 4,600 US brick-and-mortar stores by having them double as warehouses and allowing Walmart to get products to the customer faster.

COMPOSITION OF THE WORKFORCE   Through the decades, the US workforce has become more diverse. In Chapter 4, we saw the challenges managers face when managing a workforce that is diverse based on surface-level variables, including age and race, as well as deep-level variables, including differences in values, personality, and work preferences. A key challenge entails orchestrating these differences to maintain an inclusive culture that focuses on productivity.

NEW EQUIPMENT   In 1983, American engineer Charles Hull invented the first three-dimensional (3-D) printer, which is based on the technology of transforming liquid polymers into solid objects.[10] Only recently has this technology become highly refined. Now, more and more companies are using 3-D printers to create product prototypes.[11] For example, the medical industry more easily creates customized prosthetics and implants. And Apple uses 3-D printer technology to create the casings for its laptops.

Technological changes are particularly making their marks on healthcare. These technologies include advances in genomics, biotechnology, robotics, connected care, and artificial intelligence. Advances in robotic technology, for example, is changing how surgeons perform some surgical procedures. As a case in point, the Cleveland Clinic offers robotically assisted heart surgery. This technology enables cardiothoracic surgeons to use computer consoles to control surgical instruments and minimize the invasiveness of some surgeries.

EMPLOYEE ATTITUDES   A recent survey revealed that the attitudes of employees at organizations going through significant changes tend to be less favorable than at more stable companies.[12] Where change is happening, the largest differences are in attitudes toward company leadership and company image. But not all employees in changing organizations have less favorable attitudes. Those who prefer stability are less likely to try new technology or embrace change than employees who are open to change. Changing attitudes challenge managers to adopt methods to support employees through organizational changes.

Architectural design firms benefit from new 3-D printing equipment by dramatically reducing the time it takes to create handmade building models. The equipment produces accurate, highly detailed, and full-color physical 3-D models printed from digital data that help architects, contractors, and clients envision building projects.
Source: Stockbroker/MBI/Alamy Stock Photo

THE CHANGE process

LO7.2   Two very different metaphors can be used to describe the change process.[13] One metaphor envisions the organization as a large ship crossing a calm sea. The ship's captain and crew know exactly where they're going because they've made the trip many times before. Change comes in the form of an occasional storm, a

Exhibit 7-2
The Three-Step Change Process

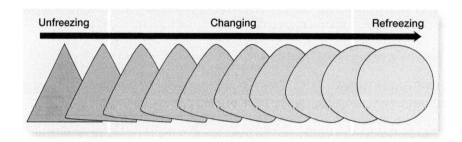

brief distraction in an otherwise calm and predictable trip. In this "calm waters" metaphor, change is seen as an occasional disruption in the normal flow of events. In another metaphor, the organization is seen as a small raft navigating a raging river with uninterrupted white-water rapids. Aboard the raft are half a dozen people who have never worked together before, who are totally unfamiliar with the river, who are unsure of their eventual destination, and who, as if things weren't bad enough, are traveling at night. In the "white-water rapids" metaphor, change is normal and expected, and managing it is a continual process. These two metaphors present very different approaches to understanding and responding to change. Let's take a closer look at each one.

The Calm Waters Metaphor

three-step change process
Unfreezing the status quo, changing to a new state, and refreezing to make the change permanent

At one time, the calm waters metaphor was fairly descriptive of the situation managers faced. It's best understood by using Kurt Lewin's **three-step change process.**[14] (See Exhibit 7-2.)

According to Lewin, successful change can be planned and requires *unfreezing* the status quo, *changing* to a new state, and *refreezing* to make the change permanent. The status quo is considered equilibrium. To move away from this equilibrium, unfreezing is necessary. Unfreezing can be thought of as preparing for the needed change. It can be done by increasing the *driving forces,* which are forces pushing for change; by decreasing the *restraining forces*, which are forces that resist change; or by combining the two approaches.

Once unfreezing is done, the change itself can be implemented. However, merely introducing change doesn't ensure that it will take hold. The new situation needs to be *refrozen* so that it can be sustained over time. Unless this last step is done, there's a strong chance that employees will revert back to the old equilibrium state—that is, the old ways of doing things. The objective of refreezing, then, is to stabilize the new situation by reinforcing the new behaviors.

Lewin's three-step process treats change as a move away from the organization's current equilibrium state. It's a calm waters scenario where an occasional disruption (a "storm") means planning and implementing change to deal with the disruption. Once the disruption has been dealt with, however, things continue on under the new changed situation. This type of environment isn't what most managers face today.

The White-Water Rapids Metaphor

An expert on weather patterns has said, "There are some times when you can predict weather well for the next fifteen days. Other times, you can only really forecast a couple of days. Sometimes you can't predict the next two hours." Today's business climate is turning out to be a lot like that two-hour weather scenario. "The pace of change in our economy and our culture is accelerating and our visibility about the future is declining."[15]

Here's what managing change might be like for you in a white-water rapids environment. The college you're attending has the following rules: Courses vary in length. When you sign up, you don't know how long a course will run. It might go for two weeks or fifteen weeks. Furthermore, the instructor can end a course at any time with no prior warning. If that isn't challenging enough, the length of the class changes each time it meets: sometimes the class lasts twenty minutes; other times, it runs for three hours. And the time of the next class meeting is set by the instructor during this class. Oh, and there's one more thing: All exams are unannounced, so you have to be ready for a test at any time. To succeed in this type of environment, you'd have to respond quickly to changing conditions. Students who are overly structured or uncomfortable with change wouldn't succeed.

Increasingly, managers are realizing that their job is much like what a student would face in such a college. The stability and predictability of the calm waters metaphor don't exist. Disruptions in the status quo are not occasional and temporary, and they are not followed by a return to calm waters. Many managers never get out of the rapids.

Amazon competes in a white-water rapids environment where major changes in technology and shopping behavior continue to reshape retailing. For instance, the company's first AmazonGo grocery, which requires no checkout and no lines, opened in Seattle in 2018. This model could potentially disrupt the entire retail grocery industry.
Source: MariaX/Shutterstock

AREAS of change

LO7.3 Have you seen (or used) the 3M Company's Command picture-hanging hooks? They're a relatively simple product consisting of plastic hooks and sticky foam strips. You can stick them anywhere and easily remove them without damaging the wall or having to use a drill. But while the product is simple, the manufacturing process to produce them isn't. The work used to be done in four different states and take 100 days. However, a couple of years ago, the company's former CEO decided to start "untangling its hairballs" by streamlining complex and complicated production processes. To do so required a number of changes. Today, those Command products are produced at a consolidated production "hub" in a third less time.[16] 3M was up for the "hairball" challenge and focused its change efforts on its people and processes.

Managers primarily focus on four areas of change: strategy, structure, technology, and people (see Exhibit 7-3).

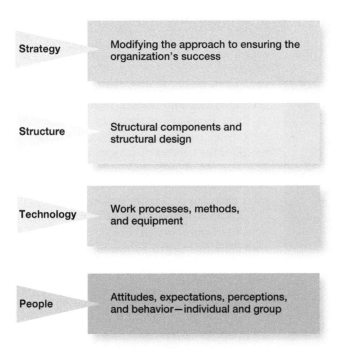

Strategy — Modifying the approach to ensuring the organization's success

Structure — Structural components and structural design

Technology — Work processes, methods, and equipment

People — Attitudes, expectations, perceptions, and behavior—individual and group

Exhibit 7-3
Four Types of Change

Strategy

Failure to change strategy when circumstances dictate can undermine a company's success. Consider the example of Ryanair, which is a regional airline based in Europe. Just more than thirty-five years old, the airline started out with a strategy to differentiate itself from the competition by offering low-cost airfares. Lower fares came with spartan cabin decor, hefty fees for baggage handling, snacks, and the use of the restroom facilities while onboard. The airline developed a poor reputation for customer service. Through the years, this strategy proved to undermine the airline's reputation and financial performance because of competitors who didn't skimp on amenities. With new, aggressive competitors, the company realized that a change in strategy was essential. At the center of the new strategy was raising customer service quality, including cutting out many extra fees. Michael O'Leary, Ryanair's CEO, admitted: "If I had only known that being nicer to our customers was good for business I would have done it years ago."[17] Had the company maintained its original strategy, Ryanair probably would no longer exist.

Structure

Any organizational change comes with risk. But changes in an organization's structure is often one of the surest ways to shake up a struggling firm. When it works, it can set the organization on the path to future success. When it doesn't, chaos can ensue. A reorganization at Microsoft is proving to be a true success story.[18]

In spite of its phenomenal success with Windows and its suite of Office products, Microsoft had lost much of its momentum when Satya Nadella took over the CEO position in 2014. The company was stagnant and rife with turf wars between business units. There was little innovation, and the company was surviving off of regular refresh cycles for Windows and Office. One of Nadella's first actions as CEO was to initiate a major restructuring. Product and platform groups were combined. His goal: do away with destructive internal competition and get business units to work together. Two years later, Nadella shook things up again by merging the Microsoft Research Group with the Bing, Cortana, and Information Platform Group teams. His goal this time was to create a 5,000-strong team of engineers and computer scientists who could innovate in artificial intelligence across the Microsoft product line. Nadella's structural changes appear to be working. They have reenergized Microsoft by stimulating innovation, improving morale and increasing employee engagement. Sales between 2014 and 2018 were up 27 percent, while Microsoft stock was up a whopping 208 percent!

Changes in the external environment or in organizational strategies often lead to changes in the organizational structure. Because an organization's structure is defined by how work gets done and who does it, managers can alter one or both of these *structural components*. For instance, departmental responsibilities can be combined, organizational levels eliminated, or the number of persons a manager supervises can be increased. More rules and procedures can be implemented to increase standardization. Or employees can be empowered to make decisions so decision making could be faster.

Another option would be to make major changes in the actual *structural design*. For instance, when Dow Chemical and DuPont merged to create DowDuPont, the goal was to cut $3 billion in costs, combine common product lines, and reorganize into three separate and more focused companies.[19] The reorganization set apart Dow, which housed products aimed at packaging, infrastructure, and consumer care; DuPont, which will focus on electronics, food-additives, biochemicals, military-protection, and safety-consulting; and Corteva, whose businesses relate to agriscience products and services.

When Microsoft CEO Satya Nadella joined the firm in 2014, he initiated a much-needed restructuring. Since then the company has been reenergized. Microsoft is now battling Amazon and Apple for the title of "America's Most Valuable Company."
Source: Ted S. Warren/AP Images

Technology

Managers can also change the technology used to convert inputs into outputs. Most early management studies dealt with changing technology. For instance, scientific management techniques involved implementing changes that would increase production efficiency. Today, technological changes usually involve the introduction of new equipment, tools, or methods; automation; or computerization.

For example, software company Visia Solutions developed a quality-assurance program for Ford Motor Company. Assembly workers in Ford's Valencia, Spain, manufacturing facility wear a small device on their wrists that enables them to ensure that vehicle specifications are correct. According to Ford of Europe's manufacturing vice president, employees only need to check a smartphone screen to assess any element of a vehicle's quality.

The future for many organizations will be replacing humans with robots. Already, thousands of companies are using robotic technology to cut costs, improve efficiency, and increase productivity. At an Orchard Supply Hardware warehouse, a chain owned by Lowe's, they are testing robots that use facial-recognition technology to identify human customers. They ask, "What are you looking for?" After customers select what they want on the robot's touch screen, it wheels away and asks the customer to follow. Similarly, Yotel, a hotel chain in London, Amsterdam, and New York City, has a robotic "staff" that can carry guests' luggage, deliver laundry, clean rooms, and make coffee.[20]

People

Changing people involves changing attitudes, expectations, perceptions, and behaviors. The popular term used to describe change methods that focus on people and the nature and quality of interpersonal work relationships is called **organizational development (OD)**.[21] Specifically, OD is a collection of change methods that try to improve organizational effectiveness and employee well-being. OD techniques value human and organizational growth, collaborative and participative processes, and a spirit of inquiry. The most popular OD techniques are described in Exhibit 7-4.

OD interventions are typically led by internal human resource specialists or outside consultants. And what might some of these interventions look like? Consultants, working with companies like Uber, Facebook, and Salesforce, have utilized a number

organizational development (OD)
Change methods that focus on people and the nature and quality of interpersonal work relationships

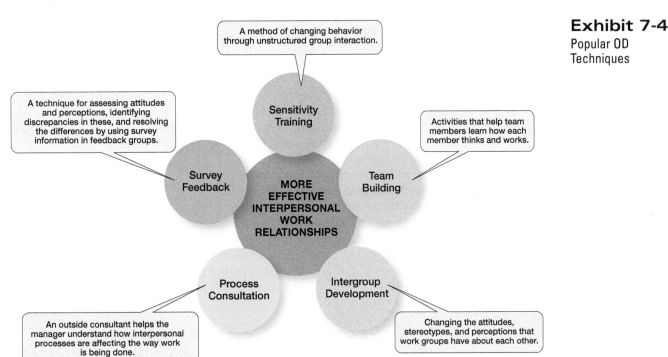

Exhibit 7-4
Popular OD Techniques

A method of changing behavior through unstructured group interaction.

A technique for assessing attitudes and perceptions, identifying discrepancies in these, and resolving the differences by using survey information in feedback groups.

Activities that help team members learn how each member thinks and works.

Sensitivity Training

Survey Feedback

Team Building

MORE EFFECTIVE INTERPERSONAL WORK RELATIONSHIPS

Process Consultation

Intergroup Development

An outside consultant helps the manager understand how interpersonal processes are affecting the way work is being done.

Changing the attitudes, stereotypes, and perceptions that work groups have about each other.

Managers at a firm in Austria use a team building competition as an organizational development method for helping employees learn to work more effectively together.
Source: Volkerpreusser/Alamy Stock Photos

of games and exercises as team-building experiences.[22] The focus is on building trust by allowing employees to be vulnerable in a low-stakes environment and to try out new ideas without the fear of criticism or rejection. These consultants rely heavily on fun activities to make the team-building exercises motivational and relevant. Examples include karaoke sessions, music video competitions, and even taking over an island and turning it into a fortress of fun.

MANAGING change

L07.4 Change is often a threat to people in organizations. The fact that organizations create job descriptions, rules, standard operating procedures, and lines of authority all reinforce maintenance of the status quo. So organizations tend to build up inertia that motivates people to resist change. Add to this people's preference for routine and predictability, and you have the ingredients for resistance to change. Let's look at why people resist change and what can be done to minimize their resistance.

Why Do People Resist Change?

Why do people resist change? The main reasons include uncertainty, habit, concern over personal loss, and the belief that the change is not in the organization's best interest.[23]

Change replaces the known with uncertainty. No matter how much you may dislike attending college, at least you know what's expected of you. When you leave college for the world of full-time employment, you'll trade the known for the unknown. Employees in organizations are faced with similar uncertainty. For example, when quality control methods based on statistical models are introduced into manufacturing plants, many quality control inspectors have to learn the new methods. Some may fear that they will be unable to do so and may develop a negative attitude toward the change or behave poorly if required to use them.

Another cause of resistance is that we do things out of habit. Every day when you go to school or work, you probably go the same way, if you're like most people. We're creatures of habit. Life is complex enough—we don't want to have to consider the full range of options for the hundreds of decisions we make every day. To cope with this complexity, we rely on habits or programmed responses. But when confronted with change, our tendency to respond in our accustomed ways becomes a source of resistance.

The third cause of resistance is the fear of losing something already possessed. Change threatens the investment you've already made in the status quo. The more people have invested in the current system, the more they are likely to resist change. Why? They fear the loss of status, money, authority, friendships, personal convenience, or other benefits they value. For instance, the Mayo Clinic in Rochester, Minnesota, implemented the use of radio-frequency identification technology (RFID) to track the location of patients, equipment, and caregivers, including doctors and nurses within the facility's emergency department.[24] The goal was to improve patient care. However, hospital management learned that some of the caregivers expressed concern with the use of RFID technology. Their concerns centered on how the data would be used in performance reviews.

A final cause of resistance is a person's belief that the change is incompatible with the goals and interests of the organization. For instance, an employee who believes that a proposed new job procedure will reduce product quality can be expected to resist the change. This type of resistance actually can be beneficial to the organization if expressed in a positive way.

Employee resistance to change is a primary reason why 70 percent of company change initiatives don't achieve their goals.[25]

Techniques for Reducing Resistance to Change

When managers see resistance to change as dysfunctional, what can they do? Several strategies have been suggested in dealing with resistance to change.[26] These approaches include education and communication, participation, facilitation and support, negotiation, manipulation and co-optation, and coercion. These tactics are summarized here and described in Exhibit 7-5. Managers should view these techniques as tools and use the most appropriate one(s), depending on the type and source of the resistance.

Let's Get REAL

The Scenario:

A health products company decides to overhaul its product lines, eliminating some products and adding some new ones. Tyler Russo manages the sales department at the company, and he's finding that his sales staff is having a difficult time with these changes. Some of the staff really liked some of the products that are no longer available, and they generally don't seem excited about the new products.

What can Tyler do to convince his staff to give the new portfolio of products a chance?

When rolling out a change within an organization, one of the most important things to do is to "lead with the why." Tyler should make sure he has clearly communicated to the team why the company has made this change: what the value of the change is to the business, the customer, and the team. This will ensure that the team is starting from a place of common language and understanding. If employees are demonstrating resistance to the change, Tyler should seek to understand their why. Why are they resistant to this change, and why specifically are they so passionate about the previous products? Often, resistance to change is due to a lack of awareness or education. Understanding their why will enable Tyler to craft his next steps accordingly. From there, Tyler should lead by example by being vocal, active, and visible in supporting the new products. Next, he can highlight reps on his team who are selling the new product and are seeing success, as well as customer success stories, to continue to reinforce the benefits of this change.

◀ **Rebecca Ross**
Manager, Customer Service

Source: Rebecca Ross

Technique	When Used	Advantage	Disadvantage
Education and communication	When resistance is due to misinformation	Clear up misunderstandings	May not work when mutual trust and credibility are lacking
Participation	When resisters have the expertise to make a contribution	Increase involvement and acceptance	Time-consuming; has potential for a poor solution
Facilitation and support	When resisters are fearful and anxiety ridden	Can facilitate needed adjustments	Expensive; no guarantee of success
Negotiation	When resistance comes from a powerful group	Can "buy" commitment	Potentially high cost; opens doors for others to apply pressure too
Manipulation and co-optation	When a powerful group's endorsement is needed	Inexpensive, easy way to gain support	Can backfire, causing change agent to lose credibility
Coercion	When a powerful group's endorsement is needed	Inexpensive, easy way to gain support	May be illegal; may undermine change agent's credibility

Exhibit 7-5
Techniques for Reducing Resistance to Change

Education and communication can reduce resistance to change by helping employees see the logic of the change effort. This technique, of course, assumes that much of the resistance lies in misinformation or poor communication. The use of social media might be useful as part of an overall communication plan. A study found that 55 percent of participants who had experienced change in the workplace expressed a desire that their employer provide more social media engagement.[27] In addition, 42 percent preferred having more face-to-face communication. These findings suggest that both the use of technology and conventional methods in communicating change should be part of a plan to deliver information about change.

Participation involves bringing those individuals directly affected by the proposed change into the decision-making process. It follows from the recognition that people don't tend to resist changes that they helped to make. Participation allows individuals to provide input, increase the quality of the process, and increase employee commitment to the final decision.

Facilitation and support involve helping employees deal with the fear and anxiety associated with the change effort. This help may include employee counseling, therapy, new skills training, or a short, paid leave of absence.

Negotiation involves exchanging something of value for an agreement to lessen the resistance to the change effort. This resistance technique may be quite useful when the resistance comes from a powerful source.

Manipulation and co-optation refer to covert attempts to influence others about the change. For instance, it may involve distorting facts to make the change appear more attractive.

Finally, *coercion* can be used to deal with resistance to change. Coercion involves the use of direct threats or force against the resisters.

CONTEMPORARY issues in managing change

L07.5 In this section, we discuss two contemporary issues in managing change: the challenge in changing an organization's culture and helping employees cope with the stress that often accompanies change.

Changing an Organization's Culture

Let's begin with the bad news: an organization's culture is very difficult to change.[28] The fact that it's made up of relatively stable and permanent characteristics tends to make it resilient to change efforts. Add in the fact that established organizations have tended to hire people who fit well with the current culture means people are well matched and comfortable with the status quo and resist change. This helps explain why it took decades to change AT&T's corporate culture after the government broke up its monopoly of the US phone business. AT&T employees had long been used to a relaxed workplace where there was no competition.[29]

Acknowledging that organizational cultures are hard to change doesn't mean that they can't be changed. They can. But successfully changing an organization's culture should be looked at as a process that can take years. And certain cultures are easier to change than others. Let's look at some of the relevant factors.

UNDERSTANDING THE SITUATIONAL FACTORS What "favorable conditions" facilitate cultural change? One is that *a dramatic crisis occurs*, such as an unexpected financial setback, the loss of a major customer, or a dramatic technological innovation by a competitor. Such a shock can weaken the status quo and make people start thinking about the relevance of the current culture. Another condition is when *leadership changes hands*. New top leadership

Royal Bank of Canada CEO David McKay (left in photo) has been instrumental in changing the bank's culture to emphasize the importance of working together and focusing on the customer.
Source: GARY HE/REUTERS/Newscom

can provide an alternative set of key values and may be perceived as more capable of responding to the crisis than the old leaders were. Another is that *the organization is young and small*. The younger the organization, the less entrenched its culture. And it's easier for managers to communicate new values in a small organization than in a large one. Finally, change favors *weak cultures*. Weak cultures are more receptive to change than strong ones because they're not as deeply rooted.[30]

MAKING CHANGES IN CULTURE If conditions are right, how do managers change culture? No single action is likely to have the impact necessary to change something ingrained and highly valued. Managers need a strategy for managing cultural change, as described in Exhibit 7-6. These suggestions focus on specific actions that managers can take.[31] Following them, however, is no guarantee that the cultural change efforts will succeed. Organizational members don't quickly let go of values that they understand and that have worked well for them in the past. As we previously noted, change, if it comes, will be slow. Also, managers must stay alert to protect against any return to old, familiar traditions.

Employee Stress

As a student, you've probably experienced stress—class projects, exams, even juggling a job and school. Then, there's the stress associated with getting a decent job after graduation. But even after you've landed that job, stress isn't likely to stop. For many employees, organizational change creates stress. An uncertain environment characterized by time pressures, increasing workloads, lack of work-life balance, mergers, and restructuring has created a large number of employees who are overworked and stressed.[32] How widespread is stress in the workplace? An American Institute of Stress survey found 40 percent of US workers reporting that their job was very or extremely stressful. Twenty-five percent said that their jobs were the number one stressor in their lives.[33]

The US workplace, of course, has no monopoly on stress. It's a worldwide phenomenon.[34] Global studies indicate that some 50 percent of workers surveyed in 16 European countries reported that stress and job responsibility have risen significantly; 35 percent of Canadian workers surveyed said they are under high job stress; in Australia, cases of occupational stress jumped 21 percent in a one-year period; and some 83 percent of call-center workers in India suffer from sleeping disorders. In Japan, where 100-hour workweeks are not uncommon, the government reported that more than 2,000 Japanese killed themselves in 2016 due to work-related stress.

WHAT IS STRESS? **Stress** is the adverse reaction people have to excessive pressure placed on them from extraordinary demands, constraints, or opportunities.[35] Stress isn't always bad. Although it's often discussed in a negative context, stress can be positive, especially when it offers a potential gain. For instance, functional stress allows an athlete, stage performer, or employee to perform at his or her highest level at crucial times.

stress
The adverse reaction people have to excessive pressure placed on them from extraordinary demands, constraints, or opportunities

Exhibit 7-6
Changing Culture

- ■ *Set the tone through management behavior;* top managers, particularly, need to be positive role models.
- ■ Create *new stories, symbols, and rituals* to replace those currently in use.
- ■ Select, promote, and support employees who *adopt* the new values.
- ■ *Redesign socialization processes* to align with the new values.
- ■ To encourage acceptance of the new values, *change the reward system.*
- ■ Replace unwritten norms with *clearly specified expectations.*
- ■ *Shake up current subcultures* through job transfers, job rotation, and/or terminations.
- ■ Work to get consensus through *employee participation* and creating a *climate with a high level of trust.*

stressors
Factors that cause stress

role conflicts
Work expectations that are hard to satisfy

role overload
Having more work to accomplish than time permits

role ambiguity
When role expectations are not clearly understood

Type A personality
People who have a chronic sense of urgency and an excessive competitive drive

Type B personality
People who are relaxed and easygoing and accept change easily

However, stress is more often associated with constraints and demands. A constraint prevents you from doing what you desire; demands refer to the loss of something desired. When you take a test at school or have your annual performance review at work, you feel stress because you confront opportunity, constraints, and demands. A good performance review may lead to a promotion, greater responsibilities, and a higher salary. But a poor review may keep you from getting the promotion. An extremely poor review might lead to your being fired.

WHAT CAUSES STRESS? Stress can be caused by personal factors and by job-related factors called **stressors**.[37] Clearly, change of any kind—personal or job related—has the potential to cause stress because it can involve demands, constraints, or opportunities. Organizations have no shortage of factors that can cause stress. Pressures to avoid errors or complete tasks in a limited time period, changes in the way reports are filed, a demanding supervisor, and unpleasant coworkers are a few examples. Let's look at five categories of organizational stressors: task demands, role demands, interpersonal demands, organization structure, and organizational leadership.

Task demands are factors related to an employee's job. They include the design of a person's job (autonomy, task variety, degree of automation), working conditions, and the physical work layout. Work quotas can put pressure on employees when their "outcomes" are perceived as excessive. The more interdependence between an employee's tasks and the tasks of others, the greater the potential for stress. *Autonomy*, on the other hand, tends to lessen stress. Jobs in which temperatures, noise, or other working conditions are dangerous or undesirable can increase anxiety. So, too, can working in an overcrowded room or in a visible location where interruptions are constant.

Role demands relate to pressures placed on an employee as a function of the particular role he or she plays in the organization. **Role conflicts** create expectations that may be hard to reconcile or satisfy. **Role overload** is experienced when the employee is expected to do more than time permits. **Role ambiguity** is created when role expectations are not clearly understood and the employee is not sure what he or she is to do.

Interpersonal demands are pressures created by other employees. Lack of social support from colleagues and poor interpersonal relationships can cause considerable stress, especially among employees with a high social need.

Organization structure can increase stress. Excessive rules or an employee's lack of opportunity to participate in decisions that affect him or her are examples of structural variables that might be potential sources of stress.

Organizational leadership represents the supervisory style of the organization's managers. Some managers create a culture characterized by tension, fear, and anxiety. They establish unrealistic pressures to perform in the short run, impose excessively tight controls, and routinely fire employees who don't measure up. This style of leadership filters down through the organization and affects all employees.

Personal factors that can create stress include family issues, personal economic problems, and inherent personality characteristics. Because employees bring their personal problems to work with them, a full understanding of employee stress requires a manager to be aware of these personal factors. Evidence also indicates that employees' personalities have an effect on how susceptible they are to stress. The most commonly used labels for these personality traits are Type A and Type B.[38]

Type A personality is characterized by a chronic sense of time urgency, an excessive competitive drive, and difficulty accepting and enjoying leisure time. The opposite of Type A is **Type B personality**. Type Bs are relaxed, easygoing, and accept change easily. Until quite recently, it was believed

High stress comes with many jobs. One of the more stressful jobs is being a trader on the New York Stock Exchange.
Source: Brendan McDermid/Reuters

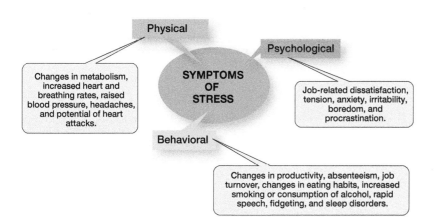

Exhibit 7-7
Symptoms of Stress

that Type As were more likely to experience stress on and off the job. A closer analysis of the evidence, however, has produced new conclusions. Studies show that only the hostility and anger associated with Type A behavior are actually associated with the negative effects of stress. And Type Bs are just as susceptible to the same anxiety-producing elements. For managers, it is important to recognize that Type A employees are more likely to show symptoms of stress, even if organizational and personal stressors are low.

WHAT ARE THE SYMPTOMS OF STRESS?   We see stress in a number of ways. For instance, an employee who is experiencing high stress may become depressed, accident prone, or argumentative; may have difficulty making routine decisions; or may be easily distracted. Employees in organizations where downsizing is occurring tend to get ill at twice the rate of employees whose jobs are secure.[39] As Exhibit 7-7 shows, stress symptoms can be grouped under three general categories: physical, psychological, and behavioral.

HOW CAN STRESS BE REDUCED?   As mentioned earlier, not all stress is dysfunctional. Because stress can never be totally eliminated from a person's life, managers want to reduce the stress that leads to dysfunctional work behavior. How? Through controlling certain job-related factors and, to a more limited extent, offering help for personal stress.[40]

Things managers can do in terms of job-related factors begin with employee selection. Managers need to make sure an employee's abilities match the job requirements. When employees are in over their heads, their stress levels are typically high. A realistic job preview during the selection process can minimize stress by reducing ambiguity over job expectations. Improved organizational communications will also keep ambiguity-induced stress to a minimum. Similarly, a performance planning program such as MBO (management by objectives) will clarify job responsibilities, provide clear performance goals, and reduce ambiguity through feedback. Job redesign is also a way to reduce stress. If stress can be traced to boredom or to work overload, jobs should be redesigned to increase challenge or to reduce the workload. Redesigns that increase opportunities for employees to participate in decisions and to gain social support also have been found to reduce stress.

Some companies—including Airbnb, Google, Etsy, Dropbox, and Salesforce—have developed unique ways to help employees manage stress.[41] The list includes on-site yoga classes, concierge services, on-site daycare, open-door dog policies, days off to volunteer, and on-site "distractions" like ping-pong tables, basketball courts, and indoor rock-climbing walls.

Stress from an employee's personal life raises two problems. First, it's difficult for the manager to control directly. Second, ethical considerations include whether the manager has the right to intrude—even in the most subtle ways—in an employee's

Workplace CONFIDENTIAL   Coping with Job Stress

We asked several dozen recent college graduates whether they had experienced job stress and, if so, what was the source. Almost all said they had. Here are a few of their responses: "I've got ridiculous deadlines to meet," "They let several people in my department go, and two of us had to absorb their work," "Business is slow and there are rumors of layoffs," and "I hoped to take my two-week vacation next month, but I can't. Too much work to do."

These recent graduates don't appear to be unusual. Numerous studies indicate that *job stress* is far and away the major source of stress for American adults. For instance, a recent survey found that 83 percent of American workers said they were stressed at work. And what was stressing them out? Their answers included unreasonable workloads, poor compensation, frustration with coworkers, commuting, working in a job that was not their first choice, poor work-life balance, lack of opportunity for advancement, and fear of being fired or laid off. Interestingly, those aged eighteen to twenty-nine indicated the highest stress levels due largely, they said, to work and job stability concerns.

So if you're among those stressing out at work, what can you do to help reduce that stress? Here's what the experts suggest:

Time management. Start with time management. As noted in Chapter 1, effective time management can allow you to be more efficient, get more things done, and help to reduce workload-based stress. We know that many people manage their time poorly. If you're well organized, you can often accomplish twice as much as the person who is poorly organized. So an understanding and utilization of basic time-management principles can help you better cope with tensions created by job demands.

Work breaks. A growing body of research shows that simply taking breaks from work at routine intervals can facilitate psychological recovery and significantly reduce stress. If you work at a desk or a fixed workstation, for both reducing stress and your general health, get up at least every half hour and walk around for a few minutes.

Deep-relaxation techniques. You can teach yourself to reduce tension through deep-relaxation techniques such as deep breathing. The objective is to reach a state of deep physical relaxation, in which you focus all your energy on the release of muscle tension.

Deep breathing is one of the simplest techniques for addressing stress. The technique requires you to avoid shallow breaths and to learn to breathe from the abdomen. This technique works on neuromuscular functioning and leads to relaxing the neuromuscular system.

An extension of deep breathing is progressive muscle relaxation. With this technique, you assume a comfortable position and begin to breathe deeply. Then you relax groups of muscles one at a time, beginning with the feet and working up.

Deep relaxation for fifteen to twenty minutes a day releases strain and provides a pronounced sense of peacefulness, as well as significant changes in heart rate, blood pressure, and other physiological factors.

Meditation. While meditation is another form of relaxation, we separate it out because of its wide popularity and long history as a stress-reducing practice. Meditation has been done for thousands of years and continues to be a well-recognized approach to stress reduction. It's a group of self-regulated techniques you use to refocus your attention through concentration to attain a subjective, even "blissful," state that proponents describe as calmness, clarity, and concentration. Although meditation is done in many forms, a popular Western variety has individuals blank out their mind and stop conscious thinking. This is often combined with a mantra or focusing on an object. Advocates of meditation report that it increases calmness and physical relaxation, improves psychological balance, and enhances overall health and well-being.

Yoga. The American Yoga Association suggests that a few yoga exercises practiced daily help to regulate breathing and relax the body. Exercises, such as the sun salutation sequence of poses, have been shown to be particularly helpful because they encourage you to breathe deeply and rhythmically.

Imagery. When life and work seem to overwhelm you, try putting your mind in a more peaceful place. Think of the most peaceful and serene location that you can envision—such as a quiet Caribbean beach, a peaceful setting in a forest, or a sailboat on a calm lake. Then close your eyes and imagine yourself there. So, using the beach example, imagine the waves gently coming ashore, the rhythmic sounds of the waves, the smell of salt air, and the warm sun on your skin. Then apply some of the relaxation techniques described previously.

Physical exercise. Physicians have recommended noncompetitive physical exercise—such as aerobics, Pilates, walking, jogging, swimming, and riding a bicycle—as a way to deal with excessive stress levels. These activities increase lung capacity, lower the resting heart rate, and provide a mental diversion from work pressures, effectively reducing work-related levels of stress.

Social support network. Finally, friends, family, or work colleagues can provide an outlet when stress levels become excessive. Expanding your social support network provides someone to hear your problems and offer a perspective on a stressful situation more objective than your own.[42]

personal life. If a manager believes it's ethical and the employee is receptive, the manager might consider several approaches. Employee *counseling* can provide stress relief. Employees often want to talk to someone about their problems, and the organization—through its managers, in-house human resource counselors, or free or low-cost outside professional help—can meet that need. A *time management program* can help employees whose personal lives suffer from a lack of planning to sort out their priorities. Still another approach is organizationally sponsored *wellness programs*. For example, Phillips 66 works with WebMD as their wellness partner and includes services such as WebMD Health Coaching. This service enables employees to have confidential phone meetings with a health expert.[43]

STIMULATING innovation

L07.6 Thomas A. Edison once said: "I find out what the world needs. Then I go ahead and try to invent it."[44] Today, innovation is the foundation of highly successful organizations. In a recent survey of global companies, 79 percent of respondents ranked innovation as either their topmost priority or a top-three priority.[45] And which companies are leading the way in innovation? The top five include Apple, Netflix, Square, Tencent, and Amazon.[46]

What's the secret to the success of these and other innovator champions? What can other managers do to make their organizations more innovative? In the following sections, we'll try to answer those questions as we discuss the factors behind innovation.

Innovation was the foundation of Thomas Edison's highly successful business enterprise. To stimulate innovation, Edison established an industrial research and development facility for creating new products and adapting them to the needs of users.
Source: Mondadori Portfolio/Getty Images

Creativity Versus Innovation

The definition of innovation varies widely, depending on who you ask. For instance, the Merriam-Webster dictionary defines innovation as "the introduction of something new" and "a new idea, method, or device; novelty." The CEO of the company that makes Bubble Wrap says, "It means inventing a product that has never existed." To the CEO of Ocean Spray, it means "turning an overlooked commodity, such as leftover cranberry skins into a consumer snack like Craisins."[47] First, we need to look at the concept of creativity. **Creativity** refers to the ability to combine ideas in a unique way or to make unusual associations between ideas.[48] A creative organization develops unique ways of working or novel solutions to problems. But creativity by itself isn't enough. The outcomes of the creative process need to be turned into useful products or work methods, which is **innovation**. Thus, the innovative organization is characterized by its ability to generate new ideas that are implemented into new products, processes, and procedures designed to be useful—that is, to channel creativity into useful outcomes. When managers talk about changing an organization to make it more creative, they usually mean they want to stimulate and nurture innovation.

creativity
The ability to combine ideas in a unique way or to make unusual associations between ideas

innovation
Taking creative ideas and turning them into useful products or work methods

Stimulating and Nurturing Innovation

There are three sets of variables that have been found to stimulate innovation. They pertain to the organization's structure, culture, and human resource practices. (See Exhibit 7-8.)

STRUCTURAL VARIABLES An organization's structure can have a huge impact on innovativeness. Research into the effect of structural variables on innovation

Exhibit 7-8

Innovation Variables

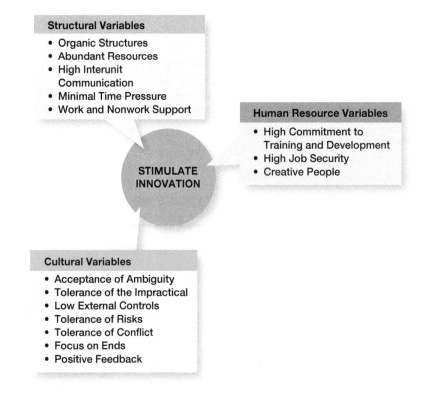

shows five things.[49] First, an organic-type structure positively influences innovation. Because this structure is low in formalization, centralization, and work specialization, it facilitates the flexibility and sharing of ideas that are critical to innovation. Second, the availability of plentiful resources provides a key building block for innovation. With an abundance of resources, managers can afford to purchase innovations, can afford the cost of instituting innovations, and can absorb failures. Third, frequent communication between organizational units helps break down barriers to innovation. Cross-functional teams, task forces, and other such organizational designs facilitate interaction across departmental lines and are widely used in innovative organizations. Fourth, innovative organizations try to minimize extreme time pressures on creative activities despite the demands of white-water rapids environments. Although time pressures may spur people to work harder and may make them feel more creative, studies show that it actually causes them to be less creative. Companies such as Google, 3M, and Hewlett-Packard actually urge staff researchers to spend a chunk of their workweek on self-initiated projects, even if those projects are outside the individual's work area of expertise. Finally, studies have shown that an employee's creative performance was enhanced when an organization's structure explicitly supported creativity. Beneficial kinds of support included things like encouragement, open communication, readiness to listen, and useful feedback.

CULTURAL VARIABLES Innovative organizations tend to have common cultural elements.[50] They encourage experimentation, set creativity goals, reward both successes and failures, and celebrate mistakes. An innovative organization is likely to have the following characteristics.

- *Accept ambiguity.* Too much emphasis on objectivity and specificity constrains creativity.
- *Tolerate the impractical.* Individuals who offer impractical, even foolish, answers to what-if questions are not stifled. What at first seems impractical might lead to innovative solutions. Encourage entrepreneurial thinking.

- *Keep external controls minimal.* Rules, regulations, policies, and similar organizational controls are kept to a minimum.
- *Tolerate risk.* Employees are encouraged to experiment without fear of consequences should they fail. Treat mistakes as learning opportunities.
- *Tolerate conflict.* Diversity of opinions is encouraged. Harmony and agreement between individuals or units are *not* assumed to be evidence of high performance.
- *Focus on ends rather than means.* Goals are made clear, and individuals are encouraged to consider alternative routes toward meeting the goals. Focusing on ends suggests that several right answers might be possible for any given problem.
- *Provide positive feedback.* Managers provide positive feedback, encouragement, and support so employees feel that their creative ideas receive attention.

Trying out the latest in Google's virtual reality technology, Colette Archer, a senior manager at PwC, appears at the opening of Europe's first PwC and Google innovation Lab in Belfast. Google nurtures a culture of innovation that tolerates risks, encourages experimentation, and views mistakes as learning opportunities. *Source: Brian Lawless/PA images/Alamy Stock Photos*

HUMAN RESOURCE VARIABLES In this category, we find that innovative organizations actively promote the training and development of their members so their knowledge remains current; offer their employees high job security to reduce the fear of getting fired for making mistakes; and encourage individuals to become **idea champions**, actively and enthusiastically supporting new ideas, building support, overcoming resistance, and ensuring that innovations are implemented. Research finds that idea champions have common personality characteristics: extremely high self-confidence, enthusiasm, persistence, and a tendency toward risk taking. They also display characteristics associated with dynamic leadership. They inspire and energize others with their vision of the potential of an innovation and through their strong personal conviction in their mission.[51]

idea champions
Individuals who actively and enthusiastically support new ideas, build support, overcome resistance, and ensure that innovations are implemented

Let's Get REAL

The Scenario:

The challenge to find new candidates is at the top of Katie Franklin's priority list. As a branch manager for a national temporary employee agency, Katie must lead her team to keep their database full of high-quality candidates to make sure the agency can quickly provide temporary employees to their clients on short notice. At the last staff meeting, Katie's team had a lot of creative ideas on how to recruit new candidates. However, a few weeks later none of the ideas have been developed and implemented. Creative ideas are great, but without implementation, they can't help the business.

How can Katie help her employees turn their creative ideas into innovative new practices?

Sounds like too many ideas with too little accountability. Bring the team back together and narrow the list of creative ideas down to a more manageable list, engaging the entire team in the dialogue. With only a few ideas to work through, delegate a leader and discuss the next best step for each one, jotting down a brief outline of action items, resources needed, and due dates. Regularly check in with the team, removing roadblocks and discussing challenges. With employee time and resources at stake, if the idea is not producing results, you will want to know early on and put those resources toward the more successful ideas.

◀ **Christina Moser**
Strategic Account Manager

Source: Christina Moser

DISRUPTIVE innovation

L07.7 In 1988, Kodak had 170,000 employees and sold 85 percent of all photo paper worldwide. Within just a few years, their business model disappeared and they were bankrupt. Photographic film went the way of the horse and buggy. Twenty-five years ago, every Main Street and shopping mall in the United States had a bookstore. Chains like Borders and Barnes & Noble had hundreds of locations, and there were additionally thousands of small bookstores scattered across America. Then along came Amazon, offering book buyers a million-plus titles at super-low prices, all accessible without leaving the comfort of home. Amazon single-handedly disrupted the brick-and-mortar bookstore. Looking ahead, the self-driving cars you'll be using in ten years may not be built by GM, Ford, or Toyota. As cars become "computers on wheels," traditional auto manufacturers may be displaced by companies like Apple, Google, and Intel. Welcome to the world of disruptive innovation!

Definition

Disruptive innovation describes innovations in products, services or processes that radically change an industry's rules of the game.[52] Oftentimes, a smaller company with fewer resources successfully challenges established companies.[53] Those smaller companies prove themselves to be disruptive by serving overlooked segments of possible consumers with products or services at relatively low prices. Although the term "disruptive innovation" is relatively new, the concept isn't. For instance, economist Joseph Schumpeter used the term "creative destruction" more than seventy-five years ago to describe how capitalism builds on processes that destroy old technologies but replaces them with new and better ones.[54] That, in essence, is disruptive innovation.

In practice, disruptive innovation has been around for centuries. Vanderbilt's railroads disrupted the sailing-ship business. Alexander Bell's telephone rang the death knell for Western Union's telegraphy. Ford and other automobile builders destroyed horse-drawn-buggy manufacturers. As Exhibit 7-9 illustrates, there is no shortage of businesses that have suffered at the expense of disruptive innovation.

It's helpful to distinguish disruptive innovation from sustaining innovation. When most of us think of innovations, we tend to think of things like the introduction of the high-definition television, back-up cameras on cars, fingerprint technology on smartphones, or Double Stuf Oreos. These are examples of **sustaining innovation** because they sustain the status quo. They represent small and incremental changes in established products rather than dramatic breakthroughs. While the original television set disrupted the radio industry, high-def TV just improved the quality of the TV picture.

Borders is among a number of chains that have closed their doors as companies such as Amazon have reinvented how people shop for books and other products.
Source: Kristoffer Tripplaar/Alamy Stock Photos

disruptive innovation
Innovations in products, services or processes that radically change an industry's rules of the game

sustaining innovation
Small and incremental changes in established products rather than dramatic breakthroughs

Why Disruptive Innovation Is Important

It's often said that "success breeds success." But success can also breed failure. How? Companies that are successful tend to grow. With growth comes expanded size. And as we'll describe, large size frequently makes successful companies vulnerable to disruptive competitors.

Large organizations create rules and regulations to standardize operations. They create multiple departments with defined areas of responsibility. And they create socialization processes—like new-employee orientations and corporate handbooks—that convey to employees "the way we do things around here." The result is that these successful organizations establish entrenched cultures and values that, on the one hand, guide employees, but, on the other hand, also act as constraints on change. Companies like Blockbuster Video, Polaroid, and Woolworths were iconic companies

Established Business	Disruptor
Compact disc	Apple iTunes
Carbon paper	Xerox copy machine
Portable radio	Sony Walkman
Sony Walkman	Apple iPod
Typewriters	IBM PC
Weekly news magazines	CNN
TV networks	Cable and Netflix
Local travel agencies	Expedia
Stockbrokers	eTrade
Traveler's checks	ATMs and Visa
Encyclopedias	Wikipedia
Newspaper classified ads	Craigslist
AM/FM radio stations	Sirius XM
Tax preparation services	Intuit's Turbo Tax
Yellow Pages	Google
Paper maps	Garmin's GPS
Paperback books	Kindle
Lawyers	LegalZoom
Taxis	Uber
Hotels	Airbnb

Exhibit 7-9

Examples of Past Disruptive Innovators

in their day that became hostage to their previous successes—and it led to their eventual decline.

New ideas for products or services that differ significantly from the status quo are a threat to the established power structure within large companies. And as we'll elaborate later, entrenched cultures tend to be threatened by disruptive ideas. For instance, when Ross Perot worked for IBM and suggested that the company move into the computer services business, he was told that IBM sold computer hardware, not services. Perot resigned, created EDS Corp. to provide computer support, and became a billionaire. Similarly, when Xerox engineers invented the computer mouse and the graphical user interface, which would ultimately become the standard for personal computers, Xerox executives dismissed these products with "we're in the copying business" and then literally gave the inventions to Steve Jobs and Apple. Jobs then featured these innovations on Apple's Mac computer.

The fact is that disruptive innovations are a threat to many established businesses, and responding with sustaining innovations isn't enough. Making incremental improvements to the BlackBerry smartphone, for instance, couldn't help its manufacturer compete against the far superior iOS and Android devices from Apple and Samsung. Of course, all "disruptive" innovations don't succeed. The radical nature of the changes they initiate implies a high level of risk. The Segway "personal transporter" was introduced with much fanfare. It was hyped as a replacement to the automobile for short trips. It didn't happen. Similarly, the Google Glass wearable computer was promoted as a hands-free disruptive replacement for a smartphone, but it failed in the marketplace.

Who's Vulnerable?

So which businesses are most vulnerable to disruptive innovations? The answer, as alluded to previously, is large, established, and highly profitable organizations. Why? Because they have the most to lose and are most vested in their current markets and technologies.

fyi

Eighty percent of executives expect their current business models to be disrupted by innovation in the near future.[55]

Successful organizations focus on what they do best. They repeat what has succeeded in the past, and they put their resources into the ventures that have the highest probability of generating maximum profits. Small markets, which typically describe those applicable to early disruptive innovations, don't fit with the growth needs of large organizations. Importantly, large organizations have distinct cultures and values that define their capabilities and limit their ability to move into new products or markets. Sears's management, for instance, might have seen a need for discount department stores in the 1970s, but it didn't have the personnel, buying channels, structure, or low-cost locations to move into this market. Upstart Walmart didn't have those limitations and was able to radically disrupt the market. Similarly, Tesla was able to conceive, design, and produce an electric car in a time frame and at a quality level that could never have been done by a Fiat Chrysler.

Disruptive innovations, especially at the beginning, typically apply to emerging or small markets and project lower profits than a firm's mainline products. And their novelty has little or no appeal to the organization's most profitable customers. Ken Olsen, founder of Digital Equipment Corporation, said in 1977, "There is no reason anyone would want a computer in their home." What he was acknowledging was that he couldn't see investing DEC resources into microcomputers when his company was making huge profits from selling much larger systems. And his customers were perfectly happy with DEC's larger systems. So large and successful companies are motivated to repeat what has succeeded in the past and invest in ideas that offer the highest probability of generating maximum profits—and those aren't disruptive innovations. This is why, for instance, VW, Honda, and Toyota were able to disrupt the US auto market by introducing compact cars. GM, Ford, and Chrysler were initially reluctant to pursue this market segment because they made their money making big cars.

Which businesses or occupations are currently in the throes of disruptive innovation? Here are a few: bank tellers (to ATMs), camera manufacturers (smartphones), financial services (to online providers), and travel agents (to online travel services). Which others may be vulnerable in the near future? Actuaries (computer algorithms), maintenance personnel (robotics), truck drivers (self-driving vehicles), model builders (3-D printers), and pipeline workers and oil drillers (renewable energy) are vulnerable.

Implications

Disruptive innovation has the potential to upend entrepreneurs, corporate managers, and even your career plans. Let's take a specific look at what the future might hold for each.

FOR ENTREPRENEURS   Think opportunity! Entrepreneurs thrive on change and innovation. Major disruptions open the door for new products and services to replace established and mature businesses. If you're looking to create a new business with a large potential upside, look for established businesses that can be disrupted with a cheaper, simpler, smaller, or more convenient substitute.

"Despite their endowments in technology, brand names, manufacturing prowess, management experience, distribution muscle, and just plain cash, successful companies populated by good managers have a genuinely hard time doing what does not fit their model for how to make money."[56] So lack of resources, which create high barriers of entry into established markets, isn't a critical liability for entrepreneurs. The small size of new entrepreneurial firms typically comes with low overhead and a minimal cost structure, which can translate into a huge competitive advantage. Large companies come with big overhead; bureaucratic rules, regulations, and hierarchies that limit flexibility and speed of response; and entrenched cultures that are highly effective at killing ideas that don't fit neatly into their current business models.

FOR CORPORATE MANAGERS   For managers in large, successful businesses, the challenge to disruptive innovation is to create an appropriate response. Contrary to popular belief, management in these organizations is not powerless. They can become disruptive innovators themselves. But the evidence is overwhelming that their disruptive response must be carried out by a separate group that is physically and structurally disconnected from the business's main operations. "With few exceptions, the only instances in which mainstream firms have successfully established a timely position in a disruptive technology were those in which the firms' managers set up an autonomous organization charged with building a new and independent business around the disruptive technology."[57] This can be achieved by either creating a new business from scratch or acquiring a small company and keeping it separate.

These separate groups are frequently referred to as **skunk works**—defined as a small group within a large organization, given a high degree of autonomy and unhampered by corporate bureaucracy, whose mission is to develop a project primarily for the sake of radical innovation. These skunk works, in effect, are entrepreneurial operations running inside a large company. Their small size allows employees to be enthusiastic about their mission and to see the impact of their efforts. To be successful, however, they can't carry the cultural values or cost structure of the main organization. They need enough autonomy that they don't have to compete with projects in the primary organization for resources.

IBM succeeded in developing a personal computer by creating a product team and locating it in Florida—some 1,200 miles from IBM's headquarters in Armonk, New York. Steve Jobs created a separate and autonomous unit at Apple to develop the Macintosh computer. And Google/Alphabet created Google X, a semisecret facility located a half mile from the company's corporate headquarters, whose team was assigned the challenge of developing a self-driving car. In contrast, Johnson & Johnson has aggressively bought numerous small companies, kept them independent, and provided them with a large degree of autonomy.

FOR CAREER PLANNING What career advice can we offer you in a disruptive world? Here are some suggestions:

Never get comfortable with a single employer. You can't build your hopes on working in one organization for your entire career. There are no longer any secure jobs, and the days of an organization providing employees with lifetime employment are mostly gone. So, your first loyalty should be to yourself and making yourself marketable.

Keep your skills current. Disruptive technologies will continue to make established jobs and professions obsolete. To keep yourself marketable, you need to keep your skills current. Learning no longer ends when you finish school. You need to make a continual commitment to learning new things.

Look for jobs that value and reward experience, relationships, and creativity. These are least likely to be disrupted by innovations in robotics, artificial intelligence, virtual reality, or other digital technologies.

You are responsible for your future. Don't assume your employer is going to be looking out for your long-term interests. Your personal skill development, career progression, and retirement plans are all decisions that you need to make. Don't delegate your future to someone else. You need to actively manage your career.

Take risks while you're young. Few people have achieved great results without taking a risk. They quit a secure job, or went back to school, or moved to a new city, or started a business. While risks don't always pay off, setbacks or failures are much easier to recover from when you're twenty-five than when you're fifty-five.

skunk works
A small group within a large organization, given a high degree of autonomy and unhampered by corporate bureaucracy, whose mission is to develop a project primarily for the sake of radical innovation

Chapter 7 PREPARING FOR: Exams/Quizzes

CHAPTER SUMMARY by Learning Objectives

LO7.1

DESCRIBE making the case for change.

Organizational change is any alteration of people, structure, or technology. A change agent acts as a catalyst and assumes responsibility for the change process. External forces that create the need for change include changing consumer needs and wants, new governmental laws, technology, and the economy. Internal forces that create a need for change include a new organizational strategy, the composition of the workforce, new equipment, and employee attitudes.

LO7.2

COMPARE and contrast views on the change process.

The calm waters metaphor suggests that change is an occasional disruption in the normal flow of events and can be planned and managed as it happens. Lewin's three-step model says change can be managed by unfreezing the status quo (old behaviors), changing to a new state, and refreezing the new behaviors. In the white-water rapids metaphor, change is ongoing and managing it is a continual process.

LO7.3

CLASSIFY areas of organizational change.

Organizational change can focus on strategy, structure, technology, or people. Changing strategy signifies a change in how managers ensure the success of the company. Changing structure involves any changes in structural components or structural design. Changing technology involves introducing new equipment, tools, or methods; automation; or computerization. Changing people involves changing attitudes, expectations, perceptions, and behaviors. Organizational development is the term used to describe change methods that focus on people and the nature and quality of interpersonal relationships.

LO7.4

EXPLAIN how to manage change.

People resist change because of uncertainty, habit, concern over personal loss, and the belief that the change is not in the organization's best interest.

The techniques for reducing resistance to change include education and communication (educating employees about and communicating to them the need for the change), participation (allowing employees to participate in the change process), facilitation and support (giving employees the support they need to implement the change), negotiation (exchanging something of value to reduce resistance), manipulation and co-optation (using negative actions to influence), and coercion (using direct threats or force).

LO7.5

DISCUSS contemporary issues in managing change.

An organization's culture is made up of relatively stable and permanent characteristics, which makes it difficult to change. Managers can take steps toward changing an organization's culture through understanding the situational factors that facilitate change. Managers must have a strategy for managing cultural change, which includes being positive role models; creating new stories, symbols, and rituals; selecting, promoting, and supporting employees who adopt the new values; redesigning socialization processes; changing the reward system; clearly specifying expectations; shaking up current subcultures; and getting employees to participate in change.

Organizational change can cause employees to experience stress. Stress is the adverse reaction people have to excessive pressure placed on them from extraordinary demands, constraints, or opportunities. To help employees deal with stress, managers can address job-related factors by making sure an employee's abilities match the job requirements, improve organizational communications, use a performance planning program, or redesign jobs. Addressing personal stress factors is trickier, but managers could offer employee counseling, time management programs, and wellness programs.

LO7.6 **DESCRIBE** techniques for stimulating innovation.

Creativity is the ability to combine ideas in a unique way or to make unusual associations between ideas. Innovation is turning the outcomes of the creative process into useful products or work methods. Important structural variables that impact innovation include an organic-type structure, abundant resources, frequent communication between organizational units, minimal time pressure, and support. Important cultural variables include accepting ambiguity, tolerating the impractical, keeping external controls minimal, tolerating risk, tolerating conflict, focusing on ends not means, and providing positive feedback. Important human resource variables include high commitment to training and development, high job security, and encouraging individuals to be idea champions.

LO7.7 **EXPLAIN** why managing disruptive innovation is important.

Disruptive innovation exists when innovations in products, services, or processes radically change an industry's rules of the game. This often occurs when a smaller company with fewer resources is able to successfully challenge established incumbent businesses. Disruptive innovation presents an asset to organizations that recognize the market potential of the technology. Companies can become a victim of disruptive innovation when they choose to conduct business as usual.

REVIEW AND DISCUSSION QUESTIONS

7-1. Why is a change agent needed for organizational change? Can a low-level employee be a change agent? Explain your answer.

7-2. Contrast the calm waters and white-water rapids metaphors of change.

7-3. What is organizational development? How do organizational development techniques support organizational change?

7-4. Why do people in organizations resist change? Provide examples an organization can take to reduce resistance to change.

7-5. Discuss the role of organizational culture in the change process. What are steps an organization can take to create a culture that supports change?

7-6. Why should organizational managers be concerned about reducing employee stress levels?

7-7. Innovation requires allowing people to make mistakes. However, being wrong too many times can be disastrous to your career. Do you agree? Why or why not? What are the implications for nurturing innovation?

7-8. Provide an example of a disruptive innovation. What impact did this innovation have on the industry?

PREPARING FOR: My Career

ETHICS DILEMMA

Workplace stress has reduced the quality of life for a large number of employees. Two-thirds of employees say they lose sleep due to work-related stress while 76% report that their personal relationships suffer due to stress from work.[58] In order to help with the negative effects of stress, many employers offer forms of wellness programs. In fact, depending on the industry involved, 39 to 63% of employees have access to wellness programs at work. Although employee assistance programs (EAPs) are available to more than half of employees in the U.S., many employees choose not to participate. Why? Many employees are reluctant to ask for help, especially if a major source of that stress is job overload or job insecurity. After all, there's still a stigma associated with stress. Employees don't want to be perceived as being unable to handle the demands of their job. Although they

may need stress management now more than ever, few employees want to admit they're stressed.

7-9. What can be done about this paradox of needing stress management assistance but being reluctant to admit it?

7-10. Do organizations *have* an ethical responsibility to help employees deal with stress? Discuss.

SKILLS EXERCISE   Developing Your Change-Management Skill

About the Skill

Managers play an important role in organizational change. That is, they often serve as a catalyst for the change—a change agent. However, managers may find that change is resisted by employees. After all, change represents ambiguity and uncertainty, or it threatens the status quo. How can this resistance to change be effectively managed? Here are some suggestions.[59]

Steps in Practicing the Skill

• *Assess the climate for change.* One major factor in why some changes succeed while others fail is the readiness for change. Assessing the climate for change involves asking several questions. The more affirmative answers you get, the more likely it is that change efforts will succeed. Here are some guiding questions:

a. Is the sponsor of the change high enough in the organization to have power to effectively deal with resistance?

b. Is senior management supportive of the change and committed to it?

c. Do senior managers convey the need for change, and is this feeling shared by others in the organization?

d. Do managers have a clear vision of how the future will look after the change?

e. Are objective measures in place to evaluate the change effort, and have reward systems been explicitly designed to reinforce them?

f. Is the specific change effort consistent with other changes going on in the organization?

g. Are managers willing to sacrifice their personal self-interests for the good of the organization as a whole?

h. Do managers pride themselves on closely monitoring changes and actions by competitors?

i. Are managers and employees rewarded for taking risks, being innovative, and looking for new and better solutions?

j. Is the organizational structure flexible?

k. Does communication flow both down and up in the organization?

l. Has the organization successfully implemented changes in the past?

m. Are employees satisfied with, and do they trust, management?

n. Is a high degree of interaction and cooperation typical between organizational work units?

o. Are decisions made quickly, and do they take into account a wide variety of suggestions?

• *Choose an appropriate approach for managing the resistance to change.* In this chapter, six strategies have been suggested for dealing with resistance to change—education and communication, participation, facilitation and support, negotiation, manipulation and co-optation, and coercion. Review Exhibit 7-5 (p. 171) for the advantages and disadvantages and when it is best to use each approach.

• *During the time the change is implemented and after the change is completed, communicate with employees regarding what support you may be able to provide.* Your employees need to know you are there to support them during change efforts. Be prepared to offer the assistance that may be necessary to help them enact the change.

Practicing the Skill

Read through the following scenario. Write down some notes about how you would handle the situation described. Be sure to refer to the suggestions for managing resistance to change.

You're the nursing supervisor at a community hospital employing both emergency room and floor nurses. Each of these teams of nurses tends to work almost exclusively with others doing the same job. In your professional reading, you've come across the concept of cross-training nursing teams and giving them more varied responsibilities, which in turn has been shown to improve patient care while lowering costs. You call the two team leaders, Sue and Scott, into your office to discuss your plan to have the nursing teams move to this approach. To your surprise, they're both opposed to the idea. Sue says she and the other emergency room nurses feel they're needed in the ER, where they fill the most vital role in the hospital. They work special hours when needed, do whatever tasks are required, and often work in difficult and stressful circumstances. They think the floor nurses have relatively easy jobs for the pay they receive. Scott, leader of the floor nurses team, tells you that his group believes the ER nurses lack the special training and extra experience that the floor nurses bring to the hospital. The floor nurses claim they have the heaviest responsibilities and do the most exacting work. Because they have ongoing contact with the patients and their families, they believe they shouldn't be pulled away from vital floor duties to help ER nurses complete their tasks. Now—what would you do?

WORKING TOGETHER **Team Exercise**

Many technology companies are known for their organizational cultures that support innovation. You've probably read about Google's expansive campus and amenities that create an environment where the company's creative staff is able to drive innovation. Get together in groups of three to four students and assume the role of the founders of a new technology start-up company. Your job is to create a work environment in your new company that will stimulate innovation. Identify the steps you will take to support creating this work environment. Include your insights on the structure, culture, and human resource practices for your new company. Be prepared to share your ideas with the class.

MY TURN TO BE A MANAGER

- Choose two organizations you're familiar with and assess whether these organizations face a calm waters or white-water rapids change environment. Write a short report

describing these organizations and your assessment of the change environment each faces. Be sure to explain your choice of change environment.

- Reflect on a significant change you've experienced in your life (for example, moving to a new school, going to college, or a family problem such as a divorce). Did you resist the change? Why? Did you use any strategies to adjust to the change? What could you have done differently? Write your reflection and make note of how you could effectively manage future changes in your life.

- Choose an organization with which you're familiar (employer, student organization, family business, etc.). Describe its culture (shared values and beliefs). Select two of those values/beliefs and describe how you would go about changing them. Put this information in a report.

- When you find yourself experiencing dysfunctional stress, write down what's causing the stress, what stress symptoms you're exhibiting, and how you're dealing with the stress. Keep this information in a journal and evaluate how well your stress reducers are working and how you could handle stress better. Your goal is to get to a point where you recognize that you're stressed and can take positive actions to deal with the stress.

- Visit www.testmycreativity.com to take an assessment to measure your creativity. What is your level of creativity in comparison with others? What are your strengths? Your weaknesses? Do you agree with the assessment?

- Research information on how to be a more creative person. Write down suggestions in a bulleted-list format and be prepared to present your information in class.

- What businesses and jobs would be disrupted if all vehicles became self-driving and car-sharing services (like Uber and Lift) were universally popular?

CASE APPLICATION 1   Change from Within at Google

In October 2018, the media reported that technology giant Google responded to what were deemed credible sexual assault claims against a former executive by paying him $90 million and praising him as he left the company.[60]

Google employees have been pushing for changes related to discrimination, harassment, and equality in the company for years through established channels: working committees, ethics councils, and employee meetings with the CEO. None of these efforts resulted in any real change, according to Meredith Whittaker, founder of Google's Open Research group.[61]

It's not that Google has never responded to employees' pleas for change. For instance, Google backed down from supplying artificial intelligence to a drone warfare project called Project Maven in the spring of 2018 after 4,000 Google employees signed a petition and a dozen employees resigned in protest.[62] And Google employees are recruited on the basis of their mission to "develop services that significantly improve the lives of as many people as possible," so employees have this mission in mind when they judge what the company is (or is not) doing.

After reading a thread of stories from Google employees that was being sent through email after the October 2018 sexual assault story was published, Claire Stapleton had had enough. Claire, a marketing manager at YouTube (an Alphabet/Google subsidiary), sent an email to a large group of employees saying that they had to do something. Employees replied to the email with ideas about what to demand of the company. These demands were transferred to a Google Doc, and hundreds of employees contributed to the document. They streamlined the document so that five demands remained that had to do with sexual harassment, discrimination, and pay and opportunity inequities for both full-time employees and contractors.

To increase the chances that Google would listen to the employee demands, plans were made to organize a day when employees would walk out of their offices together and ask for their demands to be met. On Tuesday, October 30, 2018, Google employees in two cities planned to participate in the walkout. Two days later, the number of participating cities had expanded to thirty with a field organizer in each of those cities.[63] More than 20,000 Google employees and contractors participated. Nine other offices didn't report protest participant numbers, suggesting that more than 20 percent of Google's workforce was involved in the walkout.[64]

What did Google leadership do in response? After holding a town hall meeting with employees, they took action by dropping forced arbitration for sexual harassment (but not for discrimination). They also offered sexual harassment training, which was not included in the list of demands. According to one of the walkout organizers, Google leaders tried to claim some degree of credit, saying, "This is a great walkout, and this has been such a wake-up call, and we're so happy to be now leading the industry in this."[65] The walkout organizers would like more of the employee demands to be met, but they realize that it will likely have to be the employees who keep the conversation going with company leaders.

Google isn't the only technology company that has employees leading the way toward change. Employees at Amazon have been pushing the company to stop selling facial recognition to the government, and Salesforce employees have been organizing to put an end to a company contract with Customs and Border Protection. Also, Microsoft and Amazon employees are demanding that their companies sever ties with US Immigration and Customs Enforcement.[66]

DISCUSSION QUESTIONS:

7-11. Who were the change agents at Google, and what did they do that made them change agents?

7-12. What were the internal and/or external forces for change in this case?

7-13. How did employees increase driving forces in this case?

7-14. What techniques for reducing resistance to change could employees use to help make further progress toward change?

CASE APPLICATION 2

Creating an Innovation Lab at Neiman Marcus

Scott Emmons was working for Neiman Marcus, the luxury retailer, as an enterprise architect when he realized a big gap in how their stores were handling technology. "Customers were showing up with smartphones and outgunning our own associates' capability to access relevant information that would help them on their shopping journey," Emmons said.[67]

Emmons brought the need for better addressing technology to the company and they supported his founding of the Neiman Marcus Innovation Lab (iLab) in 2012. A few years into running the iLab, Emmons realized that a new way of thinking was needed. Neiman Marcus needed to serve shoppers of the future and approach what customers might want in a new way.[68]

One of iLab's innovations for serving shoppers is the digital memory mirror that records 360-degree views of how customers look in outfits. Customers can text video recordings of these views to friends to ask them for feedback. Customers also can compare how different outfits looks side by side via video using the mirror's technology. Recently, a new augmented-reality feature was added to the memory mirrors: customers can virtually "try on" sunglasses and makeup without having to put them on in real life.[69] Memory mirrors have been installed in most of Neiman Marcus's forty-four locations across the United States.

Another related innovation is memory makeover mirrors. These mirrors record how a makeup specialist in the store applies makeup. The personalized recordings are sent to the customer to ensure they don't get home and forget the steps to follow. Customer service buttons in dressing rooms that connect to sales associates' smartphones and a "Snap Find Shop" app that allows customers to take a picture of a product and find similar styles in the store are other examples of iLab's work. These innovations have contributed to Neiman Marcus achieving four straight quarters of revenue growth through the end of 2018.[70]

Unlike other companies that create an innovation center that works separate from the rest of the company, Neiman Marcus' iLab helps other teams through the company learn from their work. They also are able to get needed resources for projects (including borrowing the work of other employees at Neiman Marcus or getting help from consultants). By offering their services to different parts of the company, they have built "a model for innovation and experimentation...they've built a culture from that, that it's okay to experiment and fail," according to Brian Solis, an analyst at Altimeter, an innovation-focused consulting firm.[71]

DISCUSSION QUESTIONS:

7-15. Why is "innovation" a more accurate word to describe Neiman Marcus's lab than "creativity"?

7-16. What structural, cultural, and/or human resource variables helped encourage innovation success at Neiman Marcus?

7-17. Has Neiman Marcus achieved disruptive innovation with their iLab's work? Why or why not?

7-18. What is an example of "sustaining innovation" in this case?

ENDNOTES

1. A. A. Armenakis and A. G. Bedeian, "Organizational Change: A Review of Theory and Research in the 1990s," *Journal of Management* 25, no. 3 (June 1999): pp. 293–315.
2. J. Muller, "Ford Embraces Car-Sharing and Electric Bikes on a Crowded Planet," *Forbes*, June 24, 2015, https://www.forbes.com/sites/joannmuller/2015/06/24/ford-embraces-car-sharing-and-electric-bikes-on-a-crowded-planet/#4291458a5e1c.
3. S. Giles, "How VUCA Is Reshaping the Business Environment, And What It Means for Innovation,"

Forbes, May 9, 2018, https://www.forbes.com/sites/sunniegiles/2018/05/09/how-vuca-is-reshaping-the-business-environment-and-what-it-means-for-innovation/#2c41d4e4eb8d.
4. J. Jargon, "Burger King Returns to Its Roots," *Wall Street Journal*, March 9, 2016, https://www.wsj.com/articles/burger-king-returns-to-its-roots-1457519402.
5. PriceWaterhouseCoopers' CEO Survey, 2019, pwc.com.
6. J. Karsten and D. M. West, "Five Emerging Battery Technologies for Electric Vehicles," *Brookings*, September 15, 2015, https://www.brookings.edu/blog/

techtank/2015/09/15/five-emerging-battery-technologies-for-electric-vehicles/.

7. US Bureau of Labor Statistics, "The Recession of 2007–2009," February 2012, https://www.bls.gov/spotlight/2012/recession/pdf/recession_bls_spotlight.pdf.

8. C. H. Wong, "China May Rein in Wage Increases to Boost Economy," *Wall Street Journal*, March 10, 2016, https://www.wsj.com/articles/china-may-rein-in-wage-rises-to-boost-economy-1457616686.

9. A. Nusca, "5 Moves Walmart Is Making to Compete With Amazon and Target," *Fortune*, September 27, 2017, http://fortune.com/2017/09/27/5-moves-walmart-is-making-to-compete-with-amazon-and-target/.

10. M. Ponsford and N. Glass, "The Night I Invented 3D Printing," *CNN*, February 14, 2014, https://www.cnn.com/2014/02/13/tech/innovation/the-night-i-invented-3d-printing-chuck-hall/index.html.

11. L. Columbus, "The State of 3D Printing, 2018," *Forbes*, May 30, 2018, https://www.forbes.com/sites/louiscolumbus/2018/05/30/the-state-of-3d-printing-2018/#38d7f0247b0a.

12. K. Chaudhary, R. Luss, and U. Shriram, "The Human Factor: How Employee Attitudes Toward Change Affect Change Management," *Towers Watson*, June 23, 2015, https://www.towerswatson.com/en-US/Insights/Newsletters/Americas/insider/2015/06/how-employee-attitudes-toward-change-affect-change-management.

13. The idea for these metaphors came from P. B. Vaill, *Managing as a Performing Art: New Ideas for a World of Chaotic Change* (San Francisco: Jossey-Bass, 1989); B. H. Kemelgor, S. D. Johnson, and S. Srinivasan, "Forces Driving Organizational Change: A Business School Perspective," *Journal of Education for Business* 75, no. 3 (January-February 2000): pp.133–137; and J. E. Dutton, S. J. Ashford, R. M. O'Neill, and K. A. Lawrence, "Moves That Matter: Issue Selling and Organizational Change," *Academy of Management Journal* (August 2001): pp.716–736.

14. K. Lewin, *Field Theory in Social Science* (New York: Harper & Row, 1951).

15. R. Safian, "Generation Flux," *Fast Company*, February 2012, p.62.

16. J. R. Hagerty, "3M Begins Untangling Its Hairballs," *Wall Street Journal*, May 17, 2012, pp. B1+; and M. Pinola, "15 Brilliant Things You Can Do with Command," *Lifehacker*, September 20, 2013, https://lifehacker.com/15-brilliant-things-you-can-do-with-command-hooks-1355369802.

17. R. Wall, "Ryanair's New Strategy: Being Nice," *Wall Street Journal*, March 13, 2016, https://www.wsj.com/articles/ryanairs-new-strategy-being-nice-1457862512.

18. L. Troyani, "3 Examples of Organizational Change Done Right," *TINYpulse*, May 25, 2017, https://www.tinypulse.com/blog/3-examples-of-organizational-change-and-why-they-got-it-right.

19. S. Norton, "Dow Chemical Digital Chief Helps Shape Massive Restructuring," *Wall Street Journal*, July 26, 2018, https://blogs.wsj.com/cio/2018/07/26/dow-chemical-digital-chief-helps-shape-massive-restructuring/.

20. L. Garfield, "7 Companies That Are Replacing Human Jobs with Robots," *Business Insider*, March 2, 2016, https://www.businessinsider.com/companies-that-use-robots-instead-of-humans-2016-2.

21. See P. F. Sorensen, T. Yaeger, and R. Narel, "The Golden Age of Organization Development Research and Knowledge," *Organization Development Journal* (Spring 2017): pp. 47–55; B. Shimoni, "A Sociological Perspective to Organization Development," *Organizational Dynamics* (July-September 2017): pp. 165–70; and D. L. Anderson, *Organization Development: The Process of Leading Organizational Change* (Thousand Oaks, CA: Sage, 2017).

22. K. Caprino, "How Companies Like Uber, Facebook and Saleforce Engage in Team-Building (It's Not What You Think)," *Forbes*, January 14, 2016, https://www.forbes.com/sites/kathycaprino/2016/01/14/how-companies-like-uber-facebook-and-salesforce-engage-in-team-building-its-not-what-you-think/#121fec703cc1.

23. See, for instance, P. Strebel, "Why Do Employees Resist Change?," *Harvard Business Review*, May-June 1996, pp.86–92; R. Kegan and L. L. Lahey, "The Real Reason People Won't Change," *Harvard Business Review*, November 2001, pp. 85–92; J. D. Ford, L. W. Ford, and A. D'Amelio, "Resistance to Change: The Rest of the Story," *Academy of Management Review* (April 2008): pp. 362–77; J. T. Jost, "Resistance to Change: A Social Psychological Perspective," *Social Research* 33, no. 2 (Fall 2015): pp. 607–36; and V. Amarantou, S. Kazakopoulou, D. Chatzoudes, and P. Chatzoglou, "Resistance to Change: An Empirical Investigation of Its Antecedents," *Journal of Organizational Change Management* 32, no. 2 (2018): pp. 426–50.

24. K. S. Pasupathy and T. R. Hellmich, "How RFID Technology Improves Hospital Care," *Harvard Business Review*, December 31, 2015, https://hbr.org/2015/12/how-rfid-technology-improves-hospital-care.

25. C. Tams, "Why We Need to Rethink Organizational Change Management," *Forbes*, January 26, 2018, https://www.forbes.com/sites/carstentams/2018/01/26/why-we-need-to-rethink-organizational-change-management/#3da23fb0e93c.

26. J. P. Kotter and L. A. Schlesinger, "Choosing Strategies for Change," *Harvard Business Review*, March-April 1979, pp. 106–14; and R. K. Smollan, "The Multi-Dimensional Nature of Resistance to Change," *Journal of Management & Organization* 17, no. 6 (November 2011): pp. 828–49.

27. S. Clayton, "Change Management Meets Social Media," *Harvard Business Review*, November 10, 2015, https://hbr.org/2015/11/change-management-meets-social-media.

28. See T. H. Fitzgerald, "Can Change in Organizational Culture Really Be Managed?," *Organizational Dynamics* 17, no. 2 (Autumn 1988): pp.5–15; Anthony, *Managing Culture* (Philadelphia: Open University Press, 1994); P. Bate, *Strategies for Cultural Change* (Boston: Butterworth-Heinemann, 1994); M. Esawi, "Changing Organizational Culture Through Constructive Confrontation of Values," *Journal of Organization and Human Behaviour* (April 2012): pp. 46–50; and J. McCalman and D. Potter, *Leading Cultural Change: The Theory and Practice of Successful Transformation* (London, UK: Kogan Page, 2015).

29. "AT&T's History of Invention and Breakups," *New York Times*, February 13, 2016, https://www.nytimes.com/interactive/2016/02/12/technology/att-history.html.

30. See, for example, R. H. Kilmann, M. J. Saxton, and R. Serpa, eds., *Gaining Control of the Corporate Culture* (San Francisco: Jossey-Bass, 1985); D. C. Hambrick and S. Finkelstein, "Managerial Discretion: A Bridge Between Polar Views of Organizational Outcomes," in *Research in Organizational Behavior*, vol. 9, eds. L. L. Cummings and B. M. Staw (Greenwich, CT: JAI Press, 1987), p.384; and J. Cresie, "Changing the Culture of Your Organization," *Law & Order*, December 2005, pp. 74–78.

31. Ibid.; and I. Levin and J. Z. Gottlieb, "Realigning Organization Culture for Optimal Performance: Six Principles & Eight Practices," *Organization Development Journal* 27, no. 4 (Winter 2009): pp. 31–46.

32. J. Reynolds, "11 Shocking Stats About Stress at Work and How to Remedy Them," *TINYpulse*, June 28, 2016, https://www.tinypulse.com/blog/stats-stress-in-the-workplace-how-to-remedy-them.

33. American Institute of Stress, "Transforming Stress Through Awareness, Education and Collaboration," January 12, 2018, https://www.stress.org/.

34. A. Oswald, "New Research Reveals Dramatic Rise in Stress Levels in Europe's Workplaces," University of Warwick (press release), July 29, 1999, https://warwick.ac.uk/newsand events/pressreleases/ne100000007552//; O. Siu, P. E. Spector, C. L. Cooper, L. Lu, and S. Yu, "Managerial Stress in Greater China: The Direct and Moderator Effects of Coping Strategies and Work Locus of Control," *Applied Psychology: An International Review* 51, no. 4 (October 2002): pp.608–632; UnionSafe, "Stressed Employees Worked to Death," August 23, 2003, unionsafe.labor.net.au/news; V. P. Sudhashree, K. Rohith, and K. Shrinivas, "Issues and Concerns of Health Among Call Center Employees," *Indian Journal of Occupational Environmental Medicine* 9, no. 3 (2005): pp.129–132; M. Conlin, "Go-Go-Going to Pieces in China," *Business Week*, April 23, 2007, p.88; "Chinese Workers Chill as Japan's Workers Stress: Report," *CNBC*, June 17, 2015, https://www.cnbc.com/2015/06/17/chinese-workers-chill-as-japans-workers-stress-report.html; and "Worked to Death," *The Week*, October 20, 2017, p. 9.

35. Adapted from the UK National Work-Stress Network website, www.workstress.net.

36. V. Lipman, "Workplace Trend: Stress Is on the Rise," *Forbes*, January 9, 2019, https://www.forbes.com/sites/victorlipman/2019/01/09/workplace-trend-stress-is-on-the-rise/#561001286e1b.

37. P. D. Bliese, J. B. Edwards, and S. Sonnentag, "Stress and Well-Being at Work: A Century of Empirical Trends Reflecting Theoretical and Societal Influences," *Journal of Applied Psychology* 102, no. 3 (March 2017): pp. 389–402.

38. Y Janjhua, "Behavior of Personality Type Toward Stress and Job Performance: A Study of Healthcare Professionals," *Journal of Family Medicine and Primary Care* 1, no. 2 (July-December 2012): pp. 109–15; T. K. Billing and P. Steverson, "Moderating Role of Type-A Personality on Stress-Outcome Relationships," *Management Decision* 51, no. 9 (2013): pp. 1893–1904; and E.-S. Shin, T.-S. Shin, and Y.-C. Cho, "Relationship of Type A Behavior Pattern and Psychosocial Stress With Fatigue Symptoms in Manufacturing Workers," *Indian Journal of Science and Technology* 9, no. 39 (October 2016).

39. Cited in G. B. White, "Job-Related Stress Can Have Fatal Consequences," *Atlantic*, February 5, 2015, https://www.atlantic.com.

40. K. M. Richardson and H. R. Rothstein, "Effects of Occupational Stress Management Intervention Programs: A Meta-Analysis," *Journal of Occupational Health Psychology* 13, no. 1 (January 2008): pp. 69–93; and S. Riva and E. Chinyio, "Stress Factors and Stress Management Interventions: The Heuristic of 'Bottom Up' an Update From a Systematic Review," *Occupational Health Science* (June 2018): pp. 127–55.

41. "Unique Ways Top Companies Help Their Employees Manage Stress," *kununu* (blog), July 13, 2017, https://transparency.kununu.com/unique-ways-top-companies-help-employees-manage-stress/.

42. C. J. Hobson and L. DeLunes, "Efficacy of Different Techniques for Reducing Stress: A Study Among Business Students in the United States," *International Journal of Management* (August 2009): pp. 186–196; M. Clayton, *Brilliant Stress Management: How to Manage Stress in Any Situation* (New York: FT Press, 2012); "Work Stress on the Rise: 8 in 10 Americans Are Stressed About Their Jobs, Survey Finds," *HuffingtonPost Healthy Living*, updated April 12, 2013, https://www.huffpost.com/entry/work-stress-jobs-americans_n_3053428; H. Hanna, *Stressaholic: 5 Steps to Transform Your Relationship with Stress* (Hoboken, NJ: Wiley, 2014); and H. Anisman, *Stress and Your Health: From Vulnerability to Resilence* (Hoboken, NJ: Wiley-Blackwell, 2015).

43. "The Fortune 100 and Their Fitness and Wellness Programs," *Health Fitness Revolution*, August 15, 2015, http://www.healthfitnessrevolution.com/fortune-100-fitness-wellness-programs/.

44. T. A. Edison, "Famous Quotations from Thomas Edison," Thomas A. Edison Innovation Foundation, https://www.thomasedison.org/, accessed March 10, 2019.

45. Cited in M. Ringel, A. Taylor, and H. Zablit, "The World's Best Innovators: 4 Things That Differentiate Them," *Rotman Magazine*, September 1, 2016, p. 85.

46. "The World's 50 Most Innovative Companies 2018," *Fast Company*, https://www.fastcompany.com/most-innovative-companies/2018.

47. L. Kwoh, "You Call That Innovation?," *Wall Street Journal*, May 23, 2012, pp. B1+.

48. These definitions are based on T. M. Amabile, *Creativity in Context* (Boulder, CO: Westview Press, 1996); and J. Cocco and M. Quttainah, "Creativity Versus Innovativeness: Exploring the Differences Between the Two Constructs May Lead to Greater Innovation in Large Firms," *International Journal of Business Management* 10, no. 11 (2015): pp. 83–93.

49. F. Damanpour, "Organizational Innovation: A Meta-Analysis of Effects of Determinants and Moderators," *Academy of Management Journal* 34, no. 3 (September 1991): pp. 555–590; G. R. Oldham and A. Cummings, "Employee Creativity: Personal and Contextual Factors at Work," *Academy of Management Journal* 39, no. 3 (June 1996): pp. 607–634; T. M. Amabile, C. N. Hadley, and S. J. Kramer, "Creativity

Under the Gun," *Harvard Business Review*, August 2002, pp. 52–61; N. Madjar, G. R. Oldham, and M. G. Pratt, "There's No Place Like Home? The Contributions of Work and Nonwork Creativity Support to Employees' Creative Performance," *Academy of Management Journal* 45, no. 4 (August 2002): pp.757–767; T. M. Egan, "Factors Influencing Individual Creativity in the Workplace: An Examination of Quantitative Empirical Research," *Advances in Developing Human Resources* 7, no. 2 (May 2005): pp.160–181; G. Hirst, D. Van Knippenberg, C. H. Chen, and C. A. Sacramento, "How Does Bureaucracy Impact Individual Creativity? A Cross-Level Investigation of Team Contextual Influences on Goal Orientation-Creativity Relationships," *Academy of Management Journal* 54, no. 3 (June 2011): pp. 624–641; T. Shukla and A. Singh, "Organizational Factors Influencing Innovation: An Empirical Investigation," *Journal of Strategic Human Resource Management* 4, no. 3 (2015): pp. 66-73; and M. Moussa, A. McMurray, and N. Muenjohn, "A Conceptual Framework of the Factors Influencing Innovation in Public Sector Organizations," *Journal of Developing Areas* 52, no. 3 (Summer 2018): pp. 231–40.

50. T. M. Amabile, *Creativity in Context*; R. Moss Kanter, "When a Thousand Flowers Bloom: Structural, Collective, and Social Conditions for Innovation in Organization," in *Research in Organizational Behavior*, vol. 10, ed. B. M. Staw and L. L. Cummings (Greenwich, CT: JAI Press, 1988), pp.169–211; D. C. Wyld and R. Maurin, "Keys to Innovation: The Right Measures and the Right Culture?," *Academy of Management Perspective* 23, no. 2 (May 2009): pp.96–98; J. Cable, "Building an Innovation Culture," *Industry Week*, March 2010, pp.32–37; S. Shellenbarger, "Better Ideas Through Failure," *Wall Street Journal*, October 27, 2011, pp. D1+; R. W. Goldfarb, "When Fear Stifles Initiative," *New York Times*, May 14, 2011, https://www.nytimes.com/2011/05/15/jobs/15pre.html; L. A. Schlesinger, C. F. Kiefer, and P. B. Brown, "New Project? Don't Analyze—Act," *Harvard Business Review*, March 2012, pp.154–158; S. J. Hogan and L. V. Coote, "Organizational Culture, Innovation, and Performance: A Test of Schein's Model," *Journal of Business Research* 67, no. 8 (August 2014): pp. 1609–21; and C. Cancialosi, "Why Culture Is the Heart of Organizational Innovation," *Forbes*, February 7, 2017, https://www.forbes.com/sites/chriscancialosi/2017/02/07/why-culture-is-the-heart-of-organizational-innovation/#7e664f3f4d76.

51. J. M. Howell and C. A. Higgins, "Champions of Change," *Business Quarterly*, Spring 1990, pp.31–32; J. M. Howell and C. A. Higgins, "Champions of Technological Innovation," *Administrative Science Quarterly* 35, no. 2 (June 1990): pp. 317–41; and J. M. Howell, C. M. Shea, and C. A. Higgins, "Champions of Product Innovations: Defining, Developing, and Validating a Measure of Champion Behavior," *Journal of Business Venturing* 20, no. 5 (September 2005): pp. 641–61.

52. See C. M. Christensen, *The Innovator's Dilemma: When New Technologies Cause Great Firms to Fail* (Boston: Harvard Business Review Press, 1997); A. W., "What Disruptive Innovation Means," The Economist Explains, *Economist*, January 25, 2015, https://www.economist.com/the-economist-explains/2015/01/25/what-disruptive-innovation-means; and A. Webb, *The Signals Are Talking: Why Today's Fringe Is Tomorrow's Mainstream* (New York: PublicAffairs Books, 2018).

53. C. M. Christensen, M. Raynor, and R. McDonald, "What is Disruptive Innovation?," *Harvard Business Review*, December 2015, pp. 44–53. For an expanded view of disruption, see J. Gans, "The Other Disruption: When Innovations Threaten the Organizational Model," *Harvard Business Review*, March 2016, pp. 78–85.

54. J. Schumpeter, *Capitalism, Socialism and Democracy* (New York: Harper & Row, 1942).

55. J. Nieminen, "50+ Statistics on Innovation—What Do the Numbers Tell Us?," Viima, October 10, 2018, https://www.viima.com/blog/innovation-stats.

56. Christensen, *The Innovator's Dilemma*, p. 228 [see note 52].

57. Ibid.

58. Ethics Dilemma based on V. Lipman, "Workplace Trend: Stress is on the Rise." Forbes, January 9, 2019,https://www.forbes.com/sites/victorlipman/2019/01/09/workplace-trend-stress-is-on-the-rise/#5e6294226e1b; "Employee Access to Wellness Programs in 2017," Bureau of Labor Statistics, January 3, 2018, https://www.bls.gov/opub/ted/2018/employee-access-to-wellness-programs-in-2017.htm; and T. Roth and J. Harter, "Unhealthy, Stressed Employees Are Hurting Your Business," *Gallup Business Journal*, May 22, 2012, https://news.gallup.com/businessjournal/154643/unhealthy-stressed-employees-hurting-business.aspx.

59. J. P. Kotter and L. A. Schlesinger, "Choosing Strategies for Change," *Harvard Business Review*, March-April 1979, pp. 106–14; and T. A. Stewart, "Rate Your Readiness to Change," *Fortune*, February 7, 1994, pp. 106–10.

60. D. Wakabayashi and K. Benner, "How Google Protected Andy Rubin, the 'Father of Android'," *New York Times*, October 25, 2018, https://www.nytimes.com/2018/10/25/technology/google-sexual-harassment-andy-rubin.html.

61. S. Ghaffary and E. Johnson, "After 20,000 Workers Walked Out, Google Said It Got the Message. The Workers Disagree," *Recode*, November 21, 2018, https://www.recode.net/2018/11/21/18105719/google-walkout-real-change-organizers-protest-discrimination-kara-swisher-recode-decode-podcast.

62. K. Conger, "Google Employees Resign in Protest Against Pentagon Contract," *Gizmodo*, May 14, 2018, https://gizmodo.com/google-employees-resign-in-protest-against-pentagon-con-1825729300.

63. Ghaffary and Johnson, "After 20,000 Workers Walked Out" [see note 61].

64. L. M. Segarra, "More Than 20,000 Google Employees Participated in Walkout Over Sexual Harassment Policy," *Fortune*, November 3, 2018.

65. Ghaffary and Johnson, "After 20,000 Workers Walked Out" [see note 61].

66. B. Tarnoff, "Can Silicon Valley Workers Rein in Big Tech From Within?," *Guardian*, August 9, 2018, https://www.theguardian.com/commentisfree/2018/aug/09/silicon-valley-tech-workers-labor-activism.

67. A. DeNisco-Rayome, "How Neiman Marcus's Top-Down Innovation Strategy Transformed Retail and Increased Revenue," *ZDNet*, August 1, 2018, https://www.zdnet.com/article/how-neiman-marcuss-top-down-innovation-strategy-transformed-retail-and-increased-revenue/.

68. B. Thau, "Why the Neiman Marcus 'IT Guy' Is My New Hero," *Forbes*, March 2, 2018, https://www.forbes.com/sites/barbarathau/2018/03/02/why-the-neiman-marcus-it-guy-is-my-new-retail-hero/#600d0a936588.

69. K. Burnham, "For 5 Pioneering Brands, the Innovation Process Is Also an Experience," *CMO.com*, May 23, 2018, https://www.cmo.com/features/articles/2018/5/15/how-5-companies-have-prioritized-innovation.html#gs.2uoblf.

70. D. Howland, "Neiman Marcus Ends Fiscal Year with Some Breathing Room," *Retail Dive*, September 18, 2018, https://www.retaildive.com/news/neiman-marcus-ends-fiscal-year-with-some-breathing-room/532617/.

71. DeNisco-Rayome, "Neiman Marcus's Top-Down Innovation Strategy" [see note 67].

A Manager's Dilemma

One of the biggest fears of a food service company manager has to be the hepatitis A virus, a highly contagious virus transmitted by sharing food, utensils, cigarettes, or drug paraphernalia with an infected person. Food service workers aren't any more susceptible to the illness than anyone else, but an infected employee can easily spread the virus by handling food, especially cold foods. The virus, which is rarely fatal, can cause flulike illness for several weeks. There is no cure for hepatitis A, but a vaccine can prevent it. Jim Brady, manager of a restaurant, is facing a serious dilemma. He recently learned one of his cooks could have exposed as many as 350 people to hepatitis A during a five-day period when he was at work. The cook was thought to have contracted the virus through an infant living in his apartment complex. Because children usually show no symptoms of the disease, they can easily pass it on to adults. Jim has a decision to make. Should he go public with the information, or should he only report it to the local health department as required by law?

Using what you learned in Part 2, and especially in Chapter 6, what would you do in this situation?

Global Sense

A boss who says, "We can try that," means the proposal has been dismissed in Japan, but the same statement means the idea is fully supported in Germany. Mexican managers who conduct business in the US find American managers to be less relationship-oriented than they are. In Mexico, doing business with someone means getting to know them personally, while American managers often want to "get down to business" without establishing a relationship first. A vice president for engineering at a major US chip manufacturer, who found one of his projects running more than a month late, felt that perhaps the company's Indian engineers "didn't understand the sense of urgency" in getting the project completed. And the manager of a team of employees from around the world didn't realize how some members had to speak in a style that was not culturally comfortable for them in order to be heard.

It's not easy being a successful global manager, especially when it comes to dealing with cultural differences. Those cultural differences have been described as an "iceberg," of which we only see the top 15 percent, mainly food, appearance, and language. Although these elements can be complicated, it's the other 85 percent of the "iceberg" that's not apparent initially that managers need to be especially concerned about. What does that include? Workplace issues

such as communication styles, priorities, role expectations, work tempo, negotiation styles, nonverbal communication, attitudes toward planning, and so forth. Understanding these issues requires developing a global mindset and skill set. Many organizations are relying on cultural awareness training to help them do just that.

Discuss the following questions in light of what you learned in Part 2:
- *What global attitude do you think would most encourage, support, and promote cultural awareness? Explain.*
- *How might legal, political, and economic differences play a role as companies design appropriate cultural awareness training for employees?*
- *Is diversity management related to cultural awareness? Discuss.*
- *Pick one of the countries mentioned above and do some cultural research on it. What did you find out about the culture of that country? How might this information affect the way a manager in that country plans, organizes, leads, and controls?*
- *What advice might you give to a manager who has little experience globally?[1]*

Continuing Case
STARBUCKS—BASICS OF MANAGING IN TODAY'S WORKPLACE

As managers manage in today's workplace, they must be aware of some specific integrative issues that can affect the way they do their job. What are these integrative managerial issues, and how does Starbucks accommodate and respond to them? In this part of the Continuing Case, we're going to look at Starbucks's external environment/organizational culture, management in a global environment, diversity, and social responsibility/ethical challenges.

Starbucks—Defining the Terrain: Culture and Environment

Managers must be aware of the terrain or broad environment within which they plan, organize, lead, and control. The characteristics and nature of this "terrain" will influence what managers and other employees do and how they do it. And more importantly, it will affect how efficiently and effectively managers do their job of coordinating and overseeing the work of other people so that goals—organizational and work-level or work-unit—can be accomplished. What does Starbucks's terrain look like, and how is the company adapting to that terrain?

An organization's culture is a mix of written and un-written values, beliefs, and codes of behavior that influence the way work gets done and the way people behave in organizations. And the distinct flavor of Starbucks's culture can be traced to the original founders' philosophies and Howard Schultz's unique beliefs about how a company should be run. The three friends (Jerry Baldwin, Gordon Bowker, and Zev Siegl) who founded Starbucks in 1971 as a store in Seattle's historic Pike Place Market district did so for one reason: They loved coffee and tea and wanted Seattle to have access to the best. They had no intention of building a business empire. Their business philosophy, although never written down, was simple: "Every company must stand for something; don't just give customers what they ask for or what they think they want; and assume that your customers are intelligent and seekers of knowledge." The original Starbucks was a company passionately committed to world-class coffee and dedicated to educating its customers, one-on-one, about what great coffee can be. It was these qualities that ignited Howard Schultz's passion for the coffee business and inspired him to envision what Starbucks could become.

The company's mission and guiding principles (which you can find at www.starbucks.com) are meant to guide the decisions and actions of company partners from top to bottom. They also have significantly influenced the organization's culture. For instance, Starbucks's culture emphasizes keeping employees motivated and content. Howard Schultz cared about the relationships he had with his employees, and Kevin Johnson has continued that sense of caring. Johnson calls his employees "partners"; as he says, "As CEO, I serve the 330,000 Starbucks partners around the world who proudly wear the green apron, a purpose that brings me joy." He understands how Starbucks depends on relationships with both employees and with customers. As he puts it, "I believe our success is defined by how we enhance the human experience not just for ourselves, but for others as well."

Starbucks's employees worldwide serve millions of customers each week. That's a lot of opportunities to either satisfy or disappoint the customer. The experiences customers have in the stores ultimately affect the company's relationships with its customers. That's why Starbucks has created a unique relationship with its employees. Starbucks provides a set of generous employee benefits, referred to as "Your Special Blend," to all employees who work more than twenty hours a week: healthcare benefits, paid sick leave, and a compensation plan that includes stock options. Starbucks's employees also can earn a bachelor's degree from Arizona State University's online course offerings at company expense. In 2018, Starbucks shared some of its savings from tax cuts to give employees raises, additional stock, and increased benefits. Johnson explained this employee-centered approach by saying, "Investing in our partners has long been our strategy." Starbucks is known for providing employees with higher pay and better benefits than many restaurants and retail companies. Schultz described this approach as, "what sets us apart and gives us a higher-quality employee, an employee that cares more."

It's clear that Starbucks cares about its employees. For instance, when Hurricanes Harvey and Irma hit in 2017, Starbucks paid employees even though they had to close 700 stores in Puerto Rico and 400 stores in Texas. Hurricane Irma affected more than 10,000 Starbucks employees. As another example, Starbucks has begun installing safe-needle disposal boxes in restrooms in some of their stores where employees have expressed concerns about being poked by needles that were thrown away by drug users. Other examples of the company's concern: Starbucks is committed to hiring 10,000 veterans by 2020 and has offered to reimburse any fees employees face as part of the "Dreamers" immigration program.

As a global company with revenues of $24.7 billion, Starbucks's executives recognize they must be aware of the impact the environment has on their decisions and actions. Starbucks actively lobbies legislators in Washington, DC on issues including global trade policies, health care costs, and tax breaks. It's something that Schultz didn't really want to do, but he recognized that such efforts are important to the company's future.

Global Challenges

You could say that Starbucks has been a global business from day one. While on a business trip in 1983 to Milan, Howard Schultz (who worked in marketing for Starbucks's original founders) experienced firsthand Italy's coffee culture and had an epiphany about how such an approach might work back home in the United States. Now, almost forty years later, Starbucks stores are found in seventy-seven countries, including stores from China and Australia to the Netherlands and Switzerland. Doing business globally, as Chapter 4 points out, can be challenging. With Starbucks stores already established on what might seem like every neighborhood corner in the US, Starbucks depends on growing globally in countries like China, Uruguay, and Italy. Starbucks was a "first mover" in China and has grown to 3,700 stores as of 2019. That makes China Starbucks's second-largest market in the world! Other companies have been competing with Starbucks in China, including the local brand Luckin Coffee. Luckin has been opening up to 300 stores per month, which is a rate that would surpass the current number of Starbucks stores in China by the end of 2019. Starbucks is countering with plans to open a store in China every fifteen hours until 2022. Luckin understands Chinese preferences—like how much delivered coffee is appreciated—and has allocated half of its stores to coffee delivery and "pick up and go" coffee outlets. Expanding Starbucks's delivery options in China to compete with Luckin has not been easy. Not only does coffee delivery cut into Starbucks's profit margins, but it involves challenges like using more durable foam lids on top of drinks to keep the beverage intact after a delivery scooter ride darting through traffic. Between Luckin and the plans of global competitors like Dunkin Brands and McDonald's to expand on a large scale in China, Starbucks has its work cut out for them.

In China and all of its global markets, Starbucks must be cognizant of the economic, legal-political, and cultural aspects that characterize those markets. For instance, in Europe—the "birthplace of café and coffee-house culture"—Starbucks experienced years of slowing sales. Starbucks sold its stores in four European countries (France, Netherlands, Belgium, and Luxemburg) to a partner company, Alesea, in 2018. In the same year, Starbucks opened its first store in Italy. The Starbucks in Milan, Italy, is one of the company's Reserve Roastery locations, which are high-end "experiential coffee palaces." The Milan store has heated marble counters, a 21-foot bronze cask suspended in the air to store coffee, and a bar serving signature Starbucks cocktails. Ironically, Milan is where Howard Schultz famously drank his first cappuccino that sparked his ideas about how to grow the company. If Starbucks can sell the "Starbucks experience"—not just coffee—with Reserve Roasteries in global locations like Milan, Shanghai, and Tokyo, some think that will be the recipe for success. Shanghai's Reserve Roastery has become a sort of "Willy Wonka for coffee" tourist destination. Customers in Shanghai can use augmented reality tools for an enhanced experience of coffee roasting right in front of them and can participate in an online/offline scavenger hunt using their phones within the store. The Shanghai location is beautifully adorned with 1,000 hand-engraved traditional Chinese stamps that tell the story of Starbucks and coffee making while offering three restaurants inside, including a pizzeria. Starbucks is hoping to figure out just how to appeal to the vast array of tastes and preferences around the world. So, as Starbucks continues its global expansion, it has to pay close attention and respect to cultural differences.

Managing Diversity and Inclusion

Not only does Starbucks attempt to be respectful of global cultural differences, it is committed to being an organization that embraces and values diversity in how it does business. The company-wide diversity strategy encompasses four areas: customers, suppliers, partners (employees), and communities.

Starbucks's attempts to make the Starbucks experience accessible to all customers and to respond to each customer's unique preferences and needs. Starbucks's supplier diversity program works to provide opportunities for developing a business relationship with women- and minority-owned suppliers. As far as its partners, the company is committed to a workplace that values and respects people from diverse backgrounds. The most current company diversity statistics available show that 45 percent of employees are minorities and 67 percent are women. And Starbucks aims to enable its partners to do their best work and to be successful in the Starbucks environment. The company supports employee resource groups (which they call "partner networks"). Some of the current ones include Starbucks Access Alliance, a forum for partners with disabilities; Starbucks Armed Forces Support Network, which supports veterans and those currently in the armed forces and their families; and the Starbucks Black Partner Network, which strengthens relationships and connections among partners of African descent. In 2018, Starbucks achieved its goal of increasing the number of women in senior leadership by 50 percent two years earlier than forecast. The company set another goal—this time, for women to be half of all senior leaders by the end of 2020. Starbucks also is making strides toward their goal of a 50 percent increase in minority representation in senior leadership positions by 2020. Finally, Starbucks supports diversity in its local neighborhoods and global communities through programs and investments that deepen its ties in those areas. To create job opportunities and a community presence, Starbucks made good on its pledge to open fifteen cafes in underserved communities by the end of 2018. Starbucks also purposefully set out to hire young people between the ages of 16 and 24, who are unemployed and not in school, as part of its Opportunity Youth program. Between 2015 and January 2019, 165,000 opportunity youth were hired at Starbucks.

Starbucks has sometimes met with challenges while attempting to embrace diversity. There were threats of a Starbucks boycott and the company's Buzz score (a measure of consumer perceptions) fell by two-thirds after Starbucks announced that it would hire 10,000 refugees. In another instance, Starbucks was criticized for closing restrooms in three cafes in Los Angeles located near homeless populations in 2016. Starbucks claimed that their restrooms were being used as showers, which made the restrooms difficult for other guests to use. But then, new criticisms arose after Starbucks implemented a company-wide policy in 2018 welcoming unpaying guests into their stores. After that guest policy update, critics voiced their concerns that some Starbucks stores would turn into destinations for both the homeless and drug users.

Social Responsibility and Ethics

Starbucks takes its social responsibility and ethical commitments seriously. In 2001, the company began issuing an annual corporate social responsibility report, which addresses the company's decisions and actions in relation to its products, society, the environment, and the workplace. These reports aren't simply a way for Starbucks to brag about its socially responsible actions, but are intended to stress the importance of doing business in a responsible way and to hold employees and managers accountable for their actions.

Starbucks focuses its corporate responsibility efforts on three main areas: ethical sourcing (buying), environmental stewardship, and community involvement. Starbucks approaches ethical sourcing from the perspective of helping the farmers and suppliers who grow and produce their products use responsible growing methods and helping them be successful, thus promoting long-term sustainability of its supply of quality coffee. The company views this as a win-win situation. The farmers have a better (and more secure) future, and Starbucks is helping create a long-term supply of a commodity they depend on.

Environmental stewardship has been one of the more challenging undertakings for Starbucks, especially considering the number of disposable containers generated by the more than 85 million customers *each week* across the globe. And front-of-the-store waste is only half the battle. Behind-the-counter waste is also generated in the form of cardboard boxes, milk jugs, syrup bottles, and, not surprisingly, coffee grounds. Even with recycling bins provided, one wrong item in a recycle bin can make the whole thing unrecyclable to a hauler. Despite this, the company has made significant strides in recycling. Starbucks has the largest number of "green stores" (energy efficient involving sustainable materials) in its industry and was the first to include post-consumer fiber in its hot cups. They introduced a more recyclable cup lid in 2017 and have plans to stop using plastic straws worldwide by 2020. Even so, 6 billion of Starbucks's single-use cups end up in landfills each year. They have pledged to double the recyclability of their cups by 2022 and have pilot tested a paper cup charge in London. Finally, Starbucks has always strived to be a good neighbor by providing a place for people to come together and by committing to supporting, financially and in other ways, the communities where its stores are located. Partners (and customers) are encouraged to get involved in volunteering in their communities. In addition, the Starbucks Foundation, which started in 1997 with funding for literacy programs in the United States and Canada, now makes grants to a wide variety of community projects and service programs.

Starbucks is also very serious about doing business ethically. In fact, it was named to the 2018 list of World's Most Ethical Companies, as it has been for twelve years in a row. From the executive level to the store level, individuals are expected and empowered to protect Starbucks's reputation through how they conduct business and how they treat others. And individuals are guided by the *Standards of Business Conduct,* a resource created for employees in doing business ethically, with integrity and honesty. These business conduct standards cover the workplace environment, business practices, intellectual property and proprietary information, and community involvement. Despite the thorough information in the standards, if partners face a situation where they're unsure how to respond or where they want to voice concerns, they're encouraged to seek out guidance from their manager, their partner resources representative, or even the corporate office of business ethics and compliance. The company also strongly states that it does not tolerate any retaliation against or victimization of any partner who raises concerns or questions.[2]

Innovation, Innovation

Starbucks has always thought "outside the box." From the beginning, it took the concept of the corner coffee shop and totally revamped the coffee experience. And the company has always had the ability to roll out new products relatively quickly. Starbucks invests heavily in research and development. It has received an Outstanding Corporate Innovator (OCI) Award for its commitment to innovation as a strategy to grow their businesses. Starbucks's System to Accelerate Results (STAR) process has enabled the company to test and measure new products and measure customer interest. *Fast Company* ranked Starbucks as a "Most Innovative" company in 2018 within the magazine's social good award division for donating 100 percent of its daily leftovers to community groups for combating hunger. Also, Starbucks was recognized by *Forbes* magazine as one of the 100 most innovative companies in the world in 2015.

Some of the areas where you can see Starbucks innovations are products, technology, and new roasteries. The popularity of energy drinks led the company to create a line of "natural" energy drinks called Refreshers. These fruity carbonated drinks are high in antioxidants and get their energy boost from unroasted green coffee extract. In 2018, the Mango Dragonfruit Refresher came on the scene with its highly "Instagrammable" bright color. The Unicorn Frappuccino drink that Starbucks rolled out for a short time in April 2017 made a splash for the company. The bright blue and purple drink that changed colors when stirred increased customer traffic into stores and also resulted in hoped-for social media attention. Since the Unicorn drink reveal, traditional Frappuccino sales at Starbucks have declined so that they make up 3 percent less of company revenue relative to a year earlier. Some industry experts say that customers want healthier drinks, while others say that Starbucks needs to show more innovation in their drink options.

Meanwhile, Starbucks has been innovating in the area of technology by streamlining mobile ordering and making Wi-Fi access in its stores easier. Starbucks also has been experimenting with ways to eventually use "smart" (self-monitoring) equipment in its stores. For example, in Starbucks's Seattle Reserve SODO store, they are pilot testing a drink-making machine called Clover X that grinds beans and brews coffee one cup at a time on demand in just 30 seconds. Starbucks also is working on refining a Digital Order Manager that allows customers to track progress on orders and to let them know when their order is ready. Starbucks has entered a partnership with Microsoft to advance in the technology realm as it relates to improving the customer experience. Finally, Starbucks's Reserve Roasteries—now located in Seattle, New York City, Milan, Shanghai, and Tokyo, with another on its way in Chicago—are a testament to the company's commitment to innovation due to their transformation of the customer experience beyond coffee.[3]

Discussion Questions

P2-1. Do you think Howard Schultz and Kevin Johnson have viewed their roles more from the omnipotent or from the symbolic perspective? Explain.

P2-2. What has made Starbucks's culture what it is? How is that culture maintained?

P2-3. Does Starbucks encourage a customer-responsive culture? An ethical culture? Explain.

P2-4. Describe some of the specific and general environmental components that are likely to impact Starbucks.

P2-5. How would you classify the uncertainty of the environment in which Starbucks operates? Explain.

P2-6. What stakeholders do you think Starbucks might be most concerned with? Why? What issue(s) might each of these stakeholders want Starbucks to address?

P2-7. If Starbucks wanted to increase the adaptability of its organizational culture due to the tough competition it is facing, what are some examples of how Starbucks could encourage more innovation and experimentation among its employees?

P2-8. What types of global economic and legal-political issues might Starbucks face as it does business globally?

P2-9. Pick one of the countries mentioned as an important target for Starbucks. Make a bulleted list of economic, political-legal, and cultural characteristics of this country and how it might affect Starbucks's operation.

P2-10. What workforce challenges might Starbucks face in China in regard to its partners?

P2-11. With more than 330,000 partners worldwide, what challenges might Starbucks face in making sure its diversity values are practiced and adhered to?

P2-12. Kevin Johnson is quoted on the Starbucks website as saying, "We aspire to be a place of inclusion, diversity, equity and accessibility." Explain what you think this means. How are these four concepts different from one another?

P2-13. What are specific ways in which Starbucks has shown top-management commitment to diversity? In what ways could Starbucks become even stronger in the area of diversity?

P2-14. Go to the company's website, www.starbucks.com, and find the latest corporate social responsibility report. Choose one of the key areas in the report (or your instructor may assign one of these areas). Describe and evaluate what the company has done in this key area.

P2-15. What do you think of Starbucks's goal to stop using plastic straws worldwide by 2020? What challenges might it face in meeting that goal? Is this merely a "public relations" promotion?

P2-16. Which of the approaches to "going green" (see Exhibit 6-3) does Starbucks utilize? Explain your choice.

P2-17. What do you think the company's use of the term *partners* instead of *employees* implies? What's your reaction to this? Do you think it matters what companies call their employees? (For instance, Walmart calls its employees *associates*.) Why or why not?

P2-18. Would you classify Starbucks's environment as more calm waters or white-water rapids? Explain. How does the company manage change in this type of environment?

P2-19. Using Exhibit 13-8) describe which innovation variables are already a part of Starbucks? To stimulate more innovative, which innovation variables could they consider adding more of?

Notes for the Part 2 Continuing Case

1. M. Lamson, "10 Tips to Develop Your Firm's Cultural Competence," Inc., July 3, 2018, https://www.inc.com/melissa-lamson/cultural-competence-your-most-valuable-business-asset.html; M. Abadi, "The Exact Same Sentence From Your Boss Can Mean 'Yes,' 'No,' or 'Maybe' Depending on the Country Where You Work," Business Insider, December 7, 2017, https://www.businessinsider.com/direct-feedback-work-depends-on-culture-2017-12; M. Smith, "The Cultural Advice Your Need Before You Take Your Business Global," Fast Company, November 29, 2018, https://www.fastcompany.com/90272039/the-cultural-advice-you-need-before-taking-your-business-global; B. Sodoma, "6 Everyday Things to Consider Before Doing Business Abroad," Forbes, November 6, 2018, https://www.forbes.com/sites/colehaan/2018/11/06/6-everyday-things-to-consider-before-doing-business-abroad/#2766db322ef9; A. Molinsky, "How to Keep a Global Team Engaged," *Harvard Business Review Digital Articles,* May 14, 2018, pp. 2–4.

2. Information from www.starbucks.com, accessed March 11, 2019; "Population of Cities in China (2019)," *World Population Review,* http://worldpopulationreview.com/countries/china-population/cities/; M. Vultaggio, "Who Is Current CEO of Starbucks? About Kevin Johnson After Howard Schultz Announces Potential 2020 Presidential Run," *Newsweek,* January 28, 2019, https://www.newsweek.com/who-current-ceo-starbucks-kevin-johnson-howard-schultz-1308360; "Morning Joe—Starbucks to Boost Worker Pay and Benefits After US Lowers Corporate Taxes," US House of Representatives documents, January 24, 2018; K. Taylor, "Drugs and Syringes Have Become Such a Problem in Starbucks Bathrooms That the Company Is Installing Needle-Disposal Boxes in Certain Locations," *Business Insider,* January 9, 2019, https://www.businessinsider.com/starbucks-workers-petition-bathroom-needle-disposal-boxes-2019-1;

J. Maze, "Starbucks Plans to Hire 10,000 Refugees," *Nation's Restaurant News,* January 31, 2017; "Starbucks Helps Staff Weather 2 Hurricanes," *Public Relations Tactics* 24, issue 10 (October 2017): p. 21; I. S. Fish, "American Companies In China Shouldn't Fear Tariffs. They Should Fear a Boycott.," *Washington Post*, April 10, 2018; "Starbucks Reports Q4 and Full Year Fiscal 2018 Results," news release, *Starbucks Stories,* November 1, 2018, https://stories.starbucks.com/press/2018/starbucks-q4-fy18-earnings/; N. Luna, "Starbucks Strikes Licensing Deal with Multi-Brand Operator in Brazil," *Nation's Restaurant News*, March 14, 2018; Lex, "Starbucks/Luckin Coffee: Trouble Brewing," *Financial Times*, July 11, 2018, https://app.ft.com/content/718049a0-84f6-11e8-a29d-73e3d454535d; T. Hancock, "Chinese Rival to Starbucks Pursues Growth at Expense of Profit," *Financial Times*, September 26, 2018, https://www.ft.com/content/29922d60-b7e2-11e8-bbc3-ccd7de085ffe; P. Mourdoukoutas, "Starbucks Worst Nightmare in China is Coming True," *Forbes*, January 21, 2019, https://www.forbes.com/sites/panosmourdoukoutas/2019/01/21/starbucks-worst-nightmare-in-china-is-coming-true/#664e37f617ec; H. Jacobs, "See Inside the World's Largest Starbucks, Where 'Coffee is Theater' and the Line Is Always Down the Block," *Business Insider*, April 22, 2018, https://www.businessinsider.com/starbucks-reserve-roastery-shanghai-china-is-worlds-biggest-2018-4; E. Schroeder, "Starbucks Restructuring Efforts Extend to Europe," *Food Business News*, October 18, 2018, https://www.foodbusinessnews.net/articles/12719-starbucks-restructuring-efforts-extend-to-europe; J. Bird, "Roasted: How China Is Showing the Way for Starbucks in the U.S.," *Forbes*, January 15, 2019, https://www.forbes.com/sites/jonbird1/2019/01/15/roasted-how-china-is-showing-the-way-for-starbucks-u-s/#31b4befdd443; "Italians Welcome First Starbucks Store with Defiance—and Curiosity," All Things Considered, *National Public Radio*, September 12, 2018, https://www.npr.org/2018/09/12/647180436/italians-welcome-first-starbucks-store-with-defiance-and-curiosity; S. Whitten, "You Don't Have to Buy a Coffee to Sit at Starbucks, but You Still Can't Nap There," *CNBC*, May 22, 2018, https://www.cnbc.com/2018/05/22/starbucks-clarifies-new-guest-policy-no-sleeping-or-drug-use.html; "How Starbucks Got Tangled Up in LA's Homelessness Crisis," All Things Considered, *National Public Radio*, May 3, 2016, https://www.npr.org/sections/thesalt/2016/05/03/476456674/how-starbucks-got-tangled-up-in-las-homelessness-crisis; L. Jennings, "Did Refugee Hiring Plan Hurt Starbucks?," *Nation's Restaurant News*, February 24, 2017, https://www.nrn.com/consumer-trends/did-refugee-hiring-plan-hurt-starbucks; B. Houck, "We're Buried in Starbucks Cups. What Are They Doing About It?," *Eater*, May 28, 2018, https://www.eater.com/2018/3/28/17172556/starbucks-cup-waste-sustainable-compost-recyclable; P. Wells, "Starbucks Jolted Higher After Plastic Straw Phase-Out Plan," *Financial Times*, July 9, 2018, https://www.ft.com/content/6503605c-8386-11e8-a29d-73e3d454535d;and J. Wernau and J. Jargon, "Starbucks Races Coffee Rival in China," *Wall Street Journal*, March 14, 2019.

3. Information from the company website, www.starbucks.com; Starbucks Stories, "Leadership," March 17, 2019, https://www.starbucks.com; M. Flager, "10 Things You Didn't Know About Kevin Johnson, Starbucks's New CEO," *Delish*, June 21, 2018, https://www.delish.com/food-news/g21753662/kevin-johnson-starbucks-ceo-facts/; P. Meyer, "Starbucks Coffee's Organizational Structure and Its Characteristics," Panmore Institute, February 14, 2019, http://panmore.com/starbucks-coffee-company-organizational-structure; J. Calfas, "Was Starbucks's Racial Bias Training Effective? Here's What These Employees Thought," *Time*, May 30, 2018, http://time.com/5294343/starbucks-employees-racial-bias-training/; K. Washington, "Starbucks, Walmart, and Amazon Offer "Free" College—But Read the Fine Print," *The Century Foundation*, October 15, 2018, https://tcf.org/content/commentary/starbucks-walmart-amazon-offer-free-college-read-fine-print/?agreed=1; "How Starbucks Does Training to Create an Unforgettable Customer Experience," *Panopto*, accessed March 17, 2019, https://www.panopto.com/blog/how-starbucks-does-training-to-create-an-unforgettable-customer-experience/; Z Meyer, "Starbucks's First US 'Signing Store' Lets Deaf Customers Order Using Sign Language," *USA Today*, October 23, 2018, https://www.usatoday.com/story/money/restaurants/2018/10/23/starbucks-sign-language-store-now-open-washington-d-c/1737022002/; Z. Weiner, "Starbucks Releases Mango Dragonfruit Refresher," *Teen Vogue*, June 19, 2018, https://www.teenvogue.com/story/starbucks-introduces-mango-dragonfruit-refresher; S. Whitten, "Starbucks Has a 'Void in Innovation' and Healthy Beverages Won't Turn the Tide," CNBC, June 24, 2018, https://www.cnbc.com/2018/06/22/starbucks-has-a-void-in-innovation-and-healthy-beverages-wont-turn-the-tide.html; N. Luna, "Starbucks Courts Digital Relationships Outside Reward Program," *Nation's Restaurant News*, March 10, 2018, https://www.nrn.com/consumer-trends/starbucks-courts-digital-relationships-outside-rewards-program.

Chapter 8   Foundations of Planning

Learning Objectives

8.1 Define the nature and purposes of planning.

8.2 Classify the types of plans organizations might use.

8.3 Identify the key contingency factors in planning.

8.4 Compare and contrast approaches to objective setting.

8.5 Discuss contemporary issues in planning.

Employability Skills Matrix (ESM)

This matrix identifies which features and end-of-chapter material will help you develop specific skills employers are looking for in job candidates.

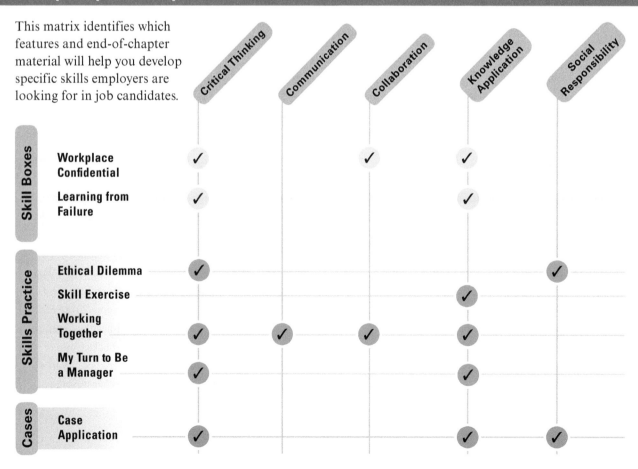

		Critical Thinking	Communication	Collaboration	Knowledge Application	Social Responsibility
Skill Boxes	Workplace Confidential	✓		✓	✓	
	Learning from Failure	✓			✓	
Skills Practice	Ethical Dilemma	✓				✓
	Skill Exercise				✓	
	Working Together	✓	✓	✓	✓	
	My Turn to Be a Manager	✓			✓	
Cases	Case Application	✓			✓	✓

There may be no more impressive example of planning than that preceding the legendary World War II Allied forces' invasion of France on June 6, 1944.[1] Typically referred to as "D-Day," it would be the largest seaborne invasion in history. Imagine what had to go into this effort. Years in the planning, stockpiles of guns, rocket weapons, and amphibious vehicles had to be secretly stored. Meanwhile, military planners had to oversee pre-invasion training, photo reconnaissance, and mapping, and then coordinate air, ground, and sea forces as well supply and transport. This, of course, was all done without modern imaging, mapping, and communication equipment. On the actual day of invasion, 4,000 ships carried troops across the English Channel under protection from a dozen battleships and thousands of aircraft. End result: All that planning for D-Day proved instrumental toward the Allied defeat of Germany.

THE *WHAT* AND *WHY* of planning

LO8.1 Contemporary organizational planning may not take on the complexity or drama of a D-Day invasion, but all managers need to understand the importance of planning. Let's start by covering the basics of planning: *What* is it? And *why* is it important?

What Is Planning?

What do we mean by the term *planning*? As we stated in Chapter 1, planning encompasses defining the organization's objectives or goals, establishing an overall strategy for achieving these goals, and developing a comprehensive hierarchy of plans to integrate and coordinate activities. It is concerned, then, with *ends* (what is to be done) as well as with *means* (how it is to be done).

Planning can be further defined in terms of whether it is informal or formal. All managers engage in planning, but it might be only the informal variety. In informal planning, nothing is written down, and there is little or no sharing of objectives with others in the organization. This describes planning in many small businesses; the owner-manager has a vision of where he or she wants to go and how he or she expects to get there. The planning is general and lacks continuity. Of course, informal planning exists in some large organizations, and some small businesses have very sophisticated formal plans.

When we use the term "planning" in this book, we are implying *formal* planning. Specific objectives are formulated covering a period of years. These objectives are committed to writing and made available to organization members. Finally, specific action programs exist for the achievement of these objectives; that is, management clearly defines the path it wants to take to get from where it is to where it wants to be.

Why Do Managers Plan?

The planning process consumes a lot of time and effort. So why should managers plan? We can give you at least four reasons:

1. *Planning provides direction* to managers and nonmanagers alike. When employees know what their organization or work unit is trying to accomplish and what they must contribute to reach goals, they can coordinate their activities, cooperate with each other, and do what it takes to accomplish those goals. Without planning, departments and individuals might work at cross-purposes and prevent the organization from efficiently achieving its goals.
2. *Planning reduces uncertainty* by forcing managers to look ahead, anticipate change, consider the impact of change, and develop appropriate responses. Although planning won't eliminate uncertainty, managers plan so they can respond effectively.

Planning contributes to the profitable performance of Recreational Equipment, Inc. Formal expansion plans have helped REI grow from one store in 1944 to become a major retailer of outdoor gear with more than 150 stores, 12,000 employees, and annual sales of over $2 billion. Shown here are employees at an REI store opening in New York City's SoHo shopping district.
Source: Matt Peyton/REI/AP Images

3. *Planning minimizes waste and redundancy.* When work activities are coordinated around plans, inefficiencies become obvious and can be corrected or eliminated.

4. *Planning establishes the goals or standards* used in controlling. When managers plan, they develop goals and plans. When they control, they see whether the plans have been carried out and the goals met. Without planning, there would be no goals against which to measure work effort or identify deviations.

Planning and Performance

Is planning worthwhile? We have more than thirty years of research that has looked at the relationship between planning and performance.[2] Although most have shown generally positive relationships, we can't say that organizations that formally plan always outperform those that don't plan. But *what* can we conclude?

First, generally speaking, formal planning is associated with positive financial results—higher profits, higher returns on assets, and so forth. Second, the *quality* of the planning process and the appropriate *implementation* of the plans probably contribute more to high performance than does the *extent* of planning. Finally, in those studies where formal planning didn't lead to higher performance, the external environment is typically the culprit. When government regulations, powerful labor unions, and similar environmental forces constrain management's options, planning will have less of an impact on the organization's performance. Why? Because management will have fewer choices for which planning can propose viable alternatives. For example, planning might suggest that a manufacturing firm produce a number of it key parts in Asia in order to compete effectively against low-cost foreign competitors. But if the firm's contract with its labor union specifically forbids transferring work overseas, the value of the firm's planning effort is significantly reduced. Dramatic shocks from the environment can also undermine the best-laid plans. Hurricane Irma in September

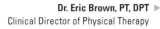

Let's Get REAL

Dr. Eric Brown, PT, DPT ▶
Clinical Director of Physical Therapy

Source: Dr. Eric Brown

The Scenario:

Leticia Reyes is a newly promoted midlevel manager at an information technology company. Executives at higher levels in the company have formulated two-year strategic plans for the company. Other midlevel managers often consider the high-level executive's strategic plans to be enough planning. They think that employees can figure out how to realize the objectives in those plans on their own. Leticia is wondering if she should put some operational plans in place that offer more specifics and a shorter time frame than two years.

What advice would you give Leticia about why and how she should put operational plans in place?

Leticia has a unique opportunity as a mid-level manager to address potential problems that may arise by implementing the operational plans within the early stages of development. This allows her to obtain feedback from her employees, gain perspective on unanticipated challenges, and refine the company's original plans. Not only will this help make the objectives more tangible for her team, it will help the company become more efficient and productive prior to the two-year deadline. It's important to remember that change is a process, not an event.

Exhibit 8-1
Types of Plans

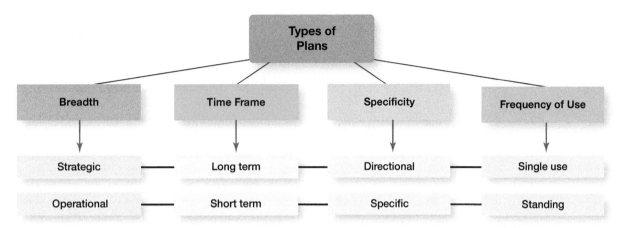

2017 destroyed much of the Florida Keys and, at the same time, destroyed the value of any formal plans that hotel managements in the Keys may have made for the 2017-2018 winter season. In conditions of such environmental uncertainty, there is no reason to expect that planners will necessarily outperform nonplanners.

TYPES of plans

LO8.2 The most popular ways to describe organizational plans are breadth (strategic versus operational), time frame (short-term versus long-term), specificity (directional versus specific), and frequency of use (single use versus standing). As Exhibit 8-1 shows, these types of plans aren't independent of one another. For instance, there is a close relationship between the short-and long-term categories and the strategic and operational categories.

Strategic Versus Operational Plans

Plans that apply to the entire organization, that establish the organization's overall objectives, and that seek to position the organization in terms of its environment are called **strategic plans**. These plans evolve from the organization's mission. A **mission** is a broad statement of an organization's purpose that provides an overall guide to what organizational members think is important. Plans should reflect the organization's mission. For instance, Walmart's mission is "to save people money so they can live better." [3]

Plans that specify the details of how the overall objectives are to be achieved are called **operational plans**. Strategic and operational plans differ in their time frame, their scope, and whether or not they include a known set of organizational objectives. Operational plans tend to cover shorter periods of time. For instance, an organization's monthly, weekly, and day-to-day plans are almost all operational. Strategic plans tend to include an extended time period—usually five years or more. They also cover a broader area and deal less with specifics. Finally, strategic plans include the formulation of objectives, whereas operational plans assume the existence of objectives. Operational plans offer ways of attaining these objectives.

Short-Term Versus Long-Term Plans

Financial analysts traditionally describe investment returns as *short-, intermediate-,* and *long-term.* **Short-term plans** cover less than one year. Any time frame beyond five years is classified as **long-term plans**. The intermediate covers the period in between. Managers have adopted the same terminology to describe plans. For clarity, we'll emphasize short-term plans and long-term plans in future discussions.

strategic plans
Plans that apply to the entire organization, that establish the organization's overall objectives, and that seek to position the organization in terms of its environment

mission
The purpose of an organization

operational plans
Plans that specify the details of how the overall objectives are to be achieved

short-term plans
Plans covering less than one year

long-term plans
Plans of five-years or more

Specific Versus Directional Plans

specific plans
Plans that are clearly defined and leave no room for interpretation

It seems intuitively correct that specific plans are always preferable to directional, or loosely guided, plans. **Specific plans** have clearly defined objectives. There is no ambiguity, no problem with misunderstandings. For example, a manager who seeks to increase his or her firm's sales by 20 percent over a given twelve-month period might establish specific procedures, budget allocations, and schedules of activities to reach that objective. These represent specific plans.

However, specific plans are not without drawbacks. They require clarity and a sense of predictability that often doesn't exist. When uncertainty is high, which requires management to maintain flexibility in order to respond to unexpected changes, then it's preferable to use directional plans.

directional plans
Plans that are flexible and set out general guidelines

Directional plans identify general guidelines. They provide focus but do not lock management into specific objectives or specific courses of action. Using Exhibit 8-2 as an example, specific plans would dictate the exact route to get from point A to point B. In contrast, directional plans would point you in the general direction but essentially leave open the specific streets to take. And point B might be a general area rather than a specifically defined destination.

Instead of a manager following a specific plan to cut costs by 4 percent and increase revenues by 6 percent in the next six months, a directional plan might aim at improving profits by 5 to 10 percent during the next six months. The flexibility inherent in directional plans is obvious. This advantage must be weighed against the loss in clarity provided by specific plans.

Only 22 perecent of employees strongly agree that leaders have a clear direction for their organization.[4]

Single-Use Versus Standing Plans

Some plans that managers develop are ongoing while others are used only once. A **single-use plan** is a one-time plan specifically designed to meet the needs of a unique situation. For instance, when Walmart wanted to expand the number of its stores in China, top-level executives formulated a single-use plan as a guide. In contrast, **standing plans** are ongoing plans that provide guidance for activities performed repeatedly. Standing plans include policies, rules, and procedures, which we defined in Chapter 2. An example of a standing plan is the nondiscrimination and anti-harassment policy developed by Microsoft. It provides guidance to Microsoft executives and staff as they make hiring plans and do their jobs.

single-use plan
A one-time plan specifically designed to meet the needs of a unique situation

standing plans
Ongoing plans that provide guidance for activities performed repeatedly

Exhibit 8-2
Specific versus directional plans

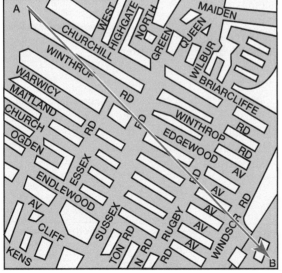

Directional Plans

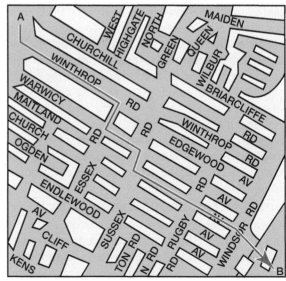

Specific Plans

CONTINGENCY factors in planning

LO8.3 In some cases, long-term plans make sense; in others, they do not. Similarly, in some situations, directional plans are more effective than specific ones. What are these situations? In this section, we identify three contingency factors that affect planning.

Level in the Organization

Exhibit 8-3 illustrates the general relationship between managerial level in an organization and the type of planning that is done. For the most part, operational planning dominates the planning activities of lower-level managers. As managers rise in the hierarchy, their planning role becomes more strategy oriented. The planning effort by the top executives of large organizations is essentially strategic. In a small business, of course, the owner-manager needs to do both.

Degree of Environmental Uncertainty

The greater the environmental uncertainty, the more plans should be directional and emphasis placed on the short term.

If rapid or important technological, social, economic, legal, or other changes are taking place, well-defined and precisely chartered routes are more likely to hinder an organization's performance than aid it. When environmental uncertainty is high, specific plans have to be altered to accommodate the changes—often at high cost and decreased efficiency. In today's highly competitive environment, where disruptors are attacking most industries, this contingency variable would suggest that plans be more flexible—hence, less specific and covering a shorter term.

Length of Future Commitments

Our final contingency factor is the **commitment concept**. This states that the more that current plans affect future commitments, the longer the time frame for which management should plan. This concept means that plans should extend far enough to see through those commitments that are made today. Planning for too long or too short a period is inefficient.

Managers are not planning for future decisions. Rather, they are planning for the future impact of the decisions that they are currently making. Decisions made today become a commitment to some future action or expenditure. For instance, in 2014, Tesla committed to building a 5.8 million square foot factory outside of Sparks, Nevada, to build batteries that will power its electric vehicles.[5] An investment of this magnitude commits Tesla to producing electric cars for decades into the future. Hence, Tesla's management should develop plans that parallel this commitment.

commitment concept
Plans should extend far enough to meet those commitments made when the plans were developed

Exhibit 8-3
Planning in the Hierarchy of Organizations

Learning from FAILURE
US Army Corps of Engineers and Hurricane Katrina

It has been described as the single most catastrophic natural disaster in American history. In August 2005, a Category 3 storm with winds of 127 mph hit New Orleans. This storm, Hurricane Katrina, killed more than 1800 people, caused more than $81 billion in damage, and devastated the city of New Orleans. Most of the damage came from flooding. And follow-up studies put the blame for the widespread flood damage directly on the US Army Corps of Engineers. They were responsible for the levee system that protected the city.

Much of New Orleans is below sea level. It depends on its levee system to keep the city dry when heavy rains and winds come. Unfortunately, the Corps failed to maintain the levees and the shipping channels surrounding the city. Erosion widened over time, and the banks that were built to protect the levees deteriorated. When Katrina hit, the levees gave way and catastrophic flooding resulted.

A federal court ruled that the Army Corps of Engineers failed to properly maintain the shipping channel linking New Orleans to the Gulf of Mexico. A judge concluded:

For over 40 years, the Corps was aware that the Reach II levee protecting [New Orleans] was going to be compromised by…continued deterioration….The Corps had an opportunity to take a myriad of actions to alleviate this deterioration or rehabilitate this deterioration and failed to do so.

Katrina provided a hard lesson for the Corps. It learned that it can't shortcut its responsibilities to the city of New Orleans. In the decade following Katrina, the Corps completed one of the world's most sophisticated hurricane protection systems to encircle New Orleans at a cost of $14.5 billion. More than 350 miles of hurricane barriers, massive new floodgates, and updated pumping stations have been built. For instance, a water gate nearly as long as a football field can now be shut during a flood event, and eleven huge diesel engines kick on to pump water out of the flooded area.[6]

OBJECTIVES: The foundation of planning

LO8.4

objectives (also called goals)
Desired outcomes for individuals, groups, or entire organizations.

Objectives are goals. We use the terms interchangeably. What do these terms mean? They refer to desired outcomes for individuals, groups, or entire organizations. They provide the direction for all management decisions and form the criterion against which actual accomplishments can be measured. It's for these reasons that they are the foundation of planning.

Stated Versus Real Objectives

stated objectives
Official statements of what an organization says—and what it wants various publics to believe—are its objectives

Stated objectives are official statements of what an organization says—and what it wants various publics to believe—are its objectives. However, stated objectives—which can be found in the organization's charter, annual report, public-relations announcements, or in public statements made by managers—are often conflicting and excessively influenced by what society believes organizations *should* do.

The conflict in stated goals exists because organizations respond to a vast array of constituencies. Unfortunately, these constituencies frequently evaluate the organization by different criteria. As a result, management is forced to say different things to different audiences. For example, a number of years ago, a major US airline was negotiating to get wage concessions from its flight attendants' union.[7] The union, not wanting to give up anything, was threatening to strike. To the union's representatives, management was saying, "If you strike, we'll dismantle the airline. By selling off aircraft and air routes, the company is worth more dead than alive." At the same time, management was trying to calm the nerves of potential passengers by saying the company was determined to fly and survive, even if its flight attendants struck. To support its intention, airline management said that it was training 1,500 people to step in if its attendants walked out. Management had explicitly presented itself in one way to the union and in another way to the public. Was one true and the other false? No. Both were true, but they were in conflict.

Did you ever read an organization's objectives as they are stated in its brochures or on its website?[8] American Express says, "We work hard every day to make American Express the world's most respected service brand." Nordstrom states that it seeks "to give customers the most compelling shopping experience possible." JetBlue's mission is "to inspire humanity—both in the air and on the ground." Chipotle says it stands for "food with integrity." These types of statements are, at best, vague and more likely representative of management's public relations skills than they are meaningful guides to what the organization is actually seeking to accomplish. In Chipotle's case, its "food with integrity" claim actually became an embarrassment when its restaurants suffered repeated outbreaks of foodborne illnesses between 2015 and 2017.[9]

It shouldn't be surprising, then, to find that an organization's stated objectives are often quite irrelevant to what actually goes on in that organization. In a corporation, for instance, one statement of objectives is issued to stockholders, another to customers, and still others to employees and to the public.

The overall objectives stated by top management should be treated for what they are: "fiction produced by an organization to account for, explain, or rationalize to particular audiences rather than as valid and reliable indications of purpose."[10] The content of objectives is substantially determined by what those audiences want to hear. Moreover, it is simpler for management to state a set of consistent, understandable objectives than to explain a multiplicity of objectives.

If you want to know what an organization's **real objectives** are, closely observe what members of the organization actually do. Actions define priorities. The university that proclaims the objectives of limiting class size, facilitating close student-faculty relations, and actively involving students in the learning process, and then puts its students into lecture halls of 300 or more, is not unusual. Nor is the automobile service center that promotes fast, low-cost repairs and then gives mediocre service at high prices. An awareness that stated and real objectives can deviate is important, if for no other reason than because it can help you to explain what might otherwise seem to be management inconsistencies.

Objectives are typically set at the top of an organization and then broken down for each level. Each department may work toward its own set of objectives, depending on its contribution to the firm.
Source: Narin Nonthamand/Shutterstock

real objectives
Objectives that an organization actually pursues, as defined by the actions of its members

Traditional Objective Setting

The traditional role of objectives is one of control imposed by an organization's top management. The president of a manufacturing firm *tells* the production vice president what he or she expects manufacturing costs to be for the coming year. The president *tells* the marketing vice president what level he or she expects sales to reach for the coming year. The city mayor *tells* his or her chief of police how much the departmental budget will be. Then, at some later point, performance is evaluated to determine whether the assigned objectives have been achieved.

The central theme in **traditional objective setting** is that objectives are set at the top and then broken down into subgoals for each level of an organization. It is a one-way process. The top imposes its standards on everyone below. This traditional perspective assumes that top management knows what's best because only it can see the "big picture."

In addition to being imposed from above, traditional objective setting is often largely nonoperational. If top management defines the organization's objectives in broad terms such as achieving "sufficient profits" or "market leadership," these ambiguities have to be turned into specifics as the objectives filter down through the organization. At each level, managers supply operational meaning to the goals. Specificity is achieved by each manager applying his or her own set of interpretations and biases. The result is that objectives lose clarity and unity as they make their way down from the top (see Exhibit 8-4).

traditional objective setting
Objectives are set at the top and then broken down into subgoals for each level of an organization

Exhibit 8-4
Traditional Objective Setting

Management by Objectives

management by objectives (MBO)
A system in which specific performance objectives are jointly determined by subordinates and their superiors, progress toward objectives is periodically reviewed, and rewards are allocated on the basis of this progress

Instead of using traditional goal setting, companies such as Adobe, GE, and Microsoft have implemented **management by objectives (MBO)**. MBO is a system in which specific performance objectives are jointly determined by subordinates and their superiors, progress toward objectives is periodically reviewed, and rewards are allocated on the basis of this progress. Rather than using goals to control, MBO uses them to motivate.

Adobe refers to its MBO program as Check In. Each year, employees and managers meet to establish goals. Then, at least every two months, employees check in with their managers to discuss their progress. At the end of the year, managers meet for a "rewards check-in" session where they discuss how well employees attained their goals, and pay increases and bonuses are awarded based on goal attainment.[11]

WHAT IS MBO?   Management by objectives is not new.[12] Its appeal lies in its emphasis on converting overall objectives into specific objectives for organizational units and individual members.

MBO makes objectives operational by devising a process by which they cascade down through the organization. As depicted in Exhibit 8-5, the organization's overall objectives are translated into specific objectives for each succeeding level—divisional, departmental, individual—in the organization. Because lower unit managers jointly participate in setting their own goals, MBO works from the "bottom up" as well as from the "top down." The result is a hierarchy that links objectives at one level to those at the next level. For the individual employee, MBO provides specific personal performance objectives. Each person, therefore, has an identified specific contribution to make to his or her unit's performance. If all the individual employees achieve their goals, then their unit's goals will be attained, and the organization's overall objectives will become a reality.

MBO'S COMMON ELEMENTS   There are four ingredients common to MBO programs. These are goal specificity, participative decision making, an explicit time period, and performance feedback.

The objectives in MBO should be concise statements of expected accomplishments. It's not adequate, for example, merely to state a desire to cut costs, improve service, or increase quality. Such desires have to be converted into tangible objectives that can be measured and evaluated. To cut departmental costs *by 7 percent*, to improve service by ensuring that all telephone orders are processed *within 24 hours of receipt*, or to increase quality by keeping returns to *less than 1 percent of sales* are examples of specific objectives.

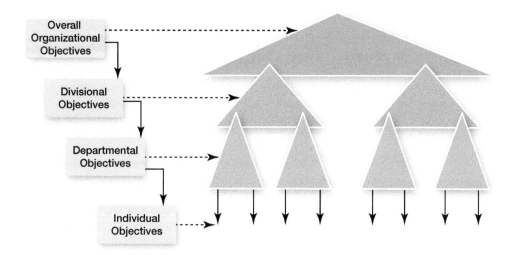

Exhibit 8-5
Planning in the Hierarchy of Organizations

In MBO, the objectives are not unilaterally set by the boss and assigned to subordinates, as is characteristic of traditional objective setting. MBO replaces these imposed goals with participatively determined goals. The employee and his or her boss jointly choose the goals and agree on how they will be achieved.

Each objective has a concrete time period in which it is to be completed. Typically, the time period is three months, six months, or a year.

The final ingredient in an MBO program is feedback on performance. MBO seeks to give continuous feedback on progress toward goals. Ideally, this is accomplished by giving ongoing feedback to individuals so they can monitor and correct their own actions. This is supplemented by periodic formal appraisal meetings in which an employee and superior can review progress toward goals and further feedback can be provided.

DOES MBO WORK? Assessing the effectiveness of MBO is a complex task. Let's begin by briefly reviewing a growing body of literature on the relationship between goals and performance.[14]

If factors such as a person's ability and acceptance of goals are held constant, evidence demonstrates that more *difficult* goals lead to higher performance. Although individuals with very difficult goals achieve them far less often than those with very easy goals, they nevertheless perform at a consistently higher level. Of course, goals can be too hard. If individuals perceive a goal to be impossible instead of challenging, their desire to achieve it decreases, and the likelihood that they will abandon it increases.

Moreover, studies consistently support the finding that *specific* hard goals produce a higher level of output than do no goals or generalized goals such as "do your best." *Feedback* also favorably affects performance. Feedback lets a person know whether his or her level of effort is sufficient or needs to be increased. It can induce a person to raise his or her goal after attaining a previous goal and can inform a person of ways in which to improve his or her performance.

The results cited above are all consistent with MBO's stress on specific goals and feedback. MBO implies, rather than explicitly states, that goals must be perceived as feasible. Research on goal setting indicates that MBO is most effective if the goals are difficult enough to require the person to do some stretching.

But what about participation? MBO strongly advocates that goals be set participatively. Does the research demonstrate that participatively set goals lead to higher performance than those assigned by a superior? Interestingly, the research comparing participatively set and assigned goals on performance has not shown any strong or consistent relationships. When goal difficulty has been held constant, assigned goals frequently do as well as participatively determined goals,

fyi

Companies that set goals quarterly using MBO earn 31 percent greater returns from their performance process than those who set goals yearly.[13]

Athletes, managers, and employees all perform better when they have specific and difficult goals.
Source: Gary Mitchell, GMP Media / Alamy Stock Photo

WORKPLACE CONFIDENTIAL When You Face a Lack of Clear Directions

Today's workplace is often described as exhibiting rapid change. New competitors pop out of nowhere. Innovative ideas disrupt established businesses. Products and services find their life cycles increasingly shortened. And employees are finding themselves having to cope with change and the ambiguity that comes with it.

While some people thrive on ambiguity, most of us find it frustrating and stressful. This is particularly true at work. What does my boss want me to do? What's a priority, and what can wait? When problems arise, whom should I see for help? How far can I go without overstepping my job responsibilities?

There are essentially two solutions to a lack of clear directions. One is a boss who offers explicit and precise guidelines. He or she tells you, in unambiguous terms, what your job entails. In your boss's leadership role, the lines of where your job responsibilities start and end are made perfectly clear to you. The other solution is a formal position description.

Reducing ambiguity can be largely facilitated by having a written position description. This is a statement of the essential components of your job—what work is to be performed, your primary duties and responsibilities, and the criteria that will be used to evaluate your performance. Most large organizations will have position descriptions available.

Ideally, your employer has a position description for your job. One might exist but you may have never received it when you took your job. If so, ask your boss or human resources department for a copy.

There is strong evidence indicating that position descriptions provide role clarity and that employees who have role clarity are much more likely to be engaged with the work they're doing. Of course, these position descriptions need to be updated regularly to reflect the changing nature of work and specific jobs. You might suggest to your boss that, following your annual performance evaluation, the two of you sit down, assess the changes that have taken place in the past year, and then update your position description to reflect if, or how, these changes have reshaped your job responsibilities.

But let's assume a position description for your job doesn't exist and your boss doesn't excel at providing you with clear directives. What then? Consider creating a position description in partnership with your boss. Explain to your boss how a detailed position description can help you do

your job better and reduce your dependence on him or her. Importantly, if this document is truly to be effective, it needs to contain shared expectations. That is, it has to be created in cooperation with your boss so he or she "owns" the final document with you.

Realistically, even with a great boss who provides clear directions or a detailed position description, there will still be times when you'll feel a lack of clear directions. Here are three suggestions that can help you through these times:

Suppress your urge to control things. No matter how much we want to control those things around us, we have to accept that there are elements of our life that we can't control. This is certainly true in relation to work. In terms of our concern here, we rarely get to choose our boss. And you may find that it's not realistic to impose structure—in the terms of a position description—in a culture where it has never existed. Add in the fact that, in many organizations, changes are occurring so rapidly that the valid life span of a position description may be only a few months or even weeks. End result: You need to learn to accept the reality that you can't control everything related to your job.

Learn to act without the complete picture. Rational decision making assumes that problems are clear and unambiguous, and that you know all possible alternatives and consequences. That's not the real world of work; hence, you will rarely, if ever, have all the information you need when making a decision. You need to accept that you will regularly face ambiguous situations and that you will have to take actions without clear directions either from your boss, colleagues, or a procedure manual.

You can make decisions based on the information you have, even if the information isn't complete. Don't be afraid to make a mistake. Often, a wrong decision is better than no decision. Don't be gun-shy, or as one executive once described a colleague: "It was always, 'ready, aim, aim, aim, aim.' He was afraid to pull the trigger!" You don't want to become characterized as someone who's afraid to do anything without your boss's direction or without first getting his or her approval. If you're going to move ahead in the organization and be seen as a leader, you will have to take assertive action under conditions of ambiguity. And that means your decisions are not always going to be proven correct. Live with it! Baseball players who fail 60 percent of the time at bat end up in the Hall of Fame.[15]

contrary to MBO ideology.[16] Therefore it isn't possible to argue for the superiority of participation as MBO proponents advocate. One major benefit from participation, however, is that it appears to induce individuals to establish more difficult goals. Thus participation may have a positive impact on performance by increasing one's goal aspiration level.

CONTEMPORARY issues in planning

L08.5 We conclude this chapter by looking at two contemporary planning topics: Monitoring what's going on in the environment to identify potential threats or opportunities; and utilizing virtual reality to improve the planning process.

Environmental Scanning

What potential changes in laws and regulations could affect our business? What technological breakthroughs might create new competitors? What new products or services are our competitors working on? Which of our competitors are talking about a possible merger? What cultural trends might indicate changing customer or client tastes? These are the kind of questions for which environmental scanning can provide answers.

Environmental scanning refers to screening large amounts of information to detect emerging trends and create a set of scenarios.[17] In the general environment, managers will be looking for political, economic, social, and technological data. Data more specific to an organization would include a firm's industry, competitors, suppliers, and customers. Exhibit 8-6 lists these environmental elements and examples of where you might get information on them.

One of the fastest-growing and important forms of environmental scanning is **competitive intelligence**, which refers to gathering information about competitors that allows managers to anticipate competitors' actions rather than merely react to them.[18] Who are our competitors? What are they doing? How will what they're doing affect us? This can be as simple as monitoring a competitor's website to see what new products they have in the pipeline. Or as aggressive as following up on a merger rumor by monitoring FAA flight plans of corporate aircraft to identify locations where competitors' executives are flying.

Competitive intelligence *isn't* corporate espionage. Advertisements, promotional materials, press releases, reports filed with government agencies, annual reports, online job postings, media reports, internet searches, and industry studies are readily accessible sources of information. Specific information on an industry and associated organizations is increasingly available through electronic databases. Managers can literally tap into this wealth of competitive information by purchasing access to databases. Attending trade shows and debriefing your own sales staff also can be good sources of information on competitors.

Airlines provide a ready example of competitive intelligence, as do professional sports teams.[19] Every day, airlines change ticket prices based on data they monitor on their competitors' routes and prices. And almost all pro baseball, football, and basketball teams now combine scouting and analytics to help coaches and managers better position their teams against opponents, shape drafting and trade decisions, and guide play choices.

environment scanning
Screening large amounts of information to detect emerging trends and create a set of scenarios

competitive intelligence
Gathering information about competitors that allows managers to anticipate competitors' actions

Seventy-seven percent of businesses find competitive intelligence to be critical to their success.[21]

What	Where
General Environment	
Political	Lobbyists; political representative
Economic	Fed minutes; financial news
Social	Social media
Technological	Patent reports
Specific Environment	
Industry	Business media; industry associations
Competitors	Web sites; others in the industry
Suppliers	Vendors
Customers	Surveys; focus groups

Exhibit 8-6
Environmental Scanning

Firms use social media, including LinkedIn, to conduct competitive intelligence in their market. This gathering of information about competitors allows managers to make important planning decisions.
Source: Alex Segre/Alamy Stock Photo

virtual reality (VR)
A three-dimensional, interactive computer-generated experience that takes place within a simulated environment

One of the most recent and important competitive intelligence sources is social media.[20] In the same way that high school students and parents use social media platforms to exchange information and opinions about potential colleges, managers can utilize sites such as LinkedIn, Facebook, and Twitter to extract opinions, patterns, and intelligence. The problem, in fact, is the availability of *too much* information. The challenge is to analyze the wealth of available data to extract information that can help managers make planning decisions. But with the right analytics, management can gain valuable information about competitors. For instance, job listings on LinkedIn might be a tip-off that a competitor is planning on adding a new location or expanding into a new product line.

Virtual Reality

It first saw light of day in science fiction. Then it found a huge market in video gaming. Now it has begun to be seen as a planning tool for managers. We're talking about **virtual reality (VR)**—a three-dimensional, interactive, computer-generated experience that takes place within a simulated environment.[22]

The future of virtual reality in organizations is huge. We can imagine it being a widely used tool for interviewing job candidates, holding virtual meetings, conducting complex job training, and previewing new office layouts. And it has potential to help managers in the planning process.[23]

As a production manager, you find yourself responsible for building a new factory or redesigning a current facility. What's the optimum design? What would plan A look like versus plan B? Instead of building a model or finding flaws after the project is complete, VR can allow you to "walk through" a simulated factory floor. It can also allow you to try different alternative designs to see which works best. For instance, VR can allow an airplane manufacturer, like Boeing, to visualize various designs without having to build expensive, full-scale prototypes.[24]

VR also has applications for financial planning. It makes it possible to visualize data in 3D displays. For instance, Virtualitics has created a virtual platform that allows managers and financial executives to view, analyze, and work collaboratively on their data in their own VR space.[25]

Chapter 8 | PREPARING FOR: Exams/Quizzes

CHAPTER SUMMARY by Learning Objectives

LO8.1

DEFINE the nature and purposes of planning.

Planning involves defining the organization's goals, establishing an overall strategy for achieving those goals, and developing plans for organizational work activities. Planning can be informal or formal. The four purposes of planning include providing direction, reducing uncertainty, minimizing waste and redundancy, and establishing the goals or standards used in controlling. Studies of the planning-performance relationship have concluded that formal planning is associated with positive financial performance, for the most part; it's more important to do a good job of planning and implementing the plans than doing more extensive planning; the external environment is usually the reason why companies that plan don't achieve high levels of performance.

L08.2 CLASSIFY the types of plans organizations might use.

Organizational plans vary in terms of breadth (strategic or operational), time frame (short-term or long-term), specificity (directional or specific), and frequency of use (single use or standing). Strategic plans apply to the entire organization and seek to position the organization in terms of its environment, while operational plans detail how objectives are to be achieved and cover shorter period of time. Long-term plans are those with a time frame beyond five years. Short-term plans cover one year or less. Specific plans have clearly defined objectives. Directional plans identify more general guidelines. A single-use plan is a one-time plan designed to meet the needs of a unique situation. Standing plans are on-going plans that provide guidance for activities performed repeatedly.

L08.3 IDENTIFY the key contingency factors in planning.

The key contingency factors in planning are the organizational level, the degree of environmental uncertainty, and the length of future commitments.

L08.4 COMPARE and contrast approaches to objective setting.

Stated objectives are official statements of what an organization says are its objectives. An organization's real objectives are what members of the organization actually do. In traditional objective setting, objectives are set at the top of the organization and then become subgoals for each organizational area. MBO (management by objectives) is a process of setting mutually agreed-upon objectives and using those objectives to evaluate employee performance. The contingency factors that affect planning are the manager's level in the organization, the degree of environmental uncertainty, and the length of future commitments.

L08.5 DISCUSS contemporary issues in planning.

One contemporary planning issue involves using environmental scanning to detect emerging trends in the firm's external environment. One form of environmental scanning, competitive intelligence, can be especially helpful in finding out what competitors are doing. Another contemporary issue in planning is utilizing virtual reality, which is a three-dimensional, interactive, computer-generated experience. Virtual reality allows managers to simulate different options being considered in the planning process.

REVIEW AND DISCUSSION QUESTIONS

8-1. Explain what studies have shown about the relationship between planning and performance.

8-2. Discuss the contingency factors that affect planning.

8-3. Will planning become more or less important to managers in the future? Why?

8-4. If planning is so crucial, why do some managers choose not to do it? What would you tell these managers?

8-5. Explain how planning involves making decisions today that will have an impact later.

8-6. How might planning in a not-for-profit organization such as the American Cancer Society differ from planning in a for-profit organization such as Coca-Cola?

8-7. What types of planning do you do in your personal life? Describe these plans in terms of being (a) strategic or operational, (b) short term or long term, and (c) specific or directional.

8-8. Provide examples of the sources of data a fruit juice drink company might gather when engaging in environmental scanning. Exhibit 8-6 may be helpful when answering this question.

PREPARING FOR: My Career

ETHICS DILEMMA

Dr. Elizabeth Johnson was meeting with her patient Bob Abernathy to review the results of medical testing after he complained that he was experiencing blurred vision. Dr. Johnson explained to Mr. Abernathy that he was suffering from a rare condition that leads to blindness. Naturally, Mr. Abernathy was upset and he asked whether there was any treatment. Unfortunately, conventional therapies were rarely effective, but Dr. Johnson discussed a relatively new medication that showed promise for preventing blindness when taken over a three-month period. She went on to tell Mr. Abernathy that his health insurance company does not pay for the treatment, costing $10,000. Mr. Abernathy visited several pharmacies to ask whether he could purchase the medication at a steeply discounted price, explaining that he has been unemployed for the past several months and has little savings. None of the pharmacies were willing to help Mr. Abernathy. Desperate to get the medication, Mr. Abernathy broke into one of the pharmacies after closing to steal the medication.

8-9. What potential ethical issues do you see here?

8-10. If you were the store manager, would you press charges? Why or why not?

SKILLS EXERCISE Making a To-Do List That Works and Using It

Do you have lots to do and limited time in which to do it? That sounds familiar, doesn't it! One tool that many successful people use is a to-do list. Lists can be useful because they: help organize and make sense of what needs to be done; keep details of work/life events; track progress; and help overcome procrastination. Making a to-do list that works and then using it is a skill that every manager needs to develop.

Steps in Practicing the Skill

- *Break project(s) into smaller tasks and prioritize those tasks.* When you have a major project to complete, spend some time up front identifying as many of the sequential tasks necessary to complete that project. Also, prioritize, prioritize, prioritize. It's the only way to get done what's most important.

- *Be realistic about your to-do list.* Whether your to-do list is daily, weekly, or monthly—or all of these—you've got to realize that interruptions will and do happen. Don't overestimate what you can get done. And you will face conflicting priorities. Reprioritize when this happens.

- *Know and pay attention to your own time and energy.* Develop your own personal routines. You know when you're the most productive. Those are the times you need to do your most important tasks. Or maybe you need to do the task you like least first. You'll want to get it done faster so you can move on to tasks that you enjoy doing.

- *Know your biggest time wasters and distractions.* We all have them, whether they're found online or on the television or elsewhere. (And you probably already know what yours are!) Also, realize you probably can't (nor do you want to) eliminate them. But do be leery of them, especially when you're trying to get something done or need to get something done.

- *Let technology be a tool, not a distraction.* Find an app (or written approach) that works FOR YOU. There are many available. And don't constantly try out new ones—that, in itself, wastes precious time. Find one that works for your needs and your personal situation and that you'll USE.

- *Conquer the email/instant messaging challenge.* Although coworkers communicate in many ways in organizations, email and instant messaging are popular *and* can be overwhelming to deal with when you're trying to accomplish work tasks. Again, you need to find what works best for you. Some ideas for "conquering" this distraction include:

  - Check only at certain times during the day.

  - Maybe avoid email first thing in the morning because it's so easy to get sidetracked.

  - Come up with a system for responding—if a response can be given in less than three minutes (or whatever time control you choose), respond immediately; if it can't, set the email/message aside for later when you have more time. And a good rule: the faster your response time, the shorter the email.

  - Weed out any "subscriptions" that you're not reading/using. You know, those you thought sounded really interesting and you end up deleting immediately anyway. So, don't even get them—unsubscribe.

  - Use your email system tools—filters that move emails to folders, canned responses, autoresponders, and so forth—to manage your email messages.

Practicing the Skill

The best way to practice this skill is to pick a project (school, work, personal) that you're facing and try to use the above suggestions. To get better at using to-do lists, you've just got to jump in, create them and, most importantly, use them to guide what you do and when you do it. Commit to making your to-do list a habit by referring to it on a daily basis for at least a month.

WORKING TOGETHER **Team Exercise**

In groups of three or four, choose a local bakery, sandwich shop, or restaurant with which members of your group are familiar. Now, look through the list of strategic objectives found at this link and choose three strategic objectives that your team believes to be important for this business: *www.clearpointstrategy.com/56-strategic-objective-examples-for-your-company-to-copy*. Why are the strategic objectives you chose important to this business? Discuss what operational plans this business could put into place to help achieve each of the strategic objectives chosen. Be prepared to discuss your view with the class.

MY TURN TO BE A MANAGER

- Practice setting goals for various aspects of your personal life, such as academics, career preparation, family, hobbies, and so forth. Set at least two short-term goals and at least two long-term goals for each area.

- For these goals that you have set, write out plans for achieving those goals. Think in terms of what you will have to do to accomplish each. For instance, if one of your academic goals is to improve your grade point average, what will you have to do to reach it?

- Write a personal mission statement. Although this may sound simple to do, it's not going to be simple or easy. Our hope is that it will be something you'll want to keep, use, and revise when necessary and that it will help you be the person you'd like to be and live the life you'd like to live. Start by doing some research on personal mission statements. There are some online resources that can guide you.

- Interview three managers about the types of planning they do. Ask them for suggestions on how to be a better planner. Write a report describing and comparing your findings.

- Choose two companies, preferably in different industries. Research the companies' websites and find examples of goals they have stated. (Hint: A company's annual report is often a good place to start.) Evaluate these goals.

- Effective managers are always screening information to look for emerging trends that might affect their industries. Start looking for trends in an industry you are interested in by subscribing to a variety of social media sources that are related to the industry.

CASE APPLICATION 1 — Capturing Anti-Trends at New Balance

New York Fashion Week is a big event in the fashion industry. It's held twice a year, providing an estimated economic impact of $887 million to the city of New York.[26] Fashion buyers come out in force to view the latest fashions, and photographers try to capture the most current fashion trends.

New Balance—the footwear company—decided to use New York Fashion Week in September 2018 to monitor trends differently than other companies have in the past. For weeks before the event, New Balance set up cameras around New York to gather data on the styles, colors, patterns, and accessories worn by people walking by. This data was used to establish an "aesthetic average," which is another way of saying fashion trends found somewhat regularly.[27]

Then, during New York Fashion Week, cameras in a booth in New York's SoHo neighborhood used machine learning to find people wearing fashion that is different from this average. New Balance partnered with VML, a global marketing firm, to come up with an algorithm that identified people who stand out from the crowd. "We want the computers to do their job," commented Craig Elimeliah, executive director of creative technology at VML. "Who knows exactly what they will identify as exceptions to trends? We can't wait to find out."[28]

When the computers identified someone with different-than-average fashion walking in the SoHo neighborhood during Fashion Week, New Balance and VML employees came out from behind the camera booth and talked with the person. This approach is part of a marketing campaign to show recognition to "those who are confidently demonstrating their unique style."[29] Each fashion-forward person identified by the cameras was given a new pair of New Balance Fresh Foam Cruz Nubuck, a new shoe developed by the company.

After additionally collecting fashion data through cameras in Toronto, Stockholm, and Madrid, New Balance hopes to use the data on trend exceptions to inform the development of new products. The computers will not use facial recognition or personal data. Instead, it will focus on exceptions to trends in the aggregate.

DISCUSSION QUESTIONS

8-11. How is New Balance's approach to environmental scanning different from how companies usually gather information about customers?

8-12. What advantages and disadvantages does New Balance's approach have compared with using traditional competitive intelligence as a source of information about fashion trends?

8-13. What legal or ethical concerns might New Balance need to think about regarding their approach to monitoring trends?

8-14. How could New Balance apply virtual reality to the data they collect in New York, Toronto, Stockholm, and Madrid?

CASE APPLICATION 2 — Living Up to Goals at Tesla

Tesla Inc. has generated a lot of excitement about producing its Model 3 sedan, its electric car "for the masses." The Model 3 begins at $35,000, while other luxury models Tesla produces cost $80,000-plus. Production on the Model 3 only started in mid-2017, but there already were 500,000 reservations for the vehicle by February 2018.[30] The challenge for Tesla was producing cars on a much bigger scale than it ever had before.

To meet this challenge, Tesla set an objective of producing 5,000 Model 3 sedans per week.[31] Tesla missed this objective at the end of 2017 due to difficulties it encountered with automation and battery-pack assembly. It took longer than expected to install more than 1,000 robots in its Fremont, California, factory. Tesla also spent over $80 million on an automated warehouse system that did not initially run smoothly.

In January 2018, Tesla postponed its objective—for the second time—of producing 5,000 Model 3 sedans per week to the end of the second quarter of 2018. Tesla was described as "entering one of the most critical phases in its history, a make-or-break period."[32] The company had to figure out how to increase production to meet its objective. If this objective wasn't reached by the end of June 2018, there might not be enough cash to maintain its operations. Raising additional cash could be difficult if investors lost confidence in a company that had repeatedly missed its production targets.

As the objective deadline at the end of June 2018 drew near, Elon Musk (Tesla's founder and CEO) had not left the Tesla factory in three days. He was sleeping on the floor under his desk. A temporary assembly line was created under a tent outdoors to help reach the production target.[33]

The hard work paid off! Tesla produced 5,031 Model 3 sedans in the final week of the second quarter of 2018. Nearly 18 percent of the 28,500 Model 3 sedans produced in the second quarter were made in the final week. Some questioned whether Tesla could sustain their progress toward their production objective in later quarters.[34] Tesla proved they were up to the challenge during the third quarter of 2018 by meeting their target. Also, their Model 3 was listed in the top 10 sedans sold in the US and was the only electric car on the list.[35]

DISCUSSION QUESTIONS

8-15. What factors made it difficult for Tesla to initially meet their stated objective of 5,000 Model 3 sedans per week? Explain why you think their stated objective should (or should not) have been different than it was.

8-16. What's the downside for setting an ambitious production objective like Tesla did for the Model 3?

8-17. What do you think Tesla's production staff felt about the 5,000-unit objective? Would it have a positive or negative impact on morale? Explain.

ENDNOTES

1. Reprinted from the August 1944 edition of *Popular Mechanics*: "How the D-Day Invasion Was Planned," *Popular Mechanics*, June 6, 2017, https://www.popularmechanics.com/military/a15909/how-d-day-was-planned-1944/.

2. See, for example, J. A. Pearce II, K. K. Robbins, and R. B. Robinson, Jr., "The Impact of Grand Strategy and Planning Formality on Financial Performance," *Strategic Management Journal* (March-April 1987): pp. 125–134; L. C. Rhyne, "Contrasting Planning Systems in High, Medium, and Low Performance Companies," *Journal of Management Studies* (July 1987): pp. 363–385; J. A. Pearce II, E. B. Freeman, and R. B. Robinson Jr., "The Tenuous Link Between Formal Strategic Planning and Financial Performance," *Academy of Management Review* (October 1987): pp. 658–675; N. Capon, J. U. Farley, and J. M. Hulbert, "Strategic Planning and Financial Performance: More Evidence," *Journal of Management Studies* (January 1994): pp. 22–38; C. C. Miller and L. B. Cardinal, "Strategic Planning and Firm Performance: A Synthesis of More Than Two Decades of Research," *Academy of Management Journal* (March 1994): pp. 1649–1685; J. Siciliano, "The Relationship Between Formal Planning and Performance," *Nonprofit Management and Leadership*, September 2006, pp. 387–403; J. Brinckmann, D. Grichnik, and D. Kapsa, "Should Entrepreneurs Plan or Just Storm the Castle? A Meta-Analysis on Contextual Factors Impacting the Business Planning-Performance Relationship in Small Firms," *Journal of Business Venturing* (January 2010): pp. 24–40; and M. R. Parke, J. M. Weinhardt, A. Brodsky, S. Tangirala, and S. E. DeVoe, "When Daily Planning Improves Employee Performance: The Importance of Planning Type, Engagement, and Interruptions," *Journal of Applied Psychology* (March 2018): pp. 300–12.

3. panmore.com.

4. R. Pendell, "Six Scary Numbers for Your Organization's C-Suite," Gallup, October 30, 2018, https://www.gallup.com/workplace/244100/scary-numbers-organization-suite.aspx.

5. J. Stewart, "This Is the Enormous Gigafactory, Where Tesla Will Build Its Future," *Wired*, July 27, 2016, https://www.wired.com/2016/07/tesla-gigafactory-elon-musk/.

6. Based on A. Hayes, "Court: Army Corps of Engineers Liable for Katrina Flooding," CNN, November 19, 2009, http://www.cnn.com/2009/US/11/18/louisiana.katrina.lawsuit/index.html; and J. Burnett, "Billions Spent on Flood Barriers, but New Orleans Still a 'Fishbowl'," All Things Considered, *NPR*, August 28, 2015, https://www.npr.org/2015/08/28/432059261/billions-spent-on-flood-barriers-but-new-orleans-still-a-fishbowl.

7. "Icahn Threatens to Dismantle TWA," *San Diego Union*, March 3, 1986, p. A1.

8. The following are from L. Kolowich, "17 Truly Inspiring Company Vision and Mission Statement Examples," https://blog.hubspot.com/marketing/inspiring-company-mission-statements.

9. J. Zarroli, "After Chipotle Outbreaks, Will 'Food with Integrity' Still Resonate?," All Things Considered, *NPR*, January 5, 2016, https://www.npr.org/secti ons/thesalt/2016/01/05/461925691/after-chipotle-outbreaks-will-food-with-integrity-still-resonate; and E. Yaverbaum, "Food with Integrity: How Chipotle Can Escape a Mess of Its Own Making," *HuffPost*, July 26, 2017, https://www.huffingtonpost.com/entry/food-with-integrity-how-chipotle-can-escape-a-mess_us_5978f141e4b09982b73761b0.

10. C. K. Warriner, "The Problem of Organizational Purpose," *Sociological Quarterly* (Spring 1965): pp. 140.

11. A. Fisher, "How Adobe Keeps Key Employees from Quitting," *Fortune*, June 16, 2015, http://fortune.com/2015/06/16/adobe-employee-retention/.

12. The concept is generally attributed to P. Drucker, *The Practice of Management* (New York: Harper & Row, 1954).

13. R. Barone, "The MBO Bonus—Definition, Tips, and Considerations," xactlycorp.com, January 19, 2017.

14. R. Rodgers and J.E. Hunter, "Impact of Management by Objectives on Organizational Productivity," *Journal of Applied Psychology* (April 1991): pp. 322–36; E. A. Locke and G. P. Latham, "Has Goal Setting Gone Wild, or Have Its Attackers Abandoned Good Scholarship?" *Academy of Management Perspectives* (February 2009): pp. 17–23; E. A. Locke and G. P. Latham, *New Developments in Goal Setting and Task Performance* (New York: Routledge, 2013); and L. E. Miller and R. M. Weiss, "Setting Goals in Different Roles: Applying Key Results From the Goal-Setting Literature," *Organization Management Journal* (January 2015): pp. 14–22.

15. Based on J. A. Breaugh and J. P. Colihan, "Measuring Facets of Job Ambiguity: Construct Validity Evidence," *Journal of Applied Psychology* (March 1994): pp. 191–202; "Position Descriptions Essential for Role Clarity and Engagement," *HR Daily* (website), July 16, 2012, https://www.hrdaily.com.au/; C. Shaw, "Dealing with Ambiguity: The New Business Imperative," *LinkedIn* (website), August 29, 2013, https://www.linkedin.com/pulse/20130829124922-284615-dealing-with-ambiguity-the-new-business-imperative/; and C. Osborn, "The Essential Skill for Career Development: Dealing with Ambiguity," The Training Associates (blog), May 7, 2018, https://thetrainingassociates.com/blog/career-development-skill-ambiguity/.

16. A. Kleingeld, H. van Mierlo, and L. Arends, "The Effect of Goal Setting on Grop Performance: A Meta-Analysis," *Journal of Applied Psychology* (November 2011): pp. 1289–1304; and S. W. Anderson, H. C. Dekker, and K. L. Sedatole, "An Empirical Examination of Goals and Performance-to-Goal Following the Introduction of an Incentive Bonus Plan with Participative Goal Setting," *Management Science* (January 2010): pp. 90–109.

17. See, for instance, C. V. Robinson and J. E. L. Simmons, "Organising Environmental Scanning: Exploring Information Source, Mode and the Impact of Firm Size," *Long Range Planning* (August 2018), pp. 526–39.

18. See, for instance, B. Gilad and M. Hoppe, "The Right Way to Use Competitive Intelligence," *Harvard Business Review*, June 16, 2016, https://hbr.org/2016/06/the-right-way-to-use-analytics-isnt-for-planning.

19. L. Calicchia, "Four Competitive Intelligence Examples from the Real World," *Kompyte* (blog), updated April 5, 2018, https://www.kompyte.com/blog/competitive-intelligence-examples/.

20. This section is based on W. He, J. Shen, X. Tian, Y Li, V. Akula, G. Yan, and R. Tao, "Gaining Competitive Intelligence from Social Media Data," *Industrial Management and Data Systems* 15, no. 9 (2015): pp. 1622–36; and I. Lee, "Social Media Analytics for Enterprises: Typology, Methods, and Processes," *Business Horizons* (March–April 2018) pp. 199–210.

21. "2018 State of Market Intelligence," Crayon, December 27, 2018, https://www.crayon.co/state-of-competitive-intelligence.

22. D. M. Ewalt, *Defying Reality: The Inside Story of the Virtual Reality Revolution* (New York: Blue Rider Press, 2018).

23. "Virtual Reality and the Planning Process," *Mayer Brown* (blog), February 5, 2018, https://www.mayerbrown.co.uk/keep-up-to-date/blog/posts/virtual-reality-and-the-planning-process/.

24. "Boeing Tests Augmented Reality in the Factory," *Boeing* (website), January 19, 2018, https://www.boeing.com/features/2018/01/augmented-reality-01-18.page.

25. "Virtualitics: Caltech & NASA Scientists Build VR/AR Analytics Platform Uisng AI & Machine Learning," *InsideBIGDATA* (website), August 5, 2017, https://insidebigdata.com/2017/08/05/virtualitics-caltech-nasa-scientists-build-vrar-analytics-platform-using-ai-machine-learning/.

26. Wikipedia, s.v. "New York Fashion Week," accessed October 1, 2018, https://en.wikipedia.org/wiki/New_York_Fashion_Week.

27. G. Lacombe, "New Balance Will Use Artificial Intelligence to Celebrate Self-Expression at New York Fashion Week," *Fashion Network* (website), August 31, 2018, https://us.fashionnetwork.com/news/New-Balance-will-use-artificial-intelligence-to-celebrate-self-expression-at-New-York-Fashion-Week,1009059.html.

28. L. Handley, "Sneaker Company New Balance Will Use A.I. at New York Fashion Week to Find ... Unfashionable People," cnbc.com, August 30, 2018.

29. E. Segran, "New Balance Is Watching You," *Fast Company*, August 29, 2018, https://www.fastcompany.com/90228083/new-balance-is-watching-you.

30. T. Higgins, "Tesla Signals Better Model 3 Output," *Wall Street Journal*, February 8, 2018.

31. T. Higgins, "Business News: Tesla Rivals Pay for Model 3 Data," *Wall Street Journal*, January 31, 2018.

32. T. Higgins, "Tesla Faces Crunch as Cash Hoard Thins," *Wall Street Journal*, March 16, 2018.

33. T. Higgins and S. Pulliam, "Deadline Places Musk in 'Production Hell'," *Wall Street Journal*, June 28, 2018.

34. C. Grant, "Tesla's Triumph Goes Only So Far." *Wall Street Journal*, July 3, 2018.

35. T. Randall and G. Coppola, "Tesla's Model 3 Is Becoming One of America's Best-Selling Sedans," *Bloomberg News,* October 3, 2018, https://www.bloomberg.com/news/articles/2018-10-03/tesla-s-model-3-is-becoming-one-of-america-s-best-selling-sedans.

Chapter 9   Managing Strategy

Learning Objectives

9.1 **Define** strategic management and explain why it's important.

9.2 **Explain** what managers do during the six steps of the strategic management process.

9.3 **Describe** the three types of corporate strategies.

9.4 **Describe** competitive advantage and the competitive strategies organizations use to get it.

Employability Skills Matrix (ESM)

This matrix identifies which features and end-of-chapter material will help you develop specific skills employers are looking for in job candidates.

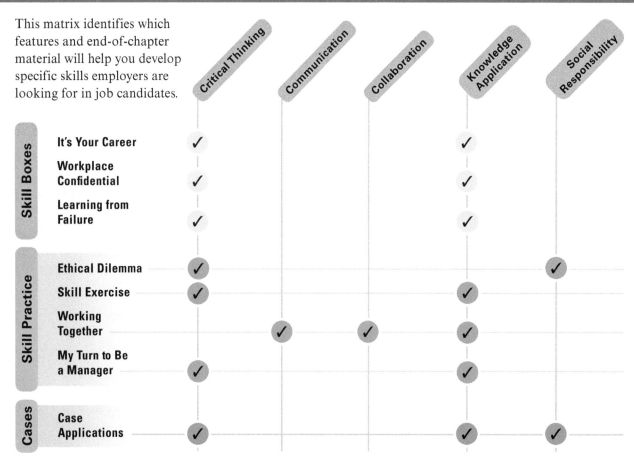

		Critical Thinking	Communication	Collaboration	Knowledge Application	Social Responsibility
Skill Boxes	It's Your Career	✓			✓	
	Workplace Confidential	✓			✓	
	Learning from Failure	✓			✓	
Skill Practice	Ethical Dilemma	✓				✓
	Skill Exercise	✓			✓	
	Working Together		✓	✓	✓	
	My Turn to Be a Manager	✓			✓	
Cases	Case Applications	✓			✓	✓

Founded in 2011, MoviePass had an interesting but, unfortunately, flawed business strategy.[1] For a flat subscription fee of $10 a month, users could get a ticket and see a single movie every day. This business model had no trouble attracting customers. In the summer of 2018, it was reported to have 3 million users. The unfortunate part was that the company had to pay the movie theaters the full price of each ticket. With tickets averaging $10 apiece, MoviePass could be paying theaters as much as $300 a month for each user.

MoviePass's management thought the potential profits would be in monetizing its users' viewing habits. But no market surfaced for this service. So the company made adjustments: cutting the number of movies that users could see to four a month, excluding certain movies and theaters, and raising prices. None of these changes seemed to work. In late 2018, the company was losing $40 million a month. In September 2019, MoviePass's management threw in the towel and shut down the company. It's business model and overall strategy had failed.

Successful managers recognize market opportunities to exploit, take steps to correct company weaknesses, or formulate new and hopefully more effective strategies to be strong competitors. How they manage those strategies will play an important role in an organization's success or failure. This chapter presents the strategic management process and reviews a variety of strategies that organizations can pursue.

WHAT is strategic management and why is it important?

LO9.1 The cell phone industry is a good place to see what strategic management is all about. BlackBerry successfully sold cellular products in the 1990s that appealed to the business market. In 2007, the introduction of Apple's iPhone posed a significant threat to BlackBerry's success. The quality of the iPhone's hardware was vastly superior to that of BlackBerry smartphones, and Apple enabled developers to create a diverse set of apps, making the iPhone more appealing to a broader audience. However, BlackBerry stayed the course by focusing on business enterprise and made little effort to help developers create apps for the BlackBerry operating system. Apple iPhone sales took off and plummeted. By 2017, Apple had 17.9 percent of the world's smartphone market. BlackBerry had 0.2 percent![2] And few businesspeople today use a BlackBerry, while Apple iPhones are everywhere.

Defining Strategic Management

Strategic management is the formulation and implementation of initiatives by top management—taking into consideration resources and environmental opportunities—that will allow the organization to achieve its goals. What are an organization's **strategies**? They're the plans for how the organization will do whatever it's in business to do, how it will compete successfully, and how it will attract and satisfy its customers in order to achieve its goals.

One term often used in strategic management is **business model**, which simply is how a company is going to make money. It focuses on two things: (1) whether customers will value what the company is providing and (2) whether the company can make any money doing that.[3] MoviePass's business model apparently failed. But Jeff Bezos pioneered a business model for selling books to consumers directly online that worked. Customers *valued* what Amazon offered. Did Amazon *make money* doing it that way? Not at first, but now, absolutely! What began as the world's biggest bookstore is now the world's biggest everything store—and one of the most

strategic management
The formulation and implementation of initiatives by top management that will allow the organization to achieve its goals

strategies
The plans for how the organization will do what it's in business to do, how it will compete successfully, and how it will attract and satisfy its customers in order to achieve its goals

business model
How a company is going to make money

Using strategic management has helped Marvel Entertainment achieve higher levels of organizational performance. When market demand for its comic books declined, the company broadened its focus from print readership to a wider audience of moviegoers by featuring Spider-Man and other comic book characters in films.
Source: COLUMBIA PICTURES/MARVEL ENTERTAINMENT/BRAMLEY, JOHN/Album/ Newscom

valuable companies in the world! These examples illustrate that as executives develop their organization's strategies, they need to assess and ensure the economic viability of their business model.

Why Is Strategic Management Important?

Marvel Entertainment, the home of Spider-Man and numerous other iconic characters, has long been the comic book world's biggest player. But in the mid-1990s the comics market crashed, Marvel went broke, and there was no superpower strong enough to stave off bankruptcy. But after restructuring, Marvel changed its approach, focusing on movies rather than paper and ink. Today, Iron Man, the Avengers, Spider-Man, and the X-Men are all billion-dollar franchises, and the company's strategic plan—to connect many of its characters in a single cinematic universe—has turned it into one of pop culture's most powerful brands. The managers behind Marvel clearly understand the importance of strategic management.[4]

Why is strategic management so important? There are three reasons. The most significant one is that it can make a difference in how well an organization performs. It helps explain why some businesses succeed and others fail, even when faced with the same environmental conditions. Research has found a generally positive relationship between strategic planning and performance.[5] In other words, it appears that organizations that use strategic management do have higher levels of performance. A second reason is the fact that managers in organizations of all types and sizes face continually changing situations. They cope with this uncertainty by using the strategic management process to examine relevant factors and decide what actions to take. Finally, strategic management is important because organizations are complex and diverse. Each part needs to work together toward achieving the organization's goals; strategic management helps do this.

Today, both business organizations and not-for-profit organizations are using strategic management. For instance, the US Postal Service (USPS) is locked in competitive battles with overnight package delivery companies, telecommunications companies, email and text messaging services, and private mailing facilities. In 2006, 213 billion pieces of mail were handled by the postal service. By 2017, that total had dropped to 149 billion, a decline of 30 percent.[6] With the loss in volume came financial losses—2017 marking the eleventh straight year of losses, with some annual losses as high as $15.9 billion.[7] USPS's executive team is using strategic management to come up with a response. One possible action plan is a revised service level schedule: six-day package delivery and five-day mail delivery. Others include streamlining and consolidating mail-processing facilities, increasing the availability of self-service in high-volume post offices, and raising rates. More recently, the USPS started offering same-day delivery service—of everything from bottled water to fresh fish—to compete with FedEx, UPS, and Amazon.com.[8] Strategic management will continue to be important to USPS's operation. Although strategic management in not-for-profits hasn't been as well researched as it has been for for-profit organizations, we know it's important for them as well.

THE STRATEGIC management process

strategic management process
A six-step process that encompasses strategic planning, implementation, and evaluation

LO9.2 The **strategic management process** (see Exhibit 9-1) is a six-step process that encompasses strategy planning, implementation, and evaluation. Although the first four steps describe the planning that must take place, implementation and evaluation are just as important! Even the best strategies can fail if management doesn't implement or evaluate them properly.

Exhibit 9-1
Strategic Management Process

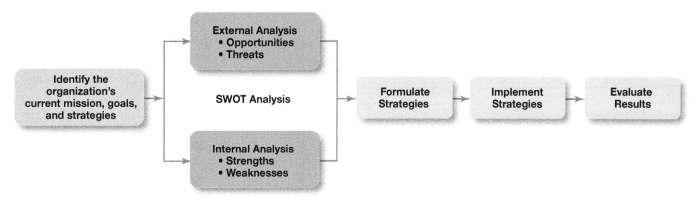

Step 1: Identifying the Organization's Current Mission, Goals, and Strategies

As noted in the previous chapter, every organization needs a mission—a statement of its purpose. Defining the mission forces managers to identify what it's in business to do. Some examples of mission statements are Patagonia's "build the best product, cause no unnecessary harm, use business to inspire and implement solutions to the environmental crisis" and Tesla's "to accelerate the world's transition to sustainable energy."[10] But these statements aren't written in stone. Sometimes management realizes they are in need of modification. For instance, Facebook's original mission statement had been "making the world open and connected." However, Facebook's problems with the spreading of disinformation encouraged it to rethink what it was about. Frustrated by an increasingly divided society, the firm's mission was refocused to not just connect the world but to bring the world closer together. Its revised mission: Give people the power to build community and bring the world closer together."[11]

What *should* a mission statement include? Exhibit 9-2 describes some typical components.

Sixty-one percent of executives admit to not being prepared for the strategic challenges they faced when they were appointed to senior leadership positions.[9]

Exhibit 9-2
Components of a Mission Statement

Source: Based on R. R. Davic, Strategic Management, *13th ed. (Upper Saddle River, NJ: Pearson Education, Inc., 2011).*

Customers:	Who are the firm's customers?
Markets:	Where does the firm compete geographically?
Concern for survival, growth, and profitability:	Is the firm committed to growth and financial stability?
Philosophy:	What are the firm's basic beliefs, values, and ethical priorities?
Concern for public image:	How responsive is the firm to societal and environmental concerns?
Products or services:	What are the firm's major products or services?
Technology:	Is the firm technologically current?
Self-concept:	What are the firm's major competitive advantage and core competencies?
Concern for employees:	Are employees a valuable asset of the firm?

Step 2: Doing an External Analysis

What impact might the following trends have for businesses?

- Cell phones are now used by customers more for data transmittal and retrieval than for phone calls, and the number of smartphones in use continues to soar.
- The unemployment rate has been declining.
- Interest rates have been rising.

We described the external environment in Chapter 3 as an important constraint on a manager's actions. Analyzing that environment is a critical step in the strategic management process. Managers do an external analysis so they know, for instance, what the competition is doing, what pending legislation might affect the organization, or what the labor supply is like in locations where it operates. In an external analysis, managers should examine the economic, demographic, political/legal, sociocultural, technological, and global components to see the trends and changes. For example, Aetna now offers customized health insurance because consumers want more control over the design and cost of their plans. The company's external analysis revealed that websites such as WebMD help many people to become more savvy healthcare consumers, and national healthcare legislation promises lower insurance costs.[12]

opportunities
Positive trends in the external environment

threats
Negative trends in the external environment

Once they've analyzed the environment, managers need to pinpoint opportunities that the organization can exploit and threats that it must counteract or buffer against. **Opportunities** are positive trends in the external environment; **threats** are negative trends.[13]

Let's take a look at ongoing strategic opportunities and threats in the pharmaceutical industry. Patent protection laws provide US pharmaceutical companies with the opportunity to recoup research and development costs and generate profits from the sale of its products. The US government grants pharmaceutical companies exclusivity and patent protection for up to 20 years. Without exclusivity provisions, pharmaceutical companies such as Wyeth Pharmaceuticals would be placed at a competitive disadvantage because other pharmaceutical companies would manufacture and distribute a therapeutically equivalent product at a lower cost. For example, Wyeth Pharmaceuticals developed Protonix, a product that treats gastroesophageal reflux disease. The company enjoyed exclusivity protection until 2011. The expiration of an exclusivity clause posed a threat for Wyeth Pharmaceuticals, yet this was an opportunity for other pharmaceutical companies to compete for market share. For instance, Teva Pharmaceuticals has been selling pantoprazole, a therapeutically generic product comparable to Protonix, at a lower price. These so-called generic alternatives are less expensive because companies that manufacture and distribute them do not have research and development costs to recoup. Many health insurance companies refuse to provide coverage for brand-name products when less-expensive generic alternatives are available, giving further advantage to companies like Teva.

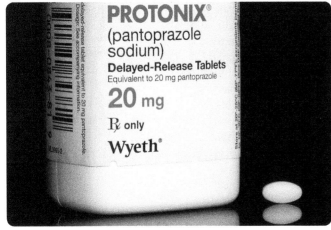

Wyeth Pharmaceuticals developed Protonix, a product that treats gastroesophageal reflux disease, and enjoyed exclusivity protection until 2011. The expiration of this exclusivity clause posed a threat for Wyeth Pharmaceuticals; yet, this was an opportunity for more pharmaceutical companies to compete for market share, by offering generic options at a lower cost to the consumer.
Source: Jb Reed/Bloomberg/Getty Images

resources
An organization's assets that are used to develop, manufacture, and deliver products to its customers

capabilities
An organization's skills and abilities in doing the work activities needed in its business

core competencies
The organization's major value-creating capabilities that determine its competitive weapons

Step 3: Doing an Internal Analysis

Now we move to the internal analysis, which provides important information about an organization's specific resources and capabilities. An organization's **resources** are its assets—financial, physical, human, and intangible—that it uses to develop, manufacture, and deliver products to its customers. They're "what" the organization has. On the other hand, its **capabilities** are its skills and abilities in doing the work activities needed in its business—"how" it does its work. The major value-creating capabilities of the organization are known as its **core competencies**.[14] Both resources and core competencies determine the organization's competitive weapons. For instance, transportation giant Norfolk Southern's CEO indicates that "we believe we have the right strategic plan to streamline operations, accelerate growth, and enhance value for shareholders."[15] The leadership plans to leverage the company's two core competencies—superior customer service and reliability—to meet the company's strategic goals.

After completing an internal analysis, managers should be able to identify organizational strengths and weaknesses. Any activities the organization does well or any unique resources that it has are called **strengths**. **Weaknesses** are activities the organization doesn't do well or resources it needs but doesn't possess.

The combined external and internal analyses are called the **SWOT analysis**, an analysis of the organization's *S*trengths, *W*eaknesses, *O*pportunities, and *T*hreats.[16] After completing the SWOT analysis, managers are ready to formulate appropriate strategies—that is, strategies that (1) exploit an organization's strengths and external opportunities, (2) buffer or protect the organization from external threats, or (3) correct critical weaknesses.

strengths
Any activities the organization does well or its unique resources

weaknesses
Activities the organization does not do well or resources it needs but does not possess

SWOT analysis
An analysis of the organization's strengths, weaknesses, opportunities, and threats

Let's Get REAL

The Scenario:

Emily's Bakery found success quickly. Emily Smith was surprised by how fast the bakery, started just three years ago, became profitable. The growth was mostly due to timing and location. She just happened to open in a busy neighborhood around the same time a competing bakery closed because the owner wanted to relocate to a new city. However, over the last few months, sales have slowed a little, and Emily has had some time to think about the future. She needs to figure out her next step and thinks maybe she needs a strategic plan for her business, but she isn't sure where to start.

How should Emily start her strategic planning process?

The strategic plan will be the company's road map that future decisions will be based on, and effectively planning the strategy at the beginning is a critical step. A starting point to begin the process is analyzing the current state of the business. This includes outlining strengths and weaknesses and identifying external factors that could pose threats or opportunities for growth. With this information, the business leader can then begin planning the desired future state by developing short- and long-term goals and aligning these with the company culture, available resources, and realistic time frames to develop an actionable plan.

◀ **Kelly Nelson**
Organizational Development and Training Manager

Source: Kelly Nelson

Step 4: Formulating Strategies

As managers formulate strategies, they need to consider the realities of the external environment and their available resources and capabilities in order to design strategies that will help an organization achieve its goals. The three main types of strategies managers will formulate include corporate, competitive, and functional. We'll describe each shortly.

Step 5: Implementing Strategies

Once strategies are formulated, they must be implemented. No matter how effectively an organization has planned its strategies, performance will suffer if the strategies aren't implemented properly.

Step 6: Evaluating Results

The final step in the strategic management process is evaluating results. How effective have the strategies been at helping the organization reach its goals? What adjustments are necessary? For example, in the early 1990s, Las Vegas faced new competition from legal gambling on riverboats and Indian reservations. In response, the city's convention bureau created a strategy to promote Las Vegas as a family destination rather than as a place for adult entertainment. The new emphasis would be on things like swimming pools, amusement parks, and shopping. After several years, an evaluation of that strategy revealed families didn't see the city as a place to bring kids, and hotels and casinos didn't want families and kids. Gambling and kids didn't mix. The return to the original adult-entertainment strategy has proven to be much more successful.[17]

IT'S YOUR CAREER

Learning Your Strengths and Weaknesses

Do you know your personal strengths and weaknesses? You need to for at least two reasons. The first is that job interviewers commonly ask what you consider your strengths and weaknesses, and you want to be prepared to answer those questions. Second, by knowing your strengths and weaknesses you can size up where you stand in your career and make good decisions about what you need to do to keep advancing.

Here are some suggestions to help you learn your strengths and weaknesses:

1. *Identify your strengths.* Your strengths are your individual personal positive attributes and characteristics. As you look at your strengths, assess the following: skills (what you are good at), interests (what you enjoy doing), educational background (what qualifications you have), your values (what things are important to you), and your personality (what characteristics you have). As you evaluate these, think in terms of what sets you apart. What things do you like to do? What things do you do well? What things do you do better than others? It's also helpful to ask others you trust what they see as your strengths.

2. *Take a look at your weaknesses.* It's sometimes hard to admit, but we all have weaknesses. What things could you improve about yourself? What are your negative personal/work habits? What things do you not like to do? What skills, training, or qualifications are you lacking, the possession of which would make you a more valuable employee? Are you lacking career direction or focus? What things do others do better than you do? Again, it's helpful to ask others you trust what they see as your weaknesses.

3. *As discussed later in this chapter's "Workplace Confidential," develop a strategy to do something about your strengths and weaknesses.* What actions can you take to get the job you want or to best meet the requirements of your current job or a promotion you're seeking? Accentuate your positives! You want to leverage, emphasize, and capitalize on your strengths.

Here's an insight that many young people don't realize: You can go a long way on just a few strengths. In school, to be an outstanding student, you have to be a generalist. You have to be good at everything: math, science, history, geography, languages, the arts, and so forth. But "the real world" pays off for specialization. You only have to excel in one or two areas to have an amazing career. So find your niche and exploit that strength.

4. *Update your list of strengths and weaknesses periodically.* As you gain new experiences and as your life circumstances change, you'll want to revise your list of strengths and weaknesses. Sharpen your self-awareness so you can craft the kind of life—professionally and personally—you want to live.

CORPORATE strategies

LO9.3 As we said earlier, organizations use three types of strategies: corporate, competitive, and functional. (See Exhibit 9-3.) Top-level managers typically are responsible for corporate strategies, middle-level managers for competitive strategies, and lower-level managers for the functional strategies. In this section, we'll look at corporate strategies.

Exhibit 9-3
Types of Organizational Strategies

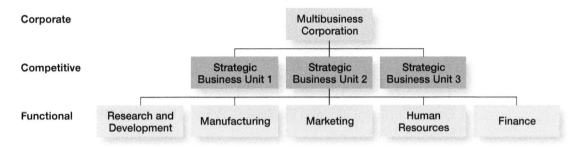

WORKPLACE CONFIDENTIAL Developing a Career Strategy

The concept of strategy is not limited to managers and organizations. You can use it to "think strategically" about your career.

Let's start by acknowledging that, if you're reading this book, you are likely either at an early point in starting to build a career or considering a new career direction. Either way, your career plans are a top priority. Here are some suggestions for helping you develop a career plan.

Start by creating your own SWOT analysis. What are your strengths? What talents have you developed that give you a comparative advantage to others? Are you good with numbers, an excellent writer, a smooth talker, an outstanding debater, uniquely creative? And what qualities can give you an edge up? Consider your work experience, education, technical knowledge, networking contacts, and personal characteristics, like your work ethic or self-discipline. Think hard about what differentiates you and what might give you an advantage. Next, consider your weaknesses. Try to be honest with yourself and identify those things that either others do better than you or that you tend to avoid. Examples might include a lack of work experience, a low GPA, lack of specific job knowledge, weak communication skills, or previous legal problems. Now move to consider opportunities and threats that you see in the job market. Where are the growth industries? Examples, for instance, might include healthcare, solar energy, artificial intelligence, counterterrorism, or internet businesses. All appear to have strong growth opportunities. Then focus on organizations within these industries that might benefit from this growth. Finally, look for geographic opportunities. What cities or towns appear to offer above-average job growth? Of course, you also want to look at the other side. Which are the declining industries, downsizing or stagnant organizations, and shrinking job markets? Integrating this analysis should provide you with a blueprint of where you're likely to find the best career opportunities.

Now, let's talk about fit. By this, we mean the match between you and specific jobs and the match between you and specific organizational cultures. The former we call the person-job fit and the latter the person-organization fit. Here's an obvious, but often overlooked, observation: Not everyone is fit for certain jobs or certain organizations. Regardless of the opportunity, one size does not fit all!

In Chapter 15, Holland's personality-job fit theory is discussed. In essence, the theory proposes six personality types and argues that people who are in jobs congruent with their personality are more satisfied with their jobs and less likely to quit. We suggest that you look over these six personalities, see which one best describes you, and use the information to guide you in selecting a job that best fits you.

The person-organization fit essentially argues that people are attracted and selected by organizations that match their values, and they leave organizations that are not compatible with their personalities. So, for instance, if you tend to be high on the extroversion scale, you're likely to fit well with aggressive and team-oriented cultures; if you're high on agreeableness, you match up better with a supportive organizational culture than one focused on aggressiveness; and if you're open to new experiences, you'll fit better into organizations that emphasize innovation rather than standardization.

One final suggestion: Don't delegate your future to someone else. You are responsible for your personal career plan, your career progression, and your eventual retirement. In the 1950s and 1960s, most people either didn't think about shaping their career to maximize their potential or assumed that this was the responsibility of their employer. Even retirement programs were essentially designed by your employer, controlled by your employer, and nontransferable between employers. While they did offer predictability, they also put control of an employee's future in the hands of the employer. In today's disruptive world, your career is in your hands. Never get comfortable with a single employer. Keep your skills current and think long term. Continually ask yourself: How will each job I take help to build a pattern of accomplishment? How will this job and my next one get me to where I eventually want to be?[18]

What Is Corporate Strategy?

A **corporate strategy** determines what businesses a company is in or wants to be in and what it wants to do with those businesses. It's based on the mission and goals of the organization and the roles that each business unit of the organization will play. We can see both of these aspects with PepsiCo, for instance. Its mission: To be the world's premier consumer products company focused on convenient foods and beverages. It pursues that mission with a corporate strategy that has put it in different businesses, including its PepsiCo Americas Beverage (beverage business), PepsiCo Americas Foods (snack and prepared foods businesses, including Frito-Lay and Quaker Oats), and its global businesses—PepsiCo Europe and PepsiCo Asia, Middle East and Africa.[19]

What Are the Types of Corporate Strategy?

The three main types of corporate strategies are growth, stability, and renewal. Let's look at each type.

GROWTH   In spite of sales of nearly $10 billion a year, you probably never heard of Nvidia. But this company, which has been a leader in hardware graphics technology for decades, recently expanded into artificial intelligence, deep learning, and automotive technology. This expansion has helped grow company sales by an astounding 45.6 percent between 2017 and 2018.[20]

A **growth strategy** is when an organization expands the number of markets served or products offered, either through its current business(es) or through new business(es). Because of its growth strategy, an organization may increase revenues, number of employees, or market share. Organizations grow by using concentration, vertical integration, horizontal integration, or diversification.

An organization that grows using *concentration* focuses on its primary line of business and increases the number of products offered or markets served in this primary business. For instance, Buick has used concentration as a strategy to work toward becoming a luxury automobile brand. In the United States, the brand's sales have increased nearly 25 percent, outselling Audi and closing the sales gap with BMW.[21] Another example of a company using concentration is Bose Corporation of Framingham, Massachusetts, which focuses on developing innovative audio products. It has become one of the world's leading manufacturers of speakers for home entertainment, automotive, and professional audio markets, with annual sales of $3.8 billion.

A company also might choose to grow by *vertical integration*, either backward, forward, or both. In backward vertical integration, the organization becomes its own supplier so it can control its inputs. For instance, Walmart built a dairy-processing plant in Indiana to supply private-label milk to hundreds of its stores at a lower cost than purchasing milk from an outside supplier.[22] In forward vertical integration, the organization becomes its own distributor and is able to control its outputs. For example, Apple has more than 500 retail stores worldwide to distribute its products.

In *horizontal integration*, a company grows by combining with competitors. For instance, Bank of America has acquired MBNA, Summit Bancorp, NationsBank, U.S. Trust, and Fleet Financial. Another example is Live Nation, the largest concert promoter in the United States, which combined operations with competitor HOB Entertainment, the operator of the House of Blues clubs. Horizontal integration has been used in a number of industries in the last few years—financial services, consumer products, airlines, department stores, and software, among others.

Finally, an organization can grow through *diversification*, either related or unrelated. Related diversification happens when a company combines with other companies in different, but related, industries. For example, Google has acquired a number of businesses (some 150 total), including YouTube, DoubleClick, Nest, and Motorola Mobility. Although this mix of businesses may seem odd, the company's "strategic fit" is its information search capabilities and efficiencies. Unrelated diversification is when a company combines with firms in different and unrelated industries. For instance, the Tata Group of India has businesses in chemicals, communications and IT, consumer products, energy, engineering, materials, and services. Again, an odd mix. But in this case, there's no strategic fit among the businesses.

STABILITY   The Boeing Company has many aspirations. One of them illustrates a stability strategy: "To continue building strength-on-strength to deliver on our existing plans and commitments."[23] A **stability strategy** is a corporate strategy in which an organization continues to do what it is currently doing. Examples of this strategy include continuing to serve the same clients by offering the same product or service, maintaining market share, and sustaining the organization's current business operations. The organization doesn't grow, but it doesn't fall behind, either.

stability strategy
A corporate strategy in which an organization continues to do what it is currently doing

RENEWAL   General Electric (GE) was once one of America's largest and most prestigious corporations. It was in dozens of different businesses—from making light bulbs and refrigerators to healthcare and aircraft leasing. After watching sales drop from $185 billion to $125 billion over a ten-year period, management reorganized the company in 2018 to focus on its aviation, power, and renewable-energy businesses.[24]

renewal strategy
A corporate strategy designed to address declining performance

When an organization is in trouble, something needs to be done. Managers need to develop strategies, called **renewal strategies**, that address declining performance. The two main types of renewal strategies are retrenchment and turnaround strategies. A *retrenchment strategy* is a short-run renewal strategy used for minor performance problems. This strategy helps an organization stabilize operations, revitalize organizational resources and capabilities, and prepare to compete once again. For instance, Biogen reduced its workforce by 11 percent to cut costs.[25] With those savings, the company has increased spending for research and development and for marketing Tecfidera, its potentially highly profitable multiple-sclerosis drug. When an organization's problems are more serious, more drastic action—a *turnaround strategy*—is needed. Managers do two things for both renewal strategies: cut costs and restructure organizational operations. However, in a turnaround strategy, these measures are more extensive than in a retrenchment strategy. For example, CIT Group's declining profits prompted management to cut costs by $125 million and sell the company's aircraft financing business unit to more effectively focus on commercial lending and leasing.[26]

Hubert Joly became Best Buy's CEO in 2012, when it was on the brink of collapse. His renewal strategy has proved highly successful. He turned his stores into mini-shops for Apple, Amazon, Google, and Microsoft. He initiated a price-matching guarantee to compete against online sites. And he made Best Buy stores into warehouses where online customers can quickly and easily pickup orders.
Source: Travis Anderson

BCG matrix
A strategy tool that guides resource-allocation decisions on the basis of market share and growth rate of SBUs

How Are Corporate Strategies Managed?

When an organization's corporate strategy encompasses a number of businesses, managers can manage this collection, or portfolio, of businesses using a tool called a corporate portfolio matrix. This matrix provides a framework for understanding diverse businesses and helps managers establish priorities for allocating resources.[27] The first portfolio matrix—the **BCG matrix**—was developed by the Boston Consulting Group and introduced the idea that an organization's various businesses could be evaluated and plotted using a 2 × 2 matrix to identify which ones offered high potential and which were a drain on organizational resources.[28] The horizontal axis represents market share (low or high), and the vertical axis indicates anticipated market growth (low or high). A business unit is evaluated using a SWOT analysis and placed in one of the four categories, which are as follows:

- Stars: High market share/High anticipated growth rate
- Cash Cows: High market share/Low anticipated growth rate
- Question Marks: Low market share/High anticipated growth rate
- Dogs: Low market share/Low anticipated growth rate

Learning from
F A I L U R E   Coke Panics after the Pepsi Challenge

Have you ever heard of "Project Kansas"? Probably not. It's the name that Coca-Cola gave to its effort to fight off competition posed by Pepsi.

The story begins with the "Pepsi Challenge" marketing campaign that had people blindly tasting two sodas and being asked, "Which tasted better?" One of these sodas was Pepsi and the other Coke. The widely played TV ads showed people largely favoring Pepsi.

The ad campaign was a smashing success. Pepsi sales surged. And Coke panicked!

Consumers who participated in the taste test said they preferred Pepsi for its sweeter taste. In spite of having maintained the same cola recipe for 99 years, Coke executives concluded that they needed to adjust their formula. And so "Project Kansas" was created to reformulate Coke.

With great fanfare in 1985, the company introduced New Coke, which was sweeter and lighter, to replace its iconic cola. Almost immediately, Coke drinkers were outraged and demanded their old Coke back.

The market had spoken, and Coke executives listened. Less than three months after the introduction of New Coke, the company brought back the original formula, with the tag Coca-Cola Classic. The Classic quickly became the company's dominant seller, and New Coke was ultimately killed off in 2002.

What did Coca-Cola's management learn from all of this? Some say, "If it ain't broke, don't fix it." Others suggest, "Think long and hard about introducing changes to a product that's a market leader, been around for a century, and loved by hundreds of millions." Still others offer, "Be calm; don't panic!"[29]

What are the strategic implications of the BCG matrix? The dogs should be sold off or liquidated, as they have low market share in markets with low growth potential. Managers should "milk" cash cows for as much as they can, limit any new investment in them, and use the large amounts of cash generated to invest in stars and question marks with strong potential to improve market share. Heavy investment in stars will help take advantage of the market's growth and help maintain high market share. The stars, of course, will eventually develop into cash cows as their markets mature and sales growth slows. The hardest decision for managers relates to the question marks. After careful analysis, some will be sold off and others strategically nurtured into stars.

COMPETITIVE strategies

L09.4 A **competitive strategy** is a strategy for how an organization will compete in its business(es).[30] For a small organization in only one line of business or a large organization that has not diversified into different products or markets, its competitive strategy describes how it will compete in its primary or main market. For organizations in multiple businesses, however, each business will have its own competitive strategy that defines its competitive advantage, the products or services it will offer, the customers it wants to reach, and the like. For example, Johnson & Johnson has different competitive strategies for its businesses, which include pharmaceuticals, medical devices, and consumer products. When an organization is in several different businesses, those single businesses that are independent and that have their own competitive strategies are referred to as **strategic business units (SBUs)**.

The Role of Competitive Advantage

Michelin has mastered a complex technological process for making superior radial tires. Apple has created the world's best and most powerful brand using innovative design and merchandising capabilities. The Ritz-Carlton hotels have a unique ability to deliver personalized customer service. Each of these companies has created a competitive advantage.

Developing an effective competitive strategy requires an understanding of **competitive advantage**, which is what sets an organization apart—that is, its

competitive strategy
An organizational strategy for how an organization will compete in its business(es)

strategic business unit (SBU)
The single independent businesses of an organization that formulate their own competitive strategies

competitive advantage
What sets an organization apart; its distinctive edge

distinctive edge.[31] That distinctive edge can come from the organization's core competencies by doing something that others cannot do or doing it better than others can do it. For example, Porsche has a competitive advantage based on its engineering and design capabilities plus its reputation for building high-quality, high-performing vehicles. Or competitive advantage can come from the company's resources because the organization has something its competitors don't have. For instance, Walmart's state-of-the-art information system allows it to monitor and control inventories and supplier relations more efficiently than its competitors, which gives Walmart lower product costs, reduced inventory carrying costs, and highly competitive pricing for its customers.

Walmart has a competitive advantage in its state-of-the-art information system that allows it to monitor and control inventories and supplier relations more efficiently than its competitors. This gives Walmart lower product costs, reduced inventory carrying costs, and highly competitive pricing for its customers.
Source: Michael Nagle/Bloomberg/Getty Images

Sustaining Competitive Advantage

Every organization has resources (assets) and capabilities (how work gets done). So what makes some organizations more successful than others? Why do some professional baseball teams consistently win championships or draw large crowds? Why do some companies consistently appear at the top of lists ranking the "best," or the "most admired," or the "most profitable"? The answer is that not every organization is able to effectively exploit its resources and to develop the core competencies that can provide it with a competitive advantage. However, it's not enough simply to create a competitive advantage. The organization must be able to *sustain* that advantage; that is, to keep its edge despite competitors' actions or evolutionary changes in the industry.[32]

Warren Buffett has popularized the term *economic moat* as a means of maintaining a competitive advantage over competitors and protecting long-term profits and market share.[33] Just as moats protected medieval castles, an economic moat acts to protect profit margins. The wider the moat, the more secure the competitive advantage. Over time, many competitive advantages can be duplicated. Many cost advantages, for instance, are vulnerable to duplication. In contrast, a patent or high switching costs provide tougher moats to cross. Apple has developed a wide moat by creating high switching costs for consumers. Once a consumer has an iPhone, an iMac, an iPad, and an Apple Watch, it's tough for Apple competitors to steal that consumer's business.

Building a sustainable "moat" isn't easy to do. Market instabilities, new technology, and other changes can challenge managers' attempts at creating a long-term, sustainable competitive advantage. However, by using strategic management, managers can better position their organizations to get a sustainable competitive advantage.

Many important ideas in strategic management have come from the work of Michael Porter.[34] One of his major contributions was explaining how managers can create a sustainable competitive advantage. An important part of doing this is an industry analysis, which is done using the five forces model.

FIVE FORCES MODEL In any industry, five competitive forces dictate the rules of competition. Together, these five forces determine industry attractiveness and profitability, which managers assess using these five factors:

1. ***Threat of new entrants.*** How likely is it that new competitors will come into the industry?
2. ***Threat of substitutes.*** How likely is it that other industries' products can be substituted for our industry's products?
3. ***Bargaining power of buyers.*** How much bargaining power do buyers (customers) have?
4. ***Bargaining power of suppliers.*** How much bargaining power do suppliers have?
5. ***Current rivalry.*** How intense is the rivalry among current industry competitors?

L.L.Bean prides itself on offering exceptional customer service, which is one product difference a firm can use as part of its differentiation strategy.
Source: Singh_lens/Shutterstock

CHOOSING A COMPETITIVE STRATEGY Once managers have assessed the five forces and done a SWOT analysis, they're ready to select an appropriate competitive strategy—that is, one that fits the competitive strengths (resources and capabilities) of the organization and the industry it's in. According to Porter, no firm can be successful by trying to be all things to all people. He proposed that managers select a strategy that will give the organization a competitive advantage, either from having lower costs than all other industry competitors or by being significantly different from competitors.

When an organization competes on the basis of having the lowest costs (costs or expenses, not prices) in its industry, it's following a *cost leadership strategy*. A low-cost leader is highly efficient. Overhead is kept to a minimum, and the firm does everything it can to cut costs. For example, you won't find many frills in Ross Stores. "We believe in "no frills"—no window displays, mannequins, fancy fixtures or decorations in our stores so we can pass more savings on to our customers."[35] Low overhead costs allow Ross to sell quality apparel and home items at 20 to 60 percent less than most department store prices, and the company is profitable.[36]

A company that competes by offering unique products that are widely valued by customers is following a *differentiation strategy*. Product differences might come from exceptionally high quality, extraordinary service, innovative design, technological capability, or an unusually positive brand image. Practically any successful consumer product or service can be identified as an example of the differentiation strategy; for instance, 3M Corporation (product quality and innovative design); Coach (design and brand image); Apple (product design); and L.L.Bean (customer service).

Although these two competitive strategies are aimed at the broad market, a third type of competitive strategy—the *focus strategy*—involves a cost advantage (cost focus) or a differentiation advantage (differentiation focus) in a narrow segment or niche. Segments can be based on product variety, customer type, distribution channel, or geographical location. For example, Denmark's Bang & Olufsen, whose revenues exceed $318 million, focuses on high-end audio equipment sales. Whether a focus strategy is feasible depends on the size of the segment and whether the organization can make money serving that segment.

What happens if an organization can't develop a cost or a differentiation advantage? Porter called that being *stuck in the middle* and warned that's not a good place to be. An organization becomes stuck in the middle when its costs are too high to compete with the low-cost leader or when its products and services aren't differentiated enough to compete with the differentiator. Getting unstuck means choosing which competitive advantage to pursue and then doing so by aligning resources, capabilities, and core competencies.

Although Porter said you had to pursue either the low cost or the differentiation advantage to prevent being stuck in the middle, additional research has shown that organizations *can* successfully pursue both a low cost and a differentiation advantage and achieve high performance.[37] Needless to say, it's not easy to pull off! You have to keep costs low *and* be truly differentiated. But a company like Southwest Airlines has been able to do it.

Before we leave this section, we want to point out the final type of strategy, the functional strategies, which are the strategies used by an organization's various functional departments to support the competitive strategy. These include marketing, finance, human resources, R&D, and the like. We don't cover specific functional strategies in this book because you'll cover them in other business courses you take.

Examples of Differentiation Strategies

We've talked about how Michelin, Walmart, Apple, 3M, and others have succeeded by differentiating themselves from the competition. In this section, we review five differentiation strategies and how they've been used for competitive advantage.

QUALITY AS A COMPETITIVE ADVANTAGE A number of well-known brands have built their success on their reputation for quality. These include Lexus, Rolex, Viking appliances, Harley-Davidson bikes, and Nordstrom. If implemented properly, quality can be a way for an organization to create a sustainable competitive advantage.[39] That's why many organizations apply quality management concepts in an attempt to set themselves apart from competitors. If a business is able to continuously improve the quality and reliability of its products, it may have a competitive advantage that can't be taken away.

INNOVATION AS A COMPETITIVE ADVANTAGE When Procter & Gamble purchased the Iams pet food business, it did what it always does—used its renowned research division to look for ways to transfer technology from its other divisions to make new products.[40] One outcome of this cross-divisional combination: a tartar-fighting ingredient from toothpaste that's included in all of its dry adult pet foods.

As this example shows, innovation strategies aren't necessarily focused on just the radical, breakthrough products. They can include applying existing technology to new uses. And organizations have successfully used both approaches. What types of innovation strategies do organizations need in today's environment? Those strategies should reflect their innovation philosophy, which is shaped by two strategic decisions: innovation emphasis and innovation timing.

Managers must first decide where the emphasis of their innovation efforts will be. Is the organization going to focus on basic scientific research, product development, or process improvement? Basic scientific research requires the most resource commitment because it involves the nuts-and-bolts work of scientific study. In numerous industries (for instance, genetic engineering, pharmaceuticals, information technology, or cosmetics), an organization's expertise in basic research is the key to a sustainable competitive advantage. However, not every organization requires this extensive commitment to scientific research to achieve high performance levels. Instead, many depend on product development strategies. In this approach, the organization takes existing technology and improves on it or applies it in new ways, just as Procter & Gamble did when it applied tartar-fighting knowledge to pet food products. Both of these first two strategic approaches to innovation (basic scientific research and product development) can help an organization achieve high levels of differentiation, which can be a significant source of competitive advantage.

Another strategic approach related to innovation differentiation is to focus on process development. Using this strategy, an organization looks for ways to improve and enhance its work processes. The organization innovates new and improved ways for employees to do their work. This innovation strategy can lead to lower costs, which, as we know, also can be a significant source of competitive advantage.

Once managers have determined the focus of their innovation efforts, they must decide their innovation timing strategy. Some organizations want to be the first with innovations, whereas others are content to follow or mimic the innovations. An organization that's first to bring a product innovation to the market or to use a new process innovation is called a **first mover**. Being a first mover has certain strategic advantages and disadvantages, as shown in Exhibit 9-4. Some organizations pursue this route, hoping to develop a sustainable competitive advantage. For example, Yum! Brands was the first major fast-food company to establish itself in China when it opened a KFC restaurant in Beijing's Tiananmen Square. Now it has more than 5,000 KFC restaurants in over 1,100 cities throughout China. Others have successfully developed a sustainable competitive advantage by being the followers in the industry. They let the first movers pioneer the innovations and then mimic their products or processes. For instance, Microsoft is rarely a first mover. It lets others incur the risks of introducing new products, then refines and improves them. Visicorp developed the first desktop spreadsheet program, but Microsoft created a superior product—Excel, for its Windows platform—with a graphical interface and more powerful features.

CUSTOMER SERVICE AS A COMPETITIVE ADVANTAGE Focusing on customer service typically means giving customers what they want, communicating effectively with them, and providing employees with customer service training.

first mover
An organization that's first to bring a product innovation to the market or to use a new process innovation

Exhibit 9-4
First Mover Advantages and
Disadvantages

Advantages

- Reputation for being innovative and an industry leader
- Cost and learning benefits
- Control over scarce resources and keeping competitors from having access to them
- Opportunity to begin building customer relationships and customer loyalty

Disadvantages

- Uncertainty over exact direction technology and market will go
- Risk of competitors imitating innovations
- Financial and strategic risks
- High development costs

Singapore Airlines considers providing exceptional customer service a priority, as demonstrated by their extensive employee training, as well as comfortable seating (and champagne) in business class.
Source: Nicky Loh/Bloomberg/Getty Images

It shouldn't surprise you that an important customer service strategy is giving customers what they want, which is a major aspect of an organization's overall marketing strategy. For instance, New Balance Athletic Shoes gives customers a truly unique product: shoes in varying widths. No other athletic shoe manufacturer has shoes for narrow or wide feet and in practically any size.[41]

Having an effective customer communication system is an important customer service strategy. Managers should know what's going on with customers. They need to find out what customers liked and didn't like about their purchase encounter—from their interactions with employees to their experience with the actual product or service. It's also important to let customers know if something is going on with the company that might affect future purchase decisions.

Finally, employees need to be trained to provide exceptional customer service. For example, Singapore Airlines is well known for its customer treatment. Employees go through extensive training to "get service right." It apparently works. Singapore Air has been voted the best airline in the world for twenty-two consecutive years.[42]

MASS CUSTOMIZATION AS A COMPETITIVE ADVANTAGE The twentieth century was significant for the popularization of mass production. What began with Henry Ford and his factories that could produce a car in ninety-three minutes in "any color you want as long as it's black," management sought efficiencies through producing standardized products en masse. Standardization and economies of scale encouraged large size and volume. However, contemporary consumers increasingly seek products and services that are customized to their needs. As a result of improvements in production methods, information technology, and supply-chain management, businesses now have the capability of providing customized offerings at mass-production prices.[43] Very importantly, these improvements have undermined the comparative advantage of large size, allowing any size businesses to produce customized products and services at mass-produced prices.

One of the early proponents of mass customization was Dell. Michael Dell believed that many computer buyers would want to customize their purchase to meet their specific needs. He customized PC-compatible computers out of stock components, sold them directly to customers, and did all of this at a lower cost than his competitors. Today, clothiers can offer customized suits at a fraction of what such suits cost twenty years ago. You can order M&M's with your own printed message. Furniture companies allow you to create unique sofas out of interchangeable components. Modular homebuilders can customize essentially standardized houses for buyers. BMW even claims that no two of its new cars are exactly identical.[44]

SOCIAL MEDIA AS A COMPETITIVE ADVANTAGE Finally, many organizations are making substantial investments in social media in order to gain a competitive advantage. For instance, the Bleacher Report, a Turner sports network, has taken a unique approach to choosing news content. The network relies on social media, including Facebook, Instagram, and Twitter, to identify the topics and sports events fans want to read about. Then, a team of sports journalists use social media to broadcast the information. Steve Minichini of the ad buying company AboveNation Media said that "Turner has smartly tapped into a new breed of sports addict, one who in this era of DraftKings and data-obsessed fandom, is constantly seeking out sports news and community chatter—and not just from traditional media players."[45] Already, the Bleacher Report has more than 10 million followers on social media and 45 million unique views in one month.[46] Turner will spend $100 million to enhance offerings. Clearly, Turner understands that using social media strategically can build competitive advantage.

Successful social media strategies should (1) help people—inside and outside the organization—connect and (2) reduce costs or increase revenue possibilities or both. More specifically, social media can provide competitive advantages in hiring, marketing, customer relations, and competitive intelligence. Social media increases your chances for finding talented, internet-literate, and well-networked job candidates. It allows you to present and promote your organization and carry your message to customers and potential customers. It allows you to interact with customers, learn their preferences, and track what they're saying about your organization. And, of course, as noted in our discussion of competitive intelligence in the previous chapter, it can alert you to actions of your competitors and give you an edge in forming a timely response.

> **fyi**
>
> Ninety-two percent of small businesses planned to increase their investment in social media platforms in 2018.[47]

Chapter 9 | PREPARING FOR: Exams/Quizzes

CHAPTER SUMMARY by Learning Objectives

LO9.1 **DEFINE** strategic management and explain why it's important.

Strategic management is what managers do to develop the organization's strategies. Strategies are the plans for how the organization will do whatever it's in business to do, how it will compete successfully, and how it will attract and satisfy its customers in order to achieve its goals. A business model is how a company is going to make money. Strategic management is important for three reasons. First, it makes a difference in how well organizations perform. Second, it's important for helping managers cope with continually changing situations. Finally, strategic management helps coordinate and focus employee efforts on what's important, which is helpful since organizations are complex and diverse.

LO9.2 **EXPLAIN** what managers do during the six steps of the strategic management process.

The six steps in the strategic management process encompass strategy planning, implementation, and evaluation. These steps include the following: (1) identify the current mission, goals, and strategies; (2) do an external analysis; (3) do an internal analysis (steps 2 and 3 collectively are known as SWOT analysis); (4) formulate strategies; (5) implement strategies; and (6) evaluate strategies. Strengths are any activities the organization does well or its unique resources. Weaknesses are activities the organization doesn't do well or resources it needs. Opportunities are positive trends in the external environment. Threats are negative trends.

LO9.3

DESCRIBE the three types of corporate strategies.

A corporate strategy determines what businesses a company is in (or wants to be in) and what it wants to do with those businesses. A growth strategy is when an organization expands the number of markets served or products offered, either through current or new businesses. The types of growth strategies include concentration, vertical integration (backward and forward), horizontal integration, and diversification (related and unrelated). A stability strategy is when an organization makes no significant changes in what it's doing. Both renewal strategies—retrenchment and turnaround—address organizational weaknesses leading to performance declines. The BCG matrix is a way to analyze a company's portfolio of businesses by looking at a business's market share and its industry's anticipated growth rate. The four categories of the BCG matrix are cash cows, stars, question marks, and dogs.

LO9.4

DESCRIBE competitive advantage and the competitive strategies organizations use to get it.

An organization's competitive advantage is what sets it apart—its distinctive edge. A company's competitive advantage becomes the basis for choosing an appropriate competitive strategy. Porter's five forces model assesses the five competitive forces that dictate the rules of competition in an industry: threat of new entrants, threat of substitutes, bargaining power of buyers, bargaining power of suppliers, and current rivalry. Porter's three competitive strategies are as follows: cost leadership (competing on the basis of having the lowest costs in the industry), differentiation (competing on the basis of having unique products that are widely valued by customers), and focus (competing in a narrow segment with either a cost advantage or a differentiation advantage). Five differentiation strategies that have been used for competitive advantage are quality, innovation, customer service, mass customization, and social media.

REVIEW AND DISCUSSION QUESTIONS

9-1. Why is strategic management important for organizations? Can an organization be successful without a strategic plan? Why or why not?

9-2. Describe the six steps in the strategic management process.

9-3. How might the process of strategy formulation, implementation, and evaluation differ for (a) large businesses, (b) small businesses, (c) not-for-profit organizations, and (d) global businesses?

9-4. Should ethical considerations be included in analyses of an organization's internal and external environments? Why or why not?

9-5. Describe the three major types of corporate strategies and how the BCG matrix is used to manage those corporate strategies.

9-6. Describe the role of competitive advantage and how Porter's competitive strategies help an organization develop competitive advantage.

9-7. "The concept of competitive advantage is as important for not-for-profit organizations as it is for for-profit organizations." Do you agree or disagree with this statement? Explain, using examples to make your case.

9-8. Describe quality, innovation, customer service, mass customization, and social media differentiation strategies.

PREPARING FOR: My Career

ETHICS DILEMMA

You were a marketing manager for We-Sell-It-All, one of the world's largest online retailers. While at a conference, the CEO of a start-up online retailer, BuyIt, offered you a job as the company's first marketing VP. Colleagues encouraged you to take the job as a step in your career advancement. You agreed and enthusiastically accepted the job offer. On your first day, the CEO asked you to do whatever is necessary to take market share from We-Sell-It-All. She emphasized *whatever is necessary* several times.

You quickly realized that the CEO wants you to share competitive information.

9-9. What do you think? Should you follow the CEO's instructions?

9-10. What ethical dilemmas are involved with sharing competitive intelligence?

9-11. What responsibilities, if any, do you have to inform your former employer about what you've been asked?

SKILLS EXERCISE   Developing Your Business Planning Skill

About the Skill
An important step in starting a business or in determining a new strategic direction is preparing a business plan.[48] Not only does the business plan aid in thinking about what to do and how to do it, but it can be a sound basis from which to obtain funding and resources.

Steps in Practicing the Skill
1. *Describe your company's background and purpose.* Provide the history of the company. Briefly describe the company's history and what this company does that's unique. Describe what your product or service will be, how you intend to market it, and what you need to bring your product or service to the market.

2. *Identify your short- and long-term goals.* What is your intended goal for this organization? Clearly, for a new company three broad objectives are relevant: creation, survival, and profitability. Specific objectives can include such things as sales, market share, product quality, employee morale, and social responsibility. Identify how you plan to achieve each objective, how you intend to determine whether you met the objective, and when you intend the objective to be met (e.g., short or long term).

3. *Do a thorough market analysis.* You need to convince readers that you understand what you are doing, what your market is, and what competitive pressures you'll face. In this analysis, you'll need to describe the overall market trends, the specific market you intend to compete in, and who the competitors are. In essence, in this section you'll perform your SWOT analysis.

4. *Describe your development and production emphasis.* Explain how you're going to produce your product or service. Include time frames from start to finish. Describe the difficulties you may encounter in this stage

as well as how much you believe activities in this stage will cost. Provide an explanation of what decisions (e.g., make or buy?) you will face and what you intend to do.

5. *Describe how you'll market your product or service.* What is your selling strategy? How do you intend to reach your customers? In this section, describe your product or service in terms of your competitive advantage and demonstrate how you'll exploit your competitors' weaknesses. In addition to the market analysis, provide sales forecasts in terms of the size of the market, how much of the market you can realistically capture, and how you'll price your product or service.

6. *Put together your financial statements.* What's your bottom line? Investors want to know this information. In the financial section, provide projected profit-and-loss statements (income statements) for approximately three to five years, a cash flow analysis, and the company's projected balance sheets. In the financial section, give thought to how much start-up costs will be and develop a financial strategy—how you intend to use funds received and how you'll control and monitor the financial well-being of the company.

7. *Provide an overview of the organization and its management.* Identify the key executives, summarizing their education, experience, and any relevant qualifications. Identify their positions in the organization and their job roles. Explain how much salary they intend to earn initially. Identify others who may assist the organization's management (e.g., company lawyer, accountant, board of directors). This section should also include, if relevant, a subsection on how you intend to deal with employees. For example, how will employees be paid, what benefits will be offered, and how will employee performance be assessed?

8. ***Describe the legal form of the business.*** Identify the legal form of the business. For example, is it a sole proprietorship, a partnership, a corporation? Depending on the legal form, you may need to provide information regarding equity positions, shares of stock issued, and the like.

9. ***Identify the critical risks and contingencies facing the organization.*** In this section, identify what you'll do if problems arise. For instance, if you don't meet sales forecasts, what then? Similar responses to such questions as problems with suppliers, inability to hire qualified employees, poor-quality products, and so on should be addressed. Readers want to see if you've anticipated potential problems and if you have contingency plans. This is the "what if" section.

10. ***Put the business plan together.*** Using the information you've gathered from the previous nine steps, it's now time to put the business plan together into a well-organized document. A business plan should contain a cover page that shows the company name, address, contact person, and numbers at which the individual can be reached. The cover page should also contain the date the business was established and, if one exists, the company logo. The next page of the business plan should be a table of contents. Here you'll want to list and identify the location of each major section and subsection in the business plan. Remember to use proper outlining techniques. Next comes the executive summary, the first section the readers will actually read. Thus, it's one of the more critical elements of the business plan, because if the executive summary is poorly done, readers may not read any further. In a two- to three-page summary, highlight information about the company, its management, its market and competition, the funds requested, how the funds will be used, financial history (if available), financial projections, and when investors can expect to get their money back (called the exit). Next come the main sections of your business plan; that is, the material you've researched and written about in steps 1 through 9. Close out the business plan with a section that summarizes the highlights of what you've just presented. Finally, if you have charts, exhibits, photographs, tables, and the like, you might want to include an appendix in the back of the business plan. If you do, remember to cross-reference this material to the relevant section of the report.

Practicing the Skill

You have a great idea for a business and need to create a business plan to present to a bank. Choose one of the following products or services, or choose a product or service of your own. Draft the parts of your plan that describe how you will price and market it (see step 5) and that identify critical risks and contingencies (see step 9).

1. Haircuts at home (you make house calls)
2. Vending machines offering only healthy products
3. Rent a pet (the joys of pet owning without all the responsibility)
4. Voice-activated house alarm

WORKING TOGETHER **Team Exercise**

In groups of three or four, look up a company in one of these industries: virtual reality, green or solar energy, or drones. Discuss what you think this company's competitive advantage is. Then, apply the five forces model to the company's industry. Brainstorm what the company could do so that they minimize any threats you identify. Is there anything the company could do to increase their bargaining power within their industry? Be prepared to share your analysis with the class.

MY TURN TO BE A MANAGER

- Using current business periodicals, find two examples of each of the corporate and competitive strategies. Write a description of what these businesses are doing and how it represents that particular strategy.

- Pick five companies from the latest version of *Fortune*'s "Most Admired Companies" list. Research these companies and identify their (a) mission statements, (b) strategic goals, and (c) strategies used.

- Consider several businesses from which you purchase products or services on a regular basis. Identify the business model for each business.

- Customer service, social media, and innovation strategies are particularly important to managers today. We described specific ways companies can pursue these strategies. Your task is to pick customer service, e-business, or innovation and find one example for each of the specific approaches in that category. For instance, if you choose customer service, find an example of (a) giving customers what they want, (b) communicating effectively with them, and (c) providing employees with customer service training. Write a report describing your examples.

CASE APPLICATION 1 — Turnaround at Chipotle

There's no other way to say it ... 2015 was just a bad year for Chipotle, the fast-casual restaurant that specializes in burritos and tacos. There were *E. coli* outbreaks in July, October, and November 2015 in different parts of the US; norovirus incidents in August and December 2015; and a salmonella problem in 17 Minnesota Chipotle restaurants in August 2015.[49] The company tried implementing new food safety measures and changed CEOs. But Chipotle's performance wasn't improving enough. In 2018, Chipotle announced that Brian Niccol would become the new CEO. Niccol had been a turnaround CEO at Taco Bell. The hope was he could do the same for Chipotle.[50]

Chipotle's stock price rose over 12 percent in February 2018, when the new CEO announcement was made. Niccol said that the company's turnaround strategy would focus on fundamentals and on innovation. He closed underperforming restaurants and re-energized Chipotle's marketing efforts. Niccol also added happy-hour items to expand when customers would eat without burdening operations too much.[51]

The innovation side of Chipotle's turnaround strategy involved a digital transformation. That is, they wanted to make mobile ordering as close to in-person ordering as possible. How did they do this? With a graphics-based system that is easy for customers and cuts down on errors for employees working the "digital make lines." Having separate lines for digital orders is meant to improve the speed that all customers experience whether they order in person or online. These improvements also were intended to help grow Chipotle's delivery sales.[52]

Digital sales grew 33 percent in the second quarter of 2018, and delivery sales increased by 300 percent. Chipotle shares were upgraded almost twelve times, and the company share price was up nearly 80 percent, since Niccol took the helm.[53]

But then 700 Chipotle customers in Ohio in August 2018 experienced food safety issues due to food being kept warm for too long. In October 2018, Chipotle share prices slipped 2 percent and analysts said they weren't optimistic that the company could meet earning expectations by 2020.

DISCUSSION QUESTIONS

9-12. In what specific ways did Chipotle follow (or not follow) the two components of renewal strategies?

9-13. If Chipotle only needed a retrenchment strategy (instead of a turnaround strategy), what might they have done?

9-14. How does Chipotle's turnaround strategy show that they paid attention (or didn't) to the external and internal analyses steps in the strategy management process?

9-15. Has Chipotle made additional progress toward their turnaround strategy since October 2018? What, if any, new challenges has the company faced?

CASE APPLICATION 2 — Saving Lives Through Strategy at RapidSOS

Michael Martin's dad fell off the roof of his home while clearing away snow. His dad tried calling 911 from his cellphone, but couldn't reach them. He had to lie in the driveway with a broken wrist and shattered hip for two hours before his wife arrived and called 911 from a landline.[54]

Michael saw that there was a clear opportunity to fill the need of connecting cellphone users with 911 more smoothly. The 911 system was developed in the late 1960s for landline phones and has not been updated for cellphones. Unlike landlines, cellphones don't provide accurate location information to 911 operators. As a result, 10,000 people are estimated to die each year.[55]

Michael created a new company, RapidSOS, and launched its 911 app, Haven, with co-founder Nick Horelik. Talking to public safety officials after the launch, Michael learned that a 911 app would be likely to experience problems. The 6,500 call centers that respond to 911 calls use different technologies and may have trouble receiving a call coming through the app.

RapidSOS refocused its efforts. Instead of an app, they focused on developing technology that would allow cell phone locations to be transmitted to 911 call centers during a phone call. Once created, the next question for RapidSOS was how to bring their technology to market. Should they work on replacing existing emergency response systems? That would involve overhauling 911 call centers and how ambulances, police, and fire professionals are mobilized to emergencies. Or should they target specific communities and then expand further to others?[56]

To decide which strategy to use, RapidSOS considered what its mission was: to allow those with a high risk for emergencies to have better access to emergency services. They first gained the support of specific patient groups, like epilepsy and domestic violence. They continued gaining the support of other groups, such as diabetes patient groups. That gained the attention of Google and Apple.[57] Google and Apple entered partnerships with RapidSOS that allowed life-saving 911 location information to be transmitted from cell phones. These partnerships allowed RapidSOS to be the first company to be able to transmit data directly into the existing 911 system. Its competitors relied on other approaches, such as connecting to a third-party call center.

DISCUSSION QUESTIONS

9-16. How does RapidSOS exemplify advantages and disadvantages of being a first mover?

9-17. What type of growth strategy did RapidSOS implement (concentration, vertical integration, horizontal integration, or diversification)? Justify your answer.

9-18. What could RapidSOS have done differently to have avoided the problems related to using an app to reach 911 operators?

9-19. How has RapidSOS's actions decreased the threat of new entrants and threat of substitutes?

ENDNOTES

1. N. Statt, "MoviePass Is No Longer Too Good to Be True," *The Verge*, April 27, 2018, https://www.theverge.com/2018/4/27/17291242/moviepass-unlimited-movie-deal-repeat-viewings-theater-blackouts; D. Seitz, "MoviePass Users Are Reporting Widespread Outages—Is the Service Dead for Good?," *Uproxx*, July 30, 2018, https://uproxx.com/movies/is-moviepass-out-of-business-app-down-dead/; S. Kaplan, "The MoviePass Business Model Just Imploded. Here's Why," *Inc.*, July 30, 2018, https://www.inc.com/soren-kaplan/the-moviepass-business-model-just-imploded-heres-why.html; and E. Millman and R.T. Watson, "It's a Wrap: MoviePass Ends Theater Subscription Service," *Wall Street Journal*, September 14, 2019, p. B1. https://www.nytimes.com/2018/12/05/business/media/moviepass-subscription-plan.html.

2. J. W. Dean Jr. and M. P. Sharfman, "Does Decision Process Matter? A Study of Strategic Decision-Making Effectiveness," *Academy of Management Journal* (April 1996): pp. 368–396; R. Price, "BlackBerry's Share of the Global Smartphone Market is Now Officially 0%," *Business Insider*, February 15, 2017, https://nordic.businessinsider.com/blackberry-smartphone-marketshare-zero-percent-gartner-q4-2016-2017-2/ (file not found); and M. deAgonia, "Review: The iPhone X Is the Best Phone for Business, Period," *Computerworld*; November 17, 2017, https://www.computerworld.com/article/3237689/review-the-iphone-x-is-the-best-phone-for-business-period.html.

3. J. Magretta, "Why Business Models Matter," *Harvard Business Review*, May 2002, pp. 86–92; B. W. Wirtz, A. Pistoia, S. Ullrich, and V. Göttel, "Business Models: Origin, Development and Future Research Perspectives," *Long Range Planning* (February 2016): pp. 36–54; and T. L. J. Broekhuizen, T. Bakker, and T. J. B. M. Postma,

"Implementing New Business Models: What Challenges Lie Ahead?," *Business Horizons* (July-August 2018): pp. 555–66.

4. R. Reiss, "How Marvel Became a Business Superhero," *Forbes*, February 1, 2010, https://www.forbes.com/2010/02/01/peter-cuneo-marvel-leadership-managing-turnaround.html#6aee24146fa1; and R. Lamble, "How Marvel Went From Bankruptcy to Billions," *Den of Geek*, April 15, 2018, https://www.denofgeek.com/us/books-comics/marvel/243710/how-marvel-went-from-bankruptcy-to-billions.

5. See, for instance, C. C. Miller and L. B. Cardinal, "Strategic Planning and Firm Performance: A Synthesis of More Than Two Decades of Research," *Academy of Management Journal* (December 1994): pp. 1649–1665; N. Capon, J. U. Farley, and J. M. Hulbert, "Strategic Planning and Financial Performance: More Evidence," *Journal of Management Studies* (January 1994): pp. 105–110. E. H. Bowman and C. E. Helfat, "Does Corporate Strategy Matter?," *Strategic Management Journal* 22 (2001): pp. 1–23; J. C. Short, D. J. Ketchen Jr., T. B. Palmer, and G. T. M. Hult, "Firm, Strategic Group, and Industry Influences on Performance," *Strategic Management Journal* (February 2007): pp. 147–167; J. Aspara, J. Hietanen, and H. Tikkanen, "Business Model Innovation vs. Replication: Financial Performance Implications of Strategic Emphases," *Journal of Strategic Marketing* (February 2010): pp. 39–56; M. Song, S. Im, H. van der Bij, and L. Z. Song, "Does Strategic Planning Enhance or Impede Innovation and Firm Performance?," *Journal of Product Innovation Management* (July 2011): pp. 503–520; M. A. Luoma, "Revisiting the Strategy-Performance Linkage: An Application of an Empirically Derived Typology of Strategy Content Areas," *Management Decision* 53, no. 5 (2015): pp. 1083–1106; and L. Heracleous and K. Werres, "On the Road to Disaster: Strategic Misalignments and Corporate Failure," *Long Range Planning* (August 2016): pp. 491–506.

6. "USPS 2018 Forecast: Declining Volumes, Higher Revenues," Official Mail Guide, https://mailomg.com/2017/11/29/usps-2018-forecast-declining-volumes-higher-revenues/ (contains a link to the US Postal Service's "Fiscal Year 2018 Integrated Financial Plan," https://mailomg.files.wordpress.com/2017/11/usps-fy18-financial-plan.pdf).

7. R. W. Miller, "Debt-Plagued U.S. Postal Service Eyes Bipartisan Bill to Solve Woes," USA Today, March 1, 2017, https://www.usatoday.com/story/news/nation/2017/03/01/debt-plagued-us-postal-service-eyes-bipartisan-bill-solve-woes/97944594/; J. Heckman, "Postal Service Forecasts 'Much-Needed Revenue' from Approved Rate Hike," *Federal News Network*, November 16, 2017, https://federalnewsnetwork.com/management/2017/11/postal-service-forecasts-much-needed-revenue-from-approved-rate-hike/; and C. Isidore, "Postal Service Losses Soar to $1.3 Billion, but Don't Blame Amazon," CNNMoney, May 11, 2018. https://money.cnn.com/2018/05/11/news/companies/postal-service-losses/index.html.

8. L. Stevens, "U.S. Postal Service Tries Hand as Fishmonger, Grocer," *Wall Street Journal* online, updated August 17, 2015, https://www.wsj.com/articles/u-s-postal-service-tries-hand-as-fishmonger-grocer-1439855940.

9. R. Carucci, "Executives Fail to Execute Strategy Because They're Too Internally Focused," *Harvard Business Review*, November 13, 2017, https://hbr.org/2017/11/executives-fail-to-execute-strategy-because-theyre-too-internally-focused.

10. L. Kolowich, "17 Truly Inspiring Company Vision and Mission Statement Examples," *HubSpot* (blog), July 9, 2018, https://blog.hubspot.com/marketing/inspiring-company-mission-statements.

11. J. Constine, "Facebook Changes Mission Statement to Bring the World Closer Together,'" *TechCrunch*, June 22, 2017, https://techcrunch.com/2017/06/22/bring-the-world-closer-together/.

12. M. Bertolini, D. Duncan, and A. Waldeck, "Knowing When to Reinvent," *Harvard Business Review* online, December 2015, https://hbr.org/2015/12/knowing-when-to-reinvent.

13. T. Saebi, L. Lien, and N. J. Foss, "What Drives Business Model Adaptation? The Impact of Opportunities, Threats and Strategic Orientation," *Long Range Planning* (October 2017): pp. 567–81.

14. C. K. Prahalad and G. Hamel, "The Core Competence of the Corporation," *Harvard Business Review*, May–June 1990, pp. 79–91; and G. Hamel and C. K. Prahalad, *Competing for the Future* (Boston: Harvard Business Review Press, 1996).

15. "Norfolk Southern Announces Further Details of Its Strategic Plan to Reduce Costs, Drive Profitability, and Accelerate Growth," on Norfolk Southern Corporation's website, accessed August 6, 2018, http://www.nscorp.com/content/nscorp/en/news/norfolk-southernannouncesfurtherdetailsofitsstrategicplantoreduc.html.

16. See, for instance, M. M. Helms and J. Nixon, "Exploring SWOT Analysis—Where Are We Now?" *Journal of Strategy and Management* 3, no. 3 (2010): pp. 215–51.

17. J. Lee, "Las Vegas Returns to Sinful Roots," CNNMoney, May 28, 2004, https://money.cnn.com/2004/05/28/news/midcaps/las_vegas/.

18. Based on W. Arthur Jr., S. T. Bell, A. J. Villado, and D. Doverspike, "The Use of Person-Organization Fit in Employment Decision-Making: An Assessment of Its Criterion-Related Validity," *Journal of Applied Psychology* (July 2006): pp. 786–801; D. A. McKay and D. M. Tokar, "The HEXACO and Five-Factor Models of Personality in Relation to RIASEC Vocational Interests," *Journal of Vocational Behavior* (October 2012): pp. 138–149; L. Quast, "How to Conduct a Personal SWOT Analysis," *Forbes*, April 15, 2013, https://www.forbes.com/sites/lisaquast/2013/04/15/how-to-conduct-a-personal-s-w-o-t-analysis/#e0a46cc28d8b; and M. Martin, "Conducting a Personal SWOT Analysis for Your Career," *Business News Daily*, November 25, 2015.

19. J. Dudovskiy, "PepsiCo Business Strategy and Competitive Advantage," Research Methodology, May 1, 2016, https://research-methodology.net/pepsico-analysis-of-corporate-strategy/.

20. P. Suciu, "Nvidia Lays Out Bold Strategy at CES," *TechNewsWorld*, January 6, 2017, https://www.technewsworld.com/story/84205.html; and "Nvidia Corp.," MarketWatch, December 30, 2018, www.marketwatch.com.

21. K. Stock, "How Boring Old Buick Is Crushing the Luxury Car Market," *Bloomberg* online, March 22, 2016, https://www.bloomberg.com/news/articles/2016-03-22/how-boring-old-buick-is-crushing-the-luxury-car-market.

22. K. Welshans, "Walmart Opens New Indiana Milk Processing Plant," *Supermarket News*, June 15, 2018, https://www.supermarketnews.com/news/walmart-opens-new-indiana-milk-processing-plant.

23. The Boeing Company, "2015 Annual Report," p. 4

24. G. Colvin, "What the Hell Happened?," *Fortune*, June 1, 2018, pp. 149–56.

25. K. Kingsbury, *"Bio*gen Retrenches, Despite Strong Quarter," *Wall Street Journal* online, October 21, 2015, https://www.wsj.com.

26. R. L. Ensign, "CIT Group to Focus on Commercial Businesses in Turnaround Plan," *Wall Street Journal* online, updated March 23, 2016, https://www.wsj.com/articles/cit-group-to-focus-on-commercial-businesses-in-turnaround-plan-1458731530.

27. D. Sull, S. Turconi, C. Sull, and J. Yoder, "Four Logics of Corporate Strategy," *MIT Sloan Management Review* (Winter 2018): pp. 136–42.

28. Boston Consulting Group, *Perspective on Experience* (Boston: Boston Consulting Group, 1970); and D. O. Madsen, "Not Dead Yet: The Rise, Fall and Persistence of the BCG Matrix," *Problems and Perspectives in Management* 15, no. 1 (2017): pp. 19–34.

29. Based on C. L. Hays, *The Real Thing: Truth and Power at the Coca-Cola Company* (NY: Random House, 2005); A. Klaassen, "New Coke: One of Marketing's Biggest Blunders Turns 25," *Ad Age*, April 23, 2010, https://adage.com/article/adages/coke-marketing-s-biggest-blunders-turns-25/143470/; and R. Gorman and S. Gould, "This Mistake from 30 Years Ago Almost Destroyed Coca-Cola," *Business Insider*, April 23, 2015, https://www.businessinsider.com/new-coke-the-30th-anniversary-of-coca-colas-biggest-mistake-2015-4.

30. H. E. Salavou, "Competitive Strategies and Their Shift to the Future," *European Business Review* 27, no. 1 (2015): pp. 80–99.

31. M. E. Porter, *Competitive Advantage: Creating and Sustaining Superior Performance* (New York: Free Press, 1985); J. Barney, "Firm Resources and Sustained Competitive Advantage," *Journal of Management* 17, no. 1 (1991): pp. 99–120; J. B. Barney, "Looking Inside for Competitive Advantage," *Academy of Management Executive* (November 1995): pp. 49–61; and C. Sigalas, "Competitive Advantage: The Known Unknown Concept," *Management Decision* 53, no. 9 (2015): pp. 2004–16.

32. B. Maury, "Sustainable Competitive Advantage and Profitability Persistence: Sources Versus Outcomes for Assessing Advantage," *Journal of Business Research* (March 2018): pp. 100–13.

33. C. Gallant, "What Is an Economic Moat?," *Investopedia*, November 20, 2017, https://www.investopedia.com/ask/answers/05/economicmoat.asp; and A. R. Sorkin, "Mogul on a Contrarian Mission to Fill in Buffett's Sacred Moat," *New York Times*, May 8, 2018, New York edition, p. B1.

34. See, for example, Porter, *Competitive Advantage* [see note 29]; and M. E. Porter, *Competitive Strategy: Techniques for Analyzing Industries and Competitors* (New York: Free Press, 1980); G. G. Dess and P. S. Davis, "Porter's (1980) Generic Strategies as Determinants of Strategic Group Membership and Organizational Performance," *Academy of Management Journal* (September 1984): pp. 467–488;. G. G. Dess and P. S. Davis, "Porter's (1980) Generic Strategies and Performance: An Empirical Examination with American Data—Part I: Testing Porter," *Organization Studies*, no. 1 (1986): pp. 37–55; G. G. Dess and P. S. Davis, "Porter's (1980) Generic Strategies and Performance: An Empirical Examination with American Data—Part II:

Performance Implications," *Organization Studies*, no. 3 (1986): pp. 255–261; M. E. Porter, "From Competitive Advantage to Corporate Strategy," *Harvard Business Review*, May–June 1987, pp. 43–59; and A. Brandenburger, "Porter's Added Value: High Indeed!," *Academy of Management Executive* (May 2002): pp. 58–60.

35. From the Ross Stores website, "About Us," https://www.rossstores.com/about-us, accessed January 11, 2019.

36. D. Trainer, "Ross Stores Shine Like a Diamond in Rough-and-Tumble Retail," *Forbes*, October 25, 2017, https://www.forbes.com/sites/greatspeculations/2017/10/25/ross-stores-shines-like-a-diamond-in-rough-and-tumble-retail/#6997e73f481c.

37. D. Miller, "The Generic Strategy Trap," *Journal of Business Strategy* (January-February 1991): pp. 37–41; S. Cappel, P. Wright, M. Kroll, and D. Wyld, "Competitive Strategies and Business Performance: An Empirical Study of Select Service Businesses," *International Journal of Management* (March 1992): pp. 1–11; and J. W. Bachmann, "Competitive Strategy: It's O.K. to Be Different," *Academy of Management Executive* (May 2002): pp. 61–65.

38. PwC, *Reinventing Innovation: Five Findings to Guide Strategy Through Execution*, PwC Innovation Benchmark, December 29, 2018, https://www.pwc.com/gr/en/publications/assets/innovation-benchmark-report.pdf.

39. R. D. Spitzer, "TQM: The Only Source of Sustainable Competitive Advantage," *Quality Progress* (June 1993): pp. 59–64; T. C. Powell, "Total Quality Management as Competitive Advantage: A Review and Empirical Study," *Strategic Management Journal* (January 1995) pp. 15–37; and H.-C. Su, S. Dhanokar, and K. Linderman, "A Competitive Advantage From the Implementation Timing of ISO Management Standards," *Journal of Operations Management* (July 2015): pp. 31–44.

40. "Innovation at Work: Is Anyone in Charge," *Wall Street Journal*, January 22, 2013, p. B14.

41. B. Stout, "Shoe Widths Explained," *ShoeStores.com* (blog), September 13, 2016, https://shoestores.com/blog/shoe-widths-explained/.

42. S-C Hoeller, "Here's Why Singapore Airlines Was Just Named the Best International Airline in the World," *Insider*, July 6, 2016, https://www.thisisinsider.com/singapore-airline-best-international-airline-2016-7; and T. Avakian, "This Airline Has Been Voted the Best in the World for the Past 22 Years," *Travel + Leisure*, updated July 12, 2017, https://www.travelandleisure.com/airlines-airports/singapore-airlines-best-international-airline.

43. F. T. Piller and M. M. Tseng (eds.), *Handbook of Research in Mass Customization and Personalization* (Singapore: World Scientific, 2010); and M. Martin, "Mass Customization: What, Why, How, and Examples," *Cleverism*, February 25, 2015, https://www.cleverism.com/mass-customization-what-why-how/.

44. Cited in P. Myerson, "The Lean Supply Chain," *IndustryWeek* (blog), August 29, 2014, https://www.industryweek.com/blog/lean-supply-chain.

45. M. Shields, "'Just Talk to a 24-Year-Old,' and You'll Know Why ESPN Is Getting Buried in One Critical Area by Bleacher Report and Barstool Sports," *Business Insider Nederland*, September 16, 2017, https://www.businessinsider.nl/

espn-losing-social-media-audience-trump-facebook-instagram-jemele-hill-bleacher-report-barstool-2017-9/.

46. M. Shields, "Turner Plans to Spend $100 Million Expanding Bleacher Report," *Wall Street Journal* online, March 24, 2016, https://www.wsj.com/articles/turner-plans-to-spend-100-million-expanding-bleacher-report-1458813601.

47. K. Herhold, "How Small Businesses Invest in Social Media in 2018," *Manifest*, May 10, 2018, https://themanifest.com/social-media/how-small-businesses-invest-social-media-2018.

48. See, for instance, C. Barrow, P. Barrow, and R. Brown, *The Business Plan Workbook: A Step-by-Step Guide to Creating and Developing a Successful Business*, 9th ed. (London, UK: Kogan Page, 2018).

49. Wikipedia, s.v., "Chipotle Mexican Grill," https://en.wikipedia.org/wiki/Chipotle_Mexican_Grill.

50. P. Wahba, "Chipotle Kickstarts Comeback by Sticking to What It Does Best," *Fortune,* July 27, 2018, http://fortune.com/2018/07/27/chipotle-turnaround/.

51. S. Halzack, "Chipotle Wisely Starts Turnaround with Low-Hanging Tacos," *Bloomberg News*, June 28, 2018, https://www.bloomberg.com/opinion/articles/2018-06-28/chipotle-revamp-wisely-goes-with-low-hanging-tacos.

52. M. Wilson, "Chipotle Is Quietly Staging a Comeback," *Fast Company*, June 1, 2018, https://www.fastcompany.com/90174266/chipotle-is-quietly-staging-a-comeback.

53. S. Whitten, "Oppenheimer Downgrades Chipotle, Says Wall Street Is 'Too Optimistic' About the Company's Earnings," Nightly Business Report, *CNBC*, October 1, 2018, http://nbr.com/2018/10/01/oppenheimer-downgrades-chipotle-says-wall-street-is-too-optimistic-about-the-companys-earnings/.

54. "This App May Lead All Apps in Saving Lives," *AlleyWatch*, July 2016, https://www.alleywatch.com/2016/07/app-may-lead-apps-saving-lives/.

55. R. Knutson, "Startup Seeks Solution for a Critical 911 Problem—Ex-FCC Leaders Join Effort to Improve Emergency System That Can't Pinpoint the Location of Cellphone Callers," *Wall Street Journal*, April 29, 2017.

56. J. Gans, E. L. Scott, and S. Stern, "Strategy for Start-Ups," *Harvard Business Review,* May-June 2018, pp. 44–51.

57. H. Detrick, "Cellphone Calls to 911 Can Be Catastrophically Bad. Apple Has a Plan to Fix Them.," *Fortune*, June 18, 2016, http://fortune.com/2016/06/18/apple-911-calls-rapidsos-cellphones/; and "Company Overview of Rapid SOS, Inc.," *Bloomberg*, https://www.bloomberg.com/research/stocks/private/snapshot.asp?privcapid=308956782.

Chapter 10   Entrepreneurial Ventures

Learning Objectives

10.1 **Define** entrepreneurship and explain why it's important.

10.2 **Explain** what entrepreneurs do in the planning process for new ventures.

10.3 **Describe** the six legal forms of organization and the choice of appropriate organizational structure.

10.4 **Describe** how entrepreneurs lead organizations.

10.5 **Explain** how managers control organizations and exit the venture.

Employability Skills Matrix

This matrix identifies which features and end-of-chapter material will help you develop specific skills employers are looking for in job candidates.

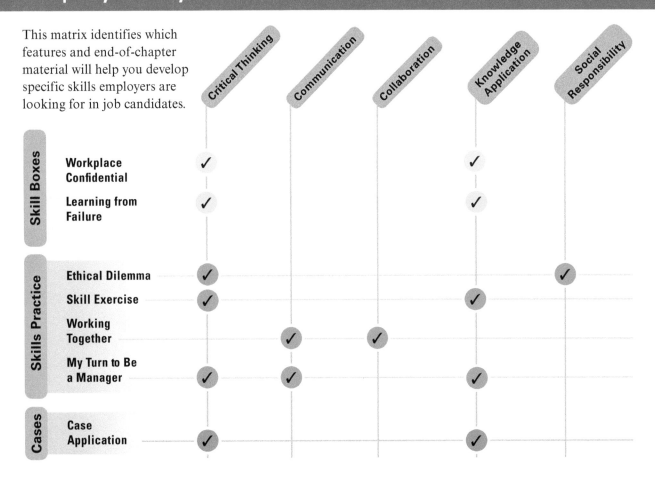

		Critical Thinking	Communication	Collaboration	Knowledge Application	Social Responsibility
Skill Boxes	Workplace Confidential	✓			✓	
	Learning from Failure	✓			✓	
Skills Practice	Ethical Dilemma	✓				✓
	Skill Exercise	✓			✓	
	Working Together		✓	✓		
	My Turn to Be a Manager	✓	✓		✓	
Cases	Case Application	✓			✓	

There are few people more deserving of the title "serial entrepreneur" than Elon Musk. His entrepreneurial career started with the creation of Zip2, a web software company, that he sold in 1999 for $340 million. This was followed by starting the online payment company X.com, which became PayPal, and was bought in 2002 by eBay for $1.5 billion. More recently, Musk founded the car company Tesla; the space transport company SpaceX; the energy services company Solar City; Neuralink, a developer of brain-computer interfaces; and The Boring Company, an infrastructure and tunnel-building construction company.

THE CONTEXT of entrepreneurship

LO10.1 For those who want to become entrepreneurs, there is a lot to know. In this chapter, we provide an overview of that knowledge. Let's begin by defining *entrepreneurship*.

What Is Entrepreneurship?

Entrepreneurship is the process of starting new businesses, generally in response to opportunities.[1] Entrepreneurs are pursuing opportunities by changing, revolutionizing, transforming, or introducing new products or services.

entrepreneurship
The process of starting new businesses, generally in response to opportunities

Are entrepreneurs and small-business owners the same thing? No.[2] There are some key differences. Entrepreneurs want to change the world. They think big and have innovative ideas. They typically have a passion that goes beyond profits. In contrast, small-business owners want to make a living. Their business is typically composed of doing something others are already doing. Where a small-business owner sees risk, the entrepreneur sees opportunity. A small-business owner, for instance, might open a bike rental shop. An entrepreneur might develop an app that would allow people to share a common set of bikes, invest in a fleet of bicycles, negotiate with communities for places to locate bike racks and his bikes, and then promote his bike-sharing app and rental business.

Why Is Entrepreneurship Important?

Entrepreneurs have given us much of what defines our current lifestyle: the microchip (Jack Kilby and Robert Noyce), the personal computer (Steve Wozniak), 24-hour news (Ted Turner), ride-sharing (Travis Kalanick and Garrett Camp), home review and referral services (Angie Hicks and Bill Oesterle), online personal shopping service (Katrina Lake), and ubiquitous social networking (Mark Zuckerberg), to name just a few. Clearly, entrepreneurship is important. You can see it in its impact on innovation, economic growth, and job creation.[3]

INNOVATION Innovating is a process of changing, experimenting, transforming, and revolutionizing, and is a key aspect of entrepreneurial activity. The "creative destruction" process that characterizes innovation leads to technological changes and employment growth. Entrepreneurial firms act as "agents of change" by providing an essential source of new and unique ideas that may otherwise go untapped.

Entrepreneurs play a disproportionate role in commercializing new products. The most radical innovations of the modern era—the airplane, the automobile, the telephone, frozen foods, air conditioning—came from the mind of an entrepreneur.

ECONOMIC GROWTH A country's ability to improve its standard of living over time depends largely on its ability to raise output per worker; that is, to increase efficiency. Entrepreneurship contributes to this goal of increased efficiency by keeping markets competitive. New businesses keep established businesses "on their toes" and push out the inefficient. New and improved products, processes, and methods of production stimulate economic growth.

Entrepreneur Salma Likupila (right) talking to a customer in her Batik dye shop in Tanzania, Africa.
Source: Mile 91/Ben Langdon/Alamy Stock Photo

As important as growth is to first-world economies, it's critical to emerging nations where a large portion of the population live in poverty. For instance, rapid economic growth has been the primary force for bringing tens of millions in India into the middle class. And it's having a dramatic effect on raising living standards in places like Kenya, Ghana, Ethiopia, Cambodia, and Senegal. Central to this improvement in living standards has been the surge in entrepreneurial ventures.[4] For instance, Bhavarlal Jain began with a pushcart in Maharashtra, India. Today, his Jain Irrigation Systems has thousands of employees providing products and services to small farmers. And Peter Chege, an entrepreneur in Nairobi, is developing and installing hydroponics systems for farmers in Kenya, Uganda, and Rwanda that allow them to significantly increase their crop yields while reducing water usage.

JOB CREATION We know that job creation is important to the overall long-term economic health of communities, regions, and nations. And the largest source of new jobs isn't big corporations. It's small businesses.[5] Small business employs 47.5 percent of the US private workforce and, in 2017, accounted for 1.9 million of the 2.1 million net new jobs created. Most revealing is that it's the new and young businesses that are the job creators, not small business per se.

The Entrepreneurial Process

Entrepreneurs must address four key steps as they start and manage their entrepreneurial ventures.

The first is *exploring the entrepreneurial context.* The context includes the realities of the current economic, political/legal, social, and work environment. It's important to look at each of these aspects of the entrepreneurial context because they determine the "rules" of the game and which decisions and actions are likely to meet with success. Also, it's through exploring the context that entrepreneurs confront the next critically important step in the entrepreneurial process—*identifying opportunities and possible competitive advantages.* We know from our definition of entrepreneurship that the pursuit of opportunities is a key to the process.

Once entrepreneurs have explored the entrepreneurial context and identified opportunities and possible competitive advantages, they need to look at the issues involved with actually bringing their entrepreneurial venture to life; that is, *starting the venture.* Included in this phase are researching the feasibility of the venture, planning the venture, organizing the venture, and launching the venture.

Finally, once the entrepreneurial venture is up and running, the last step is *managing the venture*, which an entrepreneur does by managing processes, managing people, and managing growth. We can elaborate on this process by looking at what entrepreneurs do.

What Do Entrepreneurs Do?

Describing what entrepreneurs do isn't easy because no two entrepreneurs' work activities are exactly alike. In a general sense, entrepreneurs create something new, something different. They search for change, respond to it, and exploit it.

Initially, an entrepreneur is engaged in assessing the potential for the entrepreneurial venture and then dealing with start-up issues. In exploring the entrepreneurial context, entrepreneurs gather information, identify potential opportunities, and pinpoint possible competitive advantage(s). Then, armed with this information, the entrepreneur researches the venture's feasibility—uncovering business ideas, looking at competitors, and exploring financing options.

After looking at the potential of the proposed venture and assessing the likelihood of pursuing it successfully, the entrepreneur proceeds to plan the venture. Planning includes developing a viable organizational mission and creating a well-thought-out business plan. Once these planning issues have been resolved, the entrepreneur must look at organizing the venture, which involves choosing a legal form of business organization, addressing other legal issues such as patent or copyright searches, and coming up with an appropriate organizational design for structuring how work is going to be done.

Only after these start-up activities have been completed is the entrepreneur ready to actually launch the venture. Such a launch involves setting goals and strategies and establishing the technology-operations methods, marketing plans, information systems, financial-accounting systems, and cash flow management systems.

Once the entrepreneurial venture is up and running, the entrepreneur's attention switches to managing it. What's involved with actually managing the entrepreneurial venture? An important activity is managing the various processes that are part of every business: making decisions, reacting to changes in the environment, and measuring and evaluating performance. Also, the entrepreneur must perform activities associated with managing people, including selecting and hiring, appraising and training, motivating, delegating tasks, and displaying effective leadership. Finally, the entrepreneur must manage the venture's growth, including such activities as developing and designing growth strategies, exploring various avenues for additional financing, placing a value on the venture, and perhaps even eventually exiting the venture.

A Hybrid Path to Entrepreneurship

Entrepreneurship needn't be an "all in" proposition. A hybrid path to entrepreneurship can allow you to pursue the opportunities of a new venture without the full risk and uncertainty associated with the activity.

There is no ignoring the statistics on entrepreneurial failures. They can be disheartening. A little more than 50 percent of new-venture start-ups fail in the first four years.[6] To improve those odds, you might consider a hybrid approach.

A *hybrid path to entrepreneurship* means starting a business while retaining your "day job" in an existing organization. By combining paid employment and self-employment, you can gain several advantages over jumping into full-time entrepreneurship.[7] First, since it reduces risk, it clearly has appeal to individuals who are risk averse. It, therefore, opens up the entrepreneurship "door" to many people who might otherwise forgo it. Second, the hybrid path allows entrepreneurs to test their ideas and grow in a less-pressured environment. The full-time job continues to provide a secure and ongoing income. Third, obtaining the financial assets to create a new venture is often a major barrier to starting a business. The hybrid approach can allow individuals to use income generated from their full-time job as start-up and continuing funding for their new venture. Finally, when the hybrid path is used as an interim step to full-time self-employment, studies show survival rates are much higher than for those who enter full-time self-employment straight from a waged job.

Sara Blakely, founder of Spanx and now a frequent investor on *Shark Tank*, identified an opportunity and turned it into a billion-dollar fortune.
Source: Mitch Haaseth/Walt Disney Television/ Getty Images

START-UP **and planning issues**

LO10.2 Sara Blakely was a door-to-door fax machine salesperson with a dilemma—what to wear under white slacks that would work with a pair of strappy sandals. She cut the feet off a pair of pantyhose. That eliminated lines, but the hose rolled up at her feet. From that problem came a solution: Spanx. With an initial investment of $5,000, she has created a hugely successful shapewear line of undergarments, leggings, and maternity wear that are now sold in sixty-five countries.[8]

WORKPLACE CONFIDENTIAL Dealing with Risks

Former hockey great Wayne Gretzky captured the importance of risk taking when he said, "You miss 100 percent of the shots you never take." His message: You have to risk failure to achieve success.

The easy route in life is to stay the course and not make waves. This typically means making choices that provide predictable outcomes and minimal threats to your known world: staying in the town you grew up in, keeping the same job for your entire career, going to your "regular" vacation spot every year, maintaining constant hobbies and interests, and so on. You might think that by minimizing change, you minimize risk. As you'll see, if you think that's true, there's a good chance you're wrong.

Risk has both positive and negative outcomes. Risk avoiders tend to emphasize its negative aspects. Risk seekers focus on the positives. You need to understand when to take risks, when to avoid them, and how to turn risk taking to your advantage.

Let's begin with a brief analysis of risk perception. That is, what shapes your perception of risk? There are four elements you want to consider: uncertainty, gains, losses, and your risk profile. Uncertainty reflects doubt or acknowledging the unknown. As uncertainty increases, decisions become more risky. As such, we try to avoid uncertainty or minimize its influence. We do this by accumulating as much appropriate information as possible. A potential risk outcome is derived by comparing gains and losses. Larger anticipated gains are preferred over smaller gains and smaller potential losses to larger losses. Riskiness increases as possible returns become smaller or potential losses appear larger. You want to take on risks where the potential gains exceed potential losses—and the larger the gain, the better. So you have to answer the question: Is it worth the risk? Finally, you need to take into consideration your risk profile. What's your risk tolerance? People differ in their willingness to take chances. Low-risk-seekers are likely to identify, value, and choose decision options that have low chances for failure. Right or wrong, that often means choosing alternatives that contain minimal change from the status quo. High-risk-takers, on the other hand, are more likely to identify, value, and choose alternatives that are unique and that have a greater chance of failing.

Now let's turn our attention to the positive aspects of risk. There are few truisms in life, but one is, with the exception of those lucky enough to be born into wealth, you can't achieve success in this world without taking risks. Oprah Winfrey, Jeff Bezos, Jay-Z, Angela Merkel, Ray Kroc, Rihanna, Steve Jobs, I. M. Pei—they all took risks. They quit a job, they moved to a new city, they started a business, they ran for political office. They did something that made them vulnerable and exposed themselves to rejection and failure. We're not proposing here that risk-taking guarantees success. Clearly, it doesn't. What we are saying is that it's hard to become successful without giving up some security and taking a chance.

As we noted, we all don't have the same tolerance for risk. If you see yourself as a risk taker, your concern should be focused on keeping your risk taking under control. You want to take calculated risks and avoid throwing caution to the wind. For those of you who tend to be risk-averse, the following should be relevant.

If you tend to be risk averse, remind yourself that it's easier to take risks while you're young. Setbacks and failures are much easier to recover from when you're 25 than when you're 55. In fact, in comparing risk-taking propensity among people between ages 22 and 58, it was found that both risk taking and the value placed upon risk was negatively related to age. That is, as we get older, we tend to become more conservative toward assuming risk. This is probably because older individuals perceive themselves as having more to lose. So leverage your "youth and inexperience." If you're going to quit a job or start a business, consider doing it sooner rather than later. It's easier to accept a setback when you're young, and you're more likely to become risk averse as you get older.

For those who fear failure, you need to be reminded that setbacks are not fatal. The landscape is littered with people who confronted early failure but rebounded to phenomenal success. Walt Disney was fired from the *Kansas City Star* because his editor felt he "lacked imagination and had no good ideas." Oprah Winfrey was fired from her first television job in Baltimore for getting "too emotionally invested in her stories." Sam Walton failed in his early attempts at retailing but eventually hit it big with Walmart. A film executive made the following assessment at seeing one of Fred Astaire's first screen tests: "Can't sing; can't act; slightly balding; can dance a little." Theodor Geisel, a.k.a. Dr. Seuss, had his first book rejected by 27 different publishers. And Steven Spielberg was rejected multiple times by the University of Southern California School of Cinematic Arts.

Nothing in our discussion should be interpreted as promoting unrestrained risk taking. Risk taking needs to be undertaken thoughtfully, intelligently, selectively, and with careful consideration of probabilities. Options with minimal chance of success, regardless of payoffs, are gambles and should be avoided. However, you don't want to miss opportunities with good chances of success just because they have potential for failure.[9]

The first thing that entrepreneurs like Sara Blakely must do is to identify opportunities and possible competitive advantages. Once they've identified the opportunities, they're ready to start the venture by researching its feasibility and then planning for its launch. These start-up and planning issues are what we're going to look at in this section.

Identifying Environmental Opportunities and Competitive Advantage

Jack Ma was an English teacher in China. On a visit to Seattle in 1998, he saw a computer connected to the web for the first time. On a whim, he searched for "beer." The search engine showed sites from around the world but nothing in China. He searched for "Chinese beer." Again, nothing. Ma recognized that small- and medium-sized businesses were invisible on the web. He saw an opportunity—to create a website where Chinese businesses could connect with each other. That was the impetus for what would become Alibaba, an e-commerce site that now does in excess of $40 billion a year in sales.[10]

Undoubtedly others saw that small and medium businesses in China were not being served on the internet. But Jack Ma did something about it. As we noted in the previous chapter, opportunities are positive trends in external environmental factors. These trends provide unique and distinct possibilities for innovating and creating value. Entrepreneurs need to be able to pinpoint these pockets of opportunities that a changing context provides.[11] After all, organizations do not see opportunities; individuals do. And they need to do so quickly, especially in dynamic environments, before those opportunities disappear or are exploited by others.

The late Peter Drucker, a well-known management author, identified seven potential sources of opportunity that entrepreneurs might look for in the external context.[13]

1. *The unexpected.* When situations and events are unanticipated, opportunities can be found. The event may be an unexpected success (positive news) or an unexpected failure (bad news). Either way, it may present opportunities for entrepreneurs to pursue. For instance, it came as a surprise in May 2018 when the Supreme Court struck down a prohibition on sports betting in states outside of Nevada. But Buffalo Wild Wings's management saw it as a potential opportunity. As the largest sports bar in America, the company saw itself as uniquely positioned to leverage sports gaming to enhance its business. As millennials have indicated declining interest in chain dining experiences, BWW's management envisions sports gambling as a possible way to coax them back.[14]

2. *The incongruous.* When something is incongruous, it exhibits inconsistencies and incompatibilities in the way it appears. Things "ought to be" a certain way, but aren't. When conventional wisdom about the way things should be no longer holds true, for whatever reason, opportunities are present. Entrepreneurs who are willing to "think outside the box"—that is, to think beyond the traditional and conventional approaches—may find pockets of potential profitability. Herb Kelleher, founder of Southwest Airlines, recognized incongruities in the way that commercial airlines catered to the traveling public. Most airlines focused on providing full service, including meals, to business travelers on routes between large business hubs. Ticket prices were high, but business travelers could absorb the cost. Although this approach was profitable, it ignored the opportunity to serve leisure travelers who wanted to travel between smaller cities (not business hubs). Kelleher knew that a better way was possible. His company offered lower fares with no-frill service.[15] Southwest Airlines has been profitable ever since.

3. *The process need.* What happens when technology doesn't immediately come up with the "big discovery" that's going to fundamentally change the nature of some product or service? What happens is the emergence of pockets of entrepreneurial opportunity in the various stages of the process as researchers and technicians continue to work for the monumental breakthrough. Because the full leap hasn't been possible, opportunities abound in the tiny steps. Take the medical products industry, for example. Although researchers haven't yet discovered a cure for cancer, many successful entrepreneurial biotechnology ventures have been created as knowledge about a possible cure continues to grow. Some process needs are more easily addressed. Decades ago, a variety

fyi

Eighty-six percent of new entrepreneurs start their businesses in response to an opportunity rather than the necessity of being unemployed and looking for a job.[12]

of inventors developed technology that led to the creation of ATMs in the late 1960s. As customers became more comfortable with self-service banking, ATMs became ubiquitous. Later, the internet gave way to full-service, online banking.

4. *Industry and market structures.* When changes in technology change the structure of an industry and market, existing firms can become obsolete if they're not attuned to the changes or are unwilling to change. Even changes in social values and consumer tastes can shift the structures of industries and markets. These markets and industries become open targets for nimble and smart entrepreneurs. For instance, eBay has prospered as an online intermediary between buyers and sellers. eBay's CEO says that the company's job is connecting people, not selling them things. And connect them they do! The online auction firm has more than 175 million active users.[16]

5. *Demographics.* The characteristics of the world population are changing. These changes influence industries and markets by altering the types and quantities of products and services desired and customers' buying power. Although many of these changes are fairly predictable if you stay alert to demographic trends, others aren't as obvious. Either way, significant entrepreneurial opportunities can be realized by anticipating and meeting the changing needs of the population. For example, WebMD has been successful partly because it anticipated the needs of the aging population. WebMD publishes news and information about human health and well-being for health care providers and consumers. Pharmaceutical companies also recognize the importance of demographic trends, which has led to substantial advertising on WebMD.[17]

6. *Changes in perception.* Perception is one's view of reality. When changes in perception take place, the facts do not vary, but their meanings do. Changes in perception get at the heart of people's psychographic profiles—what they value, what they believe in, and what they care about. Changes in these attitudes and values create potential market opportunities for alert entrepreneurs. For example, Airbnb cofounders Brian Chesky, Nathan Blecharczyk, and Joe Gebbia changed the perception that short-term home and apartment rentals to strangers is a bad idea. Brian Chesky said, "It's about people and experiences. At the end of the day, what we're trying to do is bring the world together. You're not getting a room, you're getting a sense of belonging."[18] In a few short years, the company began generating billions of dollars in revenue.

7. *New knowledge.* New knowledge is a significant source of entrepreneurial opportunity. Although not all knowledge-based innovations are significant, new knowledge ranks pretty high on the list of sources of entrepreneurial opportunity. It takes more than just having new knowledge, though. Entrepreneurs must be able to do something with that knowledge and to protect important proprietary information from competitors. For example, Intel pursues an entrepreneurial culture by following the latest academic research and investing heavily in R&D. The result has been the continual development of more powerful microprocessors and maintaining its position as a leading technology company.

Being alert to entrepreneurial opportunities is only part of an entrepreneur's initial efforts. He or she must also understand competitive advantage. As we discussed in Chapter 9, when an organization has a competitive advantage, it has something that other competitors don't, does something better than other organizations, or does something that others can't. Competitive advantage is a necessary ingredient for an entrepreneurial venture's long-term success and survival.

Researching the Venture's Feasibility—Ideas

Every year thousands of medical professionals enter the workforce, and 90 percent have to buy their own uniforms—called scrubs. Bland in style and poorly fitting, scrubs are a product that hasn't changed much in a century. Trina Spear (a financial specialist) and Heather Hasson (a fashion designer) had an idea: Let's design attractive, better-fitting scrubs; use high-tech fabrics; and sell them online directly to consumers. These women turned their idea into FIGS Scrubs.[19] Using Heather's experience and contacts in the fashion industry, they designed and produced a line of scrubs that were an immediate hit with nurses, doctors, and other healthcare workers. In just a few short years, they created a $100 million a year business.

It's important for entrepreneurs to research the venture's feasibility by generating and evaluating business ideas. Entrepreneurial ventures thrive on ideas. Generating ideas is an innovative, creative process. It's also one that will take time, not only in the beginning stages of the entrepreneurial venture, but throughout the life of the business. Where do ideas come from?

GENERATING IDEAS Entrepreneurs cite unique and varied sources for their ideas. One survey, for instance, found the highest responses were given to "sudden insight or chance" and "following a passion."[21]

What should entrepreneurs look for as they explore these idea sources? They should look for limitations of what's currently available, new and different approaches, advances and breakthroughs, unfilled niches, or trends and changes. A strong case can be made for using *design thinking* to generate ideas.[22] This could include cognitive exercises like drawing associations between situations, transferring something that works in one situation to a totally different situation, and rethinking the use for a product or service. This was essentially the approach that the founders of Zipcar, the ride-sharing company, used as they reconceived the car as a means of transportation, not a possession. Similarly, video games didn't take off until upstart producers saw that they were in the entertainment industry and not the toy business.

Trina Spear and Heather Hasson took their idea for a line of uniforms for medical professionals and developed a multimillion-dollar business.
Source: FIGS photo (Spear and Hasson)

Let's Get REAL

Whitney Portman ▸
Senior Marketing Communications Manager

Source: Whitney Portman

The Scenario:

Nick Rossi is excited to start working on his business plan to pursue his dream of opening a music store. He plans to sell mostly guitars, but thinks he should also sell some percussion instruments and a wide variety of accessories. However, he still has some research to do on the feasibility of his ideas. His competition is one area that he needs to explore further.

What should Nick learn about his competitors?

Learning about your competitive set is a key component to the success of your business plan. First, start with researching direct competitors, then expand to indirect competitors, either in close geographical proximity or online. How long have they been in business? What did they start out selling and how have they expanded? What's been the biggest contributors to their success and failures? You can learn a lot from those that have come before you. Then you should also consider future competitors: Are there any innovations on the horizon that would threaten your business plan? How can you safeguard against them? The goal is to determine where the unmet need is in the marketplace. What are customers looking for that the current competitive landscape does not offer? Once you can answer that question, you've identified your opportunity.

feasibility study
An analysis of the various aspects of a proposed entrepreneurial venture designed to determine its feasibility

EVALUATING IDEAS Evaluating entrepreneurial ideas revolves around personal and marketplace considerations. Each of these assessments will provide an entrepreneur with key information about the idea's potential. Exhibit 10-1 describes some questions that entrepreneurs might ask as they evaluate potential ideas.

A more structured evaluation approach that an entrepreneur should consider is a **feasibility study**—an analysis of the various aspects of a proposed entrepreneurial venture designed to determine its feasibility. Not only is a well-prepared feasibility study an effective evaluation tool to determine whether an entrepreneurial idea is a potentially successful one, it also can serve as a basis for the all-important business plan.

A feasibility study should give descriptions of the most important elements of the proposed venture and the entrepreneur's analysis of the viability of these elements. It should cover an analysis of the environment and competition as well as accounting projections, sources of funds, personnel requirements, equipment needs, the target market, and legal considerations.

Researching the Venture's Feasibility—Competitors

Part of researching the venture's feasibility is looking at the competitors. What would entrepreneurs like to know about their potential competitors? Here are some possible questions:

What types of products or services are competitors offering?

What are the major characteristics of these products or services?

What are their products' strengths and weaknesses?

How do they handle marketing, pricing, and distribution?

What do they attempt to do differently from other competitors?

Do they appear to be successful at it? Why or why not?

What are they good at?

What competitive advantage(s) do they appear to have?

What are they not so good at?

What competitive disadvantage(s) do they appear to have?

How large and profitable are these competitors?

For instance, the CEO of The Children's Place carefully examined the competition as he took his chain of children's clothing stores nationwide. Although he faced

Exhibit 10-1
Evaluating Potential Ideas

Personal Considerations	Marketplace Considerations
• Do you have the capabilities to do what you've selected?	• Who are the potential customers for your idea: who, where, how many?
• Are you ready to be an entrepreneur?	
• Are you prepared emotionally to deal with the stresses and challenges of being an entrepreneur?	• What similar or unique product features does your proposed idea have compared to what's currently on the market?
• Are you prepared to deal with rejection and failure?	• How and where will potential customers purchase your product?
• Are you ready to work hard?	
• Do you have a realistic picture of the venture's potential?	• Have you considered pricing issues and whether the price you'll be able to charge will allow your venture to survive and prosper?
• Have you educated yourself about financing issues?	
• Are you willing and prepared to do continual financial and other types of analyses?	• Have you considered how you will need to promote and advertise your proposed entrepreneurial venture?

stiff competition from the likes of GapKids, JCPenney, and Gymboree, he felt that his company's approach to manufacturing and marketing would give it a competitive edge. He was obviously right! Gymboree went bankrupt, and JCPenney is on life support.[24]

Researching the Venture's Feasibility—Financing

Historically, getting financing for a new venture was a very difficult hurdle to jump. Surprisingly, this is an area that has changed a lot in recent years. And that change has been positive for entrepreneurs.

Traditional sources of funds for entrepreneurs have been personal savings, home equity, personal loans, credit cards, and supportive family and friends. Today, there are a lot of venture capitalists competing to invest in new businesses. In just one two-week period, Letgo, an online classified ads company, raised $500 million; Actifio, a data storage company, took in $100 million; MyDreamPlus, a co-working space start-up, obtained $120 million; and Klook, a travel activity booking site, got $200 million.[25] As these examples illustrate, if an idea has merit, there is money available.

Developing a Business Plan

Once the venture's feasibility has been thoroughly researched, the entrepreneur then must look at planning the venture. The most important element in planning the venture is developing a **business plan**—a written document that summarizes a business opportunity and defines and articulates how the identified opportunity is to be seized and exploited.[26]

A good business plan is valuable. It pulls together all of the elements of the entrepreneur's vision into a single coherent document. It serves as a blueprint and road map for operating the business. And the business plan is a "living" document, guiding organizational decisions and actions throughout the life of the business, not just in the start-up stage.

If an entrepreneur has completed a feasibility study, much of the information included in it becomes the basis for the business plan. A good business plan covers six major areas: executive summary, analysis of opportunity, analysis of the context, description of the business, financial data and projections, and supporting documentation.

EXECUTIVE SUMMARY The executive summary distills the key points that the entrepreneur wants to make about the proposed entrepreneurial venture. These points might include a brief mission statement; primary goals; a brief history of the entrepreneurial venture, maybe in the form of a timeline; key people involved in the venture; the nature of the business; concise product or service descriptions; brief explanations of market niche, competitors, and competitive advantage; proposed strategies; and key financial information.

ANALYSIS OF OPPORTUNITY In this section of the business plan, an entrepreneur presents the details of the perceived opportunity. Essentially, details include (1) sizing up the market by describing the demographics of the target market, (2) describing and evaluating industry trends, and (3) identifying and evaluating competitors.

ANALYSIS OF THE CONTEXT Whereas the opportunity analysis focuses on the opportunity in a specific industry and market, the context analysis takes a much broader perspective. Here, the entrepreneur describes the broad external changes and trends taking place in the economic, political-legal, technological, and global environments.

DESCRIPTION OF THE BUSINESS In this section, an entrepreneur describes how the entrepreneurial venture is going to be organized, launched, and managed. It includes a thorough description of the mission statement; a description of the desired

fyi
- Entrepreneurs increase their success by 125 percent when they have work experience in the same sector as the business they're starting.
- Entrepreneurs who have business venture failures increase their chances of success with their next venture by 20 percent.[23]

business plan
A written document that summarizes a business opportunity and defines and articulates how the identified opportunity is to be seized and exploited

organizational culture; marketing plans, including overall marketing strategy, pricing, sales tactics, and advertising and promotion tactics; product development plans with risks and costs; operational plans including a description of proposed geographic location, facilities and needed improvements, equipment, and work flow; human resource plans including staffing, compensation, and training; and an overall schedule and timetable of events.

FINANCIAL DATA AND PROJECTIONS   No business plan is complete without financial data and projections. Financial plans should cover at least three years and contain projected income statements, *pro forma* cash flow analysis, *pro forma* balance sheets, breakeven analysis, and cost controls. If major equipment or other capital purchases are expected, the items, costs, and available collateral should be listed.

SUPPORTING DOCUMENTATION   For this important component of an effective business plan, the entrepreneur should back up his or her descriptions with charts, graphs, tables, photographs, or other visual tools. In addition, it might be important to include information (personal and work-related) about the key participants in the entrepreneurial venture.

ORGANIZING issues

LO10.3   Roy Ng, former chief operating officer at Twilio in San Francisco, California, redesigned his organization's structure by transforming it into an employee-empowered company. He wanted to drive authority down through the organization so employees were responsible for their own efforts. One way he did this was by creating employee teams to handle specific projects. He says, "Small teams allow for autonomy, rapid experimentation and innovation. Small teams have enabled Twilio's ability to grow and scale, and at the same time maintain the same level of passion, hunger, resourcefulness and productivity our founding team had on day one."[27]

Once the start-up and planning issues are complete, the entrepreneur is ready to begin the organizing stage. Three organizing issues should be addressed: the legal form of the organization, organizational design and structure, and human resource management.

Legal Forms of Organization

The first organizing decision that an entrepreneur must make is the form of legal ownership for the venture. The two primary factors affecting this decision are taxes and legal liability. An entrepreneur wants to minimize the impact of both of these factors. The right choice can protect the entrepreneur from legal liability as well as save tax dollars.

What alternatives are available? The three basic ways to organize an entrepreneurial venture are sole proprietorship, partnership, and corporation. However, when you include the variations of these basic organizational alternatives, you end up with six possible choices, each with its own tax consequences, liability issues, and pros and cons. These six choices are sole proprietorship, general partnership, limited liability partnership (LLP), C corporation, S corporation, and limited liability company (LLC). Let's briefly look at each one with their advantages and drawbacks. (Exhibit 10-2 summarizes the basic information about each organizational alternative.)

Entrepreneurs need to decide on the form of legal ownership for their venture.
Source: IQoncept/Shutterstock

SOLE PROPRIETORSHIP   A **sole proprietorship** is a form of legal organization in which the owner maintains sole and complete control over the business and is personally liable for business debts. The legal requirements for establishing a sole proprietorship consist of obtaining the necessary local business licenses and permits. In a sole proprietorship, income and losses "pass through" to the owner and are taxed at the owner's personal income tax rate. The biggest drawback, however, is the unlimited personal liability for any and all debts of the business.

sole proprietorship
A form of legal organization in which the owner maintains sole and complete control over the business and is personally liable for business debts

GENERAL PARTNERSHIP   A **general partnership** is a form of legal organization in which two or more business owners share the management and risk of the business. Even though a partnership is possible without a written agreement, the potential and inevitable problems that arise in any partnership make a written partnership agreement drafted by legal counsel highly recommended.

general partnership
A form of legal organization in which two or more business owners share the management and risk of the business

LIMITED LIABILITY PARTNERSHIP (LLP)   The **limited liability partnership (LLP)** is a legal organization composed of general partner(s) and limited partner(s). The general partners actually operate and manage the business. They are the ones who have unlimited liability. At least one general partner is necessary in an LLP, but any number of limited partners are allowed. Limited partners are usually passive investors, although they can make management suggestions to the general partners. They also have the right to inspect the business and make copies of business records. The limited partners are entitled to a share of the business's profits as agreed to in the partnership agreement and, very importantly, their risk is limited to the amount of their investment in the LLP.

limited liability partnership (LLP)
A form of legal organization consisting of general partner(s) and limited liability partner(s)

corporation
A legal business entity that is separate from its owners and managers

C CORPORATION   Of the three basic types of ownership, the corporation (also known as a C corporation) is the most complex to form and operate. A **corporation** is a legal business entity that is separate from its owners and managers. Many entrepreneurial ventures are organized as a **closely held corporation**, which, very simply, is a

closely held corporation
A corporation owned by a limited number of people who do not trade the stock publicly

Exhibit 10-2
Legal Forms of Business Organization

Structure	Ownership Requirements	Tax Treatment	Liability	Advantages	Drawbacks
Sole proprietorship	One owner	Income and losses "pass through" to owner and are taxed at personal rate	Unlimited personal liability	Low start-up costs Freedom from most regulations *Owner has direct control* All profits go to owner *Easy to exit business*	Unlimited personal liability *Personal finances at risk* Miss out on many business tax deductions *Total responsibility* May be more difficult to raise financing
General partnership	Two or more owners	Income and losses "pass through" to partners and are taxed at personal rate; *flexibility in profit-loss allocations to partners*	Unlimited personal liability	*Ease of formation* Pooled talent *Pooled resources* Somewhat easier access to financing *Some tax benefits*	*Unlimited personal liability* Divided authority and decisions *Potential for conflict* Continuity of transfer of ownership
Limited liability partnership (LLP)	Two or more owners	Income and losses "pass through" to partner and are taxed at personal rate; *flexibility in profit-loss allocations to partners*	Limited, although one partner must retain unlimited liability	Good way to acquire capital from limited partners	*Cost and complexity of forming can be high* Limited partners cannot participate in management of business without losing liability protection
C corporation	Unlimited number of shareholders; *no limits on types of stock or voting arrangements*	Dividend income is taxed at corporate and personal shareholder levels; *losses and deductions are corporate*	Limited	*Limited liability* Transferable ownership *Continuous existence* Easier access to resources	*Expensive to set up* Closely regulated *Double taxation* Extensive record keeping *Charter restrictions*
S corporation	Up to 75 shareholders; *no limits on types of stock or voting arrangements*	Income and losses "pass through" to partners and are taxed at personal rate; *flexibility in profit-loss allocation to partners*	Limited	*Easy to set up* Enjoy limited liability protection and tax benefits of partnership *Can have a tax-exempt entity as a shareholder*	Must meet certain requirements *May limit future financing options*
Limited liability company (LLC)	Unlimited number of "members"; *flexible membership arrangements for voting rights and income*	Income and losses "pass through" to partners and are taxed at personal rate; *flexibility in profit-loss allocations to partners*	Limited	Greater flexibility Not constrained by regulations on C and S corporations *Taxed as partnership, not as corporation*	Cost of switching from one form to this can be high *Need legal and financial advice in forming operating agreement*

corporation owned by a limited number of people who do not trade the stock publicly. Whereas the sole proprietorship and partnership forms of organization don't exist separately from the entrepreneur, the corporation does. The corporation functions as a distinct legal entity and, as such, can make contracts, engage in business activities, own property, sue and be sued, and of course, pay taxes. A corporation must operate in accordance with its charter and the laws of the state in which it operates.

S CORPORATION   The **S corporation** (also called a subchapter S corporation) is a specialized type of corporation that has the regular characteristics of a corporation but is unique in that the owners are taxed as a partnership as long as certain criteria are met. The S corporation has been the classic organizing approach for having the limited liability of a corporate structure without incurring corporate tax. However, this form of legal organization must meet strict criteria. If any of these criteria are violated, a venture's S status is automatically terminated.

> **S corporation**
> A specialized type of corporation that has the regular characteristics of a corporation but is unique in that the owners are taxed as a partnership as long as certain criteria are met

LIMITED LIABILITY COMPANY (LLC)   The **limited liability company (LLC)** is a hybrid between a partnership and a corporation. The LLC offers the liability protection of a corporation, the tax benefits of a partnership, and fewer restrictions than an S corporation. However, the main drawback of this approach is that it's quite complex and expensive to set up. Legal and financial advice is an absolute necessity in forming the LLC's **operating agreement**, the document that outlines the provisions governing the way the LLC will conduct business.

> **limited liability company (LLC)**
> A form of legal organization that's a hybrid between a partnership and a corporation

> **operating agreement**
> The document that outlines the provisions governing the way an LLC will conduct business

SUMMARY OF LEGAL FORMS OF ORGANIZATION   The organizing decision regarding the legal form of organization is important because it can have significant control, tax, and liability consequences. An entrepreneur needs to think carefully about what's important, especially in the areas of flexibility, taxes, and amount of personal liability in choosing the best form of organization.

Organizational Design and Structure

At some point, successful entrepreneurs find that they can't do everything themselves. More people are needed. The entrepreneur must then decide on the most appropriate structural arrangement for effectively and efficiently carrying out the organization's activities. Without some suitable type of organizational structure, the entrepreneurial venture may soon find itself in a chaotic situation.

In many small firms, the organizational structure tends to evolve with little intentional or deliberate planning by the entrepreneur. For the most part, the structure may be simple—one person does whatever is needed. As the entrepreneurial venture grows and the entrepreneur finds it increasingly difficult to go it alone, employees are brought on board to perform certain functions or duties that the entrepreneur can't handle. These individuals tend to perform those same functions as the company grows. Then, as the entrepreneurial venture continues to grow, each of these functional areas may require managers and employees.

With the evolution to a more deliberate structure, the entrepreneur faces a new set of challenges: sharing decision-making and operating responsibilities. This transition is typically one of the most difficult things for an entrepreneur to do—letting go and allowing someone else to make decisions. *After all*, he or she reasons, *how can anyone know this business as well as I do*? Also, what might have been a fairly informal, loose, and flexible atmosphere that worked well when the organization was small may no longer be effective. Many entrepreneurs are greatly concerned about keeping that "small company" atmosphere alive even as the venture grows and evolves requiring a more structured arrangement. But having a structured organization doesn't necessarily mean giving up flexibility, adaptability, and freedom. In fact, the structural design may be as fluid as the entrepreneur feels comfortable with and yet still have the rigidity it needs to operate efficiently. In Chapter 11, we will review various forms of organization structure and consider each's strengths and weaknesses. Many are well designed for use by entrepreneurs.

Human Resource Management

As an entrepreneurial venture grows, additional employees will need to be hired to handle the increased workload. As the need for more personnel increases, the entrepreneur faces numerous human resource management (HRM) issues: Two HRM issues of particular importance are employee recruitment and employee retention.

EMPLOYEE RECRUITMENT The ability of small firms to successfully recruit appropriate employees is consistently rated as one of the most important factors influencing organizational success.[28]

In the early stages, entrepreneurs typically look for individuals who "buy into" the venture's culture—individuals who have a passion for the business and fit with the personality of the founder. Unlike their corporate counterparts, who usually focus on filling a job by matching a person to the job requirements, entrepreneurs look to fill in critical skill gaps. They're looking for people who are exceptionally capable and self-motivated, flexible, and multi-skilled, and who can help grow the entrepreneurial venture.[29] Entrepreneurs emphasize matching characteristics of applicants to the values and culture of the upstart organization.

EMPLOYEE RETENTION Once hired, the challenge is to keep new employees. Founder and CEO Scott Signore of Matter Communications, a public relations agency based in Newburyport, Massachusetts, understands the importance of having good people on board and keeping them. Signore says: "There's a lot of credit to share amongst our team for embracing a healthy, energetic, fun culture that sets us apart as a PR agency."[30] For instance, one of the benefits is "Summer Fridays," which includes a beer keg on tap in the kitchen and an early closing time. Its fun culture has helped land the company a spot on the *Boston Globe's* Top Places to Work list. Katie Johnston, *Boston Globe* workplace reporter, said: "The winning companies have developed innovative ways to engage and motivate their workers, which often serves as a key factor in innovation and leads to better professional performance."[31]

A major component of whether employees stay is compensation. While traditional organizations are more likely to view compensation from the perspective of monetary rewards (base pay, benefits, and incentives), smaller entrepreneurial firms tend to take a wider view. For these firms, compensation encompasses psychological rewards, learning opportunities, and recognition in addition to monetary rewards.[32] However, as we see in many new high-tech start-ups, the potential to receive and eventually cash-in stock options can be a powerful force in retaining employees.

LEADING issues

LO10.4 The employees at the software firm ClearCompany have to be flexible. Everyone is expected to contribute ideas. CEO and cofounder Andre Lavoie said: "One way to give employees more [creative] freedom over how they work is to shift the focus from to-do lists and deadlines to goals and objectives—quantity to quality." In return, Lavoie is a supportive leader who gives his employees considerable latitude.[33]

As an entrepreneurial venture grows and people are brought on board, an entrepreneur takes on a new role—that of a leader. In this section, we want to look at what's involved with the leading function. First, we're going to look at the unique personality characteristics of entrepreneurs. Then we're going to discuss the important role entrepreneurs play in motivating employees through empowerment and leading the venture and employee teams.

Personality Characteristics of Entrepreneurs

Think of someone you know who is an entrepreneur. Maybe it's someone you personally know, or someone you've read about like Mark Zuckerberg at Facebook. How would you describe this person's personality? One of the most researched areas of entrepreneurship has been the search to determine what—if any—psychological characteristics entrepreneurs have in common, what types of personality traits entrepreneurs have that might distinguish them from nonentrepreneurs, and what traits entrepreneurs have that might predict who will be a successful entrepreneur.[34]

Successful entrepreneurs, such as Facebook CEO Mark Zuckerberg, often have personality traits that make them stand apart from others.
Source: Frederic Legrand—COMEO/ Shutterstock

Is there a general "entrepreneurial type"? No. This, however, hasn't stopped entrepreneurship researchers from listing common traits. For instance, one list of personality characteristics included the following: high level of motivation, abundance of self-confidence, ability to be involved for the long term, high energy level, persistent problem solver, high degree of initiative, ability to set goals, and moderate risk-taker. Another list of characteristics of "successful" entrepreneurs included high energy level, great persistence, resourcefulness, the desire and ability to be self-directed, and relatively high need for autonomy. A Gallup survey of nearly 200 highly successful entrepreneurs found ten strengths that all had in some quantity. They're listed in Exhibit 10-3.

While there is no general entrepreneurial type, one of the more powerful predictors of entrepreneurial intent is the possession of a **proactive personality**—these are people who have a disposition toward taking intentional action to influence their situation or environment.[35] From an entrepreneurial perspective, they firmly believe that they control the fate of their business. In terms of specific characteristics, proactive types (1) don't just see an opportunity, they take the initiative to act on it; (2) see obstacles as personal challenges to overcome; (3) strongly believe that they are masters of their own fate; (4) demonstrate persistence until they reach their goals; and (5) embrace and drive change.[36]

proactive personality
A personality trait that describes individuals who have a disposition towards taking intentional action to influence their situation or environment

The Entrepreneur as Leader

We'll discuss leadership at length in Chapter 17, but there are some unique challenges that are specific to the entrepreneur, especially in the early stages of a venture.[37] Let's begin with the recognition that the motivation to create a business and the possession of a good idea do not automatically translate into effective leadership. One of the most common causes for a new business's failure is the inability

Risk: Can manage high-risk situations; mitigating risk rather than seeking it
Knowledge: Strives to acquire in-depth information about the industry
Independence: Can manage every aspect of his/her organization
Confidence: Believes in oneself and his/her ability to succeed
Delegation: Unafraid to assign tasks to others
Determination: Strong work ethic; undeterred by failure
Relationships: Able to build mutually beneficial relationships
Selling: Speaks boldly on behalf of the organization; can influence others
Profitability: Sets clear goals; measures progress; good judge of opportunities
Disruption: Constantly has new ideas for products and services

Exhibit 10-3
Strengths of Entrepreneurs
Cited in L. Buchanan, "What It Takes," Inc., September 2018, pp. 14–15.

for the entrepreneur to provide the required leadership. Regardless of how great the idea is, the financial backing, or the demand for the product or service, if the entrepreneur can't exhibit the relevant leadership skills, the business is likely to fail. Unfortunately, the personality characteristics, skills, and motivation that it takes to lead a start-up business are rarely the same ones required to run a large, established organization.

It can help if you think of a new venture as proceeding through three stages: start-up, transition, and scaling. Each stage comes with specific challenges and leadership requirements.

At the *start-up stage*, the entrepreneur is defining the business: a general business plan is created, and the first hires are made. But the entrepreneur is the heart and soul of the business. There are no policies or procedures for new hires to follow. The entrepreneur/leader's vision is in his or her head. And the leadership style is hands-on. Employees will look to the entrepreneur for guidance, and this will place increased demands on his or her time. Meanwhile, the entrepreneur is nearly always in close proximity to "the action." He or she knows everything that is going on and expects to make most of the decisions. And because there is no history or precedents, employees are apt to expect the founder to make most of the decisions. The organization can best be described as informal, flexible, and ambiguous.

The *transition stage* is when the venture moves from an informal and loosely structured start-up into a disciplined business that can adapt to rapid expansion. Jobs become specialized and standardized policies are introduced. And this is when the entrepreneur must learn to delegate authority. Many entrepreneurs have difficulty making this transition from a "one-person does it all" style to being part of a functionally organized, professional management team. This is because it requires the entrepreneur to give up some control, and this can be very hard—sometimes impossible—for the proactive personality.

Once a venture has progressed to the *scaling stage*, much of the "uniqueness" of entrepreneurship has disappeared. At this point, the concepts of management become fairly generalizable.

Learning from
FAILURE   The Third Time Is a Charm for Vera Wang

If you know the name Vera Wang, it's probably because she's one of the world's premier fashion designers. But before her success as a designer, she had disappointments as a figure skater and a magazine editor.

As a child, Wang was an ice-skating prodigy. She trained rigorously with the hopes of someday making the US Olympic team. As a high school student, she placed in the 1968 US Figure Skating Championships. However, by her late teens, she had to accept the reality that her ability had peaked and she wasn't going to improve. There were younger skaters coming up that were going to be better than her. So she quit.

Wang went on to a fifteen-year career at *Vogue* magazine, eventually working her way up to senior fashion editor.

When she was passed over for the editor-in-chief job, she quit.

In 1989, engaged to be married, Wang became frustrated at the available selection of bridal gowns. So she designed her own. The following year she opened up her own bridal boutique in New York City. The rest, as they say, is history.

Today this successful entrepreneur is the head designer of her own brand—which includes bridal, ready-to-wear, publishing, fragrance, beauty accessories, and home decor. She says, "Don't be afraid of failing. I think not trying is worse than failing." And what has she learned from her earlier setbacks? That her strength was design and that she had the entrepreneurial skills to create and run her own firm.[38]

CONTROL issues

LO10.5 While all businesses need effective controls, a case can be made that this is more critical for new start-ups and small businesses. Why? Because they're more vulnerable to shocks or setbacks. They don't have the resources—financial, personnel, customer base—to withstand problems that large, established businesses can absorb. One slow-paying customer, a loss of a key employee, or a breakdown in the supply chain can literally put a young business on life support or even close down the venture.

Potential Control Problems and Actions

Common causes of small-business failures suggest areas that need close monitoring: inadequate cash reserves; new competitors; loss of a major customer; expanding too rapidly; poor hiring; and unwillingness to delegate.

The above should lead entrepreneurs to particularly develop controls that address these potential problems:

Keep a close eye on the numbers. Entrepreneurs who lack expertise in accounting and finance need to make sure that someone—working internally or hired from the outside—is watching expenses, cash flow, inventory costs, sales orders, receivables, payables, and the like.

Monitor the competition and potential competition. Competitive intelligence is as important to small businesses as it is to large corporations. And the ability to respond quickly to actions of the competition are critical to maintaining the new venture's viability.

Maintain regular contact with customers. Are customers satisfied with your products or service? What are their complaints or concerns? Is your marketing attracting new customers?

Monitor employee performance. Are employees performing as expected? What skills might they be lacking? What additional training do they need?

Monitor employee workloads. Are important tasks being ignored or poorly performed? Is the founder or other key people trying to do too much?

Exiting the Venture

Getting out of an entrepreneurial venture may seem to be a strange thing for entrepreneurs to do. At some point, however, the entrepreneur is likely to decide that it's time to move on.

What are the exit options?[39] There are essentially five: (1) *Merger or acquisition.* The entrepreneur sells his or her controlling interest in the business to the buying company. (2) *Selling to a friendly buyer*. This might be to a family member, a friend, or acquaintance. (3) *Initiate an IPO*. If the business has grown and proven successful, an initial public offering allows the entrepreneur to sell shares of the business to the general public. (4) *Treat it as a cash cow*. Use profits to take a large salary and bonus. "Milk" the business for as long as possible. (5) *Liquidation*. Sell off assets and close down the business.

If the entrepreneur decides to sell, what should he or she use to establish a fair price? Valuation techniques generally fall into three categories: (1) asset valuations (assets less liabilities); (2) earnings valuations, and (3) cash flow valuations. For the latter two, the price is typically calculated at some multiple of earnings or cash flow. In many cases, the entrepreneur has sacrificed much for the business and sees it as his or her "baby." Calculating the value of the business based on objective standards such as cash flow or some multiple of net profits can often feel to the founder like the business is undervalued. To obtain a fair-market price, it's best to have a comprehensive business valuation prepared by professionals.

| Chapter 10 | **PREPARING FOR:** Exams/Quizzes |

CHAPTER SUMMARY by Learning Objectives

LO10.1 **DEFINE** entrepreneurship and explain why it's important.

Entrepreneurship is the process of starting new businesses, generally in response to opportunities. Entrepreneurial ventures are different from small businesses. Entrepreneurial ventures are characterized by innovative ideas and are motivated by a passion that goes beyond profits, whereas a small business usually involves doing something that others already are doing and typically is motivated by the desire to make a living. Entrepreneurs must explore the entrepreneurial context, identify opportunities and possible competitive advantages, start the venture, and manage the venture. Entrepreneurship is important due to its impact on innovation, economic growth, and job creation.

LO10.2 **EXPLAIN** what entrepreneurs do in the planning process for new ventures.

Entrepreneurs must identify environmental opportunities and competitive advantage. They must research a venture's feasibility, first generating ideas and then evaluating ideas. Design thinking may be used to generate ideas while a structured way of evaluating ideas is through a feasibility study. A feasibility study is an analysis of the various aspects of a proposed entrepreneurial venture designed to determine its feasibility. This analysis includes looking at the competitors, determining how to get financing, and developing a business plan. The business plan should include an executive summary, an analysis of the opportunity, an analysis of the context, a description of the business, financial data and projections, and supporting documentation.

LO10.3 **DESCRIBE** the six legal forms of organization and the choice of appropriate organizational structure.

Two primary factors that affect the decision about how to organize a business are taxes and legal liability. In a sole proprietorship, the owner maintains sole and complete control over the business and is personally liable for business debts. In a general partnership, two or more owners share the management and risk of the business. A limited liability partnership is formed by general partner(s) and limited partner(s). A corporation (C corporation) is a legal business entity that is separate from its owners and managers. It is a closely held corporation when it is owned by a limited number of people who do not trade the stock publicly. An S corporation is a corporation that is unique because the owners are taxed as a partnership as long as certain criteria are met. A limited liability company (LLC) is a hybrid between a partnership and a corporation. As an organization grows, the entrepreneur must decide on an appropriate structure for the organization. The entrepreneur must also face human resource management issues such as employee recruitment and employee retention.

LO10.4 **DESCRIBE** how entrepreneurs lead organizations.

While there is no specific personality characteristic that all entrepreneurs have, researchers suggest that there are several personality traits that are more common among entrepreneurs. These include a high level of motivation, an abundance of self-confidence, the ability to be involved for the long term, and a high energy level. Entrepreneurs are often persistent problem solvers; have a high degree of initiative;

have the ability to set goals; are moderate risk-takers; possess great persistence, resourcefulness, the desire and ability to be self-directed; and have a relatively high need for autonomy. Entrepreneurs may also have a proactive personality trait, which means they are more prone to take actions to influence their environment. In the start-up stage, entrepreneurs' leadership is informal and hands-on, but it needs to involve more delegating in the transition stage. Once a venture is in the scaling stage, entrepreneurs' leadership becomes similar to leadership found in other types of organizations.

LO10.5 **EXPLAIN** how managers control organizations and exit the venture.

Entrepreneurs should develop controls that address problems related to: accounting/finance, competition, customers, employee performance, and employee workloads. When entrepreneurs decide that it's time to get out of a venture, there are five exit options they might consider: merger or acquisition, selling to a friendly buyer, initiate an initial public offering (IPO), treat it as a cash cow, or liquidation. To establish a fair price for the venture, it often is best to have a comprehensive business valuation prepared by professionals.

REVIEW AND DISCUSSION QUESTIONS

10-1. What do you think would be the hardest thing about being an entrepreneur? What do you think would be the most fun?

10-2. Why are entrepreneurs important to society?

10-3. Would a good manager be a good entrepreneur? Discuss.

10-4. Why do you think many entrepreneurs find it hard to step aside and let others manage their business?

10-5. Do you think a person can be taught to be an entrepreneur? Why or why not?

PREPARING FOR: My Career

ETHICS DILEMMA

You have started a business named Let 'US'help. Let 'US'help refers service providers who assist people to get mundane tasks done. You promise consumers that all service providers must first pass a background check and guarantee faster referrals or "your money back." Lately, the demand for services is much greater than ever anticipated, and you are working feverishly to fulfill customer requests.

To honor the money-back guarantee, you refer some providers without first conducting background checks.

10-6. What ethical dilemmas are involved with choosing not to conduct background checks?

10-7. Should you focus on providing timely placements or taking the extra time to complete background checks? Explain your answer.

SKILLS EXERCISE **Developing Grit**

Those who succeed as entrepreneurs have at least one thing in common; they possess grit.[40] Having grit means you have the perseverance and passion for long-term goals. When you have grit, you work hard and maintain effort and interest even after facing failure or adversity. Some say having grit means you have mental toughness. It is a

trait that brings together other qualities such as optimism, self-discipline, and self-motivation. You must have talent to accomplish your goals, but you must also have focused and sustained use of that talent over time in order to accomplish difficult goals. Grit helps entrepreneurs because they often face challenges and setbacks in the process of launching a venture. An entrepreneur with grit will continue working hard, even in the face of seemingly endless obstacles.

Steps in Practicing the Skill

- *Practice your resilience.* Resilience is the ability to bounce back. As you are faced with an obstacle, notice your reaction to the challenge. Are you ready to quit? If so, it is time to build your resilience. Learn from your mistake and make yourself give it another try instead of giving up.

- *Pursue your passion.* Figure out what you are passionate about in life and pursue it. Our passions inspire us and give us the internal drive to keep moving forward. Identifying and pursuing your passion can help develop your perseverance.

- *Practice positive self-talk.* Grit means you have a strong belief in yourself. By engaging in positive self-talk, you can develop the internal motivation to keep moving forward even as you face obstacles. Remind yourself of your abilities and be your own biggest cheerleader. With every challenge you face, make sure you encourage yourself to keep moving forward with a positive attitude.

- *Build in practice time.* Understand that anything significant you are going to accomplish in life is going to take time and effort. When working toward a goal, you must consider how you can practice whatever it is you are trying to accomplish. For example, if you have the dream to open a restaurant, spend some time working in other restaurants in order to really understand the business before jumping in on your own.

- *Put together a support team.* Identify some trusted friends and let them know you are working on developing grit. Share with them your future goals and what you want to work toward. Ask them to encourage you and make sure you call them for support when you are feeling like you might want to give up.

Practicing the Skill

Identify a challenging goal you would like to attain. You can start small, but make sure it is something that will test your abilities. For example, have you ever considered running a 5K race? Getting an A in your next statistics course? What is something significant you would like to accomplish? Once you set your goal, use the steps above as you work toward your goal. Once you accomplish your goal, move on to a new one. As you overcome the challenges along the way, you will find yourself developing grit. And then you can accomplish anything!

WORKING TOGETHER **Team Exercise**

Have you ever considered starting a business? Take a few minutes and brainstorm business ideas that you could start on your campus. What are problems that could be solved? Considering the idea of the sharing economy, what are things that students could share or a service you could provide for a fee? What kinds of products or services would students be willing to purchase? Get together in groups of three or four students and share your business ideas. Pick one idea to explore further. What would be your competitive advantage? Is the idea feasible? Who would be your competitors? Would it require financing to get started? Make a few notes on what you would write as an executive summary for a business plan for your idea. Be prepared to share with the class.

MY TURN TO BE A MANAGER

- To be an entrepreneur, you must first have an idea. Entrepreneurs get their ideas from many sources; however, an idea often hits when the entrepreneur steps out of his or her own comfort zone. Start by exposing yourself to new ideas and information. Ensure that you are following social media that taps into a wide variety of disciplines such as science, technology, sports, and the arts. Take as many classes outside of your own major that you can. Attend diverse events and network with people from a wide variety of backgrounds. Keep an idea journal with interesting ideas or information that you come across on a daily basis.

- Explore the innovations or business ideas of others. Visit www.springwise.com, a website that discovers and shares innovative ideas from around the world, and www.socialbusiness.org, a website that shares ideas and businesses

Rachel Nilsson, founder of Rags to Raches (now known simply as Rags), appeared on the television show *Shark Tank* seeking funding for her kids' clothing company. She cut a $200,000 deal, and within a month after her appearance, her daily sales had quintupled. The funding helped Nilsson turn her venture into a million-dollar clothing brand.
Source: Michael Desmond ABC/Walt Disney Television/Getty Images

that are creating positive social change. Add your thoughts and reflections on what you learn to your idea journal.

- Interview an entrepreneur. Ask how he or she discovered his or her business idea. What challenges did he or she face in starting the business? What do you think made the business succeed?

- Look online to find local resources or organizations that support entrepreneurs. Make a list of the resources that are available to entrepreneurs in your area.

- One of the biggest challenges start-ups face is obtaining funding. While only a very few businesses are able to obtain funding through the popular television show *Shark Tank,* you can learn a lot by watching how the "sharks" or venture capitalists on the show's panel make decisions on which ideas to invest in. Watch an episode of the show. Take note of why the sharks decide to invest in a particular business and why they let some contestants leave empty handed.

CASE APPLICATION 1

Becoming an Entrepreneur While In College with Brainz Power

Many college students pull all-nighters to study for midterms and finals. What Andrew Kozlovski noticed when he was a freshman at the University of Southern California was how many students were using Adderall to allow them to stay awake and concentrate. Andrew explained, "Kids all around me were exchanging it like money."[41] Individuals with attention deficit hyperactivity disorder (ADHD) may be prescribed Adderall to increase their attentiveness. But Andrew saw a potential national problem: 38.5 percent of college-age individuals report using ADHD medications for nonmedical reasons. In other words, they officially don't need Adderall but are using it to increase their focus.

Andrew did some research on Adderall and found out that it is highly addictive. Also, Adderall has all kinds of side effects that students taking it as a study aid often do not know. Andrew had issues with attentiveness himself, but he wondered if there was a safer option than Adderall. He immersed himself in research on natural supplements that could help focus, reduce stress, and improve overall mental health. Andrew found a lab that was licensed by the Food and Drug Administration (FDA). They were willing to create small batches of pills that used different combinations of the natural supplements on his list.[42] After some trial and error, Andrew came up with a formula and received FDA approval for it. He launched his company, Brainz Power, which sells this "non-caffeinated cognitive enhancement supplement."[43]

To get his company going, Andrew focused on connecting with potential customers via Instagram. "It's about connecting, the sales come after," Andrew said. The sales did come. Brainz Power averaged $10,000 in sales per month, rising to nearly $30,000 per month several years later.[44]

Andrew spent most of his college years working on his company. As he put it, "the hours are long. I don't sleep that much anymore. I work on the weekend. I work when all the other kids are partying ... if you think about it, I'm always busy, but I do it with a smile on my face the entire time."[45] Andrew didn't need to look for a job when he graduated from USC in May 2018. He had created his job—and a company—as a freshman.

DISCUSSION QUESTIONS

10-8. What did Andrew Kozlovski do well during the steps involved in the entrepreneurial process?

10-9. In what ways is Andrew an example of a hybrid path to entrepreneurship? Also, in what ways is he different from a typical person who takes the hybrid path to entrepreneurship?

10-10. What personality characteristics of entrepreneurs do you think Andrew has? Which of these characteristics were likely most important to his success?

10-11. What potential control problems should Andrew be aware of? What should he do to minimize these problems?

CASE APPLICATION 2

Qordoba: How Sweet It Is to Find a Solution to a Problem

The founders of the start-up Qordoba (a content management platform firm) realized that many companies have a problem. Companies need their corporate names, slogans, and brand messaging to be consistent across thousands of mentions on the internet. Just imagine the difficulty involved when a company makes a change to their messaging that requires consistency across so many hard-to-catch locations online. "This is something that used to be done completely manually, one string at a time. Very slow, very tedious, very error-prone, and we automated it," explained May Habib, Qordoba's CEO and cofounder.[46] Engineers didn't enjoy that work ... it's boring, and it's not putting their talents to good use.

Qordoba's software checks for consistency, language, and grammar. The software uses machine learning to ensure that newly created content is consistent with a company's style guide. The software even can check to make sure that the tone and emotion of newly created text is consistent with the way a company's marketing wants a message to sound.[47] And text updates can be made without engineers' help.

Originally, Qordoba planned on helping businesses translate their digital content into different languages, but they quickly figured out that a larger problem businesses faced was consistency. This problem was considered important enough that Qordoba's founders were able to get financing from venture capitalists in the Silicon Valley even though their business at first was located in Dubai. As Jennifer Fonstad, a venture capitalist who helped organize funding for Qordoba, put it, "Everyone we spoke to had this problem. The challenge was so prolific that we felt they'd hit on something."[48]

Qordoba relocated from Dubai to San Francisco. Just a few months later, they were able to raise another round of venture capital: $11.5 million. Qordoba is going to be doing a lot of hiring with these funds. They have plans to hire in areas like product development, data science, and sales.

Customers like the NBA, Marriott, Sephora, and Visa use their software. In September 2018, Qordoba was named one of Forbes's Cloud 100 Rising Stars, which means it is considered one of the top 100 privately held cloud computing companies in the world.

DISCUSSION QUESTIONS

10-12. Explain how Qordoba has an impact on the areas that show the importance of entrepreneurship (innovation, economic growth, and job creation).

10-13. Qordoba's founders identified an opportunity in the external environment when they founded the company. Which of the seven potential sources of opportunity that entrepreneurs might look for in the external context apply to the example of Qordoba?

10-14. Describe the role that financing (venture capital funding) played in Qordoba's rising success.

10-15. What leadership requirements and challenges do you think Qordoba might be dealing with now? How might those leadership requirements and challenges change for Qordoba in the future?

ENDNOTES

1. See, for instance, M. B. Low and I. C. MacMillan, "Entrepreneurship: Past Research and Future Challenges," *Journal of Management* (June 1988): pp. 139–61; S. Spinelli and R. Adams, *New Venture Creation: Entrepreneurship for the 21st Century*, 10th ed. (New York: McGraw Hill, 2016); and T. Saebi, N. J. Foss, and S. Linder, "Social Entrepreneurship Research: Past Achievements and Future Promises," *Journal of Management* (January 2019): pp. 70–95.

2. T. M. Begley and D. P. Boyd, "A Comparison of Entrepreneurs and Managers of Small Business Firms," *Journal of Management* (March 1987): pp. 99–108.

3. C. M. van Praag and P. H. Versloot, "What Is the Value of Entrepreneurship? A Review of Recent Research," *Small Business Economics* (December 2007): pp. 351–82; R. Baijal, "Four Reasons Why Entrepreneurship is Important," *Entrepreneur*, January 20, 2016, https://www.entrepreneur.com/article/269796; and Center for American Entrepreneurship, "Why Is Entrepreneurship Important?," 2017, https://www.startupsusa.org/why-is-entrepreneurship-important/.

4. S. Winter, "Fostering Entrepreneurship in Developing Countries," *World Bank*, April 30, 2012, http://blogs.worldbank.org/jobs/fostering-entrepreneurship-developing-countries; and G. Rasagam, "Why We Should Champion Entrepreneurs in Developing Countries," *World Economic Forum*, November 6, 2015, https://www.weforum.org/agenda/2015/11/why-we-should-champion-entrepreneurs-in-developing-countries/.

5. US Small Business Administration, "Small Businesses Drive Job Growth in the U.S.," news release no. 18-20.1 ADV, April 25, 2018, https://www.sba.gov/advocacy/small-businesses-drive-job-growth-us.

6. M. Mansfield, "Startup Statistics—The Numbers You Need to Know," *Small Business Trends*, updated December 26, 2018, https://smallbiztrends.com/2016/11/startup-statistics-small-business.html.

7. J. Raffiee and J. Feng, "Should I Quit My Day Job?: A Hybrid Path to Entrepreneurship," *Academy of Management Journal* (August 2014): pp. 936–63; and M. Z. Solesvik, "Hybrid Entrepreneurship: How and Why Entrepreneurs Combine Employment with Self-Employment," *Technology Innovation Management Review* (March 2017): pp. 33–41.

8. D. Wiener-Bronner, "She Was Too Short to Play Goofy. Then She Invented Spanx. Now She's a Billionaire," *CNNMoney*, April 2, 2018, https://money.cnn.com/2018/04/02/news/companies/sara-blakely-rebound/index.html.

9. Based on V. H. Vroom and B. Pahl, "Relationship Between Age and Risk Taking Among Managers," *Journal of Applied Psychology* (October 1971): pp. 399–405; J. G. March and Z. Shapira, "Managerial Perspectives on Risk and Risk-Taking," *Management Science* (November 1987): pp. 1404–1418; and J. F. Yates and E. R. Stone, "The Risk Construct," in *Risk-Taking Behavior*, ed. J. F. Yates (Chichester, UK: Wiley, 1992), pp. 1–25.

10. A. Wilkinson, "How Do the World's Leading Entrepreneurs Spot Opportunities?," *World Economic Forum*, September 10, 2015, https://www.weforum.org/agenda/2015/09/how-do-leading-entrepreneurs-spot-opportunities/.

11. J. C. Short, D. J. Ketchen Jr., C. L. Shook, and R. D. Ireland, "The Concept of 'Opportunity' in Entrepreneurship Research: Past Accomplishments and Future Challenges," *Journal of Management* (January 2010): pp. 40–65.

12. "2017 Kauffman Index of Startup Activity," Ewing Marion Kauffman Foundation, May 2017, https://www.kauffman.org/kauffman-index/reporting/startup-activity/~/media/c9831094536646528ab012dcbd1f83be.ashx.

13. P. Drucker, *Innovation and Entrepreneurship* (New York: Harper & Row, 1985).

14. J. Gay, "Chicken Wings With a Side of Sports Betting," *Wall Street Journal*, August 14, 2018, p. A12.

15. W. F. Strong, "The Airline That Started With a Cocktail Napkin," *Texas Standard*, April 20, 2016, https://www.texasstandard.org/stories/the-airline-that-started-with-a-cocktail-napkin/.

16. L. Rao, "For eBay, a New Chapter Begins," *Fortune*, July 19, 2015, http://fortune.com/2015/07/19/ebay-independence/.

17. T. Stynes, "WebMD Says Profits Rise 69%, Gives Upbeat Outlook," *Wall Street Journal*, February 23, 2016, https://www.wsj.com/articles/webmd-says-profit-rises-69-gives-upbeat-outlook-1456264442.

18. B. Helm, "Behind the Scenes: Why Airbnb Is Inc.'s Company of the Year," *Inc.*, December 2014, https://www.inc.com/magazine/201412/burt-helm/airbnb-company-of-the-year-2014.html.

19. L. Blakely, "Diagnosis: The Scrubs Market Is Comatose. The Cure? Add Fashion and Function," *Inc.*, September 2018, pp. 72–74.

20. M. Guta, "One in 7 Americans Think They Are Sitting on a Game Changing Business Idea, Survey Says," *Small Business Trends*, November 27, 2018, https://smallbiztrends.com/2018/11/startup-idea-research.html.

21. P. Reikofski, "Where 'Aha' Comes From," *Wall Street Journal*, April 29, 2013, p. R2.

22. M. Garbuio, D. Lovallo, A. Dong, N. Lin, and T. Tschang, "Demystifying the Genius of Entrepreneurship: How Design Cognition Can Help Create the Next Generation

of Entrepreneurs," *Academy of Management Learning & Education* (March 2018): pp. 41–61.

23. A. Bowman, "Essential Facts and Statistics Every Entrepreneur Must Know," *Crowdspring*, June 25, 2018, https://www.crowdspring.com/blog/entrepreneur-statistics/.

24. E. Neuborne, "Hey, Good-Looking," *Businessweek*, May 29, 2000, p. 192; and B. Unglesbee, "The Children's Place and Gymboree: A Tale of Two Specialty Retailers," *Retail Dive*, March 5, 2018, https://www.retaildive.com/news/the-childrens-place-and-gymboree-a-tale-of-two-specialty-retailers/518107/.

25. E. Griffith, "For Start-Up Investors, the Sky's the Limit," *New York Times*, August 15, 2018, New York edition, p. B1.

26. J. Rampton, "7 Steps to a Perfectly Written Business Plan," *Entrepreneur*, February 20, 2019, https://www.entrepreneur.com/article/281416.

27. C. Forrest, "How to Structure Your Startup as the Company Grows," *TechRepublic*, September 22, 2015, https://www.techrepublic.com/article/how-to-structure-your-startup-as-the-company-grows/.

28. See, for instance, J. DeMers, "The 10 Most Critical Factors That Dictate Startup Success," *Entrepreneur*, November 16, 2015, https://www.entrepreneur.com/article/252813.

29. K. Sundheim, "Entrepreneurial Recruiting: Staying Competitive When Staffing Top Talent," *Forbes*, April 4, 2013, https://www.forbes.com/sites/kensundheim/2013/04/04/entrepreneurial-recruiting-staying-competitive-when-staffing-top-talent/#2f067cb22e36.

30. "The *Boston Globe* Names PR Agency Matter Communications a Top Place to Work for 2015," November 16, 2015, https://services.businesswire.com/; and K. Johnston (ed.), "The 2017 Top Places to Work," *Boston Globe*, November 16, 2017, https://www.bostonglobe.com/magazine/2017/11/16/the-top-places-work-and-how-picked-them/G9WeCoQOotN25QeL1BXRZL/story.html.

31. "*Boston Globe* Names PR Agency" [see note 30].

32. W. Gay, "7 Workplace Benefits to Reach Top Tech Talent," *Forbes*, September 22, 2017, https://www.forbes.com/sites/wesgay/2017/09/22/workplace-benefits-tech/#706aa6c21699.

33. A. Lavoie, "The Top Thing Employees Want from Their Bosses, and It's Not a Promotion," *Entrepreneur*, March 31, 2015, https://www.entrepreneur.com/article/244437.

34. See, for instance, H. Zhao, S. E. Seibert, and G. T. Lumpkin, "The Relationship of Personality to Entrepreneurial Intentions and Performance: A Meta-Analytic Review," *Journal of Management* (March 2010): pp. 381–404; and S. P. Kerr, W. R. Kerr, and T. Xu, "Personality Traits of Entrepreneurs: A Review of Recent Literature" (Working Paper 18-047, Harvard Business School, November 2017).

35. J. M. Crant, "The Proactive Personality Scale as a Predictor of Entrepreneurial Intentions," *Journal of Small Business Management* (July 1996): pp. 42–49; R. C. Becherer and J. G. Maurer, "The Proactive Personality Disposition and Entrepreneurial Behavior Among Small Company Presidents," *Journal of Small Business Management* (January 1999): pp. 28–36; and V. P. Prabhu, "Proactive Personality and Entrepreneurial Intent: Is Entrepreneurial Self-Efficacy a Mediator or Moderator?," *International Journal of Entrepreneurial Behavior & Research* 18, no. 5 (2012): pp. 559–86.

36. D. Van Rooy, "The Little-Known Personality Trait That Predicts Entrepreneurial Success," *Inc.*, August 18, 2014, https://www.inc.com/david-van-rooy/the-little-known-personality-trait-that-predicts-entrepreneurial-success.html.

37. J. C. Picken, "From Founder to CEO: An Entrepreneur's Roadmap," *Business Horizons* (January-February 2017): pp. 7–14.

38. Based on J. Vineyard, "Vera Wang Says: Know When to Walk Away. . . And Start Something New," *Advice Week*, June 24, 2015, www.thecut.com/2015/06/vera-wang-says-know-when-to-walk-away.html

39. K. Wennberg and D. R. Detienne, "What Do We Really Mean When We Talk about 'Exit'? A Critical Review of Research on Entrepreneurial Exit," *International Small Business Journal* (February 2014): pp. 4–16; and D. R. Detienne, A. Mckelvie, and G. N. Chandler, "Making Sense of Entrepreneurial Exit Strategies: A Typology and Test," *Journal of Business Venturing* (March 2015): pp. 255–72.

40. See F. Hoque, "How Entrepreneurs Can Develop Grit, the Most Important Trait of Successful People," *Business Insider*, October 8, 2014, https://www.businessinsider.com/how-to-develop-grit-an-important-success-trait-2014-10; and A. Duckworth, *Grit: The Power of Passion and Persuasion* (New York: Scribner, 2016).

41. A. Rossow, "How a 21-Year-Old USC Entrepreneur Turned a Campus-Wide Issue into a Healthy, Thriving Business," *Forbes*, April 8, 2018, https://www.forbes.com/sites/andrewrossow/2018/04/08/how-21-year-old-usc-entrepreneur-andrew-kozlovski-turned-instagram-into-a-10000month-business/#db6a54d297ad.

42. H. Jacobs, "How a 21-Year-Old Who Makes $10,000 a Month Through an Instagram Business Spends His Money in a Typical Week," *Business Insider*, March 7, 2018, https://www.businessinsider.com/instagram-star-budgets-money-in-los-angeles-california-2018-3.

43. R. Robinson, "How to Launch a Profitable Side Hustle While You're Still In College," *Forbes*, May 11, 2018, https://www.forbes.com/sites/ryanrobinson/2018/05/11/launch-side-hustle-in-college/#6d7a14776e6a.

44. Rossow, "USC Entrepreneur Turned a Campus-Wide Issue" [see note 41].

45. Robinson, "Profitable Side Hustle" [see note 43].

46. "Qordoba Named Forbes Cloud100 SaaS Rising Star for 2018," *Qordoba* (website), September 18, 2018, https://qordoba.com/blog/qordoba-named-forbes-cloud100-saas-rising-star-2018/.

47. D. Rubinstein, "Industry Spotlight: Qordoba Brings Contextual Content to the Fore," *Software Development Times*, July 20, 2018, https://sdtimes.com/ai/ industry-spotlight-qordoba-brings-contextual-content-to-the-fore/.

48. A. Konrad, "The Startup Postmates and Visa Use to Watch Their Language Just Raised $11.5 Million to Expand," *Forbes*, October 11, 2018, https://www.forbes.com/sites/alexkonrad/2018/10/11/the-startup-postmates-and-visa-use-to-keep-their-language-consistent-just-raised-115-million-to-expand/#395b0b94768c.

PART 3 Management Practice

A Manager's Dilemma

Alan Naiman was a frugal social worker who used duct tape to repair his shoes, looked for deals at the supermarket, and chose fast-food restaurants when it was his turn to treat friends to lunch. When he died in 2018, Naiman left $11 million to child-related charities. He was especially interested in helping children who are poor, sick, disabled, or abandoned. Some say that having had an older brother who was developmentally disabled led to his passion for helping kids. Naiman used to be a banker and often worked several jobs at once. He also was a successful investor—much more successful than seemingly anyone knew—and didn't spend much money on himself.

Naiman chose to donate $2.5 million to Washington-based Pediatric Interim Care Center, which was the first organization in the nation to provide medical care to infants born to mothers who abused drugs. The center provides around-the-clock monitoring and nursing care after an infant leaves the hospital (which, for these fragile infants, is before they are ready to go home). Providing caregiver training and following the infants after they leave the center are core components to their mission. They also work at increasing community awareness about the dangers of drug abuse during pregnancy.

Social service organizations often struggle financially to provide services—with needs exceeding resources. Naiman's gift to Pediatric Interim Care Center will allow them to make a difference in the lives of babies and their families well into the future. The Center's management team wants to use the gift wisely—a definite planning, strategy, and control challenge. They started by paying off their mortgage, but now they have to think about their next steps.

Pretend you're part of that management team. Using what you've learned in the chapters on planning and strategic management in Part 3, what five things would you suggest the team focus on? Think carefully about your suggestions to the team.

Global Sense

Manufacturers have spent years building low-cost global supply chains. However, when those businesses are dependent on a global supply chain, any unplanned disruptions (political, economic, weather, natural disaster, etc.) can wreak havoc on plans, schedules, and budgets. The Indonesian earthquake/tsunami and California "Camp Fire" fires in 2018 will be looked back on by logistics, transportation, and operations managers around the globe for years to come.

Although unexpected problems in the supply chain have always existed, now the far-reaching impact of something happening not in your own facility but thousands of miles away has created additional volatility and risk for managers and organizations. For instance, when a typhoon hit near Osaka, Japan, in 2018, the Kansai International Airport was closed for more than two weeks, which affected air traffic and supplies throughout Asia. Small businesses can be especially hard hit by unplanned disruptions – 40 percent of small businesses do not reopen after a disaster. The same month that Hurricane Florence's floods in North Carolina cut freight activity by 60 percent in 2018, Coca-Cola and Mars became the first multinational companies to join the Climate-Resilient Value Chain Leaders Platform. This platform helps companies take a science-based approach to guard against climate shocks that wreck havoc with usual business activities.

Discuss the following questions in light of what you learned in Part 3:

- *You see the challenges associated with a global supply chain; what are some of the benefits of it? What can managers do to minimize the impact of such disruptions?*
- *What types of plans would be best in these unplanned events?*
- *How can managers plan effectively in dynamic environments?*
- *Could SWOT analysis be useful in these instances? Explain.*
- *How might managers use environmental scanning and virtual reality in preparing for such disasters?*[1]

Continuing Case

Starbucks—Planning

Based on Starbucks's numerous achievements, there's no doubt that managers have done their planning. Let's take a look.

Company Plans

In 2019, Starbucks had nearly 30,000 stores in seventy-seven countries. Although Starbucks increased sales and made improvements on nearly every measure of their operations in the last quarter of 2018, customer traffic in Starbucks stores in the US fell in the last two quarters of 2018 and sales growth targets have been difficult to meet since 2016. Kevin Johnson is responding by leading the company through a more measured approach toward growth than they have taken in the past. In 2019, Starbucks planned on closing 150 underperforming stores, which is three times more than they usually close in one year. Johnson views customer service improvements in existing stores as a way to increase the company's health. One of the ways Starbucks wants to achieve this is to expand delivered coffee service from almost one-quarter of its stores in the US in early 2019. Also, the company's financial plans have been reined in a bit compared to the past. In early 2019, their global same-store sales-goal increases were 3 to 4 percent (instead of 5 percent or more). Starbucks' earnings-per-share growth target has been set at 10 percent (rather than 15 to 20 percent). An important market for Starbucks's growth plans is China. Kevin Johnson has set a five-year goal of tripling revenues in China. In addition to quantitative/fiscal plans, Starbucks is focusing on increasing its product sales outside its cafés (at supermarkets, for example) and staying true to its global social responsibilities. Starbucks's ambition is to rank among the world's most admired brands and to maintain Starbucks's standing as one of the most recognized brands in the world.

Company Strategies

Starbucks has been considered a leading dynamic retail brand for more than two decades. It has been able to rise above the commodity nature of its product and become a global brand leader by reinventing the coffee experience. Over 85 million times a week, a customer receives a product (hot drink, chilled drink, food, etc.) from a Starbucks partner somewhere in the world. It's a reflection of the success that Howard Schultz had in creating something that never really existed in the United States—café life. And in so doing, he created a cultural phenomenon. Starbucks has been credited with changing what we eat and drink. It has shaped how we spend our time and money.

Starbucks has found a way to appeal to practically every customer demographic, as its customers cover a broad base. It's not just the affluent or the urban professionals, and it's not just the intellectuals or the creative types who frequent Starbucks. You'll find soccer moms, construction workers, bank tellers, and office assistants at Starbucks. And despite the high price of its products, customers pay it because they think it's worth it. What they get for that price is some of the finest coffee available commercially, custom preparation, and, of course, that Starbucks ambiance—the comfy chairs, the music, the aromas, the hissing steam from the espresso machine—all invoking that warm feeling of community and connection that Schultz experienced on his first business trip to Italy and felt instinctively could work elsewhere.

An integral part of Starbucks's measured growth strategy is its loyalty program, Starbucks Rewards. In the first quarter of 2019, Starbucks had an increase of 14 percent in its Rewards program enrollment, which was the biggest gain in three years. That membership bump resulted in a grand total of 16.3 million Rewards members. On top of this impressive feat, increasing the number of Rewards members was one of the ways that Starbucks was able to boost same-store sales—a metric that Starbucks was trying to improve—beyond projections in the first quarter of 2019.

Besides their Rewards program, Starbucks is focusing on technology as a key strategic emphasis. Starbucks has made refinements to its mobile app, making it easier to get customers to use. It's also now available to anyone—even those who are not members of its Rewards program. Starbucks can boast that it has the most popular digital payment app in the US, with 23.4 million users. That's more than the number of Apple Pay users! Further advancements are planned on the company's digital front. For example, Starbucks has plans to open twenty stores in New York City that will pilot test a digital-only payment system.

Starbucks's growth strategy in China has involved delivering coffee. Their plan now is to expand delivery in the US. As Kevin Johnson says, "We've learned a tremendous amount about delivery [in China] and we're now applying those learnings here in the US." Starbucks is working with Uber with a plan to expand delivery service to about a quarter of its US stores. This follows the pattern that Starbucks used when expanding delivery in China, which they did in a partnership with the Chinese company Alibaba.

If you're thinking that selling Starbucks outside its cafés should be another way to expand, you are absolutely correct! Nestlé paid $7.15 billion to sell Starbucks products through its distribution channels throughout the world. This partnership deal also involves Nestle working with Starbucks to develop new coffee products in the future.[2]

Discussion Questions

P3-1. Make a list of Starbucks's plans. Describe what type of plan each is. Then, describe how that plan might affect how the following employees do their job: (a) a part-time store employee—a barista—in Omaha; (b) a quality assurance technician at the company's roasting plant in Amsterdam; (c) a regional sales manager; (d) the executive vice president of global supply chain operations; and (e) the CEO.

P3-2. Discuss the types of growth strategies that Starbucks has used. Be specific.

P3-3. In what specific ways do stability and/or renewal strategies apply to Starbucks's in recent years?

P3-4. What is Starbucks doing to sustain its competitive advantage over competitors? What else might they do to continue to be competitive relative to others in their industry?

P3-5. Starbucks charges more for coffee than its Chinese competitor Luckin. Starbucks also has followed Luckin by offering coffee delivery. What kind of differentiation strategy is Starbucks currently using relative to its competitors like Luckin and McDonalds in China? What other differentiation strategies might Starbucks consider using in the future?

P3-6. How is the way that Kevin Johnson is leading Starbucks different from the way that Howard Schultz led the company as an entrepreneur-founder?

Notes for the Part 3 Continuing Case

1. Social Worker Leaves Secret $11 Million Fortune to Children's Charities," *New York Post,* December 28, 2018, https://nypost.com/2018/12/28/social-worker-leaves-secret-11-million-fortune-to-childrens-charities/;"Japan's Kansai Airport Fully Reopens 17 Days After Typhoon," *Straits Times*, September 22, 2018, https://www.straitstimes.com/asia/east-asia/japans-kansai-airport-fully-reopens-17-days-after-typhoon; C. Morris, "Hurricane Alert: 40 Percent of Small Businesses Never Recover From a Disaster," CNBC/ Survey Monkey Small Business Survey, *CNBC*, September 16, 2017, https://www.cnbc.com/2017/09/16/hurricane-watch-40-percent-of-small-businesses-dont-reopen-after-a-disaster.html; "Major Companies Join Forces to Drive Climate Resilience in Supply Chains," *BSR Insights*, September 2018, https://www.bsr.org/en/our-insights/news/major-companies-join-forces-to-drive-climate-resilience-in-supply-chains; S. Banker, "The Supply Chain in Review," *Forbes*, December 27, 2018, https://www.forbes.com/sites/stevebanker/2018/12/27/the-supply-chain-year-in-review/#7556b75223f4.

2. J. Jargon, "Starbucks CEO Kevin Johnson Reins in Predecessor's Ambitions: 'I'm Not Howard'," *Wall Street Journal*, January 8, 2019, https://www.wsj.com/articles/starbucks-ceo-kevin-johnson-reins-in-predecessors-ambitions-im-not-howard-11546857001; H. Field, "Starbucks Is Closing 150 Underperforming U.S. Locations. Here's Why." *Entrepreneur*, June 20, 2018, *https://www.entrepreneur.com/article/315463*; A. Edgecliffe-Johnson, "Starbucks' Kevin Johnson: Taking On a Founder's Brand," *Financial Times*, December 8, 2018, https://www.ft.com/content/62e2323c-f927-11e8-af46-2022a0b02a6c; P. R. La Monica, "Starbucks Has Done Just Fine Since Howard Schultz Left," *CNN Business*, February 11, 2019, https://www.cnn.com/2019/02/11/investing/starbucks-kevin-johnson-howard-schultz/index.html; R. Williams, "Starbucks Rewards Membership Jumps 14% in Q1, Highest Gain in 3 Years," *Mobile Marketer*, January 29, 2019, https://www.mobilemarketer.com/news/starbucks-rewards-membership-jumps-14-in-q1-highest-gain-in-3-years/547059/; L. Gurdus, "Starbucks CEO Confirms Alibaba Partnership, Plans to Expand Delivery to 2,000 Stores in China," *CNBC*,

August 1, 2018, https://www.cnbc.com/2018/08/02/starbucks-ceo-confirms-alibaba-partnership-china-delivery-expansion.html; A. Gray, A. Edgecliffe-Johnson, and S. Bond, "Uber to Start Delivering Starbucks," *Financial Times*, December 13, 2018, https://www.ft.com/content/9b45e8da-ff03-11e8-aebf-99e208d3e521; D. B. Kline, "Here's How Starbucks Is Driving Same-Store Sales Growth," *Motley Fool*, January 26, 2019, https://www.fool.com/investing/2019/01/26/heres-how-starbucks-is-driving-us-same-store-sales.aspx; R. Atkins, "Nestlé to Pay $7bn for Starbucks' Products," *Financial Times*, May 7, 2018, https://www.ft.com/content/e73fd2aa-51ca-11e8-b24e-cad6aa67e23e; and J. Wernau and J. Jargon, "Starbucks Fights Hot Startup in China," *Wall Street Journal*, March 13, 2019, https://www.wsj.com/articles/starbucks-struggles-to-beat-hot-startup-on-delivery-in-china-11552469400.

Chapter 11   Designing Organizational Structure

Learning Objectives

11.1 *Describe* six key elements in organizational design.

11.2 *Contrast* mechanistic and organic structures.

11.3 *Discuss* the contingency factors that favor either the mechanistic model or the organic model of organizational design.

11.4 *Describe* traditional organizational design options.

11.5 *Discuss* organizing for flexibility in the twenty-first century.

Employability Skills Matrix

This matrix identifies which features and end-of-chapter material will help you develop specific skills employers are looking for in job candidates.

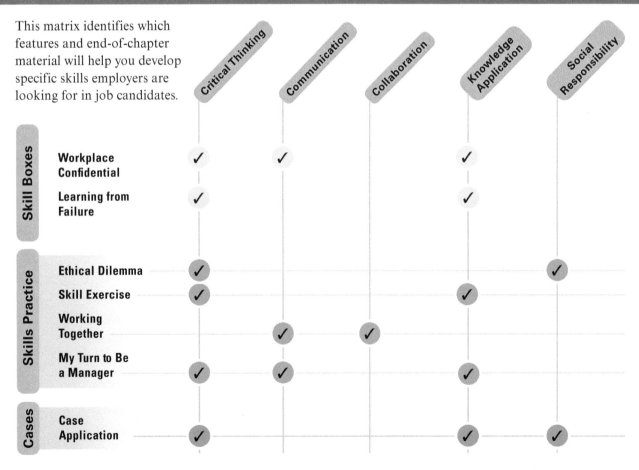

	Critical Thinking	Communication	Collaboration	Knowledge Application	Social Responsibility
Skill Boxes					
Workplace Confidential	✓	✓		✓	
Learning from Failure	✓			✓	
Skills Practice					
Ethical Dilemma	✓				✓
Skill Exercise	✓			✓	
Working Together		✓	✓		
My Turn to Be a Manager	✓	✓		✓	
Cases					
Case Application	✓			✓	✓

When you think of organizational structure, you're likely to think about things like rules and regulations, how jobs are defined, and an authority chain of command. A "well-oiled" organization is thought to have a comprehensive set of formal rules, designated departments, and a clearly defined authority hierarchy. But this needn't be the case. ING, a Dutch banking firm, has recently transitioned into a free-form structure that flattens the organization, minimizes the number of managers, and relies on small teams to get the work done. Specifically, ING has replaced its functional departments with 350 nine-person autonomous teams. They have end-to-end responsibility for handling clients' needs. The company credits this new structure with improved response speed, increased employee engagement, and higher productivity.[1]

In this chapter, we present the basics of organizing. We define the key organizing concepts and their components and how managers use these to create a variety of structures. We'll also show under what conditions a free-form structure like INGs is preferred or when a more structured hierarchy is the best choice.

SIX elements of organizational design

LO11.1 Few topics in management have undergone as much change in recent years as that of organizing and organizational structure. Managers are reevaluating traditional approaches to find new structural designs that best support and facilitate employees doing the organization's work—designs that can achieve efficiency but are also flexible.[2]

First, a few terms: In Chapter 1, we defined *organizing* as arranging and structuring work to accomplish organizational goals. **Organizational structure** is the formal arrangement of jobs within an organization. This structure, which can be shown visually in an **organizational chart**, serves many purposes. (See Exhibit 11-1.) When managers create or change the structure, they're engaged in **organizational design**, a process that involves decisions about six key elements: work specialization, departmentalization, chain of command, span of control, centralization/decentralization, and formalization.

organizational structure
The formal arrangement of jobs within an organization

organizational chart
The visual representation of an organization's structure

organizational design
Creating or changing an organization's structure

Work Specialization

Early in the twentieth century, Henry Ford became rich by doing something unique: building automobiles using an assembly line. Every worker was assigned a specific, repetitive task, such as putting on the right front wheel or installing the left front door. By dividing jobs into small standardized tasks that could be performed over and over, Ford was able to produce a car every ten seconds, using employees with relatively limited skills.[3]

Work specialization, or *division of labor*, describes the degree to which activities in the organization are divided into separate jobs. The essence of work specialization is to divide a job into several steps, each completed by a separate individual.

work specialization
Dividing work activities into separate job tasks

- Divides work to be done into specific jobs and departments.
- Assigns tasks and responsibilities associated with individual jobs.
- Coordinates diverse organizational tasks.
- Clusters jobs into units.
- Establishes relationships among individuals, groups, and departments.
- Establishes formal lines of authority.
- Allocates and deploys organizational resources.

Exhibit 11-1
Purposes of Organizing

Lacing is one of 13 separate tasks involved in hand-crafting a Wilson Sporting Goods football. The company uses work specialization in dividing job activities as an organizing mechanism that helps employees boost their productivity.
Source: Luke Sharrett/ Bloomberg/Getty Images

Specialization is a means of making the most efficient use of employees' skills and even successfully improving them through repetition. Less time is spent changing tasks, putting away tools and equipment from a prior step and getting ready for another.

Work specialization makes efficient use of the diversity of skills that workers have. In most organizations, some tasks require highly developed skills; others can be performed by employees with lower skill levels. If all workers were engaged in all the steps of, say, a manufacturing process, all would need the skills necessary to perform both the most demanding and the least demanding jobs. Thus, except when performing the most highly skilled or highly sophisticated tasks, employees would be working below their skill levels. Because skilled workers are paid more than unskilled workers and their wages tend to reflect their highest level of skill, it represents an inefficient usage of resources to pay highly skilled workers to do easy tasks.

Early proponents of work specialization believed it could lead to great increases in productivity. At the beginning of the twentieth century, that generalization was reasonable. Because specialization was not widely practiced, its introduction almost always generated higher productivity. But, as Exhibit 11-2 illustrates, a good thing can be carried too far. At some point, the human diseconomies from division of labor—boredom, fatigue, stress, low productivity, poor quality, increased absenteeism, and high turnover—exceed the economic advantages.

TODAY'S VIEW   Most managers today continue to see work specialization as important because it helps employees be more efficient. For example, McDonald's uses high work specialization to get its products made and delivered to customers efficiently and quickly—that's why it's called "fast" food. One person takes orders at the drive-through window, others cook and assemble the hamburgers, another works the fryer, another bags orders, and so forth. Such single-minded focus on maximizing efficiency has contributed to increasing productivity. In fact, at many McDonald's, you'll see a clock that times how long it takes employees to fill the order; look closer, and you'll probably see posted somewhere an order fulfillment

Exhibit 11-2
Economies and Diseconomies of Work Specialization

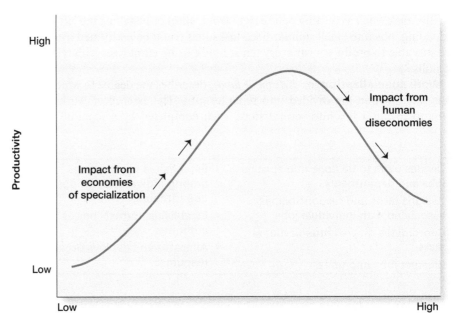

time goal. At some point, however, work specialization no longer leads to increased productivity. That's why companies such as Avery Dennison, Ford Australia, Hallmark, and American Express use minimal work specialization and instead give employees a broad range of tasks to do.

Departmentalization

Does your college have a department of student services or financial aid? Are you taking this course through a management department? After deciding what job tasks will be done by whom, common work activities need to be grouped back together so work gets done in a coordinated and integrated way. How jobs are grouped together is called **departmentalization**. Five common forms of departmentalization are used, although an organization may develop its own unique classification. (For instance, a hotel might have departments such as front desk operations, sales and catering, housekeeping, and maintenance.) Exhibit 11-3 illustrates each type of departmentalization as well as the advantages and disadvantages of each.

departmentalization
The basis by which jobs are grouped together

TODAY'S VIEW Most large organizations continue to use combinations of most or all of these types of departmentalization. For example, General Electric organizes its corporate staff along functional lines, including public relations, legal, global research, human resources, and finance. Pearson Education, publisher of this textbook, arranges its business by educational market segment (Pre-K–12, higher education, and professional) and its customers (students, professors, and workplace educators) and arranges its sales function around customers and geographic regions (for example, the United States, Europe, and Asia). Procter & Gamble relies on product departmentalization, organizing around five product categories: fabric care and home care; baby, feminine and family care; beauty; grooming; and health care.

One popular departmentalization trend is the increasing use of customer departmentalization. This approach works well because it emphasizes monitoring and responding to changes in customers' needs. Another popular trend is the use of teams, especially as work tasks have become more complex and diverse skills are needed to accomplish those tasks.

Chain of Command

Suppose you were at work and had a problem with an issue that came up. What would you do? Who would you ask for help? People need to know who their boss is. That's why the chain of command is important. The **chain of command** is the line of authority extending from upper organizational levels to lower levels, which clarifies who reports to whom. Managers need to consider it when organizing work because it helps employees with questions such as "Who do I report to?" or "Who do I go to if I have a problem?" To understand the chain of command, you have to understand three other important concepts: authority, responsibility, and unity of command.

chain of command
The line of authority extending from upper organizational levels to the lowest levels, which clarifies who reports to whom

Authority refers to the rights inherent in a managerial position to tell people what to do and to expect them to do it.[4] The early management writers distinguished between two forms of authority: line authority and staff authority. **Line authority** entitles a manager to direct the work of an employee. It is the employer–employee authority relationship that extends from the top of the organization to the lowest echelon, following the chain of command. As a link in the chain of command, a manager with line authority has the right to direct the work of employees and to make certain decisions without consulting anyone.

authority
The rights inherent in a managerial position to tell people what to do and to expect them to do it

line authority
Authority that entitles a manager to direct the work of an employee

As organizations get larger and more complex, line managers find that they do not have the time, expertise, or resources to get their jobs done effectively. In response, they create **staff authority** functions to support, assist, advise, and generally reduce some of their informational burdens. For instance, a human resource management director who cannot effectively handle managing all the activities the department needs creates a recruitment department, performance management department, and compensation and rewards department, which are staff functions.

staff authority
Positions created to support, assist, and advise those holding line authority

Exhibit 11-3

The Five Common Forms of Departmentalization

FUNCTIONAL DEPARTMENTALIZATION—Groups Jobs According to Function

+ Efficiencies from putting together similar specialties and people with common skills, knowledge, and orientations
+ Coordination within functional area
+ In-depth specialization
− Poor communication across functional areas
− Limited view of organizational goals

GEOGRAPHICAL DEPARTMENTALIZATION—Groups Jobs According to Geographic Region

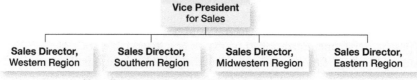

+ More effective and efficient handling of specific regional issues that arise
+ Serve needs of unique geographic markets better
− Duplication of functions
− Can feel isolated from other organizational areas

PRODUCT DEPARTMENTALIZATION—Groups Jobs by Product Line

Source: Bombardier Annual Report.

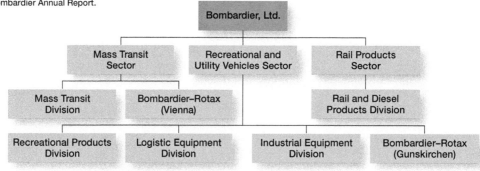

+ Allows specialization in particular products and services
+ Managers can become experts in their industry
+ Closer to customers
− Duplication of functions
− Limited view of organizational goals

PROCESS DEPARTMENTALIZATION—Groups Jobs on the Basis of Product or Customer Flow

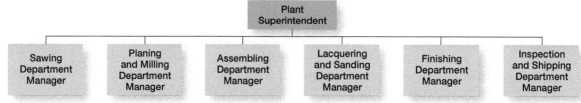

+ More efficient flow of work activities
− Can only be used with certain types of products

CUSTOMER DEPARTMENTALIZATION—Groups Jobs on the Basis of Specific and Unique Customers Who Have Common Needs

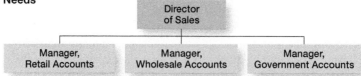

+ Customers' needs and problems can be met by specialists
− Duplication of functions
− Limited view of organizational goals

Let's Get REAL

◄ **Rebecca Ross**
Manager, Customer Success

The Scenario:

Reid Lawson cofounded a small sports marketing company that has been in business for two years. Reid and his co-founder purposely set up the company without a lot of structure. The firm's twenty employees work in project teams to flexibly meet client needs. There aren't any standard operating procedures, and there isn't any employee training either. Reid is starting to wonder if introducing some structure might be helpful. Issues cropping up on one client project are being handled very differently than other projects with the same client. As another example, lessons learned from one client project aren't being carried over to future projects.

What would you advise that Reid should do to help the company make adjustments to the level of structure in the company?

Source: Rebecca Ross

When a company or team is first starting out, it's common to operate without a lot of structure. This enables agility by creating space for the team to try different approaches, learn from them, and iterate to improve. As organizations grow, it becomes increasingly important to create a foundation of structure to scale effectively. First, Reid should clearly articulate the problem statement and define what he is solving for. Is the customer experience suffering due to the lack of knowledge sharing? Is there a loss in profitability due to internal inefficiencies? Is there a talent retention risk due to the lack of training? Next, Reid should make sure that the team is aware of the long-term goals of the organization and that he clearly communicates how this problem will prevent them from reaching their goals. From there, Reid can map out a plan that includes the specific steps that the team will take together to get to their future ideal state. He should keep in mind that behavior change is a multi-step process, and even in a small organization, a well thought out change management plan is the best way to achieve lasting results.

When managers use their authority to assign work to employees, those employees take on an obligation to perform those assigned duties. This obligation or expectation to perform is known as **responsibility**. And employees need to be held accountable for their performance. Assigning work authority without responsibility and accountability can create opportunities for abuse. Likewise, no one should be held responsible or accountable for work tasks over which he or she has no authority to complete those tasks.

Finally, the **unity of command** principle (one of Fayol's fourteen management principles—see page 26 in the Management History module) states that a person should report to only one manager. Without unity of command, conflicting demands from multiple bosses can occur.

responsibility
The obligation or expectation to perform assigned duties

unity of command
The management principle that each person should report to only one manager

TODAY'S VIEW Although early management theorists believed that chain of command, authority (line and staff), responsibility, and unity of command were essential, times have changed. Those elements are far less important today. Information technology has made such concepts less relevant. Employees can access information that used to be available only to managers in a matter of a few seconds. It also means that employees can communicate with anyone else in the organization without going through the chain of command. In addition, many employees, especially in organizations where work revolves around projects, find themselves reporting to more than one boss, thus violating the unity of command principle.[5]

Span of Control

How many employees can a manager efficiently and effectively manage? That's what **span of control** seeks to answer. The traditional view was that managers could not—and should not—directly supervise more than five or six subordinates. Any more and a manager would be overwhelmed.

span of control
The number of employees a manager can efficiently and effectively manage

WORKPLACE CONFIDENTIAL Coping with Multiple Bosses

Sue Lee was complaining about her job at a large property development company. "I work for Ted in our marketing department. But I've been assigned to help promote our new luxury condo project on Park Avenue. The project manager, Xu Xiang, thinks she's my boss. She is constantly giving me things to do, priorities, and deadlines. Meanwhile, I'm getting text messages, emails, and phone calls from Ted with conflicting requests. I wish these two would talk to each other. I only have so many hours in my day. I can't do two jobs at once. What do I do? Whose directives get priority? Did I mention that I spend most of my time on Xu's project, but Ted does my annual performance review?"

Sue's complaint is not unique. An increasing number of people are finding themselves reporting to more than one boss. In some cases, the problem is a poorly designed organization where the lines of authority aren't clearly defined and the unity-of-command principle is broken. In other cases, especially small or family-run businesses, it can be blurred authority lines with overlapping roles. In still other cases it might be the formation of temporary teams where people report to multiple bosses. But more often, nowadays, the culprit is a matrix organization structure. As noted later in this chapter, organizations are increasingly imposing project structures on top of functional departments to better manage specific businesses, regions, or product lines. In so doing, they create overlapping responsibilities. If you find yourself in one of these situations, you very well may need to deal with bosses who have different management styles or who impose conflicting directives, vague communications, or unrealistic workloads.

Multiple bosses can create multiple headaches, but three challenges stand out. First is dealing with an excessive workload. Multiple bosses often aren't aware of what others are asking of you. Whether deliberate or not, each may treat you as if you are solely working for him or her and have no other responsibilities. So two bosses might result in your having twice the workload. With three or more bosses, of course, the problem might only increase. Second is the challenge of conflicting messages. Different bosses have different expectations and different leadership styles. What do you do when you have multiple bosses wanting you to meet their deadlines "ASAP"? Finally, there is the issue of loyalty. Who do you give first priority to? Reporting to more than one person may require you to negotiate between competing demands for your time, goals, and priorities.

So what can you do if you find yourself having to cope with multiple bosses? Here are some suggestions:

Prioritize your bosses. Like it or not, you need to choose to whom your first loyalty lies. Who is more powerful, and who would hurt you the least? Make sure you know who your ultimate boss is and make sure he or she is satisfied with your work. The person who completes your reviews and decides on your compensation is typically the person who should never be ignored. Consistent with our discussion of organizational politics in Chapter 1, you want to support your boss and, when you have more than one, give first priority to the one with the most power.

Be proactive about your workload. It's your responsibility to make sure your multiple bosses are kept up to date on your workload. That includes telling each what the others have asked of you. When the load exceeds your capacity, share this information with each boss and ask for their suggestions regarding priorities.

Prioritize your workload and list. Make a list of all your ongoing tasks and projects, prioritize them, and then share this list with your bosses. The list needs to be updated regularly and communicated in weekly check-in meetings. These meetings are your best opportunity to anticipate and reconcile potential conflicts.

Set boundaries. Don't be afraid to set limits. Identify how many hours you can devote to each boss's project and how you've allocated priorities. If your bosses know ahead of time what the boundaries are, you can eliminate a lot of potential conflicts.

Get your bosses to communicate with each other. Get your bosses to talk with each other. Try to avoid becoming the vehicle through whom they communicate. It's not your job to represent each boss's agenda to the other. When there are conflicts that are directly affecting you, bring your bosses together, explain the conflicts, and encourage them to come to a resolution.

Look at the bright side. There is a positive side to multiple bosses. First, the fact that two or more bosses want you working for them says that you have valuable skills and that they trust you. Second, the complexity and ambiguity created by the absence of a single boss can allow you to expand your autonomy and influence. When you set the boundaries and define priorities, you take control over variables typically held by a boss. Finally, there is the opportunity to play one boss off against another: "Like a kid playing parents off each other, ask the person who you know will give you the answer you want."[6]

Determining the span of control is important because, to a large degree, it determines the number of levels and managers in an organization—an important consideration in how efficient an organization will be. All other things being equal, the wider or larger the span, the more efficient the organization. Here's why.

Assume two organizations both have approximately 4,100 operative employees. As Exhibit 11-4 shows, if one organization has a span of four and the other a span of eight, the organization with the wider span will have two fewer levels and approximately 800

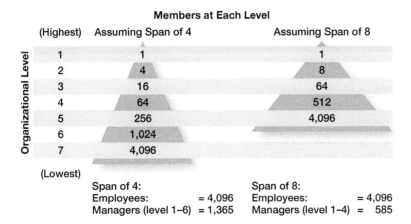

Members at Each Level

(Highest)	Assuming Span of 4	Assuming Span of 8
1	1	1
2	4	8
3	16	64
4	64	512
5	256	4,096
6	1,024	
7	4,096	

(Lowest)

Span of 4:		Span of 8:	
Employees:	= 4,096	Employees:	= 4,096
Managers (level 1–6)	= 1,365	Managers (level 1–4)	= 585

Organizational Level (vertical axis label)

Exhibit 11-4
Contrasting Spans of Control

fewer managers. At an average manager's salary of $85,000 a year, the organization with the wider span would save $68 million a year! Obviously, wider spans are more efficient in terms of cost. However, at some point, wider spans may reduce effectiveness if employee performance worsens because managers no longer have the time to lead effectively.

TODAY'S VIEW The contemporary view of span of control recognizes there is no magic number. Many factors influence the number of employees a manager can efficiently and effectively manage. These factors include the skills and abilities of the manager and the employees, as well as the characteristics of the work being done. For instance, managers with well-trained and experienced employees can function well with a wider span. Apple CEO Tim Cook has seventeen direct reports. At first glance, that seems like a lot. But Cook indicates otherwise: "If you have smart people, a strong organizational culture, and a well-defined and articulated strategy that everyone understands, you can [have] numerous direct reports because your job isn't to tell people what to do."[8] Other contingency variables that determine the appropriate span include similarity and complexity of employee tasks; the physical proximity of subordinates; the degree to which standardized procedures are in place; the sophistication of the organization's information system; the strength of the organization's culture, as Cook noted; and the preferred style of the manager.[9]

The trend in recent years has been toward larger spans of control, which is consistent with managers' efforts to speed up decision making, increase flexibility, get closer to customers, empower employees, and reduce costs. Managers are beginning to recognize that they can handle a wider span when employees are trained and experienced in their jobs and have coworkers to help with problems or questions. New technologies are also allowing organizations to widen spans by allowing managers to interact with and monitor a larger number of employees.

Centralization and Decentralization

Centralization vs. decentralization seeks to answer: "At what organizational level are decisions made?" **Centralization** is the degree to which decision making takes place at upper levels of the organization. If top managers make key decisions with little input from below, then the organization is more centralized. On the other hand, the more that lower-level employees provide input or actually make decisions, the more **decentralization** there is. Keep in mind that centralization–decentralization is not an either-or concept. The decision is relative, not absolute—that is, an organization is never completely centralized or decentralized.

Early management writers proposed that the degree of centralization in an organization depended on the situation. But they favored centralization since it maintains top-management control. Traditional organizations were structured

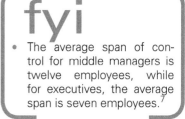

fyi

- The average span of control for middle managers is twelve employees, while for executives, the average span is seven employees.[7]

centralization
The degree to which decision making is concentrated at upper levels of the organization

decentralization
The degree to which lower-level employees provide input or actually make decisions

The span of control identifies how many people a manager can effectively supervise. All other things equal, the wider the span, the flatter the organization structure.
Source: Fotogestoeber/Alamy Stock photo

Exhibit 11-5

Centralization or Decentralization

More Centralization	More Decentralization
• Environment is stable.	• Environment is complex, uncertain.
• Lower-level managers are not as capable or experienced at making decisions as upper-level managers.	• Lower-level managers are capable and experienced at making decisions.
• Lower-level managers do not want a say in decisions.	• Lower-level managers want a voice in decisions.
• Decisions are relatively minor.	• Decisions are significant.
• Organization is facing a crisis or the risk of company failure.	• Corporate culture is open to allowing managers a say in what happens.
• Company is small.	• Company is geographically dispersed.
• Effective implementation of company strategies depends on managers retaining say over what happens.	• Effective implementation of company strategies depends on managers having involvement and flexibility to make decisions.

in a pyramid, with power and authority concentrated near the top of the organization. Given this structure, historically, centralized decisions were the most prominent, but organizations today have become more complex and responsive to dynamic changes in their environments. As such, many managers believe decisions need to be made by those individuals closest to the problems, regardless of their organizational level. Exhibit 11-5 lists some of the factors that affect an organization's use of centralization or decentralization.[10]

TODAY'S VIEW Today, managers often choose the amount of centralization or decentralization that will allow them to best implement their decisions and achieve organizational goals. What works in one organization, however, won't necessarily work in another, so managers must determine the appropriate amount of decentralization for each organization and work units within it.

As organizations have become more flexible and responsive to environmental trends, there's been a distinct shift toward decentralized decision making.[11] This trend, also known as **employee empowerment**, gives employees more authority to make decisions. (We'll address this concept more thoroughly in our discussion of leadership in Chapter 17.) In large companies especially, lower-level managers are "closer to the action" and typically have more detailed knowledge about problems and how best to solve them than top managers. For instance, decentralized management is the cornerstone of Johnson & Johnson's business model. Alex Gorsky, chairman and CEO, indicates that "our decentralized management approach acknowledges that those closest to patients and customers are in the best position to understand and address their needs."[12] The company's approach has paid off. It has three business divisions with 265 operating companies located across 60 countries, enabling Johnson & Johnson to serve more than 1 billion people per day.[13]

employee empowerment
Giving employees more authority to make decisions

Formalization

Formalization refers to how standardized an organization's jobs are and the extent to which employee behavior is guided by rules and procedures. In highly formalized organizations, there are explicit job descriptions, numerous organizational rules, and clearly defined procedures covering work processes. Employees are given little discretion over what's done, when it's done, and how it's done. However, where there is less formalization, employees have more discretion in how they do their work. Traditional management theorists favored high formalization. It was believed that work could be accomplished most efficiently when employees had extensive rules and procedures to guide them.

formalization
How standardized an organization's jobs are and the extent to which employee behavior is guided by rules and procedures

TODAY'S VIEW Although some formalization is necessary for consistency and control, many organizations today rely less on strict rules and standardization to guide and regulate employee behavior. High formalization works well when the workplace is characterized by stability and consistency. This allows rules, for instance, to be applied in a fair and consistent manner. But high formalization doesn't work very effectively in times of rapid change. And today's workplace is increasingly one having to cope with a dynamic and changing environment.

MECHANISTIC and organic structures

LO11.2 Basic organizational design revolves around two organizational forms, described in Exhibit 11-6.[14]

The **mechanistic organization** (or bureaucracy) was the natural result of combining the six elements of structure. Adhering to the chain-of-command principle ensured the existence of a formal hierarchy of authority, with each person controlled and supervised by one superior. Keeping the span of control small at increasingly higher levels in the organization created tall, impersonal structures. As the distance between the top and the bottom of the organization expanded, top management would increasingly impose rules and regulations. Because top managers couldn't control lower-level activities through direct observation and ensure the use of standard practices, they substituted rules and regulations. The early management writers' belief in a high degree of work specialization created jobs that were simple, routine, and standardized. Further specialization through the use of departmentalization increased impersonality and the need for multiple layers of management to coordinate the specialized departments.[15]

The **organic organization** is a highly adaptive form that is as loose and flexible as the mechanistic organization is rigid and stable. Rather than having standardized jobs and regulations, the organic organization's loose structure allows it to change rapidly, as needs require.[16] It has division of labor, but the jobs people do are not standardized. Employees tend to be professionals who are technically proficient and trained to handle diverse problems. They need few formal rules and little direct supervision because their training has instilled in them standards of professional conduct. For instance, a petroleum engineer doesn't need to follow specific procedures on how to locate oil sources miles offshore. The engineer can solve most problems alone or after conferring with colleagues. Professional standards guide his or her behavior. The organic organization is low in centralization so that the professional can respond quickly to problems and because top-level managers cannot be expected to possess the expertise to make necessary decisions.

In the same way that there are no pure mechanistic organizations, there are no pure organic ones either. But the trend indicates many companies today are moving strongly in the organic direction. They would include firms such as Patagonia, Zappos, Alphabet, Netflix, and Spotify.[17]

CONTINGENCY factors affecting structural choice

LO11.3 When is a mechanistic structure preferable and when is an organic one more appropriate? Let's look at the main contingency factors that influence this decision.

Regulation manuals and handbooks standardize work procedures and improve efficiency. Here Lieutenant J. G. Gerardo Arbulu, left, and Chief Aviation Boatswain's Mate Ronald Mosley reference a damage control handbook during a general quarters drill aboard the aircraft carrier USS Dwight D. Eisenhower (CVN 69).
Source: PR Library/Alamy Stock Photo

mechanistic organization
An organizational design that's rigid and tightly controlled

organic organization
An organizational design that's highly adaptive and flexible

Mechanistic	Organic
• High specialization	• Cross-functional teams
• Rigid departmentalization	• Cross-hierarchical teams
• Clear chain of command	• Free flow of information
• Narrow spans of control	• Wide spans of control
• Centralization	• Decentralization
• High formalization	• Low formalization

Exhibit 11-6
Mechanistic Versus Organic Organizations

Strategy and Structure

An organization's structure should facilitate goal achievement. Because goals are an important part of the organization's strategies, it's only logical that strategy and structure are closely linked. Alfred Chandler initially researched this relationship.[18] He studied several large US companies and concluded that changes in corporate strategy led to changes in an organization's structure that support the strategy.

Research has shown that certain structural designs work best with different organizational strategies.[19] For instance, the flexibility and free-flowing information of the organic structure works well when an organization is pursuing meaningful and unique innovations. The mechanistic organization with its efficiency, stability, and tight controls works best for companies wanting to tightly control costs.

Size and Structure

There's considerable evidence that an organization's size affects its structure.[20] Large organizations—typically considered to be those with more than 2,000 employees—tend to have more specialization, departmentalization, centralization, and rules and regulations than do small organizations. However, once an organization grows past a certain size, size has less influence on structure. Why? Essentially, once there are around 2,000 employees, it's already fairly mechanistic. Adding another 500 employees won't impact the structure much. On the other hand, adding 500 employees to an organization with only 300 employees is likely to make it more mechanistic.

To improve employee engagement, IKEA uses a flat structure within stores.
Source: Meritzo/Alamy Stock Photo

Technology and Structure

Every organization uses some form of technology to convert its inputs into outputs. For instance, CloudDDM uses 3D printers to make prototypes and product parts for corporate customers. This technology has made it possible to conduct the work with few workers. According to CloudDDM's founder, "We'll have 100 high-tech 3D printers running 24 hours, 7 days a week. And it'll need just three employees: one for each of the eight-hour shifts."[21]

The initial research on technology's effect on structure can be traced to Joan Woodward, who studied small manufacturing firms in southern England to determine the extent to which structural design elements were related to organizational success.[22] She couldn't find any consistent pattern until she divided the firms into three distinct technologies that had increasing levels of complexity and sophistication. The first category, **unit production**, described the production of items in units or small batches. The second category, **mass production**, described large-batch manufacturing. Finally, the third and most technically complex group, **process production**, included continuous-process production. A summary of her findings is shown in Exhibit 11-7.

Other studies also have shown that organizations adapt their structures to their technology depending on how routine their technology is for transforming inputs into outputs.[23] In general, the more routine the technology, the more mechanistic the structure can be, and organizations with more nonroutine technology are more likely to have organic structures.

unit production
The production of items in units or small batches

mass production
The production of items in large batches

process production
The production of items in continuous processes

Environmental Uncertainty and Structure

Some organizations face stable and simple environments with little uncertainty; others face dynamic and complex environments with a lot of uncertainty. Managers try to minimize environmental uncertainty by adjusting the organization's structure.[24]

	Unit Production	**Mass Production**	**Process Production**
Structural characteristics:	Low vertical differentiation	Moderate vertical differentiation	High vertical differentiation
	Low horizontal differentiation	High horizontal differentiation	Low horizontal differentiation
	Low formalization	High formalization	Low formalization
Most effective structure:	Organic	Mechanistic	Organic

Exhibit 11-7
Woodward's Findings on Technology and Structure

In stable and simple environments, mechanistic designs can be more effective. On the other hand, the greater the uncertainty, the more an organization needs the flexibility of an organic design. For example, the uncertain nature of the commercial air travel industry means that airlines need to be flexible. Several mergers reduced the number of major US airlines from nine to four. For instance, United and Continental merged in 2010, and American acquired US Airways in 2015. Combining airlines reduced the number of competitors and pressures to continually lower airfares.[25] The merged companies also were able to streamline corporate structure and operations.

The evidence on the environment–structure relationship helps explain why so many managers today are restructuring their organizations to be lean, fast, and flexible. Global competition, accelerated product innovation by competitors, and increased demands from customers for high quality and faster deliveries are examples of dynamic environmental forces. Mechanistic organizations are not equipped to respond to rapid environmental change and environmental uncertainty. As a result, we're seeing organizations become more organic.

TRADITIONAL organizational design options

LO11.4 When designing a structure, managers may choose one of the traditional organizational designs. These structures tend to be more mechanistic in nature. A summary of the strengths and weaknesses of each can be found in Exhibit 11-8.

simple structure
An organizational design with little departmentalization, wide spans of control, centralized authority, and little formalization

Simple Structure

Most companies start as entrepreneurial ventures using a **simple structure**, an organizational design with little departmentalization, wide spans of control, authority centralized in a single person, and little formalization.[26] As employees are added, however, most don't remain as simple structures. The structure tends to become more specialized and formalized. Rules and regulations are introduced, work becomes specialized, departments are created, levels of management are added, and the organization becomes increasingly bureaucratic. At this point, managers might choose a functional structure or a divisional structure.

An example of a simple structure is Mr. Mike's Surf Shop. A single store operation, the business is made up of four people: Mike (the owner and manager) and three sales personnel. The lack of rules, hierarchy, specialization, or departments makes this business highly organic.

Mr. Mike's Surf Shop uses a simple structure because of the shop's few employees
Source: Mia2you/Shutterstock

Exhibit 11-8
Traditional Organizational Designs

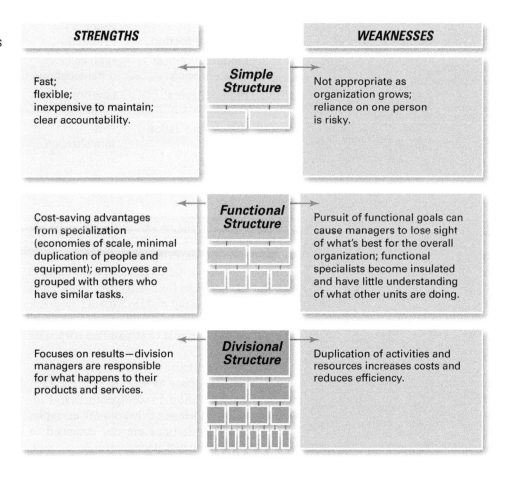

STRENGTHS		WEAKNESSES
Fast; flexible; inexpensive to maintain; clear accountability.	**Simple Structure**	Not appropriate as organization grows; reliance on one person is risky.
Cost-saving advantages from specialization (economies of scale, minimal duplication of people and equipment); employees are grouped with others who have similar tasks.	**Functional Structure**	Pursuit of functional goals can cause managers to lose sight of what's best for the overall organization; functional specialists become insulated and have little understanding of what other units are doing.
Focuses on results—division managers are responsible for what happens to their products and services.	**Divisional Structure**	Duplication of activities and resources increases costs and reduces efficiency.

functional structure
An organizational design that groups together similar or related occupational specialties

divisional structure
An organizational structure made up of separate, semiautonomous units or divisions

Functional Structure

A **functional structure** is an organizational design that groups similar or related occupational specialties together. You can think of this structure as functional departmentalization applied to the entire organization.

Divisional Structure

The **divisional structure** is an organizational structure made up of separate business units or divisions. In this structure, each division has limited autonomy, with a division manager who has authority over his or her unit and is responsible for performance. In divisional structures, however, the parent corporation typically acts as an external overseer to coordinate and control the various divisions, and often provides support services such as financial and legal. For instance, the Ford Motor Co. is organized into three divisions, each headed by an executive vice president: The Americas; Europe, Middle East, and Africa; and Asia Pacific.

ORGANIZING for flexibility in the twenty-first century

LO11.5 Many organizations are finding that traditional organizational designs often aren't appropriate for today's increasingly dynamic and complex environment. These organizations seek to be lean, flexible, and innovative; that is, to be more organic. So managers are finding creative ways to structure and organize work.[27]

Team Structures

Larry Page and Sergey Brin, cofounders of Google, created a corporate structure that organized projects around "small, tightly focused teams."[28] A **team structure** is one in which the entire organization is made up of work teams that do the organization's work.[29] In this structure, employee empowerment is crucial because no line of managerial authority flows from top to bottom. Rather, employee teams design and do work in the way they think is best, but the teams are also held responsible for all work performance results in their respective areas. Google found that its best teams share five traits: psychological safety, dependability, structure and clarity, meaningful membership, and purpose.[30]

In large organizations, the team structure complements what is typically a functional or divisional structure and allows the organization to have the efficiency of a bureaucracy *and* the flexibility that teams provide. Companies such as Amazon, Boeing, HP, Louis Vuitton, Motorola, and Xerox, for instance, extensively use employee teams to improve productivity.

> **team structure**
> An organizational structure in which the entire organization is made up of work teams

Matrix and Project Structures

Other popular contemporary designs are the matrix and project structures. The **matrix structure** assigns specialists from different functional departments to work on projects led by a project manager. (See Exhibit 11-9.) One unique aspect of this design is that it creates a *dual chain of command* because employees in a matrix organization have two bosses, their functional area manager and their product or project manager, who share authority. The project manager has authority over the functional members who are part of his or her project team in areas related to the project's goals. However, any decisions about promotions, salary recommendations, and annual reviews typically remain the functional manager's responsibility.

The matrix design "violates" the unity-of-command principle, which says that each person should report to only one boss; however, it can—and does—work effectively if both managers communicate regularly, coordinate work demands on employees, and resolve conflicts together.[31] For instance, matrix structures are common in healthcare settings. Physical therapists could be assigned to different programs. Some may help geriatric patients recover from hip replacement surgery. Others may work with trauma patients who have lost one or more limbs. All of the therapists report to the director of physical rehabilitation and to directors of their specialties.

Many organizations use a **project structure**, in which employees continuously work on projects. Unlike the matrix structure, a project structure has no formal departments where employees return at the completion of a project. Instead, employees take their specific skills, abilities, and experiences to other projects. Also, all work in project structures is performed by teams of employees. For instance, at design firm IDEO, project teams form, disband, and form again as the work requires. Employees "join" project teams because they bring needed skills and abilities to that project. Once a project is completed, however, they move on to the next one.[32]

Project structures tend to be more flexible organizational designs, without the departmentalization or rigid organizational hierarchy that can slow down making decisions or taking action. In this structure, managers serve as facilitators, mentors, and coaches. They eliminate or minimize organizational obstacles and ensure that teams have the resources they need to effectively and efficiently complete their work.

> **matrix structure**
> An organizational structure that assigns specialists from different functional departments to work on one or more projects

> **project structure**
> An organizational structure in which employees continuously work on projects

> **virtual organization**
> An organization that consists of a small core of full-time employees and outsources its major business functions

The matrix structure is an appropriate design for the dynamic and complex environment of construction projects.
Source: Morsa Images/E+/Getty Images

The Virtual Organization

Why own when you can rent? That question captures the essence of the **virtual organization** (also sometimes called the *network* or *modular* organization). It's typically a small

Exhibit 11-9

Example of a Matrix Organization

	R&D	Marketing	Customer Services (CS)	Human Resources (HR)	Finance	Information Systems (IS)
Product 1	R&D Group	Marketing Group	CS Group	HR Group	Finance Group	IS Group
Product 2	R&D Group	Marketing Group	CS Group	HR Group	Finance Group	IS Group
Product 3	R&D Group	Marketing Group	CS Group	HR Group	Finance Group	IS Group

fyi

Eighty-four percent of US employees are matrixed to some extent with 49 percent irregularly working on multiple teams.[33]

core of full-time employees that outsources its major business functions.[34] The virtual organization is highly centralized, with little or no departmentalization.

The prototype of the virtual structure is today's filmmaking organization. In Hollywood's golden era, movies were made by huge, vertically integrated corporations. Studios such as MGM, Warner Bros, and 20th Century Fox owned large movie lots and employed thousands of full-time specialists—set designers, camera people, film editors, costumers, directors, and actors. Today, most movies are made by a collection of individuals and small companies who come together and make films project by project. This structural form allows each project to be staffed with the talent best suited to its demands rather than just with the people employed by the studio. It minimizes bureaucratic overhead because there is no lasting organization to maintain. It lessens long-term risks and their costs because there is no long term—a team is assembled for a finite period and then disbanded.

The major advantage of the virtual structure is its flexibility, which allows individuals with an innovative idea and little money to successfully compete against larger, more established organizations. The structure also saves a great deal of money by eliminating permanent offices and hierarchical roles for outsourced functions. The drawbacks have become increasingly clear as popularity has grown. Virtual organizations are in a state of perpetual flux and reorganization, which means roles, goals, and responsibilities are unclear, setting the stage for increased political behavior.

Telecommuting

telecommuting
A work arrangement in which employees work at home and are linked to the workplace by computer

It was a work arrangement originally proposed as a win for both employers and employees. **Telecommuting** allowed employees to work at home and be linked to the workplace by computer.[36] For employees it meant no commutes, no colleague interruptions, and an opportunity to better balance work and personal lives. For employers, telecommuting reduces office expenses plus the potential to attract employees who otherwise wouldn't be available because of family responsibilities or physical disabilities. While not every job would be a candidate for telecommuting, almost any job that is substantially done on a computer could potentially be done by a telecommuter.

As recently as 2014, 59 percent of US employers offered telecommuting to employees.[37] This included companies like Xerox, Dell, American Express, and Apple. However, more recently, a number of major companies—IBM, Yahoo, Best Buy, Bank of America, Aetna, and Hewlett-Packard—have ended or significantly reduced their telecommuting program.[38] Why? The primary answer appears to be a desire to improve employee collaboration. Putting employees in the same physical space is believed to hasten the speed of work, build collegial relationships, and spark innovation. For many employees, having colleagues close by meets an important social need. In addition, many telecommuters admit that it's harder to stay focused and avoid distractions without the structure of an office environment.

fyi

Eighty to 90 percent of US employees would prefer to telecommute, at least part time.

• Between 2005 and 2019, telecommuting has grown by 140 percent.[35]

The fact that employees rate flexible-work programs highly suggests that telecommuting is not going to go away. It's likely to be a popular work arrangement but applicable to a more selective set of jobs and individuals.

Compressed Work Weeks

It has intuitive employee appeal: Work a day less each week for the same pay. That, essentially, is the **compressed workweek**—a workweek where employees work longer hours per day but fewer days per week. The most common arrangement is four 10-hour days (a 4–40 program), with the day off most commonly being Friday; thus providing a three-day weekend.[39]

Advocates of the compressed workweek propose that it allows workers extra time to pursue leisure activities and handle personal responsibilities; while cutting commuting time and costs—employees tend to arrive and leave at non-rush hour times, and commuting is reduced to four times a week. For employers, it can result in higher worker satisfaction, fewer absences, less turnover.

A number of large employers—Amazon, Google, Deloitte, The Gap—have experimented with four-day weeks but results have been mixed.[40] An ongoing schedule of ten-hour days can be physically and mentally draining, so initial employee enthusiasm frequently declines due to the long hours. Employees can find it difficult to arrange dependent care or transportation around the longer workday. And engaging in social activities on a weekday can be difficult when friends and family have to work. For management, the major negatives of the compressed week are coordinating scheduling and supervision.

Telecommuting allows employees to more easily balance their work and personal lives. Steven Schoonveld of Mansfield, Mass., sometimes sets up his "office" in coffee shops where he communicates with clients across the country.
Source: Tom Maguire/The Sun Chronicle/ AP Images

compressed workweek
A workweek where employees work longer hours per day but fewer days per week

---

Let's Get REAL

The Scenario:

Isabella Castillo, vice president of professional services at a consulting company that helps IT organizations deliver better service to their customers, needs help with her professional staff of sixteen consultants, who all work from home. Her problem: dealing with the realities of telecommuting—lack of direct interaction, lack of camaraderie, feeling isolated and out of the loop, etc. For their type of business, remote work makes good business sense, but how can she connect and engage her employees?

Source: Justin Kidwell

◄ **Justin Kidwell**
Management Consultant

What advice would you give Isabella?

I would focus on a few things:

1. *Making people development a strategic goal*
2. *Semiannual retreats*
3. *Leveraging technology*

Embedding people development into the performance measurement equation ensures interaction and teaming. The semiannual retreats provide a bonding environment and opportunity to gain buy-in to management priorities. Collaborative tools make phone-only meetings obsolete.

Learning from
FAILURE Working at Home Doesn't Work at IBM

In spite of the widespread popularity of telecommuting, it apparently isn't right for every job or every organization. IBM promoted the policy for several decades but, in 2017, decided that the negatives exceeded the positives and backed away.

In February 2017, some 2,600 people in IBM's marketing department, plus a number of others in IT and procurement, were informed that they could no longer telecommute. They could move to one of six IBM offices—in Atlanta, Austin, Boston, New York, Raleigh, and San Francisco—or look for a new job.

When initially introduced, IBM's management promoted the advantages of telecommuting: it cut down on workspace overhead costs while, at the same time, allowing employees more flexibility. However, at least among the company's marketing group, management recognized that times had changed. Effective marketing programs were no longer made up of independent processes but required real-time interactions. Bringing people together and promoting teamwork would likely improve speed, creativity, and productivity. While many employees affected were upset, management learned that telecommuting—at least among its marketing people—was a concept that was no longer the right answer for organizing their work tasks.[41]

Flextime

In contrast to the compressed workweek, flextime is an alternative work arrangement that appears to have staying power.

flextime
A scheduling system in which employees work a specific number of hours per week and can vary their hours of work within limits

Flexible work arrangements accommodate employees' needs and desires to achieve a balance between their work lives and personal lives. For example, work options such as compressed workweeks, flextime, and job sharing give parents the opportunity to spend time during the day with their children.
Source: Iakov Filimonov/Shutterstock

Flextime (short for flexible work time) is a scheduling system that requires employees to work a specific number of hours per week but allows them to vary their hours of work within limits.[42] In a typical flextime program, each day consists of a common core, usually six hours, with a flexibility band surrounding it. The core may be 9 a.m. to 3 p.m., with the office opening at 6 a.m. and closing at 6 p.m. Employees must be at their jobs during the common core period, but they can accumulate their other two hours around that. Some flextime programs also allow employees to accumulate extra hours and turn them into days off.

Flextime has become extremely popular. Surveys indicate a majority (54 to 56 percent) of US organizations offer some form of flextime.[43] And it seems to be a hit with both employers and employees. Twenty-three percent of organizations with flextime report an increase in productivity.[44] Many also indicate a reduction in employee tardiness and absenteeism. Among flextime workers, 53 percent cite flexible arrangements as a very important aspect of their job satisfaction, 55 percent were unlikely to look for job opportunities elsewhere within the year, and 34 percent stated that they would remain with their current employer because of flexible arrangements.[45]

The obvious drawback to flextime is that it's not applicable to every job. Among general employees, jobs that require close coordination of job tasks—such as assembly line work—and service jobs where employees have to be available during the entire 8-to-5 workday, don't readily lend themselves to flextime. And among managers and supervisors, they already have a high degree of autonomy in their jobs, so flextime's benefits have less appeal.

Job Sharing

Lynda Thomas and Hilary Cross are both CEOs at British cancer charity Macmillan.[46] How can an organization have two CEOs? The answer is that these two women *share* the same job. Thomas works from Monday until noon on

Wednesday; Cross works Wednesday at noon through Friday. This proves to work well for each—having worked their way up the organization, sharing jobs for more than a decade and a half. They both had families and only wanted a part-time job, but they also desired to progress in their careers. They partnered up in 2001 and made it to the top, sharing jobs all along the way.

Job sharing is the practice of two or more people splitting a full-time job.[48] For employers, its appeal is that it provides the opportunity to get two-for-the-price-of-one, gaining wider skills and experience than might be available in a single person. It also allows firms to attract skilled workers—for instance, retirees and parents with young children—who might not be available on a full-time basis. For employees, job sharing can increase motivation and satisfaction if they can work when they wouldn't normally be able to do so.

Like the compressed workweek, job sharing isn't widely popular. One survey found only 18 percent of US organizations offered it.[49] Reasons it's not more widely adopted include the difficulty in finding compatible partners to job-share and the historically negative perception of individuals not completely committed to their jobs and employer. However, it should be noted that a number of companies introduced job sharing during the 2007–09 Great Recession to avoid employee layoffs.[50]

The Contingent Workforce

Uber has between a million and a million and a half people worldwide working for it. But only 10,000 of them are full-time employees. The rest are contingent workers—drivers who work on their own schedules.

Uber is an example of a company that relies on **contingent workers**—freelancers, independent contractors, consultants, or other outsourced and non-permanent workers who are hired on a temporary basis. This contingent-based organization has been described as the dominant form of the future's workforce.[51]

As full-time jobs are eliminated to increase organizational flexibility and decrease costs, managers have increasingly relied on a contingent workforce to fill in as needed. A recent survey of top executives revealed that a majority of companies from a variety of industries are engaging contingent workers. For example, 81 percent of organizations in the healthcare industry use contingent workers.[52]

One of the main issues businesses face with their contingent workers, especially those who are independent contractors or freelancers, is classifying who actually qualifies as one. For instance, Uber treats its drivers as contractors. Their classification of these workers as independent contractors has caused battles in the courts. Uber drivers claim that they should be treated as employees because the company controls their work, sets compensation, and imposes vehicle standards.

While the legal status of contingent workers is likely to be in doubt for some time, the trend is clear: reliance on contingent workers will increase in the coming years. This is largely due to the increasingly dynamic environment in which organizations operate and the need to maintain maximum flexibility. When technology and new competitors are disrupting almost every business, managers don't have the luxury of being able to offer all employees long-term job security and abundant benefits. That said, the disappearance of traditional jobs may be widely exaggerated.[53] In 2017, only 10 percent of American workers were in temporary or freelance jobs.[54] So while the contingent workforce might be the dominant future, that future is likely to be at least a decade or more away.

---

fyi

Eighty-six percent of employees indicate that they value a flexible schedule, yet only 50 percent of their employers offer such flexibility.[47]

---

job sharing
The practice of having two or more people split a full-time job

contingent workers
Outsourced and non-permanent workers who are hired on a temporary basis

| Chapter 11 | **PREPARING FOR: Exams/Quizzes** |

CHAPTER SUMMARY by Learning Objectives

LO11.1

DESCRIBE six key elements in organizational design.

The key elements in organizational design are work specialization, departmentalization, chain of command, span of control, centralization–decentralization, and formalization. Work specialization is dividing work activities into separate job tasks. Work specialization can help employees be more efficient. Departmentalization is how jobs are grouped together. Today most large organizations use combinations of different forms of departmentalization. The chain of command and its companion concepts—authority, responsibility, and unity of command—were viewed as important ways of maintaining control in organizations. The contemporary view is that they are less relevant in today's organizations. The traditional view of span of control was that managers should directly supervise no more than five to six individuals. The contemporary view is that the span of control depends on the skills and abilities of the manager and the employees and on the characteristics of the situation. Centralization–decentralization is a structural decision about who makes decisions—upper-level managers or lower-level employees. Formalization concerns the organization's use of standardization and strict rules to provide consistency and control. Today, organizations rely less on strict rules and standardization to guide and regulate employee behavior.

LO11.2

CONTRAST mechanistic and organic structures.

A mechanistic organization is a rigid and tightly controlled structure. An organic organization is highly adaptive and flexible.

LO11.3

DISCUSS the contingency factors that favor either the mechanistic model or the organic model of organizational design.

An organization's structure should support the strategy. If the strategy changes, the structure also should change. An organization's size can affect its structure up to a certain point. Once an organization reaches a certain size (usually around 2,000 employees), it's fairly mechanistic. An organization's technology can affect its structure. An organic structure is most effective with unit production and process production technology. A mechanistic structure is most effective with mass production technology. The more uncertain an organization's environment, the more it needs the flexibility of an organic design.

LO11.4

DESCRIBE traditional organizational design options.

A simple structure is one with little departmentalization, wide spans of control, authority centralized in a single person, and little formalization. A functional structure groups similar or related occupational specialties together. A divisional structure is made up of separate business units or divisions.

LO11.5

DISCUSS organizing for flexibility in the twenty-first century.

In a team structure, the entire organization is made up of work teams. The matrix structure assigns specialists from different functional departments to work on one or more projects being led by project managers. A project structure is one in which employees continuously work on projects. A virtual organization consists of a small core of full-time employees and outside specialists temporarily hired as needed to work on projects.

Telecommuting is a work arrangement in which employees work at home and are linked to the workplace by computer. A compressed workweek is one in which employees work longer hours per day but fewer days per week. Flextime is a scheduling system in which employees are required to work a specific number of hours a week but are free to vary those hours within certain limits. Job sharing is when two or more people split a full-time job.

Contingent workers are temporary, freelance, or contract workers whose employment is contingent on demand for their services. Organizing issues include classifying who actually qualifies as an independent contractor; setting up a process for recruiting, screening, and placing contingent workers; and having a method in place for establishing goals, schedules, and deadlines for monitoring work performance.

REVIEW AND DISCUSSION QUESTIONS

11-1. Discuss the traditional and contemporary views of each of the six key elements of organizational design.

11-2. Would you rather work in a mechanistic or an organic organization? Why?

11-3. Contrast the three traditional organizational designs.

11-4. With the availability of advanced information technology that allows an organization's work to be done anywhere at any time, is organizing still an important managerial function? Why or why not?

11-5. Differentiate between matrix and project structures.

11-6. What structural issues might arise in managing employees' flexible work arrangements? Think about what you've learned about organizational design. How might that information help a manager address those issues?

11-7. How could a job-sharing arrangement be made effective? What would a job sharer need to do to make the arrangement work?

11-8. Why are more companies today relying on contingent workers?

PREPARING FOR: My Career

ETHICS DILEMMA

Thomas Lopez, a lifeguard in the Miami area, was fired for leaving his assigned area to save a drowning man. His employer, Jeff Ellis and Associates, which has a contract with the Florida city of Hallandale, said that by leaving his assigned patrol area uncovered, Lopez opened the company up to possible legal action. Lopez said he had no choice but to do what he did. He wasn't putting his job rules first over helping someone who desperately needed help. "I'm going

to do what I felt was right, and I did." After this story hit the media, the company offered Lopez his job back, but he declined.

11-9. What do you think? What ethical concerns do you see in this situation?

11-10. What lessons can be applied to organizational design from this story?

SKILLS EXERCISE   Developing Your Acquiring Power Skill

About the Skill
Power is a natural process in any group or organization, and to perform their jobs effectively, managers need to know how to acquire and use power.[55] Why is having power important? Because power makes you less dependent on others. When a manager has power, he or

she is not as dependent on others for critical resources. And if the resources a manager controls are important, scarce, and nonsubstitutable, her power will increase because others will be more dependent on her for those resources. (See Chapter 17 for more information on leader power.)

Steps in Practicing the Skill
You can be more effective at acquiring and using power if you use the following eight behaviors.

- *Frame arguments in terms of organizational goals.* To be effective at acquiring power means camouflaging your self-interest. Discussions over who controls what resources should be framed in terms of the benefits that will accrue to the organization; do not point out how you personally will benefit.

- *Develop the right image.* If you know your organization's culture, you already understand what the organization wants and values from its employees in terms of dress, associates to cultivate and those to avoid, whether to appear risk taking or risk aversive, the preferred leadership style, the importance placed on getting along well with others, and so forth. With this knowledge, you're equipped to project the appropriate image. Because the assessment of your performance isn't always a fully objective process, you need to pay attention to style as well as substance.

- *Gain control of organizational resources.* Controlling organizational resources that are scarce *and* important is a source of power. Knowledge and expertise are particularly effective resources to control. They make you more valuable to the organization and therefore more likely to have job security, chances for advancement, and a receptive audience for your ideas.

- *Make yourself appear indispensable.* Because we're dealing with appearances rather than objective facts, you can enhance your power by appearing to be indispensable. You don't really have *to be* indispensable, as long as key people in the organization believe that you are.

- *Be visible.* If you have a job that brings your accomplishments to the attention of others, that's great. However, if you don't have such a job, you'll want to find ways to let others in the organization know what you're doing by highlighting successes in routine reports, having satisfied customers relay their appreciation to senior executives, being seen at social functions, being active in your professional associations, and developing powerful allies who speak positively about your accomplishments. Of course, you'll want to be on the lookout for those projects that will increase your visibility.

- *Develop powerful allies.* To get power, it helps to have powerful people on your side. Cultivate contacts with potentially influential people above you, at your own level, and at lower organizational levels. These allies often can provide you with information that's otherwise not readily available. In addition, having allies can provide you with a coalition of support—if and when you need it.

- *Avoid "tainted" members.* In almost every organization, there are fringe members whose status is questionable. Their performance and/or loyalty may be suspect. Keep your distance from such individuals.

- *Support your boss.* Your immediate future is in the hands of your current boss. Because he or she evaluates your performance, you'll typically want to do whatever is necessary to have your boss on your side. You should make every effort to help your boss succeed, make her look good, support her if she is under siege, and spend the time to find out the criteria she will use to assess your effectiveness. Don't undermine your boss. And don't speak negatively of her to others.

Practicing the Skill
The following suggestions are activities you can do to practice the behaviors associated with acquiring power.

1. Keep a one-week journal of your behavior describing incidences when you tried to influence others around you. Assess each incident by asking: Were you successful at these attempts to influence them? Why or why not? What could you have done differently?

2. Review recent issues of a business periodical (such as *Bloomberg Businessweek, Fortune, Forbes, Fast Company, Industry Week,* or *The Wall Street Journal*). Look for articles on reorganizations, promotions, or departures from management positions. Find at least two articles where you believe power issues are involved. Relate the content of the articles to the concepts introduced in this skill module.

WORKING TOGETHER **Team Exercise**

Many organizations today offer telecommuting as an option for employees. However, there are many challenges in managing remote workers. It is useful to for organizations to create telecommuting guidelines to help address issues such as when and how to maintain communication with the office. Assume you are the manager of a small technology firm and you have decided to allow workers to telecommute. Consider some of the challenges you might face in managing the remote workers. Next, work in groups of three or four students to draft guidelines for telecommuters at your office. Be prepared to share your guidelines with the class.

MY TURN TO BE A MANAGER

- Find three different examples of an organizational chart. (A company's annual reports are a good place to look.) In a report, describe each of these. Try to decipher the organization's use of organizational design elements, especially departmentalization, chain of command, centralization-decentralization, and formalization.

- Survey at least ten different managers as to how many employees they supervise. Also ask them whether they feel they could supervise more employees or whether they feel the number they supervise is too many. Graph your survey results and write a report describing what you found. Draw some conclusions about span of control.

- Using current business periodicals, research matrix structures used by companies. Choose three examples of

businesses using this and describe and evaluate what each is doing.

- Visit the When Work Works website at www. whenworkworks.org. This organization works to bring research on workplace flexibility into practice. Visit the "Find Solutions" page of the website and review the guidance provided for employers. What resources are available for managers looking to create more flexible work arrangements?

CASE APPLICATION 1 — Making a Flat Organization Work at Punchkick

If you get a job at Punchkick Interactive—a digital agency that designs and builds software in Chicago—you won't have a boss. You'll not be shown an organizational chart of who reports to whom because such a chart doesn't exist. You also will be asked to choose your own job title.

As cofounder Zak Dabbas explains, growing up with no curfew taught him "that you can treat those you work alongside with all the respect in the world and trust them to make incredibly smart decisions from a place of empathy, not an org chart."[56]

Not having managers or a hierarchy worked well when there were about eight people in the company. Once the company grew to more than twenty employees, however, Punchkick's founders realized that they needed to find ways to improve how people work together.

Punchkick rolled out an "advice channel," which allows employees to share expertise. So, if employees are experiencing a challenge with a client project, they can reach out to the entire company through the advice channel and ask who has encountered a similar problem before. The company also asked employees to be sure to "touch base" with anyone who might be impacted by a decision they're making. This is not the same as getting permission—it's more about ensuring that communication has occurred before any challenges arise. Employees are evaluated by other employees via a feedback channel instead of being evaluated by only a manager.

Job titles sometimes emerge as part of using the advice channel. For instance, Abby Gartner was the "go-to" person for handling clients. She was the first person employees went to about how to address client needs. According to Dabbas, "Eventually, we said, 'Abby, let's face it; you're our head of customer experience.'"

So far, Punchkick is prospering. They have been on the Inc. 5000 list of fastest-growing privately held companies for five years in a row. Dabbas believes that having a flat organizational structure is a key ingredient to their success . . . and complementing that structure with transparency. "Everyone knows what our goals are every month and how we're tracking toward them," Dabbas explained.

Other companies without official bosses have experienced problems. Valve, a computer game development company in Seattle, officially had no bosses, but as one former employee stated, "There is actually a hidden layer of powerful management structure in the company . . . which made it feel a lot like high school."[57] Another ex-employee at Valve explained, "To succeed at Valve you need to belong to the group that has more decisional power and, even when you succeed temporarily, be certain that you have an expiration date."

DISCUSSION QUESTIONS

11-11. How would you describe Punchkick Interactive in terms of the elements of organizational design?

11-12. What are the strengths and potential areas of concern illustrated by the example of Punchkick?

11-13. What do you think makes a flat, "no boss" structure like Punchkick's work effectively? In what situations (e.g., industries, organizational sizes, employee characteristics) would this structure not work as well?

11-14. What advice would you give to Punchkick to ensure that they don't experience the problems that Valve has had?

CASE APPLICATION 2 — The Invisible Workforce at Google

Imagine being at all-company meetings where trays of hors d'oeuvres and drinks are being served, but you and the others who aren't wearing white badges are asked to return to your desks. That has been the experience of some contractors at Google. There aren't just a few contractors at Google these days. In early 2018, there were more contractors than regular employees (and there were more than 89,000 regular employees).[58]

Google spokespeople have said that they hire contractors when the company needs to fill temporary positions that arise due to events like upswings in workload or paternity leave. Contractor hiring also can be done when there is a need for a certain specialty within the company. Former Google hiring managers explain that hiring expensive engineers in fields like artificial intelligence can sometimes cost as much as $1 million per year, so contractors offer a way to bring the budget back in line. Contractors can be hired quickly—within days—whereas it can take months to hire regular employees at Google.

There are advantages to being a contractor at Google. Even though they are asked to list their association with Google as being a contractor on LinkedIn, just mentioning Google can open doors. Chris Szymczak, a former Google contractor, had several Google coworkers serve as references. "They were just immensely supportive ... the gig was a real springboard for me."

Life as a contractor has its negatives. "People look down on you even though you're doing the same work," said one former Google contractor. "You're there, but you're not there." Your work assignment can end without notice; asking contractors to hand in their laptop the next day could happen. Google views contractors' pay, benefits, and grievances to be the hiring agencies' issues. That means, for example, that experiencing verbal harassment at work is the hiring company's concern rather than Google's. There are contractor janitors at Google who make just over half of what is considered to be a "low income" level of pay in the county where Google's headquarters is located. Benefits tend be less than competitive, such as was the case for a former Google contractor who was paying $600 per month for health insurance.

A group of regular employees at Google met with the company's senior leadership recently to complain about several issues—including concerns about contractors. Yana Calou, an organizer with Coworker.org, said that many Google employees believe the experiences of contractors could be better. Calou said contractors "feel isolated, precarious, and like second-class citizens."

DISCUSSION QUESTIONS

11-15. What are the advantages of contractor workers for a) Google and b) the workers themselves?

11-16. What are the most important problems that you see with being a contractor?

11-17. How do you think the contractor hiring arrangement could be improved to realize effective outcomes for both contractors and Google?

11-18. Do you think the experiences of contractors and regular employees would have a better chance of being more similar to one another in a mechanistic or organic organizational structure? Explain the reasons for your answer.

ENDNOTES

1. McKinsey & Company, "ING's Agile Transformation," *McKinsey Quarterly*, January 2017, https://www.mckinsey.com/industries/financial-services/our-insights/ings-agile-transformation; and N. Perkin, "Agile Transformation at ING—A Case Study," agilebusinessmanifesto.com, October 25, 2017, https://agilebusinessmanifesto.com/agilebusiness/agile-transformation-at-ing/.

2. J. S. Bunderson, Y. Cantimur, and F. Rink, "Different Views of Hierarchy and Why They Matter: Hierarchy as Inequality or as Cascading Influence," *Academy of Management Journal* 59, no. 4 (August 2016): pp. 1265–89; and Richard L. Daft, *Organization Theory and Design*, 12th ed. (Boston: Cengage, 2016).

3. T. Hindle, *Guide to Management Ideas and Gurus* (London, UK: Profile Books, 2008).

4. For a discussion of authority, see W. A. Kahn and K. E. Kram, "Authority at Work: Internal Models and Their Organizational Consequences," *Academy of Management Review* 19, no. 1 (January 1994): pp. 17–50.

5. L. Weber and L. Cook, "Workers Deal With Too Many Bosses," *Wall Street Journal*, August 21, 2018, p. B1.

6. Based on L. Taylor, "How to Deal with 'Multiple Boss Madness,'" *Psychology Today*, February 23, 2011, https://www.psychologytoday.com/us/blog/tame-your-terrible-office-tyrant/201102/how-deal-multiple-boss-madness; A. Gallo, "Managing Multiple Bosses," *Harvard Business Review* (online), August 18, 2011, https://hbr.org/2011/08/managing-multiple-bosses; R. I. Sutton, *Good Boss, Bad Boss: How to Be the Best ... and Learn from the Worst* (New York: Business Plus, 2012); J. Simmons, "Who's the Boss? Answering to Multiple Bosses," *Monster*, January 1, 2015, https://www.monster.com/career-advice/article/answering-to-multiple-bosses; and M. Backman, "Multiple Bosses? Here's How to Cope," *Motley Fool*, January 15, 2018, https://www.fool.com/careers/2018/01/15/multiple-bosses-heres-how-to-cope.aspx.

7. "2017 Human Capital Benchmarking Report," Society for Human Resource Management, December 2017, https://www.shrm.org/hr-today/trends-and-forecasting/research-and-surveys/Documents/2017-Human-Capital-Benchmarking.pdf.

8. S. Lebowitz, "Apple CEO Tim Cook Now Has 17 Direct Reports—and That's Probably Too Many," *Business Insider*, July 8, 2015, https://www.businessinsider.com/apple-ceo-tim-cook-has-too-many-direct-reports-2015-7.

9. G. L. Neilson and J. Wulf, "How Many Direct Reports?," *Harvard Business Review*, April 2012, pp. 112–19.

10. See, for example, H. Mintzberg, *Power In and Around Organizations* (Upper Saddle River, NJ: Prentice Hall, 1983); and J. Child, *Organization: A Guide to Problems and Practices* (London: Kaiser & Row, 1984).

11. G. Panou, "Why Is Decentralization of Decision-Making, Becoming More Common in Contemporary Organizations?," *ResearchGate*, November 2016, https://www.researchgate.net/publication/325923403_Why_is_decentralization_of_decision-making_becoming_more_common_in_contemporary_organizations.

12. Johnson & Johnson, *Annual Report 2015*, 2016, https://www.jnj.com/_document?id=0000015a-817f-d3f1-af7e-ddffde9e0000.

13. K. King, "Johnson & Johnson: Company Overview," *Harvard Business School Open Knowledge*; December 8, 2015; https://www.hbs.org.

14. T. Burns and G. M. Stalker, *The Management of Innovation* (London: Tavistock, 1961); and D. A. Morand, "The Role of Behavioral Formality and Informality in the Enactment of Bureaucratic Versus Organic Organizations," *Academy of Management Review* 20, no. 4 (October 1995): pp. 831–72.

15. C. Feser, "Long Live Bureaucracy," *Leader to Leader*, Summer 2012, pp. 57–62; and N. Ferguson, "In Praise of Hierarchy," *Wall Street Journal*, January 6–7, 2018, p. C1.

16. M. Garbuio and N. Lin, "The Appeal of the 'Flat' Organisation—Why Some Firms Are Getting Rid of Middle Managers," *Conversation*, January 14, 2018, http://theconversation.com/the-appeal-of-the-flat-organisation-why-some-firms-are-getting-rid-of-middle-managers-88942.

17. Ibid.

18. A. D. Chandler Jr., *Strategy and Structure: Chapters in the Industrial Enterprise* (Cambridge, MA: MIT Press, 1962).

19. See, for instance, W. Chan Kim and R. Mauborgne, "How Strategy Shapes Structure," *Harvard Business Review*, September 2009, pp. 73–80; B. Grøgaard, "Alignment of Strategy and Structure in International Firms: An Empirical Examination," *International Business Review* 21, no. 3 (June 2012): pp. 397–407; R. Wilden, S. P. Gudergan, B. B. Nielsen, and I. Lings, "Dynamic Capabilities and Performance: Strategy, Structure and Environment," *Long Range Planning* 46, nos. 1–2 (February–April 2013): pp. 72–96; and E. Ford, R. Wells, and T. Reeves, "Strategy and Structure: A Learning Perspective and Analysis," *Business and Economic Research* (January 2014): pp. 1–13.

20. R. Z. Gooding and J. A. Wagner III, "A Meta-Analytic Review of the Relationship Between Size and Performance: The Productivity and Efficiency of Organizations and Their Subunits," *Administrative Science Quarterly* 30, no. 4 (December 1985): pp. 462–81.

21. P. Kavilanz, "Louisville's CloudDDM Factory: 100 Printers, 3 Employees," *CNNMoney*, May 4, 2015, https://money.cnn.com/2015/05/04/smallbusiness/cloudddm-3d-printing-factory-ups/index.html.

22. J. Woodward, *Industrial Organization: Theory and Practice* (London: Oxford University Press, 1965).

23. D. Gerwin, "Relationships Between Structure and Technology," in *Handbook of Organizational Design*, vol. 2, eds. P. C. Nystrom and W. H. Starbuck (New York: Oxford University Press, 1981), pp. 3–38; C. C. Miller, W. H. Glick, Y.-D. Wang, and G. Huber, "Understanding Technology-Structure Relationships: Theory Development and Meta-Analytic

Theory Testing," *Academy of Management Journal* 34, no. 2 (June 1991); and M. Attar and G. Temizel, "Strategic Choice Perspective to Technological Change," *European Scientific Journal* (July 2015): pp. 118–23.

24. P. Lawrence and J. W. Lorsch, *Organization and Environment: Managing Differentiation and Integration* (Boston: Harvard Business School, Division of Research, 1967); M. Yasai-Ardekani, "Structural Adaptations to Environments," *Academy of Management Review* 11, no. 1 (January 1986): pp. 9–21; and Q. Tran and Y. Tian, "Organizational Structure: Influencing Factors and Impact on a Firm," *American Journal of Industrial and Business Management* 3, no. 2 (April 2013): pp. 229–36.

25. B. Mutzabaugh, "Era of Airline Merger Mania Comes to a Close with Last US Airways Flight," USA Today, October 16, 2015, https://www.usatoday.com/story/travel/flights/todayinthesky/2015/10/15/airline-mergers-american-delta-united-southwest/73972928/.

26. H. Mintzberg, *Structure in Fives: Designing Effective Organizations* (Upper Saddle River, NJ: Prentice Hall, 1983), p. 157.

27. See, for instance, P. Puranam, O. Alexy, and M. Reitzig, "What's 'New' About New Forms of Organizing?," *Academy of Management Review* 39, no. 2 (April 2014): pp. 162–80; and T. Felin and T. C. Powell, "Designing Organizations for Dynamic Capabilities," *California Management Review* 58, no. 4 (August 2016): pp. 78–96.

28. N. Smithson, "Google's Organizational Structure & Organizational Culture," *Panmore Institute*, updated September 8, 2018, http://panmore.com/google-organizational-structure-characteristics-analysis.

29. S. H. Courtright, G. R. Thurgood, G. L. Stewart, and A. J. Pierotti, "Structural Interdependence in Teams: An Integrative Framework and Meta-Analysis," *Journal of Applied Psychology* 100, no. 6 (2015): pp. 1825–46.

30. R. Feloni, "Google Has Found That Its Most Successful Teams Have 5 Traits in Common," *Business Insider*, November 18, 2015, https://www.businessinsider.com/google-explains-top-traits-of-its-best-teams-2015-11.

31. M. Bazigos and J. Harter, "Revisiting the Matrix Organization," *McKinsey Quarterly*, no. 4 (2015): pp. 8–13.

32. T. Amabile, C. M. Fisher, and J. Pillemer, "IDEO's Culture of Helping," *Harvard Business Review*, January–February 2014, pp. 54–61.

33. Bazigos and Harter, "Revisiting the Matrix Organization" [see note 31].

34. See, for instance, K. Culo, "Virtual Organization: The Future Has Already Begun," *Media, Culture, and Public Relations*, January 2016, pp. 35–42; and S. Shekhar, *Managing the Reality of Virtual Organizations* (New York: Springer, 2016).

35. Global Workplace Analytics, "Latest Telecommuting Statistics," GlobalWorkplaceAnalytics.com, 2019.

36. Y. Blount and M. Gloet, eds., *Anywhere Working and the New Era of Telecommuting* (Hershey, PA: Business Science Reference, 2017).

37. Cited in D. Wilkie, "Has the Telecommuting Bubble Burst?," *HRMagazine*, June 2015, p. 77.

38. See, for instance, Wilkie, "Telecommuting Bubble," pp. 76–81; and J. Simons, "IBM Says No to Home Work," *Wall Street Journal*, May 19, 2017, p. A1.

39. C. A. Arbon, R. L. Facer, and L. L. Wadsworth, "Compressed Workweeks—Strategies for Successful Implementation," *Public Personnel Management* 41, no. 3 (September 2012): pp. 389–405; and B. Lufkin, "Just How Short Could We Make the Working Week?," *BBC*, August 28, 2018, http://www.bbc.com/capital/story/20180828-just-how-short-could-we-make-the-workweek.

40. A. Dembe, "The Hidden Dangers of a 4-Day Workweek," *Quartz*, March 7, 2017, https://qz.com/820467/sorry-but-a-four-day-workweek-isnt-actually-better-for-your-health/.

41. Based on C. Weller, "IBM was a Pioneer in the Work-From-Home Revolution—Now It's Cracking Down," Business Insider, March 27, 2017, https://www.businessinsider.com/ibm-slashes-work-from-home-policy-2017-3; and J. Simons, "Employers Pull Plug on Remote Work," *Wall Street Journal*, July 26, 2017, p. B1.

42. B. H. Gottlieb, E. K. Kelloway, and E. J. Barham, *Flexible Work Arrangements: Managing the Work-Family Boundary* (New York: John Wiley, 1998); and S. Yap, "Improve Employee Productivity With Flextime," *Zendesk* (blog), July 24, 2014, https://www.zendesk.com/blog/improve-employee-productivity-flextime/.

43. Society for Human Resource Management, *2016 Employee Benefits: Looking Back at 20 Years of Employee Benefits Offering in the U.S.* (Alexandria, VA: SHRM, 2016); and Society for Human Resource Management, *2016 Strategic Benefits— Flexible Work Arrangements* (Alexandria, VA: SHRM, 2016).

44. Ibid.

45. Society for Human Resource Management, *Employee Job Satisfaction and Engagement: Revitalizing a Changing Workforce* (Alexandria, VA: SHRM, 2016).

46. S. Brennan, "How Two Women Became CEOs Through Job Sharing," telegraph.co.uk, February 3, 2016.

47. "The Rise of the Social Enterprise: 2018 Deloitte Global Capital Trends," *Deloitte*, 2018, https://www2.deloitte.com/content/dam/insights/us/articles/HCTrends2018/2018-HCtrends_Rise-of-the-social-enterprise.pdf.

48. S. Driver, "The Advantages and Disadvantages of Job Sharing," *Business News Daily*, December 11, 2017, https://www.businessnewsdaily.com.

49. S. Adams, "Workers Have More Flextime, Less Real Flexibility, Study Shows," *Forbes*, May 2, 2014, https://www.forbes.com/sites/susanadams/2014/05/02/workers-have-more-flextime-less-real-flexibility-study-shows/#452c6fde7bfa.

50. S. Greenhouse, "Work-Sharing May Help Companies Avoid Layoffs," *New York Times*, June 16, 2009, https://www.nytimes.com/2009/06/16/business/economy/16workshare.html.

51. A. Srinivasan, "The Future Workforce Is Here: And It's Forcing Contingent Workforce Management to Evolve," *HR.com*, February 19, 2016, https://www.hr.com/en/topleaders/all_articles/the-future-workforce-is-here-and-it%E2%80%99s-forcing-cont_iktobbh2.html.

52. M. Ettling/SAP, "The Rise of the Contingent Worker," *Forbes*, December 19, 2014, https://www.forbes.com/sites/sap/2014/12/19/the-rise-of-the-contingent-worker/#7d3f07482a82.

53. B. Casselman, "The Exaggerated Gig Economy," *New York Times*, June 8, 2018, p. B1.

54. Ibid.

55. Based on H. Mintzberg, *Power In and Around Organizations* (Upper Saddle River, NJ: Prentice Hall, 1983), p. 24; G. Ferris, S. Davidson, and P. Perrewe, "Developing Political Skill at Work," *Training*, November 2005, pp. 40–45; and R. E. Sturm

and J. Antonakis, "Interpersonal Power: A Review, Critique, and Research Agenda," *Journal of Management* 41, no. 1 (January 2015): pp. 136–63.

56. G. Abramovich, "How This Company's Flat Org Structure Empowers Employees," *CMO.com*, June 20, 2018, https://www.cmo.com/features/articles/2018/5/23/inside-innovation-how-punchkicks-flat-org-structure-empowers-employees.html#gs.2enpei.

57. A. Spicer, "No Bosses, No Managers: The Truth Behind the 'Flat Hierarchy' Façade," Opinion, *Guardian*, July 30, 2018, https://www.theguardian.com/commentisfree/2018/jul/30/no-bosses-managers-flat-hierachy-workplace-tech-hollywood.

58. M. Bergen and J. Eidelson, "Inside Google's Shadow Workforce of Contract Laborers," *Bloomberg*, July 25, 2018, https://www.bloomberg.com/news/articles/2018-07-25/inside-google-s-shadow-workforce.

Chapter 12

Managing Human Resources

Learning Objectives

12.1 Explain the importance of human resource management and the human resource management process.

12.2 Describe the external influences that affect the human resource management process.

12.3 Discuss the tasks associated with identifying and selecting competent employees.

12.4 Explain how companies provide employees with skills and knowledge.

12.5 Describe strategies for retaining competent, high-performing employees.

12.6 Identify two important trends in organizational career development.

12.7 Discuss contemporary issues in managing human resources.

Employability Skills Matrix

This matrix identifies which features and end-of-chapter material will help you develop specific skills employers are looking for in job candidates.

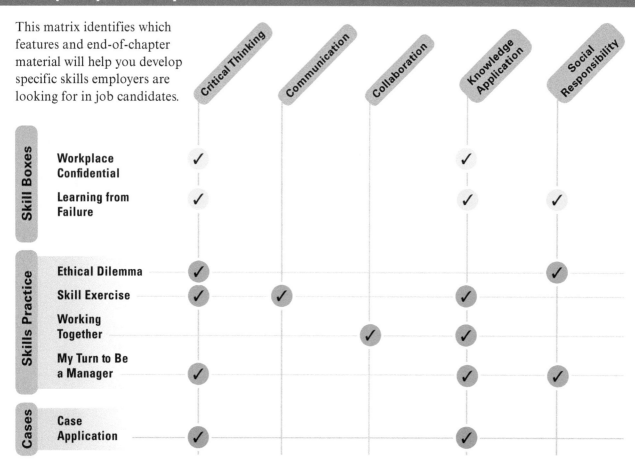

		Critical Thinking	Communication	Collaboration	Knowledge Application	Social Responsibility
Skill Boxes	Workplace Confidential	✓			✓	
	Learning from Failure	✓			✓	✓
Skills Practice	Ethical Dilemma	✓				✓
	Skill Exercise	✓	✓		✓	
	Working Together			✓	✓	
	My Turn to Be a Manager	✓			✓	✓
Cases	Case Application	✓			✓	

Walmart wants to ensure that all of its 1.4 million employees are well prepared to deal with common problems they might confront on the job. Toward that end, all employees go through two weeks of training before starting an entry-level job or a new role.

Part of Walmart's training now includes the use of virtual reality.[1] Using state-of-the-art technology, employees experience real-world scenarios through the use of a VR headset. This VR training covers three main areas: new technology, soft skills like empathy and customer service, and compliance. Training modules contain realistic content that allows associates to learn information faster than through lectures or training manuals. The headsets are linked to a video screen that additionally shows others in the classroom what the trainee is seeing so that the instructor and students can weigh in on the performance.

Walmart's commitment to employee training highlights the importance that organization's place on human resource practices. Management needs to ensure that they have the right number of people, with the right skills, in the right place, at the right time. In this chapter, we'll look at the process managers use to do just that. In addition, we'll look at some contemporary human resource issues facing managers.

Walmart incorporates virtual reality into its employee training programs. Here, Jeanelle Bass, an assistant store manager, wears virtual reality goggles while participating in an interactive session at the Walmart Academy training facility.
Source: Julio Cortez/AP Images

WHY human resource management is important

L012.1 Management experts regularly state the importance that effective human resource management (HRM) policies and practices play in an organization's performance.[2] Why is HRM important? There are at least three reasons.

First, HRM has shown to be a significant source of competitive advantage.[3] It's true for both US and international organizations. The Human Capital Index, a comprehensive study of more than 2,000 global firms, concluded that people-oriented HRM gives an organization an edge by creating superior shareholder value.[4] Another study found that 71 percent of CEOs say that their "human capital" is the key source of sustained economic value.[5]

Second, HRM is an important part of organizational strategies.[6] Outside the HR department, achieving competitive success through people means managers must change how they think about their employees and how they view the work relationship. They must work with people and treat them as partners, not just as costs to be minimized or avoided. That's what people-oriented organizations such as Southwest Airlines and W.L. Gore do.

Finally, the way organizations treat their people has been found to significantly impact organizational performance.[7] For instance, a study that tracked average annual shareholder returns of companies on *Fortune's* list of 100 Best Companies to Work For found that these companies significantly beat the S&P 500 over 10-year, 5-year, 3-year, and 1-year periods.[8]

Keep in mind that an understanding of HRM is not just the domain of people who work in an organization's human resource department. HR departments don't exist in the majority of businesses—which are small and don't have defined HR specialists. HR departments tend to exist in large firms. As a result, in smaller firms, HR activities tend to be undertaken by line managers. Additionally, even in large corporations and government organizations, most managers need to be skilled in basic HR practices such as knowledge and interpretation of labor laws and conducting employee selection interviews and performance evaluations.

Exhibit 12-1
HRM Process

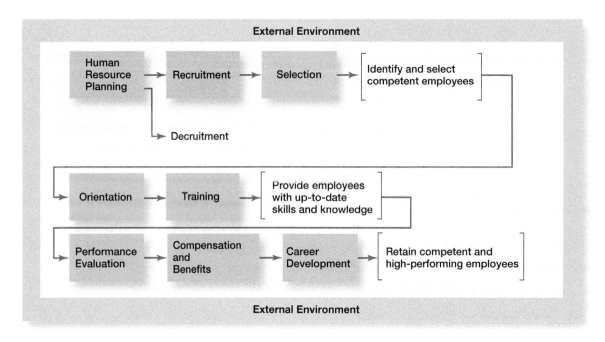

THE HUMAN RESOURCE MANAGEMENT PROCESS

To ensure that an organization has qualified people to perform the work that needs to be done, specific HRM activities need to be performed. These activities compose the HRM process. Exhibit 12-1 shows the eight activities in this process. The first three activities ensure that competent employees are identified and selected, the next two involve providing employees with up-to-date knowledge and skills, and the final three ensure that the organization retains competent and high-performing employees. Before we discuss those specific activities, we need to look at external factors that affect the HRM process.

EXTERNAL factors that affect the human resource management process

LO12.2 A strong economy makes it difficult for Employer X to find people with the skills it needs. Company Y faces a walkout by its unionized workforce over a contract dispute. And although the US federal minimum wage is $7.25 an hour, fast-food Employer Z in San Francisco is required to raise its minimum wage to $15 after new legislation is passed by the city. These are examples of how the HRM process is influenced by the external environment. In this section, we look more closely at these influences.

The Economy

The Great Recession of 2008 forced many employers to reduce costs by cutting their workforce. In many cases, employees with twenty or more years of service found that their jobs had been eliminated. Fast-forward ten years and it's another story. The economy is booming and companies struggle to find and retain skilled workers.[9] In the summer of 2018, the US unemployment rate had dropped to an eighteen-year low of 3.9 percent. Almost anyone who wanted a job could find one. And employers found themselves having to forgo business because they couldn't find workers. For instance, employers in Ames, Iowa, had a particularly hard time in 2018 as the city's jobless rate was a mere 1.5 percent.[10] Chris Nelson, who runs a century-old electrical business in Ames, couldn't find electricians. He raised wages and took on semi-retired workers to fill the gaps in his seventy-worker firm. Ron Sandlin's Patriot Transportation firm, which operates oil trucks out of Ames, boosted pay, added vacation days, and offered hiring and longevity bonuses to maintain his 600-person payroll.

As the above illustrates, the ebb and flow of the economy—with changes in the business cycle—directly affect an organization's human resources. In downturns, management is often forced to reduce staff, cut pay, and reorganize work activities. In strong economies and tight labor markets, management has to raise wages, improve benefits, seek out retirees, provide in-house training, and make other adaptations to attract and keep qualified people.

Yoon Gap-han (right), president of Hyundai Motor Co., and union leader Ha Bu-young shake hands at a signing ceremony for a wage deal.
Source: Yonhap News/YNA/Newscom

Labor Unions

In 2016, 40,000 unionized workers at Verizon walked off the job after failing to reach a new labor agreement. The strike was precipitated, in part, by outsourcing thousands of the company's jobs to Mexico, the Philippines, and the Dominican Republic.[11] In 2018, train workers in France initiated months of nationwide rolling strikes that created widespread disruption of local and regional train service. The reason for these strikes: the French government sought to overhaul the state-run railway, SNCF, which included ending job-for-life guarantees for unionized rail staff.[12] These two examples illustrate the influence of labor unions and how they can create challenges for management.

A **labor union** is an organization that represents workers and seeks to protect their interests through collective bargaining. In unionized organizations, many HRM decisions are dictated by collective bargaining agreements, which usually define things such as recruitment sources; criteria for hiring, promotions, and layoffs; training eligibility; and disciplinary practices.

Union participation rates in the US peaked in the mid-1950s, when approximately 35 percent of all wage and salary workers belonged to a union. Today, that number is down under 11 percent.[13] But don't let the fact that a minority of workers are now unionized be interpreted as meaning that they've lost their influence. They still hold dominant positions in certain businesses—for instance utilities, transportation, and warehousing—and represent a third of all workers in the public sector (including teachers, police officers, firefighters, and government workers).[14] Additionally, there is an indirect effect on nonunion workers. When unions negotiate higher salaries, expanded benefits, or enhance job security for their members, they influence labor practices for non-union organizations that have to compete against unionized firms. For instance, a new contract that increases unionized truck drivers' salaries in Buffalo by $4 an hour is likely to lead to higher wages for all truck drivers in the Buffalo area. Finally, we need to recognize that labor union membership is often considerably higher outside the US. In Germany, 17 percent of the total labor force belongs to unions. In Canada, it's 26 percent. And in Iceland, it's over 90 percent![15]

labor union
An organization that represents workers and seeks to protect their interests through collective bargaining

Laws and Rulings

Twenty-eight million dollars. That's the amount an Ohio jury awarded a former Cleveland Clinic doctor who sued the hospital for discrimination and retaliation.[16] Dr. Robert Katz, an ear, nose, and throat doctor who had worked at the clinic for two decades, claimed he was forced out at age 77 due to his age. According to Katz, a new chairman of the Head and Neck Institute pressured him to retire because he was "no longer a fit" for the hospital.

As the above example illustrates, an organization's HRM practices are governed by a country's laws, and not following those laws can be costly. (See Exhibit 12-2 for some of the important US laws that affect the HRM process.) Decisions regarding who will be hired or which employees will be chosen for a training program or what an employee's compensation will be must be made without regard to race, sex, religion, age, color, national origin, pregnancy, or disability. Exceptions can occur only in special circumstances. For instance, a community fire department can deny employment to a firefighter applicant who uses a wheelchair; but if that same individual is applying for a desk job, such as a dispatcher, the disability cannot be used as a reason to deny employment.

HRM laws and regulations clearly affect organizational practices and limit managerial discretion. And because workplace lawsuits are increasingly targeting supervisors, as well as their organizations, all managers need to know what they can and cannot do by law.[17] Trying to balance the "shoulds" and "should nots" of many laws often falls within the realm of **affirmative action**. Many US organizations have

affirmative action
Organizational programs that enhance the status of members of protected groups

Exhibit 12-2
Major HRM Laws

Sources: US Equal Employment Opportunity Commission, www.eeoc.gov; US Department of Labor, www.dol.gov; US Occupational Safety and Health Administration, www.osha.gov.

LAW OR RULING	YEAR	DESCRIPTION
Equal Employment Opportunity and Discrimination		
Equal Pay Act	1963	Prohibits pay differences for equal work based on gender
Civil Rights Act, Title VII	1964 (amended in 1972)	Prohibits discrimination based on race, color, religion, national origin, or gender
Age Discrimination in Employment Act	1967 (amended in 1978)	Prohibits discrimination against employees 40 years and older
Vocational Rehabilitation Act	1973	Prohibits discrimination on the basis of physical or mental disabilities
Americans with Disabilities Act	1990	Prohibits discrimination against individuals who have disabilities or chronic illnesses; also requires reasonable accommodations for these individuals
Compensation/Benefits		
Worker Adjustment and Retraining Notification Act	1990	Requires employers with more than 100 employees to provide 60 days' notice before a mass layoff or facility closing
Family and Medical Leave Act	1993	Gives employees in organizations with 50 or more employees up to 12 weeks of unpaid leave each year for family or medical reasons
Health Insurance Portability and Accountability Act	1996	Permits portability of employees' insurance from one employer to another
Lilly Ledbetter Fair Pay Act	2009	Changes the statute of limitations on pay discrimination to 180 days from each paycheck
Patient Protection and Affordable Care Act	2010	Penalizes employers with 50 or more employees who don't offer coverage or do not offer coverage that meets minimal value and affordability standards.
Health/Safety		
Occupational Safety and Health Act (OSHA)	1970	Establishes mandatory safety and health standards in organizations
Privacy Act	1974	Gives employees the legal right to examine personnel files and letters of reference
Consolidated Omnibus Reconciliation Act (COBRA)	1985	Requires continued health coverage following termination (paid by employee)

affirmative action programs to ensure that decisions and practices enhance the employment, upgrading, and retention of members from protected groups such as minorities, females, and the disabled. That is, through affirmative action an organization refrains from discrimination and actively seeks to enhance the status of members from protected groups.

What about HRM laws globally? Let's take a brief look at some of the federal legislation in countries such as Canada, Mexico, and Germany.

Canadian laws pertaining to HRM practices share similarities with those in the United States. The Canadian Human Rights Act prohibits discrimination on the basis of race, national or ethnic origin, color, religion, age, sex, sexual orientation, marital status, family status, disability, or conviction for an offense for which a pardon has been granted. This act governs practices throughout the country. Canada's HRM environment, however, is somewhat different from that in the United States in that it involves more decentralization of lawmaking to the provincial level. For example, discrimination on the basis of language is not prohibited anywhere in Canada except in Quebec.

In Mexico, employees are more likely to be unionized than they are in the United States. Labor matters in Mexico are governed by the Mexican Federal Labor Law. One hiring law states that an employer has twenty-eight days to evaluate a new employee's work performance. After that period, the employee is granted job security and termination is quite difficult and expensive. Those who violate the Mexican Federal Labor Law are subject to severe penalties, including criminal action that can result in steep fines and even jail sentences for employers who fail to pay, for example, the minimum wage.

Our final example, Germany, is similar to most Western European countries when it comes to HRM practices. Legislation requires companies to practice representative participation, which redistributes power within the organization, putting labor on a more equal footing with the interests of management and stockholders. The two most common forms of representative participation are work councils and board representatives. **Work councils** link employees with management. They are groups of nominated or elected employees who must be consulted when management makes decisions involving personnel. **Board representatives** are employees who sit on a company's board of directors and represent the interests of the firm's employees.

work councils
Groups of nominated or elected employees who must be consulted when management makes decisions involving personnel

board representatives
Employees who sit on a company's board of directors and represent the interests of the firm's employees

Demography

A few years back, the head of BMW's 2,500-employee power train plant in Dingolfing, Lower Bavaria, was worried about the potential inevitable future decline in productivity due to an aging workforce.[18] That's when company executives decided to redesign its factory for older workers. With input from employees, they implemented physical changes to the workplace—for instance, new wooden floors to reduce joint strain and special chairs for sitting down or relaxing for short periods—that would reduce wear and tear on workers' bodies. Other organizations worldwide are preparing for a shift as baby boomers retire. Companies are creating succession plans, bringing retirees on as consultants, and increasing cross-training efforts to prepare younger workers to fill the void. As you can see, demographic trends impact HRM practices.

Much of the change in the US workforce over the last fifty years can be attributed to federal legislation enacted in the 1960s that prohibited employment discrimination. With these laws, avenues opened up for minority and female job applicants. These two groups dramatically changed the workplace in the latter half of the twentieth century. Women, in particular, have changed the composition of the workforce—from under 30 percent of jobs in 1950 to 46.9 percent today.[19]

Workforce trends in the early twenty-first century are notable for four reasons: (1) changes in racial and ethnic composition, (2) an aging baby boomer generation, (3) an expanding cohort of Gen Y workers, and (4) skill imbalances. By 2024, Hispanics will grow from today's 13 percent of the workforce to 19.8 percent, blacks will remain steady at about 13 percent, and Asians will increase slightly from 5.6 percent to 6.6 percent. Meanwhile, as noted previously, the labor force is aging. The 55-and-older age group, which currently makes up 16.3 percent of the workforce, will increase to 24.8 percent by 2024.[20] Another group that's having a significant impact on today's workforce is Gen Y, a population group that includes individuals born from about 1978 to 1994. Gen Y has been the fastest-growing segment of the workforce—increasing from 14 percent to more than 24 percent. Finally, employers face the reality that changing technology and increasing job complexity has created an imbalance between the skills that organizations need and those that are available in the job market.[21] Two skills in high demand, but often lacking in job applicants, are digital literacy and soft skills such as communication, critical thinking, and working in teams.

These and other demographic trends are important because of the impact they're having on current and future HRM practices.

IDENTIFYING and selecting competent employees

LO12.3 The HRM process begins by assessing what human resources are needed, finding potential candidates who could fill those needs, and then culling the applicant pool down to identify the best candidates. Referring back to Exhibit 12-1, this involves three tasks: human resource planning, recruitment, and selection.

Human Resource Planning

human resource planning
Ensuring that the organization has the right number and kinds of capable people in the right places and at the right times

Human resource planning is the process by which managers ensure that they have the right number and kinds of capable people in the right places and at the right times. Through planning, organizations avoid sudden people shortages and surpluses. HR planning entails two steps: (1) assessing current human resources and (2) meeting future HR needs.

CURRENT ASSESSMENT Managers begin HR planning by inventorying data on current employees. This inventory usually includes information on each employee such as name, education, training, prior employment, languages spoken, special capabilities, and specialized skills. Sophisticated databases make getting and keeping this information quite easy.

job analysis
A process that defines jobs and the behaviors necessary to perform them

An important part of a current assessment is **job analysis**, a process that defines a job and the behaviors necessary to perform it. For instance, what are the duties of a level 3 accountant who works for General Motors? What minimal knowledge, skills, and abilities are necessary to adequately perform this job? How do these requirements compare with those for a level 2 accountant or for an accounting manager? Information for a job analysis is gathered by directly observing individuals on the job, interviewing employees individually or in a group, having employees complete a questionnaire or record daily activities in a diary, or having job "experts" (usually managers) identify a job's specific characteristics.

job description (position description)
A written statement that describes a job

Using this information from the job analysis, managers develop or revise job descriptions and job specifications. A **job description** (or *position description*) is a written statement describing a job—typically job content, environment, and conditions of employment. A **job specification** states the minimum qualifications that a person must possess to successfully perform a given job. It identifies the knowledge, skills, and aptitudes needed to do the job effectively.

job specification
A written statement of the minimum qualifications a person must possess to perform a given job successfully

MEETING FUTURE HR NEEDS Future HR needs are determined by the organization's mission, goals, and strategies. Demand for employees results from demand for the organization's products or services. After assessing both current capabilities and future needs, managers can estimate areas in which the organization will be understaffed or overstaffed. Then they're ready to proceed to the next step in the HRM process.

Recruitment and Decruitment

If employee vacancies exist, managers should use the information gathered through job analysis to guide them in **recruitment**—that is, locating, identifying, and attracting capable applicants.[22] On the other hand, if HR planning shows a surplus of employees, managers may want to reduce the organization's workforce through **decruitment**.[23]

RECRUITMENT Some organizations have interesting approaches to finding employees. For instance, McDonald's Canada held a national hiring day in April 2018. The company sought to hire 8,500 people, and interested applicants were encouraged to apply online or in person.[24] Ikea launched a cost-effective recruitment campaign in Australia. The company advertised job opportunities to its customers with a "Careers Instructions" sheet packed inside product boxes. Customers were *instructed* to apply for a job. The campaign was highly successful for generating nearly 4,300 quality applicants that yielded 280 new hires.[25]

Exhibit 12-3 lists different recruiting sources managers can use to find potential job candidates. Of these, two deserve elaboration—*referrals* because of their effectiveness, and *social media* because of its increased importance.[26]

Employee referrals top the list as the best source for finding strong applicants. One study of a thousand companies found that more than 30 percent of all hires overall and 45 percent of internal hires came through referrals.[27] Other studies have found that employee referrals also have the highest applicant to hire conversion rate—only 7 percent apply, but they account for 40 percent of all hires.[28] And additionally, referral hires have been found to have greater job satisfaction and longer tenures than hires from other sources.[29] Why are referrals such effective sources? Because current employees know both the job and the person being recommended, they tend to refer applicants who are well qualified. Also, current employees often feel their reputation is at stake and refer others only when they're confident that the person will not make them look bad.

Amazon uses job fairs to find and recruit new talent.
Source: BRIAN SNYDER/REUTERS/Newscom

recruitment
Locating, identifying, and attracting capable applicants

decruitment
Reducing an organization's workforce

Source	Advantages	Disadvantages
Internet	Reaches large numbers of people; can get immediate feedback	Generates many unqualified candidates
Employee referrals	Knowledge about the organization provided by current employee; can generate strong candidates because a good referral reflects on the recommender	May not increase the diversity and mix of employees
Company website	Wide distribution; can be targeted to specific groups	Generates many unqualified candidates
College recruiting	Large centralized body of candidates	Limited to entry-level positions
Professional recruiting organizations	Good knowledge of industry challenges and requirements	Little commitment to specific organization
Social media	Takes advantage of current employees' connections; particularly effective at reaching younger candidates	Not nearly as effective in reaching older or senior candidates

Exhibit 12-3
Recruiting Sources

WORKPLACE CONFIDENTIAL Job Search

Finding the right job is a complex task. But selecting the appropriate search channel can significantly increase your chances for success. We'll take a quick look at some of your search options. After that, we'll discuss the importance of choosing the right organization.

Your grandfather probably found jobs by looking at classified ads in the newspaper, going to an employment agency, or following up on a referral from a friend or relative. But newspaper ads have gone the way of the dinosaur, replaced by online websites; and employment agencies have been largely replaced by search firms that focus on executive and high-level professional positions. Job referrals, however, continue to be an excellent source of job openings.

Referrals from a current employee of an organization tend to provide accurate and realistic information, the kind of information you're not likely to get from a company recruiter. As a result, referrals tend to reduce unrealistic expectations. If what a motel chain ad once said is true—"the best surprise is no surprise"—you should place a high value on information provided by a current employee.

If you're nearing the completion of your college degree or are a recent graduate, consider using your college's placement service. For college graduates, college placement services have been shown to be excellent channels for securing jobs.

Where you find jobs depends on the channels employers choose. So what do employers favor? Research on employment channels has shown that employers generally favor informal sources—such as contacts and networks—for most workers but more formal channels for professionals, managers, and college graduates. Let's take a look at some of these formal channels.

Job fairs offer organizations a good opportunity to build their employment brand. Organizations like to use them to contact prospective employees and collect information and résumés. For instance, the Cleveland Clinic recently conducted three job fairs in northeast Ohio in their search to fill 500 nursing positions. Note that it's not uncommon for a job fair to include multiple employers. Typically staffed by company employees, such job fairs give you a chance to meet face-to-face with some company employees and interview with multiple employers at one site.

Many *professional organizations* operate placement services for the benefit of their members. Professional organizations serving such varied occupations as human resource management, industrial engineering, psychology, accounting, and law publish rosters of job vacancies and distribute these lists to members. It's also common practice to provide placement facilities at regional and national meetings where individuals looking for employment and organizations looking for employees can find each other.

Today, much of the job search process is done *online*. Most organizations, large and small, now use the internet to recruit new employees by adding a "careers" section to their website. One recent survey indicated that 60 percent of employers report hiring new employees from online sources. In addition to an employer's website, you'll want to check out job boards, social media, and job-search apps. Job boards allow searches by location, key words, industry, level of education, salary, and any combination of these criteria. Popular job boards include CareerBuilder.com and Monster.com. Social media sites such as Facebook and LinkedIn include "career" sections. And two apps you might want to investigate are Switch and Jobmaster. Switch is to job searches what Tinder is to dating. It provides job seekers with anonymity as they scan job postings, swiping right for positions of interest. If the user's qualifications match the employer's needs, the parties can initiate an in-app chat. Jobmaster aggregates job listings from some 1,000 job boards around the world. It has national job boards as well as boards devoted to particular professions.

Now we turn to our other concern regarding a job search: making sure that a job vacancy is right for you. Specifically, even if the job looks great and an employer extends an offer, is the organization a good match for you?

We've discussed organizational culture in several previous Workplace Confidential boxes (see Chapters 3 and 9). Consistent with those discussions, no job search can be called successful if you end up with a great job but in an organization where you don't fit. So how do you find out what an organization is really like before you actually start working there? During your interviews, read between the lines. Listen to the stories people tell about how management handled setbacks, rule breakers, nonconformists, or creative types. Does the company, for instance, reward risk taking or punish it? Listen and observe rituals that indicate what employees believe are important. And look for artifacts and symbols that can give you clues as to the kind of employee behaviors that are considered appropriate. As Yogi Berra said, "You can observe a lot just by watching." After you've sized up the organization, ask yourself: Do my personality and beliefs fit with what this organization values? In job searches, too often we focus on the title, position, and salary. They're obviously important, but finding a culture that is the right fit will significantly increase the chances that you'll be happy and successful in your job.[30]

Is there a downside to referrals? Yes. Since people tend to befriend, and hence recommend, people like themselves, referrals aren't likely to enhance diversity. As a case in point, to the degree that Silicon Valley companies rely heavily on current employees for referrals, new employees are likely to mirror current ones—that is, young, white males.

Social media is now the fastest growing source for job applicants.[31] LinkedIn, for instance, was built for recruiting and networking. And if an employer is trying to reach teenagers and young adults, more than 75 percent of them say they use Snapchat or Facebook.[32] The appeal of social media lies in its ability to expand the applicant pool, its ease for finding rich profiles on potential applicants, and the power of online connections. Using their social media connections, employees can alert their personal networks about possible job openings in their organizations.

DECRUITMENT   The other approach to controlling labor supply is decruitment, which is not a pleasant task for any manager. Decruitment options are shown in Exhibit 12-4. Although employees can be fired, other choices may be better. However, no matter how you do it, it's never easy to reduce an organization's workforce.

Selection

Once you have a pool of candidates, the next step in the HRM process is **selection**— screening job applicants to determine who is best qualified for the job. Managers need to "select" carefully since hiring errors can have significant implications.[33] Zappos CEO Tony Hsieh once estimated bad hires had cost his company "well over $100 million."[34] These costs include everything from disrupting a well-functioning team to encouraging talented colleagues to leave to the cost of hiring a replacement.

WHAT IS SELECTION?   Selection involves predicting which applicants will be successful if hired.[35] As shown in Exhibit 12-5, any selection decision can result in four possible outcomes—two correct and two errors.

A decision is correct when the applicant was predicted to be successful and proved to be successful on the job, or when the applicant was predicted to be unsuccessful and was not hired. In the first instance, we have successfully accepted; in the second, we have successfully rejected.

Problems arise when errors are made in rejecting candidates who would have performed successfully on the job (reject errors) or accepting those who ultimately perform poorly (accept errors). Given today's HR laws and regulations, reject errors can cost more than the additional screening needed to find acceptable candidates. Why? Because they can expose the organization to discrimination charges, especially if applicants from protected groups are disproportionately rejected. For instance, employment assessments used by Target Corporation were found to have disproportionately screened out black, Asian, and female applicants for exempt-level professional positions.[37] The Equal Employment Opportunity Commission said that Target violated

selection
Screening job applicants to ensure that the most appropriate candidates are hired

CEOs rate a failure to attract and retain top talent as their number one concern (even ahead of the competition or technology disruption).[36]

Option	Description
Firing	Permanent involuntary termination
Layoffs	Temporary involuntary termination; may last only a few days or extend to years
Attrition	Not filling openings created by voluntary resignations or normal retirements
Transfers	Moving employees either laterally or downward; usually does not reduce costs but can reduce intraorganizational supply–demand imbalances
Reduced workweeks	Having employees work fewer hours per week, share jobs, or perform their jobs on a part-time basis
Early retirements	Providing incentives to older and more senior employees for retiring before their normal retirement date
Job sharing	Having employees share one full-time position

Exhibit 12-4
Decruitment Options

Exhibit 12-5
Selection Decision Outcomes

	Selection Decision	
	Accept	**Reject**
Successful	Correct Decision	Reject Error
Unsuccessful	Accept Error	Correct Decision

(Later Job Performance)

Title VII of the Civil Rights Act because the tests were not sufficiently job related and consistent with business necessity. On the other hand, the costs of accept errors include the cost of training the employee, the profits lost because of the employee's incompetence, the cost of severance, and the subsequent costs of further recruiting and screening. The major emphasis of any selection activity should be reducing the probability of reject errors or accept errors while increasing the probability of making correct decisions. Managers do this by using selection tools that are both valid and reliable.

valid selection device
A selection device characterized by a proven relationship to some relevant criterion

reliable selection device
A selection device that measures the same thing consistently

VALIDITY AND RELIABILITY   A **valid selection device** is characterized by a proven relationship between the selection device and some relevant criterion. For instance, federal employment laws prohibit managers from using a test score to select employees unless clear evidence shows that, once on the job, individuals with high scores on this test outperform individuals with low test scores. The burden is on managers to support that any selection device they use to differentiate applicants is validly related to job performance.

A **reliable selection device** measures the same thing consistently. On a test that's reliable, any single individual's score should remain fairly consistent over time, assuming that the characteristics being measured are also stable. No selection device can be effective if it's not reliable. Using such a device would be like weighing yourself every day on an erratic scale. If the scale is unreliable—randomly fluctuating, say, five to ten pounds every time you step on it—the results don't mean much.

TYPES OF SELECTION TOOLS   The best-known selection tools include application forms, written and performance-simulation tests, interviews, background investigations, and in some cases, physical exams. Exhibit 12-6 lists the strengths and weaknesses of each.

A few comments need to be made regarding the quality and popularity of some of these tools. Specifically, most interviews are poor predictors of job performance, the best predictor of future performance is actual performance simulations, and social media is rapidly becoming a popular source for background information.

Job interviews continue to be one of the most popular selection tools. Few jobs are obtained without a face-to-face interview. Unfortunately, the overwhelming evidence indicates that they're not very reliable, and yet they carry a disproportionate amount of influence in the final selection decision.[38] The major problem is that most interviews tend to be unstructured—short, casual, and made up of random questions. The data gathered is typically biased and often only modestly related to future job performance. Without structure, interviewers tend to favor applicants who share their

The job interview is a selection tool McDonald's uses for job candidates in both entry-level and professional positions at its 34,000 locations worldwide. During personal interviews, the store manager shown here looks for applicants who possess good communication skills, would qualify in meeting McDonald's customer-service standards, and work well as a team member.
Source: The Idaho Statesman Joe Jaszewski/ Associated Press

Application Forms

- Almost universally used
- Most useful for gathering information
- Can predict job performance but not easy to create one that does

Written Tests

- Must be job-related
- Include intelligence, aptitude, ability, personality, and interest tests
- Are popular (e.g., personality tests; aptitude tests)
- Relatively good predictor for supervisory positions

Performance-Simulation Tests

- Use actual job behaviors
- Work sampling—test applicants on tasks associated with that job; appropriate for routine or standardized work
- Assessment center—simulate jobs; appropriate for evaluating managerial potential

Interviews

- Almost universally used
- Must know what can and cannot be asked
- Can be useful for managerial positions

Background Investigations

- Used for verifying application data—valuable source of information
- Used for verifying reference checks—not a valuable source of information

Physical Examinations

- Are for jobs that have certain physical requirements
- Mostly used for insurance purposes

Exhibit 12-6
Selection Tools

attitudes, give undue weight to negative information, and allow the order in which applicants are interviewed to influence their evaluations.[39] The good news is that structured interviews, where all candidates receive a standardized set of questions, can significantly increase reliability.[40]

One of the most reliable and valid tools for predicting an applicant's future job performance is having the candidate perform actual job-related skills.[41] Performance-simulation tests include work samples and assessment centers. **Work sample tests** are hands-on simulations of part or all the work that workers in the job routinely must perform. Each work sample element is matched with a job-performance element to measure applicants' knowledge, skills, and abilities with more specificity than written aptitude or personality tests.[42] A more elaborate set of performance-simulation tests, specifically designed to evaluate a candidate's managerial potential, is administered in **assessment centers**. Line executives, supervisors, and/or trained psychologists evaluate candidates as they go through one to several days of exercises that simulate real problems they would confront on the job.[43]

Just as social media is reshaping organizational decision making and communication, it is also becoming a popular tool in making selection decisions.[44] Social media sites like Facebook are being used to gather information and screen potential employees. But is this information helpful in improving the quality of hiring decisions? The preliminary evidence suggests not.[45] Ratings of applicants' Facebook information has been found to be unrelated to supervisor ratings of job performance or turnover rates. Additionally, this information tends to have adverse impact potential by favoring female and white applicants.

work sample tests
Hands-on simulations of part or all the work that workers in a job routinely must perform

assessment centers
A set of performance-simulation tests designed to evaluate a candidate's managerial potential

Zakiyyah Rogers ▶
Department Manager, Human
Resources

Let's Get REAL

The Scenario:

José Salinas is the HR director at a large food processor. Within the last couple of years, he has seen more frequent parental involvement in their adult child's job hunt. In fact, one candidate's parents actually contacted the company after their child got a job offer wanting to discuss their daughter's salary, relocation package, and educational reimbursement opportunities. He's not sure how to handle these occurrences.

What advice would you give José?

You may understand a parent's concern, but we cannot discuss company information with them. Our relationship is with the potential employee. Let the parent know you are willing to speak directly to their child and answer any questions they may have.

Source: Zakiyyah Rogers

REALISTIC JOB PREVIEWS When recruiters and interviewers describe their organization and the job a potential prospect will be doing, there is a tendency to focus on the positive. The logic is that a good prospect is less likely to accept a job if he or she hears negatives. The problem is that if applicants only are told the good aspects, they are likely to be disenchanted when reality sets in.[46] Bad things can happen when the information an applicant receives is excessively inflated. First, mismatched applicants probably won't self-select themselves out of the selection process. Second, inflated information builds unrealistic expectations, so new employees may quickly become dissatisfied and leave the organization. Third, new hires become disillusioned and less committed to the organization when they face the unexpected harsh realities of the job. Finally, individuals who feel they were misled during the hiring process may become problem employees.

To increase employee job satisfaction and reduce turnover, managers should consider a **realistic job preview (RJP)**, one that includes both positive and negative information about the job and the company. For instance, in addition to the positive comments typically expressed during an interview, the job applicant might be told there are limited opportunities to talk to coworkers during work hours, that promotional advancement is unlikely, or that work hours are erratic and they may have to work weekends. The evidence indicates that applicants who receive an RJP have more realistic expectations about the jobs they'll be performing and are better able to cope with the frustrating elements than applicants who receive only inflated information.

realistic job preview (RJP)
A preview of a job that provides both positive and negative information about the job and the company

PROVIDING employees with needed skills and knowledge

LO12.4 Even the most qualified new hires need to adjust to their work group and become acquainted with their new organization's culture. And, given today's rapidly changing work environment, current employees need to keep their skills up-to-date. Toward these ends, HRM uses orientation, socialization, and training programs.

Orientation and Socialization

Did you participate in some type of organized "introduction to college life" when you started school? If so, you may have been told about your school's rules and the procedures for activities such as applying for financial aid, cashing a check, or registering for classes, and you were probably introduced to some of the college administrators.

A person starting a new job needs the same type of introduction to his or her job and the organization. This introduction is called **orientation**.

There are two types of orientation. *Work unit orientation* familiarizes employees with the goals of the work unit, clarifies how their job contributes to the unit's goals, and includes an introduction to new coworkers. *Organization orientation* informs new employees about the company's goals, history, philosophy, procedures, and rules. It should also include relevant HR policies and maybe even a tour of the facilities.

Beyond just introducing new employees to an organization, management should consider its various options for helping new employees adapt to the organization's culture. As introduced in Chapter 3, these options fall under the process called *socialization*. Exhibit 12-7 lists management's options. These options can be bundled in ways to encourage employees to exhibit restrictive and regimentation behavior or to be independent and creative.[47] The more management relies on formal, collective, fixed, and serial socialization programs while emphasizing divestiture, the more likely newcomers' differences will be stripped away and replaced by standardized predictable behaviors. These *institutional* practices are common in police departments, fire departments, and other organizations that value rule following and order. Programs that are informal, individual, variable, and random while emphasizing investiture are more likely to give newcomers an innovative sense of their roles and methods of working. Creative fields such as research and development, advertising, and filmmaking rely on these *individual* practices.

It's in the best interests of both the organization and the new employee to get the person up and running in the job as soon as possible. Successful socialization results in an outsider-insider transition that makes the new employee feel comfortable, lowers the likelihood of poor work performance, and reduces the probability of a premature resignation.[48] One study revealed that 22 percent of staff turnover occurs in the first forty-five days of employment, and the cost of losing an employee in the first year amounts to about three times annual salary.[49]

Exhibit 12-7
Entry Socialization Options

Formal vs. Informal   The more a new employee is segregated from the ongoing work setting and differentiated in some way to make explicit his or her newcomer's role, the more socialization is formal. Specific orientation and training programs are examples. Informal socialization puts new employees directly into the job, with little or no special attention.

Individual vs. Collective   New members can be socialized individually. This describes how it's done in many professional offices. Or they can be grouped together and processed through an identical set of experiences, as in military boot camp.

Fixed vs. Variable   This refers to the time schedule in which newcomers make the transition from outsider to insider. A fixed schedule establishes standardized stages of transition. This characterizes rotational training programs where new hires might spend three months in each of half-dozen departments before final assignment. Variable schedules give no advance notice of their transition timetable. This describes the typical promotion system where one isn't advanced to the next stage until one is "ready."

Serial vs. Random   Serial socialization is characterized by the use of role models who train and encourage the newcomer. Apprenticeship and mentoring programs are examples. In random socialization, role models are deliberately withheld. New employees are left on their own to figure things out.

Investiture vs. Divestiture   Investiture socialization assumes that the newcomer's qualities and qualifications are the necessary ingredients for success, so these qualities and qualifications are confirmed and supported. Divestiture socialization tries to strip away certain characteristics of the recruit. Fraternity and sorority "pledges" go through divestiture rituals to shape them into the proper role.

Exhibit 12-8

Types of Training

Source: Based on "2005 Industry Report—
Types of Training," Training, December 2005,
p. 22.

TYPE	INCLUDES
General	Communication skills, computer systems application and programming, customer service, executive development, management skills and development, personal growth, sales, supervisory skills, and technological skills and knowledge
Specific	Basic life–work skills, creativity, customer education, diversity/cultural awareness, remedial writing, managing change, leadership, product knowledge, public speaking/presentation skills, safety, ethics, sexual harassment, team building, wellness, and others

Employee Training

On the whole, planes don't cause airline accidents, people do. Most collisions, crashes, and other airline mishaps—more than 50 percent of them—result from errors by the pilot or air traffic controller, or from inadequate maintenance.[50] For instance, a United Airlines pilot could have avoided a catastrophic accident while attempting to land had he listened to the copilot's warning that fuel levels were rapidly dropping. The airline recognized that this accident could have been avoided if teamwork principles were emphasized in training.[51] We cite this example and these statistics to illustrate the importance of training in the airline industry. Such maintenance and human errors could be prevented or significantly reduced by better employee training, as shown by the amazing "landing" of US Airways Flight 1549 in the Hudson River in January 2009 with no loss of life. Pilot Captain Chesley Sullenberger attributed the positive outcome to the extensive and intensive training that US Air pilots and flight crews undergo.[53]

Employee training is a key HRM activity. As job demands change, employee skills have to change with them. In 2017, US business firms spent $90.6 billion on formal employee training.[54] Managers, of course, are responsible for deciding what type of training employees need, when they need it, and what form that training should take.[55]

TYPES OF TRAINING Exhibit 12-8 describes the major types of training that organizations provide. Some of the most popular types include profession/industry-specific training, management/supervisory skills, mandatory/compliance information (such as sexual harassment, safety, etc.), and customer service training. For many organizations, employee interpersonal skills training—communication, conflict resolution, team building, customer service, and so forth—is a high priority. For example, until recently, medical schools did not teach students how to communicate with patients. Many hospitals have now taken on this responsibility as patient satisfaction becomes more important. For instance, the University of Rochester Medical Center provides one-on-one coaching to help doctors improve communication with patients.[56]

Learning the skill of rappelling is an important part of the search and rescue training for US citizen-soldiers serving in the US Army National Guard. Training teaches soldiers the skills, policies, and procedures they need in responding to domestic emergencies such as natural disasters and riots as well as international crises.
Source: Rouelle Umali/Xinhua/Alamy

TRAINING METHODS Many organizations are relying more on technology-based training methods because of their accessibility, cost, and ability to deliver information. Exhibit 12-9 provides a description of the various traditional and technology-based training methods that managers might use. Of all these training methods, experts believe that organizations will increasingly rely on e-learning, mobile applications, and virtual reality to deliver important information and to develop employees' skills.

Exhibit 12-9
Training Methods

Traditional Training Methods

On-the-job—Employees learn how to do tasks simply by performing them, usually after an initial introduction to the task.

Job rotation—Employees work at different jobs in a particular area, getting exposure to a variety of tasks.

Mentoring and coaching—Employees work with an experienced worker who provides information, support, and encouragement; also called apprenticeships in certain industries.

Experiential exercises—Employees participate in role-playing, simulations, or other face-to-face types of training.

Workbooks/manuals—Employees refer to training workbooks and manuals for information.

Classroom lectures—Employees attend lectures designed to convey specific information.

Technology-Based Training Methods

DVDs/CDs/podcasts—Employees listen to or watch selected media that convey information or demonstrate certain techniques.

Videoconferencing/teleconferencing/satellite TV—Employees listen to or participate as information is conveyed or techniques demonstrated.

E-learning—Internet-based learning where employees participate in multimedia simulations or other interactive modules.

Mobile learning—Learning delivered via mobile devices.

Virtual reality—Using VR headsets and customized software, employees learn through simulated practice.

RETAINING competent, high-performing employees

LO12.5 Evaluating employee performance has long been a basic element in HR practices. The annual review, for instance, has traditionally provided feedback to management on how well employees are doing their jobs, formed the basis for performance-based compensation decisions, and identified areas where employees might need additional supervision or training to improve performance.

Technology and changes in the workforce have encouraged some organizations to experiment with alternatives to the annual review. One such approach provides never-ending performance feedback to employees.[57] For instance, at software company Revinate, managers use goal-setting programs and apps to rate workers' progress in real time. As the senior director of customer success put it, team members receive "bite-size feedback, and lots of it."[58] Other companies—like Adobe Systems, PricewaterhouseCoopers, and Lumeris Healthcare Outcomes—are following suit. The availability of digital employee-assessment tools and the employment of younger workers who are accustomed to instant gratification and desire ongoing feedback make short, constant reviews an attractive option.

> **fyi**
>
> Employers who provide performance evaluation feedback monthly or on an ongoing basis are up to 1.5 times more effective at retaining and engaging employees than employers who provide evaluations only once a year.[59]

Performance Evaluation

Few management topics generate more controversy than performance evaluation. As the Revinate example demonstrated, some organizations have replaced the annual performance review with constant assessments. A third of US companies have now abandoned traditional annual reviews.[60] And at least thirty Fortune 500 companies have dropped formal reviews altogether and replaced them with subjective evaluations.[61] In these latter cases, complaints that formal reviews are political, biased, and punitive have tainted the value of the process.

PERFORMANCE EVALUATION METHODS Most organizations have chosen not to throw the baby out with the bathwater! They are still conducting formal performance appraisals. Exhibit 12-10 describes seven different performance appraisal methods with their advantages and disadvantages.

Exhibit 12-10
Performance Evaluation Methods

Written Essay

Evaluator writes a description of employee's strengths and weaknesses, past performance, and potential; provides suggestions for improvement.

+ Simple to use

− May be better measure of evaluator's writing ability than of employee's actual performance

Critical Incident

Evaluator focuses on critical behaviors that separate effective and ineffective performance.

+ Rich examples, behaviorally based

− Time-consuming, lacks quantification

Graphic Rating Scale

Popular method that lists a set of performance factors and an incremental scale; evaluator goes down the list and rates employee on each factor.

+ Provides quantitative data, not time-consuming

− Doesn't provide in-depth information on job behavior

BARS (Behaviorally Anchored Rating Scale)

Popular approach that combines elements from critical incident and graphic rating scale; evaluator uses a rating scale, but items are examples of actual job behaviors.

+ Focuses on specific and measurable job behaviors

− Time-consuming, difficult to develop

Multiperson Comparison

Employees are rated in comparison to others in work group.

+ Compares employees with one another

− Difficult with large number of employees, legal concerns

MBO

Employees are evaluated on how well they accomplish specific goals.

+ Focuses on goals, results oriented

− Time-consuming

360-Degree Appraisal

Utilizes feedback from supervisors, employees, and coworkers.

+ Thorough

− Time-consuming

electronic performance monitoring
Electronic instruments or devices to collect, store, analyze, and report individual or group performance

We should note that, even where formal reviews are conducted, technology is changing how performance data is collected. Increasingly, especially in jobs that are done on computers, observation by a supervisor is being replaced by **electronic performance monitoring**.[62] This is the use of electronic instruments or devices to collect, store, analyze, and report individual or group performance. For instance, this technology is being widely used in call centers where supervisors can continually track and analyze an employees' workflow in real time. Electronic monitoring systems can continually collect information on performance metrics like the average call handle time, total number of calls handled, and time on breaks. This allows supervisors to do formal performance reviews with objective data to support the evaluation. Additionally, these digital monitoring systems alert supervisors almost immediately to performance problems and allow for rapid corrective action. This is a big improvement over the annual review where supervisors may be addressing problems that occurred six or nine months ago.

Learning from
FAILURE   Forced Rankings Bomb at Microsoft

It began at General Electric and then spread to dozens of major firms. The concept—called stack ranking or forced ranking—required business-unit managers to rate all of their employees and then compare them against each other. Those that end up at the bottom of the rankings are let go. In theory, over time, annual performance evaluations using forced rankings tends to cull the organization of low-performing employees.

Here's how forced ranking works. Most employee groups are made up of above-average, average, and below-average performers. Or at least that's how this system requires managers to rate their people. The flaw, of course, is obvious: it assumes every group is normally distributed. Even though a manager might have a five-member team of superstars, the system requires rating at least one as below average and some as average. But work units are *not* typically normally distributed. So good people can, and are, thrown under the bus.

What was the original appeal of forced rankings? It pressured managers to make the tough decision of identifying and confronting poor performers—something that many managers want to avoid. But at what price? Microsoft found that in the dozen years or so that they used this system, employees went out of their way to be part of mediocre teams, compete against each other, and try to make colleagues look bad. If you're going to be judged against others, then it makes sense to do whatever you can to undermine those "others." The company's top engineers, for example, would avoid working together out of fear that it would hurt their rankings. And employees would regularly try to sabotage colleagues in order to make themselves look better.

Microsoft learned that forced rankings didn't work for them and they got rid of this system in 2012. They replaced it with a performance review system that emphasized teamwork, collaboration, and cooperation.[63]

Compensation and Benefits

Unless we're doing volunteer work, we expect to receive compensation from our employer. And developing an effective and appropriate compensation system is an important part of the HRM process. It's a key component in any organization's effort to attract and retain competent and talented individuals.

Organizational compensation can include many different types of rewards and benefits—including base wages and salaries, wage and salary add-ons, incentive payments, and other benefits and services.[64] Employee benefits commonly include offerings such as retirement benefits, health insurance, and paid time off. Many organizations are addressing the needs of their diverse workforces through offering flexible work options and family-friendly benefits to accommodate employees' needs for work-family life balance.

Some organizations offer employees some unusual, but popular, benefits. For instance, Campbell's Soup and Mercedes-Benz offer concierge services. Employees can ask a concierge to pick up dry cleaning or make dinner reservations. Employees at accounting firm Barfield, Murphy, Shank, and Smith enjoy on-site massages during tax preparation season. At Bank of America, employees receive $3,000 when they purchase a hybrid or electric car. And here's a benefit that college graduates will appreciate: student loan repayment assistance! Natixis Global Asset Management and ChowNow, an online food-ordering platform, offer repayment assistance in hopes of recruiting and retaining top talent.[65]

How do managers determine who gets paid what? Several factors influence the compensation and benefit packages that different employees receive. Exhibit 12-11 summarizes these factors, which are job-based and business- or industry-based.

A 401(k) matching program is one way a company can attract and retain quality employees. Lowes offers a competitive 401(k) package to its employees, matching the first 3 percent employees save each pay period at 100 percent, 4–5 percent will be matched at 50 percent, and 6 percent at 25 percent.
Source: Randy Duchaine/Alamy Images

Exhibit 12-11
What Determines Pay and Benefits

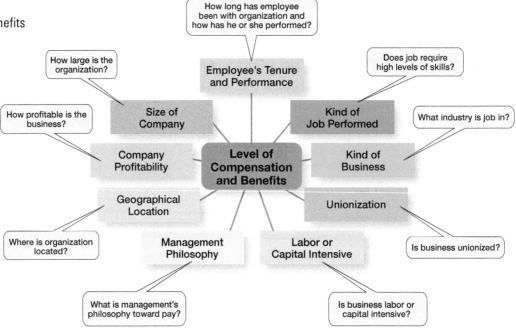

In the following sections we look at three contemporary compensation issues: skill-based vs. variable pay; bonuses vs. annual pay increases; and pay secrecy vs. transparency. Then we briefly look at benefit options and which options employees indicate they prefer.

skill-based pay
A pay system that rewards employees for the job skills they can demonstrate

SKILL-BASED VS. VARIABLE PAY **Skill-based pay** systems reward employees for the job skills and competencies they can demonstrate. Under this type of pay system, an employee's job title doesn't define his or her pay category; skills do. A wide variety of employers have established skill-focused pay programs. Many of the companies known

---

Let's Get REAL

Leya Gaynor
HR Business Partner ▶

Source: Leya Gaynor

The Scenario:

As the human resources manager at Extreme Software Solutions, Kim Yoshida has helped develop the policies and practices to manage the growing staff. As a start-up company ten years ago, the company hired mostly recent college graduates eager to work any number of hours to help get the company up and running. Now that Extreme Software Solutions is an established company, Kim has noted that many employees are starting families and she has received some requests for reduced or more flexible work schedules. At this point Kim thinks the company should consider offering family-friendly benefits.

What kind of family-friendly benefits should Kim consider?

In order to retain and maintain engagement with employees who started with the company, Kim should consider flexible work programs, benefits that enhance work-life balance, and policies that make it easier for parents to transition back into the workforce after starting a family. Some examples of these include job sharing for employees who are interested in reduced hours, working from home or remotely, an in-house day care or subsidized day care programs, and paid leave of absence after the birth or adoption of a child. The benefits put in place should not only enhance an employee's ability to get the job done based on his or her work and personal schedule, but also allow the company to continue to achieve its business goals.

to be using this kind of pay operate in manufacturing. How well do these programs work? One study found that a skill-based pay plan in a manufacturing setting increased plant productivity by 58 percent, lowered labor cost per part by 16 percent, and generated favorable quality outcomes.[66] On the other hand, many organizations use **variable pay** systems, in which an individual's compensation is contingent on performance—nearly 90 percent of US organizations use some type of variable pay plans, and about 50 percent of Asian and Latin American organizations do.[67] In Chapter 16, we'll discuss variable pay systems further as they relate to employee motivation.

Although many factors influence the design of an organization's compensation system, flexibility is a key consideration. The traditional approach to paying people reflected a more stable time when an employee's pay was largely determined by seniority and job level. Given the dynamic environments that many organizations now face, the trend is to make pay systems more flexible and to reduce the number of pay levels.

variable pay
A pay system in which an individual's compensation is contingent on performance

BONUSES VS. ANNUAL PAY INCREASES The annual pay raise has been the norm in the US for a century. But is it the best way to compensate people? Some companies and pay experts expand on the variable pay concept to propose replacing annual pay raises with one-time bonuses for selected, high-performing individuals.[68]

Much of the motivating potential of a pay raise is lost when mediocre performers get a 3 percent raise while top performers get 5 percent. Given that the pool of funds for pay raises is limited, giving increases to everyone means less for the best performers. Instead of spreading the wealth, why not give it where it will do the most good? At Novitex Enterprise Solutions, top-performing employees have earned increases of 10 percent or more. An added plus, says Novitex's service-delivery manager: "You are going to experience some healthy turnover" among low performers.[69]

PAY SECRECY VS. TRANSPARENCY Historically, employers—especially in large corporations—made a point to tell employees that they were not to share salary information. Their thinking was: a number of factors go into an individual's pay and employees don't know all those factors, so comparisons were likely to create problems. Specifically, employees were likely to question the equity of distributions, reduce their trust and loyalty to the organization, and have lower motivation and satisfaction.[70]

A new age of transparency in the US began in 2016, with an executive order.[71] Applying to organizations with contracts valued over $10,000 with the US government, the order prohibited employers from retaliating against employees for disclosure and discussion of compensation information. As a result, a number of companies—including those that do no business with the government—began reassessing their pay secrecy policies. We should expect to see more pay transparency in coming years, especially since the secrecy taboo hasn't set well with younger workers. A survey of millennials recently found that 30 percent had shared their salaries with coworkers. This compared with just 8 percent among baby boomers.[72]

BENEFIT OPTIONS Employee compensation isn't just about pay. A key factor in attracting and retaining good employees is the organization's benefit programs. Surveys of employees confirm this: 57 percent report benefits being among their top considerations in weighing a job offer; 80 percent said they would prefer additional benefits to a pay raise; and 87 percent said the right benefit package would make them less likely to leave their jobs.[73]

But what benefits do most employees want? What programs should managers be focusing on to maximize the value of these benefits? The benefits that appear to have the greatest impact on employee satisfaction are (in this order): health insurance, vacations and paid time off, and retirement plans (including pensions and 401(k) plans).[74] Additional benefits should reflect factors like the interests of employees, the organization's culture, and even a firm's location. For instance, Apple, Facebook, and Google provide shuttle bus service to take their tech workers from their homes in San Francisco to their Silicon Valley offices.[75] And Reebok provides its employees with Crossfit classes and on-site gym facilities.[76]

fyi

American executives were shocked when introduced to the Chinese start-up concept of 996: Work from 9 a.m. to 9 p.m., six days a week.[77]

CAREER DEVELOPMENT

LO12.6 Our final activity in the HRM process is career development. We discussed careers—from your perspective—in the Workplace Confidential box in Chapter 9. Here we want to briefly focus on the organization's responsibility.

In the past thirty years, the trend has been for career development to be the responsibility of employees. Where once almost all large companies like IBM and GE provided formal, multi-year training programs and ongoing career development workshops, such offerings are now far less frequent. As some authors have put it, it's each individual's responsibility to create "brand *YOU*."[78]

While the general trend is toward pushing the responsibility for career development onto employees, two important trends should be noted. First, organizations are helping employees to keep their skills current through supporting "lifetime learning." For instance, many firms offer tuition reimbursement for employees to take job-related college classes. And companies like SAS, Amazon, Bonobos, and Enterprise Rent-A-Car all offer leadership programs to prepare employees for taking on managerial responsibilities.[79] Second, companies are expanding and promoting their internship programs.[80] A three-month summer internship program is an excellent way to assess a potential employee's abilities and motivation without the cost and legal issues involved if a permanent employee fails to perform well. And interns get the chance to learn by doing and scope out whether this is an organization they want to commit to on a full-time basis. Major banks like JPMorgan, Credit Suisse, and Deutsche, for instance, take hundreds of high-potential college students during the summer before their senior year, pay them generously, put them into multiple jobs, and use this trial to determine which interns will be offered full-time jobs upon graduation.

CONTEMPORARY issues in managing human resources

LO12.7 We'll conclude this chapter by looking at two contemporary HR issues facing today's managers: sexual harassment and bullying in the workplace.

Sexual Harassment

Sexual harassment in the workplace has long been a serious issue in both public and private sector organizations. But as we noted in Chapter 5 in our discussion of gender discrimination, 2017 marked a watershed year. Behaviors that were acceptable for decades or at least given little attention—especially by people with power and influence in organizations—were replaced by a new standard: "zero tolerance."

Women, who before were afraid to speak out, are now being heard. And powerful executives, politicians, and high-profile media personalities have lost their jobs because of inappropriate sexual behaviors. This movement has made senior management of almost all organizations increasingly sensitive to claims of inappropriate behavior and aware that creating a non-threatening workplace is a must. The pendulum has swung from often "looking the other way" to aggressively researching charges and taking aggressive action against protagonists.

What exactly is **sexual harassment**? It's defined as any unwanted action or activity of a sexual nature that explicitly or implicitly affects an individual's employment, performance, or work environment. It can occur between members of the opposite sex or of the same sex.

Many problems associated with sexual harassment involve determining exactly what constitutes this illegal behavior. The EEOC defines sexual harassment this way: "Unwelcome sexual advances, requests for sexual favors, and other verbal or physical conduct of a sexual nature constitute sexual harassment when this conduct explicitly or implicitly affects an individual's employment, unreasonably interferes with an individual's work performance, or creates an intimidating, hostile or offensive work

sexual harassment
Any unwanted action or activity of a sexual nature that explicitly or implicitly affects an individual's employment, performance, or work environment

environment."[81] The EEOC has added that sexual harassment can include offensive remarks about a person's sex. For many organizations, it's the offensive or hostile environment issue that is problematic. Managers must be aware of what constitutes such an environment.

The costs for organizations of sexual harassment are high. Almost all Fortune 500 companies in the United States have had complaints lodged by employees, and at least a third have been sued.[82] Settlements can range from low thousands to the tens of millions. For instance, it cost 21st Century Fox $20 million to settle a claim by a former news anchor.[83] Sexual harassment isn't a problem just in the United States. It's a global issue. Thirty-five percent of women globally have experienced physical or sexual violence.[84]

Even though discussions of sexual harassment cases often focus on the large awards granted by a court, there are other concerns for employers. It creates an unpleasant, oftentimes hostile, work environment and undermines workers' ability to perform their job.

What can an organization do to protect itself against harassment claims? A program made up of seven elements has been suggested:[85] (1) a clear anti-harassment policy; (2) an explicit statement of prohibited behaviors that can be considered harassment; (3) a complaint procedure that encourages employees to come forward; (4) protections for complainants and witnesses against retaliation; (5) an investigative strategy that protects privacy interests of both the alleged victim and the accused offender; (6) ongoing management training and employee awareness programs; and (7) measures and processes to ensure prompt corrective action to stop ongoing harassment and appropriate disciplinary actions for offenders.

NBC Today host Matt Lauer was fired by NBC over accusations of "inappropriate sexual behavior in the workplace." 2017 marked a shift in the workplace, where behaviors that were previously accepted (or overlooked), particularly by people with power and influence in organizations, are no longer being tolerated.
Source: Nancy Kaszerman/ZUMAPRESS.com/ Alamy Live News/Alamy Stock Photo

workplace bullying
When an individual experiences a number of negative behaviors repeatedly over a period of time that results in physical or mental harm

Bullying in the Workplace

What is **workplace bullying**? It occurs when an individual experiences a number of negative behaviors repeatedly over a period of time that results in physical or mental harm.[86] Note that a single episode alone of negative behavior is not considered to be bullying. It includes verbal abuse, derogatory remarks, humiliation, intimidation, and retaliation. Some specific bullying behaviors that employees have described are: having their opinions ignored, being shouted at, having gossip or rumors spread about them, and being ridiculed in public.[87] One final element of our definition: Bullying also includes the presence of a power imbalance so that one party is at a disadvantage or unable to protect or shield themselves from the bullying.

One highly publicized case of bullying occurred at Nike.[88] The company had developed a reputation as an intense place to work, which included numerous complaints about bullying. In an attempt to try to address this culture, the company initiated an internal misconduct inquiry. It led to some high-level departures. Brand President Trevor Edwards, who had developed a reputation for humiliating subordinates through insults and disparaging comments, was fired. So were four other executives, including a woman with more than twenty years at the company.

How big a problem is bullying in the workplace? It's widespread and it's growing. Research estimates that approximately 29 percent of the US workforce has been bullied on the job.[89] In terms of impact, this is about four times more prevalent than reports of sexual harassment.[90]

Bullying has multiple real negative effects on both employees and organizations.[91] For employees, bullying increases anxiety and panic attacks, reduces self-esteem, and can even create stress-related depression. For organizations, bullying can lead to lower employee productivity, increased absences, higher turnover, and increased replacement hiring costs.

Maybe somewhat surprisingly, the US has no federal laws against bullying. In contrast, Western Europe, Canada, and Australia have specific anti-bullying policies.

The result is that, in the US, it's hard for an affected employee to bring a lawsuit based on bullying. One way around this has been when the target can demonstrate that the bullying is related to a protected discrimination class. Lawsuits have been successful when they have shown that the bullying was related, for example, to the target's race, color, disability, or sexual orientation.

Management has an obligation to create a workplace free from bullies. Unfortunately, that isn't easy. A multifaceted approach is necessary. It starts with top management's leadership. There has to be commitment by senior executives—both in words and actions. This can then be supported by formal policies, codes of conduct, awareness workshops, the creation of formal channels for victims to make their claims, prompt investigations into incidences, and well-publicized disciplinary actions against the abusers.[92]

Chapter 12 | PREPARING FOR: Exams/Quizzes

CHAPTER SUMMARY by Learning Objectives

LO12.1 **EXPLAIN** the importance of human resource management and the human resource management process.

HRM is important for three reasons. First, it can be a significant source of competitive advantage. Second, it's an important part of organizational strategies. Finally, the way organizations treat their people has been found to significantly impact organizational performance. To meet these objectives, managers rely on eight activities (Exhibit 12-1) that comprise the HRM process.

LO12.2 **DESCRIBE** the external influences that affect the human resource management process.

The external factors that most directly affect the HRM process are the economy, labor unions, legal environment, and demographic trends. The economy affects how employees view their work and has implications for how an organization manages its human resources. A labor union is an organization that represents workers and seeks to protect their interests through collective bargaining. In unionized organizations, HRM practices are dictated by collective bargaining agreements. HRM practices are governed by a country's laws and not following those laws can be costly. Demographic trends such as changes in the racial and ethnic composition of the workforce, retiring baby boomers, and an expanding cohort of Gen Y workers will also have implications for HRM practices.

LO12.3 **DISCUSS** the tasks associated with identifying and selecting competent employees.

Human resource planning is the process by which managers ensure they have the right number and kinds of capable people in the right places at the right times. A job analysis is part of the assessment process that defines a job and the behaviors necessary to perform it. A job description is a written statement describing a job and typically includes job content, environment, and conditions of employment. A job specification is a written statement that specifies the minimum qualifications a person must possess to successfully perform a given job.

Employers must cautiously screen potential job applicants. Recruitment is the process of locating, identifying, and attracting capable applicants. Decruitment involves reducing the workforce when there is a surplus in the labor supply.

Selection involves predicting which applicants will be successful if hired. A valid selection device is characterized by a proven relationship between the selection device and some relevant criterion. A reliable selection device indicates that it measures the same thing consistently. The different selection devices include application forms, written and performance-simulation tests, interviews, background investigations, and in some cases physical exams.

A realistic job preview is important because it gives an applicant more realistic expectations about the job, which in turn should increase employee job satisfaction and reduce turnover.

LO12.4 **EXPLAIN** how companies provide employees with skills and knowledge.

Orientation is important because it results in an outsider-insider transition that makes the new employee feel comfortable and fairly well adjusted, lowers the likelihood of poor work performance, and reduces the probability of an early surprise resignation.

The most popular types of training include profession/industry-specific training, management/supervisory skills, mandatory/compliance information, and customer service training. This training can be provided using traditional training methods (on the job, job rotation, mentoring and coaching, experiential exercises, workbooks/manuals, and classroom lectures) or by technology-based methods (CD/DVDs video-conferencing or teleconferencing, e-learning, mobile learning, or virtual reality).

LO12.5 **DESCRIBE** strategies for retaining competent, high-performing employees.

A performance management system establishes performance standards used to evaluate employee performance. The different performance appraisal methods are written essays, critical incidents, graphic rating scales, BARS, multiperson comparisons, MBO, and 360-degree appraisals.

The factors that influence employee compensation and benefits include the employee's tenure and performance, kind of job performed, kind of business/industry, unionization, whether it is labor or capital intensive, management philosophy, geographical location, company profitability, and size of company.

Skill-based pay systems reward employees for the job skills and competencies they can demonstrate. In a variable pay system, an employee's compensation is contingent on performance. Some companies provide one-time bonuses for high-performing individuals instead of using annual pay raises. Benefits that have the greatest impact on employee satisfaction are health insurance, vacations, and paid time off.

LO12.6 **IDENTIFY** two important trends in organizational career development.

One trend has been toward lifelong learning. In decades past, skill demands changed slowly. If someone learned a specific skill on the job, in college, or in an apprenticeship program, that skill would likely hold throughout an individual's career. That is no longer the case. To stay current, employees need to commit to continually updating their skills through lifelong learning. And organizations are providing support.

The other trend is the growth of internship programs. These provide potential employees the opportunity to learn skills and for employers to evaluate individuals without the commitment to full-time employment.

LO12.7 **DISCUSS** contemporary issues in managing human resources.

Sexual harassment is any unwanted action or activity of a sexual nature that explicitly or implicitly affects an individual's employment, performance, or work environment. Managers need to be aware of what constitutes an offensive or hostile work environment, educate employees on sexual harassment, and ensure that no retaliatory actions are taken against any person who files harassment charges.

Workplace bullying occurs when an individual experiences negative behaviors (such as verbal abuse) repeatedly over a period of time that results in physical or mental harm. Responses to bullying include a commitment by senior executives to prevent workplace bullying as well as formal policies, codes of conduct, awareness workshops, and formal channels for making claims against bullies.

REVIEW AND DISCUSSION QUESTIONS

12-1. Discuss how human resource management practices can be a source of competitive advantage for a company.

12-2. Discuss the external environmental factors that most directly affect the HRM process.

12-3. Describe the different selection devices and which work best for different jobs.

12-4. What are the benefits and drawbacks of realistic job previews? (Consider this question from the perspective of both the organization and the employee.)

12-5. Describe the different types of orientation and training and how each of the types of training might be provided.

12-6. List the factors that influence employee compensation and benefits.

12-7. Describe the different performance appraisal methods.

12-8. What, in your view, constitutes sexual harassment? Describe how companies can minimize sexual harassment in the workplace.

PREPARING FOR: My Career

ETHICS DILEMMA

It's one thing to place security cameras in the workplace or to monitor business-related emails in order to prevent intellectual property theft.[93] But, there are now so many other ways that employees can be electronically monitored at work. Software can monitor how much time is spent on social media sites and take screenshots of what workers have on-screen. There even are badges that track the tone and length of conversations between coworkers, health trackers, and fingerprint scanners.[94] Since there is a lack of consistent laws about what constitutes legal employee monitoring, many companies engage in electronic monitoring without letting employees know they are being watched. Employers don't legally need to tell employees that

they are under video surveillance.[95] If they do let employees know, it often is buried in a lengthy document that is in legal language that employees don't understand.

12-9. What are the pros and cons of monitoring employees electronically?

12-10. How might employee electronic monitoring affect employee retention, engagement, and productivity?

12-11. If employers want to electronically monitor employees, how should they do it ethically? How should they decide whether a specific monitoring practice is OK or is going too far?

SKILLS EXERCISE Developing Your Interviewing Skills

About the Skill
One human resource practice that most managers must master is interviewing candidates in the hiring process. As a manager, you need to develop your interviewing skills. The following discussion highlights the key behaviors associated with this skill.

Steps in Practicing the Skill

• *Review the job description and job specification.* Reviewing pertinent information about the job provides valuable information about how to assess the candidate.

Furthermore, relevant job requirements help to eliminate interview bias.

• *Prepare a structured set of questions to ask all applicants for the job.* By having a set of prepared questions, you ensure that the information you wish to elicit is attainable. Furthermore, if you ask all applicants similar questions, you're better able to compare their answers against a common base.

• *Before meeting an applicant, review his or her application form and résumé.* Doing so helps you to create a complete picture of the applicant in terms of what is represented on the résumé or application and what the job requires. You will also begin to identify areas to explore in the interview. That is, areas not clearly defined on the résumé or application but essential for the job will become a focal point of your discussion with the applicant.

- *Open the interview by putting the applicant at ease and by providing a brief preview of the topics to be discussed.* Interviews are stressful for job applicants. By opening with small talk (e.g., the weather), you give the person time to adjust to the interview setting. By providing a preview of topics to come, you're giving the applicant an agenda that helps the individual begin framing what he or she will say in response to your questions.

- *Ask your questions and listen carefully to the applicant's answers.* Select follow-up questions that naturally flow from the answers given. Focus on the responses as they relate to information you need to ensure that the applicant meets your job requirements. Any uncertainty you may still have requires a follow-up question to probe further for the information.

- *Close the interview by telling the applicant what's going to happen next.* Applicants are anxious about the status of your hiring decision. Be honest with the applicant

regarding others who will be interviewed and the remaining steps in the hiring process. If you plan to make a decision in two weeks or so, let the individual know what you intend to do. In addition, tell the applicant how you will let him or her know about your decision.

- *Write your evaluation of the applicant while the interview is still fresh in your mind.* Don't wait until the end of your day, after interviewing several applicants, to write your analysis of each one. Memory can fail you. The sooner you complete your write-up after an interview, the better chance you have of accurately recording what occurred in the interview.

Practicing the Skill

The most challenging part of interviewing job applicants is preparing for the interview. Practice interview preparation by writing an interview guide that includes a structured set of questions. Look up a sample job description online. Create a list of skills and qualifications that you need to assess in the interview for this job. Next, write a list of questions to assess those qualifications. Make sure you have opening questions to put the applicant at ease, a body of questions that target the skills and qualifications you noted, and closing questions.

WORKING TOGETHER **Team Exercise**

New-hire orientation is an important human resource management practice. Take a few minutes and consider the orientation that you received at your last job. Write down some notes about the orientation process. Was the orientation formal or informal? Did you learn about the organization or just your work unit? What was helpful to you? What else would have been helpful to learn or do during the orientation? If you have not held a job, think

about a job you might be qualified to apply for now. Make some notes about what you think you would need to learn during the orientation for that job. Get together in groups of three or four students and share your orientation experiences. Next, create a list of your recommended orientation program "dos and don'ts" for companies. Be prepared to share your list with the class.

MY TURN TO BE A MANAGER

- Studies show that women's salaries still lag behind men's, and even with equal opportunity laws and regulations, women are paid about 80 percent of what men are paid.[96] Do some research on designing a compensation system that would address this issue. Write up your findings in a bulleted list format.

- The American Federation of Labor and Congress of Industrial Organizations is a national trade union center and the largest federation of unions in the United States. Visit the organization's website at www.aflcio.org. Explore the website and identify issues that are of current concern for today's labor unions.

- Go to the Society for Human Resource Management website (www.shrm.org) and look for the "HR News" page. Pick one of the news stories to read. (Note: Some of these may be available only to SHRM members, but

others should be generally available.) Write a summary of the information. At the end of your summary, discuss the implications of the topic for managers.

- Find *Fortune*'s "Best Companies to Work For" list online. Read the profiles of the top companies. Identify the types of benefits and other company characteristics that are common among these companies. Collect this information in a formal report you can present to your class.

- Visit an online job board and learn about how a company posts a job. Pick any online job board, such as www.monster.com, www.careerboard.com, or a local job board in your area. Click on the "Employers" tab and read about the process to post a job.

- Work on your résumé. If you don't have one, research what a good résumé should include. If you have one already, make sure it provides specific information that explicitly describes your work skills and experience rather than meaningless phrases such as "results oriented."

- Set up a profile on LinkedIn. Make sure you use a professional photo and provide a complete profile. Click on the "Business Services" link to learn how companies can use LinkedIn in the hiring process.

- Search online for a sample sexual harassment training program. How could an organization use this training program to help prevent harassment in the workplace?

CASE APPLICATION 1 — "Moneyball for HR" at Unilever

Let's say that you want to apply for a job at Unilever, a consumer goods company that owns over 400 food and personal care brands, including Dove and VO5 shampoos, Ben & Jerry's, and Lipton.[97] One of the steps in their selection process is asking applicants to solve puzzle-like games like "betting" virtual money on how many times you can hit the space bar on your keyboard in a certain amount of time. If that sounds random, Frida Polli, an MIT-trained neuroscientist, claims that it's not. She's the founder of pymetrics, the company behind that testing experience. Polli explains that their tests can predict behaviors that are often seen in high performers. Her firm can use their algorithms to figure out where in the organization an applicant might fit (if they fit at all). This data-driven approach to hiring is like "Moneyball for HR," says Polli, making a comparison to the statistical approach that the Oakland Athletics baseball team uses to choose players as described in the book and movie *Moneyball*.[98] Besides Unilever, other clients of pymetrics include Burger King, LinkedIn, and Tesla.[99]

It's not just pymetrics that is attracting big-name clients to help with hiring. HR start-ups using high-tech applications have experienced a 138 percent increase in investment in just one year (for an expected total of $2.9 billion in 2018). Travis Kessel, senior director of recruiting at Walmart's Jet.com division, puts it this way: "When you have a 4 percent unemployment rate and a skills gap in every sense for the talent we're competing for today, you have to use data to win. The war for talent is so hot right now that you can't afford not to." Kessel seeks to move beyond the traditional applicant-evaluation approach—reviewing resumes—which entails his recruiters reviewing a resume for an average of six seconds and selecting employees who up to 30–50 percent of the time do not pan out as good hires.

Unilever points to advantages already realized by their new approach to hiring. Their HR costs went down, their applicant numbers increased by 100 percent, and they shortened the timing of their hiring process from four months to four weeks. Since this process is still so new, they don't yet know whether employees hired through this new process will be successful in the long run.

Using technology tools in human resources does not automatically lead to success. As Sjoerd Gehring, multinational pharmaceutical company Johnson & Johnson's VP of talent acquisition, explains, "A lot of my peers see a new artificial intelligence tool or a chatbot and say, 'Oh, let me add that so I can show I'm doing something with AI.' When you do that year after year, you end up with forty or fifty tools that are super disconnected and don't deliver results."

DISCUSSION QUESTIONS

12-12. Which activities in the HRM process (see Exhibit 12-1) does this Moneyball approach to HR relate to? What challenges involved in these activities does their approach seek to address?

12-13. What are the advantages and disadvantages of Unilever's approach to hiring?

12-14. What evidence will be necessary to prove that Unilever is using a valid selection device to hire employees? What evidence would make it clear that they are using a reliable selection device?

12-15. What suggestions would you provide to a company that is considering implementing an approach similar to Unilever's?

CASE
APPLICATION **2**

CASE APPLICATION 2 — Keeping Dealership Sales Staff from Leaving at Nissan

Nissan—the automobile manufacturer—no doubt considered it good news that its overall sales were up 4.4 percent as of September 2018.[100] But, it was bad news for Nissan that it had 100 percent turnover in dealership sales positions within the same year.[101] Nissan is not alone. Employee turnover in auto dealerships has been consistently increasing over the past five years, while US auto sales have been generally good.

Part of the issue is that car dealerships rely on millennials for many of their hires. Millennials often have more debt than earlier generations and are looking for stable pay.[102] How do car dealerships usually pay salespeople? Their pay is typically solely based on commission. Commissions have been shrinking as customers walk into dealerships with internet research in hand that gives customers—not salespeople—the upper hand in car negotiations. Millennials often think of car dealership sales jobs as involving lots of customer haggling and an "old boys' club"—aspects of a job that doesn't usually excite prospective hires.

One of the ways dealerships are addressing these issues is by changing how employees are paid. At some dealerships, salespeople are paid by how many vehicles they sell per month. Other dealers are increasing commission-based pay and offering monthly sales bonuses. Offering benefits, like free college tuition for employees who don't leave the company and shorter workday hours, have helped some dealers keep salespeople on the job. And those dealers who have set "no-negotiation low prices" have removed the need for salespeople to have to haggle with customers.

Since so many salespeople at dealerships are new to their jobs, they often don't know as much as they should about the cars they're selling. There is so much technology to learn about each car when you're new on the job. A Texas-based Hyundai dealership recently implemented online training for salespeople to minimize a problem that has cropped up partly due to high employee turnover: potential buyers knowing more about the cars than the salespeople themselves.

DISCUSSION QUESTIONS

12-16. How have external forces affecting the HRM process impacted car dealerships' recent experience with employee turnover?

12-17. Several of the compensation issues described in this chapter could be applied to this case. Which issues are they, and how do they apply?

12-18. Which of the dealerships' attempts at reducing turnover do you think seems most promising? What else might they do to reduce turnover?

12-19. How, if at all, could realistic job previews for potential sales staff at car dealerships help reduce turnover?

ENDNOTES

1. A. Stych, "Walmart Brings VR Training to Stores Nationwide," *Business Journals*, September 26, 2018, https://www.bizjournals.com/pacific/news/2018/09/26/walmart-brings-vr-training-to-stores-nationwide.html.
2. See, for instance, R. Wartzman and L. Crosby, "The Key Factor Driving a Company's Results: Its People," *Wall Street Journal*, August 13, 2018, p. R5.
3. A. A. Lado and M. C. Wilson, "Human Resource Systems and Sustained Competitive Advantage," *Academy of Management Review* (October 1994): pp. 699–727; J. Pfeffer, *Competitive Advantage Through People* (Boston: Harvard Business School Press, 1994); E. F. Chapman, F. A. Sisk, J. Schatten, and E. W. Miles, "Human Resource Development and Human Resource Management Levers for Sustained Competitive Advantage: Combining Isomorphism and Differentiation," *Journal of Management and Organization* (July 2018): pp. 533–50.

4. "Maximizing the Return on Your Human Capital Investment: The 2005 Watson Wyatt Human Capital Index Report," "WorkAsia 2004/2005: A Study of Employee Attitudes in Asia," and "European Human Capital Index 2002," Watson Wyatt Worldwide (Washington, DC).

5. IBM Institute for Business Value, "Leading Through Connections: Highlights of the Global Chief Executive Officer Study," IBM, 2012, https://www.ibm.com/downloads/cas/3O8OG8RL.

6. C. Y.-P. Wang and B.-S. Jaw, "Building Dynamic Strategic Capabilities: A Human Capital Perspective," *International Journal of Human Resource Management* (March 2012): pp. 1129–57.

7. M. Subramony, "A Meta-Analytic Investigation of the Relationship Between HRM Bundles and Firm Performance," *Human Resource Management* (September–October 2009): pp. 745–68; and G. Spreitzer and C. Porath, "Creating Sustainable Performance," *Harvard Business Review*, January–February 2012, pp. 92–99.

8. M. Boyle, "Happy People, Happy Returns," *Fortune*, January 11, 2006, p. 100.

9. D. J. Lynch, "'This Is Super Tight:' Companies Struggle to Find, Retain Workers in a Hot Economy," *Washington Post*, January 12, 2018, https://www.washingtonpost.com/business/economy/this-is-super-tight-companies-struggle-to-find-retain-workers-in-a-hot-economy/2018/01/12/0c1ce97e-f7cf-11e7-b34a-b85626af34ef_story.html.

10. Ibid.

11. C. Stangler, "40,000 Verizon Workers Launch One of the Biggest Strikes of the Decade," *Nation*, April 15, 2016, https://www.thenation.com/article/40000-verizon-workers-launch-one-of-the-biggest-strikes-of-the-decade/.

12. S. White and M. Cabrera, "French Train Strikes Resume as Unions Square Off with Macron," *Reuters*, April 8, 2018, https://www.reuters.com/article/us-france-reform-sncf-strike/french-train-strikes-resume-as-unions-square-off-with-macron-idUSKBN1HF04D.

13. US Bureau of Labor Statistics, "Union Members Summary," US Department of Labor, January 19, 2018.

14. A. Doyle, "Best Union Jobs in America," *Balance Careers*, April 17, 2018, https://www.thebalancecareers.com/.

15. N. McCarthy, "Which Countries Have the Highest Levels of Labor Union Membership?," *Forbes*, June 20, 2017, https://www.forbes.com/sites/niallmccarthy/2017/06/20/which-countries-have-the-highest-levels-of-labor-union-membership-infographic/#1e4f4d8933c0.

16. C. Shaffer, "Jury Slaps Cleveland Clinic Foundation with $28 Million Judgment in Age Discrimination Suit," *Cleveland.com*, April 27, 2018, https://www.cleveland.com/court-justice/2018/04/jury_awards_former_cleveland_c.html.

17. See, for instance, E. Arvedlund, "When Workers Complain: Discrimination Lawsuits Accuse Vanguard of Targeting Workers," *Philly.com*, January 15, 2016, https://www.philly.com/philly/business/20160117_When_workers_complain__Discrimination_lawsuits_accuse_Vanguard_of_targeting_workers.html.

18. C. H. Loch, F. J. Sting, N. Bauer, and J. Mauermann, "How BMW Is Defusing the Demographic Time Bomb," *Harvard Business Review*, March 2010, pp. 99–102.

19. "Women in the Workforce: United States," *Catalyst*, March 28, 2018, https://www.catalyst.org/research/women-in-the-workforce-united-states/.

20. US Bureau of Labor Statistics, "Labor Force Projections to 2024: The Labor Force Is Growing but Slowly," *Monthly Labor Review*, US Department of Labor, December 2015, https://www.bls.gov/opub/mlr/2015/article/labor-force-projections-to-2024.htm.

21. See, for instance, K. Davidson, "Hard to Find: Workers with Good 'Soft Skills,'" *Wall Street Journal*, August 31, 3016, p. B1; and J. Barrett, "The U.S. Is Facing a Critical Skills Shortage, Reskilling Can Be Part of the Solution," *LinkedIn* (blog), April 19, 2018, https://blog.linkedin.com/2018/april/19/the-u-s-is-facing-a-critical-skills-shortage-reskilling-can-be-part-of-the-solution.

22. M. Horvath, "An Integrative Model of Recruitment Source Processes and Effects," *Organizational Psychology Review* (May 2015): pp. 126–45; and R. E. Ployhart, N. Schmitt, and N. T. Tippins, "Solving the Supreme Problem: 100 Years of Selection and Recruitment at the Journal of Applied Psychology," *Journal of Applied Psychology* (March 2017): pp. 291–304.

23. P. Joynt, "Decruitment: A New Personnel Function," *International Studies of Management & Organization* (March 1982): pp. 43–53.

24. "McDonald's Canada Announces 2018 National Hiring Day," *Toronto.com*, April 4, 2018, https://www.toronto.com/news-story/8370229-mcdonald-s-canada-announces-2018-national-hiring-day/.

25. Y. Bahgat, "The Top 10 Most Innovative Recruitment Campaigns," *Zoomforth* (blog), May 18, 2015, https://blog.zoomforth.com.

26. P. Brotherton, "Social Media and Referrals Are Best Sources for Talent," *T+D*, January 2012, p. 24; and R. Maurer, "Employee Referrals Remain Top Source for Hires," *Society for Human Resource Management*, June 23, 2017, https://www.shrm.org/resourcesandtools/hr-topics/talent-acquisition/pages/employee-referrals-remains-top-source-hires.aspx.

27. Maurer, "Employee Referrals."

28. "Why Employee Referrals Are the Best Source of Hire," *Undercover Recruiter*, May 14, 2018, https://theundercoverrecruiter.com/infographic-employee-referrals-hire/.

29. Ibid.

30. Based on H. B. Sagen, J. W. Dallam, and J. R. Laverty, "Job Search Techniques as Employment Channels: Differential Effects on the Initial Employment Success of College Graduates," *Career Development Quarterly* (September 1999): pp. 74–85; L. McKelvey, marketing manager at CareerBuilder.com (presentation, Chicago, IL, July 15, 2011); and A. Grant, "Which Company Is Right for You?," *New York Times*, December 20, 2015, p. SR-7.

31. Brotherton, "Social Media and Referrals" [see note 26].

32. Cited in G. Hitt, "Companies' Social Media Strategies Should Be: Data-Led, Human and Purposeful," *Universum*, February 2017, https://universumglobal.com.

33. L. Frye, "The Cost of a Bad Hire Can Be Astronomical," *Society for Human Resource Management*, May 9, 2017, https://www.shrm.org/resourcesandtools/hr-topics/employee-relations/pages/cost-of-bad-hires.aspx.

34. Cited in F. Fatemi, "The True Cost of a Bad Hire—It's More Than You Think," *Forbes*, September 28, 2016, https://www.forbes.com/sites/falonfatemi/2016/09/28/the-true-cost-of-a-bad-hire-its-more-than-you-think/#5ab6e48a4aa4.

35. K. Youngsang and R. E. Ployhart, "The Strategic Value of Selection Practices: Antecedents and Consequences of Firm-Level Selection Practice Usage," *Academy of Management Journal* (February 2018): pp. 46–66.

36. J. Bersin, "The Ugly Side of Today's Low Unemployment Rate," *Forbes*, July 3, 2018, https://www.forbes.com/sites/joshbersin/2018/07/03/the-ugly-side-to-todays-low-unemployment-rate/.

37. C. Zillman, "Target to Pay $2.8 Million for Hiring Discrimination Charges," *Fortune*, August 24, 2015, http://fortune.com/2015/08/24/target-discriminatory-hiring/.

38. B. W. Swider, M. R. Barrick, T. B. Harris, and A. C. Stoverink, "Managing and Creating an Image in the Interview: The Role of Interviewee Initial Impressions," *Journal of Applied Psychology* (November 2011): pp. 1275–88; and D. A. Moore, "How to Improve the Accuracy and Reduce the Cost of Personnel Selection," *California Management Review* (Fall 2017): pp. 8–17.

39. M. R. Barrick, B. W. Swider, and G. L. Stewart, "Initial Evaluations in the Interview: Relationships with Subsequent Interviewer Evaluations and Employment Offers," *Journal of Applied Psychology* (November 2010): pp. 1163–72; and J. Dana, "Against Job Interviews," *New York Times*, April 9, 2017, p. SR-6.

40. M. R. Barrick, J. A. Shaffer, and S. W. DeGrassi, "What You See May Not Be What You Get: Relationships Among Self-Presentation Tactics and Ratings of Interview and Job Performance," *Journal of Applied Psychology* (November 2009): pp. 1394–1411; and J. Levashina, C. J. Hartwell, F. P. Morgeson, and M. A. Campion, "The Structured Employment Interview: Narrative and Quantitative Review of the Research Literature," *Personnel Psychology* (Spring 2014): pp. 241–93.

41. F. Lievens and F. Patterson, "The Validity and Incremental Validity of Knowledge Tests, Low-Fidelity Simulations, and High-Fidelity Simulations for Predicting Job Performance in Advanced-Level High-Stakes Selection," *Journal of Applied Psychology* (September 2011): pp. 927–40.

42. P. L. Roth, P. Bobko, and L. A. McFarland, "A Meta-Analysis of Work Sample Test Validity: Updating and Integrating Some Classic Literature," *Personnel Psychology* (December 2005): pp. 1009–37.

43. G. C. Thornton, D. E. Rupp, and B. J. Hoffman, *Assessment Center Perspectives for Talent Management Strategies*, 2nd ed. (UK: Routledge, 2015); and P. R. Sackett, O. R. Shewach, and H. N. Keiser, "Assessment Centers Versus Cognitive Ability Tests: Challenging the Conventional Wisdom on Criterion-Related Validity," *Journal of Applied Psychology* (October 2017): pp. 1435–47.

44. P. L. Roth, P. Bobko, and C. H. Van Iddekinge, "Social Media in Employee-Selection Related Decisions," *Journal of Management* (January 2016): pp. 269–98.

45. C. H. Van Iddekinge, S. E. Lanivich, and P. L. Roth, "Social Media for Selection? Validity and Adverse Impact Potential of a Facebook-Based Assessment," *Journal of Management* (November 2016): pp. 1811–35.

46. S. L. Premack and J. P. Wanous, "A Meta-Analysis of Realistic Job Preview Experiments," *Journal of Applied Psychology* (November 1985): pp. 706–20; B. M. Meglino, E. C. Ravlin, and A. S. DeNisi, "A Meta-Analytic Examination of Realistic Job Preview Effectiveness: A Test of Three Counterintuitive Propositions," *Human Resource Management* (November 2000): pp. 407–34; and Y.-L. Liu, K. A. Keeling, and K. N. Papamichail, "Maximising the Credibility of Realistic Job Preview Messages: The Effect of Jobseekers' Decision-Making Style on Recruitment Information Credibility," *International Journal of Human Resource Management* 29, no. 7 (2018) pp. 1330–64.

47. J. Van Maanen and E. Schein, "Toward a Theory of Organizational Socialization," in B. M. Staw, ed., *Research in Organizational Behavior*, vol. 1 (Greenwich, CT: JAI, 1979).

48. C. Phillips, A. Esterman, and A. Kenny, "The Theory of Organizational Socialization and Its Potential for Improving Transition Experiences for New Graduate Nurses," *Nurse Education Today* (January 2015): pp. 118–24; and A. M. Ellis, S. S. Nifadkar, T. N. Bauer, and B. Erdogan, "Newcomer Adjustment: Examining the Role of Managers' Perception of Newcomer Proactive Behavior During Organizational Socialization," *Journal of Applied Psychology* (June 2017): pp. 993–1001.

49. S. Patel, "Sujan Patel: Building Loyalty from the Beginning," *Wall Street Journal* (blog), December 24, 2014, https://blogs.wsj.com/accelerators/2014/12/24/sujan-patel-building-loyalty-from-the-beginning/.

50. L. Dearden, "The One Chart That Shows What Causes Fatal Plane Crashes," *Independent*, September 10, 2015, https://www.independent.co.uk/travel/news-and-advice/the-one-chart-that-shows-what-causes-fatal-plane-crashes-10494952.html.

51. A. Pasztor, "New United Air Pilot Training Could Raise Safety Bar for Industry," *Wall Street Journal*, January 31, 2016, https://www.wsj.com/articles/new-united-air-pilot-training-could-raise-safety-bar-for-industry-1454195812.

52. "2018 Industry Training Report," *Training*, November/December 2018, p. 21.

53. "Sully's Tale," *Air & Space/Smithsonian*, February 18, 2009, https://www.airspacemag.com/as-interview/aamps-interview-sullys-tale-53584029/; and A. Altman, "Chesley B. Sullenberger III," *Time*, January 16, 2009, http://content.time.com/time/nation/article/0,8599,1872247,00.html.

54. "2017 Training Industry Report," *Training*, December 2017, https://trainingmag.com/trgmag-article/2017-training-industry-report/.

55. B. S. Bell, S. I. Tannenbaum, J. K. Ford, R. A. Noe, and K. Kraiger, "100 Years of Training and Development Research: What We Know and Where We Should Go," *Journal of Applied Psychology* (March 2017): pp. 305–23.

56. S. Luthra, "How to Improve Doctors' Beside Manner," CNN, September 18, 2015, https://www.cnn.com/2015/09/13/health/doctor-empathy-increase/index.html.

57. R. Feintzeig, "Your Manager Wants to See You. Again," *Wall Street Journal*, May 10, 2017, p. B7.

58. Ibid.

59. Forrester Consulting, "Employee Performance Management Needs a Promotion," *Workday*, February 2018, https://www.workday.com/en-us/forms/reports/employee-performance-management-needs-a-promotion.html.

60. Cited in P. Cappelli and A. Tavis, "The Performance Management Revolution," Harvard Business Review, October 2016, pp. 58–67.

61. Cited in L. Goler, J. Gale, and A. Grant, "Let's Not Kill Performance Evaluations Yet," *Harvard Business Review*, November 2016, pp. 90–94.

62. D. P. Bhave, "The Invisible Eye? Electronic Performance Monitoring and Employee Job Performance," *Personnel Psychology* (Autumn 2014): pp. 605–35; and D. L. Tomczak, L. A. Lanzo, and H. Aguinis, "Evidence-Based Recommendations for Employee Performance Monitoring," *Business Horizons* (March-April 2018): pp. 251–59.

63. Based on S. Ovide and R. Feintzeig, "Microsoft Abandons 'Stack Ranking' of Employees," *Wall Street Journal*, November 12, 2013, https://www.wsj.com/articles/microsoft-abandons-8216stack-ranking8217-of-employees-1384279446; and S. Maier, "Microsoft Throws Employee Stack-Ranking Out the Window," *LinkedIn*, January 27, 2016, https://www.linkedin.com/pulse/microsoft-throws-employee-stack-ranking-out-window-steffen-maier/.

64. J. J. Martocchio, *Strategic Compensation: A Human Resource Management Approach*, 9th ed. (Hoboken, NJ: Pearson Education, 2017).

65. J. Berman, "More Companies Help Employees Pay Off Student Loans," *Wall Street Journal*, March 27, 2016, https://www.wsj.com/articles/more-companies-help-employees-pay-off-student-loans-1459130781.

66. B. Murray and B. Gerhart, "An Empirical Analysis of a Skill-Based Pay Program and Plant Performance Outcomes," *Academy of Management Journal* (January 1998): pp. 68–78.

67. "Compensation Programs and Practices," *WorldatWork*, January 2015, https://www.worldatwork.org/docs/research-and-surveys/Survey-Brief-Compensation-Programs-and-Practices-2014.pdf.

68. R. E. Silverman, "Companies Rethink Raises," *Wall Street Journal*, August 24, 2016, p. B1.

69. Ibid.

70. N. Janicijevic, "Pay Secrecy: Pros and Cons," *ResearchGate*, January 2016, https://www.researchgate.net/publication/312356880_Pay_secrecy_Pros_and_cons.

71. R. G. Trotter, S. R. Zacur, and L. T. Stickney, "The New Age of Pay Transparency," *Business Horizons* (July–August 2017): pp. 529–39.

72. J. Lutz, "Millennials Are Slowly Killing Salary Secrecy—And That's a Good Thing," *Forbes*, November 30, 2017, https://www.forbes.com/sites/jessicalutz/2017/11/30/millennials-are-slowly-killing-salary-secrecy-and-thats-a-good-thing/#25a619436015.

73. C. Merhar, "Do Employee Benefits Really Matter?," *PeopleKeep*, March 23, 2016, https://www.peoplekeep.com/blog/do-employee-benefits-really-matter; and "Top 20 Benefits and Perks and Why They Matter," *Glassdoor*, February 7, 2017, https://www.glassdoor.com/employers/blog/top-20-benefits-and-perks-and-why-they-matter/.

74. "Top 20 Benefits and Perks."

75. B. Goebel, "S.F. Agency Votes to Make 'Google Bus' Program Permanent," *KQED*, February 22, 2017, https://www.kqed.org/news/11328302/s-f-agency-votes-to-make-google-bus-program-permanent.

76. "Top 20 Benefits and Perks" [see note 73].

77. L. Yuan, "Silicon Valley Visits the Land of 72-Hour Workweeks," *New York Times*, November 6, 2018, p. B4.

78. J. Purkiss and D. Royston-Lee, *Brand You: Turn Your Unique Talents into a Winning Formula* (New York: FT Press, 2013).

79. I. Thottam, "10 Companies with Awesome Training and Development Programs," *Monster*, https://www.monster.com/career-advice/article/companies-with-awesome-training-development-programs; and E. Moore, "9 Companies That Offer Incredible Professional Development Programs," *Glassdoor* (blog), September 18, 2017, https://www.glassdoor.com/blog/companies-with-professional-development-programs/.

80. N. Saltikoff, "The Positive Implications of Internships on Early Career Outcomes," NACE Center, May 1, 2017, https://www.naceweb.org/job-market/internships/the-positive-implications-of-internships-on-early-career-outcomes/; and P. Loretto, "What is the Value of Doing an Internship?" *Balance Careers*, updated December 24, 2018, https://www.thebalancecareers.com/what-is-the-value-of-doing-an-internship-1986586.

81. "Sexual Harassment," *US Equal Employment Opportunity Commission*, https://www.eeoc.gov/laws/types/sexual_harassment.cfm.

82. B. Braverman, "The High Cost of Sexual Harassment," *Fiscal Times*, August 22, 2013, http://www.thefiscaltimes.com/Articles/2013/08/22/The-High-Cost-of-Sexual-Harassment.

83. M. Farber, "Where Gretchen Carlson's $20 Million Settlement Ranks Among the Biggest Sexual Harassment Cases," *Fortune*, September 6, 2016, http://fortune.com/2016/09/06/biggest-sexual-harassment-cases/.

84. M. Senthilingam, "Sexual Harassment: How It Stands Around the Globe," *CNN*, updated November 29, 2017, https://www.cnn.com/2017/11/25/health/sexual-harassment-violence-abuse-global-levels/index.html.

85. J. B. Becton, J. B. Gilstrap, and M. Forsyth, "Preventing and Correcting Workplace Harassment: Guidelines for Employers," *Business Horizons* (January–February 2017): pp. 101–11.

86. See S. Branch and J. Murray, "Workplace Bullying: Is Lack of Understanding the Reason for Inaction? *Organizational Dynamics* (October–December 2015): pp. 287–95; and D. Ferris, M. Yan, V. Lim, Y Chen, and S. Fatimah, "An Approach-Avoidance Framework of Workplace Aggression," *Academy of Management Journal* (October 2016): pp. 1777–80.

87. Branch and Murray, "Workplace Bullying."

88. M. Townsend and E. E. Deprez, "Is the Corporate Bully the Next Workplace Pariah?," *Bloomberg Businessweek*, May 14, 2018, pp. 22–23.

89. Cited in P. Agarwal, "Here Is Why We Need to Talk About Bullying in the Work Place," *Forbes*, July 29, 2018, https://www.forbes.com/sites/pragyaagarwaleurope/2018/07/29/workplace-bullying-here-is-why-we-need-to-talk-about-bullying-in-the-work-place/#3946b3663259.

90. Townsend and Deprez, "Is the Corporate Bully" [see note 88].

91. Branch and Murray, "Workplace Bullying" [see note 86].

92. Ibid.; and C. Woodrow and D. E. Guest, "Leadership and Approaches to the Management of Workplace Bullying," *European Journal of Work and Organizational Psychology* 26, no. 2 (2017): pp. 221–33.

93. V. Bolden-Barrett, "A Quarter of Tech Employees on Blind Say Their Company Conducts 'Unreasonable' Monitoring," *HR Dive*, October 16, 2018, https://www.hrdive.com/news/a-quarter-of-tech-employees-on-blind-say-their-company-conducts-unreasonab/539625/.

94. J. Burns, "Your Office Is Watching: The Ethics of Employee Monitoring," *AllHands*, September 6, 2017, https://blog.managedbyq.com/employee-monitoring-data-collection-ethics.

95. A. Rivera, "Spying on Your Employees? Better Understand the Law First," *Business News Daily*, July 30, 2018, https://www.businessnewsdaily.com/6685-employee-monitoring-privacy.html.

96. J. Calfas, "Women Have Pushed for Equal Pay for Decades. It's Sad How Little Progress We've Made," *Money*, April 10, 2018, http://money.com/money/5225986/equal-pay-day-2018-gender-wage-gap/.

97. Wikipedia, s.v., "Unilever," https://en.wikipedia.org/wiki/Unilever.

98. A. Carr, "Moneyball for Business: How AI Is Changing Talent Management," *Fast Company*, August 16, 2018, https://www.fastcompany.com/90205539/moneyball-for-business-how-ai-is-changing-talent-management.

99. "Pymetrics," https://www.pymetrics.com.

100. N. Bomey, "Honda, Toyota, Nissan Car Sales Plunge, but SUVs Rise: U.S. Auto Sales Likely Up in August," *USA Today*, September 4, 2018, https://www.usatoday.com/story/money/cars/2018/09/04/august-us-auto-sales/1188847002/.

101. A. Roberts, "Car Dealers Labor to Keep Young Workers," *Wall Street Journal*, August 24, 2018.

102. "5 Ways to Retain Millennial Employees at a Car Dealership," *OneDealer* (blog), February 6, 2018, https://www.onedealer.com/en/5-ways-retain-millennial-employees-car-dealership/.

Chapter 13

Managing Groups and Teams

Learning Objectives

13.1 Define groups and the stages of group development.

13.2 Describe the major components that determine group performance and satisfaction.

13.3 Define teams and best practices influencing team performance.

Employability Skills Matrix

This matrix identifies which features and end-of-chapter material will help you develop specific skills employers are looking for in job candidates.

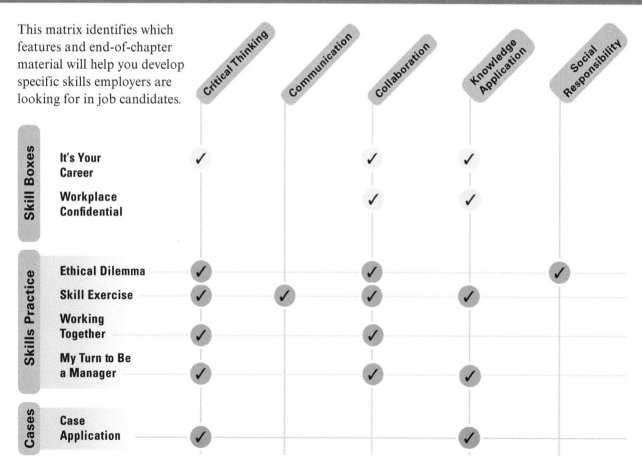

	Critical Thinking	Communication	Collaboration	Knowledge Application	Social Responsibility
Skill Boxes					
It's Your Career	✔		✔	✔	
Workplace Confidential			✔	✔	
Skills Practice					
Ethical Dilemma	✔		✔		✔
Skill Exercise	✔	✔	✔	✔	
Working Together	✔		✔		
My Turn to Be a Manager	✔		✔	✔	
Cases					
Case Application	✔			✔	

You've probably had a lot of experience working in groups—class group projects, maybe an athletic team, or a fundraising committee. In today's organizations, work is increasingly being done in teams. And this creates unique challenges for managers.

Why have teams become so popular? What do these teams look like? How can managers build effective teams? We will look at answers to these questions throughout this chapter. Before we can understand teams, however, we first need to understand some basics about groups and group behavior.

GROUPS and group development

LO13.1 Firefighters live or die on the effectiveness of their teammates. They may use different tactics and standard procedures, but fire departments all over the world depend on one common denominator: teamwork. If any member of the team fails at his or her task, lives can be lost.

While most groups in organizations don't deal with life or death situations, and managers don't literally put out fires, managers do rely on work groups to accomplish objectives. But what do we mean by the term "group"?

What Is a Group?

A **group** is defined as two or more interacting and interdependent individuals who come together to achieve specific goals. Groups can be either formal or informal. *Formal groups* are work groups defined by the organization's structure and have designated work assignments and specific tasks directed at accomplishing organizational goals. Exhibit 13-1 provides some examples. *Informal groups* are social groups. These groups occur naturally in the workplace and tend to form around friendships and common interests. For example, five employees from different departments who regularly eat lunch together are an informal group.

Stages of Group Development

Research shows that groups develop through five stages.[2] As shown in Exhibit 13-2, these five stages are *forming, storming, norming, performing,* and *adjourning.*

The **forming stage** has two phases. The first occurs as people join the group. In a formal group, people join because of some work assignment. Once they've joined, the second phase begins: defining the group's purpose, structure, and leadership. This phase involves a great deal of uncertainty as members "test the waters" to determine what types of behavior are acceptable. This stage is complete when members begin to think of themselves as part of a group.

The **storming stage** is appropriately named because of the intragroup conflict. There's conflict over who will control the group and what the group needs to be doing. During this stage, a relatively clear hierarchy of leadership and agreement on the group's direction emerge.

- **Command groups**—Groups determined by the organizational chart and composed of individuals who report directly to a given manager.
- **Task groups**—Groups composed of individuals brought together to complete a specific job task; their existence is often temporary because when the task is completed, the group disbands.
- **Cross-functional teams**—Groups that bring together the knowledge and skills of individuals from various work areas or groups whose members have been trained to do each others' jobs.
- **Self-managed teams**—Groups that are essentially independent and that, in addition to their own tasks, take on traditional managerial responsibilities such as hiring, planning and scheduling, and evaluating performance.

group
Two or more interacting and interdependent individuals who come together to achieve specific goals

forming stage
The first stage of group development in which people join the group and then define the group's purpose, structure, and leadership

storming stage
The second stage of group development, characterized by intragroup conflict

Exhibit 13-1
Examples of Formal Work Groups

Exhibit 13-2
Stages of Group Development

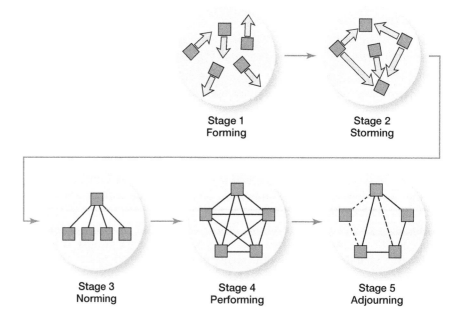

Stage 1
Forming

Stage 2
Storming

Stage 3
Norming

Stage 4
Performing

Stage 5
Adjourning

norming stage
The third stage of group development, characterized by close relationships and cohesiveness

performing stage
The fourth stage of group development when the group is fully functional and works on the group's task

adjourning
The final stage of group development for temporary groups during which group members are concerned with wrapping up activities rather than task performance

As a permanent work group in the performing stage, the kitchen staff at HILTL, a vegetarian restaurant in Zurich, prepare a dish. Everyone on the team has a strong sense of group identity and focuses their energies on creating a delectable dining experience for their guests.
Source: Bruce yuanyue Bi/Alamy Stock Photos

The **norming stage** is one in which close relationships develop and the group becomes cohesive. There's now a strong sense of group identity and camaraderie. This stage is complete when the group structure solidifies and the group has assimilated a common set of expectations (or norms) regarding member behavior.

The fourth stage is the **performing stage**. The group structure is in place and accepted by group members. Their energies have moved from getting to know and understand each other to working on the group's task. This is the last stage of development for permanent work groups. However, for temporary groups—project teams, task forces, or similar groups that have a limited task to do—the final stage is **adjourning**. In this stage, the group prepares to disband. The group focuses its attention on wrapping up activities instead of task performance. Group members react in different ways. Some are upbeat and thrilled about the group's accomplishments. Others may be sad over the loss of camaraderie and friendships.

Many of you have probably experienced these stages as you've worked on a group class project. Group members are selected or assigned and then meet for the first time. There's a "feeling out" period to assess what the group is going to do and how it's going to be done. What usually follows is a battle for control: Who's going to be in charge? Once this issue is resolved and a "hierarchy" agreed upon, the group identifies specific work that needs to be done, who's going to do each part, and dates by which the assigned work needs to be completed. General expectations are established. These decisions form the foundation for what you hope will be a coordinated group effort culminating in a successfully completed project. Once the project is complete and turned in, the group breaks up. Of course, some groups don't get much beyond the forming or storming stages. These groups may have serious interpersonal conflicts, turn in disappointing work, and get lower grades.

Does a group become more effective as it progresses through the first four stages? This may be generally true, but what makes a group effective is a complex issue. Under some conditions, high levels of conflict can be conducive to high levels of group performance. In some situations, groups in the storming stage outperform those in the norming or performing stages. Also, groups don't always proceed sequentially from one stage to the next. Sometimes, groups are storming and performing at the same time. Groups even occasionally regress to previous stages; therefore, don't assume that all groups precisely follow this process or that performing is always the most preferable stage. Think of this model as a general framework that underscores the fact that groups are dynamic entities and managers need to know the stage a group is in so they can better understand the problems and issues most likely to surface.

WORK group performance and satisfaction

L013.2 Why *are* some groups more successful than others? Why do some groups achieve high levels of performance and high levels of member satisfaction and others do not? Exhibit 13-3 presents the major factors that determine group performance and satisfaction.[3] Let's look at each.

External Conditions Imposed on the Group

Work groups are affected by the external conditions imposed on it, such as the organization's strategy, authority relationships, formal rules and regulations, availability of resources, employee selection criteria, the performance evaluation system and culture, and the general physical layout of the group's work space. For instance, a quality-improvement group at Boeing has to live with Boeing's corporate hiring criteria, budget constraints, company policies, and employee evaluation system.

Group Member Resources

A group's performance potential depends to a large extent on the resources each individual brings to the group. These resources include knowledge, abilities, skills, and personality traits, and they determine what members can do and how effectively they will perform in a group. Interpersonal skills—especially conflict management and resolution, collaborative problem solving, and communication—consistently emerge as important for high performance by work groups.[4]

Personality traits also affect group performance because they strongly influence how the individual will interact with other group members. Research has shown that traits viewed as positive in our culture (such as sociability, self-reliance, and independence) tend to be positively related to group productivity and morale. In contrast, negative personality characteristics, such as authoritarianism, dominance, and unconventionality, tend to be negatively related to group productivity and morale.[5] Some organizations recognize the importance of having the appropriate mix of personalities on a team. For instance, car review website Edmunds.com uses the results of personality testing as one consideration for assembling its executive team.[6]

Group Structure

Work groups aren't unorganized crowds. They have an internal structure that shapes members' behavior and influences group performance. The structure defines roles, norms, conformity, status systems, group size, group cohesiveness, and leadership.

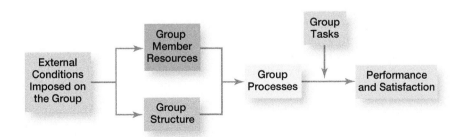

Exhibit 13-3
Group Performance/Satisfaction Model

Dark suits, dress shirts, and conservative ties for men and dark suits and tailored blouses for women is the norm for lawyers working at this law firm in New Delhi, India. In the legal industry, the norm of formal dress conveys a polished, professional image that can help lawyers command respect and inspire trust during court appearances and client meetings. *Source: The India Today Group/Getty Images*

role
Behavior patterns expected of someone occupying a given position in a social unit

norms
Standards or expectations that are accepted and shared by a group's members

Let's look at the first six of these aspects of group structure. We'll discuss leadership in Chapter 17.

ROLES   We introduced the concept of roles in Chapter 1 when we discussed what managers do. (Remember Mintzberg's managerial roles?) Of course, managers aren't the only individuals in an organization who play a variety of roles. The concept of roles applies to all employees and to their lives outside an organization as well. (Think of the various roles you play: student, friend, sibling, employee, church member, spouse or significant other, etc.)

A **role** refers to behavior patterns expected of someone occupying a given position in a social unit.[7] In a group, individuals are expected to do certain things because of their position (role) in the group. These roles are generally oriented toward either getting work done or keeping up group member morale.[8] Think about groups you've been in and the roles you played in those groups. Were you continually trying to keep the group focused on getting its work done? If so, you were performing a task accomplishment role. Or were you more concerned that group members had the opportunity to offer ideas and that they were satisfied with the experience? If so, you were performing a group member satisfaction role. Both roles are important to the group's ability to function effectively and efficiently.

NORMS   All groups have **norms**—standards or expectations that are accepted and shared by a group's members.[9] Norms dictate things such as work output levels, absenteeism, promptness, and the amount of socializing on the job.

For example, norms in Korean culture pressure workers to "pull late nights" because they feel the need to please their superiors. One observer described these workers: "They just sit in their chairs and they just watch their team leaders, and they're thinking, 'What time is he going to leave the office?'"[10] Then, there is an expectation that the boss and employees will go out for drinks, and it is important that employees participate. In Korea, drinking together helps build workplace camaraderie and trust.[11]

Although every group has its own unique set of norms, common organizational norms focus on effort and performance, dress, and loyalty. The most widespread norms are those related to work effort and performance. Work groups typically provide their members with explicit cues on how hard to work, level of output expected, when to look busy, when it's acceptable to goof off, and the like. These norms are powerful influences on an individual employee's performance. They're so powerful that you can't predict someone's performance based solely on his or her ability and personal motivation. That is, the pressure of a group's expectations can override a member's skill and drive. Dress norms frequently dictate what's acceptable to wear to work. If the norm is more formal dress, anyone who dresses casually may face subtle pressure to conform. Finally, loyalty norms can influence whether individuals work late, work on weekends, or move to locations they might not prefer to live.

CONFORMITY   Because individuals want to be accepted by groups to which they belong, they're susceptible to pressures to conform.[12] Early experiments done by Solomon Asch demonstrated the impact conformity has on an individual's judgment and attitudes.[13] In these experiments, groups of seven or eight people were asked to compare two cards held up by the experimenter. One card had three lines of different lengths and the other had one line that was equal in length to one of the three lines on the other card (see Exhibit 13-4). Each group member was to announce aloud which of the three lines matched the single line. Asch wanted to see what would happen if members began to give incorrect answers. Would pressures to conform cause

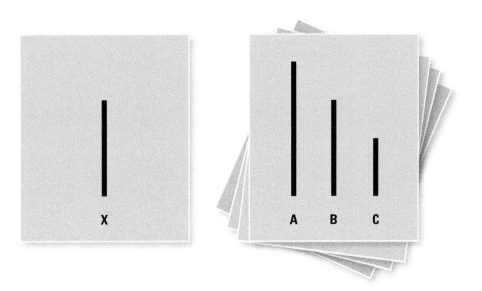

Exhibit 13-4
Examples of Asch's Cards

individuals to give wrong answers just to be consistent with the others? The experiment was "fixed" so that all but one of the members (the unsuspecting subject) were told ahead of time to start giving obviously incorrect answers after one or two rounds. Over many experiments and trials, the unsuspecting subject conformed over a third of the time.

Are these conclusions still valid? For the most part, yes.[14] Managers shouldn't ignore conformity because it can be a powerful force in groups. Group members often want to be seen as one of the group and avoid being visibly different. We find it more pleasant to agree than to be disruptive, even if being disruptive may improve the group's effectiveness. So we conform. But conformity can go too far, especially when an individual's opinion differs significantly from that of others in the group. In such a case, the group often exerts intense pressure on the individual to align his or her opinion to conform to others' opinions, a phenomenon known as **groupthink**. Groupthink seems to occur when group members hold a positive group image they want to protect and when the group perceives a collective threat to this positive image.[15] Sometimes, groupthink can lead to catastrophic outcomes. For example, NASA's so-called "go for launch" mentality is believed to have hastened the launch of the space shuttle Challenger in 1986 in spite of expressed concerns that the O-ring seal could malfunction. Unfortunately, the shuttle exploded shortly after takeoff, and investigations into this disaster revealed that the O-ring's malfunction was likely the cause.

groupthink
When a group exerts extensive pressure on an individual to align his or her opinion with others' opinions

STATUS SYSTEMS Status systems are an important factor in understanding groups.[16] **Status** is a prestige grading, position, or rank within a group. As far back as researchers have been able to trace groups, they have found status hierarchies. Status can be a significant motivator with behavioral consequences, especially when individuals see a disparity between what they perceive their status to be and what others perceive it to be.[17]

status
A prestige grading, position, or rank within a group

Status may be informally conferred by characteristics such as education, age, skill, or experience. Anything can have status value if others in the group evaluate it that way. Of course, just because status is informal doesn't mean it's unimportant or hard to determine who has it or who does not. Group members have no problem placing people into status categories and usually agree about who has high or low status.

Status is also formally conferred, and it's important for employees to believe the organization's formal status system is congruent—that is, the system shows consistency between the perceived ranking of an individual and the status symbols he or she is given by the organization. For instance, status incongruence would occur when a supervisor earns less than his or her subordinates, a desirable office is occupied by

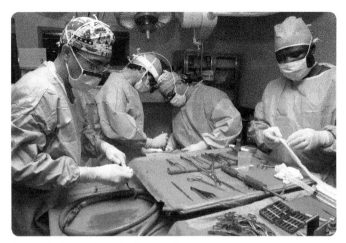

Group cohesiveness is high for this operating room surgical team at a New York hospital as it performs spinal surgery. The success of surgical and operative procedures and patients' pain control and safety requires individual expertise plus high levels of concentration, coordination, cooperation, agreement, and respect for each other among group members.
Source: David Grossman/Alamy Stock Photo

social loafing
The tendency for individuals to expend less effort when working collectively than when working individually

group cohesiveness
The degree to which group members are attracted to one another and share the group's goals

a person in a low-ranking position, or paid country club memberships are provided to division managers but not to vice presidents. Employees expect the "things" an individual receives to be congruent with his or her status. When they're not, employees can become stressed, may question the authority of their managers, or may not be motivated by job promotion opportunities.

GROUP SIZE Does the size of a group affect the group's overall performance? Yes, but the preferred size depends on what the group is attempting to accomplish.[18]

Research indicates, for instance, that small groups are faster than larger ones at completing tasks. However, for groups engaged in problem solving, large groups consistently get better results than smaller ones. What do these findings mean in terms of specific numbers? Large groups—those with a dozen or more members—are good for getting diverse input. Thus, if the goal of the group is fact finding, a larger group should be more effective. For instance, the US Department of Defense recently assembled an investigation team to determine why US military forces bombed a friendly target—a Doctors Without Borders hospital in Afghanistan—killing dozens of innocent people. A Defense official said that the investigation team included "over a dozen subject matter experts from several specialty fields."[19] Within six months, the team identified the causes of the incident, which included human error and faulty equipment. While this example illustrates the effectiveness of large teams, smaller groups—from five to seven members—are better at doing something productive with those facts.

One important research finding related to group size concerns **social loafing**, which is the tendency for an individual to expend less effort when working collectively than when working alone.[20] Social loafing may occur because people believe others in the group aren't doing their fair share or because the relationship between an individual's input and the group's output is not clear. These conditions can encourage individuals to become "free riders" and coast on the group's efforts.

The implications of social loafing are significant. When managers use groups, they need to identify individual efforts as well as the group's overall performance. If not, group productivity and individual satisfaction may decline.[21]

GROUP COHESIVENESS Cohesiveness is important because it has been found to be related to a group's productivity. Groups in which there's a lot of internal disagreement and lack of cooperation are less effective in completing their tasks than groups in which members generally agree, cooperate, and like each other. Research in this area has focused on **group cohesiveness**, or the degree to which members are attracted to a group and share the group's goals.[22]

Research has generally shown that highly cohesive groups are more effective than less-cohesive ones.[23] However, the relationship between cohesiveness and effectiveness is complex. A key moderating variable is the degree to which the group's attitude aligns with its goals or with the goals of the organization.[24] (See Exhibit 13-5.) The more cohesive the group, the more its members will follow its goals. If the goals are desirable (for instance, high output, quality work, cooperation with individuals outside the group), a cohesive group is more productive than a less-cohesive group. But if cohesiveness is high and attitudes are unfavorable (such as that low-quality work is considered acceptable by group members), productivity decreases. If cohesiveness is low, but goals are supported, productivity increases, but not as much as when both cohesiveness and support are high. When cohesiveness is low and goals are not supported, productivity is not significantly affected.

	Cohesiveness	
	High	**Low**
Alignment of Group and Organizational Goals — High	Strong Increase in Productivity	Moderate Increase in Productivity
Alignment of Group and Organizational Goals — Low	Decrease in Productivity	No Significant Effect on Productivity

Exhibit 13-5
Group Cohesiveness and Productivity

Group Processes

Next we look at the processes that go on within a work group. These processes are important to understanding work groups because they influence group performance and satisfaction positively or negatively. An example of a positive process factor is the synergy of four people on a marketing research team who are able to generate far more ideas as a group than the members could produce individually. However, the group also may have negative process factors such as social loafing, high levels of conflict, or poor communication. We'll look at two important group processes: group decision making and conflict management.

GROUP DECISION MAKING   It's a rare organization that doesn't use meetings, committees, task forces, review panels, study teams, or other similar groups to make decisions. One survey found that the average employee spends 37 percent of his or her time in meetings.[25] Another study, of CEOs, found they spend nearly three-quarters of their time in meetings.[26] Undoubtedly, a large portion of that time is spent formulating problems, developing solutions, and determining how to implement the solutions. It's possible for groups to be assigned any of the eight steps in the decision-making process we discussed in Chapter 2.

What advantages do group decisions have over individual decisions?[27] One is that groups generate more complete information and knowledge. They bring a diversity of experiences and perspectives to the decision process that an individual cannot. In addition, groups generate more diverse alternatives because they have a greater amount and diversity of information. Next, groups increase acceptance of a solution. Group members are reluctant to fight or undermine a decision they helped develop. Finally, groups increase legitimacy. Decisions made by groups may be perceived as more legitimate than decisions made by one person.

Group decisions also have their disadvantages. One is that groups almost always take more time to reach a solution than it would take an individual. Another is that a dominant and vocal minority can heavily influence the final decision. In addition, groupthink can undermine critical thinking in the group and harm the quality of the final decision. Finally, in a group, members share responsibility, but the responsibility of any single member is ambiguous.

Determining whether groups are effective at making decisions depends on the criteria used to assess effectiveness.[28] If accuracy, creativity, and degree of acceptance are important, then a group decision may work best. However, if speed and efficiency are important, then an individual decision may be the best. In addition, decision effectiveness is influenced by group size. Although a larger group provides more diverse representation, it also requires more coordination and time for members to contribute their ideas. Evidence indicates that groups of five, and to a lesser extent seven, are the most effective for making decisions.[29]

Exhibit 13-6

Creative Group Decision Making

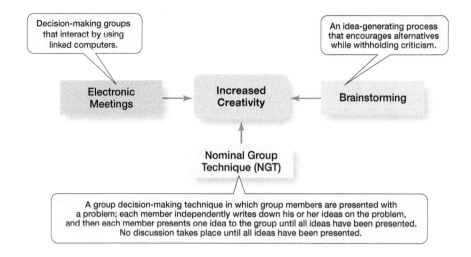

Having an odd number in the group helps avoid decision deadlocks. Also, these groups are large enough for members to shift roles and withdraw from unfavorable positions but still small enough for quieter members to participate actively in discussions.

What techniques can managers use to help groups make more creative decisions? Exhibit 13-6 describes three possibilities.

CONFLICT MANAGEMENT Another important group process is how a group manages conflict. As a group performs its assigned tasks, disagreements inevitably arise. **Conflict** is *perceived* incompatible differences resulting in some form of interference or opposition. Whether the differences are real is irrelevant. If people in a group perceive that differences exist, then there is conflict.

Three different views have evolved regarding conflict.[30] The **traditional view of conflict** argues that conflict must be avoided—that it indicates a problem within the group. Another view, the **human relations view of conflict**, argues that conflict is a natural and inevitable outcome in any group and need not be negative, but it has potential to be a positive force in contributing to a group's performance. The third and most recent view, the **interactionist view of conflict**, proposes that not only can conflict be a positive force in a group, but also that some conflict is *absolutely necessary* for a group to perform effectively.

The interactionist view doesn't suggest that all conflicts are good. Some conflicts—**functional conflicts**—are constructive and support the goals of the work group and improve its performance. Other conflicts—**dysfunctional conflicts**—are destructive and prevent a group from achieving its goals. Exhibit 13-7 illustrates the challenges facing managers at different levels of conflict.

When is conflict functional, and when is it dysfunctional? Research indicates that you need to look at the *type* of conflict.[31] **Task conflict** relates to the content and goals of the work. **Relationship conflict** focuses on interpersonal relationships. **Process conflict** refers to how the work gets done. Research shows that *relationship* conflicts are almost always dysfunctional because the interpersonal hostilities increase personality clashes and decrease mutual understanding, and the tasks don't get done. On the other hand, low levels of process conflict and low to moderate levels of task conflict are functional. For *process* conflict to be productive, it must be minimal. Otherwise, intense arguments over who should do what may become dysfunctional and can lead to uncertainty about task assignments, increase the time to complete tasks, and result in members working at cross-purposes. However, a low-to-moderate level of *task* conflict consistently has a positive effect on group performance because it stimulates discussion of ideas that help groups be more innovative.

conflict
Perceived incompatible differences that result in interference or opposition

traditional view of conflict
The view that all conflict is bad and must be avoided

human relations view of conflict
The view that conflict is a natural and inevitable outcome in any group

interactionist view of conflict
The view that some conflict is necessary for a group to perform effectively

functional conflicts
Conflicts that support a group's goals and improve its performance

dysfunctional conflicts
Conflicts that prevent a group from achieving its goals

task conflict
Conflicts over content and goals of the work

relationship conflict
Conflict based on interpersonal relationships

process conflict
Conflict over how work gets done

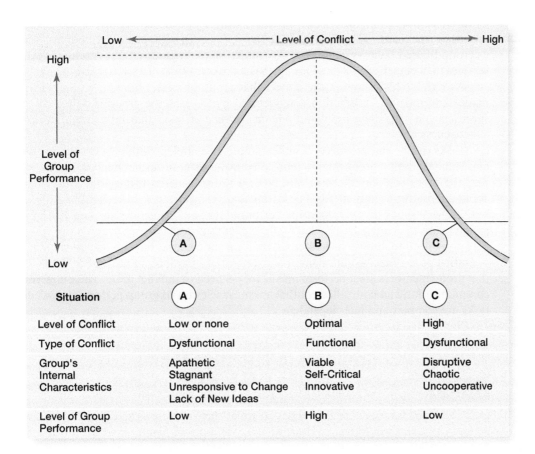

Exhibit 13-7
Conflict and Group
Performance

Situation	A	B	C
Level of Conflict	Low or none	Optimal	High
Type of Conflict	Dysfunctional	Functional	Dysfunctional
Group's Internal Characteristics	Apathetic Stagnant Unresponsive to Change Lack of New Ideas	Viable Self-Critical Innovative	Disruptive Chaotic Uncooperative
Level of Group Performance	Low	High	Low

Let's Get REAL

The Scenario:

Fran Waller is the manager of a retail store that's part of a large national chain. Many of her employees are going to school and working, but she also has some full-time employees. A conflict over vacation and holiday work schedules has been building for some time now, and it's creating a very tense atmosphere, which isn't good for customer service. She's got to resolve it NOW.

What suggestions would you give Fran for managing this conflict?

In the beginning of the year, when the vacation schedule comes out, the manager should tell all the employees that the vacation schedule is based on tenure. This will help with the arguing of the associates. To handle the issue now, she should talk to the associates who want the same weeks for their vacation, see if any of them would be willing to switch to a different week, and possibly give them a little incentive for switching. Some examples could be giving them an extra weekend off or an extra day of vacation. The same should be done with the holidays; if there are six holidays, have each associate work three. This will help maximize coverage on busy days and provide the best customer service.

◀ **Alfonso Marrese**
Retail Executive

Source: Alfonso Marrese

Group Tasks

At Hackensack University Medical Center in New Jersey, daily reviews of each patient in each nursing unit are conducted in multidisciplinary rounds by groups of nurses, case managers, social workers, and an in-hospital doctor. These groups perform tasks as varied as prescribing drugs and recommending a patient be discharged. Employee groups at Lockheed Martin's New York facility custom build complex products such as ground-based radar systems. And Accenture relies on groups to provide consulting services to clients. Each of these groups has a different type of task to accomplish.

As Exhibit 13-3 showed, the impact that group processes have on group performance and member satisfaction is moderated by the task the group is doing. More specifically, it's the *complexity* and *interdependence* of tasks that influence a group's effectiveness.[32]

Tasks can be characterized as either simple or complex. Simple tasks are routine and standardized. Complex tasks tend to be novel or nonroutine. Evidence indicates that the more complex the task, the more a group benefits from group discussion about alternative work methods. For instance, advertising agencies such as WPP Plc, a well-known agency that is responsible for branding Snickers candy bars and Kleenex, assign teams to create a brand identity for a client's products or services. Group members don't need to discuss such alternatives for a simple task, but can rely on standard operating procedures. Additionally, a high degree of interdependence among the tasks that group members must perform means they'll need to interact more. Thus, effective communication and controlled conflict are most relevant to group performance when tasks are complex and interdependent.

TURNING groups into effective teams

LO13.3 When companies like W.L. Gore, Volvo, and Kraft Foods introduced teams into their production processes in the 1970s, it made news because no one else was doing it. Today, it's just the opposite—the organization that *doesn't* use teams would be newsworthy. Without a doubt, team-based work is a core feature of today's organizations. And teams are likely to continue to be popular. Why? Research suggests that teams typically outperform individuals when the tasks being done require multiple skills, judgment, and experience.[33] Organizations are using team-based structures because they've found that teams are more flexible and responsive to changing events than traditional departments or other permanent work groups. Teams have the ability to quickly assemble, deploy, refocus, and disband. In this section, we'll discuss what a work team is, the different types of teams organizations might use, and how to develop and manage work teams.

work teams
Groups whose members work intensely on a specific, common goal using their positive synergy, individual and mutual accountability, and complementary skills

The Difference Between Groups and Teams

Most of you are probably familiar with teams, especially if you've watched or participated in organized sports events. Work *teams* differ from work *groups* and have their own unique traits (see Exhibit 13-8). Work groups interact primarily to share information and to make decisions to help each member do his or her job more efficiently and effectively. There's no need or opportunity for work groups to engage in collective work that requires joint effort. On the other hand, **work teams** are groups whose members work intensely on a specific, common goal using their positive synergy, individual and mutual accountability, and complementary skills.

Kimi Raikkonen, a Finnish racing driver, receives support from his team during a Formula 1 championship in Spain. In race car competitions, effective teamwork by pit crews is critical for success.
Source: Insidefoto srl/Alamy Stock Photo

Types of Work Teams

Teams can do a variety of things. They can design products, provide services, negotiate deals, coordinate projects, offer advice, and make decisions.[34] For instance, at Rockwell Automation's facility in North Carolina, teams are used in work process optimization projects. At Sylvania, the New Ventures Group creates cool LED-based

Work Teams	Work Groups
Leadership role is shared	One leader clearly in charge
Accountable to self and team	Accountable only to self
Team creates specific purpose	Purpose is same as broader organizational purpose
Work is done collectively	Work is done individually
Meetings characterized by open-ended discussion and collaborative problem-solving	Meetings characterized by efficiency; no collaboration or open-ended discussion
Performance is measured directly by evaluating collective work output	Performance is measured indirectly according to its influence on others
Work is decided upon and done together	Work is decided upon by group leader and delegated to individual group members
Can be quickly assembled, deployed, refocused, and disbanded	

Exhibit 13-8
Groups Versus Teams

Sources: J. R. Katzenbach and D. K. Smith, "The Wisdom of Teams," *Harvard Business Review,* July–August 2005, p. 161; and A. J. Fazzari and J. B. Mosca, "Partners in Perfection: Human Resources Facilitating Creation and Ongoing Implementation of Self-Managed Manufacturing Teams in a Small Medium Enterprise," *Human Resource Development Quarterly* (Fall 2009): pp. 353–376.

products. At Arkansas-based Acxiom Corporation, a team of human resource professionals planned and implemented a cultural change. And every summer weekend at any NASCAR race, you can see work teams in action during drivers' pit stops.[35] The four most common types of work teams are problem-solving teams, self-managed work teams, cross-functional teams, and virtual teams.

When work teams first became popular, most were **problem-solving teams**, teams from the same department or functional area involved in efforts to improve work activities or to solve specific problems. Members share ideas or offer suggestions on how work processes and methods can be improved. However, these teams are rarely given the authority to implement any of their suggested actions. For instance, a large Midwest university in the United States assembled a team of faculty members to study how to increase faculty retention. The team completed a variety of activities, including interviews with current and former faculty members. Then, members prepared a report for the university's provost in which they discussed their findings and recommendations. The decision whether to implement any of the recommendations, however, rested with the provost and not the committee.

Although problem-solving teams were helpful, they didn't go far enough in getting employees involved in work-related decisions and processes. This shortcoming led companies like GE, Google, Zappos, 3M, and Hewlett-Packard to introduce another type of team, a **self-managed work team**—a formal group of employees who operate without a manager and are responsible for a complete work process or segment. A self-managed team is responsible for getting the work done *and* for managing themselves, which usually includes scheduling work, assigning tasks to members, collective control over the pace of work, making operating decisions, and taking action on problems. For instance, General Electric uses self-managed teams at its aircraft engine plant in Bromont, Canada.[36] Employee teams decide what tasks need to be done and how they should do it. Traditional supervisory tasks such as planning and scheduling production, setting overtime and vacation policies, and improving manufacturing processes are assumed by the team. Employees from each team also sit on "councils," alongside company executives, where they participate in employee evaluation, promotion, and firing decisions.

The third type of team is the **cross-functional team**, which we introduced in Chapter 10 and defined as a work team composed of individuals from various functional specialties. Many organizations use cross-functional teams. For example, General Motors uses cross-functional teams of sculptors, systems analysts, engineers, and creative designers to come up with innovative car designs. The concept of cross-functional teams is even applied in health care. For instance, at Suburban Hospital in Bethesda, Maryland, intensive care unit (ICU) teams composed of a doctor trained

problem-solving team
A team from the same department or functional area that's involved in efforts to improve work activities or to solve specific problems

self-managed work team
A work team that operates without a manager and is responsible for a complete work process or segment

cross-functional team
A work team composed of individuals from various functional specialties

fyi

Ninety-one percent of respondents in a global study say that employees in their companies spend time working on projects outside of their functional area.[37]

in intensive care medicine, a pharmacist, a social worker, a nutritionist, the chief ICU nurse, a respiratory therapist, and a chaplain meet daily with every patient's bedside nurse to discuss and debate the best course of treatment. The hospital credits this team care approach with reducing errors, shortening the amount of time patients spend in ICU, and improving communication between families and the medical staff.[38]

The final type of team is the **virtual team**, a team that uses computer technology to link physically dispersed members and achieve a common goal. They collaborate online—using communication links such as wide-area networks, corporate social media, videoconferencing, and email—whether members are nearby or

virtual team
A work team that uses computer technology to link physically dispersed members and achieve a common goal

IT'S YOUR CAREER

Maximizing Outcomes Through Negotiation

A key to success in management and in your career is knowing how to negotiate effectively to maximize outcomes.

A young lawyer was recently asked, "So, what did you learn in three years of law school?" She replied, "Everything is negotiable!"

Lawyers aren't the only people who spend a good part of their time negotiating. Managers negotiate with employees, bosses, colleagues, suppliers, and sometimes even customers. And each of us, in our daily lives, will find ourselves having to negotiate with parents, spouses, children, friends, neighbors, and car salespersons—just to name the obvious.

We know a great deal about what effective negotiators do.[42] Here are some brief suggestions to hone your skills at negotiating:

1. *Do your homework.* Gather as much pertinent information as possible before your negotiation. Know yourself. How do you feel about negotiating? Is it something you're comfortable doing? Do you just want it to be over? Recognize your own negotiating strengths and weaknesses. But also, know who you're negotiating with before you begin. Try to assess their strengths and weaknesses. You can't make good decisions without understanding your, and the other person's, situation.

2. *Assess goals.* In addition to gauging the personal/people aspects, take the time to assess your

own goals and the other party's goals and interests. Know what you want, but also try to anticipate what the other person wants. And . . . maybe even go one step further by trying to anticipate what the other person thinks you want.

3. *Begin with a positive proposal.* Concessions tend to be reciprocated. So start with something positive. Often, if you expect more, you get more. Your optimism may become a self-fulfilling prophecy.

4. *Address problems, not personalities.* Concentrate on the negotiation issues, not on the personal characteristics of your opponent. Don't take the issues or the other person's behavior personally. Don't let the negotiation get sidetracked by personal issues that have nothing to do with what you're negotiating.

5. *Pay attention to the interpersonal aspects of the negotiation process.* Negotiating is communicating. Trust is an important part of that communication. Work at building trust by telling the truth, being trustworthy, and honoring your commitments. Also, listen with your ears and your eyes. Pay attention to important nonverbal messages, facial expressions, and voice inflections. Listen—really listen—to what the other person is saying verbally and nonverbally.

6. *Pay little attention to initial offers.* Initial offers tend to be extreme and idealistic. Treat them as such. Negotiating is a process, not a one-and-done interaction.

7. *Emphasize win-win solutions.* Frame options in terms of your opponent's interests and look for solutions that can allow both you and the person you're negotiating with to declare a victory.

continents apart.[39] For instance, SAP, a software company with more than 30,000 employees in 60 countries, relies heavily on virtual teams.[40] Its headquarters is in Germany, but the company has R&D centers in India, China, Israel, and the US. Each center has a specific area of expertise it shares with the entire company. Technology allows managers to assemble virtual teams that utilize employees from each of these specialty groups.

Creating Effective Work Teams

Teams don't always achieve high levels of performance. However, research on teams provides insights into the characteristics typically associated with effective teams.[43] We've summarized these characteristics and listed them in Exhibit 13-9.

CLEAR GOALS High-performance teams have a clear understanding of the goal to be achieved. Members are committed to the team's goals, know what they're expected to accomplish, and understand how they will work together to achieve these goals.

RELEVANT SKILLS Effective teams are composed of competent individuals who have the necessary technical and interpersonal skills to achieve the desired goals while working well together. This last point is important because not everyone who is technically competent has the interpersonal skills to work well as a team member.

MUTUAL TRUST Effective teams are characterized by high mutual trust among members. That is, members believe in each other's ability, character, and integrity.

UNIFIED COMMITMENT Unified commitment is characterized by dedication to the team's goals and a willingness to expend extraordinary amounts of energy to achieve them. Members of an effective team exhibit intense loyalty and dedication to the team and are willing to do whatever it takes to help their team succeed.

GOOD COMMUNICATION Not surprisingly, effective teams are characterized by good communication. Members convey messages, verbally and nonverbally, between each

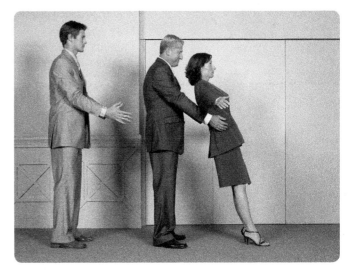

As this training exercise illustrates, mutual trust among team members is essential for success.
Source: IS195/Image Source/Alamy Stock Photo

Exhibit 13-9
Characteristics of Effective Teams

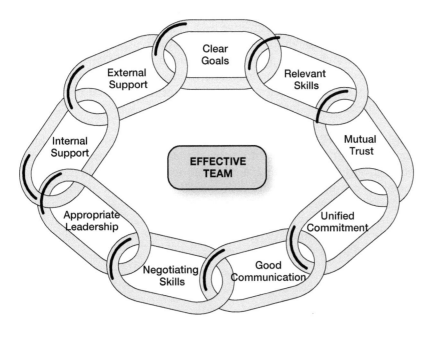

Christina Moser ▶
Strategic Account Manager

Source: Christina Moser

The Scenario:

What a mess. When Walter Smith agreed to take over managing a team of client service representatives at a financial services company, he didn't realize how poorly the team was working together. He has learned that there have been many disagreements about work responsibilities and that two team members avoid talking to each other entirely. As a result, the team is not performing well. Walter must now take steps to get the team working together again.

What can Walter do to improve the effectiveness of his team?

As a leader, begin with setting the tone for the team. Bring everyone together and explain your vision and expectations for working together. Be empathetic and explain that you want to better understand the current challenges and work together to improve it. After laying out the vision, work with each individual to detail a clear list of individual roles and responsibilities, becoming familiar with their current workload, career goals, and strengths. What might seem minor can lead to major changes, such as celebrating wins and publicly expressing your appreciation.

Be sure to also address the two embittered employees quickly or they could sabotage your efforts. Depending on the severity of their conflict, you may need to involve your HR partners in the discussion.

other in ways that are readily and clearly understood. Also, feedback helps guide team members and correct misunderstandings. Like couples who have been together for many years, members of high-performing teams are able to quickly and efficiently share ideas and feelings.

NEGOTIATING SKILLS   Effective teams are continually making adjustments as to who does what. This flexibility requires team members to possess negotiating skills. Because problems and relationships regularly change within teams, members need to be able to confront and reconcile differences.

APPROPRIATE LEADERSHIP   Effective leaders are important. They can motivate a team to follow them through the most difficult situations. How? By clarifying goals, demonstrating that change is possible by overcoming inertia, increasing the self-confidence of team members, and helping members to more fully realize their potential. Increasingly, effective team leaders act as coaches and facilitators. They help guide and support the team but don't control it.

INTERNAL AND EXTERNAL SUPPORT   The final condition necessary for an effective team is a supportive climate. Internally, the team should have a sound infrastructure, which means proper training, a clear and reasonable measurement system that team members can use to evaluate their overall performance, an incentive program that recognizes and rewards team activities, and a supportive human resource system. The right infrastructure should support members and reinforce behaviors that lead to high levels of performance. Externally, managers should provide the team with the resources needed to get the job done.

WORKPLACE CONFIDENTIAL Handling Difficult Coworkers

We've all been around people who, to put it nicely, are difficult to get along with. These people might be chronic complainers, they might be meddlers who think they know everything about everyone else's job and don't hesitate to tell you so, or they might exhibit any number of other unpleasant interpersonal characteristics. They can make your job extremely hard and your workday very stressful if you don't know how to deal with them. Being around difficult people tends to bring out the worst in all of us. What can you do? How do you learn to get along with these difficult people?

We suggest you start by recognizing that it's the behavior of the coworker that is getting to you, not the person himself or herself. Don't make this personal. Understanding the behavior will help you identify the source of the problem and how it might be solved.

Next, ask yourself: To what degree might I be contributing to the problem? The key here is just to remove any controllable factors that you might be bringing to the situation. For instance, do you tend to be moody, and if so, is that a contributing factor? If you're on a team project with the person, are you being too pushy or demanding? Since your behavior is controllable, the difficulty might be eliminated quickly by your making a few changes.

Now consider the source of your coworker's behavior. What is it, specifically, that bothers you? Put yourself in that person's shoes and attempt to see things from his or her perspective.

It's important to assess the source of your coworker's behavior. It makes a big difference whether you're dealing with just a clash of styles or whether you're facing a toxic worker. The latter has something inside—such as anger or distrust—that infects those around them. Conflicts with toxic types are more difficult to resolve.

A clash of styles might include different importance placed on promptness, deadlines, or ways of communicating. Or it might include how the two of you handle change, stressful situations, mistakes, excessive talking, or interruptions. The key here is recognizing that you're not dealing with objective states of right and wrong. Rather, the source of the difficulty is different ways of doing or seeing things.

So how do you handle differences in style? Here are some common types of difficult people you're likely to meet at work and some strategies for dealing with them.

The aggressive types. With these types, you need to stand up for yourself; give them time to run down; don't worry about being polite, jump in if you need to; get their attention carefully; speak from your own point of view; avoid a head-on fight; and be ready to be friendly.

The complainers. With the complainers, you need to listen attentively; acknowledge their concerns; be prepared to interrupt their litany of complaints; don't agree, but do acknowledge what they're saying; state facts without comment or apology; and switch them to problem solving.

The silent or nonresponsive types. With these types, you need to ask open-ended questions; use the friendly, silent stare; don't fill the silent pauses for them in conversations; comment on what's happening and help break the tension by making them feel more at ease.

The know-it-all experts. The keys to dealing with these types are to be on top of things; listen and acknowledge their comments; question firmly, but don't confront; avoid being a counterexpert; and work with them to channel their energy in positive directions.

The toxic coworker provides a tougher challenge. This person is destructive and abusive. While they often have a number of desirable traits, such as charm, leadership, and impression management skills, they also have a dark side. That dark side surfaces in one or more of three traits: psychopathy, Machiavellianism, and narcissism. Psychopathy is a personality disorder. It's characterized by a lack of remorse and empathy. Psychopaths are emotionally cold and disconnected. And unlike those who make newspaper headlines, most live relatively normal lives—including working for a living. Machiavellian types are master manipulators. They're cunning and duplicitous. Not surprisingly, they are often your boss or upper-level manager. This is because these people are very good at exhibiting charm and impressing others. The third component of toxicity is narcissism. Narcissists are highly self-centered people who are egotistical and think the world revolves around them. Studies have found that Machiavellian and narcissistic types use "soft" tactics like compliments and reason to get their way; psychopathic individuals use "hard" tactics such as assertiveness and direct manipulations.

So how do you deal with a toxic coworker? Experts suggest that the best advice is to physically distance yourself from him or her. Keep a safe distance away in order to avoid getting sucked into the toxicity. Toxic behavior is contagious! If physical avoidance isn't an option, try to distance yourself mentally and emotionally. This can best be achieved by setting boundaries. Tell your toxic coworker what you will and won't accept. It may take a lot of repetition, but hold to your boundaries. In addition, make clear the consequences if the boundaries are crossed. And be prepared to take your complaints about inappropriate behavior to your superiors. If it gets to this stage, make sure your complaint is succinct and professional. You want to make it clear which workplace rules are being broken and how this action affects yours, and others', work performance.[44]

| Chapter 13 | **PREPARING FOR: Exams/Quizzes** |

CHAPTER SUMMARY by Learning Objectives

LO13.1

DEFINE groups and the stages of group development.

A group is two or more interacting and interdependent individuals who come together to achieve specific goals. Formal groups are work groups defined by the organization's structure and have designated work assignments and specific tasks directed at accomplishing organizational goals. Informal groups are social groups.

The forming stage consists of two phases: joining the group and defining the group's purpose, structure, and leadership. The storming stage is one of intragroup conflict over who will control the group and what the group will be doing. The norming stage is when close relationships and cohesiveness develop as norms are determined. The performing stage is when group members begin to work on the group's task. The adjourning stage is when the group prepares to disband.

LO13.2

DESCRIBE the major components that determine group performance and satisfaction.

The major components that determine group performance and satisfaction include external conditions, group member resources, group structure, group processes, and group tasks.

External conditions, such as availability of resources, organizational goals, and other factors, affect work groups. Group member resources (knowledge, skills, abilities, personality traits) can influence what members can do and how effectively they will perform in a group.

Group roles generally involve getting the work done or keeping up group member morale. Group norms are standards or expectations shared by group members and dictate things such as work output levels, absenteeism, and promptness. Pressures to conform can heavily influence a person's judgment and attitudes. If carried to extremes, groupthink can be a problem. Status systems can be a significant motivator with individual behavioral consequences, especially when individuals believe others perceive their status differently than they do themselves. What size group is most effective and efficient depends on the task the group is supposed to accomplish. Cohesiveness is related to a group's productivity as a function of how aligned the group's goals are with the organization's goals.

Group decision making and conflict management are important group processes that play a role in performance and satisfaction. If accuracy, creativity, and degree of acceptance are important, a group decision may work best. Relationship conflicts are almost always dysfunctional. Low levels of process conflicts and low to moderate levels of task conflicts are functional. Effective communication and controlled conflict are most relevant to group performance when tasks are complex and interdependent.

LO13.3

DEFINE teams and best practices influencing team performance.

Characteristics of work groups include a strong, clearly focused leader; individual accountability; purpose that's the same as the broader organizational mission; individual work product; efficient meetings; effectiveness measured by influence on others; and the ability to discuss, decide, and delegate together. Characteristics of teams include shared leadership roles; individual and mutual accountability; specific team purpose; collective work products; meetings with open-ended discussion and active problem solving; performance measured directly on collective work products; and the ability to discuss, decide, and do real work.

A problem-solving team is one that's focused on improving work activities or solving specific problems. A self-managed work team is responsible for a complete work process or segment and manages itself. A cross-functional team is composed of individuals from various specialties. A virtual team uses technology to link physically dispersed members in order to achieve a common goal.

The characteristics of an effective team include clear goals, relevant skills, mutual trust, unified commitment, good communication, negotiating skills, appropriate leadership, and internal and external support.

REVIEW AND DISCUSSION QUESTIONS

13-1. Describe the different types of groups and the five stages of group development.

13-2. Explain how external conditions and group member resources affect group performance and satisfaction.

13-3. Discuss how group structure, group processes, and group tasks influence group performance and satisfaction.

13-4. Compare groups and teams.

13-5. Describe the four most common types of teams.

13-6. List the characteristics of effective teams.

13-7. Explain the role of informal (social) networks in managing teams.

PREPARING FOR: My Career

ETHICS DILEMMA

When coworkers work closely on a team project, is there such a thing as becoming too close? Not everyone thinks so. A recent survey revealed that 51 percent of employees said they have had an office romance.[45] And another survey found that workers in their 20s and 30s view workplace romances more positively than older generations do.[46] Sometimes, coworkers feel free to share personal information. For example, at one company, a team that had just finished a major project went out to lunch to celebrate. During lunch, one colleague mentioned that he was training for a twenty-mile bike race. In addition to a discussion of his new helmet and Lycra shorts, the person also described shaving his whole body to reduce

aerodynamic drag. Later, another team member said, "Why, why, why do we need to go there? This is information about a coworker, not someone I really consider a friend."

13-8. What do you think? Why do many work colleagues become romantically involved? Why do some coworkers choose to share personal information?

13-9. Should employees inform their managers about such relationships? Explain your reasoning.

13-10. What are the ethical implications of coworkers becoming romantically involved? Sharing too much information?

SKILLS EXERCISE Developing Your Coaching Skills

About the Skill
Effective work team managers are increasingly being described as coaches rather than bosses. Just like coaches, they're expected to provide instruction, guidance, advice, and encouragement to help team members improve their job performance.

Steps in Practicing the Skill

• *Analyze ways to improve the team's performance and capabilities.* A coach looks for opportunities for team members to expand their capabilities and improve performance. How? You can use the following behaviors. Observe your team members' behaviors on a day-to-day

basis. Ask questions of them: Why do you do a task this way? Can it be improved? What other approaches might be used? Show genuine interest in team members as individuals, not merely as employees. Respect them individually. Listen to each employee.

• *Create a supportive climate.* It's the coach's responsibility to reduce barriers to development and to facilitate a climate that encourages personal performance improvement. How? You can use the following behaviors. Create a climate that contributes to a free and open exchange of ideas. Offer help and assistance. Give guidance and advice when asked. Encourage your team. Be positive and upbeat. Don't use threats. Ask, "What did we learn from this that can help us in the future?" Reduce obstacles. Assure team members that you value their contribution to the team's goals. Take personal responsibility for the outcome, but don't rob team members of their full responsibility. Validate team members' efforts when they succeed. Point to what was missing when they fail. Never blame team members for poor results.

• *Influence team members to change their behavior.* The ultimate test of coaching effectiveness is whether an employee's performance improves. You must encourage ongoing growth and development. How can you do this? Try the following behaviors. Recognize and reward small improvements and treat coaching as a way of helping employees to continually work toward improvement.

Use a collaborative style by allowing team members to participate in identifying and choosing among improvement ideas. Break difficult tasks down into simpler ones. Model the qualities you expect from your team. If you want openness, dedication, commitment, and responsibility from your team members, demonstrate these qualities yourself.

Practicing the Skill

Find a friend or a classmate that you can coach on a project or assignment. Maybe it is a coworker, a new member in an organization you belong to, or a friend taking a challenging course you have already taken. Following the guidance provided above, practice your coaching skills by working with your friend or classmate to improve his or her performance.

WORKING TOGETHER **Team Exercise**

After five years as a top application developer at a software company, you are promoted to a team leader position. In this role you will lead a new team of five employees responsible for creating new products. The team must work together from idea inception to final product testing. The employees assigned to your work team have been with the company less than a year and have not worked

together before. Take a few minutes to consider some of the challenges your new role will provide. Next, work in groups of three or four students to create a plan to begin leading your new team. Review the characteristics of effective teams in Exhibit 13-9. Write down your plan to build these characteristics with your team and be prepared to share your plan with the class.

MY TURN TO BE A MANAGER

• Think of a group to which you belong (or have belonged). Trace its development through the stages of group development as shown in Exhibit 13-2. How closely did its development parallel the group development model? How might the group development model be used to improve this group's effectiveness?

• Using this same group, write a report describing the following things about this group: types of roles played by whom, group norms, group conformity issues, status system, size of group and how effective/efficient it is, and group cohesiveness.

• Using the same group, describe how decisions are made. Is the process effective? Efficient? Describe what types of conflicts seem to arise most often (relationship, process, or task) and how those conflicts are handled. Add this

information to your report on the group's development and structure.

• Select two of the characteristics of effective teams listed in Exhibit 13-9 and develop a team-building exercise for each characteristic that will help a group improve that characteristic. Be creative. Write a report describing your exercises, and be sure to explain how your exercises will help a group improve or develop that characteristic.

• Often new teams that must become productive quickly start off by writing ground rules or a team working agreement. Conduct some research on team working agreements and create a summary of what such an agreement might include. When assigned your next team project, try writing a team working agreement to kick off your project.

CASE APPLICATION **1** Making Delivery Drones a Reality at Alphabet

When X—the division of Google's parent company Alphabet—launched a team to work on delivery drones, they could have recruited members with some attention-grabbing words: How would like to work on a team where you'll be sending burritos into the sky? They didn't have to resort to a sales pitch like that, though, since being a part of this team was interesting for other reasons. It was a team that was given the freedom to work on a creative project separate from the rest of the company while using cutting-edge technology and plentiful resources. And they didn't have to show profitability right away.[47]

This team, called Project Wing, consisted of a combination of researchers, business strategy experts, engineers, and developers. An early goal for the team was to deliver defibrillator kits to heart attack victims. For the first year of the team's work, members worked on a design for a delivery drone. They didn't want the drones to have to land on the ground and then have to use a lot of power to get back into the air, so they tried to figure out a way to deliver packages while the drones hovered in the air.

It turns out this was no easy task. They had thought that packages could be lowered to the ground by a cord that would unspool from the drone while it hovered. The problem was that every package seemed to need its own system. They tried numerous other designs that didn't work until finally they came up with a system involving hooks.

Another challenge for Project Wing was air traffic management. The team initially worked on building each drone its own path in the sky from its launch to its destination. Sounds good if only Project Wing drones were in the sky, but what about airplanes? Members of Project Wing had to work closely with regulators as well as competitors to avoid crashes with other "flying objects." This kind of relationship building was not something in which project employees had experience.[48]

For the first test launches, bottled water and batteries were delivered to farmers in Australia. By Fall 2017, drones were making deliveries to homes in rural Australia where people otherwise had to drive long distances to buy groceries. Using an app, customers could order products from a pharmacy company, or they could order burritos from a restaurant called Guzman y Gomez. In 2018, Project Wing drones were working on deliveries in more densely populated areas.

The project team reached a milestone in July 2018. They "graduated" from being a team within X to being an independent business owned by Alphabet.[49]

DISCUSSION QUESTIONS:

13-11. Which of the team types apply to the Project Wing team?

13-12. How might different group development stages apply to this team? In your answer, note how making changes to the drone design might have impacted the stages of group development.

13-13. What kinds of conflict do you think might have occurred at different points described in the case? Why or why not were these kinds of conflict effective for the team?

13-14. How did the "external conditions imposed on the group" (see Exhibit 13-3) help or hinder Project Wing?

CASE APPLICATION 2 "Remote Week" at HubSpot

When Rachel Leist was working in marketing at HubSpot—a technology company headquartered in Cambridge, Massachusetts, that produces marketing and sales software—the company realized that something was happening as they grew in size.[50] Many of their teams were spread out in different locations across the globe. That meant that team meetings often were held virtually. Rachel's marketing team decided that they wanted to do something that would make not only their team work better, but also help the company learn from their experience. They came up with a special week that they named "Remote Week."

The team tried holding all their meetings via video during "Remote Week." They also made a pact to try a wide variety of meetings during this week, including cross-functional meetings, one-on-one meetings, and all-team meetings.[51] At the end of the week, they asked for feedback from everyone on the team. What did they find?

Team members realized that having someone who takes on the role of a facilitator during video meetings makes a big difference. This facilitator makes sure that everyone gets a chance to talk. The team found that sometimes facilitators would see people making "goldfish faces" (opening and closing their mouths without saying anything since they kept getting cut off by others on the team). A facilitator was just what was needed to allow everyone on the team—not just the people making these goldfish faces—to take turns talking. Facilitators also could look out for side conversations and get those to be shared with the whole group. Ensuring that everyone on the video call was in different rooms also helped to cut out side conversations.

The team realized how unplanned conversations can be incredibly helpful to their work, but they can be difficult to make happen when working virtually. The good news is they figured out a few workarounds to recreate alternatives to face-to-face conversations that happen on the fly. For starters, they made it a standard practice that team members would be ready to quickly get on a video call if someone had a question. If someone on the team couldn't make a spontaneous call, they would record a quick video so that no team members would be left out.

It also became clear that if you're not physically present, you need to do all you can to stay visible to others in the company. This means making sure that you share your thoughts during virtual meetings. Also, they use Slack at HubSpot to communicate across teams in the company. If someone has something to say about work-related projects—or even what you did over the weekend—participating in the group chat discussions on Slack keeps you in the minds of those who aren't physically working in the same location.

According to Rachel, Remote Week was a success for her team. They've been doing a better job collaborating with one another when working in different locations, and team members believe that they have improved on making sure that everyone on the team gets heard.

DISCUSSION QUESTIONS:

13-15. What type(s) of team(s) were exemplified by the team participating in "Remote Week" at HubSpot?

13-16. Explain how norms and roles were a part of making HubSpot's marketing team function well during "Remote Week."

13-17. What challenges did "Remote Week" try to address that virtual teams often have?

13-18. How is each of the characteristics of creating effective work teams relevant to virtual teams?

ENDNOTES

1. "How Leaders Spend Their Time," *Center for Management and Organization Effectiveness* (blog), January 14, 2019, https://cmoe.com/blog/how-leaders-spend-their-time/.
2. B. W. Tuckman and M. C. Jensen, "Stages of Small-Group Development Revisited," *Group and Organizational Studies* 2, no. 4 (December 1977): pp. 419–427; M. F. Maples, "Group Development: Extending Tuckman's Theory," *Journal for Specialists in Group Work* 13, no. 1 (Fall 1988): pp. 17–23; B. W. Tuckman and M. C. Jensen, "Stages of Small-Group Development Revisited," *Group Facilitation* (October 2010):

pp. 43–48; and J. M. Kiweewa, D. Gilbride, M. Luke, and T. Clingerman, "Tracking Growth Factors in Experiential Training Groups Through Tuckman's Conceptual Model," *Journal for Specialists in Group Work* 43, no. 3 (July 2018): pp. 274–96.
3. This model is based on the work of P. S. Goodman, E. Ravlin, and M. Schminke, "Understanding Groups in Organizations," in *Research in Organizational Behavior*, vol. 9, eds. L. L. Cummings and B. M. Staw (Greenwich, CT: JAI Press, 1987), pp. 124–128; J. R. Hackman, "The Design of

Work Teams," in *Handbook of Organizational Behavior,* ed. J. W. Lorsch (Upper Saddle River, NJ: Prentice Hall, 1987), pp. 315–342; G. R. Bushe and A. L. Johnson, "Contextual and Internal Variables Affecting Task Group Outcomes in Organizations," *Group and Organizational Studies* (December 1989): pp. 462–482; M. A. Campion, C. J. Medsker, and A. C. Higgs, "Relations Between Work Group Characteristics and Effectiveness: Implications for Designing Effective Work Groups," *Personnel Psychology* 46 (Winter 1993): pp. 823–850; D. E. Hyatt and T. M. Ruddy, "An Examination of the Relationship Between Work Group Characteristics and Performance: Once More into the Breach," *Personnel Psychology* 50 (Autumn 1997): pp. 553–585; and D. J. Levi, *Group Dynamics for Teams*, 5th ed. (Thousand Oaks, CA: Sage Publications, 2016).

4. M. J. Stevens and M. A. Campion, "The Knowledge, Skill, and Ability Requirements for Teamwork: Implications for Human Resource Management," *Journal of Management* 20, no. 2 (Summer 1994): pp. 503–530; and G. L. Stewart, "A Meta-Analytic Review of Relationships Between Team Design Features and Team Performance," *Journal of Management* 32, no. 1 (February 2006): pp. 29–54.

5. M. E. Shaw, *Contemporary Topics in Social Psychology* (Morristown, NJ: General Learning Press, 1976), pp. 350–351; D. C. Kinlaw, *Developing Superior Work Teams: Building Quality and the Competitive Edge* (San Diego, CA: Lexington, 1991); and V. U. Druskat and S. B. Wolff, "The Link between Emotions and Team Effectiveness: How Teams Engage Members and Build Effective Task Processes," *Academy of Management Proceedings*, August 1999.

6. T. Chamorro-Premuzic and D. Winsborough, "Personality Tests Can Help Balance a Team," *Harvard Business Review*, March 19, 2015, https://hbr.org/2015/03/personality-tests-can-help-balance-a-team.

7. O. Törnblom, K. Stålne, and S. Kjellström, "Analyzing Roles and Leadership in Organizations From Cognitive Complexity and Meaning-Making Perspectives," *Behavioral Development* 23, no. 1 (January 2018): pp. 63–80.

8. McMurry, Inc., "The Roles Your People Play," *Managing People at Work,* October 2005, p. 4; G. Prince, "Recognizing Genuine Teamwork," *Supervisory Management* (April 1989): pp. 25–36; R. F. Bales, *SYMLOG Case Study Kit* (New York: Free Press, 1980); and K. D. Benne and P. Sheats, "Functional Roles of Group Members," *Journal of Social Issues* 4 (1948): pp. 41–49.

9. See, for instance, D. Skarbek, "Prison Gangs, Norms, and Organizations," *Journal of Economic Behavior & Organization* 82, no. 1 (April 2012): pp. 96–109.

10. K. Novak, "Never Say No! South Korea's Pressure-Cooker Work Culture," *CNN*, July 23, 2015, https://www.cnn.com/2015/07/23/asia/south-korea-work-culture/index.html.

11. "South Korea's Hangover," *Al Jazeera*, February 5, 2016, https://www.aljazeera.com/programmes/101east/2016/02/south-korea-hangover-160201144455864.html.

12. L. C. Levitan and B. Berhulst, "Conformity in Groups: The Effects of Others' Views on Expressed Attitudes and Attitude Change," *Political Behavior* 38, no. 2 (June 2016): pp. 277–315.

13. S. E. Asch, "Effects of Group Pressure upon the Modification and Distortion of Judgments," in *Groups, Leadership and Men,* ed. H. Guetzkow (Pittsburgh: Carnegie Press, 1951), pp. 177–190; and S. E. Asch, "Studies of Independence and Conformity: A Minority of One Against a Unanimous Majority," *Psychological Monographs: General and Applied* 70, no. 9 (1956): pp. 1–70.

14. F. Neto, "Conformity and Independence Revisited," *Social Behavior and Personality: An International Journal* 23, no. 3 (January 1995): pp. 217–22; and C. Kondo, C. Saito, A. Deguchi, M. Hirayama, and A. Acar, "Social Conformity and Response Bias Revisited: The Influence of 'Others' on Japanese Respondents," *Human Affairs* 20, no. 4 (December 2010): pp. 356–63.

15. I. L. Janis, *Victims of Groupthink* (Boston: Houghton Mifflin, 1972); R. J. Aldag and S. Riggs Fuller, "Beyond Fiasco: A Reappraisal of the Groupthink Phenomenon and a New Model of Group Decision Processes," *Psychological Bulletin* 113, no. 3 (May 1993): pp. 533–552; and M. E. Turner and A. R. Pratkanis, "Mitigating Groupthink by Stimulating Constructive Conflict," in *Using Conflict in Organizations,* eds. C. DeDreu and E. Van deVliert (London: Sage, 1997), pp. 53–71.

16. A. Piazza and F. Castellucci, "Status in Organization and Management Theory," *Journal of Management* 40, no. 1 (January 2014): pp. 287–315.

17. H. J. van de Brake, A. Grow, and J. K. Dijkstra, "Status Inconsistency in Groups: How Discrepancies Between Instrumental and Expressive Status Result in Symptoms of Stress," *Social Science Research* 64 (May 2017): pp. 15–24.

18. See, for instance, E. J. Thomas and C. F. Fink, "Effects of Group Size," *Psychological Bulletin* 60, no. 4 (July 1963): pp. 371–384; and M. E. Shaw, *Group Dynamics: The Psychology of Small Group Behavior*, 3rd ed. (New York: McGraw-Hill, 1981).

19. P. Sonne, "Military Disciplines 16 for Errors Leading to 2015 Attack on Afghan Hospital," *Wall Street Journal*, April 29, 2016, https://www.wsj.com/articles/military-disciplines-16-for-errors-leading-to-2015-attack-on-afghan-hospital-1461945658.

20. R. C. Liden, S. J. Wayne, R. A. Jaworski, and N. Bennett, "Social Loafing: A Field Investigation," *Journal of Management* 30, no. 2 (April 2004): pp. 285–304; and X. Ying, H. Li, S. Jiang, F. Peng, and Z. Lin, "Group Laziness: The Effect of Social Loafing on Group Performance," *Social Behavior and Personality* 42, no. 3 (April 2014): pp. 465–72.

21. S. G. Harkins and K. Szymanski, "Social Loafing and Group Evaluation," *Journal of Personality and Social Psychology* 56, no. 6 (December 1989): pp. 934–941.

22. B. Mullen and C. Copper, "The Relation Between Group Cohesiveness and Performance: An Integration," *Psychological Bulletin* 115, no. 2 (March 1994): pp. 210–227; P. M. Podsakoff, S. B. MacKenzie, and M. Ahearne, "Moderating Effects of Goal Acceptance on the Relationship Between Group Cohesiveness and Productivity," *Journal of Applied Psychology* 82, no. 6 (December 1997): pp. 974–983; and C. R. Evans and K. L. Dion, "Group Cohesion and Performance: A Meta-Analysis," *Small Group Research* 22, no. 2 (December 2012): pp. 690–701.

23. See, for example, L. Berkowitz, "Group Standards, Cohesiveness, and Productivity," *Human Relations* 7 (November 1954): pp. 509–519; B. Mullen and C. Copper, "The Relation Between Group Cohesiveness and Performance: An Integration," *Psychological Bulletin* 115, no. 2 (1994): pp. 210–227; M. Casey-Campbell and M. L. Martens, "Sticking It All Together: A Critical

Assessment of the Group Cohesion-Performance Literature," *International Journal of Management Reviews* 11, no. 2 (June 2009): pp. 223–46; and L. L. Greer, "Group Cohesion: Then and Now," *Small Group Research* 43, no. 6 (December 2012): pp. 655–61.

24. S. E. Seashore, *Group Cohesiveness in the Industrial Work Group* (Ann Arbor: University of Michigan, Survey Research Center, 1954).

25. Cited in "Are Your Meetings Effective? Read This, and They Will Be!," *Teodesk* (blog), January 28, 2018, https://www.teodesk.com/blog/are-your-meetings-effective-read-this-and-they-will-be/.

26. J. Herzlich, "CEOs Spend 72% of Their Time in Meetings; Only 3% With Customers: Study," *Newsday*, August 5, 2018, https://www.newsday.com/business/meeting-ceo-harvard-business-review-1.20238680.

27. See, for instance, A. Mojzisch and S. Schulz-Hardt, "Process Gains in Group Decision Making," *Journal of Managerial Psychology* 26, no. 3 (2011): pp. 235-46.

28. See, for example, L. K. Michaelson, W. E. Watson, and R. H. Black, "A Realistic Test of Individual vs. Group Consensus Decision Making," *Journal of Applied Psychology* 74, no. 5 (1989): pp. 834–839; R. A. Henry, "Group Judgment Accuracy: Reliability and Validity of Postdiscussion Confidence Judgments," *Organizational Behavior and Human Decision Processes* 56, no. 1 (October 1993): pp. 11–27; P. W. Paese, M. Bieser, and M. E. Tubbs, "Framing Effects and Choice Shifts in Group Decision Making," *Organizational Behavior and Human Decision Processes* 56, no. 1 (October 1993): pp. 149–165; N. J. Castellan Jr., ed., *Individual and Group Decision Making* (Hillsdale, NJ: Lawrence Erlbaum Associates, 1993); S. G. Straus and J. E. McGrath, "Does the Medium Matter? The Interaction of Task Type and Technology on Group Performance and Member Reactions," *Journal of Applied Psychology* 79, no. 1 (February 1994): pp. 87–97; J. Osmani, "Group Decision-Making: Factors That Affect Group Effectiveness," *Academic Journal of Business Administration, Law and Social Sciences* 2, no. 1 (January 2016): pp. 23–38; and N. Mukherjee, L. V. Dicks, G. E. Shackelford, B. Vira, and W. J. Sutherland, "Comparing Groups vs. Individuals in Decision Making: A Systematic Review Protocol," *Environmental Evidence*, September 5, 2016, https://environmentalevidencejournal.biomedcentral.com/articles/10.1186/s13750-016-0066-7.

29. Thomas and Fink, "Effects of Group Size" [see note 18]; F. A. Shull, A. L. Delbecq, and L. L. Cummings, *Organizational Decision Making* (New York: McGraw-Hill, 1970), p. 151; P. Yetton and P. Bottger, "The Relationships Among Group Size, Member Ability, Social Decision Schemes, and Performance," *Organizational Behavior and Human Performance* 32, no. 2 (October 1983) pp. 145–159; and O. Amir, D. Amir, Y. Shahar, Y. Hart, and K. Gal, "The More the Merrier? Increasing Group Size May Be Detrimental to Decision-Making Performance in Nominal Groups," *PloS One*, February 2018, pp. 192–213.

30. S. P. Robbins, *Managing Organizational Conflict: A Nontraditional Approach* (Upper Saddle River, NJ: Prentice Hall, 1974); J. J. Dahling and M. B. Gutworth, "Loyal Rebels? A Test of the Normative Conflict Model of Constructive Deviance," *Journal of Organizational Behavior* 38, no. 8 (October 2017): pp. 1167–82; and C. Nemeth, *In Defense of Troublemakers* (New York: Basic Books, 2018).

31. F. R. C. de Wit, L. L. Greer, and K. A. Jehn, "The Paradox of Intragroup Conflict: A Meta-Analysis," *Journal of Applied Psychology* 97, no. 2 (March 2012): pp. 360–90; and F. R. C. de Wit, K. A. Jehn, and D. Scheepers, "Task Conflict, Information Processing, and Decision-Making: The Damaging Effect of Relationship Conflict," *Organizational Behavior and Human Decision Processes* 122, no. 2 (November 2013): pp. 177–89.

32. See, for example, J. R. Hackman and C. G. Morris, "Group Tasks, Group Interaction Process, and Group Performance Effectiveness: A Review and Proposed Integration," in *Advances in Experimental Social Psychology,* ed. L. Berkowitz (New York: Academic Press, 1975), pp. 45–99; R. Saavedra, P. C. Earley, and L. Van Dyne, "Complex Interdependence in Task-Performing Groups," *Journal of Applied Psychology* 78, no. 1 (February 1993): pp. 61–72; M. J. Waller, "Multiple-Task Performance in Groups," *Academy of Management Proceedings,* 1996. CD-ROM; and K. A. Jehn, G. B. Northcraft, and M. A. Neale, "Why Differences Make a Difference: A Field Study of Diversity, Conflict, and Performance in Workgroups," *Administrative Science Quarterly* 44, no. 4 (December 1999): pp. 741–763.

33. See, for example, A. C. Edmondson, *Teaming: How Organizations Learn, Innovate, and Compete in the Knowledge Economy* (San Francisco: Jossey-Bass Pfeiffer, 2015); R. Karlgaard and M. S. Malone, *Team Genius: The New Science of High-Performing Teams* (New York: HarperBusiness, 2015); J. E. Mathieu, J. R. Hollenbeck, D. van Knippenberg, and D. R. Ilgen, "A Century of Work Teams in the *Journal of Applied Psychology*," *Journal of Applied Psychology* 102, no. 3 (March 2017): pp. 452–67; and J. Gordon, *The Power of a Positive Team: Proven Principles and Practices That Make Great Teams Great* (Hoboken, NJ: Wiley, 2018).

34. See, for instance, E. Sundstrom, K. P. DeMeuse, and D. Futrell, "Work Teams: Applications and Effectiveness," *American Psychologist* 45, no. 2 (February 1990) pp. 120–133; and J. R. Hollenbeck, B. Beersma, and M. E. Schouten, "Beyond Team Types and Taxonomies: A Dimensional Scaling Conceptualization for Team Description," *Academy of Management Review* 37, no. 1 (January 2012): p. 85.

35. T. Boles, "Viewpoint—Leadership Lessons from NASCAR," *IndustryWeek,* December 21, 2004, https://www.industryweek.com/workforce/viewpoint-leadership-lessons-nascar; P. J. Kiger, "Acxiom Rebuilds from Scratch," *Workforce,* December 2002, pp. 52–55; J. S. McClenahen, "Bearing Necessities," *IndustryWeek,* October 2004, pp. 63–65; and M. Fitzgerald, "Shine a Light," *Fast Company,* April 2009, pp. 46–48.

36. V. Bolden-Barrett, "GE's Self-Managed Teams Are Raising Productivity, Employee Satisfaction," *HR Dive,* June 8, 2017, https://www.hrdive.com/news/ges-self-managed-teams-are-raising-productivity-employee-satisfaction/444498/.

37. D. Agarwal, J. Bersin, G. Lahiri, J. Schwartz, and E. Volini, "The Hyper-Connected Workplace: Will Productivity Reign?," 2108 Global Human Capital Trends, *Deloitte Insights,* March 28, 2018, https://www2.deloitte.com/insights/us/en/focus/human-capital-trends/2018/network-of-teams-connected-workplace.html.

38. J. Appleby and R. Davis, "Teamwork Used to Save Money; Now It Saves Lives," *USA Today* online, March 1, 2001, https://www.usatoday.com. See also M.-L. Wang, W.-Y. Chen,

Y.-Y. Lin, and B.-F. Hsu, "Structural Characteristics, Process, and Effectiveness of Cross-Functional Teams in Hospital: Testing the I-P-O Model," *Journal of High Technology Management Research* 21, no. 1 (January 2010): pp. 14–22.

39. L. L. Martins, L. L. Gilson, and M. T. Maynard, "Virtual Teams: What Do We Know and Where Do We Go from Here?," *Journal of Management* 30, no. 6 (December 2004): pp. 805–835; F. Siebdrat, M. Hoegl, and H. Ernst, "How to Manage a Virtual Team," *MIT Sloan Management Review*, Summer 2009, pp. 63–68; K. Ferrazzi, "Getting Virtual Teams Right," *Harvard Business Review*, December 2014, pp. 120–23; L. L. Gilson, M. T. Maynard, N. C. Jones Young, M. Vartiainen, and M. Hakonen, "Virtual Teams Research: 10 Years, 10 Themes, and 10 Opportunities," *Journal of Management* 41, no. 5 (July 2015): pp. 1313–37; and R. C. Ford, R. F. Piccolo, and L. R. Ford, "Strategies for Building Effective Virtual Teams: Trust Is Key," *Business Horizons* 60, no. 1 (January–February 2017): pp. 25–34.

40. D. DeRosa, "3 Companies with High-Performing Virtual Teams," *OnPoint Consulting* (blog), October 5, 2017, https://www.onpointconsultingllc.com/blog/3-companies-with-high-performing-virtual-teams.

41. "Remote Work by the Numbers," *SimpleTexting.com*, March 30, 2018, https://simpletexting.com/remote-work-statistics/.

42. See R. Fisher and W. L. Ury, *Getting to Yes: Negotiating Agreement Without Giving In*, rev. ed. (New York: Penguin, 2011); L. Thompson, *The Truth About Negotiations*, 2nd ed. (New York: FT Press, 2013); and R. J. Lewicki and D. M. Saunders, *Negotiation*, 7th ed. (New York: McGraw, 2014).

43. J. R. Hackman, "The Design of Work Teams," in J. Lorsch, ed., *Handbook of Organizational Behavior* (Englewood Cliffs, NJ: Prentice Hall, 1987), pp. 315–42; S. W. J. Kozlowski and D. R. Ilgen, "Enhancing the Effectiveness of Work Groups and Teams," *Psychological Science in the Public Interest* 7 (August 2006): pp. 77–124; M. Haas and M. Mortensen,

"The Secrets of Great Teamwork," *Harvard Business Review*, June 2016, pp. 70–76; and J. E. Mathieu, M. A. Wolfson, and S. Park, "The Evolution of Work Team Research Since Hawthorne," *American Psychologist* 73, no. 4 (May–June 2018): pp. 308–21.

44. Based on A. A. Cavaiola and N. J. Lavender, *Toxic Coworkers: How to Deal with Dysfunctional People on the Job* (Oakland, CA: New Harbinger Publications, 2000); M. Solomon, *Working with Difficult People* (Upper Saddle River, NJ: Prentice Hall, 2002); P. K. Jonason, S. Slomski, and J. Partyka, "The Dark Triad at Work: How *Toxic* Employees Get Their Way," *Personality and Individual Differences* (February 2012): pp. 449–453; A. Goforth, "12 of the Most Toxic Employees," *BenefitsPRO.com*, June 8, 2015, https://www.benefitspro.com/2015/06/08/12-of-the-most-toxic-employees/?slreturn=20190227140726.

45. Vault Careers, "Finding Love at Work Is More Acceptable Than Ever," *Vault*, February 11, 2015, http://www.vault.com/blog/workplace-issues/2015-office-romance-survey-results/.

46. J. Yang and V. Salazar, "Would You Date a Co-Worker?," *USA Today*, February 14, 2008, p. 1B.

47. N. Heath, "Project Wing: A Cheat Sheet On Alphabet's Drone Delivery Project," *Tech Republic*, April 4, 2018, https://www.techrepublic.com/article/project-wing-a-cheat-sheet/.

48. A. Davies, "Inside X, The Moonshot Factory Racing to Build the Next Google," *Wired*, July 11, 2018, https://www.wired.com/story/alphabet-google-x-innovation-loon-wing-graduation/.

49. "X–Wing," x.company.com.

50. Wikipedia, s.v. "HubSpot," https://en.wikipedia.org/wiki/HubSpot.

51. R. Leist, "What My Team Discovered When We All Worked Remotely for a Week," *Fast Company*, February 8, 2018, https://www.fastcompany.com/40527773/what-my-team-discovered-when-we-all-worked-remotely-for-a-week.

A Manager's Dilemma

Management theory suggests that compared to an individual, a diverse group of people will be more creative because team members will bring a variety of ideas, perspectives, and approaches to the group. For an organization like Alphabet's Google, innovation is critical to its success, and teams are a way of life. If management theory about teams is on target, then Google's research and development Hyderabad center in India should excel at innovation. Why? Because there you'll find broad diversity, even though all employees are from India. These Googlers include Indians, Sikhs, Hindus, Muslims, Buddhists, Christians, and Jains. And they speak English, Hindi, Tamil, Bengali, and more of India's twenty-two officially recognized languages. One skill Google looks for in potential hires is the ability to work as a team member. As Google continues to grow at a rapid pace, new Googlers are continually added to teams.

> *Suppose you're a manager at Google's Hyderabad facility. How would you gauge a potential hire's ability to work as a team member, and how would you maintain your team's innovation when new engineers and designers join the group?*

Global Sense

Workforce productivity. It's a performance measure that's important to managers and policy makers around the globe. Governments want their labor forces to be productive. Managers want their employees to be productive. Being productive encompasses both efficiency and effectiveness. Think back to our discussion of efficiency and effectiveness in Chapter 1. Efficiency is getting the most output from the least amount of input or resources. Or, said another way, doing things the right way. Effectiveness was doing those work activities that would result in achieving goals, or doing the right things that would lead to goal achievement. So how does workforce productivity stack up around the world? Here are some of the most recent data on six-year labor productivity growth rates from the Organisation for Economic Co-operation and

Development (OECD): Australia, 1.57 percent; Canada, 0.99 percent; Greece, –1.09 percent; Ireland, 6.12 percent; Korea, 2.09 percent; Turkey, 3.06 percent; United Kingdom, 0.23 percent; and United States, 0.36 percent. Despite fairly strong economic growth and low unemployment, workforce productivity rate growth across the globe has been relatively slow in recent years. Since the recession, labor productivity growth has been about half what it was before the last economic crisis. Companies have been hiring more employees as a way to increase productivity growth. Low unemployment rates mean that companies have been forced to hire less skilled employees than they would like. This makes productivity growth harder to achieve for companies. But what an opportunity this situation presents if you are getting into the workforce and have skills and strong productivity to offer!

> *Discuss the following questions in light of what you learned in Part 4:*
>
> - *How might workforce productivity be affected by organizational design? Look at the six key elements of organizational design.*
>
> - *What types of adaptive organizational design might be conducive to increasing worker productivity? Which might be detrimental to worker productivity?*
>
> - *How might an organization's human resource management approach affect worker productivity? How could managers use their HR processes to improve worker productivity?*
>
> - *Are teams more productive than individuals? Discuss and explain.*
>
> - *What could managers do to reduce the stress that employees feel due to pressure from managers to increase productivity growth?*[1]

Continuing Case

Starbucks—Organizing

Organizing is an important task of managers. As Starbucks continues its global expansion and pursues innovative strategic initiatives, managers must deal with the realities of continually organizing and reorganizing its work efforts.

Structuring Starbucks

Like many start-up businesses, Starbucks's original founders organized their company around a simple structure based on each person's unique strengths: Zev Siegl became the retail expert; Jerry Baldwin took over the administrative functions; and Gordon Bowker was the dreamer who called himself "the magic, mystery, and romance man." Bowker recognized from the start that a visit to Starbucks could "evoke a brief escape to a distant world." As Starbucks grew to the point where Jerry recognized that he needed to hire professional and experienced managers, Howard Schultz joined the company, bringing his skills in sales, marketing, and merchandising. When the original owners eventually sold the company to Schultz, he was able to take the company on a successful path. Kevin Johnson's transition to the president and CEO positions at Starbucks was smooth in part because he knew so much about the company. Johnson had been COO at Starbucks for two years before assuming the CEO role, and before that he served on Starbucks's board for six years. He was able to bring his leadership experience from other companies as well as sales, marketing, and operations skills.

As Starbucks has expanded, its organizational structure has changed to accommodate that growth. Starbucks's success is credited, in part, to its adaptive organizational structure, and the company prides itself on its "lean" corporate structure. Kevin Johnson is at the top of the structure and has focused on hiring a diverse team of executives from companies like Exxon Mobil, Sam's Club, Kraft Foods, Kimberly-Clark Corporation, and Macy's. Johnson realized how important it was to have an executive team in place that had experience in running divisions or functions of larger companies, and that's what he focused on bringing in to Starbucks. These senior corporate officers include the following: "C" (chief) officers, executive vice presidents, regional presidents, group presidents, and divisional vice presidents. Because being a global company is important to Starbucks's strategy, there are regional presidents for the geographic regions that Starbucks covers. Starbucks's focus on technology also is reflected in their structure. There not only is a chief technology officer, but there also are three senior vice presidents that oversee aspects of technology for Starbucks. A full description of the team of Starbucks executives and what each is responsible for can be found on the company's website.

Although the executive team provides the all-important strategic direction, the "real" work of Starbucks gets done at the company's support center, technology center, zone offices, retail stores, and roasting plants. The Seattle-based support center provides support to and assists all other aspects of corporate operations in the areas of accounting, finance, information technology, and sales and supply chain management. The Scottsdale, Arizona-based technology center focuses on the digital retail experience, including information security, business intelligence, and digital products for the company.

The zone offices oversee the regional operations of the retail stores and provide support in human resource management, facilities management, account management, financial management, and sales management. A matrix structure is used at the zone offices with each manager reporting to both a regional head and a functional department head. For example, a human resource manager working in China would report to both the China/Asia Pacific regional manager as well as the head of human resources for China and Asia Pacific. The essential link between the zone offices and each retail store is the district manager, each of whom oversees eight to ten stores. Since district managers need to be out working with the stores, they rely heavily on mobile technology that allows them to spend more time in the stores and still remain connected to their own office. These district managers have been called "the most important in the company" because it's out in the stores that the Starbucks vision and goals are being carried out. Thus, keeping those district managers connected is vital.

In the retail stores, hourly employees (baristas) service customers under the direction of shift supervisors, assistant store managers, and store managers. These managers are responsible for the day-to-day operations of each Starbucks location.

Finally, without coffee and other beverages and products to sell, there would be no Starbucks. The coffee beans are processed at the company's domestic roasting plants in Washington state, Pennsylvania, Nevada, South Carolina, Georgia, and internationally in Amsterdam. There's also a juicing facility in California, and the company set up a coffee roasting facility with Tata Global Beverages in India. At each manufacturing facility, the production team produces the coffee and other products and the distribution team manages the inventory and distribution of products and equipment to company stores.

People Management at Starbucks

Starbucks recognizes that what it's been able to accomplish is due to the quality of the people it hires. Since the beginning, Starbucks has strived to be an employer that nurtures employees and gives them opportunities to grow and be challenged. The company says it is "pro-partner" and has always been committed to providing a flexible and progressive work environment and treating one another with respect and dignity.

As Starbucks focuses on enhancing its customers' experience and expanding internationally, it needs to make sure it has the right number of the right people in the right place at the right time. What kinds of people are "right" for Starbucks? They describe their ideal employees as having the ability to create "genuine moments of connection" with customers, a willingness to learn, and an openness to getting the job done while helping fellow team members. Starbucks uses a variety of methods to attract potential partners. The company has an interactive and easy-to-use online career center. Job seekers can search and apply online for jobs in retail, corporate, and manufacturing in any geographic location. The company also has a limited number of summer internship opportunities for students at their support and technology centers in the US. But the company's efforts don't stop there.

The company's commitment to helping people in communities has led to various special hiring initiatives that focus on particular groups. For instance, Starbucks has hired 21,000 veterans and their spouses, exceeding their initial commitment to hire at least 10,000 military-related individuals by 2018. Starbucks also has hired 65,000 low-income individuals and committed to hiring 10,000 refugees by 2020. Recently, twenty-five employees who know American Sign Language were hired for Starbucks's first US-based Signing Store in Washington, DC—where you can order and communicate via sign language. Starbucks opened its first Signing Store in Malaysia in 2016.

Starbucks offers a variety of training, but their most high-profile training occurred after two African Americans were asked by store staff to leave a Starbucks café in Philadelphia when they were waiting for a friend. Starbucks closed more than 8,000 stores across the US in order to offer racial-bias training. This training included multiple videos, discussions about race and identity, information about what people of color experience on a day-to-day basis in public settings, and instructions for keeping a personal journal in the months after training. Starbucks plans on including racial-bias training in their orientation program for new employees in the future.

Starbucks also offers new employees "Starbucks Experience" classes that get them up to speed on the company's history, culture, and social responsibility practices. Unless an employee works at a remote location, the Starbucks Experience training is offered at regional training centers. To reinforce this off-site training, each store has a learning coach who guides new hires through hands-on training in the store. Further online training also is offered to support in-person training. For instance, Starbucks's "Solutions University Online Training" is intended to provide instant training at the fingertips of their many employees.

Starbucks's largest training initiative is their College Achievement Plan. This plan provides reimbursement of tuition costs for an online bachelor's degree through Arizona State University. Any Starbucks employee who has worked with the company for at least three months, works at least twenty hours per week, and doesn't already have a bachelor's degree is eligible to apply. Of the Starbucks employees who have applied to this program, 80 percent have been accepted into the program. The goal of this program—which was introduced in 2014—is to help make college affordable and accessible for its employees.

Discussion Questions

P4-1. What types of departmentalization are being used? Explain your choices. (Hint: In addition to information in the case, you might want to look at the description of corporate executives under "Leadership" on the company's website.)

P4-2. What possible problems could Starbucks encounter with their matrix structure? What could they do to try to minimize these problems?

P4-3. If Starbucks wanted to offer compressed workweeks, flextime, or job sharing, what would they need to consider? What are advantages and disadvantages of offering these employment options at Starbucks?

P4-4. Starbucks has said its goal is to expand delivery to one-quarter of its US stores and increase earnings per share by 10 percent. How will the organizing function contribute to the accomplishment of these goals?

P4-5. Starbucks has said that it wants people who have the ability to create "genuine moments of connection" with customers, a willingness to learn, and an openness to getting the job done while helping fellow team members. How does the company ensure that its hiring and selection process identifies those kinds of people?

P4-6. Evaluate Starbucks's training efforts. What other type(s) of training might be necessary?

P4-7. Pretend that you're a local Starbucks's store manager. You have three new hourly partners (baristas) joining your team. Describe the orientation you would provide these new hires.

P4-8. If Starbucks wanted to implement multiperson comparisons or 360-degree appraisals as methods of evaluating employee performance, what possible issues (both positive and negative) might arise? How might those employee performance manage-

ment methods affect how store managers manage their teams?

P4-9. Which of the company's values affect the organizing function of management? Explain how the one(s) you chose would affect how Starbucks's managers deal with (a) structural issues; (b) HRM issues; and (c) issues in managing teams. (Hint: Starbucks's values can be found on the company's website.)

Notes for the Part 4 Continuing Case

1. H. Torry and S. Chaney, "U.S. News: Worker-Productivity Gains Lag Behind," *Wall Street Journal,* November 2, 2018, p. A2; R. Majumdar, "Understanding the Productivity Paradox," Deloitte Insights, October 27, 2017, https://www2.deloitte.com/insights/us/en/economy/behind-the-numbers/decoding-declining-stagnant-productivity-growth.html; Organisation for Economic Co-operation and Development, *OECD Compendium of Productivity Indicators 2018* (Paris: OECD Publishing), https://www.oecd-ilibrary.org/economics/oecd-compendium-of-productivity-indicators-2018_pdtvy-2018-en.

Chapter 14   Managing Communication

Learning Objectives

14.1 **Define** the nature and function of communication.

14.2 **Describe** the communication process.

14.3 **Explain** how communication can flow most effectively in organizations.

14.4 **Describe** how the internet and social media affect managerial communication and organizations.

14.5 **Discuss** how to become a better communicator.

Employability Skills Matrix

This matrix identifies features and end-of-chapter material that will help you develop specific skills employers are looking for in job candidates.

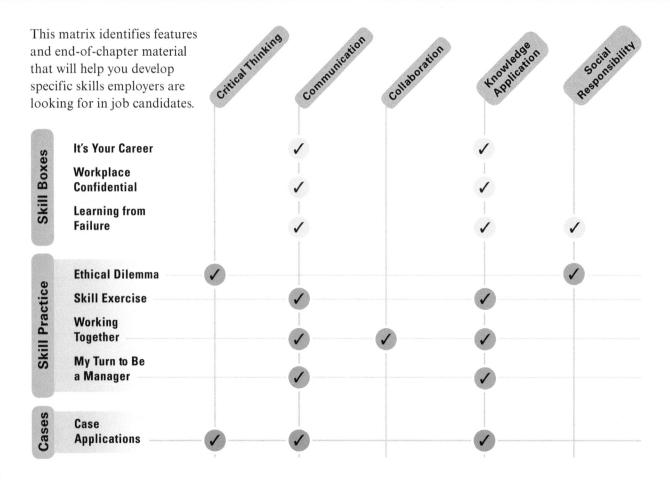

		Critical Thinking	Communication	Collaboration	Knowledge Application	Social Responsibility
Skill Boxes	It's Your Career		✓		✓	
	Workplace Confidential		✓		✓	
	Learning from Failure		✓		✓	✓
Skill Practice	Ethical Dilemma	✓				✓
	Skill Exercise		✓		✓	
	Working Together		✓	✓	✓	
	My Turn to Be a Manager		✓		✓	
Cases	Case Applications	✓	✓		✓	

Miscommunication has been shown to be one of the major sources of office conflicts, national disasters, and even international incidences. Maybe one of the most tragic examples of poor communication took place at the airport on the Spanish island of Tenerife, Canary Islands. The captain of a fully loaded KLM jumbo jet thought the air traffic controller had given him clearance for takeoff. He hadn't. That misunderstanding led the KLM plane to collide on the runway with a fully loaded Pan Am jumbo jet. The result was the deadliest accident in aviation history: 583 people lost their lives.[1]

In this chapter, we look at both interpersonal and organizational communication. We look at barriers to effective communication and ways to overcome those barriers. We close this chapter by suggesting ways that you can become a better communicator.

UNDERSTANDING communication

LO14.1 The ability to communicate effectively is a skill that must be mastered by any person who wants to be an effective manager. The importance of effective communication for managers can't be overemphasized for one specific reason: everything a manager does involves communicating. Not some things, but everything! A manager can't make a decision without information. That information has to be communicated. Once a decision is made, communication must again take place. Otherwise, no one would know that a decision was made. The best idea, the most creative suggestion, the best plan, or the most effective job redesign can't take shape without communication.

What Is Communication?

Communication is the transfer and understanding of meaning. Note the emphasis on the transfer of meaning: if information or ideas have not been conveyed, communication hasn't taken place. The speaker who isn't heard or the writer whose materials aren't read hasn't communicated. More importantly, however, communication involves the understanding of meaning. For communication to be successful, the meaning must be imparted and understood. A letter written in Spanish addressed to a person who doesn't read Spanish can't be considered communication until it's translated into a language the person does read and understand. Perfect communication, if such a thing existed, would be when a transmitted thought or idea was received and understood by the receiver exactly as it was envisioned by the sender.

Another point to keep in mind is that good communication is often erroneously defined by the communicator as agreement with the message instead of clear understanding of the message.[2] If someone disagrees with us, we assume that the person just didn't fully understand our position. In other words, many of us define good communication as having someone accept our views. But I can clearly understand what you mean and just not agree with what you say.

The final point we want to make about communication is that it encompasses both **interpersonal communication**—communication between two or more people—and **organizational communication**, which is all the patterns, networks, and systems of communication within an organization. Both types are important to managers.

Functions of Communication

Communication serves five major functions within a group or organization: management, motivation, emotional sharing, persuasion, and information exchange.[3]

Communication acts to *manage* member behavior in several ways. As we know from Chapter 11, organizations have authority hierarchies and formal guidelines that employees are expected to follow. For instance, when employees follow their job descriptions

communication
The transfer and understanding of meaning

interpersonal communication
Communication between two or more people

organizational communication
All the patterns, networks, and systems of communication within an organization

Metro General Manager Paul Wiedefeld, right, chats with an employee during a tour of track work being done on Metro's orange line in northern Virginia. Communication with employees serves the functions of information, motivation, and socialization.
Source: Ben Nuckols/AP Images

or comply with company policies, communication performs a management function. Informal communication also controls behavior. When a work group teases a member who's ignoring the norms by working too hard, they're informally communicating and managing the member's behavior.

Communication acts to *motivate* by clarifying to employees what is to be done, how well they're doing, and how they can improve their performance. As employees set specific goals, work toward those goals, and receive feedback on progress toward goals, communication is required.

For many employees, their work group is a primary source of social interaction. The communication that takes place within the group is a fundamental mechanism by which members show frustrations and satisfaction. Communication, therefore, provides for the *emotional sharing* of feelings and fulfillment of social needs.

Persuasion can be good or bad depending on if, say, a leader is trying to persuade a work group to believe in the organization's commitment to corporate social responsibility or, conversely, to persuade the work group to break the law to meet an organizational goal. These may be extreme examples, but it's important to remember that persuasion can benefit or harm an organization.

The final function of communication is *information exchange* to facilitate decision making. Communication provides the information that individuals and groups need to make decisions by transmitting the data needed to identify and evaluate choices.

THE COMMUNICATION PROCESS

LO14.2 Before communication can take place, a purpose expressed as a **message** to be conveyed must exist. It passes between a source (the sender) and a receiver. The message is converted to symbolic form (called **encoding**) and passed by way of some medium (**channel**) to the receiver, who retranslates the sender's message (called **decoding**). The result is the transfer of meaning from one person to another.[4]

Exhibit 14-1 depicts the **communication process**. This model is made up of seven elements: (1) the communication source, (2) the message, (3) encoding, (4) the channel, (5) decoding, (6) the receiver, and (7) feedback. In addition, the entire process is susceptible to **noise**—that is, disturbances that interfere with the transmission of the message (depicted in Exhibit 14-1 as lightning bolts). Typical examples of noise include illegible print, telephone static, inattention by the receiver, or the background sounds of machinery on the production floor. Remember that anything that interferes with understanding—whether internal (such as the low speaking voice of the speaker/sender) or external (like the loud voices of coworkers talking at an adjoining desk)—represents noise. Noise can create distortion at any point in the communication process.

Modes of Communicating

How do people in organizations transfer meaning among themselves? They rely on oral, written, and nonverbal communication.

message
A purpose to be conveyed

encoding
Converting a message into symbols

channel
The medium a message travels along

decoding
Retranslating a sender's message

communication process
The seven elements involved in transferring meaning from one person to another

noise
Any disturbances that interfere with the transmission of a message

Exhibit 14-1
The Communication Process

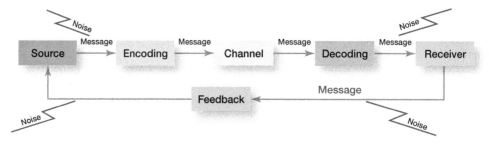

ORAL COMMUNICATION   A primary means of conveying messages is oral communication. Speeches, formal one-on-one and group discussions, and the informal rumor mill or grapevine are popular forms of oral communication.

The advantages of oral communication are speed, feedback, and exchange. We can convey a verbal message and receive a response in minimal time. If the receiver is unsure of the message, rapid feedback allows the sender to detect and correct it quickly. The exchange given through oral communication has social, cultural, and emotional components. Cultural social exchange, in which we purposely share social exchanges that transcend cultural boundaries, can build trust, cooperation, and agreement between individuals and teams.

One major disadvantage of oral communication surfaces whenever a message has to pass through a number of people: the more people, the greater the potential distortion. If you've ever played the game Telephone, you know the problem. Each person interprets the message in his or her own way. The message's content, when it reaches its destination, is often very different from the original, even when we think the message is simple and straightforward. Therefore, oral communication "chains" are generally more of a liability than an effective tool in large organizations.

WRITTEN COMMUNICATION   Written communication includes letters, email, instant messaging, blogs, organizational periodicals, and any other method that conveys written words or symbols. Written business communication today is usually conducted via letters, PowerPoint, email, text messaging, social media, apps, and blogs.

NONVERBAL COMMUNICATION   Every time we deliver a verbal message, we also impart an unspoken message. So no discussion of communication would be complete without consideration of *nonverbal communication*—which includes body movements, the intonations or emphasis we give words, and facial expressions. Body language and intonations can specifically contain powerful messages.

We could argue that every body movement has meaning, and no movement is accidental (though some are unconscious). We act out our state of being with nonverbal body language. For example, we smile to project trustworthiness, uncross our arms to appear approachable, and stand to signal authority.[5]

Body language can convey status, level of engagement, and emotional state.[6] Body language adds to, and often complicates, verbal communication. In fact, studies indicate that people read more about another's attitude and emotions from their nonverbal cues than their words! If nonverbal cues conflict with the speaker's verbal message, the cues are sometimes more likely to be believed by the listener.[7]

If you read the minutes of a meeting, you wouldn't grasp the impact of what was said the same way as if you had been there or could see the meeting on video. Why? Because there is no record of nonverbal communication, and the emphasis given to words or phrases—the intonations—is missing. Both make the meaning clearer.

Facial expressions also convey meaning. Facial expressions, along with intonations, can show arrogance, aggressiveness, fear, shyness, and other characteristics.

Barriers to Effective Communication

In our discussion of the communication process, we noted the consistent potential for distortion. What causes such distortions? In additional to the general distortions identified in the communication process, there are other barriers to effective communication.

INFORMATION OVERLOAD   **Information overload** occurs when information exceeds our processing capacity. For instance, a marketing manager goes on a week-long sales trip to Spain where she doesn't have access to her email and faces 1,000 messages on her return. Would you believe that the average

information overload
When information exceeds our processing capacity

Nonverbal communications can say a lot. Here, Serbian tennis player Novak Djokovic's nonverbal behavior tells you he is not pleased with an umpire's call.
Source: Juergen Hasenkopf/Alamy Stock Photo

worker spends thirteen hours a week dealing with emails?[8] Not surprisingly, today's employees frequently complain of information overload. The demands of keeping up with email, text messages, phone calls, meetings, and professional reading create an onslaught of data. What happens when individuals have more information than they can process? They tend to ignore, pass over, forget, or selectively choose information. Or they may stop communicating.

FILTERING   Filtering is the deliberate manipulation of information to make it appear more favorable to the receiver. For example, when a person tells his or her manager what the manager wants to hear, information is being filtered. Or if information being communicated up through organizational levels is condensed by senders, that's filtering.

How much filtering takes place tends to be a function of the number of vertical levels in the organization and the organizational culture. The more vertical levels in an organization, the more opportunities there are for filtering. As organizations use more collaborative, cooperative work arrangements, information filtering may become less of a problem. In addition, email reduces filtering because communication is more direct. Finally, the organizational culture encourages or discourages filtering by the type of behavior it rewards. The more that organizational rewards emphasize style and appearance, the more managers may be motivated to filter communications in their favor.

EMOTIONS   How a receiver feels influences how he or she interprets it. Extreme emotions are most likely to hinder effective communication. In such instances, we often disregard our rational and objective thinking processes and substitute emotional judgments.

When people feel they're being threatened, they tend to react in ways that hinder effective communication and reduce their ability to achieve mutual understanding. They become defensive—verbally attacking others, making sarcastic remarks, being overly judgmental, or questioning others' motives.

LANGUAGE   Even when we're communicating in the same language, words mean different things to different people. Age, education, and cultural background are three of the more obvious variables that influence the language a person uses and the definitions he or she gives to words.

In an organization, employees come from diverse backgrounds and have different patterns of speech. Even employees who work for the same organization but in different departments often have different **jargon**—specialized terminology or technical language that members of a group use to communicate among themselves. For instance, human resource managers discuss BFOQs (bona fide occupational qualifications) as a defense against illegal discrimination, and accounting managers use the terms LIFO and FIFO—meaning last-in, first out and first-in, first-out—as a reference to inventory-valuing methods.

SILENCE   It's easy to ignore silence or lack of communication because it's defined by the absence of information. However, this can be a serious mistake. Silence can be the message when, for instance, someone wants to communicate noninterest or the unwillingness to deal with a topic. Employees are more likely to be silent if they believe they are being mistreated by managers, are experiencing frequent negative emotions, or feel like they have less power in the organization.[9] Silence can also be a simple outcome of information overload or a delaying period for considering a response. For whatever reasons, research suggests using silence and withholding communication are common and problematic.[10]

NATIONAL CULTURE   Every aspect of global communication is influenced by cultural differences.[11] The Japanese, for instance, who have access to the latest technologies, still rely more on face-to-face communication than on written. In the US, managers

---

filtering
The deliberate manipulation of information to make it appear more favorable to the receiver

jargon
Specialized terminology or technical language that members of a group use to communicate among themselves

rely heavily on reports, memos, and other formal forms of communication. A Japanese manager extensively consults with subordinates over an issue first and draws up a formal document later to outline the agreement that was made. Executives in Latin American, Arab, and Asian countries leave much of their messages unspecified, relying on context and nonverbal cues to be understood. This is in contrast to German managers, who expect messages to be explicit and specific.

The above examples illustrate the importance of understanding and respecting differences when dealing in cross-cultural interactions—and how these differences can act as distortions to effective communication.

Overcoming the Barriers

What can managers and *you* do to be a more effective communicator? Here are five suggestions.

Communication is influenced by cultural differences. Japanese managers, for instance, typically consult with subordinates over an issue before making a final decision.
Source: Imtmphoto/Alamy Stock Photo

USE FEEDBACK Many communication problems are directly attributed to misunderstanding and inaccuracies. These problems are less likely to occur if the manager gets feedback, both verbal and nonverbal.

A manager can ask questions about a message to determine whether it was received and understood as intended. Or the manager can ask the receiver to restate the message in his or her own words. If the manager hears what was intended, understanding and accuracy should improve.

Feedback also doesn't have to be verbal. If a sales manager emails information about a new monthly sales report that all sales representatives will need to complete and some of them don't turn it in, the sales manager has received feedback. This feedback suggests that the sales manager needs to clarify the initial communication. Similarly, managers can look for nonverbal cues to tell whether someone's getting the message.

SIMPLIFY LANGUAGE Because language can be a barrier, managers should consider the audience to whom the message is directed and tailor the language to them. Remember, effective communication is achieved when a message is both *received* and *understood*. For example, a hospital administrator should try to communicate in clear, easily understood terms and to use language tailored to different employee groups. Messages to the surgical staff should be purposefully different from those used with office employees. Jargon can facilitate understanding if it's used within a group that knows what it means, but can cause problems when used outside that group.

LISTEN ACTIVELY When someone talks, we hear, but too often we don't listen. Listening is an active search for meaning, whereas hearing is passive. In listening, the receiver is also putting effort into the communication.

Many of us are poor listeners. Why? Because it's difficult, and most of us would rather do the talking. Listening, in fact, is often more tiring than talking. Unlike hearing, **active listening**, which is listening for full meaning without making premature judgments or interpretations, demands total concentration. The average person normally speaks at a rate of about 125 to 200 words per minute. However, the average listener can comprehend up to 400 words per minute.[12] The difference leaves lots of idle brain time and opportunities for the mind to wander.

active listening
Listening for full meaning without making premature judgments or interpretations

CONSTRAIN EMOTIONS It would be naive to assume that managers always communicate in a rational manner. We know that emotions can cloud and distort communication. A manager who's upset over an issue is more likely to misconstrue incoming messages and fail to communicate his or her outgoing messages clearly and accurately. What to do? The simplest answer is to calm down and get emotions under control before communicating.

IT'S YOUR CAREER

I'm Listening!

A key to success in management and in your career is knowing how to be an active listener. How well do you listen to others? Active listening requires you to concentrate on what is being said. It's more than just hearing the words. It involves a concerted effort to understand and interpret the speaker's message. Here are some insights that you'll want to remember and integrate into your efforts to be a better listener:

1. *Make eye contact.* Making eye contact with the speaker focuses your attention, reduces the likelihood that you will become distracted, and encourages the speaker.

2. *Exhibit affirmative nods and appropriate facial expressions.* Affirmative nods and appropriate facial expressions, when added to good eye contact, convey to the speaker that you're listening.

3. *Pay attention to nonverbal cues.* Sometimes, what the speaker vocalizes and how

they feel do not match. For instance, the speaker may begin by stating "It isn't a big deal ..." when, in fact, their body language shows that what they are saying is a big deal. It isn't difficult to tell when someone is anxious, angry, happy, or sad based on facial expressions.

4. *Ask questions and paraphrase what's been said.* The critical listener analyzes what he or she hears and asks questions. This behavior provides clarification, ensures understanding, and assures the speaker that you're listening. And the effective listener uses phrases such as "What I hear you saying is ..." or "Do you mean ...?" Paraphrasing is an excellent control device to check on whether you're listening carefully and to verify that what you heard is accurate.

5. *Make smooth transitions between the roles of speaker and listener.* The effective listener makes transitions smoothly from speaker to listener and back to speaker. From a listening perspective, this means concentrating on what a speaker has to say and practicing not thinking about what you're going to say as soon as you get your chance.

Let's Get REAL

Dr. Eric Brown, PT, DPT ▶
Clinical Director of Physical Therapy

Source: Dr, Eric Brown

The Scenario:

Tod Stewart distributed a memo to his employees that outlines the steps of a new process they need to follow when attracting new clients to the business. This new company policy provides guidance to employees while they are developing new business possibilities so that they act professionally and represent the company well. He told the team of employees that he manages that following this new company policy is important to do for the sake of the company's reputation. There have been a couple of instances recently when employees have not followed this new company policy, which makes Tod wonder if he could have done a better job with his communication efforts.

What should Tod do to ensure that he has effectively communicated the new process to his employees?

Change and adopting new policies can be difficult, especially when current practices and employee behaviors have been set for an extended period of time. From my personal experience, the key to helping a team adopt a new policy, plan, or procedure is in following up. By connecting personally through face-to-face meetings or through a brief conversation over the phone, a manager has an opportunity to check for understanding, answer questions, and provide further encouragement to adhere to new standards. A manager that leads by example and effectively communicates with their team will likely succeed in helping their team grow and adapt to new challenges.

WATCH NONVERBAL CUES If actions speak louder than words, then it's important to make sure your actions align with and reinforce the words that go along with them. An effective communicator watches his or her nonverbal cues to ensure that they convey the desired message.

WORKPLACE CONFIDENTIAL An Uncommunicative Boss

Many of us fantasize about having a job where our boss just leaves us alone. Out of sight, out of mind. We're free to get our work done, with an absence of bother from a boss. But be careful what you wish for! It can be very frustrating to work for someone who is uncommunicative.

We use the term "uncommunicative" to encompass a long list of behaviors you might face in the workplace. There's the absentee boss, who is never around. You have questions or concerns but no one with whom to discuss them. There's the shy or introverted boss who avoids interacting. There's the boss who hates conflicts or confrontations and who hides from the tough issues. There's also the boss who always seems too busy to talk with you. And then there's the boss who doesn't respond to tweets, emails or phone messages. You know they're being received, but it's as if they vanish into thin air. As you can see, there are lots of ways to be uncommunicative!

The following suggestions can help you deal with, and work around, an uncommunicative boss.

Ask yourself: Am I being singled out? Start by assessing whether your boss is uncommunicative with everyone or whether you've been singled out. It's possible that your boss is purposely distancing herself from you. Have you done anything to upset her? Is she purposely avoiding you? If you're annoyed or irritated with your boss, she might be picking this up and distancing herself from you in order to avoid a conflict. On the other hand, if your boss treats all her employees similarly, assume you're not being singled out. Bottom line: start by determining whether or not you may be contributing to the problem.

Does your organization's culture encourage your boss's behavior? Take a good look at your organization's culture. Does your organization encourage managers to be "hands off"? In some cases, organizations promote this behavior by the criteria they use to evaluate managers and by what they reward. For instance, a laissez-faire leadership style might be encouraged as a way to develop future managers. It may well be that, in such a culture, your boss is giving you the freedom to take on tasks and show initiative with a view toward preparing you for increased responsibilities. If most managers in your organization seem to be showing a similar, uncommunicative style, don't expect significant changes in your boss.

Are there good reasons for your boss to be uncommunicative? Look at your boss objectively. There may be good reasons for his hands-off approach. One common explanation is that he's spending his time "managing up," that is, working to get increased resources or support from those above.

Other possibilities include your boss having too much to do or too many employees to supervise. These explanations can help you better empathize with your boss's situation and better understand why he's not available.

Be proactive: Support your boss. There's an old saw: "The boss isn't always right, but he's always the boss." If you're feeling underappreciated, give your boss the benefit of the doubt. Reach out and, without fawning, take the initiative in acknowledging those things he does well and that you appreciate his efforts. There's a good chance that your positive outreach will be reciprocated. When you make the boss feel good, it increases his desire to be around you.

Share your needs with your boss. Unless you say something, there's a good chance your boss won't realize that there's a problem. Meet with your boss and frame your conversation about your needs. Be prepared to express exactly the kind of support you're seeking. Do you want to have weekly meetings with her? Do you seek quicker email responses? Don't be aggressive or pushy. Show that you're empathetic to her situation and the demands on her time; then be clear and concise about your needs.

Act, but keep your boss informed. If your efforts to improve communications fall on deaf ears, move forward on your own. Take the initiative but, very importantly, keep your boss in the loop. Even though you might not be getting any feedback, continue to give your boss brief, written status reports. If problems arise in the future, you will have at least created a paper trail to support that you were keeping your boss informed.

Look for a boss-substitute. If your boss isn't there for you, consider looking around your organization for someone who can fill the void. Find another person who can mentor and support you.

Protect yourself: Get to know your boss's boss. It rarely hurts to develop a relationship with your boss's superior. It can be as simple as just exchanging pleasantries or sharing a coffee in the lunchroom. From a political perspective, it makes sense to protect yourself and build alliances with those in power.

Turn this situation to your favor. Finally, look at the positive side. This is an opportunity for you to step up, show your initiative, and impress others in the organization. Those in nonmanagerial positions often don't get opportunities to demonstrate leadership. But if the opportunity is opened to you, don't let it get away. You can fill the void in leadership, grow your reach in the organization, make a positive impression on upper management, and possibly open the door to a promotion.[13]

EFFECTIVE organizational communication

L014.3 You've now got the basics of the communication process. In this section, we overlay an organization's structure on this framework to understand *organizational communication*. We'll look at formal versus information communication, the flow patterns of communication within organizations, organizational networks, and how management can design workplaces to enhance communication.

Formal Versus Informal

formal communication
Communication that takes place within prescribed organizational work arrangements

informal communication
Communication that is not defined by the organization's structural hierarchy

Communication within an organization is described as formal or informal. **Formal communication** refers to communication that takes place within prescribed organizational work arrangements. For example, when a manager asks an employee to complete a task, that's formal communication. Another example of formal communication occurs when an employee communicates a problem to his or her manager.

Informal communication is organizational communication not defined by the organization's structural hierarchy. When employees talk with each other in the lunch room, as they pass in hallways, or as they're working out at the company wellness facility, they engage in informal communication. Employees form friendships and communicate with each other. The informal communication system fulfills two purposes in organizations: (1) it permits employees to satisfy their need for social interaction, and (2) it can improve an organization's performance by creating alternative, and frequently faster and more efficient, channels of communication.

Direction of Flow

Let's look at the ways that organizational communication can flow: downward, upward, laterally, or diagonally.

downward communication
Communication that flows downward from a manager to employees

DOWNWARD COMMUNICATION Your boss calls you into her office and shares with you that the company auditors will be coming in next week and asks you to prepare several reports for them. This is an example of **downward communication**, which is communication that flows from a manager to employees. It's used to inform, direct, coordinate, and evaluate employees. When managers assign goals to their employees, they're using downward communication. They're also using downward communication when providing employees with job descriptions, informing them of organizational policies and procedures, pointing out problems that need attention, or evaluating their performance.

upward communication
Communication that flows upward from employees to managers

UPWARD COMMUNICATION Managers rely on their employees for information. For instance, reports are given to managers to inform them of progress toward goals or to report any problems. **Upward communication** is communication that flows from employees to managers. It keeps managers aware of how employees feel about their jobs, their coworkers, and the organization in general. Managers also rely on upward communication for ideas on how things can be improved. Some examples of upward communication include performance reports prepared by employees, suggestion boxes, employee attitude surveys, grievance procedures, manager-employee discussions, and informal group sessions in which employees have the opportunity to discuss problems with their manager or representatives of top-level management.

lateral communication
Communication that takes place among any employees on the same organizational level

LATERAL COMMUNICATION Communication that takes place among employees on the same organizational level is called **lateral communication**. In today's dynamic environment, horizontal communications are frequently needed to save time and facilitate coordination. Cross-functional teams, for instance, rely heavily on this form of

United Continental Holdings Inc. Chief Executive Officer Oscar Munoz uses downward communication when speaking to a group of his employees in Chicago.
Source: JIM YOUNG/Sipa USA/Newscom

communication interaction. However, conflicts can arise if employees don't keep their managers informed about decisions they've made or actions they've taken.

DIAGONAL COMMUNICATION **Diagonal communication** is communication that crosses both work areas and organizational levels. A credit analyst who communicates directly with a regional marketing manager about a customer's problem—note the different department and different organizational level—uses diagonal communication. Because of its efficiency and speed, diagonal communication can be beneficial. Increased email use facilitates diagonal communication. In most organizations, any employee can communicate by email with any other employee, regardless of organizational work area or level, even with upper-level managers. The downside is that diagonal interactions often leave managers out of the loop and have the potential to create conflicts.

Networks

The vertical and horizontal flows of organizational communication can be combined into a variety of patterns called **communication networks**. Exhibit 14-2 illustrates three common communication networks.

TYPES OF COMMUNICATION NETWORKS In the chain network, communication flows according to the formal chain of command, both downward and upward. The wheel network represents communication flowing between a clearly identifiable and strong leader and others in a work group or team. The leader serves as the hub through whom all communication passes. Finally, in the all-channel network, communication flows freely among all members of a work team.

The form of network you should use depends on your goal. Exhibit 14-2 also summarizes each network's effectiveness according to four criteria: speed, accuracy, the probability that a leader will emerge, and the importance of member satisfaction. One observation is immediately apparent: no single network is best for all situations.

THE GRAPEVINE We can't leave our discussion of communication networks without discussing the **grapevine**—the informal organizational communication network. The grapevine is active in almost every organization. Is it an important source of information? You bet! One survey reported that 63 percent of employees say they hear about important matters first through rumors or gossip on the grapevine.[15]

An interesting fact about grapevines are that few people are active on them. As a rule, only about 10 percent of the people in an organization act as liaisons who pass on information to more than one other person. Which individuals are active on the grapevine often depends on the message. A message that sparks the interest of an employee may stimulate him or her to tell someone else. However, another message that is perceived to be of lesser interest may never be transmitted further.

fyi

- Half of American workers use email as the primary form of communicating with co-workers.
- Only 20 percent of US workers prefer face-to-face communication or talking by phone to using email.[14]

diagonal communication
Communication that cuts across work areas and organizational levels

communication networks
The variety of patterns of vertical and horizontal flows of organizational communication

grapevine
The informal organizational communication network

Exhibit 14-2
Organizational Communication Networks

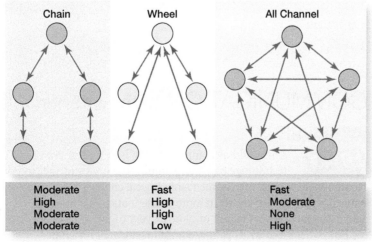

CRITERIA	Chain	Wheel	All Channel
Speed	Moderate	Fast	Fast
Accuracy	High	High	Moderate
Emergence of leader	Moderate	High	None
Member satisfaction	Moderate	Low	High

Can the grapevine be used to management's benefit? The answer is yes.[16] Given that only a small number of employees typically pass information to more than one other person, managers can analyze grapevine information and predict its flow. Certain messages are likely to follow predictable patterns. Managers might even consider using the grapevine to transmit information informally to specific individuals by "planting" messages with key people who are active on the grapevine and are likely to find a given message worth passing on.

Managers should not lose sight of the grapevine's value for identifying issues that employees consider important and that create anxiety among them. It acts as both a filter and feedback mechanism, picking up issues that employees consider relevant and planting messages that employees want passed on to upper management. For instance, the grapevine can tap employee concerns. If a rumor of a mass layoff is spreading along the grapevine and management knows the rumor to be totally false, the message still has meaning. It reflects the fears and concerns of employees and hence should not be ignored by management.

The traditional grapevine relied on face-to-face interactions or phone conversations. In the 1990s, email was added as a popular grapevine vehicle. Today's grapevine vehicle is, increasingly, social media.[17] Using Twitter, Facebook, and other popular sites, employees can share information with a wider audience than just fellow coworkers. Needless to say, the downside is that this can create unfavorable publicity for organizations or specific executives. Recent legal rulings have upheld the right of employees in private-sector organizations to discuss work conditions freely and without fear of retribution, whether the discussion takes place at the office or on a social media site. Our advice to management: create clear social media policies and make sure they are widely understood. Walmart's social media usage policy, for example, includes prohibitions against "inappropriate postings that may include discriminatory remarks, harassment, and threats of violence or similar inappropriate or unlawful conduct."[18]

Let's Get REAL

Maribel Lara ▶
Director, Account
Management

Source: Maribel Lara

The Scenario:

Alexandra Pavlou has a delicate, potentially touchy issue she needs to discuss with her team of real estate appraisers. How can she approach this discussion with care and yet address the issue frankly?

What advice would you give Alexandra?

First consider if it's an issue best addressed in several one-on-one meetings or in a group setting. Do your best to anticipate the reactions and think through how you will respond/react in turn. Be honest at the onset with your team that the forthcoming discussion(s) may make some people uncomfortable but explain why the topic is important to address.

COMMUNICATION in the internet and social media age

LO14.4 The world of communication isn't what it used to be! Although changing technology has been a significant source of the environmental uncertainty facing organizations, these same technological changes have enabled managers to coordinate employees' work efforts in more efficient and effective ways. Information technology (IT) now touches every aspect of almost every organization's operations. The implications for how, where, and when people communicate are profound.

Learning from FAILURE — GM's Catastrophic Communications Breakdown

A few inappropriate words seem to have been the cause of 124 deaths and 275 injuries. Here's the story in brief.

The Chevrolet Cobalt, built by General Motors, had a flaw. The ignition switches had a tendency to turn off by themselves, leaving the cars without power and disabling their airbags. While millions of these cars were recalled for this flaw in 2014, certain employees at GM actually became aware of the problem as early as 2004. But they didn't act. Why? Because they decided it wasn't a safety concern.

When the ignition switch failures first surfaced, it was labeled as a "customer convenience" problem. That terminology left GM management with the impression that it simply annoyed some drivers. But safety had long been a top priority at GM. The company had issued hundreds of recalls at great expense during the same decade when the problems were framed as "safety defects." Those two words always triggered a fast response. GM employees, in fact, were trained to use words like "issue," "matter," or "defect" when safety was involved. But when the ignition flaw was called a "customer convenience" problem that did "not perform to design," there was no sense of urgency. And so the flawed ignition switch continued to be installed on Cobalts, and people continued to die.

What did GM learn from this tragic communication breakdown? Clearly, it needed to improve communication. A new position, Vice President for Global Vehicle Safety, was created. And he implemented programs instructing employees how to identify safety issues and to discuss them with supervisors and executives. One such program is "Speak Up For Safety," which is designed to encourage employees to identify, report, and elevate safety issues and train them how to do so.

These corrective actions appear to be working. Three years after this story broke and new programs initiated, consumer ratings of GM vehicle quality were higher than prior to the scandal—and actually the highest the company has ever had.[19]

The 24/7 Work Environment

There was a time not so long ago when most employees rarely communicated after traditional work hours. That's because it wasn't convenient to do so. IT has made it possible to stay connected around the clock, seven days per week. For example, IT has significantly improved a manager's ability to monitor individual and team performance, has allowed employees to have more complete information to make faster decisions, and has provided employees more opportunities to collaborate and share information. In addition, IT has made it possible for people in organizations to be fully accessible, at any time, regardless of where they are. Employees don't have to be at their desk with their computers running to communicate with others in the organization.

Social Media

An executive vice president of sales tells his team of 100 district sales managers that they need to read the results of a survey regarding trends in consumer preferences. He posts the report on the company's HipChat channel created for information exchange about this subject. This allows the entire team to read the report and exchange their experiences. His employees can now read, comment, and exchange related articles on this same channel, much as they would on Facebook. This approach provides two important benefits. First, most employees send and receive dozens of business emails every day, and sometimes important emails get lost in crowded inboxes. Devoting a channel for information exchange about a specific topic can help compartmentalize the conversation. Second, the sales manager in this example is not only conveying important information, but he also is starting a useful conversation in which employees can share their experiences and make suggestions for creating competitive advantage.

A computer scientist sits in the Security Operations Center at the company headquarters and takes care of the cyber security of TÜV Rheinland and its customers. *Source: Oliver Berg/dpa/picture-alliance/ Newscom*

Creating a video portal—like on YouTube or Vimeo—but for internal audiences only is an excellent way for employees to stay up to date on colleagues, new products, and company messages.[21] For example, Textron has established an internal video portal. "It's our internal YouTube. It's the watering hole for employee-driven content. We use [it] for videos about product demos, to celebrate employee achievements and to highlight advice from company leaders."[22]

While social media offers exciting potential as a vehicle for internal communication in organizations, let's not overlook its downside: Social media is addictive. It can consume a considerable amount of employee time and undermine productivity. A recent survey found that nearly 90 percent of employees say they check social media at work. And nearly one in five said they checked social media ten times or more during the workday.[23] Unfortunately, most of those "checks" are undoubtedly external sites and have nothing to do with employee work responsibilities.

Finally, it may be called "social media," but another communication challenge posed by the internet age is the lack of personal interaction. Even when two people are communicating face-to-face, understanding is not always achieved. However, it can be especially challenging to achieve understanding and collaborate on getting work done when communication takes place in a virtual environment. Young people in Generation Z in particular have come to prefer texting, email, and social media to face-to-face communication.[24] This can create problems in the workplace when digital channels are used to convey messages that have an emotional component or sensitive information. There is a time and place for digital communication, but they are not a substitute for face-to-face communication when, for instance, the message is complex, sensitive in nature, requires confidentiality, or demands explicit feedback of understanding. Face-to-face also is preferred when it's important to build trusting relationships.

Cybersecurity

Sony Pictures Entertainment was the target of hackers who successfully obtained sensitive information about employee pay, financial information, and confidential communications about particular movie stars.[25] In another example, hackers penetrated the federal government's human resources database from which they obtained information about security clearances and health care records.[26] These security breaches are a reminder that computer networks are not impenetrable. Corporate computer and email systems should be protected against hackers and spam mail. These serious issues must be addressed if the benefits of communication technology are to be realized.

The list of companies that have had their computer systems "hacked" includes Target, Home Depot, eBay, and Equifax.[27] Tens of millions of customers were affected in each incident, and trust in these firms was seriously impacted. The fact that the typical data breach goes undetected for months opens organizations to huge potential damages.

Today, almost everything an organization does is transacted digitally. And much of this is sensitive information—employee information, customer data, financial records, and intellectual property. Between smartphones, the cloud, and the Internet of Things, organizations are vulnerable to hackers. This puts a premium on cybersecurity. While it's impossible to completely eliminate this risk, certain actions are a must.[28] These include using secure passwords; being suspicious of external downloads and emails; backing up data; securing Wi-Fi; and installing and renewing a complete antivirus, antispyware, and firewall package on every computer.

fyi

- Thirty-four percent of Americans say they had personal data compromised in the previous twelve months.
- Eighteen percent of Americans have had a social media account hacked.[29]

BECOMING a better communicator

LO14.5 Most managers will tell you that becoming an effective communicator is one ingredient of a successful career. They're right. You should always take the opportunity to improve your communication skills. In addition to listening skills, which we discussed earlier in the "It's Your Career" box, other important communication skills include persuasion, speaking, writing, and reading. Let's briefly look at each of these.

Sharpening Your Persuasion Skills

Successful managers demonstrate good persuasion skills. **Persuasion skills** enable a person to influence others to change their minds or behavior. Consider the following. Richard Branson, founder of conglomerate Virgin (including Virgin Mobile and Virgin Megastore), learned the value of persuasion at an early age. While attending boarding school, Branson launched his first business venture, creating Student magazine. But he recognized that he could not do so without the backing of investors. Branson successfully learned how to make five-minute pitches over the telephone and was quite successful at it: the magazine has been in business since 1968. What made his pitches successful? Branson said: "Any fool can make something complicated. It's hard to make something simple."[31]

Branson's comment is consistent with the research on persuasion.[32] Four of the most basic elements in successful persuasion include: (1) Be clear about the "who," "what," and "why"; (2) keep it simple; (3) think about the other person's needs, motivation, and interests when you shape your argument; and (4) appeal to the "head" and "heart" by combining both rational and emotional arguments.

persuasion skills
Skills that enable a person to influence others to change their minds or behavior

Sharpening Your Speaking Skills

By now, you have probably made many class presentations. An advantage of giving class presentations is the chance to develop speaking skills. **Speaking skills** refer to the ability to communicate information and ideas by talking so others will understand. One survey revealed that 70 percent of employees who make presentations say that good presentation skills are important to career success.[33] Yet discomfort with public speaking holds some employees back. About 20 percent of survey respondents revealed that they would avoid making presentations even if it meant "losing respect."[34] Fortunately, there are resources to help you overcome discomfort with public speaking, such as local Toastmasters clubs, which provide opportunities to make formal and impromptu speeches in a supportive environment.

Once you develop greater confidence to speak before others, it is necessary to understand the characteristics of effective speaking. Attending successful business professionals' presentations or watching them online is a good starting point. You will likely notice the following characteristics in effective speakers: authenticity, humility, brevity, and a clear understanding of the audience.[35] And to elaborate on brevity: No one ever complained about a speech being too short!

speaking skills
Skills that refer to the ability to communicate information and ideas by talking so others will understand

writing skills
Skills that entail communicating effectively in text that is most appropriate for its audience

The men and women of Toastmasters work to become more competent communicators, improve their listening skills, and learn the importance of speech "icebreakers" and visual aids. Here, Alberto Olvera-Ocampo presents his ice-breaker speech two weeks after joining the club.
Source: Alex T. Paschal/AP Images

Sharpening Your Writing Skills

Writing skills entail communicating effectively in text that is most appropriate for its audience. Our focus is on business or professional writing, in contrast to the informal writing that you might do in a journal, a letter to a friend, or a text message.

There are some fairly straightforward rules that can help you to write simply, clearly, and precisely.[36]

Think before you write. Focus on what you want to say BEFORE you start writing. This avoids meandering, wordiness, and repetition.

Be direct. Get to the point quickly.

Cut the fat. Eliminate unnecessary words.

Avoid jargon and grandiose language. Strive for clarity rather than to impress.

Be professional. Business memos, letters, and reports are different from emails, text messages, and social media comments. This is not the place for abbreviations, acronyms, or textspeak. This suggestion is particularly relevant for millennials, Generation Z, and those who live on their smartphones.

Sharpening Your Reading Skills

Employees receive an average of 122 work emails daily.[37] They also receive many written memos, reports, and policy statements. The sheer volume alone requires good reading skills. **Reading skills** entail an understanding of written sentences and paragraphs in work-related documents. If your reading skills aren't up to par—either in comprehension or speed—don't be afraid to sign up for a reading-improvement class.

reading skills
Skills that entail an understanding of written sentences and paragraphs in work-related documents

---

Chapter 14 — PREPARING FOR: Exams/Quizzes

CHAPTER SUMMARY by Learning Objectives

LO14.1 DEFINE the nature and function of communication.

Communication is the transfer and understanding of meaning. Interpersonal communication is communication between two or more people. Organizational communication includes all the patterns, networks, and systems of communication within an organization.

The functions of communication include managing employee behavior, motivating employees, providing a release for the emotional sharing of feelings and fulfillment of social needs, persuading, and providing information.

LO14.2 DESCRIBE the communication process.

The communication process contains seven elements. First, the communication *source* has a message. A message is a purpose to be conveyed. Encoding converts a message into symbols. A channel is the medium a message travels along. Decoding happens when the receiver retranslates a sender's message. Finally, feedback occurs.

People in organizations transfer meaning among themselves using oral, written, and nonverbal communication. Nonverbal communication is transmitted without words and includes body language and verbal intonation.

Barriers to effective communication include information overload and filtering. Emotions, language, silence, and national culture also create barriers. Feedback, simplified language, active listening, constraining emotions, and watching nonverbal cues can help overcome barriers.

LO14.3 EXPLAIN how communication can flow most effectively in organizations.

Formal communication is communication that takes place within prescribed organizational work arrangements. Informal communication is not defined by the organization's structural hierarchy. Communication in an organization can flow downward, upward, laterally, and diagonally.

The three communication networks include the chain, in which communication flows according to the formal chain of command; the wheel, in which communication flows between a clearly identifiable and strong leader and others in a work team; and the all-channel, in which communication flows freely among all members of a work team. The grapevine is the informal organizational communication network.

LO14.4 **DESCRIBE** how the internet and social media affect managerial communication and organizations.

Technology has changed the way we live and work. It has created a 24/7 work environment, as it is possible to stay connected around the clock and work from anywhere. Social media allows managers to communicate through one channel and encourages sharing experiences. While IT allows collaborative work, managers must be cautious that they do not overuse technology and impede creativity. Managers need to ensure that cybersecurity measures are put in place to protect computer networks from hackers.

LO14.5 **DISCUSS** how to become a better communicator.

You can become a better communicator through sharpening your persuasion, speaking, writing, and reading skills.

REVIEW AND DISCUSSION QUESTIONS

14-1. Define communication, interpersonal communication, and organizational communication. Why isn't effective communication synonymous with agreement?

14-2. What are the functions of communication?

14-3. Explain the elements of the communication process.

14-4. What are the various communication methods managers can use? What are the advantages and disadvantages of each method?

14-5. Contrast formal and informal communication.

14-6. Explain communication flow, the three common communication networks, and how managers should handle the grapevine.

14-7. How have the internet and social media changed organizational communication?

14-8. What are some specific steps you can take to become a better communicator?

PREPARING FOR: My Career

ETHICS DILEMMA

Forty-six percent of employees worry about being judged by coworkers for something they have posted on social media.[38]

Social networking websites can be fun. Staying in touch with old friends or family is one of the pleasures of joining. However, it can be challenging when colleagues or even

your boss want to "friend" you. Experts say that you should proceed with caution.[39]

14-9. What do you think? Is it okay to provide people you know in a professional sense a "window into your personal life"?

14-10. What ethical issues might arise in such a situation?

SKILLS EXERCISE Developing Your Presentation Skills

About the Skill
Managers make presentations for a variety of reasons. Whether you are sharing information about a new product or process, proposing a solution to a problem, training new employees, or selling a product to a customer, your

ability to effectively deliver a presentation is an essential communication skill. Your effectiveness as a speaker will often impact whether or not your presentation achieves the desired outcome. The good news is that with some planning and practice, you can become an engaging presenter.[40]

Steps in Practicing the Skill

* *Know your audience.* Consider your audience for the presentation. What do they already know about your presentation topic? What do they need to learn from the presentation? Are they interested in your topic? Understanding your audience and their needs can help you tailor your message and content.

* *Organize your content.* Start with an opening that allows you to connect with the audience. Include a story or scenario that engages the audience or use some data or other information to help them understand the problem at hand. For the body of the presentation, try to stick to three or four main points that you organize your information around. Have a clear closing to your presentation that leaves the audience with something to consider or remember.

* *Prepare compelling visuals.* Only use presentation slides to complement your presentation—don't make your visuals a distraction. Keep it simple; don't include too many words on your slides, or your audience will be reading instead of listening to you. Consider using graphics or photos that help illustrate your points.

* *Practice, practice, practice!* While it is fine to have note cards, you should not read the presentation. Rehearse so that you are comfortable with the content, but don't sound like you've just memorized it. Consider video recording yourself when you are rehearsing so you can identify where you need improvement.

* *Calm your nerves.* Everyone gets nervous before a presentation. Make sure you take some deep breaths and stand tall and confident. Preparation is the best antidote to nervousness.

* *Focus on your delivery.* Use a confident tone and watch out for the use of "nonwords" (ah, um, or like). Make eye contact and ask questions to engage the audience.

Practicing the Skill

Look for opportunities to deliver presentations. Volunteer to take the lead in class presentations, make presentations for organizations you are involved with, or ask your boss for an opportunity to present. Use the above guidelines to prepare and deliver your presentation. Your confidence will grow as you gain experience in giving presentations.

WORKING TOGETHER Team Exercise

Preparing for possible communication issues that arise can make you more effective at work. In groups of three or four, discuss (a) possible challenges that could arise during two of the steps involved in the communication process, (b) barriers that might occur, and (c) ways of overcoming those barriers for each of the following situations:

1. You are about to go into the first meeting as leader of a cross-functional team (a team that consists of one person from IT, one person from marketing, one person from accounting, and one person from the legal department).

2. You are working on a project with two other people, and there is a very tight project deadline approaching that you will need to uphold.

3. You need to lay off an employee due to a decline in sales and your company's need to reduce costs. You are responsible for telling the employee that he or she is going to be out of work in six weeks.

MY TURN TO BE A MANAGER

* For one day, keep track of the types of communication you use (e.g., face-to-face, text, phone, email, Skype/FaceTime). Which do you use most? Least? Were your choices of communication methods effective? Why or why not? Could they have been improved? How?

* For one day, track nonverbal communication that you notice in others. What types did you observe? Was the nonverbal communication always consistent with the verbal communication taking place? Describe.

* Survey five different managers for their advice on being a good communicator. Put this information in a bulleted list format and be prepared to present it in class.

* Improve your oral speaking skills by joining a Toastmasters Club (www.toastmasters.org). Toastmasters is a nonprofit organization that teaches public speaking through a network of clubs where you can practice giving speeches to an audience that provides feedback to help you improve your skills.

* Identify at least one company that effectively uses social media to communicate with customers and/or employees. What social media applications does the company use? Subscribe to the company's social media feeds and take notes regarding their social media communications for at least one week. What patterns do you see? What are social media messages that are effective based on the number of "likes" or "shares"?

* Given that email is a primary method of communication within most organizations, it is important to practice using it effectively. Research email etiquette and create a list of "dos and don'ts" for using email at work.

CASE APPLICATION 1

Communicating as the Company Grows at Hootsuite

Ryan Holmes is founder and CEO of Hootsuite, a Vancouver-based social media management platform company. Holmes realized that he needed to do more to improve communication within his company once it grew to over 1,000 employees. It wasn't possible to count on effective communication happening automatically. He couldn't even count on being able to talk with many coworkers in the hallway anymore since the company had become so large.

How did Hootsuite make changes to improve communication? The company set up a website that pairs employees from different departments to meet for a quick cup of coffee. Only employees who register to participate are involved in these "#RandomCoffee" matches.[41] These chats over coffee have resulted in ideas for how to solve problems at work, sparked new projects, and increased communication in the company outside of the formal organizational chart. In fact, Holmes implemented an idea that he heard from a #RandomCoffee match: each week, Holmes records a five- to ten-minute selfie-style video on his phone and shares it only with employees within the company. These videos give employees the chance to hear directly from the CEO. As Homes puts it, "It allows the entire company to get aligned on top priorities and hear what's important." Employees are encouraged to comment on the videos or ask questions. Sometimes there are only a few comments from employees, while other videos have resulted in hundreds of employee posts. Hootsuite also now holds virtual town hall meetings each quarter allowing employees from around the world to hear what's going on and weigh in. On top of that, Holmes is active on social media, which CEOs often avoid and delegate to others.

About every week or two, the company stops work at 4:00 p.m. and encourages everyone to socialize with each other in the company kitchens. In addition to socializing, they sometimes will have informal five-minute "Lightning Talks" offered by employees on topics that are usually not work related, such as "how to draw" or "Rubik's Cube art." Holmes says, "People stay for a few minutes or a few hours. It's casual and unstructured. But I know for a fact that employees connect who otherwise would never cross paths—opening up new lines of communication and bringing the team closer."

DISCUSSION QUESTIONS

14-11. In what ways do Hootsuite's communication techniques illustrate the functions of communication discussed in this chapter?

14-12. What barriers to effective communication could apply when Hootsuite employees experience the communication techniques described in this case?

14-13. Which of the five ways of overcoming barriers do Hootsuite's techniques do a good job of addressing? Which ways of overcoming barriers might need to be addressed further?

14-14. Which directions of communication flow (downward, upward, lateral, diagonal) are addressed with Hootsuite's techniques? Is there anything else they could do to be more comprehensive in addressing directions of communication flow?

CASE APPLICATION 2

Communication Challenge at Facebook

Joel Kaplan, Facebook's vice president for global public policy, sat two rows behind his friend Judge Brett Kavanaugh, during the September 27, 2018, Congressional hearing in which the judge testified about sexual assault allegations. This hearing was to determine Judge Kavanaugh's suitability for a place on the Supreme Court. When television cameras showed Kavanaugh, Kaplan was visible in the background.

Soon afterward, Facebook employees posted messages on the company's internal message boards expressing concerns. Some employees felt that Kaplan's presence appeared to be a show of support that appeared to be not only from Kaplan himself but also from Facebook. Their concern was that, as a top executive in the company, he represented the company when he sat in such a high-profile location during the hearing.

Kaplan apologized to Facebook staff the day of the hearing, acknowledging the pain he created but also saying he believes one should stand by his or her friends. As employee concerns kept pouring in on the company's internal message forums, Andrew Bosworth, a vice president at Facebook, wrote to employees: "If you need to change teams, companies, or careers to make sure your day-to-day life matches your passions, we will be sad to see you go, but we will understand. We will support you with any path you choose. But it is your responsibility to choose a path, not that of the company you work for."[42]

Some employees, including Facebook's head of human resources, thought Bosworth's comment appeared to dismiss employee concerns. In response, Bosworth wrote a post on the company message board: "I spoke at a time when I should be listening and that was a big mistake. I'm grateful to employees who shared feedback and very sorry that my actions caused employees pain and frustration when what they needed to hear was better support and understanding from leadership." Facebook continued to deal with the aftermath of these events with town hall meetings that included CEO Mark Zuckerberg and COO Sheryl Sandberg.

DISCUSSION QUESTIONS

14-15. Which of the communication networks (chain, wheel, or all-channel) was involved when workers posted concerns on Facebook's internal message boards?

14-16. In what ways was Kaplan's appearance at the congressional hearing a form of nonverbal communication?

14-17. How do you think the grapevine might have played a role in employees' reactions to Kaplan's appearance at the congressional hearing? How could the grapevine have been involved in employees' response to Bosworth's post on Facebook's internal message board?

14-18. How could Bosworth have responded more effectively to employees' concerns about Kaplan's appearance?

ENDNOTES

1. A. Moran, "Top 10 Times Miscommunication Ended in Disaster," *Career Addict*, November 6, 2014, https://www.careeraddict.com/top-10-times-miscommunication-ended-in-disaster; P. Smith, "How a Tiny Spanish Island Became the Setting for the Deadliest Plane Crash Ever," *Business Insider*, March 27, 2017, https://www.businessinsider.com/deadliest-plane-crash-history-pan-am-klm-tenerife-2017-3.

2. C. O. Kursh, "The Benefits of Poor Communication," *Psychoanalytic Review* (Summer–Fall 1971): pp. 189–208.

3. M. S. Poole, "Communication," in S. Zedeck, ed., *Handbook of Industrial and Organizational Psychology*, vol. 3 (Washington, DC: APA Books, 2010), pp. 248–70.

4. D. K. Berlo, *The Process of Communication* (New York: Holt, Rinehart & Winston, 1960), pp. 30–32.

5. C. K. Goman, "5 Body Language Tips to Increase Your Curb Appeal," *Forbes*, March 4, 2013, https://www.forbes.com/sites/carolkinseygoman/2013/03/14/5-body-language-tips-to-increase-your-curb-appeal/#7469362e6f6a.

6. A. Metallinou, A. Katsamanis, and S. Narayanan, "Tracking Continuous Emotional Trends of Participants During Affective Dyadic Interactions Using Body Language and Speech Information," *Image and Vision Computing* (February 2013): pp. 137–52.

7. J. Smith, "10 Nonverbal Cues That Convey Confidence," *Forbes*, March 11, 2013, https://www.forbes.com/sites/jacquelynsmith/2013/03/11/10-nonverbal-cues-that-convey-confidence-at-work/#37ab9fd25e13.

8. Cited in "How to Beat Email Overload in 2018," *IORG* (blog), January 16, 2018, https://iorgforum.org/blog-post/how-to-beat-email-overload-in-2018/.

9. E. W. Morrison and F. J. Milliken, "Organizational Silence: A Barrier to Change and Development in a Pluralistic World," *Academy of Management Review* (October 2000): pp. 706–25.

10. H. P. Madrid, M. G. Patterson, and P. I. Leiva, "Negative Core Affect and Employee Silence: How Differences in Activation, Cognitive Rumination, and Problem-Solving Demands Matter," *Journal of Applied Psychology* (November 2015): 1887–98; and C. Kiewitz, S. D. Restubog, M. K. Shoss, P. M. Garcia, and R. L. Tang, "Suffering in Silence: Investigating the Role of Fear in the Relationship between Abusive Supervision and Defensive Silence," *Journal of Applied Psychology* (September 2016): pp. 731–42.

11. E. Mesedahl, "Cultural Differences in Communication Styles," *International Association of Business Communicators (Boston)*, April 3, 2016, http://boston.iabc.com/2016/04/03/cultural-differences-in-communication-styles/.

12. See, for instance, S. P. Robbins and P. L. Hunsaker, Training in Interpersonal Skills, 5th ed. (Upper Saddle River, NJ: Prentice Hall, 2009), pp. 88–106.

13. Based on R. Bhattacharyya, "5 Ways to Deal with an Absentee Boss," *Economic Times*, January 16, 2015, https://economictimes.indiatimes.com/slideshows/work-career/5-ways-to-deal-with-an-absentee-boss/1-get-organised/slideshow/45905429.cms; and S. Stibitz, "Get What You Need from Your Hands-off Boss," *Harvard Business Review*, June 12, 2015, https://hbr.org/2015/06/get-what-you-need-from-your-hands-off-boss.

14. "Can We Chat? Instant Messaging Apps Invade the Workplace," *ReportLinker*, June 8, 2017, https://www.reportlinker.com/insight/instant-messaging-apps-invade-workplace.html.

15. Cited in "Shut Up and Listen," *Money*, November 2005, p. 27.

16. T. J. Grosser, V. Lopez-Kidwell, G. Labianca, and L. Ellwardt, "Hearing It Through the Grapevine: Positive and Negative Workplace Gossip," *Organizational Dynamics* (January-March 2012): pp. 52–61.

17. See, for instance, L. Potter, "Social Media, the New Grapevine of Employee Communication, Comes with Responsibility," *More with Les* (blog), January 24, 2013, https://lespotter001.wordpress.com/2013/01/24/social-media-the-new-grapevine-of-employee-communication-comes-with-responsibilities/; and P. Banerjee and S. Singh, "Managers' Perspectives on the Effects of Online Grapevine Communication: A Qualitative Inquiry," *Qualitative Report* (June 8, 2015): pp. 765–79.

18. Potter, "Social Media, the New Grapevine."

19. Based on C. Gallo, "Two Misleading Words Triggered GM's Catastrophic Communication Breakdown," *Forbes*, June 9, 2014, https://www.forbes.com/sites/carminegallo/2014/06/09/two-misleading-words-triggered-gms-catastrophic-communication-breakdown/#5d3a09f65ca0; and P. Hiebert, "General Motors Is Making More Than a Comeback," *YouGov*, October 11, 2017, https://today.

yougov.com/topics/automotive/articles-reports/2017/10/11/general-motors-record-high-consumer-perception.

20. "Share of Workers in the United States Who Check Their Work E-Mails Outside of Normal Work Hours, by Frequency," *Statista*, June 2018, https://www.statista.com.

21. See, for instance, C. Kent, "How YouTube-Like Channels Can Boost Your Internal Communication," *Ragan*, July 7, 2015, https://www.ragan.com/how-youtube-like-channels-can-boost-your-internal-communication/; S. Clayton, "Change Management Meets Social Media," *Harvard Business Review*, November 10, 2015, https://hbr.org/2015/11/change-management-meets-social-media; and A. Parrellla-Aureli, "Internal Communications Balancing Old Methods with Millennial Generation," *Workforce*, July 10, 2017, https://www.workforce.com/2017/07/10/internal-communications-balancing-old-methods-millennial-generation/.

22. C. Kent, "How YouTube-like Channels Can Boost Your Internal Communication.", www.ragan.com, Ragan Communications, Inc, July 7, 2015

23. Cited in O. Perkins, "Are You Digitally Distracted at Work?" *Cleveland Plain Dealer*, April 2, 2017, p. F1. See also S. Kim, "Managing Millennials' Personal Use of Technology at Work," *Business Horizons* (March–April 2018): pp. 261–70.

24. A. J. Agrawal, "Millennials Are Struggling with Face to Face Communication: Here's Why," *Forbes*, May 4, 2017, https://www.forbes.com/sites/ajagrawal/2017/05/04/millennials-are-struggling-with-face-to-face-communication-heres-why/#69d2176926e8.

25. C. Kang, C. Timberg, and E. Nakashima, "Sony's Hacked E-Mails Expose Spats, Director Calling Angelina Jolie a 'Brat,'" *Washington Post*, December 11, 2014, https://www.washingtonpost.com/business/economy/sonys-hacked-e-mails-expose-spats-director-calling-angelina-jolie-a-brat/2014/12/10/a799e8a0-809c-11e4-8882-03cf08410beb_story.html.

26. J. Sciutto, "OPM Government Data Breach Impacted 21.5 Million," *CNN*, July 10, 2015, https://www.cnn.com/2015/07/09/politics/office-of-personnel-management-data-breach-20-million/index.html.

27. T. Armerding, "The 17 Biggest Data Breaches of the 21st Century," *CSO Online*, January 26, 2018, https://www.csoonline.com/.

28. A. Boone, "Cyber-Security Must Be a C-Suite Priority," *Computer Fraud & Security* (February 2017): pp. 13–15; and "Ten Best Practices for Internet Security," *Verizon*, https://www.verizon.com/business/resources/ten-best-practices-for-internet-security/.

29. BusinessWire, "First Data Releases Cybersecurity Study on Personally Identifiable Information," October 17, 2018, https://www.businesswire.com/news/home/20181017005273/en/Data-Releases-Cybersecurity-Study-Personally-Identifiable-Information.

30. "2018 Workplace Learning Report," *LinkedIn Learning*, https://learning.linkedin.com/resources/workplace-learning-report-2018?trk=lilblog_02-27-18_WLR-2018-launch-blog_tl&cid=70132000001AyziAAC#.

31. C. Gallo, "Branson, Buffett Agree: This Skill Is Your Ticket to Career Success," *Forbes*, February 18, 2016, https://www.forbes.com/sites/carminegallo/2016/02/18/branson-buffett-agree-this-skill-is-your-ticket-to-career-success/.

32. T. Manning, "The Art of Successful Persuasion: Seven Skills You Need to Get Your Point Across Effectively," *Industrial and Commercial Training* (April 2012): pp. 150–58. See also R. B. Cialdini, *Influence: The Psychology of Persuasion*, rev. ed. (New York: Harper Business, 2007).

33. C. Gallo, "New Survey: 70% Say Presentation Skills Are Critical for Career Success," *Forbes*, September 25, 2014, https://www.forbes.com/sites/carminegallo/2014/09/25/new-survey-70-percent-say-presentation-skills-critical-for-career-success/#77cdef5a8890.

34. Ibid.

35. R. Bradley, "Why Public Speaking Is Linked to Being Successful," *HuffPost*, October 12, 2015, https://www.huffpost.com/entry/why-public-speaking-is-li_b_8281006?utm_hp_ref=tony-robbins.

36. C. O'Hara, "How to Improve Your Business Writing," *Harvard Business Review*, November 20, 2014, https://hbr.org/2014/11/how-to-improve-your-business-writing.

37. T. Tablyn, "We Are Beginning to Feel Crushed by the Number of Work Emails We Get," *HuffPost* (UK edition), March 23, 2016, https://www.huffingtonpost.co.uk/.

38. D. Weppler, "The State of Social Media in the Workplace 2018," *Igloo* (blog), May 2, 2018, https://www.igloosoftware.com/blog/infographic-the-state-of-social-media-in-the-workplace/.

39. N. Swanner, "Should You Connect with Colleagues on Social Media?," *Dice*, June 1, 2018, https://insights.dice.com/2018/06/01/social-media-connect-coworkers/.

40. S. Kessler, "How to Improve Your Presentation Skills," *Inc. Magazine*, February 22, 2010, https://www.inc.com/guides/how-to-improve-your-presentation-skills.html; and C. Anderson, "How to Give a Killer Presentation," *Harvard Business Review*, June 2013, https://hbr.org/2013/06/how-to-give-a-killer-presentation.

41. R. Holmes, "Communication Breakdown at Work? These 5 Hacks Transformed Our 1,000-Person Company," *Forbes*, January 18, 2018, https://www.forbes.com/sites/ryanholmes/2018/01/18/communication-breakdown-at-work-these-5-hacks-transformed-our-1000-person-company/.

42. M. Isaac, "Rifts Break Open at Facebook Over Kavanaugh Hearing," *New York Times*, October 4, 2018, https://www.nytimes.com/2018/10/04/technology/facebook-kavanaugh-nomination-kaplan.html.

Chapter 15

Understanding and Managing Individual Behavior

Employability Skills Matrix

This matrix identifies which features and end-of-chapter material will help you develop specific skills employers are looking for in job candidates.

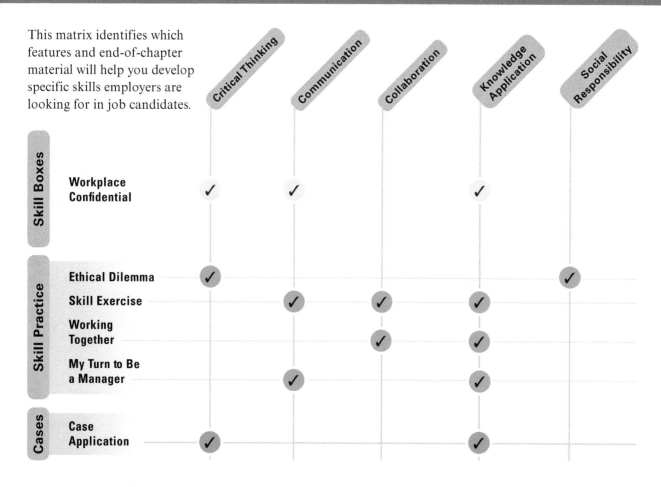

		Critical Thinking	Communication	Collaboration	Knowledge Application	Social Responsibility
Skill Boxes	Workplace Confidential	✓	✓		✓	
Skill Practice	Ethical Dilemma	✓				✓
	Skill Exercise		✓	✓	✓	
	Working Together			✓	✓	
	My Turn to Be a Manager		✓		✓	
Cases	Case Application	✓			✓	

Do you want to get a job as a business analyst at Southwest Airlines? The qualifications look like what you might expect for a similar job at Microsoft or Goldman Sachs—good verbal skills, MBA preferred, relevant experience. But Southwest additionally puts an overriding emphasis on attitude and personality.[1] The company believes its success is largely due to its hiring happy, cheerful, and engaged people who will fit in with their "fun" culture. Southwest's management hires with the view that skills can be learned but personality can't.

In this chapter, we look at employee behavior—specifically, attitudes, personality, perception, and learning. As we'll show, managers need to understand employee behavior for the insights it provides in hiring decisions, motivating staff, choosing leadership behaviors, and retaining high-performing employees.

FOCUS and goals of organizational behavior

LO15.1 The material in this and the next two chapters draws heavily on the field of study that's known as *organizational behavior (OB)*. Although it's concerned with the subject of **behavior**—that is, the actions of people—**organizational behavior** is considered more specifically with the actions of people at work.[2]

One of the challenges to understanding organizational behavior is that it addresses a number of issues that aren't obvious. Like an iceberg, a lot of organizational behavior is not visible to the naked eye. (See Exhibit 15-1.) What we tend to see when we look at organizations are their formal aspects—strategies, objectives, policies and procedures, structures, technologies, formal authority relationships, and chains of command. But just under the surface there lie a number of informal elements that managers need to understand. As we'll show, OB provides managers with considerable insights into these important, but hidden, aspects of the organization.

behavior
The actions of people

organizational behavior (OB)
The study of the actions of people at work

Focus of Organizational Behavior

Organizational behavior focuses primarily on two major areas. First, OB looks at *individual behavior*. Based predominantly on contributions from psychologists, this area includes such topics as attitudes, personality, perception, learning, and motivation. Second, OB is concerned with *group behavior*, which includes norms, roles, team building, leadership, and conflict. Our knowledge about groups comes basically

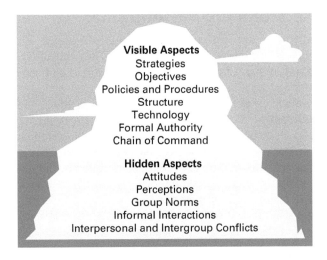

Exhibit 15-1
The "Organization as an Iceberg" Metaphor

Visible Aspects
Strategies
Objectives
Policies and Procedures
Structure
Technology
Formal Authority
Chain of Command

Hidden Aspects
Attitudes
Perceptions
Group Norms
Informal Interactions
Interpersonal and Intergroup Conflicts

Isaac Owens, a 6-year employee at Cincinnati's Coffee Emporium, enjoys a positive work environment that contributes to increased employee satisfaction and productivity.
Source: John Minchillo/AP Images

employee productivity
A performance measure of both efficiency and effectiveness

absenteeism
The failure to show up for work

turnover
The voluntary and involuntary permanent withdrawal from an organization

organizational citizenship behavior (OCB)
Discretionary behavior that is not part of an employee's formal job requirements, but which promotes the effective functioning of the organization

job satisfaction
An employee's general attitude toward his or her job

counterproductive workplace behavior
Any intentional employee behavior that is potentially damaging to the organization or to individuals within the organization

attitudes
Evaluative statements, either favorable or unfavorable, concerning objects, people, or events

cognitive component
That part of an attitude that's made up of the beliefs, opinions, knowledge, or information held by a person

affective component
That part of an attitude that's the emotional or feeling part

behavioral component
That part of an attitude that refers to an intention to behave in a certain way toward someone or something

from the work of sociologists and social psychologists. We've addressed group behavior previously. In this chapter, we'll look at individual behavior.

Goals of Organizational Behavior

The goals of OB are to *explain, predict,* and *influence* behavior. Managers need to be able to *explain* why employees engage in some behaviors rather than others, *predict* how employees will respond to various actions and decisions, and *influence* how employees behave.

What employee behaviors are we specifically concerned with explaining, predicting, and influencing? We'll focus on six: employee productivity, absenteeism, turnover, organizational citizenship behavior, job satisfaction, and counterproductive workplace behavior.

Employee productivity is a performance measure of both efficiency and effectiveness. **Absenteeism** is the failure to show up for work. It's been estimated that unscheduled absenteeism costs US employers $3,600 a year for each hourly worker and $2,650 for each salaried worker.[3] **Turnover** is the voluntary and involuntary permanent withdrawal from an organization. It can be a problem because of increased recruiting, selection, and training costs and work disruptions. And it's costly to companies—ranging from 16 percent of an unskilled worker's pay to 213 percent of a highly trained employee.[4] **Organizational citizenship behavior (OCB)** is discretionary behavior that's not part of an employee's formal job requirements but promotes the effective functioning of the organization.[5] Examples of good OCBs include helping others on one's work team, volunteering for extended job activities, avoiding unnecessary conflicts, and making constructive statements about one's work group and the organization. **Job satisfaction** refers to an employee's general attitude toward his or her job. Although job satisfaction is an attitude rather than a behavior, it's an outcome that concerns many managers because satisfied employees are more likely to show up for work, have higher levels of performance, and stay with an organization. Finally, **counterproductive workplace behavior** is any intentional employee behavior that is potentially harmful to the organization or individuals within the organization. Counterproductive workplace behavior shows up in organizations in four ways: deviance, aggression, antisocial behavior, and violence.[6] In the following sections, we'll address how an understanding of four psychological factors—employee attitudes, personality, perception, and learning—can help us explain, predict, and influence these employee behaviors.

ATTITUDES **and job performance**

LO15.2 **Attitudes** are evaluative statements—favorable or unfavorable—concerning objects, people, or events. They reflect how an individual feels about something. When a person says, "I like my job," he or she is expressing an attitude about work.

An attitude is made up of three components: cognition, affect, and behavior.[8] The **cognitive component** of an attitude refers to the beliefs, opinions, knowledge, or information held by a person (for instance, the belief that "discrimination is wrong"). The **affective component** of an attitude is the emotional or feeling part of an attitude. Using our example, this component would be reflected by the statement, "I don't like Pat because he discriminates against minorities." Finally, affect can lead to behavioral outcomes. The **behavioral component** of an attitude refers to an intention to behave in a certain way toward someone or something. To continue our example, I might choose to avoid Pat because of my feelings about him. Understanding that attitudes are made up of three components helps show their complexity. But the term *attitude* usually refers only to the affective component.

Naturally, managers aren't interested in every attitude an employee has. They're especially interested in job-related attitudes. The four most relevant to managers are job satisfaction, job involvement, organizational commitment, and employee engagement.

Job Satisfaction

As we know from our earlier definition, job satisfaction refers to a person's general attitude toward his or her job. A person with a high level of job satisfaction has a positive attitude toward his or her job. A person who is dissatisfied has a negative attitude. When people generally speak of employee attitudes, they usually are referring to job satisfaction.[9]

HOW SATISFIED ARE EMPLOYEES?   Job satisfaction levels, for the most part, tend to be rather consistent over time. For instance, US average job satisfaction levels were consistently in the 60 percent range from 1972 to 2006.[10] They did drop into the low 40s in 2010, which is generally attributable to the Great Recession.[11] By 2017, the number was 51 percent.[12]

Maybe not surprisingly, employee satisfaction is influenced by income.[13] Nearly 58 percent of individuals with a total household income above $75,000 reported feeling satisfied at work. Only 45 percent of those with income levels below $75,000 were similarly satisfied. Even though it's possible that higher pay translates into higher job satisfaction, an alternative explanation for the difference in satisfaction levels is that higher pay reflects different types of jobs. Higher-paying jobs generally require more advanced skills, give jobholders greater responsibilities, are more stimulating and provide more challenges, and allow workers more control. It's more likely that the reports of higher satisfaction among higher-income levels reflect those factors rather than the pay itself.

Finally, there are some cultural differences in job satisfaction.[14] On a six-point "job satisfaction scale," Mexico scored highest at 5.88, Scandinavian countries ranged from 5.51 to 5.72, and the US scored 5.46, while the lowest ratings went to France and South Korea at 4.89 and 4.76, respectively. Whether these differences among countries is due to the quality of the jobs or inherent cultural outlooks is unclear.

SATISFACTION AND PERFORMANCE   After the Hawthorne Studies (discussed in the Management History Module), managers believed that happy workers were productive workers. Because it wasn't easy to determine whether job satisfaction caused job performance or vice versa, some management researchers questioned that belief. However, additional research has helped clarify the relationship. We can say with some certainty that the correlation between satisfaction and performance is quite robust.[15] Individuals with higher job satisfaction perform better, and organizations with more satisfied employees tend to be more effective than those with fewer.

SATISFACTION AND ABSENTEEISM   Although research shows that satisfied employees have lower levels of absenteeism than dissatisfied employees, the relationship is moderate to weak.[16] Generally, when numerous alternative jobs are available, dissatisfied employees have high absence rates, but when there are few alternatives, dissatisfied have the same (low) rate of absence as satisfied employees.[17] And organizations that provide liberal sick leave benefits are encouraging all their employees—including those who are highly satisfied—to take days off. You can find work satisfying and yet still want to enjoy a three-day weekend if those days come free with no penalties.

SATISFACTION AND TURNOVER   The relationship between job satisfaction and turnover is stronger than that between satisfaction and absenteeism.[18] Overall, a pattern of lowered job satisfaction is the best predictor of intent to leave. Turnover also has a workplace environment connection. If the climate within an employee's immediate workplace is one of low job satisfaction leading to turnover, there will be a contagion effect. This suggests that managers consider the job satisfaction (and turnover) patterns of coworkers when assigning workers to a new area.[19]

Additionally, factors such as labor-market conditions, expectations about alternative job opportunities, and length of employment with the organization can affect an employee's decision to leave.[20] Research suggests that the level of satisfaction is less important in predicting turnover for superior performers because the organization typically does everything it can to keep them—pay raises, praise, increased promotion opportunities, and the like.[21]

A customer at Macy's values the exceptional service she receives from an associate at the store. Good service is critical for the success of the business and contributes greatly to customer satisfaction, ultimately helping to reduce employee turnover.
Source: Tomas Ovalle/AP Images for Macy's/AP Images

JOB SATISFACTION AND CUSTOMER SATISFACTION Is job satisfaction related to positive customer outcomes? For frontline employees who have regular contact with customers, the answer is "yes." Satisfied employees increase customer satisfaction and loyalty.[22] Why? In service organizations, customer retention and defection are highly dependent on how frontline employees deal with customers. Satisfied employees are more likely to be friendly, upbeat, and responsive, which customers appreciate. And because satisfied employees are less likely to leave their jobs, customers are more likely to encounter familiar faces and receive experienced service. These qualities help build customer satisfaction and loyalty.

JOB SATISFACTION AND OCB It seems logical to assume that job satisfaction should be a major determinant of an employee's organizational citizenship behavior.[23] Satisfied employees would seem more likely to talk positively about the organization, help others, and go above and beyond normal job expectations. Evidence suggests job satisfaction *is* moderately correlated with OCB; that is, people who are more satisfied with their jobs are more likely to engage in citizenship behavior.[24]

Why does job satisfaction lead to OCB? One reason is trust. Research in eighteen countries suggests that managers reciprocate employees' OCB with trusting behaviors of their own.[25] Individuals who feel that their coworkers support them are also more likely to engage in helpful behaviors than those who have antagonistic coworker relationships.[26]

JOB SATISFACTION AND COUNTERPRODUCTIVE BEHAVIOR When employees are dissatisfied with their jobs, they are likely to engage in counterproductive behaviors such as stealing, undue socializing, gossiping, absenteeism, and tardiness.[27] The problem comes from the difficulty in predicting *how* they'll respond. One person might quit. Another might respond by using work time to play computer games. And another might verbally abuse a coworker. If managers want to control the undesirable consequences of job dissatisfaction, they'd be better off attacking the problem—job dissatisfaction—than trying to control the different employee responses. A good start is understanding the source of dissatisfaction. For instance, does the employee feel that she was treated unfairly by her supervisor, or is she upset because a new company policy requires that employees pay for their uniforms? Or, does the employee feel slighted by the coworker who doesn't pull his weight?

Three other job-related attitudes we need to look at include job involvement, organizational commitment, and employee engagement.

Job Involvement and Organizational Commitment

job involvement
The degree to which an employee identifies with his or her job, actively participates in it, and considers his or her job performance to be important to self-worth

Job involvement is the degree to which an employee identifies with his or her job, actively participates in it, and considers his or her job performance to be important to his or her self-worth.[28] Employees with a high level of job involvement strongly identify with and really care about the kind of work they do. Their positive attitude leads them to contribute in positive ways to their work. High levels of job involvement have been found to be related to fewer absences, lower resignation rates, and higher employee engagement with their work.[29]

Organizational commitment is the degree to which an employee identifies with a particular organization and its goals and wishes to maintain membership in that organization.[30] Whereas job involvement is identifying with your job, organizational commitment is identifying with your employing organization. Research suggests that organizational commitment also leads to lower levels of both absenteeism and turnover and, in fact, is a better indicator of turnover than job satisfaction.[31] Why? Probably because it's a more global and enduring response to the organization than satisfaction with a particular job.[32] However, organizational commitment is less important as a work-related attitude than it once was. Employees today don't generally stay with a single organization for most of their career, and the relationship they have with their employer has changed considerably.[33] Although the commitment of *an employee to an organization* may not be as important as it once was, research about **perceived organizational support**—employees' general belief that their organization values their contribution and cares about their well-being—shows that the commitment of *the organization to the employee* can be beneficial. High levels of perceived organizational support lead to increased job satisfaction and lower turnover.[34]

organizational commitment
The degree to which an employee identifies with a particular organization and its goals and wishes to maintain membership in that organization

perceived organizational support
Employees' general belief that their organization values their contribution and cares about their well-being

Employee Engagement

Employee engagement is an employee's involvement with, satisfaction with, and enthusiasm for the work he or she does. To evaluate engagement, we might ask employees whether they have access to resources and opportunities to learn new skills, whether they feel their work is important and meaningful, and whether interactions with coworkers and supervisors are rewarding.[35] Highly engaged employees are passionate about and deeply connected to their work, and disengaged employees have essentially "checked out" and don't care. They show up for work, but have no energy or passion for it.

A number of benefits come from having highly engaged employees. First, highly engaged employees are two-and-a-half times more likely to be top performers than their less-engaged coworkers. In addition, companies with highly engaged employees have higher retention rates, which help keep recruiting and training costs low. And both of these outcomes—higher performance and lower costs—contribute to superior financial performance.[36] Managers have a lot of work to do to reap these benefits. Worldwide, only 13 percent of employees describe themselves as engaged.[37] The news is only somewhat better in the United States, where 32 percent of employees are engaged.

employee engagement
When employees are connected to, satisfied with, and enthusiastic about their jobs

Employee engagement is high at Apple, where employees are excited to be part of the growth of the company. Shown here employees applaud at the preview of a new Apple Store inside the Carnegie Library.
Source: Patrick Semansky/AP Images

Attitudes and Consistency

Have you ever noticed that people change what they say so it doesn't contradict what they do? Perhaps a friend of yours has repeatedly said that she thinks joining a sorority is an important part of college life. But then she goes through rush and doesn't get accepted. All of a sudden, she's saying that sorority life isn't all that great.

Research has generally concluded that people seek consistency among their attitudes *and* between their attitudes and behavior.[38] This tendency means that individuals try to reconcile differing attitudes and align their attitudes and behavior so they appear rational and consistent. When they encounter an inconsistency, individuals will do something to make it consistent by altering the attitudes, altering the behavior, or rationalizing the inconsistency.

As a fictional example: a campus recruiter for Enterprise Rent-A-Car who visits college campuses and sells students on the advantages of Enterprise as a good place to work would experience inconsistency if he personally believed that Enterprise had poor working conditions and few opportunities for promotion. This recruiter could, over time, find his attitudes toward Enterprise becoming more positive. He might actually convince himself by continually articulating the merits of working for the company. Another alternative is that the recruiter could become openly negative about Enterprise and the opportunities within the company for prospective applicants. The original enthusiasm the recruiter might have had would dwindle and might be replaced by outright cynicism toward the company. Finally, the recruiter might acknowledge that Enterprise is an undesirable place to work but, as a professional, realize that his obligation is to present the positive aspects of working for the company. He might further rationalize that no workplace is perfect and that his job is to present a favorable picture of the company, not to present both sides.

Cognitive Dissonance Theory

Can we assume from this consistency principle that an individual's behavior can always be predicted if we know his or her attitude on a subject? The answer isn't a simple "yes" or "no." Why? Cognitive dissonance theory.

Cognitive dissonance theory sought to explain the relationship between attitudes and behavior.[39] **Cognitive dissonance** is any incompatibility or inconsistency between attitudes or between behavior and attitudes. The theory argued that inconsistency is uncomfortable and that individuals will try to reduce the discomfort and, thus, the dissonance.

Of course, no one can avoid dissonance. You know you should floss your teeth every day but don't do it. There's an inconsistency between attitude and behavior. How do people cope with cognitive dissonance? The theory proposes that how hard we'll try to reduce dissonance is determined by three things: (1) the *importance* of the factors creating the dissonance, (2) the degree of *influence* the individual believes he or she has over those factors, and (3) the *rewards* that may be involved in dissonance.

If the factors creating the dissonance are relatively unimportant, the pressure to correct the inconsistency will be low. However, if those factors are important, individuals may change their behavior, conclude that the dissonant behavior isn't so important, change their attitude, or identify compatible factors that outweigh the dissonant ones.

How much influence individuals believe they have over the factors also affects their reaction to the dissonance. If they perceive the dissonance is something about which they have no choice, they won't be receptive to attitude change or feel a need to be. If, for example, the dissonance-producing behavior was required as a result of a manager's order, the pressure to reduce dissonance would be less than if the behavior had been performed voluntarily. Although dissonance exists, it can be rationalized and justified by the need to follow the manager's orders—that is, the person had no choice or control.

Finally, rewards also influence the degree to which individuals are motivated to reduce dissonance. Coupling high dissonance with high rewards tends to reduce the discomfort by motivating the individual to believe that consistency exists.

Attitude Surveys

Many organizations regularly survey their employees about their attitudes.[40] Exhibit 15-2 shows an example of an actual attitude survey. Typically, **attitude surveys** present employees with a set of statements or questions eliciting how they feel about their jobs, work groups, supervisors, or the organization. Ideally, the items will be designed to obtain the specific information that managers desire. An attitude score is achieved by summing up responses to individual questionnaire items. These scores can then be averaged for work groups, departments, divisions, or the organization as a whole. For instance, Ford Motor Company came up with an "Employee Satisfaction Index" to measure employee attitudes. Each year, the company measures employee satisfaction with company-offered training and their satisfaction with the recognition they receive for doing a good job. Managers use the results to develop action plans for improvement and for evaluating the success of previously implemented plans.[42]

Regularly surveying employee attitudes provides managers with valuable feedback on how employees perceive their working conditions. Policies and practices that managers view as objective and fair may not be seen that way by employees. The use of regular attitude surveys can alert

cognitive dissonance
Any incompatibility or inconsistency between attitudes or between behavior and attitudes

attitude surveys
Surveys that elicit responses from employees through questions about how they feel about their jobs, work groups, supervisors, or the organization

Satisfied employees have lower rates of turnover and absenteeism, and also perform better on the job. One way to tap satisfaction is through having employees complete attitude surveys.
Source: Chinnapong/Alamy Stock Photo

Exhibit 15-2

Sample Employee Attitude Survey

managers to potential problems and employees' intentions early so that action can be taken to prevent repercussions.

Implications for Managers

Managers should be interested in their employees' attitudes because they influence behavior. Satisfied and committed employees, for instance, have lower rates of turnover and absenteeism. If managers want to keep resignations and absences down—especially among their more productive employees—they'll want to do things that generate positive job attitudes.

Satisfied employees also perform better on the job. So managers should focus on those factors that have been shown to be conducive to high levels of employee job satisfaction: making work challenging and interesting, providing equitable rewards, creating supportive working conditions, and encouraging supportive colleagues.[43] These factors are likely to help employees be more productive.

Managers should also survey employees about their attitudes. As one study put it: "A sound measurement of overall job attitude is one of the most useful pieces of information an organization can have about its employees."[44]

Finally, managers should know that employees will try to reduce dissonance. If employees are required to do things that appear inconsistent to them or that are at odds with their attitudes, managers should remember that pressure to reduce the dissonance is not as strong when the employee perceives that the dissonance is externally imposed and uncontrollable. It's also decreased if rewards are significant enough to offset the dissonance. So the manager might point to external forces such as competitors, customers, or other factors when explaining the need to perform some work that the individual may have some dissonance about. Or the manager can provide rewards that an individual desires.

PERSONALITY

LO15.3

Some people are quiet and passive, while others are loud and aggressive. When we describe people using terms such as quiet, passive, loud, aggressive, ambitious, extroverted, loyal, tense, or sociable, we're describing their personalities. An individual's **personality** is the combination of emotional, thought, and behavioral patterns that affect how a person reacts to situations and interacts with others.

We're interested in looking at personality because, just like attitudes, it, too, affects how and why people behave the way they do. Over the years, researchers have attempted to identify those traits that best describe personality. The two most well-known approaches are the Myers-Briggs Type Indicator® (MBTI®) and the Big Five Model. In addition, other frameworks, such as the Dark Triad, explain certain aspects. We discuss each below, but let's begin with the dominant frameworks.

personality
The unique combination of emotional, thought, and behavioral patterns that affect how a person reacts to situations and interacts with others

MBTI®

The **Myers-Briggs Type Indicator® (MBTI®)** is one of the most widely used personality assessment instruments in the world.[45] This 100-question assessment asks people how they usually act or feel in different situations. On the basis of their answers,

Myers-Briggs Type Indicator (MBTI)
A personality assessment instrument that classifies people in four categories

individuals are classified as exhibiting a preference in four categories: extraversion or introversion (E or I), sensing or intuition (S or N), thinking or feeling (T or F), and judging or perceiving (J or P). These terms are defined as follows:

- *Extraversion (E) versus Introversion (I).* Individuals showing a preference for extraversion are outgoing, social, and assertive. They need a work environment that's varied and action oriented, that lets them be with others, and that gives them a variety of experiences. Individuals showing a preference for introversion are quiet and shy. They focus on understanding and prefer a work environment that is quiet and concentrated, that lets them be alone, and that gives them a chance to explore in depth a limited set of experiences.

- *Sensing (S) versus Intuition (N).* Sensing types are practical and prefer routine and order. They dislike new problems unless there are standard ways to solve them, have a high need for closure, show patience with routine details, and tend to be good at precise work. On the other hand, intuition types rely on unconscious processes and look at the "big picture." They're individuals who like solving new problems, dislike doing the same thing over and over again, jump to conclusions, are impatient with routine details, and dislike taking time for precision.

- *Thinking (T) versus Feeling (F).* Thinking types use reason and logic to handle problems. They're unemotional and uninterested in people's feelings, like analysis and putting things into logical order, are able to reprimand people and fire them when necessary, may seem hard-hearted, and tend to relate well only to other thinking types. Feeling types rely on their personal values and emotions. They're aware of other people and their feelings, like harmony, need occasional praise, dislike telling people unpleasant things, tend to be sympathetic, and relate well to most people.

- *Judging (J) versus Perceiving (P).* Judging types want control and prefer their world to be ordered and structured. They're good planners, decisive, purposeful, and exacting. They focus on completing a task, make decisions quickly, and want only the information necessary to get a task done. Perceiving types are flexible and spontaneous. They're curious, adaptable, and tolerant. They focus on starting a task, postpone decisions, and want to find out all about the task before starting it.

Combining these preferences provides descriptions of sixteen personality types, with every person identified with one of the items in each of the four pairs. Exhibit 15-3 summarizes two of them. As you can see from these descriptions, each personality type would approach work and relationships differently—neither one better than the other, just different.

The MBTI® is used in a variety of organizational settings. It is taken by over 2.5 million people each year, and more than 80 percent of the *Fortune* 100 companies use personality tests like the MBTI® to help build effective work teams.[47] For instance, a spokesperson for General Motors said that the company has been using Myers-Briggs for thirty years. And a spokesperson for Procter & Gamble said that thousands of its staff "have benefited, and are still benefiting" from taking the test.[48] In spite of its popularity, evidence is mixed about the MBTI®'s validity, with most of

Exhibit 15-3

Examples of MBTI® Personality Types

Type	Description
I–S–F–P (introversion, sensing, feeling, perceiving)	Sensitive, kind, modest, shy, and quietly friendly. Such people strongly dislike disagreements and will avoid them. They are loyal followers and quite often are relaxed about getting things done.
E–N–T–J (extraversion, intuition, thinking, judging)	Warm, friendly, candid, and decisive; also skilled in anything that requires reasoning and intelligent talk, but may sometimes overestimate what they are capable of doing.

Source: Based on I. Briggs-Myers, *Introduction to Type* (Palo Alto, CA: Consulting Psychologists Press, 1980), pp. 7–8.

Let's Get REAL

Jennifer King is excited that her company has decided to use the Myers-Briggs Type Indicator® (MBTI®) to help her manage her employees. She manages a team of creative professionals at an advertising agency. The team must work together on a variety of projects creating advertising campaigns for their clients. Her entire staff has taken the MBTI®, and she has learned a lot about her employees. However, now she is not sure what to do with this information.

How can Jennifer use the MBTI® results to improve the performance of her staff?

Jennifer could facilitate a discussion with her team (or find an experienced facilitator) to share and dissect each team member's results. She could also find ways to post the team's result near each of their work stations and/or create a one-page summary. This will allow the team to better understand and leverage each other's strengths on an ongoing basis.

◀ **Alicia Kiser**
Director of Human
Resources

Source: Alicia Kiser

the evidence stacking up against it.[49] For instance, studies have found that more than half the people who retake the test get a different result the second time.[50] As one noted psychologist said about MBTI® results, "Next time, just look at the horoscope. It is just as valid and takes less time."[51] We have described and discussed the MBTI® here, not because it's a valuable device for gaining insights into individual behavior, but because it's very likely that you'll encounter its use in organizations.

The Big Five Model

The MBTI® may lack strong supporting evidence, but an impressive body of research supports the **Big Five Model**, which proposes that five basic dimensions underlie all others and encompass most of the significant variation in human personality.[52] Test scores of these traits do a very good job of predicting how people behave in a variety of real-life situations[53] and remain relatively stable for an individual over time.[54] These are the Big Five factors:

1. *Extraversion:* The degree to which someone is sociable, talkative, assertive, and comfortable in relationships with others.
2. *Agreeableness:* The degree to which someone is good-natured, cooperative, and trusting.
3. *Conscientiousness:* The degree to which someone is reliable, responsible, dependable, persistent, and achievement oriented.
4. *Emotional stability:* The degree to which someone is calm, enthusiastic, and secure (positive) or tense, nervous, depressed, and insecure (negative).
5. *Openness to experience:* The degree to which someone has a wide range of interests and is imaginative, fascinated with novelty, artistically sensitive, and intellectual.

The Big Five Model provides more than just a personality framework. Research has shown that important

Big Five Model
Personality trait model that includes extraversion, agreeableness, conscientiousness, emotional stability, and openness to experience

Oracle CEO Safra Catz scores high on all of the personality dimensions of the Big Five Model. She is sociable, agreeable, conscientious, emotionally stable, and open to experiences. These traits have contributed to her growth at the company, where she's been employed since 1999.
Source: Albin Lohr-Jones/Consolidated News Photos/Albin Lohr-Jones-Pool via CNP-NO WIRE SERVICE/dpa picture alliance/Alamy Live News/Alamy Stock Photo

relationships exist between these personality dimensions and job performance. Here's what we know about each of the five dimensions.[55]

Extraverts perform better in jobs where high social interaction is necessary—like managerial and sales positions. They are socially dominant, "take charge" people who are usually more assertive than introverts. Extraversion is a relatively strong predictor of leadership emergence and behaviors in groups. And extraverts tend to have generally high job satisfaction and reduced burnout.

Not surprisingly, agreeable individuals are better liked than disagreeable people. They tend to perform well in interpersonally oriented jobs, such as customer service.

Conscientiousness is the best predictor of job performance. Employees who score higher in conscientiousness develop higher levels of job knowledge, probably because highly conscientious people learn more and these levels correspond with higher levels of job performance. Conscientious people have also been found to be more likely to engage in more OCB, less likely to engage in counterproductive work behaviors or think about leaving the organization, and can adapt to changing task demands and situations.

Of the Big Five traits, emotional stability is most strongly related to life satisfaction, job satisfaction, and reduced burnout and intentions to quit. People with high emotional stability can adapt to unexpected or changing demands in the workplace.

Finally, open people tend to be the most creative and innovative compared with the other traits. Open people are more likely to be effective leaders and more comfortable with ambiguity—they cope better with organizational change and are more adaptable. And openness to experience was found to be important in predicting training competency.

The Dark Triad

The traits in the Big Five model tend to be positive and desirable. With the exception of someone low on emotional stability (i.e., neurotic), organizations generally benefit when they have employees who are open, agreeable, and conscientious. But what about people with socially *undesirable* traits? Is there such a thing as a toxic employee—for example, someone who is self-absorbed, putting his or her interests ahead of the organization, or someone who is manipulative or with questionable ethics and willing to exploit situations and people? The answer appears to be "yes." Such individuals hold traits consistent with the *Dark Triad*.

Three specific traits have been identified which, together, form the **Dark Triad**.[56] They are Machiavellianism, narcissism, and psychopathy. Because each tends to be a negative trait, they've been called a *triad*, but they don't always occur together.

Machiavellianism (Mach) is named after Niccolo Machiavelli, who wrote in the sixteenth century on how to gain and manipulate power. An individual high in Machiavellianism is pragmatic, maintains emotional distance, and believes that ends can justify means. "If it works, use it" is consistent with a high Mach perspective. High-Mach employees, by manipulating others to their advantage, win in the short term at a job, but they lose those gains in the long term because they are not well liked.

Narcissism describes a person who has a grandiose sense of self-importance, requires excessive admiration, and is arrogant. These individuals have a tendency to exploit situations and people, a sense of entitlement, and a lack of empathy. They also can be hypersensitive and easy to anger. Ironically, narcissists are more likely to be chosen for leadership positions because others tend to see them as charismatic. For instance, studies have found narcissism linked to unethical behavior in CEOs.[57]

The third part of the Dark Triad is **psychopathy**. The term is used here not to connote clinical mental illness but to describe individuals who lack concern for others and lack guilt or remorse when actions cause harm. These people tend to be antisocial. And when put in leadership positions, they rely heavily on threats, manipulation, and bullying as a means to influence others.

When you see the toxic nature of people with one or more of these traits, you might ask: Why would an organization hire them? The answer is that these same

the Dark Triad
The three personality traits of Machiavellianism, narcissism, and psychopathy

Machiavellianism
A measure of the degree to which people are pragmatic, maintain emotional distance, and believe that ends justify means

narcissism
Describes a person who has a grandiose sense of self-importance, requires excessive admiration, and is arrogant

psychopathy
Describes individuals who lack concern for others and lack guilt or remorse when actions cause harm

fyi

- Narcissistic CEOs increase the likelihood of getting their company named as a defendant in a lawsuit.

- Narcissistic CEOs are not likely to settle lawsuits, even when their chance of winning isn't strong, resulting in higher costs and wasted time.[58]

people also embody many desirable traits like charm, leadership, assertiveness, and impression management skills.[59] In a condensed time period, such as an employment interview, applicants with toxic traits are very good at hiding them while, at the same time, adept at promoting their positive traits.

Additional Personality Insights

The Big Five and Dark Triad offer important, and valid, insights into personality traits. In addition, researchers have identified five singular personality traits that are powerful predictors of behavior in organizations.

LOCUS OF CONTROL   Some people believe they control their own fate. Others see themselves as pawns, believing that what happens to them in their lives is due to luck or chance. The **locus of control** in the first case is *internal*; these people believe they control their own destiny. The locus of control in the second case is *external*; these people believe their lives are controlled by outside forces.[60] Research indicates that employees who are externals are less satisfied with their jobs, more alienated from the work setting, and less involved in their jobs than those who rate high on internality.[61] A manager might also expect externals to blame a poor performance evaluation on their boss's prejudice, their coworkers, or other events outside their control; internals would explain the same evaluation in terms of their own actions.

locus of control
A personality attribute that measures the degree to which people believe they control their own fate

SELF-ESTEEM   People differ in the degree to which they like or dislike themselves, a trait called **self-esteem**.[62] Research on self-esteem (SE) offers some interesting behavioral insights. For example, self-esteem is directly related to expectations for success. Those high in SE believe they possess the ability they need to succeed at work. Individuals with high SEs will take more risks in job selection and are more likely to choose unconventional jobs than people with low SE.

The most common finding on self-esteem is that low SEs are more susceptible to external influence than high SEs. Low SEs are dependent on receiving positive evaluations from others. As a result, they're more likely to seek approval from others and are more prone to conform to the beliefs and behaviors of those they respect than high SEs. In managerial positions, low SEs will tend to be concerned with pleasing others and, therefore, will be less likely to take unpopular stands than high SEs. Finally, self-esteem has also been found to be related to job satisfaction. A number of studies confirm that high SEs are more satisfied with their jobs than low SEs.

self-esteem
An individual's degree of like or dislike for himself or herself

SELF-MONITORING   **Self-monitoring** refers to an individual's ability to adjust behavior to external, situational factors.[63]

Individuals high in self-monitoring show considerable adaptability in adjusting their behavior. They're highly sensitive to external cues and can behave differently in different situations. High self-monitors are capable of presenting striking contradictions between their public persona and their private selves. Low self-monitors can't adjust their behavior. They tend to display their true dispositions and attitudes in every situation, and there's high behavioral consistency between who they are and what they do.

Research on self-monitoring suggests that high self-monitors pay closer attention to the behavior of others and are more flexible than low self-monitors.[64] In addition, high self-monitoring managers tend to be more mobile in their careers, receive more promotions (both internal and cross-organizational), and are more likely to occupy central positions in an organization.[65] The high self-monitor is capable of putting on different "faces" for different audiences, an important trait for managers who must play multiple, or even contradicting, roles.

self-monitoring
A personality trait that measures the ability to adjust behavior to external situational factors

RISK-TAKING   People differ in their willingness to take chances. Differences in the propensity to assume or to avoid risk have been shown to affect how long it takes managers to make a decision and how much information they require before making their choice. For instance, in one study where managers worked on simulated exercises that required them to make hiring decisions, high-risk-taking managers took less time to make decisions and used less information in making their choices than low risk-taking managers.[66]

While it is generally correct to conclude that managers in organizations are risk aversive,[67] there are still individual differences on this dimension.[68] As a result, it makes sense to recognize these differences and even to consider aligning risk-taking propensity with specific job demands. For instance, a high-risk-taking propensity may lead to a more effective performance for a trader at a hedge fund. This type of job demands rapid decision making. On the other hand, this personality trait might prove a major obstacle to accountants performing auditing activities. This latter job might be better filled by someone with a low-risk-taking propensity.

PROACTIVE PERSONALITY Did you ever notice that some people take the initiative to improve their current circumstances or create new ones? These are proactive personalities.[69] Those with a **proactive personality** identify opportunities, show initiative, take action, and persevere until meaningful change occurs, unlike those who generally react to situations.

Proactive individuals have many desirable behaviors that organizations covet. They have higher levels of job performance, tend to be satisfied with their jobs, and don't need much oversight.[70] They're more likely to be seen as leaders and more likely to act as change agents in organizations, they're more likely to challenge the status quo; they have entrepreneurial abilities, and they often achieve career success.[71]

Personality Types in Different Cultures

Do personality frameworks, like the Big Five Model, transfer across cultures? Are dimensions like locus of control relevant in all cultures? Let's try to answer these questions.

The five personality factors studied in the Big Five Model appear in almost all cross-cultural studies.[72] These studies include a wide variety of diverse cultures such as China, Israel, Germany, Japan, Italy, Spain, Nigeria, Norway, Pakistan, and the United States. Differences are found in the emphasis on dimensions. The Chinese, for example, use the category of conscientiousness more often and use the category of agreeableness less often than do Americans. But a surprisingly high amount of agreement is found, especially among individuals from developed countries. As a case in point, a comprehensive review of studies covering people from the European Community found that conscientiousness was a valid predictor of performance across jobs and occupational groups.[73] Studies in the United States found the same thing.

We know that no personality type is common for a given country. You can, for instance, find high risk takers and low risk takers in almost any culture. Yet a country's culture influences the *dominant* personality characteristics of its people. We can see this effect of national culture by looking at one of the personality traits we just discussed: locus of control.

National cultures differ in terms of the degree to which people believe they control their environment. For instance, North Americans believe they can dominate their environment; other societies, such as those in Middle Eastern countries, believe life is essentially predetermined. Notice how closely this distinction parallels the concept of internal and external locus of control. On the basis of this particular cultural characteristic, we should expect a larger proportion of internals in the US and Canadian workforces than in the workforces of Saudi Arabia or Iran.

proactive personality
A personality trait that describes individuals who show initiative and take actions to influence their environments

Sisters Lucky, Dicky, and Nicky Chhetri exhibited the personality dimension of conscientiousness in starting 3 Sisters Adventure Trekking Company in Nepal. Persistence and a high achievement drive helped them not only to break into a male-dominated industry but also to grow their business by training other women to become guides. Since they started the business in 1994, they have trained close to 2,000 women in trekking and guiding, many of whom have gone on to become guides for the company.
Source: Niranjan Shrestha/AP Images

Let's Get REAL

The Scenario:

"Why can't we all just get along?" wondered Bonnie as she sat in her office. Today, she had already dealt with an employee who came in nearly every day with a complaint about something another coworker had said or done. Then, on top of that, Bonnie had to soothe over the hurt feelings of another employee who had overheard a conversation in the break room. She thought to herself, "I love being a manager, but there are days when the emotional tension in this place is too much."

◄ **Theodore Peterson**
Lead Mentor/Behavioral
Assistant

Source: Theodore Peterson

What would you tell Bonnie about emotions in the workplace and how to deal with them?

I would tell Bonnie that emotions in the workplace are always going to be present and are beyond her control. People will be people. However, don't let the emotions in the workplace affect your mood. Unfortunately, as a manager, sometimes you have to smile even when you don't feel like doing so. I would recommend Bonnie find a self-care activity that she can do outside of work, or that she take a few minutes during the workday to close the door in her office to take a few deep breaths, or to take a vacation if she has any time available. We all can feel overwhelmed, but it's all in how one deals with it that really matters.

Emotions and Emotional Intelligence

We can't leave the topic of personality without looking at the important behavioral aspect of emotions. Employees rarely check their feelings at the door to the workplace, nor are they unaffected by things that happen throughout the workday.[74] How we respond emotionally and how we deal with our emotions are typically functions of our personality.

Emotions are intense feelings directed at someone or something. They're object specific; that is, emotions are reactions to an object.[75] For instance, when a work colleague criticizes you for the way you spoke to a client, you might become angry at him. That is, you show emotion (anger) toward a specific object (your colleague). Sometimes negative feelings can be a good thing. Having bad feelings can make people think that something is wrong and motivate them to "look for external information to support your argument, to be much more rigorous about questioning your own presumptions and other people's perspectives, [and have] much more reliance on objective data."[76] Because employees bring an emotional component with them to work every day, managers need to understand the role that emotions play in employee behavior.[77]

How many emotions are there? Although you could probably name several dozen, research has identified six universal emotions: anger, fear, sadness, happiness, disgust, and surprise.[79] Do these emotions surface in the workplace? Absolutely! I get *angry* after receiving a poor performance appraisal. I *fear* that I could be laid off as a result of a company cutback. I'm *sad* about one of my coworkers leaving to take a new job in another city. I'm *happy* after being selected as employee of the month. I'm *disgusted* with the way my supervisor treats women on our team. And I'm *surprised* to find out that management plans a complete restructuring of the company's retirement program.

People respond differently to identical emotion-provoking stimuli. In some cases, differences can be attributed to a person's personality and because people vary in their ability to express emotions. For instance, you undoubtedly know people who almost never show their feelings. They rarely get angry or show rage. In contrast, you probably also know people who seem to be on an emotional roller coaster. When they're happy, they're ecstatic. When they're sad, they're deeply depressed. And two people can be in the exact same situation—one showing excitement and joy, the other remaining calm.

emotions
Intense feelings that are directed at someone or something

WORKPLACE CONFIDENTIAL An Abusive Boss

No one *wants* an abusive boss, but sometimes we end up with one. Studies estimate that about 13 percent of US workers suffer from such a boss. And this behavior appears to be most prevalent in fields such as the military and healthcare. A possible explanation is that these organizations tend to be characterized by high work demands, pressure, risk, and high costs associated with failure—all factors that can stress bosses out.

It's hoped that you'll never face an abusive boss. But if you do, you'll want to have a strategy for dealing with him or her.

Let's first clarify what we mean by an *abusive boss*. We define it as your perception that your supervisor is engaging in sustained displays of hostile verbal or nonverbal behaviors. What specific behaviors does this encompass? Here are some examples: bullying, belittling, threats, intimidation, vindictiveness, public ridiculing, and angry outbursts. Note two things about our definition. First, it's a perception. Regardless of whether your boss is actually abusive or not, if you think he is, he is. Second, our analysis isn't concerned with the occasional rant or mistreatment. The action we're concerned with is a regular feature of your boss's behavior.

Here's an interesting insight that might help you better cope. Abusive bosses are strategic. They pick and choose their targets. Studies find that they particularly like to go after those they view as weak or vulnerable. You're rarely going to see a boss throwing abuse at a powerful or well-connected member of her department. The message here is obvious: regardless of your actual confidence level, don't give the appearance that you're weak or unsure of yourself.

If you're on the receiving end of abuse at work, what can you do? Here are some options.

- *Confrontation:* Directly talk to your abusive boss to discuss the problem.
- *Passive-aggressiveness:* Indirectly express your hostility through actions such as procrastination, stubbornness, moodiness, or deliberately making half-hearted efforts to accomplish required tasks.
- *Ingratiation:* Try to win over your boss, and get him or her to "lighten up" on you, by actions such as doing favors or using flattery.
- *Seeking Support from Others:* Assuming that there is power in numbers, this approach has others acknowledge your problem and has them act in your behalf.

- *Avoidance:* Keep away from your boss and limit his or her opportunities to harass you.
- *Reframing:* Since abuse is a perception, try to mentally restructure your boss's actions in a way so that it no longer seems to be abusive.
- *Complain to Higher-ups:* Take your complaint to higher-ups in your organization to gain their support and "encourage" your boss to change his or her behavior.

Which of the above strategies do the experts suggest? Taking your complaint to upper levels in the organization is not likely to work where the culture tolerates or even supports abusive behavior. Hostile work climates *do* exist! And they encourage those with abusive tendencies to act out. So before you consider complaining to higher-ups, make sure your culture frowns on, and acts against, managers who abuse their employees.

Studies have found that the most common employee response to abuse is to avoid contact with the boss and seek social support. Not surprisingly, confrontation was the least-used strategy. But were these the most effective ways for dealing with abuse? Apparently not. Avoidance and seeking support resulted in employees experiencing negative emotions. Their stress levels were increased because this approach only increased feelings of weakness and perpetuated fear of the boss. Somewhat counterintuitively, research indicates that standing up to your boss is most related to positive emotions. It reinforces the desire to stick up for yourself, outwardly conveys that you're aware of your boss's behavior, and demonstrates that you do not find this behavior acceptable. Another counterintuitive finding was that passive-aggressiveness paid off. So it appears that bosses are less likely to go after employees if they are assertive, speak up, or perform acts of upward hostility. The evidence indicates that standing up for yourself or retaliating is less likely to make you feel like a victim. If you're firm and outspoken, you're less likely to see yourself as a victim, and it sends a message to your boss that you have a backbone and don't want to be messed with.

Keep in mind that trying to avoid your boss or reframe his or her abusive behavior does nothing toward actually resolving the problem. It merely covers it up and is likely to leave you still feeling like a victim. If you're planning on leaving your organization shortly or expect to get a new boss soon, avoidance can be effective. Otherwise, the use of avoidance or reframing doesn't change anything.[78]

However, at other times how people respond emotionally is a result of job requirements. Jobs make different demands in terms of what types and how much emotion needs to be displayed. For instance, air traffic controllers, ER nurses, and trial judges are expected to be calm and controlled, even in stressful situations. On the other hand, public-address announcers at sporting events and lawyers in a courtroom must be able to alter their emotional intensity as the need arises.

One area of emotions research with interesting insights into personality is **emotional intelligence (EI)**, the ability to notice and to manage emotional cues and information.[80] It's composed of five dimensions:

Self-awareness: The ability to be aware of what you're feeling.

Self-management: The ability to manage one's own emotions and impulses.

Self-motivation: The ability to persist in the face of setbacks and failures.

Empathy: The ability to sense how others are feeling.

Social skills: The ability to handle the emotions of others.

EI has been shown to be positively related to job performance at all levels. For instance, one study looked at the characteristics of Lucent Technologies' (now part of Nokia) engineers who were rated as stars by their peers. The researchers concluded that stars were better at relating to others. That is, it was EI, not academic intelligence, that characterized high performers. A study of Air Force recruiters generated similar findings. Top-performing recruiters exhibited high levels of EI. Despite these findings, EI has been a controversial topic in OB.[81] Supporters say EI has intuitive appeal and predicts important behavior.[82] Critics say that EI is vague, can't be measured, and has questionable validity.[83] One thing we can conclude is that EI appears to be relevant to success in jobs that demand a high degree of social interaction.

emotional intelligence (EI)
The ability to notice and to manage emotional cues and information

fyi

- Eighty-seven percent of CEOs believe a company's financial performance is tied to empathy in the workplace.
- Eighty-one percent of employees would be willing to work longer hours for an empathetic employer.[84]

Implications for Managers

About 80 percent of US private companies are using personality tests when recruiting and hiring.[85] Perhaps the major value in understanding personality differences lies in this area. Managers are likely to have higher-performing and more satisfied employees if consideration is given to matching personalities with jobs.

The best-documented personality-job fit theory was developed by psychologist John Holland, who identified six basic personality types.[86] His theory states that an employee's satisfaction with his or her job, as well as his or her likelihood of leaving that job, depends on the degree to which the individual's personality matches the job environment. Exhibit 15-4 describes the six types, their personality characteristics, and examples of suitable occupations for each.

Holland's theory proposes that satisfaction is highest and turnover lowest when personality and occupation are compatible. Social individuals should be in "people" type jobs, and so forth. The key points of this theory are that (1) intrinsic differences in personality are apparent among individuals; (2) the types of jobs vary; and (3) people in job environments compatible with their personality types should be more satisfied and less likely to resign voluntarily than people in incongruent jobs.

We covered a lot of material on personality in this section. What should managers get out of this? Here are four suggestions related to hiring:

1. Assess vocational interests in the hiring process. By successfully matching interests and job requirements, there is an increased likelihood that new hires will perform well on the job and stay with the organization.

2. If you're looking for a single personality trait that is likely to be associated with superior job performance, you're well advised to hire people who score high on conscientiousness. Individuals who score high in conscientiousness are dependable, reliable, careful, thorough, organized, hard-working, and persistent. And these attributes tend to lead to higher job performance in most occupations.

Exhibit 15-4

Holland's Personality–Job Fit

Source: Based on J. L. Holland, *Making Vocational Choices: A Theory of Vocational Personalities and Work Environments* (Odessa, FL: Psychological Assessment Resources, 1997).

TYPE	PERSONALITY CHARACTERISTICS	SAMPLE OCCUPATIONS
Realistic. Prefers physical activities that require skill, strength, and coordination	Shy, genuine, persistent, stable, conforming, practical	Mechanic, drill press operator, assembly-line worker, farmer
Investigative. Prefers activities involving thinking, organizing, and understanding	Analytical, original, curious, independent	Biologist, economist, mathematician, news reporter
Social. Prefers activities that involve helping and developing others	Sociable, friendly, cooperative, understanding	Social worker, teacher, counselor, clinical psychologist
Conventional. Prefers rule-regulated, orderly, and unambiguous activities	Conforming, efficient, practical, unimaginative, inflexible	Accountant, corporate manager, bank teller, file clerk
Enterprising. Prefers verbal activities that offer opportunities to influence others and attain power	Self-confident, ambitious, energetic, domineering	Lawyer, real estate agent, public relations specialist, small business manager
Artistic. Prefers ambiguous and unsystematic activities that allow creative expression	Imaginative, disorderly, idealistic, emotional, impractical	Painter, musician, writer, interior decorator

3. When filling jobs where successful social interaction is a major factor in performance, hire people with high emotional intelligence. This should especially apply to managerial positions.
4. Finally, take time to carefully screen job candidates—through intensive interviews, reference checks, and the like—to identify and reject individuals who hold the set of Dark Triad traits. While individuals with these traits typically come with some positive qualities, the toxic side of their personalities is likely to pollute their work environments. And when hiring mistakes are made, correct them quickly—preferably during their probationary period.

PERCEPTION

LO15.4 Maybe you've seen this in a Facebook post or on some other online source: AOCRNDICG TO RSCHEEARCH AT CMABRIGDE UINERVTISY, IT DSENO'T MTAETR WAHT OERDR THE LTTERES IN A WROD ARE, THE OLNY IPROAMTNT TIHNG IS TAHT THE FRSIT AND LSAT LTTEER BE IN THE RGHIT PCLAE. TIHS IS BCUSEAE THE HUAMN MNID DEOS NOT RAED ERVEY LTETER BY ISTLEF, BUT THE WROD AS A WLOHE. IF YOU CAN RAED. . .TIHS, PSOT IT TO YUOR WLAL. OLNY 55% OF PLEPOE CAN.[87] How'd you do in trying to read this? If you were able to make sense out of this jumbled message, that's the perceptual process at work. **Perception** is a process by which we give meaning to our environment by organizing and interpreting sensory impressions. Research on perception consistently demonstrates that

perception
A process by which we give meaning to our environment by organizing and interpreting sensory impressions

individuals may look at the same thing yet perceive it differently. One manager, for instance, can interpret the fact that her assistant regularly takes several days to make important decisions as evidence that the assistant is slow, disorganized, and afraid to make decisions. Another manager with the same assistant might interpret the same tendency as evidence that the assistant is thoughtful, thorough, and deliberate. The first manager would probably evaluate her assistant negatively; the second manager would probably evaluate the person positively. The point is that none of us sees reality. We interpret what we see and call it reality. And, of course, as the example shows, we behave according to our perceptions.

Factors That Influence Perception

How do we explain the fact that people can perceive the same thing differently? A number of factors act to shape and sometimes distort perception. These factors are in the *perceiver*, in the *target* being perceived, or in the *context* in which the perception occurs.

When a person looks at a target and attempts to interpret what he or she sees, the individual's personal characteristics will heavily influence the interpretation. These personal characteristics include attitudes, personality, motives, interests, experiences, or expectations. For instance, the perception of employees sporting tattoos differs based on age. Older workers tend to perceive tattoos in the office as inappropriate or objectionable, while younger workers don't.[88] Differences in these perceptions may be due, in part, to more young people having tattoos or knowing others who do.

The characteristics of the target being observed can also affect what's perceived. Loud people are more likely than quiet people to be noticed in a group, as are extremely attractive or unattractive individuals. The relationship of a target to its background also influences perception, as does our tendency to group close things and similar things together. You can experience these tendencies by looking at the visual perception examples shown in Exhibit 15-5. Notice how what you see changes as you look differently at each one.

Finally, the context in which we see objects or events is also important. The time at which an object or event is seen can influence perception, as can location, light, heat, color, and any number of other situational factors.

Attribution Theory

Much of the research on perception is directed at inanimate objects. Managers, however, are concerned with people. Our perceptions of people differ from our perception of inanimate objects because we make inferences about the behaviors of people that we don't make about objects. Objects don't have beliefs, motives, or intentions; people do. The result is that when we observe an individual's behavior, we try to develop explanations of why they behave in certain ways. Our perception and

Old woman or young woman?   A knight on a horse?

Exhibit 15-5
What Do You See?

attribution theory
A theory used to explain how we judge people differently depending on what meaning we attribute to a given behavior

judgment of a person's actions are significantly influenced by the assumptions we make about the person.

Attribution theory was developed to explain how we judge people differently depending on what meaning we attribute to a given behavior.[89] Basically, the theory suggests that when we observe an individual's behavior, we attempt to determine whether it was internally or externally caused. Internally caused behaviors are those believed to be under the personal control of the individual. Externally caused behavior results from outside factors; that is, the person is forced into the behavior by the situation. That determination, however, depends on three factors: distinctiveness, consensus, and consistency.

Distinctiveness refers to whether an individual displays different behaviors in different situations. Is the employee who arrived late today the same person who some employees complain of as being a "goof-off"? What we want to know is whether this behavior is unusual. If it's unusual, the observer is likely to attribute the behavior to external forces, something beyond the control of the person. However, if the behavior isn't unusual, it will probably be judged as internal.

If everyone who's faced with a similar situation responds in the same way, we can say the behavior shows *consensus*. A tardy employee's behavior would meet this criterion if all employees who took the same route to work were also late. From an attribution perspective, if consensus is high, you're likely to give an external attribution to the employee's tardiness; that is, some outside factor—maybe road construction or a traffic accident—caused the behavior. However, if other employees who come the same way to work made it on time, you would conclude that the cause of the late behavior was internal.

Finally, an observer looks for *consistency* in a person's actions. Does the person engage in the behaviors regularly and consistently? Does the person respond the same way over time? Coming in ten minutes late for work isn't perceived in the same way if, for one employee, it represents an unusual case (she hasn't been late in months), while for another employee, it's part of a routine pattern (she's late two or three times every week). The more consistent the behavior, the more the observer is inclined to attribute it to internal causes. Exhibit 15-6 summarizes the key elements of attribution theory.

One interesting finding from attribution theory is that errors or biases distort our attributions. For instance, substantial evidence supports the fact that when we make judgments about the behavior of other people, we have a tendency to *under*estimate the influence of external factors and to *over*estimate the influence of internal or personal factors.[90] This tendency is called the **fundamental attribution error** and can explain why a sales manager may attribute the poor performance of her sales representative to laziness rather than to the innovative product line introduced by a competitor. Another tendency is to attribute our own successes to internal factors, such as

fundamental attribution error
The tendency to underestimate the influence of external factors and overestimate the influence of internal factors when making judgments about the behavior of others

Exhibit 15-6
Attribution Theory

OBSERVATION	INTERPRETATION	ATTRIBUTION OF CAUSE
Does person behave this way in other situations?	**YES:** Low distinctiveness **NO:** High distinctiveness	Internal attribution External attribution
Do other people behave the same way in similar situations?	**YES:** High consensus **NO:** Low consensus	External attribution Internal attribution
Does person behave this way consistently?	**YES:** High consistency **NO:** Low consistency	Internal attribution External attribution

ability or effort, while putting the blame for personal failure on external factors, such as luck. This tendency is called the **self-serving bias** and suggests that feedback provided to employees in performance reviews will be distorted by them depending on whether it's positive or negative.[91] In some cases, these distortions can be serious. A recent survey found that employees with self-serving tendencies were 25 percent more likely to rate their bosses as abusive.[92] Obviously, these perceptions can damage reputations of nonabusive managers.

Are these errors or biases that distort attributions universal across different cultures? The evidence is mixed but most suggest that there are differences across cultures in the attributions that people make.[93] For instance, in one study, Asian managers were more likely to blame institutions or whole organizations when things went wrong, whereas Western observers believe individual managers should get blame or praise.[94] That probably explains why US newspapers feature the names of individual executives when firms do poorly, whereas Asian media report the firm as a whole has failed.

Brig. General Diana Holland challenges the gender stereotype in the military that women are too fragile to lead men. She was the first female deputy commanding general of a light infantry division and the first female commandant of cadets at West Point.
Source: Staff Sgt. Kelly Simon/AB Forces News Collection/Alamy Stock Photo

Shortcuts Used in Judging Others

Perceiving and interpreting people's behavior is a lot of work, so we use shortcuts to make the task more manageable. These techniques can be valuable when they let us make accurate interpretations quickly and provide valid data for making predictions. However, they aren't perfect. They can and do get us into trouble.

SELECTIVE PERCEPTION Any characteristic that makes a person, an object, or an event stand out will increase the probability we will perceive it. Why? Because it is impossible for us to assimilate everything we see; we can take in only certain stimuli. Thus, you are more likely to notice cars like your own, and your boss may reprimand some people and not others doing the same thing. Because we can't observe everything going on around us, we use **selective perception**. But we don't choose randomly. We make selections based on our interests, background, experience, and attitudes. Seeing what we want to see, we sometimes draw unwarranted conclusions from an ambiguous situation.

ASSUMED SIMILARITY It's easy to judge others if we assume they're similar to us. In **assumed similarity**, or the "like me" effect, the observer's perception of others is influenced more by the observer's own characteristics than by those of the person observed. For example, if you want challenges and responsibility in your job, you'll assume that others want the same. People who assume that others are like them can, of course, be right, but not always.

STEREOTYPING When we judge someone on the basis of our perception of a group he or she is part of, we're using the shortcut called **stereotyping**. For instance, "Married people are more stable employees than single persons" is an example of stereotyping. To the degree that a stereotype is based on fact, it may produce accurate judgments. However, many stereotypes aren't factual and distort our judgment.

HALO EFFECT When we form a general impression about a person on the basis of a single characteristic, such as intelligence, sociability, or appearance, we're influenced by the **halo effect**. This effect frequently occurs when students evaluate their classroom instructor. Students may isolate a single trait, such as enthusiasm, and allow their entire evaluation to be slanted by the perception of this one trait. An instructor may be quiet, assured, knowledgeable, and highly qualified, but if his classroom teaching style lacks enthusiasm, he might be rated lower on a number of other characteristics.

self-serving bias
The tendency for individuals to attribute their own successes to internal factors while putting the blame for failures on external factors

selective perception
Biased perception based on our interests, background, experience, and attitudes

assumed similarity
The assumption that others are like oneself

stereotyping
Judging a person based on a perception of a group to which that person belongs

halo effect
A general impression of an individual based on a single characteristic

CONTRAST EFFECT There's an adage among show-business entertainers to "never follow an act with kids or animals." Why? Audiences love children and animals, so you'll look bad in comparison. This example illustrates how the **contrast effect** can distort perceptions. We don't evaluate a person in isolation. Our reaction is influenced by other people we have recently encountered.

contrast effect
Potentially distorted perceptions based on comparisons to others

Implications for Managers

Managers need to recognize that their employees react to perceptions, not to reality. So whether a manager's appraisal of an employee's performance is actually objective and unbiased or whether the organization's wage levels are among the highest in the community is less relevant than what employees perceive them to be. If individuals perceive appraisals to be biased or wage levels as low, they'll behave as if those conditions actually exist. Employees organize and interpret what they see, so the potential for perceptual distortion is always present. The message is clear: pay close attention to how employees perceive both their jobs and management actions.

learning
Any relatively permanent change in behavior that occurs as a result of experience

operant conditioning
A theory of learning that says behavior is a function of its consequences

LEARNING

LO15.5 The Kansas City Chiefs of the National Football League kept veteran safety Ron Parker on the team even though his best years were behind him. He was one of a handful of former players re-signed by the Chiefs to mentor younger players and help them adjust to the Chiefs' complex schemes. "My role is to give back to the younger guys and give all the knowledge that I know to help them play the defense, to help them get better as a player," says Parker.[95]

Mentoring is a good example of the last individual behavior concept we're going to look at—learning. Learning is included in our discussion of individual behavior for the obvious reason that almost all behavior is learned. If we want to explain, predict, and influence behavior, we need to understand how people learn.

The psychologists' definition of learning is considerably broader than the average person's view that "it's what we do in school." Learning occurs all the time as we continuously learn from our experiences. A workable definition of **learning** is any relatively permanent change in behavior that occurs as a result of experience. Two learning theories help us understand how and why individual behavior occurs.

The Kansas City Chiefs of the National Football League kept veteran safety Ron Parker (number 38) on the team even though his best years were behind him. He was one of a handful of former players re-signed by the Chiefs to mentor younger players and help them adjust to the Chief's complex schemes.
Source: Frank Jansky/Icon Sportswire DCT/ Newscom

Operant Conditioning

Operant conditioning argues that behavior is a function of its consequences. People learn to behave to get something they want or to avoid something they don't want. Operant behavior is voluntary or learned behavior, not reflexive or unlearned behavior. The tendency to repeat learned behavior is influenced by reinforcement or lack of reinforcement that happens as a result of the behavior. Reinforcement strengthens a behavior and increases the likelihood that it will be repeated. Lack of reinforcement weakens a behavior and lessens the likelihood that it will be repeated.

B. F. Skinner's research widely expanded our knowledge of operant conditioning.[96] Behavior is assumed to be determined from without—that is, *learned*—rather than from within—reflexive or unlearned. Skinner argued that people will most likely engage in desired behaviors if they are positively reinforced for doing so, and rewards are most effective if they immediately follow the desired response. In addition, behavior that isn't rewarded or is punished is less likely to be repeated.

You see examples of operant conditioning everywhere. Any situation in which it's either explicitly stated or implicitly suggested that reinforcement (rewards) is contingent on some action on your part is an example of operant conditioning. Your instructor says that if you want a high grade in this course, you must perform well on tests by giving correct answers. A salesperson working on commission knows that earning a sizeable income is contingent on generating high sales in his or her territory. And, in some companies, employees with perfect attendance receive bonuses. Of course, the linkage between behavior and reinforcement can also work to teach individuals to behave in ways that work against the best interests of the organization. Assume your boss tells you that if you'll work overtime during the next three-week busy season, you'll be compensated for it at the next performance appraisal. Then, when performance appraisal time comes, you are given no positive reinforcements (such as a pay raise or bonus). What will you do the next time your boss asks you to work overtime? You'll probably refuse. Your behavior can be explained by operant conditioning: if a behavior isn't positively reinforced, the probability that the behavior will be repeated declines.

Social Learning

Individuals can also learn by observing what happens to other people and just by being told about something as well as by direct experiences. Much of what we have learned comes from watching others (models)—parents, teachers, peers, television and movie actors, managers, and so forth. This view that we can learn both through observation and direct experience is called **social learning theory**.

The influence of others is central to the social learning viewpoint. The amount of influence these models have on an individual is determined by four processes:

1. *Attentional processes.* People learn from a model when they recognize and pay attention to its critical features. We're most influenced by models who are attractive, repeatedly available, thought to be important, or seen as similar to us.
2. *Retention processes.* A model's influence will depend on how well the individual remembers the model's action, even after the model is no longer readily available.
3. *Motor reproduction processes.* After a person has seen a new behavior by observing the model, the watching must become doing. This process then demonstrates that the individual can actually do the modeled activities.
4. *Reinforcement processes.* Individuals will be motivated to exhibit the modeled behavior if positive incentives or rewards are provided. Behaviors that are reinforced will be given more attention, learned better, and performed more often.

social learning theory
A theory of learning that says people can learn through observation and direct experience

Shaping: A Managerial Tool

Because learning takes place on the job as well as prior to it, managers are concerned with how they can teach employees to behave in ways that most benefit the organization. Thus, managers will often attempt to "mold" individuals by guiding their learning in graduated steps, through a method called **shaping behavior**.

Consider the situation in which an employee's behavior is significantly different from that sought by a manager. If the manager reinforced the individual only when he or she showed desirable responses, the opportunity for reinforcement might occur too infrequently. Shaping offers a logical approach toward achieving the desired behavior. We shape behavior by systematically reinforcing each successive step that moves the individual closer to the desired behavior. So, if an employee who has chronically been a half-hour late for work comes in only twenty minutes late, we can reinforce the improvement. Reinforcement would increase as an employee gets closer to the desired behavior.

Four ways to shape behavior include positive reinforcement, negative reinforcement, punishment, and extinction. When a behavior is followed by something pleasant, such as praising an employee for a job well done, it's called *positive reinforcement.* Positive reinforcement increases the likelihood that the desired behavior will be repeated. Rewarding a response by eliminating or withdrawing something unpleasant is *negative reinforcement.* A manager who says "I won't dock your pay if you start getting to work on time" is using negative reinforcement. The desired behavior (getting to work on time) is being encouraged by the withdrawal of something unpleasant (the employee's pay

shaping behavior
The process of guiding learning in graduated steps using reinforcement or lack of reinforcement

being docked). On the other hand, *punishment* penalizes undesirable behavior and will eliminate it. Suspending an employee for two days without pay for habitually coming to work late is an example of punishment. Finally, eliminating any reinforcement that's maintaining a behavior is called *extinction.* When a behavior isn't reinforced, it gradually disappears. In meetings, managers who wish to discourage employees from continually asking irrelevant or distracting questions can eliminate this behavior by ignoring those employees when they raise their hands to speak. Soon this behavior should disappear.

Both positive and negative reinforcement result in learning. They strengthen a desired behavior and increase the probability that the desired behavior will be repeated. Both punishment and extinction also result in learning, but do so by weakening an undesired behavior and decreasing its frequency.

Implications for Managers

Employees are going to learn on the job. The only issue is whether managers are going to manage their learning through the rewards they allocate and the examples they set, or allow it to occur haphazardly. If marginal employees are rewarded with pay raises and promotions, they will have little reason to change their behavior. In fact, productive employees who see marginal performance rewarded might change their behavior. If managers want behavior A, but reward behavior B, they shouldn't be surprised to find employees learning to engage in behavior B. Similarly, managers should expect that employees will look to them as models. Managers who are consistently late to work, or take two hours for lunch, or help themselves to company office supplies for personal use should expect employees to read the message they are sending and model their behavior accordingly.

Chapter 15   PREPARING FOR: Exams/Quizzes

CHAPTER SUMMARY by Learning Objectives

LO15.1   **IDENTIFY** the focus and goals of individual behavior within organizations.

Just like an iceberg, it's the hidden organizational elements (attitudes, perceptions, norms, etc.) that make understanding individual behavior so challenging.

Organizational behavior (OB) focuses primarily on two areas: individual behavior and group behavior. The goals of OB are to explain, predict, and influence behavior.

Employee productivity is a performance measure of both efficiency and effectiveness. Absenteeism is the failure to report to work. Turnover is the voluntary and involuntary permanent withdrawal from an organization. Organizational citizenship behavior (OCB) is discretionary behavior that's not part of an employee's formal job requirements, but it promotes the effective functioning of an organization. Job satisfaction is an individual's general attitude toward his or her job. Counterproductive workplace behavior is any intentional employee behavior that is potentially harmful to the organization or individuals within the organization.

LO15.2   **EXPLAIN** the role that attitudes play in job performance.

The cognitive component refers to the beliefs, opinions, knowledge, or information held by a person. The affective component is the emotional or feeling part of an attitude. The behavioral component refers to an intention to behave in a certain way toward someone or something.

Job satisfaction refers to a person's general attitude toward his or her job. Job satisfaction positively influences productivity, lowers absenteeism levels, lowers turnover rates, promotes positive customer satisfaction, moderately promotes OCB, and helps minimize counterproductive workplace behaviors.

Job involvement is the degree to which an employee identifies with his or her job, actively participates in it, and considers his or her job performance to be important to his or her self-worth. Organizational commitment is the degree to which an employee identifies with a particular organization and its goals and wishes to maintain membership in that organization. Perceived organizational support is employees' general belief that their organization values their contribution and cares about their well-being. Employee engagement is when employees are connected to, satisfied with, and enthusiastic about their jobs.

Individuals try to reconcile attitude and behavior inconsistencies by changing their behavior, concluding that the dissonance behavior isn't so important, changing their attitude, or identifying compatible factors that outweigh the dissonant ones. Many organizations regularly survey their employees about their attitudes.

LO15.3 DESCRIBE different personality theories.

The MBTI® measures four dimensions: extraversion/introversion, sensing/intuition, thinking/feeling, and judging/perceiving. The Big Five Model consists of five personality traits: extraversion, agreeableness, conscientiousness, emotional stability, and openness to experience. The Dark Triad includes the socially undesirable traits of Machiavellianism, narcissism, and psychopathy.

Five other personality traits that help explain individual behavior in organizations are locus of control, self-esteem, self-monitoring, risk taking, and proactive personality.

How people respond emotionally and how they deal with their emotions is a function of personality. A person who is emotionally intelligent has the ability to notice and to manage emotional cues and information.

LO15.4 DESCRIBE perception and factors that influence it.

Perception is how we give meaning to our environment by organizing and interpreting sensory impressions. Because people behave according to their perceptions, managers need to understand it.

Attribution theory depends on three factors. Distinctiveness is whether an individual displays different behaviors in different situations (that is, is the behavior unusual). Consensus is whether others facing a similar situation respond in the same way. Consistency is when a person engages in behaviors regularly and consistently. Whether these three factors are high or low helps managers determine whether employee behavior is attributed to external or internal causes.

The fundamental attribution error is the tendency to underestimate the influence of external factors and overestimate the influence of internal factors. The self-serving bias is the tendency to attribute our own successes to internal factors and to put the blame for personal failure on external factors.

Shortcuts used in judging others are selective perception, assumed similarity, stereotyping, the halo effect, and the contrast effect.

LO15.5 DISCUSS learning theories and their relevance in shaping behavior.

Operant conditioning argues that behavior is a function of its consequences. If a behavior is not positively reinforced, there is a likelihood that the behavior will be repeated.

Social learning theory says that individuals learn by observing what happens to other people and by directly experiencing something.

Managers can shape behavior by using positive reinforcement (reinforcing a desired behavior by giving something pleasant), negative reinforcement (reinforcing a desired response by withdrawing something unpleasant), punishment (eliminating undesirable behavior by applying penalties), or extinction (not reinforcing a behavior to eliminate it).

REVIEW AND DISCUSSION QUESTIONS

15-1. Does the importance of knowledge of OB differ based on a manager's levels in the organization? If so, how? If not, why not? Be specific.

15-2. Explain why the concept of an organization as an iceberg is important.

15-3. Define the six important employee behaviors.

15-4. Describe the three components of an attitude and explain the five job-related and organization-related attitudes.

15-5. Contrast the MBTI® and the Big Five Model. Describe five other personality traits that help explain individual behavior in organizations.

15-6. Explain how an understanding of perception can help managers better understand individual behavior. Name three shortcuts used in judging others.

15-7. Describe the key elements of attribution theory. Discuss the fundamental attribution error and self-serving bias.

15-8. Describe operant conditioning and how managers can shape behavior.

PREPARING FOR: My Career

ETHICS DILEMMA

A new business analyst needs to be hired to work at the corporate headquarters of a retail firm. Jared and Amanda are managers in charge of the hiring decision. The candidates have been narrowed down to three possible hires: 1) Sheri, who was in the same sorority at the same college as Amanda (even though they did not overlap in their years in college), 2) Scott, who has known a good friend of Jared's for years, and 3) Stephanie who has a somewhat higher college GPA and more work experience

than either Sheri or Scott. After the interviews, Amanda thinks Sheri's interview was clearly the best, while Jared is convinced that Scott is the best candidate for the job.

15-9. What ethical issues might arise if Scott is hired? In what ways are the possible ethical issues involved in hiring Sheri different (or the same) as hiring Scott?

15-10. What steps could senior management take to minimize ethical issues in this situation?

SKILLS EXERCISE Developing Your Shaping Behavior Skill

About the Skill
In today's dynamic work environments, learning is continual. But this learning shouldn't be done in isolation or without any guidance. Most employees need to be shown what's expected of them on the job. As a manager, you must teach your employees the behaviors most critical to their and the organization's success.

Steps in Practicing the Skill
1. *Identify the critical behaviors that have a significant impact on an employee's performance.* Not everything

employees do on the job is equally important in terms of performance outcomes. A few critical behaviors may, in fact, account for the majority of one's results. These high-impact behaviors need to be identified.

2. *Establish a baseline of performance.* A baseline is obtained by determining the number of times the identified behaviors occur under the employee's present job conditions.

3. *Analyze the contributing factors to performance and their consequences.* A number of factors, such as the

norms of a group, may be contributing to the baseline performance. Identify these factors and their effect on performance.

4. *Develop a shaping strategy.* The change that may occur will entail changing some element of performance—structure, processes, technology, groups, or the task. The purpose of the strategy is to strengthen the desirable behaviors and weaken the undesirable ones.

5. *Apply the appropriate strategy.* Once the strategy has been developed, it needs to be implemented. In this step, an intervention occurs.

6. *Measure the change that has occurred.* An intervention should produce the desired results in performance behaviors. Evaluate the number of times the identified behaviors now occur. Compare these with the baseline evaluation in step 2.

7. *Reinforce desired behaviors.* If an intervention has been successful and the new behaviors are producing the desired results, maintain these behaviors through reinforcement mechanisms.

Practicing the Skill

a. Imagine that your assistant is ideal in all respects but one—he or she is hopeless at taking phone messages for you when you're not in the office. You're often in training sessions, and the calls are sales leads you want to follow up on, so you have identified taking accurate messages as a high-impact behavior for your assistant.

b. Focus on steps 3 and 4, and devise a way to shape your assistant's behavior. Identify some factors that might contribute to his or her failure to take messages—these could range from a heavy workload to a poor understanding of the task's importance (you can rule out insubordination). Then develop a shaping strategy by determining what you can change—the available technology, the task itself, the structure of the job, or some other element of performance.

c. Now plan your intervention and hold a brief meeting with your assistant in which you explain the change you expect. Recruit a friend to help you role-play your intervention. Do you think you would succeed in a real situation?

WORKING TOGETHER **Team Exercise**

Group members often have preferences about what tasks they most like to do. At least some of those preferences are a result of the personality attributes that a group member has. Groups can avoid problems when they discuss preferences early on during a group's work and assign tasks to individuals based on their preferences.

In groups of three of four, brainstorm how the different personality attributes described in this chapter could impact group members' preferences for tasks that might need to be done in a typical group project for a class in college. What kinds of tasks should be assigned to group members with which personality attributes? Which personality attributes might need to be taken into account with work that happens early on (versus later) as the group works on their project? Be prepared to discuss your thoughts with the class.

MY TURN TO BE A MANAGER

- Write down three attitudes you have. Identify the cognitive, affective, and behavioral components of those attitudes.

- Survey fifteen employees (at your place of work or at some campus office). Be sure to obtain permission before doing this anonymous survey. Ask them what rude or negative behaviors they've seen at work. Compile your findings in a report and be prepared to discuss this in class. If you were the manager in this workplace, how would you handle this behavior?

- If you've never taken a personality or career compatibility test, contact your school's testing center to see if you can take one. Once you get your results, evaluate what they mean for your career choice. Have you chosen a career that "fits" your personality? What are the implications?

- Have you ever heard of the "waiter rule"? A lot of business people think that how you treat service workers says a lot about your character and attitudes. What do you think this means? Do you agree with this idea? Why or why not? How would you be evaluated on the "waiter rule"?

- Like it or not, each of us is continually shaping the behavior of those around us. For one week, keep track of how many times you use positive reinforcement, negative reinforcement, punishment, or extinction to shape behaviors. At the end of the week, which one did you tend to use most? What were you trying to do; that is, what behaviors were you trying to shape? Were your attempts successful? Evaluate. What could you have done differently if you were trying to change someone's behavior?

- Find two companies that have been recognized for their employee engagement efforts. Compare the different strategies each company uses to build and engage their workforce. Are any the same? Different? Why do you think each company has been successful with employee engagement?

- What is your level of emotional intelligence? Google "emotional intelligence test." Select and complete a quiz. What did the results show? Are they compatible with your personal assessment of your EI?

CASE APPLICATION 1 — Employee Experience at IBM

IBM—the giant information technology company—wanted to take employee engagement to the next level. They found that employee engagement explained two-thirds of their client experience scores, which have a strong impact on their revenue.[97]

So, what did IBM do? They focused on redesigning processes to improve employees' experiences at work. They started with employee recruitment and moved through their entire time working at the company. This Employee Experience approach "required a shift in mindset," said Diane Gherson, chief human resources officer at IBM. They asked employees to co-design changes that affect them and alter processes that previously might have been overlooked.

In the past, IBM might have updated their first-day orientation class for new hires. But now, as part of their Employee Experience approach, they asked new hires for feedback about how their onboarding experience was. Comments about delays in receiving laptops or in accessing work email highlighted where changes could be made. IBM realized that to get the first-day experience right, they needed to involve their security department to ensure badges were there and work with their networking department to get email access quickly.

Beyond employees' first day of work, IBM also redesigned their employee learning platform and performance evaluation process with employee input. Their new learning-management system is organized like Netflix, with different channels and user ratings. There is a live-chat advisor who helps answer questions employees might have as they navigate the system. Their performance evaluation system was redesigned after receiving input from 100,000 employees. Employees now receive richer feedback more often and can continue to offer suggestions for improvement through internal company blogs.

Airbnb and General Electric also are leaders in Employee Experience. Employees' workspaces were redesigned at Airbnb's corporate headquarters based on employee input. Paul Davies, GE's head of Employee Experience, explained their approach as "We ask our employees, our people leaders, and our candidates what matters most to them, we listen to their stories, listening especially for emotions."[98]

DISCUSSION QUESTIONS

15-11. Why do employees with high employee engagement scores provide better customer service?

15-12. Why might a company's investments in their employees' experience result in benefits to behaviors (e.g., productivity, absenteeism, turnover) and attitudes (organizational commitment, perceived organizational support)?

15-13. What are the benefits of "listening for emotions" when asking employees what matters to them?

15-14. What do you think it would take to make an Employee Experience approach effective? What could make an Employee Experience ineffective?

CASE APPLICATION 2 — Getting Your Company's Logo as a Tattoo

If you wanted something to show for spending 25 percent of your life working for Walmart, you might get some Walmart logo wear or maybe a license plate holder for your car. Jeff Atkins decided to have Walmart's company logo tattooed on his left arm.[99]

Tattoos have become more common. Recent survey results indicate that up to 40 percent of US households include someone who has a tattoo. A study of 2,000 people in the US found that having a tattoo makes you no less employable and doesn't impact the amount of money you earn on the job.[100] Still, a tattoo of a company logo is not something you see every day.

Some people have made an in-the-moment decision to get a company logo tattoo. Mahadeva Matt Mani was at a company retreat for the consulting firm Booz & Company when they were about to be purchased by PricewaterhouseCoopers. Mahadeva sensed that the way to relieve employees' concerns about their company being bought was to get a tattoo to show his loyalty. Dave Heath, cofounder of the sock company Bombas, joked that he would get a company logo tattoo after selling the millionth pair of socks. Since they hadn't sold any socks when he made that promise, he thought he was safe. But 2.5 years later, Heath was reminded of his promise when they had sold a million socks and he got the tattoo.

Paul Bosneag thought getting a company logo tattoo would prevent him from getting laid off. Paul remembered thinking, "What kind of jerk would fire an employee that has the logo tattooed on him?" Although he hasn't been laid off, his company—Anytime Fitness Gym chain—has fired seven people who had the company logo as tattoos.

DISCUSSION QUESTIONS

15-15. Once an employee gets a company logo tattoo, how might his or her job satisfaction, job involvement, organizational commitment, absenteeism, and turnover be different from nontattooed employees? What are the reasons for any differences?

15-16. Employees might get a company logo tattoo when their attitude toward their company is positive. How does cognitive dissonance apply if their attitude towards the company changes to a negative attitude?

15-17. How could the shortcuts used in judging others (e.g., selective perception, assumed similarity, stereotyping, etc.) apply to an employee with a company logo tattoo?

15-18. Sometimes family members of employees who get company logo tattoos don't think it was smart to make a sudden decision to get that tattoo. How does attribution theory apply to how a family member might try to interpret an employee's decision to get a company logo tattoo?

ENDNOTES

1. T. Winship, "How to Get a Job at Southwest Airlines," Smarter Travel, January 14, 2016, https://www.smartertravel.com/how-to-get-a-job-at-southwest-airlines/.

2. See S. P. Robbins and T. A. Judge, *Organizational Behavior*, 18th ed. (New York: Pearson Education, 2019).

3. Cited in "Why It Matters: The Direct and Indirect Costs of Absenteeism," *TrackSmart*, January 22, 2018, http://blog.tracksmart.com/why-it-matters-the-direct-and-indirect-costs-of-absenteeism/.

4. J. S. Kantor, "High Turnover Costs Way More Than You Think," *HuffPost*, updated February 11, 2017, https://www.huffpost.com/entry/high-turnover-costs-way-more-than-you-think_b_9197238.

5. P. M. Podsakoff, S. B. MacKenzie, J. B. Paine, and D. G. Bachrach, "Organizational Citizenship Behaviors: A Critical Review of the Theoretical and Empirical Literature and Suggestions for Future Research," *Journal of Management* 26, no. 3 (June 2000): pp. 513–63; and J. A. LePine, A. Erez, and D. E. Johnson, "The Nature and Dimensionality of Organizational Citizenship Behavior: A Critical Review and Meta-Analysis," *Journal of Applied Psychology* 87, no. 1 (February 2002): pp. 52–65.

6. This definition adapted from R. W. Griffin and Y. P. Lopez, "Bad Behavior in Organizations: A Review and Typology for Future Research," *Journal of Management* (December 2005): pp. 988–1005.

7. "Work and Workplace," *Gallup*, accessed January 25, 2019, https://www.gallup.com.

8. S. J. Breckler, "Empirical Validation of Affect, Behavior, and Cognition as Distinct Components of Attitude," *Journal of Personality and Social Psychology* 47, no. 6 (May 1984): pp. 1191–1205; and S. L. Crites Jr., L. R. Fabrigar, and R. E. Petty, "Measuring the Affective and Cognitive Properties of Attitudes: Conceptual and Methodological Issues," *Personality and Social Psychology Bulletin* 20, no. 6 (December 1994): pp. 619–634.

9. T. A. Judge, H. M. Weiss, J. D. Kameyer-Mueller, and C. L. Hulin, "Job Attitudes, Job Satisfaction, and Job Affect: A Century of Continuity and of Change," *Journal of Applied Psychology* 102, no. 3 (March 2017): pp. 356–74.

10. N. A. Bowling, T. A. Beehr, and L. R. Lepisto, "Beyond Job Satisfaction: A Five-Year Prospective Analysis of the Dispositional Approach to Work Attitudes," *Journal of Vocational Behavior* 69, no. 2 (October 2006): pp. 315–30; and N. A. Bowling, M. R. Hoepf, D. M. LaHuis, and L. R. Lepisto, "Mean Job Satisfaction Levels Over Time: Are Things Bad and Getting Worse?," *Industrial-Organizational Psychologist*, April 2013, pp. 57–64.

11. L. Weber, "U.S. Workers Can't Get No (Job) Satisfaction," *Wall Street Journal*, June 18, 2014, https://blogs.wsj.com/atwork/2014/06/18/u-s-workers-cant-get-no-job-satisfaction/.

12. L. Weber, "Workers Register Highest Satisfaction on Jobs Since 2005," *Wall Street Journal*, August 30, 2018, p. B6.

13. Ibid.

14. J. H. Westover, "The Impact of Comparative State-Directed Development on Working Conditions and Employee Satisfaction," *Journal of Management & Organization* (July 2013): pp. 537–54.

15. T. A. Judge, C. J. Thoresen, J. E. Bono, and G. K. Patton, "The Job Satisfaction-Job Performance Relationship: A Qualitative and Quantitative Review," *Psychological Bulletin* 127, no. 3 (May 2001): pp. 376–407.

16. R. D. Hackett, "Work Attitudes and Employee Absenteeism: A Synthesis of the Literature," *Journal of Occupational Psychology* 62, no. 3 (September 1989): pp. 235–48; and J. F. Ybema, P. G. W. Smulders, and P. M. Bongers, "Antecedents and Consequences of Employee Absenteeism: A Longitudinal Perspective on the Role of Job Satisfaction and Burnout," *European Journal of Work and Organizational Psychology* 19, no. 1 (2010): pp. 102–24.

17. J. P. Hausknecht, N. J. Hiller, and R. J. Vance, "Work-Unit Absenteeism: Effects of Satisfaction, Commitment, Labor Market Conditions, and Time," *Academy of Management Journal* 51, no. 6 (December 2008): pp. 1123–45.

18. R. W. Griffeth, P. W. Hom, and S. Gaertner, "A Meta-Analysis of Antecedents and Correlates of Employee Turnover: Update, Moderator Tests, and Research Implications for the Next Millennium," *Journal of Management* 26, no. 3 (June 2000): pp. 463–88; and G. Chen, R. E. Ployhart, H. C. Thomas, N. Anderson, and P. D. Bliese, "The Power of Momentum: A New Model of Dynamic Relationships Between Job Satisfaction Change and Turnover Intentions," *Academy of Management Journal* 54, no. 1 (February 2011): pp. 159–81.

19. W. Felps, T. R. Mitchell, D. R. Hekman, T. W. Lee, B. C. Holtom, and W. S. Harman, "Turnover Contagion: How Coworkers' Job Embeddedness and Job Search Behaviors Influence Quitting," *Academy of Management Journal* 52, no. 3 (August 2009): pp. 545–61.

20. See, for example, J. M. Carsten and P. E. Spector, "Unemployment, Job Satisfaction, and Employee Turnover: A Meta-Analytic Test of the Muchinsky Model," *Journal of Applied Psychology* 72, no. 3 (August 1987): pp. 374–381; and C. L. Hulin, M. Roznowski, and D. Hachiya, "Alternative Opportunities and Withdrawal Decisions: Empirical and Theoretical Discrepancies and an Integration," *Psychological Bulletin* 97, no. 2 (July 1985): pp. 233–250.

21. T. A. Wright and D. G. Bonett, "Job Satisfaction and Psychological Well-Being as Nonadditive Predictors of Workplace Turnover," *Journal of Management* 33, no. 2 (April 2007): pp. 141–160; and D. G. Spencer and R. M. Steers, "Performance as a Moderator of the Job Satisfaction-Turnover Relationship," *Journal of Applied Psychology* 66, no. 4 (August 1981): pp. 511–514.

22. M. Schulte, C. Ostroff, S. Shmulyian, and A. Kinicki, "Organizational Climate Configurations: Relationships to Collective Attitudes, Customer Satisfaction, and Financial Performance," *Journal of Applied Psychology* 94, no. 3 (May 2009): pp. 618–634; and R. G. Netemeyer, J. G. Maxham III, and D. R. Lichtenstein, "Store Manager Performance and Satisfaction: Effects on Store Employee Performance

and Satisfaction, Store Customer Satisfaction, and Store Customer Spending Growth," *Journal of Applied Psychology* 95, no. 3 (May 2010): pp. 530–45.

23. Podsakoff, et al., "Organizational Citizenship Behaviors" [see note 5].

24. B. J. Hoffman, C. A. Blair, J. P. Maeriac, and D. J. Woehr, "Expanding the Criterion Domain? A Quantitative Review of the OCB Literature," *Journal of Applied Psychology* 92, no. 2 (March 2007): pp. 555–66.

25. B. S. Reiche, P. Cardona, Y.-T. Lee, M. A. Canela, E. Akinnukawe, J. P. Briscoe, H. Wilkinson, et al., "Why Do Managers Engage in Trustworthy Behaviors? A Multilevel Cross-Cultural Study in 18 Countries," *Personnel Psychology* 61, no. 1 (Spring 2014): pp. 61–98.

26. D. S. Chiaburu and D. A. Harrison, "Do Peers Make the Place? Conceptual Synthesis and Meta-Analysis of Coworker Effect on Perceptions, Attitudes, OCBs, and Performance," *Journal of Applied Psychology* 93, no. 5 (May 2008): pp. 1082–103.

27. T. A. Judge, B. A. Scott, and R. Ilies, "Hostility, Job Attitudes, and Workplace Deviance: Test of a Multilevel Model," *Journal of Applied Psychology* 91, no. 1 (January 2006): pp. 126–38; and M. Mount, R. Ilies, and E. Johnson, "Relationship of Personality Traits and Counterproductive Work Behaviors: The Mediating Effects of Job Satisfaction," *Personnel Psychology* 59, no. 3 (Autumn 2006): pp. 591–622.

28. T. M. Lodahl and M. Kejner, "The Definition and Measurement of Job Involvement," *Journal of Applied Psychology* 49, no. 1 (January 1965): pp. 24–33; and S. P. Brown, "A Meta-Analysis and Review of Organizational Research on Job Involvement," *Psychological Bulletin* 120, no. 2 (March 1996): pp. 235–55.

29. D. A. Harrison, D. A. Newman, and P. L. Roth, "How Important Are Job Attitudes? Meta-Analytic Comparisons of Integrative Behavioral Outcomes and Time Sequences," *Academy of Management Journal* 49, no. 2 (April 2006): pp. 305–325; G. J. Blau, "Job Involvement and Organizational Commitment as Interactive Predictors of Tardiness and Absenteeism," *Journal of Management* 12, no. 2 (Winter 1986): pp. 577–584; and K. Boal and R. Cidambi, "Attitudinal Correlates of Turnover and Absenteeism: A Meta-Analysis." Paper presented at the meeting of the American Psychological Association, Toronto, Canada, 1984.

30. O. N. Solinger, W. van Olffen, and R. A. Roe, "Beyond the Three-Component Model of Organizational Commitment," *Journal of Applied Psychology* 92, no. 1 (January 2008): pp. 70–83; and Z. A. Mercurio, "Affective Commitment as a Core Essence of Organizational Commitment: An Integrative Literature Review," *Human Resource Development Review* 14, no. 4 (December 2015) pp. 389–414.

31. See, for instance, P. W. Hom, R. Katerberg, and C. L. Hulin, "Comparative Examination of Three Approaches to the Prediction of Turnover," *Journal of Applied Psychology* 64, no. 3 (June 1979): pp. 280–290; R. T. Mowday, L. W. Porter, and R. M. Steers, *Employee Organization Linkages: The Psychology of Commitment, Absenteeism, and Turnover* (New York: Academic Press, 1982); H. Angle and J. Perry, "Organizational Commitment: Individual and Organizational Influence," *Work and Occupations* 10, no. 2 (May 1983): pp. 123–145; and J. L. Pierce and R. B. Dunham, "Organizational

Commitment: Pre-Employment Propensity and Initial Work Experiences," *Journal of Management* 13, no. 1 (Spring 1987): pp. 163–178.

32. L. W. Porter, R. M. Steers, R. T. Mowday, and V. Boulian, "Organizational Commitment, Job Satisfaction, and Turnover Among Psychiatric Technicians," *Journal of Applied Psychology* 59, no. 5 (October 1974): pp. 603–609.

33. D. M. Rousseau, "Organizational Behavior in the New Organizational Era," in *Annual Review of Psychology,* vol. 48, eds. J. T. Spence, J. M. Darley, and D. J. Foss (Palo Alto, CA: Annual Reviews, 1997), p. 523.

34. L. Rhoades, R. Eisenberger, and S. Armeli, "Affective Commitment to the Organization: The Contribution of Perceived Organizational Support," *Journal of Applied Psychology* (May 2001): pp. 825–36.

35. B. L. Rich, J. A. Lepine, and E. R. Crawford, "Job Engagement: Antecedents and Effects on Job Performance," *Academy of Management Journal* (April 2010): pp. 617–35.

36. "Driving Employee Engagement in a Global Workforce," *Watson Wyatt Worldwide,* 2007–2008, p. 2.

37. A. Mann and J. Harter, "The Worldwide Employee Engagement Crisis," *Gallup,* January 7, 2016, https://www. gallup.com/workplace/236495/worldwide-employee-engagement-crisis.aspx

38. See, for instance, D. J. Schleicher, J. D. Watt, and G. J. Greguras, "Reexamining the Job Satisfaction-Performance Relationship: The Complexity of Attitudes," *Journal of Applied Psychology* 89, no. 1 (February 2004): pp. 165–77; and L. R. Fabrigar, R. E. Petty, S. M. Smith, and S. L. Crites, "Understanding Knowledge Effects on Attitude-Behavior Consistency: The Role of Relevance, Complexity, and Amount of Knowledge," *Journal of Personality and Social Psychology* 90, no. 4 (April 2006): pp. 556–77.

39. L. Festinger, *A Theory of Cognitive Dissonance* (Stanford, CA: Stanford University Press, 1957); and A. S. Hinojosa, W. L. Gardner, H. J. Walker, C. Cogliser, and D. Gullifor, "A Review of Cognitive Dissonance Theory in Management Research," *Journal of Management* 43, no. 1 (January 2017): pp. 170–99.

40. See, for example, S. V. Falletta, "Organizational Intelligence Surveys," *TD,* June 2008, pp. 52–58; and K. Pritchard, "Using Employee Surveys to Attract and Retain the Best Talent," *Strategic HR Review* 13, no. 2 (2014): pp. 59–62.

41. J. Wiles, "Is It Time to Toss Out Your Old Employee Engagement Survey?," *Gartner,* November 26, 2018, https:// www.gartner.com/smarterwithgartner/is-it-time-to-toss-out-your-old-employee-engagement-survey/.

42. "Sustainability Report 2014/15," Ford Motor Company, 2015, https://corporate.ford.com/content/dam/corporate/en/company/2014-15-Sustainability-Report.pdf.

43. T. A. Judge and A. H. Church, "Job Satisfaction: Research and Practice," in *Industrial and Organizational Psychology: Linking Theory with Practice,* eds. C. L. Cooper and E. A. Locke (Oxford, UK: Blackwell, 2000); and L. Saari and T. A. Judge, "Employee Attitudes and Job Satisfaction," *Human Resource Management* 43, no. 4 (Winter 2004): pp. 395–407.

44. Harrison, Newman, and Roth, "How Important Are Job Attitudes" [see note 29].

45. I. Briggs-Myers, *Introduction to Type* (Palo Alto, CA: Consulting Psychologists Press, 1980); W. L. Gardner and M. J. Martinko, "Using the Myers-Briggs Type Indicator to Study Managers: A Literature Review and Research Agenda," *Journal of Management* 22, no. 1 (February 1996): pp. 45–83; N. L. Quenk, *Essentials of Myers-Briggs Type Indicator Assessment* (New York: Wiley, 2000); and M. Emre, *The Personality Brokers* (New York: Doubleday, 2018).

46. K. Wylde, "What's The Most Common Myers-Briggs Type? A Significant Amount of People Test As This," *Bustle*, March 8, 2018, https://www.bustle.com/p/whats-the-most-common-myers-briggs-type-a-significant-amount-of-people-test-as-this-8406913.

47. E. Bajic, "How the MBTI Can Help You Build a Stronger Company," *Forbes*, September 28, 2015, https://www.forbes.com/sites/elenabajic/2015/09/28/how-the-mbti-can-help-you-build-a-stronger-company/#190696f2d93c.

48. M. Ahmed, "Is Myers-Briggs Up to the Job?," *Financial Times*, February 11, 2016, https://www.ft.com/content/8790ef0a-d040-11e5-831d-09f7778e7377.

49. See, for instance, L. Bess and R. J. Harvey, "Bimodal Scofre Distributions and the Myers-Briggs Type Indicator: Fact or Artifact?," *Journal of Personality Assessment* 78, no. 1 (2002): pp. 176–86; and R. M. Capraro and M. M. Capraro, "Myers-Briggs Type Indicator Score Reliability Across Studies: A Meta-Analytic Reliability Generalization Study," *Educational & Psychological Measurement* 62, no. 4 (August 2002): pp. 590–602.

50. Cited in E. Harrell, "A Brief History of Personality Tests," *Harvard Business Review*, March-April 2017, p. 63.

51. D. Ariely, "When Lame Pick-Up Lines Actually Work," *Wall Street Journal*, July 19-20, 2014, p. C12.

52. O. P. John, L. P. Naumann, and C. J. Soto, "Paradigm Shift to the Integrative Big Five Trait Taxonomy: History, Measurement, and Conceptual Issues," in O. P. John, R. W. Robins, and L. A. Pervin, eds., *Handbook of Personality: Theory and Research*, 3rd ed. (New York: Guilford, 2008), pp. 114–58.

53. W. Fleeson and P. Gallagher, "The Implications of Big-Five Standing for the Distribution of Trait Manifestation in Behavior: Fifteen Experience-Sampling Studies and a Meta-Analysis," *Journal of Personality and Social Psychology* 97, no. 6 (December 2009): pp. 1097–1114.

54. T. A. Judge, L. S. Simon, C. Hurst, and K. Kelley, "What I Experienced Yesterday Is Who I Am Today: Relationship of Work Motivations and Behaviors to Within-Individual Variation in the Five-Factor Model of Personality," *Journal of Applied Psychology* 99, no. 2 (February 2014): pp. 199–221.

55. See, for instance, M. R. Barrick and M. K. Mount, "The Big Five Personality Dimensions and Job Performance: A Meta-Analysis," *Personnel Psychology* 44, no. 1 (March 1991): pp. 1–26; A. J. Vinchur, J. S. Schippmann, F. S. Switzer III, and P. L. Roth, "A Meta-Analytic Review of Predictors of Job Performance for Salespeople," *Journal of Applied Psychology* 83, no. 4 (August 1998): pp. 586–597; G. M. Hurtz and J. J. Donovan, "Personality and Job Performance Revisited," *Journal of Applied Psychology* 85, no. 6 (December 2000): pp. 869–879; T.

A. Judge, D. Heller, and M. K. Mount, "Five-Factor Model of Personality and Job Satisfaction: A Meta-Analysis," *Journal of Applied Psychology* 87, no. 3 (June 2002): pp. 530–541; and A. E. Poropat, "A Meta-Analysis of the Five-Factor Model of Personality and Academic Performance," *Psychological Bulletin* 135, no. 2 (March 2009): pp. 322–38.

56. See, for instance, D. L. Paulhus and K. M. Williams, "The Dark Triad of Personality: Narcissism, Machiavellianism, and Psychopathy," *Journal of Research in Personality* 36, no. 6 (December 2002): pp. 556–63; L. Veselka, J. A. Schermer, and P. A. Vernon, "The Dark Triad and an Expanded Framework of Personality," *Personality and Individual Differences* 53, no. 4 (September 2012): pp. 417–25; A. Furnham, S. Richards, L. Rangel, and D. N. Jones, "Measuring Malevolence: Quantitative Issues Surrounding the Dark Triad of Personality," *Personality and Individual Differences* 64 (September 2014): pp. 114–21; and P. D. Harms and S. M. Spain, "Beyond the Bright Side: Dark Personality at Work," *Applied Psychology: An International Review* 64, no. 1 (January 2015): pp. 15–24.

57. J. H. Amernic and R. J. Craig, "Accounting as a Facilitator of Extreme Narcissism," *Journal of Business Ethics* 96, no. 1 (September 2010): pp. 79–93; and B. L. Galperin, R. J. Bennett, and K. Aquino, "Status Differentiation and the Protean Self: A Social-Cognitive Model of Unethical Behavior in Organizations," *Journal of Business Ethics* 98, no. 3 (February 2011): pp. 407–24.

58. J. Sahadi, "How Narcissistic CEOs Put Companies at Risk," *CNN*; November 5, 2018, https://www.cnn.com/2018/11/05/success/narcissist-ceo/index.html.

59. P. K. Jonason, S. Slomski, and J. Partyka, "The Dark Triad at Work: How Toxic Employees Get Their Way," *Personality and Individual Differences* 52, no. 3 (February 2012): pp. 449–53.

60. J. B. Rotter, "Generalized Expectancies for Internal Versus External Control of Reinforcement," *Psychological Monographs* 80, no. 609 (1966); R. E. Johnson, C. C. Rosen, C.-H. Chang, and S.-H. Lin, "Getting to the Core of Locus of Control: Is It an Evaluation of the Self or the Environment?," *Journal of Applied Psychology* 100, no. 5 (May 2015): pp. 1568–78; and B. M. Galvin, A. E. Randel, B. J. Collins, and R. E. Johnson, "Changing the Focus (of Control): A Targeted Review of the Locus of Control Literature and Agenda for Future Research," *Journal of Organizational Behavior* 39, no. 7 (March 2018): pp. 820–33.

61. See, for instance, D. W. Organ and C. N. Greene, "Role Ambiguity, Locus of Control, and Work Satisfaction," *Journal of Applied Psychology* 59, no. 1 (February 1974): pp. 101–102; and T. R. Mitchell, C. M. Smyser, and S. E. Weed, "Locus of Control: Supervision and Work Satisfaction," *Academy of Management Journal* 18, no. 3 (September 1975): pp. 623–631.

62. See J. Brockner, *Self-Esteem at Work: Research, Theory, and Practice* (Lexington, MA: Lexington Books, 1988), chapters 1–4; N. Branden, *Self-Esteem at Work* (San Francisco: Jossey-Bass, 1998); and T. A. Judge and J. E. Bono, "Relationship of Core Self-Evaluations Traits—Self-Esteem, Generalized Self-Efficacy, Locus of Control, and Emotional Stability with Job Satisfaction and Job Performance: A

Meta-Analysis," *Journal of Applied Psychology* 86, no. 1 (January 2001): pp. 80–92.

63. See M. Snyder, *Public Appearances/Private Realities: The Psychology of Self-Monitoring* (New York: W. H. Freeman, 1987); and D. V. Day, D. J. Schleicher, A. L. Unckless, and N. J. Hiller, "Self-Monitoring Personality at Work: A Meta-Analytic Investigation of Construct Validity," *Journal of Applied Psychology* 87, no. 2 (April 2002): pp. 390–401.

64. Snyder, *Public Appearances/Private Realities*; and J. M. Jenkins, "Self-Monitoring and Turnover: The Impact of Personality on Intent to Leave," *Journal of Organizational Behavior* 14, no. 1: (January 1993): pp. 83–91.

65. M. Kilduff and D. V. Day, "Do Chameleons Get Ahead? The Effects of Self-Monitoring on Managerial Careers," *Academy of Management Journal* 37, no. 4 (August 1994): pp. 1047 1060; and A. Mehra, M. Kilduff, and D. J. Brass, "The Social Networks of High and Low Self-Monitors: Implications for Workplace Performance," *Administrative Science Quarterly* 46, no. 1 (March 2001): pp. 121–146.

66. I. L. Janis and L. Mann, *Decision Making: A Psychological Analysis of Conflict, Choice, and Commitment* (New York: Free Press, 1977).

67. N. Kogan and M. A. Wallach, "Group Risk Taking as a Function of Members' Anxiety and Defensiveness," *Journal of Personality* 35, no. 1 (March 1967): pp. 50–63.

68. J. L. Holland, *Making Vocational Choices: A Theory of Vocational Personalities and Work Environments*, 3rd ed. (Lutz, FL: Psychological Assessment Resources, 1997).

69. T. S. Bateman and J. M. Crant, "The Proactive Component of Organizational Behavior: A Measure and Correlates," *Journal of Organizational Behavior* 14, no. 2 (March 1993): pp. 103–118; and J. M. Crant, "Proactive Behavior in Organizations," *Journal of Management* 26, no. 3 (2000): pp. 435–462.

70. A. B. Bakker, M. Tims, and D. Derks, "Proactive Personality and Job Performance: The Role of Job Crafting and Work Engagement," *Human Relations* 65, no. 10 (October 2012): pp. 1359–78; K. Tornau and M. Frese, "Construct Clean-up in Proactivity Research: A Meta-Analysis on the Nomological Net of Work-Related Proactivity Concepts and Their Incremental Values," *Applied Psychology: An International Review* 62, no. 1 (January 2013): pp. 44–96; and D. M. Bergeron, T. Schroeder, and H. A. Martinez, "Proactive Personality at Work: Seeing More to Do and Doing More?," *Journal of Business and Psychology* 29, no. 1 (March 2014): pp. 71–86; and W.-D. Li, D. Fay, M. Frese, P. D. Harms, and X. Y. Gao, "Reciprocal Relationship Between Proactive Personality and Work Characteristics: A Latent Change Score Approach," *Journal of Applied Psychology* 99, no. 5 (May 2014): pp. 948–65.

71. R. C. Becherer and J. G. Maurer, "The Proactive Personality Disposition and Entrepreneurial Behavior Among Small Company Presidents," *Journal of Small Business Management* 37, no. 1 (January 1999): pp. 28–36; S. E. Seibert, M. L. Kraimer, and J. M. Crant, "What Do Proactive People Do? A Longitudinal Model Linking Proactive Personality and Career Success," *Personnel Psychology* 54, no. 4 (Winter 2001): pp. 845–874; and F. Yang and R. Chau, "Proactive Personality

and Career Success," *Journal of Managerial Psychology* 31, no. 2 (2016): pp. 467–82.

72. See, for instance, J. E. Williams, J. L. Saiz, D. L. Formyduval, M. L. Munick, E. E. Fogle, A. Adom, A. Haque, F. Neto, and J. Yu, "Cross-Cultural Variation in the Importance of Psychological Characteristics: A Seven-Year Country Study," *International Journal of Psychology* 30, no. 5 (October 1995): pp. 529–550; V. Benet and N. G. Walker, "The Big Seven Factor Model of Personality Description: Evidence for Its Cross-Cultural Generalizability in a Spanish Sample," *Journal of Personality and Social Psychology* 69, no. 4 (October 1995): pp. 701–718; R. R. McCrae and P. T. Costa Jr., "Personality Trait Structure as a Human Universal," *American Psychologist* 52, no. 5 (1997): pp. 509–516; M. J. Schmit, J. A. Kihm, and C. Robie, "Development of a Global Measure of Personality," *Personnel Psychology* 53, no. 1 (Spring 2000): pp. 153–193; J. B. Nezlek, A. Schütz, M. Schröder-Abé, and C. V. Smith, "A Cross-Cultural Study of Relationships Between Daily Social Interaction and the Five-Factor Model of Personality," *Journal of Personality* 79, no. 4 (August 2011): pp. 811–40; and D. Ispas, D. Iliescu, A. Ilie, and R. E. Johnson, "Exploring the Cross-Cultural Generalizability of the Five-Factor Model of Personality: The Romanian NEO PI-R," *Journal of Cross-Cultural Psychology* 45, no. 7 (August 2014): pp. 1074–88.

73. J. F. Salgado, "The Five Factor Model of Personality and Job Performance in the European Community," *Journal of Applied Psychology* 82, no. 1 (February 1997): pp. 30–43.

74. N. P. Rothbard and S. L. Wilk, "Waking Up on the Right or Wrong Side of the Bed: Start-of-Workday Mood, Work Events, Employee Affect, and Performance," *Academy of Management Journal* 54, no. 5 (October 2011): pp. 959–980; and N. M. Ashkanasy, R. H. Humphrey, and Q. N. Huy, "Integrating Emotions and Affect in Theories of Management," *Academy of Management Review* 42, no. 2 (April 2017) pp. 175–89.

75. N. H. Frijda, "Moods, Emotion Episodes, and Emotions," in M. Lewis and J. M. Havilland, eds., *Handbook of Emotions* (New York: Guilford Press, 1993), pp. 381–403.

76. A. North, "The Power of Bad Feelings," Op-Talk, *New York Times*, October 21, 2014, https://op-talk.blogs.nytimes.com/2014/10/21/the-power-of-feeling-bad/.

77. N. M. Ashkanasy and C. S. Daus, "Emotion in the Workplace: The New Challenge for Managers," *Academy of Management Executive* 61, no. 1 (February 2002) pp. 76–86; T.-Y. Kim, D. M. Cable, S.-P. Kim, and J. Wang, "Emotional Competence and Work Performance: The Mediating Effect of Proactivity and the Moderating Effect of Job Autonomy," *Journal of Organizational Behavior* 30, no. 7 (October 2009): pp. 983–1000; J. M. Diefendorff and G. J. Greguras, "Contextualizing Emotional Display Rules: Examining the Roles of Targets and Discrete Emotions in Shaping Display Rule Perceptions," *Journal of Management* 35, no. 4 (August 2009): pp. 880–898; J. Gooty, M. Gavin, and N. M. Ashkanasy, "Emotions Research in OB: The Challenges That Lie Ahead," *Journal of Organizational Behavior* 30, no. 6 (August 2009): pp. 833–838; and N. M. Ashkanasy and A. D. Dorris, "Emotions in the Workplace," in F. P. Morgeson, ed., *Annual Review of Organizational Psychology*

and Organizational Behavior, vol. 4 (Palo Alto, CA: Annual Reviews, 2017), pp. 67–90.

78. Based on B. J. Tepper, "Abusive Supervision in Work Organizations: Review, Synthesis, and Research Agenda," *Journal of Management* (June 2007): pp. 261–289; B. J. Tepper, et al., "On the Exchange of Hostility with Supervisors: An Examination of Self-Enhancing and Self-Defeating Perspectives," *Personnel Psychology* (Winter 2015): pp. 723–758; and J. D. Mackey, R. E. Frieder, J. R. Brees, and M. J. Martinko, "Abusive Supervision: A Meta-Analysis and Empirical Review," *Journal of Management* (July 2017) pp. 194–65.

79. H. M. Weiss and R. Cropanzano, "Affective Events Theory," in B. M. Staw and L. L. Cummings, eds., *Research in Organizational Behavior,* vol. 18 (Greenwich, CT: JAI Press, 1996), pp. 20–22.

80. This section is based on D. Goleman, *Emotional Intelligence* (New York: Bantam, 1995); D. Goleman, *Working with Emotional Intelligence* (New York: Bantam, 1999); R. Bar-On and J. D. A. Parker, eds., *The Handbook of Emotional Intelligence: Theory, Development, Assessment, and Application at Home, School, and in the Workplace* (San Francisco: Jossey-Bass, 2000); D. L. Joseph and D. A. Newman, "Emotional Intelligence: An Integrative Meta-Analysis and Cascading Model," *Journal of Applied Psychology* 95, no. 1 (January 2010): pp. 54–78; N. S. Schutte and N. M. Loi, "Connections Between Emotional Intelligence and Workplace Flourishing," *Personality and Individual Differences* 66 (August 2014): pp. 134–39; and Z. Hui-Hua and N. S. Schutte, "Personality, Emotional Intelligence and Other-Rated Task Performance," *Personality and Individual Differences* 87 (December 2015): pp. 298–301.

81. F. Walter, M. S. Cole, and R. H. Humphrey, "Emotional Intelligence? Sine Qua Non of Leadership or Folderol?," *Academy of Management Perspectives* 25, no. 1 (February 2011): pp. 45–59.

82. P. J. Jordan, N. M. Ashkanasy, and C. E. J. Härtel, "The Case for Emotional Intelligence in Organizational Research," *Academy of Management Review* 28, no. 2 (April 2003): pp. 195–197; D. L. Van Rooy and C. Viswesvaran, "Emotional Intelligence: A Meta-Analytic Investigation of Predictive Validity and Nomological Net," *Journal of Vocational Behavior* 65, no. 1 (August 2004): pp. 71–95; R. D. Shaffer and M. A. Shaffer, "Emotional Intelligence Abilities, Personality, and Workplace Performance," *Academy of Management Best Conference Paper—HR,* August 2005; and E. J. O'Boyle Jr., R. H. Humphrey, J. M. Pollack, T. H. Hawver, and P. A. Story, "The Relation Between Emotional Intelligence and Job Performance: A Meta-Analysis," *Journal of Organizational Behavior* online, June 2010, https://doi.org/10.1002/job.714.

83. M. Davies, L. Stankov, and R. D. Roberts, "Emotional Intelligence: In Search of an Elusive Construct," *Journal of Personality and Social Psychology* 75, no. 4 (October 1998): pp. 989–1015; T. Becker, "Is Emotional Intelligence a Viable Concept?," *Academy of Management Review* 28, no. 2 (April 2003) pp. 192–195; F. J. Landy, "Some Historical and Scientific Issues Related to Research on Emotional Intelligence," *Journal of Organizational Behavior* (June 2005): pp. 411–424; E. A. Locke, "Why Emotional Intelligence Is an Invalid Concept," *Journal of Organizational Behavior* 26, no. 4 (June 2005): pp. 425–431; and J. M. Conte, "A Review and Critique of Emotional Intelligence Measures," *Journal of Organizational Behavior* 26, no. 4 (June 2005): pp. 433–440.

84. K. Higginbottom, "Why Empathy Matters in the Workplace," *Forbes,* May 31, 2018, https://www.forbes.com/sites/karenhigginbottom/2018/05/31/why-empathy-matters-in-the-workplace/#4a4a0241130b.

85. L. Weber, "Today's Personality Tests Raise the Bar for Job Seekers," *Wall Street Journal,* April 14, 2015, https://www.wsj.com/articles/a-personality-test-could-stand-in-the-way-of-your-next-job-1429065001.

86. J. L. Holland, *Making Vocational Choices: A Theory of Vocational Personalities and Work Environments* (Odessa, FL: Psychological Assessment Resources, 1997); E. Cowger Jr., I. Chauvin, and M. J. Miller, "An 'Inverse' Validation of Holland's Theory," *College Student Journal* 43, no. 3 (September 2009): pp. 807–12; and H.-B. Sheu, R. W. Lent, S. D. Brown, M. J. Miller, K. D. Hennessy, and R. D. Duffy, "Testing the Choice Model of Social Cognitive Career Theory Across Holland Themes: A Meta-Analytic Path Analysis," *Journal of Vocational Behavior* 76, no. 2 (April 2010): pp. 252–64.

87. Copyright © 2012 by Matt Davis, Cambridge University. Reprinted with permission.

88. T. Priestley, "How Technology Is Changing the Perception of Tattoos in the Workplace," *Forbes,* December 10, 2015, https://www.forbes.com/sites/theopriestley/2015/12/10/how-technology-is-changing-the-perception-of-tattoos-in-the-workplace/#2336b15c5392.

89. See, for instance, H. H. Kelley, "Attribution in Social Interaction," in E. Jones et al., eds., *Attribution: Perceiving the Causes of Behavior* (Morristown, NJ: General Learning Press, 1972); M. J. Martinko, ed., *Attribution Theory: An Organizational Perspective* (Delray Beach, FL: St. Lucie Press, 1995); and M. J. Martinko, P. Harvey, and M. T. Dasborough, "Attribution Theory in the Organizational Sciences: A Case of Unrealized Potential," *Journal of Organizational Behavior* 32, no. 1 (January 2011): 144–49.

90. See A. G. Miller and T. Lawson, "The Effect of an Informational Option on the Fundamental Attribution Error," *Personality and Social Psychology Bulletin* 15, no. 2 (June 1989) pp. 194–204.

91. J. Shepperd, W. Malone, and K. Sweeny, "Exploring Causes of the Self-Serving Bias," *Social and Personality Psychology Compass* 2, no. 2 (March 2008): pp. 895–908.

92. P. Harvey, "Entitled & Self-Serving Employees Are More Likely to Accuse Bosses of Abuse," *Forbes,* December 9, 2015, https://www.forbes.com/sites/datafreaks/2015/12/09/entitled-self-serving-employees-are-more-likely-to-accuse-bosses-of-abuse/#36893f0c260a.

93. A. H. Mezulis, L. Y. Abramson, J. S. Hyde, and B. L. Hankin, "Is There a Universal Positivity Bias in Attributions? A Meta-Analytic Review of Individual, Developmental, and Cultural Differences in the Self-Serving Attributional Bias," *Psychological Bulletin* 130, no. 5 (September 2004): pp. 711–47; and C. F. Falk, S. J. Heine, M. Yuki, and K. Takemura, "Why Do Westerners Self-Enhance More Than East Asians?," *European Journal of Personality* 23, no. 3 (May 2009): pp. 183–203.

94. R. Friedman, W. Liu, C. C. Chen, and S.-C. s. Chi, "Casual Attributions for Interfirm Contract Violation: A Comparative Study of Chinese and American Commercial Arbitrators," *Journal of Applied Psychology* 92, no. 3 (March 2007): pp. 856–64.

95. B. Pryor, "They're Baaaack: Chiefs Resign Veterans to Mentor Younger Players," *Kansas City Star*, October 17, 2018, https://www.kansascity.com/sports/nfl/kansas-city-chiefs/article220189100.html.

96. B. F. Skinner, *Contingencies of Reinforcement* (East Norwalk, CT: Appleton-Century-Crofts, 1971).

97. L. Burrell, "Co-Creating the Employee Experience," *Harvard Business Review*, March-April 2018, pp. 54–58.

98. D. Surt and T. Nordstrom, "Employee Experience Vs. Engagement, And 3 Things You Should Start Thinking About Now," *Forbes*, May 18, 2018, https://www.forbes.com/sites/davidsturt/2018/05/18/employee-experience-vs-engagement-and-3-things-you-should-start-thinking-about-now/#594c907ba88f.

99. R. Feintzeig and K. Gee, "Nice Tattoo! I Didn't Know You Worked at Walmart—Devoted Employees Ink Their Company Logos on Arms, Backs, and Legs," *Wall Street Journal,* March 3, 2018, p. B1.

100. A. Beard, "A Tattoo Won't Hurt Your Job Prospects," *Harvard Business Review*, November/December 2018, pp. 30–31.

Chapter 16   Motivating Employees

Learning Objectives

16.1 **Define** motivation.
16.2 **Compare** and contrast early theories of motivation.

16.3 **Compare** and contrast contemporary theories of motivation.
16.4 **Discuss** current issues in motivation.

Employability Skills Matrix

This matrix identifies which features and end-of-chapter material will help you develop specific skills employers are looking for in job candidates.

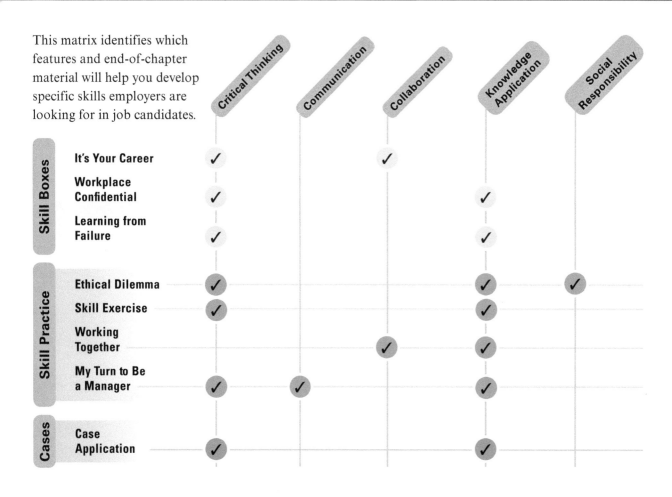

		Critical Thinking	Communication	Collaboration	Knowledge Application	Social Responsibility
Skill Boxes	It's Your Career	✓		✓		
	Workplace Confidential	✓			✓	
	Learning from Failure	✓			✓	
Skill Practice	Ethical Dilemma	✓			✓	✓
	Skill Exercise	✓			✓	
	Working Together			✓	✓	
	My Turn to Be a Manager	✓	✓		✓	
Cases	Case Application	✓			✓	

What motivates millennials? There is an increasing amount of evidence that flexibility is near the top of the list.[1] For example, Jessi Berrin, 32, works at the corporate headquarters of Baptist Health South Florida in Miami. She says, "The traditional 9-to-5 is not at all appealing to millennials... We want to work for employers who meet us where we are." She values her job because it gives her the flexibility to do things like work from home, leave work early to get to her fitness class, or come in to the office late to avoid rush-hour traffic.

While flexibility might not be an important motivator for every employee, employers who want to attract and keep millennials should consider increasing the flexibility around their organization's work arrangements.

WHAT is motivation?

LO16.1 All managers need to be able to motivate their employees, which first requires understanding what motivation is. Let's begin by pointing out what motivation isn't! Why? Because many people incorrectly view motivation as a personal trait; that is, they think some people are motivated and others aren't. Our knowledge of motivation tells us that individuals differ in motivational drive and their overall motivation varies from situation to situation. For instance, you're probably more motivated in some classes than in others.

Motivation refers to the process by which a person's efforts are energized, directed, and sustained toward attaining a goal.[2] This definition has three key elements: energy, direction, and persistence.

The *energy* element is a measure of intensity, drive, and vigor. A motivated person puts forth effort and works hard. However, the quality of the effort must be considered as well as its intensity. High levels of effort don't necessarily lead to favorable job performance unless the effort is channeled in a *direction* that benefits the organization. Effort directed toward and consistent with organizational goals is the kind of effort we want from employees. Finally, motivation includes a *persistence* dimension. We want employees to persist in putting forth effort to achieve those goals.

Motivating high levels of employee performance is an important organizational concern, and managers keep looking for answers. For instance, a Gallup Poll found a large majority of US employees—some 68 percent—are disengaged.[3] The number

motivation
The process by which a person's efforts are energized, directed, and sustained toward attaining a goal

---

IT'S YOUR CAREER

What Motivates You?

What's important to you or excites you in a job? Some say "money." Others might say "challenging work" or "fun coworkers." If you have a solid grounding in and understanding of what motivates you, it can help you make smart career and job choices.

The following is a list of twelve factors that might enter into your decision in selecting a job. Read over the list. Then rank order the items in terms of importance, with 1 being highest in importance and twelve being lowest in importance.

____ *High pay*
____ *Good working conditions*
____ *Friendly and supportive colleagues*
____ *Flexible working hours*
____ *Opportunities for growth and new challenges*
____ *Considerate boss*
____ *Inclusion in decisions that affect you*
____ *Fair and equitable treatment*
____ *Job security*
____ *Promotion potential*
____ *Excellent benefits (vacation time, retirement contributions, etc.)*
____ *Freedom and independence*

Now, compare your list with others in your class. How similar were your preferences? It's rare for lists to be exactly the same. This tells us that people differ in terms of what they value. Second, use these results to better understand what you're looking for in a job.

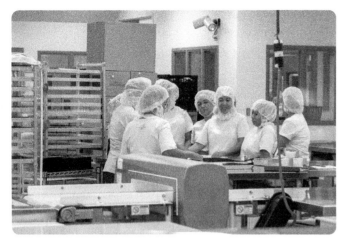

Motivators for employees of Big Island Candies in Hilo, Hawaii, include satisfying their lower-order needs of a salary, a safe job, benefits, and job security.
Source: Jim West/Alamy Stock Photo

hierarchy of needs theory
Maslow's theory that human needs—physiological, safety, social, esteem, and self-actualization—form a hierarchy and that each level in the needs hierarchy must be substantially satisfied before the next need becomes dominant

physiological needs
A person's needs for food, drink, shelter, sexual satisfaction, and other physical requirements

safety needs
A person's needs for security and protection from physical and emotional harm

social needs
A person's needs for affection, belongingness, acceptance, and friendship

esteem needs
A person's needs for internal factors such as self-respect, autonomy, and achievement, and external factors such as status, recognition, and attention

self-actualization needs
A person's need to become what he or she is capable of becoming

globally is even more disturbing—some 87 percent are not excited about their work.[4] It's no wonder then that both managers and academics want to understand and explain employee motivation.

EARLY theories of motivation

LO16.2 We begin by looking at four early motivation theories: *Maslow's hierarchy of needs, Theories X and Y, Herzberg's two-factor theory*, and *McClelland's three-needs theory*. Although more valid explanations of motivation have been developed, these early theories are important because they represent the foundation from which contemporary motivation theories were developed and because many practicing managers still use them.

Maslow's Hierarchy of Needs Theory

The best-known theory of motivation is probably Abraham Maslow's **hierarchy of needs theory**.[5] Maslow was a psychologist who proposed that within every person is a hierarchy of five needs:

1. **Physiological needs**: A person's needs for food, drink, shelter, sex, and other physical requirements.
2. **Safety needs**: A person's needs for security and protection from physical and emotional harm as well as assurance that physical needs will continue to be met.
3. **Social needs**: A person's needs for affection, belongingness, acceptance, and friendship.
4. **Esteem needs**: A person's needs for internal esteem factors such as self-respect, autonomy, and achievement and external esteem factors such as status, recognition, and attention.
5. **Self-actualization needs**: A person's needs for growth, achieving one's potential, and self-fulfillment; the drive to become what one is capable of becoming.

Maslow argued that each level in the needs hierarchy must be substantially satisfied before the next need becomes dominant. An individual moves up the needs hierarchy from one level to the next. (See Exhibit 16-1.) In addition, Maslow separated the five needs into higher and lower levels. Physiological and safety needs were considered *lower-order needs*; social, esteem, and self-actualization needs were considered *higher-order needs*. Lower-order needs are predominantly satisfied externally while higher-order needs are satisfied internally.

How does Maslow's theory explain motivation? Managers using Maslow's hierarchy to motivate employees do things to satisfy employees' needs. But the theory also says that once a need is substantially satisfied, an individual is no longer motivated

Exhibit 16-1

Maslow's Hierarchy of Needs

Source: A. H. Maslow, R. D. Frager, and J. Fadiman, *Motivation and Personality*, 3rd Edition, © 1987. Reprinted and electronically reproduced by permission of Pearson Education, Inc., Upper Saddle River, NJ.

to satisfy that need. Therefore, to motivate someone, you need to understand at what need level that person is on in the hierarchy and focus on satisfying needs at or above that level.

Maslow's needs theory was widely recognized during the 1960s and 1970s, especially among practicing managers, probably because it was intuitively logical and easy to understand. But Maslow provided no empirical support for his theory, and several studies that sought to validate it could not.[6]

McGregor's Theory X and Theory Y

Douglas McGregor proposed two assumptions about human nature: Theory X and Theory Y.[7] Very simply, **Theory X** is a negative view of people that assumes workers have little ambition, dislike work, want to avoid responsibility, and need to be closely controlled to work effectively. **Theory Y** is a positive view that assumes employees enjoy work, seek out and accept responsibility, and exercise self-direction. McGregor believed that Theory Y assumptions should guide management practice and proposed that participation in decision making, responsible and challenging jobs, and good group relations would maximize employee motivation. For example, Walmart gives workers a significant role in decision making. Store associates can provide input into what is sold locally. The company relies on associates' judgment because they interact with customers. Walmart's US CEO stated: "There is nothing I like better than hearing about your [associates'] jobs, your ideas, your hopes and dreams, and frustrations, and listening to how we can make your lives easier."[8] Clearly, this is an example of Walmart putting the philosophy of Theory Y into practice.

Unfortunately, there is no evidence to confirm that either set of assumptions is valid or that following Theory Y assumptions is the only way to motivate employees. In the real world, there are plenty of examples of effective managers who make Theory X assumptions. For instance, Apple co-founder Steve Jobs drove his staff hard and had no problem humiliating employees in staff meetings. Yet he was extremely successful in pushing his people to create innovative products and to constantly work to improve them.

Theory X
The assumption that employees dislike work, are lazy, avoid responsibility, and must be coerced to perform

Theory Y
The assumption that employees are creative, enjoy work, seek responsibility, and can exercise self-direction

Herzberg's Two-Factor Theory

Frederick Herzberg's **two-factor theory** (also called **motivation–hygiene theory**) proposes that intrinsic factors are related to job satisfaction, while extrinsic factors are associated with job dissatisfaction.[9] Herzberg wanted to know when people felt exceptionally good (satisfied) or bad (dissatisfied) about their jobs. (These findings are shown in Exhibit 16-2.) He concluded that the replies people gave when they felt good about their jobs were significantly different from the replies they gave when they felt bad. Certain characteristics were consistently related to job satisfaction (factors on

two-factor theory (motivation–hygiene theory)
The motivation theory that proposes intrinsic factors are related to job satisfaction and motivation, whereas extrinsic factors are associated with job dissatisfaction

Motivators	Hygiene Factors
• Achievement	• Supervision
• Recognition	• Company Policy
• Work Itself	• Relationship with
• Responsibility	Supervisor
• Advancement	• Working Conditions
• Growth	• Salary
	• Relationship with Peers
	• Personal Life
	• Relationship with
	Subordinates
	• Status
	• Security
Extremely Satisfied	**Neutral** **Extremely Dissatisfied**

Exhibit 16-2
Herzberg's Two-Factor Theory
Source: Based on F. Herzberg, B. Mausner, and B. B. Snyderman, *The Motivation to Work* (New York: John Wiley, 1959).

Exhibit 16-3
Contrasting Views of
Satisfaction–Dissatisfaction

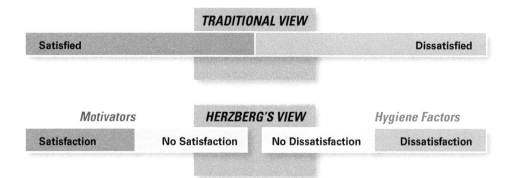

the left side of the exhibit), and others to job dissatisfaction (factors on the right side). When people felt good about their work, they tended to cite intrinsic factors arising from the job itself such as achievement, recognition, and responsibility. On the other hand, when they were dissatisfied, they tended to cite extrinsic factors arising from the job context such as company policy and administration, supervision, interpersonal relationships, and working conditions.

In addition, Herzberg believed the data suggested that the opposite of satisfaction was not dissatisfaction, as traditionally had been believed. Removing dissatisfying characteristics from a job would not necessarily make that job more satisfying (or motivating). As shown in Exhibit 16-3, Herzberg proposed that a dual continuum existed: the opposite of "satisfaction" is "no satisfaction," and the opposite of "dissatisfaction" is "no dissatisfaction."

Again, Herzberg believed the factors that led to job satisfaction were separate and distinct from those that led to job dissatisfaction. Therefore, managers who sought to eliminate factors that created job dissatisfaction could keep people from being dissatisfied but not necessarily motivate them. The extrinsic factors that remove job dissatisfaction were called **hygiene factors**. When these factors are adequate, people won't be dissatisfied, but they won't be satisfied (or motivated) either. To motivate people, Herzberg suggested emphasizing **motivators**, the intrinsic factors having to do with the job itself.

Herzberg's theory enjoyed wide popularity from the mid-1960s to the early 1980s, despite criticisms of his procedures and methodology. Although some critics said his theory was too simplistic, it has influenced how we currently design jobs, especially when it comes to job enrichment, which we'll discuss later in this chapter.

Three-Needs Theory

David McClelland and his associates proposed the **three-needs theory**, which says three acquired (not innate) needs are major motives in work.[10] These three are the **need for achievement (nAch)**, the drive to succeed and excel in relation to a set of standards; the **need for power (nPow)**, the need to make others behave in a way they would not have behaved otherwise; and the **need for affiliation (nAff)**, the desire for friendly and close interpersonal relationships. Of these three needs, the need for achievement has been researched the most.

People with a high need for achievement are striving for personal achievement rather than for the trappings and rewards of success. They have a desire to do something better or more efficiently than it's been done before.[11] They prefer jobs in which they can take personal responsibility for finding solutions to problems, in which they can receive rapid and unambiguous feedback on their performance in order to tell whether they're improving, and in which they can set moderately challenging goals. High achievers avoid what they perceive to be very easy or very difficult tasks. Also, a high need to achieve doesn't necessarily lead to being a good manager, especially in large organizations. That's because high achievers focus on their *own* accomplishments, while good managers emphasize helping *others* accomplish their goals.[12] McClelland

hygiene factors
Factors that eliminate job dissatisfaction, but don't motivate

motivators
Factors that increase job satisfaction and motivation

three-needs theory
The motivation theory that says three acquired (not innate) needs—achievement, power, and affiliation—are major motives in work

need for achievement (nAch)
The drive to succeed and excel in relation to a set of standards

need for power (nPow)
The need to make others behave in a way that they would not have behaved otherwise

need for affiliation (nAff)
The desire for friendly and close interpersonal relationships

Exhibit 16-4
TAT Pictures: Examples of pictures used for assessing levels of nAch, nAff, and nPow

Photo Source: Bill Aron/PhotoEdit

nAch: Indicated by someone in the story wanting to perform or do something better.
nAff: Indicated by someone in the story wanting to be with someone else and enjoy mutual friendship.
nPow: Indicated by someone in the story desiring to have an impact or make an impression on others in the story.

showed that employees can be trained to stimulate their achievement need by being in situations where they have personal responsibility, feedback, and moderate risks.

The other two needs in this theory haven't been researched as extensively as the need for achievement. However, studies have found that the best managers tend to be high in the need for power and low in the need for affiliation.[13]

All three of these needs can be measured by using a projective test (known as the Thematic Apperception Test or TAT), in which respondents react to a set of pictures. Each picture is briefly shown to a person who writes a story based on the picture. (See Exhibit 16-4 for some examples.) Trained interpreters then determine the individual's levels of nAch, nPow, and nAff from the stories written.

CONTEMPORARY theories of motivation

LO16.3 The theories we look at in this section represent current explanations of employee motivation. Although these theories may not be as well-known as those we just discussed, they are supported by research.[14] These contemporary motivation approaches include goal-setting theory, reinforcement theory, job design theory, equity theory, expectancy theory.

Goal-Setting Theory
We introduced the importance of goals in Chapter 8 in our discussion of planning. In this section we revisit them but through the lenses of motivation.

Before a big assignment or major class project presentation, has a teacher ever encouraged you to "just do your best"? What does that vague statement mean? Would your performance on a class project have been higher had that teacher said you needed to score a 93 percent to keep your A in the class? Research on goal-setting theory addresses these questions, and the findings, as you'll see, are impressive in terms of the effect that goal specificity, challenge, and feedback have on performance.[15]

Research provides substantial support for **goal-setting theory**, which says that specific goals increase performance and that difficult goals, when accepted, result in higher performance than do easy goals. What does goal-setting theory tell us?

goal-setting theory
The proposition that specific goals increase performance and that difficult goals, when accepted, result in higher performance than do easy goals

First, working toward a goal is a major source of job motivation. Studies on goal setting have demonstrated that specific and challenging goals are superior motivating forces.[16] Such goals produce a higher output than the generalized goal of "do your best." The specificity of the goal itself acts as an internal stimulus. For instance, when a sales rep commits to making eight sales calls daily, this intention gives him a specific goal to try to attain.

It's not a contradiction that goal-setting theory says that motivation is maximized by *difficult* goals, whereas achievement motivation (from three-needs theory) is stimulated by *moderately challenging* goals.[17] First, goal-setting theory deals with people in general, whereas the conclusions on achievement motivation are based on people who have a high nAch. Given that no more than 10 to 20 percent of North Americans are high achievers (a proportion that's likely lower in underdeveloped countries), difficult goals are still recommended for the majority of employees. Second, the conclusions of goal-setting theory apply to those who accept and are committed to the goals. Difficult goals will lead to higher performance *only* if they are accepted.

Next, will employees try harder if they have the opportunity to participate in the setting of goals? Not always. In some cases, participants who actively set goals elicit superior performance; in other cases, individuals performed best when their manager assigned goals. However, participation is probably preferable to assigning goals when employees might resist accepting difficult challenges.[19]

Finally, we know people will do better if they get feedback on how well they're progressing toward their goals because feedback helps identify discrepancies between what they have done and what they want to do. But all feedback isn't equally effective. Self-generated feedback—where an employee monitors his or her own progress—has been shown to be a more powerful motivator than feedback coming from someone else.[20]

Three other contingencies besides feedback influence the goal-performance relationship: goal commitment, adequate self-efficacy, and national culture.

First, goal-setting theory assumes an individual is committed to the goal. Commitment is most likely when goals are made public, when the individual has an internal locus of control, and when the goals are self-set rather than assigned.[21]

self-efficacy
An individual's belief that he or she is capable of performing a task

Next, **self-efficacy** refers to an individual's belief that he or she is capable of performing a task.[22] The higher your self-efficacy, the more confidence you have in your ability to succeed in a task. So, in difficult situations, we find that people with low self-efficacy are likely to reduce their effort or give up altogether, whereas those with high self-efficacy will try harder to master the challenge.[23] In addition, individuals with high self-efficacy seem to respond to negative feedback with increased effort and motivation, whereas those with low self-efficacy are likely to reduce their effort when given negative feedback.[24]

Finally, the value of goal-setting theory depends on national culture. It's well adapted to North American countries because its main ideas align reasonably well with those cultures. It assumes that subordinates will be reasonably independent (not a high score on power distance), that people will seek challenging goals (low in uncertainty avoidance), and that performance is considered important by both managers and subordinates (high in assertiveness). Don't expect goal setting to lead to higher employee performance in countries where the cultural characteristics aren't like this.

Exhibit 16-5 summarizes the relationships among goals, motivation, and performance. Our overall conclusion is that the intention to work toward hard and specific goals is a powerful motivating force. Under the proper conditions, it can lead to higher performance. However, no evidence indicates that such goals are associated with increased job satisfaction.[25]

Reinforcement Theory

reinforcement theory
The theory that behavior is a function of its consequences

reinforcers
Consequences immediately following a behavior, which increase the probability that the behavior will be repeated

Reinforcement theory says that behavior is a function of its consequences. Those consequences that immediately follow a behavior and increase the probability that the behavior will be repeated are called **reinforcers**. Reinforcement theory ignores factors

Exhibit 16-5
Goal-Setting Theory

such as goals, expectations, and needs. Instead, it focuses solely on what happens to a person when he or she does something.

In the previous chapter, we showed how managers use reinforcers to shape behavior, but the concept is also widely believed to explain motivation. To rehash, according to B. F. Skinner, people will most likely engage in desired behaviors if they are rewarded for doing so. These rewards are most effective if they immediately follow a desired behavior; and behavior that isn't rewarded, or is punished, is less likely to be repeated.[26]

Using reinforcement theory, managers can influence employees' behavior by using positive reinforcers for actions that help the organization achieve its goals. And managers should ignore, not punish, undesirable behavior. Although punishment eliminates undesired behavior faster than nonreinforcement, its effect is often temporary and may have unpleasant side effects, including dysfunctional behavior such as workplace conflicts, absenteeism, and turnover. Although reinforcement is an important influence on work behavior, it isn't the only explanation for differences in employee motivation.[27]

Designing Motivating Jobs

Because managers want to motivate individuals on the job, we need to look at ways to design motivating jobs. If you look closely at what an organization is and how it works, you'll find that it's composed of thousands of tasks. These tasks are, in turn, aggregated into jobs. We use the term **job design** to refer to the way tasks are combined to form complete jobs. The jobs people perform in an organization should not evolve by chance. Managers should design jobs deliberately and thoughtfully to reflect the demands of the changing environment; the organization's technology; and employees' skills, abilities, and preferences.[29] When jobs are designed like that, employees are motivated to work hard. Let's look at some ways that managers can design motivating jobs.

JOB ENLARGEMENT As we saw in the Management History module, job design historically has been to make jobs smaller, simpler, and more specialized. But it's difficult to motivate employees when jobs are like this. An early effort at overcoming the drawbacks of job specialization involved horizontally expanding a job through increasing **job scope**—the number of different tasks required in a job and the frequency with which these tasks are repeated. For instance, a dental hygienist's job could be enlarged so that in addition to cleaning teeth, he or she is pulling patients' files, refiling them when finished, and sanitizing and storing instruments. This type of job design option is called **job enlargement**.

Most job enlargement efforts that focus solely on increasing the number of tasks don't seem to work. As one employee who experienced such a job redesign said, "Before, I had one lousy job. Now, thanks to job enlargement, I have three lousy

job design
The way tasks are combined to form complete jobs

job scope
The number of different tasks required in a job and the frequency with which those tasks are repeated

job enlargement
The horizontal expansion of a job by increasing job scope

job enrichment
The vertical expansion of a job by adding planning and evaluating responsibilities

job depth
The degree of control employees have over their work

job characteristics model (JCM)
A framework for analyzing and designing jobs that identifies five primary core job dimensions, their interrelationships, and their impact on outcomes

skill variety
The degree to which a job requires a variety of activities so that an employee can use a number of different skills and talents

task identity
The degree to which a job requires completion of a whole and identifiable piece of work

task significance
The degree to which a job has a substantial impact on the lives or work of other people

autonomy
The degree to which a job provides substantial freedom, independence, and discretion to the individual in scheduling work and determining the procedures to be used in carrying it out

feedback
The degree to which carrying out work activities required by a job results in the individual's obtaining direct and clear information about his or her performance effectiveness

jobs!" However, research has shown that *knowledge* enlargement activities (expanding the scope of knowledge used in a job) lead to more job satisfaction, enhanced customer service, and fewer errors.[30]

JOB ENRICHMENT Another approach to job design is the vertical expansion of a job by adding planning and evaluating responsibilities—**job enrichment**. Job enrichment increases **job depth**, which is the degree of control employees have over their work. In other words, employees are empowered to assume some of the tasks typically done by their managers. Thus, an enriched job allows workers to do an entire activity with increased freedom, independence, and responsibility. In addition, workers get feedback so they can assess and correct their own performance. For instance, if our dental hygienist had an enriched job, he or she could, in addition to cleaning teeth, schedule appointments (planning) and follow up with clients (evaluating). Although job enrichment may improve the quality of work, employee motivation, and satisfaction, research evidence has been inconclusive as to its usefulness.[31]

JOB CHARACTERISTICS MODEL Even though many organizations implemented job enlargement and job enrichment programs and experienced mixed results, neither approach provided an effective framework for managers to design motivating jobs. But the **job characteristics model (JCM)** does.[32] It identifies five core job dimensions, their interrelationships, and their impact on employee productivity, motivation, and satisfaction. These five core job dimensions are:

1. **Skill variety**, the degree to which a job requires a variety of activities so that an employee can use a number of different skills and talents.
2. **Task identity**, the degree to which a job requires completion of a whole and identifiable piece of work.
3. **Task significance**, the degree to which a job has a substantial impact on the lives or work of other people.
4. **Autonomy**, the degree to which a job provides substantial freedom, independence, and discretion to the individual in scheduling the work and determining the procedures to be used in carrying it out.
5. **Feedback**, the degree to which doing work activities required by a job results in an individual obtaining direct and clear information about the effectiveness of his or her performance.

The JCM is shown in Exhibit 16-6. Notice how the first three dimensions—skill variety, task identity, and task significance—combine to create meaningful work. In other words, if these three characteristics exist in a job, we can predict that the person will view his or her job as being important, valuable, and worthwhile. Notice, too, that jobs that possess autonomy give the jobholder a feeling of personal responsibility for the results and that if a job provides feedback, the employee will know how effectively he or she is performing.

The JCM suggests that employees are likely to be motivated when they *learn* (knowledge of results through feedback) that they *personally* (experienced responsibility through autonomy of work) performed well on tasks that they *care about* (experienced meaningfulness through skill variety, task identity, or task significance).[33] The more a job is designed around these three elements, the greater the employee's motivation, performance, and satisfaction and the lower his or her absenteeism and likelihood of resigning. As the model shows, the links between the job dimensions and the outcomes are moderated by the strength of the individual's growth need (the person's desire for self-esteem and self-actualization). Individuals with a high-growth need are more likely than low-growth need individuals to experience the critical psychological states and respond positively when

Meaningful work that helps people with physical problems gives occupational therapist, Abbey Wash, considerable motivation and job satisfaction. Wash's job scores high in skill and task variety plus task significance.
Source: Jeff Siner/Charlotte Observer/TNS/ Newscom

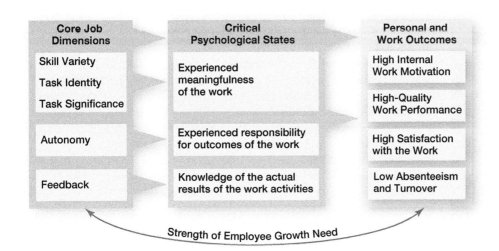

Exhibit 16-6
Job Characteristics Model
Source: "Job Characteristics Model," from *Work Redesign*, by J. R. Hackman & G. R. Oldham. Copyright © 1980 by Addison-Wesley (a division of Pearson). Reprinted with permission.

their jobs include the core dimensions. This distinction may explain the mixed results with job enrichment: individuals with low-growth need aren't likely to achieve high performance or satisfaction by having their jobs enriched.

The JCM provides specific guidance to managers for job design. These suggestions specify the types of changes most likely to lead to improvement in the five core job dimensions. You'll notice that two suggestions incorporate job enlargement and job enrichment, although the other suggestions involve more than vertical and horizontal expansion of jobs.

1. *Combine tasks.* Put fragmented tasks back together to form a new, larger work module (job enlargement) to increase skill variety and task identity.
2. *Create natural work units.* Design tasks that form an identifiable and meaningful whole to increase employee "ownership" of the work. Encourage employees to view their work as meaningful and important rather than as irrelevant and boring.
3. *Establish client (external or internal) relationships.* Whenever possible, establish direct relationships between workers and their clients to increase skill variety, autonomy, and feedback.
4. *Expand jobs vertically.* Vertical expansion gives employees responsibilities and controls that were formerly reserved for managers, which can increase employee autonomy.
5. *Open feedback channels.* Direct feedback lets employees know how well they're performing their jobs and whether their performance is improving or not.

The research into the JCM has provided a rich knowledge base for understanding how job design influences employee motivation; however, the research does not directly specify motivating jobs. What are some of the jobs people consider to be more or less meaningful?

A survey of over two million workers in twenty-four job categories provides some insights.[34] When asked, "Does your job make the world a better place," more than 70 percent of those working in healthcare, social services, education, and protective services said "yes." In contrast, fewer than 50 percent of those in food preparation services, sales, production, and office administration felt that they make the world a better place.

Research into the JCM continues. Jobs have changed since the mid-1970s, when the JCM was originally formulated. One study, for instance, found that jobs today offer greater skill variety and autonomy—but concluded that the association between the five core job characteristics and satisfaction has remained unchanged over time.[35] Other assessments have questioned whether the JCM captures the global shift from a manufacturing economy to a knowledge and service economy by failing to take into account the social dimensions of work.[36]

JOB DESIGN UPDATED In response to concerns that the JCM may not be totally appropriate for today's jobs, two emerging viewpoints have received attention. Let's take a look at each.

The first, the **relational perspective of work design**, focuses on how people's tasks and jobs are increasingly based on social relationships.[37] In jobs today, employees have more interactions and interdependence with co-workers and others both inside and outside the organization. In doing their job, employees rely more and more on those around them for information, advice, and assistance. So what does this mean for designing motivating jobs? It means that managers need to look at important components of those employee relationships such as access to and level of social support in an organization, types of interactions outside an organization, amount of task interdependence, and interpersonal feedback.

Let's look at an example of the relational perspective of work design. Have you ever called a software company's help line? Isn't your expectation that the product expert will provide straightforward answers and step-by-step instructions for addressing the problem? Of course, we all do! Microsoft understands customers' expectations. Managers help improve the customer service experience by connecting software developers with customers. In this example, the manager's goal is to have developers write software that meets technical specifications and is user friendly.

The second perspective, the **proactive perspective of work design**, says that employees are taking the initiative to change how their work is performed.[38] They're much more involved in decisions and actions that affect their work. Important job design factors according to this perspective include autonomy (which *is* part of the JCM), amount of ambiguity and accountability, job complexity, level of stressors, and social or relationship context. Each of these has been shown to influence employee proactive behavior. For instance, researchers observed cleaners at a hospital took the initiative to craft their own jobs. According to one of the researchers, "The cleaners had tons of rooms they had to clean in a very short period of time so they had very little discretion over the number of tasks they had to get done.... [T]o make it more meaningful for themselves, they would do all types of little things to help the patients and their patients' families."[39] One stream of research that's relevant to proactive work design is **high-involvement work practices**, which are designed to elicit greater input or involvement from workers.[40] The level of employee proactivity is believed to increase as employees become more involved in decisions that affect their work.

Equity Theory

If someone offered you $80,000 a year on your first job after graduating from college, you'd probably jump at the offer and report to work enthusiastic, ready to tackle whatever needed to be done, and certainly be satisfied with your pay. How would you react, though, if you found out a month into the job that a coworker—another recent graduate, your age, with comparable grades from a comparable school, and with comparable work experience—was getting $85,000 a year? You'd probably be upset! Even though in absolute terms, $80,000 is a lot of money for a new graduate to make (and you know it!), that suddenly isn't the issue. Now you see the issue as what you believe is *fair*—what is *equitable*. The term *equity* is related to the concept of fairness and equitable treatment compared with others who behave in similar ways. Evidence indicates that employees compare themselves to others and that inequities influence how much effort employees exert.[41]

Equity theory proposes that employees compare what they get from a job (outcomes) in relation to what they put into it (inputs), and then they compare their inputs-outcomes ratio with the inputs-outcomes ratios of relevant others (Exhibit 16-7). If an employee perceives her ratio to be equitable in comparison to those of relevant others, there's no problem. However, if the ratio is inequitable, she

The newly opened headquarters of the Zalando campus was created to facilitate social support, consistent with the relational perspective of work design.
Source: Jens Kalaene/dpa-Zentralbild/dpa picture alliance/Alamy Live News/Alamy Stock Photo

relational perspective of work design
An approach to job design that focuses on how people's tasks and jobs are increasingly based on social relationships

proactive perspective of work design
An approach to job design in which employees take the initiative to change how their work is performed

high-involvement work practices
Work practices designed to elicit greater input or involvement from workers

equity theory
The theory that an employee compares his or her job's input-outcomes ratio with that of relevant others and then corrects any inequity

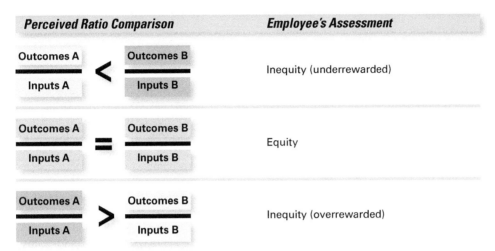

Exhibit 16-7
Equity Theory

Perceived Ratio Comparison		Employee's Assessment
$\frac{\text{Outcomes A}}{\text{Inputs A}} < \frac{\text{Outcomes B}}{\text{Inputs B}}$		Inequity (underrewarded)
$\frac{\text{Outcomes A}}{\text{Inputs A}} = \frac{\text{Outcomes B}}{\text{Inputs B}}$		Equity
$\frac{\text{Outcomes A}}{\text{Inputs A}} > \frac{\text{Outcomes B}}{\text{Inputs B}}$		Inequity (overrewarded)

views herself as underrewarded or overrewarded. When inequities occur, employees attempt to do something about it.[42] The result might be lower or higher productivity, improved or reduced quality of output, increased absenteeism, or voluntary resignation. Interestingly, people are pretty good at rationalizing over-rewarding so under-rewarding tends to have the greatest impact on behavior.

The **referent**—the other persons, systems, or selves individuals compare themselves against in order to assess equity—is an important variable in equity theory.[43] Each of the three referent categories is important. The "persons" category includes other individuals with similar jobs in the same organization but also includes friends, neighbors, or professional associates. Based on what they hear at work or read about in newspapers or trade journals, employees compare their pay with that of others. The "systems" category includes organizational pay policies, procedures, and allocation. The "selves" category refers to inputs-outcomes ratios that are unique to the individual. It reflects past personal experiences and contacts and is influenced by criteria such as past jobs or family commitments.

Originally, equity theory focused on **distributive justice**, the perceived fairness of the amount and allocation of rewards among individuals. More recent research has focused on looking at issues of **procedural justice**, the perceived fairness of the process used to determine the distribution of rewards. This research shows that distributive justice has a greater influence on employee satisfaction than procedural justice, while procedural justice tends to affect an employee's organizational commitment, trust in his or her boss, and intention to quit.[44] What are the implications for managers? They should consider openly sharing information on how allocation decisions are made, follow consistent and unbiased procedures, and engage in similar practices to increase the perception of procedural justice. By increasing the perception of procedural justice, employees are likely to view their bosses and the organization as positive even if they're dissatisfied with pay, promotions, and other personal outcomes.

Expectancy Theory

The most comprehensive explanation of how employees are motivated is **expectancy theory**.[45] Although the theory has its critics,[46] most research evidence supports it.[47]

Expectancy theory states that an individual tends to act in a certain way based on the expectation that the act will be followed by a given outcome and on the attractiveness of that outcome to the individual. It includes three variables or relationships (see Exhibit 16-8):

1. *Effort-performance linkage:* the probability perceived by the individual that exerting a given amount of effort will lead to a certain level of performance.
2. *Performance-reward linkage:* the degree to which the individual believes that performing at a particular level is instrumental in attaining the desired outcome.

referents
The persons, systems, or selves against which individuals compare themselves to assess equity

distributive justice
Perceived fairness of the amount and allocation of rewards among individuals

procedural justice
Perceived fairness of the process used to determine the distribution of rewards

expectancy theory
The theory that an individual tends to act in a certain way based on the expectation that the act will be followed by a given outcome and on the attractiveness of that outcome to the individual

Workplace confidential Feelings of Unfair Pay

For many employees, nothing is likely to act as a demotivator as much as learning that someone in their organization is getting paid more than they are for the same or similar job. Depending on your equity sensitivity, someday you might find yourself angry and frustrated because you believe you're not being fairly compensated.

Let's start with the fact that we're not all equally equity sensitive. Equity sensitivity (ES) is a term that developed out of equity theory. ES acknowledges that not all individuals are equivalently sensitive to equity. ES, therefore, is a personality trait based on an individual's preferred input-to-outcome ratios. For our purposes, we will focus on individuals who believe that they are being underrewarded relative to others. If you're not equity sensitive and you think you're underpaid, you might just want to let it go. As we'll point out, there are risks when you try to correct what you perceive as unfair pay. Sometimes the best strategy is to do nothing. Be sure that you really want to pursue the issue before you act.

If you do feel that you're being paid unfairly, you need to start by asking yourself: What's my evidence? A few organizations make employee salaries public. But that's not the norm. Especially for white-collar jobs, organizations typically don't want employees to know what others are making. In fact, in some organizations, it's a stated policy that employees are *not* to share salary information with each other. Why do organizations do this? The obvious answer is that they don't want employees making comparisons and expecting management to justify every perceived unfairness.

The above suggests that you need to do research before you want to proclaim that you're underpaid. While historically it was difficult to get accurate data for comparing salaries, the internet has changed that. Salary websites such as Glassdoor and PayScale.com provide comparative data for many jobs and in different markets.

Two questions to consider: What's your basis for concluding you're underpaid, and is there a logical explanation why you might be paid less than someone else in the same or similar job? Keep in mind that there are a lot of reasons to justify salary differences—education, skills, length of time with the organization, relevant experience, different performance ratings, location, and cost of living. There's a reason, for instance, that two insurance adjusters working for Liberty Mutual might be paid differently if one works out of New York City and the other out of Birmingham, Alabama. In the United States, gender is not a justification for paying a woman less than a man for doing the same job. The Equal Pay Act specifically prohibits wage disparities based on sex. Also, remember that most organizations have salary ranges for specific jobs and people have different skills in negotiating. Some differences in pay may be attributable to initial starting salaries that were negotiated at different times and under different conditions.

If you're convinced your pay is unfair and have the evidence to support your claim, ask yourself how much risk you're willing to take. Is it worth pursuing this, and if so, how hard do you want to push? In some organizations, the culture discourages people from comparing salaries or challenging the pay structure. And be prepared to find that your concern falls on deaf ears. Many managers fear that increasing one individual's pay because he or she complained will open up a flood of requests for pay reevaluations.

If you decide to pursue the issue, you'll need a strategy. Start by deciding to whom you are going to make your case. Don't assume your boss has solo discretion to adjust your pay. Pay structures, especially in large organizations, are carefully designed and monitored. While your boss may have some say in recommending pay increases, the final decision usually lies with the human resources department. So you should consider whether you want to present your case to your immediate boss, the human resources manager, or both.

Timing counts! That is, there are times that are better for making your case. The natural time is with your performance evaluation. A strong evaluation strengthens your hand in asking for an adjustment, especially if it is backed up with evidence suggesting that you're underpaid. And what kind of evidence makes your case and helps your boss to get approvals from his or her superiors? If you have objective data that indicates that others in your organization or community are getting paid more than you are for the same or similar job, present the facts. Additionally, elaborate on your contributions. Specifically reference your past accomplishments and what you expect to contribute in the future. Ideally, you'll have concrete evidence to make your case, such as how much you brought the organization in sales or how much you saved through increased productivity. If your job doesn't lend itself to such facts, support your case with positive comments on your accomplishments from customers, suppliers, or work colleagues.

We conclude with some things you should *not* do. (1) Don't go over your boss's head—for instance, talking with your human resources manager—without first getting your boss's approval. No manager wants to feel that you are undermining his or her authority. (2) Don't discuss your compensation with coworkers. Pay is a sensitive subject. It's best not to share salary information. Use other sources, besides coworkers, to get comparative data. (3) Don't make comparisons to a specific person in your department or organization. This is not likely to win you support from your boss or colleagues. (4) Don't go negative. Complaining or making threats rarely results in positive outcomes. And saying that you haven't had a raise in years or that you're doing twice as much work as everyone else is also likely to prove unproductive.[48]

Exhibit 16-8
Expectancy Model

3. *Attractiveness:* the importance an individual places on the potential outcome or reward that can be achieved on the job. This considers both the goals and needs of the individual.

While this might sound complex, it really isn't that difficult to visualize. It can be summed up in the following questions: How hard do I have to work to achieve a certain level of performance, and can I actually achieve that level? What reward will performing at that level of performance get me? How attractive is the reward to me, and does it help me achieve my own personal goals? Whether you are motivated to put forth effort (that is, to work hard) at any given time depends on your goals and your perception of whether a certain level of performance is necessary to attain those goals.

Let's use the classroom organization as an illustration of how one can use expectancy theory to explain motivation.

Just Born Quality Confections—makers of Peeps and Mike & Ike brands—uses expectancy theory in motivating employees to achieve annual sales goals. Sales team members shown here expected their efforts would result in winning an all-expenses-paid trip to Hawaii. But they failed to meet their goal and instead earned jackets and bomber hats and a trip to Fargo, North Dakota.
Source: Ann Arbor Miller/AP Photo

Most students prefer an instructor who tells them what is expected of them in the course. They want to know what the assignments and examinations will be like, when they are due or to be taken, and how much weight each carries in the final term grade. They also like to think that the amount of effort they exert in attending classes, taking notes, writing papers, meeting with project team members, and/or studying will be reasonably related to the grade they will make in the course. Let's assume that you, as a student, feel this way. Consider that five weeks into a class you are really enjoying (we'll call it MGT 301), an examination is given back to you. You studied hard for this exam, and you have consistently made As and Bs on exams in other courses to which you have expended similar effort. The reason you work so hard is to make top grades, which you believe are important for getting a good job upon graduation. Also, you are not sure, but you might want to go on to graduate school. Again, you think grades are important for getting into a good graduate school.

Well, the results of that five-week exam are in. The class median was 72. Ten percent of the class scored an 85 or higher and got an A. Your grade was 46; the minimum passing mark was 50. You're mad. You're frustrated. Even more, you're perplexed. How could you possibly have done so poorly on the exam when you usually score in the top range in other classes by preparing as you did for this one?

Several interesting things are immediately evident in your behavior. Suddenly, you're no longer driven to attend MGT 301 classes regularly. You find that you do not study for the course either. When you do attend classes, you daydream a lot—the result is an empty notebook instead of several pages of notes. One would probably be correct in describing you as "lacking in motivation" in MGT 301. Why did you motivation level change? You know and I know, but let's explain it in expectancy terms.

If we use Exhibit 16-8 to understand this situation, we might say the following: studying and preparing for MGT 301 (effort) are conditioned by their resulting in correctly answering the questions on the exam (performance), which will produce a high grade (reward), which will lead, in turn, to the security, prestige, and other benefits that accrue from obtaining a good job (individual goal).

The attractiveness of the outcome, which in this case is a good grade, is high. But what about the performance-reward linkage? Do you feel that the grade you received truly reflects your knowledge of the material? In other words, did the test fairly measure what you know? If the answer is yes, then this linkage is strong. If the answer is no, then at least part of the reason for your reduced motivational level is your belief that the test was not a fair measure of your performance. If the test was of the essay type, maybe you believe the instructor's grading method was poor. Was too much weight placed on a question that you thought was trivial? Maybe the instructor doesn't like you and was biased in grading your paper. These are examples of perceptions that influence the performance-reward linkage and your level of motivation.

Another possible demotivating force may be the effort-performance relationship. If, after you took the exam, you believe that you could not have passed it regardless of the amount of preparation you had done, then your desire to study will drop. Possibly the instructor wrote the exam under the assumption that you had a considerably broader background in the subject matter. Maybe the course had several prerequisites that you didn't know about, or possibly you had the prerequisites but took them several years ago. The result is the same: you place a low value on your effort leading to answering the exam questions correctly, hence your motivational level decreases, and you lessen your effort.

The key to expectancy theory is therefore understanding an individual's goal—and the linkage between effort and performance; between performance and rewards; and, finally, between rewards and individual goal satisfaction. It emphasizes payoffs, or rewards. As a result, we have to believe that the rewards an organization is offering align with what the employee wants. As a contingency model, expectancy theory recognizes that no universal principle explains what motivates individuals and thus stresses that managers understand why employees view certain outcomes as attractive or unattractive. After all, we want to reward individuals with those things they value positively. Also, expectancy theory emphasizes expected behaviors. Do employees know what is expected of them and how they'll be evaluated? Finally, the theory is concerned with perceptions. Reality is irrelevant. An individual's own perceptions of performance, reward, and goal outcomes—not the outcomes themselves—will determine his or her motivation (level of effort).

Integrating Contemporary Theories of Motivation

We've presented a number of theories in this chapter. There is a tendency, at this point, to view them independently. This is a mistake. The fact is that many of the ideas underlying the theories are complementary, and your understanding of how to motivate people is maximized when you see how the theories fit together.

Exhibit 16-9 presents a model that integrates much of what we know about motivation. Its basic foundation is the simplified expectancy model shown in Exhibit 16-8. Let's work through Exhibit 16-9, beginning at the left.

The individual effort box has an arrow leading into it. This arrow flows from the individual's goals. Consistent with goal-setting theory, this goals-effort loop is meant to illustrate that goals direct behavior.

Expectancy theory predicts that an employee will exert a high level of effort if he or she perceives a strong relationship between effort and performance, performance and rewards, and rewards and satisfaction of personal goals. Each of these relationships is, in turn, influenced by certain factors. For effort to lead to good performance, the individual must have the requisite ability to perform, and the performance evaluation system that measure the individual's performance must be perceived as being fair and objective. The performance-reward relationship will be strong if the individual perceives that it is performance (rather than seniority, personal favorites, or other criteria) that is rewarded. The final link in expectancy theory is the rewards-goals relationship. Need theories would come into play at this point. Motivation would be high

Exhibit 16-9
Integrating Contemporary
Theories of Motivation

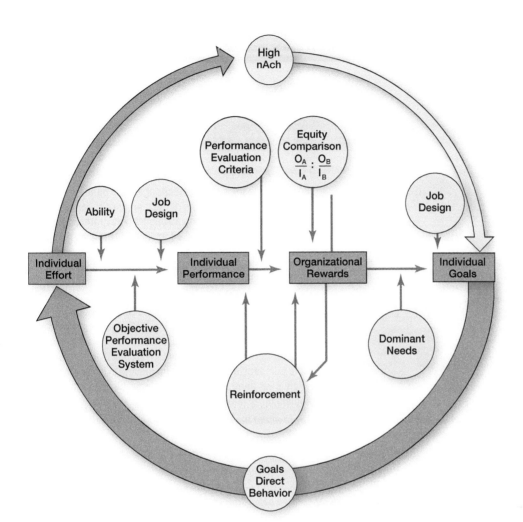

to the degree that the rewards an individual received for his or her high performance satisfied dominant needs consistent with his or her individual goals.

A closer look at the model also shows that it considers the achievement-need, reinforcement, equity, and JCM theories. The high achiever isn't motivated by the organization's assessment of his or her performance or organizational rewards, hence the jump from effort to individual goals for those with a high nAch. Remember that high achievers are internally driven as long as the jobs they're doing provide them with personal responsibility, feedback, and moderate risks. They're not concerned with the effort-performance, performance-reward, or rewards-goals linkages.

Reinforcement theory is seen in the model by recognizing that the organization's rewards reinforce the individual's performance. If managers have designed a reward system that is seen by employees as "paying off" for good performance, the rewards will reinforce and encourage continued good performance. Rewards also play a key part in equity theory. Individuals will compare the rewards (outcomes) they have received from the inputs or efforts they made with the inputs-outcomes ratio of relevant others. If inequities exist, the effort expended may be influenced.

Finally, the JCM is seen in this integrative model. Task characteristics influence job motivation at two places. First, jobs designed around the five job dimensions are likely to lead to higher actual job performance because the individual's motivation will be stimulated by the job itself; that is, they will increase the linkage between effort and performance. Second, jobs designed around the five job dimensions also increase an employee's control over key elements in his or her work.

Therefore, jobs that offer autonomy, feedback, and similar task characteristics help to satisfy the individual goals of employees who desire greater control over their work.

Let's Get REAL

Anooja Rangnekar ▶
Manager, Medicaid
Business Development

Source: Anooja Rangnekar

The Scenario:

Laura Mora is the sales manager at a solar panel installation company. Some of the members of her sales staff seem to be just getting through the day rather than putting positive energy and effort towards their jobs. These sales staff members are responsible for attracting new clients, discussing potential client needs over the phone, and visiting prospective clients on-site to determine what products would work best for them. When Laura overheard a couple of phone calls some of her staff had with potential clients recently, it seemed like her staff members provided the minimal information asked of them. Additional details about products and their benefits were not discussed. Sales at the company have been on the decline in recent months, which is yet another indicator of a possible motivation problem for at least some of her staff members.

What suggestions do you have for Laura about how she can try to improve the motivation of her employees?

There are a few strategies that Laura can use to improve the motivation of her employees:

1. *It may be the case that some of her employees are unfamiliar with the additional details and benefits of the products. Laura could conduct an all-staff training and provide training materials to help ensure all sales staff are knowledgeable about the products they are selling.*

2. *Laura could work with her team to develop training guides that the staff can refer to while they are conducting sales calls. The guides can serve as reminders to staff about the additional details about products and their benefits.*

3. *Lastly, Laura could introduce the idea of a game or friendly competition among the staff. This can help team members push one another to achieve greater results. Laura could also structure a game that incentivizes staff to compete with themselves and strive to increase sales and productivity month-over-month.*

CURRENT issues in motivation

LO16.4 Understanding and predicting employee motivation is one of the most popular areas in management research. We've introduced you to a number of motivation theories. However, contemporary theories of employee motivation are influenced by some significant workplace issues—managing cross-cultural challenges, motivating unique groups of workers, and designing appropriate rewards programs.

Managing Cross-Cultural Motivational Challenges

In today's global business environment, managers can't automatically assume motivational programs that work in one geographic location are going to work in others. Most current motivation theories were developed in the United States by

Americans and about Americans.[49] Maybe the most blatant pro-American characteristic in these theories is the strong emphasis on individualism and achievement. For instance, both goal-setting and expectancy theories emphasize goal accomplishment as well as rational and individual thought. Let's look at motivation theories to see their level of cross-cultural transferability.

Maslow's needs hierarchy argues that people start at the physiological level and then move progressively up the hierarchy in order. This hierarchy, if it has any application at all, aligns with American culture. In countries like Japan, Greece, and Mexico, where uncertainty avoidance characteristics are strong, security needs would be the foundational layer of the needs hierarchy. Countries that score high on nurturing characteristics—Denmark, Sweden, Norway, the Netherlands, and Finland—would have social needs as their foundational level.[50] We predict, for instance, that group work will be more motivating when the country's culture scores high on the nurturing criterion.

The motivation of these employees working at the research and development facility at the Daihatsu Motor plant near Jakarta, Indonesia, is influenced by their national culture. Indonesia has a strong collectivist culture, where employees are motivated less by receiving individual praise because their culture places a greater emphasis on harmony, belonging, and consensus.
Source: Kyodo/Newscom

Another motivation concept that clearly has an American bias is the achievement need. The view that a high achievement need acts as an internal motivator presupposes two cultural characteristics—a willingness to accept a moderate degree of risk (which excludes countries with strong uncertainty avoidance characteristics) and a concern with performance (which applies almost singularly to countries with strong achievement characteristics). This combination is found in countries such as the United States, Canada, and Great Britain.[51] On the other hand, these characteristics are relatively absent in countries such as Chile and Portugal.

Equity theory has a relatively strong following in the United States, which is not surprising given that US-style reward systems are based on the assumption that workers are highly sensitive to equity in reward allocations. In the United States, equity is meant to closely link pay to performance. However, evidence suggests that in collectivist cultures, especially in the former socialist countries of Central and Eastern Europe, employees expect rewards to reflect their individual needs as well as their performance.[52] Moreover, consistent with a legacy of communism and centrally planned economies, employees exhibited a greater "entitlement" attitude—that is, they expected outcomes to be greater than their inputs.[53] These findings suggest that US-style pay practices may need to be modified in some countries in order to be perceived as fair by employees.

Another research study of more than 50,000 employees around the world examined two cultural characteristics from the GLOBE framework—individualism and masculinity (see Chapter 4 for a discussion of these characteristics)—in relation to motivation.[54] The researchers found that in individualistic cultures such as the United States and Canada, individual initiative, individual freedom, and individual achievement are highly valued. In more collective cultures such as Iran, Peru, and China, however, employees may be less interested in receiving individual praise but place a greater emphasis on harmony, belonging, and consensus. They also found that in masculine (achievement/assertive) cultures such as those in Japan and Slovakia, the focus is on material success. Those work environments are designed to push employees hard and then reward top performers with high earnings. However, in more nurturing cultures such as Sweden and the Netherlands, smaller wage gaps among employees are common, and employees are likely to have extensive quality-of-life benefits.

Despite these cross-cultural differences in motivation, some cross-cultural consistencies are evident. In a study of employees in thirteen countries, the top motivators included (ranked from number one on down) being treated with respect, work-life balance, the type of work done, the quality of people worked with, the quality of the organization's leadership, base pay, working in an environment where good service can be provided to others, long-term career potential, flexible working arrangements, learning and development opportunities, benefits, promotion opportunities, and incentive pay or bonuses.[55] And other studies have shown that the desire for interesting work seems important to almost all workers, regardless of their national culture. For instance, employees in Belgium, Britain, Israel, and the United States ranked "interesting work" number one among 11 work goals. It was ranked either second or third in Japan, the Netherlands, and Germany.[56] Similarly, in a study comparing job-preference outcomes among graduate students in the United States, Canada, Australia, and Singapore, growth, achievement, and responsibility were rated the top three and had identical rankings.[57] Both studies suggest some universality to the importance of intrinsic factors identified by Herzberg in his two-factor theory. Another recent study examining workplace motivation trends in Japan also seems to indicate that Herzberg's model is applicable to Japanese employees.[58]

Motivating Unique Groups of Workers

Employees come into organizations with different needs, personalities, skills, abilities, interests, and aptitudes. They have different expectations of their employers and different views of what they think their employer has a right to expect of them. And they vary widely in what they want from their jobs. Given these differences, how can managers do an effective job of motivating the unique groups of employees found in today's workforce? One thing is to understand the motivational requirements of these groups, including diverse employees, professionals, and contingent workers.

MOTIVATING A DIVERSE WORKFORCE To maximize motivation among today's workforce, managers need to think in terms of *flexibility.* For instance, studies tell us that men place more importance on having autonomy in their jobs than women. In contrast, the opportunity to learn, convenient and flexible work hours, and good interpersonal relations are more important to women.[59] Millennials value social relationships and, in contrast to older workers, are likely to enjoy being part of a team.[60] Managers need to recognize that what motivates a single mother with two dependent children who's working full time to support her family may be very different from the needs of a single part-time employee or an older employee who is working only to supplement his or her retirement income. A diverse array of rewards is needed to motivate employees with such diverse needs. For instance, many organizations have developed flexible work arrangements—such as compressed workweeks, flextime, and job sharing, which we discussed in Chapter 11—that recognize different needs. Another job alternative we also discussed earlier is telecommuting. However, keep in mind that not all employees embrace the idea of telecommuting. Some workers relish the informal interactions at work that satisfy their social needs and are a source of new ideas.

Do flexible work arrangements motivate employees? Although such arrangements might seem highly motivational, both positive and negative relationships have been found. For instance, a study that looked at the impact of telecommuting on job satisfaction found that job satisfaction initially increased as the extent of telecommuting increased, but as the number of hours spent telecommuting increased, job satisfaction started to level off, decreased slightly, and then stabilized.[61]

MOTIVATING PROFESSIONALS In contrast to a generation ago, the typical employee today is more likely to be a professional with a college degree than a blue-collar factory worker. What special concerns should managers be aware of when trying to motivate a team of engineers at Intel's India Development Center, software designers at SAS Institute in North Carolina, or a group of consultants at Accenture in Singapore?

Professionals are different from nonprofessionals.[62] They have a strong and long-term commitment to their field of expertise. To keep current in their field, they need to regularly update their knowledge, and because of their commitment to their profession, they rarely define their workweek as 8 a.m. to 5 p.m., five days a week.

What motivates professionals? Money and promotions typically are low on their priority list. Why? They tend to be well paid and enjoy what they do. In contrast, job challenge tends to be ranked high. They like to tackle problems and find solutions. Their chief reward is the work itself. An interesting stream of research has focused on the "flow experience."[63] *Flow* is a state of total absorption in one's work, where individuals lose their sense of time and awareness of surrounding activities. It appears to apply most directly to professionals. Managers can maximize flow among professional employees by designing jobs that are challenging, provide opportunities for using creativity, and allow full utilization of employees' skills. The irony of flow is that it's self-motivating. The tasks themselves stimulate high levels of performance.

Lastly, keep in mind that professionals tend to be focused on their work as their central life interest, whereas nonprofessionals typically have other interests outside of work that can compensate for needs not met on the job. This suggests that professionals are less likely to stay in jobs that lack challenge, variety, or fail to fully utilize their skills.

Managers of home rental website Airbnb motivate the firm's young employees at its San Francisco headquarters with an open and collaborative work environment that promotes teamwork and a sense of community and stimulates innovation. Employees have the freedom to work where they want and enjoy amenities such as a cafeteria, nap room, library, yoga classes, organic lunches, and $2,000 each year for personal travel.
Source: Ed Reeve-VIEW/Alamy Stock Photo

MOTIVATING CONTINGENT WORKERS   We discussed in Chapter 11 the increased number of contingent workers employed by organizations. There's no simple solution for motivating these employees. For that small set of individuals who prefer the freedom of their temporary status, the lack of stability may not be an issue. In addition, temporariness might be preferred by highly compensated physicians, engineers, accountants, or financial planners who don't want the demands of a full-time job. But these individuals are the exceptions. For the most part, temporary employees are not temporary by choice.

What will motivate involuntarily temporary employees? An obvious answer is the opportunity to become a permanent employee. In cases in which permanent employees are selected from a pool of temps, the temps will often work hard in hopes of becoming permanent. A less-obvious answer is the opportunity for training. The ability of a temporary employee to find a new job is largely dependent on his or her skills. If an employee sees that the job he or she is doing can help develop marketable skills, then motivation is increased. From an equity standpoint, when temps work alongside permanent employees who earn more and get benefits too for doing the same job, the performance of temps is likely to suffer. Separating such employees or perhaps minimizing interdependence between them might help managers counteract potential problems.[64]

How do these issues influence contingent workers' job satisfaction? Research shows that differences in job satisfaction between contingent and permanent workers is not significant until we consider the particular contingent work arrangements—temporary employee versus independent contractor.[65] Temporary workers are less satisfied than permanent workers. This difference may be explained by the fact that most temporary employees do not receive benefits such as paid vacation and are paid lower wages than earned by comparably skilled permanent workers. In contrast, independent contractors are about as equally satisfied as permanent workers. Why? Organizations are more likely to recognize the importance of independent contractors' contributions because they're mostly highly skilled individuals. For instance, management consultants are well educated and have a proven track record of success.

Designing Appropriate Rewards Programs

We conclude this chapter by looking at three reward programs designed to increase employee motivation.

OPEN-BOOK MANAGEMENT   Bettina Hein, founder of video technology company Pixability, learned a lesson about secrecy.[66] In her first company, she lost the trust of her employees when they thought business was doing well and then she announced major layoffs. "It was so painful that from that day onward we opened all our books to everyone."[67] When she started Pixability, she adopted open book management from day one.

open-book management
A motivational approach in which an organization's financial statements are shared with all employees

In **open-book management**, senior executives share key financial information with all employees so they will be motivated to make better decisions about their work and better able to understand the implications of what they do, how they do it, and the ultimate impact on the bottom line.[68] Ideally, employees begin to think like owners rather than hired hands.

The goal of open-book management is to get employees to think like an owner by seeing the impact their decisions have on financial results. Since many employees don't initially have the knowledge or background to understand the financials, they have to be taught how to read and understand the organization's financial statements. Once employees have this knowledge, however, managers can regularly share the numbers with them. By sharing this information, employees begin to see the link between their efforts, level of performance, and operational results.

Open-book management particularly aligns well with the needs of today's millennial employees. A survey of millennials found that the most valued characteristics they sought in a boss was honesty and integrity.[69] So open-book management appears to appeal to new entrants to the workforce.

EMPLOYEE RECOGNITION PROGRAMS Laura makes $11 an hour working at her fast-food job in Pensacola, Florida, and the job isn't very challenging or interesting. Yet Laura talks enthusiastically about the job, her boss, and the company that employs her. "What I like is the fact that Guy [her supervisor] appreciates the effort I make. He compliments me regularly in front of the other people on my shift, and I've been chosen Employee of the Month twice in the past six months. Did you see my picture on that plaque on the wall?" Organizations are increasingly realizing what Laura knows: recognition programs can increase motivation.

employee recognition program
a plan to encourage specific behaviors by formally appreciating specific employee contributions

An **employee recognition program** is a plan to encourage specific behaviors by formally appreciating specific employee contributions.[71] These programs range from a spontaneous and private thank-you to widely publicized formal programs in which the procedures for attaining recognition are clearly identified. Everett Clinic in Washington State, for instance, uses a combination of local and centralized initiatives to encourage managers to recognize employees.[72] Employees and managers give "Hero Grams" and "Caught in the Act" cards to colleagues for exceptional accomplishments at work. Part of the incentive is simply to receive recognition, but there are also drawings for prizes based on the number of cards a person receives.

As companies and government organizations face tighter budgets, non-financial incentives become more attractive. A recent survey of organizations found that 89 percent had some type of program to recognize worker achievements.[73] Another survey found that 12 percent of employees say they receive frequent appreciation for a job well done; 7 percent of employees say their company is excellent at showing appreciation for great work.[74] And do employees think these programs are important? Yes! In a survey conducted a few years ago, a wide range of employees was asked what they considered the most powerful workplace motivator. Their response? Recognition, recognition, and more recognition![75]

An obvious advantage of recognition programs is that they are inexpensive. Praise is free! With or without financial rewards, they can be highly motivating to employees.

PAY-FOR-PERFORMANCE Nick Garcia is a college student. Last summer he had a job walking up and down the stairs of Progressive Field during Cleveland Indian baseball games selling peanuts. The peanuts sold for $5 a bag and Nick got $1 for each one he sold. On a good day, he'd make himself over $200. On a poor day, it was more like $50. Nick received no base pay, no minimum wage, and no guarantees. He had, what we would call, a pure pay-for-performance job. The more peanuts he sold (performance), the more money he made (pay).

Pay-for-performance programs are compensation plans that vary with some measure of individual or organizational performance.[76] These programs have long been used to compensate salespeople and executives, but the scope of variable-pay jobs has broadened. Some 94 percent of employers now have some form of variable pay plan.[77]

pay-for-performance programs
Compensation plans that vary with some measure of individual or organizational performance

Examples of pay-for-performance programs would include piece-rate pay plans, merit-based pay, profit-sharing, and lump-sum bonuses. What differentiates these forms of pay from more traditional compensation plans is that instead of paying a person for *time* on the job, pay is adjusted to reflect some performance measure. These performance measures might include such things as individual productivity, team or work group productivity, departmental productivity, or the overall organization's profit performance.

Pay-for-performance is probably most compatible with expectancy theory. Individuals should perceive a strong relationship between their performance and the rewards they receive for motivation to be maximized. If rewards are allocated only on nonperformance factors—such as seniority, job title, or across-the-board pay raises—then employees are likely to reduce their efforts. From a motivation perspective, making some or all of an employee's pay conditional on some performance measure focuses his or her attention and effort toward that measure, then reinforces the continuation of the effort with a reward. If the employee's team's or organization's performance declines, so does the reward. Thus, there's an incentive to keep efforts and motivation strong. The key, in expectancy terms, is ensuring a strong performance-reward relationship so employees feel that their greater performance will yield them rewards that they value.[78]

But do these programs work? For the most part, the answer is yes. Merit and bonus pay, in particular, have been shown to be positively associated with future employee performance.[79] But as the "Learning from Failure" box in this chapter shows, pay-for-performance is not right for all organizations.

Let's Get REAL

The Scenario:

The associates at Footwear Unlimited are paid minimum wage, but they can increase their pay with commissions on sales that they ring up. As a result, the associates work hard to greet customers and help them find the right shoe sizes. However, Christy Jefferson, the store manager, is concerned that the current commission plan discourages employees from working as a team. She has noticed that some associates won't help others since only one associate will receive the commission for a sale. Further, associates seem to be ignoring some duties around the store such as straightening displays.

Should Christy consider a different approach than pay-for-performance?

◀ **Matt O'Rourke**
Supply Chain Engineer

Source: Matt O'Rourke

Don't accept an environment that discourages teamwork; strong teams are a key factor in achieving business results. Rather than reward individual sales, Christy should consider modifying the pay-for-performance plan to incorporate team goals. A bonus could be paid to the team for achieving critical results such as total number of sales for a period of time or a non-monetary reward for straightening up the store. A strong team and company culture is worth the change in approach.

Learning from
F A I L U R E NSPS: Pay-for-Performance Gone Bad

In 2008, the US Department of Defense introduced the National Security Personnel System (NSPS). This was the first pay-for-performance system implemented in a large federal department.

The goal of NSPS was to make job performance a predominant factor in determining employee pay. Rather than longevity, favoritism, or political clout, pay increases would be allocated based on merit. Supervisors and employees would work together to create an annual appraisal plan; then supervisors would use the appraisal to later evaluate each employee. And at the end of each appraisal year, an employee's pay increase would be determined on how well he or she met the plan.

Unfortunately, NSPS didn't work. After trying it for three years, Congress ended the program. They concluded that NSPS was trying to fit a square peg into a round hole.

What went wrong? It appears the likely answer was trying to apply a concept in government that was designed more for the private sector. Pay-for-performance makes sense in organizations and jobs with clear objectives and precise ways of measuring. For instance, it can be effective with objectives like sales targets, on-time delivery, number of clients seen per day, or number of days needed to shoot a movie. Most DOD jobs didn't lend themselves easily to such objective measurement. Employees complained that their job objectives were too broad to be accurately measured, and that subjectively gave managers wide latitude when it came to ratings. But maybe more importantly, in contrast to the business sector, most government jobs come with a narrow and limited salary range. So managers have little discretion when it comes to allocating raises. When top performers get a $40-a-month raise and weak performers get $20, there isn't a lot of motivation provided by the "pay" in pay-for-performance.

What did the DOD learn from the failure of NSPS? Management concepts that work in the private sector don't necessarily transfer successfully to the public sector.[80]

Chapter 16 **PREPARING FOR: Exams/Quizzes**

CHAPTER SUMMARY by Learning Objectives

LO16.1

DEFINE motivation.

Motivation is the process by which a person's efforts are energized, directed, and sustained toward attaining a goal.

The *energy* element is a measure of intensity, drive, or vigor. The high level of effort needs to be *directed* in ways that help the organization achieve its goals. Employees must *persist* in putting forth effort to achieve those goals.

LO16.2

COMPARE and contrast early theories of motivation.

In Maslow's hierarchy, individuals move up the hierarchy of five needs (physiological, safety, social, esteem, and self-actualization) as needs are substantially satisfied. A need that's substantially satisfied no longer motivates.

A Theory X manager believes people don't like to work or won't seek out responsibility so they have to be threatened and coerced to work. A Theory Y manager assumes people like to work and seek out responsibility, so they will exercise self-motivation and self-direction.

Herzberg's Two-Factor Theory proposed that intrinsic factors associated with job satisfaction were what motivated people. Extrinsic factors associated with job dissatisfaction simply kept people from being dissatisfied. Managers who eliminate factors that create job dissatisfaction do not necessarily motivate employees – they may just keep people from being dissatisfied.

Three-needs theory proposed three acquired needs that are major motives in work: need for achievement, need for affiliation, and need for power.

LO16.3

COMPARE and contrast contemporary theories of motivation.

Goal-setting theory says that specific goals increase performance, and difficult goals, when accepted, result in higher performance than easy goals. Important points in goal-setting theory include intention to work toward a goal as a major source of job motivation; specific hard goals that produce higher levels of output than generalized goals; participation in setting goals as often (but not always) preferable to assigning goals; feedback that guides and motivates behavior, especially self-generated feedback; and contingencies that affect goal setting—goal commitment, self-efficacy, and national culture. Self-efficacy refers to an individual's belief that he or she is capable of performing a task. People with high self-efficacy often will maintain effort throughout a task and achieve higher performance as a result.

Reinforcement theory says that behavior is a function of its consequences. To motivate, use positive reinforcers to reinforce desirable behaviors. Ignore undesirable behavior rather than punishing it.

Job enlargement involves horizontally expanding job scope by adding more tasks or increasing how many times the tasks are done. Job enrichment vertically expands job depth by giving employees more control over their work. The job characteristics model says five core job dimensions (skill variety, task identity, task significance, autonomy, and feedback) are used to design motivating jobs. Another job design approach proposed looking at relational aspects and proactive aspects of jobs.

Equity theory focuses on how employees compare their inputs-outcomes ratios to relevant others' ratios. A perception of inequity will cause an employee to do something about it. Distributive justice has a greater influence on employee satisfaction than procedural justice while procedural justice affects an employee's organizational commitment, trust in his or her boss, and intention to quit.

Expectancy theory says an individual tends to act in a certain way based on the expectation that the act will be followed by a desired outcome. Expectancy is the effort-performance linkage (will exerting a given amount of effort lead to a certain level of performance?); instrumentality is the performance-reward linkage (achieving at a certain level of performance will get me a specific reward); and valence is the attractiveness of the reward (is it the reward that I want?).

LO16.4

DISCUSS current issues in motivation.

Managers must cope with three current motivation issues: managing cross-cultural challenges, motivating unique groups of workers, and designing appropriate rewards programs.

Most motivational theories were developed in the United States and have a North American bias. Some theories (Maslow's needs hierarchy, achievement need, and equity theory) don't work well for other cultures. However, the desire for interesting work seems important to all workers, and Herzberg's motivator (intrinsic) factors may be universal.

Managers face challenges in motivating unique groups of workers. A diverse workforce is looking for flexibility. Professionals want job challenge and are motivated by the work itself. Designing professional jobs so that workers experience flow (total absorption in one's work) often results in high levels of performance. Contingent workers want the opportunity to become permanent or to receive skills training.

Open-book management is when financial statements (the books) are shared with employees who have been taught what they mean. Employee recognition programs consist of personal attention, approval, and appreciation for a job well done. Pay-for-performance programs are variable compensation plans that pay employees on the basis of some performance measure.

REVIEW AND DISCUSSION QUESTIONS

16-1. What is motivation? Explain the three key elements of motivation.

16-2. Describe each of the four early theories of motivation.

16-3. How do goal-setting, reinforcement, and equity theories explain employee motivation?

16-4. What are the different job design approaches to motivation?

16-5. Explain the three key linkages in expectancy theory and their role in motivation.

16-6. What challenges do managers face in motivating today's workforce?

16-7. Describe open-book management, employee recognition, and pay-for-performance programs.

16-8. Can an individual be too motivated? Discuss.

PREPARING FOR: My Career

ETHICS DILEMMA

Advocates of open-book management point to the advantages of getting employees to think like owners and to be motivated to make better decisions about how they do their work once they see how their decisions impact financial results. However, is there such a thing as "too much openness?" At some companies, employees not only have access to company financial details but also to staff performance reviews and individual pay information.[81]

16-9. What do you think? What are the pros and cons of such an approach?

16-10. What potential ethical issues do you see here? How might managers address these ethical issues?

SKILLS EXERCISE Developing Your Motivating Employees Skill

About the Skill

Because a simple, all-encompassing set of motivational guidelines is not available, the following suggestions draw on the essence of what we know about motivating employees.

Steps in Practicing the Skill

* *Recognize individual differences.* Almost every contemporary motivation theory recognizes that employees are not homogeneous. They have different needs. They also differ in terms of attitudes, personality, and other important individual variables.

* *Match people to jobs.* A great deal of evidence shows the motivational benefits of carefully matching people to jobs. People who lack the necessary skills to perform successfully will be at a disadvantage.

* *Use goals.* You should ensure that employees have hard, specific goals and feedback on how well they're doing in pursuit of those goals. In many cases, these goals should be participatively set.

* *Ensure goals are perceived as attainable.* Regardless of whether goals are actually attainable, employees who see goals as unattainable will reduce their effort. Be sure, therefore, that employees feel confident that increased efforts can lead to achieving performance goals.

* *Individualize rewards.* Because employees have different needs, what acts as a reinforcer for one may not do so for another. Use your knowledge of employee differences to individualize the rewards over which you have control. Some of the more obvious rewards that you can allocate include recognition, pay, promotions, autonomy, and the opportunity to participate in goal setting and decision making.

* *Link rewards to performance.* You need to make rewards contingent on performance. Rewarding factors other than performance will only reinforce the importance of those other factors. Key rewards such as pay increases and promotions should be given for the attainment of employees' specific goals.

* *Check the system for equity.* Employees should perceive that rewards or outcomes are equal to the inputs given. On a simplistic level, experience, ability, effort, and other obvious inputs should explain differences in pay, responsibility, and other obvious outcomes.

* *Don't ignore money.* It's easy to get so caught up in setting goals, creating interesting jobs, and providing opportunities for participation that you forget that money is a major reason why most people work. Thus, the allocation of performance-based wage increases, piece-work bonuses, employee stock ownership plans, and other pay incentives are important in determining employee motivation.

Practicing the Skill

Create a motivational plan for each of the groups of employees listed. Include ideas on what kinds of rewards or incentives would be appropriate for each group.

a. Fast-food workers
b. Software development engineers
c. High school teachers
d. Construction site workers

WORKING TOGETHER **Team Exercise**

What motivates you to work hard? Consider a job you've held in the past or an organization you've been involved in. What about the job or work with the organization was motivating? Or, if you weren't motivated, what was missing? What could management or organizational leaders have done differently? Get into groups of three or four students and share your reflections. Identify some common themes of effective motivators and be prepared to share your ideas with the class.

MY TURN TO BE A MANAGER

- A good habit to get into if you don't already do it is goal setting. Set goals for yourself using the suggestions from goal-setting theory. Write these down and keep them in a notebook or in a folder on your phone. Track your progress toward achieving these goals.

- Describe a task you've done recently for which you exerted a high level of effort. Explain your behavior, using any three of the motivation approaches described in this chapter.

- Pay attention to times when you're highly motivated and times when you're not as motivated. Write down a description of these. What accounts for the difference in your level of motivation?

- Interview three managers about how they motivate their employees. What have they found that works the best? Write up your findings in a report and be prepared to present it in class.

- Using the job characteristics model, redesign the following jobs to be more motivating: retail store sales associate, utility company meter reader, and server at a restaurant. In a written report, describe for each job at least two specific actions you would take for each of the five core job dimensions.

- Do some serious thinking about what you want from your job after graduation. Using the list of job factors in the "What Motivates You" *It's Your Career* feature near the beginning of the chapter, make a list of what's important to you. Think about how you will discover whether a particular job will help you get those things.

- Find three different examples of employee recognition programs from organizations with which you're familiar or from articles that you find. Write a report describing your examples and evaluating what you think about the various approaches.

- Have you ever participated in a pay-for-performance program? If not, ask your friends and find someone who has participated in such a program. Consider your or your friend's program. Was it effective in motivating employees? Why or why not? How could the program be improved?

| CASE APPLICATION **1** | Motivating Employees Who Love the Outdoors at REI |

REI, the outdoor retailer, has become a regular on Fortune's "100 Best Companies to Work For" list. The year 2018 was the twenty-first consecutive year that the company was recognized on Fortune's list.[82] REI also won a Glassdoor's Employees' Choice Award in 2018.[83] Both awards are based on employees' opinions about what it's like working for their companies. One employee's Glassdoor review described how, at REI, there are "fellow co-workers who really, really love their jobs and love working there, and want you to love working there too."[84]

REI designed some of their benefits to appeal to employees with outdoor interests. For instance, there are "Yay Days"—two paid days each year for employees to participate in a favorite outdoor activity or help maintain outdoor spaces. "People literally use [Yay Days] to go have fun in the outdoors. When you request your Yay Day, you tell your manager what you're doing with it," explained Raquel Karls, Senior Vice

President of Human Resources at REI.[85] The company also started the #OptOutside perk several years ago. This is an additional day off with pay on Black Friday, a day that the company now closes its stores to encourage employees and customers to enjoy the outdoors rather than work or shop.

There are other benefits that aren't outdoor-oriented, but also enhance the experience of being a REI employee. REI offers up to six weeks of paid parental leave. There are annual incentive plans, company contributions to employee retirement plans, and tuition reimbursement offerings. All employees get a 50 percent discount on REI brands. If you work at least twenty hours per week, you are provided with health insurance. And once an employee works at REI for fifteen years, they receive four weeks of paid sabbatical time in addition to vacation time.[86]

DISCUSSION QUESTIONS

16-11. In what ways could the work environment at REI help satisfy one of the needs in Three-Needs theory?

16-12. How could the outdoor-oriented benefits offered at REI apply to expectancy theory?

16-13. What else could REI do to improve how they motivate their employees?

16-14. What are advantages and disadvantages of hiring employees at REI who might not be as outdoor-oriented as other employees?

CASE APPLICATION 2 — Motivating Under Constraints at Televerde

Most of the employees at Televerde, a technology-focused business-to-business marketing firm, wear orange to work every day. It's not a company-mandated uniform or an unusual approach to fashion. It's what they have to wear because they are prison inmates! These Televerde employees (all are women) work by phone securing sales leads for large technology companies. Inmates who have worked at Televerde are much less likely to return to prison upon being released (their recidivism rate is 80 percent lower than the national average). And they have helped Televerde become highly successful with a compound annual growth rate of 8.5 percent over the last decade.[87]

Televerde's inmate employees are paid more than most prison jobs, but prison regulations mandate that they can't be paid more than the federal minimum wage. Prisons also don't allow employees to earn raises, bonuses, or promotions. That means that motivational techniques used at Televerde cannot rely entirely on money. So, how are inmates motivated at Televerde?

New employees are told that "as soon as you come through that door, you are a coworker, not an inmate." Employees are called by name (not by their inmate number). Newcomers are told of the professional development opportunities available to them, including a professional book club, eligibility for scholarships to pay for higher education, and a six-month series of training workshops in the year before they are released to help with transition. They are also eligible to work at Televerde's corporate office upon release.

There are numerous milestones that employees must clear as part of their training, including presenting a business plan, making practice phone calls with mentors, and passing exams. Performance goals and employee progress toward those goals are written on a whiteboard for all to see. The objective of the whiteboard is to allow employees to measure their performance against an objective standard. Televerde discourages employees from comparing their performance against each other, which would create competition and a lack of cohesion.

Employees receive frequent one-on-one feedback from trainers and recognition is provided for deserved accomplishments. Any time an employee secures a sales lead, she rings a bell signaling both employees and managers to applaud. Employees earn award certificates for excellent performance and they tend to display these certificates in their workspaces. As one employee put it, it's through these expressions of earned respect "that we gain confidence. And the more confident you become inside, the more confident you sound on the phone. ... So of course that brings more success and then more confidence, and it feeds on itself in a positive snowball effect." Twenty-five percent of inmate employees continue working for the company after they are released from prison. But that's not the only place where they might work. As Televerde CEO Jim Hooker said, "These women can walk into any job at market prices."[88]

DISCUSSION QUESTIONS

16-15. Analyze this case using the integrative model in Exhibit 16-9.

16-16. How might self-efficacy increase for inmates who work at Televerde?

16-17. In what ways could the relational perspective of work design be applied to Televerde's approach? Are there other aspects of this perspective that Televerde might consider adding to what they already do?

16-18. What would be an example of how Televerde might implement a high-involvement work practice to complement what they currently do?

ENDNOTES

1. Jessi Berrin , "2017 looks like it will be a big year for workplace flexibility" Miami herald, JANUARY 01, 2017; C. K. Goodman, "Workplace Flexibility to Gain Traction in '17," The Cleveland Plain Dealer, January 8, 2107, p. F3.

2. See, for instance, R. M. Steers, R. T. Mowday, and D. L. Shapiro, "The Future of Work Motivation Theory," *Academy of Management Review* 29, no. 3 (July 2004): pp. 379–87; C. C. Pinder, *Work Motivation in Organizational Behavior*, 2nd ed. (London, UK: Psychology Press, 2008); and R. Kanfer, M. Frese, and R. E. Johnson, "Motivation Related to Work: A Century of Progress," *Journal of Applied Psychology* 102, no. 3 (March 2017): pp. 338–55.

3. A. Mann and J. Harter, "The Worldwide Employee Engagement Crisis," *Gallup*, January 7, 2016, https://www.gallup.com/workplace/236495/worldwide-employee-engagement-crisis.aspx.

4. Ibid.

5. A. Maslow, *Motivation and Personality* (New York: McGraw-Hill, 1954); A. Maslow, D. C. Stephens, and G. Heil, *Maslow on Management* (New York: John Wiley & Sons, 1998); and R. J. Taormina and J. H. Gao, "Maslow and the Motivation Hierarchy: Measuring Satisfaction of the Needs," *American Journal of Psychology* 126, no. 2 (Summer 2013): pp. 155–57.

6. See, for example, D. T. Hall and K. E. Nongaim, "An Examination of Maslow's Need Hierarchy in an Organizational Setting," *Organizational Behavior and Human Performance* 3, no. 1 (February 1968): pp. 12–35; E. E. Lawler III and J. L. Suttle, "A Causal Correlational Test of the Need Hierarchy Concept," *Organizational Behavior and Human Performance* 7, no. 2 (April 1972): pp. 265–287; R. M. Creech, "Employee Motivation," *Management Quarterly*, Summer 1995, pp. 33–39; J. Rowan, "Maslow Amended," *Journal of Humanistic Psychology* 38, no. 1 (Winter 1998): pp. 81–92; J. Rowan, "Ascent and Descent in Maslow's Theory," *Journal of Humanistic Psychology* 39, no. 3 (Summer 1999): pp. 125–133; and M. L. Ambrose and C. T. Kulik,

"Old Friends, New Faces: Motivation Research in the 1990s," *Journal of Management* 25, no. 3 (June 1999): pp. 231–92; S. Fowler, "What Maslow's Hierarchy Won't Tell You About Motivation," *Harvard Business Review*, November 26, 2014, https://hbr.org/2014/11/what-maslows-hierarchy-wont-tell-you-about-motivation; and T. Bridgman, S. Cummings, and J.A. Ballard, "Who Built Maslow's Pyramid? A History of the Creation of Management Studies' Most Famous Symbol and Its Implications for Management Education," *Academy of Management Learning & Education* 18, no. 1 (2019): pp. 81–98.

7. D. McGregor, *The Human Side of Enterprise* (New York: McGraw-Hill, 1960). For an updated description of Theories X and Y, see an annotated edition with commentary of *The Human Side of Enterprise* (McGraw-Hill, 2006); G. Heil, W. Bennis, and D. C. Stephens, *Douglas McGregor, Revisited: Managing the Human Side of Enterprise* (New York: Wiley, 2000); and S. Gurbuz, F. Sahin, and O. Koksal, "Revisiting of Theory X and Y: A Multilevel Analysis of the Effects of Leaders' Managerial Assumptions on Followers' Attitudes," *Management Decision*, vol. 52, no. 10 (2014): pp. 1888–1906.

8. P. Wahba, "One Way Walmart Is Motivating Workers: Less Celine Dion on the PA System," *Fortune*, June 3, 2015, http://fortune.com/2015/06/03/walmart-employees/.

9. F. Herzberg, B. Mausner, and B. Snyderman, *The Motivation to Work* (New York: John Wiley, 1959); F. Herzberg, *The Managerial Choice: To Be Effective or to Be Human*, rev. ed. (Salt Lake City: Olympus, 1982); and N. Bassett-Jones and G. C. Lloyd, "Does Herzberg's Motivation Theory Have Staying Power?" *The Journal of Management Development* 24, no. 10 (2005): pp. 929–43.

10. D. C. McClelland, *The Achieving Society* (New York: Van Nostrand Reinhold, 1961); J. W. Atkinson and J. O. Raynor, *Motivation and Achievement* (Washington, DC: Winston, 1974); D. C. McClelland, *Power: The Inner Experience* (New York: Irvington, 1975); and M. J. Stahl, *Managerial and Technical Motivation: Assessing Needs for Achievement, Power, and Affiliation* (New York: Praeger, 1986).

Part 5 Leading

11. McClelland, *The Achieving Society.*
12. McClelland, *Power* [see note 10]; D. C. McClelland and D. H. Burnham, "Power Is the Great Motivator," *Harvard Business Review*, March-April 1976, pp. 100–110.
13. "McClelland: An Advocate of Power," *International Management*, July 1975, pp. 27–29.
14. Ambrose and Kulik, "Old Friends, New Faces" [see note 6]; L. Porter, G. Bigley, and R. Steers, *Motivation and Work Behavior*, 7th ed. (New York: McGraw-Hill/Irwin, 2003); Steers, Mowday, and Shapiro, "Future of Work Motivation Theory" [see note 2]; and E. A. Locke and G. P. Latham, "What Should We Do About Motivation Theory? Six Recommendations for the Twenty-First Century," *Academy of Management Review* 29, no. 3 (July 2004): pp. 388–403.
15. E. A. Locke and G. P. Latham, "Building a Practically Useful Theory of Goal Setting and Task Motivation," *American Psychologist* 57, no. 9 (September 2002): pp. 705–17; E. A. Locke and G. P. Latham, "New Directions in Goal-Setting Theory," *Current Directions in Psychological Science* 15, no. 5 (October 2006): pp. 265–68; and A. Kleingeld, H. van Mierlo, and L. Arends, "The Effect of Goal Setting on Group Performance: A Meta-Analysis," *Journal of Applied Psychology* 96, no. 6 (November 2011): pp. 1289–304.
16. J. C. Naylor and D. R. Ilgen, "Goal Setting: A Theoretical Analysis of a Motivational Technique," in *Research in Organizational Behavior*, vol. 6, ed. B. M. Staw and L. L. Cummings (Greenwich, CT: JAI Press, 1984), pp. 95–140; and G. P. Latham, "The Motivational Benefits of Goal-Setting," *Academy of Management Perspectives* 18, no. 4 (November 2004): pp. 126–129.
17. Ibid.
18. C. Comaford, "Why Leaders Need to Embrace Employee Motivation," *Forbes*, January 20, 2018, https://www.forbes.com/sites/christinecomaford/2018/01/20/why-leaders-need-to-embrace-employee-motivation/#356a26812725.
19. J. A. Wagner III, "Participation's Effects on Performance and Satisfaction: A Reconsideration of Research and Evidence," *Academy of Management Review* 19, no. 2 (April 1994): pp. 312–330; J. George-Falvey, "Effects of Task Complexity and Learning Stage on the Relationship Between Participation in Goal Setting and Task Performance," *Academy of Management Proceedings*, 1996, CD-ROM; T. D. Ludwig and E. S. Geller, "Assigned Versus Participative Goal Setting and Response Generalization: Managing Injury Control Among Professional Pizza Deliverers," *Journal of Applied Psychology* 82, no. 2 (April 1997): pp. 253–261; S. G. Harkins and M. D. Lowe, "The Effects of Self-Set Goals on Task Performance," *Journal of Applied Social Psychology* 30, no. 1 (January 2000): pp. 1–40; and Kleingeld, Van Mierlo, and Arends, "The Effect of Goal Setting" [see note 15].
20. J. M. Ivancevich and J. T. McMahon, "The Effects of Goal Setting, External Feedback, and Self-Generated Feedback on Outcome Variables: A Field Experiment," *Academy of Management Journal* 25, no. 2 (June 1982): pp. 359–372; and E. A. Locke, "Motivation Through Conscious Goal Setting," *Applied and Preventive Psychology* 5, no. 2 (Spring 1996): pp. 117–24.
21. J. R. Hollenbeck, C. R. Williams, and H. J. Klein, "An Empirical Examination of the Antecedents of Commitment to Difficult Goals," *Journal of Applied Psychology* 74, no. 1 (February 1989): pp. 18–23; see also J. C. Wofford, V. L. Goodwin, and S. Premack, "Meta-Analysis of the Antecedents of Personal Goal Level and of the Antecedents and Consequences of Goal Commitment," *Journal of Management*, September 1992, pp. 595–615; M. E. Tubbs, "Commitment as a Moderator of the Goal-Performance Relation: A Case for Clearer Construct Definition," *Journal of Applied Psychology* 78, no. 1 (February 1993): pp. 86–97; J. W. Smither, M. London, and R. R. Reilly, "Does Performance Improve Following Multisource Feedback? A Theoretical Model, Meta-Analysis, and Review of Empirical Findings," *Personnel Psychology* 58, no. 1 (Spring 2005): pp. 171–203.
22. Y. Gong, J.-C. Huang, and J.-L. Farh, "Employee Learning Orientation, Transformational Leadership, and Employee Creativity: The Mediating Role of Employee Self-Efficacy," *Academy of Management Journal* 52, no. 2 (August 2009): pp. 765–778; M. E. Gist, "Self-Efficacy: Implications for Organizational Behavior and Human Resource Management," *Academy of Management Review* 12, no. 3 (July 1987): pp. 472–485; and A. Bandura, *Self-Efficacy: The Exercise of Control* (New York: Freeman, 1997).
23. E. A. Locke, E. Frederick, C. Lee, and P. Bobko, "Effect of Self-Efficacy, Goals, and Task Strategies on Task Performance," *Journal of Applied Psychology* 69, no. 2 (May 1984): pp. 241–251; M. E. Gist and T. R. Mitchell, "Self-Efficacy: A Theoretical Analysis of Its Determinants and Malleability," *Academy of Management Review* 17, no. 2 (April 1992): pp. 183–211; A. D. Stajkovic and F. Luthans, "Self-Efficacy and Work-Related Performance: A Meta-Analysis," *Psychological Bulletin* 124, no. 2 (September 1998): pp. 240–261; and A. Bandura, "Cultivate Self-Efficacy for Personal and Organizational Effectiveness," in *Handbook of Principles of Organizational Behavior*, ed. E. Locke (Malden, MA: Blackwell, 2004), pp. 120–136.
24. A. Bandura and D. Cervone, "Differential Engagement in Self-Reactive Influences in Cognitively-Based Motivation," *Organizational Behavior and Human Decision Processes* 38, no. 1 (August 1986): pp. 92–113; and R. Ilies and T. A. Judge, "Goal Regulation Across Time: The Effects of Feedback and Affect," *Journal of Applied Psychology* 90, no. 3 (May 2005): pp. 453–467.
25. See J. C. Anderson and C. A. O'Reilly, "Effects of an Organizational Control System on Managerial Satisfaction and Performance," *Human Relations* 34, no. 6 (June 1981): pp. 491–501; and J. P. Meyer, B. Schacht-Cole, and I. R. Gellatly, "An Examination of the Cognitive Mechanisms by Which Assigned Goals Affect Task Performance and Reactions to Performance," *Journal of Applied Social Psychology* 18, no. 5 (May 1988): pp. 390–408.
26. B. F. Skinner, *Science and Human Behavior* (New York: Free Press, 1953); and Skinner, *Beyond Freedom and Dignity* (New York: Knopf, 1972).
27. The same data, for instance, can be interpreted in either goal-setting or reinforcement terms, as shown in E. A. Locke, "Latham vs. Komaki: A Tale of Two Paradigms," *Journal of Applied Psychology* 65, no. 1 (February 1980): pp. 16–23. For an argument on the power of rewards to kill interest and motivation, see A. Kohn, *Punished by Rewards: The Trouble with Gold Stars, Incentive Plans, A's, Praise, and Other Bribes* (Boston: Houghton Mifflin, 2018).
28. R. Carucci, "What Not to Do When You're Trying to Motivate Your Team," *Harvard Business Review*, July 16, 2018, pp. 2–4.

29. See, for example, R. W. Griffin, "Toward an Integrated Theory of Task Design," in *Research in Organizational Behavior*, vol. 9, eds. L. L. Cummings and B. M. Staw (Greenwich, CT: JAI Press, 1987), pp. 79–120; G.R. Oldham and Y. Fried, "Job Design Research and Theory: Past, Present, and Future," *Organizational Behavior and Human Decision Processes* 136 (September 2016) pp. 20–35; S. K. Parker, A. Van den Broeck, and D. Holman, "Work Design Influences: A Synthesis of Multilevel Factors that Affect the Design of Jobs," *Academy of Management Annals* 11, no. 1 (January 2017): pp. 267–308; S. K. Parker, F. P. Morgeson, and G. Johns, "One Hundred Years of Work Design Research: Looking Back and Looking Forward," *Journal of Applied Psychology* 102, no. 3 (March 2017): pp. 403–20.

30. M. A. Campion and C. L. McClelland, "Follow-Up and Extension of the Interdisciplinary Costs and Benefits of Enlarged Jobs," *Journal of Applied Psychology* 78, no. 3 (June 1993): pp. 339–351; and Ambrose and Kulik, "Old Friends, New Faces" [see note 6].

31. See, for example, J. R. Hackman and G. R. Oldham, *Work Redesign* (Reading, MA: Addison-Wesley, 1980); Miner, *Theories of Organizational Behavior*, pp. 231–266; R. W. Griffin, "Effects of Work Redesign on Employee Perceptions, Attitudes, and Behaviors: A Long-Term Investigation," *Academy of Management Journal* 34, no. 2 (June 1991): pp. 425–435; J. L. Cotton, *Employee Involvement* (Newbury Park, CA: Sage, 1993), pp. 141–172; Ambrose and Kulik, "Old Friends, New Faces" [see note 6]; and Oldham and Fried, "Job Design Research" [see note 29].

32. J. R. Hackman and G. R. Oldham, "Development of the Job Diagnostic Survey," *Journal of Applied Psychology* 60, no. 2 (April 1975): pp. 159–170; J. R. Hackman and G. R. Oldham, "Motivation Through the Design of Work: Test of a Theory," *Organizational Behavior and Human Performance* 16, no. 2 (August 1976): pp. 250–279; Oldham and Fried, "Job Design Research" [see note 29]; and L. A. Wegman, B. J. Hoffman, N. T. Carter, J. M. Twenge, and N. Guenole, "Placing Job Characteristics in Context: Cross-Temporal Meta-Analysis of Changes in Job Characteristics Since 1975," *Journal of Management* 33, no. 1 (January 201), pp. 352–86.

33. J. R. Hackman, "Work Design," in *Improving Life at Work*, eds. R. Hackman and J. L. Suttle (Glenview, IL: Scott, Foresman, 1977), p. 129; and Ambrose and Kulik, "Old Friends, New Faces" [see note 6].

34. "Most and Least Meaningful Jobs," *PayScale*, accessed December 15, 2018, https://www.payscale.com/data-packages/most-and-least-meaningful-jobs.

35. Wegman et al., "Placing Job Characteristics" [see note 32].

36. Oldman and Fried, "Job Design Research" [see note 29].

37. See, for instance, A. M. Grant and S. K. Parker, "Redesigning Work Design Theories: The Rise of Relational and Proactive Perspectives," *Academy of Management Annals* 3, no. 1 (January 2009): pp. 317–75; and Y. Freeny and M.R. Fellenz, "Work Engagement, Job Design and the Role of the Social Context at Work: Exploring Antecedents From a Relational Perspective," *Human Relations* 66, no. 11 (November 2013): pp. 1427–45.

38. Grant and Parker, "Redesigning Work Design Theories."

39. V. Giang, "Why Innovative Companies Like Google Are Letting Employees Craft Their Own Jobs," *Fast Company*, April 29, 2016, https://www.fastcompany.com/3059345/why-innovative-companies-like-google-are-letting-employees-craft-their-own-jobs.

40. R. D. Mohr and C. Zoghi, "High-Involvement Work Design and Job Satisfaction," *Industrial and Labor Relations Review* 61, no. 3 (April 2008): pp. 275–296; J. Camps and R. Luna-Arocas, "High Involvement Work Practices and Firm Performance," *International Journal of Human Resource Management* 20, no. 5 (May 2009): pp. 1056–1077; P. Boxall and K. Macky, "Research and Theory on High-Performance Work Systems: Progressing the High-Involvement Stream," *Human Resource Management Journal* 19, no. 1 (January 2009): pp. 3–23; P. Bockerman, A. Bryson, and P. Llmakunnas, "Does High Involvement Management Improve Worker Wellbeing?," *Journal of Economic Behavior & Organization* 84, no. 2 (November 2012): pp. 660–680; and C. Maden, "Linking High Involvement Human Resource Practices to Employee Proactivity: The Role of Work Engagement and Learning Goal Orientation," *Personnel Review* 44, no. 5 (August 2015): pp. 720–38.

41. J. S. Adams, "Inequity in Social Exchanges," in *Advances in Experimental Social Psychology*, vol. 2, ed. L. Berkowitz (New York: Academic Press, 1965), pp. 267–300; Ambrose and Kulik, "Old Friends, New Faces" [see note 6]; and T. Menon and L. Thompson, "Envy at Work," *Harvard Business Review*, April 2010, pp. 74–79.

42. See, for example, P. S. Goodman and A. Friedman, "An Examination of Adams' Theory of Inequity," *Administrative Science Quarterly* 16, no. 3 (September 1971): pp. 271–288; M. R. Carrell, "A Longitudinal Field Assessment of Employee Perceptions of Equitable Treatment," *Organizational Behavior and Human Performance* 21, no. 1 (February 1978): pp. 108–118; E. Walster, G. W. Walster, and W. G. Scott, *Equity: Theory and Research* (Boston: Allyn & Bacon, 1978); R. G. Lord and J. A. Hohenfeld, "Longitudinal Field Assessment of Equity Effects on the Performance of Major League Baseball Players," *Journal of Applied Psychology* 64, no. 1 (February 1979): pp. 19–26; J. E. Dittrich and M. R. Carrell, "Organizational Equity Perceptions, Employee Job Satisfaction, and Departmental Absence and Turnover Rates," *Organizational Behavior and Human Performance* 24, no. 1 (August 1979): pp. 29–40; and J. Greenberg, "Cognitive Reevaluation of Outcomes in Response to Underpayment Inequity," *Academy of Management Journal* 32, no. 1 (March 1989): pp. 174–184.

43. P. S. Goodman, "An Examination of Referents Used in the Evaluation of Pay," *Organizational Behavior and Human Performance* 12, no. 2 (October 1974): pp. 170–195; S. Ronen, "Equity Perception in Multiple Comparisons: A Field Study," *Human Relations* 39, no. 4 (April 1986): pp. 333–346; R. W. Scholl, E. A. Cooper, and J. F. McKenna, "Referent Selection in Determining Equity Perception: Differential Effects on Behavioral and Attitudinal Outcomes," *Personnel Psychology* 40, no. 1 (Spring 1987): pp. 113–127; and C. T. Kulik and M. L. Ambrose, "Personal and Situational Determinants of Referent Choice," *Academy of Management Review* 17, no. 2 (April 1992): pp. 212–237.

44. See, for example, R. C. Dailey and D. J. Kirk, "Distributive and Procedural Justice as Antecedents of Job Dissatisfaction and Intent to Turnover," *Human Relations* 45, no. 3 (March 1992): pp. 305–316; D. B. McFarlin and P. D. Sweeney, "Distributive and Procedural Justice as Predictors of Satisfaction with Personal and Organizational Outcomes,"

Academy of Management Journal 35, no. 3 (August 1992): pp. 626–637; M. A. Konovsky, "Understanding Procedural Justice and Its Impact on Business Organizations," *Journal of Management* 26, no. 3 (March 2000): pp. 489–511; J. A. Colquitt, "Does the Justice of One Interact with the Justice of Many? Reactions to Procedural Justice in Teams," *Journal of Applied Psychology* 89, no. 4 (August 2004): pp. 633–646; J. Brockner, "Why It's So Hard to Be Fair," *Harvard Business Review,* March 2006, pp. 122–129; B. M. Wiesenfeld, W. B. Swann Jr., J. Brockner, and C. A. Bartel, "Is More Fairness Always Preferred? Self-Esteem Moderates Reactions to Procedural Justice," *Academy of Management Journal* 50, no. 5 (October 2007): pp. 1235–1253; A. H. Y. Hon, J. Yang, and L. Lu, "A Cross-Level Study of Procedural Justice Perceptions," *Journal of Managerial Psychology* 26, no. 8 (November 2011) pp. 700–15; and C. M. Bell and C. Khoury, "Organizational Powerlessness, Dehumanization, and Gendered Effects of Procedural Justice," *Journal of Managerial Psychology* 31, no. 2 (March 2016): pp. 570–85.

45. V. H. Vroom, *Work and Motivation* (New York: John Wiley, 1964); and W. Van Eerde and H. Thierry, "Vroom's Expectancy Models and Work-Related Criteria: A Meta-Analysis," *Journal of Applied Psychology* 81, no. 5 (October 1996): pp. 575–86.

46. See, for example, H. G. Heneman III and D. P. Schwab, "Evaluation of Research on Expectancy Theory Prediction of Employee Performance," *Psychological Bulletin* 78, no. 1 (July 1972): pp. 1–9; and L. Reinharth and M. Wahba, "Expectancy Theory as a Predictor of Work Motivation, Effort Expenditure, and Job Performance," *Academy of Management Journal* 18, no. 3 (September 1975): pp. 502–537.

47. See, for example, V. H. Vroom, "Organizational Choice: A Study of Pre- and Postdecision Processes," *Organizational Behavior and Human Performance* 1, no. 2 (April 1966): pp. 212–225; L. W. Porter and E. E. Lawler III, *Managerial Attitudes and Performance* (Homewood, IL: Richard D. Irwin, 1968); Van Eerde and Thierry, "Vroom's Expectancy Models" [see note 45]; and Ambrose and Kulik, "Old Friends, New Faces" [see note 6].

48. Based on E. W. Miles, J. D. Hatfield, and R. C. Husman, "The Equity Sensitive Construct: Potential Implications for Worker Performance," *Journal of Management* 14, no. 4 (December 1989): pp. 581–588; R. Rueff, "Tips on How to Approach Suspected Pay Inequity," *Glassdoor* (blog), March 11, 2009, https://www.glassdoor.com/blog/tips-on-how-to-approach-suspected-pay-inequity/; A. Doyle, "What Can You Do When Your Co-Workers Are Paid More Money?," *Career Tool Belt*, June 15, 2015, https://www.careertoolbelt.com/what-can-you-do-when-your-co-workers-are-paid-more-money/; and "How to Ask for a Raise," *Forbes*, November 5, 2015, https://www.forbes.com/sites/rent/2015/11/05/how-to-ask-for-a-raise/#7556e7c5497e.

49. N. J. Adler with A. Gundersen, *International Dimensions of Organizational Behavior*, 5th ed. (Cincinnati, OH: South-Western College Publishing, 2008).

50. G. Hofstede, "Motivation, Leadership and Organization: Do American Theories Apply Abroad?" *Organizational Dynamics* 90, no. 1 (Summer 1980): p. 55.

51. Ibid.

52. J. K. Giacobbe-Miller, D. J. Miller, and V. I. Victorov, "A Comparison of Russian and U.S. Pay Allocation Decisions, Distributive Justice Judgments and Productivity Under Different Payment Conditions," *Personnel Psychology* 51, no. 1 (Spring 1998): pp. 137–163.

53. S. L. Mueller and L. D. Clarke, "Political-Economic Context and Sensitivity to Equity: Differences Between the United States and the Transition Economies of Central and Eastern Europe," *Academy of Management Journal* 41, no. 3 (June 1998): pp. 319–329.

54. S. D. Sidle, "Building a Committed Global Workforce: Does What Employees Want Depend on Culture?," *Academy of Management Perspective* 23, no. 1 (February 2009): pp. 79–80; and G. A. Gelade, P. Dobson, and K. Auer, "Individualism, Masculinity, and the Sources of Organizational Commitment," *Journal of Cross-Cultural Psychology* 39, no. 5 (2008): pp. 599–617.

55. P. Brotherton, "Employee Loyalty Slipping Worldwide; Respect, Work-Life Balance Are Top Engagers," *Talent Development,* February 2012, p. 24.

56. I. Harpaz, "The Importance of Work Goals: An International Perspective," *Journal of International Business Studies* 21, no. 1 (First Quarter 1990): pp. 75–93.

57. G. E. Popp, H. J. Davis, and T. T. Herbert, "An International Study of Intrinsic Motivation Composition," *Management International Review* 26, no. 3 (Third Quarter 1986): pp. 28–35.

58. R. W. Brislin, B. MacNab, R. Worthley, F. Kabigting Jr., and B. Zukis, "Evolving Perceptions of Japanese Workplace Motivation: An Employee-Manager Comparison," *International Journal of Cross-Cultural Management* 5, no. 1 (April 2005): pp. 87–104.

59. J. R. Billings and D. L. Sharpe, "Factors Influencing Flextime Usage Among Employed Married Women," *Consumer Interests Annual* 45 (1999): pp. 89–94; and Harpaz, "Importance of Work Goals" [see note 56].

60. See, for instance, E. Parry and P. Urwin, "Generational Differences in Work Values: A Review of Theory and Evidence," *International Journal of Management Reviews* 13, no. 1 (March 2011): pp. 79–96.

61. T. D. Golden and J. F. Veiga, "The Impact of Extent of Telecommuting on Job Satisfaction: Resolving Inconsistent Findings," *Journal of Management* 31, no. 2 (April 2005): pp. 301–318.

62. See, for instance, M. Alpert, "The Care and Feeding of Engineers," *Fortune*, September 21, 1992, pp. 86–95; G. Poole, "How to Manage Your Nerds," *Forbes ASAP*, December 1994, pp. 132–136; T. J. Allen and R. Katz, "Managing Technical Professionals and Organizations: Improving and Sustaining the Performance of Organizations, Project Teams, and Individual Contributors," *Sloan Management Review,* Summer 2002, pp. S4–S5; and S. R. Barley and G. Kunda, "Contracting: A New Form of Professional Practice," *Academy of Management Perspectives* (February 2006): pp. 45–66.

63. See, for instance, M. Csikszentmihalyi, *Finding Flow* (New York: Basic Books, 1997); N. Baumann and D. Scheffer, "Seeking Flow in the Achievement Domain: The Achievement Flow Motive Behind Flow Experience," *Motivation and Emotion* 35, no. 3 (September 2011): pp. 267–84; and M. Barros, F. M. Araujo-Moreira, L. C. Trevelin, and R. Radel, "Flow Experience and the Mobilization of Attentional Resources," *Cognitive, Affective & Behavioral Neuroscience* 18, no. 4 (August 2018) pp. 810–23.

64. C. E. Connelly and D. G. Gallagher, "Emerging Trends in Contingent Work Research," *Journal of Management* 30, no. 6 (November 2004): pp. 959–983; M. L. Kraimer, S. J. Wayne, R. C. Liden, and R. T. Sparrowe, "The Role of Job Security in Understanding the Relationship Between Employees' Perceptions of Temporary Workers and Employees' Performance," *Journal of Applied Psychology* 90, no. 2 (March 2005): pp. 389–398; J. P. Broschak and A. Davis-Blake, "Mixing Standard Work and Nonstandard Deals: The Consequences of Heterogeneity in Employment Arrangements," *Academy of Management Journal* 49, no. 2 (April 2006): pp. 371–393; and A. Moore, "Temporary Lure," *Talent Development*, September 2016, p. 12.

65. C. L. Wilkin, "I Can't Get No Job Satisfaction: Meta-analysis Comparing Permanent and Contingent Workers," *Journal of Organizational Behavior*, January 2013, pp. 47–64.

66. A. Verasai, "Companies That Swear by Open Book Management," *HR Digest*, October 13, 2016, https://www.thehrdigest.com/companies-swear-open-book-management/.

67. Ibid.

68. See, for instance, B. Fotsch and J. Case, "The Business Case for Open-Book Management," *Forbes*, July 25, 2017, https://www.forbes.com/sites/fotschcase/2017/07/25/the-business-case-for-open-book-management/#5f560a725883; and M. Weinstein, "Is Open-Book Management Right for Your Company?," *Training*, March 16, 2018, https://trainingmag.com/open-book-management-right-your-company/.

69. Cited in Weinstein, "Is Open-Book Management Right."

70. Fotsch and Case, "The Business Case" [see note 68].

71. L. E. Tetrick and C. R. Haimann, "Employee Recognition," in A. Day, E. K. Kelloway, and J. J. Hurrell Jr., eds., *Workplace Well-Being: How to Build Psychologically Healthy Workplaces* (Hoboken, NJ: Wiley, 2014), pp. 161–74.

72. L. Shepherd, "Special Report on Rewards and Recognition: Getting Personal," *Workforce Management*, September 2010, pp. 24-29.

73. "Trends in Employee Recognition," A Report by WorldatWork, May 2015.

74. K. Piombino, "Infographic: Only 12% of Workers Get Frequent Appreciation," January 4, 2013, https://www.hrcommunication.com.

75. Cited in S. Caudron, "The Top 20 Ways to Motivate Employees," *Industry Week,* April 3, 1995, pp. 15–16. See also B. Nelson, "Try Praise," *Inc.,* September 1996, p. 115; and J. Wiscombe, "Rewards Get Results," *Workforce,* April 2002, pp. 42–48.

76. G.T. Milkovich, J.M. Newman, and B. Gerhart, *Compensation*, 12th ed. (New York: McGraw-Hill, 2017).

77. "Incentive Pay Practices: Privately Held Companies," WorldatWork, February 2016, https://www.worldatwork.org/docs/research-and-surveys/survey-brief-incentive-pay-practices-survey-privately-held-companies-1115.pdf.

78. J. H. Han, K. M. Bartol, and S. Kim, "Tightening Up the Performance-Reward Linkage: Roles of Contingent Reward Leadership and Profit-Sharing in the Cross-Level Influence of Individual Pay-for-Performance," *Journal of Applied Psychology* 100, no. 2 (March 2015): pp. 417–30.

79. A. J. Nyberg, J. R. Pierper, and C. O. Trevor, "Pay-for-Performance's Effect on Future Employee Performance: Integrating Psychological and Economic Principles Toward a Contingency Perspective," *Journal of Management* 42, no. 7 (November 2016): pp. 1753–83.

80. Based on W. R. Ginsberg, "Pay-for-Performance: Lessons From the National Security Personnel System," Congressional Research Service Report for Congress, December 18, 2009; and M. Hardy, "NSPS: Anatomy of a Failure," *FCW*, July 22, 2011, https://fcw.com/articles/2011/07/25/feat-pay-for-performance-sidebar.aspx.

81. L. Weber and R. E. Silverman, "Workers Share Their Salary Secrets," *Wall Street Journal*, April 17, 2013, p. B1; R. E. Silverman, "Psst ... This Is What Your Co-Worker Is Paid," *Wall Street Journal*, January 30, 2013, p. B6; and R. E. Silverman, "My Colleague, My Paymaster," *Wall Street Journal*, April 4, 2012, p. B1.

82. "REI Co-op Makes Fortune 100 Best Companies to Work For List for 21st Consecutive Year," *PR Newswire*, February 15, 2018, https://www.prnewswire.com/news-releases/rei-co-op-makes-fortune-100-best-companies-to-work-for-list-for-21st-consecutive-year-300599633.html.

83. A. Cain, "One of the Best Companies in America Gives Employees 'Yay Days' to Take Off Work—But They Can't Be Used for Just Anything," *Business Insider*, February 27, 2018, https://www.businessinsider.com/rei-jobs-vacation-2018-2.

84. "REI," Glassdoor Employee Reviews, accessed February 8, 2019, https://www.glassdoor.com.

85. Cain, "One of the Best Companies" [see note 83].

86. "REI Co-op Pay and Benefits," https://rei.jobs.

87. K. Rogers, "Do Your Employees Feel Respected?," *Harvard Business Review*, July-August 2018, pp. 62–70.

88. H. Ringle, "This Tech Company That Hires Incarcerated Women Expands to Europe, Hiring in Phoenix," *Phoenix Business Journal*, June 17, 2016, https://www.bizjournals.com/phoenix/blog/techflash/2016/06/this-tech-company-that-hires-incarcerated-women.html.

Chapter 17 Being an Effective Leader

Employability Skills Matrix

This matrix identifies which features and end-of-chapter material will help you develop specific skills employers are looking for in job candidates.

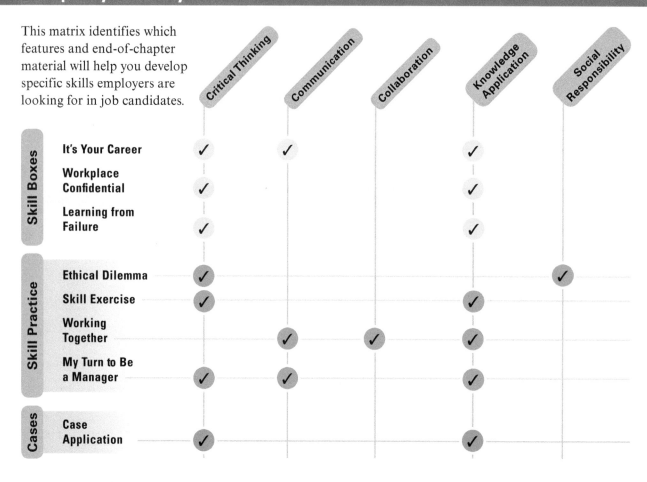

		Critical Thinking	Communication	Collaboration	Knowledge Application	Social Responsibility
Skill Boxes	It's Your Career	✓	✓		✓	
	Workplace Confidential	✓			✓	
	Learning from Failure	✓			✓	
Skill Practice	Ethical Dilemma	✓				✓
	Skill Exercise	✓			✓	
	Working Together		✓	✓	✓	
	My Turn to Be a Manager	✓	✓		✓	
Cases	Case Application	✓			✓	

Dr. Delos "Toby" Cosgrove is a cardiac surgeon by training, having performed more than 22,000 operations. But in 2004, he switched roles to become president and CEO of the Cleveland Clinic. He held that position until he retired at the end of 2017. In those thirteen years, the clinic opened locations in Toronto and Abu Dhabi, increased visits from 2.8 million to 7.1 million, and grew revenues from $3.7 billion to $8.5 billion.[1]

Cosgrove's leadership was critical in leading the clinic's dramatic growth, expansion, and status as the number two hospital in the US. Among his accomplishments were reorganizing clinical services into a patient-centered model of care designed around organs and diseases rather than doctors; and implementing "new ways for patients to access care anytime, anywhere, with walk-in appointments, and virtual visits by phone or tablet."

Let's begin this chapter by clarifying who leaders are and what leadership is.

WHO are leaders, and what is leadership?

LO17.1 Our definition of a **leader** is someone who can influence others and who has managerial authority. **Leadership** is a process of leading a group and influencing that group to achieve its goals. It's what leaders do.

Are all managers leaders? Because leading is one of the four management functions, yes, ideally, all managers *should* be leaders. Thus, we're going to study leaders and leadership from a managerial perspective.[2] However, even though we're looking at these from a managerial perspective, we're aware that groups often have informal leaders who emerge. Although these informal leaders may be able to influence others, they have not been the focus of most leadership research and are not the types of leaders we're studying in this chapter.

Leaders and leadership, like motivation, are organizational behavior topics that have been researched a lot. Most of that research has been aimed at answering the question: *What is an effective leader?* Let's look at some early leadership theories that attempted to answer that question.

leader
Someone who can influence others and who has managerial authority

leadership
A process of influencing a group to achieve goals

EARLY leadership theories

LO17.2 People have been interested in leadership since they started coming together in groups to accomplish goals. However, it wasn't until the early part of the twentieth century that researchers actually began to formally study leadership. These early leadership theories focused on the *leader* (leadership trait theories) and how the *leader interacted* with his or her group members (leadership behavior theories).

Leadership Traits

Researchers at the universities of Florida and North Carolina reported that taller men, compared to shorter men, tended to possess higher levels of social esteem, become successful leaders, earn more money, and have greater career success.[3] What does a study of height have to do with trait theories of leadership? Well, that's also what leadership trait theories have attempted to do—identify certain traits that all leaders have.

Leadership research in the 1920s and 1930s focused on isolating leader traits—that is, characteristics—that would differentiate leaders from nonleaders. Some of the traits studied included physical stature, appearance, social class, emotional stability, fluency of speech, and sociability. Despite the best efforts of researchers, it proved impossible to identify a set of traits that would *always* differentiate a leader (the person) from a nonleader. Maybe it was a bit optimistic to think that a set

Exhibit 17-1

Ten Traits Associated with Leadership

1. **Drive.** Leaders exhibit a high effort level. They have a relatively high desire for achievement, they are ambitious, they have a lot of energy, they are tirelessly persistent in their activities, and they show initiative.

2. **Desire to lead.** Leaders have a strong desire to influence and lead others. They demonstrate the willingness to take responsibility.

3. **Honesty and integrity.** Leaders build trusting relationships with followers by being truthful or nondeceitful and by showing high consistency between word and deed.

4. **Self-confidence.** Followers look to leaders for an absence of self-doubt. Leaders, therefore, need to show self-confidence in order to convince followers of the rightness of their goals and decisions.

5. **Intelligence.** Leaders need to be intelligent enough to gather, synthesize, and interpret large amounts of information, and they need to be able to create visions, solve problems, and make correct decisions.

6. **Job-relevant knowledge.** Effective leaders have a high degree of knowledge about the company, industry, and technical matters. In-depth knowledge allows leaders to make well-informed decisions and to understand the implications of those decisions.

7. **Extraversion.** Leaders are energetic, lively people. They are sociable, assertive, and rarely silent or withdrawn.

8. **Proneness to guilt.** Guilt proneness is positively related to leadership effectiveness because it produces a strong sense of responsibility for others.

9. **Emotional intelligence.** Empathetic leaders can sense others' needs, listen to what followers say (and don't say), and read the reactions of others.

10. **Conscientiousness.** People who are disciplined and able to keep commitments have an apparent advantage when it comes to leadership.[4]

of consistent and unique traits would apply universally to all effective leaders, no matter whether they were in charge of Procter & Gamble, the Moscow Ballet, the country of France, a local collegiate chapter of Alpha Chi Omega, a McDonald's franchise, or Oxford University. However, later attempts to identify traits consistently associated with *leadership* (the process of leading, not the person) were more successful. Ten traits shown to be associated with effective leadership are described briefly in Exhibit 17-1.

Researchers eventually recognized that traits alone were not sufficient for identifying effective leaders, since explanations based solely on traits ignored the interactions of leaders and their group members as well as situational factors. Possessing the appropriate traits only made it more likely that an individual would be an effective leader. Therefore, leadership research from the late 1940s to the mid-1960s concentrated on the preferred behavioral styles that leaders demonstrated. Researchers wondered whether something unique in what effective leaders *did*—in other words, in their *behavior*—was the key.

Leadership Behaviors

Carter Murray, CEO of the advertising agency FCB, once told a colleague, "Look, I think you're amazing, incredibly talented and you can do even more than you think in your wildest dreams. And I am not going to manage you to do that. You will determine that yourself."[5] In contrast, Martha Stewart, founder of Martha Stewart Living Omnimedia, was known for her demanding leadership approach. It was reported that she micromanaged employees and treated them as a commodity.[6] These two leaders, as you can see, behaved in two very different ways. What do we know about leader behavior and how can it help us in our understanding of what an effective leader is?

Researchers hoped that the **behavioral theories of leadership** would provide more definitive answers about the nature of leadership than did the trait theories.[7] The four main leader behavior studies are summarized in Exhibit 17-2.

behavioral theories of leadership
Theories that identify behaviors that differentiate effective leaders from ineffective leaders

Exhibit 17-2
Behavioral Theories of Leadership

	Behavioral Dimension	**Conclusion**
University of Iowa	*Democratic style:* involving subordinates, delegating authority, and encouraging participation *Autocratic style:* dictating work methods, centralizing decision making, and limiting participation *Laissez-faire style:* giving group freedom to make decisions and complete work	Democratic style of leadership was most effective, although later studies showed mixed results.
Ohio State	*Consideration:* being considerate of followers' ideas and feelings *Initiating structure:* structuring work and work relationships to meet job goals	High–high leader (high in consideration and high in initiating structure) achieved high subordinate performance and satisfaction, but not in all situations.
University of Michigan	*Employee oriented:* emphasized interpersonal relationships and taking care of employees' needs *Production oriented:* emphasized technical or task aspects of job	Employee-oriented leaders were associated with high group productivity and higher job satisfaction.
Managerial Grid	*Concern for people:* measured leader's concern for subordinates on a scale of 1 to 9 (low to high) *Concern for production:* measured leader's concern for getting job done on a scale of 1 to 9 (low to high)	Leaders performed best with a 9,9 style (high concern for production and high concern for people).

UNIVERSITY OF IOWA STUDIES The University of Iowa studies explored three leadership styles to find which was the most effective.[8] The **autocratic style** described a leader who dictated work methods, made unilateral decisions, and limited employee participation. The **democratic style** described a leader who involved employees in decision making, delegated authority, and used feedback as an opportunity for coaching employees. Finally, the **laissez-faire style** leader let the group make decisions and complete the work in whatever way it saw fit. The researchers' results seemed to indicate that the democratic style contributed to both good quantity and quality of work.

Had the Iowa group found the answer to the question of the most effective leadership style? Unfortunately, it wasn't that simple. Later studies of the autocratic and democratic styles showed mixed results. For instance, the democratic style sometimes produced higher performance levels than the autocratic style, but at other times it didn't. However, more consistent results were found when a measure of employee satisfaction was used. Group members were more satisfied under a democratic leader than under an autocratic one.[9]

Now leaders had a dilemma. Should they focus on achieving higher performance or on achieving higher member satisfaction? This recognition of the dual nature of a leader's behavior—that is, focus on the task and focus on the people—was also a key characteristic of the other behavioral studies.

THE OHIO STATE STUDIES The Ohio State studies identified two important dimensions of leader behavior.[10] Beginning with a list of more than 1,000 behavioral dimensions, the researchers eventually narrowed it down to just two that accounted for most of the leadership behavior described by group members. The first was called **initiating structure**, which referred to the extent to which a leader defined his or her role and the roles of group members in attaining goals. It included behaviors that involved attempts to organize work, work relationships, and goals. The second was called **consideration**, which was defined as the extent to which a leader had work relationships characterized by mutual trust and respect for group members' ideas and feelings. A leader who was high in consideration helped group members with personal problems, was friendly

autocratic style
A leader who dictates work methods, makes unilateral decisions, and limits employee participation

democratic style
A leader who involves employees in decision making, delegates authority, and uses feedback as an opportunity for coaching employees

laissez-faire style
A leader who lets the group make decisions and complete the work in whatever way it sees fit

initiating structure
The extent to which a leader defines his or her role and the roles of group members in attaining goals

consideration
The extent to which a leader has work relationships characterized by mutual trust and respect for group members' ideas and feelings

Apple's former senior vice president of retail Angela Ahrendts is an employee-oriented leader. Her compassionate and nurturing behavior toward subordinates helps them realize their full potential, inspires them to succeed, and results in their loyalty and job satisfaction. Caring for her employees has contributed to Ahrendts' success as an entrepreneur and business leader. She has recently left Apple and is now on the board at Airbnb, where she's been charged with building community among customers.
Source: Then Chih Wey/Xinhua/Alamy Live News/Alamy Stock Photo

high–high leader
A leader high in both initiating structure and consideration behaviors

managerial grid
A two-dimensional grid for appraising leadership styles

Fiedler contingency model
A leadership theory proposing that effective group performance depends on the proper match between a leader's style and the degree to which the situation allows the leader to control and influence

and approachable, and treated all group members as equals. He or she showed concern for (was considerate of) his or her followers' comfort, well-being, status, and satisfaction. Research found that a leader who was high in both initiating structure and consideration (a **high–high leader**) sometimes achieved high group task performance and high group member satisfaction, but not always.

UNIVERSITY OF MICHIGAN STUDIES Leadership studies conducted at the University of Michigan at about the same time as those done at Ohio State also hoped to identify behavioral characteristics of leaders that were related to performance effectiveness. The Michigan group also came up with two dimensions of leadership behavior, which they labeled employee-oriented and production-oriented.[11]

Leaders who were *employee-oriented* were described as emphasizing interpersonal relationships. The *production-oriented* leaders, in contrast, tended to emphasize the task aspects of the job. Unlike the other studies, the Michigan researchers concluded that leaders who were employee-oriented were able to get high group productivity and high group member satisfaction.

THE MANAGERIAL GRID The behavioral dimensions from these early leadership studies provided the basis for the development of a two-dimensional grid for appraising leadership styles. This **managerial grid** used the behavioral dimensions "concern for people" (the vertical part of the grid) and "concern for production" (the horizontal part of the grid) and evaluated a leader's use of these behaviors, ranking them on a scale from 1 (low) to 9 (high).[12] Although the grid had eighty-one potential categories into which a leader's behavioral style might fall, only five styles were named: impoverished management (1,1, or low concern for production, low concern for people), task management (9,1, or high concern for production, low concern for people), middle-of-the-road management (5,5, or medium concern for production, medium concern for people), country club management (1,9, or low concern for production, high concern for people), and team management (9,9, or high concern for production, high concern for people). Of these five styles, the researchers concluded that managers performed best when using a 9,9 style. Unfortunately, the grid offered no answers to the question of what made a manager an effective leader; it only provided a framework for conceptualizing leadership style. In fact, little substantive evidence supports the conclusion that a 9,9 style is most effective in all situations.[13]

Leadership researchers were discovering that predicting leadership success involved something more complex than isolating a few leader traits or preferable behaviors. They began looking at situational influences; specifically, which leadership styles might be suitable in different situations and what these different situations might be.

CONTINGENCY theories of leadership

LO17.3 "The corporate world is filled with stories of leaders who failed to achieve greatness because they failed to understand the context they were working in."[14] In this section, we examine three contingency theories—Fiedler, Hersey-Blanchard, and path-goal—that focus on context. Each looks at defining leadership style and the situation and attempts to answer the *if-then* contingencies (that is, *if* this is the context or situation, *then* this is the best leadership style to use).

The Fiedler Model

The first comprehensive contingency model for leadership was developed by Fred Fiedler.[15] The **Fiedler contingency model** proposed that effective group performance depended on properly matching the leader's style and the amount of control and influence in the situation. The model was based on the premise that a certain leadership style would be most effective in different types of situations. The keys were to (1) define those leadership styles and the different types of situations and then (2) identify the appropriate combinations of style and situation.

Fiedler proposed that a key factor in leadership success was an individual's basic leadership style, either task-oriented or relationship-oriented. To measure a leader's style, Fiedler developed the **least-preferred coworker (LPC) questionnaire**. This questionnaire contained eighteen pairs of contrasting adjectives—for example, pleasant–unpleasant, cold–warm, boring–interesting, or friendly–unfriendly. Respondents were asked to think of all the coworkers they had ever had and to describe that one person they *least enjoyed* working with by rating him or her on a scale of 1 to 8 for each of the eighteen sets of adjectives (the 8 always described the positive adjective out of the pair, and the 1 always described the negative adjective out of the pair).

If the leader described the least-preferred coworker in relatively positive terms (in other words, a "high" LPC score), then the respondent was primarily interested in good personal relations with coworkers and the style would be described as *relationship-oriented*. In contrast, if you saw the least-preferred coworker in relatively unfavorable terms (a low LPC score), you were primarily interested in productivity and getting the job done; thus, your style would be labeled as *task-oriented*. Fiedler did acknowledge that a small number of people might fall between these two extremes and not have a cut-and-dried leadership style. One other important point is that Fiedler assumed a person's leadership style was fixed and stable, regardless of the situation. In other words, if you were a relationship-oriented leader, you'd always be one, and the same would be true for being task-oriented.

After an individual's leadership style had been assessed through the LPC, it was time to evaluate the situation in order to match the leader with the situation. Fiedler's research uncovered three contingency dimensions that defined the key situational factors in leader effectiveness.

- **Leader–member relations**: the degree of confidence, trust, and respect employees have for their leader; rated as either good or poor.
- **Task structure**: the degree to which job assignments are formalized and structured; rated as either high or low.
- **Position power**: the degree of influence a leader has over activities such as hiring, firing, discipline, promotions, and salary increases; rated as either strong or weak.

Each leadership situation was evaluated in terms of these three contingency variables, which, when combined, produced eight possible situations that were either favorable or unfavorable for the leader. (See Exhibit 17-3.) Categories I, II, and III were classified as highly favorable for the leader. Categories IV, V, and VI were moderately favorable for the leader. And categories VII and VIII were described as highly unfavorable for the leader.

Once Fiedler had described the leader variables and the situational variables, he had everything he needed to define the specific contingencies for leadership effectiveness. To do so, he studied 1,200 groups where he compared relationship-oriented versus task-oriented leadership styles in each of the eight situational categories. He concluded that task-oriented leaders performed better in very favorable situations and in very unfavorable situations. (See the top of Exhibit 17-3, where performance is shown on the vertical axis and situation favorableness is shown on the horizontal axis.) On the other hand, relationship-oriented leaders performed better in moderately favorable situations.

Because Fiedler treated an individual's leadership style as fixed, only two ways could improve leader effectiveness. First, you could bring in a new leader whose style better fit the situation. For instance, if the group situation was highly unfavorable but was led by a relationship-oriented leader, the group's performance could be improved by replacing that person with a task-oriented leader. The second alternative was to change the situation to fit the leader. This could be done by restructuring tasks; by

least-preferred coworker (LPC) questionnaire
A questionnaire that measures whether a leader is task or relationship oriented

leader–member relations
One of Fiedler's situational contingencies that describes the degree of confidence, trust, and respect employees have for their leader

task structure
One of Fiedler's situational contingencies that describes the degree to which job assignments are formalized and structured

position power
One of Fiedler's situational contingencies that describes the degree of influence a leader has over activities such as hiring, firing, discipline, promotions, and salary increases

Exhibit 17-3
The Fiedler Model

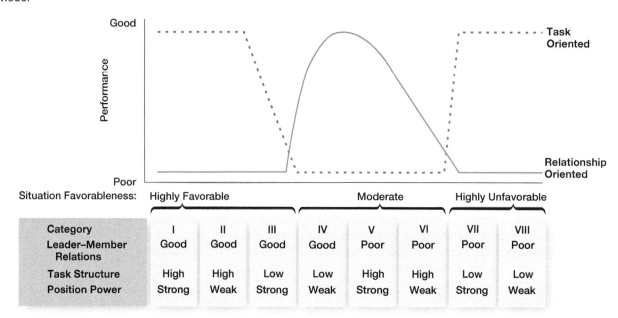

increasing or decreasing the power that the leader had over factors such as salary increases, promotions, and disciplinary actions; or by improving leader–member relations.

Research testing the overall validity of Fiedler's model has shown considerable evidence to support the model.[16] However, his theory wasn't without critics. The major criticism is that it's probably unrealistic to assume that a person can't change his or her leadership style to fit the situation. Effective leaders can, and do, change their styles. Another is that the LPC wasn't very practical. Finally, the situation variables were difficult to assess.[17] In spite of these shortcomings, the Fiedler model showed that effective leadership style needed to reflect situational factors.

Hersey and Blanchard's Situational Leadership Theory

Paul Hersey and Ken Blanchard developed a leadership theory that has gained a strong following among management development specialists.[18] This model, called **situational leadership theory (SLT)**, is a contingency theory that focuses on followers' readiness. Before we proceed, two points need clarification: why a leadership theory focuses on the followers and what is meant by the term *readiness*.

The emphasis on the followers in leadership effectiveness reflects the reality that it *is* the followers who accept or reject the leader. Regardless of what the leader does, the group's effectiveness depends on the actions of the followers. This important dimension has been overlooked or underemphasized in most leadership theories. And **readiness**, as defined by Hersey and Blanchard, refers to the extent to which people have the ability and willingness to accomplish a specific task.

SLT uses the same two leadership dimensions that Fiedler identified: task and relationship behaviors. However, Hersey and Blanchard go a step further by considering each as either high or low and then combining them into four specific leadership styles, described as follows:

- *Telling* (high task–low relationship): The leader defines roles and tells people what, how, when, and where to do various tasks.
- *Selling* (high task–high relationship): The leader provides both directive and supportive behavior.

- *Participating* (low task–high relationship): The leader and followers share in decision making; the main role of the leader is facilitating and communicating.
- *Delegating* (low task–low relationship): The leader provides little direction or support.

The final component in the model is the four stages of follower readiness:

- *R1:* People are both *unable and unwilling* to take responsibility for doing something. Followers aren't competent or confident.
- *R2:* People are *unable but willing* to do the necessary job tasks. Followers are motivated but lack the appropriate skills.
- *R3:* People are *able but unwilling* to do what the leader wants. Followers are competent, but don't want to do something.
- *R4:* People are both *able and willing* to do what is asked of them.

SLT essentially views the leader–follower relationship as being like that of a parent and a child. Just as a parent needs to relinquish control when a child becomes more mature and responsible, so, too, should leaders. As followers reach higher levels of readiness, the leader responds not only by decreasing control over their activities but also by decreasing relationship behaviors. The SLT says if followers are at R1 (*unable* and *unwilling* to do a task), the leader needs to use the telling style and give clear and specific directions; if followers are at R2 (*unable* and *willing*), the leader needs to use the selling style and display high task orientation to compensate for the followers' lack of ability and high relationship orientation to get followers to "buy into" the leader's desires; if followers are at R3 (*able* and *unwilling*), the leader needs to use the participating style to gain their support; and if employees are at R4 (both *able* and *willing*), the leader doesn't need to do much and should use the delegating style.

SLT has intuitive appeal. It acknowledges the importance of followers and builds on the logic that leaders can compensate for ability and motivational limitations in their followers. However, research efforts to test and support the theory generally have been disappointing.[19] Possible explanations include internal inconsistencies in the model as well as problems with research methodology. Despite its appeal and wide popularity, we have to be cautious about any enthusiastic endorsement of SLT.

Dan Reynolds, leader of the group Imagine Dragons, uses the participative approach of the path-goal theory. His approach to songwriting is that each member writes songs constantly and works on putting together their songs as a group. Reynolds strives to create a shared environment in which band members work together as a unit.
Source: Derek Storm/Everett Collection/Alamy Stock Photo

Path-Goal Model

Another approach to understanding leadership is Robert House's **path-goal theory**, which states that it's the leader's job to provide followers with information, support, or other resources necessary to achieve goals. Path-goal theory takes key elements from the expectancy theory of motivation.[20] The term *path-goal* is derived from the belief that effective leaders remove the roadblocks and pitfalls so that followers have a clearer path to help them get from where they are to the achievement of their work goals.

House identified four leadership behaviors:

- *Directive leader:* Lets subordinates know what's expected of them, schedules work to be done, and gives specific guidance on how to accomplish tasks.
- *Supportive leader:* Shows concern for the needs of followers and is friendly.
- *Participative leader:* Consults with group members and uses their suggestions before making a decision.
- *Achievement-oriented leader:* Sets challenging goals and expects followers to perform at their highest level.

In contrast to Fiedler's view that a leader couldn't change his or her behavior, House assumed that leaders are flexible and can display any or all of these leadership styles depending on the situation.

As Exhibit 17-4 illustrates, path-goal theory proposes two situational or contingency variables that moderate the leadership behavior–outcome relationship: those in the *environment* that are outside the control of the follower (factors including task

path-goal theory
A leadership theory that says the leader's job is to assist followers in attaining their goals and to provide direction or support needed to ensure that their goals are compatible with the goals of the group or organization

Exhibit 17-4
Path-Goal Model

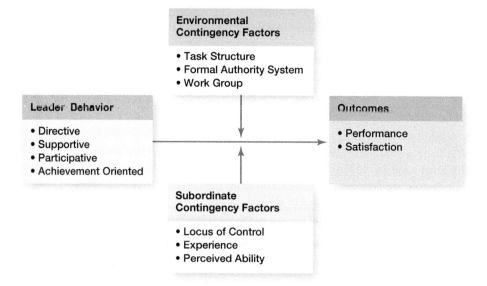

structure, formal authority system, and the work group) and those that are part of the personal characteristics of the *follower* (including locus of control, experience, and perceived ability). Environmental factors determine the type of leader behavior required if subordinate outcomes are to be maximized; personal characteristics of the follower determine how the environment and leader behavior are interpreted. The theory proposes that a leader's behavior won't be effective if it's redundant with what the environmental structure is providing or is incongruent with follower characteristics. For example, some predictions from path-goal theory are:

- Directive leadership leads to greater satisfaction when tasks are ambiguous or stressful than when they are highly structured and well laid out. The followers aren't sure what to do, so the leader needs to give them some direction.
- Supportive leadership results in high employee performance and satisfaction when subordinates are performing structured tasks. In this situation, the leader only needs to support followers, not tell them what to do.
- Directive leadership is likely to be perceived as redundant among subordinates with high perceived ability or with considerable experience. These followers are quite capable, so they don't need a leader to tell them what to do.
- The clearer and more bureaucratic the formal authority relationships, the more leaders should exhibit supportive behavior and de-emphasize directive behavior. The organizational situation has provided the structure as far as what is expected of followers, so the leader's role is simply to support.
- Directive leadership will lead to higher employee satisfaction when there is substantive conflict within a work group. In this situation, the followers need a leader who will take charge.
- Subordinates with an internal locus of control will be more satisfied with a participative style. Because these followers believe they control what happens to them, they prefer to participate in decisions.
- Subordinates with an external locus of control will be more satisfied with a directive style. These followers believe that what happens to them is a result of the external environment, so they would prefer a leader who tells them what to do.
- Achievement-oriented leadership will increase subordinates' expectancies that effort will lead to high performance when tasks are ambiguously structured. By setting challenging goals, followers know what the expectations are.

A review of the research to test path-goal theory suggests mixed support.[21] To summarize the model, however, an employee's performance and satisfaction are likely to be positively influenced when the leader chooses a leadership style that compensates for shortcomings in either the employee or the work setting. However, if the leader spends time explaining tasks that are already clear or when the employee has the ability and experience to handle them without interference, the employee is likely to see such directive behavior as redundant or even insulting.

CONTEMPORARY views of leadership

LO17.4 What are the latest views of leadership? Given the widespread interest in the topic of leadership, you won't be surprised to learn that there are a number of new and interesting directions in leadership research. We review a number of them in the following pages.

Leader–Member Exchange (LMX) Theory

Have you ever been in a group in which the leader had "favorites" who made up his or her in-group? If so, that's the premise behind leader–member exchange (LMX) theory.[22] **Leader–member exchange theory (LMX)** says leaders create in-groups and out-groups, and those in the in-group will have higher performance ratings, less turnover, and greater job satisfaction.

LMX theory suggests that early on in the relationship between a leader and a given follower, a leader will implicitly categorize a follower as an "in" or as an "out." That relationship tends to remain fairly stable over time. Leaders also encourage LMX by rewarding those employees with whom they want a closer linkage and punishing those with whom they do not.[23] For the LMX relationship to remain intact, however, both the leader and the follower must invest in the relationship.

It's not exactly clear how a leader chooses who falls into each category, but evidence shows that in-group members have demographic, attitude, personality, and even gender similarities with the leader, or they have a higher level of competence than out-group members.[24] The leader does the choosing, but the follower's characteristics drive the decision.

Research on LMX has been generally supportive. It appears that leaders do differentiate among followers; that these disparities are not random; and followers with in-group status will have higher performance ratings, engage in more helping or "citizenship" behaviors at work, and report greater satisfaction with their boss.[25]

Charismatic Leadership

Richard Branson, founder of the Virgin Group, is a person who exudes energy, enthusiasm, and drive. He has pursued his vision for Virgin with serious intensity and has demonstrated an ability to inspire his employees as it expanded into an array of different businesses—from music to space travel. Branson is what we call a **charismatic leader**—that is, someone to whom followers attribute heroic or extraordinary leadership abilities when they observe certain behaviors and tend to give power.[26]

A number of authors have attempted to identify personal characteristics of the charismatic leader.[27] The most comprehensive analysis identified five such characteristics: they have a vision, the ability to articulate that vision, a willingness to take risks to achieve that vision, a sensitivity to both environmental constraints and follower needs, and behaviors that are out of the ordinary.[28]

An increasing body of evidence shows impressive correlations between charismatic leadership and high performance and satisfaction among followers.[29] Although one study found that charismatic CEOs had no impact on subsequent organizational performance, charisma is still believed to be a desirable leadership quality.[30] But we can't ignore that charisma has a potential downside. Charismatic leaders who are larger than life don't necessarily act in the best interests of their organizations.[31] Research has shown that

leader–member exchange theory (LMX)
The leadership theory that says leaders create in-groups and out-groups and those in the in-group will have higher performance ratings, less turnover, and greater job satisfaction

charismatic leader
Someone to whom followers attribute heroic or extraordinary leadership abilities when they observe certain behaviors and tend to give power

Richard Branson, founder of the Virgin Group, has demonstrated an ability to inspire his employees as Virgin has expanded into an array of different businesses—from music to space travel. Branson is the model of a charismatic leader.
Source: Kristin Callahan/Everett Collection/ Alamy Stock Photo

individuals who are narcissistic are also higher in some behaviors associated with charismatic leadership. Many charismatic—but corrupt—leaders have allowed their personal goals to override the goals of their organizations. Charismatic leaders at Enron, Tyco, WorldCom, and HealthSouth recklessly used organizational resources for their personal benefit and unethically violated laws to inflate stock prices, and then cashed in millions of dollars in personal stock options. Hopefully the corrupt charismatic leaders at these organizations stand out largely because they're the exceptions.

If charisma is desirable, can people learn to be charismatic leaders? Or are charismatic leaders born with their qualities? Although a small number of experts still think that charisma can't be learned, most believe that individuals can be trained to exhibit charismatic behaviors.[32] For example, researchers have succeeded in teaching undergraduate students to "be" charismatic. How? They were taught to articulate a far-reaching goal, communicate high performance expectations, exhibit confidence in the ability of subordinates to meet those expectations, and empathize with the needs of their subordinates; they learned to project a powerful, confident, and dynamic presence; and they practiced using a captivating and engaging voice tone. The researchers also trained the student leaders to use charismatic nonverbal behaviors, including leaning toward the follower when communicating, maintaining direct eye contact, and having a relaxed posture and animated facial expressions. In groups with these "trained" charismatic leaders, members had higher task performance, higher task adjustment, and better adjustment to the leader and to the group than did group members who worked in groups led by noncharismatic leaders.

One last thing we should say about charismatic leadership is that it may not always be needed to achieve high levels of employee performance. It may be most appropriate when the follower's task has an ideological purpose or when the environment involves a high degree of stress and uncertainty.[33] This distinction may explain why, when charismatic leaders surface, it's more likely to be in politics, religion, or wartime, or when a business firm is starting up or facing a survival crisis. For example, Martin Luther King Jr. used his charisma to bring about social equality through nonviolent means, and Steve Jobs achieved unwavering loyalty and commitment from Apple's technical staff in the early 1980s by articulating a vision of personal computers that would dramatically change the way people lived.

Transformational-Transactional Leadership

Many early leadership theories viewed leaders as **transactional leaders**; that is, leaders who lead primarily by using social exchanges (or transactions). Transactional leaders guide or motivate followers to work toward established goals by exchanging rewards for their productivity.[34] But another type of leader—a **transformational leader**—stimulates and inspires (transforms) followers to achieve extraordinary outcomes. Examples include Jim Goodnight of SAS Institute and Reed Hastings at Netflix. They pay attention to the concerns and developmental needs of individual followers; they change followers' awareness of issues by helping those followers look at old problems in new ways; and they are able to excite, arouse, and inspire followers to exert extra effort to achieve group goals.

Transactional and transformational leadership shouldn't be viewed as opposing approaches to getting things done.[35] Transformational leadership develops from transactional leadership. Transformational leadership produces levels of employee effort and performance that go beyond what would occur with a transactional approach alone. Moreover, transformational leadership is more than charisma because the transformational leader attempts to instill in followers the ability to question not only established views but also those views held by the leader.[36]

The evidence supporting the superiority of transformational leadership over transactional leadership is overwhelmingly impressive. For instance, studies that looked at managers in different settings, including the military and business, found that transformational leaders were evaluated as more effective, higher performers, more promotable than their transactional counterparts, and more interpersonally

transactional leaders
Leaders who lead primarily by using social exchanges (or transactions)

transformational leaders
Leaders who stimulate and inspire (transform) followers to achieve extraordinary outcomes

fyi

Forty-seven percent of employees with uninspiring leaders (those at or below the 10th percentile on inspiring and motivating others) say they have considered quitting.[37]

Learning from
FAILURE The Firing of Steve Jobs at Apple

Some stories are so good that they're hard to believe. Steve Jobs's story at Apple is one of those. He co-founded the company, got fired, and then came back to save it.

Jobs and Steve Wozniak founded Apple in 1976. Wozniak handled the technical stuff and Jobs was the ideas guy and took care of the business side. As the company grew, they brought in professional management to oversee operations. In 1983, Jobs personally recruited then-PepsiCo CEO John Sculley to take over the helm at Apple. But Jobs and Sculley quickly butted heads. Sculley saw Jobs as a zealot who was more concerned with turning out beautiful products than making money. Sculley cut heavily into Jobs's responsibilities. Their conflict reached a peak in 1985, with company sales in decline. Jobs went to Apple's board of directors to protest constraints that Sculley was placing on Jobs. The board sided with Sculley, and Jobs was essentially ousted.

Sculley proved unable to turn the Apple "ship" around. Under Sculley, Apple turned out flops like the Newton MessagePad, a personal assistant device that was ahead of its time and just didn't function very well. The board fired Sculley in 1993. Over the next several years, new CEOs were hired, but the company continued its decline.

In 1996, the board realized its mistake and reached out to Jobs. In the interim, he had created a small PC maker, NeXT. Apple bought NeXT and brought back Jobs as its "interim" CEO. Two years later, the "interim" title was dropped and Jobs was back in the driver's seat. The rest is history. Jobs oversaw the resurgence of Apple with innovative products like the iMac, iPod, iPhone, and iPad—and turned it into the most valuable company in the world. Apple's board had learned that Jobs was truly a unique talent and that it was OK to admit they had made a mistake in ever letting him go.[38]

sensitive.[39] In addition, evidence indicates that transformational leadership is strongly correlated with lower turnover rates and higher levels of productivity, employee satisfaction, creativity, goal attainment, follower well-being, and corporate entrepreneurship, especially in start-up firms.[40]

Authentic Leadership

The late Senator John McCain and the former CEO of Home Depot, Frank Blake, are examples of authentic leaders. McCain never shirked from his moral standards, nor was he afraid to oppose the majority. Blake took responsibility for a data breach of the company's computer systems that led to the theft of 56 million credit card numbers. This theft happened just before Blake's retirement, and he could have easily left the crisis for the new CEO to deal with.

Authentic leadership focuses on the moral aspects of being a leader. **Authentic leaders** know who they are, know what they believe in, and act on those values and beliefs openly and candidly. More specifically, authentic leaders have been found to possess four qualities: they're self-aware, transparent, openly solicit views that challenge their deeply held positions, and guided by strong moral standards.[41] They're also typically humble.

The combination of these qualities lead followers to consider them as ethical people and trust them as a result. When leaders practice what they preach, or act on their values openly and candidly, followers tend to develop a strong affective commitment and trust in their leader and, to a lesser degree, to improve their performance and organizational citizenship behavior.[42]

authentic leadership
Leaders who know who they are, know what they believe in, and act on those values and beliefs openly and candidly

Mary Barra, CEO of General Motors, is an ethical leader. She is placing public safety ahead of profits after the company's installation of faulty ignition switches in millions of vehicles.
Source: Tom Williams/CQ Roll Call/Newscom

Ethical Leadership

Shortly after becoming CEO of General Motors, Mary Barra faced a character-defining choice: Should she take responsibility for the company's installation of faulty ignition switches in millions of vehicles even though she was not

CEO at the time? Barra chose to take the high road: "I want to start by saying how sorry personally and how sorry General Motors is for what has happened."[43] She then appointed Jeff Boyer as the vice president of global safety. Barra said that "if there are any obstacles in his way, Jeff has the authority to clear them. If he needs any additional resources, he will get them."[44] Mary Barra is an example of an ethical leader because she is placing public safety ahead of profits. She is holding culpable employees accountable, and she stands behind her employees by creating a culture in which they feel that they could and should do a better job.

Leadership is not value-free. In assessing its effectiveness, we need to address the *means* that a leader uses to achieve goals as well the content of those goals. The role of the leader in creating the ethical expectations for all members is crucial.[45] Ethical top leadership influences not only direct followers but spreads all the way down the command structure as well, because top leaders set expectations and expect lower-level leaders to behave consistent with ethical guidelines.[46]

Leaders rated as highly ethical tend to be evaluated very positively by their subordinates, who are also more satisfied and committed to their jobs, and experience less strain and turnover intentions.[47] Followers of such leaders are also more motivated, perform better, and engage in more organizational citizenship behaviors and fewer counterproductive work behaviors.[48]

Servant Leadership

servant leadership
Leadership that goes beyond self-interest and focuses on opportunities to help followers grow and develop

An extension of ethical leadership has recently gotten the attention of leadership researchers. The concept is called **servant leadership**.[49] Servant leaders go beyond their self-interest and focus on opportunities to help followers grow and develop. What's unique about servant leadership is that, relative to other approaches to leadership, it puts the needs of followers ahead of attending to one's own needs. Its specific characteristics include caring about followers' personal problems and well-being; empowering followers with responsibility and decision-making influence; helping subordinates grow and succeed; and serving as a model of integrity.[50]

Syliva Metayer, CEO of Sodexo Corporate Services Worldwide, provides an example of servant leadership. "I've been CEO for 18 months, so I'm learning," says Metayer. "I'm learning that to be a CEO is to be a servant. My main job is to support our employees, and be a support to our clients and to our consumers."[51] Other, more notable examples of servant leaders include Martin Luther King Jr., Nelson Mandela, Mother Teresa, and Mahatma Gandhi.

Dr. Martin Luther King, Jr. provides an example of servant leadership, which is defined as leadership that goes beyond self-interest and focuses on opportunities to help followers grow and develop.
Source: GL Archive/Alamy Stock Photo

One study of seventy-one general managers of restaurants in the US and over 1,000 of their employees found that servant leaders tend to create a culture of service, which in turn improves restaurant performance and enhances employees attitudes and performance by increasing employees' identification with the restaurant.[52] Another study of Chinese hairstylists found similar results, with servant leadership predicting customer satisfaction and stylists' service performance.[53]

One interesting aside is that servant leadership may be more prevalent and effective in certain cultures.[54] When asked to draw images of leaders, for example, US subjects tended to draw them in front of the group, giving orders to followers. Singaporeans, in contrast, tended to draw leaders at the back of the group, acting more to gather a group's opinions together and then unifying them from the rear. This suggests that the East Asian prototype is more like a servant leader, which might mean servant leadership is more effective in these cultures.

Followership

Here's a statement beyond debate: You can't be a leader without any followers! So leaders can only be as effective as their ability to engage followers. However, it's only recently that students of leadership have begun considering the role of followers in the leadership process.[55]

The leader–follower interaction is two-way. First, it's obvious that leaders need to motivate and engage their followers to achieve end goals. But often overlooked is the fact that followers influence the attitudes, aptitudes, and behaviors of leaders.[56] The two need to work together to move the collective forward.[57]

The recent attention on followership has underscored that leadership is a process that emerges from a relationship between leaders and followers who are bound together as part of the same social group. For success, followers need a set of skills that are complementary to those of the leader.[58]

What defines a good follower? Through most of the 20th century, the answer was unquestioned obedience and deference to a leader. But today, when leaders engage in less unilateral decision making and more collaboration, great followership is characterized by a different set of qualities:[59]

1. **They can manage themselves.** Effective followers are self-directed. They are self-motivated and can work without close supervision.
2. **They are strongly committed to a purpose outside themselves.** Effective followers are committed to something—a cause, a product, a work team, an idea, an organization—in addition to the care of their own lives. Most people like working with colleagues who are emotionally, as well as physically, committed to their work.
3. **They are enthusiastic.** They approach their work with a positive attitude. They "buy into" their leader's vision.
4. **They build their competence and focus their efforts for maximum impact.** Effective followers master skills that will be useful to their organization, and they hold higher performance standards than their job or work group requires.
5. **They are courageous, honest, and credible.** Effective followers establish themselves as independent, critical thinkers whose knowledge and judgment can be trusted. They hold high ethical standards, give credit where credit is due, and aren't afraid to admit their mistakes.

INTEGRATING THEORIES OF LEADERSHIP

LO17.5 We've introduced a number of leadership theories in this chapter. Let's try to see what commonalities might exist between these theories, how they might be complementary or overlap, and how they can be integrated to help you better understand what makes an effective leader.

TRAITS. Let's begin with traits. Although there is no single trait or set of traits that are unique to leaders, several traits seem to regularly appear in research studies of leaders. We noted ten of them in Exhibit 17-1. Of these, the most powerful appear to be intelligence, emotional intelligence, and conscientiousness.[60] But these traits may more accurately reflect the *perception* of leadership rather than actual leadership *effectiveness.* Our conclusion is that even if traits play a role in defining leaders, their role is small and dependent on situational factors.

BEHAVIORS. The behavioral theories we discussed focused on a number of dimensions: democratic, autocratic, and laissez-faire styles; directive and participative; initiating structure and consideration; employee-oriented and production-oriented; concern for people and concern for production. Even the most cursory review of these dimensions suggests considerably overlap, if not redundancy. In addition, transitional, transformational, charismatic, and leader-member exchange theories all include leadership behaviors.

Efforts to streamline these behaviors have found that three metacategories encompass almost all of these:[61]

Task-oriented behavior. This describes transactional leader behavior, initiating structure, directive behavior, and production orientation.

Relations-oriented behavior. This describes leaders who care about their followers' needs, treats members equally, and who are friendly and approachable. This would describe consideration, a democratic style, employee and people oriented, participative behavior, transformational leadership, and LMX's in-group.

Change-oriented behavior. This leader behavior includes communicating a vision of change, encouraging innovative thinking, and risk-taking. It's a major component of both transformational and charismatic leadership.

Using these three behaviors, researchers have found that relations-oriented leadership accounted for most of the differences in both employee commitment and job performance.[62]

In terms of reducing redundancy and confusion, efforts at comparing ethical and authentic leadership with transformational leadership found considerable overlap. Specifically, it appears that transformational leadership encompasses almost all of the same variables as ethical and authentic leadership.[63] So while both authentic and ethical leadership may help understand a few focused employee outcomes, they don't "offer much that transformational leadership does not already provide."[64] Meanwhile, transformational leadership does appear to be related to employee commitment, trust, satisfaction, and performance.

CONTINGENCY FACTORS.   There is no shortage of contingency factors that have been introduced to help explain when leaders are most likely to be effective. Some, however, appear to be more relevant. We'll look at four.

A follower's *experience* appears important. The more experience an employee has, the less dependent he or she is on a leader. It appears a leader's guidance is particularly important when an employee is new. But experienced employees don't require close supervision and are likely to find task-oriented behavior by a leader as unnecessary or even insulting.

A followers' *ability* also appears important. Like experience, high levels of ability allow employees to perform their work with minimal supervision.

Culture has consistently shown to be a highly relevant contingency variable in leadership.[65] *Organizational culture* shapes what leadership style is appropriate. Regardless of a leader's predisposition, what's defined as "appropriate" in a prison or military organization is likely to be very different than in a consulting firm or an academic department in a university. *National culture* also shapes what's appropriate and acceptable. The same relations-oriented style that's appropriate and effective in Sweden is likely to be seen as weak and ineffective in Mexico.

LEADERSHIP issues in the twenty-first century

LO17.6 Today's leaders face some important issues. In this section, we look at several of them.

Managing Power

Where do leaders get their power—that is, their right and capacity to influence work actions or decisions? Five sources of leader power have been identified: legitimate, coercive, reward, expert, and referent.[66]

Legitimate power and authority are the same. Legitimate power represents the power a leader has as a result of his or her position in the organization. Although people in positions of authority are also likely to have reward and coercive power, legitimate power is broader than the power to coerce and reward.

Coercive power is the power a leader has to punish or control. Followers react to this power out of fear of the negative results that might occur if they don't comply. Managers typically have some coercive power, such as being able to suspend or demote employees or to assign them work they find unpleasant or undesirable.

Reward power is the power to give positive rewards. A reward can be anything a person values, such as money, favorable performance appraisals, promotions, interesting work assignments, friendly colleagues, and preferred work shifts or sales territories.

Expert power is power based on expertise, special skills, or knowledge. If an employee has skills, knowledge, or expertise that's critical to a work group, that person's expert power is enhanced.

Finally, **referent power** is the power that arises because of a person's desirable resources or personal traits. It develops out of admiration of another and a desire to be like that person. Referent power explains why celebrities are paid millions of dollars to endorse products in commercials. Marketing research shows that people like Ariana Grande, Kim Kardashian, and LeBron James have the power to influence your choice of beauty products and athletic shoes.

Most effective leaders rely on several different forms of power to affect the behavior and performance of their followers. For example, the commanding officer of one of Australia's state-of-the-art submarines, the HMAS *Sheean*, employs different types of power in managing his crew and equipment. He gives orders to the crew (legitimate), praises them (reward), and disciplines those who commit infractions (coercive). As an effective leader, he also strives to have expert power (based on his expertise and knowledge) and referent power (based on his being admired) to influence his crew.

Developing Credibility and Trust

We saw the importance trust plays in a variety of leadership theories. In fact, it's probably fair to say that a lack of credibility and trust is likely to undermine leadership. But how can leaders build credibility and trust? Let's start with making sure we know what the terms mean and why they're so important.

The main component of credibility is honesty. Surveys show that honesty is consistently singled out as the number one characteristic of admired leaders. "Honesty is absolutely essential to leadership. If people are going to follow someone willingly, whether it be into battle or into the boardroom, they first want to assure themselves that the person is worthy of their trust."[68] In addition to being honest, credible leaders are competent and inspiring. They are personally able to effectively communicate

legitimate power
The power a leader has as a result of his or her position in the organization

coercive power
The power a leader has to punish or control

reward power
The power a leader has to give positive rewards

expert power
Power that's based on expertise, special skills, or knowledge

referent power
Power that arises because of a person's desirable resources or personal traits

When employees trust their leaders:

- 23 percent of employees offer more ideas and solutions
- 21 percent of employees are willing to work longer hours[67]

WORKPLACE CONFIDENTIAL A Micromanaging Boss

Micromanaging has been described as "probably the most common complaint about a boss." What exactly is *micromanaging*, and what can you do if you find yourself working for a micromanager?

A micromanaging boss is someone who wants to control every particular aspect, down to the smallest detail, of your work. For you, it can be very frustrating, stressful, and demoralizing. What are some signs that your boss may be micromanaging you? He checks on your progress multiple times a day, asks for frequent updates, tells you how to complete tasks, is obsessed with meaningless details, or becomes irritated if you make a decision without consulting him first. But just because your boss monitors your work doesn't mean he's a micromanager. Every manager has a responsibility for controlling activities for which he or she is responsible. And good managers are detail oriented. The difference is that micromanagers obsess on details, lose sight of priorities, and behave as if they don't trust you. Good managers, on the other hand, understand the value of delegation. Unfortunately, you might not always have one of these.

There's a long list of reasons why your boss might be micromanaging you. That list would include insecurity, lack of trust in others, risk aversion, or lack of confidence in your ability. Additionally, other reasons might be having too little to do, thinking he or she is being helpful, or just being a control freak.

Self-assessment. If you feel that your boss is micromanaging you, the place to start is with self-assessment. Ask yourself: "Is it *me*?" Is there any reason your boss might feel the need to micromanage? For instance, have you shown up late to work? Have you missed some deadlines? Have you been distracted at work lately? Have you made mistakes that have reflected negatively on your boss? Start your assessment by making sure that your boss's behavior isn't rational and reasonable.

New to the job. The next question to ask is: Are either you or your boss new on the job? If you're new, your boss may just be temporarily monitoring your work until he or she is confident of your ability and you prove yourself. If your boss is new, either to her current position or in her first managerial position, you will want to give her some slack as she adjusts. Micromanaging is not uncommon among new managers

who, with little experience, are fearful of delegation and being held accountable for results. And experienced managers, in a new position, may be overly controlling until they're confident of your abilities. So if either you or your boss is new, you might want to give it some time.

Changing conditions. A final step before you take any action should be to assess whether conditions have changed. If your boss's micromanaging behavior is a change from her past behavior, consider whether it might be justified by changing conditions. Is your organization going through layoffs? Is there a major reorganization going on? Has your boss been given additional projects with pressing deadlines? Has your boss got a new boss? Any of these types of conditions can increase stress and lead your boss to micromanaging. If the conditions creating stress are temporary, her strong oversight behavior may be just short term.

Talk to your boss. If you've come to the conclusion that your boss's behavior isn't temporary and it's creating difficulties for you to do your job properly, you and your boss need to talk.

It's very possible your boss is unaware that there's a problem. In a nonconfrontational voice, specifically explain how his oversight is impacting your work, creating stress, and making it harder for you to perform at your full capabilities. You want to show him that you've got things under control and that you know what his expectations are.

Keep your boss updated. In addition to talking to your boss, you want to alleviate any concerns she might have that work isn't being done correctly or that she might be unable to answer questions about your work progress. This is best achieved by regularly updating her on your work's status. No boss likes surprises, especially ones that might reflect negatively on her management skills. This can best be achieved by proactively providing your boss with updates before they're requested.

Reinforce your boss's positive behaviors. When your boss leaves you alone, let her know you appreciate her hands-off approach. Thank her for trusting you. By positively reinforcing her trust, you increase the probability that she'll demonstrate more of that behavior. Over time, when combined with your regular updates and your solid performance, you're very likely to see a decline in the micromanaging behavior.[69]

credibility
The degree to which followers perceive someone as honest, competent, and able to inspire

trust
The belief in the integrity, character, and ability of a leader

their confidence and enthusiasm. Thus, followers judge a leader's **credibility** in terms of his or her honesty, competence, and ability to inspire.

Trust is closely entwined with the concept of credibility, and, in fact, the terms are often used interchangeably. **Trust** is defined as the belief in the integrity, character, and ability of a leader. Followers who trust a leader are willing to be vulnerable to the leader's actions because they are confident that their rights and interests will not be abused.[70] Research has identified five dimensions that make up the concept of trust:[71]

- *Integrity:* honesty and truthfulness
- *Competence:* technical and interpersonal knowledge and skills
- *Consistency:* reliability, predictability, and good judgment in handling situations
- *Loyalty:* willingness to protect a person, physically and emotionally
- *Openness:* willingness to share ideas and information freely

IT'S YOUR CAREER

How to Be Seen as Trustworthy

To be seen as trustworthy is an obvious asset. As a leader, what can you do to get others to trust you? It's no simple task, but the evidence indicates certain actions help to build trusting relationships:[73]

1.   Be open. Mistrust comes as much from what people don't know as from what they do know. Keep people informed, make the criteria on how decisions are made overtly clear, explain the rationale for your decisions, be candid about problems, and fully disclose relevant information.

2.   Be fair. Before making decisions or taking actions, consider how others will perceive them in terms of objectivity and fairness. Give credit where it's due, be objective and impartial in performance appraisals, and pay attention to equity perceptions in reward distributions.

3.   Speak your feelings. Leaders who convey only hard facts come across as cold and distant. If you share your feelings, others will see you as real and human.

4.   Tell the truth. Truth is an inherent part of integrity. Once you have lied and been found out, your ability to gain and hold trust is largely diminished. People are generally more tolerant of learning something they "don't want to hear" than finding out that their leader lied to them.

5.   Show consistency. People want predictability. Mistrust comes from not knowing what to expect. Let your central values and beliefs guide your actions. This increases consistency and builds trust.

6.   Fulfill your promises. Trust requires that people believe you are dependable, so make sure you keep your word and commitments.

7.   Maintain confidences. People trust those who are discreet and upon whom they can rely. They need to feel assured that you will not discuss their confidences with others or betray that confidence. If people perceive you as someone who leaks personal confidences or someone who can't be depended on, you won't be perceived as trustworthy.

Of these five dimensions, integrity seems to be the most critical when someone assesses another's trustworthiness.[72] Both integrity and competence were seen in our earlier discussion of leadership traits to be consistently associated with leadership. Workplace changes have reinforced why such leadership qualities are important. For instance, the trends toward empowerment and self-managed work teams have reduced many of the traditional control mechanisms used to monitor employees. If a work team is free to schedule its own work, evaluate its own performance, and even make its own hiring decisions, trust becomes critical. Employees have to trust managers to treat them fairly, and managers have to trust employees to conscientiously fulfill their responsibilities.

Also, leaders have to increasingly lead others who may not be in their immediate work group or may even be physically separated—members of cross-functional or virtual teams, individuals who work for suppliers or customers, and perhaps even people who represent other organizations through strategic alliances. These situations don't allow leaders the luxury of falling back on their formal positions for influence. Many of these relationships, in fact, are fluid and fleeting, so the ability to quickly develop trust and sustain that trust is crucial to the success of the relationship.

Why is it important that followers trust their leaders? Research has shown that trust in leadership is significantly related to positive job outcomes, including job performance, organizational citizenship behavior, job satisfaction, and organizational commitment.[74]

Now, more than ever, managerial and leadership effectiveness depends on the ability to gain the trust of followers.[75] Downsizing, financial challenges, and the increased use of temporary employees have undermined employees' trust in their leaders and shaken the confidence of investors, suppliers, and customers. Today's leaders are faced with the challenge of rebuilding and restoring trust with employees and with other important organizational stakeholders.

Matt Ramos ▶
Director of Marketing

Let's Get REAL

The Scenario:

Adhita Chopra is stumped. Three months ago, he was assigned to lead a team of phone app designers, and although no one has come out and said anything directly, he feels like his team doesn't trust him. They have been withholding information and communicating only selectively when asked questions. And they have persistently questioned the team's goals and strategies and even Adhita's actions and decisions. How can he build trust with his team?

What advice would you give Adhita?

Trust in the workplace is always a tricky subject. I've seen a similar situation unfold once before. If Adhita feels this, but hasn't heard it directly, he's probably right. Earning trust at work comes down to three things: being good at what you do, being passionate about your work and the people around you, and having the ability to listen and follow through. Adhita should make sure he's producing top-notch work and set up weekly one-on-one meetings with the team. Hard work and careful listening will see Adhita through this.

Leading Virtual Teams

We briefly described virtual teams in Chapter 13. Because they lack the "face-to-face" feature of other types of teams, they provide a unique challenge to managers. Specifically, how do you lead people who are physically separated and might be in different time zones, geographic locations, or residing in a different culture?

We can't ignore the reality that today's managers and their employees are increasingly linked by networks rather than geographical proximity. Working remotely is a rapidly spreading trend. For instance, a recent Gallup survey found 43 percent of employed Americans said they spent at least some time working remotely.[76] Emerging technologies allow people to work from almost any location. Obvious examples include managers who regularly use email or video calls to communicate with their staff, managers overseeing virtual projects or teams, and managers whose telecommuting employees are linked to the office by a computer at home. These managers need to become effective virtual leaders—who use email, instant messaging, phone conferences, web-enabled meetings, and technologies like Skype and FaceTime to communicate effectively.[77]

What's missing in virtual interactions that provide challenges to the virtual leader? There's a lack of physical contact, it's difficult to achieve work group cohesion, there is no opportunity for direct supervision, and there is often a time difference. But the central issue is communication.

In face-to-face communication, harsh words can be softened by nonverbal action. A smile and supporting body language, for instance, can lessen the blow behind strong words like *disappointed, unsatisfactory, inadequate,* or *below expectations.* That nonverbal component doesn't exist online or in a phone call. Because they lack emotions and feelings, an email or text-message exchange can easily lead to escalations of conflicts that would never occur had the parties been face-to-face. Online leaders also need to be sure the tone of their message correctly reflects the emotions they want to send. Is the message formal or informal? Does it match the verbal style of the sender? Does it convey the appropriate level of importance or urgency? And online leaders need to choose an appropriate style of communication. Many inexperienced virtual leaders use the same style with their bosses that they use with their staff, with unfortunate consequences. Or they selectively use digital communications to "hide" when delivering bad news.

The informal interaction that typically takes place in face-to-face environments—usually described as "water cooler talk"—is absent or at least restricted in a virtual world. Much of an on-site leader's interaction with his or her group is often accomplished at the personal level in these informal settings. They are instrumental as means for a leader to express his or her personality, demonstrate enthusiasm, build trust, and for bonding. Successful virtual leaders, however, have found a substitute in social media. Using Facebook and similar outlets, virtual leaders can share interests, experiences, and gossip, as well as work-related documents, pictures, video, and the like.

Any discussion of virtual leadership needs to also consider the possibility that the digital age can turn nonleaders into leaders. Some managers, whose face-to-face leadership skills are less than satisfactory, may shine online. Their talents may lie in their writing skills and ability to read the messages behind written communiqués. A virtual environment works *against* people with strong verbal skills and *for* those with writing skills.

U.S. Naval Forces Europe-Africa Fleet Master Chief Raymond Kemp Sr. speaks to a multinational group of senior enlisted leaders during the Combined Joint Maritime Enlisted Leadership Development Program (ELDP), Back Bone University.
Source: AB Forces News Collection/ Alamy Stock Photo

Finally, there is the challenge of developing effective virtual interpersonal skills. The idea of virtual interpersonal skills may, at first glance, seem like an oxymoron. *Interpersonal skills* implies social interaction. *Virtual* refers to a decoupling of space where events happen. But virtual leaders do need interpersonal skills—except they're just different than those required for face-to-face contacts. Virtual interpersonal skills are likely to include the abilities to communicate support and leadership through written words on a computer, smartphone, or tablet; to read emotions in others' written messages; and to develop good phone skills. And for the virtual leader, good writing skills are rapidly becoming an extension of interpersonal skills.

Leadership Training

Organizations around the globe spend billions of dollars, yen, and euros on leadership training and development. In the United States alone, it has been estimated that companies spend more than $87 billion a year on formal training and development.[78] These efforts take many forms—from $50,000 leadership programs offered by universities such as Harvard and organizations such as Disney to sailing experiences at the Outward Bound School.

Is leadership training effective? A number of individual studies have been done on leadership effectiveness with mixed results.[79] However, a recent comprehensive review of over 300 studies found very encouraging results when certain conditions are met. It was found that leadership training composed of multiple sessions and combining information, demonstration, and practice-methods was effective in creating real behavioral change and in positively influencing organizational and subordinate outcomes.[80]

More specifically, there is some consensus about characteristics of effective leadership training. One is contextualization (ensuring that learning is set in the strategy and culture of the organization), and another is personalization (enabling participants to seek out learning related to their aspirations).[81]

First, let's recognize the obvious. Some people don't have what it takes to be a leader. Period. For instance, evidence indicates that leadership training is more likely to be successful with individuals who are high self-monitors rather than with low self-monitors. Such individuals have the flexibility to change their behavior as different situations may require. In addition, organizations may find that individuals with higher levels of a trait called "motivation to lead" are more receptive to leadership development opportunities.[82]

What kinds of things can individuals learn that might be related to being a more effective leader? It may be a bit optimistic to think that "vision-creation" can be taught, but implementation skills can be taught. People can be trained to develop "an understanding about content themes critical to effective visions."[83] We can also teach skills such as trust-building and mentoring. And leaders can be taught situational analysis skills. They can learn how to evaluate situations, how to modify situations to make them fit better with their style, and how to assess which leader behaviors might be most effective in given situations.

When Leadership May Not Be Important

Despite the belief that some leadership style will always be effective regardless of the situation, leadership may not always be important! Data from numerous studies collectively demonstrate that, in many situations, whatever actions leaders exhibit are irrelevant. Certain individual, job, and organizational variables can act as *substitutes* for leadership or *neutralize* the leader's effect to influence his or her followers.[85]

Neutralizers make it impossible for leader behavior to make any difference to follower outcomes. They negate the leader's influence. Substitutes, on the other hand, make a leader's influence not only impossible but also unnecessary. They act as a replacement for the leader's influence. For instance, characteristics of employees such as their experience, training, "professional" orientation, or indifference toward organizational rewards can substitute for, or neutralize the effect of, leadership. Experience and training can replace the need for a leader's support or ability to create structure and reduce task ambiguity. Jobs that are inherently unambiguous and routine or that are intrinsically satisfying may place fewer demands on the leadership variable. And organizational characteristics like explicit formalized goals, rigid rules and procedures, and cohesive work groups can also replace formal leadership.

Chapter 17 | PREPARING FOR: Exams/Quizzes

CHAPTER SUMMARY by Learning Objectives

LO17.1 | DEFINE leader and leadership.

A leader is someone who can influence others and who has managerial authority. Leadership is a process of leading a group and influencing that group to achieve its goals. Managers should be leaders because leading is one of the four management functions.

LO17.2 | COMPARE and contrast early theories of leadership.

Early attempts to define leader traits were unsuccessful, although later attempts found eight traits associated with leadership.

The University of Iowa studies explored three leadership styles. The only conclusion was that group members were more satisfied under a democratic leader than under an autocratic one. The Ohio State studies identified two dimensions of leader behavior—initiating structure and consideration. A leader high in both those dimensions at times achieved high group task performance and high group member satisfaction, but not always. The University of Michigan studies looked at employee-oriented leaders and production-oriented leaders. They concluded that leaders who were employee oriented could get high group productivity and high group member satisfaction. The managerial grid looked at leaders' concern for production and concern for people and identified five leader styles. Although it suggested that a leader who was high in concern for production and high in concern for people was the best, there was no substantive evidence for that conclusion.

As the behavioral studies showed, a leader's behavior has a dual nature: a focus on the task and a focus on the people.

LO17.3

DESCRIBE the three major contingency theories of leadership.

Fiedler's model attempted to define the best style to use in particular situations. He measured leader style—relationship oriented or task oriented—using the least-preferred coworker questionnaire. Fiedler also assumed a leader's style was fixed. He measured three contingency dimensions: leader–member relations, task structure, and position power. The model suggests that task-oriented leaders performed best in very favorable and very unfavorable situations, and relationship-oriented leaders performed best in moderately favorable situations.

Hersey and Blanchard's situational leadership theory focused on followers' readiness. They identified four leadership styles: telling (high task–low relationship), selling (high task–high relationship), participating (low task–high relationship), and delegating (low task–low relationship). They also identified four stages of readiness: unable and unwilling (use telling style), unable but willing (use selling style), able but unwilling (use participative style), and able and willing (use delegating style).

The path-goal model developed by Robert House identified four leadership behaviors: directive, supportive, participative, and achievement oriented. He assumed that a leader can and should be able to use any of these styles. The two situational contingency variables were found in the environment and in the follower. Essentially, the path-goal model says that a leader should provide direction and support as needed; that is, structure the path so the followers can achieve goals. The path-goal model proposes that a leader's behavior won't be effective if it's redundant with what the environmental structure is providing or is incongruent with follower characteristics.

LO17.4

DESCRIBE contemporary views of leadership.

Leader–member exchange theory (LMX) says that leaders create in-groups and out-groups and that those in the in-group will have higher performance ratings, less turnover, and greater job satisfaction.

A charismatic leader is an enthusiastic and self-confident leader whose personality and actions influence people to behave in certain ways. People can learn to be charismatic.

A transactional leader exchanges rewards for productivity while a transformational leader stimulates and inspires followers to achieve goals. Transformational leaders have been associated with better outcomes than transactional leaders.

Authentic leadership focuses on the moral aspects of being a leader. Authentic leaders also openly solicit views that challenge their own positions and are self-aware, transparent, and humble. Ethical leaders create a culture in which employees feel that they could and should do a better job. Servant leaders go beyond their self-interest and focus on opportunities to help followers grow and develop.

Followership recognizes the role of followers in the leadership process. Not only do leaders need to motivate followers, but followers also influence the attitudes and behaviors of leaders.

LO17.5

COMPARE the various theories of leadership for their validity.

If traits play a role in defining leaders, their role is small and dependent on situational factors. In terms of behaviors, relationship-oriented leadership appears to account for most of the differences in both employee commitment and job performance. And transformational leadership encompasses almost all of the same variables as ethical and authentic leadership. Among contingency factors, the most relevant appear to be follower's experience and ability, organizational culture, and national culture.

LO17.6

DISCUSS twenty-first century issues affecting leadership.

The five sources of a leader's power are legitimate (authority or position), coercive (punish or control), reward (give positive rewards), expert (special expertise, skills, or knowledge), and referent (desirable resources or traits).

Today's leaders face the issues of managing power, developing trust, leading virtual teams, and becoming an effective leader through leadership training.

REVIEW AND DISCUSSION QUESTIONS

17-1. What does each of the four theories on leadership behavior say about leadership?

17-2. Explain Fiedler's contingency model of leadership.

17-3. How do situational leadership theory and path-goal theory each explain leadership?

17-4. What is leader–member exchange theory, and what does it say about leadership?

17-5. Differentiate between transactional and transformational leaders and between ethical and servant leaders.

17-6. What are the five sources of a leader's power?

17-7. Do you think most managers in real life use a contingency approach to increase their leadership effectiveness? Explain.

17-8. Why is trust between leaders and employees important? How can a leader build trust?

PREPARING FOR: My Career

ETHICS DILEMMA

Have you ever watched the show *Undercover Boss*? It features a company's "boss" working undercover in his or her own company to find out how the organization really works. Typically, the executive works undercover for a week, and then the employees the leader has worked with are summoned to company headquarters and either rewarded or punished for their actions. Bosses from organizations ranging from Waste Management and White Castle to NASCAR and Family Dollar have participated.

17-9. What do you think? Is it ethical for a leader to go undercover in his or her organization? Why or why not?

17-10. What ethical issues could arise? How could managers deal with those issues?

SKILLS EXERCISE   Choosing an Effective Group Leadership Style Skill

About the Skill

Effective leaders are skillful at helping the groups they lead be successful as the group goes through various stages of development. No leadership style is consistently effective. Situational factors, including follower characteristics, must be taken into consideration in the selection of an effective leadership style. The key situational factors that determine leadership effectiveness include stage of group development, task structure, position power, leader–member relations, the work group, employee characteristics, organizational culture, and national culture.

Steps in Practicing the Skill

You can choose an effective leadership style if you use the following six suggestions.

* ***Determine the stage in which your group or team is operating: forming, storming, norming, or performing.*** Because each team stage involves specific and different issues and behaviors, it's important to know in which stage your team is. *Forming* is the first stage of group development, during which people join a group and then help define the group's purpose, structure, and leadership.

Storming is the second stage, characterized by intragroup conflict. *Norming* is the third stage, characterized by close relationships and cohesiveness. *Performing* is the fourth stage, when the group is fully functional.

* ***If your team is in the forming stage, you want to exhibit certain leader behaviors.*** These include making certain that all team members are introduced to one another, answering member questions, working to establish a foundation of trust and openness, modeling the behaviors you expect from the team members, and clarifying the team's goals, procedures, and expectations.

* ***If your team is in the storming stage, you want to exhibit certain leader behaviors.*** These behaviors include identifying sources of conflict and adopting a mediator role, encouraging a win-win philosophy, restating the team's vision and its core values and goals, encouraging open discussion, encouraging an analysis of team processes in order to identify ways to improve, enhancing team cohesion and commitment, and providing recognition to individual team members as well as the team.

- *If your team is in the norming stage, you want to exhibit certain leader behaviors.* These behaviors include clarifying the team's goals and expectations, providing performance feedback to individual team members and the team, encouraging the team to articulate a vision for the future, and finding ways to publicly and openly communicate the team's vision.

- *If your team is in the performing stage, you want to exhibit certain leader behaviors.* These behaviors include providing regular and ongoing performance feedback, fostering innovation and innovative behavior, encouraging the team to capitalize on its strengths, celebrating achievements (large and small), and providing the team whatever support it needs to continue doing its work.

- *Monitor the group for changes in behavior and adjust your leadership style accordingly.* Because a group is not a static entity, it will go through up periods and down periods. You should adjust your leadership style to the needs of the situation. If the group appears to need more direction from you, provide it. If it appears to be functioning at a high level on its own, provide whatever support is necessary to keep it functioning at that level.

Practicing the Skill

The following suggestions are activities you can do to practice the behaviors in choosing an effective leadership style.

1. Think of a group or team to which you currently belong or of which you have been a part. What type of leadership style did the leader of this group appear to exhibit? Give some specific examples of the types of leadership behaviors he or she used. Evaluate the leadership style. Was it appropriate for the group? Why or why not? What would you have done differently? Why?

2. Observe a sports team (either college or professional) that you consider extremely successful and one that you would consider not successful. What leadership styles appear to be used in these team situations? Give some specific examples of the types of leadership behaviors you observe. How would you evaluate the leadership style? Was it appropriate for the team? Why or why not? To what degree do you think leadership style influenced the team's outcomes?

WORKING TOGETHER Team Exercise

After reading about the different leadership traits and behaviors, make a list of those you think a good leader possesses. Considering your own leadership ability, what skills or traits do you need to develop to become a better leader? Once you have your list, get together with three or four other students to brainstorm strategies to develop your leadership abilities. What are some steps you can take (particularly while still in college) to develop yourself as a leader? Following your discussion, each student should write a brief personal leadership development plan.

MY TURN TO BE A MANAGER

- Think of the different organizations to which you belong. Note the different styles of leadership used by the leaders in these organizations. Write a paper describing these individual's style of leading (no names, please) and evaluate the styles being used.

- Write down three people you consider effective leaders. Make a bulleted list of the characteristics these individuals exhibit that you think make them effective leaders.

- Think about the times you have had to lead. Describe your own personal leadership style. What could you do to improve your leadership style? Come up with an action plan of steps you can take. Put all this information into a brief paper.

- Managers say that, increasingly, they must use influence to get things done. Do some research on the art of persuasion. Make a bulleted list of suggestions you find on how to improve your skills at influencing others.

- Here's a list of leadership skills. Choose two and develop a training exercise that will help develop or improve that skill: building employee communities; building teams; coaching and motivating others; communicating with impact, confidence, and energy; leading by example; leading change; making decisions; providing direction and focus; and valuing diversity.

- Select one of the topics in the section on leadership issues in the twenty-first century. Do some additional research on the topic, and put your findings in a bulleted list that you are prepared to share in class. Be sure to cite your sources.

- Interview three managers about what they think it takes to be a good leader. Write up your findings in a report and be prepared to present it in class.

- Try out your leadership skills! Volunteer for a leadership position with an organization you are involved in.

CASE APPLICATION 1

Transforming the Fashion Industry at Stitch Fix

Katrina Lake planned on being a doctor. It never came to be. Instead, her career started with a job in consulting followed by work at a venture fund and then business school.[86] After business school, Lake launched Stitch Fix—the online subscription-based personal styling fashion service. She's been immensely successful since then. She is the youngest female business founder and CEO to ever take a company public and she now runs a $3 billion business.[87] Lake made the Forbes list of 40 under 40 in 2016 and has been named as one of America's richest self-made women.[88]

It hasn't always been an easy road for Stitch Fix. Venture capitalists were not quick to invest in the company. As one put it, "I don't see why this is better than the personal shopper my wife goes to at Saks." Never mind that most people don't use personal shoppers and Stitch Fix was opening up personal shopping to the mass market for the first time. The company ended up with less investment than it officially needed, but Lake believed it forced the company, early on, to focus on profitability.

As CEO, Lake is involved in strategic decisions that impact the company. But she also makes the time to offer five or six style recommendations to clients each week. As Lake puts it, "It's valuable because I can see who our clients are. I can see how our inventory looks today.... It gives me more insight into areas in the assortment that, yes, we have data around it, but experiencing it firsthand is sometimes even better. It also gives me a sense of a stylist's experience."[89]

When Stitch Fix went public in November 2017, Lake was holding her young son in her arms while ringing the Nasdaq Opening Bell. The media made a big deal about this, but Lake says the moment was unplanned. "I was doing it because that's who I am and that was a normal thing for me to do. In retrospect, I wish I had been smart enough to plan for it, because I understand why it meant a lot to people ... to start to break down those barriers around who you are as an executive, who you are in raising a family and who you are personally, is something I feel really privileged to have been a part of."

Lake has become involved in helping to develop the next generation of female company founders as a mentor and coach. She says, "There just aren't enough great examples of different types of people that are at the top. I feel a lot of responsibility in making sure that others can see themselves there."

DISCUSSION QUESTIONS:

17-11. What examples are provided in this case for how Katrina Lake exhibited authentic leadership?

17-12. What has Katrina Lake done that likely allowed her to develop credibility and trust as a leader?

17-13. In what ways has Katrina Lake demonstrated behaviors that indicate servant leadership? What could she do to exemplify servant leadership even more?

17-14. Lake's Stitch Fix is thought to have transformed the fashion industry by making personal shopping more affordable and less time-consuming. If Lake has been a transformational leader with her followers, what kinds of behaviors would she have exhibited?

When Steve Kerr first became the coach of the Golden State Warriors basketball team, he saw the need for some changes. He wanted to steer away from the tendency for new leaders to announce that they want to change the culture, since that can be insulting. Instead, Kerr focused on key areas, such as that the team was last in their league in the number of passes. Kerr set a goal for the team to get to the top five teams in passes by striving for 300 passes per game.[90] Kerr's efforts seemed to pay off. During Kerr's first season as the Golden Warriors' coach, the team had their best record in the team's sixty-nine-year history and one of the best seasons in NBA history.[91]

The very next season, Kerr had terrible back pain. It was so bad, in fact, that he missed the first forty-three games of the season. Kerr relied on his top assistant, Luke Walton, to coach in his absence. The team's record with Walton at the helm was incredible: 39 wins, 4 losses. During the playoffs in a later season, another assistant (Mike Brown) oversaw 12 wins and no losses. While Walton and Brown certainly deserve credit for their efforts, Kerr had worked on developing and empowering both assistants and provided advice as a mentor.[92]

When the Golden State Warriors struggled in early 2018, Kerr decided that what was needed was for the players to coach themselves. On the morning of a game against the Phoenix Suns in February 2018, Andre Iguodala was put in charge of a practice and JaVale McGee oversaw the computer while other players analyzed film during a team meeting. Then, in the game that evening, Iguodala, David West, and Draymond Green took turns coaching during timeouts while Green (who was injured) was in charge of overseeing the team during much of a game. Kerr explained these coaching moves in these words: "I have not reached them for the last month. They're tired of my voice. I'm tired of my voice. ... We just figured it was probably a good night to pull a trick out of the hat and do something different. ... As coaches, our job is to nudge them in the right direction, guide them, but we don't control them. They determine their own fate." That trick seemed to work. That night, the Warriors beat the Suns by more than 40 points.[93]

Another aspect of Kerr's leadership is that he stands up for what he believes in. Reporters have asked him questions about how current events are affecting his team. He easily could have dismissed the questions, especially when they were asked of him shortly before a game. Most coaches are silent when asked controversial questions out of concern about what team owners or sponsors will think. Instead, Kerr took the time to explain his position and what he thinks is right. As Bob Myers, the Warriors' general manager, puts it, "There is no hidden agenda to Steve, it's 'I will say what I feel and speak my mind and I'm going to try to live in that manner and try to back it up'."[94]

DISCUSSION QUESTIONS:

17-15. What leadership models, theories, or concepts do you see in this case? List and describe.

17-16. What situational conditions or leadership actions do you think are necessary for it to be effective to let players coach themselves?

17-17. What does this case suggest about followership (and about how leaders might relate to followers)?

17-18. What are the advantages and disadvantages involved in speaking up on current events? In what ways does this approach help and/or hurt Kerr's strength as a leader?

ENDNOTES

1. M. Crowley, "How a World-Class Surgeon Found the One Leadership Trait Many Businesses Are Missing," *Fast Company*, August 14, 2014, https://www.fastcompany.com/3034315/how-a-world-class-heart-surgeon-found-the-one-leadership-trait-many-busin; Z. Budryk, "Cleveland Clinic's Toby Cosgrove on Critical Skills and Traits for Healthcare Leaders," *FireceHealthcare*, March 23, 2016, https://www.fiercehealthcare.com/healthcare/cleveland-clinic-s-toby-cosgrove-critical-skills-and-traits-for-healthcare-leaders; and "Toby Cosgrove, M.D., Announces His Decision to Transition from President, CEO Role," *Cleveland Clinic Newsroom* (news release), May 1, 2017, https://newsroom.clevelandclinic.org/2017/05/01/toby-cosgrove-m-d-announces-decision-transition-president-cco-role/.

2. Most leadership research has focused on the actions and responsibilities of managers and extrapolated the results to leaders and leadership in general.

3. T. A. Judge and D. M. Cable, "The Effect of Physical Height on Workplace Success and Income: Preliminary Test of a Theoretical Model," *Journal of Applied Psychology* 89, no. 3 (June 2004): pp. 428–441; and J. Pinsker, "The Financial Perks of Being Tall," *Atlantic*, May 18, 2015, https://www.theatlantic.com/business/archive/2015/05/the-financial-perks-of-being-tall/393518/.

4. Based on T. A. Judge, J. E. Bono, R. Ilies, and M. W. Gerhardt, "Personality and Leadership: A Qualitative and Quantitative Review," *Journal of Applied Psychology* 87, no. 4 (August 2002): pp. 765–780; R. H. Humphrey, J. M. Pollack, and T. H. Hawver, "Leading with Emotional Labor," *Journal of Managerial Psychology* 23, no. 2 (2008): pp. 151–68; D. S. Derue, J. D. Nahrgang, N. Wellman, and S. E. Humphrey, "Trait and Behavioral Theories of Leadership: An Integration and Meta-Analytic Test of Their Relative Validity," *Personnel Psychology* 64, no. 1 (Spring 2011): pp. 7–52; S. V. Marinova, H. Moon, and D. Kamdar, "Getting Ahead or Getting Along? The Two-Facet Conceptualization of Conscientiousness and Leadership Emergence," *Organization Science* 24, no. 4 (September–October 2012): pp. 1257–76; and R. L. Schaumberg and F. J. Flynn, "Uneasy Lies the Head That Wears the Crown: The Link Between Guilt Proneness and Leadership," *Journal of Personality and Social Psychology* 103, no. 2 (August 2012): pp. 327–342.

5. A. Bryant, "Carter Murray Giving Talented People Room to Bloom," *New York Times*, May 13, 2016, https://www.nytimes.com/2016/05/15/business/carter-murray-giving-talented-people-room-to-bloom.html.

6. N. Nayab, "A Review of Companies with Autocratic Leadership," *Bright Hub Project Management*, July 29, 2015, https://www.brighthubpm.com/resource-management/77233-examples-of-companies-with-autocratic-leadership/.

7. D. S. DeRue, J. D. Nahrgang, N. Wellman, and S. E. Humphrey, "Trait and Behavioral Theories of Leadership: An Integration and Meta-Analytic Test of Their Relative Validity," *Personnel Psychology* 64, no. 1 (Spring 2011): pp. 7–52.

8. K. Lewin and R. Lippitt, "An Experimental Approach to the Study of Autocracy and Democracy: A Preliminary Note," *Sociometry* 1, no. 3/4 (1938): pp. 292–300; K. Lewin, "Field Theory and Experiment in Social Psychology: Concepts and Methods," *American Journal of Sociology* 44 (1939): pp. 868–896; K. Lewin, L. Lippitt, and R. K. White, "Patterns of Aggressive Behavior in Experimentally Created Social Climates," *Journal of Social Psychology* 10 (1939): pp. 271–301; and L. Lippitt, "An Experimental Study of the Effect of Democratic and Authoritarian Group Atmospheres," *University of Iowa Studies: Child Welfare* 16, no. 3 (1940) pp. 43–195.

9. B. M. Bass, *Stogdill's Handbook of Leadership* (New York: Free Press, 1981), pp. 289–299. See also N. Bhatti, G. M. Maitlo, N. Shaikh, M. A. Hashmi, and F. M. Shaikh, "The Impact of Autocratic and Democratic Leadership Style on Job Satisfaction," *International Business Research* 5, no. 2 (February 2012): pp. 192–201.

10. R. M. Stogdill and A. E. Coons, eds., *Leader Behavior: Its Description and Measurement*, Research Monograph no. 88 (Columbus: Ohio State University, Bureau of Business Research, 1951). For an updated literature review of Ohio State research, see S. Kerr, C. A. Schriesheim, C. J. Murphy, and R. M. Stogdill, "Toward a Contingency Theory of Leadership Based upon the Consideration and Initiating Structure Literature," *Organizational Behavior and Human Performance* 12, no. 1 (August 1974): pp. 62–82; B. M. Fisher, "Consideration and Initiating Structure and Their Relationships with Leader Effectiveness: A Meta-Analysis," in F. Hoy, ed., *Proceedings of the 48th Annual Academy of Management Conference*, Anaheim, California, 1988, pp. 201–205; T. A. Judge, R. F. Piccolo, and R. Ilies, "The Forgotten Ones? The Validity of Consideration and Initiating Structure in Leadership Research," *Journal of Applied Psychology* 89, no. 1 (February 2004): pp. 36–51; and L. S. Lambert, B. J. Tepper, J. C. Carr, D. T. Holt, and A. J. Barelka, "Forgotten but Not Gone: An Examination of Fit Between Leader Consideration and Initiating Structure Needed and Received," *Journal of Applied Psychology* 97, no. 5 (September 2012): pp. 913–930.

11. R. Kahn and D. Katz, "Leadership Practices in Relation to Productivity and Morale," in *Group Dynamics: Research and Theory*, 2nd ed., eds. D. Cartwright and A. Zander (Elmsford, NY: Row, Paterson, 1960).

12. R. R. Blake and J. S. Mouton, *The Managerial Grid III* (Houston: Gulf Publishing, 1984).

13. L. L. Larson, J. G. Hunt, and R. N. Osborn, "The Great Hi-Hi Leader Behavior Myth: A Lesson from Occam's Razor," *Academy of Management Journal* 19, no. 4 (December 1976): pp. 628–641; and P. C. Nystrom, "Managers and the Hi-Hi Leader Myth," *Academy of Management Journal* 21, no. 2 (June 1978): pp. 325–331.

14. W. G. Bennis, "The Seven Ages of the Leader," *Harvard Business Review*, January 2004, p. 52.

15. F. E. Fiedler, *A Theory of Leadership Effectiveness* (New York: McGraw-Hill, 1967). For a more current discussion of the model, see R. G. Lord, D. V. Day, S. J. Zaccaro, B. J. Avolio, and A. H. Eagly, "Leadership in Applied Psychology: Three Waves of Theory and Research," *Journal of Applied Psychology* 102, no. 3 (March 2017): pp. 434–51.

16. L. H. Peters, D. D. Hartke, and J. T. Pholmann, "Fiedler's Contingency Theory of Leadership: An Application of the Meta-Analysis Procedures of Schmidt and Hunter," *Psychological Bulletin* 97, no. 2 (March 1985): pp. 274–285; C. A. Schriesheim, B. J. Tepper, and L. A. Tetrault, "Least

Preferred Coworker Score, Situational Control, and Leadership Effectiveness: A Meta-Analysis of Contingency Model Performance Predictions," *Journal of Applied Psychology* 79, no. 4 (August 1994): pp. 561–573; and R. Ayman, M. M. Chemers, and F. Fiedler, "The Contingency Model of Leadership Effectiveness: Its Levels of Analysis," *Leadership Quarterly* 6, no. 2 (Summer 1995): pp. 147–167.

17. See E. H. Schein, *Organizational Psychology*, 3rd ed. (Upper Saddle River, NJ: Prentice Hall, 1980), pp. 116–117; and B. Kabanoff, "A Critique of Leader Match and Its Implications for Leadership Research," *Personnel Psychology* 34, no. 4 (Winter 1981): pp. 749–764.

18. P. Hersey and K. Blanchard, "So You Want to Know Your Leadership Style?," *Training and Development Journal* 28, no. 2 (February 1974): pp. 1–15; and P. Hersey, K. H. Blanchard, and D. E. Johnson, *Management of Organizational Behavior: Leading Human Resources*, 10th ed. (New York: Pearson, 2013).

19. See, for instance, E. G. Ralph, "Developing Managers' Effectiveness: A Model with Potential," *Journal of Management Inquiry* 13, no. 2 (June 2004): pp. 152–163; C. L. Graeff, "Evolution of Situational Leadership Theory: A Critical Review," *Leadership Quarterly* 8, no. 2 (Summer 1997): pp. 153–170; C. F. Fernandez and R. P. Vecchio, "Situational Leadership Theory Revisited: A Test of an Across-Jobs Perspective," *Leadership Quarterly* 8, no. 1 (Spring 1997): pp. 67–84; R. P. Vecchio, C. R. Bullis, and D. M. Brazil, "The Utility of Situational Leadership Theory—a Replication in a Military Setting," *Small Group Research* 37, no. 5 (October 2006): pp. 407–24; and G. Thompson and R. P. Vecchio, "Situational Leadership Theory: A Test of Three Versions," *Leadership Quarterly* 20, no. 5 (October 2009): pp. 837–48.

20. R. J. House, "A Path-Goal Theory of Leader Effectiveness," *Administrative Science Quarterly* 16, no. 3 (September 1971): pp. 321–338; R. J. House and T. R. Mitchell, "Path-Goal Theory of Leadership," *Journal of Contemporary Business* 4, no. 3 (Autumn 1974) p. 86; and R. J. House, "Path-Goal Theory of Leadership: Lessons, Legacy, and a Reformulated Theory," *Leadership Quarterly* 7, no. 2 (Fall 1996): pp. 323–352.

21. M. L. Dixon and L. K. Hart, "The Impact of Path-Goal Leadership Styles on Work Group Effectiveness and Turnover Intention," *Journal of Managerial Issues* 22, no. 1 (Spring 2010): pp. 52–69; J. C. Wofford and L. Z. Liska, "Path-Goal Theories of Leadership: A Meta-Analysis," *Journal of Management* 19, no. 4 (Winter 1993) pp. 857–876; A. Sagie and M. Koslowsky, "Organizational Attitudes and Behaviors as a Function of Participation in Strategic and Tactical Change Decisions: An Application of Path-Goal Theory," *Journal of Organizational Behavior* 15, no. 1 (January 1994) pp. 37–47; and R. R. Vecchio, J. E. Justin, and C. L. Pearce, "The Utility of Transactional and Transformational Leadership for Predicting Performance and Satisfaction within a Path-Goal Theory Framework," *Journal of Occupational and Organizational Psychology* 81, no. 1 (March 2008): pp. 71–82.

22. G. B. Graen and M. Uhl-Bien, "Relationship-Based Approach to Leadership: Development of Leader–Member Exchange (LMX) Theory of Leadership over 25 Years: Applying a Multi-Domain Perspective," *Leadership Quarterly* 6, no. 2 (Summer 1995): pp. 219–247; R. C. Liden, R. T. Sparrowe, and S. J. Wayne, "Leader–Member Exchange Theory: The Past and Potential for the Future," in *Research in Personnel and Human Resource Management*, vol. 15, ed. G. R. Ferris (Greenwich, CT: JAI Press, 1997), pp. 47–119; R. Martin, Y. Guillaume, G. Thomas, A. Lee, and O. Epitropaki, "Leader-Member Exchange (LMX) and Performance: A Meta-Analytic Review, *Personnel Psychology* 69, no. 1 (Spring 2016): pp. 67–121; and X.-P. Chen, W. He, and L.-C. Weng, "What Is Wrong with Treating Followers Differently? The Basis of Leader-Member Exchange Differentiation Matters," *Journal of Management* 44, no. 3 (March 2018): pp. 946–71.

23. R. C. Liden and G. Graen, "Generalizability of the Vertical Dyad Linkage Model of Leadership," *Academy of Management Journal* 23, no. 3 (September 1980): pp. 451–465; R. C. Liden, S. J. Wayne, and D. Stilwell, "A Longitudinal Study of the Early Development of Leader–Member Exchanges," *Journal of Applied Psychology* 78, no. 4 (August 1993): pp. 662–674; S. J. Wayne, L. J. Shore, W. H. Bommer, and L. E. Tetrick, "The Role of Fair Treatment and Rewards in Perceptions of Organizational Support and Leader–Member Exchange," *Journal of Applied Psychology* 87, no. 3 (June 2002): pp. 590–598; and S. S. Masterson, K. Lewis, and B. M. Goldman, "Integrating Justice and Social Exchange: The Differing Effects of Fair Procedures and Treatment on Work Relationships," *Academy of Management Journal* 43, no. 4 (August 2000): pp. 738–748.

24. D. Duchon, S. G. Green, and T. D. Taber, "Vertical Dyad Linkage: A Longitudinal Assessment of Antecedents, Measures, and Consequences," *Journal of Applied Psychology* 71, no. 1 (February 1986): pp. 56–60; Liden, Wayne, and Stilwell, "A Longitudinal Study"; M. Uhl-Bien, "Relationship Development as a Key Ingredient for Leadership Development," in *Future of Leadership Development*, eds. S. E. Murphy and R. E. Riggio (Mahwah, NJ: Lawrence Erlbaum, 2003), pp. 129–147; R. Vecchio and D. M. Brazil, "Leadership and Sex-Similarity: A Comparison in a Military Setting," *Personnel Psychology* 60, n o. 2 (Summer 2007): pp. 303–335; and V. L. Goodwin, W. M. Bowler, and J. L. Whittington, "A Social Network Perspective on LMX Relationships: Accounting for the Instrumental Value of Leader and Follower Networks," *Journal of Management* 35, no. 4 (August 2009): pp. 954–980.

25. See, for instance, C. R. Gerstner and D. V. Day, "Meta-Analytic Review of Leader–Member Exchange Theory: Correlates and Construct Issues," *Journal of Applied Psychology* 82, no. 6 (December 1997) pp. 827–844; R. Ilies, J. D. Nahrgang, and F. P. Morgeson, "Leader–Member Exchange and Citizenship Behaviors: A Meta-Analysis," *Journal of Applied Psychology* 92, no. 1 (January 2007): pp. 269–277; Z. Chen, W. Lam, and J. A. Zhong, "Leader–Member Exchange and Member Performance: A New Look at Individual-Level Negative Feedback-Seeking Behavior and Team-Level Empowerment Culture," *Journal of Applied Psychology* 92, no. 1 (January 2007): pp. 202–212; Z. Zhang, M. Wang, and J. Shi, "Leader-Follower Congruence in Proactive Personality and Work Outcomes: The Mediating Role of Leader-Member Exchange," *Academy of Management Journal* 55, no. 1 (February 2012): pp. 111–130; and R. Martin, G. Thomas, A. Legood, and S.D. Russo, "Leader-Member Exchange (LMX) Differentiation and Work Outcomes: Conceptual Clarification and Critical Review,"

Journal of Organizational Behavior 39, no. 2 (February 2018): pp. 151–68.

26. R. J. House, "A 1976 Theory of Charismatic Leadership," in *The Cutting Edge,* eds. J. G. Hunt and L.L. Larson (Carbondale, IL: Southern Illinois University Press, 1977), pp. 189-207. See also J. Antonakis, N. Bastardoz, P. Jacquart, and B. Shamir, "Charisma: An Ill-Defined and Ill-Measured Gift," *Annual Review of Organizational Psychology and Organizational Behavior* 3 (2016): pp. 293–319.

27. J. A. Conger and R. N. Kanungo, "Behavioral Dimensions of Charismatic Leadership," in J. A. Conger, R. N. Kanungo et al., *Charismatic Leadership* (San Francisco: Jossey-Bass, 1988), pp. 78–97; G. Yukl and J. M. Howell, "Organizational and Contextual Influences on the Emergence and Effectiveness of Charismatic Leadership," *Leadership Quarterly* 10, no. 2 (Summer 1999): pp. 257–283; J. M. Crant and T. S. Bateman, "Charismatic Leadership Viewed from Above: The Impact of Proactive Personality," *Journal of Organizational Behavior* 21, no. 1 (February 2000): pp. 63–75; F. Walter and H. Bruch, "An Affective Events Model of Charismatic Leadership Behavior: A Review, Theoretical Integration, and Research Agenda," *Journal of Management* 35, no. 6 (December 2009): pp. 1428–1452; and A. Pentland, "We Can Measure the Power of Charisma," *Harvard Business Review*, January-February 2010, pp. 34–35.

28. J. A. Conger and R. N. Kanungo, *Charismatic Leadership in Organizations* (Thousand Oaks, CA: Sage, 1998).

29. Walter and Bruch, "An Affective Events Model" [see note 27]; K. S. Groves, "Linking Leader Skills, Follower Attitudes, and Contextual Variables via an Integrated Model of Charismatic Leadership," *Journal of Management* 31, no. 2 (April 2005): pp. 255–277; A. H. B. deHoogh, D. N. den Hartog, P. L. Koopman, H. Thierry, P. T. van den Berg, J. G. van der Weide, and C. P. M. Wilderom, "Leader Motives, Charismatic Leadership, and Subordinates' Work Attitudes in the Profit and Voluntary Sector," *Leadership Quarterly* 16, no. 1 (February 2005): pp. 17–38; J. M. Howell and B. Shamir, "The Role of Followers in the Charismatic Leadership Process: Relationships and Their Consequences," *Academy of Management Review* 30, no. 1 (January 2005): pp. 96–112; J. A. Conger, R. N. Kanungo, and S. T. Menon, "Charismatic Leadership and Follower Effects," *Journal of Organizational Behavior* 21, no. 7 (2000): pp. 747–767; R. W. Rowden, "The Relationship Between Charismatic Leadership Behaviors and Organizational Commitment," *Leadership & Organization Development Journal* 21, no. 1 (January 2000): pp. 30–35; G. P. Shea and C. M. Howell, "Charismatic Leadership and Task Feedback: A Laboratory Study of Their Effects on Self-Efficacy," *Leadership Quarterly* 10, no. 3 (Fall 1999): pp. 375–396; S. A. Kirkpatrick and E. A. Locke, "Direct and Indirect Effects of Three Core Charismatic Leadership Components on Performance and Attitudes," *Journal of Applied Psychology* 81, no. 1 (February 1996): pp. 36–51; D. A. Waldman, B. M. Bass, and F. J. Yammarino, "Adding to Contingent-Reward Behavior: The Augmenting Effect of Charismatic Leadership," *Group & Organization Studies* 15, no. 4 (December 1990): pp. 381–394; and R. J. House, J. Woycke, and E. M. Fodor, "Charismatic and Noncharismatic Leaders: Differences in Behavior and Effectiveness," in Conger and Kanungo, *Charismatic Leadership*, pp. 103–104.

30. B. R. Agle, N. J. Nagarajan, J. A. Sonnenfeld, and D. Srinivasan, "Does CEO Charisma Matter? An Empirical Analysis of the Relationships Among Organizational Performance, Environmental Uncertainty, and Top Management Team Perceptions of CEO Charisma," *Academy of Management Journal* 49, no. 1 (February 2006): pp. 161–174.

31. See, for instance, J. A. Raelin, "The Myth of Charismatic Leaders," *Training & Development* 57, no. 2 (March 2003): pp. 47–54; D. Tourish, *The Dark Side of Transformational Leadership: A Critical Perspective* (London: Routledge, 2013); and E. Zehndorfer, *Charismatic Leadership: The Role of Charisma in the Global Financial Crisis* (London: Routledge, 2016).

32. J. Antonakis, M. Fenley, and S. Liechti, "Learning Charisma," *Harvard Business Review*, June 2012, pp. 127–130; J. Antonakis, M. Fenley, and S. Liechti, "Can Charisma Be Taught? Tests of Two Interventions," *Academy of Management Learning & Education* 10, no. 3 (September 2011): pp. 374–396; R. Birchfield, "Creating Charismatic Leaders," *Management*, June 2000, pp. 30–31; S. Caudron, "Growing Charisma," *Industry Week*, May 4, 1998, pp. 54–55; and J. A. Conger and R. N. Kanungo, "Training Charismatic Leadership: A Risky and Critical Task," in Conger and Kanungo, *Charismatic Leadership*, pp. 309–323.

33. J. G. Hunt, K. B. Boal, and G. E. Dodge, "The Effects of Visionary and Crisis-Responsive Charisma on Followers: An Experimental Examination," *Leadership Quarterly* 10, no. 3 (Fall 1999): pp. 423–448; R. J. House and R. N. Aditya, "The Social Scientific Study of Leadership: Quo Vadis?," *Journal of Management* 23, no. 3 (1997): pp. 316–323; and R. J. House, "A 1976 Theory of Charismatic Leadership," in J. G. Hunt & L. L. Larson, eds., *Leadership: The Cutting Edge* (Carbondale, IL: Southern Illinois University, 1977): pp. 189–207.

34. B. M. Bass and R. E. Riggio, *Transformational Leadership*, 2nd ed. (Mahwah, NJ: Lawrence Erlbaum Associates, Inc., 2006), p. 3.

35. B. M. Bass, "Leadership: Good, Better, Best," *Organizational Dynamics* 13, no. 3 (Winter 1985): pp. 26–40; and J. Seltzer and B. M. Bass, "Transformational Leadership: Beyond Initiation and Consideration," *Journal of Management* 16, no. 4 (December 1990): pp. 693–703.

36. B. J. Avolio and B. M. Bass, "Transformational Leadership, Charisma, and Beyond" (working paper, School of Management, State University of New York at Binghamton, 1985), p. 14.

37. J. Folkman, "The Shocking Statistics Behind Uninspiring Leaders," *Forbes*, November 20, 2018, https://www.forbes.com/sites/joefolkman/2018/11/20/the-shocking-statistics-behind-uninspiring-leaders/#7d6d7b0a2b65.

38. J. J. Hater and B. M. Bass, "Supervisors' Evaluation and Subordinates' Perceptions of Transformational and Transactional Leadership," *Journal of Applied Psychology* 73, no. 4 (November 1988): pp. 695–702; B. M. Bass and B. J. Avolio, "Developing Transformational Leadership: 1992 and Beyond," *Journal of European Industrial Training* 14, no. 5 (January 1990): p. 23; B. M. Bass and R. E. Riggio, *Transformational Leadership*, 2nd ed. (Mahwah, NJ: Lawrence Erlbaum, 2006); B. J. Hoffman, B. H. Bynum, R. F. Piccolo, and A. W. Sutton, "Person-Organization Value Congruence: How Transformational Leaders Influence Work Group Effectiveness," *Academy of Management Journal* 54, no. 4 (August 2011): pp. 779–796; G. Wang, I.-S. Oh, S. H. Courtright, and A. E. Colbert, "Transformational

Leadership and Performance Across Criteria and Levels: A Meta-Analytic Review of 25 Years of Research," *Group & Organization Management* 36, no. 2 (April 2011): pp. 223–270.

39. R. T. Keller, "Transformational Leadership and the Performance of Research and Development Project Groups," *Journal of Management* 18, no. 3 (September 1992): pp. 489–501; T.A. Judge and R.F. Piccolo, "Transformational and Transactional Leadership: A Meta-Analytic Test of Their Relative Validity," *Journal of Applied Psychology* 89, no. 5 (October 2004): pp. 755–68; Y. Ling, Z. Simsek, M. H. Lubatkin, and J. F. Veiga, "Transformational Leadership's Role in Promoting Corporate Entrepreneurship: Examining the CEO-TMT Interface," *Academy of Management Journal* 51, no. 3 (June 2008): pp. 557–576; and Wang, Oh, Courtright, and Colbert, "Transformational Leadership."

40. Based on "How Steve Jobs Got Fired From His Own Company," *ABC News*, October 6, 2011, https://abcnews.go.com; and M. Weinberger, "This Is Why Steve Jobs Got Fired From Apple—And How He Came Back to Save the Company," *Business Insider*, July 31, 2017, https://www.businessinsider.com/steve-jobs-apple-fired-returned-2017-7.

41. L. L. Neider and C. A. Schriesheim, "The Authentic Leadership Inventory (ALI): Development and Empirical Tests," *Leadership Quarterly* 22, no. 6 (December 2011): pp. 1146-64; and B. J. Avolio, T. Wernsing, and W. L. Gardner, "Revisiting the Development and Validation of the Authentic Leadership Questionnaire: Analytical Clarifications," *Journal of Management* 44, no. 2 (February 2018): pp. 399-411.

42. H. Leroy, F. Anseel, W. L. Gardner, and L. Sels, "Authentic Followership, Basic Need Satisfaction, and Work Role Performance," *Journal of Management* 41, no. 6 (September 2015): pp. 1677–97; T. Simons, H. Leroy, V. Collewaert, and S. Masschelein, "How Leader Alignment of Words and Deeds Affects Followers: A Meta-Analysis of Behavioral Integrity Research," *Journal of Business Ethics* 132, no. 4 (December 2015): pp. 831–44; and C. Gill and A. Caza, "An Investigation of Authentic Leadership's Individual and Group Influence on Follower Reponses," *Journal of Management* 44, no. 2 (February 2018): pp. 530–54.

43. G. Loftus, "Mary Barra's Leadership Legacy," *Forbes*, March 19, 2014, https://www.forbes.com/sites/geoffloftus/2014/03/19/mary-barras-leadership-legacy/#543f26f45301.

44. Ibid.

45. J. Stouten, M. van Dijke, and D. DeCremer, "Ethical Leadership: An Overview and Future Perspectives," *Journal of Personnel Psychology* 11, no. 1 (January 2012): pp. 1–6.

46. J. M. Schaubroeck, S. T. Hannah, B. J. Avolio, S. W. J. Kozlowski, R.G. Lord, et al., "Embedding Ethical Leadership Within and Across Organization Levels," *Academy of Management Journal* 55, no. 5 (October 2012): pp. 1053–78.

47. T. W. H. Ng and D. C. Feldman, "Ethical Leadership: Meta-Analytic Evidence of Criterion-Related and Incremental Validity," *Journal of Applied Psychology* 100, no. 3 (May 2015) pp. 948–65.

48. Ibid.

49. D. van Dierendonck, "Servant Leadership: A Review and Synthesis," *Journal of Management* 37, no. 4 (July 2011): pp. 1228–61; D. L. Parris and J. W. Peachey, "A Systematic Literature Review of Servant Leadership Theory in Organizational Contexts," *Journal of Business Ethics* 113, no. 3 (March 2013): pp. 377–93; and N. Eva, M. Robin, S. Sendjaya, D. van Dierendonck, and R. C. Liden, "Servant Leadership: A Systematic Review and Call for Future Research," *Leadership Quarterly* 30, no. 1 (February 2019): pp. 111–32.

50. R. C. Liden, S. J. Wayne, J. D. Meuser, J. Hu, J. Wu, and C. Liao, "Servant Leadership: Validation of a Short Form of the SL-28," *Leadership Quarterly* 26, no. 2 (April 2015): pp. 254–69.

51. M. Schwantes, "The World's 10 Top CEOs (They Lead in a Totally Unique Way)," *Inc.*, March 29, 2017, https://www.inc.com/marcel-schwantes/heres-a-top-10-list-of-the-worlds-best-ceos-but-they-lead-in-a-totally-unique-wa.html.

52. R. C. Liden, S. J. Wayne, C. Liao, and J. D. Meuser, "Servant Leadership and Serving Culture: Influence of Individual and Unit Performance," *Academy of Management Journal* 57, no. 5 (October 2014): pp. 1434–52.

53. Z. Chen, J. Zhu, and M. Zhou, "How Does a Servant Leader Fuel the Service Fire? A Multilevel Model of Servant Leadership, Individual Self Identity, Group Competition Climate, and Customer Service Performance," *Journal of Applied Psychology* 100, no. 2 (March 2015): pp. 511–21.

54. T. Menon, J. Sim, J. Ho-Ying Fu, C. Chiu, and Y. Hong, "Blazing the Trail versus Trailing the Group: Culture and Perceptions of the Leader's Position," *Organizational Behavior and Human Decision Processes* 113, no. 1 (September 2010): pp. 51–61.

55. See, for instance, M. Uhl-Bien, R. E. Riggio, K. B. Lowe, and M. K. Carsten, "Followership Theory: A Review and Research Agenda," *Leadership Quarterly* 25, no. 1 (February 2014): pp. 83–104.

56. D. J. Brown, "In the Minds of Followers: Follower-Centric Approaches to Leadership" in J. Antonakis and D. Day, eds., *the Nature of Leadership*, 3rd ed. (Thousand Oaks, CA: Sage, 2017), p. 82.

57. R. E. Riggio, "Followership Research: Looking Back and Looking Forward," *Journal of Leadership Education* 13, no. 4 (December 2014): p. 16.

58. M. Hurwitz and S. Hurwitz, *Leadership Is Half the Story: A Fresh Look at Followership, Leadership, and Collaboration* (Toronto: Rotman-UTP, 2018).

59. R. Kelley, "In Praise of Followers," *Harvard Business Review*, November 1988, pp. 141–48; I. Chaleff, *The Courageous Follower: Standing Up To and For Our Leaders* (San Francisco: Berrett-Koehler, 1995); and G. Ramazzina, "Don't Forget the Importance of Followership," *TD*, July 2017, p. 71.

60. Lord, Day, Zaccaro, Avolio, and Eagly, "Leadership in Applied Psychology," p. 441 [see note 15].

61. L. Borgmann, J. Rowold, and K.C. Bormann, "Integrating Leadership Research: A Meta-Analytical Test of Yukl's Meta-Categories of Leadership," *Personnel Review* 45, no. 6 (2016): pp. 340–366.

62. Ibid.

63. J. E. Hoch, W. H. Bommer, J. H. Dulebohn, and D. Wu, "Do Ethical, Authentic, and Servant Leadership Explain Variance Above and Beyond Transformational Leadership? A Meta-Analysis," *Journal of Management* 44, no. 2 (February 2018): pp. 501–29.

64. Ibid., p. 523.

65. P. Dorfman, M. Javidan, P. Hanges, A. Dastmalchian, and R. House, "GLOBE: A Twenty Year Journey Into the Intriguing World of Culture and Leadership," *Journal of World Business* 47, no. 4 (October 2012): pp. 504–18; D. D. Warrick, "What Leaders Need to Know About Organizational Culture,"

Business Horizons 60, no. 3 (May-June 2017): pp. 395–404; and E. H. Schein, *Organizational Culture and* Leadership, 5th ed. (San Francisco: Jossey-Bass, 2017).

66. See J. R. P. French Jr. and B. Raven, "The Bases of Social Power," in *Group Dynamics: Research and Theory*, eds. D. Cartwright and A. F. Zander (New York: Harper & Row, 1960), pp. 607–623; P. M. Podsakoff and C. A. Schriesheim, "Field Studies of French and Raven's Bases of Power: Critique, Reanalysis, and Suggestions for Future Research," *Psychological Bulletin* 97, no. 3 (May 1985): pp. 387–411; and R. A. Turner and K. F. Schabram, "The Bases of Power Revisited: An Interpersonal Perceptions Perspective," *Journal of Occupational Psychology* 12, no. 1 (March 2012): pp. 9–18.

67. "The 2018 Trust Outlook," Trust Edge Leadership Institute, https://trustedge.com/wp-content/uploads/2018/02/2018-Trust-Outlook.pdf.

68. J. M. Kouzes and B. Z. Posner, *Credibility: How Leaders Gain and Lose It, and Why People Demand It* (San Francisco: Jossey-Bass, 1993), p. 14.

69. Based on R. D. White, "The Micromanagement Disease: Symptoms, Diagnosis, and Cure," *Public Personnel Management* 39, no. 1 (Spring 2010): pp. 71–76; G. Campbell, "Confronting Micromanaging Bosses," *Nursing Management* 41, no. 9 (September 2010): p. 56; Amy Gallo, "Stop Being Micromanaged," *Harvard Business Review*, September 22, 2011, https://hbr.org/2011/09/stop-being-micromanaged; and P. Ganeshan-Singh, "7 Ways to Survive Working for a Micromanaging Boss," *PayScale*, October 29, 2014, https://www.payscale.com/career-news/2014/10/7-ways-to-survive-working-for-a-micromanaging-boss.

70. Based on F. D. Schoorman, R. C. Mayer, and J. H. Davis, "An Integrative Model of Organizational Trust: Past, Present, and Future," *Academy of Management Review* 32, no. 2 (April 2007): pp. 344–354; R. C. Mayer, J. H. Davis, and F. D. Schoorman, "An Integrative Model of Organizational Trust," *Academy of Management Review* 20, no. 3 (July 1995): p. 712; and L. T. Hosmer, "Trust: The Connecting Link Between Organizational Theory and Philosophical Ethics," *Academy of Management Review* 20, no. 2 (April 1995): p. 393.

71. P. L. Schindler and C. C. Thomas, "The Structure of Interpersonal Trust in the Workplace," *Psychological Reports* 73, no. 2 (October 1993): pp. 563–573.

72. H. H. Tan and C. S. F. Tan, "Toward the Differentiation of Trust in Supervisor and Trust in Organization," *Genetic, Social, and General Psychology Monographs* 126, no. 2 (May 2000): pp. 241–260.

73. See, for example, F. Bartolome, "Nobody Trusts the Boss Completely—Now What?," *Harvard Business Review*, March–April 1989, pp. 135–142; K. T. Dirks and D. L. Ferrin, "Trust in Leadership: Meta-Analytic Findings and Implications for Research and Practice," *Journal of Applied Psychology* 87, no. 4 (August 2002): pp. 611–628; and J. K. Butler Jr., "Toward Understanding and Measuring Conditions of Trust: Evolution of a Conditions of Trust Inventory," *Journal of Management* 17, no. 3 (September 1991): pp. 643–663.

74. H. H. Brower, S. W. Lester, M. A. Korsgaard, and B. R. Dineen, "A Closer Look at Trust Between Managers and Subordinates: Understanding the Effects of Both Trusting and Being Trusted on Subordinate Outcomes," *Journal of Management* 35, no. 2 (April 2009): pp. 327–347; R. C. Mayer and M. B. Gavin, "Trust in Management and Performance:

Who Minds the Shop While the Employees Watch the Boss?," *Academy of Management Journal* 48, no. 5 (October 2005): pp. 874–888; and Dirks and Ferrin, "Trust in Leadership."

75. P. H. Kim, K. T. Dirks, and C. D. Cooper, "The Repair of Trust: A Dynamic Bilateral Perspective and Multilevel Conceptualization," *Academy of Management Review* 34, no. 3 (July 2009): pp. 401–422; R. Zemke, "The Confidence Crisis," *Training*, June 2004, pp. 22–30; J. A. Byrne, "Restoring Trust in Corporate America," *BusinessWeek*, June 24, 2002, pp. 30–35; S. Armour, "Employees' New Motto: Trust No One," *USA Today*, February 5, 2002, p. 1B; J. Scott, "Once Bitten, Twice Shy: A World of Eroding Trust," *New York Times*, April 21, 2002, p. WK5; and J. Brockner, P. A. Siegel, J. P. Daly, T. Tyler, and C. Martin, "When Trust Matters: The Moderating Effect of Outcome Favorability," *Administrative Science Quarterly* 42, no. 3 (September 1997): p. 558.

76. N. Chokshi, "Out of the Office: More People Are Working Remotely, Survey Finds," *New York Times*, February 15, 2017, https://www.nytimes.com/2017/02/15/us/remote-workers-work-from-home.html.

77. The following is based on B. J. Avolio and S. S. Kahai, "Adding the 'E' to E-Leadership: How It May Impact Your Leadership," *Organizational Dynamics* 31, no. 4 (January 2003): pp. 325–38; S. J. Zaccaro and P. Bader, "E-Leadership and the Challenges of Leading E-Teams: Minimizing the Bad and Maximizing the Good," *Organizational Dynamics* 31, no. 4 (January 2003): pp. 381–85; C. L. Snellman, "Virtual Teams: Opportunities and Challenges for e-Leaders," *Social and Behavioral Sciences* 110, no. 24 (January 2014): pp. 1251–61; G. B. Schmidt, "Virtual Leadership: An Important Leadership Context," *Industrial and Organizational Psychology* 7, no. 2 (June 2014): pp. 182–87; and L. L. Gilson, M. T. Maynard, N. C. J. Young, M. Vartiainen, and M. Hakonen, "Virtual Teams Research: 10 Years, 10 Themes, 10 Opportunities," *Journal of Management* 41, no. 5 (July 2015): pp. 1313–37.

78. L. Freifield, "2018 Training Industry Report," *Training*, November 30, 2018, https://trainingmag.com/trgmag-article/2018-training-industry-report/.

79. See, for example, J. Barling, T. Weber, and E. K. Kelloway, "Effects of Transformational Leadership Training on Attitudinal and Financial Outcomes: A Field Experiment," *Journal of Applied Psychology* 81, no. 6 (December 1996) pp. 827–832; D. V. Day, "Leadership Development: A Review in Context," *Leadership Quarterly* 11, no. 4 (Winter 2000): pp. 581–613; and D. S. DeRue and N. Wellman, "Developing Leaders via Experience: The Role of Developmental Challenge, Learning Organization, and Feedback Availability," *Journal of Applied Psychology* 94, no. 4 (July 2009): pp. 859–875.

80. C. N. Lacerenza, D. L. Reyes, S. L. Marlow, D. L. Joseph, and E. Salas, "Leadership Training Design, Delivery, and Implementation: A Meta-Analysis," *Journal of Applied Psychology* 102, no. 12 (December 2017): pp. 1686–718.

81. G. Petriglieri, "How to Really Customize Leadership Development," *Harvard Business Review*, February 18, 2016, https://hbr.org/2016/02/how-to-really-customize-leadership-development.

82. K. Y. Chan and F. Drasgow, "Toward a Theory of Individual Differences and Leadership: Understanding the Motivation to Lead," *Journal of Applied Psychology* 86, no. 3 (June 2001): pp. 481–498.

83. M. Sashkin, "The Visionary Leader," in *Charismatic Leadership*, eds. J. A. Conger, R. N. Kanungo et al. (San Francisco: Jossey-Bass, 1988), p. 150.

84. "Interesting Statistics about Effective Leadership," *Bloom Leadership* (blog), October 9, 2018, http://www.bloomleaders.com/blog/2018/10/9/interesting-statistics-about-effective-leadership.

85. S. Kerr and J. M. Jermier, "Substitutes for Leadership: Their Meaning and Measurement," *Organizational Behavior and Human Performance* 22, no. 3 (December 1978): pp. 375–403; J. P. Howell and P. W. Dorfman, "Leadership and Substitutes for Leadership Among Professional and Nonprofessional Workers," *Journal of Applied Behavioral Science* 22, no. 1 (1986): pp. 29–46; J. P. Howell, D. E. Bowen, P. W. Dorfman, S. Kerr, and P. M. Podsakoff, "Substitutes for Leadership: Effective Alternatives to Ineffective Leadership," *Organizational Dynamics* 19, no. 1 (Summer 1990): pp. 21 38; P. M. Podsakoff, B. P. Niehoff, S. B. MacKenzie, and M. L. Williams, "Do Substitutes for Leadership Really Substitute for Leadership? An Empirical Examination of Kerr and Jermier's Situational Leadership Model," *Organizational Behavior and Human Decision Processes* 54, no. 1 (February 1993): pp. 1–44; Y.-C. Wu, "An Exploration of Substitutes for Leadership: Problems and Prospects," *Social Behavior and Personality* 38, no. 5 (June 2010): pp. 583–95; and G. Hussain, W. K. W. Ismail, M. A. Rashid, and F. Nisar, "Substitutes for Leadership: Alternative Perspectives," *Management Research Review* 39, no. 5 (May 2016): pp. 546–68.

86. D. Gelles, "A Prominent Presence in Silicon Valley," *New York Times*, June 3, 2018, p. BU-5.

87. M. Forbes, "How Stitch Fix's Katrina Lake Built a $3 Billion Business," *Forbes*, August 9, 2018, https://www.forbes.com/sites/moiraforbes/2018/08/09/katrina-lake-billion-dollar-business/.

88. Wikipedia, s.v. "Katrina Lake," last modified February 20, 2019, 19:53, https://en.wikipedia.org/wiki/Katrina_Lake.

89. N. LaPorte, "Stitch Fix CEO Katrina Lake Talks Data, Amazon—And Hot Tubs," *Fast Company*, February 27, 2018, https://www.fastcompany.com/40525485/stitch-fix-ceo-katrina-lake-talks-data-styling-and-hot-tubs.

90. J. Coronado, "Key Leadership Lessons from Steve Kerr," *Design Impact*, September 5, 2018.

91. Wikipedia, s.v. "Steve Kerr," last modified April 10, 2019, 16:19, https://en.wikipedia.org/wiki/Steve_Kerr.

92. A. Mendler, "What Leaders Can Learn from Steve Kerr," *Forbes*, July 10, 2018, https://www.forbes.com/sites/forbesbusinessdevelopmentcouncil/2018/07/10/what-leaders-can-learn-from-steve-kerr/#78776c1604e0.

93. J. Bariso, "By Doing Something No One Expected, Golden State Warriors Coach Steve Kerr Taught a Brilliant Leadership Lesson," *Inc.*, February 13, 2018, https://www.inc.com/justin-bariso/golden-state-warriors-coach-steve-kerr-unorthodox-move-brilliant-lesson-leadership-emotional-intelligence.html.

94. L. Carpenter, "He Would Be An Incredible President. Steve Kerr is US Sports' Voice of Reason," *Guardian*, June 8, 2018, https://www.theguardian.com/sport/2018/jun/08/steve-kerr-golden-state-warriors-coach-political-views.

PART 5

Management Practice

A Manager's Dilemma

How would you feel as a new employee if your boss asked you to do something and you had to admit that you didn't know how to do it? Most of us would probably feel pretty inadequate and incompetent. Now imagine how strange and uncomfortable it would be if, after experiencing such an incident, you went home with the boss because you were roommates and have been friends since fourth grade. That's the situation faced by John, Glen, and Kurt. John and Kurt are employees at a software company that their friend Glen and three others started. The business now has thirty-nine employees, and the "friends" are finding out that mixing work and friendships can be tricky. At home, they're equals. They share a three-bedroom condo and divide up housework and other chores. However, at work, equality is out the door. Glen is John's boss, and Kurt's boss is another company manager. Recently, the company moved into a new workspace. As part of the four-person management team, Glen has a corner office with windows. However, John was assigned a cubicle and is annoyed at Glen for not standing up for him when offices were assigned. But John didn't complain because he didn't want to get an office only because of his friendship with Glen. Another problem brewing is that the roommates compete to outlast one another at working late. Kurt's boss is afraid that he's going to burn out. Other awkward moments arise whenever the company's performance is discussed. When Glen wants to get something off his chest about work matters, he has to stop himself. And then there's the "elephant in the room." If the software company is ever bought out by a larger company, Glen (and his three partners) stand to profit dramatically, thereby creating some interesting emotional issues for the roommates. Although it might seem easy to say the solution is to move, real estate is too expensive and, besides that, these guys are good friends.

Put yourself in Glen's shoes. Using what you've learned in Part 5 about communication, individual behavior, employee motivation, and leadership, how would you handle this situation?

Global Sense

As you discovered in this part of the text, employee engagement is an important focus for managers. Managers want their employees to be connected to, satisfied with, and enthusiastic about their jobs; that is, to be engaged. Why is employee engagement so important? The level of employee engagement serves as an indicator of organizational health and ultimately business results. The latest available data on global employee engagement levels showed that only 15 percent of employees (surveyed from 155 countries) were engaged in their jobs, 66 percent were not engaged, and 18 percent were actively disengaged. That is, only 15 percent of employees worldwide say they're passionate about and deeply connected to their work. The region of East Asia showed the lowest proportion of engaged employees at 6 percent. The global regions of the United States and Canada showed the highest levels of employee engagement at around 34 percent. Latin America was the next highest employee engagement region, with 27 percent of engaged employees. And the highest level of active disengagement of employees is in the MENA region—Middle East and North Africa.[1]

So what can managers do to get and keep employees engaged? Some important efforts include providing opportunities for career advancement, offering recognition, and having a good organization reputation.

Discuss the following questions in light of what you learned in Part 5.

- *What role do you think external factors, such as the economy or a country's culture, play in levels of employee engagement? Discuss.*
- *What role does an organization's motivational programs play in whether an employee is engaged or not? Discuss.*
- *How might a manager's leadership style affect an employee's level of engagement? Discuss.*
- *What could a manager do in the way he or she communicates to affect an employee's level of engagement?*
- *You're a manager of a workplace that has different "generations." How will you approach engaging your employees? Do you think Gen Y employees (born between 1980 and 1994) and Gen Z (born between 1995 and 2015) will tend to be more difficult to "engage"? Discuss.*

Continuing Case

Starbucks—Leading

Once people are hired or brought into organizations, managers must oversee and coordinate their work so that organizational goals can be pursued and achieved. This is the leading function of management. Managing people successfully means understanding their attitudes, behaviors, personalities, individual efforts, motivation, conflicts, and more. Starbucks has worked hard to create a workplace environment in which employees (partners) are *encouraged to* and *want to* put forth their best efforts. Kevin Johnson believes that people everywhere have the same desire—to find purpose in their work—and Starbucks's partners are able to find this purpose by enhancing the human experience.

Communication at Starbucks

Keeping organizational communication flowing at Starbucks starts at the top. Kevin Johnson regularly visits stores, which he started doing in his previous role at Starbucks as chief operating officer and continues now as CEO. Not only does this give him an up-close view of what's happening out in the field, it gives partners a chance to talk with the top guy in the company. Johnson has initiated "Partner Connection Tours," which start with partners sharing their life journeys and then move on to discussions about other matters on their minds. According to Johnson, the Partner Connection Tours have taught him to "listen with his heart" and better understand what is going on in the company. Johnson also has held open forums in order to reach out to more employees in a question-and-answer setting. Lastly, not only does Johnson use the live broadcast feature of Starbucks's internal social media tool (Workplace) to connect with store managers, but 80 percent of store managers use this tool to communicate with partners and other Starbucks managers.

Most people would probably consider the biggest challenge so far during Kevin Johnson's tenure as CEO to be the situation at a Philadelphia Starbucks in 2018 involving two African Americans who were asked to leave the store and were arrested while waiting for a friend. Johnson flew out to Philadelphia the day after the incident, met with the men, issued an apology video, met with the police commissioner and mayor, and fired the store manager. He also was the one who suggested that Starbucks close all of their US stores for racial bias training. In doing so, Johnson said he realized how it was time to do what had been done previously at Starbucks in 2008, when all US stores were closed to retrain baristas on the coffee experience. In 2008, it was about reaffirming what it meant to provide a customer experience around coffee. Fast forward to 2018, and closing stores for the day was about reaffirming the company's "commitment to creating a safe and welcoming environment for every customer."

Starbucks—Focus on Individuals

Even with some 330,000 full- and part-time partners around the world, one thing that's been important to Kevin Johnson is the relationship he has with employees. Johnson recognizes that taking care of its partners is a key way to ensure that these partners ensure a positive customer experience. In fact, Johnson notes that he understands how reducing employee turnover at the store level affects how well those employees connect to customers. Starbucks has an employee turnover rate that is a mere 20 percent of the industry average. Starbucks estimates that it costs them over $2,000 every time an hourly employee leaves. So, keeping turnover low also is very good for the company's bottom line.

One way Starbucks demonstrates the concern it has for its employees is through administering an attitude survey called Partner Perspectives. It measures overall satisfaction and engagement—the degree to which partners are connected to the company. It's been an effective way for Starbucks to show that it cares about what its employees think. For example, a partner survey indicated that it was important to employees to have more flexibility in what they can wear to work. Starbucks first changed the dress code to allow visible tattoos (except those on the face and throat), small nose studs, and larger piercings of the earlobe based on partner survey feedback. Then, in 2016, Starbucks partners were allowed to dye their hair any color, wear muted-color shirts in colors other than just white and black, wear dark-wash jeans, and don fedoras and beanies. Starbucks has tried to strike a balance between the company's brand and reputation on the one hand and being responsive to employees on the other hand.

Starbucks does well in how it takes care of its employees but also has areas that could be improved. On Glassdoor.com, Starbucks employees give the company 3.8 stars out of 5. Employees frequently comment about liking the benefits and opportunities for advancement. Yet the fast-paced environment of most Starbucks stores is something that can be challenging and is commented on by many of Starbucks's partners. A former Starbucks shift supervisor explained in a case heard by the California Supreme Court that Starbucks instructed its supervisors to clock out before completing tasks needed to close their stores. Supervisors clocked out before submitting sales and inventory data to headquarters, walking coworkers to their cars, activating the store alarm, and locking up for the night. The court ruled that Starbucks needed to pay supervisors for these tasks, and Starbucks has followed through on this.

Starbucks states that it wants employees who have the ability to create "genuine moments of connection" with customers, a willingness to learn, and an openness to getting the job done while helping fellow team members. As you can see, this "ideal" Starbucks partner should have individual strengths and should be able to work as part of a team. In the retail store setting, especially, individuals must work together as a team to provide the experience that customers expect.

Starbucks—Motivating Employees

A story from Howard Schultz's childhood provides some clues into what has shaped Starbucks's philosophy about how to treat people. Schultz's father worked hard at various blue-collar jobs. However, when he didn't work, he didn't get paid. When his father broke his ankle when Howard was seven years old, the family "had no income, no health insurance, no worker's compensation, nothing to fall back on." The image of his father with his leg in a cast, unable to work, left a lasting impression on the young Schultz. Many years later, when his father died of lung cancer, "he had no savings, no pension, and more important, he had never attained fulfillment and dignity from work he found meaningful." The sad realities of the types of work environments his father endured had a powerful effect on Howard, and he vowed that if he were "ever in a position where I could make a difference, I wouldn't leave people behind." And those personal experiences have shaped the way that Starbucks cares for its partners to this day—the relationships and commitments the company has with each and every employee.

One of the best reflections of how Starbucks treats its eligible part- and full-time partners is its Total Pay package, which includes competitive base pay, bonuses, a comprehensive health plan, paid-time-off plans, a stock equity reward program, a generous retirement savings program, reimbursement for an online bachelor's degree from Arizona State University, and partner perks (which includes a pound of coffee each week). Although specific benefits differ between regions and countries, all Starbucks international partners share the "Total Pay" philosophy. For instance, in Malaysia and Thailand, partners are provided extensive training opportunities to further their careers in addition to health insurance, paid vacation, sick leave, and other benefits. In Turkey, the "Total Pay" package for Starbucks's partners includes transportation subsidies and access to a company doctor, who provides free treatment. And, in China, full-time partners receive a monthly housing allowance and are eligible for a sabbatical (called a "Career Coffee Break").

Partner (employee) recognition is important to Starbucks. The company has several formal recognition programs in place that partners can use as tools to encourage, reward, and inspire one another. There are a whole host of performance-based awards for individuals and for teams, anniversary awards, and company-wide awards (like Partner of the Quarter). These programs range from formal company awards to informal special acknowledgments given by coworkers (which they call "Green Apron Awards").

To assist partners who are facing particularly difficult circumstances (such as natural disaster, fire, or illness), the company has a CUP (Caring Unites Partners) fund that provides financial support. After Hurricane Harvey in 2017, more than 2,000 partners in the Texas region received more than $1 million in assistance from the CUP fund. In China, Starbucks has set aside CUP funds starting in 2017 for a Parent Care program. This program provides critical illness insurance for parents of full-time employees working in mainland China. Understanding the culturally important role that parents play in China, Starbucks wanted to reduce the financial burden that many of its partners otherwise would bear if their parents become seriously ill. This kind of focus on partners' needs extends back to founder Howard Schultz's promise not to allow employees to experience financial hardship due to illness or injury the way his father's injury created difficulties in his family growing up.

In 2018, Starbucks was listed among the 50 best places to work by *Inc.* magazine (ranked 21 on the list) and also was ranked on Glassdoor's list of the 100 best companies to work for. Starbucks has not been on *Fortune* magazine's 100 Best Companies to Work For list since 2013, but it was included on that list for fifteen years in a row prior to that

year. Like many companies, Starbucks had to make some difficult strategic decisions during tough economic periods, such as closing underperforming stores. Despite the challenges, it's a testament to Starbucks's treatment of its partners that it has made lists that are based on employee reviews and ratings in recent years and made *Fortune*'s Top 100 list for fifteen years straight. With recent decisions to increase wages, relax the dress code, and increase benefits for sick leave, there is a potential for higher ratings in the near future.

Starbucks—Fostering Leadership

To Howard Schultz, being a great leader means identifying a path your organization needs to follow and then creating enough confidence in your people so they follow that path and don't take an easier route. He also said leaders, particularly of growing companies, need to stay true to those values and principles that have guided how their business is done and not let those values be compromised by ambitions of growth. Kevin Johnson's take on leadership is very similar to Schultz's. When talking about his leadership at Starbucks, Johnson repeatedly mentions how important it is to him to stay true to the mission and values of Starbucks every single day. When figuring out what needs to be done to steer the company, it's a question of how well it accomplishes Starbucks' mission of inspiring and nurturing the human spirit.

Kevin Johnson frequently tells the story of a turning point that has defined the direction he continues to take as a leader. While he was the CEO of Juniper Networks, a technology company, Johnson was diagnosed with skin cancer (melanoma). He continued to prioritize business over his health until one day, while waiting in an airport, he realized how he had his priorities mixed up. He cancelled his flight and scaled back his work with a promise to himself to only "do things that are joyful." This incident in his life likely informed Starbucks's decision to provide paid benefits to employees who need to take time off to take care of sick family members. Johnson also says that his changed approach to life has allowed him to move from being a leader who "intellectually" understood business to someone who has grown to understand the business of Starbucks from an emotional standpoint too. This emotional understanding of Starbucks is important to his leadership, Johnson says, since Starbucks is a company that is "about the heart" as it works to fulfill its mission.

Starbucks recognizes the importance of having individuals with excellent leadership skills throughout the company. In addition to providing leadership development training for upper-level managers, Starbucks encourages leadership development skills by training for partners who have been identified as particularly good ambassadors of customer service. This training has been provided in an off-site conference format. In addition, Starbucks offers to managers at all organizational levels additional training courses that develop them further as leaders.[2]

Discussion Questions

P5-1. Which of the functions of communication do you think Kevin Johnson uses when he is involved in a Partner Connection Tour? Are the communication functions any different when he uses the internal social media tool Workplace? Discuss.

P5-2. What potential barriers to effective communication might apply to employees working in a busy Starbucks café? What could a store manager do to minimize those barriers?

P5-3. Besides asking employees for their opinions through attitude surveys, what else could managers at Starbucks do to ensure that employees have as positive attitudes as possible?

P5-4. Look at the description of the types of people Starbucks seeks. What individual behavior issues might arise in managing these types of people? (Think in terms of attitudes, personality, etc.) What work team issues might arise? (Think in terms of what makes teams successful. Hint: Can a person be self-motivated and passionate *and* be a good team player?)

P5-5. Discuss the "ideal" Starbucks employee in terms of the various personality trait theories.

P5-6. Describe the workplace environment Starbucks has tried to create. What impact might such an environment have on motivating employees?

P5-7. Using the Job Characteristics Model in Exhibit 16–6, redesign a part-time hourly worker's job to be more motivating. Do the same with a store manager's job.

P5-8. Describe Kevin Johnson's leadership style. Would his approach be appropriate in other types of organizations? Why or why not?

P5-9. What is Starbucks doing "right" with respect to the leading function? Are they doing anything "wrong?" Explain.

P5-10. Which of the company's mission and values (see website) influence the leading function of management? Explain how the one(s) you chose would affect how Starbucks' managers deal with (a) communication issues, (b) individual behavior issues, (c) motivational techniques, and (d) leadership styles or approaches.

Notes for the Part 5 Continuing Case

1. J. Harter, "Employee Engagement on the Rise in the U.S.," *Gallup*, August 26, 2018, https://news.gallup.com/poll/241649/employee-engagement-rise.aspx; "The State of the Global Workplace," *Gallup*, 2017, accessed March 18, 2019, https://www.gallup.com/workplace/238079/state-global-workplace-2017.aspx?utm_source=link_wwwv9&utm_campaign=item_231668&utm_medium=copy#formheader.

2. Information from www.starbucks.com, March 2019; M. Vultaggio, "Who is Current CEO of Starbucks? About Kevin Johnson After Howard Schultz Announces Potential 2020 Presidential Run," *Newsweek*, January 28, 2019, https://www.newsweek.com/who-current-ceo-starbucks-kevin-johnson-howard-schultz-1308360; D. Gelles, "Starbucks's CEO Comes Into the Light," *New York Times*, June 18, 2018, p. B1; "Watch: Starbucks CEO Kevin Johnson on Innovation and Empathy," *Fast Company*, October 26, 2017, https://www.fastcompany.com/40482678/live-now-starbucks-ceo-keving-johnson-on-innovation-and-empathy; A. Bradford, "Employee Engagement in Every Cup—A Starbucks Case Study," Social Media for Business Performance, University of Waterloo, May 28, 2018, http://smbp.uwaterloo.ca/2018/05/employee-engagement-in-every-cup-a-starbucks-case-study/; H. Halzack, "The CEO of Starbucks Just Passed His Biggest Leadership Test Yet," *Bloomberg*, April 18, 2018, https://www.bloomberg.com/opinion/articles/2018-04-18/starbucks-ceo-kevin-johnson-aces-this-leadership-test; K. Taylor, "'They'd Rather Us Be Machines': Starbucks Baristas Reveal the Worst Parts of Working There," *Business Insider*, May 26, 2017, https://www.businessinsider.com/worst-parts-of-working-at-starbucks-2017-5; L. Nagele-Piazza, "Calif. High Court: Starbucks Must Pay Workers to Close Store," *Society for Human Resource Management*, July 27, 2018, https://www.shrm.org/resourcesandtools/legal-and-compliance/state-and-local-updates/pages/california-high-court-said-starbucks-must-pay-workers-to-close-store.aspx; D. Wilkie, "Blue Hair Topped By a Beanie? Both Now OK at Starbucks," *Society for Human Resource Management*, July 29, 2016, https://www.shrm.org/resourcesandtools/hr-topics/employee-relations/pages/starbucks,-dyed-hair-.aspx; D. Percival, "Starbucks' Approach to Employee Engagement," *Medium*, July 14, 2017, https://medium.com/@dperciv1/starbucks-approach-to-employee-engagement-3e2830bbffb3; P. Economy, "Facebook, Southwest, Delta, Apple, and Starbucks Among 50 Best Places to Work in 2018," *Inc.*, July 12, 2018, https://www.inc.com/peter-economy/facebook-southwest-delta-apple-starbucks-among-50-best-places-to-work-in-2018.html; P. Schrodt, "The 100 Best Places to Work in 2018 – and the Jobs They Have Open Right Now," *Money*, December 6, 2017, http://money.com/money/5047491/the-100-best-places-to-work-in-2018/; "Starbucks to Help Chinese Employees Pay for Aging Parents' Health Care," *Fast Casual*, April 11, 2017, https://www.fastcasual.com/news/starbucks-to-help-chinese-employees-pay-for-aging-parents-health-care/; "Starbucks—Creating Excitement for Training," *Root Inc.*, accessed March 21, 2019, https://www.rootinc.com/case_studies/starbucks-creating-excitement-training/.

Chapter 18   Monitoring and Controlling

Learning Objectives

18.1 *Explain* the nature and importance of control.

18.2 *Describe* the three steps in the control process.

18.3 *Explain* how organizational and employee performance are measured.

18.4 *Describe* tools used to measure organizational performance.

18.5 *Discuss* contemporary issues in control.

Employability Skills Matrix

This matrix identifies which features and end-of-chapter material will help you develop specific skills employers are looking for in job candidates.

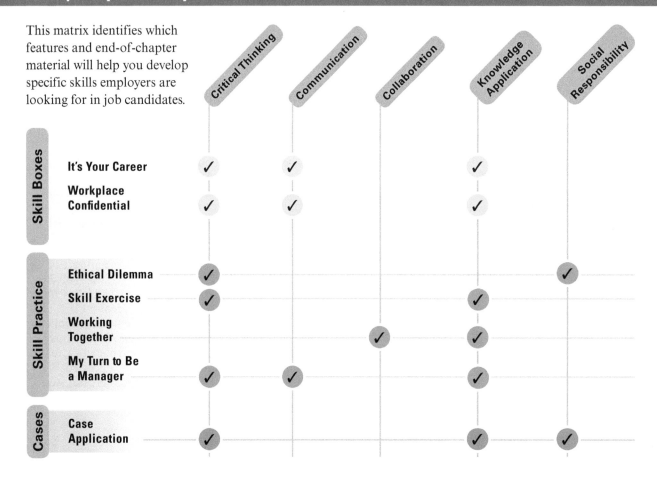

	Critical Thinking	Communication	Collaboration	Knowledge Application	Social Responsibility
Skill Boxes					
It's Your Career	✓	✓		✓	
Workplace Confidential	✓	✓		✓	
Skill Practice					
Ethical Dilemma	✓				✓
Skill Exercise	✓			✓	
Working Together			✓	✓	
My Turn to Be a Manager	✓	✓		✓	
Cases					
Case Application	✓			✓	✓

*Suraj Samaroo worked as a call-center employee at an IKEA in Maryland.[1]
After mastering the furniture company's phone and mail-order system,
Samaroo began issuing himself refunds for purchases made by customers that
were never actually returned. He covered up his scheme by altering inventory
records. In less than a year he stole almost $400,000.*

*The US Social Security Administration mistakenly paid 740 deceased
beneficiaries approximately $17 million in retirement benefits.[2]*

*An airport security screening audit revealed a startling statistic: auditors
were able to move fake explosives and weapons past security screeners 95
percent of the time.[3]*

*The above are examples of poor organizational controls. They illustrate that
no matter how effective an organization's plans or tight its structure, there
exists the possibility that things can go awry. In this chapter, we show how
control systems are critical to ensure that an organization successfully achieves
its goals.*

WHAT is controlling, and why is it important?

LO18.1 *Controlling* is the final step in the management process. But what do we specifically mean by the term?

What Is Controlling?

Controlling is the process of monitoring, comparing, and correcting work performance. Managers cannot really know whether their units are performing properly until they have evaluated what activities have been done and have compared the actual performance with the desired standard. Effective controls, therefore, ensure that activities are completed in ways that lead to the attainment of goals. And the effectiveness of controls is determined by how well they help employees and managers achieve their goals.[4]

Applying controls in organizations is nothing new. Accounting and auditing practices, for instance, have been found to be present in ancient China and Egypt. In more modern times, the writings of Frederick Taylor, Henri Fayol, and Max Weber (see the Management History module following Chapter 1) in the early twentieth century was directly concerned with the need to enact controls with the advent of an industrial economy. Concepts such as scientifically training workers, creating lines of authority, and imposing formal rules and regulations were introduced so as to ensure that work was completed consistent with goals established by management.

controlling
Management function that involves monitoring, comparing, and correcting work performance

Why Is Controlling Important?

Planning can be done, an organization structure can be created to facilitate efficient achievement of goals, and employees motivated through effective leadership. Still, there's no assurance that activities are going as planned and that the goals employees and managers are working toward are, in fact, being attained. Control is important, therefore, because it's the final link in the functional chain of management. The value of the control function can be seen in three specific areas: planning, empowering employees, and protecting the workplace.

In Chapter 8, we described goals, which provide specific direction to employees and managers as the foundation of planning. However, just stating goals or having employees accept goals doesn't guarantee that the necessary actions to accomplish those goals have been taken. As the old saying goes, "The best-laid plans of mice and men oft go awry." The effective manager follows up to ensure that what employees are supposed to do is, in fact, being done and goals are being achieved. Controlling provides a critical link back to planning. (See Exhibit 18-1.)

The second reason controlling is important is because of employee empowerment. Many managers are reluctant to empower their employees because they fear something will go wrong for which they would be held responsible. Thus many managers

Exhibit 18-1
Planning-Controlling Link

Exhibit 18-1
Planning-Controlling Link

might be tempted to do things themselves and avoid delegating. This reluctance to delegate, however, can be reduced if managers develop an effective control system. Such a control system can provide information and feedback on the performance of employees to whom they have delegated authority. An effective control system is therefore important because managers need to delegate authority; but because they are held ultimately responsible for the decisions that their employees make, managers also need a feedback mechanism.

The final reason controls are important is to protect the organization and its assets. Today's environment brings heightened threats from natural disasters, financial scandals, workplace violence, global supply chain disruptions, security breaches, and even possible terrorist attacks. It's management's responsibility to protect the organization's assets against such threats. Comprehensive controls and backup plans will help assure minimal work disruptions.

THE control process

L018.2   The **control process** consists of three separate and distinct steps: (1) *measuring* actual performance; (2) *comparing* actual performance against a standard; and (3) taking *managerial action* to correct deviations or inadequate standards (see Exhibit 18-2). Before we consider each step in detail, you should be aware that the control process assumes that standards of performance *already exist*. These standards are the specific objectives against which progress can be measured. They are created in the planning function. If managers use MBO, then objectives are, by definition, tangible, verifiable, and measurable. In such instances, these objectives are the standards against which progress is measured and compared. If MBO is not practiced, then standards are the specific performance indicators that management uses. Our point is that these standards are developed in the planning function; planning must *precede* control.

Step 1: Measuring Actual Performance

To determine what actual performance is, a manager must first get information about it. Thus, the first step in control is measuring. Let's consider *how* we measure and *what* we measure.

HOW WE MEASURE   Five sources of information used by managers to measure and report actual performance are personal observation, statistical reports, self-monitoring computers, oral reports, and written reports.

control process
A three-step process of measuring actual performance, comparing actual performance against a standard, and taking managerial action to correct deviations or inadequate standards

Exhibit 18-2
The Control Process

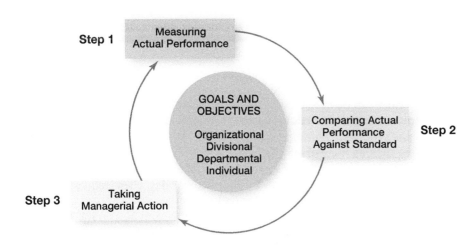

Personal observation provides firsthand, intimate knowledge of the actual activity—information that is not filtered through others. It permits intensive coverage because minor as well as major performance activities can be observed as well as opportunities for the manager to "read between the lines." Management-by-walking-around can pick up omissions, facial expressions, and tones of voice that may be missed by other sources. Unfortunately, in a time when quantitative information suggests objectivity, personal observation is often considered an inferior information source. It is subject to perceptual biases—what one manager sees, another might not. Personal observation also consumes a good deal of time. Finally, this method suffers from obtrusiveness. Employees might interpret a manager's overt observation as a sign of a lack of confidence in them or of mistrust.

Managers increasingly rely on *statistical reports* for measuring actual performance. It includes computer outputs, graphs, bar charts, and numerical displays of any form that managers may use for assessing performance. Although statistical data is easy to visualize and effective for showing relationships, they provide limited information about an activity. Statistics report on only a few key areas and often ignore other important factors.

Self-monitoring computers may well be the information source of the future. The computerization of everything—sometimes referred to as the Internet of Things—is reshaping the manager's role in the control process. Sensors in smartphones, machinery, robotics, tracking devices, and the like collect data and initiate corrective action or alert management to a problem. Human intervention becomes an option rather than a necessity as computers sense, think, and act. How effective these controls are is still too early to determine. One concern is how employees respond to a technology that can monitor their every movement, from every stroke on their computer keyboard to their whereabouts in the building.

Oral reports encompasses information acquired through conferences, meetings, one-to-one conversations, or telephone calls. Although information is filtered, oral reports are fast, allow for feedback, and permit language expression and tone of voice, as well as words themselves, to convey meaning.

Actual performance may also be measured by *written reports*. They are slower yet more formal than first- or secondhand oral reports. This formality also often means greater comprehensiveness and conciseness than is found in oral reports. In addition, written reports are usually easy to catalogue and reference.

WHAT WE MEASURE *What* we measure is probably more critical to the control process than *how* we measure. The selection of the wrong criteria can result in serious dysfunctional consequences.[5] An example that makes this point occurred a number of years ago.[6] A consultant hired by a city noticed that as soon as the city's police officers came on duty, they took their patrol cars to the highway that ran through town and raced back and forth from one edge of town to the other. While this had little to do with effective policing, it all made sense when the consultant learned that the city council was measuring police effectiveness by how many miles were racked up on the patrol cars' odometers.

Some control criteria can be used for any management situation. For instance, all managers deal with people, so criteria such as employee satisfaction or turnover and absenteeism rates can be measured. Keeping costs within budget is also a fairly common control measure. Other control criteria should recognize the different activities that managers supervise. For instance, a manager at a pizza delivery location might use measures such as number of pizzas delivered per day, average delivery time for phone orders versus online orders, or number of coupons redeemed. A manager in a governmental agency might use applications typed per day, client requests completed per hour, or average time to process paperwork.

Most jobs and activities can be expressed in tangible and measurable terms. When a performance indicator can't be stated in quantifiable terms, managers should look for and use subjective measures. Although such measures may have limitations, they're better than no standards at all and ignoring the control function.

Step 2: Comparing Actual Performance Against the Standard

The comparing step determines the variation between actual performance and the standard. Although some variation in performance can be expected in all activities, it's critical to determine an acceptable **range of variation** (see Exhibit 18-3). Deviations outside this range need attention. Let's work through an example.

Chris Tanner is a sales manager for Green Earth Gardening Supply, a distributor of specialty plants and seeds in the Pacific Northwest. Chris prepares a report during the first week of each month that describes sales for the previous month, classified by product line. Exhibit 18-4 displays both the sales goals (standard) and actual sales figures for the month of June. After looking at the numbers, should Chris be concerned? Sales were a bit higher than originally targeted, but does that mean there were no significant deviations? That depends on what Chris thinks is *significant*; that is, outside the acceptable range of variation. Even though overall performance was generally quite favorable, some product lines need closer scrutiny. For instance, if sales of heirloom seeds, flowering bulbs, and annual flowers continue to be over what was expected, Chris might need to order more product from nurseries to meet customer demand. Because sales of vegetable plants were 15 percent below goal, Chris may need to run a special on them. As this example shows, both

range of variation
The acceptable parameters of variance between actual performance and the standard

Exhibit 18-3
Acceptable Range of Variation

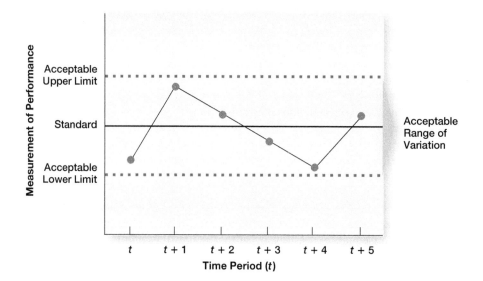

Product	Standard	Actual	Over (Under)
Vegetable plants	1,075	913	(162)
Perennial flowers	630	634	4
Annual flowers	800	912	112
Herbs	160	140	(20)
Flowering bulbs	170	286	116
Flowering bushes	225	220	(5)
Heirloom seeds	540	672	132
Total	3,600	3,777	177

Exhibit 18-4
Green Earth Gardening Supply—June Sales

overvariance and undervariance may require managerial attention, which is the third step in the control process.

Step 3: Taking Managerial Action

Managers can choose among three possible courses of action: do nothing, correct the actual performance, or revise the standards. Because "do nothing" is self-explanatory, let's look at the other two.

CORRECT ACTUAL PERFORMANCE   Sports coaches understand the importance of correcting actual performance. During a game, they'll often correct a player's actions. But if the problem is recurring or encompasses more than one player, they'll devote time during practice before the next game to correcting the actions. That's what managers need to do as well.

If the source of the variation has been deficient performance, the managers will want to take corrective action. Examples of such corrective action might include changes in strategy, structure, compensation practices, or training programs; the redesign of jobs; or the replacement of personnel.

A manager who decides to correct actual performance has to make another decision: Should he or she take immediate or basic corrective action? **Immediate corrective action** corrects problems at once and gets performance back on track. **Basic corrective action** asks how and why performance has deviated and then proceeds to correct the source of the deviation. It's not unusual for managers to rationalize that they don't have the time to take basic corrective action and, therefore, must be content to perpetually "put out fires" with immediate actions. Effective managers, however, analyze deviations and, when the benefits justify it, take the time to permanently correct significant variances between standard and actual performance.

immediate corrective action
Corrective action that corrects problems at once to get performance back on track

basic corrective action
Corrective action that looks at how and why performance deviated before correcting the source of deviation

REVISE THE STANDARD   It's possible that the variance was a result of an unrealistic standard—too low or too high a goal. In such cases, the standard needs the corrective action, not the performance. If performance consistently exceeds the goal, then a manager should look at whether the goal is too easy and needs to be raised. On the other hand, managers must be cautious about revising a standard downward. It's natural to blame the goal when an employee or a team falls short. For instance, students who get a low score on a test often attack the grade cutoff standards as too high. Rather than accept the fact that their performance was inadequate, they will argue that the standards are unreasonable. Likewise, salespeople who don't meet their monthly quota often want to blame what they think is an unrealistic quota. It may be true that standards are too high, resulting in significant variance and acting to demotivate those employees being assessed against it. But keep in mind that if employees or managers don't meet the standard, the first thing they are likely to attack is the standard itself. If you believe the standard is realistic, hold your ground. Explain your position, reaffirm to the employee or manager that you expect future performance to improve, and then take the necessary corrective action to turn that expectation into reality.

Exhibit 18-5
Managerial Decisions in the
Control Process

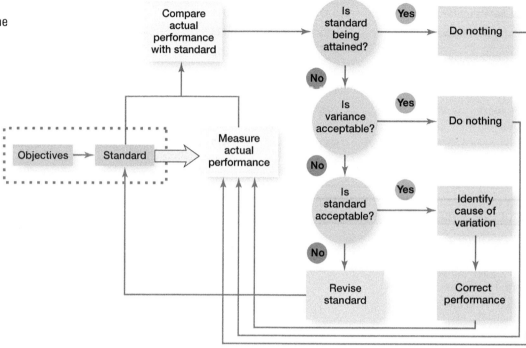

Summary

Exhibit 18-5 summarizes the decisions a manager makes in controlling. The standards evolve out of objectives, but because objectives are developed during planning, they are tangential to the control process. The process is essentially a continuous flow between measuring, comparing, and managerial action. Depending on the results of the comparing stage, management's courses of action are to do nothing, correct the performance, or revise the standard.

CONTROLLING for organizational and employee performance

LO18.3 Cost efficiency. The length of time customers are kept on hold. Customer satisfaction with service provided. These are just a few of the important performance indicators that executives in the intensely competitive call-center service industry measure. To make good decisions, managers in this industry want and need this type of information so they can manage organizational and employee performance.

What Is Organizational Performance?

When you hear the word *performance,* what do you think of? A summer evening concert by a local community orchestra? An Olympic athlete striving for the finish line in a close race? A Southwest Airlines ramp agent in Fort Myers, Florida, loading passengers as efficiently as possible in order to meet the company's twenty-minute gate turnaround goal? **Performance** is all of these things. It's the end result of an activity. And whether that activity is hours of intense practice before a concert or race or carrying out job responsibilities as efficiently and effectively as possible, performance is what results from that activity.

Managers are concerned with **organizational performance**—the accumulated results of all the organization's work activities. It's a multifaceted concept, but managers need to understand the factors that contribute to organizational performance.

performance
The end result of an activity

organizational performance
The accumulated results of all the organization's work activities

Measures of Organizational Performance

It's not by accident that NBA basketball players are taking a lot more three-point shots than they did a few years back.[7] In 2012, the average NBA team was taking 18.4 three-point shots per game. In 2017, the average was up nearly 50 percent to 27 shots. Using data science and data analytics, team analysts showed that while a three-point shot had only a 35 percent chance of going in, it still led to more points than a two-point shot taken closer to the basket. In this case, data analysis acted as a performance measure and helped coaches improve their organization's performance.

In this section, we look at three commonly used measures of organizational performance: organizational productivity, organizational effectiveness, and industry rankings.

ORGANIZATIONAL PRODUCTIVITY **Productivity** is the amount of goods or services produced divided by the inputs needed to generate that output. Organizations and individual work units want to be productive. They want to produce the most goods and services using the least amount of inputs. Output is measured by the sales revenue an organization receives when goods are sold (selling price × number sold). Input is measured by the costs of acquiring and transforming resources into outputs.

It's management's job to increase this ratio. Of course, the easiest way to do this is to raise prices of the outputs. But in today's competitive environment, that may not be an option. For instance, it is difficult for Walmart to meet its objective of "Everyday Low Prices" because it has increased pay for 1.2 million workers and is facing intense competition from retailers such as Costco.[8] The only other option, then, is to decrease the inputs side. How? By being more efficient in performing work and thus decreasing the organization's expenses. Walmart has been pressuring product suppliers to lower their prices in an effort to reduce expenses and maintain competitive store pricing.[9]

ORGANIZATIONAL EFFECTIVENESS **Organizational effectiveness** is a measure of how appropriate organizational goals are and how well those goals are met. That's the bottom line for managers, and it's what guides managerial decisions in designing strategies and work activities and in coordinating the work of employees.

INDUSTRY AND COMPANY RANKINGS Industry and company rankings are a popular way for managers to measure their organization's performance. And there's no shortage of these rankings, as Exhibit 18-6 shows. Rankings are determined by specific performance measures, which are different for each list. For instance, *Fortune*'s

Houston Rocket guard James Harden is regularly among the NBA's top 3-point shooters. The Rockets' coaches encourage team members to shoot 3-point shots rather than 2-point shots because the former provides a statistical advantage.
Source: Troy Taormina/USA TODAY Sports/ Newscom

productivity
The amount of goods or services produced divided by the inputs needed to generate that output

organizational effectiveness
A measure of how appropriate organizational goals are and how well those goals are being met

Fortune (www.fortune.com)	*IndustryWeek* (www.industryweek.com)
Fortune 500	*IndustryWeek* 1000
Global 500	*IndustryWeek* US 500
World's Most Admired Companies	50 Best Manufacturers
100 Best Companies to Work For	*IndustryWeek* Best Plants
100 Fastest-Growing Companies	
Forbes (www.forbes.com)	**Customer Satisfaction Indexes**
World's Largest Public Companies	American Customer Satisfaction Index— University of Michigan Business School
INC. (www.inc.com)	Customer Satisfaction Measurement Association
Fastest-growing private companies	

Exhibit 18-6
Popular Industry and Company Rankings

Best Companies to Work For are chosen by answers given by thousands of randomly selected employees on a questionnaire called "The Great Place to Work® Trust Index®" and on materials filled out by thousands of company managers, including a corporate culture audit created by the Great Place to Work Institute. These rankings give managers (and others) an indicator of how well their company performs in comparison to others. Wegmans Food Markets is an example of a great place to work. It has been on the *Fortune* list every year since 1998.[10] It is not surprising that 96 percent of Wegmans's employees said that they have great bosses and great rewards, and 97 percent indicated that the work atmosphere is great.[11]

IT'S YOUR CAREER
How to Be a Pro at Giving Feedback

A key to success in management and in your career is knowing how to be effective at giving feedback.
Everyone needs feedback! If you want people to do their best, they need to know what they're doing well and what they can do better. That's why providing feedback is such an important skill to have. But being effective at giving feedback is tricky! That's why we often see managers either (a) not wanting to give feedback or (b) giving feedback in such a way that it doesn't result in anything positive.

You can feel more comfortable with and be more effective at providing feedback if you use the following specific suggestions:[12]

1. **Be straightforward by focusing on specific behaviors.** Feedback should be specific rather than general. Avoid such statements as "You have a bad attitude" or "I'm really impressed with the good job you did." They're vague and although they provide information, they don't tell the recipient enough to correct the "bad attitude" or on what basis you concluded that a "good job" had been done so the person knows what behaviors to repeat or to avoid.

2. **Be realistic.** Focus your feedback on what can be changed. When people get comments on things over which they have no control, it can be frustrating.

3. **Keep feedback impersonal.** Feedback, particularly the negative kind, should be descriptive rather than judgmental or evaluative. No matter how upset you are, keep the feedback focused on job-related behaviors and never criticize someone personally because of an inappropriate action.

4. **Keep feedback goal oriented.** Feedback should not be given primarily to "blow off steam" or "unload" on another person. If you have to say something negative, make sure it's directed toward the recipient's goals. Ask yourself whom the feedback is supposed to help. If the answer is you, bite your tongue and hold the comment. Such feedback undermines your credibility and lessens the meaning and influence of future feedback.

5. **Know when to give feedback—make it well timed.** Feedback is most meaningful to a recipient when there's a very short interval between his or her behavior and the receipt of feedback about that behavior. Moreover, if you're particularly concerned with changing behavior, delays in providing feedback on the undesirable actions lessen the likelihood that the feedback will be effective in bringing about the desired change. Of course, making feedback prompt merely for the sake of promptness can backfire if you have insufficient information, if you're angry, or if you're otherwise emotionally upset. In such instances, "well timed" could mean "somewhat delayed."

6. **Ensure understanding.** Make sure your feedback is concise and complete so that the recipient clearly and fully understands the communication. It may help to have the recipient rephrase the content of your feedback to find out whether it fully captured the meaning you intended.

7. **Watch your body language, tone of voice, and facial expressions.** Your body language and tone of voice can speak louder than words. Think about what you want to communicate, and make sure your body language supports that message.

PROBLEM TYPE	EXAMPLES OF EACH
Attendance	Absenteeism, tardiness, abuse of sick leave
On-the-Job Behaviors	Insubordination, failure to use safety devices, alcohol or drug abuse
Dishonesty	Theft, lying to supervisors, falsifying information on employment application or on other organizational forms
Outside Activities	Criminal activities, unauthorized strike activities, working for a competing organization (if no-compete clause is part of employment)

Exhibit 18-7
Types of Discipline Problems and Examples of Each

Controlling for Employee Performance

Managers need to make sure employees' work efforts are of the quantity and quality needed to accomplish organizational goals. Thus the need to impose controls. It's particularly important for managers to deliver effective performance feedback and to be prepared, if needed, to use **disciplinary actions**—actions taken by a manager to enforce the organization's work standards and regulations.[13] Let's look first at effective performance feedback.

DELIVERING EFFECTIVE PERFORMANCE FEEDBACK Throughout the semester, do you keep track of all your scores on homework, exams, and papers? If you do, why do you want to know that information? For most of us, it's because we like to know where we stand in terms of where we'd like to be and what we'd like to accomplish in our work. We like to know how we're doing. This similarly applies in the workplace. Managers need to provide their employees with feedback so that the employees know where they stand in terms of their job performance. The "It's Your Career" box on the previous page offers specific suggestions for how to give effective feedback.

Sometimes performance feedback doesn't work. An employee's performance may continue to be an issue. Under those circumstances, disciplinary actions may be necessary to address the problems.

USING DISCIPLINARY ACTIONS Most employees do their jobs well and never need formal correction. Yet, sometimes it's needed. Exhibit 18-7 lists some common types of work discipline problems and examples of each. In those circumstances, it's important for a manager to know what the organization's policies are on discipline. Most organizations require managers to follow a progressive disciplinary action policy. **Progressive disciplinary action** is intended to ensure that the minimum penalty appropriate to the offense is imposed. It typically progresses through five steps: oral warning; initial written warning; final written warning; termination review or suspension; and, in the most serious cases, a dismissal letter that states the reason for dismissal.[15] From a legal standpoint, challenges by employees to organizational disciplinary actions have typically gone in favor of management when the disciplinary actions have been carefully documented and followed the progressive steps.[16]

fyi

Managers spend 26 percent of their time per week coaching underperforming employees.[14]

disciplinary actions
Actions taken by a manager to enforce the organization's work standards and regulations

progressive disciplinary action
Discipline that moves sequentially through steps to ensure that the minimum penalty to an offense is imposed

TOOLS for measuring organizational performance

LO18.4 All managers need appropriate tools for monitoring and measuring organizational performance. Before describing some specific types of control tools, let's look at three different types of control: feedforward, concurrent, and feedback.

WORKPLACE CONFIDENTIAL Responding to an Unfair Performance Review

A recent survey of 1,000 full-time employees, all born after 1980, found a great deal of frustration with their performance reviews. Sixty-two percent, for instance, felt "blindsided" by their reviews; 74 percent frequently felt unsure as to what their managers thought of their performance; 22 percent called in sick because they were anxious about their reviews; and 28 percent reacted to their reviews by looking for another job. Our conclusion: it's very possible that sometime in your career you'll experience frustration as a result of your performance review.

It might surprise you to learn that most bosses actually dislike performance reviews. Why? First, managers are often uncomfortable discussing performance weaknesses directly with employees because they fear a confrontation when presenting negative feedback. Second, many employees become defensive when their weaknesses are pointed out. It's not uncommon for employees to challenge the evaluation by criticizing the manager or redirecting blame to someone else. Finally, employees tend to have an inflated assessment of their own performance. Statistically speaking, half of all employees must be below-average performers. But the evidence indicates that the average employee's estimate of his or her performance level generally falls around the 75th percentile. So even when managers are providing good news, employees are likely to perceive it as not good enough!

Here are some suggestions on how best to handle a performance evaluation that you feel isn't fair:

Listen closely to what your boss is saying. The place to begin is to listen carefully to the specifics in your review. What exactly is your boss saying? Don't interrupt your boss as she goes over your review. You specifically want to have clarity on the negative comments. Let your boss complete her review and make sure you understand her concerns before you initiate a response.

Be prepared to accept that there might be truth in some or all of the negative comments. As we noted above, we have a tendency to overestimate our own performance level. Your boss's assessment may be more accurate than your self-evaluation.

Stay calm and cool, and avoid being defensive. Control your emotions and your tongue. Don't get angry and say something you'll regret. Don't react by diverting blame, giving excuses, or getting into a debate with your boss. As you seek clarity, pay attention to your tone so it doesn't appear that you're challenging the truthfulness of her feedback. At this point, just treat her negative comments as constructive criticism.

Ask what you can do to improve. Asking for suggestions on what you might do to improve can work for you in two ways. First, it shows your acceptance of the criticism. Second, it indicates your willingness to change.

Request more feedback between reviews. Once you understand the content of your performance review and what you need to improve, you should talk to your boss about the possibility of getting more feedback between formal reviews. The goal should be to eliminate surprises in your annual review. You want to know if you're underperforming as soon as your boss is concerned so you can correct the problem quickly. The idea is to discourage your boss from accumulating performance problems, then unloading them in the annual review.

Do you want to push back? What if you take issue with your boss's assessment? If you're convinced your boss's evaluation if unfair, you have a serious decision to make. Do you let the evaluation go or do you challenge it? Both have risks. Ignoring a negative review may begin your boss's effort to terminate your employment. On the other hand, challenging your boss's assessment could escalate a conflict that has long-term career implications.

If you truly feel your review is unfair, there is always a possibility to change the decision in your favor. However, before you protest your boss's decision, consider your organization's culture and talk to your colleagues to assess how those who have challenged a bad performance review in the past were treated.

Challenging your performance appraisal. If you decide to challenge your performance appraisal, here are a few suggestions: (1) Request a copy of your appraisal so you can better process the information. (2) Determine what exact aspects of the appraisal you disagree with. (3) Schedule a meeting with your boss to provide your evidence in support of your position. (4) If the meeting with your boss fails to achieve the ends you desire, present your case to your Human Resources department—but let your boss know ahead of time of your intention.

Writing a rebuttal. If you decide to challenge your review, you will want to write up a formal rebuttal. It should be short and to the point. Don't attack your boss or the organization. Stay positive and respectful, and control your anger or other negative emotions. Finally, address only the specific issues within the review that you feel were unfair.

The worst-case scenario. If you see that your performance review is really just a precursor to being let go, don't despair. This may be an opportunity in disguise. It might just be the impetus you need to find your true calling. As we have described throughout this book, there is no shortage of people who turned being "fired" into a success story. Thomas Edison was dismissed from his night-shift telegraph operator job at Western Union. Robert Redford was sacked from a manual labor job at Standard Oil. Madonna was let go after only one day as a counter clerk at Dunkin' Donuts. And early in his career, billionaire Mark Cuban was fired from his job as a computer-store salesman.[17]

Let's Get REAL

The Scenario:

Malik Green knows today is going to be challenging. As the manager of the pool at the local community center, safety is his top priority. Today he must give a disciplinary action to a part-time lifeguard who failed to follow safety procedures during a shift change at the pool. While he knows he needs to give the employee a warning, he is nervous about the disciplinary meeting. He wants to make sure he provides a clear warning and also encourages the lifeguard to use proper safety procedures moving forward.

What advice can you give Malik about giving the disciplinary action?

Prepare yourself for the conversation by having your talking points clearly defined to explain the logic behind your coaching of the policy. It is important to explain the reasoning behind the safety procedures being enforced. By doing so, the manager earns credibility that the culture he or she desires to create is built from commitment rather than compliance. Give the employee an opportunity to ask questions, define your expectations, and be sure the policy being enforced is clearly understood.

◄ **Kevin Krossber**
Director of Operations

Source: Kevin Krossber

Feedforward/Concurrent/Feedback Controls

Managers can implement controls *before* an activity begins, *during* the time the activity is going on, and *after* the activity has been completed.[18] The first type is called feedforward control; the second, concurrent control; and the last, feedback control (see Exhibit 18-8).

FEEDFORWARD CONTROL The most desirable type of control—**feedforward control**—prevents problems because it takes place before the actual activity.[19] For instance, hospital emergency rooms are looking to prevent mistakes such as an eighteen-year-old with fever and chills being sent home from the emergency room with Tylenol and later dying of sepsis, a blood infection; or a forty-two-year-old woman with chest pains being discharged, only to suffer a heart attack two hours later. Medical experts know that a serious ailment can look a lot like something else in the hubbub and chaos of the ER. So that's why many are setting protocols and oversights in place to prevent these kinds of mistakes.[20] When McDonald's opened its first restaurant in Moscow, it sent company quality-control experts to help Russian farmers learn techniques for growing high-quality potatoes and to help bakers learn processes for baking high-quality breads. Why? McDonald's demands consistent product quality no matter the geographical location. They want a cheeseburger in Moscow to taste like one in Omaha. Still another example of feedforward control is the scheduled preventive maintenance programs on nuclear power plants done by energy companies. These programs are designed to detect and prevent malfunctions that might lead to an accident.

The key to feedforward controls is taking managerial action *before* a problem occurs. That way, problems can be prevented rather than having to correct them after any damage (poor-quality products, lost customers, lost revenue, etc.) has already been done. However, these controls require timely and accurate information that isn't always easy to get. Thus, managers frequently end up using the other two types of control.

feedforward control
Control that takes place before a work activity is done

McDonald's uses feedforward control to ensure consistent product quality no matter the geographical location. When the global chain opened its first restaurant in Moscow, it sent company quality control experts to help Russian farmers learn techniques for growing high-quality potatoes and to help bakers learn processes for baking high-quality breads.
Source: Heorshe/Alamy Stock Photo

Exhibit 18-8
Types of Control

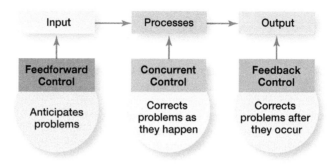

concurrent control
Control that takes place while a work
activity is in progress

CONCURRENT CONTROL **Concurrent control**, as its name implies, takes place while a work activity is in progress. For example, upholsterers for Rolls-Royce vehicles remove blemishes on leather hides before fitting them to the seat frames. The ongoing monitoring of material quality and proper assembly at every stage virtually eliminates producing a substandard product.

The best-known form of concurrent control is direct supervision. For example, Michael Bowman, former CEO of Valley Forge Casino Resort, worked alongside housekeepers to clean guest rooms.[21] He observed that it was taking too long to travel from one room to the next. By observing and listening to the housekeepers, Bowman learned that lengthy wait times for elevators were slowing them down. One housekeeper offered a solution: "Just block this elevator off from 7:00 in the morning until 9:00, so we just have it for the top floors."[22] Implementing this suggestion led to more rooms being cleaned on a timely basis. Harry Herington, CEO of information service provider NIC Inc., visits NIC branches across the US on his motorcycle to meet with his employees and see operations up-close. He calls his initiative "Ask the CEO."[23] All managers can benefit from using concurrent control, but especially first-line managers, because they can correct problems before they become too costly.

feedback control
Control that takes place after a work
activity is done

FEEDBACK CONTROL The most popular type of control relies on feedback. In **feedback control**, the control takes place *after* the activity is done. Most of the major automobile manufacturers, for instance, have extensive quality control departments that inspect cars as they come off the assembly line. Cars that don't meet quality standards are identified and sent back for correction. Note that with feedback quality control, problems are found after the fact. And that's the major problem with this type of control. By the time a manager has the information, the problems have already occurred, leading to waste, damage, and/or additional costs. However, in many work areas, feedback is the only viable type of control.

Feedback controls have two advantages. First, feedback gives managers meaningful information on how effective their planning efforts were. Feedback that shows little variance between standard and actual performance indicates that the planning was generally on target. If the deviation is significant, a manager can use that information to formulate new plans. Second, feedback can enhance motivation. People want to know how well they're doing, and feedback provides that information.

Let's now turn to look at some specific control tools that managers can use.

Financial Controls

Every business wants to earn a profit. To achieve this goal, managers need financial controls. For instance, they might analyze quarterly income statements for excessive expenses. They might also calculate financial ratios to ensure that sufficient cash is available to pay ongoing expenses, that debt levels haven't become too high, or that assets are used productively.

Exhibit 18-9 summarizes some of the most popular ratios used for financial control. Liquidity ratios measure an organization's ability to meet its current debt

Exhibit 18-9
Popular Financial Ratios

Objective	Ratio	Calculation	Meaning
Liquidity	Current ratio	$\dfrac{\text{Current assets}}{\text{Current liabilities}}$	Tests the organization's ability to meet short-term obligations
	Acid test	$\dfrac{\text{Current assets less inventories}}{\text{Current liabilities}}$	Tests liquidity more accurately when inventories turn over slowly or are difficult to sell
Leverage	Debt to assets	$\dfrac{\text{Total debt}}{\text{Total assets}}$	The higher the ratio, the more leveraged the organization
	Times interest earned	$\dfrac{\text{Profits before interest and taxes}}{\text{Total interest charges}}$	Measures how many times the organization is able to meet its interest expenses
Activity	Inventory turnover	$\dfrac{\text{Sales}}{\text{Inventory}}$	The higher the ratio, the more efficiently inventory assets are used
	Total asset turnover	$\dfrac{\text{Sales}}{\text{Total assets}}$	The fewer assets used to achieve a given level of sales, the more efficiently management uses the organization's total assets
Profitability	Profit margin on sales	$\dfrac{\text{Net profit after taxes}}{\text{Total sales}}$	Identifies the profits that are generated
	Return on investment	$\dfrac{\text{Net profit after taxes}}{\text{Total assets}}$	Measures the efficiency of assets to generate profits

obligations. Leverage ratios examine the organization's use of debt to finance its assets and whether it's able to meet the interest payments on its debt. Activity ratios assess how efficiently a company uses its assets. Finally, profitability ratios measure how efficiently and effectively the company uses its assets to generate profits. These ratios are calculated using selected information from the organization's two primary financial statements (the balance sheet and the income statement), which are then expressed as a percentage or ratio. Because you've probably studied these ratios in accounting or finance courses, or will in the near future, we aren't going to elaborate on how they're calculated. We mention them here to remind you that managers use such ratios as internal control tools.

Budgets are both planning and control tools. (See the Planning and Control Techniques module for more information on budgeting.) When a budget is formulated, it's a planning tool because it indicates which work activities are important and what and how much resources should be allocated to those activities. But budgets are also used for controlling, because they provide managers with quantitative standards against which to measure and compare resource consumption. If deviations are significant enough to require action, the manager examines what has happened and tries to uncover why. With this information, necessary action can be taken.

Information Controls

Guests who stayed at a Sheraton, Westin, W Hotels, St. Regis, Four Points, Aloft, Le Méridien, Tribute, or Element hotel between 2014 and September 2018 got a shock in November 2018. The Marriott-owned Starwood hotel brands revealed that its reservation system had been hacked and personal information on up to 500 million of its guests had been stolen.[24] This information included names, addresses, phone numbers, birthdates, email addresses, and encrypted credit card details. In some cases, travel histories and passport numbers were also taken. Needless to say, this was a huge embarrassment to Marriott and a black mark on the company's reputation.

Alicia Kiser ▶
Director of Human Resources

Source: Alicia Kiser

The Scenario:

Since she opened a boutique chocolate shop, Elyse Chung has been at the shop at all times when it has been open. She recognizes that it would be healthy for her to occasionally not be at the shop during operating hours. The three employees that she has hired know what needs to be done and have proven to be worthy of her trust.

What would you suggest to Elyse to help her feel that her shop is under control even when she isn't there?

While it sounds as though Elyse can count on her employees to handle the responsibility of managing the shop in her absence, it is always prudent to have processes and governance in place. Elyse should implement procedures for crucial components to running the operations of the shop—such as opening, closing, register reconciliation, and ordering—with checklists that need to be completed each day, so that these procedures can be audited. Elyse also should ensure she communicates to her employees her expectations and the consequences connected to not suitably managing the operations of the shop while she is out.

Marriott's experience is not unique. Similar attacks have occurred in the computer systems at Equifax, eBay, Target, and American Express. Protecting information is creating increasing demands for comprehensive information controls.

Managers deal with information controls in two ways: (1) as a tool to help them control other organizational activities and (2) as an organizational area they need to control.

HOW IS INFORMATION USED IN CONTROLLING? Managers need the right information at the right time and in the right amount to monitor and measure organizational activities and performance.

In measuring actual performance, managers need information about what is happening within their area of responsibility and about the standards in order to be able to compare actual performance with the standards. They also rely on information to help them determine if deviations are acceptable. Finally, they rely on information to help them develop appropriate courses of action. Most of the information tools managers use come from the organization's management information system.

A **management information system (MIS)** is a system used to provide managers with needed information on a regular basis. In theory, this system can be manual or computer based, although almost all organizations today have computer-supported applications. The term *system* in MIS implies order, arrangement, and purpose. Further, an MIS focuses specifically on providing managers with *information* (processed and analyzed data), not merely *data* (raw, unanalyzed facts). A library provides a good analogy. Although it can contain millions of volumes, a library doesn't do you any good if you can't find what you want quickly. That's why librarians spend a great deal of time cataloging a library's collections and ensuring that materials are returned to their proper locations. Organizations today are like well-stocked libraries. The issue is not a lack of data; instead, the issue is whether an organization has the ability to process that data so that the right information is available to the right person when he or she needs it. An MIS collects data and turns them into relevant information for managers to use.

management information system (MIS)
A system used to provide management with needed information on a regular basis

Chief engineer Ryan Egan demonstrates a new smart thermostat system installed at Chicago's riverside Sheraton hotel that will cut energy bills by $136,000 a year. This management information system will help the company operate at the highest levels of safety, efficiency, and reliability.
Source: Mira oberman/afp/Getty Images

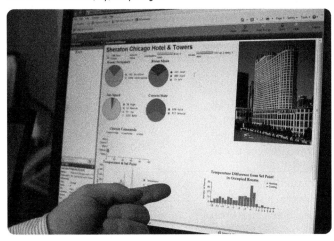

CONTROLLING INFORMATION A survey shows that 60 percent of companies had a network security breach in the past year.[25] Because information is critically important to everything an organization does, managers must have comprehensive and secure controls in place to protect that information. Such controls can range from data encryption to system firewalls to data backups. Problems can lurk in places that an organization might not have considered, like blogs, search engines, and Twitter accounts. Sensitive, defamatory, confidential, or embarrassing organizational information has found its way into search engine results. For instance, after Sony Pictures Entertainment's email servers were hacked, unflattering comments about numerous actors, directors, and producers showed up in Web searches.[26] Equipment such as tablet and laptop computers, smartphones, and even RFID tags are vulnerable to viruses and hacking. Needless to say, information controls should be monitored regularly to ensure that all possible precautions are in place to protect important information.

Balanced Scorecard

The **balanced scorecard** approach is a way to evaluate organizational performance from more than just the financial perspective.[27] A balanced scorecard typically looks at four areas that contribute to a company's performance: financial, customer, internal processes, and people/innovation/growth assets. According to this approach, managers should develop goals in each of the four areas and then measure whether the goals are being met.

Although a balanced scorecard makes sense, managers will tend to focus on areas that drive their organization's success and use scorecards that reflect those strategies.[28] For example, if strategies are customer centered, then the customer area is likely to get more attention than the other three areas. Yet, you can't focus on measuring only one performance area because others are affected as well. For instance, the United Kingdom treasury recommends that financial firms link executive teams to gender balance.[29] This recommendation is based on several studies that showed more diverse leadership leads to better financial returns. At IBM Global Services in Houston, managers developed a scorecard around an overriding strategy of customer satisfaction. However, the other three areas support that central strategy. The division manager described it as follows: "The internal processes part of our business is directly related to responding to our customers in a timely manner, and the learning and innovation aspect is critical for us since what we're selling our customers above all is our expertise. Of course, how successful we are with those things will affect our financial component."[30]

Benchmarking of Best Practices

We mentioned the Cleveland Clinic before as world renowned for delivering high-quality health care, with a top-ranked heart program that attracts patients from around the world. But what you may not realize is that it's also a model of cost-effective healthcare.[31] It could serve as a model for other healthcare organizations looking to be more effective and efficient.

Managers in such diverse industries as healthcare, education, and financial services are discovering what manufacturers have long recognized—the benefits of **benchmarking**, which is identifying, analyzing, and adopting the best practices from other organizations that lead to their superior performance.[32] Benchmarking seeks to identify various **benchmarks**, the standards of excellence against which to measure and compare. For instance, Target Corporation benchmarked Amazon by mimicking its online offerings, including recurring diaper delivery, free shipping, and member discounts.[33] And many firms use peer companies to benchmark their executive compensation.[34]

balanced scorecard
A performance measurement tool that looks at performance from more than just the financial perspective

benchmarking
Identifying, analyzing, and adopting the best practices from other organizations that lead to their superior performance

benchmark
The standard of excellence against which to measure and compare

The Cleveland Clinic is world renowned for delivering high-quality health care, with a top-ranked heart program that attracts patients from around the world. It's also a model of cost-effective health care and can serve as a benchmark for other health care organizations looking to be more effective and efficient.
Source: Mark Kanning/Alamy Stock Photo

Exhibit 18-10
Suggestions for Internal
Benchmarking

1. ***Connect best practices to strategies and goals.*** The organization's strategies and goals should dictate what types of best practices might be most valuable to others in the organization.
2. ***Identify best practices throughout the organization.*** Organizations must have a way to find out what practices have been successful in different work areas and units.
3. ***Develop best practices reward and recognition systems.*** Individuals must be given an incentive to share their knowledge. The reward system should be built into the organization's culture.
4. ***Communicate best practices throughout the organization.*** Once best practices have been identified, that information needs to be shared with others in the organization.
5. ***Create a best practices knowledge-sharing system.*** There needs to be a formal mechanism for organizational members to continue sharing their ideas and best practices.
6. ***Nurture best practices on an ongoing basis.*** Create an organizational culture that reinforces a "we can learn from everyone" attitude and emphasizes sharing information.[36]

At its most basic, benchmarking means learning from others. As a tool for monitoring and measuring organizational performance, benchmarking can be used to identify specific performance gaps and potential areas of improvement. And one of its primary benefits is that it allows management to gain an *independent* perspective on how well its organization is performing compared to others. But best practices aren't just found externally.

Sometimes those best practices can be found inside the organization and just need to be shared. One fertile area for finding good performance improvement ideas is an employee suggestion box. Best practices frequently already exist within an organization but often go unidentified and unnoticed. In today's environment, organizations seeking high performance levels can't afford to ignore such potentially valuable information. Some examples of internal benchmarks might include comparing the energy efficiency of your data centers against your most efficient center, comparing the revenue per employee for different business units, and comparing IT costs as a percentage of revenue for different business units.[35] Exhibit 18-10 provides some suggestions for internal benchmarking.

CONTEMPORARY issues in control

LO18.5 In this section, we look at five contemporary control issues: social media as a control tool, global differences in control, workplace privacy, employee theft, and corporate governance.

Social Media as a Control Tool

In the mid-1970s, New York City Mayor Abe Beame was famous for continually asking, "How 'm I doin?" If New York's mayor would ask that question today, he need only checkout social media sites to find the answer. Governments, along with businesses, are finding that social media can be a valuable tool for providing feedback on operations and services.[37] During the huge California fires that ravaged northern and southern California in 2018, government officials and rescue personnel relied on social media for information on where people were stranded, escape routes, and where best to direct resources.[38]

The potential of social media as a control tool is seen during two flooding events in the UK.[39] City officials were uncertain of peak depths and flood extents. Data from Twitter provided information that allowed officials to identify with detail and accuracy where the greatest problems were and to alert citizens.

Customers, clients, and citizens are congregating on social media. As a result, businesses and government agencies want to be there in order to leverage this medium for feedback on what their organizations are doing well and where they are lacking. Twenty years ago, if management wanted feedback from customers on the quality of their products or services, they did mail or phone surveys. Today, while those surveys are still widely used, they can be supplemented by monitoring social media for candid comments and assessments.

Global Differences in Control

The concepts of control that we've been discussing are appropriate for an organization whose work units are not geographically separated or culturally distinct. But control techniques can be quite different for different countries. The differences are primarily in the measurement and corrective action steps of the control process. In a global corporation, managers of foreign operations tend to be less controlled by the home office, if for no other reason than the distance, keeping managers from being able to observe work directly. Because distance creates a tendency to formalize controls, such organizations often rely on extensive formal reports for control, most of which are communicated electronically.

Technology's impact on control is also seen when comparing technologically advanced nations with less technologically advanced countries. Managers in countries where technology is more advanced often use indirect control devices such as computer-generated reports and analyses in addition to standardized rules and direct supervision to ensure that work activities are going as planned. In less technologically advanced countries, however, managers tend to use more direct supervision and highly centralized decision making for control.

Managers in foreign settings also need to be aware of constraints on investigating complaints and corrective actions they can take. Some countries' laws prohibit closing facilities, laying off employees, taking money out of the country, or bringing in a new management team from outside the country.

Another control challenge for global managers is comparability. For instance, a company that manufactures apparel in Cambodia might produce the same products at a facility in Scotland. However, the Cambodian facility might be more labor intensive than its Scottish counterpart to take advantage of lower labor costs in Cambodia. This difference makes it hard to compare, for instance, labor costs per unit.

Finally, global organizations need to have controls in place for protecting their workers and other assets during times of global turmoil and disasters. For instance, when the earthquake/tsunami hit Japan in 2011, companies scrambled to activate their disaster management plans. In the volatile Middle East, many companies have had to evacuate workers during times of crisis. The best time to be prepared is before an emergency occurs with feedforward controls.

Workplace Privacy

Do workers have a right to privacy at their job? You might be surprised at the answer. Employers can (and many do), among other things, read your email (even those marked "personal" or "confidential"), tap your telephone, monitor your work by computer, monitor you in an employee bathroom or dressing room, and track your whereabouts in a company vehicle.

One survey indicates that 66 percent of US companies monitor internet use, 45 percent log keystrokes, and 43 percent track emails.[41] There are consequences for employees who inappropriately surf the web or use email. And some companies do not limit monitoring computer use to just the

Many managers monitor employee email and computer usage. This is because many employees use the Internet for personal use at work, costing billions of dollars in lost work productivity annually. Also, managers want to monitor for any inappropriate workplace behavior that could trigger a lawsuit or create a hostile workplace environment.
Source: Frederic Cirou/PhotoAlto sas/Alamy Stock Photo

office. For instance, UPS tracks the location of delivery drivers, driving speed, and the number of daily deliveries. Their efforts have paid off. Tracking has allowed the company to deliver 1.4 million more packages per day with 1,000 fewer drivers.[42]

Some 26 percent of companies have fired an employee for email misuse; 26 percent have fired workers for misusing the internet; 6 percent have fired employees for inappropriate cell phone use; 4 percent have fired someone for instant messaging misuse; and 3 percent have fired someone for inappropriate text messaging.[43]

Why do managers feel they need to monitor what employees are doing? Employees are hired to work, not to surf the web checking stock prices, watching online videos, playing fantasy baseball, or shopping for presents for family or friends. A recent survey of adult Americans found that 50 percent admit to using the internet for personal use while at work.[44] This recreational on-the-job web surfing is thought to cost billions of dollars in lost work productivity annually.

Another reason why managers monitor employee email and computer usage is that they don't want to risk being sued for creating a hostile workplace environment because of offensive messages or an inappropriate image displayed on a coworker's computer screen. Concerns about racial or sexual harassment are one reason companies might want to monitor or keep backup copies of all email. Electronic records can help establish what actually happened so managers can react quickly.

Finally, managers want to ensure that company secrets aren't being leaked. In addition to typical email and computer usage, companies are monitoring instant messaging and banning camera phones in the office. Managers need to be certain that employees are not, even inadvertently, passing information on to others who could use that information to harm the company.

Because of the potentially serious costs, and given the fact that many jobs now entail computers, organizations have workplace monitoring policies. Such policies should control employee behavior in a nondemeaning way, and employees should be informed about those policies.

Employee Theft

At the Saks flagship store in Manhattan, a twenty-three-year-old sales clerk was caught ringing up $130,000 in false merchandise returns and putting the money onto a gift card.[45] And such practices regularly occur at other retailers.

Would you be surprised to find that up to 85 percent of all organizational theft and fraud is committed by employees, not outsiders?[46] And it's a costly problem—estimated in the US to be $50 billion a year.[47]

Employee theft is defined as any unauthorized taking of company property by employees for their personal use.[48] It can range from embezzlement to fraudulent filing of expense reports to removing equipment, parts, software, or office supplies from company premises. Although retail businesses have long faced serious potential losses from employee theft, loose financial controls at startups and small companies and the ready availability of information technology have made employee stealing an escalating problem in all kinds and sizes of organizations. Managers need to educate themselves about this control issue and be prepared to deal with it.[49]

Why do employees steal? The answer depends on whom you ask.[50] Experts in various fields—industrial security, criminology, clinical psychology—have different perspectives. The industrial security people propose that people steal because the opportunity presents itself through lax controls and favorable circumstances. Criminologists say it's because people have financial-based pressures (such as personal financial problems) or vice-based pressures (such as gambling debts). And the clinical psychologists suggest that people steal

employee theft
Any unauthorized taking of company property by employees for their personal use

Most organizational theft is committed by employees such as Alexander Didenko, manager of the Krasnopresnensky office of the Russian bank Sberbank, who here is being detained in the case of theft of more than 28 billion rubles (774 million dollars) from Russia's International Industrial Bank.
Source: Tass/Itar-Tass News Agency/Alamy Stock Photo

FEEDFORWARD	CONCURRENT	FEEDBACK
Use careful prehiring screening.	Treat employees with respect and dignity.	Make sure employees know when theft or fraud has occurred—not naming names but letting people know this is not acceptable.
Establish specific policies defining theft and fraud and discipline procedures.	Openly communicate the costs of stealing.	Use the services of professional investigators.
Involve employees in writing policies.	Let employees know on a regular basis about their successes in preventing theft and fraud.	Redesign control measures.
Educate and train employees about the policies.	Use video surveillance equipment if conditions warrant.	Evaluate your organization's culture and the relationships of managers and employees.
Have a professional review of your internal security controls.	Install "lock-out" options on computers, telephones, and email. Use corporate hotlines for reporting incidences. Set a good example.	

Exhibit 18-11

Controlling Employee Theft

Based on A. H. Bell and D. M. Smith, "Protecting the Company Against Theft and Fraud," *Workforce Management Online,* December 3, 2000; J. D. Hansen, "To Catch a Thief," *Journal of Accountancy,* March 2000, pp. 43–46; and J. Greenberg, "The Cognitive Geometry of Employee Theft," in *Dysfunctional Behavior in Organizations: Nonviolent and Deviant Behavior,* eds. S. B. Bacharach, A. O'Leary-Kelly, J. M. Collins, and R. W. Griffin (Stamford, CT: JAI Press, 1998), pp. 147–193.

because they can rationalize whatever they're doing as being correct and appropriate behavior ("everyone does it," "they had it coming," "this company makes enough money and they'll never miss anything this small," "I deserve this for all that I put up with," and so forth).[51] Regardless of the motive, what can managers do?

The concept of feedforward, concurrent, and feedback control is useful for identifying measures to deter or reduce employee theft. Exhibit 18-11 summarizes several possible managerial actions.

Corporate Governance

As chief executive at CBS, Leslie Moonves was one of the most powerful media heads in Hollywood. That, of course, should never have excused his more than twenty-year history of sexual misconduct. What made this disconcerting for CBS shareholders is that senior executives at CBS and selected members of the company's board of directors knew of Moonves's behavior and, out of loyalty to him, chose to ignore it.[52] Going back to as far as 1997, reports of Moonves's behavior had been reported to the Los Angeles Police Department. Multiple CBS executives knew this, yet chose to say nothing. The board finally acted—firing Moonves in 2018. This provides a clear example of corporate governance failure.

Corporate governance, the system used to govern a corporation so that the interests of corporate owners are protected, failed abysmally at CBS, as it has at many companies caught in various scandals. In an effort to improve corporate behavior and better protect their firms, senior management at an increasing number of companies have pushed for reforms.[53] Three areas where reform has taken place are changing the role of boards of directors, improving financial reporting, and expanding compliance offices.

corporate governance
The system used to govern a corporation so that the interests of corporate owners are protected

THE ROLE OF BOARDS OF DIRECTORS The original purpose of a board of directors was to have a group, independent from management, looking out for the interests of shareholders who were not involved in the day-to-day management of the organization. However, it hasn't always worked out that way. Board members are often selected by management and expected to be loyal and supportive of management's interests.

Senate Banking Chairman Paul S. Sarbanes and Financial Services ranking Democrat John LaFalce congratulate each other at the conclusion of the House Senate conference meeting during which the Sarbanes-Oxley Act passed with near unanimous support.
Source: Scott J. Ferrell/Congressional Quarterly/Newscom

corporate compliance
The process of making sure an organization and its employees follow the laws, regulations, standards, and ethical practices

compliance officer
The person responsible for ensuring an organization conducts its business in full compliance with all national and internal laws and regulations

This type of "quid pro quo" arrangement has changed. The Sarbanes-Oxley Act of 2002 puts greater demands on board members of publicly traded companies in the United States to do what they were empowered and expected to do.[54] To help boards do this better, the Business Roundtable—representing business leaders from every sector of the US economy—has developed a document outlining principles of corporate governance.[55] Its focus is on a commitment to governance practices that increase integrity, accountability, and effective engagement between public companies, boards of directors, and investors.

FINANCIAL REPORTING AND THE AUDIT COMMITTEE In addition to expanding the role of boards of directors, the Sarbanes-Oxley Act also called for more disclosure and transparency of corporate financial information. In fact, the CEO and CFO of public companies in the United States are now required to certify their companies' financial results. Such changes have led to better information—that is, information that is more accurate and reflective of a company's financial condition.

COMPLIANCE OFFICES AND POSITIONS In response to increased regulations, most large organizations have created a compliance office, appointed a senior executive as a compliance officer, and established corporate compliance policies.

Corporate compliance is the process of making sure your company and employees follow the laws, regulations, standards, and ethical practices that apply to your organization.[56] It covers both internal policies and rules and federal and state laws. Compliance policies are overseen by a **compliance officer**. This person's role is to ensure that your company conducts its business in full compliance with all national and internal laws and regulations that pertain to your specific industry, as well as professional standards, accepted business practices, and internal standards.

Pharmaceutical giant Bayer offers an example of a compliance policy.[57] It outlines Bayer's principles of business conduct. Among those principles are: to compete fairly in every market; to act with integrity in all business dealings; to balance economic growth with ecological and social responsibility; to keep accurate books and records; to treat all employees with fairness and respect; and to safeguard and respect company intellectual property.

Chapter 18 | PREPARING FOR: Exams/Quizzes

CHAPTER SUMMARY by Learning Objective

LO18.1 EXPLAIN the nature and importance of control.

Controlling is the process of monitoring, comparing, and correcting work performance. As the final step in the management process, controlling provides the link back to planning.

Control is important because (1) it's the only way to know if goals are being met, and if not, why; (2) it provides information and feedback so managers feel comfortable empowering employees; and (3) it helps protect an organization and its assets against threats and work disruptions.

LO18.2 DESCRIBE the three steps in the control process.

The three steps in the control process are measuring, comparing, and taking action. Measuring involves deciding how to measure actual performance and what to measure.

Actual performance can be measured by personal observation, statistical reports, self-monitoring computers, oral reports, and written reports. Comparing involves looking at the variation between actual performance and the standard (goal). Deviations outside an acceptable range of variation need attention.

Taking managerial action can involve doing nothing, correcting the actual performance, or revising the standards. Doing nothing is self-explanatory. Correcting the actual performance can involve different corrective actions, which can either be immediate or basic. Standards can be revised by either raising or lowering them.

LO18.3

EXPLAIN how organizational and employee performance are measured.

Organizational performance is the accumulated results of all the organization's work activities. Three frequently used organizational performance measures include (1) productivity, the amount of goods or services produced divided by the inputs needed to generate that output; (2) effectiveness, a measure of how appropriate organizational goals are and how well those goals are being met; and (3) industry and company rankings compiled by various business publications.

Employee performance is controlled through effective performance feedback and through disciplinary actions, when needed. Most organizations prefer that managers enact progressive disciplinary action, which is intended to ensure that the minimum penalty appropriate to the offense is imposed.

LO18.4

DESCRIBE tools used to measure organizational performance.

Feedforward controls take place before a work activity is done and are intended to prevent problems. Concurrent controls take place while a work activity is being done. Feedback controls take place after a work activity is done.

Financial controls that managers can use include financial ratios (liquidity, leverage, activity, and profitability) and budgets.

Managers approach information controls in two ways. Information control can be used as a tool to help them control other organizational activities and as an organizational area they need to control.

One information control managers can use is a management information system (MIS), which provides managers with needed information on a regular basis. Others include comprehensive and secure controls such as data encryption, system firewalls, and data backups that protect the organization's information.

Balanced scorecards provide a way to evaluate an organization's performance in four different areas rather than just from the financial perspective. Benchmarking provides control by finding the best practices among competitors or noncompetitors and from inside the organization itself.

LO18.5

DISCUSS contemporary issues in control.

Five management control issues are social media as a control tool, global differences in control, workplace privacy, employee theft, and corporate governance. For each of these issues, managers need to have policies in place to control inappropriate actions and ensure that work is getting done efficiently and effectively.

Social media provides rapid, candid feedback on operations and services. Social media often supplements customer surveys to indicate what organizations are doing well and where they are lacking.

Global differences in control are primarily in the areas of measuring and taking corrective actions. Organizations should clearly communicate to managers and employees how to approach and respond to routine and nonroutine situations within and outside the home country.

Employees who use the internet and social media for personal use are not entitled to privacy. Managers monitor employee email and computer usage due to lost productivity costs, risk of being sued for offensive messages, and fear of company secrets being leaked. Employees should be informed about companies' workplace monitoring policies.

Employee theft is costly to organizations. Procedures for monitoring theft and the consequences for committing a theft should be clearly explained to employees.

Corporate governance is the system used to govern a corporation so that the interests of corporate owners are protected. A board of directors looks out for the interests of shareholders. The Sarbanes-Oxley Act called for more disclosure and transparency of corporate financial information. Most large companies have created a corporate compliance office in order to ensure that business complies with laws and regulations.

REVIEW AND DISCUSSION QUESTIONS

18-1. What are the three steps in the control process? Describe in detail.

18-2. What is organizational performance?

18-3. Contrast feedforward, concurrent, and feedback controls.

18-4. Discuss the various types of tools used to monitor and measure organizational performance.

18-5. Explain the balanced scorecard approach to evaluating organizational performance.

18-6. Why is control important to customer interactions?

18-7. In Chapter 7 we discussed the white-water rapids view of change, which refers to situations in which unpredictable change is normal and expected and managing it is a continual process. Do you think it's possible to establish and maintain effective standards and controls in this type of environment? Discuss.

18-8. "Every individual employee in an organization plays a role in controlling work activities." Do you agree with this statement, or do you think control is something that only managers are responsible for? Explain.

PREPARING FOR: My Career

ETHICS DILEMMA

Cyber Monday falls on the first Monday following the Thanksgiving holiday. During Cyber Monday, employers find that a significant number of employees are surfing the web for holiday deals. A recent survey revealed that 64 percent of professionals planned on shopping online during working hours. Even though 53 percent of managers in the technology sector would prefer that employees not shop online while at work, 76 percent admitted that their company policies do not forbid it.[58]

18-9. What problems do you see here, especially as it relates to control?

18-10. How would you handle this? How could organizations make sure they're addressing work controls ethically?

SKILLS EXERCISE Managing Challenging Employees

About the Skill

In Chapter 13, we provided some advice on handling difficult coworkers. Difficult people can be even more challenging to manage. In this section, we expand on the ideas provided in Chapter 13 to provide further guidance in honing your skill as a manager in working with difficult people.

Almost all managers will, at one time or another, have to manage employees who are difficult. There is no shortage of characteristics that can make someone difficult to work with. Some examples include people being short-tempered, demanding, abusive, angry, defensive, complaining, intimidating, aggressive, narcissistic, arrogant, and rigid. Successful managers have learned how to manage difficult people and minimize their negative impact on fellow employees.

Steps in Practicing the Skill

No single approach is always effective in dealing with difficult people. However, we can offer several suggestions that are likely to lessen the angst caused by a difficult employee and may have some influence in reducing their difficult behavior.

- *Don't let your emotions rule.* Our first response to a difficult person is often emotional. We get angry. We show frustration. We want to lash out at them or "get even" when we think they've insulted or demeaned us. This response is not likely to reduce your angst and may escalate the other person's negative behavior. So fight your natural tendencies and keep your cool. Stay rational and thoughtful. At worst, while this approach may not improve the situation, it is also unlikely to encourage and escalate the undesirable behavior.

- *Attempt to limit contact.* If possible, try to limit your day-to-day interactions with the difficult employee. When appropriate, use communication channels—like email and text messaging—that minimize face-to-face contact and verbal intonations.

- *Try polite confrontation.* As a manager it is your responsibility to address the behavior. Let them know that you're aware of their behavior, that you find it

unacceptable, and that you won't tolerate it. For people who are unaware of the effect their actions have on you, confrontation might awaken them to altering their behavior. For those who are acting purposefully, taking a clear stand might make them think twice about the consequences of their actions.

- *Practice positive reinforcement.* We know that positive reinforcement is a powerful tool for changing behavior. Rather than criticizing undesirable behavior, try reinforcing desirable behaviors with compliments or other positive comments. This focus will tend to weaken and reduce the exhibiting of the undesirable behaviors.[59]

Practicing the Skill

Consider a difficult person you have had to deal with in the past: Someone you've worked with? Another student? Write down the person's behaviors that you found challenging or difficult. Consider the strategies that you used to deal with this person. What worked? What didn't work? Using the steps above, what could you do differently to work more effectively with this person? Now, think about what you would do if you were a manager and this person was your direct report. Write down the steps you could take to effectively manage this person and also limit the negative impact of this person's behavior on other employees.

WORKING TOGETHER **Team Exercise**

Providing effective feedback is an important control technique for any manager. In groups of three or four, building on the scenarios below, take turns being the person to provide feedback to another group member while the other group members watch and listen. After each person provides feedback based on a scenario below, discuss as a group how effective the feedback was provided as well as how it could be improved using the suggestions included in the "It's Your Career" box.

Use the following scenarios to provide feedback. Add details (that you make up) when providing feedback regarding the scenario you choose:

1. The employee hasn't been managing time well, which is affecting the department's ability to complete projects effectively for clients.

2. The employee has been underperforming in the last month. You have discussed this with the employee once before. The problem has persisted despite this earlier conversation.

3. Your department has a technological device that is shared among all members of the department. After using the device, you are supposed to return it to a central location for others to use. The employee has been using the device and not returning it, which has disrupted the workflow of other department members.

4. The employee tends to do what he or she is told, but does not take initiative beyond those requests.

MY TURN TO BE A MANAGER

- You have a major class project due in a month. Identify some performance measures you could use to help determine whether the project is going as planned and will be completed efficiently (on time) and effectively (with high quality).

- How could you use the concept of control in your personal life? Be specific. (Think in terms of feedforward, concurrent, and feedback controls as well as specific controls for the different aspects of your life—school, work, family relationships, friends, hobbies, etc.)

- Survey thirty people as to whether they have experienced office rage. Ask them specifically whether they have experienced any of the following: yelling or other verbal abuse from a coworker, yelling at coworkers themselves, crying over work-related issues, seeing someone purposely damaging equipment or furniture, seeing physical violence in the workplace, or striking a coworker. Compile your findings in a table. Are you surprised at the results? Be prepared to present these in class.

- Pretend you're the manager of a customer call center for timeshare vacations. What types of control measures would you use to see how efficient and effective an employee is? How about measures for evaluating the entire call center?

- Disciplining employees is one of the least favorite tasks of managers, but it is something that all managers have to do. Survey three managers about their experiences with employee discipline. What types of employee actions have caused the need for disciplinary action?

What disciplinary actions have they used? What do they think is the most difficult thing to do when disciplining employees? What suggestions do they have for disciplining employees?

- Exhibit 18-6 lists several industry and company ranking lists. Find the website for 3 lists and identify the performance measures that are used to determine the rankings on each. Are there any similar measures? Any unique measures? Summarize your findings in a brief report.

CASE APPLICATION 1 — Bug Bounty Hackers at General Motors

When General Motors (GM) decided to start a bug bounty program—paying hackers to find computer bugs in the company's information systems—they purposely tried to avoid other companies' mistakes with such programs. Uber ended up paying hackers more than ten times the amount that they had originally allotted, partly to avoid hackers destroying customer data they had downloaded.[60] Uber made changes to their bug bounty program after that, making it more clear what hackers should not do. Uber's experience showed the potential problems that can occur when hackers try to profit from the problems they find.

GM didn't want to face the challenges involved in overpaying, underpaying, or getting into arguments whether a payment was deserved for its bounty hackers. In fact, GM didn't pay bounty hackers at all at first. During the first stage in the GM program, hackers who reported bugs were given a direct link to GM's security team. "Having that reporting system in place sent the message to hackers that the company was serious about security," said Jeff Massimilla, a GM cybersecurity executive. After two years of building relationships with hackers, GM started paying for bugs. Just two years later, the select group of hackers in the company's bug bounty program had found 700 bugs.

GM's bug bounty program is only one part of its three-prong approach to cybersecurity. What are the other prongs? Their staff includes twenty-five to thirty "white hat hackers" who sometimes are called ethical hackers.[61] White hat hackers' work focuses on ensuring that a company's information systems aren't subject to security breaches. GM also works with third-party companies that hire more white hat hackers. They have to use the bounty program and third-party companies in addition to full-time internal hackers, since there is a shortage of white hat hackers.

White hat hackers not only need technical skills, but they also need to be trusted to work for the benefit of the companies that employ them. People with hacking skills often would rather not work for just one company and like flexibility and working from home. GM's three-prong approach also was designed to catch more bugs. "If you have so many different perspectives coming together, it's very different than having your own internal hackers who are all probably trained using the same processes," said Massimilla.[62]

DISCUSSION QUESTIONS

18-11. Bug bounty programs and hiring white hat hackers are forms of information controls. What are other forms of information controls mentioned in the chapter?

18-12. When a bug is found through a bug bounty program, do you think managers are more likely to take immediate corrective action or basic corrective action? What are the reasons for your answer?

18-13. What are the dangers versus the benefits of hiring hackers? Why have companies decided that there are more benefits than dangers in accomplishing the process of controlling via hiring hackers?

Posting for Just Other Employees to See

When Walmart wanted to find a way to connect employees throughout the company—including those who do not sit at desks and might not use email—they turned to a known social media platform, Facebook. Only they didn't use the same Facebook that employees are used to. They launched Workplace by Facebook, which is a separate application that has the look of Facebook. The hope is that the familiar interface increases employees' use of Workplace.

What can Walmart employees do with their Workplace app? It's intended to be a platform for exchanging ideas and giving employees a voice. It also allows managers to have another view into what is going on in their stores. Employees across the country can communicate with each other by posting pictures of in-store product displays and sharing what has worked well in their store.[63] If a new product is rolled out on a trial basis in a few select stores, stories about how to make that product a success can be shared.

There's also the possibility of employees' ideas being implemented at rapid speed as a result of Workplace posts. Take what happened at Starbucks. It was because of an employee's post on Starbucks's Workplace site that the company made a decision in just one day to add a new beverage to their menu. A store manager shared via Workplace that his store was selling a lot of a beverage featured on Instagram, but he and his coworkers didn't have an exact recipe. Other store managers chimed in how much they were selling of the same beverage. Marketing managers who kept up with the discussion on Workplace made a decision that very day to provide an official recipe for the drink and get it on the menu right away. Usually a decision like that would take months, but they were able to make the change especially quickly due to the combination of Instagram and Workplace.[64]

Employees' accomplishments and success stories also can be shared with others in a company. That sharing promotes employee engagement and reduces employee turnover.[65] Workplace "usually replaces mailing lists, newsletters, intranets that no one is using. And the behavior we want to replace is the CEO sending an email that no one replies to. That new generation of CEOs want feedback,"[66] explains Julien Codorniou, Workplace director.

Social media use by employees can lead to problems, like accidentally disclosing confidential information.[67] But Workplace is different since it's not for those outside of the company to see. The problem of employees using company time to view ads is not an issue since the app doesn't have ads. Instead it generates revenue based on subscription fees by charging companies $3 per month per employee.

DISCUSSION QUESTIONS

18-14. How did Starbucks use social media as a control tool?

18-15. In what ways does employees' use of Workplace allow employers to monitor employees' activities at work in both positive and potentially negative ways?

18-16. How could Workplace have an impact on organizational performance?

18-17. Some employees might not feel drawn to using Workplace. What do you think managers might need to do to increase the chances that employees would choose to use Workplace?

ENDNOTES

1. J. Bilski, "Workers Gone Wild: 7 Outrageous Cases of Employee Fraud," *CFO Daily News*, July 13, 2018, http://www.cfodailynews.com/workers-gone-wild-7-outrageous-cases-of-employee-fraud/.

2. E. Harrington, "Social Security Paid 740 Dead People at Least $17.1 Million," Washington Free Beacon, March 13, 2015, https://freebeacon.com/issues/social-security-paid-740-dead-people-at-least-17-1-million/.

3. R. Nixon, "Airport Security Delays Won't End Soon, T.S.A. Chief Says," *New York Times*, May 25, 2016, https://www.nytimes.com/2016/05/26/us/politics/airport-security-delays-wont-end-soon-tsa-chief-says.html.

4. For a review of organizational control, see L. B. Cardinal, M. Kreutzer, and C. C. Miller, "An Aspirational View of Organizational Control Research: Re-Invigorating Empirical Work to Better Meet the Challenges of the 21st Century Organizations," *Academy of Management Annals* 11, no, 2 (June 2017): pp. 559–92.

5. S. Kerr, "On the Folly of Rewarding A, While Hoping for B," *Academy of Management Journal* (December 1975): pp. 769–783; and T. A. Wright, R. W. Stackman, J. Hollwitz, and A. S. DeGroat, "Further Thoughts on Kerr's 'Folly' and Repeat Offenses: Where We Are, Have Been, and Are Going," *Journal of Management Inquiry* 27, no. 3 (July 2018): pp. 316–24.

6. "The Cop-Out Cops," *National Observer*, August 3, 1974.

7. D. Kopf, "Data Analytics Have Made the NBA Unrecognizable," *Quartz*, October 18, 2017, https://qz.com/1104922/data-analytics-have-revolutionized-the-nba/; and R. Anderson, "How the NBA Uses Data & Analytics," *Medium*, August 16, 2018, https://medium.com/@randerson112358/how-the-nba-uses-data-analytics-6eac3c43a096.

8. C. Isidore, "1 Million Walmart Workers Get a Raise on Saturday," *CNN*, February 18, 2016, https://money.cnn.com/2016/02/18/news/companies/walmart-worker-pay-raise/index.html; and P. Ziobro and S. Ng, "Wal-Mart Ratchets Up Pressure on Suppliers to Cut Prices," *Wall Street Journal*, March 31, 2015, https://www.wsj.com/articles/wal-mart-ratchets-up-pressure-on-suppliers-to-cut-prices-1427845404.

9. Ziobro and Ng, "Wal-Mart Ratchets Up."

10. "Fortune's 100 Best Companies to Work For 2018," *Fortune*, accessed March 5, 2019, fortune.com.

11. "What Employees Say," *Great Places to Work*, reviews.greatplacetowork.com/wegmans-food-markets.

12. Based on C. R. Mill, "Feedback: The Art of Giving and Receiving Help," in *The Reading Book for Human Relations Training*, eds. L. Porter and C. R. Mill (Bethel, ME: NTL Institute for Applied Behavioral Science, 1976); S. Bishop, *The Complete Feedback Skills Training Book* (Aldershot, UK: Gower Publishing, 2000); and A. Tugend, "You've Been Doing a Fantastic Job. Just One Thing ...," *New York Times*, April 5, 2013, https://www.nytimes.com/2013/04/06/your-money/how-to-give-effective-feedback-both-positive-and-negative.html.

13. A. H. Jordan and P. G. Audia, "Self-Enhancement and Learning from Performance Feedback," *Academy of Management Review* 37, no. 2 (April 2012): pp. 211–231; D. Busser, "Delivering Effective Performance Feedback," *T&D*, April 2012, pp. 32–34; and "U.S. Employees Desire More Sources of Feedback for Performance Reviews," *T&D*, February 2012, p. 18.

14. J. Burnett, "Survey: Managers Spend 26% of Their Time Coaching Bad Employees," *Ladders*, May 16, 2018, https://www.theladders.com/career-advice/survey-managers-spend-more-than-10-hours-a-week-on-poorly-performing-employees.

15. "Apply This Fair and Firm 5-Step Progressive Discipline Policy," *TCA Regional News*, November 3, 2016.

16. P. Falcone, "Progressive Discipline: Answers to More of Your Common Questions," *HR News*, August 11, 2017.

17. Based on S. P. Robbins, *The Truth About Managing People*, 3rd ed. (Upper Saddle River, NJ: Pearson Education, 2013), pp. 199–201; "How to Handle an Unfair or Negative Performance Review at Work," *HubPages*, November 5, 2014, https://hubpages.com; "Survey: Performance Reviews Drive One in Four Millennials to Search for a New Job or Call in Sick," Newstex finance and accounting blogs, October 28, 2015; and "How to Write a Rebuttal to an Unfair Performance Review," *Law Office of Arkady Itkin*, November 16, 2015, http://www.arkadylaw.com/employment-law-blog/how-to-write-a-rebuttal-to-unfair-performance-review.

18. See, for instance, A. Fowler, "Feedback and Feedforward as Systematic Frameworks for Operations Control," *International Journal of Operations & Production Management* 19, no. 2 (1999): pp. 182–204.

19. H. Koontz and R. W. Bradspies, "Managing Through Feedforward Control," *Business Horizons* 15, no. 3 (June 1972): pp. 25–36.

20. L. Landro, "Hospitals Overhaul ERs to Reduce Mistakes," *Wall Street Journal,* May 10, 2011, p. D3.

21. J. M. Von Bergen, "CEO Lesson: Walking in the Workers' Shoes," philly.com, September 21, 2015, http://www.philly.com/philly/blogs/jobs/INQ_Jobbing_CEO-lesson-Walking-in-the-workers-shoes-hotels-Valley-Forge-Bowman.html.

22. Ibid.

23. S. Vozza, "10 Unique Ways Leaders Bond with Employees," *Fast Company*, September 18, 2015, https://www.fastcompany.com/3050651/10-unique-ways-leaders-bond-with-employees.

24. N. Perlroth, A. Tsang, and A. Satariano, "Marriott Hacking Exposes Data of Up to 500 Million Guests," *New York Times*, November 30, 2018, https://www.nytimes.com/2018/11/30/business/marriott-data-breach.html.

25. B. Acohido, "To Be a Hacker, You'd Better Be Sneaky," *USA Today,* February 28, 2013, p. 2B.

26. M. Boardman, "Angelina Jolie Blasted as 'Minimally Talented Spoiled Brat' by Producer Scott Rudin in Leaked Sony Emails," *Us Weekly*, December 10, 2014, https://www.usmagazine.com/celebrity-news/news/angelina-jolie-called-spoiled-brat-by-scott-rudin-in-leaked-emails-20141012/.

27. H. Sundin, M. Granlund, and D. A. Brown, "Balancing Multiple Competing Objectives with a Balanced Scorecard," *European Accounting Review* 19, no. 2 (2010): pp. 203–246; T. Leahy, "Tailoring the Balanced Scorecard," *Business Finance,* August 2000, pp. 53–56; K. Hendricks, M. Hora, L. Menor, and C. Wiedman, "Adoption of the Balance Scorecard: A Contingency Variables Analysis," *Canadian Journal of Administrative Sciences* 29, no. 2 (June 2012): pp. 124–138; R. Gibbons and R. S. Kaplan, "Formal Measures in Informal Management: Can a Balanced Scorecard Change a Culture?," *American Economic Review* 105, no. 5 (May 2015): pp. 447–51;

and J. Llach, L. Bagur, J. Perramon, and F. Marimon, "Creating Value Through the Balanced Scorecard: How Does It Work?," *Management Decision* 55, no. 10 (2017): pp. 2181–99.

28. Leahy, "Tailoring the Balanced Scorecard."

29. M. Lemos Stein, "The Morning Risk Report: U.K. Report Highlights Gender Issues," *Wall Street Journal* (blog), March 24, 2016, https://blogs.wsj.com/riskandcompliance/2016/03/24/the-morning-risk-report-u-k-report-highlights-gender-issues/.

30. Ibid.

31. See, for instance, J. Merlino and A. Raman, "Health Care's Service Fanatics," *Harvard Business Review*, May 2013, pp. 108–16; and J. K. Stoller, "The Cleveland Clinic: A Distinctive Model of American Medicine," *Annals of Translational Medicine* 2, no. 4 (April 2014) p. 33.

32. V. Ferreira de Castro and E. M. Frazzon, "Benchmarking of Best Practices: An Overview of the Academic Literature," *Benchmarking: An International Journal* 24, no. 3 (2017): pp. 750–74; and A.-L. Ghete, L.-L. Cioca, and R. Belu, "Benchmarking in Manufacturing Companies," *FAIMA Business & Management Journal*, March 2018, pp. 45–51.

33. P. Ziobro, "Target Fills Its Cart with Amazon Ideas," *Wall Street Journal,* November 12, 2013, pp. B1+.

34. M. Murphy, "Some Compensation Peer Groups Draw a Crowd," *Wall Street Journal*, November 24, 2015, https://blogs.wsj.com/cfo/2015/11/24/some-compensation-peer-groups-draw-a-crowd/.

35. J. Spacey, "Six Types of Internal Benchmarking," *Simplicable*, April 26, 2017, https://simplicable.com/new/internal-benchmarking.

36. Based on T. Leahy, "Extracting Diamonds in the Rough," *Business Finance*, August 2000.

37. M. W. Graham, E. J. Avery, and S. Park, "The Role of Social Media in Local Government Crisis Communications," *Public Relations Review* 41, no. 3 (September 2015): pp. 386–94.

38. C. Miller, "Does Social Media Belong in Today's Fire Service?," *Fire Fighter Nation*, July 30, 2018, https://www.firefighternation.com/articles/2018/07/does-social-media-belong-in-today-s-fire-service.html.

39. L. Smith, "Assessing the Utility of Social Media as a Data Source for Flood Risk Management Using a Real-Time Modeling Framework," *Journal of Flood Risk Management* 10, no. 3 (September 2017): pp. 370–80.

40. "90% of Social Media Users Reach Out to Retailers. Why Social Media is Your Secret Weapon.," *V12*, August 5, 2018, https://www.v12data.com/blog/90-percent-social-media-users-reach-out-retailers-why-social-media-your-secret-weapon/.

41. B. Chloe, "The Rising Trend of Employee Spying at Workplace," *TheOneSpy* (blog), March 13, 2018, https://www.theonespy.com/rising-trend-of-employee-spying-at-workplace/.

42. "The Rise of Workplace Spying," *The Week*, July 5, 2015, https://theweek.com/articles/564263/rise-workplace-spying.

43. L. Petrecca, "Feel Like Someone's Watching? You're Right," *USA Today,* March 17, 2010, pp. 1B+.

44. "Half of Americans Use the Internet for Personal Reasons While at Work, Says Findlaw.com Survery," Thomson Reuters, November 23, 2015, https://www.thomsonreuters.com/en/press-releases/2015/november/americans-use-internet-personal-reasons-at-work-findlaw-survey.html.

45. S. Greenhouse, "Shoplifters? Studies Say Keep an Eye on Workers," *New York Times*, December 30, 2009.

46. A. M. Bell and D. M. Smith, "Theft and Fraud May Be an Inside Job," *Workforce*, December 3, 2000. https://www.workforce.com/2000/05/15/theft-and-fraud-may-be-an-inside-job/.

47. "Employee Theft Costs U.S. Businesses $50 Billion per Year," *Security*, November 1, 2017, https://www.securitymagazine.com/articles/88432-employee-theft-costs-us-businesses-50-billion-per-year.

48. J. Greenberg, "The STEAL Motive: Managing the Social Determinants of Employee Theft," in *Antisocial Behavior in Organizations*, eds. R. Giacalone and J. Greenberg (Newbury Park, CA: Sage, 1997), pp. 85–108.

49. B. P. Niehoff and R. J. Paul, "Causes of Employee Theft and Strategies That HR Managers Can Use for Prevention," *Human Resource Management* 39, no. 1 (March 2000): pp. 51–64; B. E. Litzky, K. A. Eddleston, and D. L. Kidder, "The Good, the Bad, and the Misguided: How Managers Inadvertently Encourage Deviant Behaviors," *Academy of Management Executive* 20, no. 1 (February 2006): pp. 91–103;

and S. Peters and B. Maniam, "Corporate Fraud and Employee Theft: Impacts and Costs on Business," *Journal of Business and Behavioral Sciences* 28, no. 2 (Fall 2016): pp. 104–17.

50. This section is based on J. Greenberg, *Behavior in Organizations: Understanding and Managing the Human Side of Work,* 8th ed. (Upper Saddle River, NJ: Prentice Hall, 2003), pp. 329–330.

51. "Why Employees Steal, and How to Handle It," *HR Specialist*, April 13, 2016, https://www.thehrspecialist.com/23224/why-employees-steal-and-how-to-handle-it.

52. J. B. Stewart, "CBS Report on Moonves Cites Failure of Oversight," *New York Times*, December 5, 2018, p. B1.

53. See, for instance, G. Subramanian, "Corporate Governance 2.0," *Harvard Business Review*, March 2015, https://hbr.org/2015/03/corporate-governance-2-0; and N. Zhong, S. Wang, and R. Yang, "Does Corporate Governance Enhance Common Interests of Shareholders and Primary Stakeholders?," *Journal of Business Ethics* 141, no. 2 (March 2017): pp. 411–31.

54. D. Salierno, "Boards Face Increased Responsibility," *Internal Auditor,* June 2003, pp. 14–15; and T. Clarke, "The Widening Scope of Directors' Duties: The Increasing Impact of Corporate Social and Environmental Responsibility," *Seattle University Law Review* 39, no. 2 (2016): pp. 531–78.

55. "Business Roundtable Applauds Release of Commonsense Principles of Corporate Governance 2.0," *Business Roundtable*, October 18, 2018, https://www.businessroundtable.org/business-roundtable-applauds-release-of-commonsense-principles-of-corporate-governance-20.

56. "What Is Corporate Compliance and Why It's Important," *PowerDMS*, April 5, 2018, https://www.powerdms.com/blog/what-corporate-compliance-is-why-compliance-is-important/.

57. W. Baumann, "Corporate Compliance Policy: Conducting the Business According to Applicable Law and Company Rules," Bayer AG website, https://www.bayer.com/en/corporate-compliance-policy.aspx.

58. "Over Half of Tech Leaders Don't Want Staff to Shop Online at Work, but 64 Percent of Employees Plan on 'Workshopping' This Holiday Season." *Robert Half*, November 15, 2018, http://rh-us.mediaroom.

com/2018-11-15-Over-Half-Of-Tech-Leaders-Dont-Want-Staff-To-Shop-Online-At-Work-But-64-Percent-Of-Employees-Plan-On-Workshopping-This-Holiday-Season.

59. Based on N. Pelusi, "Dealing with Difficult People," *Psychology Today*, September–October 2006, pp. 68–69; and R. I. Sutton, *The No Asshole Rule: Building a Civilized Workplace and Surviving One That Isn't* (New York: Business Plus, 2007).

60. R. McMillan, "Software Bugs Have a Bounty on Their Heads," *Wall Street Journal*, May 29, 2018, https://www.wsj.com/articles/software-bugs-have-a-bounty-on-their-heads-1527646200.

61. J. L. Lareau, "Hottest Auto Job in Town: Hacking: Finding Security Flaws Helps Prevent Malicious Attacks," *Detroit Free Press*, August 20, 2018, https://www.freep.com/.

62. A. Loten and J. Stone, "GM Calls in the Bug Bounty Hunters," *Wall Street Journal Pro Cyber Security*, August 7, 2018.

63. N. Levy, "WalMart Joins 'Workplace by Facebook,' Boosting Social Giant's Collaboration Tools," *GeekWire*, September

26, 2017, https://www.geekwire.com/2017/walmart-joins-workplace-facebook-boosting-social-giants-collaboration-tools/.

64. "Walmart and Workplace by Facebook," *Prepp*, accessed February 22, 2019, https://prepp.io/walmart-and-workplace-by-facebook/.

65. L. Bizzi, "Employees Who Use Social Media For Work Are More Engaged—But Also More Likely to Leave Their Jobs," *Harvard Business Review*, May 17, 2018, https://hbr.org/2018/05/employees-who-use-social-media-for-work-are-more-engaged-but-also-more-likely-to-leave-their-jobs.

66. P. Olyson, "Facebook's Workplace Takes On Slack with AI, Newsfeeds–and Zero Ads," *Forbes*, October 11, 2018, https://www.forbes.com/sites/parmyolson/2018/10/11/facebooks-workplace-takes-on-slack-with-ai-newsfeedsand-zero-ads/#6a9382a51269.

67. S. Marquez, "Should Companies Let Employees Use Social Media While at Work?," *Wall Street Journal*, May 29, 2018, https://www.wsj.com/articles/should-companies-let-employees-use-social-media-at-work-1527645780.

Planning and Control Techniques *Module*

Managers at the Disney World Magic Kingdom and Disneyland theme parks decided to charge higher ticket prices during peak visiting times and lower prices during less busy times. The higher prices minimized excessive crowds and provided a better customer experience. By lowering prices at other times, management sought to attract price-sensitive consumers to the parks. Disney spokesperson Jacquee Wahler said, "We continue to evolve the way we think about managing demand—particularly during our busiest seasons—in order to deliver a world-class experience for our guests."[1] This approach by Disney is an example of demand pricing. If it works, Disney expects to increase revenue and improve customer satisfaction.

As this example shows, managers use planning tools and techniques to help their organizations be more efficient and effective. In this module, we discuss three categories of basic planning tools and techniques: techniques for assessing the environment, techniques for allocating resources, and contemporary planning techniques.

TECHNIQUES for assessing the environment

In our description of the planning and strategic management processes in Chapters 8 and 9, we discussed the importance of assessing the organization's environment. Two techniques help managers do that: environmental scanning and forecasting.

Environmental Scanning

How can managers become aware of significant environmental changes, such as a new law in Germany permitting shopping for "tourist items" on Sunday; the increased trend of counterfeit consumer products in South Africa; the precipitous decline in the working-age populations in Japan, Germany, and Italy; or the decrease in family size in Mexico? Managers in both small and large organizations use environmental scanning. As we discussed in Chapter 8, environmental scanning is an important element of the strategic planning process. The goal is to detect emerging trends by screening of large amounts of information to anticipate and interpret changes in the environment. Research has shown that companies that use environmental scanning have higher performance.[2]

There are two fast-growing areas of environmental scanning: competitor intelligence and global scanning. As we discussed in Chapter 8, competitor intelligence is a process by which organizations gather information about their competitors and get answers to questions such as: Who are they? What are they doing? How will what they're doing affect us? Let's look at an example of how one organization used competitor intelligence in its planning. Dun & Bradstreet (D&B), a leading provider of business information, has an active business intelligence division. The division manager received a call from an assistant vice president for sales in one of the company's geographic territories. This person had been on a sales call with a major customer and the customer happened to mention in passing that another company had visited and made a major presentation about its services. It was interesting because, although D&B had plenty of competitors, this particular company wasn't one of them. The manager gathered together a team that sifted through dozens of sources (research services, Internet, personal contacts, and other external sources) and quickly became convinced that there was something to this; that this company was "aiming its guns right at us." Managers at D&B jumped into action to develop plans to counteract this competitive attack.[3] However, jumping into action is not always a prudent choice. Competitive intelligence may also suggest that disengagement from a course of action is most appropriate. For instance, in a survey of managers, one respondent stated that competitive intelligence "identified only a single competitor, while determining others did not have the business case to continue a pursuit."[4]

Competitor intelligence experts suggest that 80 percent of what managers need to know about competitors can be found out from their own employees, suppliers, customers, and online searches.[5] Competitor intelligence doesn't have to involve spying. Advertisements, promotional materials, press releases, reports filed with government agencies, annual reports, job listings, newspaper reports, and industry studies are examples of readily accessible sources of information. Attending trade shows and debriefing the company's sales force can be other good sources of competitor information. Many firms regularly buy competitors' products and have their own engineers study them (i.e., *reverse engineering*) to learn about new technical innovations. In addition, many corporate web pages include new product information and other press releases.

Managers need to be careful about the way competitor information is gathered to prevent any concerns about whether it's legal or ethical. Competitor intelligence becomes illegal corporate spying when it involves the theft of proprietary materials or trade secrets by any means. The Economic Espionage Act makes it a crime in the United States to engage in economic espionage or to steal a trade secret. But espionage is a global problem. For example, U.S. Steel claims that Chinese government hackers broke into its servers and stole proprietary plans for developing new steel technology.[6] The difficult decisions about competitive intelligence arise because often there's a fine line between *legal and ethical* and *legal but unethical.* Some people or companies will go to any lengths—some unethical—to get information about competitors.

Global scanning is another type of environmental scanning that's particularly important. Because world markets are complex and dynamic, managers have expanded the scope of their scanning efforts to gain vital information on global forces that might affect their organizations. The value of global scanning to managers, of course, largely depends on the extent of the organization's global activities. For a company with significant global interests, global scanning can be quite valuable. For instance, Carnival Cruise Lines actively strives to expand the number of itineraries to more regions of the world. Their efforts have paid off. A Carnival cruise ship sailed from the United States to Cuba, making it the first passenger excursion by a US-based cruise operator in more than fifty years.[7] All the while, other US cruise lines were still negotiating access with the Cuban government.[8]

Because the sources that managers use for scanning the domestic environment are too limited for global scanning, managers must globalize their perspectives. For instance, they can subscribe to information-clipping services that review world newspapers and business periodicals and provide summaries of desired information. Also, numerous electronic services will provide topic searches and automatic updates in global areas of special interest to managers.

Forecasting

The second technique managers can use to assess the environment is forecasting. Forecasting is an important part of planning, and managers need forecasts that will allow them to predict future events effectively and in a timely manner. Environmental scanning establishes the basis for **forecasts**, which are predictions of outcomes. Virtually any component in an organization's environment can be forecasted. Let's look at how managers forecast and the effectiveness of those forecasts.

forecasts
Predictions of outcomes

FORECASTING TECHNIQUES Forecasting techniques fall into two categories: quantitative and qualitative. **Quantitative forecasting** applies a set of mathematical rules to a series of past data to predict outcomes. These techniques are preferred when managers have sufficient hard data that can be used. **Qualitative forecasting**, in contrast, uses the judgment and opinions of knowledgeable individuals to predict outcomes. Qualitative techniques typically are used when precise data are limited or hard to obtain. Exhibit PC-1 describes some popular forecasting techniques.

quantitative forecasting
Forecasting that applies a set of mathematical rules to a series of past data to predict outcomes

qualitative forecasting
Forecasting that uses the judgment and opinions of knowledgeable individuals to predict outcomes

Exhibit PC-1
Forecasting Techniques

Technique	Description	Application
Quantitative		
Time series analysis	Fits a trend line to a mathematical equation and projects into the future by means of this equation	Predicting next quarter's sales on the basis of four years of previous sales data
Regression models	Predicts one variable on the basis of known or assumed other variables	Seeking factors that will predict a certain level of sales (e.g., price, advertising expenditures)
Econometric models	Uses a set of regression equations to simulate segments of the economy	Predicting change in car sales as a result of changes in tax laws
Economic indicators	Uses one or more economic indicators to predict a future state of the economy	Using change in GNP to predict discretionary income
Substitution effect	Uses a mathematical formula to predict how, when, and under what circumstances a new product or technology will replace an existing one	Predicting the effect of streaming video services on the sale of Blu-ray players
Qualitative		
Jury of opinion	Combines and averages the opinions of experts	Polling the company's human resource managers to predict next year's college recruitment needs
Sales force composition	Combines estimates from field sales personnel of customers' expected purchases	Predicting next year's sales of industrial lasers
Customer evaluation	Combines estimates from established customers' purchases	Surveying major car dealers by a car manufacturer to determine types and quantities of products desired

Today, many organizations collaborate on forecasts using an approach known as CPFR, which stands for collaborative planning, forecasting, and replenishment.[9] CPFR provides a framework for the flow of information, goods, and services between retailers and manufacturers. Each organization relies on its own data to calculate a demand forecast for a particular product. If their respective forecasts differ by a certain amount (say, 10 percent), the retailer and manufacturer exchange data and written comments until they arrive at a more accurate forecast. Such collaborative forecasting helps both organizations do a better job of planning.

FORECASTING EFFECTIVENESS The goal of forecasting is to provide managers with information that will facilitate decision making. Despite its importance to planning, managers have had mixed success with it.[10] In a survey of inventory managers of multinational corporations, 70 percent of the respondents said their understanding of inventory management strategies was good; forecasting accuracy ranged between 56 and 75. However, efforts to improve accuracy did not always pay off.[11] Forty percent of the respondents reported improvements to the accuracy of forecasting after adopting inventory management software. Results of a survey on financial forecasting accuracy showed that 39 percent of financial executives said they could reliably forecast revenues only one quarter out. Even more disturbing is that 16 percent of those executives said they were "in the dark" about revenue forecasts.[12] But it is important to try to make forecasting as effective as possible because research shows that a company's forecasting ability can be a distinctive competence.[13] Here are some suggestions for making forecasting more effective.[14]

First, it's important to understand that forecasting techniques are most accurate when the environment is not rapidly changing. The more dynamic the environment, the more likely managers are to forecast ineffectively. Also, forecasting is relatively ineffective in predicting nonseasonal events such as recessions, unusual occurrences, discontinued operations, and the actions or reactions of competitors. Next, use simple forecasting methods. They tend to do as well as, and often better than, complex methods that may mistakenly confuse random data for meaningful information. Next, look at involving more people in the process. At Fortune 100 companies, it's not unusual to have 1,000 to 5,000 managers providing forecasting input. These businesses are finding that as more people are involved in the process, the more the reliability of the outcomes improves.[15] Next, compare every forecast with "no change." A no-change forecast is accurate approximately half the time. Next, use *rolling* forecasts that look twelve to eighteen months ahead, instead of using a single, static forecast. These types of forecasts can help managers spot trends better and help their organizations be more adaptive in changing environments.[16] It's also important to not rely on a single forecasting method. Make forecasts with several models and average them, especially when making longer-range forecasts. Next, don't assume you can accurately identify turning points in a trend. What is typically perceived as a significant turning point often turns out to be simply a random event. And, finally, remember that forecasting *is* a managerial skill and, as such, can be practiced and improved. Forecasting software has made the task somewhat less mathematically challenging, although the "number crunching" is only a small part of the activity. Interpreting the forecast and incorporating that information into planning decisions is the challenge facing managers.

TECHNIQUES **for allocating resources**

Once an organization's goals have been established, there's a need for **resources**—the assets of the organization (financial, physical, human, and intangible). How can managers allocate these resources effectively and efficiently so that organizational goals are met? Although managers can choose from a number of techniques for allocating resources (many of which are covered in accounting, finance, and operations management courses), we'll briefly discuss four techniques here: budgeting, scheduling, breakeven analysis, and linear programming.

resources
An organization's assets—including financial, physical, human, and intangible—that are used to develop, manufacture, and deliver products to its customers

Budgeting

Most of us have had some experience, as limited as it might be, with budgets. We probably learned at an early age that unless we allocated our "revenues" carefully, our weekly allowance was spent on "expenses" before the week was half over.

budget
A numerical plan for allocating resources to specific activities

A **budget** is a numerical plan for allocating resources to specific activities. Managers typically prepare budgets for revenues, expenses, and large capital expenditures such as equipment. It's not unusual, though, for budgets to be used for improving time, space, and use of material resources. These types of budgets substitute nondollar numbers for dollar amounts. Such items as person-hours, capacity utilization, or units of production can be budgeted for daily, weekly, or monthly activities. Exhibit PC-2 describes the different types of budgets that managers might use.

Why are budgets so popular? Probably because they're applicable to a wide variety of organizations and work activities within organizations. We live in a world in which almost everything is expressed in monetary units. Dollars, rupees, pesos, euros, yuan, yen, and the like are used as a common measuring unit within a country. That's why monetary budgets are a useful tool for allocating resources and guiding work in such diverse departments as manufacturing and information systems or at various levels in an organization. Budgets are one planning technique that most managers use—regardless of organizational level. It's an important managerial activity because it forces financial discipline and structure throughout the organization. However, many managers don't like preparing budgets because they feel the process is time-consuming, inflexible, inefficient, and/or ineffective.[17] How can the budgeting process be improved? Exhibit PC-3 provides some suggestions. Now that we understand the importance and types of budgets, how do organizations set them?

budgeting
The process of allocating resources to pay for designated future costs

Budgeting is the process of allocating resources to pay for designated future costs. There are two common approaches to setting budgets: incremental budgeting and zero-base budgeting.

Exhibit PC-2
Types of Budgets

Source: Based on *Production and Operations Management,* by R. S. Russell and B. W. Taylor III. Upper Saddle River, NJ: Prentice-Hall, Inc., 1966.

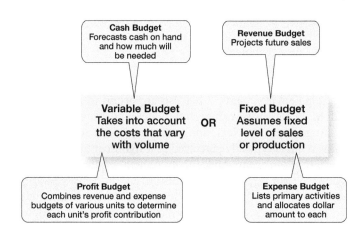

Exhibit PC-3
How to Improve Budgeting

- Collaborate and communicate.
- Be flexible.
- Goals should drive budgets—budgets should not determine goals.
- Coordinate budgeting throughout the organization.
- Use budgeting/planning software when appropriate.
- Remember that budgets are tools.
- Remember that profits result from smart management, not because you budgeted for them.

until the foundation is laid. How can managers schedule such a complex project? The program evaluation and review technique (PERT) is highly appropriate for such projects.

A **PERT network** is a flowchart diagram that depicts the sequence of activities needed to complete a project and the time or costs associated with each activity.[22] With a PERT network, a manager must think through what has to be done, determine which events depend on one another, and identify potential trouble spots. PERT also makes it easy to compare the effects alternative actions might have on scheduling and costs. Thus, PERT allows managers to monitor a project's progress, identify possible bottlenecks, and shift resources as necessary to keep the project on schedule.

To understand how to construct a PERT network, you need to know four terms. **Events** are end points that represent the completion of major activities. **Activities** represent the time or resources required to progress from one event to another. **Slack time** is the amount of time an individual activity can be delayed without delaying the whole project. The **critical path** is the longest or most time-consuming sequence of events and activities in a PERT network. Any delay in completing events on this path would delay completion of the entire project. In other words, activities on the critical path have zero slack time.

Developing a PERT network requires that a manager identify all key activities needed to complete a project, rank them in order of occurrence, and estimate each activity's completion time. Exhibit PC-6 explains the steps in this process.

Most PERT projects are complicated and include numerous activities. Such complicated computations can be done with specialized PERT software. However, let's work through a simple example. Assume you're the superintendent at a construction company and have been assigned to oversee the construction of an office building. Because time really is money in your business, you must determine how long it will take to get the building completed. You've determined the specific activities and events. Exhibit PC-7 outlines the major events in the construction project and your estimate of the expected time to complete each. Exhibit PC-8 shows the actual PERT network based on the data in Exhibit PC-7. You've also calculated the length of time that each path of activities will take:

A-B-C-D-I-J-K (44 weeks)

A-B-C-D-G-H-J-K (50 weeks)

A-B-C-E-G-H-J-K (47 weeks)

A-B-C-F-G-H-J-K (47 weeks)

Your PERT network shows that if everything goes as planned, the total project completion time will be fifty weeks. This is calculated by tracing the project's critical

PERT network
A flowchart diagram showing the sequence of activities needed to complete a project and the time or cost associated with each

events
End points that represent the completion of major activities in a PERT network

activities
The time or resources needed to progress from one event to another in a PERT network

slack time
The amount of time an individual activity can be delayed without delaying the whole project

critical path
The longest sequence of activities in a PERT network

---

1. *Identify every significant activity that must be achieved for a project to be completed.* The accomplishment of each activity results in a set of events or outcomes.
2. *Determine the order in which these events must be completed.*
3. *Diagram the flow of activities from start to finish, identifying each activity and its relationship to all other activities.* Use circles to indicate events and arrows to represent activities. This results in a flowchart diagram called a PERT network.
4. *Compute a time estimate for completing each activity.* This is done with a weighted average that uses an *optimistic* time estimate (t_o) of how long the activity would take under ideal conditions, a *most likely* estimate (t_m) of the time the activity normally should take, and a *pessimistic* estimate (t_p) that represents the time that an activity should take under the worst possible conditions. The formula for calculating the expected time (t_e) is then

$$t_e = \frac{t_o + 4t_m + t_p}{6}$$

5. *Using the network diagram that contains time estimates for each activity, determine a schedule for the start and finish dates of each activity and for the entire project.* Any delays that occur along the critical path require the most attention because they can delay the whole project.

Exhibit PC-6
Steps in Developing a PERT Network

Exhibit PC-7
Events and Activities in
Constructing an Office Building

Event	Description	Expected Time (in weeks)	Preceding Event
A	Approve design and get permits	10	None
B	Dig subterranean garage	6	A
C	Erect frame and siding	14	B
D	Construct floor	6	C
E	Install windows	3	C
F	Put on roof	3	C
G	Install internal wiring	5	D, E, F
H	Install elevator	5	G
I	Put in floor covering and paneling	4	D
J	Put in doors and interior decorative trim	3	I, H
K	Turn over to building management group	1	J

Exhibit PC-8
PERT Network for Constructing
an Office Building

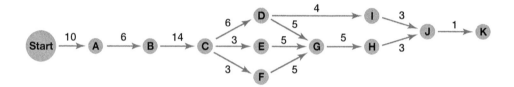

path (the longest sequence of activities), A-B-C-D-G-H-J-K, and adding up the times. You know that any delay in completing the events on this path would delay the completion of the entire project. Taking six weeks instead of four to put in the floor covering and paneling (Event I) would have no effect on the final completion date. Why? Because that event isn't on the critical path. However, taking seven weeks instead of six to dig the subterranean garage (Event B) would likely delay the total project. A manager who needed to get back on schedule or to cut the fifty-week completion time would want to concentrate on those activities along the critical path that could be completed faster. How might the manager do this? He or she could look to see if any of the other activities *not* on the critical path had slack time in which resources could be transferred to activities that *were* on the critical path.

Breakeven Analysis

Managers at Glory Foods want to know how many units of their new BBQ Beef Jerky must be sold in order to break even—that is, the point at which total revenue is just sufficient to cover total costs. **Breakeven analysis** is a widely used resource allocation technique to help managers determine breakeven point.

Breakeven analysis is a simple calculation, yet it's valuable to managers because it points out the relationship between revenues, costs, and profits. To compute breakeven point *(BE)*, a manager needs to know the unit price of the product being sold *(P)*, the variable cost per unit *(VC)*, and total fixed costs *(TFC)*. An organization breaks even when its total revenue is just enough to equal its total costs. But total cost has two parts: fixed and variable. *Fixed costs* are expenses that do not change regardless of volume. Examples include insurance premiums, rent, and property taxes. *Variable costs* change in proportion to output and include raw materials, labor costs, and energy costs.

breakeven analysis
A technique for identifying the point at which total revenue is just sufficient to cover total costs

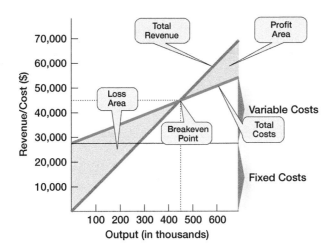

Breakeven point can be computed graphically or by using the following formula:

$$BE = \frac{TFC}{P - VC}$$

This formula tells us that (1) total revenue will equal total cost when we sell enough units at a price that covers all variable unit costs, and (2) the difference between price and variable costs, when multiplied by the number of units sold, equals the fixed costs. Let's work through an example.

Assume that Randy's Photocopying Service charges $0.10 per photocopy. If fixed costs are $27,000 a year and variable costs are $0.04 per copy, Randy can compute his breakeven point as follows: $27,000 ÷ ($0.10 − $0.04) = 450,000 copies, or when annual revenues are $45,000 (450,000 copies × $0.10). This same relationship is shown graphically in Exhibit PC-9.

As a planning tool, breakeven analysis could help Randy set his sales goal. For example, he could determine his profit goal and then calculate what sales level is needed to reach that goal. Breakeven analysis could also tell Randy how much volume has to increase to break even if he's currently operating at a loss or how much volume he can afford to lose and still break even.

Linear Programming

Maria Sanchez manages a manufacturing plant that produces two kinds of cinnamon-scented home fragrance products: wax candles and a wood-chip potpourri sold in bags. Business is good, and she can sell all of the products she can produce. Her dilemma: Given that the bags of potpourri and the wax candles are manufactured in the same facility, how many of each product should she produce to maximize profits? Maria can use **linear programming** to solve her resource allocation problem.

Although linear programming can be used here, it can't be applied to all resource allocation problems because it requires that resources be limited, that the goal be outcome optimization, that resources can be combined in alternative ways to produce a number of output mixes, and that a linear relationship exist between variables (a change in one variable must be accompanied by an exactly proportional change in the other).[23] For Maria's business, that last condition would be met if it took exactly twice the amount of raw materials and hours of labor to produce two of a given home fragrance product as it took to produce one.

What kinds of problems can be solved with linear programming? Some applications include selecting transportation routes that minimize shipping costs, allocating a limited advertising budget among various product brands, making the optimal assignment of people among projects, and determining how much of each product to make with a limited number of resources. Let's return to Maria's problem and see how linear programming could help her solve it. Fortunately, her problem is relatively

linear programming
A mathematical technique that solves resource allocation problems

Exhibit PC-10

Production Data for
Cinnamon-Scented Products

Department	Number of Hours Required (per unit)		Monthly Production Capacity (in hours)
	Potpourri Bags	Scented Candles	
Manufacturing	2	4	1,200
Assembly	2	2	900
Profit per unit	$10	$18	

simple, so we can solve it rather quickly. For complex linear programming problems, managers will use computer software programs designed specifically to help develop optimizing solutions.

First, we need to establish some facts about Maria's business. She has computed the profit margins on her home fragrance products at $10 for a bag of potpourri and $18 for a scented candle. These numbers establish the basis for Maria to be able to express her *objective function* as maximum profit $= 10P + \$18S$, where P is the number of bags of potpourri produced and S is the number of scented candles produced. The objective function is simply a mathematical equation that can predict the outcome of all proposed alternatives. In addition, Maria knows how much time each fragrance product must spend in production and the monthly production capacity (1,200 hours in manufacturing and 900 hours in assembly) for manufacturing and assembly. (See Exhibit PC-10.) The production capacity numbers act as *constraints* on her overall capacity. Now Maria can establish her constraint equations:

$$2P + 4S \le 1,200$$
$$2P + 2S \le 900$$

Of course, Maria can also state that $P \ge 0$ and $S \ge 0$ because neither fragrance product can be produced in a volume less than zero.

Maria has graphed her solution in Exhibit PC-11. The shaded area represents the options that don't exceed the capacity of either department. What does this mean? Well, let's look first at the manufacturing constraint line BE. We know that total manufacturing capacity is 1,200 hours, so if Maria decides to produce all potpourri bags, the maximum she can produce is 600 (1,200 hours ÷ 2 hours required to produce a bag of potpourri). If she decides to produce all scented candles, the maximum she can produce is 300 (1,200 hours ÷ 4 hours required to produce a scented candle). The other constraint Maria faces is that of assembly, shown by line DF. If Maria decides to produce all potpourri bags, the maximum she can assemble is 450 (900 hours production capacity ÷ 2 hours required to assemble). Likewise, if Maria decides to produce all scented candles, the maximum she can assemble is also 450 because the scented candles also take 2 hours to assemble. The constraints imposed by these capacity limits establish Maria's *feasibility region*. Her optimal resource allocation will be defined at

Exhibit PC-11

Graphical Solution to Linear
Programming Problem

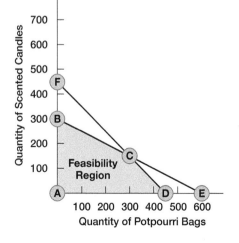

one of the corners within this feasibility region. Point C provides the maximum profits within the constraints stated. How do we know? At point A, profits would be 0 (no production of either potpourri bags or scented candles). At point B, profits would be $5,400 (300 scented candles × $18 profit and 0 potpourri bags produced = $5,400). At point D, profits would be $4,500 (450 potpourri bags produced × $10 profit and 0 scented candles produced = $4,500). At point C, however, profits would be $5,700 (150 scented candles produced × $18 profit and 300 potpourri bags produced × $10 profit = $5,700).

CONTEMPORARY planning techniques

Trade tariffs on Chinese goods. Escalating interest rates. Terrorist attacks. Category 4 hurricanes. Disruptive competitors. Today's managers face the challenges of planning in an environment that's both dynamic and complex. Two planning techniques appropriate for this type of environment are project management and scenarios. Both techniques emphasize *flexibility*, something that's important to making planning more effective and efficient in this type of organizational environment.

Project Management

Different types of organizations, from manufacturers such as Coleman and Boeing to software design firms such as SAS and Microsoft, use projects. A **project** is a one-time-only set of activities that has a definite beginning and ending point in time. Projects vary in size and scope—from the 2-mile-long traffic tunnel under downtown Seattle to a sorority's holiday formal. **Project management** is the task of getting a project's activities done on time, within budget, and according to specifications.[24]

More and more organizations are using project management because the approach fits well with the need for flexibility and rapid response to perceived market opportunities. For instance, India's Tata Motors relied on project management to develop and manufacture a subcompact car to be competitive with similar models from Hyundai and Toyota. Girish Wagh, senior vice president for program planning and project management for passenger vehicles, said that Tata's Tiago (new car model) is "one of the important launches from Tata Motors' passenger car business and the first step towards our transformation."[25]

When organizations undertake projects that are unique, have specific deadlines, contain complex interrelated tasks requiring specialized skills, and are temporary in nature, these projects often do not fit into the standardized planning procedures that guide an organization's other routine work activities. Instead, managers use project management techniques to effectively and efficiently accomplish the project's goals.

PROJECT MANAGEMENT PROCESS   In the typical project, work is done by a project team whose members are assigned from their respective work areas to the project and who report to a project manager. The project manager coordinates the project's activities with other departments. When the project team accomplishes its goals, it disbands, and members move on to other projects or back to their permanent work area.

The essential features of the project planning process are shown in Exhibit PC-12. The process begins by clearly defining the project's goals. This step is necessary because the manager and the team members need to know what's expected. All activities in the project and the resources needed to do them must then be identified. What materials and labor are needed to complete the project? This step may be time-consuming and complex, particularly if the project is unique and the managers have no history or experience with similar projects. Once the activities have been identified, the sequence of completion needs to be determined. What activities must be completed before

project
A one-time-only set of activities that has a definite beginning and ending point in time

project management
The task of getting a project's activities done on time, within budget, and according to specifications

Exhibit PC-12
Project Planning Process

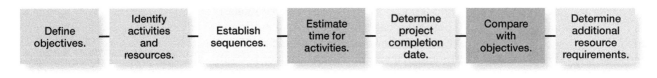

Define objectives. — Identify activities and resources. — Establish sequences. — Estimate time for activities. — Determine project completion date. — Compare with objectives. — Determine additional resource requirements.

Source: Based on R. S. Russell and B. W. Taylor III, eds., *Production and Operations Management,* 7th ed. (Hoboken, NJ: Wiley, 2011).

others can begin? Which can be done simultaneously? This step often uses flowchart diagrams such as a Gantt chart, a load chart, or a PERT network. Next, the project activities need to be scheduled. Time estimates for each activity are done, and these estimates are used to develop an overall project schedule and completion date. Then the project schedule is compared to the goals, and any necessary adjustments are made. If the project completion time is too long, the manager might assign more resources to critical activities so they can be completed faster.

Today, the project management process can take place online, as a number of web-based software packages are available. These packages cover aspects from project accounting and estimating to project scheduling and bug and defect tracking.

THE ROLE OF THE PROJECT MANAGER The temporary nature of projects makes managing them different from, say, overseeing a production line or preparing a weekly tally of costs on an ongoing basis. The one-shot nature of the work makes project managers the organizational equivalent of a hired gunman. There's a job to be done. It has to be defined—in detail. And the project manager is responsible for how it's done. The complexity of some projects warrant hiring project management firms. For instance, a Canadian mining company and a Chinese investment firm are considering whether to open a molybdenum mine near Boise, Idaho. Both companies have contracted with MCC8 Group Company, a firm that specializes in the management of overseas mineral and exploration development, to conduct a feasibility study.[26] MCC8 will assign several project managers to oversee this feasibility study, including geologists and environmental impact experts.

Even with the availability of sophisticated computerized and online scheduling programs and other project management tools, the role of project manager remains difficult because he or she is managing people who typically are still assigned to their permanent work areas. The only real influence project managers have is their communication skills and their power of persuasion. Additionally, team members seldom work on just one project. They're usually assigned to two or three at any given time. So project managers end up competing with each other to focus a worker's attention on his or her particular project.

Scenario Planning

scenario
A consistent view of what the future is likely to be

A **scenario** is a consistent view of what the future is likely to be.[27] Developing scenarios also can be described as *contingency planning*; that is, if this event happens, then we need to take these actions. For instance, when environmental scanning revealed that the Trump administration planned to pressure China to reform its trade policies by imposing tariffs, executives at U.S. Steel began assessing the possible consequences on their firm. What would be the effect of a 10 percent tariff on imported steel from China? What would be the effect of a 25 percent tariff? What if China retaliated and imposed a 10 percent tariff on steel coming into China? Based on these individual scenarios, management would be prepared to implement new strategies to get and keep its competitive position.

Although scenario planning is useful in anticipating events that *can be* anticipated, it's difficult to forecast random events—the major surprises and aberrations that can't be foreseen. For instance, an outbreak of deadly and devastating tornadoes in Kansas and Oklahoma in May 2016 was a scenario that could not be anticipated. The disaster recovery planning that took place after the storms was effective because this type of scenario had been experienced before. A response had already been planned and people knew what to do. But the planning challenge comes from those totally unexpected events. For instance, the shooting of a doctor by a patient's family member in a Boston hospital was unexpected and a total shock to many organizations already concerned about workplace safety. Scenario planning was of little use because no one could have envisioned this scenario. As difficult as it may be for managers to anticipate and deal with these random events, they're not totally vulnerable to the consequences. One suggestion identified by risk experts as particularly important is to have an early warning system in place. (A similar idea is the tsunami warning systems in the Pacific and in Alaska, which alert officials to potentially dangerous tsunamis and give them time to take action.) Early warning indicators for organizations can give managers advance notice of potential risks and changes so they can take action. Then, managers need to have appropriate responses (plans) in place if these unexpected events occur. For instance, five large banks, including Bank of America and Capital One, own Early Warning Services (EWS).[28] EWS enables banks to easily exchange information about a customer's potential risk in an effort to fight fraud.

REVIEW AND DISCUSSION QUESTIONS

PC-1. Describe the different approaches to assessing the environment.

PC-2. Describe the four techniques for allocating resources.

PC-3. How does PERT network analysis work?

PC-4. Why is flexibility so important to today's planning techniques?

PC-5. What is project management, and what are the steps managers use in planning projects?

PC-6. "It's a waste of time and other resources to develop a set of sophisticated scenarios for situations that may never occur." Do you agree or disagree? Support your position.

PC-7. Do intuition and creativity have any relevance in quantitative planning tools and techniques? Explain.

PC-8. The *Wall Street Journal* and other business periodicals often carry reports of companies that have not met their sales or profit forecasts. What are some reasons a company might not meet its forecast? What suggestions could you make for improving the effectiveness of forecasting?

PC-9. In what ways is managing a project different from managing a department or other structured work area? In what ways are they the same?

PC-10. What might be some early warning signs of (a) a new competitor coming into your market, (b) an employee work stoppage, or (c) a new technology that could change demand for your product?

ENDNOTES

1. Burke, "Your Ticket to Disney May Cost More—or Less—Depending on When You Go," *MarketWatch*, February 29, 2016, https://www.marketwatch.com/story/how-disneys-dynamic-pricing-could-benefit-some-consumers-2015-10-05.

2. S. C. Jain, "Environmental Scanning in U.S. Corporations," *Long Range Planning* 17, no. 2 (April 1984): pp. 117–128; L. M. Fuld, *Monitoring the Competition* (New York: John Wiley & Sons, 1988); E. H. Burack and N. J. Mathys, "Environmental Scanning Improves Strategic Planning," *Personnel Administrator* (April 1989): pp. 82–87; R. Subramanian, N. Fernandes, and E. Harper, "Environmental Scanning in U.S. Companies: Their Nature and Their Relationship to Performance," *Management International Review* 33, no. 3 (July 1993): pp. 271–286; K. Kumar, R. Subramanian, and K. Strandholm, "Competitive Strategy, Environmental Scanning and Performance: A Context Specific Analysis of Their Relationship," *International Journal of Commerce and Management* 11, no. 1 (Spring 2001): pp. 1–18; V. K. Garg, B. A. Walters, and R. L. Priem, "Chief Executive Scanning Emphases, Environmental Dynamism, and Manufacturing Firm Performance," *Strategic Management Journal* 24, no./8 (August 2003): pp. 725–744; H. Y. Wong, J.-Y. Hung, "Environmental Scanning Literature—Past, Present, and Future Research Propositions," *International Journal of Business Environment* 5, no. 1 (2012): pp. 30–50; and E. J. Blageski Jr. and C. R. Rossetto, "Environmental Scanning, Strategic Behavior, Organizational Characteristics, and Performance in Small Firms," *Journal of Information Systems and Technology Management* 11, no. 3 (September 2015): pp. 611–28.

3. C. Davis, "Get Smart," *Executive Edge,* October-November 1999, pp. 46–50.

4. B. Gilad and L. M. Fuld, "Only Half of Companies Actually Use the Competitive Intelligence They Collect," *Harvard Business Review*, January 26, 2016, https://hbr.org/2016/01/only-half-of-companies-actually-use-the-competitive-intelligence-they-collect.

5. B. Ettore, "Managing Competitive Intelligence," *Management Review*, October 1995, pp. 15–19.

6. J. W. Miller, "U.S. Steel Accuses China of Hacking," *Wall Street Journal*, April 28, 2016, https://www.wsj.com/articles/u-s-steel-accuses-china-of-hacking-1461859201.

7. Associated Press, "First U.S. Cruise in Decades Arrives in Cuba," *Wall Street Journal*, May 2, 2016, https://www.wsj.com/articles/first-u-s-cruise-in-decades-arrives-in-cuba-1462202835.

8. Ibid.

9. R. L. Hollmann, L. F. Scavarda, A. Marcio, and T. Thome, "Collaborative Planning, Forecasting and Replenishment: A Literature Review," *International Journal of Productivity and Performance Management* 64, no. 7 (2015): pp. 971–93; F. Panahifar, C. Heavey, P. J. Byrne, and H. Fazlollahtabar, "A Framework for Collaborative Planning, Forecasting and Replenishment (CPFR)," *Journal of Enterprise Information Management* 28, no. 6 (October 2015): pp. 838–71; and C. A. Hill, G. P. Zhang, and K. E. Miller, "Collaborative Planning, Forecasting, and Replenishment and Firm Performance: An Empirical Evaluation," *International Journal of Production Economics* 196 (February 2018): pp. 12–23.

10. See G. Hamel and C. K. Prahalad, "Competing for the Future," *Harvard Business Review*, July–August 1994, pp. 122–128; F. Elikai, W. Hall Jr., and P. P. Elikai, "Managing and Improving the Forecasting Process," *Journal of Business Forecasting Methods & Systems* 18, no. 1 (Spring 1999): pp. 15–19; and L. Lapide, "New Developments in Business Forecasting," *Journal of Business Forecasting Methods & Systems* (Summer 1999): pp. 13–14.

11. L. Cecere, "What Drives Inventory Effectiveness in a Market-Driven World?," *Supply Chain Insights*, October 27, 2015, https://supplychaininsights.com/what-drives-inventory-effectiveness-in-a-market-driven-world/.

12. V. Ryan, "Future Tense," *CFO,* December 2008, pp. 37–42.

13. R. Durand, "Predicting a Firm's Forecasting Ability: The Roles of Organizational Illusion of Control and Organizational Attention," *Strategic Management Journal* 24, no. 9 (September 2003): pp. 821–838.

14. Elikai and Hall Jr., "Managing and Improving" [see note 10]; and N. Pant and W. H. Starbuck, "Innocents in the Forest: Forecasting and Research Methods," *Journal of Management* 16, no. 2 (June 1990): pp. 433–460; M. A. Giullian, M. D. Odom, and M. W. Totaro, "Developing Essential Skills for Success in the Business World: A Look at Forecasting," *Journal of Applied Business Research* (Summer 2000): pp. 51–65; T. Leahy, "Turning Managers into Forecasters," *Business Finance,* August 2002, pp. 37–40; A. Stuart, "Imperfect Futures," *CFO,* July–August 2009, pp. 48–53; C. L. Jain and M. Covas, "Thinking About Tomorrow," *Wall Street Journal,* July 7, 2008, p. R10+; and J. Katz, "Forecasts Demand Change," *Industry Week,* May 2010, pp. 26–29.

15. Leahy, "Turning Managers into Forecasters."

16. J. Hope, "Use a Rolling Forecast to Spot Trends," *Harvard Business School Working Knowledge,* March 13, 2006, https://hbswk.hbs.edu/archive/use-a-rolling-forecast-to-spot-trends.

17. J. Mariotti, "Surviving the Dreaded Budget Process," *IW,* August 17, 1998, p. 150; G. J. Nolan, "The End of Traditional Budgeting," *Bank Accounting & Finance* (Summer 1998): pp. 29–36; A. Kennedy and D. Dugdale, "Getting the Most from Budgeting," *Management Accounting,* February 1999, pp. 22–24; "Budgeting Processes: Inefficiency or Inadequate?," *Management Accounting,* February 1999, p. 5; J. Fanning, "Businesses Languishing in a Budget Comfort Zone?," *Management Accounting,* July–August 1999, p. 8; T. Leahy, "Necessary Evil," *Business Finance*, November 1999, pp. 41–45; T. Leahy, "The Top 10 Traps of Budgeting," *Business Finance,* November 2001, pp. 20–26; J. Hope and R. Fraser, "Who Needs Budgets?," *Harvard Business Review,* February 2003, pp. 108–115; and E. Krell, "The Case Against Budgeting," *Business Finance,* July 2003, pp. 20–25.

18. R. Knutson, "Verizon Set to Slash $10 Billion in Costs," *Wall Street Journal*, September 15, 2017, p. B1.

19. S. C. Kavanagh, "Zero-Base Budgeting," Government Finance Officers Association and the City of Calgary, Alberta, 2011, https://www.gfoa.org/zero-base-budgeting.

20. S. Callaghan, K. Hawke, and C. Mignerey, "Five Myths (and Realities) About Zero-Based Budgeting," *McKinsey & Company*, October 2014, https://www.mckinsey.com/business-functions/strategy-and-corporate-finance/our-insights/five-myths-and-realities-about-zero-based-budgeting.

21. J. Geraldi and T. Lechter, "Gantt Charts Revisited," *International Journal of Managing Projects in Business* 5, no. 4 (September 2012): pp. 578–94.

22. P. N. Modi, S. Modi, and R. Modi, *PERT and CPM*, 6th ed. (New Delhi: Standard Book House, 2018).

23. M. J. Panik, *Linear Programming and Resource Allocation Modeling* (Hoboken, NJ: Wiley, 2019).

24. See E. W. Larson and C. F. Gray, *Project Management: The Managerial Process* (New York: McGraw-Hill, 2018); and H. Kerzner, *Project Management: A Systems Approach to Planning, Scheduling and Controlling*, 12th ed. (Hoboken, NJ: Wiley, 2018).

25. S. Choudhury, "This Is How Much Tata Motor's Tiago Costs in India," India Real Time (blog), *Wall Street Journal*, April 6, 2016, https://blogs.wsj.com/indiarealtime/2016/04/06/this-is-how-much-tata-motors-tiago-costs-in-india/.

26. Associated Press, "Canadian, Chinese Companies Sign Deal on Proposed Idaho Mine," *New York Times*, June 9, 2016.

27. N. Konno, I. Nonaka, and J. Ogilvy, "Scenario Planning: The Basics," *World Futures* 70, no, 1 (January 2014): pp. 28–43; R. Ramirez, S. Churchhouse, J. Hoffman, and A. Palermo, "Using Scenario Planning to Reshape Strategy," *MIT Sloan Management Review*, Summer 2017, pp. 31–37; and J. J. Oliver and E. Parrett, "Managing Future Uncertainty: Reevaluating the Role of Scenario Planning," *Business Horizons* 61, no. 2 (March-April 2018), pp. 339–52.

28. L. Phillips, "EWS Can Stop You from Opening a Bank Account," *Rebuild Credit Scores*, updated January 21, 2019, https://rebuildcreditscores.com/early-warning-services/.

Managing Operations *Module*

Divergent 3D plans to change the way cars are produced.[1] The typical auto factory is the size of forty or fifty football fields and costs between $500 million and $1 billon to build. To justify that investment, these factories have to produce hundreds of thousands of cars a year. Divergent 3D's founder, Kevin Czinger, thinks small. He promises to build a factory no bigger than a large grocery store, for just over $50 million, that can produce 20,000 cars a year. Relying on large-scale 3-D metal printers, laser cutters, and assembly robots, Czinger says he'll be able to deliver low-carbon vehicles, in small and highly customizable batches, at a cost of about $6,700 less than today's typical factory.

Czinger's vision isn't just idle talk. He's already created a mini-factory in suburban Los Angeles where he's built a sporty-looking motorcycle and a sleek sports car using his innovative methods. And his firm is teaming up with France's Groupe PSA, the maker of Peugeot and Citroen vehicles, to work on a number of development projects.

Divergent 3D is an example of the rapid change that is taking place on factory floors around the world. In this module, we review the topic of operations management and describe the ways technology is changing the ways goods and services are produced.

THE role of operations management

operations management
The transformation process that converts resources into finished goods and services

What is **operations management**? The term refers to the transformation process that converts resources into finished goods and services. Exhibit MO-1 portrays this process in a simplified fashion. The system takes in inputs—people, technology, capital, equipment, materials, and information—and transforms them through various processes, procedures, work activities, and so forth into finished goods and services. Because every unit in an organization produces something, managers need to be familiar with operations management concepts in order to achieve goals efficiently and effectively.

Operations management is important to organizations and managers for three reasons: (1) it encompasses both services and manufacturing; (2) it's important in effectively and efficiently managing productivity; and (3) it plays a strategic role in an organization's competitive success.

Services and Manufacturing

With a menu that offers more than 200 items, The Cheesecake Factory restaurants rely on a finely tuned production system.[2] One food-service consultant says, "They've evolved with this highly complex menu combined with a highly efficient kitchen."[3]

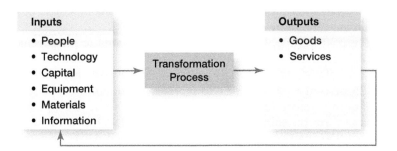

Exhibit MO-1
The Operations System

Every organization produces something. Unfortunately, this fact is often overlooked except in obvious cases such as in the manufacturing of cars, cell phones, or lawn mowers. After all, **manufacturing organizations** produce physical goods. It's easy to see the transformation process at work in these types of organizations because raw materials are turned into recognizable physical products. But the transformation process isn't as readily evident in **service organizations** that produce nonphysical outputs in the form of services. For instance, hospitals provide medical and healthcare services that help people manage their personal health, airlines provide transportation services that move people from one location to another, military forces provide defense capabilities, and the list goes on. These service organizations also transform inputs into outputs, although the transformation process isn't as easily recognizable as that in manufacturing organizations. Take a university, for example. University administrators bring together inputs—professors, books, academic journals, technology materials, computers, classrooms, and similar resources—to transform "unenlightened" students into educated and skilled individuals who are capable of making contributions to society.

The reason we're making this point is that the US economy, and to a large extent the global economy, is increasingly dominated by the creation and sale of services. Most of the world's developed countries are predominantly service economies. In the United States, for instance, almost 80 percent of all economic activity is services, and in the European Union it's over 71 percent. In lesser-developed countries, the services sector is less important. For instance, in Chad, it accounts for only 30 percent of economic activity; in the Democratic Republic of the Congo, 26 percent; and in Timor-Leste, about 17 percent.[4]

manufacturing organizations
Organizations that produce physical goods

service organizations
Organizations that produce nonphysical products in the form of services

Managing Productivity

One jetliner has roughly 4 million parts. Efficiently assembling such a finely engineered product requires intense focus. Boeing and Airbus, the two major global manufacturers, have copied techniques from Toyota. However, not every technique can be copied because airlines demand more customization than do car buyers and significantly more rigid safety regulations apply to jetliners than to cars. Yet, advances in manufacturing technology are enabling Boeing to significantly increase its ability to turn out custom jetliners. The company planned to increase the production of its model 737 aircraft from forty-two planes per month to fifty-seven per month in 2019.[5]

Some organizations, like Adidas, are planning manufacturing plants that will replace workers with robots altogether.[6] One study estimates that manufacturing facilities that rely on robots will cut labor costs by 33 percent in South Korea and 25 percent in the United States and Taiwan.[7]

Although most organizations don't make products that have 4 million parts and most organizations can't function without people, improving productivity has become a major goal in virtually every organization. For countries, high productivity can lead to economic growth and development. Employees can receive higher wages and company profits can increase without causing inflation. For individual organizations, increased productivity gives them a more competitive cost structure and the ability to offer more competitive prices.

Over the past decade, businesses have made dramatic improvements to increase their efficiency. For example, at Changying Precision Technology Company in China, technology has enabled the company to lower its manufacturing defect rate from 25 percent to 5 percent and increase production capacity from 8,000 units per month to more than 21,000 units.[8] And it's not just in manufacturing that companies are pursuing productivity gains. Les Clos, a French restaurant located in San Francisco, uses a smartphone app called Allset, which enables patrons to book their table, preorder food, and pay for it. Shortly after adopting Allset, Les Clos saw a 30 percent increase in lunch orders and a 25 percent increase in sales.[9]

Productivity is a composite of people and operations variables. To improve productivity, managers must focus on both. The late W. Edwards Deming, a renowned quality expert, believed that managers, not workers, were the primary source of increased productivity. Some of his suggestions for managers included planning for the long-term future, never being complacent about product quality, understanding whether problems were confined to particular parts of the production process or stemmed from the overall process itself, training workers for the job they're being asked to perform, raising the quality of line supervisors, and requiring workers to do quality work.[10] Deming understood the interplay between people and operations. High productivity can't come solely from good "people management." The truly effective organization will maximize productivity by successfully integrating people into the overall operations system.

Strategic Role of Operations Management

Modern manufacturing originated over 100 years ago in the United States, primarily in Detroit's automobile factories. The success that US manufacturers experienced during World War II led manufacturing executives to believe that troublesome production problems had been conquered. So these executives focused, instead, on improving other functional areas, such as finance and marketing, and paid little attention to manufacturing.

However, as US executives neglected production, managers in Japan, Germany, and other countries took the opportunity to develop modern, technologically advanced facilities that fully integrated manufacturing operations into strategic planning decisions. The competition's success realigned world manufacturing leadership. US manufacturers soon discovered that foreign goods were made not only less expensively but also with better quality. Finally, by the late 1970s, US executives recognized they were facing a true crisis and responded. They invested heavily in improving manufacturing technology, increased the corporate authority and visibility of manufacturing executives, and began incorporating existing and future production requirements into the organization's overall strategic plan. Today, successful organizations recognize the crucial role that operations management plays as part of the overall organizational strategy to establish and maintain global leadership.[11]

The strategic role that operations management plays in successful organizational performance can be seen clearly as more organizations move toward managing their operations from a value chain perspective.

VALUE chain management

The concepts of value chain management have transformed operations management strategies and turned organizations around the world into finely tuned models of efficiency and effectiveness, strategically positioned to exploit competitive opportunities. But what do we mean by the term *value chain management*? To understand, we need to break it down into its components.

What is Value Chain Management?

Every organization needs customers if it's going to survive and prosper. Even a not-for-profit organization must have "customers" who use its services or purchase its products. Customers want some type of value from the goods and services they purchase or use, and these customers decide what has value. Organizations must provide that value to attract and keep customers. **Value** is defined as the performance characteristics, features, and attributes and any other aspects of goods and services for which customers are willing to give up resources (usually money). For example, when you purchase a new pair of Australian sheepskin Ugg boots online at Zappos, a Wendy's bacon cheeseburger at a drive-through, or a haircut from your local hair salon, you're exchanging money in return for the value you need or desire from these products—keeping your feet warm *and* fashionable during winter's cold weather, alleviating your lunchtime hunger pangs, or looking professionally groomed.

How *is* value provided to customers? Through transforming raw materials and other resources into some product or service that end users need or desire when, where, and how they want it. However, that seemingly simple act of turning varied resources into something that customers value and are willing to pay for involves a vast array of interrelated work activities performed by different participants (suppliers, manufacturers, and even customers)—that is, it involves the value chain. The **value chain** is the entire series of organizational work activities that add value at each step from raw materials to finished product. In its entirety, the value chain can encompass the supplier's suppliers to the customer's customer.[12] For instance, consider the value chain from growing macadamia nuts to selling macadamia nut cookies in a grocery store. The chain begins with a farmer who grows the macadamia nuts, picks them from trees, and sells them to a processing plant. The added value is the increase in the farmer's income for selling macadamia nuts and the material and labor costs for growing and picking them. The processing plant removes the shells, discards rotten nuts, and sells the rest to a bakery. The added value created by the processing plant is the difference between the cost of buying the macadamia nuts and the price at which these are sold to the bakery. The bakery adds value by blending the nuts with the cookie dough, baking the cookies, and selling them to the grocery store for a profit. The grocer adds value by buying the cookies from the bakery, transporting them to the store, stocking the shelves, and selling them for a profit.

Value chain management is the process of managing the sequence of activities and information along the entire value chain. In contrast to supply chain management, which is *internally* oriented and focuses on efficient flow of incoming materials to the organization, value chain management is *externally* oriented and focuses on both incoming materials and outgoing products and services. Although supply chain management is efficiency oriented (its goal is to reduce costs and make the organization more productive), value chain management is effectiveness oriented and aims to create the highest value for customers.[13] The relationship between Magna International and General Motors illustrates the benefits of improving value chain management. Magna manufactures front and rear bumper covers for GM vehicles. After Magna moved from Ohio to a facility near the GM assembly plant in Michigan, GM saved millions of dollars in purchase costs.[14] By moving closer to GM, Magna no longer needs to maintain a costly storage facility and incur high fuel costs for transport. In turn, the cost savings enables Magna to sell bumper covers to GM at a lower price.

Goal of Value Chain Management

Who has the power in the value chain? Is it the suppliers providing needed resources and materials? After all, they have the ability to dictate prices and quality. Is it the manufacturer who assembles those resources into a valuable product or service? Their contribution in creating a product or service is quite obvious. Is it the distributor that makes sure the product or service is available where and when the customer needs it? Actually, it's none of these! In value chain management, ultimately customers are the

value
The performance characteristics, features, and attributes, and any other aspects of goods and services for which customers are willing to give up resources

value chain
The entire series of organizational work activities that add value at each step from raw materials to finished product

value chain management
The process of managing the sequence of activities and information along the entire value chain

ones with power. They're the ones who define what value is and how it's created and provided. Using value chain management, managers hope to find that unique combination that offers customers solutions to truly meet their unique needs incredibly fast and at a price that can't be matched by competitors.

With these factors in mind, then, the goal of value chain management is to create a value chain strategy that meets and exceeds customers' needs and desires and allows for full and seamless integration among all members of the chain. A good value chain involves a sequence of participants working together as a team, each adding some component of value—such as faster assembly, more accurate information, better customer response and service, and so forth—to the overall process. The better the collaboration among the various chain participants, the better the customer solutions. When value is created for customers and their needs and desires are satisfied, everyone along the chain benefits. For example, at Johnson Controls Inc., managing the value chain started first with improved relationships with internal suppliers, then expanded out to external suppliers and customers. As the company's experience with value chain management improved, so did its connection with its customers, which ultimately paid off for all its value chain partners.[15]

Benefits of Value Chain Management

Collaborating with external and internal partners in creating and managing a successful value chain strategy requires significant investments in time, energy, and other resources, and a serious commitment by all chain partners. Given these demands, why would managers ever choose to implement value chain management? There are at least four benefits of value chain management: improved procurement, improved logistics, improved product development, and enhanced customer order management.[16]

Value Chain Strategy

Exhibit MO-2 shows the six main requirements of a successful value chain strategy: coordination and collaboration, technology investment, organizational processes, leadership, employees, and organizational culture and attitudes.

COORDINATION AND COLLABORATION For the value chain to achieve its goal of meeting and exceeding customers' needs and desires, collaborative relationships among all chain participants must exist. Each partner must identify things he or she may not value but that customers do. Sharing information and being flexible as far as who in the value chain does what are important steps in building coordination and collaboration. This sharing of information and analysis requires open communication among the various value chain partners.

TECHNOLOGY INVESTMENT Successful value chain management isn't possible without a significant investment in information technology. The payoff from this

Exhibit MO-2

Value Chain Strategy Requirement

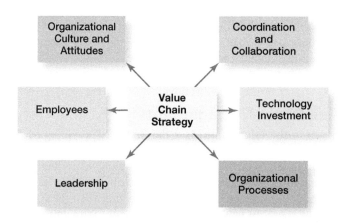

investment, however, is that information technology can be used to restructure the value chain to better serve end users. For example, each year the Houston-based food distributor Sysco ships 21.5 million tons of produce, meats, prepared meals, and other food-related products to restaurants, cafeterias, and sports stadiums. To get all that food safely to the right place at the right time, Sysco relies on a complex web of software, databases, scanning systems, and robotics.[17]

ORGANIZATIONAL PROCESSES   Value chain management radically changes organizational processes—that is, the ways that organizational work is done. When managers decide to manage operations using value chain management, old processes are no longer appropriate. All organizational processes must be critically evaluated from beginning to end to see where value is being added. Non-value-adding activities should be eliminated. Questions such as "Where can internal knowledge be leveraged to improve the flow of material and information?" "How can we better configure our product to satisfy both customers and suppliers?" "How can the flow of material and information be improved?" and "How can we improve customer service?" should be asked for each and every process.

Three important conclusions can be made about organizational processes. First, better demand forecasting is necessary *and* possible because of closer ties with customers and suppliers. For example, in an effort to make sure that Listerine was on the store shelves when customers wanted it (known in the retail industry as *product replenishment rates*), Walmart and Pfizer's Consumer Healthcare Group collaborated on improving product demand forecast information. Through their mutual efforts, the partners boosted Walmart's sales of Listerine, an excellent outcome for both supplier and retailer. Customers also benefited because they were able to purchase the product when and where they wanted it.

Second, selected functions may need to be done collaboratively with other partners in the value chain. This collaboration may even extend to sharing employees. For instance, Coca-Cola Hellenic Bottling Company places employees in grocery stores, where they work with store employees to prepare the merchandising and placement of Coca-Cola products on the shelves.

Finally, new measures are needed for evaluating performance of various activities along the value chain. Because the goal in value chain management is meeting and exceeding customers' needs and desires, managers need a better picture of how well this value is being created and delivered to customers. For example, when Nestlé USA implemented value chain management, it redesigned its metrics system to focus on one consistent set of measurements—including, for instance, accuracy of demand forecasts and production plans, on-time delivery, and customer-service levels—that allowed them to more quickly identify problem areas and take actions to resolve them.[18]

LEADERSHIP   Successful value chain management isn't possible without strong and committed leadership. From top organizational levels to lower levels, managers must support, facilitate, and promote the implementation and ongoing practice of value chain management. Managers must seriously commit to identifying what value is, how that value can best be provided, and how successful those efforts have been. A culture where all efforts are focused on delivering superb customer value isn't possible without a serious commitment on the part of the organization's leaders.

Also, it's important that managers outline expectations for what's involved in the organization's pursuit of value chain management. Ideally, managers start with a vision or mission statement that expresses the organization's commitment to identifying, capturing, and providing the highest possible value to customers. Then, managers should clarify expectations regarding each employee's role in the value chain. But clear expectations aren't just important for internal partners. Being clear about expectations also extends to external partners.

EMPLOYEES/HUMAN RESOURCES   When new employees at the Thermo Fisher Scientific plant in Marietta, Ohio, have work-related questions, they can consult with a member of the facility's "Tree of Knowledge." The "tree" is actually a bulletin board with pictures of employees who have worked at the plant for decades.[19]

Employees play an important role in value chain management. The three main human resource requirements for value chain management are flexible approaches to job design, an effective hiring process, and ongoing training.

Flexibility is the key to job design in value chain management. Traditional functional job roles—such as marketing, sales, accounts payable, customer service, and so forth—won't work. Instead, jobs must be designed around work processes that create and provide value to customers. It takes flexible jobs and flexible employees. For instance, at Nordson Corporation's facility in Swainsboro, Georgia, workers are trained to do several different tasks, which isn't all that uncommon in many manufacturing plants. What's unique about this facility is that even salaried employees are expected to spend four hours every month building products on the shop floor.[20]

In a value chain organization, employees may be assigned to work teams that tackle a given process and may be asked to do different things on different days depending on need. In such an environment, where customer value is best delivered through collaborative relationships that may change as customer needs change and where processes or job descriptions are not standardized, an employee's ability to be flexible is critical. Therefore, the organization's hiring process must be designed to identify those employees who have the ability to learn and adapt.

Finally, the need for flexibility also requires a significant investment in continual and ongoing employee training. Whether that training involves learning how to use information technology software, how to improve the flow of materials throughout the chain, how to identify activities that add value, how to make better decisions faster, or how to improve any other number of potential work activities, managers must see to it that employees have the knowledge and tools they need to do their jobs efficiently and effectively.

ORGANIZATIONAL CULTURE AND ATTITUDES The last requirement for value chain management is having a supportive organizational culture and attitudes. From our extensive description of value chain management, you could probably guess the type of organizational culture that's going to support its successful implementation. Those cultural attitudes include sharing, collaborating, openness, flexibility, mutual respect, and trust. These attitudes encompass not only the internal partners in the value chain, but extend to external partners as well.

CURRENT issues in managing operations

We close out our discussion of operations management by looking at six contemporary operations' issues: technology in general, robotics, quality management, specific quality goals, mass customization, and creating a lean organization.

Technology's Role in Operations Management

Global positioning systems (GPS) are changing a number of enterprises from shipping to shopping, from health care to law enforcement, and even farming.[21] GPS was originally invented for military use to track weapons and personnel as they moved. Now GPS is being used to track shipping fleets, revitalize consumer products such as watches or photos, and monitor parolees or sex offenders.

Smart companies are looking at ways to harness technology to improve operations management. For instance, many fast-food companies are competing to see who can provide faster and better service to drive-through customers. With drive-through now representing a huge portion of sales, faster and better delivery can be a significant competitive edge. Wendy's has added awnings to some of its menu boards and replaced some of the text with pictures. Others use confirmation screens, a technology that helped McDonald's boost accuracy by more than 11 percent. Technology used by two national chains tells managers how much food they need to prepare by counting vehicles in the drive-through line and factoring in demand for current promotional and popular staple items. Even Domino's is using a point-of-sale system to attract customers and streamline online orders.[22]

Operations managers need systems that can reveal available capacity, status of orders, and product quality while products are in the process of being manufactured, not just after the fact. To connect more closely with customers, production must be synchronized across the enterprise. To avoid bottlenecks and slowdowns, the production function must be a full partner in the entire business system.

What's making such extensive collaboration possible is technology. Technology is also allowing organizations to control costs, particularly in the areas of predictive maintenance, remote diagnostics, and utility cost savings. For instance, internet-compatible equipment increasingly contains embedded web servers that can communicate proactively—that is, if a piece of equipment breaks or reaches certain preset parameters indicating that it's about to break, it asks for help. Some devices have the ability to initiate email or signal a pager at a supplier, the maintenance department, or contractor describing the specific problem and requesting parts and service.[23]

The emphasis should be on working together with all the organization's business functions to find solutions to customers' business problems. Even service providers understand the power of technology for these tasks. For example, Southwest Airlines upgraded its cockpit software, enabling its pilots to fly precise satellite-based navigation approaches to airports, thus saving fuel, reducing delays, and cutting noise.[24]

The Robots Are Coming!

The robots are coming and they'll be replacing humans in a variety of jobs.[25] While this statement is a threat to millions of workers, it nevertheless is fairly accurate. Moreover, this is not something that is coming in some distant future. It's here and it's changing the face of operations management.

Robots have become ubiquitous on factory floors. But they're also picking items at Amazon fulfillment centers and sorting grapes in Napa Valley. So what does this mean for management and future labor markets?

First, the jobs that are being replaced tend to be ones that are physically tasking or mind-numbing—jobs that most people would prefer *not* to do. Second, in most cases, robots won't be taking human jobs. Rather, they'll be taking on parts of jobs that humans have been doing. They'll be augmenting humans to make job performance more effective and efficient. For instance, surgeons will be using robots to perform complex surgical procedures with more precision, flexibility, and control. Surgeons' jobs won't be going away. They'll just be able to do their jobs better.

Quality Management

What is *quality*? When you consider a product or service to have quality, what does that mean? Does it mean that the product doesn't break or quit working—that is, that it's reliable? Does it mean that the service is delivered in a way that you intended? Does it mean that the product does what it's supposed to do? Or does quality mean something else? We're going to define **quality** as the ability of a product or service to reliably do what it's supposed to do and to satisfy customer expectations.

A reminder: For a specific discussion of *Total Quality Management*, see the History Module that follows Chapter 1.

How is quality achieved? A good way to answer this is by looking at quality through the management functions—planning, organizing, leading, and controlling.

quality
The ability of a product or service to reliably do what it's supposed to do and to satisfy customer expectations

PLANNING FOR QUALITY Managers must have quality improvement goals and strategies and plans to achieve those goals. Goals can help focus everyone's attention toward some objective quality standard. For instance, the *Forbes Travel Guide* rates hotels on a star system, with five stars representing the highest quality. Hotels must earn high ratings on 800 standards to earn the five-star highest rating.

A quality plan is a document that specifies quality standards, practices, resources, specifications, and the sequence of activities relevant to a particular product or service.[26] For instance, in a manufacturing firm that machines metal parts, its quality plan might be made up of applicable procedures, a description of material standards, specific workmanship standards, and the measurement tolerances acceptable.[27]

ORGANIZING AND LEADING FOR QUALITY   Because quality improvement initiatives are carried out by organizational employees, it's important that managers look at how they can best organize and lead them. For instance, at the Moosejaw, Saskatchewan, plant of General Cable Corporation, every employee participates in continual quality assurance training. In addition, the plant manager believes in giving employees the information they need to do their jobs better. He says, "Giving people who are running the machines the information is just paramount. You can set up your cellular structure, you can cross-train your people, you can use lean tools, but if you don't give people information to drive improvement, there's no enthusiasm." This company shares production data and financial performance measures with all employees.[28]

Organizations with extensive and successful quality improvement programs tend to rely on two important people approaches: cross-functional work teams and self-directed, or empowered, work teams. Because achieving product quality is something in which all employees from upper to lower levels must participate, it's not surprising that quality-driven organizations rely on well-trained, flexible, and empowered employees.

CONTROLLING FOR QUALITY   Quality improvement initiatives aren't possible without having some way to monitor and evaluate their progress. Whether it involves standards for inventory control, defect rate, raw materials procurement, or other operations management areas, controlling for quality is important. For instance, at the Northrup Grumman Corporation plant in Rolling Meadows, Illinois, several quality controls have been implemented, such as automated testing and IT that integrates product design and manufacturing and tracks process quality improvements. Also, employees are empowered to make accept/reject decisions about products throughout the manufacturing process. The plant manager explains, "This approach helps build quality into the product rather than trying to inspect quality into the product."[29]

Quality Goals

To publicly demonstrate their quality commitment, many organizations worldwide have pursued challenging quality goals—the two best known being ISO 9001 and Six Sigma.

ISO 9001:2015   **ISO 9001** is the international quality management standard established by the International Organization for Standardization, which sets uniform guidelines for processes to ensure that products conform to customer and regulatory requirements.[30] These standards cover everything from contract review to product design to product delivery.

The ISO 9001 standards have become the internationally recognized standard for evaluating and comparing companies in the global marketplace. In fact, this type of certification can be a prerequisite for doing business globally. More than a million organizations from more than 160 countries have applied the ISO 9001 standard requirements to their quality management systems. And achieving ISO 9001 certification provides proof that a quality operations system is in place.

SIX SIGMA   Motorola popularized the use of stringent quality standards more than thirty years ago through a trademarked quality improvement program called Six Sigma. Very simply, **Six Sigma** is a quality program designed to reduce defects to help

---

ISO 9001
A series of international quality management standards that set uniform guidelines for processes to ensure products conform to customer and regulatory requirements

Six Sigma
A quality program designed to reduce defects and help lower costs, save time, and improve customer satisfaction

lower costs, save time, and improve customer satisfaction.[31] It's based on the statistical standard that establishes a goal of no more than 3.4 defects per million units or procedures. Six Sigma uses a common platform of knowledge, practices, and quality resources to increase an organization's effectiveness.

What does the name mean? Sigma is the Greek letter that statisticians use to define a standard deviation from a bell curve. The higher the sigma, the fewer the deviations from the norm—that is, the fewer the defects. At One Sigma, two-thirds of whatever is being measured falls within the curve. Two Sigma covers about 95 percent. At Six Sigma, you're about as close to defect-free as you can get. Although it's an extremely high standard to achieve, many quality-driven businesses are using it and benefiting from it. For instance, McKesson, a healthcare information technology company, saved $150 million and achieved 99.98 percent order accuracy following Six Sigma.[32] Other well-known companies pursuing Six Sigma include ITT Industries, GE, Dow Chemical, 3M Company, American Express, Sony Corporation, Nokia Corporation, and Johnson & Johnson.

Mass Customization

The term *mass customization* seems an oxymoron. However, the design-to-order concept is becoming an important operations management issue for today's managers. **Mass customization** provides consumers with a product when, where, and how they want it.[33] Companies as diverse as BMW, Ford, Levi Strauss, Mattel, and Dell are adopting mass customization to maintain or attain a competitive advantage. Mass customization requires flexible manufacturing techniques and continual customer dialogue. Technology plays an important role in both.

With flexible manufacturing, companies have the ability to quickly readjust assembly lines to make products to order. Using technology such as computer-controlled factory equipment, intranets, industrial robots, barcode scanners, 3-D printers, and logistics software, companies can manufacture, assemble, and ship customized products with customized packaging to customers in incredibly short timeframes. Warby Parker is a good example of a company that uses flexible manufacturing techniques and technology to create custom eyeglasses to customers' specifications.

Technology also is important in the continual dialogue with customers. Using extensive databases, companies can keep track of customers' likes and dislikes. And the internet has made it possible for companies to have ongoing dialogues with customers to learn about and respond to their exact preferences. For instance, on Amazon's website, customers are greeted by name and can get personalized recommendations of books and other products. The ability to customize products to a customer's desires and specifications starts an important relationship between the organization and the customer. If the customer likes the product and it provides value, he or she is more likely to be a repeat customer.

> **mass customization**
> Providing customers with a product when, where, and how they want it

Creating a Lean Organization

An intense focus on customers is also important in order to be a **lean organization**, which is an organization that understands what customers want, identifies customer value by analyzing all activities required to produce products, and then optimizes the entire process from the customer's perspective.[34] Lean organizations drive out all activities that fail to add value in customers' eyes. The goals are to improve quality, eliminate waste, reduce time, and reduce total costs. Critical to achieving these goals is a commitment to continuous improvement.

Companies like United Parcel Service, LVMH Moet Hennessy Louis Vuitton, and Harley-Davidson have pursued lean operations. "Lean operations adopt a philosophy of minimizing waste by striving for perfection through continuous learning, creativity, and teamwork."[35]

> **lean organization**
> An organization that understands what customers want, identifies customer value by analyzing all activities required to produce products, and then optimizes the entire process from the customer's perspective

REVIEW AND DISCUSSION QUESTIONS

MO-1. What is operations management?

MO-2. Do you think that manufacturing or service organizations have the greater need for operations management? Explain.

MO-3. What is a value chain, and what is value chain management? What is the goal of value chain management? What are the benefits of value chain management?

MO-4. What is required for successful value chain management? What obstacles exist to successful value chain management?

MO-5. How could you use value chain management in your everyday life?

MO-6. How does technology play a role in manufacturing?

MO-7. What are ISO 9001 and Six Sigma?

MO-8. Describe lean management and explain why it's important.

MO-9. How might operations management apply to other managerial functions besides control?

ENDNOTES

1. A. Ohnsman and J. Muller, "Honey, I Shrunk the Factory," *Forbes*, December 12, 2017, pp. 48–52.
2. A. Lutz, "4 Reasons the Cheesecake Factory Is Crushing the Competition," *Business Insider*, March 23, 2015, https://www.businessinsider.com/cheesecake-factorys-strategy-for-success-2015-3.
3. D. McGinn, "Faster Food," *Newsweek,* April 19, 2004, pp. E20–E22.
4. *World Factbook 2017–2018,* 2018, available online at cia.gov/library/publications/the-world-factbook.
5. J. Dwyer-Lindgren, "Boeing Will Boost 737 Production, Slow 777 Rates," *USA Today*, January 28, 2016, https://www.usatoday.com/story/travel/flights/todayinthesky/2016/01/28/boeing-boost-737-production-but-slow-777-rates/79450198/.
6. M. Sheahan, "Adidas Aims to Open Automated Shoe Factory in Germany in 2016," *Reuters*, October 20, 2015, https://www.reuters.com/article/us-adidas-robots/adidas-aims-to-open-automated-shoe-factory-in-germany-in-2016-idUSKCN0SE1RL20151020.
7. Associated Press, "Robots Replacing Human Factory Workers at Faster Place," *Los Angeles Times*, February 10, 2015, https://www.latimes.com/business/la-fi-robots-jobs-20150211-story.html.
8. PTI, "China Sets Up First Unmanned Factory; All Processes Are Operated by Robots," *Economic Times*, July 27, 2015, https://economictimes.indiatimes.com/news/international/business/china-sets-up-first-unmanned-factory-all-processes-are-operated-by-robots/articleshow/48238331.cms.
9. A. J. Agrawal, "How Retail and Restaurants Can Use Apps to Effectively Market Their Business," *Forbes*, December 30, 2015, https://www.forbes.com/sites/ajagrawal/2015/12/30/how-retail-and-restaurants-can-use-apps-to-effectively-market-their-business/#130859f22cd4.
10. W. E. Deming, "Improvement of Quality and Productivity Through Action by Management," *National Productivity Review* 1, no. 1 (Winter 1981): pp. 12–22.

11. "The Future of Manufacturing 2009," *Industry Week,* November 2009, pp. 25–31; T. D. Kuczmarski, "Remanufacturing America's Factory Sector," *Businessweek*, September 9, 2009, https://www.bloomberg.com/businessweek/innovate/content/sep2009/id2009099_517814.htm; and J. Hagel III, J. Seely Brown, D. Kulasooriya, C. A. Giffi, and M. Chen, "The Future of Manufacturing: Making Things in a Changing World," *Deloitte Insights*, March 31, 2015, https://www2.deloitte.com/insights/us/en/industry/manufacturing/future-of-manufacturing-industry.html.
12. A. Martel and W. Klibi, *Designing Value-Creating Supply Chain Networks* (New York: Springer, 2018).
13. A. Agnihotri, "The Role of the Upper Echelon in the Value Chain Management," *Competitiveness Review* 24, no. 3 (2014): pp. 240–55.
14. D. Sedgwick, "Suppliers Start Moving Closer to GM Plants," *Automotive News*, November 17, 2014, https://www.autonews.com/article/20141117/OEM10/311179991/suppliers-start-moving-closer-to-gm-plants.
15. T. Stevens, "Integrated Product Development," *Industry Week,* June 2002, pp. 21–28; and H. Armstrong, "Frank Vorrath, Johnson Controls: 'We Are Undergoing a Bi-Modal Transformation'," *Supply Chain Movement*, October 31, 2016, https://www.supplychainmovement.com/frank-vorrath-johnson-controls-we-are-undergoing-a-bi-modal-transformation/.
16. O. Durden, "What Are the Benefits of Value Chain Management?," *Chron*, updated November 5, 2018, https://smallbusiness.chron.com/benefits-value-chain-management-70083.html.
17. J. L. Yang, "Veggie Tales," *Fortune,* June 8, 2009, pp. 25–30.
18. G. Taninecz, "Forging the Chain," *Industry Week,* May 15, 2000, pp. 40–46.
19. J. Katz, "Empowering the Workforce," *Industry Week,* January 2009, p. 43.
20. D. Blanchard, "In the Rotation," *Industry Week*, January 2009, p. 42.

21. D. Joseph, "The GPS Revolution: Location, Location, Location," *Businessweek*, May 27, 2009, https://www.bloomberg.com/news/articles/2009-05-27/the-gps-revolution-location-location-location.

22. S. Anderson/Associated Press, "Restaurants Gear Up for Window Wars," *Springfield (Missouri) News-Leader,* January 27, 2006, p. 5B; and J. Maze, "5 Lessons From Domino's Comeback," *Restaurant Business*, January 18, 2018, https://www.restaurantbusinessonline.com/financing/five-lessons-dominos-comeback.

23. C. Mims, "Factories of the Future," *The Week*, December 2, 2016, p. 38.

24. S. McCartney, "A Radical Cockpit Upgrade Southwest Fliers Will Feel," *Wall Street Journal,* April 1, 2010, p. D1.

25. This section is based on A. Kessler, "The Robots Are Coming: Welcome Them," *Wall Street Journal*, August 23, 2016, p. A11; J. Kaplan, "Don't Fear the Robots," *Wall Street Journal*, July 22-23, 2017, p. C3; and J. Morrissey, "When Robots Join the Work Force," *New York Times*, December 16, 2018, p. F2.

26. "Quality Plans," *ASQ*, December 10, 2018, https://asq.org.

27. Ibid.

28. J. S. McClenahen, "Prairie Home Companion," *Industry Week,* October 2005, pp. 45–46.

29. T. Vinas, "Zeroing In on the Customer," *Industry Week,* October 2004, pp. 61–62.

30. D. Hoyle, *ISO 9000 Quality Systems Handbook*, 7th ed. (UK: Routledge, 2018). See also P. Chatzoglou, D. Chatzoudes, and N. Kipraios, "The Impact of ISO 9000 Certification on Firms' Financial Performance," *International Journal of Operations & Production Management* 35, no. 1 (2015): pp. 145–74.

31. T. Pyzdek and P. A. Keller, *The Six Sigma Handbook*, 5th ed. (New York: McGraw-Hill, 2019).

32. "The Healthcare Supply Chain Top 25 for 2015," *Gartner*, November 18, 2015, https://www.gartner.com/doc/3169736/healthcare-supply-chain-top-.

33. See, for instance, T. Blecker and G. Friedrich, eds., *Mass Customization: Challenges and Solutions* (New York: Springer, 2006); and F. S. Fogliatto, G. J. C. da Silveira, and D. Borenstein, "The Mass Customization Decade: An Updated Review of the Literature," *International Journal of Production Economics* 138, no. 1 (July 2012): pp. 14–25.

34. J. Heizer and B. Render, *Operations Management*, 10th ed. (Upper Saddle River, NJ: Prentice Hall, 2011), p. 636; S. Minter, "Measuring the Success of Lean," *Industry Week*, February 2010, pp. 32–35; and E. Rosen, "The Efficiencies of Lean Manufacturing," *New York Times*, December 16, 2018, p. F2.

35. Heizer and Render, *Operations Management*.

PART 6

Management Practice

A Manager's Dilemma

What comes to mind when you think of IKEA? You might have memories of following your parents through an IKEA maze-like store with the promise of Swedish meatballs at the end of the trip. The Swedish-based company is known for its flat-packed furniture, minimalist style, and affordability. IKEA's purpose, to "create a better everyday life" for people through build-it-yourself furniture, has been a successful strategy. Founded over seventy years ago, IKEA has 190,000 employees working in over 400 stores in 49 countries. Its yearly revenue is approximately $41 billion—that's a lot of furniture! All this sounds like life for IKEA should continuously be a smooth ride. But, it wasn't when several children were seriously hurt by one of its dresser designs that tipped over. After one child fatality, IKEA was responsible for the largest furniture recall in the world *ever*. They recalled 29 million furniture items in a recall that was three times bigger than the next largest furniture recall in history. IKEA also rolled out a massive communication campaign about the recall and offered wall mountings for dressers for customers who did not want to return their furniture. Then, there was another child fatality by a dresser that was not wall mounted.

> *Pretend you're part of the management team. Using what you've learned in this part on monitoring and controlling, what five things would you suggest the team focus on? Think carefully about your suggestions to the team.*

Global Sense

This is a story about the global economy. It's about markets, politics, and public opinion. And as US jobs—especially white-collar and professional jobs—continue to be outsourced and offshored, the story hits closer and closer to home. Although the terms *offshoring* and *outsourcing* are often used interchangeably, they do mean different things. *Offshoring* is relocating business processes (production and services) from one country to another. *Outsourcing* is moving noncore activities from being done internally to being done externally by an entity that specializes in that activity.

One of the realities of a global economy is that to be competitive, strategic decision makers must look for the best places to do business. If a car can be made more cheaply in Mexico, maybe it should be. If a telephone inquiry can be processed more cheaply in India or the Philippines, maybe it should be. And if programming code can be written more cheaply in China or Russia, maybe it should be. Almost any professional job that can be done outside the organization is up for grabs. There's nothing political or philosophical about the reason for shipping jobs elsewhere. The bottom line is that it can save companies money. But there's a price to be paid in terms of angry and anxious employees. So are offshoring and outsourcing bad?

Critics say "yes." It's affecting jobs once considered "safe" across a wider range of professional work activities. And the offshoring and outsourcing have taken place at a breathtaking pace. What this means is that the careers many college students are preparing for may not sustain them in the long run. This structural change in the US economy also means that the workforce is likely to face frequent career changes and downward pressures on wages.

Proponents say "no." Their argument is based on viewing economic development as a ladder with every country trying to climb to the next rung. And it's foolish to think that the United States has reached the top of the ladder with nowhere else to go. Although people fear that educated US workers will face the same fate as blue-collar workers, whose jobs shifted to lower-cost countries, the truth is that the United States currently still has a competitive advantage in innovation; although that may be in jeopardy. The US may have a trade deficit when it comes to goods (and a shortage of skilled labor that is needed in today's manufacturing processes). But the US still has a trade surplus when it comes to services.

Trends overall seem to have steered away from US firms deciding to bring their manufacturing operations back to the US (what it is called "reshoring"). Tariffs have not had a clear effect on the offshoring and outsourcing numbers yet either. It's safe to say that offshoring and outsourcing is a reality that is not disappearing any time soon. This means that offshoring and outsourcing is another example of why decision makers need to be aware of the context within which their organizations are doing business.

> *Discuss the following questions:*
> - *How are offshoring and outsourcing similar? How are they different?*
> - *What arguments do critics use to say offshoring and outsourcing are bad?*
> - *What arguments do proponents use to say offshoring and outsourcing are not bad?*
> - *How does the decision to offshore and outsource affect monitoring and controlling activities?*
> - *Is it just manufacturers that deal with these decisions/issues? Discuss.[1]*

Continuing Case
Starbucks—Controlling

Managers must monitor work activities to make sure they're being done as planned and correct any significant deviations. At Starbucks, managers control various functions, activities, processes, and procedures to ensure that desired performance standards are achieved at all organizational levels.

Controlling the Coffee Experience

Why has Starbucks been so successful? Although many factors have contributed to its success, one significant factor is its ability to provide customers with a unique product of the highest quality delivered with exceptional service. And managers need controls to help monitor and evaluate what's being done and how it's being done. Starbucks's managers use different types of controls to ensure that the company meets its goals. These controls include transaction controls, security controls, employee controls, and organizational performance controls.

Every week, an average of 85 million customers make purchases at a Starbucks store somewhere in the world. These transactions between partners and customers—the exchange of products for money—are the major source of sales revenue for Starbucks. Measuring and evaluating the efficiency and effectiveness of these transactions for both walk-in customers and customers at drive-through windows is important. Starbucks has been doing drive-through transactions for a number of years, but there is a push to add much more. Customers aren't looking to Starbucks as a place to sit and work as much as they used to due to an increase in shared workspace options and greater ease in finding free Wi-Fi. Instead, many customers want speed and convenience. So, 80 percent of new stores are including a drive-through window. In stores with drive-through windows, 70 percent of sales come from drive-through customers. The focus of these transactions is on both speed and quality—a different metric than for walk-in transactions. When a customer walks into a store and orders, he can step aside while the order is being prepared; that's not possible in a drive-through line. Besides, Starbucks takes longer to deliver orders to its customers relative to competitors. McDonald's, Dunkin Donuts, and even Panera Bread (with its lengthier food menu) have shorter drive-through delivery times than Starbucks. Recognizing these limitations, the company is taking steps to improve its drive-through service, such as using screens that allow customers to see their order and make corrections before driving up to the window, showing baristas' faces on video screens to maintain a human connection, and making improvements to their mobile app to speed up ordering.

Starbucks has new challenges as they expand their delivery services. Customers who order by delivery want their coffee at the right temperature, looking and tasting the same as if they ordered it in a Starbucks store. Starbucks' delivery service in the US has been expanding through a partnership with Uber Eats. It's important to Starbucks that this partnership results in coffee that is delivered at the same level of quality as coffee consumed in a Starbucks café. Concerns include: What if an Uber Eats delivery vehicle has to stop suddenly or gets stuck in traffic? Rather than working alone, Starbucks will need to work in cooperation with Uber Eats to ensure that delivery is fast and provides the same quality standards as in-store offerings.

Starbucks also ensures control over customers' experiences through social media. In fact, Starbucks responds to customer feedback with an average of 155 tweets per day (99 percent of those tweets are replies to customer tweets). For example, customers vented their frustration on Twitter when Starbucks' mobile app "crashed" one morning. Starbucks didn't just respond by fixing the technical glitch. A company spokesperson also got the word out to customers via Twitter quickly that they were working on the problem and thanked customers for their patience.

Security is also an important issue for Starbucks. Keeping company assets (such as people, equipment, products, financial information, and so forth) safe and secure requires security controls. All partners share the responsibility to follow all safety rules and practices; to cooperate with officials who enforce those rules and practices; to take necessary steps to protect themselves and other partners; to attend required safety training; and to report immediately all accidents, injuries, and unsafe practices or conditions. When hired, each partner is provided with a manual that covers safety, security, and health standards and is trained on the requirements outlined in the manual. In addition, managers receive ongoing training about these issues and are expected to keep employees up-to-date on any changes. And at any time, any partner can contact the Partner & Asset Protection Department for information and advice.

One security area that has been particularly important to Starbucks has been cybersecurity. Starbucks is known for being an early adopter of a bug bounty program that provides incentives to security experts when they identify cybersecurity problems that affect the company. Soon after Starbucks began offering bug bounty incentives, a security expert identified bugs in Starbucks's website. The problems identified included that hackers could get customers' credit card information, hijack customer accounts, and change customers' passwords. By continuing their bug bounty program, Starbucks is able to identify and resolve cybersecurity problems quickly.

Although Starbucks's control methods are well thought out, some thefts occur and are not detected right away. For instance, a Starbucks store manager in Wisconsin admitted to stealing store deposits that totaled over $37,000 over three months of time in order to pay off student loans and credit card debt. Theft problems can come from customers too. Two customers in northern California were suspected of stealing other customers' laptops in at least three Starbucks stores over a three-month period. Since trust is so important to customers' perceptions and to Starbucks' reputation, putting a stop quickly to any form of theft is an important task for Starbucks to take.

Exemplary customer service is a top priority at Starbucks. Partners are encouraged to strive to make every customer's experience pleasant and fulfilling and to treat customers with respect and dignity. What kinds of employee controls does Starbucks use to ensure that this happens? Partners are trained in and are required to follow all proper procedures relating to the storage, handling, preparation, and service of Starbucks's products. In addition, partners are told to notify their managers immediately if they see anything that suggests a product may pose a danger to the health or safety of themselves or of customers. Partners also are taught the warning signs associated with possible workplace violence and how to reduce their vulnerability if faced with a potentially violent situation. In either circumstance where product or partner safety and security are threatened, store managers have been trained in the appropriate steps to take if such situations occur.

The final types of control that are important to Starbucks's managers are performance and financial controls. Starbucks uses the typical financial control measures (such as revenue growth and operating income), but also looks at same-store sales growth as a performance standard. Starbucks directed their attention toward improving same-store growth in late 2018 and was able to realize a 4 percent increase by early 2019. They did this by shifting cleaning duties to after stores close, automating processes that used to take time away from customers, and increasing their digital sales.

One continual challenge is trying to control store operating costs. There's a fine balance between keeping costs low and keeping quality high. Some costs are beyond the company's control (such as the rising cost of rent and coffee beans). Other costs—like employee benefits and digital advancements—are part of Starbucks's mission and strategy, so they are thought to be necessary. To offset costs, Starbucks recently increased the price of its regular drip coffee by 10 to 20 cents per cup, or about a 10 percent increase. The challenge is how to keep costs as low as possible so as not to force price increases.

In addition to the typical financial measures, corporate governance procedures and guidelines are an important part of Starbucks's financial controls, as they are at any public corporation. The company has identified guidelines for its board of directors with respect to responsibilities, processes, procedures, and expectations.

Starbucks's Value Chain: From Bean to Cup

The steaming cup of coffee placed in a customer's hand at any Starbucks starts as coffee beans (berries) plucked from fields of coffee plants. From harvest to storage to roasting to retail to cup, Starbucks is dependent on each participant in its value chain.

Starbucks offers a selection of coffees from around the world, and its coffee buyers personally travel to the coffee-growing regions of Latin America, Africa/Arabia, and Asia/Pacific to select and purchase the highest-quality *arabica* beans. Once the beans arrive at any one of the company's five roasting facilities in the United States (and one in

Amsterdam), Starbucks' master professional roasters take over. These individuals know coffee and do their "magic" in balancing flavors and creating the company's rich signature roast coffee. There are many potential challenges to "transforming" the raw material into the product and experience that customers have come to expect. Weather, shipping and logistics, technology, and political instability are examples of factors with potential impact.

One issue Starbucks gives high priority to is environmental protection. For instance, Starbucks has accelerated its efforts towards developing a greener cup for its beverages by 2022. Their plan to phase out plastic straws by 2020 will result in eliminating more than one billion straws worldwide. They also have set the goal of increasing their number of environmentally certified retail stores by 2025. And they already have been investing in solar farms, like one in North Carolina that supplies solar power to 600 Starbucks stores across more than six states. To minimize Starbucks's environmental footprint throughout its supply chain, suppliers are asked to sign a code of conduct that deals with certain expectations in business standards and practices.[2]

Discussion Questions

P6-1. What might need to be different in Starbucks's control process as a result of their shift to including more drive-through windows in their stores? What specific measures of performance might be needed with drive-through service that are not as relevant to inside-store sales? What are control issues that Starbucks may need to address related to its out-of-store delivery offerings?

P6-2. How could Starbucks use social media to practice effective levels of feedforward control, concurrent control, and feedback control?

P6-3. What companies might make good benchmarks for Starbucks? Why? What companies might want to benchmark Starbucks? Why?

P6-4. What "red flags" might indicate significant deviations from standard for (a) an hourly partner, (b) a store manager, (c) a district manager, (d) the executive vice president of finance, and (e) the CEO? Are there any similarities? Why or why not?

P6-5. Using the company's most current financial statements, calculate the following financial ratios: current, debt to assets, inventory turnover, total asset turnover, profit margin on sales, and return on investment. What do these ratios tell managers?

P6-6. Can Starbucks manage the uncertainties in its value chain? If so, how? If not, why not?

Notes for the Part 6 Continuing Case

1. K. Schwab, "IKEA's Killer Dressers and America's Hidden Recall Crisis," *Fast Company*, February 14, 2019, https://www.fastcompany.com/90298511/ikeas-

killer-dressers-and-americas-hidden-recall-crisis; J. Brownlee, "The 5 Biggest Furniture Recalls in U.S. History (And How IKEA Compares)," *Fast Company*, July 5, 2016, https://www.fastcompany. com/3061528/the-5-biggest-furniture-recalls-in-us-history-and-how-ikea-compares; M. Jarrett and Q. N. Huy, "IKEA's Success Can't Be Attributed to One Charismatic Leader," *Harvard Business Review*, February 2, 2018, https://hbr.org/2018/02/ikeas-success-cant-be-attributed-to-one-charismatic-leader; Wikipedia, s.v. "IKEA," last modified April 12, 2019, 01:10, https://en.wikipedia.org/wiki/IKEA; "Chinese Companies Shifting to Other Countries to Avoid US Tariffs," *IndustryWeek*, September 12, 2018, https://www.industryweek.com/trade/chinese-companies-shifting-other-countries-avoid-us-tariffs; M. L. Corbat, "America Has a Surplus in Services," Opinion, *Wall Street Journal*, November 13, 2018, https://www.wsj.com/articles/america-has-a-surplus-in-services-1542154242; and S. Banker, "U.S. Manufacturers Are Not Reshoring," *Forbes*, July 11, 2018, https://www.forbes.com/sites/stevebanker/2018/07/11/u-s-manufacturers-are-not-reshoring/#663da412460c.

2. L. Patton, "Starbucks Embraces the Drive-Thru," *Bloomberg*, April 24, 2018, https://www.bloomberg.com/news/articles/2018-04-24/as-starbucks-embraces-the-drive-thru-a-few-speed-traps-ahead; M. Maynard, "Starbucks, Trailing Dunkin,' Tim's and McDonald's, Wants to Speed Up Its Drive-Thru," *Forbes*, April 24, 2018, https://www.forbes.com/sites/michelinemaynard/2018/04/24/starbucks-trailing-dunkin-tims-and-mcdonalds-wants-to-speed-up-its-drive-thru/#73269aa0446f; M. Glynn, "Racine Woman Accused of Stealing Thousands from Starbucks," *WTMJ-Milwaukee*, November 10, 2017, https://www.tmj4.com/news/local-news/racine-woman-accused-of-stealing-thousands-from-starbucks; P. Hegarty, "Video Shows Thieves Stealing Laptops from Starbucks Customers in Alameda," *Mercury News*, October 3, 2017, https://www.mercurynews.com/2017/10/03/video-shows-thieves-stealing-laptops-from-starbucks-customers-in-alameda/; Q. Fottrell, "Starbucks Drops to Lowest Consumer-Perception Level Since November 2015," *Market Watch*, April 21, 2018, https://www.marketwatch.com/story/starbucks-drops-to-lowest-consumer-perception-level-since-november-2015-2018-04-18; K. Boyer, "Behind the Scenes at Starbucks Supply Chain Operations, Its Plan, Source, Make and Deliver," *Supply Chain 24/7*, September 20, 2013, https://www.supplychain247.com/article/behind_the_scenes_at_starbucks_supply_chain_operations; N. Spector, "Bummed by Starbucks' Price Hike? Here's How Much It Costs to Make Your Coffee," *NBC News*, June 11, 2018, https://www.nbcnews.com/better/business/bummed-starbucks-price-hike-here-s-how-much-it-costs-ncna881821; J. Maze, "Was Starbucks' Price Hike a Good Idea?," *Restaurant Business*, June 8, 2018, https://www.restaurantbusinessonline.com/financing/was-starbucks-price-hike-good-idea; D. B. Kline, "Here's How Starbucks Is Driving U.S. Same-Store Sales Growth," *Motley Fool*, January 26, 2019, https://www.fool.com/investing/2019/01/26/heres-how-starbucks-is-driving-us-same-store-sales.aspx; H. Lalley, "Starbucks' Mobile App Goes Down," *Restaurant Business*, August 20, 2018, https://www.restaurantbusinessonline.com/technology/starbucks-mobile-app-goes-down; K. Ravi, "8 Ways Starbucks Creates an Enviable Social Media Strategy," *Unmetric*, March 28, 2018, https://blog.unmetric.com/starbucks-social-media-strategy; and "Cream, Sugar, and Security Bugs: Another Starbucks Vulnerability," *adaware*, February 23, 2017, https://www.adaware.com/blog/cream-sugar-and-security-bugs-another-starbucks-vulnerability.

Glossary

A

Absenteeism The failure to show up for work

Active listening Listening for full meaning without making premature judgments or interpretations

Activities The time or resources needed to progress from one event to another in a PERT network

Adjourning The final stage of group development for temporary groups during which group members are concerned with wrapping up activities rather than task performance

Affective component That part of an attitude that's the emotional or feeling part

Affirmative action Organizational programs that enhance the status of members of protected groups

Artificial intelligence Using the power of computers to replicate the reasoning functions of humans

Assessment centers A set of performance-simulation tests designed to evaluate a candidate's managerial potential

Association of Southeast Asian Nations (ASEAN) A trading alliance of 10 Southeast Asian nations

Assumed similarity The assumption that others are like oneself

Attitude surveys Surveys that elicit responses from employees through questions about how they feel about their jobs, work groups, supervisors, or the organization

Attitudes Evaluative statements, either favorable or unfavorable, concerning objects, people, or events

Attribution theory A theory used to explain how we judge people differently depending on what meaning we attribute to a given behavior

Authentic leadership Leaders who know who they are, know what they believe in, and act on those values and beliefs openly and candidly

Authority The rights inherent in a managerial position to tell people what to do and to expect them to do it

Autocratic style A leader who dictates work methods, makes unilateral decisions, and limits employee participation

Autonomy The degree to which a job provides substantial freedom, independence, and discretion to the individual in scheduling work and determining the procedures to be used in carrying it out

B

Balanced scorecard A performance measurement tool that looks at performance from more than just the financial perspective

Basic corrective action Corrective action that looks at how and why performance deviated before correcting the source of deviation

BCG matrix A strategy tool that guides resource-allocation decisions on the basis of market share and growth rate of SBUs

Behavior The actions of people

Behavioral component That part of an attitude that refers to an intention to behave in a certain way toward someone or something

Behavioral theories of leadership Theories that identify behaviors that differentiate effective leaders from ineffective leaders

Benchmark The standard of excellence against which to measure and compare

Benchmarking Identifying, analyzing, and adopting the best practices from other organizations that lead to their superior performance

Bias A tendency or preference toward a particular perspective or ideology

Big data Huge and complex sets of data

Big Five Model Personality trait model that includes extraversion, agreeableness, conscientiousness, emotional stability, and openness to experience

Board representatives Employees who sit on a company's board of directors and represent the interests of the firm's employees

Bounded rationality Decision making that's rational but limited (bounded) by an individual's ability to process information

Breakeven analysis A technique for identifying the point at which total revenue is just sufficient to cover total costs

Budget A numerical plan for allocating resources to specific activities

Budgeting The process of allocating resources to pay for designated future costs

Bureaucracy A form of organization characterized by division of labor, a clearly defined hierarchy, detailed rules and regulations, and impersonal relationships

Business model How a company is going to make money

Business plan A written document that summarizes a business opportunity and defines and articulates how the identified opportunity is to be seized and exploited

C

Capabilities An organization's skills and abilities in doing the work activities needed in its business

Centralization The degree to which decision making is concentrated at upper levels of the organization

Chain of command The line of authority extending from upper organizational levels to the lowest levels, which clarifies who reports to whom

Change agent Someone who acts as a catalyst and assumes the responsibility for managing the change process

Channel The medium a message travels along

Charismatic leader Someone to whom followers attribute heroic or extraordinary leadership abilities when they observe certain behaviors and tend to give power

Classical approach First studies of management, which emphasized rationality and making organizations and workers as efficient as possible

Classical view The view that management's only social responsibility is to maximize profits

Closed systems Systems that are not influenced by and do not interact with their environment

Closely held corporation A corporation owned by a limited number of people who do not trade the stock publicly

Code of ethics A formal statement of an organization's primary values and the ethical rules it expects its employees to follow

Coercive power The power a leader has to punish or control

Cognitive component That part of an attitude that's made up of the beliefs, opinions, knowledge, or information held by a person

Cognitive dissonance Any incompatibility or inconsistency between attitudes or between behavior and attitudes

Commitment concept Plans should extend far enough to meet those commitments made when the plans were developed

Communication networks The variety of patterns of vertical and horizontal flows of organizational communication

Communication process The seven elements involved in transferring meaning from one person to another

Communication The transfer and understanding of meaning

Competitive advantage What sets an organization apart; its distinctive edge

Competitive strategy An organizational strategy for how an organization will compete in its business(es)

Competitive intelligence Gathering information about competitors that allows managers to anticipate competitors' actions

Compliance officer The person responsible for ensuring an organization conducts its business in full compliance with all national and internal laws and regulations

Compressed workweek A workweek where employees work longer hours per day but fewer days per week

Conceptual skills The ability to think and to conceptualize about abstract and complex situations

Concurrent control Control that takes place while a work activity is in progress

Conflict Perceived incompatible differences that result in interference or opposition

Consideration The extent to which a leader has work relationships characterized by mutual trust and respect for group members' ideas and feelings

Contingency approach A management approach that recognizes organizations as different, which means they face different situations (contingencies) and require different ways of managing

Contingent workers Outsourced and non-permanent workers who are hired on a temporary basis

Contrast effect Potentially distorted perceptions based on comparisons to others

Control process A three-step process of measuring actual performance, comparing actual performance against a standard, and taking managerial action to correct deviations or inadequate standards

Controlling Management function that involves monitoring, comparing, and correcting work performance

Core competencies The organization's major value-creating capabilities that determine its competitive weapons

Corporate compliance The process of making sure an organization and its employees follow the laws, regulations, standards, and ethical practices

Corporate governance The system used to govern a corporation so that the interests of corporate owners are protected

Corporate strategy An organizational strategy that determines what businesses a company is in or wants to be in, and what it wants to do with those businesses

Corporation A legal business entity that is separate from its owners and managers

Counterproductive workplace behavior Any intentional employee behavior that is potentially damaging to the organization or to individuals within the organization

Creativity The ability to combine ideas in a unique way or to make unusual associations between ideas

Credibility The degree to which followers perceive someone as honest, competent, and able to inspire

Critical path The longest sequence of activities in a PERT network

Cross-functional team A work team composed of individuals from various functional specialties

Crowdsourcing Relying on a network of people outside the organization's traditional set of decision makers to solicit ideas via the internet

D

Decentralization The degree to which lower-level employees provide input or actually make decisions

Decision A choice among two or more alternatives

Decision criteria Criteria that define what's important or relevant to resolving a problem

Decisional roles Managerial roles that revolve around making choices

Decoding Retranslating a sender's message

Decruitment Reducing an organization's workforce

Deep learning Use of algorithms to create a hierarchical level of artificial neural networks that simulate functions of the human brain

Deep-level diversity Differences in values, personality, and work preferences

Democratic style A leader who involves employees in decision making, delegates authority, and uses feedback as an opportunity for coaching employees

Departmentalization The basis by which jobs are grouped together

Design thinking Approaching management problems as designers approach design problems

Diagonal communication Communication that cuts across work areas and organizational levels

Directional plans Plans that are flexible and set out general guidelines

Disciplinary actions Actions taken by a manager to enforce the organization's work standards and regulations

Discrimination When someone acts out their prejudicial attitudes toward people who are the targets of their prejudice

Disruptive innovation Innovations in products, services or processes that radically change an industry's rules of the game

Distributive justice Perceived fairness of the amount and allocation of rewards among individuals

Division of labor (job specialization) The breakdown of jobs into narrow and repetitive tasks

Divisional structure An organizational structure made up of separate, semiautonomous units or divisions

Downward communication Communication that flows downward from a manager to employees

Dysfunctional conflicts Conflicts that prevent a group from achieving its goals

E

Effectiveness Doing those work activities that will result in achieving goals

Efficiency Getting the most output from the least amount of inputs or resources

Ego strength A personality measure of the strength of a person's convictions

Electronic performance monitoring Electronic instruments or devices to collect, store, analyze, and report individual or group performance

Emotional intelligence (EI) The ability to notice and to manage emotional cues and information

Emotions Intense feelings that are directed at someone or something

Employee empowerment Giving employees more authority to make decisions

Employee engagement When employees are connected to, satisfied with, and enthusiastic about their jobs

Employee productivity A performance measure of both efficiency and effectiveness

Employee recognition program A plan to encourage specific behaviors by formally appreciating specific employee contributions

Employee resource groups A voluntary, employee-led subgroup within an organization that shares distinctive qualities, interests, or goals

Employee theft Any unauthorized taking of company property by employees for their personal use

Encoding Converting a message into symbols

Entrepreneurship The process of starting new businesses, generally in response to opportunities

Environment Institutions or forces that are outside the organization and potentially affect the organization's performance

Environmental complexity The number of components in an organization's environment and the extent of the organization's knowledge about those components

Environmental scanning Screening large amounts of information to detect emerging trends and create a set of scenarios

Environmental uncertainty The degree of change and complexity in an organization's environment

Equity theory The theory that an employee compares his or her job's input-outcomes ratio with that of relevant others and then corrects any inequity

Esteem needs A person's needs for internal factors such as self-respect, autonomy, and achievement, and external factors such as status, recognition, and attention

Ethics Principles, values, and beliefs that define what is right and wrong behavior

Ethnicity The social and culture factors—including nationality, regional culture, and ancestry—that define the groups a person belongs to

Ethnocentric attitude The parochial belief that the best work approaches and practices are those of the home country

European Union (EU) A union of 28 European nations created as a unified economic and trade entity

Events End points that represent the completion of major activities in a PERT network

Evidence-based management (EBMgt) The systematic use of the best available evidence to improve management practice

Expectancy theory The theory that an individual tends to act in a certain way based on the expectation that the act will be followed by a given outcome and on the attractiveness of that outcome to the individual

Expert power Power that's based on expertise, special skills, or knowledge

Exporting Making products domestically and selling them abroad

F

Feasibility study An analysis of the various aspects of a proposed entrepreneurial venture designed to determine its feasibility

Feedback control Control that takes place after a work activity is done

Feedback The degree to which carrying out work activities required by a job results in the individual's obtaining direct and clear information about his or her performance effectiveness

Feedforward control Control that takes place before a work activity is done

Fiedler contingency model A leadership theory proposing that effective group performance depends on the proper match between a leader's style and the degree to which the situation allows the leader to control and influence

Filtering The deliberate manipulation of information to make it appear more favorable to the receiver

First-line (frontline) managers Managers at the lowest level of management who manage the work of non-managerial employees

Flextime (or flexible work hours) A scheduling system in which employees work a specific number of hours per week and can vary their hours of work within limits

Forecasts Predictions of outcome

Foreign subsidiary Directly investing in a foreign country by setting up a separate and independent production facility or office

Formal communication Communication that takes place within prescribed organizational work arrangements

Formalization How standardized an organization's jobs are and the extent to which employee behavior is guided by rules and procedures

Forming stage The first stage of group development in which people join the group and then define the group's purpose, structure, and leadership

Franchising An organization gives another organization the right to use its name and operating methods

Free market economy An economic system in which resources are primarily owned and controlled by the private sector

Functional conflicts Conflicts that support a group's goals and improve its performance

Functional structure An organizational design that groups together similar or related occupational specialties

Fundamental attribution error The tendency to underestimate the influence of external factors and overestimate the influence of internal factors when making judgments about the behavior of others

G

Gantt chart A scheduling chart developed by Henry Gantt that shows actual and planned output over a period of time

General administrative theory An approach to management that focuses on describing what managers do and what constitutes good management practice

General environment Everything outside the organization

General partnership A form of legal organization in which two or more business owners share the management and risk of the business

Geocentric attitude A world-oriented view that focuses on using the best approaches and people from around the globe

Glass ceiling The invisible barrier that limits the level to which women and minorities can advance within an organization

Global company An MNC that centralizes management and other decisions in the home country

Globalization Refers to a process by which organizations develop influence or operations across international borders

Global Leadership and Organizational Behavior Effectiveness (GLOBE) program The research program that studies cross-cultural leadership behaviors

Global sourcing Purchasing materials or labor from around the world wherever it is cheapest

Goal-setting theory The proposition that specific goals increase performance and that difficult goals, when accepted, result in higher performance than do easy goals

Grapevine The informal organizational communication network

Green management Managers consider the impact of their organization on the natural environment

Group cohesiveness The degree to which group members are attracted to one another and share the group's goals

Group Two or more interacting and interdependent individuals who come together to achieve specific goals

Groupthink When a group exerts extensive pressure on an individual to align his or her opinion with others' opinions

Growth strategy A corporate strategy that's used when an organization wants to expand the number of markets served or products offered, either through its current business(es) or through new business(es)

H

Halo effect A general impression of an individual based on a single characteristic

Hawthorne Studies A series of studies during the 1920s and 1930s that provided new insights into individual and group behavior

Heuristics Shortcuts that managers use to simplify or speed up decision making

Hierarchy of needs theory Maslow's theory that human needs—physiological, safety, social, esteem, and self-actualization—form a hierarchy and that each level in the needs hierarchy must be substantially satisfied before the next need becomes dominant

High-involvement work practices Work practices designed to elicit greater input or involvement from workers

High–high leader A leader high in both initiating structure and consideration behaviors

Human relations view of conflict The view that conflict is a natural and inevitable outcome in any group

Human resource planning Ensuring that the organization has the right number and kinds of capable people in the right places and at the right times

Hygiene factors Factors that eliminate job dissatisfaction, but don't motivate

I

Idea champions Individuals who actively and enthusiastically support new ideas, build support, overcome resistance, and ensure that innovations are implemented

Immediate corrective action Corrective action that corrects problems at once to get performance back on track

Importing Acquiring products made abroad and selling them domestically

Incremental budgeting Process starting with the current budget from which managers decide whether they need additional resources and the justification for requesting them

Industrial revolution A period during the late eighteenth century when machine power was substituted for human power, making it more economical to manufacture goods in factories than at home

Informal communication Communication that is not defined by the organization's structural hierarchy

Information overload When information exceeds our processing capacity

Informational roles Managerial roles that involve collecting, receiving, and disseminating information

Initiating structure The extent to which a leader defines his or her role and the roles of group members in attaining goals

Innovation Taking creative ideas and turning them into useful products or work methods

Interactionist view of conflict The view that some conflict is necessary for a group to perform effectively

International Monetary Fund (IMF) An organization of 189 countries that provides temporary loans to its members, facilitates international trade, and seeks to promote economic growth and reduce poverty.

Interpersonal communication Communication between two or more people

Interpersonal roles Managerial roles that involve people and other duties that are ceremonial and symbolic in nature

Interpersonal skills The ability to work well with other people individually and in a group

Intuitive decision making Making decisions on the basis of experience, feelings, and accumulated judgment

ISO 9001 A series of international quality management standards that set uniform guidelines for processes to ensure products conform to customer and regulatory requirements

J

Jargon Specialized terminology or technical language that members of a group use to communicate among themselves

Job analysis A process that defines jobs and the behaviors necessary to perform them

Job characteristics model (JCM) A framework for analyzing and designing jobs that identifies five primary core job dimensions, their interrelationships, and their impact on outcomes

Job depth The degree of control employees have over their work

Job description (position description) A written statement that describes a job

Job design The way tasks are combined to form complete jobs

Job enlargement The horizontal expansion of a job by increasing job scope

Job enrichment The vertical expansion of a job by adding planning and evaluating responsibilities

Job involvement The degree to which an employee identifies with his or her job, actively participates in it, and considers his or her job performance to be important to self-worth

Job satisfaction An employee's general attitude toward his or her job

Job scope The number of different tasks required in a job and the frequency with which those tasks are repeated

Job sharing The practice of having two or more people split a full-time job

Job specification A written statement of the minimum qualifications a person must possess to perform a given job successfully

Joint venture A specific type of strategic alliance in which the partners agree to form a separate, independent organization for some business purpose

L

Labor union An organization that represents workers and seeks to protect their interests through collective bargaining

Laissez-faire style A leader who lets the group make decisions and complete the work in whatever way it sees fit

Lateral communication Communication that takes place among any employees on the same organizational level

Leader Someone who can influence others and who has managerial authority

Leader–member exchange theory (LMX) The leadership theory that says leaders create in-groups and out-groups and those in the in-group will have higher performance ratings, less turnover, and greater job satisfaction

Leader–member relations One of Fiedler's situational contingencies that describes the degree of confidence, trust, and respect employees have for their leader

Leadership A process of influencing a group to achieve goals

Leading Management function that involves working with and through people to accomplish organizational goals

Lean organization An organization that understands what customers want, identifies customer value by analyzing all activities required to produce products, and then optimizes the entire process from the customer's perspective

Learning Any relatively permanent change in behavior that occurs as a result of experience

Least-preferred coworker (LPC) questionnaire A questionnaire that measures whether a leader is task or relationship oriented

Legitimate power The power a leader has as a result of his or her position in the organization

Licensing An organization gives another organization the right to make or sell its products using its technology or product specifications

Limited liability company (LLC) A form of legal organization that's a hybrid between a partnership and a corporation

Limited liability partnership (LLP) A form of legal organization consisting of general partner(s) and limited liability partner(s)

Line authority Authority that entitles a manager to direct the work of an employee

Linear programming A mathematical technique that solves resource allocation problems

Load chart A modified Gantt chart that schedules capacity by entire departments or specific resources

Locus of control A personality attribute that measures the degree to which people believe they control their own fate

Long-term plans Plans of five years or more

M

Machiavellianism A measure of the degree to which people are pragmatic, maintain emotional distance, and believe that ends justify means

Machine learning A method of data analysis that automates analytical model building

Management by objectives (MBO) A system in which specific performance objectives are jointly determined by subordinates and their superiors, progress toward objectives is periodically reviewed, and rewards are allocated on the basis of this progress

Management by walking around A term used to describe when a manager is out in the work area interacting directly with employees

Management Coordinating and overseeing the work activities of others so their activities are completed efficiently and effectively

Management information system (MIS) A system used to provide management with needed information on a regular basis

Manager Someone who coordinates and oversees the work of other people so organizational goals can be accomplished

Managerial grid A two-dimensional grid for appraising leadership styles

Managerial roles Specific actions or behaviors expected of and exhibited by a manager

Manufacturing organizations Organizations that produce physical goods

Mass customization Providing customers with a product when, where, and how they want it

Mass production The production of items in large batches

Matrix structure An organizational structure that assigns specialists from different functional departments to work on one or more projects

Mechanistic organization An organizational design that's rigid and tightly controlled

Mentoring A process whereby an experienced (typically senior) organizational member (a mentor) provides advice and guidance to a less-experienced member (a protégé)

Message A purpose to be conveyed

Middle managers Managers between first-line managers and the top level of the organization

Mission The purpose of an organization

Motivation The process by which a person's efforts are energized, directed, and sustained toward attaining a goal

Motivators Intrinsic factors having to do with the job itself

Multidomestic corporation An MNC that decentralizes management and other decisions to the local country

Multinational corporation (MNC) A broad term that refers to any and all types of international companies that maintain operations in multiple countries

Myers-Briggs Type Indicator (MBTI) A personality assessment instrument that classifies people in four categories

N

National culture The values and attitudes shared by individuals from a specific country that shape their behavior and beliefs about what is important

Narcissism Describes a person who has a grandiose sense of self-importance, requires excessive admiration, and is arrogant

Nationalism Refers to patriotic ideals and policies that glorify a country's values

Need for achievement (nAch) The drive to succeed and excel in relation to a set of standards

Need for affiliation (nAff) The desire for friendly and close interpersonal relationships

Need for power (nPow) The need to make others behave in a way that they would not have behaved otherwise

Noise Any disturbances that interfere with the transmission of a message

Nonprogrammed decisions Unique and nonrecurring decisions that require a custom-made solution

Nonverbal communication Communication transmitted without words

Norming stage The third stage of group development, characterized by close relationships and cohesiveness

Norms Standards or expectations that are accepted and shared by a group's members

North American Free Trade Agreement (NAFTA) An agreement among the Mexican, Canadian, and US governments in which barriers to trade have been eliminated

O

Objectives (also called goals) Desired outcomes for individuals, groups, or entire organizations.

Omnipotent view of management The view that managers are directly responsible for an organization's success or failure

Open systems Systems that interact with their environment

Open-book management A motivational approach in which an organization's financial statements are shared with all employees

Operant conditioning A theory of learning that says behavior is a function of its consequences

Operating agreement The document that outlines the provisions governing the way an LLC will conduct business

Operational plans Plans that specify the details of how the overall objectives are to be achieved

Operations management The transformation process that converts resources into finished goods and services

Opportunities Positive trends in the external environment

Organic organization An organizational design that's highly adaptive and flexible

Organisation for Economic Co-operation and Development (OECD) An international economic organization that helps its 36 member countries achieve sustainable economic growth and employment

Organization A deliberate arrangement of people to accomplish some specific purpose

Organizational behavior (OB) The study of the actions of people at work

Organizational change Any alteration of people, structure, or technology in an organization

Organizational chart The visual representation of an organization's structure

Organizational citizenship behavior (OCB) Discretionary behavior that is not part of an employee's formal job requirements, but which promotes the effective functioning of the organization

Organizational commitment The degree to which an employee identifies with a particular organization and its goals and wishes to maintain membership in that organization

Organizational communication All the patterns, networks, and systems of communication within an organization

Organizational culture The shared values, principles, traditions, and ways of doing things that influence the way organizational members act and that distinguish the organization from other organizations

Organizational design Creating or changing an organization's structure

Organizational development (OD) Change methods that focus on people and the nature and quality of interpersonal work relationships

Organizational effectiveness A measure of how appropriate organizational goals are and how well those goals are being met

Organizational performance The accumulated results of all the organization's work activities

Organizational structure The formal arrangement of jobs within an organization

Organizing Management function that involves arranging and structuring work to accomplish the organization's goals

Orientation Introducing a new employee to his or her job and the organization

P

Parochialism Viewing the world solely through your own perspectives, leading to an inability to recognize differences between people

Path-goal theory A leadership theory that says the leader's job is to assist followers in attaining their goals and to provide direction or support needed to ensure that their goals are compatible with the goals of the group or organization

Pay-for-performance programs Compensation plans that vary with some measure of individual or organizational performance

Perceived organizational support Employees' general belief that their organization values their contribution and cares about their well-being

Perception A process by which we give meaning to our environment by organizing and interpreting sensory impressions

Performance management system Establishes performance standards used to evaluate employee performance

Performance The end result of an activity

Performing stage The fourth stage of group development when the group is fully functional and works on the group's task

Personality The unique combination of emotional, thought, and behavioral patterns that affect how a person reacts to situations and interacts with others

Persuasion skills Skills that enable a person to influence others to change their minds or behavior

PERT network A flowchart diagram showing the sequence of activities needed to complete a project and the time or cost associated with each

Physiological needs A person's needs for food, drink, shelter, sexual satisfaction, and other physical requirements

Planned economy An economic system in which economic decisions are planned by a central government

Planning Management function that involves setting goals, establishing strategies for achieving those goals, and developing plans to integrate and coordinate activities

Policy A guideline for making decisions

Polycentric attitude The view that the managers in the host country know the best work approaches and practices for running their business

Position power One of Fiedler's situational contingencies that describes the degree of influence a leader has over activities such as hiring, firing, discipline, promotions, and salary increases

Prejudice A preconceived belief, opinion, or judgment toward a person or a group of people

Principles of management Fundamental rules of management that could be applied in all organizational situations and taught in schools

Proactive personality A personality trait that describes individuals who are more prone to take actions to influence their environments

Proactive perspective of work design An approach to job design in which employees take the initiative to change how their work is performed

Problem A discrepancy between an existing and a desired condition

Problem-solving team A team from the same department or functional area that's involved in efforts to improve work activities or to solve specific problems

Procedural justice Perceived fairness of the process used to determine the distribution of rewards

Procedure A series of sequential steps used to respond to a well-structured problem

Process conflict Conflict over how work gets done

Process production The production of items in continuous processes

Productivity The amount of goods or services produced divided by the inputs needed to generate that output

Programmed decision A repetitive decision that can be handled by a routine approach

Progressive disciplinary action Discipline that moves sequentially through steps to ensure that the minimum penalty to an offense is imposed

Project A one-time-only set of activities that has a definite beginning and ending point in time

Project management The task of getting a project's activities done on time, within budget, and according to specifications

Project structure An organizational structure in which employees continuously work on projects

Psychopathy Describes individuals who lack concern for others and lack guilt or remorse when actions cause harm

O

Qualitative forecasting Forecasting that uses the judgment and opinions of knowledgeable individuals to predict outcomes

Quality The ability of a product or service to reliably do what it's supposed to do and to satisfy customer expectations

Quantitative approach The use of quantitative techniques to improve decision making

Quantitative forecasting Forecasting that applies a set of mathematical rules to a series of past data to predict outcomes

R

Race Physical characteristics, such as bone structure, skin, or eye color, that people use to identify themselves

Range of variation The acceptable parameters of variance between actual performance and the standard

Rational decision making Describes choices that are logical and consistent and maximize value

Readiness The extent to which people have the ability and willingness to accomplish a specific task

Reading skills Skills that entail an understanding of written sentences and paragraphs in work-related documents

Realistic job preview (RJP) A preview of a job that provides both positive and negative information about the job and the company

Real objectives Objectives that an organization actually pursues, as defined by the actions of its members

Recruitment Locating, identifying, and attracting capable applicants

Referent power Power that arises because of a person's desirable resources or personal traits

Referents The persons, systems, or selves against which individuals compare themselves to assess equity

Reinforcement theory The theory that behavior is a function of its consequences

Reinforcers Consequences immediately following a behavior, which increase the probability that the behavior will be repeated

Relational perspective of work design An approach to job design that focuses on how people's tasks and jobs are increasingly based on social relationships

Relationship conflict Conflict based on interpersonal relationships

Reliable selection device A selection device that measures the same thing consistently

Renewal strategy A corporate strategy designed to address declining performance

Resources An organization's assets that are used to develop, manufacture, and deliver products to its customers

Responsibility The obligation or expectation to perform assigned duties

Reward power The power a leader has to give positive rewards

Role ambiguity When role expectations are not clearly understood

Role Behavior patterns expected of someone occupying a given position in a social unit

Role conflicts Work expectations that are hard to satisfy

Role overload Having more work to accomplish than time permits

Rule An explicit statement that tells managers what can or cannot be done

S

S corporation A specialized type of corporation that has the regular characteristics of a C corporation but is unique in that the owners are taxed as a partnership as long as certain criteria are met

Safety needs A person's needs for security and protection from physical and emotional harm

Satisfice Solutions that are satisfactory and sufficient or "good enough"

Scenario A consistent view of what the future is likely to be

Scheduling Detailing what activities have to be done, the order in which they are to be completed, who is to do each, and when they are to be completed

Scientific management An approach that involves using the scientific method to find the "one best way" for a job to be done

Selection Screening job applicants to ensure that the most appropriate candidates are hired

Selective perception Biased perception based on our interests, background, experience, and attitudes

Self-actualization needs A person's need to become what he or she is capable of becoming

Self-efficacy An individual's belief that he or she is capable of performing a task

Self-esteem An individual's degree of like or dislike for himself or herself

Self-managed work team A work team that operates without a manager and is responsible for a complete work process or segment

Self-monitoring A personality trait that measures the ability to adjust behavior to external situational factors

Self-serving bias The tendency for individuals to attribute their own successes to internal factors while putting the blame for failures on external factors

Servant leadership Leadership that goes beyond self-interest and focuses on opportunities to help followers grow and develop

Service organizations Organizations that produce non-physical products in the form of services

Sexual harassment Any unwanted action or activity of a sexual nature that explicitly or implicitly affects an individual's employment, performance, or work environment

Shaping-behavior The process of guiding learning in graduated steps using reinforcement or lack of reinforcement

Short-term plans Plans covering less than one year

Simple structure An organizational design with little departmentalization, wide spans of control, centralized authority, and little formalization

Single-use plan A one-time plan specifically designed to meet the needs of a unique situation

Situational leadership theory (SLT) A leadership contingency theory that focuses on followers' readiness

Six Sigma A quality program designed to reduce defects and help lower costs, save time, and improve customer satisfaction

Skill variety The degree to which a job requires a variety of activities so that an employee can use a number of different skills and talents

Skill-based pay A pay system that rewards employees for the job skills they can demonstrate

Skunk works A small group within a large organization, given a high degree of autonomy and unhampered by corporate bureaucracy, whose mission is to develop a project primarily for the sake of radical innovation

Slack time The amount of time an individual activity can be delayed without delaying the whole project

Social entrepreneur Social entrepreneurship An entrepreneurial activity with an embedded social purpose

Social learning theory A theory of learning that says people can learn through observation and direct experience

Social loafing The tendency for individuals to expend less effort when working collectively than when working individually

Social media Forms of electronic communication through which users create online communities to share ideas, information, personal messages, and other content

Social needs A person's needs for affection, belongingness, acceptance, and friendship

Social obligation Meeting economic and legal responsibilities and no more

Social responsibility A firm's obligation, beyond that required by the law and economics, to pursue long-term goals that are good for society

Social responsiveness Adapting to changing societal conditions

Socialization A process that helps new employees learn the organization's way of doing things

Socioeconomic view The view that management's social responsibility goes beyond making profits to include protecting and improving society's welfare

Sole proprietorship A form of legal organization in which the owner maintains sole and complete control over the business and is personally liable for business debts

Span of control The number of employees a manager can efficiently and effectively manage

Speaking skills Skills that refer to the ability to communicate information and ideas in talking so others will understand

Specific environment The part of the environment consisting of crucial constituencies or stakeholders that can positively or negatively influence an organization's effectiveness.

Specific plans Plans that are clearly defined and leave no room for interpretation

Stability strategy A corporate strategy in which an organization continues to do what it is currently doing

Staff authority Positions created to support, assist, and advise those holding line authority

Standing plans Ongoing plans that provide guidance for activities performed repeatedly

Stated objectives Official statements of what an organization says—and what it wants various publics to believe—are its objectives

Status A prestige grading, position, or rank within a group

Stereotyping Judging a person based on a perception of a group to which that person belongs

Storming stage The second stage of group development, characterized by intragroup conflict

Strategic alliance A partnership between an organization and foreign company partner(s) in which both share resources and knowledge in developing new products or building production facilities

Strategic business unit (SBU) The single independent businesses of an organization that formulate their own competitive strategies

Strategic leadership The ability to anticipate, envision, maintain flexibility, think strategically, and work with others in the organization to initiate changes that will create a viable and valuable future for the organization

Strategic management process A six-step process that encompasses strategic planning, implementation, and evaluation

Strategic management The formulation and implementation of initiatives by top management that will allow the organization to achieve its goals

Strategic plans Plans that apply to the entire organization, that establish the organization's overall objectives, and that seek to position the organization in terms of its environment

Strategies The plans for how the organization will do what it's in business to do, how it will compete successfully, and how it will attract and satisfy its customers in order to achieve its goals

Strengths Any activities the organization does well or its unique resources

Stress The adverse reaction people have to excessive pressure placed on them from extraordinary demands, constraints, or opportunities

Stressors Factors that cause stress

Strong cultures Organizational cultures in which the key values are intensely held and widely shared

Structured problems Straightforward, familiar, and easily defined problems

Surface-level diversity Easily perceived differences that may trigger certain stereotypes, but that do not necessarily reflect the ways people think or feel

Sustaining innovation Small and incremental changes in established products rather than dramatic breakthroughs

SWOT analysis An analysis of the organization's strengths, weaknesses, opportunities, and threats

Symbolic view of management The view that much of an organization's success or failure is due to external forces outside managers' control

System A set of interrelated and interdependent parts arranged in a manner that produces a unified whole

T

Task conflict Conflicts over content and goals of the work

Task identity The degree to which a job requires completion of a whole and identifiable piece of work

Task significance The degree to which a job has a substantial impact on the lives or work of other people

Task structure One of Fiedler's situational contingencies that describes the degree to which job assignments are formalized and structured

Team structure An organizational structure in which the entire organization is made up of work teams

Technical skills Job-specific knowledge and techniques needed to proficiently perform work tasks

Telecommuting A work arrangement in which employees work at home and are linked to the workplace by computer

The Dark Triad The three personality traits of Machiavellianism, narcissism, and psychopathy

Theory X The assumption that employees dislike work, are lazy, avoid responsibility, and must be coerced to perform

Theory Y The assumption that employees are creative, enjoy work, seek responsibility, and can exercise self-direction

Therbligs A classification scheme for labeling basic hand motions

Threats Negative trends in the external environment

Three-needs theory The motivation theory that says three acquired (not innate) needs—achievement, power, and affiliation—are major motives in work

Three-step change process Unfreezing the status quo, changing to a new state, and refreezing to make the change permanent

Top managers Managers at or near the upper levels of the organization structure who are responsible for making organization-wide decisions and establishing the strategy and goals that affect the entire organization

Total quality management (TQM) A philosophy of management that is driven by continuous improvement and responsiveness to customer needs and expectations

Traditional objective setting Objectives are set at the top and then broken down into subgoals for each level of an organization

Traditional view of conflict The view that all conflict is bad and must be avoided

Transactional leaders Leaders who lead primarily by using social exchanges (or transactions)

Transformational leaders Leaders who stimulate and inspire (transform) followers to achieve extraordinary outcomes

Transnational or borderless organization An MNC in which artificial geographical barriers are eliminated

Trust The belief in the integrity, character, and ability of a leader

Turnover The voluntary and involuntary permanent withdrawal from an organization

Two-factor theory (motivation-hygiene theory) The motivation theory that intrinsic factors are related to job satisfaction and motivation, whereas extrinsic factors are associated with job dissatisfaction

Type A personality People who have a chronic sense of urgency and an excessive competitive drive

Type B personality People who are relaxed and easygoing and accept change easily

U

Unit production The production of items in units or small batches

Unity of command The management principle that each person should report to only one manager

Universality of management The reality that management is needed in all types and sizes of organizations, at all organizational levels, in all organizational areas, and in organizations, no matter where located

Unstructured problems Problems that are new or unusual and for which information is ambiguous or incomplete

Upward communication Communication that flows upward from employees to managers

V

Valid selection device A selection device characterized by a proven relationship to some relevant criterion

Value chain management The process of managing the sequence of activities and information along the entire value chain

Value chain The entire series of organizational work activities that add value at each step from raw materials to finished product

Value The performance characteristics, features, and attributes, and any other aspects of goods and services for which customers are willing to give up resources

Values Basic convictions about what is right and wrong

Variable pay A pay system in which an individual's compensation is contingent on performance

Virtual organization An organization that consists of a small core of full-time employees and outsources its major business functions

Virtual reality A three-dimensional, interactive computer-generated experience that takes place within a simulated environment

Virtual team A work team that uses computer technology to link physically dispersed members and achieve a common goal

VUCA An acronym describing an environment of nonstop volatility, uncertainty, complexity, and ambiguity

W

Weaknesses Activities the organization does not do well or resources it needs but does not possess

Whistle-blowing An act of an individual within an organization who discloses information in order to report and correct corruption

Work councils Groups of nominated or elected employees who must be consulted when management makes decisions involving personnel

Workplace bullying When an individual experiences a number of negative behaviors repeatedly over a period of time that results in physical or mental harm

Work specialization Dividing work activities into separate job tasks

Work teams Groups whose members work intensely on a specific, common goal using their positive synergy, individual and mutual accountability, and complementary skills

Workforce diversity The ways in which people in an organization are different from and similar to one another

Work sample tests Hands-on simulation of part of all the work that workers in a job routinely must perform

World Bank A financial institution that provides assistance to developing countries.

World Economic Forum Annual meeting that brings together several thousand of the world's leaders to find solutions to economic, social, and political problems.

World Trade Organization (WTO) A global organization of 164 countries that deals with the rules of trade among nations

Writing skills Skills that entail communicating effectively in text as appropriate for the needs of the audience

Z

Zero-base budgeting (ZBB) Process starting with an established point of zero rather than using the current budget as the basis for adding, modifying, or subtracting resources

Name Index

Organization Index

Subject Index